CRIMINAL LAW AND ITS PROCESSES

CASES AND MATERIALS

CRIMINAL LAW AND ITS PROCESSES

CASES AND MATERIALS

SEVENTH EDITION

Sanford H. Kadish
Alexander F. and May T. Morrison
Professor of Law, Emeritus
University of California, Berkeley

Stephen J. Schulhofer
Julius Kreeger Professor of Law and Criminology
University of Chicago

PUBLISHERS

1185 Avenue of the Americas, New York, NY 10036
www.aspenpublishers.com

Permissions
Aspen Publishers
1185 Avenue of the Americas
New York, NY 10036

Printed in the United States of America
ISBN 0-7355-1990-0
2 3 4 5 6 7 8 9 0

Library of Congress Cataloging-in-Publication Data
Kadish, Sanford H.
Criminal law and its processes : cases and materials / Sanford H. Kadish, Stephen J. Schulhofer. — 7th ed.
p. cm.
Includes bibliographical references and index.
ISBN 0-7355-1990-0
1. Criminal law — United States — Cases.
I. Schulhofer, Stephen J. II. Title.
KF9218.K3 2001
345.73 — dc21
00-053609

About Aspen Publishers

Aspen Publishers, headquartered in New York City, is a leading information provider for attorneys, business professionals, and law students. Written by preeminent authorities, our products consist of analytical and practical information covering both U.S. and international topics. We publish in the full range of formats, including updated manuals, books, periodicals, CDs, and online products.

Our proprietary content is complemented by 2,500 legal databases, containing over 11 million documents, available through our Loislaw division. Aspen Publishers also offers a wide range of topical legal and business databases linked to Loislaw's primary material. Our mission is to provide accurate, timely, and authoritative content in easily accessible formats, supported by unmatched customer care.

To order any Aspen Publishers title, go to *www.aspenpublishers.com* or call 1-800-638-8437.

To reinstate your manual update service, call 1-800-638-8437.

For more information on Loislaw products, go to *www.loislaw.com* or call 1-800-364-2512.

For Customer Care issues, e-mail CustomerCare@aspenpublishers.com; call 1-800-234-1660; or fax 1-800-901-9075.

Aspen Publishers
A Wolters Kluwer Company

SUMMARY OF CONTENTS

CONTENTS

CHAPTER 2

THE JUSTIFICATION OF PUNISHMENT 95

CHAPTER 3

DEFINING CRIMINAL CONDUCT — THE ELEMENTS OF JUST PUNISHMENT 173

CHAPTER 6

THE SIGNIFICANCE OF RESULTING HARM 517

CHAPTER 8

EXCULPATION 749

PREFACE

We have tried in this edition to freshen the material while at the same time maintaining close continuity with it. Thus we have left unaltered the basic organization, tone, and perspective of the book. We have replaced relatively few of the major cases, only doing so to improve teachability or to introduce new developments. Most of the changes have been in the reorganization of some chapters and in the Notes and Problems, where we try to present the most interesting ideas in the non-case literature, as well as new issues of importance.

Why *substantive criminal law?* We conceive of a criminal law course as serving the ends of both general legal education and training in the criminal law in particular. There are, as we see it, three chief ways the course can contribute to the general legal education of the law student. One way is to provide a vehicle for the close reading of statutory texts — primarily the Model Penal Code, but also state statutory formulations — to help balance the emphasis on case law in the first-year curriculum.

The second way is to introduce the student to the operation of a system of rules and principles designed to apportion blame and responsibility in accordance with our moral norms, subject to the practical restraints of a functioning system. While the criminal law is the primary institution serving this function, fault and wrongdoing each play a role in determining liability throughout the law. Hence some understanding of the analytical elements in assessing blame for a person's conduct or for the conduct of another, and of the concepts of excuse and justification, is an important element in a lawyer's legal education.

The third way the criminal law course serves the purposes of general legal education is by enlarging insight into the potentialities and limitations of the law as an instrument of social control. We have in mind the hard problems encountered in using the law for this purpose: the difficulty of giving legal form to the compromises made necessary when goals conflict; the creation of institutional arrangements — judicial and administrative — appropriate to the goals sought; the limitations — moral and practical — on the use of the law as a means of social control; the relation of legal controls to other social processes.

The substantive criminal law provides an unusually suitable introduction to these pervasive problems of the law. The ends criminal law serves involve social and human values of the highest order. Its means, entailing the imposition of brute force on the lives of individuals, are potentially the most destructive and abusive to be found within the legal system. The issues it raises and the setting in which it raises them are compelling and vivid. Its institutions are acutely controversial and often controverted. And one of its underlying themes is the momentous issue of the reconciliation of authority and the individual. As Professor Herbert Wechsler has written:

> Whatever views one holds about the penal law, no one will question its importance in society. This is the law on which men place their ultimate reliance for protection against all the deepest injuries that human conduct can inflict on individuals and institutions. By the same token, penal law governs the strongest force that we permit official agencies to bring to bear on individuals. Its promise as an instrument of safety is matched only by its power to destroy. If penal law is weak or ineffective, basic human interests are in jeopardy. If it is harsh or arbitrary in its impact, it works a gross injustice on those caught within its toils. The law that carries such responsibilities should surely be as rational and just as law can be. Nowhere in the entire legal field is more at stake for the community or for the individual.[1]

What of the course's narrower purpose of training students in the criminal law in particular? Here there are two main pedagogic objectives. One is to furnish a solid foundation for those who will, in greater or lesser degree, participate directly in the processes of the criminal law. This foundation does not require mastery of the full range of technical skills and information held by the practicing criminal lawyer or administrator, but rather the development of confidence in handling principles and rules — judge-made or statutory — through knowledge about the larger implications of the doctrines and institutions of the criminal law. The second purpose is to create in law school graduates who will have little occasion to practice criminal law an understanding of the problems of the criminal law. As influential members of their communities — and more directly as judges, legislators, or teachers — lawyers versed in the principles of criminal law can bring an informed intelligence to the challenge of solving some of the most vexing problems of our times.[2]

Revisions for the seventh edition. In the procedural sections (Chapter 1), we have streamlined the materials but have retained those fundamentals of criminal trial procedure that we consider essential for understanding the issues in substantive criminal law (rules of evidence, burden of proof, presumptions, and the role of the jury). These topics can now be covered in several classes. We believe that a brief but intensive treatment of this material at the outset of the course adds immeasurably to the student's appreciation of the concrete setting in which substantive law issues arise and the practical considerations that so often influence those debates. We have retained in Chapter 1 a substantial but more tightly edited section dealing with the ethical responsibilities of the criminal defense attorney. The themes of this section are central to the study and practice of law, and we believe that students can profit from exposure to these themes early and often in their legal education.

The growing complexity and importance of sentencing procedure and sentencing guidelines pose a dilemma for an introductory criminal law course. The subject is too important to be ignored but too complex to be covered comprehensively. We have sought to strike an appropriate balance by providing in Chapter 2 both a textual summary of current sentencing procedures and a principal case that can serve as a focal point for discussion in class. Though brief and tightly edited, the material is sufficient to illustrate for students the mechanics of how guidelines work, as well as the tough jurisprudential issues underlying them.

1. Herbert Wechsler, The Challenge of a Model Penal Code, 65 Harv. L. Rev. 1097, 1087-98 (1952).

2. For a fuller discussion of the role of the criminal law course in a law school curriculum, see Sanford H. Kadish, Why Substantive Criminal Law — A Dialogue, 29 Clev. St. L. Rev. 1 (1980).

In the substantive sections we have updated the cases, added Notes and Problems dealing with issues of current concern, and done some reorganization of the material. For example, we have tried in the provocation section and the mental disorder chapter to tighten (as well as lighten) the presentation of material, and in the rape chapter to cover some of the expanding issues, as well as to permit sustained attention to statutory drafting and interpretation. Among the new principal cases are City of Chicago v. Morales (vagueness and new strategies of policing); Commonwealth v. Fischer (mistake of fact in rape); State v. Guthrie (premeditation); People v. Kevorkian (assisted suicide and causation); Public Committee Against Torture v. State of Israel (necessity defense); and Washington v. Glucksberg (euthanasia).

As in previous editions, the substantive materials continue to focus on imparting an understanding of what is often called the "general part" of the criminal law — that is, those basic principles and doctrines that come into play across the range of specific offenses (for example, actus reus, mens rea, and the various justifications and excuses). We believe that mastery of the detailed elements of many particular crimes is not an appropriate goal for a basic criminal law course. Nevertheless, we have found that understanding of the basic principles is enhanced by testing their applications and interactions in the context of particular offenses. Accordingly, we examine in detail three offense categories: rape (Chapter 4), homicide (Chapter 5), and theft (Chapter 9). The chapter on rape provides an opportunity to focus on the definitional elements of a major crime in a context that has become the focus of acute controversy because of changing perceptions and changing social values. The theme of the homicide chapter is the task of legislative grading of punishment in a particularly challenging area. The theft chapter explores the significance of history and the continued impact of old doctrinal categories on the resolution of thoroughly modern difficulties in defining the boundaries of the criminal law.

Use of the materials in diverse teaching formats. Over the years, law schools have experimented with a variety of formats for the basic criminal law course. Although the year-long five- or six-hour course remains common, some schools offer criminal law as a four- or even three-hour course, and some schedule the course in the first or second semester or even in the second or third years. Under these circumstances, a short book designed to be taught straight through, without adjustments or deletions, is bound to prove unsatisfactory for many users. In preparing the seventh edition, we have sought to edit the materials tightly enough to avoid significant surplusage for the average course, but we have not attempted to preempt all possible judgments about inclusion and exclusion. Rather, we thought it essential to allow for teachers to select topics that accord with their own interests and with the curricular arrangements at their own schools. Thus, we have aspired to create a flexible teaching tool, one that reflects the rich diversity of the subject. For the five- or six-hour, year-long course, the book can be taught straight through, perhaps with some minor deletions. For a four-hour course, and especially in the case of a three-hour course, substantial omissions will be necessary. The Teachers Manual presents detailed suggestions for appropriate coverage and focus, together with specific suggestions for sequencing and class-by-class assignments.

Collateral Reading. There are a number of useful readings for students interested in pursuing further the questions developed in this casebook. Some of the suggestions that follow may no longer be in print, but they are available in virtually all law libraries.

Comprehensive Works: The following publications should be of considerable use to the student:

American Law Institute, Model Penal Code and Commentaries (1980-1985). This is a 6-volume set containing the text and supporting commentaries of the Model Penal Code. The commentaries constitute the most comprehensive available examination of the American substantive criminal law.

Encyclopedia of Crime and Justice (S. H. Kadish ed., Macmillan and Free Press, 1983). This work contains relatively short treatments, written by experts for the general lay reader, on virtually all the subjects covered in this casebook. It should prove particularly helpful for orientation and perspective. A second edition is in preparation under the editorship of Professor Joshua Dressler.

Textbooks: There are several conventional textbooks that are useful for review purposes:

Wayne LaFave, *Criminal Law* (West Publishing Co., 3d ed. 2000). A widely used hornbook; comprehensive and heavily footnoted.

Joshua Dressler, *Understanding Criminal Law* (Matthew Bender, 2d ed. 1995). A shorter textbook, available in paperback; its coverage largely focuses on the subjects covered in this casebook.

In addition, students may wish to consult English materials. Professor Glanville Williams has written two outstanding accounts of the criminal law: *Criminal Law: The General Part* (2d ed. 1961) and *Textbook of Criminal Law* (2d ed. 1983). The latter addressed specifically to law students.

Monographs: The following books deal selectively with aspects of the criminal law:

George Fletcher, *Rethinking Criminal Law* (Little, Brown, 1978): A comparative and theoretical treatment of the criminal law that is critical of dominant thinking in the field. See also Fletcher's more recent *Basic Concepts of Criminal Law* (Oxford Univ. Press, 1998).

H. L. A. Hart, *Punishment and Responsibility* (Oxford University Press, 1968): A collection of powerfully argued essays that have had a great influence on contemporary thinking concerning issues of punishment and excuse.

Sanford H. Kadish, *Blame and Punishment*—Essays in the Criminal Law (Macmillan, 1987): Authored by one of the editors of this casebook, a collection of essays, most of which grew out of the experience of teaching prior editions.

Herbert Packer, *The Limits of the Criminal Sanction* (Stanford, 1968): A classic treatment of the problems of criminalization and the theory of punishment.

Style. Citations in the footnotes and text of extracted material have been omitted when they did not seem useful for pedagogical purposes, and we have not used ellipses or other signals to indicate such deletions. Ellipses are used, however, to indicate omitted text material. Where we have retained footnotes in readings and quotations, the original footnote numbers are preserved. Our own footnotes to excerpts and quotations from other works are designated by letters, while footnotes to our own Notes are numbered consecutively throughout each chapter.

Acknowledgments: Sanford Kadish gratefully acknowledges the support provided for his research by former Dean Herma Hill Kay through the Alexander F. and May T. Morrison Chair at Boalt Hall. Stephen Schulhofer gratefully acknowledges the support provided for his research by the Dwight P. Green Sr. Fund for Studies in Criminal Justice at the University of Chicago Law School. In addition, we wish to express our thanks to a number of people who have provided invaluable assistance to each of us:

To Ms. Amatullah Alaji-Sabrie (Berkeley), and Ms. Brenda Burns and Ms. Sharon Mikulich (Chicago) for their excellent secretarial support.

To our students, Jin Kim and Chandra Fienen (Berkeley) and Greg Brown, John Pfaff, and Eric Rinehart (Chicago) for their research assistance.

To our wives, June (Berkeley) and Laurie Wohl (Chicago), yet again, for their cheerful forbearance.

SHK
SJS
February 2001

ACKNOWLEDGMENTS

The authors would like to acknowledge the permission of the authors, publishers, and copyright holders of the following publications for permission to reproduce excerpts herein:

Allen, Francis A., The Erosion of Legality in American Criminal Justice: Some Latter-Day Adventures of the Nulla Poena Principle, 29 Arizona Law Review 387 (1987). Copyright © 1987 by the Arizona Board of Regents. Reprinted by permission.

Alschuler, Albert W., The Prosecutor's Role in Plea Bargaining, 36 University of Chicago Law Review 50 (1968). Reprinted by permission.

American Bar Association, Model Code of Professional Responsibility and Model Rules of Professional Conduct. Copyright © by the American Bar Association. All rights reserved. Reprinted with permission.

American Law Institute, Model Penal Code and Commentaries (Tentative Drafts No. 4, 1955, No. 10, 1960). Copyright © 1955, 1960 by the American Law Institute. Reprinted by permission of the American Law Institute.

American Law Institute, Model Penal Code and Commentaries (1985). Copyright © 1955, 1960, 1962, 1980, 1985 by the American Law Institute. Reprinted by permission of the American Law Institute.

Andenaes, Johannes, General Prevention — Illusion or Reality?, 43 Journal of Criminal Law, Criminology & Police Science 176 (1952). Reprinted by special permission of Northwestern University School of Law.

Andenaes, Johannes, The General Preventive Effects of Punishment, 114 University of Pennsylvania Law Review 949 (1966). Copyright © by the University of Pennsylvania Law Review and reprinted with their permission and that of Fred B. Rothman & Co.

Armour, Jody D., Race Ipsa Loquitur: Of Reasonable Racists, Intelligent Beyesians, and Involuntary Negrophobes, 46 Stanford Law Review 781 (1994). Copyright © 1994 by the Board of Trustees of the Leland Stanford Jr. University and reprinted with their permission and that of Fred B. Rothman & Co.

Ashworth, A. J., The Doctrine of Provocation, 35 Cambridge Law Journal 292 (1976). Copyright © 1976 by Cambridge University Press. Reprinted with the permission of Cambridge University Press.

Austin, J. L., A Plea for Excuses, 57 Proceedings of the Aristotelian Society (1956-1957). Copyright © 1956 by The Aristotelian Society. Reprinted by courtesy of the editor.

Bedau, Hugo, Innocence and the Death Penalty, The Death Penalty in America: Current Controversies (H. Bedau ed., 1997). Reprinted by permission of Oxford University Press.

Berger, Joseph, Goetz Case: Commentary on Nature of Urban Life, The New York Times, June 18, 1987. Copyright© 1987 by the New York Times Company. Reprinted by permission.

Boldt, Richard, The Construction of Responsibility in the Criminal Law, 140 University of Pennsylvania Law Review 2245 (1992). Copyright © the University of Pennsylvania Law Review and reprinted by their permission and that of Fred B. Rothman & Co.

Brickey, Kathleen, Rethinking Corporate Liability Under the Model Penal Code, 19 Rutgers Law Journal 593 (1988). Reprinted by permission.

Brown, Sharon Morey & Nicholas J. Wittner, Criminal Law (1978 Annual Survey of Michigan Law), 25 Wayne Law Review 335 (1979). Reprinted by permission.

Bucy, Pamela H., Corporate Ethos: A Standard for Imposing Corporate Criminal Liability, 75 Minnesota Law Review 1095 (1991). Reprinted by permission.

Butler, Paul, Racially Based Jury Nullification: Black Power in the Criminal Justice System, 105 Yale Law Journal 677 (1995). Reprinted by permission of The Yale Law Journal Company and William S. Hein Company from The Yale Law Journal, Vol. 105, pages 677-725.

Carter, Stephen L., When Victims Happen to be Black, 97 Yale Law Journal 420 (1988). Reprinted by permission.

Chapman, Stephen, Court Upholds America's Right to Hang Out, excerpts from article appearing on June 13, 1999. Copyrighted 1999, Chicago Tribune Corporation. All rights reserved. Used with permission.

Coffee, Jr., John C., Hush!: The Criminal Status of Confidential Information After McNally and Carpenter and the Enduring Problem of Overcriminalization, 26 American Criminal Law Review 121 (1988). Reprinted with permission of the publisher, Georgetown University and American Criminal Law Review. Copyright © 1988.

Cohen, Morris, Moral Aspects of the Criminal Law, 49 Yale Law Journal 987, 1012-1014 (1940). Reprinted by permission of Yale Law Journal and Fred B. Rothman & Co.

Coleman, Doriane, Individualizing Justice Through Multiculturalism: The Liberals' Dilemma. This article originally appeared at 96 Columbia Law Review 1093 (1996). Reprinted by permission.

Comment on *Stephenson,* 31 Michigan Law Review 659 (1933). Reprinted by permission of the Michigan Law Review.

Conley, John, William M. O'Barr, E. Allen Lind, The Power of Language: The Presentational Style in the Courtroom. [1978] Duke Law Journal 1375. Copyright © 1978 by Duke University School of Law. Reprinted by permission.

Dan-Cohen, Meir, Actus Reus, in 1 Encyclopedia of Crime and Justice 15 (1983). Copyright © 1983 by The Free Press. Reprinted by permission of The Gale Group.

Delgado, Richard, "Rotten Social Background": Should the Criminal Law Recognize a Defense of Severe Environmental Deprivation?, 3 Law and Inequality 9 (1985). Reprinted by permission.

Denning, Alfred T., Freedom Under the Law (1949). Reprinted by permission of Sweet & Maxwell Ltd.

Devlin, Sir Patrick, The Enforcement of Morals (1959). Copyright © 1959 by Oxford University Press. Reprinted by permission of Oxford University Press.

DiIulio, Jr., John, Prisoners Are A Bargain By Any Measure, excerpts from an article appearing January 16, 1996. Copyright © 1996 by the New York Times Company. Reprinted by permission.

Donohue, John J. & Peter Seligman, Allocating Resources among Prisons and Social Programs in the Battle against Crime, 27 J. Legal Stud. 1 (1998). Copyright © 1998 by The University of Chicago. All rights reserved.

Dressler, Joshua, Rethinking Heat of Passion: A Defense in Search of a Rationale, 73 Journal of Criminal Law and Criminology 421 (1982). Reprinted by special permission of Northwestern University School of Law, Journal of Criminal Law and Criminology.

Durkheim, Emile, The Division of Labor in Society (George Simpson translator 1964). Reprinted with the permission of The Free Press, a division of Simon & Schuster, Inc.

Dworkin, G. & G. Blumenfeld, Punishments for Intentions, 75 Mind 396 (1966). Copyright © 1966 by Oxford University Press. Reprinted with permission of Oxford University Press.

Edgar, Harold, Mens Rea, in 3 Encyclopedia of Crime and Justice, Copyright © 1983 by The Free Press. Reprinted by permission of The Gale Group.

Estrich, Susan R., Defending Women, 88 Michigan Law Review 1430 (1990). Reprinted by permission.

Estrich, Susan R., Palm Beach Stories, 11 Law & Philosophy 5 (1992). Reprinted with kind permission of Kluwer Academic Publishers.

Estrich, Susan R., Real Rape (1987). Reprinted by permission of the publishers, Cambridge, Mass: Harvard University Press. Copyright © 1987 by the President and Fellows of Harvard College.

Faigman, David, (Note), The Battered Women Syndrome and Self-Defense, 72 Virginia Law Review 619 (1986). Reprinted with permission of the Virginia Law Review and Fred B. Rothman & Co.

Fischel, Daniel R. & Alan O. Sykes, Civil RICO After *Reves:* An Economic Commentary, [1993] Supreme Court Review 157. Copyright © 1995 by The University of Chicago. All Rights Reserved. Reprinted by permission.

Fletcher, George P., Blackmail: The Paradigmatic Crime, 141 University of Pennsylvania Law Review 1617 (1993). Copyright © by the University of Pennsylvania Law Review and reprinted by their permission and that of Fred B. Rothman & Co.

Fletcher, George P., Reflections on Felony-Murder, 12 Southwestern University Law Review 413 (1981). Reprinted by permission.

Fletcher, George P., Rethinking Criminal Law (1978). Copyright © 1978 by George P. Fletcher. Reprinted by permission of Aspen Law and Business Publishers and the author.

Frankel, Marvin, excerpts from Criminal Sentences: Law Without Order (1973). Copyright © 1972, 1973 by Marvin E. Frankel. Reprinted by permission of Hill & Wang a division of Farrar, Straus & Giroux.

Freedman, Monroe H., Lawyers' Ethics in an Adversary System (1975). Reprinted by permission of the author.

Ginsburg, Douglas and Paul Schechtman, Blackmail: An Economic Analysis of the Law, 141 University of Pennsylvania Law Review 1873 (1993). Copyright © by the University of Pennsylvania Law Review. Reprinted by permission of University of Pennsylvania Press and Fred B. Rothman & Co.

Goodhart, Arthur, Possession of Drugs and Absolute Liability, 84 Law Quarterly Review 382 (1968). Reprinted by permission of Sweet & Maxwell Ltd.

Gordon, Margaret T. and Stephanie Riger, The Female Fear: The Social Cost of Rape (1991). Reprinted with the permission of The Free Press, A Division of Simon & Schuster, Inc. Copyright © 1989 by Margaret T. Gordon and Stephanie Riger.

Gordon, Wendy J., Truth and Consequences: The Force of Blackmail's Central Case, 141 University of Pennsylvania Law Review 1741 (1993). Copyright © by the author and reprinted with her permission and that of University of Pennsylvania Law Review and Fred B. Rothman & Co.

Hall, Jerome, Theft, Law and Society (2d ed. 1952). Published by Michie, Bobbs-Merrill, Inc. Reprinted by permission of the publisher and the author.

Harcourt, Bernard, The Collapse of the Harm Principle, 90 Journal of Criminal Law and Criminology 109 (1999). Reprinted by special permission of Northwestern University School of Law, Journal of Criminal Law and Criminology.

Hart, H. L. A., Legal Responsibility and Excuses, In Determinism and Freedom (1958) (ed. Sidney Hook). Copyright © 1958. Reprinted by permission of Ernest Hook, MD.

Hart, H. L. A., Law, Liberty and Morality (1963). Reprinted by permission of Stanford University Press.

Hart, H. L. A. & A. Honoré, Causation in the Law (2 ed. 1985). Reprinted by permission of Oxford University Press.

Hazard, Geoffrey C., Jr., Criminal Justice System: Overview, in 2 Encyclopedia of Crime and Justice 450 (1983). Copyright © 1983 by The Free Press. Reprinted by permission of Simon & Schuster Macmillan.

Hill, Alfred, Vagueness and Police Discretion: The Supreme Court in a Box, 51 Rutgers Law Review 1289 (1999). Reprinted by permission.

Holtzman, Elizabeth, Premenstrual Symptoms: No Legal Defense, 60 St. Johns Law Review 712 (1986). Reprinted by permission.

Horder, Jeremy, Provocation and Responsibility (1992). Copyright © 1992. Reprinted by permission.

Hughes, Graham, Criminal Responsibility, 16 Stanford Law Review 470 (1964). Copyright © 1964 by the Board of Trustees of the Leland Stanford Jr. University and reprinted with their permission and that of Fred B. Rothman & Co.

Husak, Douglas N. & George C. Thomas, III, Date Rape, Social Convention and Reasonable Mistakes, 11 Law & Philosophy 95 (1992). Reprinted with kind permission of Kluwer Academic Publishers.

Jeffries, John Calvin, Jr. & Paul B. Stephan, Defenses, Presumptions and Burdens of Proof in the Criminal Law, 88 Yale Law Journal 1325 (1979). Reprinted by permission of The Yale Law Journal Company and William S. Hein Company from The Yale Law Journal, Volume 88, pages 1325-1347.

Johnson, Phillip E., Strict Liability: The Prevalent View, in 4 Encyclopedia of Crime and Justice 1518 (1983). Copyright © 1983 by The Free Press. Reprinted by permission.

Johnson, Phillip E., The Unnecessary Crime of Conspiracy, 61 California Law Review 1137 (1973). Copyright © 1973 by the California Law Review, Inc., Reprinted by permission of Fred B. Rothman & Company.

Kadish, Sandford H., Letting Patients Die: Legal and Moral Reflections, 80 California Law Review 857 (1992). Copyright © 1992 by California Law Review, Inc. Used with permission.

Kadish, Sanford H., Blame and Punishment: Essay in the Criminal Law (1987). Reprinted with permission of Macmillan, Inc.

Kadish, Sanford H., Complicity, Cause and Blame: A Study in the Interpretation of Doctrine, 73 California Law Review 323 (1985). Copyright © 1985 by California Law Review, Inc. Used with permission.

Kadish, Sanford H., The Crisis of Overcriminalization, 374 Annals 157 (1967). Reprinted by permission of The American Academy of Political and Social Science.

Kadish, Sanford H., The Decline of Innocence, 26 Cambridge Law Journal 273 (1968). Copyright © 1968 by Cambridge University Press. Reprinted by permission.

Kadish, Sanford H., Respect for Life and Regard for Rights in the Criminal Law, 64 California Law Review 871 (1976). Copyright © 1976 by California Law Review, Inc. Reprinted by permission.

Kadish, Sanford H., A Theory of Complicity, in Issues in Contemporary Legal Philosophy, The Influence of H. L. A. Hart (R. Gavison ed. 1987). Copyright © 1987 Oxford University Press. Reprinted by permission of Oxford University Press.

Kahan, Dan, Ignorance of the Law is Excuse — But Only for the Virtuous, 96 Michigan Law Review 127 (1997). Reprinted by permission of the Michigan Law Review and the author.

Kalven, Harry & Zeisel, Hans, The American Jury (1966). Reprinted by permission of Aspen Law & Business.

Kamisar, Yale, A Law to Stay the Cold Hand of Dr. Death, excerpts from an article appearing in the Legal Times (March 8, 1993). Copyright © 2000 NLP ID Company. All rights reserved. Reprinted with permission of *Legal Times,* 1730 M Street, NW, Suite 802, Washington, DC 20036.

Kant, Immanuel, The Philosophy of Law (1974 ed. W. Hastie tr. 1887). Reprinted by permission of Augustus M. Kelley Publishers.

Keisel, D., Who Saw This Happen — States Move to Make Crime Bystanders Responsible, 69 American Bar Association Journal 1208 (1983). Reprinted with permission from the ABA Journal, The Lawyer's Magazine, published by the American Bar Association.

Kelman, Mark, Strict Liability: An Unorthodox View, in 4 Encyclopedia of Crime and Justice 1512 (1983). Copyright © 1983 by The Free Press. Reprinted by permission of The Gale Group.

Kennedy, Randall L., Race, Crime and the Law (1997). Copyright © 1997 by Randall Kennedy. Used by permission of Pantheon Books, a Division of Random House, Inc.

Kleinig, John, Good Samaritanism, Philosophy & Public Affairs 5, No. 4 (Summer 1976). Copyright © 1976 by Princeton University Press. Reprinted with permission of Princeton University Press.

Lefstein, Norman, Legal Ethics, 1 Criminal Justice 27, Issue No. 2 (American Bar Association, Summer 1986). Reprinted by permission.

Lempert, Richard O., Deterrence and Desert: An Assessment of the Moral Bases for Capital Punishment, 79 Michigan Law Review 1177 (1981). Reprinted by permission.

Lewis, Anthony, excerpts from an article appearing in the International Herald Tribune (June 20, 1978). Copyright © 1978 by The New York Times Company. Reprinted by permission.

Lindgren, James, Unraveling the Paradox of Blackmail, 84 Colum. L. Rev. 670 (1984). This article originally appeared at 84 Columbia Law Review 670 (1984). Reprinted by permission.

Luban, David, Contrived Ignorance, 87 Georgetown Law Review 957 (1999). Reprinted with permission of the publisher, Georgetown University and Georgetown Law Journal. Copyright © 1999.

Lynch, Gerard E., RICO: The Crime of Being a Criminal, Parts I & II, 87 Columbia Law Review 920 (1987). This article originally appeared at 87 Columbia Law Review 661 (1987). Reprinted by permission.

Mackie, J. L., Retributivism: A Test Case for Ethical Objectivity. Published by permission of Mrs. Joan Mackie. All rights to further publication reserved.

Mair, George, What Works — Nothing or Everything?, Research Bulletin (Great Britain, Home Office, Research and Statistics Dept.) No. 30, 1991. Crown copyright reproduced with the permission of the Controller of HMSO.

McCord, David and Sandra Lyons, Moral Reasoning and the Criminal Law: The Example of Self Defense, 30 American Criminal Law Review 97 (1992). Reprinted with permission of the publisher, Georgetown University and American Criminal Law Review. Copyright © 1992.

Moore, Jennifer, Corporate Culpability and the Federal Sentencing Guidelines, 34 Arizona Law Review 744 (1992). Copyright © 1992 by the Arizona Board of Regents. Reprinted by permission.

Moore, Michael S., Law and Psychiatry: Rethinking the Relationship (1984). Copyright © 1984 by Cambridge University Press. Reprinted with the permission of Cambridge University Press.

Moore, Michael., excerpts from The Moral Worth of Retributivism, in Responsibility, Character and Emotions 179 (F. Schoeman, ed., 1987). Copyright © 1987 by Cambridge University Press. Reprinted by permission.

Morris, Herbert, On Guilt and Innocence (1976). Copyright © 1976 by The Regents of the University of California. Reprinted by permission of author.

Morris, Norval R., An Australian Newsletter, [1955] Criminal Law Review 290. Reprinted with permission of Sweet & Maxwell Ltd.

Morris, Norval R., Psychiatry and the Dangerous Criminal, 41 Southern California Law Review 514 (1968). Reprinted by permission.

Morris, Norval R., Somnambulistic Homicide: Ghosts, Spiders and North Koreans, 5 Res Judicatae 29 (1951). Reprinted by permission of the publisher.

Morse, Stephen J., Undiminished Confusion in Diminished Capacity, 75 Journal of Criminal Law and Criminology 1 (1984). Reprinted by special permission of Northwestern University School of Law, Journal of Criminal Law and Criminology and the author.

Murphy, Jeffrie, Marxism and Retribution, 2 Philosophy & Public Affairs 217 (Spring 1973). Copyright © 1973 Princeton University Press. Reprinted by permission of Princeton University Press.

New York State Task Force on Life and the Law, When Death Is Sought: Assisted Suicide and Euthanasia in the Medical Context, 1994. New York State Department of Health, Health Education Services, Task Force Reports.

Noonan, John T., Book Review, 29 Stanford Law Review 363 (1977). Copyright

© 1977 by the Board of Trustees of Leland Stanford Jr. University, Reprinted by permission.

Note, A Rationale of the Law Aggravated Theft, 54 Columbia Law Review 84 (1954). This article originally appeared at 54 Columbia Law Review 84 (1954). Reprinted by permission.

Note, Developments in the Law — Corporate Crime: Regulating Corporate Behavior through Criminal Sanction, 92 Harvard Law Review 1227 (1979). Copyright © 1979 by the Harvard Law Review Association. Reprinted by permission.

Pearce, R. (Jack), Theft by False Promises, 101 University of Pennsylvania Law Review 967 (1953). Copyright © 1953 by the University of Pennsylvania Law Review. Reprinted by permission.

Perry, Samuel, Allen Frances & John Clarkin, A DSM-III Casebook of Differential Therapeutics (1985). Reprinted by permission.

Pillsbury, Samuel, Crimes of Indifference, 49 Rutgers Law Review 105 (1996). Reprinted by permission.

Pillsbury, Samuel, Judging Evil: Rethinking the Law of Murder and Manslaughter (1998), New York University Press. Copyright © 1998. Reprinted by permission.

Pillsbury, Samuel, Evil and the Law of Murder, 24 U. C. Davis Law Review 437 (1990). Copyright © 1990 by the Regents of University of California. Reprinted by permission.

Radzinowicz, Leon & J. W. C. Turner, A Study of Punishment I: Introductory Essay, 21 Canadian Bar Review 91 (1943). Reprinted by permission of the Canadian Bar Review.

Rapaport, Elizabeth, The Death Penalty and Gender Discrimination, 25 Law & Society Review 367 No. 2 (1991). Reprinted by permission of the Law and Society Association.

Restak, Richard, The Fiction of the "Reasonable Man," Washington Post, May 17, 1987. Reprinted by permission of the author.

Robertson, John, Respect for Life in Bioethical Dilemmas, 45 Cleveland State Law Review 329 (1997). Reprinted by permission.

Robinson, Paul H. & John Darley, The Utility of Desert, 91 Northwestern University Law Review. Reprinted by special permission of Northwestern University School of Law, Law Review and the author. Copyright © Paul H. Robinson.

Salmond, J. W., Jurisprudence (1930, 8th ed.) Copyright © 1930. Reprinted with permission of Sweet & Maxwell Ltd.

Schneider, Elizabeth, Describing and Changing: Women's Self-Defense Work and the Problem of Expert Testimony on Battering, 9 Women's Rights Law Reporter 195 (1986). Reprinted with permission of the author.

Schulhofer, Stephen J., Attempt, in Encyclopedia of Crime and Justice 97 (1983). Copyright © by The Free Press. Reprinted by permission of The Gale Group.

Schulhofer, Stephen J., Due Process of Sentencing, 128 University of Pennsylvania Law Review 733 (1980). Copyright © 1980 by the University of Pennsylvania Law Review. Reprinted by permission of the publisher and the author.

Schulhofer, Stephen J., "Taking Sexual Autonomy Seriously: Rape Law and Beyond," 11 Law and Philosophy 35 (1992). Reprinted with kind permission of Kluwer Academic Publishers.

Schulhofer, Stephen J., The Gender Question in Criminal Law, 7 Social Philosophy and Public Policy 105 (1990). © Social Philosophy & Policy 1990. Reprinted with permission of Blackwell Publishers.

Schulhofer, Stephen J., Harm and Punishment: A Critique of Emphasis on the Results of Conduct in the Criminal Law, 122 University of Pennsylvania Law Review 1497 (1974). Copyright © 1974 University of Pennsylvania Law Review. Reprinted by permission of the publisher and William S. Hein & Company, Inc.

Schulhofer, Stephen J., excerpts from Sexual Bargaining, in Unwanted Sex: The Culture Of Intimidation And The Failure Of Law (1998). Reprinted by permission of the publishers Cambridge, Mass.: Harvard University Press, Copyright © 1998 by the President and Fellows of Harvard College.

Sentelle, David D., RICO: The Monster That Ate Jurisprudence, pp. 5-13 of the Lecture to the CATO Institute, Oct. 18, 1989. Reprinted by permission.

Smith, J. C., Liability for Omission in Criminal Law, 14 Legal Studies 88 (1984). Copyright Society of Public Teachers of Law. Reprinted by permission.

Smith, John C., Comment on R. v. Thornton, 1996 Criminal Law Review 597. Reprinted by permission of Sweet & Maxwell Ltd.

Smith, John C., Comment on Morhall, 1995 Criminal Law Review 891. Reprinted by permission of Sweet & Maxwell Ltd.

Smith John C., Two Problems in Criminal Attempts, 70 Harvard Law Review 422. Copyright © 1957 by the Harvard Law Review Association. Reprinted by permission.

Stanko, Elizabeth A., Intimate Intrusions (1985). Reprinted by permission of Thomson Publishing Services Ltd.

Steiker, Carol S., Jordan M. Steiker, Sober Second Thoughts: Reflections on Two Decades of Constitutional Regulation of Capital Punishment, 109 Harvard Law Review 355 (1995). Reprinted by permission.

Stone, Alan A., Law, Psychiatry and Morality (1984). Reprinted by permission of the author and the American Psychiatric Press, Inc.

Sykes, Gresham M., The Society of Captives (1971). Copyright © 1971 by Princeton University Press. Reprinted by permission of Princeton University Press.

Tebo, Margaret, Guilty By Reason of Title, 70 American Bar Association Journal 44 (May 2000). Copyright © by the American Bar Association. All rights reserved. Reprinted with permission from the ABA Journal, The Lawyer's Magazine, published by the American Bar Association.

Thomas, Clarence, Crime and Punishment — and Personal Responsibility. Reprinted with permission.

Tomkovicz, James, The Endurance of the Felony-Murder Rule: A Study of the Forces That Shape Our Criminal Law, 51 Washington & Lee Law Review 1429 (1994). Reprinted by permission.

Underwood, Barbara D., The Thumb on the Scales of Justice: Burdens of Persuasion in Criminal Cases, 86 Yale Law Journal 1299 (1977). Reprinted by permission of The Yale Law Journal Company and William S. Hein Company from The Yale Law Journal, Vol. 86, pages 1299-1348.

Von Hirsch, Andrew, and Lisa Maher, Should Penal Rehabilitationism Be Revived, Criminal Justice Ethics, Vol. 11, No. 1 (Winter/Spring 1992), pages 25–30. Reprinted by permission of The Institute for Criminal Justice Ethics, 555 West 57th Street, Suite 601, New York, NY, 10019-1029.

Wasserstrom, Richard, Lawyers as Professionals: Some Moral Issues, 5 Human Rights 1 (1975). Reprinted by permission.

Williams, Glanville, Criminal Law: The General Part (2d edition 1961). Reprinted by permission of Sweet & Maxwell Ltd.

Williams, Glanville, Finis for Novus Actus, 48 Cambridge Law Journal 391 (1989). Reprinted by permission of Cambridge University Press.

Williams, Glanville, The Mental Element in Crime (1965). Copyright © The Magnes Press. Reprinted by permission.

Williams, Glanville, Police Control of Intending Criminals, [1955] Criminal Law Review 6. Reprinted by permission of Sweet & Maxwell Ltd.

Williams, Glanville, Textbook of the Criminal Law (2d ed. 1983). Reprinted with permission of Sweet & Maxwell Ltd.

Williams, Glanville, The Unresolved Problem of Recklessness, 8 Legal Studies 74 (1988). Copyright Society of Public Teachers of Law. Reprinted by permission.

Yeager, Daniel B., A Radical Community of Aid: A Rejoinder to Opponents of Affirmative Duties to Help Strangers, 71 Washington University Law Quarterly 1 (1993). Reprinted with permission.

Younger, Irving, The Facts of a Cases, 3 University of Arkansas at Little Rock Law Review 345 (1980). Reprinted by permission.

Zimring, Franklin E., Making the Punishment Fit the Crime: A Consumer's Guide to Sentencing Reform. Hastings Center Report, December 1976. Reproduced by permission. Copyright © The Hastings Center.

CRIMINAL LAW AND ITS PROCESSES

CASES AND MATERIALS

CHAPTER 1

HOW GUILT IS ESTABLISHED

A. THE STRUCTURE OF THE CRIMINAL JUSTICE SYSTEM

PRESIDENT'S COMMISSION ON LAW ENFORCEMENT AND THE ADMINISTRATION OF JUSTICE, THE CHALLENGE OF CRIME IN A FREE SOCIETY

7-12, 91-107, 127-137, 141-150 (1967)[1]

Any criminal justice system is an apparatus society uses to enforce the standards of conduct necessary to protect individuals and the community. It operates by apprehending, prosecuting, convicting, and sentencing those members of the community who violate the basic rules of group existence. The action taken against lawbreakers is designed to serve three purposes beyond the immediately punitive one. It removes dangerous people from the community; it deters others from criminal behavior; and it gives society an opportunity to attempt to transform lawbreakers into law-abiding citizens. What most significantly distinguishes the system of one country from that of another is the extent and the form of the protections it offers individuals in the process of determining guilt and imposing punishment. Our system of justice deliberately sacrifices much in efficiency and even in effectiveness in order to preserve local autonomy and to protect the individual. . . .

The criminal justice system has three separately organized parts — the police, the courts, and corrections — and each has distinct tasks. However, these parts are by no means independent of each other. What each one does and how it does it has a direct effect on the work of the others. The courts must deal, and can only deal, with those whom the police arrest; the business of corrections is with those delivered to it by the courts. How successfully corrections reforms convicts determines whether they will once again become police business and influences the

1. For convenience of exposition, we have added some headings and altered the sequence of certain paragraphs in this excerpt. Though criminal justice problems have changed in many respects since the publication of this report, it provides a useful overview of the organization and functioning of the criminal justice system, and the passages excerpted here are still accurate as descriptions of current conditions. Where appropriate, we have provided more recent information in brackets and in the footnotes. Except as otherwise noted, current statistics were drawn from U.S. Dept. of Justice, Bureau of Justice Statistics, Sourcebook of Criminal Justice Statistics—1998 (1999), and Federal Bureau of Investigation, Uniform Crime Reports — 1998 (1999).

sentences the judges pass; police activities are subject to court scrutiny and are often determined by court decisions. And so reforming or reorganizing any part or procedure of the system changes other parts or procedures. . . . A study of the system must begin by examining it as a whole. . . .

I. Agencies and Officials of the Criminal Justice System

A. The Police

At the very beginning of the process — or, more properly, before the process begins at all — something happens that is . . . seldom recognized by the public: law enforcement policy is made by the policeman. For policemen cannot and do not arrest all the offenders they encounter. It is doubtful that they arrest most of them. A criminal code, in practice, is not a set of specific instructions to policemen but a more or less rough map of the territory in which policemen work. How an individual policeman moves around that territory depends largely on his personal discretion.

That a policeman's duties compel him to exercise personal discretion many times every day is evident. Crime does not look the same on the street as it does in a legislative chamber. How much noise or profanity makes conduct "disorderly" within the meaning of the law? When must a quarrel be treated as a criminal assault: at the first threat or at the first shove or at the first blow, or after blood is drawn, or when a serious injury is inflicted? How suspicious must conduct be before there is "probable cause," the constitutional basis for an arrest? Every policeman, however complete or sketchy his education, is an interpreter of the law.

Every policeman, too, is an arbiter of social values, for he meets situation after situation in which invoking criminal sanctions is a questionable line of action. It is obvious that a boy throwing rocks at a school's windows is committing the statutory offense of vandalism, but it is often not at all obvious whether a policeman will better serve the interests of the community and of the boy by taking the boy home to his parents or by arresting him. Who are the boy's parents? Can they control him? Is he a frequent offender who has responded badly to leniency? Is vandalism so epidemic in the neighborhood that he should be made a cautionary example? With juveniles especially, the police exercise great discretion.

Finally, the manner in which a policeman works is influenced by practical matters: the legal strength of the available evidence, the willingness of victims to press charges and of witnesses to testify, the temper of the community, the time and information at the policeman's disposal. Much is at stake in how the policeman exercises this discretion. If he judges conduct not suspicious enough to justify intervention, the chance to prevent a robbery, rape, or murder may be lost. If he overestimates the seriousness of a situation or his actions are controlled by panic or prejudice, he may hurt or kill someone unnecessarily. His actions may even touch off a riot.

It is in the cities that . . . social tensions are the most acute, that riots occur, that crime rates are the highest, that the fear of crime and the demand for effective action against it are the strongest. It is in the cities that a large proportion of American policemen work and that a large proportion of police money is spent. Though there are 40,000 separate law enforcement agencies in the Nation, 55 of them, the police departments of the cities of more than 250,000 population, employ almost one-third of all police personnel. . . .

The current police-population ratio of 1.7 policemen per thousand citizens obscures the many differences from city to city and region to region. Even the big-city ratio of 2.3 per thousand is misleading, for in San Diego there are 1.07 policemen per thousand citizens and in Boston 4.04.

There appears to be no correlation between the differing concentrations of police and the amount of crime committed, or the percentage of known crimes solved, in the various cities.[a]

At the same time it is apparent that, nationwide, the number of police has not kept pace with the relocation of the population and the attendant increases in crime and police responsibility. . . .

[By 1996 the national police-population ratio had risen to 2.3 police officers per thousand citizens and a total of 3.0 police employees, including civilian employees, per thousand. But there were still wide variations from city to city and from region to region.] . . .

B. PROSECUTORS

The key administrative officer in the processing of cases is the prosecutor. Theoretically the examination of the evidence against a defendant by a judge at a preliminary hearing, and its reexamination by a grand jury, are important parts of the process. Practically they seldom are because a prosecutor seldom has any difficulty in making a prima facie case against a defendant. [M]uch more often than not grand juries indict precisely as prosecutors ask them to. The prosecutor wields almost undisputed sway over the pretrial progress of most cases. He decides whether to press a case or drop it. He determines the specific charge against a defendant. When the charge is reduced, as it is in as many as two-thirds of all cases in some cities, the prosecutor is usually the official who reduces it. . . .

The prosecutor's discretion to decide what charge to bring against, and what disposition to recommend for, an offender is indicative of his crucial position in the law enforcement system. . . . Except for the judge he is the most influential court official.

Yet many prosecutors in this country are part-time officers. They generally are elected or selected on a partisan political basis and serve for relatively short terms.[b] In many places the office traditionally has been a stepping-stone to higher political office or the bench. Prosecutors in most places are so poorly paid that they must, and are expected to, engage in private law practice. This creates inevitable conflicts between the demands of the office and of private practice. It can lead to undesirable potential conflicts of interest in dealings with other attorneys, judges, and members of the community. As the participation of defense

a. An important study, based on experimental variations in Kansas City police patrol patterns, has provided substantial support for this hypothesis. See G. Kelling et al., The Kansas City Preventive Patrol Experiment: A Technical Report (1974). — Eds.

b. As of 1996, over 95 percent of all chief prosecutors were elected officials; only the federal government and four states (Alaska, Connecticut, Delaware, and New Jersey) chose their chief prosecutors by appointment. Large cities always have a chief prosecutor employed full-time and a large staff of full-time assistants, but overall 25 percent of American jurisdictions do not have a full-time chief prosecutor, and 40 percent of the chief prosecutors have no legal assistants. See U.S. Dept. of Justice, Bureau of Justice Statistics, Prosecutors in State Courts, 1996, pp. 1-3 (July 1998). — Eds.

counsel in criminal cases grows, the need to improve the quality of the prosecution becomes increasingly urgent. . . .

C. THE JUDICIARY

The Magistrate

In direct contrast to the policeman, the magistrate before whom a suspect is first brought usually exercises less discretion than the law allows him. He is entitled to inquire into the facts of the case, into whether there are grounds for holding the accused. He seldom does. He seldom can. The more promptly an arrested suspect is brought into magistrate's court, the less likelihood there is that much information about the arrest other than the arresting officer's statement will be available to the magistrate. Moreover many magistrates, especially in big cities, have such congested calendars that it is almost impossible for them to subject any case but an extraordinary one to prolonged scrutiny. . . .

Judges

The quality of the judiciary in large measure determines the quality of justice. It is the judge who tries disputed cases and who supervises and reviews negotiated dispositions. Through sentencing the judge determines the treatment given to an offender. Through the exercise of his administrative power over his court he determines its efficiency, fairness, and effectiveness. No procedural or administrative reforms will help the courts, and no reorganizational plan will avail unless judges have the highest qualifications, are fully trained and competent, and have high standards of performance.

Selection of Judges. Methods for the selection of judges vary from jurisdiction to jurisdiction, and some States use different methods of selection for upper court judges than for lower court judges. In [28] States judges are appointed either by the Governor or the legislature; in some of these States they are first appointed and then must run for election on their records; in [14] States they are elected without party labels, and in [8] States they are elected on a partisan basis. In a number of States there is a professional or nonpartisan screening process that develops an identified group of professionally qualified persons from which all nominations or appointments are made, or that reviews proposed nominations or appointments for professional competence. Sometimes this process is required by State constitution or statute; sometimes it is informal. Sometimes it is employed for all judges, sometimes only for certain kinds of judges. It is employed least often in the States in which judges are elected in partisan contests. . . .

The Lower Courts

In many big cities the congestion that produces both undue delay and unseemly haste is vividly exemplified in the lower courts — the courts that dispose of cases that are typically called "misdemeanors" or "petty offenses," and that process the first stages of felony cases. The importance of these courts in the prevention or deterrence of crime is incalculably great, for these are the courts that process the overwhelming majority of offenders. . . .

The Nation's court system was designed originally for small, rural communities. The basic unit of court organization in most States remains the county, and about two-thirds of the counties in this country still are predominantly rural in nature. But most Americans live in an urban environment, in large communities with highly mobile populations that are being subjected to particular stress. It is the urban courts that particularly need reform. . . .

[U]ntil legislation [in 1966] increased the number of judges, the District of Columbia Court of General Sessions had four judges to process the preliminary stages of more than 1,500 felony cases, 7,500 serious misdemeanor cases, and 38,000 petty offenses and an equal number of traffic offenses per year. An inevitable consequence of volume that large is the almost total preoccupation in such a court with the movement of cases. The calendar is long, speed often is substituted for care, and casually arranged out-of-court compromise too often is substituted for adjudication. Inadequate attention tends to be given to the individual defendant, whether in protecting his rights, sifting the facts at trial, deciding the social risk he presents, or determining how to deal with him after conviction. . . . [This problem remains equally serious or even more serious today. In 1998, there were an average of 3766 criminal case dispositions per judge. In a single year (1995) the average number of felony case filings per judge was 487 in Los Angeles, 516 in San Francisco, and 776 in Denver.]

D. CORRECTIONS

The correctional apparatus to which guilty defendants are delivered is in every respect the most isolated part of the criminal justice system. Much of it is physically isolated . . . in rural areas, remote from the courts where the institutions' inmates were tried and from the communities where they lived. The correctional apparatus is isolated in the sense that its officials do not have everyday working relationships with officials from the system's other branches, like those that commonly exist between policemen and prosecutors, or prosecutors and judges. . . . Finally, it is isolated from the public partly by its invisibility and physical remoteness; partly by the inherent lack of drama in most of its activities, but perhaps most importantly by the fact that the correctional apparatus is often used — or misused — by both the criminal justice system and the public as a rug under which disturbing problems and people can be swept.

The most striking fact about the correctional apparatus today is that, although the rehabilitation of criminals is presumably its major purpose, the custody of criminals is actually its major task. On any given day there are well over a million people being "corrected" in America, two-thirds of them on probation or parole and one-third of them in prisons or jails. However, prisons and jails are where four-fifths of correctional money is spent and where nine-tenths of correctional employees work.

[This situation has persisted. There are now nearly two million prisoners in federal and state custody at any given time, but these account for only 30 percent of the total offenders subject to "correction"; more than 4.1 million offenders are on probation or parole.

[The population subject to criminal justice correction has grown at a striking rate. At the end of 1998, more than 5.9 million people (one of every 38 American adults) were subject to some form of criminal justice system control, including 3.4 million offenders on probation (a 27 percent increase since 1990) and 705,000 offenders on parole (a 25 percent increase since 1990). The growth in prison populations has been especially striking. There were 1.2 million offenders in state or federal prisons, an increase of 69 percent since 1990 and 265 percent since 1980.[c] In addition, at mid-year 1999 there were a record 606,000 inmates held in local jails, an increase of 50 percent since 1990.[d]

[The precipitous growth of the corrections system has had a particularly severe impact on young black males. Recent studies in the District of Columbia suggest that at any one time, 42 percent of the city's black males aged 18 to 35 are subject to some form of criminal justice system control (incarceration, probation, parole, or bond for release pending disposition of criminal charges).[e] For Baltimore the corresponding figure is 56 percent.[f] For an inner city black male, the lifetime risk of arrest and incarceration may approach 90 percent.[g]]

[F]ewer than one-fifth of the people who work in State prisons and local jails have jobs that are not essentially either custodial or administrative in character. Many jails have nothing but custodial and administrative personnel. Of course many jails are crowded with defendants who have not been able to furnish bail and who are not considered by the law to be appropriate objects of rehabilitation because it has not yet been determined that they are criminals who need it.

What this emphasis on custody means in practice is that the enormous potential of the correctional apparatus for making creative decisions about its treatment of convicts is largely unfulfilled. This is true not only of offenders in custody but of offenders on probation and parole. Most authorities agree that while probationers and parolees need varying degrees and kinds of supervision, an average of no more than 35 cases per officer is necessary for effective attention; 97 percent of all officers handling adults have larger caseloads than that. . . .

II. Criminal Justice Procedures

A. Overview of the Steps in the Criminal Justice Process

The popular, or even the lawbook, theory of everyday criminal process oversimplifies in some respects and overcomplicates in others what usually happens. That theory is that when an infraction of the law occurs, a policeman finds, if he can, the probable offender, arrests him and brings him promptly before a magistrate. If the offense is minor, the magistrate disposes of it forthwith; if it is serious, he holds the defendant for further action and admits him to bail. The case then is turned over to a prosecuting attorney who charges the defendant with a specific statutory crime. This charge is subject to review by a judge at a preliminary hearing of the evidence and in many places if the offense charged is a felony, by a grand jury that can dismiss the charge, or affirm it by delivering it to a

c. See U.S. Dept. of Justice, Bureau of Justice Statistics, Probation and Parole in the United States, 1998, p. 1 (Aug. 1999). — Eds.

d. See U.S. Dept. of Justice, Bureau of Justice Statistics, Prison and Jail Inmates at Midyear 1999, p. 2 (April 2000). — Eds.

e. See Jerome G. Miller, Hobbling a Generation: Young African American Males in D.C.'s Criminal Justice System (Natl. Center on Institutions & Alternatives 1992); Mark Mauer, Young Black Men and the Criminal Justice System: A Growing National Problem 8 (The Sentencing Project 1990). — Eds.

f. Jerome G. Miller, Hobbling a Generation: Young African American Males in the Criminal Justice System of America's Cities: Baltimore, Maryland (Natl. Center on Institutions & Alternatives 1992). — Eds.

g. Miller, supra footnote f. — Eds.

judge in the form of an indictment. If the defendant pleads "not guilty" to the charge he comes to trial; the facts of his case are marshaled by prosecuting and defense attorneys and presented, under the supervision of a judge, through witnesses, to a jury. If the jury finds the defendant guilty, he is sentenced by the judge to a term in prison, where a systematic attempt to convert him into a law-abiding citizen is made, or to a term of probation, under which he is permitted to live in the community as long as he behaves himself.

Some cases do proceed much like that, especially those involving offenses that are generally considered "major": serious acts of violence or thefts of large amounts of property. However, not all major cases follow this course, and, in any event, the bulk of the daily business of the criminal justice system consists of offenses that are not major — of breaches of the peace, crimes of vice, petty thefts, assaults arising from domestic or street-corner or barroom disputes. These and most other cases are disposed of in much less formal and much less deliberate ways. . . .

B. THE INITIAL STAGES OF A CRIMINAL CASE

Investigation

When patrol fails to prevent a crime or apprehend the criminal while he is committing it, the police must rely upon investigation. Every sizable department has a corps of investigative specialists — detectives — whose job is to solve crimes by questioning victims, suspects, and witnesses, by accumulating physical evidence at the scene of the crime, and by tracing stolen property or vehicles associated with the crime. In practically every department the caseloads carried by detectives are too heavy to allow them to follow up thoroughly more than a small percentage of the cases assigned them. In other words, a great many cases are unsolved by default — or, at least, time will not permit a determination of whether or not they are solvable. . . .

In the present state of police knowledge and organization many crimes are, in fact, not solvable. In the great majority of cases, personal identification by a victim or witness is the *only* clue to the identity of the criminal. The Commission analyzed 1,905 crimes reported during January of 1966 in Los Angeles, which has a notably well-trained and efficient police department. The police were furnished a suspect's name in 349 of these cases, and 301 were resolved either by arrest or in some other way — either the victim would not prosecute, subsequent investigation disclosed that the reported crime was not actually a crime, or a prosecutor declined to press the case. Of the 1,375 crimes for which no suspect was named, only 181 cases were cleared. Since crimes against the person are more likely to be named-suspect crimes than crimes against property, it is natural that a much higher proportion of them are solved. In 1965, 78 percent of reported serious crimes against property were never solved. . . .

[FBI statistics for 1997 indicate that of the violent crimes (murder, aggravated assault, forcible rape, and robbery) reported or otherwise known to the police, 48 percent were cleared by an arrest. Of the serious property crimes (burglary, motor vehicle theft, and other larceny-theft), only 18 percent of the offenses known to the police were cleared by an arrest. For cities over one million population, only 38 percent of violent offenses and 11 percent of serious property offenses were cleared.] . . .

The Diversion of Cases before Charge

The limited statistics available indicate that approximately one-half of those arrested are dismissed by the police, a prosecutor, or a magistrate at an early stage of the case. Some of these persons are released because they did not commit the acts they were originally suspected of having committed, or cannot be proved to have committed them, or committed them on legally defensible grounds. The police can arrest on "probable cause," while conviction requires proof "beyond a reasonable doubt." Therefore, some justified arrests cannot lead to prosecution and conviction.

However, others who are released probably did commit the offenses for which they were arrested. In some instances offenders who could and should be convicted are released simply because of an overload of work, or inadequate investigation in the prosecutor's office. In other cases the police, or more often prosecutors, have exercised [discretion] to decline to prosecute offenders . . . who present clear medical, mental, or social problems that can be better dealt with outside the criminal process. . . . First offenders are often dealt with in this way. So are persons whose offenses arise from drinking or mental problems, if the offenses are minor. So are many cases of assault or theft within families or among friends, of passing checks with insufficient funds, of shoplifting when restitution is made, of statutory rape when both boy and girl are young, of automobile theft by teenagers for the purpose of joyriding. . . .

Pretrial Release

One-half or more of the defendants who are brought into a police or magistrate's court are released or convicted and sentenced within 24 hours of their arrest. The cases of the remainder, including all those against whom the accusation of a serious crime can be maintained, await final disposition for days or weeks or sometimes months, depending on the prosecutor's caseload, the gravity and complexity of the case, and the condition of the calendar in the court that will hear it.

The magistrate is empowered to decide whether or not such defendants will be released pending trial. [Traditionally, the device most often used to free an untried defendant and at the same time assure his or her appearance for trial was money bail. In this system, still in use in many areas, the court fixes the amount of a bond to be posted in cash or by a secured pledge; defendants able to post the required amount win their release and recover the sum upon appearance for trial. Defendants unable to raise the required amount usually attempt to secure the services of a bail-bond agency, which posts the necessary bond in return for a fixed fee, typically 10 percent of the total bail. In this system the bondsman's obligations are satisfied upon the defendant's appearance, but the 10 percent charge has to be paid by the defendant in any event.

[The money bail system is unsatisfactory in many respects. It results in confinement of large numbers of untried defendants, solely on account of inability to raise the required amounts. For those who can raise funds to pay the bondsman's fee, the system provides release but no financial incentive to appear. And in many localities the relationships between bail-bond agencies and court officials have been a source of malfeasance and corruption.

[During the 1960s and 1970s bail-reform projects were initiated in numerous cities around the country. The principal aims of these projects were to ascertain the kinds of community ties that would make defendants safe candidates for release without financial guarantees, to establish procedures for expeditiously collecting the information necessary to identify such defendants, and to develop a better system of financial guarantees for defendants who could not qualify for release on any other basis. Pretrial release projects now functioning in more than 100 cities assist the local magistrates in identifying defendants who can be released without money bail and often provide follow-up to help insure that the defendant returns for any scheduled appearances. When money bail is used, many jurisdictions now follow a "10 percent plan," under which the defendant is permitted to post directly with the court 10 percent of the face amount of the bail bond, and most or all of this sum is refundable when the defendant appears for trial. These reforms led to dramatic increases in the proportion of defendants released rather than detained for trial.[h] Nevertheless, traditional money bail survives in many localities as the primary avenue of pretrial release.

[The Bail Reform Act of 1984, 18 U.S.C. §§1341-1350, expressly authorizes preventive detention prior to trial in federal criminal prosecutions, on a finding that "no condition or conditions [of release] will reasonably assure the appearance of the [defendant] as required and the safety of any other person and the community." §3142(e). The Supreme Court upheld the constitutionality of the preventive detention provisions in United States v. Salerno, 481 U.S. 739 (1987).]

C. THE GUILTY PLEA

Most defendants who are convicted — as many as 90 percent in some jurisdictions — are not tried. They plead guilty, often as the result of negotiations about the charge or the sentence. . . . A plea negotiation can be, and often is in a minor case, a hurried conversation in a courthouse hallway. In grave cases it can be a series of elaborate conferences over the course of weeks in which facts are thoroughly discussed and alternatives carefully explored. Most often the negotiations are between a prosecutor and defense counsel, but sometimes a magistrate or a police officer or the defendant himself is involved. In some courts there are no plea negotiations at all. There almost never are negotiations in the cases of petty offenders. And, of course, many guilty pleas are not the result of negotiations. . . .

D. THE TRIAL

. . . The cases decided at trial are only a small fraction of the total of cases, but they are most important to the process because they set standards for the conduct of all cases. The trial decides the hard legal issues, and reviews and rules on claims of official abuse. . . .

E. SENTENCING . . .

Although the criminal trial on the issue of guilt is a strictly formal procedure, the determination of what is to be done with a convicted offender is often a rather informal one. A judge, when he sentences, needs facts about the offender and his offense. Both will be absent in those many instances when conviction has resulted

h. For example, from 1962 to 1971, the percentage of defendants who were detained throughout the period prior to trial dropped from 52 percent to 33 percent in felony cases and from 21 percent to only 12 percent in major misdemeanor cases. See W. Thomas, Bail Reform in America (1976). — Eds.

A general view of The Criminal Justice System

This chart seeks to present a simple yet comprehensive view of the movement of cases through the criminal justice system. Procedures in individual jurisdictions may vary from the pattern shown here. The differing weights of line indicate the relative volumes of cases disposed of at various points in the system, but this is only suggestive since no nationwide data of this sort exists.

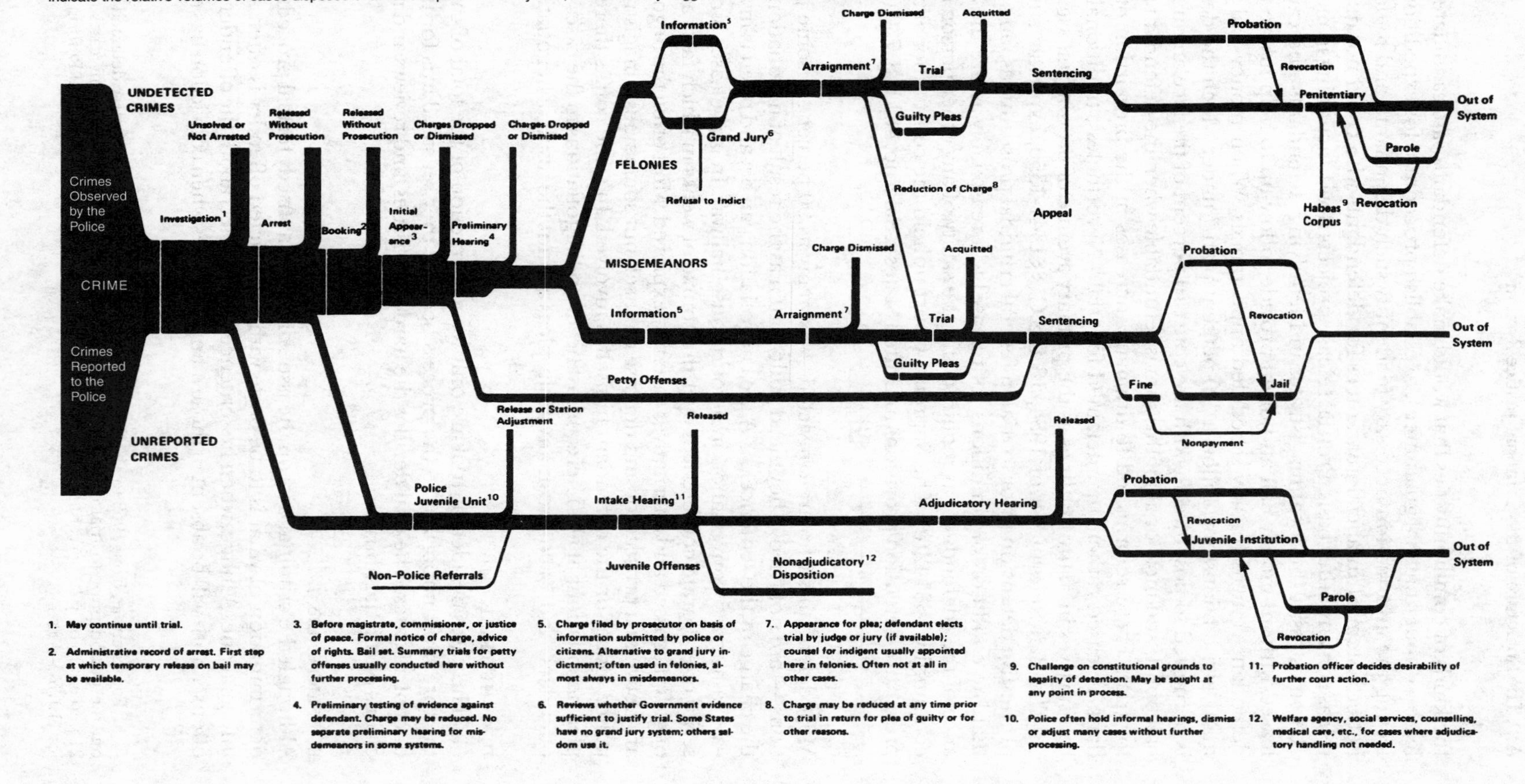

1. May continue until trial.
2. Administrative record of arrest. First step at which temporary release on bail may be available.
3. Before magistrate, commissioner, or justice of peace. Formal notice of charge, advice of rights. Bail set. Summary trials for petty offenses usually conducted here without further processing.
4. Preliminary testing of evidence against defendant. Charge may be reduced. No separate preliminary hearing for misdemeanors in some systems.
5. Charge filed by prosecutor on basis of information submitted by police or citizens. Alternative to grand jury indictment; often used in felonies, almost always in misdemeanors.
6. Reviews whether Government evidence sufficient to justify trial. Some States have no grand jury system; others seldom use it.
7. Appearance for plea; defendant elects trial by judge or jury (if available); counsel for indigent usually appointed here in felonies. Often not at all in other cases.
8. Charge may be reduced at any time prior to trial in return for plea of guilty or for other reasons.
9. Challenge on constitutional grounds to legality of detention. May be sought at any point in process.
10. Police often hold informal hearings, dismiss or adjust many cases without further processing.
11. Probation officer decides desirability of further court action.
12. Welfare agency, social services, counselling, medical care, etc., for cases where adjudicatory handling not needed.

from a plea of guilty and the court lacks, or has inadequate facilities for preparing, presentence reports. The judge then must rely on the necessarily incomplete and biased oral statements of the prosecutor, defense counsel, and defendant.

III. THE FLOW OF CASES THROUGH THE SYSTEM

[The chart presented on the previous page, taken from the report of the President's Commission at page 8, sets forth in simplified form the flow of cases through the criminal justice system and dramatically illustrates the filtering process through which the vast majority of all cases are winnowed out prior to trial.]

GEOFFREY C. HAZARD, JR., CRIMINAL JUSTICE SYSTEM: OVERVIEW, in 2 Encyclopedia of Crime and Justice 450, 454-456 (S. H. Kadish ed. 1983): [In this essay, the author identifies four significant characteristics of the criminal justice system.] First, [the system] is required to deal with a large and never-ending flow of cases. Even though the system attempts to individualize its response to each offender, and in theory is supposed to treat each case as though it stood alone under the law, the process is in fact one of mass production. This is not to say that the system was planned as a mass-production system. Quite the contrary, many difficulties with it arise from the discrepancy between the fact of mass production and the ideal that each case can be considered on its own merit.

A second general observation is that the system is pervaded by exercise of loosely controlled discretion, which is both systemic and particular. Systemically, discretion is exercised to mediate between the high incidence of crime and the modest resources available to respond to it. Decisions must be made as to the allocation of the system's resources. These decisions . . . often . . . are not based upon open deliberation. Thus, for example, no legislative act or mayoral directive says that the police shall devote intensive effort to investigating crimes against police officers, or that they shall deal with rape only where the victim is willing to carry the prosecution all the way through, but such policies in fact exist in most communities. . . .

Exercise of discretion is particular in that subsystems and individual officials within the system have a high degree of autonomy in performing their functions. A policeman is assigned a beat, but the patrol of the beat is usually under minimal supervision from superior police officers; the patrolman's allocation of time and effort is not subject to anything like the direction given an ordinary office or production-line worker, for example. In prosecutor's offices, individual deputy prosecutors generally have considerable discretion in deciding on the types and quality of cases that should be fully prosecuted. . . . [J]udges . . . have broad professional discretion in the exercise of their functions, particularly in sentencing. . . .

Taken as a whole, the system is subject to pervasive formal legal controls, but it is also characterized by the pervasive exercise of unsupervised discretion. There are dynamic relationships between these two phenomena: because legal rules so thoroughly govern official action, it is assumed that the official actions are under control and that higher administrative controls are unnecessary; and the rigidity of legal controls creates incentives to seek waivers, a fact that in turn entails exercise of discretion.

[A third point concerns balkanization.] The administrative structure of the criminal justice system is extremely decentralized. There are about forty thousand different public police forces in the United States, one for almost every city and for many villages, and usually a separate one in every county. In some large cities there are several different police agencies, such as transit police or housing police, in addition to the municipal police as such. In virtually all states, the prosecutorial function is centered at the county level in the office of the district attorney. Many large cities have a further division of prosecutorial authority in that municipal legal departments prosecute misdemeanors. The judiciary is usually organized along county lines. . . . In any case, the work load of judges and supporting court staff is unbalanced and poorly managed in many jurisdictions.

The correctional system is sharply divided in almost all states between local authorities and state authorities. . . .

The foregoing description if anything understates the lack of administrative coordination in criminal justice. A complete account would require describing the separation between various federal criminal justice agencies and their state counterparts, and between state-level criminal justice agencies, such as the state police and the state attorney general's office, and their local counterparts. It would also describe how these separations impede vital routines, such as controlling the flow of cases from one subsystem to another, coordinating allocation of resources, and using common terminology and comparable statistics. . . .

[A fourth] generalization is that the degree of professionalism and competence in the broadest sense varies considerably throughout the country. The variance is probably much less than it was around 1960, and certainly less than it was in 1930. The day of the bumpkin sheriff or of the judge who is law unto himself has virtually passed. Modern communication and interaction disseminate techniques and standards of performance despite administrative boundaries. Nevertheless, variance remains and has important consequences. "Professionalism" implies certain values, particularly impersonality, neutrality, and formal rationality in goals and techniques. The fact that professionalism is unevenly distributed among various elements in the system indicates, among other things, that there are corresponding differences of public opinion on the underlying issues of value.

B. THE PROCESS OF PROOF

1. *An Overview of Criminal Trial Procedure*

IRVING YOUNGER, THE FACTS OF A CASE, 3 U. Ark. L. Rev. 345, 345-347 (1980): The phrase is "the facts of a case." In that or some variant form each of us heard it during the first class we attended on the first day of our first term at law school. "Mr. Smith," the instructor in torts may have said, "what were the facts in Brown v. Kendall?" Or in property, "Miss Jones, state the facts of Armory v. Delamirie." And we palpitatingly did. . . . "The facts were," recites Mr. Smith, "that Kendall tried to separate two fighting dogs by beating them with a stick. He raised the stick over his shoulder and struck Brown in the eye. Brown sued Kendall for the resulting damages." "In the *Armory* case," says Miss Jones, "a chimney sweep found a jewel in the dust. He took it to a jeweler to be examined and when the jeweler refused to return it, sued for it in King's Bench." Mr. Smith and Miss Jones know that these are the facts of the case because the opinion in the casebook says they are. How the author of the opinion came by those facts is a question beyond their fathoming on that first day of law school, and understandably. . . . The facts, we tend to think at the beginning, are like acorns on an oak tree. When they are ripe, they drop to the ground. If you want some, just bend down and pick them up. Observe how they are arranged. Should they fall into the pattern we designate "negligence," Brown wins his suit against Kendall. If the pattern is that of one of the bundle of rights called "property," Armory prevails over Delamirie. Why, there's nothing to it but learning the patterns. That, I repeat, is what we tend to think at the beginning. It is what teachers of the law seem to have thought for a very long time.

With experience and reflection comes a deeper comprehension. Facts do not grow on trees, we learn. They must be investigated and proved. Cases are more often won before a jury than in the appellate courtroom. Sometimes the facts fall into a preexisting pattern, but sometimes a pattern is devised to their configuration, in accordance with whatever their arrangement happens to be. The facts, in short, are just as obscure as the law, just as malleable, just as controversial, and in determining the outcome of a lawsuit or the elaboration of a rule, more important than paltry logic.

RICHARD M. MARKUS, A THEORY OF TRIAL ADVOCACY, 56 Tulane L. Rev. 95, 97-99 (1981): Commentators have variously described a trial as an attempt to transport jurors to the time and place of the disputed event, to recreate the disputed event or at least to explain that event with maximum accuracy. All of these descriptions are more metaphorical than material. A trial presents selected witnesses who recite selected portions of their respective memories, concerning selected observations of the disputed event. These multiple selections are referred to here as the abstraction process. At each stage of the abstraction process, the tale is blurred or altered by inadvertent or deliberate errors. . . .

The event itself comprises unlimited detail. . . . Manifestly, the recited data are a fraction of the remembered data, which is a fraction of the observed data, which is a fraction of the total data for the event.

NOTE ON CREDIBILITY PROBLEMS

Guilt probably turns more frequently on the resolution of disputes about the facts than it turns on the resolution of subtle legal questions about the meaning or scope of a penal prohibition. Accordingly, a major aspect of the jury's fact-finding function is to decide which witnesses are telling the truth. But how does the jury make these credibility determinations? In the classic courtroom dramas of stage and screen, the false witness gives himself away by shifty eyes, a sweaty brow, or a mass of obvious contradictions; if not, cross-examination brilliantly exposes the lie. In everyday trials, the need to choose among conflicting stories is just as pressing, but the clues to truth are more elusive. The jury's crucial credibility findings become problematic. Consider the following studies.

New York Task Force on Women in the Courts, Report 183-186 (N.Y. Office of Court Administration 1986): Witnesses' testimony is the principal ingredient of the factfinding process. To be credited, the witness must be credible. Credibility, in turn, may not always depend on the witness's objective candor and reliability for, as Justice Benjamin N. Cardozo once observed: "The forces of which Judges . . . avail to shape the form and the content of their judgments" include "the likes and dislikes, the predilections and the prejudices, the complex of instincts and emotions and habits and convictions, which make the man, whether he be litigant or judge."[290]

Women have long been stereotyped by society as impulsive, emotional, irrational, and unpredictable. In a courtroom setting this may translate into women being presumptively viewed as incredible witnesses. . . . The Task Force heard compelling testimony at the public hearings from lawyers, legislators, lay advocates and scholars that women litigants' claims are subject to undue skepticism in New York's Courts. [Elsewhere in its report (at 183 n. 289) the Task Force noted:] There is a substantial body of social science research showing that in a variety of contexts, both women and men perceive women as being less credible than men in all of the senses of the term as defined here, and that recent years have by no means eliminated these attitudes despite the many other advances towards equality. A Kent State University Professor in 1985 [conducted an] experiment in which 150 male and 150 female subjects were randomly assigned to read an essay with the author's name indicated as either John T. McKay, J. T. McKay or Joan T. McKay and asked to rate it on such qualities as persuasiveness, intellectual depth and style. Although the essays were identical, those believed to have been written by "Joan" consistently received lower ratings from male and female readers than those believed to have been written by "John" or "J. T."

John M. Conley, William M. O'Barr & E. Allan Lind, The Power of Language: Presentational Style in the Courtroom, [1978] Duke L.J. 1375, 1375-1386: The rules of evidence control the content of testimony that may be introduced at trial. Those same rules, however, place relatively few constraints on *how* testimony is presented once it is deemed admissible. . . .

In order to discover the various testimony styles that occur frequently in trials, the authors conducted an extensive study of the speaking styles of actual courtroom witnesses. With the permission of the court, all criminal trials in the Superior Court of Durham County, North Carolina during the summer of 1974 were tape recorded. . . .

One empirically derived "style" of courtroom speech was . . . characterized by the frequent use of words and expressions that convey a lack of forcefulness in speaking. Among the specific features of this style is the abundant use of *hedges* (prefatory remarks such as "I think" and "It seems like"; appended remarks like "you know"; and modifiers such as "kinda" and "sort of"); *hesitation forms* (words and sounds that carry no substantive meaning but only fill possible speech pauses, such as "uh" "um" and "well"); *polite forms* (for example, the use of "sir" and "please"); and *question intonation* (making a declarative statement with rising intonation so as to convey uncertainty). An additional feature of this style is the frequent use of *intensifiers* (for example, "very," "definitely" and "surely") — words

290. B. Cardozo, The Nature of the Judicial Process at p. 167 (Yale Univ. 1921). . . .

that, though they normally increase the force of an assertion, may be so overused that they suggest that the speaker is not to be taken seriously in their absence. These features tended to occur together in the taped testimony, comprising a definite style in the delivery of testimony.

. . . A review of the tapes and notes of the trials revealed that witnesses of low social status — the poor and uneducated — were most likely to use this style of testimony. Female witnesses used the style more frequently than men. Because the incidence of use of this style was more common among those with little social power, it was termed the "powerless" style of testimony.

In marked contrast to the powerless style is a more straightforward manner of testifying. Those witnesses in the taped trials whose social status in court was higher — for example, well-educated, white collar men and expert witnesses of both sexes — tended to use a style that exhibited relatively few features of the powerless style. . . . [W]itnesses using one style were in fact perceived differently than witnesses using the other style. [I]n comparison to those who heard . . . testimony in the powerless style, those who heard . . . the powerful style indicated that they believed the witness more . . . and thought that she was more competent, more intelligent and more trustworthy. . . .

NOTE ON "NEGOTIATING" THE FACTS

The great majority of criminal convictions are the result of guilty pleas entered without any formal factfinding. Does the guilty plea system produce results different from those that would occur at trial? To be more specific, does it convict defendants who are in fact innocent (*and* would be acquitted) or convict defendants who committed the offense but could not be found guilty beyond a reasonable doubt at trial? Does the plea negotiation process produce convictions for offenses significantly different from the crimes a defendant may actually have committed? For the many observers who are inclined to give affirmative answers to these questions, the entire body of substantive criminal law may seem a supreme irrelevance; up to 90 percent of all convictions are obtained by guilty pleas, and these convictions are seen as the outcome of hurried horse-trading rather than the thoughtful application of complex legal principles to the known facts. What is the practical significance of substantive law in a world dominated by plea bargaining? Consider the following comments.

Donald Newman, Conviction 216 (1966): A charge reduction or sentence promise is not ordinarily a result of personal influence of the lawyer with the prosecutor or judge. The strength of a lawyer's argument for a charge reduction depends in good part on how strong a professional case he can make for the appropriateness of the lesser charge and doubtful convictability on the higher count. . . . In short, the full-blown negotiated plea is not merely an appeal for mercy; it is an adversary process and the lawyer serves the function of the guilty defendant's advocate.

Arnold Enker, Perspectives on Plea Bargaining, in President's Commission on Law Enforcement and the Administration of Justice, Task Force Report: The Courts 113-114 (1967): [C]oncern over the possibility that a negotiated plea can result in an erroneous judgment of conviction assumes a frame of reference by which the accuracy of the judgment is to be evaluated. It assumes an objective truth existing in a realm of objective historical fact which it is the sole function of our process to discover. Some, but by no means all, criminal cases fit this image. For example, this is a relatively accurate description of the issues at stake in a case in which the defendant asserts a defense of mistaken identity. . . .

But not all criminal cases fit the above picture. . . . Much criminal adjudication concerns the passing of value judgments on the accused's conduct as is obvious where negligence, recklessness, reasonable apprehension of attack, use of unnecessary force, and the like are at issue. Although intent is thought of as a question of fact, it too can represent a judgment of degrees of fault, for example, in cases where the issue is whether the defendants entertained intent to defraud or intent to kill. In many of these cases, objective truth is more ambiguous, if it exists at all. Such truth exists only as it emerges from the fact-determining process, and accuracy in this context really means relative equality of results as between defendants similarly situated and relative congruence between the formal verdict and our understanding of society's less formally expressed evaluation of such conduct.

The negotiated plea can, then, be an accurate process in this sense. So long as the judgment of experienced counsel as to the likely jury result is the key element entering into the bargain, substantial congruence is likely to result. Once we recognize that what lends rationality to the factfinding process in these instances lies not in an attempt to discover objective truth but in the devising of a process to express intelligent judgment, there is no inherent reason why plea negotiation need be regarded any the less rational or intelligent in its results.

Indeed, it may be that in some instances plea negotiation leads to more "intelligent" results. A jury can be left with the extreme alternatives of guilty of a crime of the highest degree or not guilty of any crime, with no room for any intermediate judgment. And this is likely to occur in just those cases where an intermediate judgment is the fairest and most "accurate" (or most congruent).

Clearly, the line between responsibility and irresponsibility due to insanity is not as sharp as the alternatives posed to a jury would suggest. . . . The very visibility of a trial process may be one factor that prevents us from offering the jury [a] compromise in order to preserve the symbolism of uniform rules evenly applied. The low visibility of the negotiated plea allows this compromise which may be more rational and congruent than the result we are likely to arrive at after a trial. While the desire to protect the symbolism of legality and the concern over lay compromises may warrant limiting the jury to extreme alternative[s], it does not follow that to allow the defendant to choose such a compromise is an irrational or even a less rational procedure.

Albert W. Alschuler, The Prosecutor's Role in Plea Bargaining, 36 U. Chi. L. Rev. 50, 71-79 (1968): Professor Enker suggests that the insanity defense raises problems that frequently merit a compromise solution. Such a solution was provided in the publicized case of William Heirens, a seventeen-year-old college student who pleaded guilty to three separate murders and was sentenced to three consecutive life terms. . . .

William Heirens' culpability under traditional legal standards was doubtful, yet both the defendant and society were deprived of an authoritative resolution of this issue. Heirens is today an inmate of the Stateville Penitentiary, although no one has determined on the basis of the evidence that a prison is where Heirens belongs. Society devised the insanity defense precisely to avoid such distressing spectacles. Like other legal issues, the defense was designed to be tried, not compromised. . . .

Finally, consider the case that District Attorney [Arlen] Specter advances to illustrate his concept of "variable guilt." . . . :

> The dictum that "justice and liberty are not the subjects of bargaining and barter" does not fit the realities of a typical barroom killing. . . .
>
> There is ordinarily sufficient evidence of malice and deliberation in such cases for the jury to find the defendant guilty of murder in the first degree, which [in Pennsylvania] carries either life imprisonment or death in the electric chair. Or, the conceded drinking by the defendant may be sufficient to nullify specific intent . . . to make the case second degree murder, which calls for a maximum of 10 to 20 years in jail. From all the prosecutor knows by the time the cold carbon copies of the police reports reach the District Attorney's office, the defendant may have acted in "hot blood," which makes the offense only voluntary manslaughter with a maximum penalty of 6 to 12 years. And, the defense invariably produces testimony showing that the killing was pure self-defense.
>
> When such cases are submitted to juries, a variety of verdicts are returned, which leads to the inescapable conclusion of variable guilt. Most of those trials result in convictions for second degree murder or voluntary manslaughter. The judges generally impose sentences with a minimum range of 5 to 8 years and a maximum of 10 to 20 years. That distilled experience enables the assistant district attorney and the defense lawyer to bargain on the middle ground of what experience has shown to be "justice" without the defense running the risk of the occasional first degree conviction . . . and without the Commonwealth tying up a jury room for 3 to 5 days and running the risk of acquittal.[62]

This argument seems to rest on the notion that when a man has seen one barroom killing, he has seen them all. [Yet] Specter's argument is a forceful one. In the homicide area particularly, . . . the distinctions drawn by the criminal code . . . sometimes prove too fine for workable, everyday application.

. . . If the perspective of these practitioners is sound, the best solution to the defects they perceive in the trial system does not lie in a shift from trial procedures to off-stage compromises. It lies instead in a simplification of the criminal code to reflect "everyday reality" rather than common-law refinement. [Moreover,] it seems doubtful that plea negotiation can eliminate the irrationalities of the criminal code without substituting more serious irrationalities of its own. . . . Most barroom killings seem to end in bargained pleas to voluntary manslaughter; but some end in bargained pleas to second degree murder; some end in bargained pleas to various categories of felonious assault; and I know of one barroom shooting that was resolved by a guilty plea to the crime of involuntary manslaughter, which, under the circumstances, seemed to be the last crime in the code of which the defendant might be guilty. It is therefore not clear that plea negotiation leads to greater uniformity of result than trial by jury.

Juries, of course, have biases, but the rules of evidence attempt to direct their

62. Specter, Book Review, 76 Yale L.J. 604, 606-07 (1967) (D. Newman, Conviction).

attention to relevant issues. There are no rules of evidence in plea negotiation; individual prosecutors may be influenced not only by a desire to smooth out the irrationalities of the criminal code but by thoroughly improper considerations that no serious reformer of the penal code would suggest. . . . Juries may react differently to the circumstances of indistinguishable crimes, but at least they react to the circumstances of the crimes. A jury is unlikely to seek conviction for the sake of conviction, to respond to a defense attorney's tactical pressures, to penalize a defendant because he has taken an inordinate share of the court's and the prosecutor's time, to do favors for particular defense attorneys in the hope of future cooperation, or to attempt to please victims and policemen for political reasons.

NOTE ON FORMAL TRIAL PROCEDURE

Section A of this Chapter describes the organization of the criminal justice system and typical pretrial procedures. To introduce our examination of the trial stage itself, the present Note briefly summarizes the typical course of a formal criminal trial. Naturally, the procedure followed in some jurisdictions or in particular cases may differ in points of detail from that set out in this preliminary overview.

A formal trial typically begins with the selection of the jury. A panel of prospective jurors (called a *venire*) enters the courtroom, and the judge describes the nature of the case and the identity of the parties so that any prospective jurors who are personally involved may be excused. Prospective jurors are then questioned individually by the judge or by opposing counsel to determine possible bias. On the basis of this questioning (called *voir dire*) prospective jurors may be excused *for cause,* and both prosecution and defense may remove a certain number of the panel, without showing cause, by exercising *peremptory challenges.* When the requisite number of acceptable jurors (usually 12) has been obtained by this procedure, the panel is sworn.

Now the presentation of the case begins. Usually the indictment is read to the jury; the prosecutor then makes an opening statement outlining the facts she plans to prove. Defense counsel also may make an opening statement. Claims made in these statements do not constitute *evidence;* they serve only to help the jury understand the testimony about to be presented. In many jurisdictions, motions relating to the scope or validity of the indictment and motions to suppress evidence must be made a certain number of days prior to trial. In others, such motions can be made at the outset of the trial. If the judge grants a motion to dismiss the indictment, the case will terminate at this point. Otherwise the trial goes forward, although motions may be made or renewed as the trial proceeds.

Next the prosecution calls its witnesses. The presentation of their testimony often evokes objections from counsel, and the judge must decide the bounds of permissible testimony under complex rules of evidence. We examine some of these rules in the sections to follow. When the prosecution has completed the presentation of its evidence, the defense may choose to stand on the *presumption of innocence* and move for a *directed verdict* or *judgment of acquittal* on the ground that the charges have not been proved beyond a reasonable doubt. If such a motion is not made, or if the motion is made and denied, the defense may decide to offer its own evidence (through the defendant or other witnesses). The prosecution then will have an opportunity to present further evidence in rebuttal. When both sides have rested, having completed the presentation of their evidence, opposing counsel may make a closing argument to the jury. Ordinarily the prosecution's closing argument is presented first (because it bears the burden of proof), and the prosecutor is usually allowed an opportunity for rebuttal after the closing argument of the defense.

At this point the work of the opposing parties has been completed. The judge now intercedes with his most important contribution to the proceedings — the instructions to the jury. The judge may begin with a summary of the evidence; ordinarily, however, judicial comment on the evidence tends to be cautious and limited. Formal instructions on the law, however, are always given, and they are typically quite detailed. The instructions serve both as a guide for the jury's deliberations and as a focal point for challenges on appeal in the event of a conviction. Usually the instructions cover formal procedures and responsibilities of the jurors (for example, how to elect a foreperson, when to refrain from discussing the case with other jurors or outsiders), matters related to the weight or relevance of particular kinds of testimony, and, above all, detailed explanations of the substantive criminal law applicable to the case, including specification of the facts necessary to establish the offense and definitions of legal concepts that the jury is called on to apply.

The jury at last retires to deliberate. Its verdict of guilty or not guilty on each charge must be reached by a substantial majority (and usually by unanimity). After a verdict of guilty and the imposition of sentence (usually by the judge), the trial terminates. There may of course be an appeal. If it finds trial errors, the reviewing court may reverse the conviction and order another trial, since American double jeopardy principles generally do not bar the retrial of a defendant who has successfully appealed her conviction.[2] A verdict of not guilty terminates the proceedings and is not subject to appeal or review of any kind, regardless of whether flagrant errors prejudicial to the prosecution occurred at trial.[3] When the jury is unable to agree by the requisite majority on a verdict of either guilty or not guilty (a hung jury case), a *mistrial* is declared, and the defendant then may be retried at the prosecutor's discretion.

Such, in rough outline, is the procedure by which guilt must be established when a criminal case is fully litigated through the formal trial stage. Of course, as we have already seen, guilt can be (and often is) established by entry of a guilty plea before the trial stage is ever reached.

Comprehensive treatment of all important aspects of trial procedure lies beyond the province of this book. Nevertheless, a book devoted primarily to the substantive law should provide an introduction to some of the central features of the process of proof, in order to illuminate the actual context in which crim-

2. Burks v. United States, 437 U.S. 1 (1978). The English practice is somewhat different. In that country, when a reviewing court finds prejudicial error, the conviction is "quashed," and ordinarily no retrial is permitted. Criminal Appeal Act, ch. 19, §2(2)-(3). But the English courts have discretion to order a new trial when "the interests of justice so require." Id. §7.

3. To avoid this difficulty many states provide for rulings prior to the start of trial on significant issues of law and permit the prosecutor to appeal an adverse ruling at that point. For discussion of prosecution appeals, see James A. Strazzella, The Relationship of Double Jeopardy to Prosecution Appeals, 73 Notre Dame L. Rev. 1 (1997).

inal law is applied and the ways in which the procedural system shapes (and in turn is shaped by) the substantive content of the criminal law. In the remaining sections of this chapter we undertake such an exploration.

2. *The Presentation of Evidence*

INTRODUCTORY NOTES

1. The order of proof. At trial the evidence is presented in accordance with a formally prescribed order. The prosecution first calls witnesses in an effort to prove the elements of the offense charged. As we have just seen, page •• supra, the case may terminate at this point if the prosecution fails to sustain its preliminary burden of proof. If not, the defense may then call witnesses in an effort to refute the prosecution's *case-in-chief* or to establish some *affirmative defense.* The prosecution then has an opportunity to recall witnesses or to call new witnesses solely for purposes of *rebuttal,* that is, to refute evidence offered by the defense. The defense in turn is afforded a chance to meet by *rejoinder* any matters introduced in the prosecutor's rebuttal.

Within these stages the examination of each witness follows a similar pattern. The witness is first questioned by the party that called the witness (*direct examination*), and afterward the opposing party has an opportunity to question that witness (*cross-examination*). Further questioning by the first party (*re-direct*) and by the opposing side (*re-cross*) may follow.

2. Relevance. The rules governing the admissibility of evidence are extremely detailed and complex. For present purposes, it will be useful to begin by focusing on one obvious but deceptively simple requirement that has pervasive importance, the rule of relevancy. First, evidence is *never* admissible if it is irrelevant. The converse cannot be stated so categorically. Relevant evidence is *generally* admissible, but there are many exceptions to this principle. Before turning to these exceptions, we must first be clear about the meaning of *relevancy.*

Evidence is considered relevant for purposes of the rules of evidence only if it is both *probative* and *material,* and these are precise terms of art. Evidence is probative only if it tends to establish the proposition for which it is offered or — to be precise — if the proposition is more likely to be true given the evidence than it would be without the evidence. Thus, if the proposition to be proved is that *H* was the person who killed his wife *W,* evidence of a motive (that is, that *H* stood to inherit a substantial estate on *W*'s death) is probative. Of course, the existence of the motive does not, by itself, make it probable that *H* is the killer, but *H* is more likely to be the killer if he had a motive than if he did not; this greater likelihood is all that is required to establish probative value.

Probative value alone is often thought of as synonymous with relevancy. But relevancy for purposes of the rules of evidence requires in addition that the proposition that the evidence tends to prove be one that will affect the outcome of the case under applicable law. So, for example, evidence in a homicide prosecution that defendant acted in self-defense is material because under the substantive law self-defense is a defense. But evidence that the deceased consented to be killed is not material, because under the substantive law consent by the victim is not a defense to a homicide charge. Thus, evidence may be excluded as irrelevant for one of two distinct reasons — either because the evidence does not tend to establish the proposition in question or because that proposition is not material to the outcome of the case. The materiality requirement means that the first prerequisite for determining the relevancy and hence the admissibility of evidence is a command of the substantive law of crimes.

We may sum up what we have so far said about relevancy by quoting the formulation used in the Federal Rules of Evidence:

RULE 401

"Relevant evidence" means evidence having any tendency to make the existence of any fact that is of consequence to the determination of the action more probable or less probable than it would be without the evidence.

RULE 402

All relevant evidence is admissible, except as otherwise provided. . . . Evidence which is not relevant is not admissible.

3. Privilege. Under what circumstances is relevant evidence *not* admissible? The law of evidence embodies dozens of distinct rules requiring the exclusion of relevant evidence. For example, the various rules relating to *privilege* give individuals the right to withhold certain kinds of testimony, often in order to protect particular interests of a witness or specially important relationships with others.

One of the most important privileges is the privilege against self-incrimination. The Fifth Amendment provides: "[N]or shall [any person] be compelled in any criminal case to be a witness against himself." The Supreme Court has construed this provision to imply that the government cannot require a criminal defendant to take the witness stand, cannot invite a jury to draw adverse inferences from a defendant's refusal to testify, and cannot in any other way compel the defendant to disclose potentially incriminating facts about the case. These principles are of great significance for the substantive criminal law. They not only make the prosecutor's task more difficult than it otherwise would be, but they pose an especially difficult barrier when the defendant's own frame of mind is an essential part of what the prosecutor must prove. The effect of the privilege against self-incrimination is to place largely beyond the government's reach the best (and sometimes the only) source of information about these especially elusive state-of-mind facts. As a result, substantive criminal law must constantly confront the questions whether government should be obliged to prove state-of-mind facts, and if so, what kinds of evidence will satisfy that obligation.

4. Other exclusionary rules: prejudice. Like the rules of privilege, many other rules of evidence operate to exclude relevant evidence. We will consider some of these rules in connection with the substantive crimes for which they have the greatest significance.[4] The balance of the present section is devoted to explor-

4. The hearsay rule and one of its important exceptions are explored in connection with conspiracy law, pages 671-678 infra. Special restrictions intended to protect the privacy of a witness are examined in connection with the materials on rape, pages 375-386 infra.

ing one rather open-ended rule — the rule that evidence must be excluded whenever its probative value is outweighed by its *prejudicial effect.* This exclusionary rule is of pervasive importance in the substantive criminal law, and we will encounter it repeatedly in the chapters that follow. The principle of weighing probative value against prejudicial effect is particularly central to developing doctrines in such areas as rape shield laws, the adequacy of victim provocation in homicide, battered spouse evidence, and testimony concerning intoxication, diminished capacity, and the insanity defense. As a foundation for the study of such topics throughout this book, the present section considers the problem of prejudicial effect in depth, in a context of recurring importance for criminal prosecutions — the rules concerning use of evidence of other crimes.

The term *prejudicial effect* has a rather technical meaning. To pursue the example previously mentioned, suppose that in *H*'s murder prosecution testimony is offered to the effect that shortly before the discovery of *W*'s bullet-ridden body, *H* was seen running from the scene carrying a smoking revolver. This testimony will undoubtedly be quite harmful to *H*'s chances for acquittal, but it will not be prejudicial, in the technical sense, because its harmfulness flows solely from its legitimate probative value. Evidence is considered prejudicial only when it is likely to affect the result in some *improper* way. Thus, prejudice is involved if the jury is likely to overestimate the probative value of the evidence or if the evidence will arouse undue hostility toward one of the parties.

The next case illustrates the application of these principles and their relationship to basic conceptions of criminal responsibility.

PEOPLE v. ZACKOWITZ

New York Court of Appeals
254 N.Y. 192, 172 N.E. 466 (1930)

[Defendant was convicted of first-degree murder and sentenced to death.]

CARDOZO, C.J. On November 10, 1929, shortly after midnight, the defendant in Kings county shot Frank Coppola and killed him without justification or excuse. A crime is admitted. What is doubtful is the degree only.

Four young men, of whom Coppola was one, were at work repairing an automobile in a Brooklyn street. A woman, the defendant's wife, walked by on the opposite side. One of the men spoke to her insultingly, or so at least she understood him. The defendant, who had dropped behind to buy a newspaper, came up to find his wife in tears. He was told she had been insulted, though she did not then repeat the words. Enraged, he stepped across the street and upbraided the offenders with words of coarse profanity. He informed them, so the survivors testify, that "if they did not get out of there in five minutes, he would come back and bump them all off." Rejoining his wife, he walked with her to their apartment house located close at hand. He was heated with liquor which he had been drinking at a dance. Within the apartment he induced her to tell him what the insulting words had been. A youth had asked her to lie with him, and had offered her two dollars. With rage aroused again, the defendant went back to the scene of the insult and found the four young men still working at the car. In a statement to the police, he said that he had armed himself at the apartment with a twenty-five calibre automatic pistol. In his testimony at the trial he said that this pistol had been in his pocket all the evening. Words and blows followed, and then a shot. The defendant kicked Coppola in the stomach. There is evidence that Coppola went for him with a wrench. The pistol came from the pocket, and from the pistol a single shot, which did its deadly work. . . .

At the trial the vital question was the defendant's state of mind at the moment of the homicide. Did he shoot with a deliberate and premeditated design to kill? Was he so inflamed by drink or by anger or by both combined that, though he knew the nature of his act, he was the prey to sudden impulse, the fury of the fleeting moment?[a] If he went forth from his apartment with a preconceived design to kill, how is it that he failed to shoot at once? How reconcile such a design with the drawing of the pistol later in the heat and rage of an affray? These and like questions the jurors were to ask themselves and answer before measuring the defendant's guilt. Answers consistent with guilt in its highest grade can reasonably be made. Even so, the line between impulse and deliberation is too narrow and elusive to make the answers wholly clear. The sphygmograph records with graphic certainty the fluctuations of the pulse. There is no instrument yet invented that records with equal certainty the fluctuations of the mind. At least, if such an instrument exists, it was not working at midnight in the Brooklyn street when Coppola and the defendant came together in a chance affray. With only the rough and ready tests supplied by their experience of life, the jurors were to look into the workings of another's mind, and discover its capacities and disabilities, its urges and inhibitions, in moments of intense excitement. Delicate enough and subtle is the inquiry, even in the most favorable conditions, with every warping influence excluded. There must be no blurring of the issues by evidence illegally admitted and carrying with it in its admission an appeal to prejudice and passion.

Evidence charged with that appeal was, we think, admitted here. . . . Almost at the opening of the trial the People began the endeavor to load the defendant down with the burden of an evil character. He was to be put before the jury as a man of murderous disposition. To that end they were allowed to prove that at the time of the encounter and at that of his arrest he had in his apartment, kept there in a radio box, three pistols and a teargas gun. There was no claim that he had brought these weapons out at the time of the affray, no claim that with any of them he had discharged the fatal shot. He could not have done so, for they were all of different calibre. The end to be served by laying the weapons before the jury was something very different. The end was to bring persuasion that here was a man of vicious and dangerous propensities, who because of those propensities was more likely to kill with deliberate and premeditated design than a man of irreproachable life and amiable manners. Indeed, this is the very ground on which the introduction of the evidence is now explained and defended. The District Attorney tells us in his brief that the possession of the weapons character-

a. Under New York law, a deliberate and premeditated killing would be first-degree murder, while a killing in "the fury of the fleeting moment" would be second-degree murder. At the time of the *Zackowitz* decision the former offense was punishable by death and the latter by imprisonment from a minimum of 20 years to a maximum of life. N.Y. Penal Law §§1045, 1048 (Penal Code of 1909, as amended 1928). For current penalty provisions in New York and other representative states, see pages 390-395 infra. —Eds.

ized the defendant as "a desperate type of criminal," a "person criminally inclined." The dissenting opinion, if it puts the argument less bluntly, leaves the substance of the thought unchanged. "Defendant was presented to the jury as a man having dangerous weapons in his possession, making a selection therefrom and going forth to put into execution his threats to kill." The weapons were not brought by the defendant to the scene of the encounter. They were left in his apartment where they were incapable of harm. In such circumstances, ownership of the weapons, if it has any relevance at all, has relevance only as indicating a general disposition to make use of them thereafter, and a general disposition to make use of them thereafter is without relevance except as indicating a "desperate type of criminal," a criminal affected with a murderous propensity. . . .

If a murderous propensity may be proved against a defendant as one of the tokens of his guilt, a rule of criminal evidence, long believed to be of fundamental importance for the protection of the innocent, must be first declared away. Fundamental hitherto has been the rule that character is never an issue in a criminal prosecution unless the defendant chooses to make it one. In a very real sense a defendant starts his life afresh when he stands before a jury, a prisoner at the bar. There has been a homicide in a public place. The killer admits the killing, but urges self-defense and sudden impulse. Inflexibly the law has set its face against the endeavor to fasten guilt upon him by proof of character or experience predisposing to an act of crime. . . . The principle back of the exclusion is one, not of logic, but of policy. There may be cogency in the argument that a quarrelsome defendant is more likely to start a quarrel than one of milder type, a man of dangerous mode of life more likely than a shy recluse. The law is not blind to this, but equally it is not blind to the peril to the innocent if character is accepted as probative of crime. "The natural and inevitable tendency of the tribunal — whether judge or jury — is to give excessive weight to the vicious record of crime thus exhibited, and either to allow it to bear too strongly on the present charge, or to take the proof of it as justifying a condemnation irrespective of guilt of the present charge" (Wigmore, Evidence, vol. 1, §194, and cases cited).

A different question would be here if the pistols had been bought in expectation of this particular encounter. They would then have been admissible as evidence of preparation and design. A different question would be here if they were so connected with the crime as to identify the perpetrator, if he had dropped them, for example, at the scene of the affray. They would then have been admissible as tending to implicate the possessor (if identity was disputed), no matter what the opprobrium attached to his possession. Different, also, would be the question if the defendant had been shown to have gone forth from the apartment with all the weapons on his person. To be armed from head to foot at the very moment of an encounter may be a circumstance worthy to be considered, like acts of preparation generally, as a proof of preconceived design. There can be no such implication from the ownership of weapons which one leaves behind at home.

The endeavor was to generate an atmosphere of professional criminality. It was an endeavor the more unfair in that, apart from the suspicion attaching to the possession of these weapons, there is nothing to mark the defendant as a man of evil life. . . . If his own testimony be true, he had gathered these weapons together as curios, a collection that interested and amused him. Perhaps his explanation of their ownership is false. There is nothing stronger than mere suspicion to guide us to an answer. Whether the explanation be false or true, he should not have been driven by the People to the necessity of offering it. Brought to answer a specific charge, and to defend himself against it, he was placed in a position where he had to defend himself against another, more general and sweeping. He was made to answer to the charge, pervasive and poisonous even if insidious and covert, that he was a man of murderous heart, of criminal disposition. . . .

The judgment of conviction should be reversed, and a new trial ordered.

POUND, J. (dissenting). . . .

The People may not prove against a defendant crimes not alleged in the indictment committed on other occasions than the crime charged as aiding the proofs that he is guilty of the crime charged unless such proof tends to establish (1) motive; (2) intent; (3) absence of mistake or accident; (4) a common scheme or plan embracing the commission of two or more crimes so related to each other that proof of the one tends to establish the other; (5) the identity of the person charged with the commission of the crime on trial. These exceptions are stated generally and not with categorical precision and may not be all-inclusive. None of them apply here nor were the weapons offered under an exception to the general rule. They were offered as a part of the transaction itself. The accused was tried only for the crime charged. The real question is whether the matter relied on has such a connection with the crime charged as to be admissible on any ground. If so, the fact that it constitutes another distinct crime does not render it inadmissible. . . .

As the District Attorney argues in his brief, if defendant had been arrested at the time of the killing and these weapons had been found on his person, the People would not have been barred from proving the fact, and the further fact that they were nearby in his apartment should not preclude the proof as bearing on the entire deed of which the act charged forms a part. Defendant was presented to the jury as a man having dangerous weapons in his possession, making a selection therefrom and going forth to put into execution his threats to kill; not as a man of a dangerous disposition in general, but as one who, having an opportunity to select a weapon to carry out his threats, proceeded to do so. . . .

The judgment of conviction should be affirmed.

NOTES ON ZACKOWITZ

1. On the facts of *Zackowitz,* we may assume that the killing was intentional. The principal issue at trial was whether the killing was "deliberate" (that is, whether the intent to kill was formulated before the shot, making the crime first-degree murder) or whether the killing was instead "impulsive" (that is, whether the intent to kill was formulated during the final scuffle, making the crime second-degree murder). Does defendant's possession of the weapons have some bearing on this issue? Recall that very slight probative value is usually sufficient to render evidence admissible; for example, evidence that Zackowitz stood to inherit money from the victim would undoubtedly be admissible as tending to show a motive for a deliberate killing. Does the evidence of weapons possession have at least that much probative value?

2. If the weapons evidence was relevant, as Judge (later Justice) Cardozo seems to assume, are there convincing reasons for excluding it? Cardozo stresses that the issue in the case was a "delicate" and "subtle" one. Under these circumstances was it not particularly important for the jury to have access to as much relevant evidence as possible? In which case will the trier of fact be better able to evaluate what actually happened: when it knows about the weapons, knows the defendant's explanation for them, and has a chance to judge the credibility of that explanation or when — as *Zackowitz* requires — all of this information is withheld?

NOTES ON "OTHER-CRIMES" EVIDENCE UNDER CURRENT LAW

1. *The general rule and its foundations.* Subject to certain exceptions to be explored below, the basic principle invoked by the majority in *Zackowitz* appears to enjoy universal acceptance: Other crimes (and indeed any other kind of evidence designed to show "bad character") may not be introduced in order to show that the accused had an evil disposition and thus was more likely to have committed the offense charged.

Rules 403 and 404(b) of the Federal Rules of Evidence illustrate one rigorous statement of these principles:

RULE 403 . . .

> Although relevant, evidence may be excluded if its probative value is substantially outweighed by the danger of unfair prejudice, confusion of the issues, or misleading the jury, or by considerations of undue delay, waste of time, or needless presentation of cumulative evidence.

RULE 404 . . .

> (b) Other crimes, wrongs, or acts. Evidence of other crimes, wrongs, or acts is not admissible to prove the character of a person in order to show action in conformity therewith. It may, however, be admissible for other purposes, such as proof of motive, opportunity, intent, preparation, plan, knowledge, [identity], or absence of mistake or accident. . . .

What is the justification for these principles? McCormick states that such evidence "is not irrelevant, but in the setting of jury trial the danger of prejudice outweighs the probative value." C. McCormick, Evidence §190, at 447 (2d ed. 1972). See also Michelson v. United States, 335 U.S. 469, 475-476 (1948): "The inquiry is not rejected because character is irrelevant; on the contrary it is said to weigh too much with the jury and to so overpersuade them as to prejudge one with a bad general record and deny him a fair opportunity to defend against a particular charge." Undoubtedly, this statement holds true in a very wide range of contexts. But there can be situations in which the danger of prejudice is arguably insufficient to justify the exclusion. And when a judge tries the case without a jury, the danger that the evidence will exert improper influence on the result seems considerably less. Should the rule of inadmissibility be abandoned when the case is tried to a judge?[5] Or are there other, perhaps more basic, reasons for restricting the admissibility of other-crimes evidence?

Consider how the criminal process would be affected if the prosecution were free to support its case by proving previous instances of criminal conduct by the accused. The defendant, who of course is contesting the charges of the present indictment, may deny having committed the other crimes as well. In particular, if the prosecution has not already obtained a formal conviction for the other crimes (that was the case in *Zackowitz,* for example), the entire focus of the trial could be diverted by the dispute about whether the other crimes were in fact committed.

Even if the defendant admits to committing other crimes or the other crimes are easily proved by a record of prior convictions, the defendant may feel called upon to explain the background of the other offenses or to claim extenuating circumstances. (This too happened in *Zackowitz.*) The vice here is not simply that time and attention may be diverted from the main issue in the case. It is also that a defendant should not be forever obliged to explain prior transgressions in order to dispel suspicions of further misconduct. Thus, a person who has suffered conviction and sentence is said to have "paid his debt to society"; the slate should be wiped clean. Cardozo alludes to these concerns when he states: "In a very real sense a defendant starts his life afresh when he stands before a jury, a prisoner at the bar. . . . Whether the explanation [for Zackowitz's possession of the weapons] be true or false, he should not have been driven by the People to the necessity of offering it."

Whether or not a defendant has already "paid his debt" for the prior offense, basic assumptions about criminal responsibility are tested when the focus of the trial becomes centered on the defendant's general character rather than on his behavior in a discrete situation. To be sure, a trial designed to determine a defendant's responsibility for particular events often must explore many circumstances of his life, but ultimately the events themselves are at issue, the concrete behavior precisely specified in the charges. The criminal trial usually is not viewed as a vehicle for passing judgment on the whole person. Again, Cardozo alludes to this principle: "Brought to answer a specific charge, [the defendant] had to defend himself against another, more general and sweeping[,] . . . pervasive and poisonous even if insidious and covert, that he was a man of murderous heart, or criminal disposition." Consider Gerard E. Lynch, RICO: The Crime of Being a Criminal, Parts III & IV, 87 Colum. L. Rev. 920, 934-936 (1987):

> [T]he model of crime based on specific incidents or acts [is] associated with a particular conception of the individual as a moral actor. . . . The individual is implicitly conceived not only as free in principle to act in accordance with or in violation of defined norms, but also as free at any given moment to make choices at odds with any consistent character that may be deduced from his prior acts. To infer that a defendant committed the particular offense for which he is being tried from the fact that he has previously committed other crimes of a generally similar nature — or, worse still, other crimes of an entirely different nature — is not only

5. Courts have differed in their treatment of other-crimes evidence in nonjury trials. A. Leo Levin & Harold K. Cohen, The Exclusionary Rules in Nonjury Criminal Cases, 119 U. Pa. L. Rev. 905 (1971).

unfair, but inconsistent with a fundamental supposition that criminal behavior is punishable because it represents a free choice at a particular moment in time to commit an immoral act.

Questions: To what extent are the values described fundamental to a just system of criminal law? Are they, for example, more important than the most accurate possible determination of the truth? Should they apply with as much force in proceedings to determine sentence (or the *degree* of the offense in *Zackowitz*) as they do when the issue is guilt versus innocence?[6] Consider the extent to which these values in fact *are* respected, or flouted, by the doctrines of criminal law examined in the remainder of this section and throughout this book.

2. *Exceptions to the rule.* Situations in which other-crimes evidence might be admissible are mentioned by the court in *Zackowitz,* and the dissenting opinion presents five specific "exceptions" to the rule of exclusion. Thus, for example, if a defendant is prosecuted for the murder of *V,* evidence that the defendant previously committed a robbery witnessed by *V* will be admissible — not to show that the defendant was generally disposed to violence but rather to show his *motive* for this particular killing. Similarly, evidence that the defendant had previously stolen the pistol with which *V* was shot will be admissible — not to show the defendant's disposition to crime but to help *identify* him as the killer. Many other exceptions could be given.

Technically speaking, these situations do not involve exceptions to the rule of exclusion because, properly stated, that rule renders other-crimes evidence inadmissible only when offered "to prove the character of a person in order to show action in conformity therewith." Fed. R. Evid. 404(b). In other words, the rule itself does not bar the use of other-crimes evidence for some purpose *other than* that of suggesting that he acted in conformity with a bad character. See Estelle v. McGuire, 502 U.S. 62 (1991); People v. Vandervliet, 444 Mich. 52, 508 N.W.2d 114 (1993).

When evidence of other crimes is not offered to prove propensity, and therefore is not barred by Rule 404(b), the evidence nonetheless may run afoul of some other prohibition. In particular, evidence offered to prove motive, identity, or other nonpropensity matters will be barred by Rule 403 if its prejudicial effect substantially outweighs its probative value. Evidence, even when relevant, must be excluded when it "tends to subordinate reason to emotion in the fact-finding process." United States v. Queen, 132 F.3d 991, 997 (4th Cir. 1997). When other-crimes evidence is both highly relevant and highly inflammatory, courts face a dilemma; in such cases, the Supreme Court has held, judges must consider using factual stipulations or other alternative methods for conveying the essential facts to the jury in less prejudicial fashion. Old Chief v. United States, 519 U.S. 172 (1997).

Treatises on evidence discuss various legitimate uses of other-crimes evidence — that is, uses for some purpose *other than* that of suggesting that the defendant may have committed the crime because he or she has a bad character. Nevertheless it is not always easy to tell whether the evidence links the defendant to the crime in some legitimate way or whether it simply suggests a crimi-

6. For exploration of the question whether punishment should be tailored to the character of the offender rather than the seriousness of the offense, see Chapter 2 infra.

nal propensity. The problem consistently provides a large volume of litigation, and Rule 404(b) has become one of the most-often cited provisions in the Federal Rules of Evidence. For helpful discussions, see Miguel Angel Mendez, California's New Law on Character Evidence: Evidence Code Section 352 and the Impact of Recent Psychological Studies, 31 U.C.L.A.L. Rev. 1003 (1984); Richard Uviller, Evidence of Character to Prove Conduct: Illusion, Illogic and Injustice in the Courtroom, 130 U. Pa. L. Rev. 845 (1982). Consider the following important exceptions.

(*a*) *The signature exception.* Evidence of other crimes committed by the defendant is admissible when the other crimes are "so nearly identical in method as to earmark them as the handiwork of the accused. . . . The device used must be so unusual and distinctive as to be like a signature." McCormick, page 26 supra, §190, at 449. The most famous illustration of this rule is the "brides in the bath" case, Rex v. Smith, 84 Cr. App. (K.B.) 137 (1915). The defendant's wife was found drowned in her bathtub shortly after she had executed a will in his favor. At his trial for her murder, the prosecution was allowed to prove that after this wife's death the defendant made two subsequent marriages, both of which had ended when the new bride, shortly after making a will in the defendant's favor, was found drowned in her bath. Here the uniqueness of the modus operandi gave the other crimes strong probative value in helping to identify Smith as the cause of his first wife's death.

Notice the assumption that the two other incidents *were* crimes. In *Smith* the prosecution probably could not prove guilt beyond a reasonable doubt in any one incident taken by itself. But in order for evidence to be admissible, the facts necessary to make that evidence relevant need not be proved beyond a reasonable doubt; proof of those facts by a preponderance of the evidence is sufficient. Thus, in *Smith,* if there is a likelihood of guilt (that is, a 51 percent chance) in each instance considered separately, and if the incidents can then be considered together, the jury might be convinced beyond a reasonable doubt of the defendant's guilt in all three incidents.

Should the prosecution be permitted to present as "other crimes," under any of the various exceptions, evidence concerning charges for which the defendant has been *acquitted*? Applying the principle that admissibility requires only proof by a preponderance that other crimes occurred, the Supreme Court held in Dowling v. United States, 493 U.S. 342, 348-349 (1990), that an acquittal (which implied only a reasonable doubt) did not bar subsequent prosecutors from offering evidence that the defendant was guilty of the prior charges. Thus, so long as the other crimes can be offered for some purpose other than proving propensity, the defendant is in effect forced to relitigate his guilt in the prior incidents; Cardozo's rule that a defendant on trial "starts his life afresh" can be nullified.

Because the various exceptions can so easily defeat the values that the other-crimes rule serves, it becomes critical to assure that other-crimes evidence is being used for some purpose *other than* that of suggesting a criminal propensity. In "signature" cases, courts often have difficulty determining whether the pattern of criminality is sufficiently unusual. In State v. Hills, 761 So. 2d 516 (La. 2000), the court said that a pattern of prior crimes can qualify for admissibility under the signature exception only when the crimes are "so peculiarly distinctive that one must logically say they are the work of the same person." Consider the following cases, in all of which the trial judges admitted the other-crimes evidence.

Does that evidence suggest a distinctive signature or at most only a propensity to commit offenses of some general type?

(*i*) *H* and *M* are charged with committing a series of three robberies over a five-month period. In all three cases two armed men, wearing handkerchiefs over their faces, used an employees' entrance to enter stores shortly after closing time, forced some of the employees to lie down on the floor, and fled with large amounts of cash. Should the prosecution be permitted to prove that two years earlier *H* and *M* had robbed two restaurants in the same fashion? See People v. Haston, 444 P.2d 91 (1969); cf. People v. Howard, 708 N.E.2d 1212 (Ill. App. 1999).

(*ii*) The defendant was convicted of burglary and murder and sentenced to death. The charge involved a midnight break-in at the home of a 74-year-old woman. The house was ransacked, and a TV set, a radio, and a ring were stolen; the woman, brutally beaten about the face and body, later died. Four weeks after the crime a search at the defendant's home turned up the three stolen items, but there was little other evidence to connect him to the crime. Two months before this crime, at a location four blocks away, there was a break-in, near midnight, at the home of an 84-year-old woman. The house was ransacked; the woman was severely beaten about the face but recovered. In that offense, the defendant was identified as the perpetrator, his palm print was found in the victim's house, and he was convicted of the crime. Should the prosecution be permitted to prove this earlier offense for purposes of identifying the defendant as the perpetrator of the later one? One of the appellate court judges considered this a case where the "similarities are confined to relatively insignificant details that would likely be common elements regardless of who had committed the crimes." Another judge concluded that the crimes were "so close in time and geographic proximity and so similar in gratuitous brutality . . . as to naturally show that the person who committed one also committed the other." A third said that "[t]he two incidents here were as nearly similar as human events will allow." Who was right? See Commonwealth v. Bryant, 530 A.2d 83, 86, 88-89 (Pa. 1987).

(*b*) *Sex offenses.* The Violent Crime Control and Law Enforcement Act of 1994 amended the Federal Rules of Evidence by adding the following provision (Fed. R. Evid. 413(a)):

> In a criminal case in which the defendant is accused of an offense of sexual assault, evidence of the defendant's commission of another offense or offenses of sexual assault is admissible, and may be considered for its bearing on any matter to which it is relevant.

An analogous provision (Fed. R. Evid. 414(a)) rendered the defendant's commission of child molestation admissible in a prosecution for other acts of child molestation. Evidence of prior sex crimes can be admitted under Rules 413-414 only when the evidence also passes the Rule 403 requirement that its prejudicial effect not outweigh its probative value. United States v. Guardia, 135 F.3d 1326 (10th Cir. 1998). With this safeguard in place, most courts have held, the admission of evidence of prior sex crimes does not amount to an unconstitutional denial of due process. People v. Falsetta, 986 P.2d 182 (Cal. 1999); Enjady v. United States, 134 F.3d 1427 (10th Cir. 1998). Nonetheless, the policy justifications for Rules 413-414 remain hotly contested.

What is the basis for treating prior sexual acts differently from other evidence of bad character or criminal propensity? Can an exception to the rule of exclusion be justified on the ground that sexual misconduct has greater value than other misconduct in predicting future behavior? Or should the rule of exclusion be applied even *more* strictly, on the ground that evidence of prior sexual misconduct has especially strong prejudicial effects?

For an in-depth examination of the issues, see Katharine K. Baker, Once a Rapist? Motivational Evidence and Relevancy in Rape Law, 110 Harv. L. Rev. 563 (1997). Professor Baker charges that "Rule 413's proponents rely on antiquated notitions of rapists as rare, depraved psychopaths who have some sort of perverse psychological need for sex." The empirical evidence, she argues, indicates that convicted rapists are much less likely to repeat their crimes than are convicted larcenists and burglars. Professor Baker concludes that Rule 413 is misguided because it "relies on outmoded and demonstrably false stereotypes of who rapes, what rape is, and why rape might be different from other crimes." Id. at 565, 578, 589.

In accord with Professor Baker's analysis, the Judicial Conference of the United States, the policy-making body of the federal judiciary chaired by Chief Justice Relinquist, sharply criticized the new rules and urged Congress to repeal them. The Judicial Conference concluded that "the new rules, which are not supported by empirical evidence, could diminish significantly the protections that have safeguarded persons accused in criminal cases," and noted that the rules posed a "danger of convicting a criminal defendant for past, as opposed to charged, behavior or for being a bad person." The Judicial Conference also noted that its conclusions about the undesirability of Rules 413 and 414 reflected a "highly unusual unanimity" of the judges, lawyers, and academics who serve on its advisory committees. See 56 Crim. L. Rptr. 2139-40 (Feb. 15, 1995). Nonetheless, Congress has declined to modify or repeal the new rules.

Several states have recently adopted special rules, modeled on Federal Rule 413, for admitting evidence of prior sex crimes, and other states have long permitted the use of such evidence on the theory that a defendant's "lustful disposition" was especially probative in sex-offense prosecutions. In most states, however, the usual rule excluding evidence of prior misconduct continues to be applied just as strictly in rape trials as in other kinds of prosecutions, and in a few states legislative changes similar to Rules 413-414 have been held to violate the state constitution. E.g., State v. Burns, 978 S.W.2d 759 (Mo. 1998). See Comment, Fairness to the Victim: Federal Rules of Evidence 413 and 414 Admit Propensity Evidence in Sexual Offender Trials, 35 Houston L. Rev. 1729, 1765-1772 (1999); David P. Bryden & Roger C. Park, "Other Crimes" Evidence in Sex Offense Cases, 78 Minn. L. Rev. 529 (1994); Sara Sun Beale, Prior Similar Acts in Prosecutions for Rape and Child Sex Abuse, 4 Crim. L. Forum 307 (1993).

(*c*) *The impeachment exception.* In all of the situations so far discussed, the question has been whether the prosecution can use evidence of other crimes as part of its case-in-chief. Even when the other-crimes evidence is clearly inadmissible for this purpose, if the accused chooses to testify in his own defense, then the prosecution generally will be permitted to ask about the other crimes in its cross-examination of the accused and to introduce other-crimes evidence in its rebuttal for purposes of impeaching the defendant's testimony. In theory, the other-crimes evidence may not be used to provide affirmative support for the prosecution's case. It may be considered only for purposes of judging the credibility of the defendant's testimony, and the jury will be so instructed.

The rationale of the impeachment exception appears to be that a person convicted of crime may be less trustworthy and more likely to give false testimony than a citizen with a "clean" record.[7] Whatever the soundness of this rationale when the previous misconduct involves perjury or similar crimes of dishonesty, its invocation in the case of other crimes can border on the absurd. In a prosecution for burglary, previous burglary convictions are clearly inadmissible for the purpose of showing the defendant's disposition to commit this crime, but if the defendant claims to have been elsewhere at the time, the burglary convictions will generally be held admissible to show a possibility that the defendant may be disposed to perjury!

In recent years an increasing number of courts have recognized the injustice of this unqualified exception for impeachment use of prior offenses; these courts require admissibility to be determined on a case-by-case basis, weighing such factors as the recency of the prior offense, whether the crime involved dishonesty, and whether the crime was so similar to that charged as to enhance the danger of prejudice.[8] Even in these limited terms, the impeachment exception presents a striking anomaly. If the defendant is prosecuted for perjury, previous convictions for perjury or other dishonest behavior cannot be introduced as part of the prosecution's case-in-chief in order to show the defendant's propensity to lie under oath. But whenever a defendant chooses to testify, the prior convictions become admissible precisely for that purpose.

To what extent does the impeachment exception impair the values reflected in the general rule against use of other-crimes evidence? Does it matter whether these values are preserved only when the defendant chooses not to testify?[9]

The impeachment exception is premised on the assumption that the jury will consider the other crimes *only* for the limited purpose of judging credibility and will not treat the other crimes as affirmative evidence of guilt. Is this a plausible assumption? Lawyers and social scientists have studied the question but have not reached definitive conclusions. The Note that follows explores the effectiveness of cautionary instructions and collects some of the available findings. The problem immediately at hand is to understand how the rules concerning other-crimes evidence actually function, but questions about the effectiveness of jury instructions are central to understanding the actual impact of all the elaborately crafted rules of criminal law and evidence that the jury is called upon to apply.

NOTE ON THE EFFECTIVENESS OF JURY INSTRUCTIONS

When other-crimes evidence has been introduced for impeachment purposes, a typical instruction to the jury might read as follows (1 E. Devitt & C. Blackmar, Federal Jury Practice and Instructions §11.12 (4th ed. 1992)):

7. At common law a person convicted of treason, felony, or other crime of infamy or dishonesty (crimen falsi) was disqualified from testifying as a witness. In the mid-1800s, when common law jurisdictions moved to remove the absolute disqualification, they generally provided by statute that prior convictions of the witness could be introduced for purposes of impeachment. See 2 J. Wigmore §§519-520 (3d ed. 1940); 3A J. Wigmore §§986-987 (Chadbourn rev. 1970).

8. See Gordon v. United States, 383 F.2d 936 (D.C. Cir. 1967) (Burger, J.). See also Fed. R. Evid. 609.

9. It is sometimes said that, by deciding to testify, a defendant *chooses* to put his character in issue. Is this convincing? See State v. Santiago, 53 Hawaii 254, 492 P.2d 657 (1971).

> Evidence of a defendant's previous conviction of a crime may be considered by the jury only insofar as it may affect the credibility of the defendant as a witness and must never be considered as any evidence of [his] [her] guilt of the crime for which the defendant is now on trial.

Such an instruction calls on the jury to perform an intellectual task that is bound to run counter to the jury's natural inclinations. Indeed the rule generally excluding other-crimes evidence is premised on the assumption that such evidence *is* relevant to guilt and is very difficult for the jury to keep in perspective once it becomes known. Thus jurors may be strongly tempted to disregard the instruction, even if they are able to grasp the subtle distinction it asks them to draw. The problem arises over and over in the administration of the complex body of rules that ostensibly govern the criminal process. Yet just as the jury creates the need for many of these complicated rules, the nature of the jury raises doubts about whether subtle or counter-intuitive instructions actually affect the outcome of the case.

Experienced judges confronting this question have expressed sharply divergent views about the effectiveness of jury instructions. Sometimes the courts suggest that there is no practical alternative to reliance on instructions and therefore that the effectiveness of such instructions must be assumed. In Spencer v. Texas, 385 U.S. 554, 565 (1967), the Supreme Court expressed its faith in "the ability of juries to approach their task responsibly and to sort out discrete issues given to them under proper instructions. . . ."[10] Others have been more skeptical. Chief Justice Warren once wrote that "it flouts human nature to suppose that a jury would not consider a defendant's previous trouble with the law in deciding whether he has committed the crime charged against him." Id. at 575 (dissenting opinion). Justice Jackson warned: "The naive assumption that prejudicial effects can be overcome by instructions to the jury . . . all practicing lawyers know to be unmitigated fiction." Krulewitch v. United States, 336 U.S. 440, 453 (1949) (concurring opinion), reprinted at pages 720-724 infra. In Dunn v. United States, 307 F.2d 883, 886 (5th Cir. 1962), the court was even more pessimistic:

> [O]ne cannot unring a bell; after the thrust of the saber it is difficult to say forget the wound; and finally, if you throw a skunk into the jury box, you can't instruct the jury not to smell it.

10. *Spencer* involved a challenge to the procedure followed under Texas habitual criminal statutes. The statutes provided for enhanced punishment for those convicted of crime who were shown to have been convicted of other crimes in the past. When the prosecution sought to invoke the enhanced-punishment provisions, the prior offenses would be alleged in the indictment and proved at trial. Thus the jurors trying the current charge would learn of the prior offenses, even though they would be instructed that those offenses could not be considered in determining the defendant's guilt for the present offense. The Court held that the Texas procedure was consistent with due process, rejecting the defendant's argument that the state should be required to postpone all reference to the prior offenses until after a verdict of conviction is rendered. *Spencer* was explicitly reaffirmed in Marshall v. Lonberger, 459 U.S. 422, 438 n. 6 (1983). Four justices argued that *Spencer* should be reexamined.

In a few discrete areas, the Court has held that cautionary instructions are inadequate to eliminate particularly severe prejudicial effects. For example, in Jackson v. Denno, 378 U.S. 368 (1964), the Court held unconstitutional a New York procedure under which juries were required to determine the voluntariness of a confession and instructed that in passing on the question of guilt they should disregard the confession if it was found involuntary. The Court held that in order to insure that an involuntary confession did not contribute to the verdict, the trial judge must make a preliminary determination outside the jury's presence and exclude any confession found involuntary.

In recent years social scientists have undertaken studies to determine where the truth lies, but the results have been mixed. A study of pretrial publicity found that volunteer "jurors" exposed to a sensational newspaper account of the case were much more likely to convict, but among jurors instructed to disregard the newspaper accounts, the difference in conviction rates disappeared.[11] In contrast, researchers found that exposure to a legally inadmissible confession significantly increased the likelihood of a guilty verdict when other evidence was weak and that instructions to disregard the confession had no significant effect on the likelihood of conviction.[12] Studies focusing on the impact of juror exposure to a defendant's record of prior convictions often find that evidence of previous similar offenses substantially increases the lilelihood of conviction and that cautionary instructions remove little or none of the prejudicial effect. Defendants afforded a cautionary instruction are much more likely to be convicted than those whose prior record is not mentioned at all.[13]

To the extent that cautionary instructions fail to eradicate prejudicial effects, the result could be due, in part, to jurors' inability to *understand* the subtle distinctions that such instructions sometimes require. Several studies have produced disturbing evidence that jurors often do not grasp the judge's explanations of legal concepts. One study found that the average juror understands less than half of the judge's instructions on the law.[14] Part of this problem may lie in the phraseology used, rather than in the intrinsic complexity of the concepts.

QUESTIONS ON JURY INSTRUCTIONS

Whatever the available evidence may suggest about the usefulness of jury instructions, there clearly remain substantial doubts about whether instructions are as fully effective in practice as they are assumed to be in theory. What are the implications of this situation? Granted that jury instructions function imperfectly (at best), what is the alternative?

One pragmatic approach has been to consider changes in trial procedure that might enhance the effectiveness of instructions. For example, the wording of instructions could be improved so that their meaning is more clearly explained to the jury.[15] Beyond this, when a judge tells a jury to disregard evidence, should

11. Rita James Simon, The Effects of Newspapers on the Verdicts of Potential Jurors, in R. Simon, The Sociology of Law 617-627 (1968). To the same effect, see Robin Reed, Jury Simulation: The Impact of Judge's Instructions and Attorney Tactics on Decisionmaking, 71 J. Crim. L. & Criminology 68 (1980).

12. See Sarah Tanford & Steven Penrod, Social Inference Processes in Juror Judgments of Multiple Offense Trials, 47 J. Personality & Soc. Psych. 749 (1984); Saul M. Kassin & Lawrence S. Wrightsman, Coerced Confessions, Judicial Instruction and Mock Juror Verdicts, 11 J. Applied Soc. Psych. 489 (1981).

13. See Joel D. Lieberman & Bruce D. Sales, What Social Science Teaches Us About the Jury Instruction Process, 3 Psychol., Pub. Pol. & L. 589, 601-602 (1997).

14. Alan Reifman, Spencer Grusick & Phoebe C. Ellsworth, Real Jurors' Understanding of the Law in Real Cases, 16 L. & Hum. Behav. 539 (1992). See also Bradley Saxton, How Well Do Jurors Understand Jury Instructions?, 33 Land & Water L. Rev. 59 (1998).

15. A proposal for clarifying jury instructions and translating them into plain English is developed in William E. Schwartzer, Communicating with Juries: Problems and Remedies, 69 Cal. L. Rev. 731 (1981). See also Larry Heuer & Steven D. Penrod, Instructing Jurors: A Field Experiment with Written and Preliminary Instructions, 13 L. & Human Behavior 409 (1989); Lawrence J. Severance, Edith Greene, & Elizabeth F. Loftus, Toward Criminal Jury Instructions that Jurors Can Understand, 75 J. Crim. L. & C. 198 (1984). The last source includes empirical tests showing that linguistically simplified instructions improve juror comprehension of legal concepts.

she explain *why* the law considers the evidence misleading? The standard cautionary instructions tend to be rather perfunctory. For ways to convey a more forceful message, see Albert W. Alschuler, Courtroom Misconduct by Prosecutors and Trial Judges, 50 Tex. L. Rev. 629, 652-654 (1972).

Can ameliorative reforms cure the difficulties of overly cumbersome jury instructions, or is the basic problem more fundamental? Note that jury instructions are necessary in the first place only because we want citizens without special training to participate and at the same time we want their decisions to conform to law. Do these partially inconsistent desires require a system that is simply too complex to function properly? This problem can be reconsidered in connection with the materials on other countries' approaches to lay participation. See page 60 infra.

3. *Proof Beyond a Reasonable Doubt*

INTRODUCTORY NOTES

1. *The constitutional rule and its foundations.* In In re Winship, 397 U.S. 358, 364 (1970), the Supreme Court held that "the Due Process Clause protects the accused against conviction except upon proof beyond a reasonable doubt of every fact necessary to constitute the crime charged." The Court explained the fundamental importance of this standard of proof as follows (id. at 363-364).

> The reasonable-doubt standard . . . is a prime instrument for reducing the risk of convictions resting on factual error. The standard provides concrete substance for the presumption of innocence — that bedrock "axiomatic and elementary" principle whose "enforcement lies at the foundation of the administration of our criminal law." . . .
>
> The accused during a criminal prosecution has at stake interests of immense importance, both because of the possibility that he may lose his liberty upon conviction and because of the certainty that he would be stigmatized by the conviction. Accordingly, a society that values the good name and freedom of every individual should not condemn a man for commission of a crime when there is reasonable doubt about his guilt. . . .
>
> Moreover, use of the reasonable-doubt standard is indispensable to command the respect and confidence of the community in applications of the criminal law. It is critical that the moral force of the criminal law not be diluted by a standard of proof that leaves people in doubt whether innocent men are being condemned. It is also important in our free society that every individual going about his ordinary affairs have confidence that his government cannot adjudge him guilty of a criminal offense without convincing a proper factfinder of his guilt with utmost certainty.

In a concurring opinion Mr. Justice Harlan added (id. at 371-372):

> If . . . the standard of proof for a criminal trial were a preponderance of the evidence rather than proof beyond a reasonable doubt, there would be a smaller risk of factual errors that result in freeing guilty persons, but a far greater risk of factual errors that result in convicting the innocent. Because the standard of proof affects the comparative frequency of these two types of erroneous outcomes, the choice of the standard to be applied in a particular kind of litigation should, in a rational world, reflect an assessment of the comparative social disutility of each.
>
> When one makes such an assessment, the reason for different standards of proof

in civil as opposed to criminal litigation becomes apparent. In a civil suit between two private parties for money damages, for example, we view it as no more serious in general for there to be an erroneous verdict in the defendant's favor than for there to be an erroneous verdict in the plaintiff's favor. . . .

In a criminal case, on the other hand, we do not view the social disutility of convicting an innocent man as equivalent to the disutility of acquitting someone who is guilty. . . . In this context, I view the requirement of proof beyond a reasonable doubt in a criminal case as bottomed on a fundamental value determination of our society that it is far worse to convict an innocent man than to let a guilty man go free.

2. *How burden-of-proof problems arise.* Problems relating to the reasonable-doubt standard can surface in many different ways. The issue normally arises first at the close of the prosecution's case. If the judge decides that the evidence raises a reasonable doubt about guilt *as a matter of law* (an elusive concept explored in the next note), the judge must direct a verdict for the defendant. The same problem of assessing the sufficiency of the evidence may be presented to the judge again at the close of all the evidence (when the defendant may again move for a directed verdict); it will be a central concern of the jurors in their deliberations; and it may arise again on appeal (when the defendant may seek reversal on the basis of insufficient evidence).

3. *Legal sufficiency: reasonable doubt as a matter of law.* Courts often have difficulty determining whether the evidence is insufficient as a matter of law. In a sense the judges must give the defendant the *benefit of the doubt.* If there is a reasonable doubt, then a guilty verdict would seem improper. On the other hand, before taking a case away from the jury (or reversing a jury's verdict), judges must resolve all evidentiary doubts against the proponent of the motion; in this sense the courts must give the *prosecution* the benefit of the doubt on the question whether its evidence does prove guilt beyond a reasonable doubt. The following comment from the opinion in Curley v. United States, 160 F.2d 229, 232-233 (D.C. Cir. 1947), helps clarify this elusive problem and explains the test that judges apply to determine evidentiary sufficiency:

[It is sometimes said] that unless the evidence excludes the hypothesis of innocence, the judge must direct a verdict . . . [and] that if the evidence is such that a reasonable mind might fairly conclude either guilt or innocence, a verdict of guilt must be reversed on appeal. But obviously neither of those translations is the law. Logically the ultimate premise of that thesis is that if a reasonable mind might have a reasonable doubt, there is, therefore, a reasonable doubt. That is not true. . . .

The functions of the jury include the determination of the credibility of witnesses, the weighing of the evidence, and the drawing of justifiable inferences of fact from proven facts. It is the function of the judge to deny the jury any opportunity to operate beyond its province: The jury may not be permitted to conjecture merely, or to conclude upon pure speculation or from passion, prejudice or sympathy. The critical point in this boundary is the existence or non-existence of a reasonable doubt as to guilt. If the evidence is such that reasonable jurymen must necessarily have such a doubt, the judge must require acquittal, because no other result is permissible within the fixed bounds of jury consideration. But if a reasonable mind might fairly have a reasonable doubt or might fairly not have one, the case is for the jury, and the decision is for the jurors to make. . . .

The true rule, therefore, is that a trial judge, in passing upon a motion for directed verdict of acquittal, must determine whether upon the evidence, giving full play to the right of the jury to determine credibility, weigh the evidence, and draw

> justifiable inferences of fact, a reasonable mind might fairly conclude guilt beyond a reasonable doubt. . . . If he concludes that either of the two results, a reasonable doubt or no reasonable doubt, is fairly possible, he must let the jury decide the matter.

4. Factual sufficiency: explaining reasonable doubt. The problem of evidentiary sufficiency arises not only for judges but for the jury, and the instructions accordingly must tell the jury how it should evaluate the evidence. Empirical studies confirm that jurors convict more readily when instructed under a more-likely-than-not standard than when instructed under the reasonable doubt standard,[16] and courts must protect the jury against any instruction that might dilute the latter standard. Accordingly, a conviction must be reversed for error in explaining the reasonable doubt standard to the jury, even when the appellate court does not find the evidence insufficient as a matter of law.

(*a*) In McCullough v. State, 657 P.2d 1157 (Nev. 1983), the trial judge had explained degrees of proof to the jury in terms of "a scale of zero to ten." He placed the preliminary hearing standard of probable cause at one and the burden of persuasion in civil trials at just over five. He then described beyond a reasonable doubt as "seven and a half, if you had to put it on a scale." The Nevada Supreme Court reversed, stating (id. at 1159): "The concept of reasonable doubt is inherently qualitative. Any attempt to quantify it may impermissibly lower the prosecution's burden of proof, and is likely to confuse rather than clarify."

(*b*) Courts often get into trouble when attempting to explain "reasonable doubt" in qualitative terms. In Cage v. Louisiana, 498 U.S. 39 (1990), the trial judge in a first-degree murder prosecution had instructed the jury that "a reasonable doubt [must be] founded upon a real tangible substantial basis and not upon mere caprice and conjecture. It must be such doubt as would give rise to a grave uncertainty. . . . A reasonable doubt is not a mere possible doubt. It is an actual substantial doubt. . . . What is required is not an absolute or mathematical certainty, but a moral certainty." The Supreme Court reversed the conviction, holding that the references to "grave uncertainty," "substantial doubt," and "moral certainty" improperly diluted the *Winship* standard.

(*c*) A traditionally accepted definition of reasonable doubt is the following, which is required by Cal. Penal Code §1096:

> Reasonable doubt is . . . not a mere possible doubt; because everything relating to human affairs, and depending on moral evidence, is open to some possible or imaginary doubt. It is that state of the case which, after the entire comparison and consideration of all the evidence, leaves the minds of the jurors in that condition that they cannot say they feel an abiding conviction, to a moral certainty, of the truth of the charge.

This language is drawn verbatim from an 1850 jury instruction given by Massachusetts Chief Justice Lemuel Shaw, see Commonwealth v. Webster, 59 Mass. 295, 320 (1850), and it is still in widespread use today. What is the meaning, to a modern juror, of "moral evidence" and "moral certainty"? Does the instruction meet the requirements of *Winship* and Cage v. Louisiana?

16. See Barbara D. Underwood, The Thumb on the Scales of Justice: Burdens of Persuasion in Criminal Cases, 86 Yale L.J. 1299, 1309-1311 (1977); Rita James Simon & Linda Mahan, Quantifying Burdens of Proof, 5 L. & Soc. Rev. 319 (1971). For exploration of the impact of jury instructions generally, see pages 32-34 supra.

In Sandoval v. California, 511 U.S. 1 (1994), the Court distinguished *Cage* and upheld the constitutionality of the California instruction. The court conceded that "the phrase 'moral evidence' is not a mainstay of the modern lexicon," and that "moral certainty is ambiguous" but concluded that the instruction as a whole gave sufficient content to the reasonable doubt requirement. Several concurring justices agreed that use of the nineteenth century phrases was not unconstitutional, but they urged states to choose more comprehensible modern language.

(*d*) Because reasonable doubt is difficult to explain correctly, several courts consider it preferable to give the jury no explanation at all. In United States v. Walton, 207 F.3d 694 (4th Cir. 2000), a jury that had received no explanation of reasonable doubt sent the judge a note asking him to define it. After the judge refused, the jury convicted. The Fourth Circuit affirmed, stating that trying to explain things will "confuse rather than clarify." Is this an appropriate solution to the problem?

5. Subsidiary issues. An important aspect of the overall sufficiency of the evidence is the burden of proof on particular subsidiary issues in the case. Even though the prosecution must prove guilt beyond a reasonable doubt, the state is sometimes permitted to allocate the burden of persuasion on these subsidiary issues to the defense. In situations involving allocation issues, the prosecution normally will concede that it has not proved a particular point beyond a reasonable doubt; the question will be whether it must do so.

The next section explores the issues raised by efforts to change the allocation of the burden of proof.

a. Allocating the Burden of Proof

PATTERSON v. NEW YORK

Supreme Court of the United States
432 U.S. 197 (1977)

JUSTICE WHITE delivered the opinion of the Court. . . .

After a brief and unstable marriage, the appellant, Gordon Patterson, Jr., became estranged from his wife, Roberta. Roberta resumed an association with John Northrup, a neighbor to whom she had been engaged prior to her marriage to appellant. On December 27, 1970, Patterson borrowed a rifle from an acquaintance and went to the residence of his father-in-law. There, he observed his wife through a window in a state of semiundress in the presence of John Northrup. He entered the house and killed Northrup by shooting him in the head.

Patterson was charged with second-degree murder. In New York there are two elements of this crime: (1) "intent to cause the death of another person"; and (2) "caus[ing] the death of such person or of a third person." Malice aforethought is not an element of the crime. In addition, the State permits a person accused of murder to raise an affirmative defense that he "acted under the influence of extreme emotional disturbance for which there was a reasonable explanation or excuse."[a]

a. The relevant provisions of the New York Penal Code may be found at pages 393-394 infra. —EDS.

New York also recognizes the crime of manslaughter. A person is guilty of manslaughter if he intentionally kills another person "under circumstances which do not constitute murder because he acts under the influence of extreme emotional disturbance." Appellant confessed before trial to killing Northrup, but at trial he raised the defense of extreme emotional disturbance.

The jury was instructed as to the elements of the crime of murder. Focusing on the element of intent, the trial court charged:

> [Y]ou must not expect or require the defendant to prove to your satisfaction that his acts were done without the intent to kill. Whatever proof he may have attempted, however far he may have gone in an effort to convince you of his innocence or guiltlessness, he is not obliged, he is not obligated to prove anything. It is always the People's burden to prove his guilt, and to prove that he intended to kill in this instance beyond a reasonable doubt.

The jury was further instructed, consistently with New York law, that the defendant had the burden of proving his affirmative defense by a preponderance of the evidence. The jury was told that if it found beyond a reasonable doubt that appellant had intentionally killed Northrup but that appellant had demonstrated by a preponderance of the evidence that he had acted under the influence of extreme emotional disturbance, it had to find appellant guilty of manslaughter instead of murder.

The jury found appellant guilty of murder. Judgment was entered on the verdict, and the Appellate Division affirmed. While appeal to the New York Court of Appeals was pending, this Court decided Mullaney v. Wilbur, 421 U.S. 684 (1975), in which the Court declared Maine's murder statute unconstitutional. Under the Maine statute, a person accused of murder could rebut the statutory presumption that he committed the offense with "malice aforethought" by proving that he acted in the heat of passion on sudden provocation. The Court held that this scheme improperly shifted the burden of persuasion from the prosecutor to the defendant and was therefore a violation of due process. In the Court of Appeals appellant urged that New York's murder statute is functionally equivalent to the one struck down in *Mullaney* and that therefore his conviction should be reversed.

The Court of Appeals rejected appellant's argument. . . . This appeal ensued. . . .

In determining whether New York's allocation to the defendant of proving the mitigating circumstances of severe emotional disturbance is consistent with due process, it is . . . relevant to note that this defense is a considerably expanded version of the common-law defense of heat of passion on sudden provocation and that at common law the burden of proving the latter, as well as other affirmative defenses — indeed, "all . . . circumstances of justification, excuse or alleviation" — rested on the defendant. 4 W. Blackstone, Commentaries *201. This was the rule when the Fifth Amendment was adopted, and it was the American rule when the Fourteenth Amendment was ratified.

In 1895 the common-law view was abandoned with respect to the insanity defense in federal prosecutions. Davis v. United States, 160 U.S. 469 (1895). This ruling had wide impact on the practice in the federal courts with respect to the burden of proving various affirmative defenses, and the prosecution in a majority of jurisdictions in this country sooner or later came to shoulder the burden of proving the sanity of the accused and of disproving the facts constituting other affirmative defenses, including provocation. *Davis* was not a constitutional ruling, however, as Leland v. Oregon, [343 U.S. 790 (1952)], made clear.

At issue in Leland v. Oregon was the constitutionality under the Due Process Clause of the Oregon rule that the defense of insanity must be proved by the defendant beyond a reasonable doubt. Noting that *Davis* "obviously establish[ed] no constitutional doctrine," the Court refused to strike down the Oregon scheme, saying that the burden of proving all elements of the crime beyond reasonable doubt, including the elements of premeditation and deliberation, was placed on the State under Oregon procedures and remained there throughout the trial. To convict, the jury was required to find each element of the crime beyond a reasonable doubt, based on all the evidence, including the evidence going to the issue of insanity. Only then was the jury "to consider separately the issue of legal sanity per se. . . ." This practice did not offend the Due Process Clause even though among the 20 States then placing the burden of proving his insanity on the defendant, Oregon was alone in requiring him to convince the jury beyond a reasonable doubt. . . .

[After the decision in *Mullaney,* supra,] the Court confirmed that it remained constitutional to burden the defendant with proving his insanity defense when it dismissed, as not raising a substantial federal question, a case in which the appellant specifically challenged the continuing validity of Leland v. Oregon. . . . Rivera v. Delaware, 429 U.S. 877 (1976). . . .

We cannot conclude that Patterson's conviction under the New York law deprived him of due process of law. The crime of murder is defined by the statute, which represents a recent revision of the state criminal code, as causing the death of another person with intent to do so. The death, the intent to kill, and causation are the facts that the State is required to prove beyond a reasonable doubt if a person is to be convicted of murder. No further facts are either presumed or inferred in order to constitute the crime. . . . It seems to us that the State satisfied the mandate of *Winship* [page 35 supra,] that it prove beyond a reasonable doubt "every fact necessary to constitute the crime with which [Patterson was] charged."

. . . New York did no more than *Leland* and *Rivera* permitted it to do. . . . Under those cases, once the facts constituting a crime are established beyond a reasonable doubt, based on all the evidence including the evidence of the defendant's mental state, the State may refuse to sustain the affirmative defense of insanity unless demonstrated by a preponderance of the evidence. . . .

We are unwilling to reconsider *Leland* and *Rivera.* But even if we were to hold that a State must prove sanity to convict once that fact is put in issue, it would not necessarily follow that a State must prove beyond a reasonable doubt every fact, the existence or nonexistence of which it is willing to recognize as an exculpatory or mitigating circumstance affecting the degree of culpability or the severity of the punishment. Here, in revising its criminal code, New York provided the affirmative defense of extreme emotional disturbance, a substantially expanded version of the older heat-of-passion concept; but it was willing to do so only if the facts making out the defense were established by the defendant with sufficient certainty. The State was itself unwilling to undertake to establish the absence of those facts beyond a reasonable doubt, perhaps fearing that proof would be too difficult and that too many persons deserving treatment as murderers would escape that punishment if the evidence need merely raise a reasonable doubt about the defendant's emotional state. It has been said that the new criminal code of New York contains some 25 affirmative defenses which exculpate or mitigate but which must be established by the defendant to be operative.[10] The Due Process Clause, as we see it, does not put New York to the choice of abandoning those defenses or undertaking to disprove their existence in order to convict of a crime which otherwise is within its constitutional powers to sanction by substantial punishment.

The requirement of proof beyond a reasonable doubt in a criminal case is "bottomed on a fundamental value determination of our society that it is far worse to convict an innocent man than to let a guilty man go free." *Winship,* 397 U.S., at 372 (Harlan, J., concurring). . . . While it is clear that our society has willingly chosen to bear a substantial burden in order to protect the innocent, it is equally clear that the risk it must bear is not without limits. . . . Due process does not require that every conceivable step be taken, at whatever cost, to eliminate the possibility of convicting an innocent person. . . .

It is . . . very likely true that fewer convictions of murder would occur if New York were required to negative the affirmative defense at issue here. But in each instance of a murder conviction under the present law, New York will have proved beyond a reasonable doubt that the defendant has intentionally killed another person, an act which it is not disputed the State may constitutionally criminalize and punish. If the State nevertheless chooses to recognize a factor that mitigates the degree of criminality or punishment, we think the State may assure itself that the fact has been established with reasonable certainty. To recognize at all a mitigating circumstance does not require the State to prove its nonexistence in each case in which the fact is put in issue, if in its judgment this would be too cumbersome, too expensive, and too inaccurate.[11] . . .

This view may seem to permit state legislatures to reallocate burdens of proof by labeling as affirmative defenses at least some elements of the crimes now defined in their statutes. But there are obviously constitutional limits beyond which the States may not go in this regard. "[I]t is not within the province of a legislature to declare an individual guilty or presumptively guilty of a crime." McFarland v. American Sugar Rfg. Co., 241 U.S. 79, 86 (1916). The legislature cannot "validly command that the finding of an indictment, or mere proof of

10. The State of New York is not alone in this result: "Since the Model Penal Code was completed in 1962, some 22 states have codified and reformed their criminal laws. At least 12 of these jurisdictions have used the concept of an 'affirmative defense' and have defined that phrase to require that the defendant prove the existence of an 'affirmative defense' by a preponderance of the evidence. . . ." Low & Jeffries, DICTA: Constitutionalizing the Criminal Law?, 29 Va. Law Weekly, No. 18, p. 1 (1977). Even so, the trend over the years appears to have been to require the prosecution to disprove affirmative defenses beyond a reasonable doubt. The split among the various jurisdictions varies for any given defense. . . .

11. The drafters of the Model Penal Code would, as a matter of policy, place the burden of proving the nonexistence of most affirmative defenses, including the defense involved in this case, on the prosecution once the defendant has come forward with some evidence that the defense is present. The drafters recognize the need for flexibility, however, and would, in "some exceptional situations," place the burden of persuasion on the accused. "Characteristically these are situations where the defense does not obtain at all under existing law and the Code seeks to introduce a mitigation. Resistance to the mitigation, based upon the prosecution's difficulty in obtaining evidence, ought to be lowered if the burden of persuasion is imposed on the defendant. Where that difficulty appears genuine and there is something to be said against allowing the defense at all, we consider it defensible to shift the burden in this way." ALI, Model Penal Code §1.13, Comment, p. 113 (Tent. Draft No. 4, 1955). . . .

the identity of the accused, should create a presumption of the existence of all the facts essential to guilt." Tot v. United States, 319 U.S. 463, 469 (1943). . . .

It is urged that Mullaney v. Wilbur necessarily invalidates Patterson's conviction. In *Mullaney* the charge was murder, which the Maine statute defined as the unlawful killing of a human being "with malice aforethought, either express or implied." The trial court instructed the jury that the words "malice aforethought" were most important because "malice aforethought is an essential and indispensable element of the crime of murder." Malice, as the statute indicated and as the court instructed, could be implied and was to be implied from "any deliberate, cruel act committed by one person against another suddenly . . . or without a considerable provocation," in which event an intentional killing was murder unless by a preponderance of the evidence it was shown that the act was committed "in the heat of passion, on sudden provocation." The instructions emphasized that "'malice aforethought and heat of passion on sudden provocation are two inconsistent things'; thus, by proving the latter the defendant would negate the former." . . . This Court . . . unanimously [held] that Wilbur's due process rights had been invaded by the presumption casting upon him the burden of proving by a preponderance of the evidence that he had acted in the heat of passion upon sudden provocation.

Mullaney's holding, it is argued, is that the State may not permit the blameworthiness of an act or the severity of punishment authorized for its commission to depend on the presence or absence of an identified fact without assuming the burden of proving the presence or absence of that fact, as the case may be, beyond a reasonable doubt. In our view, the *Mullaney* holding should not be so broadly read. . . . The Maine Supreme Judicial Court made it clear that . . . malice, in the sense of the absence of provocation, was part of the definition of that crime. Yet malice, i.e., lack of provocation, was presumed and could be rebutted by the defendant only by proving by a preponderance of the evidence that he acted with heat of passion upon sudden provocation. . . .

As we have explained, nothing was presumed or implied against Patterson. . . . The judgment of the New York Court of Appeals is affirmed.

JUSTICE POWELL, with whom JUSTICE BRENNAN and JUSTICE MARSHALL join, dissenting. . . .

Mullaney held invalid Maine's requirement that the defendant prove heat of passion. The Court today, without disavowing the unanimous holding of *Mullaney,* approves New York's requirement that the defendant prove extreme emotional disturbance. The Court manages to run a constitutional boundary line through the barely visible space that separates Maine's law from New York's. It does so on the basis of distinctions in language that are formalistic rather than substantive. . . .

Maine's statute was invalid, the Court reasons, because it "defined [murder] as the unlawful killing of a human being 'with malice aforethought, either express or implied.'" . . . *Winship* was violated only because this "fact" — malice — was "presumed" unless the defendant persuaded the jury otherwise by showing that he acted in the heat of passion. New York, in form presuming no affirmative "fact" against Patterson, and blessed with a statute drafted in the leaner language of the 20th century, escapes constitutional scrutiny unscathed even though the effect on the defendant of New York's placement of the burden of persuasion is exactly the same as Maine's.

This explanation of the *Mullaney* holding bears little resemblance to the basic rationale of that decision. . . . The test the Court today establishes allows a legislature to shift, virtually at will, the burden of persuasion with respect to any factor in a criminal case, so long as it is careful not to mention the nonexistence of that factor in the statutory language that defines the crime. . . .

With all respect, this type of constitutional adjudication is indefensibly formalistic. . . . What *Winship* and *Mullaney* had sought to teach about the limits a free society places on its procedures to safeguard the liberty of its citizens becomes a rather simplistic lesson in statutory draftsmanship. Nothing in the Court's opinion prevents a legislature from applying this new learning to many of the classical elements of the crimes it punishes. . . .[8]

The Court understandably manifests some uneasiness that its formalistic approach will give legislatures too much latitude in shifting the burden of persuasion. And so it issues a warning that "there are obviously constitutional limits beyond which the States may not go in this regard." . . . But if the State is careful to conform to the drafting formulas articulated today, the constitutional limits are anything but "obvious." This decision simply leaves us without a conceptual framework for distinguishing abuses from legitimate legislative adjustments of the burden of persuasion in criminal cases.

It is unnecessary for the Court to retreat to a formalistic test for applying *Winship*. Careful attention to the *Mullaney* decision reveals the principles that should control in this and like cases. *Winship* held that the prosecution must bear the burden of proving beyond a reasonable doubt "the existence of every fact necessary to constitute the crime charged." In *Mullaney* we concluded that heat of passion was one of the "facts" described in *Winship* — that is, a factor as to which the prosecution must bear the burden of persuasion beyond a reasonable doubt. We reached that result only after making two careful inquiries. First, we noted that the presence or absence of heat of passion made a substantial difference in punishment of the offender and in the stigma associated with the conviction. Second, we reviewed the history, in England and this country, of the factor at issue. Central to the holding in *Mullaney* was our conclusion that heat of passion "has been, almost from the inception of the common law of homicide, the single most important factor in determining the degree of culpability attaching to an unlawful homicide."

Implicit in these two inquiries are the principles that should govern this case. The Due Process Clause requires that the prosecutor bear the burden of persuasion beyond a reasonable doubt only if the factor at issue makes a substantial difference in punishment and stigma. The requirement of course applies a fortiori if the factor makes the difference between guilt and innocence. But a substantial difference in punishment alone is not enough. It also must be shown that in the Anglo-American legal tradition the factor in question historically has held that level of importance. If either branch of the test is not met, then the legislature retains its traditional authority over matters of proof. . . .

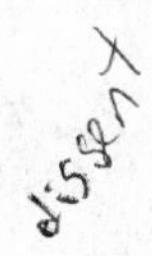

8. For example, a state statute could pass muster under the only solid standard that appears in the Court's opinion if it defined murder as mere physical contact between the defendant and the victim leading to the victim's death, but then set up an affirmative defense leaving it to the defendant to prove that he acted without culpable mens rea. The State, in other words, could be relieved altogether of responsibility for proving *anything* regarding the defendant's state of mind, provided only that the face of the statute meets the Court's drafting formulas. . . .

I hardly need add that New York's provisions allocating the burden of persuasion as to "extreme emotional disturbance" are unconstitutional when judged by these standards. "Extreme emotional disturbance" is, as the Court of Appeals recognized, the direct descendant of the "heat of passion" factor considered at length in *Mullaney*. . . . The presence or absence of extreme emotional disturbance makes a critical difference in punishment and stigma, and throughout our history the resolution of this issue in fact, although expressed in somewhat different terms, has distinguished manslaughter from murder.

The Court beats its retreat from *Winship* apparently because of a concern that otherwise the federal judiciary will intrude too far into substantive choices concerning the content of a State's criminal law. The concern is legitimate, but misplaced. . . . [W]here a State has chosen to retain the traditional distinction between murder and manslaughter, as have New York and Maine, the burden of persuasion must remain on the prosecution with respect to the distinguishing factor, in view of its decisive historical importance. But nothing in *Mullaney* or *Winship* precludes a State from abolishing the distinction between murder and manslaughter and treating all unjustifiable homicide as murder.[13] In this significant respect, neither *Winship* nor *Mullaney* eliminates the substantive flexibility that should remain in legislative hands.

Moreover, it is unlikely that more than a few factors — although important ones — for which a shift in the burden of persuasion seriously would be considered will come within the *Mullaney* holding. . . . New ameliorative affirmative defenses, about which the Court expresses concern, generally remain undisturbed by the holdings in *Winship* and *Mullaney* — and need not be disturbed by a sound holding reversing Patterson's conviction.

Furthermore, as we indicated in *Mullaney*, even as to those factors upon which the prosecution must bear the burden of persuasion, the State retains an important procedural device to avoid jury confusion and prevent the prosecution from being unduly hampered. The State normally may shift to the defendant the burden of production, that is, the burden of going forward with sufficient evidence "to justify [a reasonable] doubt upon the issue." If the defendant's evidence does not cross this threshold, the issue — be it malice, extreme emotional disturbance, self-defense, or whatever — will not be submitted to the jury. . . .

NOTES AND QUESTIONS

1. The burden of production versus the burden of persuasion. Rules allocating the burden of proof deal with two distinct problems. The first concerns allocating

13. Perhaps under other principles of due process jurisprudence, certain factors are so fundamental that a State could not, as a substantive matter, refrain from recognizing them so long as it chooses to punish given conduct as a crime. . . . But substantive limits were not at issue in *Winship* or *Mullaney*, and they are not at issue here.

Even if there are no constitutional limits preventing the State, for example, from treating all homicides as murders punishable equally regardless of mitigating factors like heat of passion or extreme emotional disturbance, the *Winship/Mullaney* rule still plays an important role. The State is then obliged to make its choices concerning the substantive content of its criminal laws with full awareness of the consequences, unable to mask substantive policy choices by shifts in the burden of persuasion. See Fletcher, Two Kinds of Legal Rules: A Comparative Study of Burden-of-Persuasion Practices in Criminal Cases, 77 Yale L.J. 880, 894 (1968). . . .

the burden of coming forward with enough evidence to put a certain fact in issue. This is commonly referred to as the burden of *production*. The second problem concerns allocating the burden of convincing the trier of fact. This is commonly referred to as the burden of *persuasion*. With respect to most elements of most crimes, the prosecution bears *both* burdens. That is, the prosecution must introduce enough evidence not only to put the facts in issue but also to persuade the trier of fact beyond a reasonable doubt. In some instances state law may require the defense to bear both burdens, and *Patterson* deals with the question of when this is constitutionally permissible. But note that an intermediate position is possible: State law might allocate the burden of *production* to the defense but the burden of *persuasion* to the prosecution. For example, the state might provide that a defendant seeking acquittal on grounds of duress must introduce some evidence of duress,[17] but that once this is done, the prosecution must prove the absence of duress beyond a reasonable doubt. In this situation it is sometimes said (confusingly) that the defendant bears the initial burden of proof and that, once duress is at issue, the burden *shifts* to the prosecution. Or it may be said that absence of duress is *presumed*, but that when evidence of duress is introduced the presumption is *rebutted* or simply *disappears*. All these expressions are equivalent to the more straightforward statement that the defendant bears the burden of production and the prosecution the burden of persuasion.

When the defendant bears the burden of production on an issue, the issue is commonly referred to as an *affirmative defense*. In some states, when an issue is designated an affirmative defense, the defendant must bear the burdens of both production and persuasion, but it is common practice to treat burdens of production and persuasion as separate issues. Thus, the defendant may bear the burden of persuasion on *some* affirmative defenses, but with respect to others he may bear *only* the burden of production. Under the Model Penal Code, the defendant generally bears only the burden of production, and once an affirmative defense is raised, the prosecution must disprove it beyond a reasonable doubt. See Model Penal Code §1.12(2)(a), Appendix.

When the defendant bears the burden of production, how much evidence is necessary to satisfy that burden so that the prosecution will be required to disprove the claim beyond a reasonable doubt? Most courts require that the evidence be sufficient to raise at least a reasonable doubt on the matter. See Frazier v. Weatherholtz, 572 F.2d 994 (4th Cir. 1978). When the defense produces evidence sufficient to satisfy the threshold requirements, it becomes necessary to determine which party must bear the burden of persuading the trier of fact.

2. *Allocating the burden of persuasion: the basis of* Patterson. Are states free to allocate the burden of persuasion however they choose, or does the reasoning of *Patterson* suggest some limits? Consider the following problems.

(*a*) *The formal structure of the statute.* Suppose that (as is commonly the case)

17. With respect to certain special defenses, notably alibi and insanity, states sometimes require that the defendant give notice of the claim by pleading it prior to trial. Typically, however, the defendant need not raise the defense by a formal pleading, even when he has the burden of production. Note also that the prosecutor's case may itself contain evidence sufficient to put some defense in issue. For example, testimony that defendant shot the deceased during a quarrel may include at least some evidence supportive of a self-defense claim. The burden of production is then satisfied even if the evidence is not offered by the defense itself. When we say that the defendant bears the burden of production we mean not that defense witnesses must produce the evidence directly but only that the defense will lose on the issue if some evidence is not produced.

state law defines murder as an "unlawful killing with malice aforethought." Under such a statute a justification like self-defense presumably renders a killing lawful and thus negates one of the definitional elements of murder. Does this mean that the constitution forbids imposing the burden of persuasion on the defendant on the self-defense issue? Should the result be different if state law explicitly describes self-defense as an affirmative defense; if state law expressly imposes the burden of persuasion on the defendant; or only if the word *unlawful* is absent from the language defining murder? Why should constitutional requirements turn on distinctions of this kind? Compare Wynn v. Mahoney, 600 F.2d 448 (4th Cir. 1979) (placing burden on defendant is unconstitutional because in North Carolina "unlawfulness" is an element of murder), with Williams v. Mohn, 462 F. Supp. 756 (N.D. W. Va. 1978) (opposite result because in West Virginia "unlawfulness" not an element of murder).

(*b*) *Liberalizing and nonliberalizing changes in the law.* In *Patterson* the affirmative defense involved "a substantially expanded version of the older heat-of-passion concept," and the Court stressed the need for permitting the states flexibility in this situation. But what if, after *Patterson,* a state shifts to the defendant a burden of persuasion previously imposed on the prosecution and does not enlarge the scope of the defense? Should it matter whether the traditional defense might otherwise have been restricted or repealed?

3. Should the greater power include the lesser? The *Patterson* majority assumed that New York could eliminate the "extreme emotional disturbance" defense altogether, a point conceded by Justice Powell's dissent. If this is so, how can there be any serious challenge to the constitutionality of recognizing the defense only in diluted form, that is, when the defendant can prove it? Several commentators argue that "the greater power should include the lesser."[18] Under this analysis the constitutionality of imposing a burden of persuasion on the defendant would not depend on either the formal structure of the statute or the kind of historical analysis emphasized in the dissent. Rather, states would be free to reallocate burdens of persuasion relating to any fact that is not a constitutionally mandated prerequisite to just punishment, but conversely, states would be required to prove a fact beyond a reasonable doubt if punishment would be impermissible (or excessive, violating Eighth Amendment proportionality requirements) as applied to conduct not involving that fact. See, e.g., Ronald Allen, The Restoration of *In re Winship:* A Comment on Burdens of Persuasion in Criminal Cases after Patterson v. New York, 76 Mich. L. Rev. 30 (1977). Consider the following comments.

John C. Jeffries Jr. & Paul B. Stephan, Defenses, Presumptions and Burdens of Proof in the Criminal Law, 88 Yale L.J. 1325, 1345-1347 (1979): The chief justification for proof beyond a reasonable doubt in general has always been thought to be that it enhances the certainty of the factual findings needed for criminal conviction. . . . The trouble is that this rationale does not justify the rule for which it is offered. Implementing the presumption of innocence — whether on an ac-

18. The originator of the greater-includes-the-lesser argument in this context is generally thought to be Justice Holmes, who advanced it in his opinion for the Court in Ferry v. Ramsey, 277 U.S. 88 (1928).

tual or a symbolic level — requires that *something* be proved beyond a reasonable doubt. It does not, however, speak to the question of *what* that something must be. . . . In our view, these rationales extend only so far as the substantive issue at stake is thought to be an essential ingredient of the state's case. When, in contrast, the state considers a gratuitous defense, that is, one that it may grant or deny as it sees fit, a constitutional insistence on proof beyond a reasonable doubt no longer makes sense. Such a rule would purport to preserve individual liberty and the societal sense of commitment to it by forcing the government *either* to disprove the defense beyond a reasonable doubt *or* to eliminate the defense altogether. The latter solution results in an extension of penal liability despite the presence of mitigating or exculpatory facts. It is difficult to see this result as constitutionally compelled and harder still to believe that it flows from a general policy, whether actual or symbolic, in favor of individual liberty. . . .

The trouble lies in trying to define justice in exclusively procedural terms. *Winship*'s insistence on the reasonable doubt standard is thought to express a preference for letting the guilty go free rather than risking conviction of the innocent. This value choice, however, cannot be implemented by a purely procedural concern with burden of proof. Guilt and innocence are substantive concepts. Their content depends on the choice of facts determinative of liability. If this choice is remitted to unconstrained legislative discretion, no rule of constitutional procedure can restrain the potential for injustice. . . .

Barbara D. Underwood, The Thumb on the Scales of Justice: Burdens of Persuasion in Criminal Cases, 86 Yale L.J. 1299, 1312-1313, 1321-1324 (1977): [The author challenges the "greater includes the lesser" argument on several grounds. First, she argues, adjusting burdens of proof is an inappropriate way of compromising disputes over the proper reach of substantive law. Second, this approach tends to obscure the substantive commands of the law. Excerpts from the discussion of these two points follow.]

[First, s]uppose that a legislature has decided to prohibit the possession of certain narcotic drugs. Suppose further that there is a controversy over a proposal to exempt from punishment those who possess narcotics solely for their personal use. Proponents and opponents of the defense might well seek an intermediate position that would recognize a defense for some, but not all, of those who possess for personal use. One possibility for substantive compromise would be to exempt from punishment only those who possess specified small quantities for personal use. Another possibility would be to exempt only those who possess for personal use in the privacy of their homes. Each of these compromises, by redefining the prohibited conduct, seeks to accommodate differing views about the harm caused, or the harm threatened, or the culpability of the actor in various situations. . . .

A substantive disagreement about whether to recognize a defense [of possession solely for personal use] amounts to a disagreement about whether the person with the proposed defense is less suitable than other offenders for specified criminal sanctions. By shifting the burden of persuasion [on the personal-use issue] to the defendant, a legislature limits the defense to those for whom the evidence is most abundant. That group, however, is not necessarily the least culpable, least harmful, or least deterrable. . . . An exception [to the reasonable-doubt rule] designed solely for the purpose of compromise would subvert the policies of the rule, without accomplishing an appropriate compromise of substantive disagreements. . . .

[Second, a]lthough popular understanding of the substantive law is notoriously deficient, rules about proof at trial are even less accessible to popular understanding than rules about conduct in society. One consequence of that fact is that . . . unusual rules of proof, even more than unusual substantive laws, are likely to trap an unsuspecting public into reliance on a false idea of the law. . . . This is an argument for truth-in-labeling.

For scholarship critical of *Patterson*'s "greater includes the lesser" approach, see Scott E. Sunby, The Reasonable Doubt Rule and the Meaning of Innocence, 40 Hastings L.J. 457 (1989); Donald A. Dripps, The Constitutional Status of the Reasonable Doubt Rule, 75 Cal. L. Rev. 1665 (1987). Both authors argue that the due process clause should be construed to require proof beyond a reasonable doubt for any fact that makes a significant difference in the authorized range of punishment.

4. Nongratuitous defenses. In *Patterson* the affirmative defense was "gratuitous," in the sense that the state could have eliminated the defense completely. Should the state's freedom to shift the burden of proof extend to defenses that are *not* gratuitous? Consider, for example, the insanity defense. There is a long-standing debate (see pages 902-905 infra) over the question whether some form of an insanity defense is constitutionally mandated. Yet in Rivera v. Delaware (discussed in *Patterson,* page 40 supra), the court summarily dismissed a challenge to a Delaware law that required the defendant to bear the burden of proving insanity. Should *Rivera* be read as holding, by implication, that states are free to eliminate the insanity defense completely? If not, what is the justification for permitting states to avoid the reasonable doubt requirement and to "dilute" a defense that may be constitutionally mandated?

In connection with these questions consider Martin v. Ohio, 480 U.S. 228 (1987). The defendant shot her husband in what she claimed was an act of self-defense. She was charged with aggravated murder, which is defined under Ohio law as a killing "purposely, and with prior calculation and design." Ohio law also provides that self-defense is a complete defense when "the defendant was not at fault in creating the situation giving rise to the argument; [and] had an honest belief that she was in imminent danger of death or great bodily harm and that her only means of escape from such danger was in the use of such force. . . ." At trial, the jury was instructed that the prosecution had to prove beyond a reasonable doubt all the elements of aggravated murder, but that the defendant was required to prove her self-defense claim by a preponderance of the evidence. The defendant's aggravated murder conviction was upheld by the Supreme Court. Writing for the majority, Justice White said (id. at 233-235):

> The State did not exceed its authority in defining the crime of murder as purposely causing the death of another with prior calculation or design. It did not seek to shift to Martin the burden of proving any of those elements, and the jury's verdict reflects that none of her self-defense evidence raised a reasonable doubt about the state's proof that she purposefully killed with prior calculation and design. . . .
>
> Petitioner submits that there can be no conviction under Ohio law unless the defendant's conduct is unlawful and that because self-defense renders lawful what

> would otherwise be a crime, unlawfulness is an element of the offense that the state must prove by disproving self-defense. [B]ut the Ohio courts hold that the unlawfulness in cases like this is the conduct satisfying the elements of aggravated murder — an interpretation of state law that we are not in a position to dispute. The . . . the necessary mental state for aggravated murder under Ohio law is the specific purpose to take life pursuant to prior calculation and design.

Justice Powell, writing for the four dissenters, argued that the defense claim of imminently necessary self-defense was inherently inconsistent with the prosecution claim of killing "by prior calculation and design." As a result, he argued, the instruction requiring the defendant to prove self-defense was in direct conflict with the instruction requiring the prosecution to prove aggravated murder beyond a reasonable doubt. As to this point, the majority asserted (id. at 235) that "the instructions were sufficiently clear to convey to the jury that the state's burden of proving prior calculation did not shift."

Note that no problem of conflicting instructions would be present if murder were simply defined as an intentional killing (without prior calculation or design). Yet no member of the Court challenged Justice White's assertion, supra, that "[t]he State did not exceed its authority in defining the crime of murder as purposely causing the death of another. . . ." Is this so clear? Could a state constitutionally abolish the defense of self-defense altogether? Could the state condemn as a murderer, and sentence to long-term imprisonment, a person who kills when such an act is the only available means to avoid an unlawful threat of imminent death?[19]

5. *Sentencing enhancements.* Legislatures often define a crime and then specify, in a separate sentencing section, that the range of punishments to be imposed, or the minimum punishment that must be imposed, will depend on certain characteristics of the offense committed (such as whether a firearm was used; whether a given quantity of drugs was involved). Usually the judge determines at a sentencing hearing whether such circumstances exist and then imposes sentence accordingly. The procedure at the sentencing hearing is relatively informal, and the judge need only determine by a preponderance of the evidence any facts crucial to fixing the sentence. See McMillan v. Pennsylvania, 477 U.S. 79 (1986), and the materials in Chapter 2, page 150 infra.

Clearly, this technique affords an easy way to ease the burden of compliance with the requirement of proof beyond a reasonable doubt — facts that dictate a large increase in punishment can be established merely by a preponderance of the evidence. But this technique is available only when the facts at issue are merely "sentencing factors," rather than elements of a separate offense. For facts of the latter sort, as *Mullaney* holds, nothing less than proof beyond a reasonable doubt will suffice. A technical question of statutory structure therefore takes on great importance and offers a rich field for litigation — when is a fact that enhances the sentence merely a sentencing factor and when is it an element of a separate, aggravated offense?

20. The issue was raised in Rowe v. Debruyn, 17 F.3d 1047 (7th Cir. 1994), where, under Indiana prison regulations, a prisoner was disciplined even though his assault on another prisoner was necessary to resist being raped. A majority held that even if a person has a constitutional right to use physical force in self-defense, that right does not extend to prisons, where the use of violence against violence would disserve order and safety in prison life. The dissent argued that the right of self-defense is so fundamental that it must extend to all contexts, within as well as outside prisons.

The federal carjacking statute, 18 U.S.C. §2119, provides that whoever takes an automobile from another person by force or intimidation "shall . . . be imprisoned not more than 15 years [but] if serious bodily injury . . . results, [shall be] imprisoned not more than 25 years." In Jones v. United States, 526 U.S. 225 (1999), the Court held that this provision sets forth distinct offenses and that "serious bodily injury" was an element of the aggravated offense; accordingly the defendant had a right to have that fact determined by the jury beyond a reasonable doubt.

In Castillo v. United States, 120 S. Ct. 2090 (2000), the Court considered a federal statute that imposed a mandatory sentence enhancement of 5 years for committing a crime with an ordinary firearm and 30 years for committing a crime with a machine gun; the Court again held that the statute created separate crimes and that use of a "machine gun" was an offense element that must be proved beyond a reasonable doubt. The Court stressed that the crucial fact was not too complicated to be resolved at the trial phase and that the severity of the additional sentence that would result also created a strong ground for treating the fact as an offense element rather than as a mere sentencing factor. Though states presumably can still avoid the reasonable-doubt requirement by sufficiently clear statutory drafting, the Supreme Court seems increasingly inclined to resolve any ambiguity in favor of requiring the higher burden of proof.

6. How should a state exercise its discretion? Even where *Patterson* leaves a state free to impose a burden of persuasion on the defendant, the decision does not imply that the state must do so or should do so. State legislatures (or state courts, when statutes do not control) must decide what is desirable with respect to each defense of this kind. Those making the choice usually consider whether the defendant would have more access to the relevant evidence, whether a defendant's claim would be difficult to refute beyond a reasonable doubt, and whether placing the burden of persuasion on the prosecution would prevent recognition of a new or expanded substantive defense. Burden-of-proof questions therefore should be reconsidered in light of problems associated with particular substantive law doctrines.

7. Further reading. For a useful analysis of the early American decisions and a comparison to French and German approaches, see George Fletcher, Two Kinds of Legal Rules: A Comparative Study of Burden-of-Persuasion Practices in Criminal Cases, 77 Yale L.J. 880 (1968). See also Fernand N. Dutile, The Burden of Proof in Criminal Cases: A Comment on the *Mullaney-Patterson* Doctrine, 55 Notre Dame Law. 380 (1980); Marina Angel, Substantive Due Process and the Criminal Law, 9 Loy. Chi. L.J. 61, 93-111 (1977).

b. Presumptions

As the preceding section shows, the prosecution's burden of proof often can be eased by defining an offense in such a way that the burden of proving certain facts can be assigned to the defense. Another device that can ease the prosecutor's burden is the *presumption.* The presumption can come into play even when the state has not (or cannot) exercise the *Patterson* option of reallocating the burden of proof. Suppose, for example, that murder is defined as an *intentional* killing. The state might hesitate to redefine murder as including all killing (with lack of intent relevant only as an affirmative defense). Can the state instead choose to retain intent as a required element of murder, but then provide that the existence of the necessary intent will be *presumed* from some other fact (for example, from the use of a deadly weapon)? This section considers the significance of "presumptions" and the constitutional limits on their use.

NOTES ON PRESUMPTIONS

1. The terminology of presumptions. Professor Charles McCormick wrote (Evidence §342, at 802-803 (2d ed. 1972)): "One ventures the assertion that 'presumption' is the slipperiest member of the family of legal terms, except its first cousin, 'burden of proof.' One author has listed no less than eight senses in which the term has been used by the courts." To understand the significance of a presumption, one cannot simply resort to a dictionary but must focus on the precise effect of the presumption at trial. True presumptions concern an inference of fact to be drawn from some other fact in evidence. Normally there must, at a minimum, be some rational connection between the fact proved and the other fact to be inferred from it. But such common presumptions as the *presumption of innocence* do not function in this evidentiary sense at all. We shall call them *misnamed presumptions.*

(*a*) *Misnamed presumptions.* It is commonly said that a defendant in a criminal case is "presumed innocent until proven guilty." Is this because there is some "rational connection," a "more-often-than-not" relationship between being charged as defendant and being innocent? Obviously not: The vast majority of criminal defendants are ultimately found guilty, and indeed the filing of an indictment requires a formal finding of probable guilt. The presumption of innocence does not concern the drawing of rational inferences from facts in evidence but rather is simply a traditional way of stating that the prosecution bears the burden of proving guilt beyond a reasonable doubt. Similarly, it is common to state that an intentional killing is "presumed to be unlawful," unless the defendant produces evidence of some justification. What is normally meant is that the defendant has the burden of production (and possibly the burden of persuasion) on the issue of justification. As we have seen earlier in this chapter, pages 35-50 supra, there are constitutional limitations applicable here, but the applicable tests do not involve the requirement of some "rational connection." It could be that intentional killings are often, even half the time, committed in self-defense: A true presumption — an evidentiary inference of no self-defense — would surely be unconstitutional, but a presumption that serves only to allocate the burden of production is permitted.

(*b*) *True presumptions.* True presumptions deal with inferences drawn from a fact actually proved (the *basic fact*) to some other critical fact (the *presumed fact*). Typically the presumed fact is one on which the prosecution bears the burden of persuasion. The presumption makes this burden easier to carry.

A presumption may ease the prosecution's burden in several distinct ways. For example, a presumption might *allow* the jury to draw the inference from basic to presumed fact, or instead the presumption might *require* the jury to draw the inference. The former are often called *permissive* presumptions or permissive inferences; the latter are often called *mandatory* presumptions. Presumptions may also differ in the extent to which they remain effective after the defense offers rebuttal evidence to negate the presumed fact.[21] At one extreme a presumption requiring an inference to be drawn might remain in effect no matter how much evidence was offered to refute the presumed fact. A presumption of this kind is often called a *conclusive presumption:* In effect it is not a presumption at all because it establishes a substantive rule rendering the basic fact determinative and the presumed fact legally irrelevant. (Do you see why?) At the other extreme, the effect of a presumption might be entirely eliminated once the defense produces a rather small quantum of evidence. A presumption of this kind has precisely the same effect as a rule allocating the burden of production (do you see why?), and once that production burden is satisfied, the so-called presumption has no impact at all on the burden of persuasion.

Other presumptions retain some force even after rebuttal evidence is introduced, but the range of possible variations is wide. For the sake of convenience we will divide the true presumptions into two major categories: First are the *mandatory-but-rebuttable* presumptions. Here the jury will be told that upon proof of the basic fact, it *must* find the presumed fact, unless a given quantum of rebuttal evidence is forthcoming. Second, we have *permissive inferences.* Here the jury will be told that upon proof of the basic fact it *may* (but is not required) to find the presumed fact. Thus, the jury may reject the presumed fact even if no rebuttal is offered, and it may find the presumed fact even if extensive rebuttal is offered.

2. Constitutional limitations. The Supreme Court has developed standards governing the constitutionality of conclusive presumptions, mandatory-but-rebuttable presumptions, and permissive inferences.

(*a*) Because a conclusive presumption in effect renders the presumed fact legally immaterial, such a presumption will be unconstitutional whenever the presumed fact is constitutionally required for conviction. A related principle applies when the presumed fact, though not constitutionally mandated, has been made relevant by the state's own definition of an offense. *Patterson* appears to prohibit states from identifying a fact as a required element and then evading its responsibility to prove the fact beyond a reasonable doubt. Thus a conclusive presumption of intent would be unconstitutional, even though the state presumably could replace the intent element with whatever lesser facts were thought sufficient to justify the conclusive presumption.

(*b*) In County Court v. Allen, 442 U.S. 140 (1979), the Supreme Court developed rules applicable to mandatory presumptions and permissive inferences. The Court said that a mandatory presumption (one that the jury is required to accept in the absence of defense rebuttal) would pass muster only if, over the generality of cases, it held true beyond a reasonable doubt. In contrast, a permissive inference would pass muster if it was "more likely than not" to hold true on the facts of the particular case.

3. Is the standard applied to permissive inferences consistent with the requirement of proof beyond a reasonable doubt? The question is important because crucial elements of an offense are often established with the aid of such inferences. For example, courts often instruct that knowledge of the stolen char-

21. Note that the defense also may offer evidence to challenge the existence of the basic fact. Since the presumption cannot come into play until the trier of fact is satisfied that the *basic* fact exists, refuting the basic fact will always render the presumption inoperative.

acter of goods can be inferred from unexplained possession, or that possession and control of an illegal substance can be inferred from the defendant's presence on the premises where it is found. Consider the facts of *County Court:* Four persons, three adult males and a 16-year-old girl, riding in a Chevrolet, were stopped for speeding on the New York Thruway. Two large-caliber handguns were seen through the window of the car by the investigating police officer. The weapons were in an open handbag on either the front floor or the front seat of the car on the passenger side where the girl was sitting, and she admitted that the handbag was hers. All four people in the car were charged with illegal possession of the handguns, and at trial the judge instructed the jurors that upon proof of the presence of a firearm in an automobile, they were permitted to infer possession by all persons then occupying the vehicle. All four defendants were convicted, and the Supreme Court affirmed.

Question: If the inference in *County Court* is no better than rational (more likely than not), then is the jury in effect permitted to find the presumed fact (that is, possession) on a mere preponderance of the evidence? How can such a permissive inference be reconciled with *Winship* and *Mullaney*? In *County Court,* Justice Stevens wrote for the majority (442 U.S. at 167):

> There is no more reason to require a permissive statutory presumption to meet a reasonable doubt standard before it may be permitted to play any part in a trial than there is to require that degree of probative force for other relevant evidence before it may be admitted. As long as it is clear that the presumption is not the sole and sufficient basis for a finding of guilt, it need only satisfy the [more likely than not] test. . . .

4. Sandstrom v. Montana, 442 U.S. 510 (1979), involved a prosecution for "deliberate homicide." Under Montana law one element of the offense was an intent to kill. The defendant admitted the act of killing but introduced evidence suggesting that the act was not intentional. The jury was instructed that "[t]he law presumes that a person intends the ordinary consequences of his voluntary acts." On appeal from the conviction, the prosecution contended that the quoted language (which was not otherwise explained to the jury) established either a permissive inference or at most only a mandatory presumption rebuttable by "some" evidence and that under either interpretation the presumption satisfied applicable standards. The Supreme Court unanimously reversed. The Court held that the jurors might have understood the instruction either as establishing a conclusive presumption (that is, that intent was deemed to be established regardless of the defendant's proof) or as shifting the burden of persuasion (that is, requiring the defendant to prove the lack of intent by at least a preponderance of the evidence). In either event the presumption violated *Winship,* page 35 supra, and *Mullaney,* page 39 supra, because state law specifically made intent an element of the offense. The Court accordingly did not reach the question whether the instruction would pass muster if it were coupled with language clearly rendering its effect permissive or mandatory-but-rebuttable.

PROBLEMS

1. Leverett was prosecuted for negligent homicide after his vehicle struck and killed a pedestrian. The judge instructed the jury that "[i]f there was at that time [a blood-alcohol] concentration of 0.10 or more, it shall be presumed that the person was under the influence of alcohol. Such presumption is rebuttable." Was the instruction constitutionally permissible? See State v. Leverett, 245 Mont. 124, 799 P.2d 119 (1990).

2. Consider the facts of Francis v. Franklin, 471 U.S. 307, 309-312 (1985):

> Raymond Lee Franklin, then 21 years old and imprisoned for offenses unrelated to this case, sought to escape custody on January 17, 1979, while he and three other prisoners were receiving dental care at a local dentist's office. The four prisoners were secured by handcuffs to the same 8-foot length of chain as they sat in the dentist's waiting room. At some point Franklin was released from the chain, taken into the dentist's office and given preliminary treatment, and then escorted back to the waiting room. As another prisoner was being released, Franklin, who had not been reshackled, seized a pistol from one of the two officers and managed to escape. He forced the dentist's assistant to accompany him as a hostage.
>
> . . . They came to the home of the victim, one Collie. Franklin pounded on the heavy wooden front door of the home and Collie, a retired 72-year-old carpenter, answered. Franklin was pointing the stolen pistol at the door when Collie arrived. As Franklin demanded his car keys, Collie slammed the door. At this moment Franklin's gun went off. The bullet traveled through the wooden door and into Collie's chest killing him. Seconds later the gun fired again. The second bullet traveled upward through the door and into the ceiling of the residence.
>
> Hearing the shots, the victim's wife entered the front room. In the confusion accompanying the shooting, the dental assistant fled and Franklin did not attempt to stop her. Franklin entered the house, demanded the car keys from the victim's wife, and added the threat "I might as well kill you." When she did not provide the keys, however, he made no effort to thwart her escape. . . . Failing to obtain a car, Franklin left and remained at large until nightfall.
>
> Shortly after being captured, Franklin made a formal statement to the authorities in which he admitted that he had shot the victim but emphatically denied that he did so voluntarily or intentionally. He claimed that the shots were fired in accidental response to the slamming of the door. He was tried in the Superior Court of Bibb County, Georgia, on charges of malice murder[1] — a capital offense in Georgia — and kidnapping. His sole defense to the malice murder charge was a lack of the requisite intent to kill. To support his version of the events Franklin offered substantial circumstantial evidence tending to show a lack of intent. He claimed that the circumstances surrounding the firing of the gun, particularly the slamming of the door and the trajectory of the second bullet, supported the hypothesis of accident, and that his immediate confession to that effect buttressed the assertion. He also argued that his treatment of every other person encountered during the escape indicated a lack of disposition to use force.
>
> [The trial judge instructed the jury that "the defendant enters upon his trial with the presumption of innocence in his favor and this presumption . . . remains with him throughout the trial, unless it is overcome by evidence sufficiently strong to satisfy you of his guilt . . . beyond a reasonable doubt."] On the dispositive issue of intent, the trial judge instructed the jury as follows:
>
>> . . . A person shall not be found guilty of any crime committed by misfortune or accident where it satisfactorily appears there was no criminal scheme

1. The malice murder statute at the time in question provided: "A person commits murder when he unlawfully and with malice aforethought, either express or implied, causes the death of another human being. . . . Malice shall be implied where no considerable provocation appears and where all the circumstances of the killing show an abandoned and malignant heart."

> or undertaking or intention or criminal negligence. The acts of a person of sound mind and discretion are presumed to be the product of the person's will, but the presumption may be rebutted. A person of sound mind and discretion is presumed to intend the natural and probable consequences of his acts, but the presumption may be rebutted. A person will not be presumed to act with criminal intention but the trier of facts, that is, the Jury, may find criminal intention upon a consideration of the words, conduct, demeanor, motive and all other circumstances connected with the act for which the accused is prosecuted.

[The jury] returned a verdict of guilty. The next day Franklin was sentenced to death for the murder conviction.

On appeal, what should be the result?

4. *The Role of the Jury*

DUNCAN v. LOUISIANA

Supreme Court of the United States
391 U.S. 145 (1968)

JUSTICE WHITE delivered the opinion of the Court.

Appellant, Gary Duncan, was convicted of simple battery in the Twenty-fifth Judicial District Court of Louisiana. Under Louisiana law simple battery is a misdemeanor, punishable by two years' imprisonment and a $300 fine. Appellant sought trial by jury, but because the Louisiana Constitution grants jury trials only in cases in which capital punishment or imprisonment at hard labor may be imposed, the trial judge denied the request. Appellant was convicted and sentenced to serve 60 days in the parish prison and pay a fine of $150. Appellant sought review in the Supreme Court of Louisiana, asserting that the denial of jury trial violated rights guaranteed to him by the United States Constitution. The Supreme Court [of Louisiana denied review.] We noted probable jurisdiction. . . .

While driving on Highway 23 in Plaquemines Parish on October 19, 1966, [appellant] saw two younger cousins engaged in a conversation by the side of the road with four white boys. Knowing his cousins, Negroes who had recently transferred to a formerly all-white high school, had reported the occurrence of racial incidents at the school, Duncan stopped the car, got out, and approached the six boys. . . . The testimony was in dispute on many points, but the witnesses agreed that appellant and the white boys spoke to each other, that appellant encouraged his cousins to break off the encounter and enter his car, and that appellant was about to enter the car himself for the purpose of driving away with his cousins. The whites testified that just before getting in the car appellant slapped Herman Landry, one of the white boys, on the elbow. The Negroes testified that appellant had not slapped Landry, but had merely touched him. The trial judge concluded that the State had proved beyond a reasonable doubt that Duncan had committed simple battery, and found him guilty.

. . . Because we believe that trial by jury in criminal cases is fundamental to the American scheme of justice, we hold that the Fourteenth Amendment guarantees a right of jury trial in all criminal cases which — were they to be tried in a federal court — would come within the Sixth Amendment's guarantee. Since we

holding

consider the appeal before us to be such a case, we hold that the Constitution was violated when appellant's demand for jury trial was refused.

The history of trial by jury in criminal cases has been frequently told. It is sufficient for present purposes to say that by the time our Constitution was written, jury trial in criminal cases had been in existence in England for several centuries and carried impressive credentials traced by many to Magna Carta. Its preservation and proper operation as a protection against arbitrary rule were among the major objectives of the revolutionary settlement which was expressed in the Declaration and Bill of Rights of 1689. . . .

The guarantees of jury trial in the Federal and State Constitutions reflect a profound judgment about the way in which law should be enforced and justice administered. A right to jury trial is granted to criminal defendants in order to prevent oppression by the Government. Those who wrote our constitutions knew from history and experience that it was necessary to protect against unfounded criminal charges brought to eliminate enemies and against judges too responsive to the voice of higher authority. The framers of the constitutions strove to create an independent judiciary but insisted upon further protection against arbitrary action. Providing an accused with the right to be tried by a jury of his peers gave him an inestimable safeguard against the corrupt or overzealous prosecutor and against the compliant, biased, or eccentric judge. If the defendant preferred the common-sense judgment of a jury to the more tutored but perhaps less sympathetic reaction of the single judge, he was to have it. Beyond this, the jury trial provisions in the Federal and State Constitutions reflect a fundamental decision about the exercise of official power — a reluctance to entrust plenary powers over the life and liberty of the citizen to one judge or to a group of judges. . . . The deep commitment of the Nation to the right of jury trial in serious criminal cases as a defense against arbitrary law enforcement qualifies for protection under the Due Process Clause of the Fourteenth Amendment, and must therefore be respected by the States. . . .

We are aware of the long debate, especially in this century, among those who write about the administration of justice, as to the wisdom of permitting untrained laymen to determine the facts in civil and criminal proceedings. [M]ost of the controversy has centered on the jury in civil cases. [A]t the heart of the dispute have been express or implicit assertions that juries are incapable of adequately understanding evidence or determining issues of fact and that they are . . . little better than a roll of dice. Yet, the most recent and exhaustive study of the jury in criminal cases concluded that juries do understand the evidence and come to sound conclusions in most of the cases presented to them and that when juries differ with the result at which the judge would have arrived, it is usually because they are serving some of the very purposes for which they were created and for which they are now employed.[26]

The State of Louisiana urges that holding that the Fourteenth Amendment assures a right to jury trial will cast doubt on the integrity of every trial conducted without a jury. . . . We would not assert, however, that every criminal trial — or any particular trial — held before a judge alone is unfair or that a defendant may never be as fairly treated by a judge as he would be by a jury. Thus we hold no constitutional doubts about the practices, common in both federal

26. Kalven & Zeisel, [The American Jury (1966)].

and state courts, of accepting waivers of jury trial and prosecuting petty crimes without extending a right to jury trial. However, the fact is that in most places more trials for serious crimes are to juries than to a court alone; a great many defendants prefer the judgment of a jury to that of a court. Even where defendants are satisfied with bench trials, the right to a jury trial very likely serves its intended purpose of making judicial or prosecutorial unfairness less likely.

Louisiana's final contention is that even if it must grant jury trials in serious criminal cases, the conviction before us is valid and constitutional because here the petitioner was tried for simple battery and was sentenced to only 60 days in the parish prison. We are not persuaded. It is doubtless true that there is a category of petty crimes or offenses which is not subject to the Sixth Amendment jury trial provision and should not be subject to the Fourteenth Amendment jury trial requirement here applied to the States. . . .

We need not, however, settle in this case the exact location of the line between petty offenses and serious crimes. It is sufficient for our purpose to hold that a crime punishable by two years in prison is, based on past and contemporary standards in this country, a serious crime and not a petty offense. Consequently, appellant was entitled to a jury trial and it was error to deny it. . . .

Reversed and remanded.

JUSTICE HARLAN, with whom JUSTICE STEWART joins, dissenting. . . .

[There] is a wide range of views on the desirability of trial by jury, and on the ways to make it most effective when it is used; there is also considerable variation from State to State in local conditions such as the size of the criminal caseload, the ease or difficulty of summoning jurors, and other trial conditions bearing on fairness. We have before us, therefore, an almost perfect example of a situation in which the celebrated dictum of Mr. Justice Brandeis should be invoked. It is, he said, "one of the happy incidents of the federal system that a single courageous state may, if its citizens choose, serve as a laboratory. . . ." New State Ice Co. v. Liebmann, 285 U.S. 262, 280, 311 (dissenting opinion). This Court, other courts, and the political process are available to correct any experiments in criminal procedure that prove fundamentally unfair to defendants.

NOTES

1. *The scope of the right to jury trial.* Justice Frankfurter once wrote that "[n]o changes or chances can alter the content of the verbal symbol of 'jury'— a body of twelve men who must reach a unanimous conclusion if the verdict is to go against the defendant." Rochin v. California, 342 U.S. 165, 170 (1952). Except for the limitation to males, which had passed away long before Frankfurter reiterated it, this statement expressed a nearly universal view about what was meant by a jury. Nevertheless, in Williams v. Florida, 399 U.S. 78, 86 (1970), the Court said that the decision to fix the size of the jury at 12 "appears to have been a historical accident, unrelated to the great purposes that gave rise to the jury" and held that a 6-member jury satisfied the constitutional requirement.[22] In Apodaca v. Oregon, 406 U.S. 404 (1972), the Court held that unanimity was not re-

22. In Ballew v. Georgia, 435 U.S. 223 (1978), the Court held that a 5-person jury did not fulfill the constitutional jury trial requirement.

quired in state criminal trials, so long as a substantial majority of the jury supports the verdict. The Court in that case upheld guilty verdicts obtained by 11–1 and 10–2 votes, without ruling explicitly on whether a smaller majority could also be sufficiently substantial.[23]

Duncan had raised, but not resolved, the question of what may be deemed a "petty offense," for which the Sixth Amendment jury trial guarantee would be inapplicable. In Baldwin v. New York, 399 U.S. 66 (1970), the Court held that no offense may be deemed petty where imprisonment for more than 6 months is authorized. In such cases a defendant has a constitutional right to jury trial, whether or not imprisonment is in fact likely to be imposed.

2. The effect of jury trial on the criminal justice system. (*a*) The entire texture of the trial is influenced by the existence of the jury. Instead of addressing arguments to one law-trained person, the lawyers address themselves to 12 lay people. Obviously, lawyers believe that nonlegal factors will influence the jury and attempt, with some success, to put such matters before it.

(*b*) Because lay people may not assess items of proof as carefully as the law-trained, Anglo-American law includes an elaborate structure of rules providing for the exclusion of certain evidence at the trial.

(*c*) The judge is judge of the law; the jury decides questions of fact. The legal system must characterize the nature of a given question: Is it a question of law or of fact?

(*d*) Judges must formulate for jurors' use an acceptable statement of applicable legal rules, though these rules may be the most difficult imaginable. When significant errors are made in stating these rules, a conviction must be reversed and a new trial must be held.

3. The policies served (and disserved) by jury trial. The Court in *Duncan* summarizes the principal reasons why it regards the availability of trial by jury as an essential component of fair procedure. Is it clear that the advantages of jury trial outweigh its costs or that experimentation with different kinds of factfinding procedures should be considered intolerable? Consider the following comments.

Glanville Williams, The Proof of Guilt 271-272 (3d ed. 1963): [I]t is an understatement to describe a jury, with Herbert Spencer, as a group of twelve people of average ignorance. There is no guarantee that members of a particular jury may not be quite unusually ignorant, credulous, slow-witted, narrow-minded, biased or temperamental. The danger of this happening is not one that can be removed by some minor procedural adjustment; it is inherent in the English notion of a jury as a body chosen from the general population at random.

Dale W. Broeder, The Functions of the Jury — Facts or Fictions?, 21 U. Chi. L. Rev. 386, 413-417 (1947): From the time of the Alien and Sedition Acts, the government's attempted inroads on civil rights seem to have received the enthusiastic support of jurors. . . .

But the case against the criminal jury as a protector of individual liberty ex-

23. In Burch v. Louisiana, 441 U.S. 130 (1979), the Court held that a 5-1 vote did not satisfy constitutional requirements. Thus, where states elect to use a 6-person jury, the verdict must be unanimous. The opinions in *Apodaca* suggest that for *federal* criminal trials, a majority of the Court would continue to view unanimity as constitutionally mandated. In any event, Rule 31(a) of the Federal Rules of Criminal Procedure requires a unanimous verdict in federal prosecutions.

tends further than to contests between government and citizens opposed to its policies. Minority groups have often suffered at the hands of jurymen. Wholesale acquittals of lynch-law violators, convictions of Negroes on the slightest evidence, and numerous other occurrences which have now almost become a part of the jury tradition might be instanced as examples. . . .

Aside from the incidental psychological functions which the criminal jury is alleged to perform, the sole remaining virtue claimed for it lies in its ability to make allowances for the circumstances of the particular case — to dispense with a rule of law. As noted previously, however, law-dispensing is a two-edged sword, and there is no current means of ascertaining which way it more often swings. It may seriously be doubted whether entrusting the jury with law-dispensing powers is justified. While flexibility of legal administration is desirable, it would seem that the necessary exceptions to the normal rules could with better reason be fashioned by the legislature or court.

Harry Kalven & Hans Zeisel, The American Jury 7-9 (1966): The [jury] controversy centers around three large issues. First, there is a series of collateral advantages and disadvantages that are often charged against, or pointed to on behalf of, the jury as an institution. In this realm fall such positive points as that the jury provides an important civic experience for the citizen; that, because of popular participation, the jury makes tolerable the stringency of certain decisions; that, because of its transient personnel, the jury acts as a sort of lightning rod for animosity and suspicion which otherwise might center on the more permanent judge; and that the jury is a guarantor of integrity, since it is said to be more difficult to reach twelve men than one. Against such affirmative claims, serious collateral disadvantages have been urged, chiefly that the jury is expensive; . . . that jury service imposes an unfair tax and social cost on those forced to serve; and that, in general, exposure to jury duty disenchants the citizen and causes him to lose confidence in the administration of justice.

Second, there is a group of issues that touch directly on the competence of the jury. . . . On the one hand, it is urged that the judge, as a result of training, discipline, recurrent experience, and superior intelligence, will be better able to understand the law and analyze the facts than laymen, selected from a wide range of intelligence levels, who have no particular experience with matters of this sort, and who have no durable official responsibility. On the other hand, it is argued that twelve heads are inevitably better than one; that the jury as a group has wisdom and strength which need not characterize any of its individual members; that it makes up in common sense and common experience what it may lack in professional training, and that its very inexperience is an asset because it secures a fresh perception of each trial, avoiding the stereotypes said to infect the judicial eye.

The third group of issues about the jury goes to what is perhaps the most interesting point. The critics complain that the jury will not follow the law, either because it does not understand it or because it does not like it, and that thus only a very uneven and unequal administration of justice can result from reliance on the jury; indeed, it is said that the jury is likely to produce that government by man, and not by rule of law, against which Anglo-American political tradition is so steadfastly set.

This same flexibility of the jury is offered by its champions as its most endearing and most important characteristic. The jury, it is said, is a remarkable device for insuring that we are governed by the spirit of the law and not by its letter; for insuring that rigidity of any general rule of law can be shaped to justice in the particular case. One is tempted to say that what is one man's equity is another man's anarchy.

4. The symbolic implications of decision-making by jury. Consider George C. Harris, The Communitarian Function of the Criminal Jury Trial and the Rights of the Accused, 74 Neb.L.Rev. 804, 805 (1995):

> [There is] a public interest in trial by jury in criminal cases that is distinct from the public's interest in a fair trial for the accused or the reliable determination of guilt and innocence. This separate public interest derives from what can be called the criminal jury's "communitarian" function. The communitarian function of public trial by jury in criminal cases can be divided into three related aspects: 1) a democratic vehicle for community participation in government in general and the criminal justice system in particular; 2) a means by which the community is educated regarding our system of justice; and 3) a ritual by which the faith of the community in the administration of justice is maintained.

Question: Suppose that the defendant prefers *not* to be tried by a jury. Should the defendant's preference control, or should the community's interest in jury decision-making trump the defendant's perception of the procedure most likely to afford him a fair trial? See Harris, supra, at 810-20.[24]

5. Lay adjudicators in other countries. Other legal systems use different means to provide for lay participation. For discussion of current uses of criminal jury trial in Australia, Canada, Ireland, New Zealand and Scotland, as well as such civil-law countries as Japan, Russia, and Spain, see Symposium on The Common Law Jury, 62 L. & Contemp. Prob. 1 (1999). Consider the following comment.

Glanville Williams, The Proof of Guilt 254-256, 307 (3d ed. 1963): So great was the prestige of the British jury that it was transplanted to one Continental country after another as a symbol of new-found political freedom. . . .

[E]fforts to acclimatise jury trial have generally met with indifferent success, partly because of a failure to settle satisfactorily the relative provinces of judge and jury. Perhaps another contributing factor was the failure to apply the restrictive rules of the law of evidence (particularly in respect of the character of the accused) which English experience had shown to be necessary. . . . The strong tendency on the Continent of late years has been to replace the jury by lay justices or assessors, sitting with the judges and sharing with them the responsibility of deciding both fact and law and determining sentence. These lay justices may, as in France since 1941, bear the name of a jury and be very close to the English jury in being chosen at random from the community, differing, however, in that they sit on the Bench for a whole session and constitute a joint tribunal with the professional judges; or they may, as in Sweden, be somewhat similar to the English justices of the peace, being lay magistrates specially chosen to serve

24. American jurisdictions are closely divided on the question of whether a defendant may, over the prosecutor's objection, insist on a *non*-jury trial. Compare Commonwealth v. Wharton, 435 A.2d 158 (Pa. 1981), with Singer v. United States, 380 U.S. 24 (1965).

for a period of office and not merely for a particular case or short series of cases; in Sweden the choice of magistrates is made by election. . . .

Looking at these strains and stresses of the jury system in other countries, we may find the comparative success of the English jury is not in its ability to nullify unpopular laws, nor in its superior ability to ascertain facts, but in the fact that our system of summing up enables the judge to give the jury a lead,[a] which the jury follow sufficiently often to give an appearance of reliability to the mode of trial. It need hardly be pointed out that this explanation of the jury's success is not one that yields any very strong argument for a continuation of the system.

6. *The behavior of the jury in the United States.* The empirical study referred to by the Court in *Duncan,* Harry Kalven & Hans Zeisel, The American Jury (1966), represents an effort to determine the extent to which juries decide cases differently from the way judges would and to determine the sources of such differences. The entire book warrants careful reading in connection with efforts to understand the impact of jury trial in American criminal cases.[25] The authors find that judges and juries disagree in roughly 25 percent of jury trial cases. In a small portion of these (2 percent of the total cases), the jury convicts when the judge would acquit; in 17 percent of all cases the jury acquits when the judge would convict; in roughly 6 percent of the cases the jury "hangs" (fails to agree on a verdict). Id. at 56-57.

The authors examine in great depth the possible reasons for judge-jury disagreement. They conclude that of the various factors apparently involved, differences in assessing the evidence in close cases played a significant role. They attributed 79 percent of the disagreements to this source. The other major factors that helped account for disagreement were jury sentiments about the law (50 percent of the cases), jury sentiments about the defendant (22 percent), facts only the judge knew (5 percent), and disparity of counsel (8 percent). Id. at 111. Often there was more than one reason for disagreement in a case. In fact, the closeness of the evidence usually appeared with one of the other reasons, so that this factor apparently "liberated the jury to respond to non-evidentiary factors." Id. at 106. It thus appeared that jury sentiment about the law was one of the most significant considerations, and this factor of course lies close to the heart of the jury's function as a guarantor of lenity and equity in dispensing criminal justice. The study suggests that "in cases having a de minimus cast or a note of contributory fault or provocation . . . the jury will exercise its de facto powers to write these equities into the criminal law." Id. at 285. Other sentiments about the law that appeared to have significant impact included "impatience with the nicety of the law's boundaries hedging the privilege of self-defense" (id.

a. This role for the judge is generally not seen in the United States. In most American states, judicial commentary on the evidence is viewed as a violation of state constitutional or statutory provisions making the jury the exclusive trier of fact, and even in jurisdictions that permit such commentary, judges must be careful not to give a "one-sided rendition" of the case. Nancy Jean King, The American Criminal Jury, 62 L. & Contemp. Prob. 41, 47-48 (1999).—Eds.

25. For a critique of the methodology employed in this ground-breaking study, see Michael H. Walsh, The American Jury: A Reassessment, 79 Yale L.J. 142 (1969). Studies examining jury attitudes toward specific legal doctrines are discussed infra in the corresponding sections of this book. For an exploration of recent empirical research, with particular attention to the issues of provocation, self-defense and insanity, see Norman J. Finkel, Commonsense Justice: Jurors' Notions of the Law (1995).

at 241) and resistance to the enforcement of a few unpopular laws, primarily hunting, liquor, gambling, and drunken-driving laws. While the study provides extensive evidence of jury nullification, it also should be noted that judge and jury *agreed* in 75 percent of the cases, that only half the disagreement cases involved jury sentiments about the law, and that these sentiments usually (78 percent of the time, id. at 113) emerged in combination with other factors, principally the closeness of the evidence. The authors thus observe that the "jury's war with the law is now a polite one" (id. at 76) and conclude (at 498):

> The jury thus represents a uniquely subtle distribution of official power, an unusual arrangement of checks and balances. It represents also an impressive way of building discretion, equity and flexibility into a legal system. Not the least of the advantages is that the jury, relieved of the burdens of creating precedent, can bend the law without breaking it.

Notice that in *Duncan* the Court, referring to Kalven and Zeisel, says that when juries differ from the judge "it is usually because they are serving some of the very purposes for which they were created." Does this mean that the jury's equity-dispensing function is constitutionally protected and that procedures designed to minimize nullification would be unconstitutional?

UNITED STATES v. DOUGHERTY

United States Court of Appeals, District of Columbia Circuit
473 F.2d 1113 (1972)

LEVENTHAL, J. Seven of the so-called "D.C. Nine" bring this joint appeal from convictions arising out of their unconsented entry into the Washington office of the Dow Chemical Company, and their destruction of certain property therein. [The defendants had disrupted Dow's operations in an attempt to publicize their opposition to the Vietnam War. They then sought to use their criminal trial as a platform to further publicize their views. They made efforts to transform the trial into a "political fray" and attempted to argue to the jury that they should be acquitted because their actions were morally justified.] . . . [A]fter a six-day trial, the seven were each convicted of two counts of malicious destruction. . . .

Appellants urge [that] the judge erroneously refused to instruct the jury of its right to acquit appellants without regard to the law and the evidence, and refused to permit appellants to argue that issue to the jury. . . .

[Appellants] say that the jury has a well-recognized prerogative to disregard the instructions of the court even as to matters of law, and that they accordingly have the legal right that the jury be informed of its power. . . .

There has evolved in the Anglo-American system an undoubted jury prerogative-in-fact, derived from its power to bring in a general verdict of not guilty in a criminal case, that is not reversible by the court. The power of the courts to punish jurors for corrupt or incorrect verdicts . . . was repudiated in 1670 when Bushell's Case, 124 Eng. Rep. 1006 (C.P. 1670), discharged the jurors who had acquitted William Penn of unlawful assembly. Juries in civil cases became subject to the control of ordering a new trial; no comparable control evolved for acquittals in criminal cases.

The pages of history shine on instances of the jury's exercise of its prerogative to disregard uncontradicted evidence and instructions of the judge. Most often commended are the 18th century acquittal of Peter Zenger of seditious libel, on the plea of Andrew Hamilton, and the 19th century acquittals in prosecutions under the fugitive slave law. The values involved drop a notch when the liberty vindicated by the verdict relates to the defendant's shooting of his wife's paramour, or purchase during Prohibition of alcoholic beverages. . . .

The existence of an unreviewable and unreversible power in the jury, to acquit in disregard of the instructions on the law given by the trial judge, has for many years co-existed with legal practice and precedent upholding instructions to the jury that they are required to follow the instructions of the court on all matters of law. . . .

The rulings [in the early cases] did not run all one way, but rather precipitated "a number of classic exchanges on the freedom and obligations of the criminal jury."[36] This was, indeed, one of the points of clash between the contending forces staking out the direction of the government of the newly established Republic. . . . As the distrust of judges appointed and removable by the king receded, there came increasing acceptance that under a republic the protection of citizens lay not in recognizing the right of each jury to make its own law, but in following democratic processes for changing the law. . . .

Since the jury's prerogative of lenity . . . introduces a "slack into the enforcement of law, tempering its rigor by the mollifying influence of current ethical conventions," it is only just, say appellants, that the jurors be so told. It is unjust to withhold information on the jury power of "nullification," since conscientious jurors may come, ironically, to abide by their oath as jurors to render verdicts offensive to their individual conscience, to defer to an assumption of necessity that is contrary to reality.

This so-called right of jury nullification is put forward in the name of liberty and democracy, but its explicit avowal risks the ultimate logic of anarchy. This is the concern voiced by Judge Sobeloff in United States v. Moylan, 417 F.2d 1002, 1009 (4th Cir. 1969): "To encourage individuals to make their own determinations as to which laws they will obey and which they will permit themselves as a matter of conscience to disobey is to invite chaos. No legal system could long survive if it gave every individual the option of disregarding with impunity any law which by his personal standard was judged morally untenable. . . ." [T]he advocates of jury "nullification" apparently assume that the articulation of the jury's power will not extend its use or extent, or will not do so significantly or obnoxiously. Can this assumption fairly be made? . . .

The way the jury operates may be radically altered if there is alteration in the way it is told to operate. The jury knows well enough that its prerogative is not limited to the choices articulated in the formal instructions of the court. The jury gets its understanding as to the arrangements in the legal system from more than one voice. . . .

When the legal system relegates the information of the jury's prerogative to an essentially informal input, it is not being duplicitous, chargeable with chicane and intent to deceive. The limitation to informal input is, rather, a governor to

36. M. R. Kadish and S. H. Kadish, On Justified Rule Departures by Officials, 59 Calif. L. Rev. 905, 914 (1971).

avoid excess: the prerogative is reserved for the exceptional case, and the judge's instruction is retained as a generally effective constraint. We "recognize a constraint as obligatory upon us when we require not merely reason to defend our rule departures, but damn good reason."[49] The practicalities of men, machinery and rules point up the danger of articulating discretion to depart from a rule, that the breach will be more often and casually invoked. We cannot gainsay that occasionally jurors uninstructed as to the prerogative may feel themselves compelled to the point of rigidity. The danger of the excess rigidity that may now occasionally exist is not as great as the danger of removing the boundaries of constraint provided by the announced rules. . . .

Moreover, to compel a juror involuntarily assigned to jury duty to assume the burdens of mini-legislator or judge, as is implicit in the doctrine of nullification, is to put untoward strains on the jury system. It is one thing for a juror to know that the law condemns, but he has a factual power of lenity. To tell him expressly of a nullification prerogative, however, is to inform him, in effect, that it is he who fashions the rule that condemns. That is an overwhelming responsibility, an extreme burden for the jurors' psyche. And it is not inappropriate to add that a juror called upon for an involuntary public service is entitled to the protection, when he takes action that he knows is right, but also knows is unpopular, either in the community at large or in his own particular grouping, that he can fairly put it to friends and neighbors that the was merely following the instructions of the court. . . .

[W]hat is tolerable or even desirable as an informal, self-initiated exception, harbors grave dangers to the system if it is opened to expansion and intensification through incorporation in the judge's instruction. . . .

BAZELON, C.J., concurring in part and dissenting in part. . . .

[T]he Court apparently concedes — although in somewhat grudging terms — that the power of nullification is a "necessary counter to case-hardened judges and arbitrary prosecutors," and that exercise of the power may, in at least some instances, "enhance the over-all normative effect of the rule of law." We could not withhold that concession without scoffing at the rationale that underlies the right to jury trial in criminal cases, and belittling some of the most legendary episodes in our political and jurisprudential history.

The sticking point, however, is whether or not the jury should be told of its power to nullify the law in a particular case. Here, the trial judge not only denied a requested instruction on nullification, but also barred defense counsel from raising the issue in argument before the jury. The majority affirms that ruling. I see no justification for, and considerable harm in, this deliberate lack of candor.

[T]he justification for this sleight-of-hand lies in a fear that an occasionally noble doctrine will, if acknowledged, often be put to ignoble and abusive purposes — or, to borrow the Court's phrase, will "run the risk of anarchy." . . . The Court assumes that these abuses are most likely to occur if the doctrine is formally described to the jury by argument or instruction. . . . It seems substantially more plausible to me to assume that the very opposite is true. . . .

[T]he Court takes comfort in the fact that informal communication to the

49. Kadish and Kadish, supra, note 36, 59 Calif. L. Rev. at 926. [The "damn-good-reason" position is criticized in Alan Scheflin & Jon Van Dyke, Jury Nullification: The Contours of a Controversy, 43 L. & Contemp. Prob. 51, 98-108 (1980). — EDS.]

jury "generally convey[s] adequately enough the idea of prerogative, of freedom in an occasional case to depart from what the judge says." . . . [But if] awareness is preferable to ignorance, then I simply do not understand the justification for relying on a haphazard process of informal communication whose effectiveness is likely to depend, to a large extent, on whether or not any of the jurors are so well-educated and astute that they are able to receive the message. If the jury should know of its power to disregard the law, then the power should be explicitly described by instruction of the court or argument of counsel. . . .

NOTES AND QUESTIONS ON NULLIFICATION

1. Empirical studies have probed the impact of nullification instructions. One pair of studies[26] considered the effect of instructing mock juries that "nothing would bar them from acquitting the defendant if they feel that the law . . . would produce an inequitable or unjust result." In a case involving a nurse tried for the "mercy" killing of a terminally ill cancer patient, mock juries given the nullification instruction were, predictably, less likely to convict than mock juries not given the instruction. But, unexpectedly, the instructed mock juries were *more* likely to convict in a homicide case involving a drunk driver who struck and killed a pedestrian. In deliberations, mock juries spent less time discussing the evidence and more time discussing the defendant's character when a nullification instruction had been given.

2. The federal courts and nearly all the states follow *Dougherty* and refuse to permit instructions informing the jury of its nullification power. See, e.g., United States v. Edwards, 101 F.3d 17 (2d Cir. 1996); State v. Hatori, 990 P.2d 115 (Haw. App. 1999).

In three states the approach rejected in *Dougherty* still survives through constitutional provisions that the jury shall be the judge of the law as well as the fact. Ga. Const. art. 1, §1, ¶11(a); Ind. Const. art. 1, §19; Md. Const., Decl. of Rights, art. 23. In Georgia, however, courts have tended to confine the effect of the provision, for example by upholding a charge that the jurors are the judges of the law but are obliged to apply the court's instructions to the facts and by forbidding defense counsel to argue to the jury that it should disregard the law. See State v. Freeman, 444 S.E.2d 80 (Ga. 1994); Drummond v. State, 326 S.E.2d 787 (Ga. App. 1985). Current practice in Indiana and Maryland is summarized in Richard St. John, Note, License to Nullify: The Democratic and Constitutional Deficiencies of Authorized Jury Lawmaking, 106 Yale L.J. 2563 (1997).

3. The *Dougherty* court appears to believe that the jury's nullification power is desirable, so long as it is not exercised too often. Compare State v. Ragland, 105 N.J. 189, 519 A.2d 1361, 1371-1372 (1986):

> [J]ury nullification . . . is absolutely inconsistent with the most important value of Western democracy, that we should live under a government of laws and not of men. . . . With jury nullification, [the jurors] are told, either explicitly or implicitly,

26. Irwin A. Horowitz, The Impact of Judicial Instructions, Arguments, and Challenges on Jury Decision Making, 12 L. & Hum. Beh. 439 (1988); Irwin A. Horowitz, The Effect of Jury Nullification Instruction on Verdicts and Jury Functioning in Criminal Trials, 9 L. & Hum. Beh. 25 (1985).

that *they* are the law, . . . and that if they want to, they may convict every poor man and acquit every rich man; convict the political opponent but free the crony; put the long-haired in jail but the crew-cut on the street; imprison the black and free the white; or, even more arbitrarily, just do what they please whenever they please.

One of the biggest problems in the administration of criminal justice is the inequality of its enforcement. . . . Absolutely nowhere in the system is there some notion that someone should have the power, arbitrarily, to pick and choose who shall live and who shall die. But that is precisely what jury nullification is: the power to undo everything that is precious in our system of criminal justice, the power to act arbitrarily to convict one and acquit another where there is absolutely no apparent difference between the two. It is a power, unfortunately, that is there, that this Court cannot terminate, but a power that should be restricted as much as possible.

. . . The lengths to which we go to exclude irrelevant evidence, the expenditures made to protect defendants from juror prejudice, the energy, study, and work devoted to a particular prosecution, all of these are prodigious. Having gone through that process, admired by us both for its thoroughness and its goals, astonishing to others for its devotion to fairness and reason, it is incomprehensible that at the very end we should tell those who are to make the judgment that they may do so without regard to anything that went before and without guidance as to why they should disregard what went on before, and without the obligation of explaining why they so disregarded everything. . . .

Jury nullification is an unfortunate but unavoidable power. It should not be advertised, and, to the extent constitutionally permissible, it should be limited.

Professor Andrew D. Leipold agrees that nullification is undesirable, but he challenges the *Ragland* court's premise that the nullification power is unavoidable. Professor Leipold argues that procedural doctrines protecting the nullification power (such as the rule barring prosecution appeal from unjustified acquittals) impede the truth-seeking function of the criminal process. He would restrict the de facto nullification power by authorizing prosecution appeals (a view that would require reversal of current double jeopardy case law);[27] at the same time, he would permit explicit instructions authorizing nullification in cases involving de minimis harms, and prosecution appeal from an acquittal on that ground (if made explicit by a jury's special verdict) would be barred. See Leipold, Rethinking Jury Nullification, 82 Va. L. Rev. 253 (1996).

A diametrically opposed view is developed in Sherman J. Clark, The Courage of Our Convictions, 97 Mich. L. Rev. 2381 (1999). Professor Clark argues that jury trials "serve as a means through which we as a community take responsibility for — own up to — inherently problematic judgments regarding the blameworthiness or culpability of our fellow citizens." Id. He suggests, accordingly, that "procedures governing the criminal jury trial [should] engender in jurors a sense of personal responsibility for the fate of the accused." Id. at 2382. He recommends that jurors be instructed in a way that stresses their responsibility for their decision and makes them aware of their nullification power, without expressly encouraging them to use it — for example by telling the jurors (id. at 2446) that "the responsibility for this decision is entirely yours and . . . you will not be required to explain or justify your verdict except to your own conscience."

4. *Constraining jury nullification.* If jury nullification is usually or (as the *Rag-*

27. E.g., United States v. Ball, 163 U.S. 662 (1896).

land court argues) always undesirable, how far can courts go to discourage it? In a civil suit, the judge can set aside a jury verdict for one party and enter judgment notwithstanding the verdict (often called "judgment n.o.v.") for the other side. But the Supreme Court has held that in a criminal case, a judgment n.o.v. for the prosecution violates the defendant's Sixth Amendment right to trial by jury. Connecticut v. Johnson, 460 U.S. 73, 84 (1983). Are other judicial efforts to prevent nullification similarly barred by the Sixth Amendment? Consider these situations:

(*a*) In People v. Fernandez, 31 Cal. Rptr. 677 (Ct. App. 1994), the jurors interrupted their deliberations to send the judge a note in which they stated their belief that the defendant had committed battery with serious bodily injury and then asked whether they nonetheless had the power to acquit on that charge and instead return a verdict of guilty on the lesser offense of assault. The trial judge simply replied, "No." The court of appeal held that this response was not error.

(*b*) In People v. Engelman, 92 Cal. Rptr. 2d 416 (Cal. App. 2000), the defendant was convicted of robbery after the trial judge instructed the jury: "[S]hould it occur that any juror refuses to deliberate or expresses an intention to disregard the law . . . , it is the obligation of the other jurors to immediately advise the Court of the situation." The appellate court held that the instruction was proper, rejecting the defendant's argument that the instruction would pressure jurors in the minority to acquiesce in the majority view or to abandon any intention to nullify.

United States v. Thomas, 116 F.3d 606 (2d Cir. 1997), was a prosecution of several African-American defendants charged with conspiracy to distribute cocaine. During deliberations, several jurors informed the trial judge that Juror No. 5, the sole African-American on the panel, was refusing to follow the judge's instructions, was calling his fellow jurors "racists," and was adamantly holding out for acquittal. The judge interrupted the deliberations and conducted interviews with each of the jurors. According to several of them, Juror No. 5 had said he thought the government's evidence was unreliable, and Juror No. 5 told the judge that he needed "substantial evidence" of guilt. But several other jurors testified that Juror No. 5 had said he favored acquittal because the defendants were black and had committed the alleged crimes out of economic necessity. The trial judge accepted the latter account and dismissed Juror No. 5 on the ground that he would not convict "no matter what the evidence was" and had "preconceived . . . economic [or] social reasons [for acquittal] that are totally improper." The remaining jurors then unanimously convicted.

On appeal, the court, per Cabranes, J., "categorically reject[ed] the idea that jury nullification is desirable or that courts may permit it to occur when it is within their authority to prevent it." The court held that the Constitution permits removal whenever there is unambiguous evidence of a juror's refusal to follow the judge's instructions. The court reversed the convictions, however, on the narrow ground that Juror No. 5's intentions were ambiguous and that there was "some possibility" he had based his vote on his view of the evidence.

Questions: If jury departures from the law are so unequivocally bad, why should the defendant have a constitutional right to jury trial in the first place? Was *Duncan* wrongly decided? Conversely, if the jury's equity-dispensing function is central to its constitutional role, how can it be proper for a trial judge to remove jurors who reveal their intent to exercise that function? And what effect will the existence of such a removal power have on jurors' ability to express their views candidly during deliberation? For discussion of the issues, compare Nancy S. Marder, The Myth of the Nullifying Jury, 93 Nw. U.L. Rev. 877, 947-952 (1999) (criticizing *Thomas*), with Nancy J. King, Silencing Nullification Advocacy Inside and Outside the Courtroom, 65 U. Chi. L. Rev. 433, 438-491 (1998) (supporting the *Thomas* approach).

(*c*) The Fully Informed Jury Association is a Montana-based organization supported by a politically diverse array of protest groups, including anti-abortion activists, supporters of alternative medicines, and opponents of laws regulating firearms, marijuana, motorcycle helmets, prostitution and the right to die. See King, supra at 434; Marder, supra at 942. Through a national newsletter, website, and handbills distributed at courthouses, the FIJA seeks to spread awareness of the nullification power and encourage its use. At many courthouses throughout the country, FIJA distributes pro-nullification literature to potential and actual jurors, and encourages them to call an 800 number to hear a recorded message describing what one juror discovered were "more rights than what was read to me by the judge."[28]

Recall that in *Dougherty,* the majority considered formal nullification instructions unnecessary, in part because "the jury gets its understanding . . . from more than one voice"; the court concluded that awareness of the nullification power can best come from "informal input." Are FIJA's activities therefore legitimate and perhaps even desirable? Many judges and other court officials apparently do not think so. FIJA activists who contact jurors or engage in leafleting at the courthouse have been charged with jury tampering, obstruction of justice, and contempt of court, even though FIJA's informational materials are not alleged to be incorrect or misleading.[29] Municipalities have also responded to FIJA's efforts by enacting new laws to more tightly restrict contact with potential jurors in or near the courthouse.[30] Freedom of speech principles do not prohibit reasonable restrictions on advocacy within a fixed distance from decision-making sites like courthouses or voting booths.[31] But First Amendment considerations aside, why should it be a crime to give a juror truthful information about her rights and responsibilities? If society wants to block both formal and informal sources of information about the jury's equity-dispensing role, why bother having a jury at all? For analysis of judicial efforts to silence nullification advocacy, see King, supra 492-99.

5. Sentencing information. Does it follow from *Dougherty* that a judge not only may refuse to inform the jury of its nullification power but also may refuse to inform the jury about the severity of the sentence that a defendant faces upon conviction? The question has become increasingly important with the proliferation of mandatory minimum sentencing laws, which often dictate long terms of imprisonment for possession of small quantities of drugs, even when the defendant is a first offender. Nearly all courts hold that because the jury's role is solely to determine the facts relevant to guilt, the jury has no legitimate concern with the consequences of a conviction. E.g., Shannon v. United States, 512 U.S. 573

28. Turney v. State, 936 P.2d 533, 537 n. 4 (Alaska 1997).
29. E.g., Turney, supra.
30. See, e.g., Fully Informed Jury Ass'n. v. San Diego, 1996 US App. LEXIS 4254 (9th Cir.) (upholding restrictions).
31. Burson v. Freeman, 504 U.S. 191 (1992).

(1994); United States v. Chesney, 86 F.3d 564 (6th Cir. 1996). Compare United States v. Datcher, 830 F. Supp. 411, 414-418 (M.D. Tenn. 1993):

> [R]espect for nullification flows from the role of the jury as the "conscience of the community" in our criminal justice system. [T]he essential purpose of the jury trial [is] "to prevent oppression by the Government." And it is this essential purpose that is to be used in determining the constitutional requirements of a jury trial.
>
> When measured by this standard, a defendant's right to inform the jury of that information essential "to prevent oppression by the Government" is clearly of constitutional magnitude. [T]o deny a jury information necessary to such oversight is . . . to defeat the central purpose of the jury system.
>
> Argument against allowing the jury to hear information that might lead to nullification evinces a fear that the jury might actually serve its primary purpose, that is, it evinces a fear that the community might in fact think a law unjust. The government, whose duty it is to seek justice and not merely conviction, should not shy away from having a jury know the full facts and law of a case. . . .
>
> Overly harsh punishments were the impetus to development of jury nullification. Institution of the jury system was meant to protect against unjust punishment perpetrated by government, not merely unjust conviction. . . .
>
> No instruction on jury nullification was requested by the defendant, and none would be given if it were requested. . . . But Mr. Datcher is entitled to have the jury perform its full oversight function, and informing the jury of possible punishment is essential to this function. The court finds no good reason for opposing candor.

6. Suppose that the jurors are instructed, over the defendant's *objection,* that they are the judges of the law as well as the facts. Does such an instruction subject the defendant to capricious judgment and violate his right to be tried in accordance with ascertainable law? See Wyley v. Warden, 372 F.2d 742 (4th Cir. 1967); Isaacs v. State, 31 Md. App. 604, 358 A.2d 273 (1976).

7. *Race-based nullification.* In Detroit, Washington, D.C., parts of New York City, and several other urban centers, observers have claimed that jury nullification is becoming more common, especially in drug prosecutions involving African-American defendants. See Marder, supra note 4(b) at 899-901. Consider the following comments:

Paul Butler, Racially Based Jury Nullification: Black Power in the Criminal Justice System, 105 Yale L.J. 677 (1995). Considering the costs of law enforcement to the black community and the failure of white lawmakers to devise significant nonincarcerative responses to black antisocial conduct, it is the moral responsibility of black jurors to emancipate some guilty black outlaws. . . . I hope that the destruction of the status quo will not lead to anarchy, but rather to the implementation of certain noncriminal ways of addressing antisocial conduct. . . .

According to [some], whom I will call law enforcement enthusiasts, . . . it is in the best interest of the black community to have more, rather than less, [law enforcement]. Allowing criminals to live unfettered in the community would harm, in particular, the black poor, who are disproportionately the victims of violent crime. Indeed, the logical conclusion of the enthusiasts' argument is that African-Americans would be better off with more, not fewer, black criminals behind bars.

To my mind, the enthusiasts embrace law enforcement too uncritically: They are blind to its opportunity costs. . . .[W]hen locking up black men means that "violent criminals . . . who attack those most vulnerable" are off the streets, most people — including most law enforcement critics — would endorse the incarceration. But what about when locking up a black man has no or little net effect on public safety, when, for example, the crime with which he was charged is victimless? . . .

There is no question that jury nullification is subversive of the rule of law. . . . To borrow a phrase from the D.C. Circuit, jury nullification "betrays rather than furthers the assumptions of viable democracy. . . ." [But] "democracy," as practiced in the United States, has betrayed African-Americans far more than they could ever betray it. . . .

Because the United States is both a democracy and a pluralist society, it is important that diverse groups appear to have a voice in the laws that govern them. Allowing black people to serve on juries strengthens "public respect for our criminal justice system and the rule of law." . . . But what of the black juror who endorses racial critiques of American criminal justice? Such a person holds no "confidence in the integrity of the criminal justice system." If she is cognizant of the implicit message that the Supreme Court believes her presence sends, she might not want her presence to be the vehicle for that message. . . . In a sense, the black juror [who nullifies] engages in an act of civil disobedience, except that her choice is better than civil disobedience because it is lawful. Is the black juror's race-conscious act moral? Absolutely. It would be farcical for her to be the sole color-blind actor in the criminal process, especially when it is her blackness that advertises the system's fairness. . . .

In cases involving violent *malum in se* crimes like murder, rape, and assault, jurors should consider the case strictly on the evidence presented, and, if they have no reasonable doubt that the defendant is guilty, they should convict. For nonviolent *malum in se* crimes such as theft or perjury, nullification is an option that the juror should consider, although there should be no presumption in favor of it. A juror might vote for acquittal, for example, when a poor woman steals from Tiffany's, but not when the same woman steals from her next-door neighbor. Finally, in cases involving nonviolent, *malum prohibitum* offenses, including "victimless" crimes like narcotics offenses, there should be a presumption in favor of nullification. . . . Black people have a community that needs building, and children who need rescuing, as long as a person will not hurt anyone, the community needs him there to help. . . .

I am not encouraging anarchy. Instead, I am reminding black jurors of their privilege to serve a higher calling than law: justice. . . . I hope that there are enough of us out there, fed up with prison as the answer to black desperation and white supremacy, to cause retrial after retrial, until, finally, the United States "retries" its idea of justice.

Randall L. Kennedy, Race, Crime, and the Law 301-310 (1996): [J]ury nullification is an exceedingly poor means for advancing the goal of a racially fair administration of criminal law. . . . Jury nullification as typically implemented is a low-visibility, highly ambiguous protest unlikely to focus the attention of the public clearly on social problems in need to reform. [Moreover, if] a large number of blacks clearly engage in "guerrilla warfare" as jurors, their action might call into question the right of blacks to be selected for jury service on precisely the same terms as others. Widespread adoption of Butler's proposal would likely give rise to measures designed to exclude prospective nullifiers from juries, measures that would result almost certainly in the disproportionate exclusion of blacks. . . .

Butler exudes keen sympathy for nonviolent drug offenders and similar criminals. By contrast, Butler is inattentive to the aspirations, frustrations, and fears of law-abiding people compelled by circumstances to live in close proximity to the criminals for whom he is willing to urge subversion of the legal system. Butler simply overlooks the sector of the black law-abiding population that desires more rather than less prosecution and punishment for all types of criminals. . . .

If a large number of blacks have views on the administration of criminal law that are counter to Butler's, why worry about his proposal? . . . [I]t would not take many people to wreak havoc with the jury system. The unanimity requirement renders juries uniquely susceptible to disruption by a resolute cadre of nullifiers. . . .

The most fundamental reason to oppose Professor Butler's call for racially selective jury nullification is that it is based on a sentiment that is regrettably widespread in American culture: an ultimately destructive sentiment of racial kinship that prompts individuals of a given race to care more about "their own" than people of another race. [Butler] assumes that it is proper for prospective black jurors to care more about black communities than white communities, that it is proper for black jurors to be more concerned with the fate of black defendants than white defendants, and that it is proper for black jurors to be more protective of the property (and perhaps the lives?) of black people than white people. Along that road lies moral and political disaster. The disaster includes not only increasing but, worse, legitimizing the tendency of people to privilege in racial terms "their own." Some will say that this racial privileging has already happened and is, in any event, inevitable. The situation can and will get worse, however, if Butler's plan and the thinking behind it gains adherents. His program, although animated by a desire to challenge racial injustice, would demolish the moral framework upon which an effective, attractive, and compelling alternative can and must be built.

For further discussion of Professor Butler's proposals, see Darryl K. Brown, Jury Nullification Within the Rule of Law, 81 Minn. L. Rev. 1149, 1185-91 (1997); Andrew D. Leipold, The Dangers of Race-Based Jury Nullification, 44 UCLA L. Rev. 109 (1996); Marder, supra note 4(b), at 937-43.

8. Further reading. Other useful discussions of nullification appear in Jeffrey Abramson, We the Jury 57-95 (1994); Mortimer Kadish & Sanford Kadish, Discretion to Disobey 37-94 (1973); Albert W. Alschuler & Andrew G. Deiss, A Brief History of the Criminal Jury in the United States, 61 U. Chi. L. Rev. 867, 902-921 (1994); Robert F. Schopp, Verdicts of Conscience: Nullification and Necessity As Jury Responses to Crimes of Conscience, 69 So. Cal. L. Rev. 2039 (1996).

NOTES AND QUESTIONS ON INCONSISTENT VERDICTS

1. The problem and the prevailing solution. When a prosecution involves several separate counts, it sometimes happens that the jury's verdict on one count will be irreconcilably in conflict with its verdict on another count. Consider, for example, DeSacia v. State, 469 P.2d 369 (Alaska 1970). The defendant's reckless driving forced another vehicle off the road, and both the driver (Hogan) and passenger (Evangelista) in the other vehicle were killed. The defendant was prosecuted on two counts of manslaughter; the jury convicted on the count charging manslaughter of Evangelista but acquitted on the count charging manslaughter of Hogan. Because the defendant's conduct had endangered the two victims in precisely the same way, he was in principle guilty of manslaughter either in both cases or in neither. Should the inconsistent verdicts nevertheless be allowed to stand?

In the *DeSacia* case, the court noted that the verdict of acquittal was final; any relitigation of that count would violate the double jeopardy clause. But the court set aside the conviction on the other count, explaining that such action was necessary to assure that the conviction was not the product of jury confusion or irrationality. The court therefore remanded for a new trial on the count relating to the death of Evangelista. Some courts go even further. In People v. Klingenberg, 665 N.E.2d 1370 (Ill. 1996), the court not only set aside the inconsistent conviction but also held that retrial on that charge was barred. The court noted (id. at 1376) that "the jury, by its acquittal on another [charge], has rejected an essential element needed to support the conviction" and reasoned that double jeopardy principles should preclude the prosecution from attempting to establish that missing element on retrial.

Most American jurisdictions reject these approaches, however. The federal courts and the great majority of state courts permit the inconsistent conviction to stand. See Eric L. Muller, The Hobgoblin of Little Minds? Our Foolish Law of Inconsistent Verdicts, 111 Harv. L. Rev. 771, 787-788 (1998).

Which approach seems more faithful to the premises of jury trial? If the jury is expected to give voice to the rough common sense of the community, isn't the *DeSacia* court's desire for logic out of place? Do inconsistent verdicts facilitate the exercise of the jury's leniency or do they encourage compromise *convictions* on counts about which the jury may not really be persuaded beyond a reasonable doubt? In United States v. Powell, 469 U.S. 57, 65 (1984), the Supreme Court noted:

> Inconsistent verdicts . . . present a situation where "error," in the sense that the jury has not followed the court's instructions, most certainly has occurred, but it is unclear whose ox has been gored. Given this uncertainty, and the fact that the Government is precluded from challenging the acquittal, it is hardly satisfactory to allow the defendant to receive a new trial on the conviction as a matter of course. . . . For us, the possibility that the inconsistent verdicts may favor the criminal defendant as well as the Government militates against review of such convictions at the defendant's behest.

2. *Criticism of the prevailing approach.* The *Powell* Court's assumptions have drawn sharp criticism. Professor Andrew Leipold notes that "[f]or every case where the jury extends mercy to a deserving defendant, there may well be another (or two, or five others) where the verdict is based on improper considerations." Leipold, Rethinking Jury Nullification, 82 Va. L. Rev. 253, 304 (1996). Professor Muller, supra note at 1, at 795, argues that "by refusing to disturb inconsistent verdicts, the Court is buying a chance for lenity [benefiting defendants] — for all the Court knows, a remote chance — at the price of protecting jury confusion, mistake, and compromise." He adds (id. at 798) that "when a jury

returns an inconsistent verdict, there is a significant chance that the jury has breached its constitutional duty to apply the reasonable doubt standard." Professor Muller concludes that fundamental trial values require courts to set aside inconsistent convictions unless the evidence supporting the conviction is so overwhelming that any jury error can be deemed harmless.

Questions: Would approaches restricting inconsistent verdicts impair the jury's function as a safety valve for tempering the law's rigid logic? One answer may simply be that the defendant will not complain, because the rule leads only to reversal of the illogical conviction. But what if the prosecution seeks an instruction, in a case like *DeSacia,* that the jury must either acquit on both counts or convict on both counts? Does the result in *DeSacia* in effect require such an instruction in future cases? If so, would the defendant then be justified in claiming that the instruction improperly constrained the jury's equity-dispensing function?

In connection with these problems, consider whether it was entirely a coincidence that the *DeSacia* jury convicted for the death of Evangelista, who was a passenger, but acquitted for the death of Hogan, the other driver. As we shall see, contributory negligence ordinarily is not a defense in a criminal prosecution, see page 429 infra, but the Kalven and Zeisel study, page 59 supra, at 242-257, showed that jury nullification often occurred when contributory fault by the victim was involved. If this factor played a role in the acquittal with respect to Hogan, then wasn't the jury — to quote from Duncan v. Louisiana, page 56 supra — "serving some of the very purposes for which [it was] created"? Or are the dangers identified by Professor Muller (jury confusion, mistake, inappropriate compromise, and disregard of the reasonable-doubt requirement) more substantial than the risk of chilling the jury's equity-dispensing function?

3. Inconsistency in nonjury trials. Jurisdictions that permit inconsistent verdicts in jury trials must decide whether to follow the same approach when an inconsistent acquittal and conviction are rendered by a judge. Some courts hold such inconsistency unacceptable. See, e.g., United States v. Maybury, 274 F.2d 899 (2d Cir. 1960). Are the reasons for tolerating inconsistent jury verdicts applicable in trials before a judge? If it is sound to protect the jury's equity-dispensing power, why should a judge not have the same power?

5. *The Role of Counsel*

MONROE FREEDMAN,
LAWYERS' ETHICS IN AN ADVERSARY SYSTEM*

3-4, 27-42 (1975)

[T]he adversary process has its foundations in respect for human dignity, even at the expense of the search for truth[.] I do not mean to deprecate the search for truth or to suggest that the adversary system is not concerned with it. On the contrary, truth is a basic value, and the adversary system is one of the most efficient and fair methods designed for determining it. . . . Nevertheless, the point that I now emphasize is that in a society that honors the dignity of the individual, the high value that we assign to truth-seeking is not an absolute, but may on occasion by subordinated to even higher values. . . .

*Professor Freedman provides an expanded analysis of these issues in Understanding Lawyers' Ethics (1990).

Is it ever proper for a criminal defense lawyer to present perjured testimony? One's instinctive response is in the negative. On analysis, however, it becomes apparent that the question is an exceedingly perplexing one. My own answer is in the affirmative.

At the outset, we should dispose of some common question-begging responses. The attorney, we are told, is an officer of the court, and participates in a search for truth. Those propositions, however, merely serve to state the problem in different words: As an officer of the court, participating in a search for truth, what is the attorney obligated to do when faced with perjured testimony? That question cannot be answered properly without an appreciation of the fact that the attorney functions in an adversary system of criminal justice which . . . imposes special responsibilities upon the advocate.

First, the lawyer is required to determine "all relevant facts known to the accused," because "counsel cannot properly perform their duties without knowing the truth." The lawyer who is ignorant of any potentially relevant fact "incapacitates himself to serve his client effectively," because "an adequate defense cannot be framed if the lawyer does not know what is likely to develop at trial."

Second, the lawyer must hold in strictest confidence the disclosures made by the client in the course of the professional relationship. . . . If this were not so, the client would not feel free to confide fully, and the lawyer would not be able to fulfill the obligation to ascertain all relevant facts. . . .

Third, the lawyer is an officer of the court, and his or her conduct before the court "should be characterized by candor."

As soon as one begins to think about those responsibilities, it becomes apparent that the conscientious attorney is faced with what we may call a trilemma — that is, the lawyer is required to know everything, to keep it in confidence, and to reveal it to the court. . . .

If we recognize that professional responsibility requires that an advocate have full knowledge of every pertinent fact, then the lawyer must seek the truth from the client, not shun it. That means that the attorney will have to dig and pry and cajole, and, even then, the lawyer will not be successful without convincing the client that full disclosure to the lawyer will never result in prejudice to the client by any word or action of the attorney. That is particularly true in the case of the indigent defendant, who meets the lawyer for the first time in the cell block or the rotunda of the jail. The client did not choose the lawyer, who comes as a stranger sent by the judge, and who therefore appears to be part of the system that is attempting to punish the defendant. It is no easy task to persuade that client to talk freely without fear of harm. [T]he truth can be obtained only by persuading the client that it would be a violation of a sacred obligation for the lawyer ever to reveal a client's confidence. Of course, once the lawyer has thus persuaded the client of the obligation of confidentiality, that obligation must be respected scrupulously.

Assume the following situation. Your client has been falsely accused of a robbery committed at 16th and P Streets at 11:00 P.M. He tells you at first that at no time on the evening of the crime was he within six blocks of that location. However, you are able to persuade him that he must tell you the truth and that doing so will in no way prejudice him. He then reveals to you that he was at 15th and P Streets at 10:55 that evening, but that he was walking east, away from the scene of the crime, and that, by 11:00 P.M., he was six blocks away. At the trial, there are two prosecution witnesses. The first mistakenly, but with some degree of persuasiveness, identifies your client as the criminal. At that point the prosecution's case depends upon that single witness, who might or might not be believed. The second prosecution witness is an elderly woman who is somewhat nervous and who wears glasses. She testifies truthfully and accurately that she saw your client at 15th and P Streets at 10:55 P.M. She has corroborated the erroneous testimony of the first witness and made conviction extremely likely. However, on cross-examination her reliability is thrown into doubt through demonstration that she is easily confused and has poor eyesight. Thus, the corroboration has been eliminated, and doubt has been established in the minds of the jurors as to the prosecution's entire case.

The client then insists upon taking the stand in his own defense, not only to deny the erroneous evidence identifying him as the criminal, but also to deny the truthful, but highly damaging, testimony of the corroborating witness who placed him one block away from the intersection five minutes prior to the crime. Of course, if he tells the truth and thus verifies the corroborating witness, the jury will be more inclined to accept the inaccurate testimony of the principal witness, who specifically identified him as the criminal. . . .

The most obvious way to avoid the ethical difficulty is for the lawyer to withdraw from the case, at least if there is sufficient time before trial for the client to retain another attorney. The client will then go to the nearest law office, realizing that the obligation of confidentiality is not what it has been represented to be, and withhold incriminating information or the fact of guilt from the new attorney. In terms of professional ethics, the practice of withdrawing from a case under such circumstances is difficult to defend, since the identical perjured testimony will ultimately be presented. Moreover, the new attorney will be ignorant of the perjury and therefore will be in no position to attempt to discourage the client from presenting it. Only the original attorney, who knows the truth, has that opportunity, but loses it in the very act of evading the ethical problem.

The difficulty is all the more severe when the client is indigent. In that event, the client cannot retain other counsel, and in many jurisdictions it is impossible for appointed counsel or a public defender to withdraw from a case except for extraordinary reasons. Thus, the attorney can successfully withdraw only by revealing to the judge that the attorney has received knowledge of the client's guilt,* or by giving the judge a false or misleading reason for moving for leave to withdraw. However, for the attorney to reveal knowledge of the client's guilt would be a gross violation of the obligation of confidentiality, particularly since it is entirely possible in many jurisdictions that the same judge who permits the attorney to withdraw will subsequently hear the case and sentence the defendant. Not only will the judge then have personal knowledge of the defendant's guilt before the trial begins, but it will be knowledge of which the newly appointed counsel for the defendant will very likely be ignorant. . . .

Another solution that has been suggested is that the attorney move for leave to withdraw and that, when the request is denied, the attorney then proceed with the case, eliciting the defendant's testimony and arguing the case to the jury in the ordinary fashion. Since that proposal proceeds on the assumption that

* The typical formula is for the attorney to advise the judge of "an ethical problem." The judge understands that to mean that the client is insisting upon a perjured alibi over the lawyer's objections. In one case, the judge incorrectly drew that inference when the lawyer's ethical concern was with the fact that the client wanted to enter a guilty plea despite the fact that he was innocent.

the motion will be denied, it seems to me to be disingenuous. If the attorney avoids the ethical problem, it is only by passing it on to the judge. Moreover, the client in such a case would then have grounds for appeal on the basis of deprivation of due process and denial of the right to counsel, since the defendant would have been tried before, and sentenced by, a judge who had been informed by the defendant's own lawyer that the defendant is guilty both of the crime charged and of perjury. . . .

Another unsuccessful effort to deal with the problem appears in the ABA Standards Relating to the Defense Function. . . . Section 7.7 of the Standards requires that the lawyer "must confine his examination to identifying the witness as the defendant and permitting him to make his statement." That is, the lawyer "may not engage in direct examination of the defendant . . . in the conventional manner." Thus, the client's story will become part of the record, although without the attorney's assistance through direct examination. The general rule, of course, is that in closing argument to the jury "the lawyer may argue all reasonable inferences from the evidence in the record." Section 7.7 also provides, however, that the defense lawyer is forbidden to make any reference in closing argument to the client's testimony.

There are . . . critical flaws in that proposal. [E]xperienced trial attorneys have often noted that jurors assume that the defendant's lawyer knows the truth about the case, and that the jury will frequently judge the defendant by drawing inferences from the attorney's conduct in the case. There is, of course, only one inference that can be drawn if the defendant's own attorney turns his or her back on the defendant at the most critical point in the trial, and then, in closing argument, sums up the case with no reference to the fact that the defendant has given exculpatory testimony. . . . Ironically, the Standards reject any solution that would involve informing the judge, but then propose a solution that, as a practical matter, succeeds in informing not only the judge but the jury as well.

It would appear that the ABA Standards have chosen to resolve the trilemma by maintaining the requirements of complete knowledge and of candor to the court, and sacrificing confidentiality. Interestingly, however, that may not in fact be the case. I say that because the Standards fail to answer a critically important question: Should the client be told about the obligation imposed by Section 7.7? That is, the Standards ignore the issue of whether the lawyer should say to the client at the outset of their relationship: "I think it's only fair that I warn you: If you should tell me anything incriminating and subsequently decide to deny the incriminating facts at trial, I would not be able to examine you in the ordinary manner or to argue your untrue testimony to the jury." . . . Obviously, any other course would be a betrayal of the client's trust, since everything else said by the attorney in attempting to obtain complete information about the case would indicate to the client that no information thus obtained would be used to the client's disadvantage. On the other hand, the inevitable result of [this] position would be to caution the client not to be completely candid with the attorney. That, of course, returns us to resolving the trilemma by maintaining confidentiality and candor, but sacrificing complete knowledge. . . . I continue to stand with those lawyers who hold that "the lawyer's obligation of confidentiality does not permit him to disclose the facts he has learned from his client which form the basis for his conclusion that the client intends to perjure himself." What that means — necessarily, it seems to me — is that the criminal defense attorney, however unwillingly in terms of personal morality, has a professional responsibility as an advocate in an adversary system to examine the perjurious client in the ordinary way and to argue to the jury, as evidence in the case, the testimony presented by the defendant.

JOHN NOONAN, BOOK REVIEW, 29 Stan. L. Rev. 363-366 (1977): Can an honest person practice regularly as a criminal defense lawyer in the United States? . . . Dean Freedman's implicit answer to [this question] is "no.". . .

Under our constitutional system, the right to counsel in a criminal case cannot be denied. The right to counsel includes the right to give one's lawyer in confidence all of the facts that one subjectively believes are relevant to one's defense. These two propositions are incontestable. From them, Dean Freedman concludes that one has a right to appear as a witness for oneself and to be examined by one's counsel, whether the story one is telling is true or false. The attorney who is unable to dissuade his client from perjury must proceed by presenting the testimony and arguing the case to the jury in the normal fashion. To say that counsel must or even may withdraw or not conduct the examination if his client insists on perjuring himself is, Dean Freedman contends, to deny the constitutional right. To support his contention he has the . . . proclaimed practice of 90 percent of the lawyers answering a survey in the District of Columbia.

Dean Freedman is very American in implying that what is required by the Constitution of the United States must be morally good, and his use of common practice to establish morality only transfers to the field of legal ethics an argument frequently used as to sexual morality. Both standards, however, are parochial. The Constitution of the United States once required the return of fugitive slaves. Dean Freedman himself is not at all happy with common practice as the criterion when he discusses the practices of prosecutors. . . . Rejecting the criteria Dean Freedman uses here, I continue to believe that the presentation of perjury to a court is fraud whether it is done by concocting a document, hiring a witness, or presenting one's own lying client as a truthteller. If, as Dean Freedman maintains, criminal law practice cannot be carried on otherwise, then honest persons cannot engage in it.

Yet ours, Dean Freedman might point out, is not an ordinary trade. It is socially indispensable. Moreover, it is indispensable to the defense of human dignity. Without counsel, the defendant in a criminal case stands naked before the power of the state. Is not the object of criminal trial procedure as much the preservation of the dignity of the defendant as the discovery of the truth? If it is, counsel performs a noble role, and if those who do in fact perform this role assert that only by cooperating in perjury can they accomplish it, should not their noble role justify their aid to falsehood?

The importance of preserving human dignity . . . I willingly grant. But it seems strange to me to build on this foundation a defense of lying. "Only if I can tell my shabby falsehood with your help can I retain my sense of human worth" is what we must take to be the plea of each incriminated defendant who wants to testify falsely. I have difficulty grasping how accepting such an appeal preserves the dignity of the accused. . . .

Dean Freedman rightly points out that the attorney's difficulty is particularly acute when the client is indigent, since he cannot retain other counsel. Moreover, in many jurisdictions appointed counsel or the public defender may only withdraw from a case for extraordinary reasons, which would necessarily require revealing the client's perjurious intent to the very judge before whom he will be tried and sentenced. But Dean Freedman ignores an alternative to the problem: Allow the attorney to withdraw without breaching the confidence and if prejudicial inferences are likely to be drawn, assign both a new judge and a new attorney. . . .

Yet the problem remains, says Freedman, since the client, "realizing that the obligation of confidentiality is not what it has been represented to be," will withhold incriminating information or the fact of guilt from the new attorney and perjured testimony will be presented by an unwitting attorney. This may be true, but there is a crucial difference this time around: neither the first nor the second attorney has knowingly acquiesced in perjury, a result of no small importance in preserving the integrity of a truth-seeking system. . . .

The principle I espouse excludes the use of perjury even in the "hard cases" that Dean Freedman has appealingly constructed. Consequently I answer the first question in this review differently from the answer implicit in Lawyers' Ethics in an Adversary System.

NOTES

1. The American Bar Association has adopted Model Rules of Professional Conduct to prescribe standards for lawyers in matters related to ethics and professional responsibility. Many states have enacted the Model Rules (along with various local amendments) as legally enforceable rules of conduct. See ABA, Annotated Model Rules of Professional Conduct (as Amended to February 1997). Rules 1.6 and 3.3 of the Model Rules resolve the problems of candor, honesty, and confidentiality as follows:

RULE 1.6 CONFIDENTIALITY OF INFORMATION

(a) A lawyer shall not reveal information relating to representation of a client unless the client consents after consultation, . . . except as stated in paragraph (b).

(b) A lawyer may reveal such information to the extent the lawyer reasonably believes necessary:

(1) to prevent the client from committing a criminal act that the lawyer believes is likely to result in imminent death or substantial bodily harm; or

(2) to establish a claim or defense on behalf of the lawyer in a controversy between the lawyer and the client. . . .

RULE 3.3 CANDOR TOWARD THE TRIBUNAL

(a) A lawyer shall not knowingly:

(1) make a false statement of material fact or law to a tribunal;

(2) fail to disclose a material fact to a tribunal when disclosure is necessary to avoid assisting a criminal or fraudulent act by the client; . . . or

(4) offer evidence that the lawyer knows to be false. If a lawyer has offered material evidence and comes to know of its falsity, the lawyer shall take reasonable remedial measures.

(b) The duties stated in paragraph (a) continue to the conclusion of the proceeding, and apply even if compliance requires disclosure of information otherwise protected by Rule 1.6. . . .

The Commentary to Rule 3.3[32] states:

> While it is agreed that the lawyer should seek to persuade the client to refrain from perjurious testimony, there has been dispute concerning the lawyer's duty when that persuasion fails [and when withdrawal is not possible.]
>
> Three resolutions of this dilemma have been proposed. One is to permit the accused to testify by a narrative without guidance through the lawyer's questioning. This compromises both contending principles; it exempts the lawyer from the duty to disclose false evidence but subjects the client to an implicit disclosure of information imparted to counsel. Another suggested resolution, of relatively recent origin, is that the advocate be entirely excused from the duty to reveal perjury if the perjury is that of the client. This is a coherent solution but makes the advocate a knowing instrument of perjury.
>
> The other resolution of the dilemma is that the lawyer must reveal the client's perjury if necessary to rectify the situation. . . . [A]n accused should not have a right to assistance of counsel in committing perjury. . . .
>
> If withdrawal will not remedy the situation or is impossible, the advocate should make disclosure to the court. It is for the court then to determine what should be done — making a statement about the matter to the trier of fact, ordering a mistrial or perhaps nothing. . . . If there is an issue whether the client has committed perjury, the lawyer cannot represent the client in resolution of the issue and a mistrial may be unavoidable. . . .
>
> The general rule — that an advocate must disclose the existence of perjury with respect to a material fact, even that of a client — applies to defense counsel in criminal cases, as well as in other instances. However, the definition of the lawyer's ethical duty in such a situation may be qualified by constitutional provisions for due process and the right to counsel in criminal cases. . . . The obligation of the advocate under these Rules is subordinate to such a constitutional requirement.

2. Should it follow under the Model Code that the attorney must, at the outset of the representation, advise the client of the limitation on the confidentiality of attorney-client communications? Professor Norman Lefstein, the reporter for a related ABA Committee on Standards Relating to the Defense Function, urges that such advice be given. See Lefstein, The Criminal Defendant Who Proposes Perjury, 6 Hofstra L. Rev. 665, 687-691 (1978). Could such a warning inhibit full disclosure and effective defense planning for the defendant who may have a legitimate defense?

3. What is the significance of the last paragraph of the ABA Commentary? Consider the case that follows.

NIX v. WHITESIDE

Supreme Court of the United States
475 U.S. 157 (1986)

CHIEF JUSTICE BURGER delivered the opinion of the Court.

. . . Whiteside and two others went to one Calvin Love's apartment seeking marihuana. [An argument] ensued. At one point, Love directed his girlfriend to get his "piece," and at another point got up, then returned to his bed. According

32. ABA, Model Rules of Professional Conduct, Rule 3.3, Comment at 330-332 (2d ed. 1992).

to Whiteside's testimony, Love then started to reach under his pillow and moved toward Whiteside. Whiteside stabbed Love in the chest, inflicting a fatal wound.

Whiteside was charged with murder. [He gave Robinson, his appointed counsel,] a statement that he had stabbed Love as the latter "was pulling a pistol from underneath the pillow on the bed." Upon questioning by Robinson, however, Whiteside indicated that he had not actually seen a gun, but that he was convinced that Love had a gun. No pistol was found on the premises. . . . Robinson interviewed Whiteside's companions who were present during the stabbing and none had seen a gun during the incident. Robinson advised Whiteside that the existence of a gun was not necessary to establish the claim of self defense, and that only a reasonable belief that the victim had a gun nearby was necessary. . . .

About a week before trial, during preparation for direct examination, Whiteside for the first time told Robinson . . . that he had seen something "metallic" in Love's hand. When asked about this, Whiteside responded that "in Howard Cook's case there was a gun. If I don't say I saw a gun I'm dead." Robinson told Whiteside that such testimony would be perjury and repeated that it was not necessary to prove that a gun was available but only that Whiteside reasonably believed that he was in danger. On Whiteside's insisting that he would testify that he saw "something metallic" Robinson told him, according to Robinson's testimony,

> we could not allow him to [testify falsely] because that would be perjury, and as officers of the court we would be suborning perjury if we allowed him to do it; . . . I advised him that if he did do that it would be my duty to advise the Court of what he was doing and that I felt he was committing perjury; also, that I probably would be allowed to attempt to impeach that particular testimony.

Robinson also indicated he would seek to withdraw from the representation if Whiteside insisted on committing perjury.

Whiteside testified in his own defense at trial and stated that he "knew" that Love had a gun and that he believed Love was reaching for a gun and he had acted swiftly in self defense. On cross examination, he admitted that he had not actually seen a gun in Love's hand. Robinson presented evidence that Love had been seen with a sawed-off shotgun on other occasions, that the police search of the apartment may have been careless, and that the victim's family had removed everything from the apartment shortly after the crime. Robinson presented this evidence to show a basis for Whiteside's asserted fear that Love had a gun.

The jury returned a verdict of second-degree murder and Whiteside moved for a new trial, claiming that he had been deprived of a fair trial by Robinson's admonitions not to state that he saw a gun or "something metallic."...

The Supreme Court of Iowa affirmed respondent's conviction. That court held that the right to have counsel present all appropriate defenses does not extend to using perjury, and that an attorney's duty to a client does not extend to assisting a client in committing perjury. [T]he Iowa court concluded that not only were Robinson's actions permissible, but were required. The court commended [Robinson] "for the high ethical manner in which this matter was handled."

Whiteside then petitioned for a writ of habeas corpus. . . .

The United States Court of Appeals for the Eighth Circuit . . . directed that the writ of habeas corpus be granted. The Court of Appeals accepted the findings of the trial judge, affirmed by the Iowa Supreme Court, that trial counsel believed with good cause that Whiteside would testify falsely. . . . Nevertheless, the court reasoned that an intent to commit perjury, communicated to counsel, does not alter a defendant's right to effective assistance of counsel and that Robinson's admonition to Whiteside that he would inform the court of Whiteside's perjury constituted a threat to violate the attorney's duty to preserve client confidences. According to the Court of Appeals, this threatened violation of client confidences breached the standards of effective representation set down in Strickland v. Washington, 466 U.S. 668 (1984). . . .

In *Strickland,* we recognized counsel's duty of loyalty and his "overarching duty to advocate the defendant's cause." Plainly, that duty is limited to legitimate, lawful conduct compatible with the very nature of a trial as a search for truth. Although counsel must take all reasonable lawful means to attain the objectives of the client, counsel is precluded from taking steps or in any way assisting the client in presenting false evidence or otherwise violating the law. This principle has consistently been recognized in most unequivocal terms by expositors of the norms of professional conduct since the first Canons of Professional Ethics were adopted by the American Bar Association in 1908. . . .

These principles have been carried through to contemporary codifications[4] of an attorney's professional responsibility. Disciplinary Rule 7-102 of the Model Code of Professional Responsibility (1980), entitled "Representing a Client Within the Bounds of the Law," provides that

> (A) In his representation of a client, a lawyer shall not: . . .
> (4) Knowingly use perjured testimony or false evidence. . . .
> (7) Counsel or assist his client in conduct that the lawyer knows to be illegal or fraudulent.

This provision has been adopted by Iowa, and is binding on all lawyers who appear in its courts. The more recent Model Rules of Professional Conduct (1983) similarly admonish attorneys to obey all laws in the course of representing a client:

> RULE 1.2 SCOPE OF REPRESENTATION . . .
>
> (d) A lawyer shall not counsel a client to engage, or assist a client, in conduct that the lawyer knows is criminal or fraudulent. . . .

Both the Model Code of Professional Conduct and the Model Rules of Professional Conduct also adopt the specific exception from the attorney-client privi-

4. There currently exist two different codifications of uniform standards of professional conduct. The Model Code of Professional Responsibility was originally adopted by the American Bar Association in 1969, and was subsequently adopted (in many cases with modification) by nearly every state. The more recent Model Rules of Professional Conduct were adopted by the American Bar Association in 1983. Since their promulgation by the American Bar Association, the Model Rules have been adopted by 11 States. . . . Iowa is one of the States that adopted a form of the Model Code of Professional Responsibility, but has yet to adopt the Model Rules.

[The 1969 Model Code remains in force in many states. By one recent count, 41 states had adopted the Model Rules of Professional Conduct, though often with significant amendments. See ABA/BNA Lawyers' Manual on Professional Conduct, Vol. 13, no. 11, p. 181 (June 25, 1997).—EDS.]

lege for disclosure of perjury that his client intends to commit or has committed. DR 4-101(C)(3) (intention of client to commit a crime); Rule 3.3 (lawyer has duty to disclose falsity of evidence even if disclosure compromises client confidences). Indeed, both the Model Code and the Model Rules do not merely *authorize* disclosure by counsel of client perjury; they *require* such disclosure. See Rule 3.3(a)(4); DR 7-102(B)(1).... This special duty of an attorney to prevent and disclose frauds upon the court derives from the recognition that perjury is as much a crime as tampering with witnesses or jurors by way of promises and threats, and undermines the administration of justice....

It is universally agreed that at a minimum the attorney's first duty when confronted with a proposal for perjurious testimony is to attempt to dissuade the client from the unlawful course of conduct.... Similarly, the Model Rules and the commentary, as well as the Code of Professional Responsibility adopted in Iowa expressly permit withdrawal from representation as an appropriate response of an attorney when the client threatens to commit perjury....[6]

The essence of the brief amicus of the American Bar Association reviewing practices long accepted by ethical lawyers, is that under no circumstances may a lawyer either advocate or passively tolerate a client's giving false testimony.... The suggestion sometimes made that "a lawyer must believe his client not judge him" in no sense means a lawyer can honorably be a party to or in any way give aid to presenting known perjury.

Considering Robinson's representation of respondent in light of these accepted norms of professional conduct, we discern no failure to adhere to reasonable professional standards. . . . Nothing counsel did in any way undermined Whiteside's claim that he believed the victim was reaching for a gun.... Whiteside did testify, and he was "restricted" or restrained only from testifying falsely....

Paradoxically, even while accepting the conclusion of the Iowa trial court that Whiteside's proposed testimony would have been a criminal act, the Court of Appeals held that Robinson's efforts to persuade Whiteside not to commit that crime were improper, *first,* as forcing an impermissible choice between the right to counsel and the right to testify; and *second,* as compromising client confidences because of Robinson's threat to disclose the contemplated perjury.

Whatever the scope of a constitutional right to testify, it is elementary that such a right does not extend to testifying *falsely*. . . . Robinson's admonitions to his client can in no sense be said to have forced respondent into an *impermissible*

6. In the evolution of the contemporary standards promulgated by the American Bar Association, an early draft reflects a compromise suggesting that when the disclosure of intended perjury is made during the course of trial, when withdrawal of counsel would raise difficult questions of a mistrial holding, counsel had the option to let the defendant take the stand but decline to affirmatively assist the presentation of perjury by traditional direct examination. Instead, counsel would stand mute while the defendant undertook to present the false version in narrative form in his own words unaided by any direct examination. This conduct was thought to be a signal at least to the presiding judge that the attorney considered the testimony to be false and was seeking to disassociate himself from that course. Additionally, counsel would not be permitted to discuss the known false testimony in closing arguments. See ABA Standards for Criminal Justice, 4-7.7 (2d ed. 1980). Most courts treating the subject rejected this approach and insisted on a more rigorous standard. The Eighth Circuit in this case and the Ninth Circuit have expressed approval of the "free narrative" standards.

The Rule finally promulgated in the current Model Rules of Professional Conduct rejects any participation or passive role whatever by counsel in allowing perjury to be presented without challenge.

choice . . . for there was no *permissible* choice to testify falsely. . . . When an accused proposes to resort to perjury or to produce false evidence, one consequence is the risk of withdrawal of counsel.

. . . Similarly, we can discern no breach of professional duty in Robinson's admonition to respondent that he would disclose respondent's perjury to the court. An attorney's duty of confidentiality, which totally covers the client's admission of guilt, does not extend to a client's announced plans to engage in future criminal conduct. In short, the responsibility of an ethical lawyer, as an officer of the court and a key component of a system of justice, dedicated to a search for truth, is essentially the same whether the client announces an intention to bribe or threaten witnesses or jurors or to commit or procure perjury. No system of justice worthy of the name can tolerate a lesser standard. . . . Since there has been no breach of any recognized professional duty, it follows that there can be no deprivation of the right to assistance of counsel under the *Strickland* standard. . . .

Reversed.

JUSTICE BRENNAN, concurring in the judgment.

This Court has no constitutional authority to establish rules of ethical conduct for lawyers practicing in the state courts. . . .

Unfortunately, the Court seems unable to resist the temptation of sharing with the legal community its vision of ethical conduct. But let there be no mistake; the Court's essay regarding what constitutes the correct response to a criminal client's suggestion that he will perjure himself is pure discourse without force of law. . . . Lawyers, judges, bar associations, students and others should understand that the problem has not now been "decided."

JUSTICE BLACKMUN, with whom JUSTICE BRENNAN, JUSTICE MARSHALL, and Justice Stevens join, concurring in the judgment. . . .

Whether an attorney's response to what he sees as a client's plan to commit perjury violates a defendant's Sixth Amendment rights may depend on many factors: how certain the attorney is that the proposed testimony is false, the stage of the proceedings at which the attorney discovers the plan, or the ways in which the attorney may be able to dissuade his client, to name just three. The complex interaction of factors, which is likely to vary from case to case, makes inappropriate a blanket rule that defense attorneys must reveal, or threaten to reveal, a client's anticipated perjury to the court. Except in the rarest of cases, attorneys who adopt "the role of the judge or jury to determine the facts," pose a danger of depriving their clients of the zealous and loyal advocacy required by the Sixth Amendment.

I therefore am troubled by the Court's implicit adoption of a set of standards of professional responsibility for attorneys in state criminal proceedings. [T]his Court's responsibility extends only to ensuring that the restrictions a State enacts do not infringe a defendant's federal constitutional rights. . . . Because I conclude that the respondent in this case failed to show such an effect, I join the Court's judgment that he is not entitled to federal habeas relief.

JUSTICE STEVENS, concurring in the judgment.

Justice Holmes taught us that a word is but the skin of a living thought. A "fact" may also have a life of its own. From the perspective of an appellate judge, after a case has been tried and the evidence has been sifted by another judge, a particular fact may be as clear and certain as a piece of crystal or a small diamond. A trial lawyer, however, must often deal with mixtures of sand and clay. . . .

As we view this case, it appears perfectly clear that respondent intended to commit perjury, that his lawyer knew it, and that the lawyer had a duty — both to the court and to his client, for perjured testimony can ruin an otherwise meritorious case — to take extreme measures to prevent the perjury from occurring. The lawyer was successful and, from our unanimous and remote perspective, it is now pellucidly clear that the client suffered no "legally cognizable prejudice."

Nevertheless, beneath the surface of this case there are areas of uncertainty that cannot be resolved today. A lawyer's certainty that a change in his client's recollection is a harbinger of intended perjury — as well as judicial review of such apparent certainty — should be tempered by the realization that, after reflection, the most honest witness may recall (or sincerely believe he recalls) details that he previously overlooked. Similarly, the post-trial review of a lawyer's pre-trial threat to expose perjury that had not yet been committed — and, indeed, may have been prevented by the threat — is by no means the same as review of the way in which such a threat may actually have been carried out. Thus, one can be convinced — as I am — that this lawyer's actions were a proper way to provide his client with effective representation without confronting the much more difficult questions of what a lawyer must, should, or may do after his client has given testimony that the lawyer does not believe.

NORMAN LEFSTEIN, LEGAL ETHICS, 1 Crim. Justice 27, 28-30 (ABA 1986): The majority opinion's "essay" [in *Nix*] contains a shocking misstatement of the law pertaining to client perjury. In its zeal to advise the nation's defense attorneys that they should inform judges whenever their clients propose to commit perjury, the Court did not seriously consider the ABA's former policy on the subject, i.e., permitting the defendant to testify by making a narrative statement and prohibiting counsel from arguing the defendant's testimony to the jury. The only reference to standard 7.7 is in a footnote, in which it is said that "[m]ost courts treating the subject rejected this approach and insisted on a more rigorous standard. . . ." This statement is not accurate.

Three cases are cited by the Court in support of its observation that standard 7.7 was rejected by most courts. Remarkably, [none] of the cases [is on point]. . . .

Even more startling than the Court's use of [these] cases is its failure to cite any of the numerous appellate decisions that have endorsed standard 7.7's free narrative approach. . . .

In the wake of the *Nix* decision, what should defense counsel do when confronted by a client determined to lie under oath? Obviously, counsel must try to dissuade the client from seeking to present false testimony. If this effort fails, an appropriate next step is for counsel to seek to withdraw from the case. But if withdrawal from the case is not feasible because, for example, the perjury dilemma arises during the midst of trial or if withdrawal is denied by the judge, counsel must decide on another approach.

Regardless of the precise course finally adopted, counsel should not under any circumstances aid the defendant in presenting testimony that counsel knows to be false. . . .

It does not necessarily follow, however, that a defendant's proposed perjury should be expressly revealed to the judge. If disclosure of a defendant's intent to commit perjury will not violate the Sixth Amendment, as the Court holds in

Nix, permitting defendant to present his or her story in a narrative fashion will not do so either. . . . Admittedly, [the free narrative approach] implicitly informs the judge and perhaps the jury that the client's testimony is untrue. The defendant especially may be disadvantaged when the attorney fails to argue the defendant's version of the case to the jury. . . . But if this is a problem for the defendant, it is one for which the defendant clearly is responsible by insisting on presenting perjury.

Furthermore, compared to the alternative of advising the judge that defendant proposes to commit perjury, the free narrative approach has much to commend it. Most importantly, it avoids the confusion and confrontation that arise when an attorney informs a judge that the defendant plans to testify perjuriously. If, for example, counsel tells the judge that defendant's testimony will be false, the defendant will most likely deny counsel's allegation. How should the judge and defense attorney then respond? One possibility would be for the judge, relying on defense counsel's statements, to deny defendant the opportunity to be sworn as a witness — a solution seemingly endorsed in the *Nix* opinion. . . . However, if despite defense counsel's statements, the judge permits defendant to testify, counsel is faced with the dilemma of deciding how to conduct direct examination. If defendant is examined like any other witness, defense counsel conceivably could be charged with suborning perjury. . . . An alternative would be for counsel to invite the defendant to make a narrative statement, which is probably what counsel should have done in the first place. Finally, no matter what happens after defense counsel informs the judge that the client plans to testify falsely, all trust and confidence between counsel and client will be destroyed.

NOTES AND QUESTIONS ON CLIENT PERJURY

1. Disclosure: when and how. Both *Nix* and Model Rule 3.3 stress that the attorney whose client is about to commit perjury *must* disclose that fact to the court. How should the lawyer fulfill this obligation? Can the attorney stand up during the trial and state, in front of the jury: "The testimony you are about to hear is false"? Why not?

(*a*) Consider Lowery v. Cardwell, 575 F.2d 727 (9th Cir. 1978). During a murder trial before a judge sitting without a jury, the defendant flatly denied shooting the deceased. Defense counsel then requested a recess and in chambers, without the defendant present, moved to withdraw. When counsel refused to state the reason for the motion, the trial judge denied it. Back in court, defense counsel asked defendant no further questions, and in closing argument he made no reference to her denial of having fired the fatal shots. The court of appeals found that counsel's actions amounted to "an unequivocal announcement" that the defendant had committed perjury. The court then ruled that because the announcement had placed counsel in open opposition to his client and had disabled the fact finder from ruling on the merits of the case, the defendant had been deprived of a fair trial. The court added (id. at 730): "If in truth the defendant has committed perjury (a fact we do not know in this case) she does not by that falsehood forfeit her right to a fair trial."

Questions: Does the result in *Lowery* remain sound after *Nix?* Could defense counsel now argue that his "unequivocal announcement" of perjury was precisely the step that *Nix* approved? If not, what action would *Nix* permit or require under the circumstances of *Lowery?*

(*b*) When the trier of fact is a jury, can defense counsel avoid the *Lowery* problem by making the disclosure to the judge outside the presence of the jury? Note that the judge not only makes important evidentiary rulings at trial but also imposes sentence after conviction. Moreover, under United States v. Grayson, 438 U.S. 41 (1978), a sentencing judge is permitted to impose a higher punishment on the basis of her belief that the defendant testified falsely at trial. If disclosure of perjury to the trier of fact is unduly prejudicial, isn't there a similar problem in disclosing perjury to the judge even in a jury trial?

(*c*) *Nix* offers some support for the argument that disclosure does not impair a fair trial because there is nothing unfair about penalizing the defendant who commits perjury. On this view, it might be argued that the defendant in *Lowery* received a fair trial, even though the disclosure was made to a judge who was sitting as the trier of fact. But how do we know that the defendant in *Lowery* did commit perjury? Should defense counsel have the power to make this determination unilaterally? If a hearing is held, who should represent the defendant at the hearing? Who should preside at the hearing?

2. *After disclosure.* When the relationship between defense counsel and client breaks down prior to trial, the judge will often permit counsel to withdraw. But when a conflict arises during trial, withdrawal will seldom be permitted. How should the ethical defense attorney proceed if she fails to dissuade her client from perjury and fails to obtain leave to withdraw? *Nix,* which presented the perjury problem in a different context, has not settled the matter. Several competing approaches are being advanced.

(*a*) The National Association of Criminal Defense Lawyers, endorsing the position of Professor Monroe Freedman, argues that when the defense attorney fails to dissuade his client from committing perjury, the Sixth Amendment right to effective assistance of counsel requires the attorney to elicit the false testimony and argue it to the jury in the usual way.[33] Can this approach be reconciled with the *Nix* court's reading of the Sixth Amendment?

(*b*) An alternative is the so-called free narrative approach — the client testifies without his attorney's aid and the attorney does not argue the testimony to the jury. Jurisdictions are widely split on the propriety of this approach. Florida explicitly prohibits it.[34] The California courts have held that the free narrative approach, while not ideal, does not deny the constitutional right to effective assistance of counsel.[35] The District of Columbia bar has adopted the ABA's 1983 Model Rules, but has added an amendment stating that when counsel cannot withdraw or dissuade the client from testifying, the free narrative approach is permissible.[36]

(*c*) *Nix* condemns the free narrative approach and insists on a "more rigorous standard" (supra page 83-84 n. 6). What would the more rigorous approach be? Should the attorney simply refuse to participate at all? In Florida Bar v.

33. Natl. Assn. of Criminal Defense Lawyers, Formal Op. 92-2 (1992), quoted in John Wesley Hall, Jr., Professional Responsibility of the Criminal Lawyer §24.17, at 223-239 (Cum. Supp. 1993).
34. See Re Rules Regulating the Fla. Bar, 494 So. 2d 977 (Fla. 1986) (Rule 4-3.3 and Comment).
35. People v. Guzman, 45 Cal. 3d 915, 755 P.2d 917 (1988).
36. D.C. Rules Ann., Rules of Prof. Conduct, §3.3(b) (Michie 1993).

Rubin, 549 So. 2d 1000 (Fla. 1989), defense counsel had refused to proceed on a free narrative basis after his withdrawal motion was denied, and he served 30 days for contempt of court. Subsequently, the Florida Supreme Court reprimanded him for unethical conduct. The court said that even though the free narrative approach was prohibited under the Florida Code of Professional Responsibility, defense counsel should have proceeded on that basis when the trial court ordered him to do so; the trial court's order would have afforded him a defense if an effort had been made to discipline him for participating on a free narrative basis.

Questions: Was the trial court justified in ordering Rubin to proceed? If not, what steps would be proper in a jurisdiction that outlaws the free narrative approach?

3. Further reading. A detailed procedure for responding to client perjury situations is developed in Carol T. Rieger, Client Perjury: A Proposed Resolution of the Constitutional and Ethical Issues, 70 Minn. L. Rev. 121 (1985). See also Monroe H. Freedman, Understanding Lawyers' Ethics 109-141 (1990).

NOTE ON PROBLEMS ARISING "WITHIN THE BOUNDS OF THE LAW"

Despite the wide range of disagreement reflected in the preceding materials, all participants in the debate accept that in principle an attorney should not use illegal means to further a client's interests. No one would argue that a zealous defense attorney should attempt to shoot (or even bribe) the prosecution's chief witness. Professor Freedman stresses that defense counsel should always attempt to dissuade her client from perjury. Disagreement arises when the attorney can avoid illegality only by compromising some other contending principle; putting this somewhat special problem to one side, all agree that zealous representation must remain "within the bounds of the law."[37]

Does it follow that ethical counsel may (and indeed *must,* to be truly effective) use all helpful tactics that *are* within the bounds of the law? Even after we have ruled out illegal means, is it not still troublesome for an attorney to exercise her special training and skills, to use all of her best effort, in order to promote a result that she knows to be socially harmful? Consider the following comments.

MARK M. ORKIN, DEFENCE OF ONE KNOWN TO BE GUILTY

1 Crim. L.Q. 170, 172-175 (1958)

Dr. Johnson, as usual, resumed the question with judicial finality: "We asked of the practice of law. Sir William Forbes said he thought an honest lawyer should never undertake a cause which he was satisfied was not a just one. Sir (said

37. The 1969 Model Rules state (EC 7-1) that "[t]he duty of a lawyer . . . is to represent his client zealously within the bounds of the law." In the 1983 Model Code, Rule 1.3 provides that "[a] lawyer shall act with reasonable diligence . . . ," and the Comment (ABA Model Rules, supra page 80 n. 29, at 41) states that "[a] lawyer should act with commitment and dedication to the interests of the client and with zeal in advocacy. . . ."

Mr. Johnson), a lawyer has no business with the justice or injustice of the cause which he undertakes, unless his client asks his opinion and then he is bound to give it honestly. The justice or injustice of the cause is to be decided by the judge. Consider, Sir, what is the purpose of courts of justice? It is, that every man may have his cause fairly tried, by men appointed to try causes. A lawyer is not to tell what he knows to be a lie: he is not to produce what he knows to be a false deed; but he is not to usurp the province of the jury and of the judge, and determine what shall be the effect of evidence — what shall be the result of legal argument. . . . If lawyers were to undertake no causes till they were sure they were just, a man might be precluded altogether from a trial of his claim, though, were it judicially examined, it might be found a very just claim."[1] . . .

MONROE FREEDMAN, LAWYERS' ETHICS IN AN ADVERSARY SYSTEM

43-49 (1975)

More difficult than the question of whether the criminal defense lawyer should present known perjury, is the question of whether the attorney should cross-examine a witness who is testifying accurately and truthfully, in order to make the witness appear to be mistaken or lying. The issue was raised effectively in a symposium on legal ethics through the following hypothetical case.

The accused . . . is charged with rape. . . . The alleged victim is the twenty-two-year-old daughter of a local bank president. She is engaged to a promising young minister in town. The alleged rape occurred in the early morning hours at a service station some distance from town, where the accused was employed as an attendant. That is all you know about the case when you have your first interview with your client.

At first the accused will not talk at all. You assure him that you cannot help him unless you know the truth and that he can trust you to treat what he says as confidential. He then says that he had intercourse with the young woman, but that she "consented in every way." . . . He says that on the night in question she came in for gas; they talked; and she invited him into the car. One thing led to another and, finally, to sexual intercourse. . . .

The accused tells you he was tried for rape in California four years ago and acquitted. He has no previous convictions. . . .

You learn that the victim has had affairs with two local men from good families. . . . Jones, apparently a bitterly disappointed and jealous suitor, readily states that he frequently had intercourse with the victim, and describes her behavior toward strange men as scandalous. He once took her to a fraternity dance, he says, and, having noticed she had been gone for some time, discovered her upstairs with Smith, a fraternity brother, on a bed in a state of semi-undress. He appears eager to testify and he states that the girl got what she'd always been asking for. You believe Jones, but are somewhat repelled by the disappointed suitor's apparent willingness to smear the young woman's reputation.

Suppose the accused, after you press him, admits that he forced himself on the victim and admits that his first story was a lie. He refuses to plead guilty to the

1. Boswell's Life of Johnson, vol. 5, pp. 28-29.

charge or any lesser charge. He says that he can get away with his story, because he did once before in California.

Should the defense lawyer use the information supplied by Jones to impeach the young woman and, if necessary, call Jones as a witness?

One of the panelists who spoke to that question was Chief Justice (then Judge) Burger. The Chief Justice first discussed the question in terms of "basic and fundamental rules." One of those rules, which he characterized as "clear-cut and unambiguous," is that "a lawyer may never, under any circumstances, knowingly . . . participate in a fraud on the court." That rule, he said, "can never admit of any exception, under any circumstances," and no other consideration "can ever justify a knowing and conscious departure" from it. . . .

After that powerful rhetoric, Chief Justice Burger's response to the question posed is a matter of some astonishment. The function of an advocate, and "particularly the defense advocate in the adversary system," is to use "all the legitimate tools available to test the truth of the prosecution's case." Therefore, he concluded, "the testimony of bad repute of the complaining witness, being recent and not remote in point of time, is relevant to her credibility." The Chief Justice was even more explicit in the question period following the panel discussion: he considers it ethical to cast doubt on the woman's credibility by destroying her reputation, even though the lawyer knows that she is telling the truth.

That, of course, is sanction for nothing less than a deliberate attempt to perpetrate a fraud upon the finder of fact. The lawyer knows that the client is guilty and that the prosecutrix is truthful. In cross-examining, the lawyer has one purpose, and one purpose only: to make it appear, contrary to fact, that the prosecutrix is lying in testifying that she was raped.

There is only one difference in practical effect between presenting the defendant's perjured alibi — which the Chief Justice considers to be clearly improper — and impeaching the truthful prosecutrix. In both cases, the lawyer participates in an attempt to free a guilty defendant. In both cases, the lawyer participates in misleading the finder of fact. In the case of the perjured witness, however, the attorney asks only nonleading questions, while in the case of impeachment, the lawyer takes an active, aggressive role, using professional training and skills, including leading questions, in a one-on-one attack upon the client's victim. The lawyer thereby personally and directly adds to the suffering of the prosecutrix, her family, and the minister to whom she is engaged. In short, under the euphemism of "testing the truth of the prosecution's case," the lawyer communicates, to the jury and to the community, the most vicious of lies.

That case takes us to the heart of my disagreement with the traditional approach to dealing with difficult questions of professional responsibility. That approach has two characteristics. First, in a rhetorical flourish, the profession is committed in general terms to all that is good and true. Then, specific questions are answered by uncritical reliance upon legalistic norms, regardless of the context in which the lawyer may be acting, and regardless of the motive and the consequences of the act. Perjury is wrong, and therefore no lawyer, in any circumstance, should knowingly present perjury. Cross-examination, however, is good, and therefore any lawyer, under any circumstances and regardless of the consequences, can properly impeach a witness through cross-examination. The system of professional responsibility that I have been advancing, on the other hand, is one that attempts to deal with ethical problems in context.

Let us return, then, to the case involving the street robbery at 16th and P Streets, in which the defendant has been wrongly identified as the criminal, but correctly identified by the nervous, elderly woman who wears eyeglasses, as having been only a block away five minutes before the crime took place.[a] [T]he lawyer could take the position that since the woman is testifying truthfully and accurately, she should not be made to appear to be mistaken or lying. But if a similar course were to be adopted by every lawyer who learned the truth through confidential disclosures from the client, such disclosures would soon cease to be made. . . .

Obviously, however, the rape case is a much harder one, because the injury done to the prosecutrix is far more severe than the more limited humiliation of the public-spirited and truthful witness in the case of the street robbery. In addition, in the rape case, the lawyer is acting pursuant to a manifestly irrational rule, that is, one that permits the defense to argue that the prosecutrix is the kind of person who would have sexual intercourse with a stranger because she has had sexual relations with two men whom she knew in wholly different social circumstances. Irrational or not, however, in those jurisdictions in which the defense of unchastity is still the law, the attorney is bound to provide it on the client's behalf. For the lawyer who finds the presentation of that defense, and perhaps others in rape cases, to go beyond what he or she can in good conscience do, there are two courses that should be followed. The first is to be active in efforts to reform the law in that regard; the second is to decline to accept the defense of rape cases, on the grounds of a conflict of interest (a strong personal view) that would interfere with providing the defendant with his constitutional right to effective assistance of counsel.

RICHARD WASSERSTROM, LAWYERS AS PROFESSIONALS: SOME MORAL ISSUES

5 Human Rights 1, 5-15 (1975)

Conventional wisdom has it that where the attorney-client relationship exists, . . . it is often appropriate and many times even obligatory for the attorney to do things that, all other things being equal, an ordinary person need not, and should not do. What is characteristic of this role of a lawyer is the lawyer's required indifference to a wide variety of ends and consequences that in other contexts would be of undeniable moral significance. . . . Provided that the end sought is not illegal, the lawyer is, in essence, an amoral technician whose peculiar skills and knowledge in respect to the law are available to those with whom the relationship of client is established. The question . . . is whether this particular and pervasive feature of professionalism is itself justifiable. At a minimum, I do not think any of the typical, simple answers will suffice.

. . . The received view within the profession (and to a lesser degree within the society at large) is that having once agreed to represent the client, the lawyer is under an obligation to do his or her best to defend that person at trial, irrespective, for instance, even of the lawyer's belief in the client's innocence. [I]t is thought both appropriate and obligatory for the attorney to put on as vigorous

a. See page 74 supra.—Eds.

and persuasive a defense of a client believed to be guilty as would have been mounted by the lawyer thoroughly convinced of the client's innocence. I suspect that many persons find this an attractive and admirable feature of the life of a legal professional. . . .

But part of the difficulty is that the irrelevance of the guilt or innocence of an accused client by no means exhausts the altered perspective of the lawyer's conscience, even in criminal cases. For in the course of defending an accused, an attorney may have, as a part of his or her duty of representation, the obligation to invoke procedures and practices which are themselves morally objectionable and of which the lawyer in other contexts might thoroughly disapprove. . . . For example, in California, the case law permits a defendant in a rape case to secure in some circumstances an order from the court requiring the complaining witness, that is the rape victim, to submit to a psychiatric examination before trial. For no other crime is such a pretrial remedy available. . . . I think such a rule is wrong and is reflective of the sexist bias of the law in respect to rape. . . . Nonetheless, it appears to be part of the role-differentiated obligation of a lawyer for a defendant charged with rape to seek to take advantage of this particular rule of law — irrespective of the independent moral view he or she may have of the rightness or wrongness of such a rule.

Nor, it is important to point out, is this peculiar, strikingly amoral behavior limited to the lawyer involved with the workings of the criminal law. . . . Suppose that a client desires to make a will disinheriting her children because they opposed the war in Vietnam. Should the lawyer refuse to draft the will because the lawyer thinks this a bad reason to disinherit one's children? [T]he accepted view within the profession is that these matters are just of no concern to the lawyer qua lawyer. The lawyer need not of course agree to represent the client (and that is equally true for the unpopular client accused of a heinous crime), but there is nothing wrong with representing a client whose aims and purposes are quite immoral. And having agreed to do so, the lawyer is required to provide the best possible assistance, without regard to his or her disapproval of the objective that is sought.

. . . In this way, the lawyer as professional comes to inhabit a simplified universe which is strikingly amoral — which regards as morally irrelevant any number of factors which nonprofessional citizens might take to be important, if not decisive, in their everyday lives. . . .

[O]ne feature of this simplified, intellectual world is that it is often a very comfortable one to inhabit. To be sure, on occasion, a lawyer may find it uncomfortable to represent an extremely unpopular client. On occasion, too, a lawyer may feel ill at ease invoking a rule of law or practice which he or she thinks to be an unfair or undesirable one. Nonetheless, for most lawyers, most of the time, pursuing the interests of one's clients is an attractive and satisfying way to live in part just because the moral world of the lawyer is a simpler, less complicated, and less ambiguous world than the moral world of ordinary life. There is, I think, something quite seductive about being able to turn aside so many ostensibly difficult moral dilemmas and decisions with the reply: but that is not my concern; my job as a lawyer is not to judge the rights and wrong of the client or the cause; it is to defend as best I can my client's interests. . . .

But there is, of course, also an argument which seeks to demonstrate that it is good and not merely comfortable for lawyers to behave this way.

It is good, so the argument goes, that the lawyer's behavior and concomitant point of view are role-differentiated because the lawyer qua lawyer participates in a complex institution which functions well only if the individuals adhere to their institutional roles. . . .

When an individual is charged with having committed a crime, the trial is the mechanism by which we determine in our society whether or not the person is in fact guilty. Just imagine what would happen if lawyers were to refuse, for instance, to represent persons whom they thought to be guilty. . . . The private judgment of individual lawyers would in effect be substituted for the public, institutional judgment of the judge and jury. The amorality of lawyers helps to guarantee that every criminal defendant will have his or her day in court. . . .

[A]rguments that support the role-differentiated amorality of the lawyer on institutional grounds can succeed only if the enormous degree of trust and confidence in the institutions themselves is itself justified. . . . But the less certain we are entitled to be of either the rightness or the self-corrective nature of the larger institutions of which the professional is a part, the less apparent it is that we should encourage the professional to avoid direct engagement with the moral issues as they arise. And we are, today, I believe, certainly entitled to be quite skeptical both of the fairness and of the capacity for self-correction of our larger institutional mechanisms, including the legal system. . . .

Second, it is clear that there are definite character traits that the professional such as the lawyer must take on if the system is to work. What is less clear is that they are admirable ones. Even if the role-differentiated amorality of the professional lawyer is justified by the virtues of the adversary system, this also means that the lawyer qua lawyer will be encouraged to be competitive rather than cooperative; aggressive rather than accommodating; ruthless rather than compassionate; and pragmatic rather than principled. . . .

Third, there is a special feature of the role-differentiated behavior of the lawyer that distinguishes it from the comparable behavior of other professionals. What I have in mind can be brought out through the following question: Why is it that it seems far less plausible to talk critically about the amorality of the doctor, for instance, who treats all patients irrespective of their moral character than it does to talk critically about the comparable amorality of the lawyer? Why is it that it seems so obviously sensible, simple and right for the doctor's behavior to be narrowly and rigidly role-differentiated, i.e., just to try to cure those who are ill? And why is it that at the very least it seems so complicated, uncertain, and troublesome to decide whether it is right for the lawyer's behavior to be similarly role-differentiated?[a]

The answer, I think, is twofold. To begin with . . . it is, so to speak, intrinsically good to try to cure disease, but in no comparable way is it intrinsically good to

a. Consider John Kaplan & Jon R. Waltz, The Trial of Jack Ruby 5 (1965): "Oswald slumped, moaning, to the floor while policemen piled in from all sides to drag down his assailant. . . . Within four minutes of the shooting an ambulance arrived, and . . . rushed Oswald to the Parkland Memorial Hospital. There, in an emergency room just across the hall from the one in which President Kennedy had been pronounced dead two days before, a twelve-man surgical team — the majority of whom would probably have considered as somehow immoral any lawyer who attempted to save Oswald's life by defending him in court — opened Oswald's chest and massaged his heart in relays. . . . Two of the doctors who struggled to preserve Oswald's life had rendered similar service to the expiring President." — Eds.

try to win every lawsuit or help every client realize his or her objective.[b] In addition . . . , the lawyer's behavior is different in kind from the doctor's. The lawyer — and especially the lawyer as advocate — directly says and affirms things. The lawyer makes the case for the client. He or she tries to explain, persuade and convince others that the client's cause should prevail. . . . If the lawyer actually believes everything that he or she asserts on behalf of the client, then it appears to be proper to regard the lawyer as in fact embracing and endorsing the points of view that he or she articulates. If the lawyer does not in fact believe what is urged by way of argument, if the lawyer is only playing a role, then it appears to be proper to tax the lawyer with hypocrisy and insincerity. To be sure, actors in a play take on roles and say things that the characters, not the actors, believe. But we know it is a play and that they are actors. The law courts are not, however, theaters, and the lawyers both talk about justice and they genuinely seek to persuade. . . . [T]he lawyer's words, thoughts, and convictions are, apparently, for sale. . . . The verbal, role-differentiated behavior of the lawyer qua advocate puts the lawyer's integrity into question in a way that distinguishes the lawyer from the other professionals.

Fourth, . . . even if on balance the role-differentiated character of the lawyer's way of thinking and acting is ultimately deemed to be justifiable within the system on systemic instrumental grounds, it still remains the case that we do pay a social price for that way of thought and action. For to become and to be a professional, such as a lawyer, is to incorporate within oneself ways of behaving and ways of thinking that shape the whole person. . . .

NOTE

The questions raised by Wasserstrom are central to the work of all lawyers. The issues remain extremely controversial among academics and within the legal profession generally. For commentary that is critical of the highly role-differentiated standards of prevailing legal ethics, see Alan H. Goldman, The Moral Foundations of Professional Ethics (1980); William H. Simon, The Ethics of Criminal Defense, 91 Mich. L. Rev. 1703 (1993). Prominent discussions that largely support a role-differentiated standard and zealous advocacy on behalf of criminal defendants (including those who are guilty) include David Luban, Are Criminal Defenders Different?, 91 Mich. L. Rev. 1729 (1993); Charles J. Ogletree, Jr., Beyond Justifications: Seeking Motivations to Sustain Public Defenders, 106 Harv. L. Rev. 1239 (1993); Charles Fried, The Lawyer as Friend: The Moral Foundations of the Lawyer-Client Relation, 85 Yale L.J. 1060 (1976). A comprehensive treatment of the issues appears in David Luban, Lawyers and Justice (1988).

b. See also William Simon, Homo Psychologicus: Notes on a New Legal Formalism, 32 Stan. L. Rev. 487, 501-502 (1980): "The analogies to such roles as doctor and priest are fundamentally misleading. For unlike the relations defined by these roles, the lawyer-client relation is fundamentally impersonal and other-regarding. . . . In the case of doctors and priests, the principal impact of the professional's activity occurs within the professional relation in the form of the change which the patient or penitent undergoes. But in the case of lawyers, the principal impact occurs *outside* the professional relation. The client benefits only to the extent that outsiders are affected." — Eds.

CHAPTER 2

THE JUSTIFICATION OF PUNISHMENT

A. WHAT IS PUNISHMENT?

INTRODUCTORY NOTE

The proper justification for criminal punishment is a subject of continuing controversy in jurisprudence and criminal law. In Section B below we examine the issues in detail. But before exploring the terms of that debate, which can occasionally seem a bit abstract, we believe it necessary for students to have in mind a concrete conception of what criminal punishment *is*. For example, we will want to consider whether it is justified, in order to promote effective deterrence, to impose "criminal punishment" on those who cause certain kinds of serious harm, even when we cannot prove that they caused the harm deliberately or negligently. In examining that question, it is essential to keep in mind exactly what that "criminal punishment" will consist of.

In broad outline, the principal forms of criminal punishment are familiar. Punishment may consist of a fine, probation, imprisonment or, in especially serious cases, the death penalty. Less obviously, the conviction itself is a form of punishment, carrying with it a social stigma, a barrier to future employment, and a risk of enhanced punishment in the event of a future offense.

Contemporary courts are now actively developing "intermediate sanctions" less harsh than imprisonment but more severe than probation. These include weeks or months of home detention, mandated community service, or "intensive-supervision" probation (which often includes mandatory counseling or drug treatment).

Imprisonment, of course, represents the quintessential criminal punishment. Though not inflicted in every case, it is almost always an option that the judge has discretion to impose. And even when not imposed, imprisonment remains in the background as a possible consequence of any failure to meet conditions of a fine, probation, or intermediate sanction.

The meaning of imprisonment is obvious and yet, for most of us, unfamiliar. The remaining materials in this section present some aspects of what incarceration entails in contemporary America, with a particular focus on the large, medium- to high-security prison that is now typical. A sense of what imprisonment means in practice can serve as a preface to a discussion of the circumstances under which it is ever justified to inflict this kind of sanction.

GRESHAM M. SYKES, THE SOCIETY OF CAPTIVES

65-75 (1971)

The Deprivation of Goods and Services . . .

[T]here are a number of prison officials who will argue that some inmates are better off in prison, in strictly material terms, than they could ever hope to be in the rough-and-tumble economic life of the free community. Possibly this is so, but . . . [t]he average inmate finds himself in a harshly Spartan environment which he defines as painfully depriving. . . . In modern Western culture, material possessions are so large a part of the individual's conception of himself that to be stripped of them is to be attacked at the deepest layers of personality. . . .

The Deprivation of Heterosexual Relationships

Unlike the prisoner in many Latin-American countries, the inmate of the maximum security prison in New Jersey does not enjoy the privilege of so-called conjugal visits. And in those brief times when the prisoner is allowed to see his wife, mistress, or "female friend," the women must sit on one side of a plate glass window and the prisoner on the other, communicating by means of a phone under the scrutiny of a guard. . . . [I]t is clear that the lack of heterosexual intercourse is a frustrating experience for the imprisoned criminal and that it is a frustration which weighs heavily and painfully on his mind during his prolonged confinement. . . .[a]

The Deprivation of Security

However strange it may appear that society has chosen to reduce the criminality of the offender by forcing him to associate with more than a thousand other criminals for years on end, there is one meaning of this involuntary union which is obvious — the individual prisoner is thrown into prolonged intimacy with other men who in many cases have a long history of violent, aggressive behavior. It is a situation which can prove to be anxiety-provoking even for the hardened recidivist and it is in this light that we can understand the comment of an inmate of the New Jersey State Prison who said, "The worst thing about prison is you have to live with other prisoners."

The fact that the imprisoned criminal sometimes views his fellow prisoners as "vicious" or "dangerous" may seem a trifle unreasonable. Other inmates, after all, are men like himself, bearing the legal stigma of conviction. But even if the

a. Although Sykes' discussion focuses on the plight of the heterosexual prisoner, gay men often suffer serious problems as well. In some prisons, gays are especially likely to become targets for rape and other abuses. — Eds.

individual prisoner believes that he himself is not the sort of person who is likely to attack or exploit weaker and less resourceful fellow captives, he is apt to view others with more suspicion. And . . . regardless of the patterns of mutual aid and support which may flourish in the inmate population, there are a sufficient number of outlaws within this group of outlaws to deprive the average prisoner of that sense of security which comes from living among men who can be reasonably expected to abide by the rules of society. . . .

An important aspect of this disturbingly problematical world is the fact that the inmate is acutely aware that sooner or later he will be "tested"— that someone will "push" him to see how far they can go and that he must be prepared to fight for the safety of his person and his possessions. If he should fail, he will thereafter be an object of contempt, constantly in danger of being attacked by other inmates who view him as an obvious victim, as a man who cannot or will not defend his rights. And yet if he succeeds, he may well become a target for the prisoner who wishes to prove himself, who seeks to enhance his own prestige by defeating the man with a reputation for toughness. Thus both success and failure in defending one's self against the aggressions of fellow captives may serve to provoke fresh attacks and no man stands assured of the future.

The prisoner's loss of security arouses acute anxiety, in short, not just because violent acts of aggression and exploitation occur but also because such behavior constantly calls into question the individual's ability to cope with it. . . . These uncertainties constitute an ego threat for the individual forced to live in prolonged intimacy with criminals, regardless of the nature or extent of his own criminality; . . . the prison inmate can never feel safe.

NOTES

***1.** Prison violence.* Accurate estimates of the prevalence of rape and other serious assaults in prisons are difficult to obtain, and informed observers are to some extent divided in their opinions. The situation undoubtedly varies from prison to prison. Overall there seems little question that the threat of violent attack is a significant, and sometimes extremely serious, problem for the American prisoner.[1] Some observers are especially pessimistic. See, e.g., Kathleen Engel & Stanley Rothman, Prison Violence and the Paradox of Reform, 73 The Public Interest 91 (Fall 1983): "Men's prisons across the country are besieged by violence. . . . The realities of today's prisons are grim indeed." Similarly, in United States v. Bailey, 444 U.S. 394, 420-422 (1980), Justice Blackmun, dissenting, commented:

> The complaints that this Court, and every other American appellate court, receives almost daily from prisoners about conditions of incarceration, about filth, about

1. See Anthony E. Bottoms, Interpersonal Violence and Social Order in Prisons, in 26 Crime & Justice 205, 268-272 (M. Tonry & J. Petersilia, eds., 1999); Stephen D. Sowle, A Regime of Social Death: Criminal Punishment in the Age of Prisons, 21 N.Y.U. Rev. L. & Soc. Change 497 (1994). Professor Sowle describes, in addition, the psychologically dehumanizing effects of long-term isolation and sensory deprivation for prisoners assigned to solitary confinement. For a searing account of the brutalizing impact of long-term imprisonment, see Jack Henry Abbott, In the Belly of the Beast: Letters from Prison (1981).

> homosexual rape, and about brutality are not always the mouthings of the purely malcontent. The Court itself acknowledges that the conditions these respondents complained about do exist. . . . And the Government concedes: "In light of prison conditions that even now prevail in the United States, it would be the rare inmate who could not convince himself that continued incarceration would be harmful to his health or safety."

One factor contributing to the prevalence of prison violence is that when constitutional litigation in the 1960s and 1970s restricted the ability of prison guards to discipline inmates through summary corporal punishments, prisoners became harder to control, and in many prisons the reduction in brutality perpetrated by guards was more than offset by the increase in abuses perpetrated by inmates. See James B. Jacobs, New Perspectives on Prisons and Imprisonment 57 (1983); Engel & Rothman, supra at 91. Few prison administrators or reformers advocate a return to the days of freewheeling, unrestricted disciplinary powers for prison guards. But to have both a safe prison and due process restrictions on official discipline requires improvements in prison design and significantly higher ratios of guards to prisoners; these steps imply substantial increases in per-prisoner expenditures that legislatures hesitate to authorize and that courts cannot easily enforce. As a result, inmate violence persists in many prisons, despite court decrees and conscientious efforts by prison administrators to control it.

Nonetheless, a number of knowledgeable observers suggest that the problem of violence may no longer be so acute, at least in many prisons.[2] One long-term Louisiana inmate has written:[3]

> While [rapes] used to be a regular feature of life here at the Louisiana State Penitentiary, they are now a rare occurrence. . . . In 1976, Federal District Court Judge E. Gordon West ordered a massive crackdown on overall violence at the prison, which paved the way for the allocation of money, manpower, and sophisticated electronic equipment to do the job. Since then, *any* kind of violence at all between inmates elicits swift administrative reprisal and certain prosecution. This, more than anything else, has made Angola [prison] safe for the average youngster coming into the prison today.

2. *Crowding*. One characteristic of American prisons that is important both as a cause of prison violence and as a serious problem in its own right is pervasive overcrowding. Overcrowded conditions have proved highly resistant to reform efforts because rising rates of incarceration and lengthening sentences have far outstripped the willingness and ability of states to build new prisons. Although efficient prison management requires prisons to operate significantly below their full capacity levels,[4] at year end 1998 the federal system was operating at 27 percent above capacity, and 37 states were likewise operating well above their capacity levels. The California prison system, one of the nation's largest, held an inmate population equal to 203 percent of its capacity.[5] Forty states and more

2. See, e.g, Bottoms, supra footnote 1, at 225-227, 239-241; Norval Morris, The Modern Prison, in David Rothman & Norval Morris, eds., The History of Imprisonment (1995).
3. Walter Rideau, The Sexual Jungle, quoted in Morris, supra footnote 2.
4. See U.S. Dept. of Justice, Bureau of Justice Statistics, Prisoners in 1998, at 8 (1999).
5. Id. On the ambiguities in the concept of prison "capacity" and the difficulties in measuring it accurately, see Franklin E. Zimring, Are State Prisons *Under*crowded?, 4 Fed. Sent. Rptr. 347 (May/June 1992).

than 500 localities were under court orders to reduce overcrowding that had been held to violate federal or state constitutions,[6] but as inmate admissions rise and construction lags, courts are often reluctant to order the release of violent offenders. As a result, severely overcrowded conditions have persisted on a "temporary" basis in most states since the 1970s.[7] A surge in prison construction during the 1990s was accompanied by a nearly equivalent surge in incarceration rates, with the result that overcrowding in state prisons declined somewhat, but not dramatically.[8]

3. Women in prison. During the past decade, the number of women in prison has grown much faster than the number of men; the female prisoner population nearly doubled from 1990 to 1998. But women still represent less than 7 percent of the total prison population.[9]

Physical danger from other inmates, though occasionally a concern in women's prisons, is generally a less serious problem than it is in men's prisons. But women inmates face other difficulties. Recent reports indicate that in many states, prison guards frequently subject female prisoners under their control to rape and other forms of sexual exploitation. See Stephen J. Schulhofer, Unwanted Sex 201-205 (1998); Human Rights Watch, All Too Familiar: Sexual Abuse of Women in U.S. State Prisons (1996). In addition, because most states have few women's prisons, female prisoners are likely to be sent much farther from their homes and families than male prisoners are. And women's prisons typically afford far fewer educational and vocational programs than men's prisons do. For a discussion of the problems, see Nicole Hahn Rafter, Partial Justice: Women, Prisons, and Social Control (2d ed. 1990).

4. Different kinds of prisons. The foregoing descriptions of prison life focus primarily on conditions in medium- and high-security institutions. Although these kinds of prisons are now the most common destination for the incarcerated offender, other types of custodial institutions remain important. Some minimum-security prisons and "prison camps" operate without guard towers or walls, and afford dormitory-type rooms along with modestly good recreational facilities. In contrast, prisons in the maximum-security category typically feature high walls, long blocks of barred cells, and highly overcrowded conditions. Although many minimum-security prisoners avoid the worst forms of violence and degradation, some of the other consequences of imprisonment described by Sykes are probably inherent in any form of incarceration. To some extent, of course, imprisonment is *supposed to be* unpleasant. To what extent should society seek to moderate or reinforce the pains that are intrinsic to penal confinement?

5. "Civil" sanctions. Some forms of involuntary confinement are classified as "civil" measures rather than criminal punishments. Civil commitment of the mentally ill is a prominent example. The distinction between civil and criminal measures (or between "regulation" and "punishment") has enormous practical importance. Before imposing "punishment," the government must comply with stringent safeguards, including the requirement of proof beyond a reasonable doubt. And the duration of "punishment" is limited by the perceived imperative

6. Kerry L. Pyle, Note: Prison Employment, A Long-Term Solution to the Overcrowding Crisis, 77 B.U. L. Rev. 151, 152 n.12 (1997).
7. Id., at 151-160.
8. See U.S. Dept. of Justice, supra footnote 4, at 9.
9. Id., at 5.

(moral, statutory and constitutional) of proportionality to an offender's fault. In a "civil" proceeding, in contrast, the burden of proof is typically lower, many other safeguards of criminal procedure do not apply, and the defendant may face loss of liberty for an indefinite period, potentially for life.

What features make a proceeding "civil" rather than criminal? Government cannot escape the usual criminal law restrictions simply by attaching the "civil" label to a sanction that is punitive in its purpose or effect. To determine whether a nominally civil measure is really punishment (and thus whether criminal law safeguards apply), courts must consider:[10]

> [w]hether the sanction involves an affirmative disability or restraint, whether it has historically been regarded as a punishment, whether it comes into play only on a finding of *scienter,* whether its operation will promote the traditional aims of punishment — retribution and deterrence, whether the behavior to which it applies is already a crime, whether an alternative purpose to which it may rationally be connected is assignable for it, and whether it appears excessive in relation to the alternative purpose assigned.

Involuntary commitment of the mentally ill, for the protection of themselves or others, is universally considered a civil proceeding. The person committed has a right to treatment, and he must be released when he is no longer mentally ill or dangerous. Nonetheless, such a person may, if not cured, find himself confined for life. See page 882 infra.

Other restrictions on liberty are more difficult to classify. In the early 1990s, many states enacted Sexually Violent Predator (SVP) laws in order to permit long-term confinement of sex offenders who finish serving their criminal sentences. The typical SVP law permits indefinite commitment of persons who are not mentally ill, on the basis of a finding that they have a "mental abnormality" or "personality disorder" and are "likely to engage in predatory acts of sexual violence." SVP laws typically do not bar the provision of treatment, but many of them acknowledge that the SVP condition is difficult or impossible to treat.[11]

Can an offender be committed under such a law, after he has served his sentence, without violating the rule against double jeopardy? Can such a law be applied retroactively to a person whose sex offense was committed before the law was enacted? Can a person be adjudicated as an SVP and committed indefinitely, without proof beyond a reasonable doubt that future sexual misconduct is "likely"? If the SVP proceeding is properly classified as civil, the answer to all these questions is "yes." In Kansas v. Hendricks, 521 U.S. 346 (1997), the Supreme Court upheld the "civil" classification of one such law. The Court emphasized that under the Kansas regime, inmates are not subject to punitive conditions of confinement and are entitled to immediate release whenever it is determined that they are no longer dangerous; four dissenting Justices argued that the Kansas regime should nonetheless be considered criminal because treatable inmates had been afforded little or no treatment and because the committing authorities were not required to consider using less restrictive means of social protection, short of incarceration.

10. Kennedy v. Mendoza-Martinez, 372 U.S. 144, 168-169 (1963).

11. See Stephen J. Schulhofer, Two Systems of Social Protection: Comments on the Civil-Criminal Distinction, with Particular Reference to Sexually Violent Predator Laws, 7 J. Contemp. Leg. Issues 69 (1996).

Similar issues arise under laws that require convicted sex offenders, upon release from prison, to register with local police. Such laws, modeled on the "Megan's Law" first enacted in New Jersey, typically require the police to make such registration lists publicly available. In many instances, police must also notify schools, day care centers, and local residents of the offender's presence in the community. Should such laws be considered "civil" measures to which criminal law safeguards do not apply? In New Jersey, Megan's Law was upheld as a "civil" measure only after the state supreme court required modifications to restrict the degree of public disclosure, depending on whether the offender was found to pose a low, medium, or high risk of re-offending. See E. B. v. Verniero, 119 F.3d 107 (3d Cir. 1997). And even with this limitation, several courts hold that public disclosure is unconstitutional in the absence of a careful adversary procedure to determine the ex-offender's level of risk. E.g., Paul P. v. Farmer, 92 F. Supp. 2d 410 (D.N.J. 2000); People v. David W., 733 N.E.2d 206 (N.Y. 2000). In contrast, a Tennessee version of Megan's Law was upheld as a civil measure even though it imposed no limits on public disclosure of information about ex-offenders who had registered. Cutshall v. Sundquist, 193 F.3d 466 (6th Cir. 1999).

B. WHY PUNISH?

INTRODUCTORY NOTE

Punishment, as we have seen, is the social practice of intentionally inflicting suffering on certain individuals. This section examines the purposes that this practice is thought to serve and whether any of them (or only some) can *justify* punishment.[12]

Broadly speaking, the justifications for punishment fall into two large groups, retributive and utilitarian. "[A] retributivist claims that punishment is justified because people deserve it; a utilitarian believes that justification lies in the useful purposes that punishment serves."[13] Retributive rationales are essentially backward-looking, as they seek to justify punishment on the basis of the offender's behavior in the past. Utilitarian rationales are essentially forward-looking, as they seek to justify punishment on the basis of the good consequences it is expected to produce in the future.

Part 1 of this section presents a variety of views concerning the justifications for punishment, organized around the ideas of retribution and the three main utilitarian purposes (prevention, rehabilitation and incapacitation). Part 2 of this section presents specific cases that provide concrete settings for examining the general ideas introduced in Part 1.

As a framework for both Parts, consider the following statutory statements concerning the purposes of punishment.

12. There is a large literature on the subject of punishment. For a valuable introductory treatment, see Kent Greenawalt, Punishment, in 4 Encyclopedia of Crime and Justice 1336 (S. Kadish ed., 1983). Bibliographies may be found in Herbert Morris, Freedom and Responsibility 546-547 (1961); K. Pecarovich, Bibliography of Responsibility, 49 L. & Contemp. Prob. 277 (1986). The ideas of Professor H. L. A. Hart have been especially influential. His essays are contained in Punishment and Responsibility (1968).

13. Greenawalt, Punishment, supra footnote 12, at 1336.

MODEL PENAL CODE: *Section 1.02.* (1) The general purposes of the provisions governing the definition of offenses are: (a) to forbid and prevent conduct that unjustifiably and inexcusably inflicts or threatens substantial harm to individual or public interests; (b) to subject to public control persons whose conduct indicates that they are disposed to commit crimes; . . . (e) to differentiate on reasonable grounds between serious and minor offenses.

(2) The general purposes of the provisions governing the sentencing and treatment of offenders are: (a) to prevent the commission of offenses; (b) to promote the correction and rehabilitation of offenders; (c) to safeguard offenders against excessive, disproportionate or arbitrary punishment. . . .

NEW YORK PENAL LAW: *Section 1.05.* The general purposes of the provisions of this chapter are: . . .

5. To insure the public safety by preventing the commission of offenses through the deterrent influence of the sentences authorized, the rehabilitation of those convicted, and their confinement when required in the interests of public protection.

CALIFORNIA PENAL CODE: *Section 1170.* The Legislature finds and declares that the purpose of imprisonment for crime is punishment. This purpose is best served by terms proportionate to the seriousness of the offense with provision for uniformity in the sentences of offenders committing the same offense under similar circumstances. The Legislature further finds and declares that the elimination of disparity and the provision of uniformity of sentences can best be achieved by determinate sentences fixed by statute in proportion to the seriousness of the offense as determined by the Legislature to be imposed by the court with specified discretion.

1. *Perspectives on Punishment*

a. Retribution

i. What Is Retribution?

IMMANUEL KANT, THE PHILOSOPHY OF LAW (W. Hastie tr. 1887): The right of administering punishment is the right of the sovereign as the supreme power to inflict pain upon a subject on account of a crime committed by him. . . .

Judicial or juridical punishment (*poena forensis*) is to be distinguished from natural punishment (*poena naturalis*), in which crime as vice punishes itself, and does not as such come within the cognizance of the legislator. Juridical punishment can never be administered merely as a means of promoting another good either with regard to the criminal himself or to civil society, but must in all cases be imposed only because the individual on whom it is inflicted *has committed a crime.* For one man ought never to be dealt with merely as a means subservient to the purpose of another, nor be [treated as though he were subject to the law of property.] Against such treatment his inborn personality has a right to protect him, even although he may be condemned to lose his civil personality. He must first be found guilty and *punishable,* before there can be any thought of drawing from his punishment any benefit for himself or his fellow-citizens. The penal law is a categorical imperative; and woe to him who creeps through the serpent-windings of utilitarianism to discover some advantage that may discharge him from the justice of punishment, or even from the due measure of it, according to the Pharisaic maxim: "It is better that *one* man should die than that the whole people should perish." For if justice and righteousness perish, human life would no longer have any value in the world. What, then, is to be said of such a proposal as to keep a criminal alive who has been condemned to death, on his being given to understand that if he agreed to certain dangerous experiments being performed upon him, he would be allowed to survive if he came happily through them? It is argued that physicians might thus obtain new information that would be of value to the commonweal. But a court of justice would repudiate with scorn any proposal of this kind if made to it by the medical faculty; for justice would cease to be justice if it were bartered away for any consideration whatever.

But what is the mode and measure of punishment which public justice takes as its principle and standard? It is just the principle of equality, by which the pointer of the scale of justice is made to incline no more to the one side than the other. It may be rendered by saying that the undeserved evil which any one commits on another is to be regarded as perpetrated on himself. Hence it may be said: "If you slander another, you slander yourself; if you steal from another, you steal from yourself; if you strike another, you strike yourself; if you kill another, you kill yourself." This is the right of retaliation (*jus talionis*); and properly understood, it is the only principle which in regulating a public court, as distinguished from mere private judgment, can definitely assign both the quality and the quantity of a just penalty. All other standards are wavering and uncertain; and on account of other considerations involved in them, they contain no principle conformable to the sentence of pure and strict justice. . . .

But how then would we render the statement: "If you *steal* from another, you steal from yourself"? In this way, that whoever steals anything makes the property of all insecure; he therefore robs himself of all security in property, according to the right of retaliation. Such a one has nothing, and can acquire nothing, but he has the will to live; and this is only possible by others supporting him. But as the state should not do this gratuitously, he must for this purpose yield his powers to the state to be used in penal labour; and thus he falls for a time, or it may be life, into a condition of slavery. But whoever has committed murder must *die*. There is, in this case, no juridical substitute or surrogate that can be given or taken for the satisfaction of justice. There is no *likeness* or proportion between life, however painful, and death; and therefore there is no equality between the crime of murder and the retaliation of it but what is judicially accomplished by the execution of the criminal. His death, however, must be kept free from all maltreatment that would make the humanity suffering in his person loathsome or abominable. Even if a civil society resolved to dissolve itself with the consent of all its members — as might be supposed in the case of a people inhabiting an island resolving to separate and scatter themselves through the whole world — the last murderer lying in the prison ought to be executed before the resolution was carried out. This ought to be done in order that every one may realize the desert of his deeds, and that bloodguiltiness may not remain upon the people; for otherwise they might all be regarded as participators in the murder as a public violation of justice.

2 JAMES FITZJAMES STEPHEN, A HISTORY OF THE CRIMINAL LAW OF ENGLAND 81-82 (1883 ed.): [T]he sentence of the law is to the moral sentiment of the public in relation to any offence what a seal is to hot wax. It converts into a permanent final judgment what might otherwise be a transient sentiment. The mere general suspicion or knowledge that a man has done something dishonest may never be brought to a point, and the disapprobation excited by it may in time pass away, but the fact that he has been convicted and punished as a thief stamps a mark upon him for life. In short, the infliction of punishment by law gives definite expression and a solemn ratification and justification to the hatred which is excited by the commission of the offence, and which constitutes the moral or popular as distinguished from the conscientious sanction of that part of morality which is also sanctioned by the criminal law. The criminal law thus proceeds upon the principle that it is morally right to hate criminals, and it confirms and justifies that sentiment by inflicting upon criminals punishments which express it. . . . I am also of opinion that this close alliance between criminal law and moral sentiment is in all ways healthy and advantageous to the community. I think it highly desirable that criminals should be hated, that the punishments inflicted upon them should be so contrived as to give expression to that hatred, and to justify it so far as the public provision of means for expressing and gratifying a healthy natural sentiment can justify and encourage it. . . . The doctrine that hatred and vengeance are wicked in themselves appears to me to contradict plain facts, and to be unsupported by any argument deserving of attention. . . . The unqualified manner in which they have been denounced is in itself a proof that they are deeply rooted in human nature. No doubt they are peculiarly liable to abuse, and in some states of society are commonly in excess of what is desirable, and so require restraint rather than excitement, but unqualified denunciations of them are as ill-judged as unqualified denunciations of sexual passion. The forms in which deliberate anger and righteous disapprobation are expressed, and the execution of criminal justice is the most emphatic of such forms, stand to the one set of passions in the same relation in which marriage stands to the other.[a]

ROYAL COMMISSION ON CAPITAL PUNISHMENT, Minutes of Evidence, Ninth Day, Dec. 1, 1949, Memorandum Submitted by the Rt. Hon. Lord Justice Denning, 207: Whilst everyone agrees that crimes must be punished, there is profound disagreement as to the form which punishment should take. Many are inclined to test the efficacy of punishment solely by its value as a deterrent: but this is too narrow a view. Punishment is the way in which society expresses its denunciation of wrong doing: and, in order to maintain respect for law, it is essential that the punishment inflicted for grave crimes should adequately reflect the revulsion felt by the great majority of citizens for them. It is a mistake to consider the objects of punishment as being deterrent or reformative or preventive and nothing else. If that were so, we should not send to prison a man who was

a. Stephen put this idea more pointedly in the first, 1863, edition of A History of the Criminal Law of England, Volume 2, p. 99: "The criminal law stands to the passion of revenge in much the same relation as marriage to the sexual appetite." There is a story that on an examination a student (one presumes English) once put the idea as follows: "Stephen maintains that marriage is to love what punishment is to crime." See Cross, The Making of English Criminal Law, (6) Sir James Fitzjames Stephen [1976] Crim. L. Rev. 652, 654. — Eds.

guilty of motor manslaughter, but only disqualify him from driving; but would public opinion be content with this? The truth is that some crimes are so outrageous that society insists on adequate punishment, because the wrong-doer deserves it, irrespective of whether it is a deterrent or not. . . . Some cases are so outrageous that, irrespective of the value of the death penalty as a deterrent, the great bulk of the community consider that the only fitting penalty is death. In my view the ultimate justification of any punishment is, not that it is a deterrent, but that it is the emphatic denunciation by the community of a crime: and from this point of view, there are some murders which, in the present state of public opinion, demand the most emphatic denunciation of all, namely the death penalty.

JOEL FEINBERG, DOING AND DESERVING 98, 100-105 (1970): [P]unishment is a conventional device for the expression of attitudes of resentment and indignation, and of judgments of disapproval and reprobation, on the part either of the punishing authority himself or of those "in whose name" the punishment is inflicted. Punishment, in short, has a *symbolic significance* largely missing from other kinds of penalties. . . .

It is much easier to show that punishment has a symbolic significance than to state exactly what it is that punishment expresses. At its best, in civilized and democratic countries, punishment surely expresses the community's strong *disapproval* of what the criminal did. Indeed, it can be said that punishment expresses the *judgment* (as distinct from any emotion) of the community that what the criminal did was wrong. I think it is fair to say of our community, however, that punishment generally expresses more than judgments of disapproval; it is also a symbolic way of getting back at the criminal, of expressing a kind of vindictive resentment. To any reader who has in fact spent time in a prison, I venture to say, even Professor Gardner's strong terms — "hatred, fear, or contempt for the convict" — will not seem too strong an account of what imprisonment is universally taken to express. Not only does the criminal feel the naked hostility of his guards and the outside world — that would be fierce enough — but that hostility is self-righteous as well. His punishment bears the aspect of legitimized vengefulness. . . .

If we reserve the less dramatic term "resentment" for the various vengeful attitudes and the term "reprobation" for the stern judgment of disapproval, then perhaps we can characterize *condemnation* (or denunciation) as a kind of fusing of resentment and reprobation. . . .

The relation of the expressive function of punishment to its various central purposes is not always easy to trace. Symbolic public condemnation added to deprivation may help or hinder deterrence, reform, and rehabilitation — the evidence is not clear. On the other hand, there are other functions of punishment, often lost sight of in the preoccupation with deterrence and reform, that presuppose the expressive function and would be difficult or impossible without it.

Authoritative disavowal. Consider the standard international practice of demanding that a nation whose agent has unlawfully violated the complaining nation's rights should punish the offending agent. For example, suppose that an airplane of nation A fires on an airplane of nation B while the latter is flying over international waters. Very likely high authorities in nation B will send a note of protest to their counterparts in nation A demanding, among other things, that the transgressive pilot be punished. Punishing the pilot is an emphatic, dramatic, and well-understood way of *condemning* and thereby *disavowing* his act. . . .

Symbolic nonacquiescence: "Speaking in the name of the people." . . . In the state of Texas, so-called paramour killings were regarded by the law as not merely mitigated, but completely justifiable. Many humanitarians, I believe, will feel quite spontaneously that a great injustice is done when such killings are left unpunished. . . . The demand for punishment in cases of this sort may . . . represent the feeling that paramour killings deserve to be *condemned,* that the law in condoning, even approving of them, speaks for all citizens in expressing a wholly inappropriate attitude toward them. For in effect the law expresses the judgment of the "people of Texas," in whose name it speaks, that the vindictive satisfaction in the mind of a cuckolded husband is a thing of greater value than the very life of his wife's lover. The demand that paramour killings be punished may simply be the demand that this lopsided value judgment be withdrawn and that the state *go on record* against paramour killings. . . . Punishment no doubt would also help deter killers. This too is a desideratum and a closely related one, but it is not to be identified with reprobation; for deterrence might be achieved by a dozen other techniques, from simple penalties and forfeitures to exhortation and propaganda; but effective public denunciation and, through it, symbolic nonacquiescence in the crime seem virtually to require punishment. . . .

EMILE DURKHEIM, THE DIVISION OF LAW IN SOCIETY 62-63 (W. D. Halls transl., 1984): Although [punishment] proceeds from an entirely mechanical reaction and from . . . passionate emotion, for the most part unthinking, it continues to play a useful role. But that role is not the one commonly perceived. It does not serve, or serves only very incidentally, to correct the guilty person or to scare off any possible imitators. . . . Its real function is to maintain inviolate the cohesion of society by sustaining the common consciousness in all its vigour. If that consciousness were thwarted . . . , it would necessarily lose some of its power, were an emotional reaction from the community not forthcoming to make good that loss. Thus there would result a relaxation in the bonds of social solidarity. The consciousness must therefore be conspicuously reinforced the moment it meets with opposition. The sole means of doing so is to give voice to the unanimous aversion that the crime continues to evoke, and this by an official act, which can only mean suffering inflicted upon the wrongdoer. Thus, although a necessary outcome of the causes that give rise to it, this suffering is not a gratuitous act of cruelty. It is a sign indicating that the sentiments of the collectivity are still unchanged, that the communion of minds sharing the same beliefs remains absolute, and in this way the injury that the crime has inflicted upon society is made good. This is why it is right to maintain that the criminal should suffer in proportion to his crime, and why theories that deny to punishment any expiatory character appear, in the minds of many, to subvert the social order. In fact such theories could only be put into practice in a society from which almost every trace of the common consciousness has been expunged. Without this necessary act of satisfaction what is called the moral consciousness could not be preserved. Thus, without being paradoxical, we may state that punishment is above all intended to have its effect upon honest people. Since it serves to heal the wounds inflicted upon the collective sentiments, it can only fulfil this role where such sentiments exist, and in so far as they are active. Undoubtedly, by forestalling in minds already distressed any further weakening of the collective psyche, punishment can indeed prevent such attacks from multiplying. But such a result, useful though it is, is merely a particular side-effect. In short, to visualise an exact idea of punishment, the two opposing theories that have been advanced must be reconciled: The one sees in punishment an expiation, the other conceives it as a weapon for the defence of society. Certainly it does fulfil the function of protecting society, but this is because of its expiatory nature. Moreover, if it must be expiatory, this is not because suffering redeems error by virtue of some mystic strength or another, but because it cannot produce its socially useful effect save on this one condition.[a]

MICHAEL S. MOORE, THE MORAL WORTH OF RETRIBUTION, in F. Schoeman, ed., Responsibility, Character and Emotions 179 (1987): *Retributivism* is the view that punishment is justified by the moral culpability of those who receive it. A retributivist punishes because, and only because, the offender deserves it. Retributivism thus stands in stark contrast to utilitarian views that justify punishment of past offenses by the greater good of preventing future offenses. It also contrasts sharply with rehabilitative views, according to which punishment is justified by the reforming good it does the criminal.

Less clearly, retributivism also differs from a variety of views that are often paraded as retributivist, but that in fact are not. . . . The leading confusions seem to me to be [several].

1. First, retributivism is sometimes identified with a particular measure of punishment such as *lex talionis,* an eye for an eye, or with a kind of punishment such as the death penalty. Yet retributivism answers a question prior to the questions to which these could be answers. True enough, retributivists at some point have to answer the "how much" and "what type" questions for specific offenses, and they are committed to the principle that punishment should be graded in proportion to desert; but they are not committed to any particular penalty scheme nor to any particular penalty as being deserved. Separate argument is needed to answer these "how much" and "what type" questions, *after* one has described why one is punishing at all. It is quite possible to be a retributivist and to be against both the death penalty and *lex talionis,* the idea that crimes should be punished by like acts being done to the criminal.

2. . . . [R]etributivism is *not* "the view that only the guilty are to be punished." A retributivist will subscribe to such a view, but that is not what is distinctive about retributivism. The distinctive aspect of retributivism is that the moral desert of an offender is a *sufficient* reason to punish him or her; the principle [that only the guilty may be punished makes] such moral desert only a *necessary* con-

a. Compare David Garland, Punishment and Modern Society 80 (1990):

> Clearly punishment does perform certain 'functions' — it sanctions certain kinds of rules, restrains certain kinds of conduct, expresses certain felt emotions, and reaffirms specific forms of authority and belief. But these rules, conducts, emotions, beliefs, and authorities need not be coterminous with 'society' or [promote] social harmony. [W]hat is 'functional' from one point of view may be dysfunctional from another. Durkheim's work is deficient . . . in ignoring the role of power differentials in the maintenance of social order and underplaying penality's capacity to function as an amoral instrument of regulation. — Eds.

dition of punishment. Other reasons — typically, crime prevention reasons — must be added to moral desert, in this view, for punishment to be justified. Retributivism has no room for such additional reasons. That future crime might also be prevented by punishment is a happy surplus for a retributivist, but no part of the justification for punishing.

3. Retributivism is not the view that punishment of offenders satisfies the desires for vengeance of their victims. . . . A retributivist can justify punishment as deserved even if the criminal's victims are indifferent (or even opposed) to punishing the one who hurt them. Indeed, a retributivist should urge punishment on all offenders who deserve it, even if *no* victims wanted it.

4. [R]etributivism is not the view that the preferences of all citizens (not just crime victims) should be satisfied. A preference utilitarian might well believe, as did Sir James Fitzjames Stephen, that punishment should be exacted "for the sake of gratifying the feeling of hatred — call it revenge, resentment, or what you will — which the contemplation of such [criminal] conduct excites in healthily constituted minds . . . ," or that "the feeling of hatred and the desire of vengeance . . . are important elements of human nature which ought . . . to be satisfied in a regular public and legal manner." Yet a retributivist need not believe such things, but only that morally culpable persons should be punished, irrespective of what other citizens feel, desire, or prefer.

5. [R]etributivism is not the view that punishment is justified because without it vengeful citizens would take the law into their own hands. . . . Punishment for a retributivist is not justified by the need to prevent private violence, which is an essentially utilitarian justification. Even in the most well-mannered state, those criminals who deserve punishment should get it, according to retributivism.

6. Nor is retributivism to be confused with denunciatory theories of punishment. In this latter view punishment is justified because punishment is the vehicle through which society can express its condemnation of the criminal's behavior. This is a utilitarian theory, not a retributive one, for punishment is in this view to be justified by the good consequences it achieves — either the psychological satisfactions denunciation achieves, or the prevention of private violence, or the prevention of future crimes through the education benefits of such denunciation. A retributivist justifies punishment by none of these supposed good consequences of punishing. . . .

Retributivism is a very straightforward theory of punishment: We are justified in punishing because and only because offenders deserve it. Moral culpability ("desert") is in such a view both a sufficient as well as a necessary condition of liability to punitive sanctions. Such justification gives society more than merely a right to punish culpable offenders. It does this, making it not unfair to punish them, but retributivism justifies more than this. For a retributivist, the moral culpability of an offender also gives society the *duty* to punish. Retributivism, in other words, is truly a theory of justice such that, if it is true, we have an obligation to set up institutions so that retribution is achieved.

ii. Views on Retribution

HERBERT MORRIS, ON GUILT AND INNOCENCE 33-34 (1976): I want to . . . set . . . out two complex types of institutions both of which are designed to maintain some degree of social control. In the one a central concept is punishment for wrongdoing and in the other the central concepts are control of dangerous individuals and treatment of disease.

Let us first turn attention to the institutions in which punishment is involved. The institutions I describe will resemble those we ordinarily think of as institutions of punishment; they will have, however, additional features we associate with a system of just punishment.

Let us suppose that men are constituted roughly as they now are, with a rough equivalence in strength and abilities, a capacity to be injured by each other and to make judgments that such injury is undesirable, a limited strength of will, and a capacity to reason and to conform conduct to rules. Applying to the conduct of these men are a group of rules, ones I shall label "primary," which closely resemble the core rules of our criminal law, rules that prohibit violence and deception and compliance with which provides benefits for all persons. These benefits consist of noninterference by others with what each person values, such matters as continuance of life and bodily security. The rules define a sphere for each person then, which is immune from interference by others. Making possible this mutual benefit is the assumption by individuals of a burden. The burden consists in the exercise of self-restraint by individuals over inclinations that would, if satisfied, directly interfere or create a substantial risk of interference with others in proscribed ways. If a person fails to exercise self-restraint even though he might have and gives in to such inclinations, he renounces a burden which others have voluntarily assumed and thus gains an advantage which others, who have restrained themselves, do not possess. This system, then, is one in which the rules establish a mutuality of benefit and burden and in which the benefits of noninterference are conditional upon the assumption of burdens.

Connecting punishment with the violation of these primary rules, and making public the provision for punishment, is both reasonable and just. First, it is only reasonable that those who voluntarily comply with the rules be provided some assurance that they will not be assuming burdens which others are unprepared to assume. Their disposition to comply voluntarily will diminish as they learn that others are with impunity renouncing burdens they are assuming. Second, fairness dictates that a system in which benefits and burdens are equally distributed have a mechanism designed to prevent a maldistribution in the benefits and burdens. Thus, sanctions are attached to noncompliance with the primary rules so as to induce compliance with the primary rules among those who may be disinclined to obey. In this way the likelihood of an unfair distribution is diminished.

Third, it is just to punish those who have violated the rules and caused the unfair distribution of benefits and burdens. A person who violates the rules has something others have — the benefits of the system — but by renouncing what others have assumed, the burdens of self-restraint, he has acquired an unfair advantage. Matters are not even until this advantage is in some way erased. Another way of putting it is that he owes something to others, for he has something that does not rightfully belong to him. Justice — that is punishing such individuals — restores the equilibrium of benefits and burdens by taking from the individual what he owes, that is, exacting the debt. It is important to see that the equilibrium may be restored in another way. Forgiveness — with its legal analogue of a pardon — while not the righting of an unfair distribution by making one pay his debt is, nevertheless, a restoring of the equilibrium by forgiving the debt. Forgiveness may be viewed, at least in some types of cases, as a gift after the fact, erasing a debt, which had the gift been given before the fact, would not have created a debt. But the practice of pardoning has to proceed sensitively, for it may endanger in a way the practice of justice does not, the maintenance of an equilibrium of benefits and burdens. If all are indiscriminately pardoned less incentive is provided individuals to restrain their inclinations, thus increasing the incidence of persons taking what they do not deserve.

JEREMY BENTHAM, AN INTRODUCTION TO THE PRINCIPLES OF MORALS AND LEGISLATION, in Bentham & Mill, The Utilitarians 162, 166 (Dolphin Books, 1961): The general object which all laws have, or ought to have, in common, is to augment the total happiness of the community; and therefore, in the first place, to exclude, as far as may be, every thing that tends to subtract from that happiness: in other words, to exclude mischief.

But all punishment is mischief: all punishment in itself is evil. Upon the principle of utility, if it ought at all to be admitted, it ought only to be admitted in as far as it promises to exclude some greater evil.

It is plain, therefore, that in the following cases punishment ought not to be inflicted.

1. Where it is *groundless:* where there is no mischief for it to prevent; the act not being mischievous upon the whole.

2. Where it must be *inefficacious:* where it cannot act so as to prevent the mischief.

3. Where it is *unprofitable;* or too expensive: where the mischief it would produce would be greater than what it prevented.

4. Where it is *needless:* where the mischief may be prevented, or cease of itself, without it: that is, at a cheaper rate. . . .

JEFFRIE MURPHY, MARXISM AND RETRIBUTION

2 Phil. & Pub. Aff. 217 (1973)

> ***Is it not a delusion to substitute for the individual with his real motives, with multifarious social circumstances pressing upon him, the abstraction of "free will"— one among the many qualities of man for man himself? . . . Is there not a necessity for deeply reflecting upon an alteration of the system that breeds these crimes, instead of glorifying the hangman who executes a lot of criminals to make room only for the supply of new ones?***
>
> *Karl Marx, Capital Punishment,*
> *N.Y. Daily Tribune, Feb. 18, 1853*

In outline . . . I want to argue that when Marx challenges the material adequacy of the retributive theory of punishment, he is suggesting that it presupposes a certain view of man and society that is false. . . .

In trying to develop this case, I shall draw primarily upon Willem Bonger's Criminality and Economic Conditions (1916), one of the few sustained Marxist analyses of crime and punishment. . . .

Put bluntly, his theory is as follows. Criminality has two primary sources: (1) need and deprivation on the part of disadvantaged members of society, and (2) motives of greed and selfishness that are generated and reinforced in competitive capitalistic societies. Thus criminality is economically based — either directly in the case of crimes from need, or indirectly in the case of crimes growing out of motives or psychological states that are encouraged and developed in capitalistic society. In Marx's own language, such an economic system alienates men from themselves and from each other. It alienates men from themselves by creating motives and needs that are not "truly human." It alienates men from their fellows by encouraging a kind of competitiveness that forms an obstacle to the development of genuine communities. . . . [Bonger] argues that moral relations and moral restraint are possible only in genuine communities characterized by bonds of sympathetic identification and mutual aid resting upon a perception of common humanity. . . . In the absence of reciprocity in this rich sense, moral relations among men will break down and criminality will increase. Within bourgeois society, then, crimes are to be regarded as normal, and not psychopathological, acts. That is, they grow out of need, greed, indifference to others, and sometimes even a sense of indignation — all, alas, perfectly typical human motives. . . .

No doubt this claim will strike many as extreme and intemperate — a sample of the old-fashioned Marxist rhetoric that sophisticated intellectuals have outgrown. Those who are inclined to react in this way might consider just one sobering fact: of the 1.3 million criminal offenders handled each day by some agency of the United States correctional system, the vast majority (80 percent on some estimates) are members of the lowest 15-percent income level — that percent which is below the "poverty level" as defined by the Social Security Administration. Unless one wants to embrace the belief that all these people are poor because they are bad, it might be well to reconsider Bonger's suggestion that many of them are "bad" because they are poor. . . . At what points will this challenge the credentials of the contractarian retributive theory . . . ?

. . . If Bonger is correct, much criminality is motivated by greed, selfishness, and indifference to one's fellows; but does not the whole society encourage motives of greed and selfishness ("making it," "getting ahead"), and does not the competitive nature of the society alienate men from each other and thereby encourage indifference — even, perhaps, what psychiatrists call psychopathy? . . . There is something perverse in applying principles that presuppose a sense of community in a society which is structured to destroy genuine community.

Related to this is the whole allocation of benefits in contemporary society. The retributive theory really presupposes what might be called a "gentlemen's club" picture of the relation between man and society — i.e., men are viewed as being part of a community of shared values and rules. The rules benefit all concerned and, as a kind of debt for the benefits derived, each man owes obedience to the rules. In the absence of such obedience, he deserves punishment in the sense that he owes payment for the benefits. For, as a rational man, he can see that the rules benefit everyone (himself included) and that he would have selected them in the original position of choice. . . .

But to think that [this] applies to the typical criminal, from the poorer classes, is to live in a world of social and political fantasy. [T]hey certainly would be hard-pressed to name the benefits for which they are supposed to owe obedience. If justice, as both Kant and Rawls suggests, is based on reciprocity, it is hard to see what these persons are supposed to reciprocate for. . . .

Consider one example: A man has been convicted of armed robbery. On investigation, we learn that he is an impoverished black whose whole life has been one of frustrating alienation from the prevailing socio-economic structure — no job, no transportation if he could get a job, substandard education for his children, terrible housing and inadequate health care for his whole family, condescending-tardy-inadequate welfare payments, harassment by the police but no real protection by them against the dangers in his community, and near total exclusion from the political process. Learning all this, would we still want to talk — as many do — of his suffering punishment under the rubric of "paying a debt to society"? Surely not. Debt for what? I do not, of course, pretend that all criminals can be so described. But I do think that this is a closer picture of the typical criminal than the picture that is presupposed in the retributive theory — i.e., the picture of an evil person who, of his own free will, intentionally acts against those just rules of society which he knows, as a rational man, benefit everyone including himself.

But what practical help does all this offer, one may ask. How should we design our punitive practices in the society in which we now live? [I]t does not seem to help simply to say that our society is built on deception and inequity. How can Marx help us with our real practical problem? The answer, I think, is that he cannot and obviously does not desire to do so. For Marx would say that we have not focused (as all piecemeal reform fails to focus) on what is truly the real problem. And this is changing the basic social relations. Marx is the last person from whom we can expect advice on how to make our intellectual and moral peace with bourgeois society. . . .

[Bonger] suggests, near the end of his book, that in a properly designed society all criminality would be a problem "for the physician rather than the judge." But this surely will not do. The therapeutic state, where prisons are called hospitals and jailers are called psychiatrists, simply raises again all the old problems about the justification of coercion and its reconciliation with autonomy that we faced in worrying about punishment. The only difference is that our coercive practices are now surrounded with a benevolent rhetoric which makes it even harder to raise the important issues. Thus the move to therapy, in my judgment, is only an illusory solution — alienation remains and the problem of reconciling coercion with autonomy remains unsolved. . . .

Perhaps, then, we may really be forced seriously to consider a radical proposal. If we think that institutions of punishment are necessary and desirable, and if we are morally sensitive enough to want to be sure that we have the moral right to punish before we inflict it, then we had better first make sure that we have restructured society in such a way that criminals genuinely do correspond to the only model that will render punishment permissible — i.e., make sure that they are autonomous and that they do benefit in the requisite sense. Of course, if we did this then — if Marx and Bonger are right — crime itself and the need to punish would radically decrease if not disappear entirely.[a]

a. For other inquiries into Marxist criminal theory, see Jeffrey Reiman, the Marxian Critique of Criminal Justice, 6 Crim. Just. Ethics 30 (1987); Luigi Ferrajoli & Daniel Zolo, Marxism and the Criminal Question, 4 L. & Phil. 71 (1985). — Eds.

JOHN L. MACKIE, RETRIBUTION: A TEST CASE FOR ETHICAL OBJECTIVITY, in Joel Feinberg & Hyman Gross, eds., Philosophy of Law 677 (1991): *[R]etribuo* in Latin means "I pay back." But surely the central notion is not that the criminal repays a debt, pays something back to society, but that someone else pays the criminal back for what he has done. Punitive retribution is the repaying of harm with harm, as reward is the repaying of benefit with benefit. We can class as an essentially retributivist approach any that sees at least some prima facie rightness in the repaying of evil with evil, especially a proportionate evil.

. . . But this is a very dark saying. *Why* should it be so? Is there any way in which we can make sense of this curious principle, at least by relating it to [a] network of other moral ideas? . . .

Repayment: How does the criminal's suffering or deprivation pay anything to society? No doubt repaying a debt often hurts the person who pays it, but it does not follow that anything that hurts someone amounts to his repaying a debt. . . . So this account is simply incoherent unless it is transformed into a theory of reparations, which are not punishment, or into the satisfaction theory which . . . is consequentialist and will not explain retributivism.

Annulment: This notion . . . goes back at least to Hegel. . . . Hegel's idea seems to be that as long as a criminal goes scot-free, the crime itself still exists, still flourishes, but when the criminal is adequately punished the crime itself is somehow wiped out. It is not, therefore, by any sort of repayment or restitution that "right is restored," but just by trampling on the previously flourishing crime. But this notion is simply incoherent: there is no comprehensible way in which a penalty wipes out an otherwise still-existing crime. . . .

Kant's remark that if the "last murderer" is not executed blood-guilt will adhere to the people . . . might be . . . understood as something like an anticipation of Hegel's notion of annulment. The guilt, the badness, of the crime is still floating around as long as the criminal is unpunished, and by letting him go free the people would share in this guilt as accessories after the act. But to suppose that this guilt is extinguished by the carrying out of the penalty requires the incomprehensible Hegelian notion of annulment, and to say that the people would be accessories if they did not punish the criminal presupposes, and therefore cannot explain, the principle that the crime in itself morally requires the penalty.

Fair play: Here the suggestion is that the various members of society are all in competition with one another, a competition governed by rules. The criminal has gained an unfair advantage by breaking the rules; to restore fairness this advantage must be taken away from him. Unlike our last two approaches, this one is not incoherent; it makes perfectly good sense in certain contexts. It has its clearest exemplification in the award of a penalty in football . . . when there has been a foul. . . . It is also retributivist in our basic sense of being retrospective; the justification is complete when the penalty has been imposed; fairness has then (roughly at least) been restored, irrespective of whether there are or are not any further desirable consequences. The trouble with this approach, however, is that it has little relation to most cases of punishment. Any serious attempt to apply it would lead to bizarre results, not at all well correlated with what is thought of as desert or degree of wrongness or guilt. . . . Thus if a businessman has secured a contract worth $100,000, but has exceeded the speed limit in order to get to the relevant appointment on time, he should presumably be fined $100,000, whereas a fine of $1 would be enough for someone who murders a blind cripple to rob him of $1. And so on. Unsuccessful attempts at murder (or anything else) should not be punished at all. . . .

What is basically wrong with the fair play approach . . . is that it focuses on the advantage that may have been gained by the criminal in some sort of social competition, whereas the point of punishment surely lies not in this but in wrongness of his act and the harm that he has done or tried to do. . . .

Every one of these approaches fails completely to supply any coherent expansion or explanation of the retributivist principle, and, as far as I know, there are no others on offer. On the other hand it is plain that a considerable number of people have what would be called an intuition that a wrong action in itself calls for the infliction of suffering or deprivation on the agent. . . .

In conclusion, therefore, I maintain that it is easy to understand why we have a deeply ingrained tendency to see wrong actions as calling for penalties and some sorts of good actions as calling for reward. Though retributive principles cannot be defended, with any plausibility, as allegedly objective moral truths, retributive attitudes can be readily understood and explained as sentiments that have grown up and are sustained partly through biological processes, and partly through analogous sociological ones.

MICHAEL S. MOORE, LAW AND PSYCHIATRY 238-243 (1984): Once one grants that there are two sorts of prima facie justifications of punishment — effecting a net social gain (utilitarian) and giving just deserts (retributivist) — one can also see that in addition to the two pure theories of punishment there can also be mixed theories. [T]he popular form of mixed theory asserts that . . . punishment is justified if and only if it achieves a net social gain *and* is given to offenders who deserve it. Giving just deserts and achieving a net social gain, in such a case, are each individually necessary but only jointly sufficient conditions justifying punishment.

It is standard fare in the philosophy of punishment to assert, by way of several thought experiments, counterexamples to the utilitarian thesis that punishment is justified if and only if some net social gain is achieved. . . . [I]t might be recalled that D. B. Cooper successfully skyjacked an aircraft some years ago, and that this successful, unsolved crime apparently encouraged the mass of skyjackings that have cost so much in terms of dollars, lives, and convenience. Cooper wore large sunglasses in his escapade, and there was accordingly only a very limited description available of him. Imagine that shortly after his skyjacking we had the benefit of the knowledge we now have by hindsight, and we decided that it would be better to punish someone who looked like Cooper (and who had no good alibi) in order to convince others that skyjacking did not pay. For a consistent utilitarian, there is a net social gain that would be achieved by punishing such an innocent person, and there is no a priori reason that the net social gain in such a case might not outweigh the harm that is achieved by punishing an innocent person. . . .

The arguments against the pure utilitarian theory of punishment do not by themselves drive one into retributivism. For one can alleviate the injustice of the pure utilitarian theory of punishment by adopting the mixed theory. Since under the mixed theory the desert of the offender is a necessary condition of punishment, it will follow from the mixed theory that in each [counterexample] (where punishment is not deserved), punishment should not be given. . . .

There is . . . another sort of thought experiment that tests whether one truly believes the mixed theory, or is in fact a pure retributivist. [Consider] State v. Chaney [infra page 143]. . . .

The thought experiment such a case begins to pose for us is as follows: Imagine in such a case that after the rape but before sentencing the defendant has gotten into an accident so that his sexual desires are dampened to such an extent that he presents no further danger of rape; if money is also one of his problems, suppose further that he has inherited a great deal of money, so that he no longer needs to rob. Suppose, because of both of these facts, we are reasonably certain that he does not present a danger of either forcible assault, rape, robbery, or related crimes in the future. Since Chaney is (by hypothesis) not dangerous, he does not need to be incapacitated, specially deterred, or reformed. Suppose further that we could successfully pretend to punish Chaney, instead of actually punishing him, and that no one is at all likely to find out. Our pretending to punish him will thus serve the needs of general deterrence and maintain social cohesion, and the cost to the state will be less than if it actually did punish him. Is there anything in the mixed theory of punishment that would urge that Chaney nonetheless should really be punished? I think not, so that if one's conclusion is that Chaney and people like him nonetheless should be punished, one will have to give up the mixed theory of punishment. . . .

If one follows the predicted paths through these thought experiments, the end result is that one finds oneself, perhaps surprisingly, to be a retributivist. We might call this an argument through the back door for retributivism, because the argument does not assert in any positive way the correctness of retributivism. It only asserts that the two theories of punishment truly competitive with retributivism, namely, the pure utilitarian theory and the mixed theory, are each unacceptable to us. That leaves retributivism as the only remaining theory of punishment we can accept. . . .

Hugh Bedau has recently reminded us . . . that the retributivist faces a familiar dilemma:

> Either he appeals to something else — some good end — that is accomplished by the practice of punishment, in which case he is open to the criticism that he has nonretributivist, consequentialist justification for the practice of punishment. Or his justification does not appeal to something else, in which case it is open to the criticism that it is circular and futile.

In this respect, however, retributivism is no worse off than any other nonutilitarian theories in ethics, each of which seeks to justify an institution or practice not by the good consequences it may engender, but rather by the inherent rightness of the practice. The justification for any such theories is one that appeals to both our particular judgments and our more general principles, in order to show that the theory fits judgments that on reflection we are sure of, and principles that on reflection we are proud of.

b. Prevention

INTRODUCTORY NOTE

Prevention theories furnish a widely accepted rationale of the practice of punishment. According to these theories, punishment should be designed not to exact retribution on convicted offenders but to prevent the commission of future offenses. Theorists distinguish between the effect of punishment as a general deterrent and its effect as a specific deterrent. Punishment acts as a *general deterrent* insofar as the threat of punishment deters potential offenders in the general community. It acts as a *specific deterrent* insofar as the infliction of punishment on convicted defendants leaves *them* less likely to engage in the crime.[14] Modern theory also emphasizes prevention through *moral influence*—the broader effect of punishment in inculcating and maintaining habits of law-abiding conduct in the general population.

In considering prevention, we will focus on three sets of problems. The first arises in considering traditional conceptions of deterrence: To what extent are criminals and would-be criminals actually dissuaded from crime by the risks of conviction and imprisonment, and what is the morality of punishing some offenders in order to deter others? The second concerns the means employed: Can the stigmatizing effects of punishment be harnessed to achieve effective deterrence *without* imprisonment? The third arises in considering theories of moral influence: How important is the moralizing effect and what conditions must be imposed on punishment in order for moral influence to operate successfully?

i. Deterrence Through the Threat of Imprisonment

JEREMEY BENTHAM, PRINCIPLES OF PENAL LAW, Pt. II, bk. 1, ch. 3, in J. Bentham's Works 396, 402 (J. Bowring ed. 1843): Pain and pleasure are the great springs of human action. When a man perceives or supposes pain to be the consequence of an act, he is acted upon in such a manner as tends, with a certain force, to withdraw him, as it were, from the commission of that act. If the apparent magnitude, or rather value of that pain be greater than the apparent magnitude or value of the pleasure or good he expects to be the consequence of the act, he will be absolutely prevented from performing it. The mischief which would have ensued from the act, if performed, will also by that means be prevented. . . .

The observation of rules of proportion between crimes and punishments has been objected to as useless, because they seem to suppose, that a spirit of calculation has place among the passions of men, who, it is said, never calculate. But dogmatic as this proposition is, it is altogether false. In matters of importance every one calculates. Each individual calculates with more or less correctness, according to the degrees of his information, and the power of the motives which actuate him, but all calculate. It would be hard to say that a madman does not calculate. Happily, the passion of cupidity, which on account of its power, its constancy, and its extent, is most formidable to society, is the passion which is most given to calculation. This, therefore, will be more successfully combated, the more carefully the law turns the balance of profit against it.

14. For a study of the extent to which the doctrines of the criminal law (e.g., intent, attempt, justification, and excuse) are explainable on deterrence theories, see Steven Shavell, Criminal Law and the Optimal Use of Nonmonetary Sanctions as a Deterrent, 85 Colum. L. Rev. 1232 (1985), especially pp. 1247-1259. See also Richard Posner, An Economic Theory of the Criminal Law, 85 Colum. L. Rev. 1193 (1985).

NOTES ON THE RATIONAL-ACTOR MODEL

1. Do Criminals Calculate? Like Bentham, modern scholars who favor the economic approach to law posit that potential criminals consciously or subconsciously calculate costs and benefits, even in the context of "crimes of passion." Others argue that for the most important kinds of criminal behavior, perpetrators do not calculate at all or calculate only in bizarre ways, ignoring ordinary sorts of benefits and costs (including punishment). Consider these comments:

Richard A. Posner, Economic Analysis of Law 242-243 (5th ed. 1998): A person commits a crime because the expected benefits of the crime to him exceed the expected costs. . . .

The notion of the criminal as a rational calculator will strike many readers as unrealistic, especially when applied to criminals having little education or to crimes not committed for pecuniary gain. But . . . a better test of a theory than the realism of its assumptions is its predictive power. A growing empirical literature on crime has shown that criminals respond to changes in opportunity costs, in the probability of apprehension, in the severity of punishment, and in other relevant variables as if they were indeed the rational calculators of the economic model — and this regardless of whether the crime is committed for pecuniary gain or out of passion, or by well educated or poorly educated people.[1]

James Q. Wilson, Thinking About Crime 120 (rev. ed. 1983): The observed fact . . . that states in which the probability of going to prison for robbery is low are also states which have high rates of robbery can be interpreted in one of two ways. It can mean either that the higher robbery rates are the results of the lower imprisonment rates (and thus evidence that deterrence works) or that the lower imprisonment rates are caused by the higher robbery rates. [A] state that is experiencing . . . a rapidly rising robbery rate . . . arrests, convicts, and imprisons more and more robbers . . . , but it cannot quite keep up. [P]rosecutors and judges respond by letting more robbers off without a prison sentence, or perhaps without even a trial. . . . As a result, the proportion of arrested robbers who go to prison goes down while the robbery rate goes up. In this case, we ought to conclude, not that prison deters robbers, but that high robbery rates 'deter' prosecutors and judges.

James Gilligan, Violence 94-96, 102-110 (1996): [A]n underlying theory of violence, which I call the "rational self-interest" theory[,] . . . pervades our criminal justice system. [It] assumes that those who engage in violence do so for reasons of rational self-interest and common sense: [They] do not want to go to prison, do not want to be subjected to physical violence themselves, and do not want to die. They will do anything to avoid any of these fates, and all we need do to prevent violence is to threaten to punish those who would commit such acts with greater violence of our own, such as imprisonment and capital punishment.

1. For recent summaries of the empirical literature on the rational-choice model of criminal behavior, see Isaac Ehrlich, Crime, Punishment, and the Market for Offenses, 10 J. Econ. Perspectives 43, 55-63 (Winter 1996); D. J. Pyle, The Economic Approach to Crime and Punishment, 6 J. Interdisciplinary Stud. 1, 4-8 (1995). For an illustrative empirical study, see Steven D. Levitt, The Effect of Prison Population Size on Crime Rates: Evidence From Prison Overcrowding Litigation, 111 Q. J. Econ. 319 (1996).

[T]his theory [is] based on complete and utter ignorance of what violent people are actually like. [There is an] endless legion of mass murderers and assassins, both "public" and "private," who are as ready to be killed as to kill —whose rage is so passionate and so blinding that it has caused the subjective distinction between killing and being killed to be all but obliterated and meaningless.

[M]uch of what appears anomalous, inexplicable, and incomprehensible about violence (whether individual or collective) is not anomalous at all, but all too ominously exactly what we might expect — given a certain set of conditions. [E]ven when it seems motivated by "rational" self-interest, [violence] is the end product of a series of irrational, self-destructive, and unconscious motives. . . .

[W]hen men feel sufficiently impotent and humiliated, the usual assumptions one makes about human behavior and motivation, such as the wish to eat when starving, the wish to live or stay out of prison at all costs, no longer hold. [T]he "instinct of (physiological) self-preservation" does not hold when one approaches the point of being so overwhelmed by shame that one can only preserve one's self (as a psychological entity) by sacrificing one's body (or those of others).

Mark S. Fleisher, Beggars & Thieves: Lives of Urban Street Criminals 4-14, 184 (1995): The lives of [street] hustlers, without exception, began in unloving families . . . with often violent but always neglectful and unloving parents. . . .

Some scholars and policymakers think the career concept is useful in the formation of crime-control policy; however, the reification of street deviance as a career shields outsiders from seeing the disorder, dysfunction, and irrationality of deviant behavior. [I]n the daily lives of hustlers, order and planning and design are absent. Hustlers' lives are created less by design than by default. . . . Common expressions of physical violence and verbal assaults, irrational problem-solving, self-destructive behavior (substance abuse), social irresponsibility (adolescent truancy; the inability to hold a job or even seek employment), the inability to meet even simple requirements for peaceful social interactions (poor adjustment to school and work situations outside controlled institutional settings), and other things as well, are expressions of harsh early-life experiences that permanently affected their worldview. . . .

These hustlers' economic lives are a series of defaults, not career choices. [T]hey satisfy their needs in the easiest, most familiar ways. They steal from sleeping drunks and passersby, shoplift at local stores, sell small quantities of heroin and rock cocaine, panhandle, and even steal cash and drugs from each other. Their life trajectory was set in motion decades earlier in early childhood, and they can't stop it now.

2. How do rational actors respond to the threat of punishment? Bentham assumes that crime can be deterred by insuring that its expected costs exceed its expected benefits. Would it be "efficient," then, to punish all offenses by imprisonment for life? Bentham's answer is that for trivial offenses, the cost of imprisonment for society would exceed the benefits in terms of the minor offenses that would be deterred. But then why not impose life imprisonment in the case of all very serious offenses, such as rape or armed robbery? A further difficulty is that if armed robbery is subject to the highest possible punishment, the offender would suffer no additional punishment for committing additional robberies or for killing all possible witnesses.[15] A "three strikes and you're out" rule may have perverse effects for similar reasons.[16] Modern practitioners of the economic approach note that the rational actor's behavioral responses are complicated in other ways as well. Consider, for example, the "income" effect. Severe punishments are intended to induce rational actors to shift from illegal to legal pursuits. But if severe punishment raises an addict's cost of buying the drugs he requires, he may have to commit more predatory crimes (robbery and burglary) in order to finance his habit.[17] For detailed exploration of these and related problems, see Neal Kumar Katyal, Deterrence's Difficulty, 95 Mich. L. Rev. 2385 (1997).

3. *Certainty versus severity.* The two plausible ways to increase the direct deterrent effect of punishment are, first, to increase the risk of conviction, and second, to increase the severity of punishment. The first of these alternatives appears to be the more effective, although it is also the more difficult to implement. It is important to note, moreover, that increased enforcement does not by itself result directly in increased general deterrence. Since the effectiveness of the threat of punishment must be judged from the viewpoint of the potential criminal, certainty of punishment is important only as it contributes to the appearance of certainty.

Increased severity of punishment has a more doubtful deterrent effect. A panel of the National Academy of Sciences concluded in 1993 that a 10 percent increase in the probability of apprehension would prevent twice as much violent crime as the same increase in the severity of punishment.[18] Consider Johannes Andenaes, The General Preventive Effects of Punishment, 114 U. Pa. L. Rev. 949, 965-970 (1966):

> It seems reasonable to conclude that as a general rule, though not without exceptions, the general preventive effect of the criminal law increases with the growing severity of penalties. Contemporary dictatorships display with almost frightening clarity the conformity that can be produced by a ruthlessly severe justice.
>
> However, it is necessary to make two important reservations. In the first place, as we indicated when discussing the risk of detection, what is decisive is not the actual practice but how this practice is conceived by the public. Although little research has been done to find out how much the general public knows about the penal system, presumably most people have only vague and unspecified notions. Therefore, only quite substantial changes will be noticed. Only rarely does a single sentence bring about significant preventive effects.
>
> In the second place, the prerequisite of general prevention is that the law be en-

15. Bentham notes: "Where two offenses are in conjunction, the greater offense ought to be subjected to severer punishment, in order that the delinquent may have a motive to stop at the lesser." Jeremy Bentham, The Theory of Legislation 201 (1975).

16. Consider Neal Kumar Katyal, Deterrence's Difficulty, 95 Mich L. Rev. 2385, 2394 (1997): "If offenders know that, on their third offense, they will be jailed for life, they may be less likely to commit that third offense; but if they do, they might make it a drastic one."

17. See Posner, supra at 266; Stephen J. Schulhofer, Solving the Drug Enforcement Dilemma: Lessons from Economics, 1994 U. Chi. Legal Forum 207.

18. Albert J. Reiss, Jr. & Jeffrey A. Roth, eds., Understanding and Preventing Violence: Report of the National Research Panel on the Understanding and Control of Violence 6 (1993).

forced. Experience seems to show that excessively severe penalties may actually reduce the risk of conviction, thereby leading to results contrary to their purpose.[a]

4. Ethical constraints? Are there any moral limits to the use of punishment for deterrent purposes? If punishing an offender would have no deterrent effect, it would presumably be unjust — a gratuitous infliction of suffering. How much proof should be required to establish whether deterrence would or would not be achieved? Who should bear the burden of proof? If deterrent effects are uncertain, is punishment morally justified?

Is it just to single out particular offenders for greater punishment, solely on the ground that doing so offers special deterrence benefits? Offenses committed by celebrities or well-known public officials are likely to capture public attention, and the punishments they receive are likely to be well publicized. Should exceptionally severe punishment be imposed in cases that receive substantial media attention, in order to maximize the perceived severity of the criminal justice system (and thus the deterrent impact) while minimizing the cost of the sanctions imposed overall? See Frank Zimring & Gordon Hawkins, Deterrence: The Legal Threat in Crime Control 35-50 (1973).

ii. Deterrence Through Stigma and Expressive Condemnation

INTRODUCTORY NOTE

Problems concerning the *forms* of punishment must be kept distinct from problems concerning the *purposes* for which any particular punishment is imposed. Imprisonment, for example, may be imposed to exact retribution, to deter, or to incapacitate the offender. (Imprisonment was once viewed as a means of rehabilitating the offender,[19] but this is seldom seen as a plausible or significant goal of imprisonment today.) Probation, in contrast, is usually seen primarily as a means of rehabilitation, but when the terms of probation include harsh restrictions, probation may in part serve the purposes of retribution and deterrence. And any criminal conviction carries a stigma that may serve retributive and deterrent purposes as well.

In recent years, judges who consider probation an insufficient penalty have sometimes imposed "formal shaming" as a criminal sanction. Offenders convicted of drunk driving have been required to affix to their cars a bumper sticker proclaiming their offense; newspapers have published the names of men convicted of patronizing prostitutes; and offenders have been required to make a public apology or to perform community service while wearing a sign describing

a. See Neal Kumar Katyal, Deterrence's Difficulty, 95 Mich L. Rev. 2385, 2450-2451 (1997):

> [When penalties are high,] the public may not be willing to turn lawbreakers in, police and prosecutors may not want to prosecute, and jurors may not vote to convict. [One researcher] found that Nebraska's severe punishment for bad checks hampered enforcement and conviction. In Colorado, by contrast, he found that fewer bad checks were written because the punishment was weaker but enforcement was more consistent. — Eds.

19. See George Fisher, The Birth of the Prison Retold, 104 Yale L. J. 1235 (1995).

their crime. See Stephen P. Garvey, Can Shaming Punishments Educate?, 65 U. Chi. L. Rev. 733 (1998); Toni M. Massaro, Shame, Culture, and American Criminal Law, 89 Mich. L. Rev. 1880, 1883 (1991).

Are shaming sanctions a good idea? Are they likely to be used as substitutes for imprisonment, or will judges impose them on offenders who would otherwise get alcohol treatment, psychological counseling, or straight probation? Are shaming sanctions effective, or are they likely to be counterproductive? Recall that Professor Feinberg, in the excerpt at page 105 supra, states that expressive condemnation "may help or hinder deterrence." Why would the infliction of shame *hinder* deterrence? Consider these comments:

DAN M. KAHAN, WHAT DO ALTERNATIVE SANCTIONS MEAN?, 63 U. Chi. L. Rev. 591, 638 (1996): What we know about deterrence should make us confident that shaming penalties will be reasonably effective by virtue of their character as degradation ceremonies.

The consequences of shaming penalties are extremely unpleasant. Those who lose the respect of their peers often suffer a crippling diminishment of self-esteem. Moreover, criminal offenders are as likely to be shunned in the marketplace as they are in the public square, leading to serious financial hardship. . . . It stands to reason, then, that shaming penalties, which abstract disgrace from the afflictive dimension of formal sanctions, should compare favorably with imprisonment as a deterrent.

TONI M. MASSARO, SHAME, CULTURE, AND AMERICAN CRIMINAL LAW, 89 Mich. L. Rev. 1880, 1919-1921 (1991): The anticipated effect of public shaming is a downward change in status, coupled with symbolic and actual shunning of the offender by others. . . . Once the offender's status is changed, though, she may have a reduced incentive to avoid the behaviors that triggered the demotion. This is especially true when, as is the case in modern American criminal courts, there is no public ritual, ceremony, or other procedure for *reestablishing* or regaining the lost status. Modern shaming, like modern punishment in general, is not "reintegrative."[a] The stigmatized offender thus may "drift" toward subcultures that are more accepting of her particular norm violations. [T]hen shaming not only may not promote specific deterrence or rehabilitative ends, it may defeat them.

JAMES GILLIGAN, VIOLENCE 110-111 (1996): I have yet to see a serious act of violence that was not provoked by the experience of feeling shamed and humiliated, disrespected and ridiculed, and that did not represent the attempt to prevent or undo this "loss of face" — no matter how severe the punishment, even if it includes death. . . . [T]hese men mean it literally when they say they would rather kill or mutilate others, be killed or mutilated themselves, than live without pride, dignity, and self-respect. . . . The emotion of shame is the primary or ultimate cause of all violence.

JAMES Q. WHITMAN, WHAT IS WRONG WITH INFLICTING SHAME SANCTIONS?, 107 Yale L.J. 1055, 1087-1092 (1998): [T]here are *two* aspects to what

a. For efforts to develop a model that emphasizes the "reintegrative" dimension, see John Braithwaite, Crime, Shame and Reintegration (1989) — Eds.

is troubling about shame sanctions: their effect on the offender and their effect on the crowd. [S]hame sanctions involve a dangerous willingness, on the part of the government, to delegate part of its enforcement power to a fickle and uncontrolled general populace. . . .

Shame sanctions, in this regard, are very different from prisons or fines. However much prisons may have declined into chaos, they are in principle controllable. However monstrous they may have become, we all agree that the state has the duty to manage them: to establish rules, to call review boards, to answer complaints in court. None of that apparatus exists to control the enforcement of shame. . . . [A] system of shaming . . . means abandoning [courts'] duty to be the imposers of *measured* punishment. . . .

[Thus,] shame sanctions lend themselves to a politics of stirring up demons. . . . We have worked, over two liberal centuries, to build an ethic of businesslike politics that denies our officials the authority to pluck on the bass strings of public psychology and that makes criminal law the province of trained and disciplined officers. Over many generations of ugly experience, we have worked to build a democratic government that acknowledges the importance of an ethic of restraint and sobriety. The new shame sanctions tend to undermine that ethic. . . .

iii. Moral Influence

JOHANNES ANDENAES, GENERAL PREVENTION — ILLUSION OR REALITY?, 43 J. Crim. L., Criminology & Police Science 176, 179-180 (1952): By general prevention we mean the ability of criminal law and its enforcement to make citizens law-abiding. . . . General prevention may depend on the mere frightening or deterrent effect of punishment — the risk of discovery and punishment outweighing the temptation to commit crime. . . . Later theory puts much stress on the ability of penal law to arouse or strengthen inhibitions of another sort. In Swedish discussion the *moralizing* — in other words the *educational* — function has been greatly stressed. The idea is that punishment as a concrete expression of society's disapproval of an act helps to form and to strengthen the public's moral code and thereby creates conscious and unconscious inhibitions against committing crime. Unconscious inhibitions against committing forbidden acts can also be aroused without appealing to the individual's concepts of morality. Purely as a matter of habit, with fear, respect for authority or social imitation as connecting links, it is possible to induce favorable attitudes toward this or that action and unfavorable attitudes toward another action. . . .

We can say that punishment has three sorts of general-preventive effects: It may have a *deterrent* effect, it may strengthen *moral inhibitions* (a *moralizing* effect), and it may stimulate habitual *law-abiding conduct*. I have reason to emphasize this, since many of those who are most skeptical of general prevention think only of the deterrent effect. Even if it can be shown that conscious fear of punishment is not present in certain cases, this is by no means the same as showing that the secondary effects of punishment are without importance. To the lawmaker, the achievement of inhibition and habit is of greater value than mere deterrence. For these apply in cases where a person need not fear detection and punishment, and they can apply without the person even having knowledge of the legal prohibition.

LOUIS MICHAEL SEIDMAN, SOLDIERS, MARTYRS, AND CRIMINALS: UTILITARIAN THEORY AND THE PROBLEM OF CRIME CONTROL, 94 YALE L.J. 315, 336-338 (1984): Our most important collective institution for teaching [moral inhibitions] is the criminal law. The symbolism and ritual associated with the criminal trial as well as the traditions surrounding criminal penalties make the criminal law an especially powerful tool for communicating blame. [B]lame not only makes the threat of other punishment credible, but also provides a kind of deterrence that other punishment cannot achieve. [M]oral condemnation is a unique sanction because it inflicts suffering on individuals even when the conduct is otherwise efficient. Indeed, the condemnation is moral in character precisely because we are blaming an individual for preferring pleasure to pain in a situation where he should be obeying a categorical imperative.

PAUL H. ROBINSON & JOHN M. DARLEY, THE UTILITY OF DESERT, 91 Nw. U.L. Rev. 453, 468-478 (1997): More than because of the threat of legal punishment, people obey the law (1) because they fear the disapproval of their social group if they violate the law, and (2) because they generally see themselves as moral beings who want to do the right thing as they perceive it. In social science, these two factors are referred to as (1) compliance produced by normative social influence, and (2) behavior produced by internalized moral standards and rules. . . .

The evidence reviewed suggests that the influences of social group sanctions and internalized norms are the most powerful determinants of conduct, more significant than the threat of deterrent legal sanctions. But, we argue, the law is not irrelevant to the operation of these powerful forces. Criminal law . . . influences the powerful social forces of normative behavior control through its central role in the creation of shared norms. . . . [C]riminal law enforcement and adjudication activities send daily messages to all who read or hear about them. . . . Further, every adjudication offers an opportunity to confirm the exact nature of the norm or to signal a shift or refinement of it. . . .

The passage and subsequent failure of National Prohibition shows the law's limited ability to change norms even when the change is supported by a significant portion of the public. . . . The law is, rather, a vehicle by which the community debates, tests, and ultimately settles upon and expresses its norms. . . . The act of criminalization sometimes nurtures the norm, as does faithful enforcement and prosecution, and over time the community view may mature into a strong consensus. . . . We have seen the process at work recently in enhancing prohibitory norms against sexual harassment, hate speech, drunk driving, and domestic violence. It has also been at work in diluting existing norms against homosexual conduct, fornication, and adultery. . . .[a]

Perhaps more than any other society, ours relies on the criminal law for norm-nurturing. Our greater cultural diversity means that we cannot expect a stable pre-existing consensus on the contours of condemnable conduct that is found in more homogeneous societies. . . . [W]e share no religion or other arbiter of morality that might perform this role. Our criminal law is, for us, the place we express our shared beliefs of what is truly condemnable. . . .

The criminal law also has a second effect in . . . gaining compliance with its

a. The problem of determining what conduct should be punished is discussed at page 156-171 infra. — EDS.

demands. If it has developed a reputation as a reliable statement of existing norms, people will be willing to defer to its moral authority in cases where there exists some ambiguity as to the wrongfulness of the contemplated conduct. . . .

There is evidence, largely collected and analyzed by Tyler, that people are inclined to accept the law as a source of moral authority that they themselves should take seriously. . . . He notes: ". . . . If authorities can tap into such feelings, their decisions will be more widely followed."[53]

Tyler reviews a number of studies that suggest that the level of commitment to obey the law is proportional to what Tyler calls the law's perceived "legitimacy." . . . [I]f one regards the law as a legitimate source of rules, if it has what we have called "moral credibility," then one should be more likely to regard the law's judgments about right and wrong actions as an appropriate input to one's own moral thinking; in turn, one should be more likely to obey the law. . . .

But the criminal law can only hope to shape moral thinking or to have people follow its rules in ambiguous cases if it has earned a reputation as an institution whose focus is morally condemnable conduct. . . . A criminal law that is seen as having a different criterion for criminalization — such as criminalization whenever the greater penalties of criminal law can provide useful deterrents — is not likely to gain such a reputation. . . .

Our central point is this: The criminal law's power in nurturing and communicating societal norms and its power to have people defer to it in unanalyzed cases is directly proportional to criminal law's moral credibility. If criminalization or conviction (or decriminalization or refusal to convict) is to have an effect in the norm-nurturing process, it will be because the criminal law has a reputation for criminalizing and punishing only that which deserves moral condemnation, and for decriminalizing and not punishing that which does not. . . .

Enhancing the criminal law's moral credibility requires, more than anything, that the criminal law make clear to the public that its overriding concern is doing justice. Therefore, the most important reforms for establishing the criminal law's moral credibility may be those that concern the rules by which criminal liability and punishment are distributed. The criminal law must earn a reputation for (1) punishing those who deserve it under rules perceived as just, (2) protecting from punishment those who do not deserve it, and (3) where punishment is deserved, imposing the amount of punishment deserved, no more, no less. Thus, for example, the criminal law ought to maintain a viable insanity defense that excuses those who are perceived as not responsible for their offense, ought to avoid the use of strict liability (imposing liability in the absence of a culpable state of mind), and ought to limit the use of non-exculpatory defenses. In other words, it ought to adopt rules that distribute liability and punishment according to desert, even if a non-desert distribution appears in the short-run to offer the possibility of reducing crime.

The point is that every deviation from [desert] can incrementally undercut the criminal law's moral credibility, which in turn can undercut . . . its power to gain compliance by its moral authority. Thus, contrary to the apparent assumptions of past utilitarian debates,[57] such deviations from desert are not cost free,

53. [Tom R. Tyler, Why People Obey the Law (1990)], at 60.

57. Consider Shavell's assertion: "Whether or not a party will actually commit an act . . . depends on his perception of the possibility that he will suffer a sanction, either monetary or nonmonetary. A party will commit an act if, and only if, the expected sanction would be less than the expected

and their cost must be included in the calculation when determining which distribution of liability will most effectively reduce crime.

c. Rehabilitation

LEON RADZINOWICZ & J. W. CECIL TURNER, A STUDY OF PUNISHMENT I: INTRODUCTORY ESSAY

21 Canadian B. Rev. 91, 91-97 (1943)

[I]n the past 150 years . . . our penal policy is seen to move in three main stages. In the earliest the salient feature is a crude utilitarianism aiming at the reduction of crime through the weapon of terror. The following passage indicates how this doctrine inspired the legislator.

"If a man injured Westminster Bridge, he was hanged. If he appeared disguised on a public road, he was hanged. If he cut down young trees; if he shot rabbits; if he stole property valued at five shillings; if he stole anything at all from a bleach field; if he wrote threatening letters to extort money; if he returned prematurely from transportation; for any of these offenses he was immediately hanged."

The attitude of the contemporary moralist is well illustrated by the views expressed by the Reverend Sydney Smith, Editor of the Edinburgh Review in the eighteen-thirties, in the following quotations:

"The real and only test, in short, of a good prison system is the diminution of offences by the terror of the punishment. . . . In prisons which are really meant to keep the multitude in order, and to be a terror to evil-doers, there must be no sharing of profits — no visiting friends — no education but religious education — no freedom of diet — no weavers' looms or carpenters' benches. There must be a great deal of solitude; coarse food; a dress of shame; hard, incessant, irksome, eternal labour; a planned and regulated and unrelenting exclusion of happiness and comforts." . . .

Speaking generally, . . . there was no acceptance of any principle that the severity of punishment should be equated to the gravity of the offence. This principle became prominent in the second stage, when the doctrine of retribution took a leading place in contemporary thought on penal questions and therefore the crimes have to be graded according to their gravity and the punishments correspondingly graded so as to fit the crime in each case. The major assumption on which this conception rests is that every individual in the State has certain fundamental rights as a human being, which should not be forfeited by the fact that he may have committed a crime.

Certain thinkers in Europe had drawn attention to the evils which resulted from the policy of terror, especially when, as often, it allowed too great a discretion to the tribunals and also too great freedom to those who carried out the sentences of the tribunals. As a safeguard against this danger it was felt that the individual should be protected by the establishment of legal rules which would

---

private benefits. If he decides not to commit an act, he will be said to be deterred." Steven Shavell, Criminal Law and the Optimal Use of Nonmonetary Sanctions as a Deterrent, 85 Colum. L. Rev. 1232, 1235 (1985). Certainly if one believes, as Shavell does, that only the threatened sanction affects a person's decision whether to commit an offense, then the extent to which the distribution of sanctions deviates from that perceived as deserved is irrelevant to the calculations. . . .

closely define the nature and the amount of punishment which should be administered for each crime. . . .

[W]hereas the liberal doctrine of equality protected the individual against the arbitrary cruelties of the policy of terror, it tended to assume that all individuals have the same powers of resistance to temptation and that each will deserve the same punishment for the same crime, and moreover will react in the same way to that punishment. Thus it may be said that the liberal theory standardised individuals and concerned itself little or not at all with what at the present day is so closely studied, namely the variations of individual personality. According to this idea the primary consideration in determining the punishment to be imposed is the intrinsic nature of the particular crime which the delinquent has committed.

This development marks a revulsion against the defects which were detected in the brutality of the earlier period but in its turn it was found to be insufficiently effective to reduce adequately the volume of crime. . . .

The new approach which characterises the third period involved a fuller appreciation of the necessity of studying the personality of the offender if the disease of crime was to be successfully attacked. This led to the introduction of measures which adopted and regulated the punishment deemed appropriate for defined groups of offenders, in general without any special regard to the particular character of the crimes which they might commit.

MICHAEL MOORE, LAW AND PSYCHIATRY 234-235 (1984): Rehabilitation is perhaps the most complex of the theories of punishment, because it involves two quite different ideals of rehabilitation that are usually confused. . . .

The first sort of rehabilitative ideal is one that is achieved when we make criminals safe to return to the streets. This sort of rehabilitative theory justifies punishment, not by appeal to how much better off criminals will be at the end of the process, but rather by how much better off all of us will be if "treatment" is completed because the streets will be that much safer. Such a theory seeks to rehabilitate criminals only as a cost effective means of shortening the expensive incarceration that would otherwise be necessary to protect us all against crime. The second sort of rehabilitative ideal. . . . seeks to rehabilitate offenders not just so they can be returned safely to the streets, but so they can lead flourishing and successful lives. Such a theory justifies punishment, not in the name of all of us, but rather in the offenders' own name; since it does so in their name, but contrary to their own expressed wishes (few offenders want to be punished), this kind of rehabilitative theory is paternalistic in character.

This paternalistic type of rehabilitative theory has no proper part to play in any theory of punishment, even in the minimal sense of constituting a prima facie justification of punishment. There are three reasons why this is so. First, such a paternalistic reform theory allocates scarce societal resources away from other, more deserving groups that want them (such as retarded and autistic children or the poor), to a group that hardly can be said to deserve such favored status and, moreover, does not want such "benefits." . . . Second, in any political theory according high value to liberty, paternalistic justifications are themselves to be regarded with suspicion. Criminals are not in the standard classes in society for which paternalistic state intervention is appropriate, such as the severely disordered, the young, or others whose capacity for rational choice is diminished. . . . Third, such recasting of punishment in terms of "treatment" for the good of the criminal makes possible a kind of moral blindness that is dangerous in itself. As C. S. Lewis pointed out some years ago, adopting a "humanitarian" conceptualization of punishment makes it easy to inflict treatments and sentences that need bear no relation to the desert of the offender. We may do more to others "for their own good" than we ever allow ourselves to do when we see that it is really for our good that we act.

NOTE

The actual effects of rehabilitation efforts have been questioned. In an important 1974 paper (Robert Martinson, What Works? — Questions and Answers About Prison Reform, 36 Pub. Interest 22 (1974)), the author concluded: "With few and isolated exceptions, the rehabilitative efforts that have been reported so far have no appreciable effect on recidivism" (p. 25). Martinson quickly withdrew that conclusion, having found evidence that some programs do reduce recidivism for some offenders under some circumstances.[20] Subsequent research provided further support for this cautiously optimistic view.[21] Nonetheless, the conclusion that "nothing works" had become fixed in the public mind, and it has proved difficult to dislodge. Consider George Mair, What Works — Nothing or Everything?, Home Office [Great Britain], Research Bulletin #30 (1991):

> [It] has been confidently assumed . . . that community-based sentences (as well as imprisonment) have no effect in terms of reducing re-offending. . . . "Nothing Works," however, is a doctrine with no real foundations. . . .
>
> [N]owhere does Martinson state unequivocally that "Nothing Works"; his own summary of the evidence was not set out without qualifications. . . . [And] given the evidence he considers, Martinson's summary itself goes a little too far in its negativity. The article is littered with phrases such as "hard to interpret," "no clear evidence," [etc.] A reading which takes full account of such cautionary notes would come to a suitably cautious conclusion.
>
> [But] Martinson — quite unintentionally — found a remarkably receptive audience from both sides of the political spectrum in the U.S.A. On the right, the period from the second half of the sixties into the seventies was seen as a time of serious disorder and instability; Vietnam, black power and youth protest were seen to threaten the traditional order. And out of all this "crime assumed new meaning and significance . . . [it] became a codeword for all that was wrong with American society." The right, therefore, welcomed Martinson's attack on the rehabilitative ideal which was seen as being soft on offenders and looked forward to new, tougher methods of punishing criminals. The perspective from the left was, of course, rather different. Here, the benevolence of the state was subject to sustained questioning, a process which inevitably touched upon criminal justice. Rehabilitation and treatment became suspect; they were criticised as theoretically faulty, discriminatory and unjust, and the unfettered discretion entrusted to criminal justice professionals was attacked as leading to abuse of power and injustice. . . .
>
> Another important factor in the rapid acceptance of the idea that "Nothing

20. Robert Martinson, New Findings, New Views: A Note of Caution Regarding Sentencing Reform, 7 Hofstra L. Rev. 243 (1979).

21. See Michael Vitiello, Reconsidering Rehabilitation, 65 Tulane L. Rev. 1011 (1991).

Works" was undoubtedly the seductive clarity of a neat and simple formula. . . . [C]omplex realities . . . rarely have clear-cut solutions. And dealing with offenders effectively is not a simple process. "Nothing Works" was clear and unvarnished, it was a simple lesson which could be easily learned. . . .

[Nonetheless,] Martinson's argument is fundamentally flawed in two ways: first, by reliance upon recidivism as the sole measure of success of a sentence; and second, by a failure to address the issue of how sentences are implemented and operate in practice. . . . If, for example, a considerable number of the disposals investigated in the research reports included in Martinson's analysis had failed to be properly implemented as planned, had been starved of resources, had used badly trained and uncommitted staff, and had been studied in the first year or so of operation, would it be any surprise that the sentences had failed? Only by studying how a sentence or treatment programme has been put into practice . . . [can we] understand more clearly *why* a penal measure may be working successfully or — equally important — why it may be failing. . . . And how should those measures which show no change be interpreted? Some authors place them in the successful category while others consider them as failures.[a] [O]ptimistic details are all too often missed or lost in re-analysis.

Controversy continues over the effectiveness of rehabilitation programs, and some researchers remain quite pessimistic.[22] Most, however, concur in Professor Michael Vitiello's assessment that "some offenders are amenable to rehabilitation and . . . social scientists can identify those offenders by the use of objective criteria."[23] Programs most often prove effective when they make available a variety of social and psychological services and focus primarily on high-risk offenders;[24] some successful programs have reduced recidivism by 27-90 percent.[25] For discussion of the features most often associated with effective programs, see Edward J. Letessa, What Works in Correctional Intervention, 23 So. Ill. U. L. J. 415 (1999).

ANDREW VON HIRSCH & LISA MAHER, SHOULD PENAL REHABILITATIONISM BE REVIVED?, Criminal Justice Ethics pp. 25, 26-29 (Winter/Spring 1992): [T]he "whys" of treatment (that is, the processes by which successes are achieved) are seldom understood. Without knowing the processes by which experimental programs produce given outcomes, it is difficult to tell which features "work," and will continue to work, when programs are extended beyond experimental groups and implemented more widely.

Programs appear to have better prospects for success when they focus on selected subgroups of offenders, carefully screened for amenability. Such a screening approach, however, necessarily limits the scope for rehabilitation. . . . Treat-

a. If the recidivism rate for offenders placed in a community-based treatment program is no different from the rate for comparable offenders in prison, the program arguably should be considered a "success," to the extent that it produces the same outcomes in a less harsh and less expensive manner. — Eds.

22. E.g., Steven P. Lab & John T. Whitehead, From "Nothing Works" to "The Appropriate Works," 28 Criminology 405 (1990), arguing that the great majority of rehabilitation programs have proved ineffective.

23. Vitiello, supra note 21, at 1037.

24. Daniel H. Antonowicz & Robert R. Ross, Essential Components of Successful Rehabilitation Programs for Offenders, 38 Intl. J. Offender Therapy & Comp. Criminology 97 (1994); D. A. Andrews, Ivan Zinger, et al., Does Correctional Treatment Work?, 28 Criminology 369 (1990).

25. Antonowicz & Ross, supra, at 102.

ments do not (and are not likely to) exist, however, that can be relied upon to decide sentences routinely. . . .

Success depends, also, on the resources available for implementation. The programs that succeed tend to be well-funded, well-staffed, and vigorously implemented. These features are easiest to achieve when the program is tried in an experimental setting. When the same programs are carried out more widely, program quality tends to deteriorate. . . .

Some new advocates of penal rehabilitationism . . . stress its humaneness. . . . Treatment programs, however, seldom aim merely at social service. Their objective, instead, is recidivism prevention. . . . To accomplish that crime-preventive aim, the intervention may well have to be more drastic. It will take more to get the drug-abusing robber to stop committing further robberies than to teach him/her a skill. . . . Consider offenders convicted of crimes of intermediate or lesser gravity. A proportionate sanction for such offenses should be of no more than moderate severity. What of a rehabilitative response? That would depend on how much intervention, and how long, is required to alter the offender's criminal propensities — and to succeed, the intervention may have to be quite substantial (as in the just-noted case of drug treatments).

Cullen and Gilbert . . . argue for a return to a treatment model, on grounds that other models (for example, desert) have led to harsh results.[29] How supportable are such claims? . . . That legislatively mandated "deserved" penalties were harsh in California may be attributable, perhaps, to the character of criminal-justice politics in that state. . . . Were California to return to a rehabilitative ethos, it is far from certain (given California's politics) how "humane" or benevolent the results would be.

Some new rehabilitationists' rejection of other models, such as desert, is based on a "socially critical" perspective: how the rationale is likely to be implemented in a society characterized by race, class, and gender inequalities. Such a critique, however, cuts both ways: one also needs to consider how rehabilitationism might be implemented in such an unpropitious social setting. . . .

Treatment . . . can seldom rely on criteria relating to the blameworthiness of the conduct; whether the offender is amenable to a particular treatment depends, instead, on his/her social and personal characteristics. This creates the potential problem of fairness: one is using criminal punishment, a blame-conveying response, and yet deciding the intervention on the basis of those personal and social variables that have little to do with how reprehensible the behavior is. . . . [I]t needs to be explained what role, if any, the degree of blameworthiness of the conduct should have.

One possibility would be to give proportionality a limiting role: The seriousness of the criminal conduct would set upper and lower bounds on the quantum of punishment — within which rehabilitation could be invoked to fix the sentence. That kind of solution requires one to specify . . . how narrow or broad the offense-based limits on the sentence should be. Here, one faces the familiar dilemma; the narrower one sets those limits, the less room there would be for treatment considerations; whereas the wider one sets the limits, the more one would need to worry about seemingly disparate or disproportionate responses.

Another possibility would be to try to dispense with notions of proportionality

29. F. Cullen & K. Gilbert, Reaffirming Rehabilitation (1982).

altogether. Such a strategy, however, would pose its own difficulties. It would, first, have to be explained how it is justifiable to employ punishment — a blaming institution—without regard to the blameworthiness of the conduct. Or, if one proposes to eliminate the censuring element in punishment, it needs to be explained how this may possibly be accomplished. (The juvenile justice system, for example, long purported to convey no blame, but who was fooled?) Second, the absence of significant proportionality constraints could open the way for abuses of the kind that discredited the old rehabilitation — for example, long-term, open-ended intervention against those deemed to be in special need of treatment. (One thinks of the young car thief who was confined for sixteen years at Patuxent Institution because he refused to talk to the therapists.) One might hope that we are more sophisticated now about the therapeutic value of such interventions — but is such hope enough without principled restraints upon rehabilitative responses?

The most dangerous temptation is to treat the treatment ethos as a kind of edifying fiction: If we only act as though we cared — and minister treatment to offenders as a sign of our caring — a more humane penal system will emerge. No serious inquiry is needed, on this view, about the criteria for deciding what constitutes a humane penal system or about how a renewed treatment emphasis could achieve its intended effects or lead to reasonably just outcomes.

Such thinking is a recipe for failure. It is likely to cause the new treatment ethos to be rejected once its specifics (or lack of them) are subject to critical scrutiny. And it could do no more good than the old, largely hortatory treatment ethic: Create a facade of treatment behind which decision makers act as they choose.

d. Incapacitation

JOHN J. DIIULIO JR, PRISONS ARE A BARGAIN, BY ANY MEASURE

New York Times, January 16, 1996, p. A17

All 30 Republican governors elected or re-elected in 1994 promised to get tough on crime. Most, like George Pataki of New York, are keeping their word. But several, like Tommy Thompson of Wisconsin, who has said he would build no more prisons, are quietly promoting plans to put more convicted criminals back on the streets. Most experts applaud Governor Thompson's new-found "wisdom" and lament Governor Pataki's "hard-line" approach. As these experts love to repeat, "incarceration is not the answer."

If incarceration is not the answer, what, precisely, is the question? If the question is how to prevent at-risk youths from becoming stone-cold predators in the first place, then, of course, incarceration is no solution. But if the question is how to restrain known convicted criminals from murdering, raping, robbing, assaulting and stealing, then incarceration is a solution, and a highly cost-effective one.

On average, it costs about $25,000 a year to keep a convicted criminal in prison. For that money, society gets four benefits: Imprisonment punishes offenders and expresses society's moral disapproval. It teaches felons and would-be felons a lesson: Do crime, do time. Prisoners get drug treatment and education.

And, as the columnist Ben Wattenberg has noted, "A thug in prison can't shoot your sister."

. . . [P]risons pay big dividends even if all they deliver is relief from the murder and mayhem that incarcerated felons would be committing if free. Harvard economist Anne Piehl and I found that prisoners in New Jersey and Wisconsin committed an average of 12 crimes a year when free, excluding all drug crimes. . . . Patrick A. Langan calculated that tripling the prison population from 1975 to 1989 may have reduced "violent crime by 10 to 15 percent below what it would have been," thereby preventing a "conservatively estimated 390,000 murders, rapes, robberies and aggravated assaults in 1989 alone." . . . [T]he violent crimes committed each year will cost victims and society more than $400 billion in medical bills, lost days from work, lost quality of life — and lost life. . . . All told, research shows it costs society at least twice as much to let a prisoner loose than to lock him up. Compared with the human and financial toll of revolving-door justice, prisons are a real bargain.

Prison definitely pays, but there's one class of criminal that is an arguable exception: low-level, first-time drug offenders. Most drug felons in state prisons do not fit that description [but] it makes no sense to lock away even one drug offender whose case could be adjudicated in special drug courts and handled less expensively through intensively supervised probation featuring no-nonsense drug treatment and community service. Thus, . . . Governor Thompson should pursue whatever "alternative to incarceration" policies he fancies subject to one condition: He should agree to make public in a timely fashion the complete histories of all criminals released from custody because of his "reforms." All elected leaders should reckon that those who break their promises to protect society from career criminals can count on voters to shorten their political careers.

NOTES

1. Estimating the benefits. DiIulio and others argue that "it costs society at least twice as much to let a prisoner loose than to lock him up." But critics contend that these claims rest on greatly exaggerated estimates of the number of crimes averted by incarcerating offenders who are not sentenced to prison now. Note DiIulio's claim that "prisoners in New Jersey and Wisconsin committed an *average* of 12 crimes a year when free" (emphasis added). Does this mean that extending an offender's sentence for an additional year will avert 12 crimes? Consider John J. Donohue III & Peter Seligman, Allocating Resources Among Prisons and Social Programs in the Battle against Crime, 27 J. Legal Stud. 1, 10-12 (1998):

> A common error among researchers . . . is to assume (implicitly) that those released from prison in any year are a random sample of all prisoners, when they in fact tend to be the less serious criminals. The problem stems from the failure to distinguish between the average number of crimes committed by the total *stock* of prisoners and the mean criminality of the group of prisoners who are poised to leave prison (the annual *flow* of releasees). . . . If there is a positive correlation between sentence length and prior record, as seems likely, then the cohort of released prisoners will tend to have lower than average [rates of offending]. Thus, the crimes prevented by keeping the current group of released prisoners incarcerated

for an additional year will tend to be less than the average number of crimes committed by all prisoners — and probably dramatically so.

[Studies like DiIulio's] assume that incarcerating a prisoner for an additional year will reduce crime by the number of crimes that the prisoner committed in the year prior to his incarceration. This may be plausible for some crimes but is certainly not true for others. Many crimes are committed by criminal rings or gangs; under these circumstances, the loss of one gang member will probably just lead to the recruitment of another.

[M]ost criminals do not commit offenses uniformly over their entire adult lifetimes. Instead, criminal behavior is disproportionately concentrated over a much shorter period, typically in the late teens and early twenties. This fact has obvious implications for the efficacy of imprisonment as a means of controlling crime. Consider a 20-year-old who committed 40 crimes in the year prior to receiving a 10-year sentence. Simply multiplying 40 crimes/year by 10 years suggests that imprisoning this person would forestall 400 crimes over the next 10 years. But if the prisoner's criminal career would in any case have ended at age 25, the true crime reduction is only 200, and 5 years of the 10-year sentence produce no incapacitative benefit.

2. *Selective incapacitation.* If across-the-board increases in prison sentences are an overinclusive and inefficient method of crime prevention, a more cost-effective strategy might involve efforts to target the particular offenders most likely to commit serious crimes at high rates. Consider Jacqueline Cohen, Incapacitating Criminals: Recent Research Findings, U.S. Dept. of Justice, Natl. Institute of Justice, Research in Brief (December 1983):

It is frequently observed that a small number of offenders commits a disproportionately large number of offenses. If prison resources can be effectively targeted to high-rate offenders, it should be possible to achieve current, or improved, levels of crime control with reduced numbers in prison. The key to such a policy rests on an ability to identify high-rate offenders prospectively, and at relatively early stages in their careers.

Recent selective incapacitation research has stimulated considerable controversy. Some of the debate has focused on ethical implications of selective incapacitation and some has focused on limitations of the existing research.

Ethical Concerns

A key element of selective incapacitation is that some offenders would be imprisoned for a longer period than others convicted of the same offense, because of predictions about their *future* criminality. Reactions to selective incapacitation proposals are influenced by differing views about the purposes of criminal punishments. Proponents argue that persons convicted of crimes can justly receive any lawful sentence (unless, perhaps, it is so disproportionately severe as to be unjust), and that holding some offenders longer than others for predictive reasons raises no significant ethical problems. Moreover, proponents point out that existing sentencing is implicitly incapacitative: presumably, most judges and other officials base their decisions in part on their beliefs about an offender's future dangerousness. From this perspective, selective incapacitation policies are preferable to existing practice because predictions of future crime would no longer be ad hoc and idiosyncratic, but would be based upon the best available scientific evidence.

Some critics argue against selective incapacitation in principle: punishment should be *deserved* and two persons who have committed the same offense deserve equal punishment. If selective incapacitation means that one person will be held longer than another because of predictions of future crimes, it is unjust.

Other critics — including people who in principle do not object to unequal punishments — offer other objections:

1. It is *unfair* to punish people for crimes they have not yet committed, and might not commit if released.
2. It is unjust to incarcerate (or further incarcerate) people on the basis of predictions of future crime because those predictions are too often *wrong* — typically two out of three persons so identified are "false positives," people who would not have committed future crimes even if released.
3. Many of the variables in prediction formulas raise other policy or ethical questions. For example, several of the RAND variables involved juvenile records, which many believe should not be admissible in relation to adult prosecutions. For another example, the RAND formula includes employment information, which many would exclude from consideration at sentencing, along with education and similar factors, as class-based variables that, in effect, discriminate against the poor.
4. Many prediction variables, like education, employment, and residential stability, are associated with race: some minorities are on average less well educated and less stably employed than the white majority. Building such variables into sentencing standards, while not intended to punish minorities more severely, would have that effect. . . .

EMPIRICAL PROBLEMS IN PREDICTION

Efforts at predicting future crimes have not been very successful. In recent review of efforts to predict violence, John Monahan (1981) reports that the best predictions have false-positive rates of over 60 percent; of every three individuals predicted to be violent in the future, two were *not* observed to be violent.

. . . Given the crucial issues of low predictive accuracy and the tentativeness of the estimated impacts characterizing this research, there is as yet no sound basis for implementing selective incapacitation policies.[a]

3. Taking credit for the 1990s? From 1988 to 1998, American prison populations soared from 800,000 to 1.8 million, an increase of 125 percent. During the same period crime rates fell dramatically; in cities of more than one million inhabitants, for example, the homicide rate fell by 55 percent from 1991 to 1998.[26] Many attribute these crime-control successes to the incapacitation effect of the prison population boom. But many competing explanations have been offered, including demographic trends, community policing innovations, the waning of the crack epidemic, and even the possibility that legalized abortion may have re-

a. For in-depth discussion of the ethical and empirical issues, see Jacqueline Cohen, Selective Incapitation: An Assessment, 1984 U. Ill. L. Rev. 253, and Leonard J. Long, Rethinking Selective Incapacitation: More at Stake than Controlling Violent Crime, 62 U.M.K.C.L. Rev. 107 (1993). For further review of empirical data, see Jacqueline Cohen & Jose A. Canela-Cacho, Incapacitation and Violent Crime (Natl. Academy of Sciences 1994). — EDS.

26. U.S. Dept of Justice, Bureau of Justice Statistics, Homicide Trends in the United States: 1998 Update (March 2000).

duced the number of "unwanted" children who began reaching their crime-prone teen years during this period.[27] Efforts to sort out the impact of these diverse factors are necessarily speculative and imprecise; one careful study suggests that increases in incarceration rates in California may have produced roughly a 15 percent decrease in the volume of crime, but the reductions occurred primarily in burglaries and larcenies; no substantial incapacitation benefit was detected for homicide, robbery, and assault.[28]

4. *Cost-effective alternatives?* Three years after declaring that "prisons are a bargain," Professor DiIulio qualified his position. In a 1999 article, he insisted that increasing the incarceration rate was a justified policy in 1996 (when there were 1.6 prisoners nationwide),[29] but with the U.S. prison and jail population near the two million mark, he argued, "the nation has 'maxed out' on the public-safety value of incarceration" and "[t]he justice system is becoming less capable of distributing sanctions and supervision rationally, especially where drug offenders are concerned." Accordingly, DiIulio maintained, "[i]t's time for policy makers to change focus, aiming for zero prison growth," and devoting more resources to drug treatment and effective supervision of offenders on probation and parole. Signaling that his changed assessment was the result of more than just a shift in the cost-benefit calculus, DiIulio concluded, "In the end, whether or not we achieve this goal [of zero prison growth] will be a profound measure not merely of how nimble we are when it comes to managing public safety cost-effectively, but also of how decent we are, despite our many differences, when it came to loving all God's children unconditionally."[30]

Consider Donohue & Seligman, supra note 1, at 30-43:

> It is frequently noted that it costs more to house someone in prison . . . than it would to send them to Harvard College for the same length of time. The statement is usually followed by an admonition to spend the money up front on educating the potential criminals, making it unnecessary to send them to prison down the road. [But] we immediately run up against two central problems. The first: are there programs that can actually reduce criminality? The second is the problem of targeting. [T]here is no reliable way of identifying who is likely to become a serious criminal, and certainly no way to make accurate predictions early enough to be useful in assigning 3-year-old children to preschool. The result is that any money saved by reducing the number of people in prison must necessarily be spread across a large pool of potential incarcerees, which limits the amounts available to be spent on each recipient. . . .
>
> [We estimate] that a 50 percent increase in future incarceration for today's 3-year-olds would cost between $5.6 and $8 billion (in present dollars) and that it would reduce crime by 5-15 percent. [W]e are now in a position to explore the costs and benefits of an alternative policy: stopping the growth in incarceration and redirecting the $5.6-$8 billion toward crime reduction programs such as preschool education or job training. . . . For example, these saved resources could fund a Perry Preschool-type program for between 376,000 and 540,000 students, which is roughly 10-14 percent of all 3-year-olds.

27. See John J. Donohue III & Steven Levitt, Legalized Abortion and Crime, Stanford Law School, Olin Law & Economics Program, Paper No. 177, Q. J. Econ. (forthcoming, 2001).

28. Frank Zimring & Gordon Hawkins, Incapacitation 100-127 (1995).

29. U.S. Dept. of Justice, Bureau of Justice Statistics, Prison and Jail Inmates at Midyear 1999, (April 2000), p. 2.

30. John J. DiIulio, Jr., Two Million Prisoners Are Enough, Wall Street Journal, March 12, 1999.

On its face, widespread adoption of the Perry Preschool program looks most promising, in large part because the initial program was deemed to have reduced crime by 40 percent. . . . Assuming that a broad-based program could reduce crime among program participants by only 20 percent (that is, at half the rate of the original Perry program), the overall reduction in crime would be 9.3 percent — even under pessimistic assumptions about resource availability. In sum, halting the growth of the prison population and shifting the resources to a Perry Preschool-type program that was only *one-half* as effective at reducing crime as the original Perry Preschool could still reduce crime while realizing a social savings. . . .

[W]e must note that the strategy we have outlined might be politically difficult to implement. [P]reschool programs impose costs today and yield benefits in 15-20 years, which is not an appealing formula for most politicians. Thus, shifting resources from incarceration to social programs may not be a politically sustainable policy. [Nonetheless,] our point is simply that there may be scope for welfare-increasing large-scale interventions and that society should begin the process of trying to see whether such interventions can actually be carried out on a meaningful scale, rather than unthinkingly committing itself to a policy of massive prison construction without a full awareness of all of its attendant financial and human costs.

2. *Case Studies*

REGINA v. DUDLEY AND STEPHENS

Queen's Bench Division
14 Q.B.D. 273 (1884)

LORD COLERIDGE, C.J. The two prisoners, Thomas Dudley and Edwin Stephens, were indicted for the murder of Richard Parker on the high seas on the 25th of July in the present year. They were tried before my Brother Huddleston at Exeter on the 6th of November, and, under the direction of my learned Brother, the jury returned a special verdict, the legal effect of which has been argued before us, and on which we are now to pronounce judgment. The special verdict . . . is as follows.

That on July 5, 1884, the prisoners, Thomas Dudley and Edward [sic] Stephens, with one Brooks, all able-bodied English seamen, and the deceased also an English boy, between seventeen and eighteen years of age, the crew of an English yacht, a registered English vessel, were cast away in a storm on the high seas 1,600 miles from the Cape of Good Hope, and were compelled to put into an open boat belonging to the said yacht. That in this boat they had no supply of water and no supply of food, except two 1 lb. tins of turnips, and for three days they had nothing else to subsist upon. That on the fourth day they caught a small turtle, upon which they subsisted for a few days, and this was the only food they had up to the twentieth day when the act now in question was committed. That on the twelfth day the remains of the turtle were entirely consumed, and for the next eight days they had nothing to eat. That they had no fresh water, except such rain as they from time to time caught in their oilskin capes. That the boat was drifting on the ocean, and was probably more than 1,000 miles away from land. That on the eighteenth day, when they had been seven days without food and five without water, the prisoners spoke to Brooks as to what should be done if no succour came, and suggested that some one should be sacrificed to save the rest, but Brooks dissented, and the boy, to whom they were understood to refer, was not consulted. That on the 24th of July, the day before the act now in question, the prisoner Dudley proposed to Stephens and Brooks that lots should be cast who should be put to death to save the rest, but Brooks refused to consent, and it was not put to the boy, and in point of fact there was no drawing of lots. That on the day the prisoners spoke of their families, and suggested it would be better to kill the boy that their lives should be saved, and Dudley proposed that if there was no vessel in sight by the morrow morning the boy should be killed. That next day, the 25th of July, no vessel appearing, Dudley told Brooks that he had better go and have a sleep, and made signs to Stephens and Brooks that the boy had better be killed. The prisoner Stephens agreed to the act, but Brooks dissented from it. That the boy was then lying at the bottom of the boat quite helpless and extremely weakened by famine and by drinking sea water, and unable to make any resistance, nor did he ever assent to his being killed. The prisoner Dudley offered a prayer asking forgiveness for them all if either of them should be tempted to commit a rash act, and that their souls might be saved. That Dudley, with the assent of Stephens, went to the boy, and telling him that his time was come, put a knife into his throat and killed him then and there; that the three men fed upon the body and blood of the boy for four days; that on the fourth day after the act had been committed the boat was picked up by a passing vessel, and the prisoners were rescued, still alive, but in the lowest state of prostration. That they were carried to the port of Falmouth, and committed for trial at Exeter. That if the men had not fed upon the body of the boy they would probably not have survived to be so picked up and rescued, but would within four days have died of famine. That the boy, being in a much weaker condition, was likely to have died before them. That at the time of the act in question there was no sail in sight, nor any reasonable prospect of relief. That under these circumstances there appeared to the prisoners every probability that unless they then fed or very soon fed upon the boy or one of themselves they would die of starvation. That there was no appreciable chance of saving life except by killing some one for the others to eat. That assuming any necessity to kill anybody, there was no greater necessity for killing the boy than any of the other three men. But whether upon the whole matter by the jurors found the killing of Richard Parker by Dudley and Stephens be felony and murder the jurors are ignorant, and pray the advice of the Court thereupon, and if upon the whole matter the Court shall be of opinion that the killing of Richard Parker be felony and murder, then the jurors say that Dudley and Stephens were each guilty of felony and murder as alleged in the indictment. . . .

From these facts, stated with the cold precision of a special verdict, it appears sufficiently that the prisoners were subject to terrible temptation, to sufferings which might break down the bodily power of the strongest man, and try the conscience of the best. Other details yet more harrowing, facts still more loathsome and appalling, were presented to the jury, and are to be found recorded in my learned Brother's notes. But nevertheless this is clear, that the prisoners put to death a weak and unoffending boy upon the chance of preserving their own lives by feeding upon his flesh and blood after he was killed, and with the certainty of depriving *him* of any possible chance of survival. The verdict finds in terms that "if the men had not fed upon the body of the boy they would *probably* not have survived," and that "the boy being in a much weaker condition was *likely* to have died before them." They might possibly have been picked up next day by a passing ship; they might possibly not have been picked up at all; in either case it is obvious that the killing of the boy would have been an unnecessary and profitless act. It is found by the verdict that the boy was incapable of resistance, and, in fact, made none; and it is not even suggested that his death was due to any violence on his part attempted against, or even so much as feared by, those who killed him. Under these circumstances the jury say that they are ignorant whether those who killed him were guilty of murder, and have referred it to this Court to determine what is the legal consequence which follows from the facts which they have found. . . .

[T]he real question in the case [is] whether killing under the circumstances set forth in the verdict be or not be murder. The contention that it could be anything else was, to the minds of us all, both new and strange, and we stopped the Attorney General in his negative argument in order that we might hear what could be said in support of a proposition which appeared to us to be at once dangerous, immoral, and opposed to all legal principle and analogy. . . . First it is said that it follows from various definitions of murder in books of authority, which definitions imply, if they do not state, the doctrine, that in order to save your own life you may lawfully take away the life of another, when that other is neither attempting nor threatening yours, nor is guilty of any illegal act whatever towards you or any one else. But if these definitions be looked at they will not be found to sustain this contention. . . .

It is . . . clear . . . that the doctrine contended for receives no support from the great authority of Lord Hale. It is plain that in his view the necessity which justified homicide is that only which has always been and is now considered a justification. . . . Lord Hale regarded the private necessity which justified, and alone justified, the taking the life of another for the safeguard of one's own to be what is commonly called "self-defence." (Hale's Pleas of the Crown, i. 478.)

But if this could be even doubtful upon Lord Hale's words, Lord Hale himself has made it clear. For in the chapter in which he deals with the exemption created by compulsion or necessity he thus expresses himself: — "If a man be desperately assaulted and in peril of death, and cannot otherwise escape unless, to satisfy his assailant's fury, he will kill an innocent person then present, the fear and actual force will not acquit him of the crime and punishment of murder, if he commit the fact [sic], for he ought rather to die himself than kill an innocent; but if he cannot otherwise save his own life the law permits him in his own defence to kill the assailant, for by the violence of the assault, and the offence committed upon him by the assailant himself, the law of nature, and necessity, hath made him his own protector. . . ." (Hale's Pleas of the Crown, vol. i. 51.)

But, further still, Lord Hale in the following chapter deals with the position asserted by the casuists, and sanctioned, as he says, by Grotius and Puffendorf, that in a case of extreme necessity, either of hunger or clothing; "theft is no theft, or at least not punishable as theft, as some even of our own lawyers have asserted the same." "But," says Lord Hale, "I take it that here in England, that rule, at least by the laws of England, is false; and therefore, if a person, being under necessity for want of victuals or clothes, shall upon that account clandestinely and animo furandi steal another man's goods, it is felony, and a crime by the laws of England punishable with death." (Hale, Pleas of the Crown, i. 54.) If, therefore, Lord Hale is clear — as he is — that extreme necessity of hunger does not justify larceny, what would he have said to the doctrine that it justified murder? [The opinion then reviewed other early text writers and found that none of them supported the defendants' contentions.]

Is there, then, any authority for the proposition which has been presented to us? Decided cases there are none. . . . The American case cited by my Brother Stephen in his Digest, from Wharton on Homicide, in which it was decided, correctly indeed, that sailors had no right to throw passengers overboard to save themselves, but on the somewhat strange ground that the proper mode of determining who was to be sacrificed was to vote upon the subject by ballot, can hardly, as my Brother Stephen says, be an authority satisfactory to a court in this country.[a] . . .

The one real authority of former time is Lord Bacon, who . . . lays down the law as follows:—"Necessity carrieth a privilege in itself. Necessity is of three sorts.—necessity of conservation of life, necessity of obedience, and necessity of the act of God or of a stranger. First of conservation of life; if a man steals viands to satisfy his present hunger, this is no felony nor larceny. So if divers be in danger of drowning by the casting away of some boat or barge, and one of them get to some plank, or on the boat's side to keep himself above water, and another to save his life thrust him from it, whereby he is drowned, this is neither se defendendo nor by misadventure, but justifiable."[b] . . . Lord Bacon was great even as a lawyer; but it is permissible to much smaller men, relying upon principle and on the authority of others, the equals and even the superiors of Lord Bacon as lawyers, to question the soundness of his dictum. There are many conceivable states of things in which it might possibly be true, but if Lord Bacon meant to lay down the broad proposition that man may save his life by killing, if necessary, an innocent and unoffending neighbour, it certainly is not law at the present day. . . .

Now it is admitted that the deliberate killing of this unoffending and unresisting boy was clearly murder, unless the killing can be justified by some well-recognised excuse admitted by the law. It is further admitted that there was in this case no such excuse, unless the killing was justified by what has been called "necessity." But the temptation to the act which existed here was not what the law has ever called necessity. Nor is this to be regretted. Though law and morality are not the same, and many things may be immoral which are not necessarily illegal, yet the absolute divorce of law from morality would be of fatal consequence; and such divorce would follow if the temptation to murder in this case were to be held by law an absolute defence of it. It is not so. To preserve one's life is generally speaking a duty, but it may be the plainest and the highest duty to sacrifice it. War is full of instances in which it is a man's duty not to live, but to die. The duty, in case of shipwreck, of a captain to his crew, of the crew to the passengers, of soldiers to women and children, as in the noble case of the *Birkenhead;* these duties impose on men the moral necessity, not of the preservation, but of the sacrifice of their lives for others, from which in no country, least of all, it is to be hoped, in England, will men ever shrink, as indeed, they have not

a. Lord Coleridge is referring to United States v. Holmes, 26 F. Cas. 360, 1 Wall. Jr. 1 (C.C.E.D. Pa. 1842), which is summarized at page 823 infra — EDS.

b. The omitted first sentence with which Bacon introduced the passage quoted read as follows:

> The law chargeth no man with default where the act is compulsory and not voluntary, and where there is not a consent and election: and therefore, if either there be an impossibility for a man to do otherwise, or so great a perturbation of the judgment and reason as in presumption of law man's nature cannot overcome, such necessity carrieth a privilege in itself.

Shedding, Ellis & Heath, The Works of Francis Bacon 343 (1859). — EDS.

shrunk. It is not correct, therefore, to say that there is any absolute or unqualified necessity to preserve one's life. *Necesse est ut eam, non ut vivam,*[c] is a saying of a Roman officer quoted by Lord Bacon himself with high eulogy in the very chapter on necessity to which so much reference has been made. It would be a very easy and cheap display of commonplace learning to quote from Greek and Latin authors, from Horace, from Juvenal, from Cicero, from Euripides, passage after passage, in which the duty of dying for others has been laid down in glowing and emphatic language as resulting from the principles of heathen ethics; it is enough in a Christian country to remind ourselves of the Great Example whom we profess to follow. It is not needful to point out the awful danger of admitting the principle which has been contended for. Who is to be the judge of this sort of necessity? By what measure is the comparative value of lives to be measured? Is it to be strength, or intellect, or what? It is plain that the principle leaves to him who is to profit by it to determine the necessity which will justify him in deliberately taking another's life to save his own. In this case the weakest, the youngest, the most unresisting, was chosen. Was it more necessary to kill him than one of the grown men? The answer must be "No"—

> *So spake the Fiend, and with necessity,*
> *The tyrant's plea, excused his devilish deeds.*

It is not suggested that in this particular case the deeds were "devilish," but it is quite plain that such a principle once admitted might be made the legal cloak for unbridled passion and atrocious crime. There is no safe path for judges to tread but to ascertain the law to the best of their ability and to declare it according to their judgment; and if in any case the law appears to be too severe on individuals, to leave it to the Sovereign to exercise that prerogative of mercy which the Constitution has intrusted to the hands fittest to dispense it.

It must not be supposed that in refusing to admit temptation to be an excuse for crime it is forgotten how terrible the temptation was; how awful the suffering; how hard in such trials to keep the judgment straight and the conduct pure. We are often compelled to set up standards we cannot reach ourselves, and to lay down rules which we could not ourselves satisfy. But a man has no right to declare temptation to be an excuse, though he might himself have yielded to it, nor allow compassion for the criminal to change or weaken in any manner the legal definition of the crime. It is therefore our duty to declare that the prisoners' act in this case was wilful murder, that the facts as stated in the verdict are no legal justification of the homicide; and to say that in our unanimous opinion the prisoners are upon this special verdict guilty of murder.[1]

The Court then proceeded to pass sentence of death upon the prisoners.[2]

c. "It is necessary to go [to war], not to live."—EDS.

1. My brother Grove has furnished me with the following suggestion, too late to be embodied in the judgment but well worth preserving: "If the two accused men were justified in killing Parker, then if not rescued in time, two of the three survivors would be justified in killing the third, and of the two who remained the stronger would be justified in killing the weaker, so that three men might be justifiably killed to give the fourth a chance of surviving."— C.

2. This sentence was afterwards commuted by the Crown to six months' imprisonment.

NOTE

For discussion of the background of *Dudley and Stephens,* see Neil Hanson, The Custom of the Sea (2000); A. W. B. Simpson, Cannibalism and the Common Law (1984). As both authors detail, cannibalism was an accepted fact of life, before the era of modern communications and rescue capabilities, when seamen found themselves stranded far from help. Through most of the nineteenth century, such cases were treated as tragedies, either celebrated or discreetly ignored; the survivors were received with sympathy or perverse fascination but were seldom considered candidates for prosecution. The "custom of the sea" (cannibalism) was so well established that Dudley talked freely about the episode with an apparently clear conscience. But British officials, concerned that the custom of the sea set a potentially bad precedent, determined to make a test case of the incident, and the prosecution of Dudley and Stephens ensued. See also Allen D. Boyer, Crime, Cannibalism and Joseph Conrad: The Influence of *Regina v. Dudley and Stephens* on Lord Jim, 20 Loy. L.A. L. Rev. 9 (1986).

UNITED STATES v. BERGMAN

United States District Court, S.D.N.Y.
416 F. Supp. 496 (1976)

FRANKEL, J. Defendant is being sentenced upon his plea of guilty to two counts of an 11-count indictment. . . . It seems fitting now to report in writing the reasons upon which the court concludes that defendant must be sentenced to a term of four months in prison.

Defendant appeared until the last couple of years to be a man of unimpeachably high character, attainments, and distinction. A doctor of divinity and an ordained rabbi, he has been acclaimed by people around the world for his works of public philanthropy, private charity, and leadership in educational enterprises. Scores of letters have come to the court from across this and other countries reporting debts of personal gratitude to him for numerous acts of extraordinary generosity. . . . In addition to his good works, defendant has managed to amass considerable wealth in the ownership and operation of nursing homes, in real estate ventures, and in a course of substantial investments.

Beginning about two years ago, investigations of nursing homes in this area, including questions of fraudulent claims for Medicaid funds, drew to a focus upon this defendant among several others. The results that concern us were the present indictment and two state indictments. After extensive pretrial proceedings defendant embarked upon elaborate plea negotiations with both state and federal prosecutors. A state guilty plea and the instant plea were entered in March of this year. . . . As part of the detailed plea arrangements, it is expected that the prison sentence imposed by this court will comprise the total covering the state as well as the federal convictions.

For purposes of the sentence now imposed, the precise details of the charges, and of defendant's carefully phrased admissions of guilt, are not matters of prime importance. Suffice it to say that the plea on Count One (carrying a maximum of five years in prison and a $10,000 fine) confesses defendant's knowing and wilful participation in a scheme to defraud the United States in various ways, including the presentation of wrongfully padded claims for payments under the Medicaid program to defendant's nursing homes. Count Three, for which the guilty plea carries a theoretical maximum of three more years in prison and another $5,000 fine, is a somewhat more "technical" charge. Here, defendant admits to having participated in the filing of a partnership return which was false and fraudulent in failing to list people who had bought partnership interests from him in one of his nursing homes, had paid for such interests, and had made certain capital withdrawals.

The conspiracy to defraud, as defendant has admitted it, is by no means the worst of its kind. . . . At the same time, the sentence, as defendant has acknowledged, is imposed for two federal felonies including, as the more important, a knowing and purposeful conspiracy to mislead and defraud the Federal Government.

[D]efense counsel urge that no licit purpose could be served by defendant's incarceration. Some of these arguments are plainly sound; others are not.

The court agrees that this defendant should not be sent to prison for "rehabilitation." Apart from the patent inappositeness of the concept to this individual, this court shares the growing understanding that no one should ever be sent to prison *for rehabilitation.* That is to say, nobody who would not otherwise be locked up should suffer that fate on the incongruous premise that it will be good for him or her. Imprisonment is punishment. . . . If someone must be imprisoned — for other, valid reasons — we should seek to make rehabilitative resources available to him or her. But the goal of rehabilitation cannot fairly serve in itself as grounds for the sentence to confinement.

Equally clearly, this defendant should not be confined to incapacitate him. He is not dangerous. It is most improbable that he will commit similar, or any, offenses in the future. There is no need for "specific deterrence."

Contrary to counsel's submissions, however, two sentencing considerations demand a prison sentence in this case:

First, the aim of *general deterrence,* the effort to discourage similar wrongdoing by others through a reminder that the law's warnings are real and that the grim consequence of imprisonment is likely to follow from crimes of deception for gain like those defendant has admitted.

Second, the related, but not identical, concern that any lesser penalty would, in the words of the Model Penal Code, §7.01(1)(c), "depreciate the seriousness of the defendant's crime."

Resisting the first of these propositions, defense counsel invoke Immanuel Kant's axiom that "one man ought never to be dealt with merely as a means subservient to the purposes of another." . . .

[We] take the widely accepted stance that a criminal punished in the interest of general deterrence is not being employed "*merely* as a means. . . ." Reading Kant to mean that every man must be deemed *more* than the instrument of others, and must "always be treated as an end in himself," the humane principle is not offended here. Each of us is served by the enforcement of the law — not least a person like the defendant in this case, whose wealth and privileges, so long enjoyed, are so much founded upon law. . . .

But the whole business, defendant argues further, is guesswork; we are by no means certain that deterrence "works." . . . It would be better, to be sure, if we had more certainty and precision. Lacking these comforts, we continue to include among our working hypotheses a belief (with some concrete evidence in its support) that crimes like those in this case — deliberate, purposeful, continuing, non-impulsive, and committed for profit — are among those most likely to be generally deterrable by sanctions. . . .

The idea of avoiding depreciation of the seriousness of the offense implicates two or three thoughts. . . . It should be proclaimed by the court's judgment that the offenses are grave, not minor or purely technical. Some attention must be paid to the demand for equal justice; it will not do to leave the penalty of imprisonment a dead letter as against "privileged" violators while it is employed regularly, and with vigor, against others. There probably is in these conceptions an element of retributiveness, as counsel urge. And retribution, so denominated, . . . remains a factor. . . . [W]e have not yet reached a state, supposing we ever should, in which the infliction of punishments for crime may be divorced generally from ideas of blameworthiness, recompense, and proportionality.

Resisting prison above all else, defense counsel included in their thorough memorandum on sentencing two proposals for what they call a "constructive," and therefore a "preferable" form of "behavioral sanction." One is a plan for Dr. Bergman to create and run a program of Jewish vocational and religious high school training. The other is for him to take charge of a "Committee on Holocaust Studies," again concerned with education at the secondary school level. . . .

[Both] of the carefully formulated "sanctions" in the memorandum involve work of an honorific nature, not unlike that done in other projects to which the defendant has devoted himself in the past. It is difficult to conceive of them as "punishments" at all. . . . The seriousness of the crimes to which Dr. Bergman has pled guilty demands something more than "requiring" him to lend his talents and efforts to further philanthropic enterprises. . . .

The criminal behavior, as has been noted, is blatant in character and unmitigated by any suggestion of necessitous circumstance or other pressures difficult to resist. . . . Viewed against the maxima Congress ordained, and against the run of sentences in other federal criminal cases, it calls for more than a token sentence.

On the other side are factors that take longer to enumerate. Defendant's illustrious public life and works are in his favor, though diminished, of course, by what this case discloses. . . .

Given . . . that this is a first offense, by a man no longer young and not perfectly well, where danger of recidivism is not a concern — it verges on cruelty to think of confinement for a term of years. We sit, to be sure, in a nation where prison sentences of extravagant length are more common than they are almost anywhere else. By that light, the term imposed today is not notably long. For this sentencing court, however, for a nonviolent first offense involving no direct assaults or invasions of others' security (as in bank robbery, narcotics, etc.), it is a stern sentence. For people like Dr. Bergman, who might be disposed to engage in similar wrongdoing, it should be sufficiently frightening to serve the major end of general deterrence. For all but the profoundly vengeful, it should not depreciate the seriousness of his offenses.

Much of defendant's sentencing memorandum is devoted to the extensive barrage of hostile publicity to which he has been subjected during the years before and since his indictment. . . .

Defendant's . . . point about his public humiliation is the frequently heard contention that he should not be incarcerated because he "has been punished enough." . . . Defendant's notoriety should not in the last analysis serve to lighten, any more than it may be permitted to aggravate, his sentence. The fact that he has been pilloried by journalists is essentially a consequence of the prestige and privileges he enjoyed before he was exposed as a wrongdoer. . . . It is not possible to justify the notion that this mode of nonjudicial punishment should be an occasion for leniency not given to a defendant who never basked in such an admiring light at all. The quest for both the appearance and the substance of equal justice prompts the court to discount the thought that the public humiliation serves the function of imprisonment. . . .

[The court imposed a sentence of four months' imprisonment.]

NOTE

Compare the *Bergman* case with that of former Reagan White House deputy chief of staff Michael K. Deaver. On September 23, 1988, Deaver received a 3-year suspended prison sentence for three counts of lying under oath to a congressional committee and a grand jury that were investigating his lobbying activities. He could have been sentenced to 15 years' imprisonment. Deaver was also fined $100,000, placed on probation, and ordered to perform 1,500 hours of community service. The judge acknowledged that Deaver knew his testimony was false but noted that Deaver's alcoholism was a "distraction from exercising the judgment required" to tell the truth to Congress. Philip Shenon, Deaver Gets Fine of $100,000 and a Suspended Sentence, N.Y. Times, Sept. 24, 1988, at A1, A9. Before he was sentenced, Deaver pled for mercy: "This entire matter . . . has taken a terrible toll on me, my family, my friends and my business. . . . I would only ask that you offer me a chance to contribute to my community and to my country." "Calling Mr. Deaver's false statements a 'crime of circumstance and opportunity,' the judge said a prison term would probably not deter other perjurers. 'Nor would a prison term serve to rehabilitate Michael Deaver.'" Id.

Representative John Dingell (D-Michigan), who was heading the committee Deaver lied to, criticized the lenient sentence: "An ordinary citizen who steals a Social Security check . . . goes to jail, but someone of wealth and influence who lies to a grand jury and Congress has little to fear." Id.

STATE v. CHANEY

Supreme Court of Alaska
477 P.2d. 441 (1970)

RABINOWITZ, J. Appellee Donald Scott Chaney was indicted on two counts of forcible rape and one count of robbery. After trial by jury, appellee was found guilty on all three counts. The superior court imposed concurrent one-year terms of imprisonment and provided for parole in the discretion of the parole board. The State of Alaska has appealed from the judgment and commitment which was entered by the trial court. . . . In such circumstances, the [law] prohibit[s] any increase in the sentence which was passed by the trial court although this court may express its approval or disapproval of the sentence in a written opinion. . . .

Under Alaska's Constitution, the principles of reformation and necessity of protecting the public constitute the touchstones of penal administration. . . . Within the ambit of this constitutional phraseology are found the objectives of rehabilitation . . . , isolation . . . , deterrence of the offender himself . . . , as well as deterrence of other members of the community [and] reaffirmation of societal norms for the purpose of maintaining respect for the norms themselves. . . .

We now turn to the facts of the case at bar. At the time appellee committed the crimes of forcible rape and robbery, he was an unmarried member of the United States Armed Forces stationed at Fort Richardson, near Anchorage, Alaska. Appellee was born in 1948, the youngest of eight children. His youth was spent on the family's dairy farm in Washington County, Maryland. He played basketball on the Boonsboro High School team, was a member of Future Farmers of America and the Boy Scouts. Appellee did not complete high school, having dropped out one month prior to graduation. After a series of varying types of employment, appellee was drafted into the United States Army in 1968. At sentencing, it was disclosed that appellee did not have any prior criminal record, was not a user of drugs, and was only a social drinker.

From the record that has been furnished, it appears that appellee and a companion picked up the prosecutrix at a downtown location in Anchorage. After driving the victim around in their car, appellee and his companion beat her and forcibly raped her four times. During this same period of time, the victim's money was removed from her purse. Upon completion of these events, the prosecutrix was permitted to leave the vehicle to the accompaniment of dire threats of reprisals if she attempted to report the incident to the police.

The presentence report which was furnished to the trial court prior to sentencing contains appellee's version of the rapes. According to appellee, he felt "that it wasn't rape as forcible and against her will on my part." As to his conviction of robbery, appellee states: "I found the money on the floor of the car afterwards and was planning on giving it back, but didn't get to see the girl." At the time of sentencing, appellee told the court that he "didn't direct any violence against the girl."

The Division of Corrections, in its presentence report, recommended appellee be incarcerated and parole be denied. The assistant district attorney who appeared for the state at the time of sentencing recommended that appellee receive concurrent seven-year sentences with two years suspended on the two rape convictions, and that the appellee be sentenced to a consecutive five-year term of imprisonment on the robbery conviction, and that this sentence be suspended and appellee be placed on probation during this period of time. At the time of sentencing, a representative of the Division of Corrections recommended that appellee serve two years on each of the rape convictions and that appellee be sentenced to two years suspended with probation as to the robbery conviction. In his opinion, there was "an excellent possibility of . . . early parole." Counsel for appellee concurred in the Division of Corrections' recommendation. As was indicated at the outset, the trial court imposed concurrent one-year terms of imprisonment and provided for parole at the discretion of the parole board.[21] The trial judge further recommended that appellee be placed in a minimum security facility. . . .

21. These were minimum sentences under the applicable statutes. Rape carries a potential range of imprisonment from 1 to 20 years while a conviction of robbery can result in imprisonment from 1 to 15 years.

In imposing this sentence, the trial judge remarked that he was "sorry that the [military] regulations would not permit keeping [appellee] . . . in the service if he wanted to stay because it seems to me that is . . . a better setup for everybody concerned than putting him in the penitentiary." At a later point in his remarks, the trial judge said:

> Now as a matter of fact, I have sentenced you to a minimum on all 3 counts here but there will be no problem as far as I'm concerned for you to be paroled at the first day the Parole Board says that you're eligible for parole. . . . [If] the Parole Board should decide 10 days from now that you're eligible for parole and parole you, it's entirely satisfactory with the court.

[W]e express our disapproval of the sentence which was imposed by the trial court in the case at bar. In our opinion, the sentence was too lenient considering the circumstances surrounding the commission of these crimes. It further appears that several significant goals of our system of penal justice were accorded little or no weight by the sentencing court.

Forcible rape and robbery rank among the most serious crimes. In the case at bar, the record reflects that the trial judge explicitly stated, on several occasions, that he disbelieved appellee and believed the prosecutrix's version of what happened after she entered the vehicle which was occupied by appellee and his companion. Considering both the jury's and the trial judge's resolution of this issue of credibility, and the violent circumstances surrounding the commission of these dangerous crimes, we have difficulty in understanding why one-year concurrent sentences were thought appropriate.

Review of the sentencing proceedings leads to the impression that the trial judge was apologetic in regard to his decision to impose a sanction of incarceration. Much was made of appellee's fine military record and his potential eligibility for early parole. On the one hand, the record is devoid of any trace of remorse on appellee's part. Seemingly all but forgotten in the sentencing proceedings is the victim of appellee's rapes and robbery. On the other hand, the record discloses that the trial judge properly considered the mitigating circumstance that the prosecutrix, who at the time did not know either appellee or his companion, voluntarily entered appellee's car. But the crux of our disapproval of the sentence stems from what we consider to be the trial judge's de-emphasis of several important goals of criminal justice.

In view of the circumstances of this record, we think the sentence imposed is not well calculated to achieve the objective of reformation of the accused. Considering the apologetic tone of the sentencing proceedings, the court's endorsement of an extremely early parole, and the concurrent minimum sentences which were imposed for these three serious felonies, we fail to discern how the objective of reformation was effectuated. At most, appellee was told that he was only technically guilty and minimally blameworthy, all of which minimized the possibility of appellee's comprehending the wrongfulness of his conduct.

We also think that the sentence imposed falls short of effectuating the goal of community condemnation, or the reaffirmation of societal norms for the purpose of maintaining respect for the norms themselves. In short, knowledge of the calculated circumstances involved in the commission of these felonies and the sentence imposed could lead to the conclusion that forcible rape and robbery are not reflective of serious antisocial conduct. Thus, respect for society's condemnation of forcible rape and robbery is eroded and reaffirmation of these societal norms negated.

We believe that a . . . sentence of imprisonment for a substantially longer period of imprisonment than the one-year sentence which was imposed would unequivocally bring home to appellee the seriousness of his dangerously unlawful conduct, would reaffirm society's condemnation of forcible rape and robbery, and would provide the Division of Corrections of the State of Alaska with the opportunity of determining whether appellee required any special treatment prior to his return to society.

UNITED STATES v. JACKSON

United States Court of Appeals, 7th Circuit
835 F.2d 1195 (1987)

EASTERBROOK, J. Thirty minutes after being released from prison, to which he had been sent on conviction of two bank robberies, Dwight Jackson robbed another bank. He was let out as part of a "work release program" and returned to his old line of work. Told to get a job, he decided to do a bank job. A passer-by saw a suspicious person flee the bank and noted the license plate of the car. . . . Jackson was back in prison before the sun set on the day of his release. His principal sentence — life in prison without possibility of parole — came under a statute forbidding possession of weapons by career criminals, 18 U.S.C. App. §1202. . . .

Section 1202 provided that anyone "who . . . possesses . . . any firearm and who has three previous [felony] convictions for robbery or burglary, or both, . . . shall be fined not more than $25,000 and imprisoned not less than fifteen years, and, notwithstanding any other provision of law, the court shall not suspend the sentence of, or grant a probationary sentence to, such person . . . , and such person shall not be eligible for parole with respect to the sentence imposed under this subsection." Jackson, who had been convicted of four armed bank robberies and one armed robbery, brandished his revolver and robbed the Continental Bank of Oakbrook Terrace, Illinois, on May 30, 1986, while this statute was in force. . . .

Jackson . . . concedes that the statute permitted the imposition of any term of years but insists that it allowed only determinate numbers of years and therefore did not authorize a life sentence. When parole is forbidden, however, a judge may use either method to reach the same result. Jackson was 35 when he committed the crime. Unless there are startling advances in geriatric medicine, a long term of imprisonment (say, 60 years) and life are the same sentence; it would be silly to read the statute as authorizing one but not the other. . . .

The imposition of life in prison on Jackson was permissible. The selection of a sentence within the statutory range is essentially free of appellate review. Armed bank robbery on the day of release — following earlier armed robbery convictions back to 1973 — marked Jackson as a career criminal. Specific deterrence had failed. The court was entitled to consider general deterrence and incapacitation. Although life without possibility of parole is the upper end of the scale of sanctions (short of capital punishment), the statute reflects a judgment that career criminals who persist in possessing weapons should be dealt with most severely. . . . If this sentence is unduly harsh, the holder of the clemency power may supply a remedy. . . . Affirmed.

Posner J., concurring. I join the opinion and judgment of the court; but I think the sentence Jackson received is too harsh and I think it appropriate to point this out even though he presents no ground on which we are authorized to set aside an excessively severe sentence.

Jackson is unquestionably a dangerous and hardened criminal. He has been convicted of armed robbery four times (three were bank robberies — all of the same bank!); in each robbery he was carrying a loaded gun. I do not mean to denigrate the gravity of his offenses by pointing out that he has never inflicted a physical injury; but that fact is relevant to deciding whether the sheer enormity of his conduct warrants imprisonment for the rest of his life as a matter of retributive justice. It does not. Few murderers, traitors, or rapists are punished so severely. . . . The grounds for the sentence in this case must be sought elsewhere.

One ground, the one articulated by the district judge, is the need to prevent Jackson from committing further crimes. There is little doubt that if he were released tomorrow he would commit a bank robbery, perhaps on the same day. But it is extremely unlikely that if he were released 25 or 30 years from now (he is 35 years old) he would resume his career as a bank robber. We know that criminal careers taper off with age, although with the aging of the population and the improvements in the health of the aged the fraction of crimes committed by the elderly is rising. Crimes that involve a risk of physical injury to the criminal are especially a young man's game. In 1986 more than 62 percent of all persons arrested for robbery . . . were below the age of 25, and only 3.4 percent were 60 years old or older. . . . Bank robbery in particular, I suspect, is a young man's crime. A bank robber must be willing to confront armed guards and able to make a quick getaway. To suppose that if Jackson is fortunate enough to live on in prison into his seventies or eighties it would still be necessary to detain him lest he resume his life of crime after almost a lifetime in prison is too speculative to warrant imprisoning him until he dies of old age. . . .

The remaining possibility is that this savage sentence is proper *pour encourager les autres*. Indeed, deterrence is the surest ground for punishment, since retributive norms are so unsettled and since incapacitation may, by removing one offender from the pool of offenders, simply make a career in crime more attractive to someone else. . . . Thus, even if one were sure that Jackson would be as harmless as a mouse in the last 10, or 15, or 20 years of his life, his sentence might be justified if the example of it were likely to deter other people, similarly situated, from committing such crimes. This is possible, but speculative; it was not mentioned by the district judge.

We should ask how many 35 year olds would rob a bank if they knew that if they were caught it would mean 20 years in prison with no possibility of parole (the sentence I would have given Jackson if I had been the sentencing judge), compared to the number who would do so if it would mean life in prison. Probably very few would be deterred by the incremental sentence. Bank robbery is a crime of acquisition, not of passion; the only gains are financial — and are slight (in 1986 the average "take" from a bank robbery was $2,664). The net gains, when the expected cost of punishment is figured in, must be very small indeed. Clearance rates for bank robbery are very high; of all bank robberies investigated by the FBI during 1978 and 1979 . . . , 69 percent had been cleared by arrest by 1982. Conviction rates are high (90 percent in federal prosecutions for bank robbery) and average punishments severe (more than 13 years for federal defendants). It's a losers' game at best. Persons who would go ahead and rob a bank in the face of my hypothetical 20-year sentence are unlikely to be deterred by tightening the punishment screws still further. A civilized society locks up such people until age makes them harmless but it does not keep them in prison until they die.

NOTES AND QUESTIONS

1. In a subsequent proceeding the sentencing judge denied a motion for reduction of sentence, stating that Judge Posner's concerns had not persuaded him to reconsider. The sentencing judge mentioned, among other factors, that Jackson had persisted in denying his guilt; that his prior record, in addition to seven armed robbery convictions, included an attempt to murder his army colonel in Vietnam and an assault on a sergeant; and that the possession of firearms by this "incorrigible and hostile recidivist" created a distinct possibility that severe injury or death could result from any future criminal conduct. See United States v. Jackson, 780 F. Supp. 1508 (N.D. Ill. 1991).

2. What sentence *should* be imposed on Jackson? For what purpose?

3. *"Three strikes and you're out."* Several states have enacted or considered legislation providing that upon conviction of a felony (or *violent* felony) after two prior felony convictions, a defendant must be sentenced to life imprisonment without possibility of parole. What purpose is such a sentence intended to serve? Do the additional benefits of a life sentence in such cases (compared, for example, to a 15-year or 20-year sentence) justify the additional costs? See Michael Vitiello, Three Strikes: Can We Return to Rationality, 87 J. Crim. L & C. 395 (1997).

4. *Problem.* Consider the following presentence report adapted from 93 Cal. Rptr., Appendix at 25-26 (1970):

OFFENSE: BURGLARY SECOND

Defendant broke into a pharmacy and removed several containers of drugs from a locked cabinet. He was apprehended shortly thereafter and readily admitted the offense, and two others of a similar nature.

Prior Criminal History

1985-87	County X	Juvenile offenses	Probation
8/89	County X	Battery	5 days county jail
3/91	County X	Burglary	2 years probation
4/92	County X	Burglary	60 days county jail
1/93	County X	Sale of narcotics	Sent to California Rehabilitation Center
4/94	CRC	Released on parole	Discharged from parole in April 1997
3/99	County X	Present offense	

CASE HISTORY INFORMATION

This 29-year-old man of Latin-American laboring class ancestry was born and raised in a large urban community in Southern California, the oldest of three children. He was 12 years old when his father died, and his mother subsequently supported the family by performing domestic labor, unskilled factory work and by welfare. One sister had been institutionalized in a mental hospital, while his youngest sister, now age 24, has become a nurse.

Defendant has an exceptionally high IQ and has done very well in high school and in college which he is currently attending during the day. As a youngster, he had a series of offenses as part of a juvenile gang including petty theft and burglary, for which he was made a ward of the court. He began using marijuana at the age of 15 and later graduated to using heroin. His offenses as a young adult were related to his narcotic addiction since he was stealing to try to finance his drug habit. Finally in 1983, he was committed to the California Rehabilitation Center where he spent the ensuing 15 months in treatment. Institutional officials at CRC commented favorably about his active involvement in the treatment program and he was paroled to a job in Northern California. Significantly he managed to refrain from the use of drugs for a three-year period, which led to his successful discharge from parole in 1987. Furthermore, in the almost two years since his discharge from parole there was no record of any offenses except the present ones.

He was married at the age of 19 and one child was born to that union. The marriage was dissolved after his son was born and he assumes full responsibility for not having sufficient maturity at the time to adequately act as a husband and father. When he has not been institutionalized, he has made efforts to contribute to the support of his child.

For the past three years, he has been working nights at a semiskilled job while attending college during the daytime. He has completed three and one-half years of college in business administration and his verified academic record is excellent. He hopes to become a business executive.

Case Evaluation

This is a young adult who, despite a poor start, has striven in recent years to assume a productive role in society. His present offense is related to narcotics which he started using again approximately three months ago. He is very bright and verbal and attributes his present predicament to an exceptionally stressful situation caused by the pressures of working full time coupled with keeping up with a demanding college program. He does not have a heavy drug habit at this time since he attempted to limit his drug use in his most recent encounter. His return to the CRC program[a] is not recommended by the probation officer who prepared the court report on the grounds that he has derived all the benefits that their program has to offer. The District Attorney and arresting narcotics officer feel he is a menace to society and should be sent to prison. They note that he committed several offenses and would have committed more if he hadn't been caught.

In most states the sentencing options available in a case of this sort would include fine or probation, short-term imprisonment in a county jail (with little or no facilities for vocational training, drug treatment, or other rehabilitation), or longer term confinement in state prison (where facilities and rehabilitation programs are normally better). Also available in most jurisdictions are special drug rehabilitation programs involving a mixture of confinement, probation, and medical and psychological treatment.

Question: What sentence should be imposed in this case? For what purpose?

a. The CRC (California Rehabilitation Center) program provided for confinement in a special facility oriented toward intensive treatment of offenders with drug-related problems. Similar programs exist in many other states. — Eds.

NOTES ON THE ALLOCATION OF SENTENCING AUTHORITY

Until the 1970s, the punishment decision was entrusted almost entirely to the discretion of the trial judge. Statutory limits on sentences, the charging authority of the prosecutor, and the releasing authority of the parole board qualified the trial judge's power, but the individual judge formally controlled the penalty. That situation still prevails in the great majority of the states, but many have moved to limit the trial judge's power (1) by mandating specified punishments, (2) by establishing an administrative agency to promulgate guidelines channeling the choice of sentence in particular cases, or (3) by providing for appellate review of trial-court sentencing. See Kevin R. Reitz, The Status of Sentencing Guideline Reforms in the U.S., Overcrowded Times, December 1999, pp. 1, 8-10. Authority to determine the actual punishment has always been divided to some degree, and today the divisions are more complex and less uniform among the states than in the past. The present Notes provide a brief introduction to these developments.

1. The traditional sentencing system. The organization of sentencing authority that was found in virtually all jurisdictions before 1970 is described in Franklin Zimring, Making the Punishment Fit the Crime: A Consumer's Guide to Sentencing Reform, Hastings Center Rep. 13-14 (Dec. 1976):

> The best single phrase to describe the allocation of sentencing power in state and federal criminal justice is "multiple discretion." Putting aside the enormous power of the police to decide whether to arrest, and to select initial charges, there are four separate institutions that have the power to determine criminal sentences — the legislature, the prosecutor, the judge, and the parole board or its equivalent.
>
> The *legislature* sets the range of sentences legally authorized after conviction for a particular criminal charge. Criminal law in the United States is noted for extremely wide ranges of sentencing power, . . . with extremely high maximum penalties and very few limits on how much less than the maximum can be imposed. In practice, then, most legislatures delegate their sentencing powers to other institutions. . . .
>
> The *prosecutor* is not normally thought of as an official who has, or exercises, the power to determine punishment. In practice, however, the prosecutor is the most important institutional determinant of a criminal sentence. . . . He has the legal authority in most systems to determine the specific offense for which a person is to be prosecuted, and this ability to select a charge can also broaden or narrow the range of sentences that can be imposed upon conviction. In congested urban court systems (and elsewhere) he has the absolute power to reduce charges in exchange for guilty pleas and to recommend particular sentences to the court as part of a "plea bargain"; rarely will his recommendation for a lenient sentence be refused in an adversary system in which he is supposed to represent the punitive interests of the state.
>
> The *judge* has the power to select a sentence from the wide range made available by the legislature for any charge that produces a conviction. His powers are discretionary — within this range of legally authorized sanctions his selection cannot be appealed, and is not reviewed. . . . On occasion, the legislature will provide a mandatory minimum sentence, such as life imprisonment for first-degree murder, that reduces the judge's options once a defendant has been convicted of that particular offense. In such cases the prosecutor and judge retain the option to charge or convict a defendant for a lesser offense in order to retain their discretionary power. More often the judge has a wide range of sentencing choices and, influenced by the prosecutor's recommendation, will select either a single sentence (such as two

years) or a minimum and maximum sentence (not less than two nor more than five years) for a particular offender.

The *parole* or *correctional authority* normally has the power to modify judicial sentences to a considerable degree. When the judge pronounces a single sentence, such as two years, usually legislation authorizes release from prison to parole after a specified proportion of the sentence has been served. When the judge has provided for a minimum and maximum sentence, such as two to five years, the relative power of the correctional or parole authority is increased, because it has the responsibility to determine at what point in a prison sentence the offender is to be released. The parole board's decision is a discretionary one, traditionally made without guidelines or principles of decision.

2. Disaffection with the traditional approach. The system of broad, unstructured sentencing discretion has come under attack from diverse perspectives. Some object that the inconsistencies and uncertainties associated with discretion undermine deterrence and permit undue leniency. Others see discretion as permitting vindictively harsh punishments and invidious discrimination among offenders. A particularly influential critique of the traditional sentencing structure is that of then-Judge Marvin Frankel, Criminal Sentences: Law Without Order 5, 9-11, 17-23 (1973):

> [T]he almost wholly unchecked and sweeping powers we give to judges in the fashioning of sentences are terrifying and intolerable for a society that professes devotion to the rule of law. . . .
>
> The . . . problem of excessive judicial power reflects a congeries of causes, advertent and accidental. To look only at the most important and positive of these, the prevalent thesis of the last hundred years or so has been that the treatment of criminals must be "individualized." The Mikado's boast, we have proudly thought, was silly; the punishment in a civilized society must fit the unique criminal, not the crime. . . . The ideal of individualized justice is by no means an unmitigated evil, but it must be an ideal of justice *according to law.* This means we just reject individual distinctions — discriminations, that is — unless they can be justified by relevant tests capable of formulation and application with sufficient objectivity to ensure that the results will be more than the idiosyncratic ukases of particular officials, judges or others. . . . The judges simply are not good enough — nobody could be — to redress the fundamental absurdities of the system. . . .
>
> [S]weeping penalty statutes allow sentences to be "individualized" not so much in terms of defendants but mainly in terms of the wide spectrums of character, bias, neurosis, and daily vagary encountered among occupants of the trial bench. It is no wonder that wherever supposed professionals in the field — criminologists, penologists, probation officers, and, yes, lawyers and judges — discuss sentencing, the talk inevitably dwells upon the problem of "disparity." . . . The evidence is conclusive that judges of widely varying attitudes on sentencing, administering statutes that confer huge measures of discretion, mete out widely divergent sentences where the divergences are explainable only by the variations among the judges, not by material differences in the defendants or their crimes. . . .
>
> [T]he tragic state of disorder in our sentencing practices is not attributable to any unique endowments of sadism or bestiality among judges as a species. [Judges] may be somewhat calmer, more dispassionate, and more humane than the average of people across the board. But nobody has the experience of being sentenced by "judges in general." The particular defendant on some existential day confronts a specific judge. The occupant of the bench on that day may be punitive, patriotic, self-righteous, guilt-ridden, and more than customarily dyspeptic. The vice in our

system is that all such qualities have free rein as well as potentially fatal impact upon the defendant's finite life.

Such individual, personal powers are not evil only, or mainly, because evil people may come to hold positions of authority. The more pervasive wrong is that a regime of substantially limitless discretion is by definition arbitrary, capricious, and antithetical to the rule of law. . . .

3. The "determinate sentencing" alternative. In response to the problems just described and to public demand for harsher, more consistent punishments, many jurisdictions have replaced the traditional, discretionary systems with some form of "determinate" sentencing, in which possibilities for release on parole are reduced or eliminated and the range of sentences authorized after conviction is greatly narrowed — either by statutory categories or by guidelines that a judicial council or administrative agency promulgates. The traditional approach conferring wide discretion on the sentencing judge remains the norm in most states, but as of 1999 nine states had adopted legally enforceable guidelines to narrow the sentencing judge's discretion, and another seven states had adopted voluntary or "advisory" guidelines. See Reitz, supra, at 8. Of particular interest, sentencing in the federal courts is now governed by a guideline system that is far more detailed and restrictive than any adopted thus far in the states.

4. The federal sentencing guidelines. In 1984 Congress abolished parole for all federal criminal convictions and created a United States Sentencing Commission charged with promulgating guidelines for judges to use in federal sentencing decisions. See 28 U.S.C. §991-998. The Commission must establish sentencing categories based on specific combinations of offense and offender characteristics and identify a narrow range of authorized sentences (with no more than a 25 percent spread between minimum and maximum terms of imprisonment) for each category. See 28 U.S.C. §994(b). Judges normally must impose a sentence within the authorized range. See 18 U.S.C. §3553:

> (a) *Factors To Be Considered in Imposing a Sentence.*— The court shall impose a sentence sufficient, but not greater than necessary, to comply with the purposes set forth in paragraph (2) of this subsection. The court, in determining the particular sentence to be imposed, shall consider —
>
> (1) the nature and circumstances of the offense and the history and characteristics of the defendant;
>
> (2) the need for the sentence imposed —
>
> (A) to reflect the seriousness of the offense, to promote respect for the law, and to provide just punishment for the offense;
>
> (B) to afford adequate deterrence to criminal conduct;
>
> (C) to protect the public from further crimes of the defendant; and
>
> (D) to provide the defendant with needed educational or vocational training, medical care, or other correctional treatment in the most effective manner; . . .
>
> (4) the kinds of sentence and the sentencing range established for the applicable category of offense committed by the applicable category of defendant as set forth in the guidelines that are issued by the Sentencing Commission. . . .
>
> (b) *Application of Guidelines in Imposing a Sentence.*— The court shall impose a sentence of the kind, and within the range, referred to in subsection (a)(4) unless the court finds that there exists an aggravating or mitigating circumstance of a kind, or to a degree, not adequately taken into consideration by the Sentencing

Commission in formulating the guidelines that should result in a sentence different from that described. . . .

The guidelines promulgated by the Commission took effect in 1987. This complex set of rules for calculating federal sentences runs over 400 pages and has been amended annually. For a useful introduction, see Stephen Breyer, The Federal Sentencing Guidelines and the Key Compromises upon which They Rest, 17 Hofstra L. Rev. 1 (1988). Although the guidelines probably have reduced unwarranted disparities in punishment, at least for certain kinds of cases, they remain controversial. Prominent concerns are that the guidelines arguably: (1) create new kinds of disparity in the process of eliminating the old ones, (2) can be overly rigid and thus prevent appropriate individualization of sentences, and (3) can overly restrict the use of probation and require sentences that many critics consider too severe. The issues are explored in Kate Stith & José Cabranes, Fear of Judging: Sentencing Guidelines in the Federal Courts (1998); Reitz, supra, at 11-14; Daniel J. Freed, Federal Sentencing in the Wake of Guidelines: Unacceptable Limits on the Discretion of Sentencers, 101 Yale L.J. 1681 (1992); Stephen J. Schulhofer, Assessing the Federal Sentencing Process: The Problem Is Uniformity, Not Disparity, 29 Am. Crim. L. Rev. 833 (1992).

The next case illustrates one kind of problem that arises under the guidelines, and the complex relationship between penal theories and their implementation in actual cases.

UNITED STATES v. JOHNSON

United States Court of Appeals, 2d Circuit
964 F.2d 124 (1992)

OAKES, J. . . . In the spring of 1989, Cheryl Purvis, a payroll clerk at the Bronx V.A. Hospital, told her co-worker Cynthia Johnson and two others about a scheme Purvis had concocted to steal money by inflating paychecks. By writing pay increases for herself and others on a standard pay adjustment form . . . Purvis was able to secure inflated paychecks. Johnson and the others accepted Purvis's offer to inflate their paychecks, and shortly thereafter Johnson began offering the same to other hospital employees. In return, Purvis and Johnson received fifty percent kickbacks from the employees whose paychecks they inflated. In all, fifteen employees participated in the scheme, receiving a total of approximately $89,222.

The criminal complaint against Purvis and Johnson charged them with stealing money from the government in violation of 18 U.S.C. §641 (1988). The indictment added a charge of bribery in violation of 18 U.S.C. §201 (1988), because the defendants' conduct, while at essence a theft, insofar as it involved the acceptance of kickbacks fitted within the statutory definition of bribery. After a jury trial, the defendants were convicted on all counts. . . .

Judge Patterson calculated Johnson's sentence as follows. The base offense level for the bribery counts, under U.S.S.G. [U.S. Sentencing Guidelines] §2C1.1(a), was ten. The judge then added two levels because Johnson committed more than one bribe, id. §2C1.1(b)(1); added five levels because the total amount of the bribes exceeded $40,000, id. §§2C1.1(b)(2)(A), 2F1.1(b)(1) (F);

added four levels for Johnson's role as an organizer of the criminal activity, id. §3B1.1(a); and added two levels for obstruction of justice, id. §3C1.1. These adjustments increased the offense level by thirteen levels, from ten to twenty-three.[a]

The court then proceeded to decrease the offense level. Because Johnson's crime, though technically classifiable as a bribery, "more closely resembl[ed] theft than bribery," the court subtracted two levels. The court deducted one more level because the proceeds of the crime were divided with Purvis. Turning to Johnson's family circumstances, Judge Patterson made the following findings:

> The defendant is a single mother. . . . Her [institutionalized] daughter, age 21 is . . . the mother of a six-year-old child who currently resides with the defendant. Also residing with the defendant in Florida is her son, Lamont, and two children aged six and five, as well as her youngest child, who is five months old. The father of this child is unemployed and resides in Queens, New York. . . . There are no signs of use [of] drugs or alcohol, and she apparently has no mental or emotional health problems.

Concluding that Johnson was solely responsible for the upbringing of four young children, Judge Patterson deducted ten levels. Thus, a total downward departure of thirteen levels yielded a final offense level of ten. The court sentenced Johnson to six months of home detention, followed by three years of supervised release, and restitution of $27,973.

The government would have us hold that family circumstances, taken alone, can never justify a downward departure. . . . The government's argument relies almost entirely on a policy statement issued by the Sentencing Commission, which provides that "[f]amily ties and responsibilities . . . are not ordinarily relevant in determining whether a sentence should be outside the applicable guideline range." U.S.S.G. §5H1.6, p.s. . . .

Congress explicitly provided for sentencing departures in the Sentencing Reform Act of 1984. A district court, according to the statute, may depart from the applicable guideline range if it finds a circumstance "not adequately taken into consideration by the Sentencing Commission in formulating the guidelines." 18 U.S.C. §3553(b) (1988). Policy statements, inasmuch as they are issued by the Commission itself, give a strong indication of what the Commission has, in fact, considered. . . .

The policy statement of U.S.S.G. §5H1.6 . . . leads us to the unsurprising conclusion that the Commission took ordinary family responsibilities into account when formulating the Guidelines. The Sentencing Commission understood that many defendants shoulder responsibilities to their families, their employers, and their communities. Disruption of the defendant's life, and the concomitant diffi-

a. The guidelines specify that the authorized sentencing range (in months of imprisonment) is 6-12 months at level 10, 33-41 months at level 20, and 46-57 months at level 23. Where the guideline range is 0-6 months, a judge is permitted to grant probation; where the range is 6-12 months, the judge may grant probation only on condition that the offender serve the minimum term in home detention, community confinement (such as a halfway house or drug treatment center), or intermittent confinement (e.g., spending weekends in jail); where the guideline range is 12-18 months or higher, the entire sentence must be served in prison. See U.S.S.G. §5C1.1. — Eds.

culties for those who depend on the defendant, are inherent in the punishment of incarceration. The Commission made this clear by explaining that such disruption of the defendant's exercise of responsibility, as a general matter, should not be cause for downward departure. . . .

Extraordinary circumstances, however, are by their nature not capable of adequate consideration. They therefore may constitute proper grounds for departure. Policy statement 5H1.6 does not alter this conclusion, but simply reinforces what we would have expected in any case: . . . ordinary family circumstances do not justify departure, but *extraordinary* family circumstances may. . . .

Such extraordinary family circumstances were present in United States v. Alba, 933 F.2d 1117 (2d Cir. 1991). There, the defendant and his wife cared for their four- and eleven-year-old daughters and the defendant's disabled father and paternal grandmother. Noting the special situation of this "close-knit family whose stability depends on [the defendant's] continued presence," we let stand the sentencing court's finding that "incarceration in accordance with the Guidelines might well result in the destruction of an otherwise strong family unit" and its conclusion "that these circumstances were sufficiently extraordinary in this case to support a downward departure." . . .

To confirm that parental responsibilities can be extraordinary, we need look no further than the circumstances faced by Cynthia Johnson. She faced more than the responsibilities of an ordinary parent, more even than those of an ordinary single parent. Johnson was solely responsible for the upbringing of her three young children, including an infant, and of the young child of her institutionalized daughter. The number, age and circumstances of these children all support the finding that Johnson faced extraordinary parental responsibilities. Johnson's situation, in fact, is substantially more compelling than that of the defendant in *Alba,* whose children were ages four and eleven, and whose spouse could care for their children and elderly dependents.

The rationale for a downward departure here is not that Johnson's family circumstances decrease her culpability, but that we are reluctant to wreak extraordinary destruction on dependents who rely solely on the defendant for their upbringing. Judge Patterson made it clear that the departure was not on behalf of the defendant herself, but on behalf of her family:

> In view of the special circumstances of the defendant — I shouldn't say "defendant," I should say of the "defendant's family," which, as the court sees it, is a family in which the mother is the sole link between the children, the six-month-old child . . . and having the father in Queens who does not contribute to the support of the five- and six-year-old children, . . . a 17-year-old boy having a father who does not contribute to his support, and a six-year-old grandchild whom the mother is unable to keep because of the circumstances of her having another child, at the age of 21, and living in an institution . . . I'm going to reduce the level.

A week later, at Purvis's sentencing, the court explained the Johnson departure: "I did feel that those children being without a mother for an extended period of time was a hardship on them, not on her, hardship on them, and that was extraordinary grounds for a departure."

. . . [W]e are satisfied that Judge Patterson's departure was reasonable.

Accordingly, the judgment of the district court is affirmed.

NOTES

1. According to what theory of punishment does Johnson's family situation warrant a reduction in her sentence?

2. Johnson's co-defendant, Cheryl Purvis, was also a first offender. Judge Patterson placed her at guideline level 18 (which specifies a sentence range of 27-33 months), and he sentenced her to 27 months in prison, followed by supervised release for 2 years, and restitution of $20,183. Was Purvis a victim of sentencing "disparity"?

3. Problems. (a) Smith is a lawyer convicted of helping a client "launder" money and perpetrate a tax fraud. Based on the dollar amounts involved and other factors, Smith's guideline range is 51-63 months. Smith is currently supporting his 2 children, aged 2 and 9, and his wife, who is unable to work because of a back ailment. All of Smith's assets have been exhausted defending against the charges. If he is sent to prison, his wife and children will probably have to go on welfare. Does Smith's family situation warrant a reduction in his sentence?

(b) Jones carries a quantity of cocaine from New Jersey to New York, where she is arrested by federal agents. Based on the quantity of the drug and other factors, the guideline range is 33-41 months' imprisonment. While awaiting trial Jones gets pregnant, and when she appears before the judge for sentencing, she is due to deliver her baby in 6 months. Guideline §5H1.4 states that a defendant's physical condition is "not ordinarily relevant," but it does not refer explicitly to pregnancy. Should Jones's pregnancy affect the length of her sentence? Alternatively, should Jones be permitted to defer the start of her imprisonment until after the baby is born? Note that after the birth, if no member of Jones's family is able to care for her baby, it may be necessary to place the baby in foster care or an institution. In that event, should Jones qualify for a reduction in sentence on the basis of her family responsibilities? See United States v. Pozzy, 902 F.2d 133, 138-139 (1st Cir. 1990); Myrna C. Raeder, Gender and Sentencing: Single Moms, Battered Women and Other Sex-Based Anomalies in the Gender-Free World of the Federal Sentencing Guidelines, 20 Pepp. L. Rev. 905, 945-962 (1993).

C. WHAT TO PUNISH?

INTRODUCTORY NOTE

It is obvious that our society does not subject to criminal punishment all conduct that is antisocial or otherwise undesirable. Criminal punishment is only one of many sanctions available to induce compliance with preferred norms of conduct. A society may attempt to discourage undesired conduct by taxing it; it may provide for civil liability, including injunctive relief at the behest of a public agency or an injured party; it may establish an agency to govern such behavior through licenses, rules, and regulations; or, for, reasons practical or principled, it may leave it to be dealt with by private social pressures.

When is criminal punishment the appropriate choice? What is there about the nature of punishment that may make it unsuitable for certain kinds of conduct?

For an introduction to the problems of the reach of the criminal law, consider the use of the criminal law to deal with sexual misconduct. This area has witnessed revolutionary changes in the last generation. Criminal prohibitions long imbedded in American laws — on sex outside of marriage, unconventional sex practices, and homosexuality (though not prostitution) — have been lifted in many jurisdictions. Following the lead of the Model Penal Code, recently revised state penal codes have declined to prohibit adultery and fornication. Model Penal Code and Commentaries, Note to §213.6 at 439 (1980). Laws prohibiting adult consensual homosexuality have also changed, though more slowly. The Model Penal Code Commentary states (id. at 372-373):

> As of that date [1955], the Model Penal Code exclusion of criminal penalties for consensual sodomy was without precedent in this country.
>
> Many European nations had excepted private sexual behavior from their penal laws and Great Britain has since followed suit by enacting the recommendations of the Wolfenden Commission in 1967. In 1961, Illinois became the first American jurisdiction to adopt the Model Code position. A number of other states have taken this step in recent revisions, and . . . even though many states still punish consensual sodomy, most modern revision efforts effect a substantial reduction in the gravity of sanctions authorized for such behavior.

For a survey of state law, see Richard A. Posner & Katharine B. Silbaugh, A Guide to America's Sex Laws (1996).

New York Revised Penal Law: Section 1.05. The general purposes of the provisions of this chapter: 1. To proscribe conduct which unjustifiably and inexcusably causes or threatens substantial harm to individual or public interests.

Criminal Justice Reform Act of 1973, S. 1, 93d Cong., 1st Sess.: Section 1-1A.2. General Purposes: The purpose of this code is to establish order with justice so that the nation and its people may be secure in their persons, property, relationships, and other interests. This code aims at the articulation of the nation's fundamental system of values and its vindication through the imposition of merited punishment.

Louis B. Schwartz, The Proposed Federal Criminal Code, Comparison of S. 1 and the Recommendations of the National Commission on Reform of Federal Criminal Laws 10 (Feb. 19, 1973) (mimeo): S. 1 injects a new, false, and dangerous notion that the criminal code "aims at the articulation of the nation's fundamental system of public values" and its vindication through punishment. A criminal code necessarily falls far short of expressing the nation's morality. Many things are evil or undesirable without being at all appropriate for imprisonment: lying, overcharging for goods and services, marital infidelity, lack of charity or patriotism. Nothing has been more widely recognized in modern criminal law scholarship than the danger of creating more evil by ill-considered use of the criminal law than is caused by the target misconduct. Accordingly, the failure to put something under the ban of the penal code is not an expression of a favorable "value" of the nonpenalized behavior. It is a fatal confusion of values to see the Criminal Code as anything but a list of those most egregious misbehaviors, which, according to a broad community consensus, can be usefully dealt with by social force.

BOWERS v. HARDWICK

Supreme Court of the United States
478 U.S. 186 (1986)

JUSTICE WHITE delivered the opinion of the Court.

In August 1982, respondent was charged with violating the Georgia statute criminalizing sodomy[1] by committing that act with another adult male in the bedroom of respondent's home. After a preliminary hearing, the District Attorney decided not to present the matter to the grand jury unless further evidence developed.

Respondent then brought suit in the Federal District Court, challenging the constitutionality of the statute insofar as it criminalized consensual sodomy. He asserted that he was a practicing homosexual, that the Georgia sodomy statute, as administered by the defendants, placed him in imminent danger of arrest, and that the statute for several reasons violates the Federal Constitution. . . .

A divided panel of the Court of Appeals for the Eleventh Circuit [held] that the Georgia statute violated respondent's fundamental rights because his homosexual activity is a private and intimate association that is beyond the reach of state regulation by reason of the Ninth Amendment and the Due Process Clause of the Fourteenth Amendment. . . . We agree with the State that the Court of Appeals erred. . . .

This case does not require a judgment on whether laws against sodomy between consenting adults in general, or between homosexuals in particular, are wise or desirable. . . . The issue presented is whether the Federal Constitution confers a fundamental right upon homosexuals to engage in sodomy and hence invalidates the laws of the many states that still make such conduct illegal and have done so for a very long time. . . .

[R]espondent would have us announce, as the Court of Appeals did, a fundamental right to engage in homosexual sodomy. This we are quite unwilling to do. . . . It is true that despite the language of the Due Process Clauses of the Fifth and Fourteenth Amendments, which appears to focus only on the processes by which life, liberty, or property is taken, the cases are legion in which those Clauses have been interpreted to have substantive content, subsuming rights that to a great extent are immune from federal or state regulation or proscription. Among such cases are those recognizing rights that have little or no textual support in the constitutional language. [As examples, the Court here mentioned, among other cases, Meyer v. Nebraska, 262 U.S. 390 (1923) (dealing with child rearing and education); Loving v. Virginia, 388 U.S. 1 (1967) (right to marry); and Roe v. Wade, 410 U.S. 113 (1973) (right to abortion).] . . .

In Palko v. Connecticut, 302 U.S. 319, 325, 326 (1937), it was said that this category includes those fundamental liberties that are "implicit in the concept of ordered liberty," such that "neither liberty nor justice would exist if [they]

1. Ga. Code Ann. §16-6-2 (1984) provides, in pertinent part, as follows:

(a) A person commits the offense of sodomy when he performs or submits to any sexual act involving the sex organs of one person and the mouth or anus of another. . . .
(b) A person convicted of the offense of sodomy shall be punished by imprisonment for not less than one nor more than 20 years. . . .

were sacrificed." A different description of fundamental liberties appeared in Moore v. East Cleveland, 431 U.S. 494, 503, (1977) (opinion of Powell, J.), where they are characterized as those liberties that are "deeply rooted in this Nation's history and tradition."

It is obvious to us that neither of these formulations would extend a fundamental right to homosexuals to engage in acts of consensual sodomy. Proscriptions against that conduct have ancient roots. Sodomy was a criminal offense at common law and was forbidden by the laws of the original thirteen States when they ratified the Bill of Rights. In 1868, when the Fourteenth Amendment was ratified, all but 5 of the 37 States in the Union had criminal sodomy laws. In fact, until 1961, all 50 States outlawed sodomy, and today, 24 States and the District of Columbia continue to provide criminal penalties for sodomy performed in private and between consenting adults. Against this background, to claim that a right to engage in such conduct is "deeply rooted in this Nation's history and tradition" or "implicit in the concept of ordered liberty" is, at best, facetious. . . .

Even if the conduct at issue here is not a fundamental right, respondent asserts that there must be a rational basis for the law and that there is none in this case other than the presumed belief of a majority of the electorate in Georgia that homosexual sodomy is immoral and unacceptable. This is said to be an inadequate rationale to support the law. The law, however, is constantly based on notions of morality, and if all laws representing essentially moral choices are to be invalidated under the Due Process Clause, the courts will be very busy indeed. Even respondent makes no such claim, but insists that majority sentiments about the morality of homosexuality should be declared inadequate. We do not agree, and are unpersuaded that the sodomy laws of some 25 States should be invalidated on this basis.

Reversed.

CHIEF JUSTICE BURGER, concurring.

I join the Court's opinion, but I write separately to underscore my view that in constitutional terms there is no such thing as a fundamental right to commit homosexual sodomy.

. . . Decisions of individuals relating to homosexual conduct have been subject to state intervention throughout the history of Western civilization. Condemnation of those practices is firmly rooted in Judaeo-Christian moral and ethical standards. . . . To hold that the act of homosexual sodomy is somehow protected as a fundamental right would be to cast aside millennia of moral teaching. . . .

JUSTICE BLACKMUN, with whom JUSTICE BRENNAN, JUSTICE MARSHALL, and JUSTICE STEVENS join, dissenting.

This case is [not] about "a fundamental right to engage in homosexual sodomy," as the Court purports to declare. . . . Rather, this case is about "the most comprehensive of rights and the right most valued by civilized men," namely, "the right to be let alone." Olmstead v. United States, 277 U.S. 438, 478 (1928) (Brandeis, J., dissenting).

The statute at issue, Ga. Code Ann. §16-6-2 (1984), denies individuals the right to decide for themselves whether to engage in particular forms of private, consensual sexual activity. . . . I believe we must analyze respondent's claim in the light of the values that underlie the constitutional right to privacy. If that right means anything, it means that, before Georgia can prosecute its citizens for making choices about the most intimate aspects of their lives, it must do more than assert that the choice they have made is an "'abominable crime not fit to be named among Christians,'" Herring v. State, 119 Ga. 709, 721, 46 S.E. 876, 882 (1904).

[T]he Court's almost obsessive focus on homosexual activity is particularly hard to justify in light of the broad language Georgia has used. Unlike the Court, the Georgia Legislature has not proceeded on the assumption that homosexuals are so different from other citizens that their lives may be controlled in a way that would not be tolerated if it limited the choices of those other citizens. Rather, Georgia has provided that "[a] person commits the offense of sodomy when he performs or submits to any sexual act involving the sex organs of one person and the mouth or anus of another." The sex or status of the persons who engage in the act is irrelevant as a matter of state law. . . . Michael Hardwick's standing may rest in significant part on Georgia's apparent willingness to enforce against homosexuals a law it seems not to have any desire to enforce against heterosexuals. But his claim that §16-6-2 involves an unconstitutional intrusion into his privacy and his right of intimate association does not depend in any way on his sexual orientation. . . .

Only the most willful blindness could obscure the fact that sexual intimacy is "a sensitive, key relationship of human existence, central to family life, community welfare, and the development of human personality." The fact that individuals define themselves in a significant way through their intimate sexual relationships with others suggests, in a Nation as diverse as ours, that there may be many "right" ways of conducting those relationships, and that much of the richness of a relationship will come from the freedom an individual has to *choose* the form and nature of these intensely personal bonds. . . .

[N]either of the two general justifications for §16-6-2 that petitioner has advanced warrants dismissing respondent's challenge for failure to state a claim.

First, petitioner asserts that the acts made criminal by the statute may have serious adverse consequences for "the general public health and welfare," such as spreading communicable diseases or fostering other criminal activity. Inasmuch as this case was dismissed by the District Court on the pleadings, it is not surprising that the record before us is barren of any evidence to support petitioner's claim. In light of the state of the record, I see no justification for the Court's attempt to equate the private, consensual sexual activity at issue here with the "possession in the home of drugs, firearms, or stolen goods," to which [this Court] refused to extend its protection. None of the behavior so mentioned . . . can properly be viewed as "[v]ictimless": drugs and weapons are inherently dangerous, and for property to be "stolen," someone must have been wrongfully deprived of it. Nothing in the record before the Court provides any justification for finding the activity forbidden by §16-6-2 to be physically dangerous, either to the persons engaged in it or to others.[4]

4. Although I do not think it necessary to decide today issues that are not even remotely before us, it does seem to me that a court could find simple, analytically sound distinctions between certain private, consensual sexual conduct, on the one hand, and adultery and incest (the only two vaguely specific "sexual crimes" to which the majority points), on the other. For example, marriage, in addition to its spiritual aspects, is a civil contract that entitles the contracting parties to a variety of governmentally provided benefits. A State might define the contractual commitment necessary to become eligible for these benefits to include a commitment of fidelity and then punish individuals for breaching that contract. Moreover, a State might conclude that adultery is likely to injure

The core of petitioner's defense of §16-6-2, however, is that respondent and others who engage in the conduct prohibited by §16-6-2 interfere with Georgia's exercise of the "right of the Nation and of the States to maintain a decent society." Essentially, petitioner argues, and the Court agrees, that the fact that the acts described in §16-6-2 "for hundreds of years, if not thousands, have been uniformly condemned as immoral" is a sufficient reason to permit a State to ban them today.

I cannot agree that either the length of time a majority has held its convictions or the passions with which it defends them can withdraw legislation from this Court's scrutiny. . . .

The assertion that "traditional Judeo-Christian values proscribe" the conduct involved cannot provide an adequate justification for §16-6-2. That certain, but by no means all, religious groups condemn the behavior at issue gives the State no license to impose their judgments on the entire citizenry. The legitimacy of secular legislation depends instead on whether the State can advance some justification for its law beyond its conformity to religious doctrine. Thus, far from buttressing his case, petitioner's invocation of Leviticus, Romans, St. Thomas Aquinas, and sodomy's heretical status during the Middle Ages undermines his suggestion that §16-6-2 represents a legitimate use of secular coercive power. A State can no more punish private behavior because of religious intolerance than it can punish such behavior because of racial animus. "The Constitution cannot control such prejudices, but neither can it tolerate them. Private biases may be outside the reach of the law, but the law cannot, directly or indirectly, give them effect." Palmore v. Sidoti, 466 U.S. 429, 433 (1984). . . .

Nor can §16-6-2 be justified as a "morally neutral" exercise of Georgia's power to "protect the public environment," [Paris Adult Theatre Slaton, 413 U.S. 49, 68-69 (1973)]. [T]he mere fact that intimate behavior may be punished when it takes place in public cannot dictate how States can regulate intimate behavior that occurs in intimate places. [T]he mere knowledge that other individuals do not adhere to one's value system cannot be a legally cognizable interest, let alone an interest that can justify invading the houses, hearts, and minds of citizens who choose to live their lives differently.

NOTE

Although the majority in *Bowers* found that the federal constitution does not create a right to engage in homosexual sodomy, several state courts have ruled that their own constitutions do. See, e.g., Lawrence v. State, 2000 WL 729417 (Tex. Ct. App. 2000); Gryczan v. State, 942 P.2d 112 (Mont. 1997); Wasson v. State, 842 S.W.2d 487 (Ky. 1992). In Georgia, the supreme court has held that the state constitution gives consenting adults the right to engage in private, non-

third persons, in particular, spouses and children of persons who engage in extramarital affairs. With respect to incest, a court might well agree with respondent that the nature of familial relationships renders true consent to incestuous activity sufficiently problematical that a blanket prohibition of such activity is warranted. Notably, the Court makes no effort to explain why it has chosen to group private, consensual homosexual activity with adultery and incest rather than with private, consensual heterosexual activity by unmarried persons or, indeed, with oral or anal sex within marriage.

commercial acts of sodomy, Powell v. State, 510 S.E.2d 18 (Ga. 1998), but that commercial solicitation of sodomy remains prohibited. Howard v. State 527 S.E.2d 242 (Ga. 2000).

HOME OFFICE, SCOTTISH HOME DEPARTMENT, REPORT OF THE COMMITTEE ON HOMOSEXUAL OFFENSES AND PROSTITUTION (WOLFENDEN REPORT)

9-10, 20-21, 79-80 (1957)

48. [W]e have reviewed the existing provisions of the law in relation to homosexual behaviour between male persons. We have found that with the great majority of these provisions we are in complete agreement. We believe that it is part of the function of the law to safeguard those who need protection by reason of their youth or some mental defect, and we do not wish to see any change in the law that would weaken this protection. Men who commit offences against such persons should be treated as criminal offenders. Whatever may be the causes of their disposition or the proper treatment for it, the law must assume that the responsibility for the overt acts remains theirs, except where there are circumstances which it accepts as exempting from accountability. Offences of this kind are particularly reprehensible when the men who commit them are in positions of special responsibility or trust. We have been made aware that where a man is involved in an offence with a boy or youth the invitation to the commission of the act sometimes comes from him rather than from the man. But we believe that even when this is so that fact does not serve to exculpate the man.

49. It is also part of the function of the law to preserve public order and decency. We therefore hold that when homosexual behavior between males takes place in public it should continue to be dealt with by the criminal law. . . .

52. [W]e have reached the conclusion that legislation which covers acts [committed between adults in private] goes beyond the proper sphere of the law's concern. We do not think that it is proper for the law to concern itself with what a man does in private unless it can be shown to be so contrary to the public good that the law ought to intervene in its function as the guardian of that public good. . . .

61. . . . There remains one additional . . . argument which we believe to be decisive, namely, the importance which society and the law ought to give to individual freedom of choice and action in matters of private morality. Unless a deliberate attempt is to be made by society, acting through the agency of the law, to equate the sphere of crime with that of sin, there must remain a realm of private morality and immorality which is, in brief and crude terms, not the law's business. To say this is not to condone or encourage private immorality. On the contrary, to emphasise the personal and private nature of moral or immoral conduct is to emphasise the personal and private responsibility of the individual for his own actions, and that is a responsibility which a mature agent can properly be expected to carry for himself without the threat of punishment from the law. . . .[a]

a. Ten years after the publication of the recommendations of the Wolfenden Report, Parliament repealed criminal penalties for homosexual acts committed in private by consenting adults in England. Sexual Offenses Act, Pt. II, ch. 60 (1967). —Eds.

PATRICK DEVLIN, THE ENFORCEMENT OF MORALS

2, 4, 6-10, 13-14, 17 (1965)

What is the connection between crime and sin and to what extent, if at all, should the criminal law of England concern itself with the enforcement of morals and punish sin or immorality as such?

The statements of principle in the Wolfenden Report provide an admirable and modern starting-point for such an inquiry. . . .

I must admit that I begin with a feeling that a complete separation of crime from sin . . . would not be good for the moral law and might be disastrous for the criminal. But can this sort of feeling be justified as a matter of jurisprudence? And if it be a right feeling how should the relationship between the criminal and the moral law be stated? Is there a good theoretical basis for it, or is it just a practical working alliance, or is it a bit of both? . . .

The criminal law of England has from the very first concerned itself with moral principles. A simple way of testing this point is to consider the attitude which the criminal law adopts towards consent.

Subject to certain exceptions inherent in the nature of particular crimes, the criminal law has never permitted consent of the victim to be used as a defence. In rape, for example, consent negatives an essential element. But consent of the victim is no defence to a charge of murder. It is not a defence to any form of assault that the victim thought his punishment well deserved and submitted to it; to make a good defence the accused must prove that the law gave him the right to chastise and that he exercised it reasonably. Likewise, the victim may not forgive the aggressor and require the prosecution to desist; the right to enter a nolle prosequi belongs to the Attorney-General alone.

Now, if the law existed [solely] for the protection of the individual, there would be no reason why he should avail himself of it if he did not want it. The reason why a man may not consent to the commission of an offence against himself beforehand or forgive it afterwards is because it is an offence against society. . . .

Thus, if the criminal law were to be reformed so as to eliminate from it everything that was not designed to preserve order and decency or to protect citizens (including the protection of youth from corruption), it would overturn a fundamental principle. It would also end a number of specific crimes. Euthanasia, or the killing of another at his own request, suicide, attempted suicide and suicide pacts, dueling, abortion, incest between brother and sister, are all acts which can be done in private and without offence to others and need not involve the corruption or exploitation of others. . . .

I think it is clear that the criminal law as we know it is based upon moral principle. In a number of crimes its function is simply to enforce a moral principle and nothing else. . . .

In jurisprudence, as I have said, everything is thrown open to discussion and, in the belief that they cover the whole field, I have framed three interrogatories addressed to myself to answer:

1. Has society the right to pass judgement at all on matters of morals? Ought there, in other words, to be a public morality, or are morals always a matter for private judgment?
2. If society has the right to pass judgment, has it also the right to use the weapon of the law to enforce it?

3. If so, ought it to use that weapon in all cases or only in some; and if only in some, on what principles should it distinguish? . . .

The language used in . . . the Wolfenden Report suggest[s] the view that there ought not to be a collective judgment about immorality per se. Is this what is meant by "private morality" and "individual freedom of choice and action"? . . . In truth, the Report takes it for granted that there is in existence a public morality which condemns homosexuality and prostitution. What the Report seems to mean by private morality might perhaps be better described as private behaviour in matters of morals.

This view — that there is such a thing as public morality — can also be justified by a priori argument. What makes a society of any sort is community of ideas, not only political ideas but also ideas about the way its members should behave and govern their lives; these latter ideas are its morals. Every society has a moral structure as well as a political one: or rather, since that might suggest two independent systems, I should say that the structure of every society is made up both of politics and morals. . . .

[W]ithout shared ideas on politics, morals, and ethics no society can exist. . . . If men and women try to create a society in which there is no fundamental agreement about good and evil they will fail; if having based it on common agreement, the agreement goes, the society will disintegrate. For society is not something that is kept together physically; it is held by the invisible bonds of common thought. If the bonds were too far relaxed the members would drift apart. A common morality is part of the bondage. The bondage is part of the price of society; and mankind, which needs society, must pay its price. . . .

Society is entitled by means of its laws to protect itself from dangers, whether from within or without. Here again I think that the political parallel is legitimate. The law of treason is directed against aiding the king's enemies and against sedition from within. The justification for this is that established government is necessary for the existence of society and therefore its safety against violent overthrow must be secured. But an established morality is as necessary as good government to the welfare of society. Societies disintegrate from within more frequently than they are broken up by external pressures. There is disintegration when no common morality is observed and history shows that the loosening of moral bonds is often the first state of disintegration, so that society is justified in taking the same steps to preserve its moral code as it does to preserve its government and other essential institutions. The suppression of vice is as much the law's business as the suppression of subversive activities; it is no more possible to define a sphere of private morality than it is to define one of private subversive activity. . . .

Nothing should be punished by the law that does not lie beyond the limits of tolerance. It is not nearly enough to say that a majority dislike a practice; there must be a real feeling of reprobation. Those who are dissatisfied with the present law on homosexuality often say that the opponents of reform are swayed simply by disgust. If that were so it would be wrong, but I do not think one can ignore disgust if it is deeply felt and not manufactured. Its presence is a good indication that the bounds of toleration are being reached. Not everything is to be tolerated. No society can do without tolerance, indignation, and disgust; they are the forces behind the moral law, and indeed it can be argued that if they or something like them are not present the feelings of society cannot be weighty enough to deprive the individual of freedom of choice. . . . Every moral judgment, unless it claims a divine source, is simply a feeling that no right-minded man could behave in any other way without admitting that he was doing wrong. . . . There is, for example, a general abhorrence of homosexuality. We should ask ourselves in the first instance whether looking at it calmly and dispassionately, we regard it as a vice so abominable that its mere presence is an offence. If that is the genuine feeling of the society in which we live, I do not see how society can be denied the right to eradicate it. . . .

NOTES

1. In the course of his argument, Lord Devlin observes (at 176) that if the law were to be reformed along the lines of the Wolfenden Report "it would overturn a fundamental principle" and "would also end a number of specific crimes," including "euthanasia, or the killing of another at his request, suicide, attempted suicide and suicide pacts, dueling, abortion, incest between brother and sister." In the United States, while the Supreme Court has declined to hold sodomy laws unconstitutional (Bowers v. Hardwick, supra), homosexual practices are no longer a crime in many states. Moreover, even where they are still criminal, enforcement practices have informally decriminalized them. And, indeed, some of the consequences Lord Devlin predicted would follow a decriminalization of homosexual practices have occurred in the years since his lecture. A more accepting attitude to suicide has emerged: Attempted suicide has long ceased to be criminal in virtually all jurisdictions, and laws against helping another to commit suicide, while still on the books of half the states, have been increasingly subject to constitutional attack. (These issues are explored infra pages 832-842.) In addition, abortion is now constitutionally protected in the United States. Roe v. Wade, 410 U.S. 113 (1973). Are these developments relevant to Lord Devlin's thesis? Do they strengthen it or weaken it?

2. Consent to serious physical assault is uniformly held to constitute no defense. See Regina v. Brown, [1993] 2 All E.R. 75, declining to make an exception for voluntary sadomasochistic wounding, on the ground that consent is a defense to assault only in a restricted class of cases, such as necessary surgery and regulated sports. See Law Commission Consultation Paper No. 139, Consent in the Criminal Law (H.M.S.O. 1995). The same is true in the United States. See, e.g., People v. Samuels, 250 Cal. App. 2d 501 (Ct. App. 1967). A comment on this case in 81 Harv. L. Rev. 1339, 1340 (1968), observes:

> Surgeons who perform an operation at the request of a patient as well as sports participants who injure opponents in the course of competition appear to be in no danger of conviction. On the other hand, assaults involving aberrant behavior or conduct with no apparent social utility are often held to be criminal without regard to the consent of the victim if the force used has as its probable result bodily injury.

Question: Is the distinction between boxing and consensual sadomasochistic beatings a tenable one?

3. Devlin argued that the function of disallowing victim consent as a defense is "to enforce a moral principle and nothing else"— the moral principle being the sanctity of human life and physical integrity of the person. Compare H. L. A. Hart, Law, Liberty, and Morality 31 (1963), stating (id. at 31) that the

> rules excluding the victim's consent as a defense to charges of murder or assault may perfectly well be explained as a piece of paternalism, designed to protect individuals against themselves. Mill no doubt might have protested against a paternalistic policy of using the law to protect even a consenting victim from bodily harm nearly as much as he protested against laws used merely to enforce positive morality; but this does not mean that these two policies are identical.

To what extent can the distinctions that courts have made as to when to recognize consent as a defense (discussed in the preceding note) be explained on grounds of paternalism rather than legal moralism? Is it physical injury to persons, even consenting persons, that the courts are protecting against or physical harm in the course of immoral behavior?[31]

4. Lord Devlin argues that criminal prohibitions express a social consensus on moral standards. But often what law expresses is not consensus but rather the symbolic interim victory of one set of contending forces over another. See Joseph Gusfield, On Legislating Morals: The Symbolic Process of Designating Deviancy, 56 Cal. L. Rev. 54, 58-59 (1968):

> Affirmation through law and governmental acts expresses the public worth of one subculture's norms relative to those of others, demonstrating which cultures have legitimacy and public domination. Accordingly it enhances the social status of groups carrying the affirmed culture and degrades groups carrying that which is condemned as deviant. . . . My analysis of the American temperance movement has shown how the issue of drinking and abstinence became a politically significant focus for the conflicts between Protestant and Catholic, rural and urban, native and immigrant, middle class and lower class in American society, as an abstinent Protestant middle class attempted to control the public affirmation of morality in drinking. Victory or defeat thus symbolized the status and power of the opposing cultures. . . .

5. Professor Joel Feinberg discusses the proper limits of the criminal sanction in a multi-volumed treatise entitled The Moral Limits of the Criminal Law. Volume 4, Harmless Wrongdoing (1988), deals most directly with the issue of legal enforcement of purely moral standards.

6. In Bernard E. Harcourt, The Collapse of the Harm Principle, 90 J. Crim. L. & Cr. 109 (1999), the author argues that the debate over punishing in the absence of harm has become inconsequential because of the variety of harms discovered in so-called morals offenses. He concludes (192-193):

> During the past two decades, the proponents of regulation and prohibition of a wide range of human activities — activities that have traditionally been associated with moral offense — have turned to the harm argument. Catharine MacKinnon has focused on the multiple harms to women and women's sexuality caused by pornography. The broken windows theory of crime prevention has emphasized how

31. For further discussion, largely critical of Devlin's thesis, see Hart Social Solidarity and the Enforcement of Morality, 35 U. Chi. L. Rev. 1 (1967); D. Don Welch, Legitimate Government Purposes and State Enforcement of Morality, 1993 Univ. Ill. L. Rev. 67; Ronald Dworkin, Lord Devlin and the Enforcement of Morals, 75 Yale L.J. 986 (1966). For recent defenses of his thesis, see Gerald Dworkin, Devlin Was Right: Law and the Enforcement of Morality, 40 Wm. & Mary L. Rev. 909 (1999); Jeffrie Murphy, Moral Reasons and the Limitation of Liberty, 40 Wm. & Mary L. Rev. 947 (1999).

minor crimes, like prostitution and loitering, cause major crimes, neighborhood decline, and urban decay. The harm associated with the spread of AIDS has been used to justify increased regulation of homosexual and heterosexual conduct. The new temperance movement in Chicago and the quality-of-life initiative in New York City have focused on the harmful effects of liquor establishments and public drunks on neighborhoods and property values. The debate on drugs has focused on the harms caused by drug use and the harms caused by the war on drugs. . . .

This shift has significantly changed the structure of the debate over the legal enforcement of morality. The original pairing of the harm and legal moralist arguments in the nineteenth century offered two competing ways to resolve a dispute. Legal moralists could argue that the immorality of the offense was sufficient to enforce a prohibition, and the proponents of the harm principle could argue that the lack of harm precluded legal enforcement. . . . Today the debate is characterized by a cacophony of competing harm arguments without any way to resolve them. There is no longer an argument within the structure of the debate to resolve the competing claims of harm. The original harm principle was never equipped to determine the relative importance of harms. . . .

The collapse of the harm principle may ultimately be beneficial. It may help us realize that there is probably harm in most human activities and, in most cases, on both sides of the equation — on the side of the persons harmed by the purported moral offense, but also on the side of the actor whose conduct is restricted by the legal enforcement of morality.

Sanford H. Kadish, The Crisis of Overcriminalization, 374 The Annals 157 (1967): My objective is to call attention to matters of the hardest concreteness and practicality, which should be of as much concern . . . to a Devlin as to the staunchest libertarian; namely, the adverse consequences to effective law enforcement of attempting to achieve conformity with private moral standards through use of the criminal law.

The classic instance of the use of the criminal law purely to enforce a moral code is the laws prohibiting extra-marital and abnormal sexual intercourse between a man and a woman. [It is conceded] that there is no effort to enforce these laws. The traditional function of the criminal law, therefore — to curtail socially threatening behavior through the threat of punishment and the incapacitation and rehabilitation of offenders — is quite beside the point. Thurman Arnold surely had it right when he observed that these laws "are unenforced because we want to continue our conduct, and unrepealed because we want to preserve our morals."

But law enforcement pays a price for using the criminal law in this way. First, the moral message communicated by the law is contradicted by the total absence of enforcement; for while the public sees the conduct condemned in words, it also sees in the dramatic absence of prosecutions that it is not condemned in deed. Moral adjurations vulnerable to a charge of hypocrisy are self-defeating no less in law than elsewhere. Second, the spectacle of nullification of the legislature's solemn commands is an unhealthy influence on law enforcement generally. It tends to breed a cynicism and an indifference to the criminal-law processes which augment tendencies toward disrespect for those who make and enforce the law, a disrespect which is already widely in evidence. . . .

Finally, these laws invite discriminatory enforcement against persons selected for prosecution on grounds unrelated to the evil against which these laws are purportedly addressed. . . .

The criminalization of consensual adult homosexuality represents another attempt to legislate private morality. . . . One major reason for the ineffectiveness of these laws is that the private and consensual nature of the conduct precludes . . . any substantial deterrent efficacy. . . . There are no complainants, and only the indiscreet have reasons for fear. Another reason is the irrelevance of the threat of punishment. Homosexuality involves not so much a choice to act wickedly as the seeking of normal sexual fulfillment in [ways] preferred by the individual for reasons deeply rooted in his development. . . .

On the other hand, the use of the criminal law has been attended by grave consequences. . . . To obtain evidence, police are obliged to resort to behavior which tends to degrade and demean both themselves personally and law enforcement as an institution. [No] one can lightly accept a criminal law which requires for its enforcement that officers of the law sit concealed in ceilings, their eyes fixed to "peepholes," searching for criminal sexuality in the lavatories below, or that they loiter suggestively around public toilets or in corridors hopefully awaiting a sexual advance. Such conduct corrupts both citizenry and police and reduces the moral authority of the criminal law, especially among those liable to be treated in an arbitrary fashion. The complaint of the critical that the police have more important things to do with their time is amply attested by the several volumes of the National Crime Commission's reports.

The offense of prostitution creates similar problems. Although there are social harms beyond private immorality in commercialized sex — spread of venereal disease, exploitation of the young, and the affront of public solicitation, for example — the blunt use of the criminal prohibition has proven ineffective and costly. Prostitution has perdured in all civilizations; indeed, few institutions have proven as hardy. The inevitable conditions of social life unfailingly produce the supply to meet the ever-present demand. . . . The costs, on the other hand, . . . are similar to those entailed in enforcing the homosexual laws — diversion of police resources; encouragement of use of illegal means of police control (which, in the case of prostitution, take the form of knowingly unlawful harassment arrests to remove suspected prostitutes from the streets; and various entrapment devices, usually the only means of obtaining convictions); degradation of the image of law enforcement; discriminatory enforcement against the poor; and official corruption.

To the extent that spread of venereal disease, corruption of the young, and public affront are the objects of prostitution controls, it would require little ingenuity to devise modes of social control short of the blanket criminalization of prostitution which would at the same time prove more effective and less costly for law enforcement. Apparently, the driving force behind prostitution laws is principally the conviction that prostitution is immoral. Only the judgment that the use of the criminal law for verbal vindication of our morals is more important than its use to protect life and property can support the preservation of these laws as they are. . . .

Laws against gambling and narcotics present serious problems for law enforcement. Despite arrests, prosecutions and convictions, and increasingly severe penalties, the conduct seems only to flourish. The irrepressible demand for gambling and drugs, like the demand for alcohol during Prohibition days, survives the condemnation of the criminal law. Whether or not the criminal restriction operates paradoxically, as some have thought, to make the conduct more attractive, it is clear that the prohibitions have not substantially eliminated the demand.

Nor have the laws and enforcement efforts suppressed sources of supply. No one with an urge to gamble in any fair-sized city of this country has far to go to place an illegal bet. And in the case of narcotics, illicit suppliers enter the market to seek the profits made available by . . . the criminal law's reduction of legitimate sources of supply, while "pusher"-addicts distribute narcotics as a means of fulfilling their own needs. Risk of conviction, even of long terms of imprisonment, appears to have little effect. Partly, this is because the immediate and compelling need of the "pusher"-addict for narcotics precludes any real attention to the distant prospect of conviction and imprisonment. For large-scale suppliers, who may not be addicts, the very process of criminalization and punishment serves to raise the stakes — while the risk becomes greater, so do the prospects of reward. . . .

Our indiscriminate policy of using the criminal law against selling what people insist on buying has spawned large-scale, organized systems, often of national scope, comprising an integration of the stages of production and distribution of the illicit product on a continuous and thoroughly businesslike basis. Not only are these organizations especially difficult for law enforcement to deal with; they have the unpleasant quality of producing other crimes as well. . . . To enhance their effectiveness, these organized systems engage in satellite forms of crime, of which bribery and corruption of local government are the most far-reaching in their consequences. Hence the irony that, in some measure, crime is encouraged and successful modes of criminality are produced by the criminal law itself. . . .

There is, finally, a cost of inestimable importance, . . . the substantial diversion of police, prosecutorial, and judicial time, personnel, and resources. At a time when the volume of crime is steadily increasing [and] the burden on law-enforcement agencies is becoming more and more onerous, . . . releasing enforcement resources from the obligation to enforce the vice laws must be taken seriously. Indeed, in view of the minimal effectiveness of enforcement measures in dealing with vice crimes and the tangible costs and disadvantages of that effort, the case for this rediversion of resources to more profitable purposes becomes commanding. It seems fair to say that in few areas of the criminal law have we paid so much for so little.

NOTES ON OTHER PROBLEMS OF CRIMINALIZATION

The materials just presented suggest the difficulty of deciding whether certain conduct should be made criminal. The minimum lesson they teach is that the undesirability of certain conduct, even in the eyes of most people, is not a sufficient reason to criminalize it. What kinds of harm should suffice to justify criminalization? Other important problems of drawing the line between criminal and non-criminal conduct include the following:

1. Suicide. Statutes making suicide (or attempted suicide) criminal have disappeared. Indeed, there is increasing authority that it is unconstitutional to inflict life-saving treatment on a person who prefers to die rather than receive the treatment. See Cruzan v. Director, Missouri Department of Health, 497 U.S. 261 (1990). But Model Penal Code §210.5 and about half the states prohibit assisting another to commit suicide. Can this legislation be defended? Are the concerns that arise where one person helps another to commit suicide different from those involved where a physician aborts treatment at the request of the patient? Is the threat of a criminal sanction an appropriate response to such concerns? These issues are explored in connection with the issue of justification, page 832 infra.

2. *Maternal fetal abuse.* In December 1988, Jennifer Johnson was hospitalized after overdosing on crack cocaine. She was pregnant at the time and admitted using cocaine and marijuana throughout her pregnancy. In January she informed her doctor that she had used cocaine that morning while she was in labor. She was arrested and convicted of delivering cocaine to her daughter during the 60 to 90 seconds after the daughter's birth, before the umbilical cord was detached. Her conviction was overturned by the Florida Supreme Court, which held that the legislature had not intended "delivery" to include drugs passed through the umbilical cord. Johnson v. State, 602 S. 2d 1288 (Fla. 1992). On similar facts, the South Carolina Supreme Court upheld the child-abuse conviction (and eight-year prison sentence) imposed on a mother for ingesting crack cocaine during the third trimester of her pregnancy. The court ruled that a viable fetus is a "child" within the meaning of the South Carolina child-abuse statute. Whitner v. State, 492 S.E.2d 777 (S.C. 1997).[32]

The woman in such a case already commits a crime in ingesting the drug. But should we make it an additional crime with further penalties where the woman is pregnant or the fetus is born damaged or stillborn? Of course, the harm the drug inflicts on infants is clear. But is the criminal sanction a good way to address this problem? Will the threat of additional penalties add to the deterrent threat of the drug laws already in existence? Can we fairly criminalize a pregnant woman ingesting illegal drugs without also criminalizing other forms of fetal neglect, like excessive consumption of alcohol, aspirin or caffeine, or inadequate diet or improper activities? Does the focus on abuse of certain drugs have an unfairly disparate impact on the poor? Would criminalization discourage drug-addicted women from seeking prenatal care? See Dorothy E. Roberts, Punishing Drug Addicts Who Have Babies: Women of Color, Equality, and the Right of Privacy, 104 Harv. L. Rev. 1419 (1991); Lynn M. Paltrow, Pregnant Drug Users, Fetal Persons, and the Threat to *Roe v. Wade,* 62 Albany L. Rev. 999 (1999).

3. *Products Liability.* Should the criminal law enforce standards of products liability, or should issues of product safety be left to the tort law? Consider, for example, recent revelations concerning certain Firestone tires and the Ford Explorer sport utility vehicle on which they were commonly installed. Firestone acknowledged that the tires were seriously defective. Moreover, news reports alleged: (1) that the defects, either alone or in conjunction with alleged design defects in the Ford Explorer, caused roll-over accidents in which dozens of drivers and passengers were killed; and (2) that Firestone executives were aware of the tire defects (and their role in causing the roll-overs) years before the problem was revealed to Ford or to the general public.[33]

Should Firestone and/or its responsible executives be liable for criminally

32. To date, the South Carolina approach appears to be unique; other state courts have ruled, in a variety of settings, that an expectant mother cannot be prosecuted for causing death or injury to her fetus. E.g., State v. Deborah Z., 596 N.W.2d 490, 494 n.5 (Wis. App. 1999); State v. Ashley, 701 So. 2d 338 (Fla. 1997) (quashing charges against teenager who shot herself in stomach in successful attempt to kill her fetus); cf. Whitner, supra at 781-782 (collecting cases).

33. See, e.g., N.Y. Times, Sept. 20, 2000, p. A1.

negligent homicide in connection with the resulting deaths? If homicide convictions cannot be sustained, should some other statute impose criminal liability for marketing a defective product under such circumstances? Responding to the Ford-Firestone situation, one bill, introduced by Senator John McCain, would make it a federal crime punishable by up to 10 years' imprisonment "knowingly and willfully to introduce a motor vehicle or motor vehicle equipment into interstate commerce with a safety-related defect" that harms or kills someone.[34] Is the McCain proposal sound?

Consider first the argument in favor of the criminal sanction: Consumers have a right to be free from hazardous products. This right is not adequately protected by the tort law, which allows manufacturers to make a defective product if paying off the victims is cheaper than fixing the problem. Such transactions are improper because we can put no price on human safety; society must express that judgment by punishing corporations that violate their basic duty of producing safe products. One commentator concludes that "[a]bsent potential criminal responsiblity for marketing a defective product, the value of human life is reduced to mere cost analysis."[35] An economist notes, moreover, that tort compensation can be inadequate because the injured victim (who may not be the consumer who purchased the product) is *forced* to forego his entitlement to bodily safety and has no opportunity to negotiate the price at which the "sale" of this entitlement will occur. From this perspective, a rule allowing the manufacturer to impose a lower level of safety on potential accident victims (in return for compensating the victims) is no more "efficient" than a rule allowing a thief to forcibly transfer property to himself, subject only to a civil obligation to pay fair compensation.[36]

Compare the arguments against criminal liability: Any fine levied by statute would be far smaller than the potential tort liability for each accident. Therefore, fear of monetary penalties would not add a significant deterrent. The deterrent effect would therefore rest on the stigma involved. That stigma will unfairly fall on all persons associated with the corporation, and furthermore, a judge cannot vary the degree of stigma based on the culpability or deterrability of the offense. Stigma is therefore not likely to be an effective tool. Furthermore, the complicated issues involved in such prosecutions guarantee trials that last for months and cost millions of dollars, resources that might be better used combatting other crimes. Finally, there is a more basic problem: Consumers do not want safety at any cost. They may prefer not to pay for the extra safety.[37]

For exploration of these issues, see F. Cullen, Corporate Crime Under Attack: The Ford Pinto Case and Beyond (1987); Kathleen Brickey, Death in the Workplace: Corporate Liability for Criminal Homicide, 2 Notre Dame J. L. Ethics & Pub. Pol. 753 (1987).

34. See Dick Thornburgh, Sue but Don't Prosecute, N.Y. Times, Sept. 20, 2000.

35. Note, Corporate Homicide: A New Assault on Corporate Decision-Making, 54 Notre Dame Law. 911, 923-924 (1979).

36. Phillip Cook, The Use of Criminal Sanctions to Regulate Product Safety: Comment on Wheeler, 13 J. Legal Stud. 619 (1984).

37. The arguments against criminal liability in this context are developed in Dick Thornburgh, Sue but Don't Prosecute, N.Y. Times, Sept. 20, 2000; Malcolm E. Wheeler, The Use of Criminal Statutes to Regulate Product Safety, 13 J. Legal Stud. 593 (1984).

CHAPTER 3

DEFINING CRIMINAL CONDUCT — THE ELEMENTS OF JUST PUNISHMENT

A. INTRODUCTION

The material in this section is informed by the view that three principles limit the distribution of punishment: culpability, proportionality, and legality. These principles correspond to three of the general purposes stated in §1.02(1) of the Model Penal Code governing the definition of offenses: "to safeguard conduct that is without fault from condemnation as criminal" (culpability), "to give fair warning of the nature of the conduct declared to constitute an offense" (legality), and "to differentiate on reasonable grounds between serious and minor offenses" (proportionality).

How faithful is the system of justice in the United States to the three principles identified here? When departures from them occur, what are the circumstances that are said to justify them and are they adequate?

B. CULPABILITY

1. *Actus Reus — Culpable Conduct*

a. The Requirement of Overt and Voluntary Conduct

MARTIN v. STATE

Alabama Court of Appeals
31 Ala. App. 334, 17 So. 2d 427 (1944)

SIMPSON, J. Appellant was convicted of being drunk on a public highway, and appeals. Officers of the law arrested him at his home and took him onto the highway, where he allegedly committed the proscribed acts, viz., manifested a drunken condition by using loud and profane language.

The pertinent provisions of our statute are: "Any person who, while intoxicated or drunk, appears in any public place where one or more persons are present, . . . and manifests a drunken condition by boisterous or indecent conduct, or loud and profane discourse, shall, on conviction, be fined," etc. Code 1940, Title 14, Section 120.

Under the plain terms of this statute, a voluntary appearance is presupposed. The rule has been declared, and we think it sound, that an accusation of drunkenness in a designated public place cannot be established by proof that the accused, while in an intoxicated condition, was involuntarily and forcibly carried to that place by the arresting officer. . . .

Conviction of appellant was contrary to this announced principle and, in our view, erroneous. . . .

Reversed and rendered.

NOTES

1. What was the basis for the decision in the *Martin* case? Did it rest on the language of the statute, or was some more basic principle at work? The court seemed to say it was the former: "Under the plain terms of the statute, a voluntary appearance is presupposed." We can test that conclusion by supposing a statute without the requirement that the person *appear.* For example: "Any person who, while drunk, engages in boisterous or indecent conduct, or loud and profane discourse in a public place where one or more persons are present is guilty of an offense." Would it be appropriate to convict Martin under such a statute? After all, however he got into the public place, he voluntarily committed the prohibited actions while there.

On the other hand, suppose all the statute required was that the person be found drunk in a public place. Here too, the language of the statute would on its face support a conviction. But if Martin had done nothing beyond being in the public place to which the police brought him, would his conviction be acceptable? Would it be just?

2. In considering the foregoing questions compare the following case with Model Penal Code, §2.01(1).

Winzar v. Chief Constable of Kent, The Times, March 28, 1983, at 20. The Queen's Bench Divisional Court upheld a conviction of defendant for having been found drunk on the highway in contravention of the Licensing Act of 1872. He had been taken to a hospital in the area, but then asked to leave when the hospital doctor determined that he was drunk. The police were called later when he was noticed slumped on a seat in the hospital corridor. The Times report of the decision of Lord Justice Goff continues:

> The police arrived and placed the appellant in a police car stationed on the hospital forecourt in Westcliff Road, whereupon he was taken to Ramsgate police station and charged with being found drunk in the highway called Westcliff Road. It was submitted for the appellant that his momentary, and involuntary presence on the highway provided him a defence to the charge. [But] it was enough to show that the appellant had been present in the highway, was drunk and was perceived as such. The words "found drunk" [in the statute] meant "perceived to be drunk." The fact that his presence there was not of his own volition and was momentary made no difference. . . .

Model Penal Code, Section 2.01(1): A person is not guilty of an offense unless his liability is based on conduct which includes a voluntary act or the omission to perform an act of which he is physically capable.

If the Model Penal Code were the law, would it be possible to convict Winzar? How about Martin, if the statute had not been construed to require a voluntary appearance? In such a case would the Model Penal Code have required a reversal anyway, or would the case be distinguishable from the *Winzar* case?

3. The implication in *Martin* is that after arresting him the police officers *physically* "took him onto the highway." Suppose instead they had instructed him to accompany them out onto the highway and that he did so. Would this also be a case where Martin did not act, or a case where Martin merely had a very difficult choice to make? Would the defense available in the *Martin* case still be available to him? If not, would he have any other defense? See the section on duress, page 845 infra.

PEOPLE v. NEWTON

California District Court of Appeal
8 Cal. App. 3d 359, 87 Cal. Rptr. 394 (1970)

RATTIGAN, J. Huey P. Newton appeals from a judgment convicting him of voluntary manslaughter.

[Newton was charged with the murder of John Frey, a police officer who died of bullet wounds received in a struggle with defendant. A jury found him guilty of voluntary manslaughter.

[Frey stopped a car driven by Newton and ordered him out of the car, and an altercation ensued. From the testimony of the prosecution's witnesses, it appeared that Newton had drawn a gun, and, in the struggle for its possession, the gun went off and wounded Heanes, another police officer. The struggle continued, and Heanes fired a shot at Newton's midsection. At some point, Newton wrested the gun away and fired several fatal shots point-blank at Frey. He then ran away. Shortly afterward, Newton appeared at a hospital emergency room, seeking treatment for a bullet wound in the abdomen.

[Newton testified that he had carried no gun. According to his account, the struggle began when Frey struck him for protesting his arrest. As he stumbled backwards, Frey drew a revolver. At this point, he felt a "sensation like . . . boiling hot soup had been spilled on my stomach," and heard an "explosion," then a "volley of shots." He remembered "crawling . . . a moving sensation," but nothing else until he found himself at the entrance of Kaiser Hospital with no knowledge of how he arrived there. He expressly testified that he was "unconscious or semiconscious" during this interval, that he was "still only semiconscious" at the hospital entrance, and that — after recalling some events at Kaiser Hospital — he later "regained consciousness" at another hospital.]

The defense called Bernard Diamond, M.D., who testified that defendant's recollections were "compatible" with the gunshot wound he had received; and that

> [a] gunshot wound which penetrates in a body cavity, the abdominal cavity or the thoracic cavity is very likely to produce a profound reflex shock reaction, that is

quite different than a gunshot wound which penetrates only skin and muscle and it is not at all uncommon for a person shot in the abdomen to lose consciousness and go into this reflex shock condition for short periods of time up to half an hour or so.

Defendant asserts prejudicial error in the trial court's failure to instruct the jury on the subject of *unconsciousness* as a defense to a charge of criminal homicide. . . .

Although the evidence of the fatal affray is both conflicting and confused as to who shot whom and when, some of it supported the inference that defendant had been shot in the abdomen before he fired any shots himself. Given this sequence, defendant's testimony of his sensations when shot — supplemented to a degree, as it was, by Dr. Diamond's opinion based upon the nature of the abdominal wound — supported the further inference that defendant was in a state of unconsciousness when Officer Frey was shot.

Where not self-induced, as by voluntary intoxication or the equivalent (of which there is no evidence here . . .), unconsciousness is a complete defense to a charge of criminal homicide. (Pen. Code, §26, subd. 5; . . .) "Unconsciousness," as the term is used in the rule just cited, need not reach the physical dimensions commonly associated with the term (coma, inertia, incapability of locomotion or manual action, and so on); it can exist — and the above-stated rule can apply — where the subject physically acts in fact but is not, at the time, conscious of acting. The statute underlying the rule makes this clear,[11] as does one of the unconsciousness instructions originally requested by defendant.[12] Thus, the rule has been invoked in many cases where the actor fired multiple gunshots while inferably in a state of such "unconsciousness" . . . including some in which the only evidence of "unconsciousness" was the actor's own testimony that he did not recall the shooting. . . .

Where evidence of involuntary unconsciousness has been produced in a homicide prosecution, the refusal of a requested instruction on the subject, and its effect as a complete defense if found to have existed, is prejudicial error. . . .

NOTES AND QUESTIONS

1. The Model Penal Code approach. As we just saw, the Model Penal Code §2.01(1) excludes liability in the absence of a voluntary act, but does the Code define what voluntary action is? How would the *Newton* case be decided under the Code?

The theory behind excluding liability in the absence of a voluntary action is explained as follows (Model Penal Code and Commentaries, Comment to §2.01 at 214-215 (1985)):

> That penal sanctions cannot be employed with justice unless these requirements are satisfied seems wholly clear. It is fundamental that a civilized society does not

11. Penal Code section 26 provides in pertinent part that "All persons are capable of committing crimes except those belonging to the following classes: . . . Five — Persons who *committed the act charged without being conscious thereof.*" (Italics added.)

12. CALJIC 71-C, which read in pertinent part as follows:
"Where a person *commits an act without being conscious thereof,* such act is not criminal even though, if committed by a person who was conscious, it would be a crime. . . ." (Italics added.)

punish for thoughts alone. Beyond this, the law cannot hope to deter involuntary movement or to stimulate action that cannot physically be performed; the sense of personal security would be undermined in a society where such movement or inactivity could lead to formal social condemnation of the sort that a conviction necessarily entails. People whose involuntary movements threaten harm to others may present a public health or safety problem, calling for therapy or even for custodial commitment; they do not present a problem of correction.

2. *Distinguishing between voluntary and involuntary acts.* What does it mean to say that an act is involuntary, in situations other than the paradigmatic ones in which a person physically forces the movements of another or in which one's body is in the grip of a spasm or reflex? In Bratty v. Attorney-General [1963] A.C. 386, 409-410 (H.L. 1961), Lord Denning stated as follows:

> No act is punishable if it is done involuntarily: and an involuntary act in this context — some people nowadays prefer to speak of it as "automatism" — means an act which is done by the muscles without any control by the mind such as a spasm, a reflex action or a convulsion; or an act done by a person who is not conscious of what he is doing such as an act done whilst suffering from concussion or whilst sleep-walking. . . . The term "involuntary act" is, however, capable of wider connotations: and to prevent confusion it is to be observed that in the criminal law an act is not to be regarded as an involuntary act simply because the doer does not remember it. . . . Nor is an act to be regarded as an involuntary act simply because the doer could not control his impulse to do it. When a man is charged with murder, and it appears that he knew what he was doing, but he could not resist it, then his assertion "I couldn't help myself" is no defence in itself. . . . Nor is an act to be regarded as an involuntary act simply because it is unintentional or its consequences are unforeseen. When a man is charged with dangerous driving, it is no defence for him to say, however truly, "I did not mean to drive dangerously."

See also J. F. Stephen, 2 A History of the Criminal Law of England 102 (1883): "A criminal walking to execution is under compulsion if any man can be said to be so, but his motions are just as much voluntary as if he [were] going to leave his place of confinement and regain his liberty. He walks to his death because he prefers it to be being carried."

Consider the following problems.

(a) *Habit.* The Model Penal Code expressly declares that a habitual action done without thought is to be treated as a voluntary action. Why should this be so? Consider, for example, a person who, immediately after announcing to her husband that she plans to drive downtown before going to her office, gets into her car and starts driving her habitual route to the office instead of heading downtown. Or consider a person who continues to say "You know" before every other sentence, despite having firmly resolved never again to use that abominable locution. Why should these habits be treated as voluntary acts?

(b) *Possession.* Suppose a smuggler surreptitiously places a packet of heroin into the baggage of a respectable-looking traveler, in the expectation that the latter will not be searched and that he, the smuggler, will later retrieve the drugs through some ruse. Suppose further that the respectable traveler is searched, the drugs are discovered, and she is charged with illegal possession. Model Penal Code §2.01(4) provides that possession is an act only if the person is aware she has the thing she is charged with possessing. The majority of courts also treat possession as requiring knowledge, even where the statute prohibiting possession is silent on the issue of scienter. See United States v. Anderson, 885 F.2d 1248 (5th Cir. 1989); Dawkins v. State, 313 Md. 638, 547 A.2d 1041 (1988). Some courts hold, particularly where the penalty is not severe, that it is sufficient that the defendant should have known. See United States v. Garrett, 984 F.2d 1402 (5th Cir. 1993), where the court observed:

> Like many people trying to catch a plane around the holidays, [defendant] was in a hurry. Unlike most, she forgot that she had a gun in her purse, or so she says. The principal question . . . is whether the federal statute that criminalizes this conduct requires any degree of mens rea as an element of the offense. We hold that a "should have known" standard applies.

In a few jurisdictions, however, drug possession statutes are interpreted as dispensing with any need to show that the defendant knew or should have known of the presence of the drugs. See, e.g., State v. Cleppe, 96 Wash. 2d 393, 635 P.2d 435 (1981).

(c) Hypnosis. Are actions taken while a person is in a hypnotic trance voluntary actions? There are few decisions on the subject. See People v. Marsh, 170 Cal. App. 2d 284, 338 P.2d 495 (1959), where the defense was rejected by the jury.

The Model Penal Code took the position that the acts of a hypnotized subject are not voluntary, stating (Model Penal Code and Commentaries, Comment to §2.01 at 221 (1985)):

> The widely held view that the hypnotized subject will not follow suggestions which are repugnant to him was deemed insufficient to warrant treating his conduct while hypnotized as voluntary; his dependency and helplessness are too pronounced.

See Comment (Mary C. Bonnema), "Trance on Trial": An Exegesis of Hypnotism and Criminal Responsibility, 39 Wayne L. Rev. 1299 (1993).

(d) Somnambulism. Should acts done during sleepwalking be treated as involuntary? Consider Norval Morris, Somnambulistic Homicide: Ghosts, Spiders, and North Koreans, 5 Res Judicatae 29, 29-30 (1951):

> Mrs. Cogdon was charged with the murder of her only child, a daughter called Pat, aged nineteen. . . . Describing the relationship between Pat and her mother, Mr. Cogdon testified: "I don't think a mother could have thought any more of her daughter. I think she absolutely adored her." On the conscious level, at least, there was no reason to doubt Mrs. Cogdon's deep attachment to her daughter.
>
> To the charge of murdering Pat, Mrs. Cogdon pleaded not guilty. Her story, though somewhat bizarre, was not seriously challenged by the Crown, and led to her acquittal. She told how, on the night before her daughter's death she had dreamt that their house was full of spiders and that these spiders were crawling all over Pat. In her sleep, Mrs. Cogdon left the bed she shared with her husband, went into Pat's room and awakened to find herself violently brushing at Pat's face, presumably to remove the spiders. . . .
>
> The morning after the spider dream she told her doctor of it. He gave her a sedative and, because of the dream and certain previous difficulties she had reported, discussed the possibility of psychiatric treatment. That evening [there] was some desultory conversation . . . about the war in Korea, and just before she put out her

light Pat called out to her mother, "Mum, don't be so silly worrying about the war, it's not on our front door step yet."

Mrs. Cogdon went to sleep. She dreamt that "the war was all around the house," that the soldiers were in Pat's room, and that one soldier was on the bed attacking Pat. This was all of the dream that she could later recapture. Her first "waking" memory was of running from Pat's room, out of the house to the home of her sister who lived next door. When her sister opened the front door Mrs. Cogdon fell into her arms crying, "I think I've hurt Pattie."

In fact Mrs. Cogdon had, in her somnambulistic state, left her bed, fetched an axe from the woodheap, entered Pat's room, and struck her two accurate forceful blows on the head with the blade of the axe, thus killing her.

Mrs. Cogdon's story was supported by the evidence of her physician, a psychiatrist, and a psychologist. The burden of the evidence of all three, which was not contested by the prosecution, was that Mrs. Cogdon was suffering from a form of hysteria with an overlay of depression and that she was of a personality in which such dissociated states as fugues, amnesias, and somnambulistic acts are to be expected. They agreed that she was not psychotic and that if she had been awake at the time of the killing no defence could have been spelt out under the *M'Naughten Rules* [defining the terms of the defense of legal insanity]. They hazarded no statement as to her motives, the idea of defence of the daughter being transparently insufficient. However, the psychologist and the psychiatrist concurred in hinting that the emotional motivation lay in an acute conflict situation in her relations with her own parents; that during marital life she suffered very great sexual frustration; and that she over-compensated for her own frustration by over-protection of her daughter. Her exaggerated solicitude for her daughter was a conscious expression of her subconscious emotional hostility to her, and the dream ghosts, spiders, and Korean soldiers were projections of that aggression. . . .

At all events the jury believed Mrs. Cogdon's story. [S]he was acquitted because the act of killing itself was not, in law, regarded as her act at all.

3. Legal Insanity. The relationship between the defenses of involuntarily act and legal insanity is explored infra page 914. For the moment, it's important to be aware of the differing legal consequences of these two defenses. First is the matter of burden of proof. Since the presence of a voluntary act is a necessary element of a crime, the prosecution bears the burden of proof beyond a reasonable doubt. The defense of legal insanity, however, does not necessarily preclude the presence of the elements of a crime, so that the burden of proving legal insanity may, and often is, placed upon the defendant. See page 894, infra. Second is the matter of disposition. The effect of the acquittal of Mrs. Cogdon, for example, in the previous note is that she is immediately discharged without further supervision over her conduct. If, however, she had been acquitted on grounds of legal insanity, she would have been subject to commitment or other protective or therapeutic protocols. See infra page 852.

4. Problem. Can there be situations in which the defendant may be held criminally liable even though the action immediately causing the harm was clearly involuntary — for example, epileptic reflexes? Consider People v. Decina, 2 N.Y.2d 133, 139-140, 138 N.E.2d 799, 803-804 (1956):

The indictment states essentially that defendant, *knowing* "that he was subject to epileptic attacks or other disorder rendering him likely to lose consciousness for a considerable period of time," was culpably negligent "in that he consciously undertook to and *did operate* his Buick sedan on a public highway" (emphasis supplied) and "while so doing" suffered such an attack which caused said automobile "to travel at a fast and reckless rate of speed, jumping the curb and driving over the sidewalk" causing the death of 4 persons. In our opinion, this clearly states a violation of section 1053-a of the Penal Law. . . . ["A person who operates or drives any vehicle of any kind in a reckless or culpably negligent manner, whereby a human being is killed is guilty of criminal negligence in the operation of a vehicle resulting in death."]

Assuming the truth of the indictment, as we must on a demurrer, this defendant knew he was subject to epileptic attacks and seizures that might strike at any time. He also knew that a moving motor vehicle uncontrolled on a public highway is a highly dangerous instrumentality capable of unrestrained destruction. With this *knowledge,* and without anyone accompanying him, he deliberately took a chance by making a conscious choice of a course of action, in disregard of the consequences which he knew might follow from his conscious act, and which in this case did ensue. How can we say as a matter of law that this did not amount to culpable negligence within the meaning of section 1053-a?

To hold otherwise would be to say that a man may freely indulge himself in liquor in the same hope that it will not affect his driving, and if it later develops that ensuing intoxication causes dangerous and reckless driving resulting in death, his unconsciousness or involuntariness at that time would relieve him from prosecution under the statute. His awareness of a condition which he knows may produce such consequences as here, and his disregard of the consequences, renders him liable for culpable negligence, as the courts below have properly held. To have a sudden sleeping spell, an unexpected heart or other disabling attack, without any prior knowledge or warning thereof, is an altogether different situation.

5. Why does the law distinguish between nonactions and excused actions? Professor J. G. Murphy, in Involuntary Acts and Criminal Liability, 51 Ethics 332 (1971), points out that there are two basic situations in which human actions "misfire." One is where actions are done mistakenly, accidentally, compulsorily, or under duress. The other is where the action misfires in a more basic way—such as in cases of seizures, convulsions, reflex movements, and somnambulism. In the first group of cases, we speak of mitigating the actor's responsibility or of excusing the act. In the second group of cases, however, we do not think of excuse but rather that no human action occurred at all—"talk of excuse here seems to make no more sense than would talk of excusing a rock for falling on one's head." Indeed, this dichotomy is reflected in the organization of this casebook. The second group of cases is at issue here; problems of mistake and accident are dealt with in the section on mens rea that follows, and problems of excuse generally are dealt with in Chapter 8, Section B.

The distinction between these two categories of actions misfiring can have important legal consequences. As we shall see, it may make a difference in cases of strict liability, where ignorance or accident is ruled out as a defense but where the defense of no action (that is, no voluntary action) may serve as a defense. See page 248 infra. The distinction may also matter in cases involving the defenses based on severe mental disturbance. See Note 3, supra.

Question: Is there a rational justification for distinguishing these two classes of cases? Compare the views of Professor Murphy in the article just cited with those of Professor Hart in Punishment and Responsibility 90-112 (1968).

6. The foregoing and other problems of the criminal law with respect to the requirement of an action are discussed in Michael S. Moore, Act and Crime — The Philosophy of Action and its Implications for the Criminal Law (1993).

NOTE ON INNOCENT ACTS AND CULPABLE THOUGHTS

As we have seen, the absence of an *act* precludes culpability. In such a case, there is physical action, but it is discounted because there is no mental disposition to take such action, let alone a criminal disposition. Now consider two similar, but actually distinguishable, situations in which the absence of an appropriate action is sometimes said to preclude criminality.

1. First, consider the case in which there is external behavior accompanied by a criminal disposition, but the external behavior is, looked at from an objective view, wholly innocent. Consider these examples:

A soldier during battle shoots and kills an enemy soldier believing that his victim is his own sergeant.

A man has sexual intercourse with a woman over the age of consent, though he believes that she is underage.

Defendant deliberately shoots and kills victim, unaware that at that very instant victim was about to kill him.

Does the principle that requires a voluntary act or any other principle preclude imposing punishment in these cases? These problems are discussed more fully at page 585 infra in connection with the defense of impossibility to a charge of an attempt to commit a crime.

For a discussion of these and related questions, see G. Williams, Criminal Law: The General Part 22-27 (2d ed. 1961).

2. Second, consider the case in which there is no external behavior, but there is a criminal disposition. An example is the situation in which a person, who conceives a criminal plot in his or her mind, takes no action to further the plot. In such a case, is it the principle that conditions criminality on a voluntary act that precludes criminality, or is it some other principle? Criminality is said to be precluded in this case by the maxim *cogitationis poenam nemo patitur* (no one is punishable solely for his thoughts). What is the root justification of this principle? Consider the following comments.

*4 William Blackstone, Commentaries *21:* Indeed, to make a complete crime, cognizable by human laws, there must be both a will and an act. For though, in *foro conscientiae*, a fixed design or will to do an unlawful act is almost as heinous as the commission of it, yet, as no temporal tribunal can search the heart, or fathom the intentions of the mind, otherwise than as they are demonstrated by outward actions, it therefore cannot punish for what it cannot know. For which reason in all temporal jurisdictions an overt act, or some open evidence of an intended crime, is necessary, in order to demonstrate the depravity of the will, before the man is liable to punishment.

2 James Fitzjames Stephen, A History of the Criminal Law of England 78 (1833): Sinful thoughts and dispositions of mind might be the subject of confession and of penance, but they were never punished in this country by ecclesiastical criminal proceedings. The reasons for imposing this great leading restriction upon the sphere of criminal law are obvious. If it were not so restricted it would be utterly intolerable; all mankind would be criminals, and most of their lives would be passed in trying and punishing each other for offences which could never be proved.

G. Dworkin & G. Blumenfeld, Punishments for Intentions, 75 Mind 396, 401 (1966): What would a system of laws embodying a rule providing for the punishment of intentions look like? When would punishment be administered? As soon as we find out the agent's intentions? But how do we know he will not change his mind? Furthermore, isn't the series — fantasying, wishing, desiring, wanting, intending — a continuum, making it a rather hazy matter to know just when a person is intending rather than wishing? This last objection has two aspects, the difficulty of the authorities distinguishing between fantasying, wishing, etc. and even more importantly the difficulties the individual would have in identifying the nature of his emotional and mental set. Would we not be constantly worried about the nature of our mental life? Am I only wishing my mother-in-law were dead? Perhaps I have gone further. The resultant guilt would tend to impoverish and stultify the emotional life.

Glanville Williams, Criminal Law: The General Part 2 (2d ed. 1961): Better reasons for the rule would be (1) the difficulty of distinguishing between daydream and fixed intention in the absence of behavior tending towards the crime intended, and (2) the undesirability of spreading the criminal law so wide as to cover a mental state that the accused might be too irresolute even to begin to translate into action.

Abraham Goldstein, Conspiracy to Defraud the United States, 68 Yale L.J. 405, 405-406 (1959): Rooted in skepticism about the ability either to know what passes through the minds of men or to predict whether antisocial behavior will follow from antisocial thoughts, the act requirement serves a number of closely-related objectives: it seeks to assure that the evil intent of the man branded a criminal has been expressed in a manner signifying harm to society; that there is no longer any substantial likelihood that he will be deterred by the threat of sanction; and that there has been an identifiable occurrence so that multiple prosecution and punishment may be minimized.

3. The common law requires an act as well as an accompanying state of mind (mens rea) and does not generally consider a verbal declaration of the mens rea a sufficient act in itself. But words are a kind of act and are treated as such for some purposes. In cases of treason, conspiracy, or aiding and abetting, for example, words are sufficient to constitute the actus reus of the crime. Is this consistent with the doctrine that a person is not criminally liable for his or her thoughts alone?

b. Omissions

INTRODUCTION

The requirement of voluntary choice applicable to actions, just discussed, applies to omissions as well. Omissions, however, raise additional problems. Pope

v. State and the materials that follow it, pages 183-190, deal with the traditional reluctance of our criminal law to impose liability for omissions even where the failure to act is clearly immoral. Jones v. State and the materials that follow, pages 190-197, explore the most general exception to this position, namely, where the law imposes a legal duty to act. Finally, the material from Barber v. Superior Court, page 198 to the end of the section, consider the defensibility of the act/omission distinction in the context of the assisted suicide debate.

POPE v. STATE

Maryland Court of Appeals
284 Md. 309, 396 A.2d 1054 (1979)

ORTH, J. Joyce Lillian Pope was found guilty by the court in the Circuit Court for Montgomery County under the 3rd and 5th counts of a nine count indictment, no. 18666. The 3rd count charged child abuse, presenting that "on or about April 11, 1976, . . . while having the temporary care, custody and responsibility for the supervision of Demiko Lee Norris, a minor child under the age of eighteen years [she] did unlawfully and feloniously cause abuse to said minor child in violation of Article 27, Section 35A of the Annotated Code of Maryland. . . ." The 5th count charged misprision of felony under the common law, alleging that on the same date she "did unlawfully and willfully conceal and fail to disclose a felony to wit: the murder of Demiko Lee Norris committed by Melissa Vera Norris on April 11, 1976, having actual knowledge of the commission of the felony and the identity of the felon, with the intent to obstruct and hinder the due course of justice and to cause the felon to escape unpunished. . . ."

[Melissa Norris, a young mother with a three-month-old infant, was suffering from a serious mental illness and given to episodes of violent religious frenzy. The defendant (Mrs. Pope) took Norris and her child into her house one Friday night after church services because they had no other place to go. During the weekend Mrs. Pope fed them both and looked after the child in a variety of ways. On Sunday afternoon Melissa went into a frenzy, claiming she was God and that Satan had hidden himself in the body of her child. In Mrs. Pope's presence she savagely beat and ripped and tore at the infant, doing it violent and serious injury. During this prolonged period Mrs. Pope did nothing to try to protect the child, to call the authorities, or to seek medical assistance. She went to church with Melissa and later brought her back to her home where she spent the night. At some point in the evening the infant died from the beating.]

[A] person may be convicted of the felony of child abuse created by §35A[a] as a principal in the first degree upon evidence legally sufficient to establish that the person

a. Article 27, Section 35A, insofar as it is relevant to this case, reads as follows:
"(a) Penalty. Any parent, adoptive parent or other person who has the permanent or temporary care or custody or responsibility for the supervision of a minor child under the age of eighteen years who causes abuse to such minor child shall be guilty of a felony and upon conviction shall be sentenced to not more than fifteen years in the penitentiary.
"(b) Definitions. Wherever used in this section, unless the context clearly indicates otherwise; . . . 7. 'Abuse' shall mean any . . . physical injury or injuries sustained by a child as a result of cruel or inhumane treatment or as a result of malicious act or acts by any parent, adoptive parent or other person who has the permanent or temporary care or custody or responsibility for supervision of a minor child. . . ."—EDS.

(1) was (a) the parent of, or (b) the adoptive parent of, or (c) in loco parentis to, or (d) responsible for the supervision of a minor child under the age of eighteen years, AND

(2) caused, by being in some manner accountable for, by act of commission or omission, abuse to the child in the form of (a) physical injury or injuries sustained by the child as the result of (i) cruel or inhumane treatment, or (ii) malicious act or acts by such person, . . .

. . . Pope's lack of any attempt to prevent the numerous acts of abuse committed by the mother over a relatively protracted period and her failure to seek medical assistance for the child, although the need therefor was obviously compelling and urgent, could constitute a cause for the further progression and worsening of the injuries which led to the child's death. In such circumstances, Pope's omissions constituted in themselves cruel and inhumane treatment within the meaning of the statute. See State v. Fabritz, 276 Md. 416, 348 A.2d 275 (1975). It follows that Pope would be guilty of child abuse *if her status brought her within the class of persons specified by the statute.* It being clear that she was neither the child's parent nor adoptive parent, and there being no evidence sufficient to support a finding that she had "the permanent or temporary care or custody" of the child so as to be in loco parentis to the child, the sole question is whether she had "responsibility for the supervision of" the child in the circumstances. If she had such responsibility the evidence was legally sufficient to find her guilty of child abuse as a principal in the first degree.

The State would have us translate compassion and concern, acts of kindness and care, performance of maternal functions, and general help and aid with respect to the child into responsibility for the supervision of the child. The crux of its argument is that although Pope was not under any obligation to assume responsibility for the supervision of the child at the outset, "once she undertook to house, feed, and care for [the mother and child], she did accept the responsibility and came within the coverage of the statute." But the mother was always present. Pope had no right to usurp the role of the mother even to the extent of responsibility for the child's supervision. . . . It would be most incongruous that acts of hospitality and kindness, made out of common decency and prompted by sincere concern for the well-being of a mother and her child, subjected the Good Samaritan to criminal prosecution for abusing the very child he sought to look after. . . .

The evidence does not show why Pope did not intervene when the mother abused the child or why she did not, at least, timely seek medical assistance, when it was obvious that the child was seriously injured. . . . But Pope's conduct, during and after the acts of abuse, must be evaluated with regard for the rule that although she may have had a strong moral obligation to help the child, she was under no legal obligation to do so unless she then had responsibility for the supervision of the child as contemplated by the child abuse statute. She may not be punished as a felon under our system of justice for failing to fulfill a moral obligation, and the short of it is that she was under no legal obligation. . . . We hold that the evidence was not sufficient in law to prove that Pope fell within that class of persons to whom the child abuse statute applies. Thus it is that the judgment of the trial court that she was a principal in the first degree in the commission of the crime of child abuse was clearly erroneous and must be set aside.

The mental or emotional state of the mother, whereby at times she held herself out as God, does not change the result. We see no basis in the statute for an interpretation that a person "has" responsibility for the supervision of a child, if that person believes or may have reason to believe that a parent is not capable of caring for the child. There is no right to make such a subjective judgment in order to divest parents of their rights and obligations with respect to their minor children, and therefore, no obligation to do so. . . .

There is an understandable feeling of outrage at what occurred, intensified by the fact that the mother, who actually beat the child to death, was held to be not responsible for her criminal acts. But it is the law, not indignation, which governs. The law requires that Pope's conviction of the felony of child abuse be set aside as clearly erroneous due to evidentiary insufficiency. . . .

We assume, *arguendo*, that misprision of felony was a crime under the common law of England, and that it became the law of this State pursuant to Art. 5 of the Declaration of Rights. The question is whether it is to be deemed an indictable offense in Maryland today. . . .

We are satisfied, considering its origin, the impractical and indiscriminate width of its scope, its other obvious deficiencies, and its long non-use, that it is not now compatible with our local circumstances and situation and our general code of laws and jurisprudence. Maintenance of law and order does not demand its application, and, overall, the welfare of the inhabitants of Maryland and society as enjoyed by us today, would not be served by it. If the Legislature finds it advisable that the people be obligated under peril of criminal penalty to disclose knowledge of criminal acts, it is, of course, free to create an offense to that end, within constitutional limitations, and, hopefully, with adequate safeguards. We believe that the common law offense is not acceptable by today's standards, and we are not free to usurp the power of the General Assembly by attempting to fashion one that would be. We hold that misprision of felony is not a chargeable offense in Maryland.

We have reversed Pope's conviction of the felony of child abuse because the evidence was insufficient to sustain the verdict. She may not be tried again for that crime.

As we have held that the crime of misprision of felony does not now exist in Maryland, Pope may not, of course, be retried on a charge of that crime.

Pope moved that we strike from the State's brief and appendix a selection from the Year Book of 1484 written in Medieval Latin and references thereto. The State provided no translation and conceded a total lack of knowledge of what it meant. The motion is granted.

NOTES

1. Bystander indifference. Consider the incidents recounted in Diane Kiesel, Who Saw this Happen, 69 A.B.A.J. 1208 (1983):

> Shocking news accounts of the alleged gang rape of a woman in a Massachusetts tavern, while patrons gaped and cheered, have caused some state legislatures to consider making it a crime for witnesses to rapes and other felonies not to report them to police. . . .

In May, Rhode Island enacted a law making it a misdemeanor punishable by up to one year in jail, a $500 fine or both for anyone, other than the victim, to fail to report to police a rape that takes place in his or her presence. . . .

If the gang rape in March at the New Bedford, Mass., tavern happened as the witnesses said, it was unquestionably heinous and revolting. But some say the answer does not lie in laws like the one passed in Rhode Island. That measure was opposed by, surprisingly enough, the Rhode Island Rape Crisis Center, which raised questions about rape victims' privacy. The Rhode Island chapter of the American Civil Liberties Union also opposed it, citing constitutional and practical objections. Others think such statutes may be valid but ineffective. "These statutes will be no more effective than jaywalking laws," said Arthur Miller, Harvard law professor and television law commentator. "But that doesn't mean we shouldn't legislate in this area. It would give legal effect to a moral principle that we are our brother's keeper."

The public outcry in the New Bedford situation recalled the uproar that followed the 1964 murder of Catherine "Kitty" Genovese in Queens, N.Y. The young bar manager was stabbed to death on the street in her middle-class neighborhood in an attack that lasted some 35 minutes. Witnesses peered through their curtains and did nothing. The assailant followed Genovese from her parking lot toward her apartment building as she came home from work about 3:20 A.M. He started stabbing her, then fled when she screamed for help. But when her calls went unheeded, he returned to strike again. After the second assault he headed for his car and drove away while Genovese slowly crawled to her apartment doorway. Amazingly, the killer returned a third time, repeated his attack, and Genovese died. The first call to police was not made until 3:40 A.M. The man who finally called said he waited because he "didn't want to get involved."

2. *How to explain bystander indifference?* Consider Daniel B. Yeager, A Radical Community of Aid: A Rejoinder to Opponents of Affirmative Duties to Help Strangers, 71 Wash. U.L.Q. 1, 15 (1993):

Why those who see others in danger so often do nothing is unclear. In the case of witnesses to crimes, danger — real or imagined — and fear of retaliation account for some failures to intervene or notify authorities. In addition, because emergencies are, for most of us, exotic, a bystander's lack of opportunity for planning and rehearsal and the difficulty of quickly selecting the appropriate type of intervention might make her assistance less likely. . .

The presence of other bystanders may reduce each potential rescuer's individual sense of responsibility to the imperiled, and increase the probability of free-riding. Each is lulled into a state of "pluralistic ignorance," which induces multiple bystanders to interpret others' nonaction as a sign of no danger. Despite the apparent incentive that risk-sharing would provide to potential co-intervenors, because of social inhibitions that arise in groups, people are more prone to respond to another's distress when alone than when accompanied by other witnesses.

Bystanders thus face a "choice of nightmares": fail to intervene and experience the empathic distress of watching another human being suffer, the guilt of failing to live up to a minimal threshold of decency, and the shame of having that failure witnessed by others; or, intervene and risk retaliation by an assailant, the ridicule and derision of nonintervening bystanders, and the threat of being mistaken for the cause of the harm. Moreover, the victim may spurn, attack, or become completely dependent on the rescuer, while the legal system may enlist the rescuer as a witness subject to innumerable encounters with police, lawyers and judges. The nightmare then may be most easily resolved by convincing oneself that the victim is not imperiled.

3. Misprision of felony. As Judge Orth notes in *Pope,* the common law offense of misprision of felony is not a crime in American jurisdictions. Congress did enact a misprision of felony statute in 1909, 18 U.S.C. §4, but this requires active concealment of a known felony; merely failing to report is not sufficient. United States v. Johnson, 546 F.2d 1225 (5th Cir. 1977). Although the *Pope* case rejected misprision of felony as "not acceptable by today's standards," the offense is quite common in European jurisdictions. And a number of states have adopted statutes that revive misprision of felony, in substance, if not in name, at least for serious crimes. For example, Florida punishes the failure to report a sexual battery, Fla. Stat. Ann. §794.027; Massachusetts punishes the failure to report a rape, homicide, or robbery, Mass. Gen. Laws Ann. Ch. 268, §40; Washington punishes failure to report all crimes involving violence, Wash. Rev. Code Ann. §9.69. Additionally, all American jurisdictions require physicians and members of other designated professions to report child abuse; the vast majority of jurisdictions make failure to do so a misdemeanor. Irving Sloan, Child Abuse: Governing Law and Legislation 22-23, 43-45 (1983). Question: Is it time to revive the common law crime of misprision of felony?

JOHN KLEINIG, GOOD SAMARITANISM

5 Phil. & Pub. Aff. 382 (1976)

In the Russian Criminal Code of 1845 and, since then, in almost every continental European country, the failure to be a Good Samaritan has been declared a criminal offense. The glaring exceptions to this trend have been those countries within the Anglo-American legal tradition. . . . Though the position is slowly changing in torts, the criminal law situation remains substantially the same. "The law does not compel active benevolence between man and man. It is left to one's conscience whether he shall be the Good Samaritan or not." . . . In attempting to understand the current Anglo-American position with regard to Good Samaritan legislation, it is instructive to look at some of the debate which has led to it, since it has not come about without opposition. . . .

Bentham . . . in his Introduction to the Principles of Morals and Legislation, asked the question: "In cases where the person is in danger, why should it not be made the duty of every man to save another from mischief, when it can be done without prejudicing himself, as well as abstain from bringing it on him?" Undoubtedly, he felt that no satisfactory answer could be given. . . .

Mill, who on matters of social policy remained close to Bentham, . . . points out that there are also "many positive acts for the benefit of others" which a person may "rightly be compelled to perform." Among these he includes

> certain acts of individual beneficence, such as saving a fellow creature's life, or interposing to protect the defenceless against ill-usage, things which whenever it is obviously a man's duty to do, he may rightfully be made responsible to society for not doing. A person may cause evil to others not only by his actions but by his inaction, and in either case he is justly accountable to them for the injury.

On Mill's view, it is our duty to render aid because, by not doing so, we *harm another.* . . .

The most influential reaction came from Lord Macaulay et al. In their *Notes on the Indian Penal Code,* . . . Macaulay criticized the proposal of an offense of homicide by omission. . . . The problem as Macaulay sees it is to draw the line between harm-producing omissions which ought to be legally proscribed, and those which ought not. He has no doubt that there are cases of each, even where the imperiled person dies. If a gaoler omits to supply a prisoner with food; if an official omits to warn travelers that the river is too high to ford; if the owner of a dog which is attacking someone omits to call it off; and death results, the person who failed to act is guilty of murder. But, if a man omits to give alms to a starving beggar; if a surgeon refuses to go from Calcutta to Meerut to perform a life-saving operation; if one traveler omits to warn others that the river is too high to ford; if a passer-by omits to call off the attacking dog; and death results, the person who failed to act is not guilty of murder. Macaulay . . . [is] prepared to grant that a rich man who lets a beggar die at his feet is morally worse than some for whom severe punishment was prescribed. "But we are unable to see where, if we make such a man legally punishable, we can draw the line." How rich is rich enough, and how much can be required? If it takes a thousand rupees to save the beggar's life, should the rich man be required to provide it? If not, where is the line to be drawn? And if the potential Good Samaritan is not a rich man, how much should he be required to give? Macaulay therefore proposes that omissions which cause or threaten harm be punishable only where they are, "on other grounds, illegal." In other words, only where there are already existing legal duties to aid should the failure to aid be indictable. . . .

What are the consequences of Good Samaritan legislation so feared by Macaulay and other opponents? On the surface it looks like a problem of legal draftsmanship. Such are the differences between men and circumstances that no workable formula for specifying those occasions on which a Samaritan ought to be legally required to render aid can be produced. . . . Livingston's criterion,[a] that aid ought to be mandatory when it can be given "without personal danger or pecuniary loss," is considered to be open to serious objection. The surgeon summoned from Calcutta to Meerut might profit financially, and the trip might present no greater dangers than staying in Bengal, but it might still be extremely inconvenient for him: "He is about to proceed to Europe immediately, or he expects some members of his family by the next ship, and wishes to be at the presidency to receive them." If he refuses to go, he is no "murderer," and a good sight better than another who, "enjoying ample wealth, should refuse to disburse an anna to save the life of another." On Livingston's criterion, the latter but not the former should go free.

About the best that could be said for this argument is that it shows the inadequacy of Livingston's criterion. But it does not do much more. It does nothing to show that if Good Samaritan legislation is introduced, unreasonable sacrifices of welfare and interests will be demanded of Samaritans. As is the case with Good Samaritan provisions in those countries that already have them, the Samaritan will be required only to take reasonable steps to give or procure aid for the imperiled person. Judgments of reasonableness are not impossible of determination, and are the bread and butter of the courts. . . .

a. The reference is to the failed penal code for Louisiana drafted by Edward Livingston in 1826. See Sanford H. Kadish, Codifiers of the Criminal Law, 78 Colum. L. Rev. 1098 (1978).—Eds.

However, I think another, rather different fear underlies Macaulay's opposition to Good Samaritan legislation. Made explicit by later writers, it is basically the fear that Good Samaritan legislation will substantially diminish freedom. In a culture steeped in individualism, nothing produces more hysteria than measures which encroach on individual liberty. "You owe me nothing; I owe you nothing. You stay out of my way, and I'll stay out of yours." That is an extreme expression, but it constitutes an important thread within the Anglo-American sociomoral fabric. . . .

The freedom to pursue one's interests is not, as Mill and Bentham clearly saw, unlimited. Where the pursuit of one's interests is a causal factor in another's harm, or threatens additional harm, as in Bad Samaritanism, we have the important beginnings of a case for justifiable state interference. . . .[b]

NOTES

***1.** State of the Law.* A handful of states, including Rhode Island, Vermont, and Wisconsin, have enacted Good Samaritan statutes, which make it criminal to refuse to rescue a person in emergency situations. See, e.g., Vt. Stat. Ann. tit. 12, §519:

> A person who knows that another is exposed to grave physical harm shall, to the extent that the same can be rendered without danger or peril to himself or without interference with important duties owed to others, give reasonable assistance to the exposed person unless that assistance or care is being provided by others. [Penalty $200 fine.]

The Rhode Island statute is similar but imposes the duty only at the scene of an accident and provides a penalty of up to six months imprisonment and $500 fine. R.I. Gen. Laws §11-56-1 (1998).

European countries have long used the criminal law to enforce a duty to aid another in distress. An example is Article 323c of the German Criminal Code:

> Whoever does not render help in cases of accident, common danger or necessity although help is needed and can be provided in the circumstances without danger of serious injury to the person and without violation of other important duties, will be punished by imprisonment up to one year or by fine.

A comparable statute is the French Criminal Code, which permits imprisonment up to five years.[1]

***2.** The Vaugeness Problem.* California Penal Law §368(a) is part of a multifaceted

b. For further discussion, see Daniel B. Yeager, A Radical Community of Aid: A Rejoinder to Opponents of Affirmative Duties to Help Strangers, 71 Wash. U.L.Q. 1 (1993); F. R. Denton, The Case Against a Duty to Rescue, 4 Canadian J. L. & Juris. 101 (1991); Richard Epstein, A Theory of Strict Liability 2 J. Leg. Stud. 151, 197-204 (1973). A comprehensive examination of this and related issues is Steven J. Heyman, Foundations of the Duty to Rescue, 47 Vand. L. Rev. 673 (1994). See also Michael Menlowe and Alexander McCall (eds.), The Duty of Rescue: The Jurisprudence of Aid (1993).—Eds.

1. See Andrew Ashworth & Eva Steiner, Criminal Omissions and Public Duties: The French Experience, 10 Leg. Stud. 153 (1990); Peter Agonic & Heidi Rifkin, Comment, Criminal Liability for Failure to Rescue: A Brief Survey of French and American Law, 8 Touro Intl. L. Rev. 93 (1998).

legislative response to the problem of neglect of the elderly. It imposes felony liability upon "any person who . . . willfully permits . . . any elder or dependent adult . . . to suffer . . . unjustifiable pain or mental suffering." *Any* person? In People v. Heitzman, 9 Cal. 4th 189, 886 P.2d 1229 (1994), the court considered the application of this statute to a daughter for failing to prevent the egregious and fatal neglect of her father by her siblings who were living with him. (The siblings were successfully prosecuted for involuntary manslaughter and were not involved in this appeal.) While the defendant lived separately from her father, she had visited from time to time and was aware of the neglect. The prosecution contended that the language should be given its literal meaning, namely, as imposing a blanket duty on everyone to prevent the abuse of any elder (so long, presumably, as the person could be found to have acted "willfully"). Is there any difficulty with this position? A majority of the court thought so, stating, at 1235 and 1240:

> [A] statutory interpretation imposing such a duty on every person . . . would extend the potential for criminal liability to, for example, a delivery person who, having entered a private home, notices an elder in a disheveled or disoriented state and purposefully fails to intervene. . . . [C]ontrary to constitutional requirements, neither the language nor subsequent judicial construction of section 368(a) provides adequate notice to those who may be under a duty to prevent the infliction of abuse on an elder. Moreover, the statute fails to provide a clear standard for those charged with enforcing the law. Although the selective prosecution of defendant does not conclusively demonstrate the presence of arbitrary or discriminatory enforcement of the statute, it arguably lends support to the view that the potential exists for such impermissible enforcement.

The court concluded that in order to save the constitutionality of the statute it should be interpreted as imposing liability only on those who, under existing tort principles, have a duty to control the conduct of the individual who is directly responsible for the abuse. This would exclude such people as the delivery person as well as the daughter. Since she did not live with her father she had no legal duty to care for him; nor did she have a legal duty to control her siblings' abuse of him.

Question: Why should there be any problem of notice to the citizenry or to prosecutors of what is forbidden so long as the language is taken on its face as the prosecution urged? Is "any person" lacking in clarity? What might have been the court's real objection to a literal reading of the statute? The minority opinion found it enough to save the statute from the defect of vagueness that it imposed liability only in cases where the defendant's failure to prevent the abuse constituted criminal negligence. What might be the objection to this position?

JONES v. UNITED STATES

United States Court of Appeals, District of Columbia Circuit
308 F.2d 307 (1962)

WRIGHT, J. [Defendant was found guilty of involuntary manslaughter through failure to provide for Anthony Lee Green, which failure resulted in his death.

The deceased was the 10-month-old illegitimate baby of Shirley Green. He was placed with the defendant, a family friend. Shirley Green lived in the house with defendant for some of the time, but there was conflict in the evidence as to how long. There was also conflict as to whether or not the defendant was paid for taking care of the baby. The medical evidence was uncontested that the defendant had ample means to provide food and medical care.]

Appellant . . . takes exception to the failure of the trial court to charge that the jury must find beyond a reasonable doubt, as an element of the crime, that appellant was under a legal duty to supply food and necessities to Anthony Lee. . . .

The problem of establishing the duty to take action which would preserve the life of another has not often arisen in the case law of this country. The most commonly cited statement of the rule is found in People v. Beardsley, 150 Mich. 206, 113 N.W. 1128, 1129:

> The law recognizes that under some circumstances the omission of a duty owed by one individual to another, where such omission results in the death of the one to whom the duty is owing, will make the other chargeable with manslaughter. . . . This rule of law is always based upon the proposition that the duty neglected must be a legal duty, and not a mere moral obligation. It must be a duty imposed by law or by contract, and the omission to perform the duty must be the immediate and direct cause of death. . . .

There are at least four situations in which the failure to act may constitute breach of a legal duty. One can be held criminally liable: first, where a statute imposes a duty to care for another; second, where one stands in a certain status relationship to another;[9] third, where one has assumed a contractual duty to care for another; and fourth, where one has voluntarily assumed the care of another and so secluded the helpless person as to prevent others from rendering aid.

It is the contention of the Government that either the third or the fourth ground is applicable here. However, it is obvious that in any of the four situations, there are critical issues of fact which must be passed on by the jury — specifically in this case, whether appellant had entered into a contract with the mother for the care of Anthony Lee or, alternatively, whether she assumed the care of the child and secluded him from the care of his mother, his natural protector. On both of these issues, the evidence is in direct conflict, appellant insisting that the mother was actually living with appellant and Anthony Lee, and hence should have been taking care of the child herself, while Shirley Green testified she was living with her parents and was paying appellant to care for both children.

In spite of this conflict, the instructions given in the case failed even to suggest the necessity for finding a legal duty of care. The only reference to duty in the instructions was the reading of the indictment which charged, inter alia, that the [defendant] "failed to perform [her] legal duty." A finding of legal duty is

9. 10 A.L.R. 1137 (1921) (parent to child); Territory v. Manton, 8 Mont. 95, 19 P. 387 (husband to wife); Regina v. Smith, 8 Carr. & P. 153 (Eng. 1837) (master to apprentice); United States v. Knowles, 26 Fed. Cas. 800 (No. 15,540) (ship's master to crew and passengers); cf. State v. Reitze, 86 N.J.L. 407, 92 A. 576 (innkeeper to inebriated customers).

the critical element of the crime charged and failure to instruct the jury concerning it was plain error. . . .

Reversed and remanded.

NOTES

1. There is nothing conceptually problematic in a statute making it criminal to fail to act in certain situations. Indeed such statutes are common. The issue is only the desirability of imposing such obligations, as in the example of the Good Samaritan laws just considered. The *Jones* case, however, presents a different issue: Where a crime is defined in terms of producing a result (like homicide, which prohibits "killing" another person, or child abuse laws, which prohibit abusing a child), when may a person who fails to act to avert the prohibited result be said to have produced it?

Jones reflects the general Anglo-American position that unless a penal statute specifically requires a particular action to be performed, criminal liability for omission arises only when the law of torts or some other law concerning civil liability imposes a duty to act in the circumstances. This is a position also taken by the Model Penal Code in §2.01(3) (liability for an omission only when "a duty to perform the omitted act is otherwise imposed by law").

2. Most cases where liability for homicide is imposed for a failure to act are, like the *Jones* case, cases of involuntary manslaughter. Such a case, however, might be murder if the defendant intentionally refused aid with the intention of achieving the death of the decedent, or with full knowledge of a great risk that the decedent would die as a result. For example, in Commonwealth v. Pestinikas, 617 A.2d 1339 (Pa. Super. Ct. 1992), defendant permitted a 92-year-old person to die of starvation after agreeing to feed him and knowing there was no other way for him to obtain food. He was convicted of murder in the third degree.

3. As *Pope* and *Jones* illustrate, a person who is not a child's parent, guardian, or caretaker ordinarily cannot be convicted on the basis of a failure to protect the child from abuse by a third party. But the child's *mother* can be, and often is, convicted of child abuse or homicide when she fails to protect her child from battering or sexual assault inflicted by a male member of the household. See Dorothy E. Roberts, Motherhood and Crime, 79 Iowa L. Rev. 95 (1993). Because the duty of parent to child is well established, convictions of this sort pose no novel conceptual problems. But such convictions can sometimes pose a practical problem. Consider Commonwealth v. Cardwell, 515 A.2d 311 (Pa. Super. 1986). Defendant Julia Cardwell lived with her daughter Alicia and Clyde Cardwell, who was Julia's husband and Alicia's stepfather. For 4 years, beginning in 1979 (when Alicia was about 11 years old), Clyde sexually abused Alicia. In October 1983 Alicia told her mother Julia about the assaults. Ten months later Alicia ran away from home. Julia was convicted of child abuse for failing to take sufficient steps in the interim to protect her daughter:

> In those ten months, Julia's only actions directed at protecting her daughter consisted of: writing two letters to Clyde that did little more than express her knowledge of and anger at his abuse of Alicia; applying for Alicia to transfer schools; and moving some of her and Alicia's clothing to Julia's mother's house. We note that

> the remedy of moving to Julia's mother's house was tragically frustrated by the destruction by fire of that house in May 1984, but the fact remains that Julia took no further steps to relieve her daughter's desperate situation in the four months that ensued from May 1984 until Alicia ran away from home in September 1984.

The court's opinion mentioned, without comment, several further details:

> Alicia testified that she and Julia were afraid of Clyde, that Clyde beat up Julia on one occasion, that he threw and broke things in the house, that he had punched a number of holes in the walls of the house, and that he carried a .357 magnum pistol, which he kept on the mantelpiece.

Nonetheless the court upheld the conviction, noting:

> The affirmative performance required . . . cannot be met simply by showing any step at all toward preventing harm, however incomplete or ineffectual. An act which will negate intent is not necessarily one which will provide a successful outcome. However, the person charged with the duty of care is required to take steps that are reasonably calculated to achieve success. Otherwise, the meaning of "duty of care" is eviscerated.

A concurring judge conceded that "Julia's real choices in view of her not unreasonable fear of her husband were limited and difficult — she could report her husband to the authorities, she could take her daughter and leave the marital home, or she could send her daughter away." The judge nonetheless concurred in affirming the conviction because Julia "unquestionably endangered her daughter's welfare by doing nothing to prevent the child's continued abuse."

Questions: How should Clyde's violence toward Julia affect the extent of her duty to prevent him from harming her child? The strict requirements for a duress defense are not met, as we shall see, infra page 845. See also Heather R. Skinazi, Not Just a "Conjured Afterthought": Using Duress as a Defense for Battered Women who "Fail to Protect," 85 Calif. L. Rev. 993 (1997). To what extent should a mother be forced to risk her own life in order to avoid criminal liability for injuries inflicted intentionally by her spouse or boyfriend? See Bran A. Liang and Wendy L. Macfarlane, Murder by Omission: Child Abuse and the Passive Parent, 36 Harv. J. Legis. 397 (1999). Consider Roberts, supra, at 111-113:

> Women who fail to protect their children from violence are often victims of violence themselves. . . .
>
> Courts, however, have not asked how this web of violence affects the mother's liability. They presume that a woman's obligation to her children always takes precedence over her own interest in independence and physical safety. Feminists have criticized people who ask battered women "Why didn't you leave?" because this question fails to recognize the physical, social, and legal constraints that keep women in violent homes. Courts slowly are beginning to acknowledge these constraints in self-defense cases.
>
> These impediments do not seem to matter, however, when mothers [fail to protect] abused children. Judges assume that a woman's maternal instinct to protect her children from harm overcomes any barriers to escape.

PROBLEMS

How can we explain the recourse to the law of civil liability to determine criminal liability? What are the circumstances in which a duty to act has been held to exist? On what criteria should such determinations be made? Consider the following cases.

1. People v. Beardsley, 150 Mich. 206, 113 N.W. 1128 (1907). Beardsley spent a weekend at his home with a woman not his wife. During this period the woman took a fatal dose of morphine tablets. Beardsley failed to call a physician to help her. She died, and he was charged and convicted of manslaughter. The court reversed the conviction because defendant owed deceased no legal duty, whatever his moral duty. The court stated (113 N.W. at 1131):

> It is urged by the prosecutor that the respondent "stood towards this woman for the time being in the place of her natural guardian and protector, and as such owed her a clear legal duty which he completely failed to perform." The fact that this woman was in his house created no such legal duty as exists in law and is due from a husband towards his wife, as seems to be intimated by the prosecutor's brief. Such an inference would be very repugnant to our moral sense.

Questions: What if the relationship between defendant and deceased had been more permanent? Suppose, for example, they had been living together for some time. Would it depend on whether a common law marriage could be made out and whether the common law marriage were recognized in the jurisdiction? And why do you suppose Beardsley didn't call for help?

Today, the grudging reading of duty in *Beardsley* as restricted to a man and woman who are legally married is widely thought to be greatly outmoded and unlikely to be followed. See e.g., Arthur Leavens, A Causation Approach to Criminal Omissions, 78 Calif. L. Rev. 547, 561 (1988); State ex rel. Kuntz v. Montana Thirteenth Judicial District Court, 995 P.2d 951, 956 (Mont. 2000); State v. Miranda, 715 A.2d 680, 682 (Conn. 1998). So whether failing to save another is a crime or not would seem to depend on changing social mores as particular judges from time to time interpret them. Should this be a worry?

2. Regina v. Stone and Dobinson, [1977] Q.B. 354, 357-358. The two defendants were Stone, a 67-year-old ex-miner, and Dobinson, his 43-year-old housekeeper and mistress. In 1972, Stone's 61-year-old sister, Fanny, came to live with the defendants, paying them a small amount each week for rent. She had been living with her sister, Rosy, but "[f]or some reason, probably because Rosy could not tolerate her any longer, she had decided to leave." Fanny constantly worried about her weight and would often hide in her room for days. In 1975, she developed severe *anorexia nervosa* and stopped eating anything but "biscuits and pop." She refused to tell the defendants the name of her doctor, fearing she would be "put away." Stone and Dobinson tried to find her doctor but were unsuccessful. They also tried once to find another doctor. However, once that attempt failed, they took no other steps to help Fanny, not even mentioning her condition to the social worker who came periodically to help with Stone's mentally retarded son. Meanwhile, Fanny had retired permanently to her bed. Several weeks later, she died in terrible degradation from the lack of nursing care.

The defendants were both convicted of manslaughter, and their conviction was affirmed on appeal. The court held that the defendants had assumed a duty of care:

> Whether Fanny was a lodger or not she was a blood relative of the appellant Stone; she was occupying a room in his house; Mrs. Dobinson had undertaken the duty of trying to wash her. . . . They tried to get a doctor; they tried to discover the previous doctor.

Questions: On what basis is *Stone and Dobinson* distinguishable from *Beardsley?* Did Stone's duty come from being a blood relative,[2] or from the fact that Fanny was a lodger rather than a guest? Is Dobinson liable because, by washing the deceased and once trying to contact a doctor, she assumed a duty of care? Would she have been liable if she had never tried to help at all? Professor Glanville Williams has criticized the reasoning in this case while defending its holding. He argues that the decision should be grounded on a rule of law that an occupier of a house must take reasonable steps to save the life of a fellow occupant. Textbook of the Criminal Law 264-265 (2d ed. 1983).

3. People v. Oliver, 210 Cal. App. 3d 138, 258 Cal. Rptr. 138 (1989). Defendant Oliver met Cornejo, already intoxicated, at a bar. She invited Cornejo to her house where he asked for a spoon to ingest some heroin. She gave it to him, and he repaired to the bathroom and ingested the drug. Immediately thereafter, he passed out in her living room. Unable to rouse him, she returned to the bar. When her daughter later discovered Cornejo and telephoned her mother for instructions, Oliver told her to drag him outside and put him behind a shed where he wouldn't be seen by neighbors. When Oliver returned later with a boyfriend, she saw Cornejo still lying there. The next morning, seeing he was still there and now thinking he might be dead, she left instructions for her daughter to call the police. The police found Cornejo dead, the result of morphine poisoning. Oliver was then charged and convicted of involuntary manslaughter under an instruction that allowed the jury to find guilt on a criminal negligence theory. The court of appeal affirmed, rejecting defendant's argument that as a matter of law she did not owe decedent any duty to seek medical care, and stating (210 Cal. App. 3d at 149):

> We conclude that the evidence of the combination of events which occurred between the time appellant left the bar with Cornejo through the time he fell to the floor unconscious, established as a matter of law a relationship which imposed upon appellant a duty to seek medical aid. At the time appellant left the bar with Cornejo, she observed that he was extremely drunk, and drove him to her home. In so doing, she took him from a public place where others might have taken care to prevent him from injuring himself, to a private place — her home — where she alone could provide such care. To a certain, if limited, extent, therefore, she took charge of a person unable to prevent harm to himself. (Rest. 2d Torts §324.) [a] She

2. The only familial relationships that create a legal duty of care are parent to minor child and spouse to spouse. Wayne LaFave, Criminal Law 215 (3d ed. 2000).

a. Section 324 of the Restatement (Second) of Torts provides in part: "One who, being under no duty to do so, takes charge of another who is helpless adequately to aid or protect himself is subject to liability to the other for any bodily harm caused to him by (a) the failure of the actor to exercise reasonable care to secure the safety of the other while within the actor's charge. . . ." The then allowed Cornejo to use her bathroom, without any objection on her part, to inject himself with narcotics, an act involving the definite potential for fatal consequences. When Cornejo collapsed to the floor, appellant should have known that her conduct had contributed to creating an unreasonable risk of harm for Cornejo — death. At that point, she owed Cornejo a duty to prevent that risk from occurring by summoning aid, even if she had not previously realized that her actions would lead to such risk. (Rest. 2d Torts §321.) [b] Her failure to summon any medical assistance whatsoever and to leave him abandoned outside her house warranted the jury finding a breach of that duty.

Questions: Do the sections of the Restatement of Torts relied on by the court support the court's conclusion? What if the facts were the same except that the decedent used the spoon without asking Oliver's permission? Except that he had a heart seizure while visiting her? How do you account for the differing results in *Beardsley* and this case?

NOTE ON THE DUTY OF ONE WHO CREATES ANOTHER'S PERIL

One who culpably places another in peril has a duty to assist the imperiled person. That much is pretty standard and not problematic. Many such cases would hardly be thought of as cases of omission. If a person intentionally throws a nonswimmer into a pool and lets that person drown, we should say simply that she killed him, rather than that she failed in her duty to save him. But other cases of imperiling can be more troublesome. These are cases where either the creation of the peril cannot be said to have caused the death, or where the person was not at fault in creating the peril. Following are some matters to think about in this connection:

a. In Jones v. State, 220 Ind. 384, 43 N.E.2d 1017 (1942), the defendant raped a child of 12, who, "distracted by pain and grief," fell or jumped into a creek where she drowned. The defendant intentionally abstained from rescuing her although able to do so without risk to himself. The supreme court affirmed a conviction of second-degree murder, stating: "Can it be doubted that one who by his own overpowering criminal act has put another in danger of drowning has the duty to preserve her life?" 43 N.E.2d at 1018.

b. Adam runs with reckless abandon full tilt beside a swimming pool and crashes into Tina who is pushed into a child who is in turn thrown into the water. Adam's duty to save the child is clear. But how about Tina? Is she in the same position as some innocent bystander who is free to ignore the child's peril, or is

---

principle is qualified by Good Samaritan statutes in most states which protect many categories of interveners from liability for simple negligence. See Prosser and Keeton on the Law of Torts 378 n.57 (5th ed. 1984); Eric Brandt, Good Samaritan Laws — The Legal Placebo: A Current Analysis, 17 Akron L. Rev. 303 (1983). — Eds.

b. Section 321 of the Restatement (Second) of Torts provides: "(1) If the actor does an act, and subsequently realizes or should realize that it has created an unreasonable risk of causing physical harm to another, he is under a duty to exercise reasonable care to prevent the risk from taking effect. (2) The rule stated in Subsection (1) applies even though at the time of the act the actor has no reason to believe that it will involve such a risk." — Eds.

she to be treated like Adam? Is the former correct because she did no action, culpable or otherwise? Then suppose a different case, that Tina herself walked into the child, though wholly without any fault on her part. Here, her actions caused the child's peril. But does the fact that they were nonculpable leave her in the same position as an innocent bystander?

c. Consider the observations of Professor J. C. Smith in Liability for Omissions in Criminal Law, 14 Leg. Stud. 88, 94 (1984):

> [I]n Green v. Cross [(1910) 103 L.T. 279] . . . the defendant inadvertently caught a dog in a trap. At the time when he found the animal trapped and in pain, he had committed no offence. But if he then failed to take steps which he might reasonably have been expected to take to release it from its misery, he was guilty of causing it to be ill-treated, abused and tortured, contrary to the Cruelty to Animals Act 1849. Other interests call, *a fortiori,* for similar protection. . . .
>
> Suppose that, on leaving my office on Friday evening, I lock the storeroom door, reasonably believing the room to be empty. I then hear movement inside and realize that I have locked in a colleague and that he will be imprisoned there for the weekend unless I unlock the door and let him out. Surely my omission to do so would render me liable for false imprisonment (in criminal as well as civil law); and it should be no answer that locking the door was an entirely lawful and reasonable act.
>
> Suppose, again, that without any fault on my part, I were to knock a small child into the notorious shallow pool — he was careening along not looking where he was going until we collided. Surely the lenience of the common law does not extend so far as to permit me to walk off, leaving him to drown when I could easily have saved him.
>
> I venture, therefore, to suggest a general principle: . . . Whenever the defendant's act, though without his knowledge, imperils the person, liberty or property of another, or any other interest protected by the criminal law, and the defendant becomes aware of the events creating the peril, he has a duty to take reasonable steps to prevent the peril from resulting in the harm in question.

Do you agree with Professor Smith? Why should a wholly innocent accident serve to create a duty to help another where none would exist in the absence of the accident?

d. In State *ex rel.* Kuntz v. Montana Thirteenth Judicial District Court, 995 P.2d 951 (Mont. 2000), Bonnie Kuntz and her live-in boyfriend got into an angry dispute. At some point the boyfriend became physically abusive. He grabbed her by the hair, shook her and began slamming her into the stove. Kuntz was able to grasp a kitchen knife, which she thrust into her boyfriend's chest. The boyfriend collapsed and fell face-down on the porch in a pool of blood. Kuntz rolled him over and found him unresponsive, though still alive. She took the car keys from his pocket and drove to a friend's home several miles away without making any effort to secure medical help. Someone else subsequently called for assistance, but when the medics arrived the boyfriend was dead. On these facts, and assuming Kuntz's stabbing her boyfriend was an act of justifiable self-defense, can she be found guilty of negligent homicide for failing to call for medical assistance? Does this case fall within the general principle suggested by Professor Smith in the excerpt just above? The Montana Supreme Court held for liability on the facts stated. Do you agree?

BARBER v. SUPERIOR COURT

California District Court of Appeal
147 Cal. App. 3d 1006, 195 Cal. Rptr. 484 (1983)

[After a preliminary hearing, the magistrate dismissed murder and conspiracy charges against two physicians. The superior court set aside the magistrate's order and reinstated the complaint. The physicians then petitioned the court of appeal for review of the decision of the superior court.]

COMPTON, A.J. . . . Deceased Clarence Herbert underwent surgery. [W]hile in the recovery room, Mr. Herbert suffered a cardio-respiratory arrest. He was revived by a team of physicians and nurses and immediately placed on life support equipment.

Within the following three days, it was determined that Mr. Herbert was in a deeply comatose state. [Tests] indicated that Mr. Herbert had suffered severe brain damage, leaving him in a vegetative state, which was likely to be permanent. At that time petitioners [his physicians] informed Mr. Herbert's family of their opinion as to his condition and chances for recovery. While there is some dispute as to the precise terminology used by the doctors, it is clear that they communicated to the family that the prognosis for recovery was extremely poor. At that point, the family convened and drafted a written request to the hospital personnel stating that they wanted "all machines taken off that are sustaining life" (sic). As a result, petitioners, either directly or as a result of orders given by them, caused the respirator and other life-sustaining equipment to be removed. Mr. Herbert continued to breathe without the equipment but showed no signs of improvement. . . . After two more days had elapsed, petitioners, after consulting with the family, ordered removal of the intravenous tubes which provided hydration and nourishment. From that point until his death, Mr. Herbert received nursing care which preserved his dignity and provided a clean and hygienic environment.

The precise issue for determination by this court is whether the evidence presented before the magistrate was sufficient to support his determination that petitioners should not be held to answer to the charges of murder, and conspiracy to commit murder. . . . "Murder is the *unlawful* killing of a human being, . . . with malice aforethought." . . .

[W]e accept the superior court judge's analysis that if petitioners unlawfully and intentionally killed Mr. Herbert, the malice could be presumed regardless of their motive.

The use of the term "unlawful" in defining a criminal homicide is generally to distinguish a criminal homicide from those homicides which society has determined to be "justifiable" or "excusable." Euthanasia, of course, is neither justifiable nor excusable in California. . . .

As a predicate to our analysis of whether the petitioners' conduct amounted to an "unlawful killing," we conclude that the cessation of "heroic" life support measures is not an affirmative act but rather a withdrawal or omission of further treatment. Even though these life support devices are, to a degree, "self-propelled," each pulsation of the respirator or each drop of fluid introduced into the patient's body by intravenous feeding devices is comparable to a manually administered injection or item of medication. Hence "disconnecting" of the mechanical devices is comparable to withholding the manually administered injection or medication. Further we view the use of an intravenous administration of nourishment and fluid, under the circumstances, as being the same as the use of the respirator or other form of life support equipment. . . .

There is no criminal liability for failure to act unless there is a legal duty to act. Thus the critical issue becomes one of determining the duties owed by a physician to a patient who has been reliably diagnosed as in a comatose state from which any meaningful recovery of cognitive brain function is exceedingly unlikely. . . .

A physician has no duty to continue treatment, once it has proved to be ineffective. Although there may be a duty to provide life-sustaining machinery in the *immediate* aftermath of a cardio-respiratory arrest, there is no duty to continue its use once it has become futile in the opinion of qualified medical personnel. . . .

Of course, the difficult determinations that must be made under these principles [are] the point at which further treatment will be of no reasonable benefit to the patient, who should have the power to make that decision and who should have the authority to direct termination of treatment. No precise guidelines as to when and how these decisions should be made can be provided by this court since this determination is essentially a medical one to be made at a time and on the basis of facts which will be unique to each case. . . .

[T]he patient's interests and desires are the key ingredients of the decision making process. . . . When the patient, however, is incapable of deciding for himself, because of his medical condition or for other reasons, there is no clear authority on the issue of who and under what procedure is to make the final decision. . . .

Under the circumstances of this case, the wife was the proper person to act as a surrogate for the patient with the authority to decide issues regarding further treatment, and would have so qualified had judicial approval been sought. There is no evidence that there was any disagreement among the wife and children. Nor was there any evidence that they were motivated in their decision by anything other than love and concern for the dignity of their husband and father. . . .

In summary we conclude that the petitioners' omission to continue treatment under the circumstances, though intentional and with knowledge that the patient would die, was not an unlawful failure to perform a legal duty. . . . The superior court erred in determining that as a matter of law the evidence required the magistrate to hold petitioners to answer.

AIREDALE NHS TRUST v. BLAND, [1993] All E.R. 821 (H.L.): [The House of Lords faced the question whether artificial feeding and antibiotic drugs may lawfully be withheld from an insensate patient with no hope of recovery, when it is known that without the treatment the patient will shortly die. The House of Lords answered the question in the affirmative. Lord Goff stated in his address:]

[T]he law draws a crucial distinction between cases in which a doctor decides not to provide, or to continue to provide, for his patient treatment or care which could or might prolong his life and those in which he decides, for example, by administering a lethal drug, actively to bring his patient's life to an end. . . . [T]he former may be lawful, either because the doctor is giving effect to his patient's wishes by withholding the treatment or care, or even in certain circumstances in which . . . the patient is incapacitated from stating whether or not he gives his consent. But it is not lawful for a doctor to administer a drug to his patient to bring about his death, even though that course is prompted by a humanitarian desire to end his suffering, however great that suffering may be. So to act is to cross the Rubicon which runs between on the one hand the care of the living patient and on the other hand euthanasia — actively causing his death to avoid or to end his suffering. Euthanasia is not lawful at common law. It is of course well known that there are many responsible members of our society who believe that euthanasia should be made lawful; but that result could, I believe, only be achieved by legislation which expresses the democratic will that so fundamental a change should be made in our law, and can, if enacted, ensure that such legalized killing can only be carried out subject to appropriate supervision and control. It is true that the drawing of this distinction may lead to a charge of hypocrisy, because it can be asked why, if the doctor, by discontinuing treatment, is entitled in consequence to let his patient die, it should not be lawful to put him out of his misery straight away, in a more humane manner, by a lethal injection, rather than let him linger on in pain until he dies. But the law does not feel able to authorize euthanasia, even in circumstances such as these, for, once euthanasia is recognized as lawful in these circumstances, it is difficult to see any logical basis for excluding it in others.

At the heart of this distinction lies a theoretical question. Why is it that the doctor who gives his patient a lethal injection which kills him commits an unlawful act and indeed is guilty of murder, whereas a doctor who, by discontinuing life support, allows his patient to die may not act unlawfully and will not do so if he commits no breach of duty to his patient? Professor Glanville Williams has suggested (see Textbook of Criminal Law (2nd edn, 1983), p. 282) that the reason is that what the doctor does when he switches off a life support machine "is in substance not an act but an omission to struggle" and that "the omission is not a breach of duty by the doctor, because he is not obliged to continue in a hopeless case."

I agree that the doctor's conduct in discontinuing life support can properly be categorized as an omission. It is true that it may be difficult to describe what the doctor actually does as an omission, for example where he takes some positive step to bring the life support to an end. But discontinuation of life support is, for present purposes, no different from not initiating life support in the first place. In each case, the doctor is simply allowing his patient to die in the sense that he is desisting from taking a step which might, in certain circumstances, prevent his patient from dying as a result of his pre-existing condition; and as a matter of general principle an omission such as this will not be unlawful unless it constitutes a breach of duty to the patient. I also agree that the doctor's conduct is to be differentiated from that of, for example, an interloper who maliciously switches off a life support machine because, although the interloper may perform exactly the same act as the doctor who discontinues life support, his doing so constitutes interference with the life-prolonging treatment then being administered by the doctor. Accordingly, whereas the doctor, in discontinuing life support, is simply allowing his patient to die of his pre-existing condition, the interloper is actively intervening to stop the doctor from prolonging the patient's life, and such conduct cannot possibly be categorized as an omission.

The distinction appears, therefore, to be useful in the present context in that it can be invoked to explain how discontinuance of life support can be differentiated from ending a patient's life by a lethal injection. But in the end the reason for that difference is that, whereas the law considers that discontinuance of life support may be consistent with the doctor's duty to care for his patient, it does not, for reasons of policy, consider that it forms any part of his duty to give his patient a lethal injection to put him out of his agony.

NOTE

The distinction in the medical context between letting die and killing is also widely accepted in the United States, and the Supreme Court has endorsed this distinction by upholding its constitutionality against an equal protection challenge. Vacco v. Quill, 521 U.S. 793 (1997) (New York does not violate the Equal Protection Clause of the Fourteenth Amendment by allowing the withdrawal of life-sustaining treatment while criminalizing assisted suicide).

JOHN ROBERTSON, RESPECT FOR LIFE IN BIOETHICAL DILEMMAS — THE CASE OF PHYSICIAN-ASSISTED SUICIDE, 45 Cleveland St. L. Rev. 329, 333-335 (1997): [T]he central issue that remains is whether . . . the moral or social threat to respect for human life is greater from physician-assisted suicide than it is from our widely accepted current practices of nontreatment? This question is key because most opponents of physician-assisted suicide accept the patient's right to refuse life-saving medical treatment. They distinguish the two cases by citing the importance of the active/passive distinction. Opponents of physician-assisted suicide emphasize that overriding the patient's choice to refuse treatment requires a direct imposition or intrusion on the patient, while assisted suicide and active euthanasia entails a person having something done to them. Proponents of a right to physician-assisted suicide, on the other hand, claim there is no significant moral difference between the two. If causing death by foregoing or removing medical treatment is justified, then causing death by writing a lethal prescription for the patient, or even administering a lethal injection, should also be permitted. . . .

The moral distinction between killing and letting die — between actively and passively causing death — has been examined by many bioethicists, philosophers, and lawyers. Most have concluded that the distinction between active and passive, on which opponents so heavily rest, is a distinction without a significant enough moral difference to support the great weight that opponents of physician-assisted suicide have placed on it. From the perspective of the affected individual, the sought for end — the relief of suffering and demise — is the same regardless of whether the immediate cause of death is described as active or passive, killing or letting die. If a competent and informed patient knowingly consents, it does not matter morally whether the physician then withholds further treatment or writes a prescription for lethal drugs which the patient then administers to herself. . . .

The line drawn by opponents of assisted suicide between active and passive is also vulnerable to a charge of inconsistency or arbitrariness. It is difficult to know in practice why one thing is labeled active or even arbitrary and therefore not permitted, and another is labeled passive and permitted. A lethal injection is active, yet an injection to treat pain that turns out to be lethal because it also depresses respiration, is not thought of as active killing, even though it is often done with the knowledge or even intention that providing pain relief will hasten death. Withdrawing treatment is said to be passive, yet many acts of withdrawal are quite active, for example, "pulling the plug" is literally an act. One cannot easily distinguish in all significant respects removing ventilators or feeding tubes from the act of writing a prescription for a drug, which the patient will later take on her own. Finally, because the interest in conserving resources exists in both cases, threats to the poor and elderly to end their life prematurely may be as great with decisions to withhold treatment as they are with asking physicians to write prescriptions for drugs that patients later use to commit suicide.

CRUZAN v. DIRECTOR, MISSOURI DEPT. OF PUBLIC HEALTH, 497 U.S. 261 (1989): [The Supreme Court upheld the decision of the Missouri Supreme Court to decline to order that Nancy Cruzan, a person in permanent vegetative state, be removed from a naso-gastric mechanism that was providing her nourishment. The majority decision, while assuming a person has a constitutionally protected liberty interest in refusing unwanted medical treatment, held that a State was free to require clear and convincing evidence of the patient's consent. Justice Scalia concurred separately. In a portion of his opinion he addressed the argument that removing Cruzan from the equipment at the request of her family (on her behalf) would not be suicide because she would be bringing about her death "not by any affirmative act but by merely declining treatment that provides nourishment." He replied (296-97)]

> Suicide, it is said, consists of an affirmative act to end one's life; refusing treatment is not an affirmative act "causing" death, but merely a passive acceptance of the natural process of dying. I readily acknowledge that the distinction between action and inaction has some bearing upon the legislative judgment of what ought to be prevented as suicide — though even there it would seem to me unreasonable to draw the line precisely between action and inaction, rather than between various forms of inaction. It would not make much sense to say that one may not kill oneself by walking into the sea, but may sit on the beach until submerged by the incoming tide; or that one may not intentionally lock oneself in a cold storage locker, but may refrain from coming indoors when the temperature drops below freezing. . . . Starving oneself to death is no different from putting a gun to one's temple as far as the common-law definition of suicide is concerned; the cause of death in both cases is the suicide's conscious decision to "pu[t] an end to his own existence." 4 Blackstone, Commentaries *189.

Question: On this view is it possible to distinguish a patient who rejects medical attention, knowing that he will die without it, from the traditional suicide? Note that both Scalia and Robertson, in the previous excerpt, both reject the action/inaction distinction, but come out differently. For Robertson it means that assisted suicide is as constitutionally protected as rejecting life-sustaining medication. For Scalia it means that the legislature may regulate refusing treatment as freely as it may regulate conventional suicides.

2. *Mens Rea — Culpable Mental States*

a. Basic Conceptions

INTRODUCTORY NOTE

The criminal law constitutes a description of harms that society seeks to prohibit by threat of criminal punishment. At the same time, the criminal law includes an elaborate body of qualifications to these prohibitions and threats, based on the absence of fault. A common usage is to express all of these qualifications to liability in terms of the requirement of mens rea. This usage is the thought behind the classic maxim, *actus non facit reum, nisi mens sit rea.* Or in Blackstone's translation, "an unwarrantable act without a vicious will is no crime at all." The vicious will was the mens rea; essentially it refers to the blameworthiness entailed in choosing to commit a criminal wrong. One way the requirement of mens rea may be rationalized is on the common sense view of justice that blame and punishment are inappropriate and unjust in the absence of choice.[3] So viewed, a great variety of defenses to criminal liability may be characterized as presenting mens rea defenses — involuntary act, duress, legal insanity, accident, mistake, for example.

This all-encompassing usage of mens rea may be referred to as mens rea in its general sense. For present purposes we propose to identify a narrower usage of mens rea, which may be referred to as mens rea in its special sense. In this special sense, mens rea refers only to the mental state required by the definition of the offense to accompany the act that produces or threatens the harm.

Not all possible mental states are relevant to the law's purposes. Whether the defendant acted regretfully, arrogantly, eagerly, hopefully, and so forth may be relevant for a judge contemplating the sentence to be imposed. But the mental states relevant to defining criminal conduct and differentiating degrees of culpability are much more limited in our legal system. Indeed, mental state is something of a misnomer. The concern of the criminal law is with the level of intentionality with which the defendant acted, in other words, with what the defendant intended, knew, or should have known when he acted.

Consider some examples: an attempt to commit a crime consists of an act that comes close to its commission done with the *purpose* that the acts constituting the crime be committed. Unlawful assembly is the act of joining with a group in a public place with *intent* to commit unlawful acts. Larceny consists of the appropriation of another's property, *knowing* that it is not your own, with *intent* to deprive the owner or possessor of it permanently. Receiving stolen goods is a crime when one receives stolen goods *knowing* they are stolen. Manslaughter is the killing of another by an act done with the *awareness* of a substantial and unjustifiable risk of doing so.

That the absence of the mens rea, in this special sense of the required mental state, precludes liability in all of these cases is of course the merest tautology. This is the way these crimes are defined. But it is important to see that they are

3. This view, of course, is only one way of looking at the problem. H. L. A. Hart has given it its clearest expression. See his Punishment and Responsibility 28 (1968).

so defined because the special mens rea element is crucial to the description of the conduct we want to make criminal. And description is crucial insofar as it is regarded as important to exclude from the definition of criminality what we do not want to punish as criminal. To revert to the examples just given, it would not be regarded as appropriate to make criminal the taking of another's property when the taker believed honestly that he or she was taking his or her own property. Neither would it make sense to make persons guilty of receiving stolen goods when they neither knew nor had occasion to know that the goods were stolen. And surely we should see nothing criminal in joining a group in a public place, apart from the intent to commit unlawful acts.

The mental element required by the definition of any crime, therefore, is of central concern. This subsection on basic conceptions and terminology is designed to help the student identify and distinguish the various kinds of mental states that may be used in the definition of crimes. In the subsections that follow, we explore the issue of mistake, which, though logically related to the definition of the mental element, has to some degree produced its own body of doctrine.

Of course, these subsections will not conclude our considerations of mens rea in the special sense of levels of intentionality. The issue will be encountered at many points in this course — notably in the definition of specific crimes (for example, culpable homicides, attempt, conspiracy, rape, theft) and in some of the defenses to criminal liability, such as voluntary intoxication. It will be apparent as we encounter the issue of mens rea in these various contexts that legislatures have often left the mental element undefined or have treated it ambiguously, while courts have as often failed to analyze it with precision. This subsection on terminology should help provide a vocabulary and an analytic framework for understanding and assessing what Justice Jackson has called "the variety, disparity and confusion of [the courts'] definitions of the requisite but elusive mental element." Morissette v. United States, 342 U.S. 246, 252 (1952).

REGINA v. CUNNINGHAM

Court of Criminal Appeal
[1957] 2 Q.B. 396

BYRNE, J., read the following judgment. The appellant was convicted at Leeds Assizes upon an indictment framed under section 23 of the Offences against the Person Act, 1861, which charged that he unlawfully and maliciously caused to be taken by Sarah Wade a certain noxious thing, namely, coal gas, so as thereby to endanger the life of the said Sarah Wade.

The facts were that the appellant was engaged to be married and his prospective mother-in-law was the tenant of a house, No. 7A, Bakes Street, Bradford, which was unoccupied, but which was to be occupied by the appellant after his marriage. Mrs. Wade and her husband, an elderly couple, lived in the house next door. At one time the two houses had been one, but when the building was converted into two houses a wall had been erected to divide the cellars of the two houses, and that wall was composed of rubble loosely cemented.

On the evening of January 17, 1957, the appellant went to the cellar of No. 7A,

Bakes Street, wrenched the gas meter from the gas pipes and stole it, together with its contents, and in a second indictment he was charged with the larceny of the gas meter and its contents. To that indictment he pleaded guilty and was sentenced to six months' imprisonment. In respect of that matter he does not appeal.

The facts were not really in dispute, and in a statement to a police officer the appellant said: "All right, I will tell you. I was short of money. I had been off work for three days, I got eight shillings from the gas meter. I tore it off the wall and threw it away." Although there was a stop tap within two feet of the meter the appellant did not turn off the gas, with the result that a very considerable volume of gas escaped, some of which seeped through the wall of the cellar and partially asphyxiated Mrs. Wade, who was asleep in her bedroom next door, with the result that her life was endangered.

At the close of the case for the prosecution, Mr. Brodie, who appeared for the appellant at the trial and who has appeared for him again in this court, submitted that there was no case to go to the jury, but the judge, quite rightly in our opinion, rejected this submission. The appellant did not give evidence.

The act of the appellant was clearly unlawful and therefore the real question for the jury was whether it was also malicious within the meaning of section 23 of the Offences against the Person Act, 1861.

Before this court, Mr. Brodie has taken three points, all dependent upon the construction of that section. Section 23 provides:

> Whosoever shall unlawfully and maliciously administer to or cause to be administered to or taken by any other person any poison or other destructive or noxious thing, so as thereby to endanger the life of such person, or so as thereby to inflict upon such person any grievous bodily harm, shall be guilty of felony. . . .

Mr. Brodie argued, first, that mens rea of some kind is necessary. Secondly, that the nature of the mens rea required is that the appellant must intend to do the particular kind of harm that was done, or, alternatively, that he must foresee that that harm may occur yet nevertheless continue recklessly to do the act. Thirdly, that the judge misdirected the jury as to the meaning of the word "maliciously." . . .

[T]he following principle was propounded by the late Professor C. S. Kenny in the first edition of his Outlines of Criminal Law published in 1902; . . .

> In any statutory definition of a crime, malice must be taken not in the old vague sense of wickedness in general but as requiring either (1) An actual intention to do the particular kind of harm that in fact was done; or (2) recklessness as to whether such harm should occur or not (i.e., the accused has foreseen that the particular kind of harm might be done and yet has gone on to take the risk of it). It is neither limited to nor does it indeed require any ill will towards the person injured. . . .

We think that this is an accurate statement of the law. . . . In our opinion the word "maliciously" in a statutory crime postulates foresight of consequence.

In his summing-up Oliver, J., directed the jury as follows:

> You will observe that there is nothing there about "with intention that that person should take it." He has not got to intend that it should be taken; it is sufficient that

by his unlawful and malicious act he causes it to be taken. What you have to decide here, then, is whether, when he loosed that frightful cloud of coal gas into the house which he shared with this old lady, he caused her to take it by his unlawful and malicious action. "Unlawful" does not need any definition. It is something forbidden by law. What about "malicious"? "Malicious" for this purpose means wicked—something which he has no business to do and perfectly well knows it. "Wicked" is as good a definition as any other which you would get.

The facts . . . are these. . . . [T]he prisoner quite deliberately intended to steal the money that was in the meter . . . broke the gas meter away from the supply pipes and thus released the main supply of gas at large into that house. When he did that he knew that this old lady and her husband were living next door to him. The gas meter was in a cellar. The wall which divided his cellar from the cellar next door was a kind of honeycomb wall through which gas could very well go, so that when he loosed that cloud of gas into that place he must have known perfectly well that gas would percolate all over the house. If it were part of this offense—which it is not—that he intended to poison the old lady, I should have left it to you to decide, and I should have told you that there was evidence on which you could find that he intended that, since he did an action which he must have known would result in that. As I have already told you, it is not necessary to prove that he intended to do it; it is quite enough that what he did was done unlawfully and maliciously.

With the utmost respect to the judge, we think it is incorrect to say that the word "malicious" in a statutory offence merely means wicked. We think the judge was, in effect, telling the jury that if they were satisfied that the appellant acted wickedly—and he had clearly acted wickedly in stealing the gas meter and its contents—they ought to find that he had acted maliciously in causing the gas to be taken by Mrs. Wade so as thereby to endanger her life.

In our view, it should have been left to the jury to decide whether, even if the appellant did not intend the injury to Mrs. Wade, he foresaw that the removal of the gas meter might cause injury to someone but nevertheless removed it. We are unable to say that a reasonable jury, properly directed as to the meaning of the word "maliciously" in the context of section 23, would without doubt have convicted.

In these circumstances this court has no alternative but to allow the appeal and quash the conviction.

Conviction quashed.

REGINA v. FAULKNER, 13 Cox Crim. Cas. 550, 555, 557 (1877): [Defendant was a sailor aboard the ship *Zemindar.* While on the high seas he went to the forecastle hold to steal some rum and lit a match in order to see better in the dark hold. Some of the rum caught fire and the fire spread, injuring him and completely destroying the ship. He was convicted by a jury of violating the Malicious Damage Act by maliciously setting fire to the ship (arson) upon an instruction by the judge that "although the prisoner had no actual intention of burning the vessel, still, if they found he was engaged in stealing the rum, and that the fire took place in the manner above stated, they ought to find him guilty." In stating the case for the Court for Crown Cases Reserved, the judge observed: "It was conceded that the prisoner had no actual intention of burning the vessel, and I was not asked to leave any question to the jury as to the prisoner's knowing the probable consequences of his act, or as to his reckless conduct." The conviction for arson of the ship was quashed.]

BARRY, J. A broad proposition has been contended for by the Crown, namely, that if, while a person is engaged in committing a felony, or, having committed it, is endeavoring to conceal his act, or prevent or spoil waste consequent on that act, he accidentally does some collateral act, which if done wilfully would be another felony either at common law or by statute, he is guilty of the latter felony. I am by no means anxious to throw any doubt upon, or limit in any way, the legal responsibility of those who engage in the commission of felony, or acts mala in se; but I am not prepared without more consideration to give my assent to so wide a proposition. I shall not pronounce any opinion, as I shall consider myself bound for the purpose of this case by the authority of Reg. v. Pembliton (12 Cox C.C. 607).[a] That case must be taken as deciding that to constitute an offence under the Malicious Injuries to Property Act, sect. 51, the act done must be in fact intentional and wilful, although the intention and will may (perhaps) be held to exist in, or be proved by, the fact that the accused knew that the injury would be the probable result of his unlawful act, and yet did the act reckless of such consequences. The present indictment charges the offence to be under the 42nd section of the same Act, and it is not disputed that the same construction must be applied to both sections. The jury were, in fact, directed to give a verdict of guilty upon the simple ground that the firing of the ship, though accidental, was caused by an act done in the course of, or immediately consequent upon, a felonious operation, and no question of the prisoner's malice, constructive or otherwise, was left to the jury. I am of opinion that, according to Reg. v. Pembliton, that direction was erroneous, and that the conviction should be quashed.

FITZGERALD, J. I concur in opinion with my brother Barry, and for the reasons he has given, that the direction of the learned judge cannot be sustained in law, and that therefore the conviction should be quashed. Counsel for the prosecution in effect insisted that the defendant, being engaged in the commission of, or in an attempt to commit a felony, was criminally responsible for every result that was occasioned thereby, even though it was not a probable consequence of his act or such as he could have reasonably foreseen or intended. No authority has been cited for a proposition so extensive, and I am of opinion that it is not warranted by law.

NOTE

The following text and commentary of the Model Penal Code on culpability requirements (mental elements) is of great importance and should be studied

a. Defendant was convicted under §51 of the Malicious Damage Act for unlawfully and maliciously breaking a window. It appeared that defendant resumed a running fight with his opponents, after they had been thrown out of a public house, by throwing a stone at them from across the street. The stone missed and broke a window of the public house. The jury convicted despite a finding that he did not intend to break the window. Conviction was quashed by the Court for Crown Cases Reserved on the ground that intention or at least recklessness as to the window breaking had to be established. — EDS.

with care. The significance of the commentary will be increasingly apparent as the student progresses through the materials. It should be reviewed as the need arises.

MODEL PENAL CODE

SECTION 2.02. General Requirements of Culpability

[See Appendix.]

MODEL PENAL CODE AND COMMENTARIES, COMMENT TO §2.02 AT 229-241 (1985): 1. *Objective.* This section expresses the Code's basic requirement that unless some element of mental culpability is proved with respect to each material element of the offense, no valid criminal conviction may be obtained. . . .

The section further attempts the extremely difficult task of articulating the kinds of culpability that may be required for the establishment of liability. It delineates four levels of culpability: purpose, knowledge, recklessness and negligence. It requires that one of these levels of culpability must be proved with respect to each "material element" of the offense, which may involve (1) the nature of the forbidden conduct, (2) the attendant circumstances, or (3) the result of conduct.[1] The question of which level of culpability suffices to establish liability must be addressed separately with respect to each material element, and will be resolved either by the particular definition of the offense or the general provision of this section.

The purpose of articulating these distinctions in detail is to . . . dispel the obscurity with which the culpability requirement is often treated when such concepts as "general criminal intent," "mens rea," "presumed intent," "malice," "wilfulness," "scienter" and the like have been employed. What Justice Jackson called "the variety, disparity and confusion" of judicial definitions of "the requisite but elusive mental element" in crime should, insofar as possible, be rationalized by a criminal code.

The Model Code's approach is based upon the view that clear analysis requires that the question of the kind of culpability required to establish the commission of the offense be faced separately with respect to each material element of the crime. The Code provision on rape will afford an illustration. Under Section 213.1(1), a purpose to effect the sexual relation is clearly required. But other circumstances are also made relevant by the definition of the offense. The victim['s] consent to sexual relations would, of course, preclude the crime. Must the defendant's purpose have encompassed the [fact that] she opposed his will? [This is an] entirely different [question]. Recklessness may be sufficient for [this

1. Section 1.13(9) defines an "element of an offense" to include conduct, attendant circumstances or results that are included in the description of the offense, that negative an excuse or justification for an offense, or that negative a defense under the statute of limitations or establish jurisdiction or venue. Section 1.13(10) defines the concept of "material element" to include all elements except those that relate exclusively to statutes of limitation, jurisdiction, venue, and the like. The "material elements" of offenses are thus those characteristics (conduct, circumstances, result) of the actor's behavior that, when combined with the appropriate level of culpability, will constitute the offense.

circumstance] of the offense, although purpose is required with respect to the sexual result that is an element of the offense.

It should also be noted that, as indicated in Section 1.13, the concept of "material element" to which these requirements adhere includes facts that negative an excuse or justification as well as the facts included in the definition of the crime. Thus, in a charge of murder, the level of culpability required to be proved normally focuses upon that element of the crime that involves the result of the defendant's conduct, namely the death of the victim. The law requires knowledge or purpose, as the case may be, usually with that element in view. However, when one considers the defense of self-defense, it is not unusual to provide that the defendant's belief in the necessity to save himself must have rested upon reasonable grounds. As to the element of death of the victim, in short, purpose or knowledge will suffice for conviction; as to the elements of self-defense, negligence will deprive the defendant of his defense.

Failure to face the question of culpability separately with respect to each of these ingredients of the offense results in obvious confusion, as does the failure to consider the defense as a "material element" in the total description of the crime. To call murder a "specific intent" crime or to say that it requires an "intent to kill" does not speak with clarity to the issue of what the defendant must have believed, and how carefully he must have formed his belief, in order to successfully claim self-defense. Considering facts that negative an excuse or justification as material elements of the offense, moreover, focuses attention on an obviously relevant grading factor when it comes to assessment of the seriousness of the crime the defendant has committed. . . .

2. *Purpose and Knowledge.* In defining the kinds of culpability, the Code draws a narrow distinction between acting purposely and knowingly, one of the elements of ambiguity in legal usage of the term "intent." Knowledge that the requisite external circumstances exist is a common element in both conceptions. But action is not purposive with respect to the nature or result of the actor's conduct unless it was his conscious object to perform an action of that nature or to cause such a result. It is meaningful to think of the actor's attitude as different if he is simply aware that his conduct is of the required nature or that the prohibited result is practically certain to follow from his conduct.[6]

It is true, of course, that this distinction is inconsequential for most purposes of liability: acting knowingly is ordinarily sufficient. But there are areas where the discrimination is required and is made under traditional law, which uses the awkward concept of "specific intent." This is true in treason, for example, insofar as a purpose to aid the enemy is an ingredient of the offense, and in attempts, complicity and conspiracy, where a true purpose to effect the criminal result is requisite for liability.[a] . . .

6. As pointed out in the preliminary study of the subject for the Brown Commission, the distinction is "between a man who wills that a particular act or result takes place and another who is merely willing that it should take place." 1 Brown Commn. Working Papers 124.

a. Consider United States v. Bennie Stewart, 41 C.M.R. 58 (1969), where the Court of Military Appeals set aside a plea of guilty to desertion with intent to avoid hazardous duty. The court found the plea improvident on the ground that the defendant's statements to the court-martial suggested that while he knew he would miss hazardous duty by his unauthorized absence, he did not absent himself for that reason (at 59): "In our opinion, there is a fundamental difference between pleading guilty to such a desertion charge because one intends to avoid hazardous duty and pursuing

3. *Recklessness.* An important discrimination is drawn between acting either purposely or knowingly and acting recklessly. As the Code uses the term, recklessness involves conscious risk creation. It resembles acting knowingly in that a state of awareness is involved, but the awareness is of risk, that is of a probability less than substantial certainty; the matter is contingent from the actor's point of view.[13] Whether the risk relates to the nature of the actor's conduct, or to the existence of the requisite attendant circumstances, or to the result that may ensue, is immaterial; the concept is the same, and is thus defined to apply to any material element.

The risk of which the actor is aware must of course be substantial in order for the recklessness judgment to be made. The risk must also be unjustifiable. Even substantial risks, it is clear, may be created without recklessness when the actor is seeking to serve a proper purpose, as when a surgeon performs an operation that he knows is very likely to be fatal but reasonably thinks to be necessary because the patient has no other, safer chance. Some principle must, therefore, be articulated to indicate the nature of the final judgment to be made after everything has been weighed. Describing the risk as "substantial" and "unjustifiable" is useful but not sufficient, for these are terms of degree, and the acceptability of a risk in a given case depends on a great many variables. Some standard is needed for determining *how* substantial and *how* unjustifiable the risk must be in order to warrant a finding of culpability. There is no way to state this value judgment that does not beg the question in the last analysis; the point is that the jury must evaluate the actor's conduct and determine whether it should be condemned. . . .

4. *Negligence.* The fourth kind of culpability is negligence. It is distinguished from purposeful, knowing or reckless action in that it does not involve a state of awareness. A person acts negligently under this subsection when he inadvertently creates a substantial and unjustifiable risk of which he ought to be aware. He is liable if given the nature and degree of the risk, his failure to perceive it is, considering the nature and purpose of the actor's conduct and the circumstances known to him, a gross deviation from the care that would be exercised by a reasonable person in his situation. As in the case of recklessness, both the substantiality of the risk and the elements of justification in the situation form the relevant standards of judgment. And again it is quite impossible to avoid tautological articulation of the final question. The tribunal must evaluate the actor's failure of perception and determine whether, under all the circumstances, it was serious enough to be condemned. The jury must find fault, and must find that it was substantial and unjustified; that is the heart of what can be said in legislative terms. . . .

---

the same course only because one believes that a consequence of his act was the avoidance of hazardous duty, regardless of intent." But see United States v. Johnson, 24 M.J. 101 (Ct. Mil. App. 1987) where "intent" to injure or interfere with national defense was construed to mean "knowing that the result is practically certain to follow."—Eds.

13. With respect to result elements, one cannot of course "know" infallibly that a certain result will follow from engaging in conduct, and thus to some extent "knowledge," when applied to result elements, includes a contingency factor as well. This is expressed definitionally in terms of whether the actor is "practically certain" that the result will follow.

SANTILLANES v. NEW MEXICO, 115 N.M. 215, 849 P.2d 358 (1993). [Defendant cut his 7-year-old nephew's neck with a knife during an altercation and was convicted of child abuse under a statue defining child abuse as including "negligently, . . . causing . . . a child to be . . . placed in a situation that may endanger the child's life or health. . . ." The trial court refused a proposed instruction patterned after the definition of criminal negligence in Model Penal Code Section 2.02(2)(d) (1985). Instead it gave the jury a standard definition of negligence sufficient to support civil liability: "An act, to be 'negligence,' must be one which a reasonably prudent person would foresee as involving an unreasonable risk of injury to himself or to another and which such a person, in the exercise of ordinary care, would not do." The Supreme Court found this instruction erroneous, stating:] "The issue in this case . . . is when the legislature has included but not defined the mens rea element in a criminal statute, here the term 'negligently,' what degree of negligence is required. [O]ur interpretation of this criminal statute requires that the term 'negligently' be interpreted to require a showing of criminal negligence instead of ordinary civil negligence. . . . [W]hen moral condemnation and social opprobrium attach to the conviction of a crime, the crime should typically reflect a mental state warranting such contempt. . . .

"We construe the intended scope of the statute as aiming to punish conduct that is morally culpable. . . . We interpret the mens rea element of negligence in the child abuse statute, therefore, to require a showing of criminal negligence instead of ordinary civil negligence."

NOTES

***1.** Offense Elements.* In the Model Penal Code schema, then, one of the "four levels of culpability . . . must be proved in respect to each 'material element' of the offense, which may involve (1) the nature of the forbidden conduct, (2) the attendant circumstances, or (3) the result of conduct." See the paraphrase of §§1.13(9) and (10) in footnote 1 of the Model Penal Code Commentary, supra. This does not mean, however, that all of the four levels of culpability are appropriate choices for each of the three kinds of material element.

To illustrate, compare the definitions of "purposely" and "knowingly" in §2.02(2)(a) and (b), which have to be phrased differently depending on which of the three kinds of material elements it is associated with. Consider "purposely." While one can speak of an actor purposely engaging in certain conduct or causing a certain result, one can't speak of the actor acting purposely with respect to a fact, except in the sense that the actor is aware of it or hopes for it, which is how the Model Penal Code drafts the section. And consider "knowingly." While one can speak of an actor knowing the nature of his conduct or knowing of some attendant circumstance, one can't speak of the actor knowing that a result will happen. The reason, of course, is that while you can be aware of what you're doing or of what is, you can't be aware of what will be, only of its probability. So the Model Penal Code requires for "knowingly" that the actor be "practically certain" his conduct will cause the result in §2.02(b)(ii). But it is also open to the drafter to define "knowingly" less strictly for certain purposes, as the Model Penal Code does in §2.02(7), where knowledge of "high probability" is made enough, so long as the actor actually believes the circumstance does not exist. The reason for this loosening of the knowledge requirement is to address the problem of so-called "willful ignorance," which we will reach shortly.

2. *Exercises:* There follow some non–Model Penal Code definitions of crimes. As an exercise, it is suggested that the student identify the material elements of each crime (nature of the conduct, attendant circumstances, and result), determine the mens rea required by the definition, and determine the mens rea that would be required if the Model Penal Code's general principles of interpretation were applicable (for example, §2.02(2)-(4)).

Burglary (N.Y. Penal Law §140.25):

> A person is guilty of burglary in the second degree when he knowingly enters or remains unlawfully in a building with intent to commit a crime therein, and when . . . [t]he building is a dwelling.

Burglary (Cal. Penal Code §§459-460):

> Every person who enters any house, room, apartment . . . or other building . . . with intent to commit grand or petit larceny or any felony is guilty of burglary.
>
> . . . Every burglary of an inhabited dwelling house . . . is burglary of the first degree.
>
> . . . All other kinds of burglary are burglary of the second degree.

Destruction of Property (D.C. Code Ann. §22-3108):

> Whoever maliciously cuts down or destroys by girding or otherwise, any standing or growing vine, bush, shrub, sapling, or tree on the land of another, . . . shall, if the value of the thing destroyed or the amount of the damage done . . . is fifty dollars or more, be imprisoned for not less than 180 days nor more than three years. . . .

Destruction of Property (N.Y. Penal Law §145.10):

> A person is guilty of criminal mischief in the second degree when with intent to damage property of another person, and having no right to do so nor any reasonable ground to believe that he has such right, he damages property of another person in an amount exceeding one thousand five hundred dollars.

3. *Influence of the Code.* The mens rea proposals of the Model Penal Code have had considerable influence on criminal law reform. Paul Robinson, A Brief History of Distinctions in Criminal Culpability, 31 Hastings L. Rev. 815, 816 (1980), concludes that "since the drafting of the Model Penal Code, nearly three-fourths of the states have revised their criminal codes. Recognizing the value of the

Code's culpability structure, approximately seventy percent of those states . . . have adopted an essentially identical system."

Two critiques of the sufficiency of the Model Penal Code mens rea provisions are Kenneth W. Simons, Rethinking Mental States, 72 B.U.L. Rev. 463 (1992); Paul Robinson & Jane Grall, Element Analysis in Defining Criminal Liability: The Model Penal Code and Beyond, 35 Stan. L. Rev. 681 (1983).

4. *Purpose, knowledge, intention, and motive: (a)* What is the significance of the actor's motive? Does it differ from the Model Penal Code's concept of purpose? Consider Glanville Williams, The Mental Element in Crime 10, 14 (1965). The author defines intention in terms of desiring a consequence: "A consequence is intended when it is desired to follow as the result of the actor's conduct." He then cautions:

> [T]he consequence need not be desired as an end in itself; it may be desired as a means to another end. . . . There may be a series of ends, each a link in a chain of purpose. Every link in the chain, when it happens, is an intended consequence of the original act. Suppose that a burglar is arrested when breaking into premises. It would obviously be no defence for him to say that his sole intention was to provide a nurse for his sick daughter, and for that purpose to take money from the premises, but that he had no desire or intention to deprive anyone of anything. Such an argument would be fatuous. He intended (1) to steal money (2) in order to help his daughter. These are two intentions, and the one does not displace the other. English lawyers call the first an "intent" and the second a "motive"; this is because the first (the intent to steal) enters into the definition of burglary and is legally relevant, while the second (the motive of helping the daughter) is legally irrelevant, except perhaps in relation to sentence. Although the verbal distinction between "intention" and "motive" is convenient, it must be realized that the remoter intention called motive is still an intention.

(b) It is generally agreed that "hardly any part of the penal law is more definitely stated than that motive is irrelevant to criminal liability." Jerome Hall, Principles of Criminal Law 88 (2d ed. 1960). Yet motive in the sense of "the remoter intention," to use Professor Williams's phrase, is commonly regarded as highly relevant to sentence. Why should it be that motive is regarded as relevant to sentencing but not to liability? A common response is that "it is impracticable to make allowance for individual, idiosyncratic motives" in defining criminal liability. Mark Thornton, Intention in Criminal Law, 5 Can. J. L. & Juris. 177, 180-181 (1992). But consider Douglas Husak, Motive and Criminal Liability, 8 Crim. Just. Ethics 3-14 (1989). The author offers several examples of situations in which the law actually does make motive relevant to criminal liability. Crimes defined in terms of doing an act with some further intention (specific intent) turn on the motive of the action, in the sense that the reason for the action is relevant to whether the crime was committed. For example, breaking into a dwelling is not burglary unless it is done for the purpose of (with the motive of) committing a felony within the dwelling. So also with defenses based on the rationale of justification insofar as they require that the defendant have acted with a proper motive, for example, self-defense. Motive is also relevant to determine the liability of a person who disconnects a terminal patient from a life support system — if the motive is beneficent the behavior will often be treated as an omission to continue preserving life and, in the absence of a duty to do so, not criminal. But if

the motive is otherwise (an heir seeking her inheritance, a burglar, and so on), the behavior will be treated as culpable homicide. See Barber v. Superior Court, supra page 198 and notes following. In addition, particular statutes may make motive determinative of criminality or punishment. An example of the latter is so-called "hate crimes" statutes that make a crime of violence against a person subject to greater punishment if it is invidiously motivated against certain classes of persons. See Paul H. Robinson, Hate Crimes: Crimes of Motive, Character, or Group Terror?, 1992/1993 Annual Survey of American Law 605.

For further discussion of motive see Martin Gardner, The Mens Rea Enigma: Observations on the Role of Motive in the Criminal Law Past and Present, 1993 Utah L. Rev. 635.

(c) Suppose a desperate husband finally, after long resistance, yields to the pleas of his bed-ridden and incurably ill wife to leave poison by her bedside so that she might take her life. Assume he wants her to live and prays she does not drink the poison, but is moved to leave it for her out of respect for her dignity as a person. Is he guilty of violating §210.5 of the Model Penal Code, which provides: "A person who purposely aids or solicits another to commit suicide is guilty of a felony. . . ."? Was it the husband's purpose (his "conscious object," as the Model Penal Code defines the term, §2.02(2)(a)) to aid his wife to commit suicide? Or was his conscious object to please his wife, though knowing it would (or might) help her to commit suicide. Or is it more accurate to say his conscious object was to please his wife *by* helping her to commit suicide? Suppose he had poured the poison down her throat in response to the identical pleas and for the identical reasons — would he have poisoned her purposely, or only knowingly?

5. *Purpose, intention, and "wishing."* Is there a difference between wishing and intending? Suppose a person makes a gift of an airplane ticket to someone, hoping that the plane will crash and kill her. Assume it does, and the traveler is killed. Could it be said that defendant intentionally (or purposely) killed her?

Consider what difference it would make, if any, to your answer if:

(a) the defendant knew that the chances of the plane's crashing were exceedingly remote, but he was given to taking long shots; or
(b) the defendant believed the plane would crash because his astrologer predicted it would; or
(c) the defendant believed it would crash because he knew that a group of terrorists had targeted it.

6. *Recklessness and awareness.* The Model Penal Code distinguishes two kinds of culpable unintentional actions, those that are reckless and those that are negligent. Negligence is less culpable because the actor only acts inadvertently; the person should have been aware of the danger, but was not. The fault is inattentiveness. Recklessness is more culpable because the actor was aware of the danger but acted anyway. The fault is choosing to run the risk.

So the crucial factor distinguishing these levels of culpability is awareness. But awareness of precisely what? The Model Penal Code requires for reckless conduct that the person "consciously disregards a substantial and unjustifiable risk" that some circumstance exists or that some result will follow from his conduct.

Does this mean that the actor must be aware (i) that there is a risk, (ii) that the risk is substantial, *and* (iii) that the risk is unjustifiable? Or does it mean only that the actor must be aware that there is some risk, which the jury finds to be substantial and unjustifiable? Or could it mean that the actor must be aware that there is a substantial risk, which the jury finds to be unjustifiable?

Grammatically, the Model Penal Code appears to require conscious awareness as to all three of the crucial factors. But is this interpretation tenable in practice? Consider a person who regards himself as an extraordinarily skillful driver. Finding himself in a hurry, he drives in a manner that creates an outrageously high risk of killing someone. He believes, however, that there is little risk because of his expertise as a driver. He drove negligently, but did he drive recklessly? See David Trieman, Recklessness and the Model Penal Code, 9 Am. J. Crim. L. 283, 361-371 (1981), for a helpful analysis of this issue.

Consider the observations of Glanville Williams on these issues in The Unresolved Problem of Recklessness, 8 Legal Stud. 74, 77 (1988):

> [The subjective] theory [of recklessness] has to deal with the awkward customer who undertook a course of conduct that he knew would involve serious risks if performed by someone not highly skilled, but thought that he himself possessed sufficient skill to eliminate danger. One's reaction to this general situation depends upon the specific facts. If the defendant is a doctor who acted in good faith but lacked sufficient skill, one would not want to characterize him as subjectively reckless. But, in contrast, take *Shimmen*'s case [84 Cr. App. R. 7 (1986)]. The defendant, who held a green belt and yellow belt in the Korean art of self-defence, was demonstrating his skill to his friends. To do this, he made as if to strike a plate-glass window with his foot; however, his kick broke the window. A Divisional Court held that he was guilty of criminal damage by recklessness, since he 'was aware of the kind of risk which would attend his act if he did not take adequate precautions,' even though he believed he had taken enough precautions to eliminate or minimise risk. . . .
>
> On subjective principles the court was wrong in saying that a person who believes he has taken enough precautions to eliminate risk is to be held guilty of recklessness merely because he perceived a risk before taking the precautions. If Shimmen thought he had eliminated risk, he was not subjectively reckless, but the court might have remitted the case to the magistrates with an instruction to decide whether he thought he had eliminated or merely mitigated the risk. This was a case where the defendant needed to be cross-examined. 'Would you have kicked with such force towards your girl friend's or wife's or your baby's head, relying on your ability to stop within an inch of it? No? Then you knew that there was some risk of your boot travelling further than you intended.' A person may be convinced of his own skill, and yet know that on rare (perhaps very rare) occasions it may fail him. In the case at bar, the victim, the owner of the window, did not agree to the demonstration of skill. [T]he actor has no right to impose any foreseen risk on him, beyond those associated with the ordinary business of life. He could be given a hot time in the witness-box if he says that in his opinion there was literally no risk.

Question: Would this basis for finding recklessness in the *Shimmen* case be possible under the Model Penal Code's definition of recklessness?

7. *"Specific intent" and "general intent."* Though the Model Penal Code does not use the concepts *specific intent* and *general intent,* they have been used extensively in non–Model Penal Code jurisdictions and in England, and they have been the

source of endless confusion in the courts. To provide an introduction to this terminology, this Note gives examples of the usage of these concepts and translates their apparent meanings into their nearest equivalents in the Model Penal Code vocabulary of culpable mental states. The translation has to be rough, however, because "general" and "specific" intent are often used inconsistently or applied loosely to entire crimes (for example, "bigamy is a general intent crime"; "larceny is a specific intent crime"), even though different culpability states ("intents") can and often do apply to different elements of such crimes. The point is made and examples given in the Model Penal Code Commentary excerpt reprinted supra page 208.

(a) Perhaps the least mysterious and most common usage of specific intent is to identify those actions that must be done with some specified further purpose in mind. The nearest Model Penal Code equivalent would be purpose as to some objective. For example, burglary requires (roughly) that a person break and enter, not simply knowingly or on purpose, but with the further objective of committing a felony inside. Without proof of that further objective, there can be no conviction for burglary. It is therefore common to describe burglary as a "specific intent crime"; the description is accurate in the sense that conviction for burglary requires proof of that further ("specific") purpose to commit a felony inside the building. Similarly, assault with intent to kill requires (roughly) that a person commit a battery upon another with the specific further purpose of killing that person. Without proof of that further purpose, a case of assault with intent to kill must fail. Accordingly, it is likewise common to describe assault with intent to kill as a "specific intent crime."

May the person in the above examples be convicted of some other crime, even without proof of the specified further intention? Yes. He can be convicted of a crime that requires only a "general" intent. But what is that? "General" intent can mean a number of different things, but in this context it generally means that the defendant can be convicted if he did what in ordinary speech we would call an intentional action. So in the first example, the actor who broke into a building would be guilty of trespass, a general intent crime; so long as he acted intentionally, in the sense that he knew the nature of the acts he performed, he would be guilty, without proof that he desired any particular further consequence. Similarly, in the second example, the actor would be guilty of simple battery, a general intent crime, regardless of whether he desired any further consequence to follow from his actions.

(b) Another usage of specific intent is to describe a crime that requires the defendant to have actual knowledge (that is, subjective awareness) of some particular fact or circumstance. Take the crime of bigamy, which prohibits a married person from remarrying while still legally married to his or her spouse. Must it be shown that the defendant knew her husband was still alive? If so, the crime would be called a specific intent crime; if not, it would be called a general intent crime. In the latter case, some lesser mental state than knowledge would suffice — perhaps negligence or recklessness, or perhaps none at all beyond the mental element necessarily entailed in engaging in a voluntary action. In Model Penal Code parlance, therefore, general intent crimes include those that do not require the prosecution to prove that the defendant knew of the existence of some factual element of the crime. But the "general intent" designation does not

determine whether the crime requires proof of negligence or recklessness as to that element.

These usages are just the main ones. There are others. It will be instructive for students as they encounter these terms to consider precisely how they are being used, whether they are in effect equivalent to one of the mens rea concepts used in the Model Penal Code, and whether the court has sound reasons for giving those terms whatever meaning it implicitly or explicitly gives them.

PROBLEM

In United States v. Neiswender, 590 F.2d 1269 (4th Cir. 1979), the defendant was convicted of obstruction of justice under 18 U.S.C. §1503, which provided, "Whoever . . . corruptly or by threats or force, or by any threatening letter or communication, influences, obstructs, or impedes, or endeavors to influence, obstruct, or impede, the due administration of justice" shall be fined not more than $5,000 or imprisoned not more than five years or both. The prosecution established at the trial that the defendant approached Mr. Weiner, the lawyer defending former Maryland governor Marvin Mandel in a much publicized criminal prosecution, and said that he had contact with a juror sitting on the Mandel case through whom he could ensure that the trial "would come out the right way" for a fee of $2,000. The lawyer promptly informed the United States Attorney and the judge presiding over the Mandel trial. Government agents, posing as associates of Mandel's lawyer, sought to identify the supposedly corrupt juror, but to no avail: The prosecution was unable to establish the truth of defendant's representations to Mandel's counsel. On appeal, the defendant contended that the government thus failed to prove an essential element of the statutory crime — the "endeavor," or specific intent, to undermine judicial processes. All it established was a fraudulent attempt to obtain money by deception. *Question:* Should this contention be sustained?

The court summarized the opposing arguments of the parties as follows.

> The government concedes that the defendant's primary intent was one to defraud. It urges, however, that every man intends the natural consequences of his acts. Had Neiswender convinced Weiner that he had a juror under his control and induced Weiner to participate in the scheme, the natural consequence would have been to reduce Weiner's efforts in defending his client. This debilitating effect on defense counsel would have altered the normal course of trial and prejudiced the client. This "natural consequence," the government contends, would have obstructed the due administration of justice.
>
> Neiswender has a rejoinder to this argument. In his view, while operation of the time-honored "natural consequences" rule might normally suffice to establish specific intent, it should play no role in this case. Neiswender contends that whatever force a presumed intention has must give way to actual intent. Here Neiswender's motivation was directly at odds with any design to obstruct justice since a guilty verdict would have revealed Neiswender's fraud. It was in his best interest for Weiner to press hard in his efforts to obtain an acquittal. Indeed, the evidence suggests that Neiswender recognized this fact for, during negotiations with Weiner's "associate," he insisted that defense counsel were "not to slouch in their duties" and "were to give it the full effect."

The court upheld the conviction, stating:

> We see no need to undertake an extended excursion into the subtleties of specific intent. In our view, the defendant need only have had knowledge or notice that success in his fraud would have likely resulted in an obstruction of justice. Notice is provided by the reasonable foreseeability of the natural and probable consequences of one's acts. [While this rule is a fiction it] is grounded upon sound policy, for, as outlined above, a rule focusing on foreseeable, rather than intended, consequences operates in sensible and fair fashion to deter the conduct sought to be avoided and to punish those whose actions are blameworthy, even though undertaken for purposes that may or may not be culpable.

For a critical review of *Neiswender,* see Note (Joseph DeMarco), A Funny Thing Happened on the Way to the Courthouse: Mens Rea, Document Destruction, and the Federal Obstruction of Justice Statute, 67 N.Y.U.L. Rev. 570 (1992).

HOLLOWAY v. UNITED STATES

Supreme Court of the United States
526 U.S. 1 (1999)

JUSTICE STEVENS delivered the opinion of the Court.

Carjacking "with the intent to cause death or serious bodily harm" is a federal crime.[1] The question presented in this case is whether that phrase requires the Government to prove that the defendant had an unconditional intent to kill or harm in all events, or whether it merely requires proof of an intent to kill or harm if necessary to effect a carjacking. Most of the judges who have considered the question have concluded, as do we, that Congress intended to criminalize the more typical carjacking carried out by means of a deliberate threat of violence, rather than just the rare case in which the defendant has an unconditional intent to use violence regardless of how the driver responds to his threat. . . .

Two considerations strongly support the conclusion that a natural reading of the text is fully consistent with a congressional decision to cover both species of intent. First, the statute as a whole reflects an intent to authorize federal prosecutions as a significant deterrent to a type of criminal activity that was a matter of national concern. . . .

Second, it is reasonable to presume that Congress was familiar with the cases and the scholarly writing that have recognized that the "specific intent" to commit a wrongful act may be conditional. . . . The facts of the leading case on the point are strikingly similar to the facts of this case. In People v. Connors, 253 Ill. 266, 97 N.E. 643 (1912), the Illinois Supreme Court affirmed the conviction [for assault with intent to kill] of a union organizer who had pointed a gun at a worker and threatened to kill him forthwith if he did not take off his overalls and quit work. The Court held that the jury had been properly instructed that the "specific intent to kill" could be found even though that intent was "coupled

1. The statute provides:

"Whoever, with the intent to cause death or serious bodily harm takes a motor vehicle that has been transported, shipped, or received in interstate or foreign commerce from the person or presence of another by force and violence or by intimidation, or attempts to do so, shall—

"(1) be fined under this title or improsoned not more than 15 years, or both."

with a condition" that the defendant would not fire if the victim complied with his demand. That holding has been repeatedly cited with approval by other courts and by scholars. Moreover, it reflects the views endorsed by the authors of the Model Criminal Code. The core principle that emerges from these sources is that a defendant may not negate a proscribed intent by requiring the victim to comply with a condition the defendant has no right to impose. . . .

JUSTICE SCALIA, dissenting. . . .

In customary English usage the unqualified word "intent" does not usually connote a purpose that is subject to any conditions precedent except those so remote in the speaker's estimation as to be effectively non-existent — and it never connotes a purpose that is subject to a condition which the speaker hopes will not occur, [which is the] sort of "conditional intent" that is at issue in this case. . . .

If I have made a categorical determination to go to Louisiana for the Christmas holidays, it is accurate for me to say that I intend to go to Louisiana. And that is so even though I realize that there are some remote and unlikely contingencies — "acts of God," for example — that might prevent me. . . . But is not common usage — indeed, it is an unheard-of usage — to speak of my having an "intent" to do something, when my plans are contingent upon an event that is not virtually certain, and that I hope will not occur. When a friend is seriously ill, for example, I would not say that "I intend to go to his funeral next week." I would have to make it clear that the intent is a conditional one: "I intend to go to his funeral next week if he dies." The carjacker who intends to kill if he is met with resistance is in the same position: he has an "intent to kill if resisted"; he does not have an "intent to kill." . . .

There are of course innumerable federal criminal statutes containing an intent requirement. . . . Consider, for example, 21 U.S.C. §841, which makes it a crime to possess certain drugs with intent to distribute them. Possession alone is also a crime, but a lesser one, see §844. Suppose that a person acquires and possesses a small quantity of cocaine for his own use, and that he in fact consumes it entirely himself. But assume further that, at the time he acquired the drug, he told his wife not to worry about the expense because, if they had an emergency need for money, he could always resell it. If conditional intent suffices, this person, who has never sold drugs and has never "intended" to sell drugs in any normal sense, has been guilty of possession with intent to distribute. . . . These examples make it clear, I think, that the doctrine of conditional intent cannot reasonably be applied across-the-board to the criminal code. I am unaware that any equivalent absurdities result from reading "intent" to mean what it says — a conclusion strongly supported by the fact that the Government has cited only a single case involving another federal statute, from over two centuries of federal criminal jurisprudence, applying the conditional-intent doctrine (and that in circumstances where it would not at all have been absurd to require real intent).[1] The course selected by the Court, of course — "intent" is sometimes conditional and sometimes not — would require us to sift through these statutes one-by-one,

1. The one case the Government has come up with is Shaffer v. United States, 308 F.2d 654 (C.A.5 1962), which upheld a conviction of assault "with intent to do bodily harm" where the defendant had said that if any persons tried to leave the building within five minutes after his departure "he would shoot their heads off," 308 F.2d, at 655. In my view, and in normal parlance, the defendant did not "intend" to do bodily harm, and there would have been nothing absurd about holding to that effect. . . .

making our decision on the basis of . . . ephemeral distinctions of "congressional purpose." . . .

NOTES AND QUESTIONS

1. Model Penal Code. The Model Penal Code is in accord with the Court's interpretation. Section 2.02(6) provides: "When a particular purpose is an element of an offense, the element is established although such purpose is conditional, unless the condition negatives the harm or evil sought to be prevented by the law defining the offense." Consider whether the condition "negatives the harm or evil sought to be prevented by the law defining the offense" in the following hypotheticals:

(i) Defendant enters another's home with intent to steal, but only if he finds something worth stealing. Burglary?

(ii) Defendant takes another's property intending keep it, unless his inheritance comes through. Larceny? (Larceny requires taking with intention not to return.)

(iv) Defendant takes property intending to keep it, but only if it turns out to be his own. Larceny?

2. Some brainteasers. Suppose John meets Chris at the local bus station and announces (and means it) that he will kill her if she doesn't take the next bus out of town. Assume four different scenarios.

(i) John is unarmed at the time he makes the threat;

(ii) John is carrying a firearm in his pocket at the time;

(iii) John is pointing the firearm at Chris,

(iv) John fires his gun at Chris but the gun misfires.

It would seem that in (i) there is no assault, and that in (iv) there is a straightforward assault with intent to kill (also an attempted murder). But how should we describe the two in-between situations, (ii) and (iii)?

One approach is through language usage. The archetypal assault with an intent to kill is a present attack on the person of the victim for the purpose of killing him. But when a defendant announces that he will make such an attack unless the victim complies with some unlawful demand, perhaps his action is most accurately described as an assault, not with intent to kill, but with an intent to (later) assault with intent to kill if the victim does not comply. Another approach is to ask whether the person who tells another he will kill her then and there unless she leaves town (John in scenario iii) is equal in culpability and dangerousness to the person who shoots her with the intention of killing her (John in scenario iv). Is he?

UNITED STATES v. JEWELL

United States Court of Appeals, 9th Circuit
532 F.2d 697 (1976)

BROWNING, J. [Defendant was convicted of knowingly transporting marijuana in his car from Mexico to the United States.]

It is undisputed that appellant entered the United States driving an automobile in which 110 pounds of marijuana worth $6,250 had been concealed in a secret compartment between the trunk and rear seat. Appellant testified that he did not know the marijuana was present. There was circumstantial evidence from which the jury could infer that appellant had positive knowledge of the presence of the marijuana, and that his contrary testimony was false. On the other hand there was evidence from which the jury could conclude that appellant spoke the truth — that although appellant knew of the presence of the secret compartment and had knowledge of facts indicating that it contained marijuana, he deliberately avoided positive knowledge of the presence of the contraband to avoid responsibility in the event of discovery. If the jury concluded the latter was indeed the situation, and if positive knowledge is required to convict, the jury would have no choice consistent with its oath but to find appellant not guilty even though he deliberately contrived his lack of positive knowledge. Appellant urges this view. . . .

Appellant tendered an instruction that to return a guilty verdict the jury must find that the defendant knew he was in possession of marijuana. The trial judge rejected the instruction because it suggested that "absolutely, positively, he has to know that it's there." . . .

The court told the jury that the government must prove beyond a reasonable doubt that the defendant "knowingly" brought the marijuana into the United States . . . and that he "knowingly" possessed the marijuana. . . . The court continued:

> The Government can complete their burden of proof by proving, beyond a reasonable doubt, that if the defendant was not actually aware that there was marijuana in the vehicle he was driving when he entered the United States his ignorance in that regard was solely and entirely a result of his having made a conscious purpose to disregard the nature of that which was in the vehicle, with a conscious purpose to avoid learning the truth.

The legal premise of these instructions is firmly supported by leading commentators here and in England. . . . The substantive justification for the rule is that deliberate ignorance and positive knowledge are equally culpable. The textual justification is that in common understanding one "knows" facts of which he is less than absolutely certain. To act "knowingly," therefore, is not necessarily to act only with positive knowledge, but also to act with an awareness of the high probability of the existence of the fact in question. When such awareness is present, "positive" knowledge is not required.

This is the analysis adopted in the Model Penal Code. Section 2.02(7) states:

> When knowledge of the existence of a particular fact is an element of an offense, such knowledge is established if a person is aware of a high probability of its existence, unless he actually believes that it does not exist.

As the Comment to this provision explains,

> Paragraph (7) deals with the situation British commentators have denominated "wilful blindness" or "connivance," the case of the actor who is aware of the prob-

able existence of a material fact but does not satisfy himself that it does not in fact exist.

. . . Appellant's narrow interpretation of "knowingly" is inconsistent with the Drug Control Act's general purpose to deal more effectively "with the growing menace of drug abuse in the United States." Holding that this term introduces a requirement of positive knowledge would make deliberate ignorance a defense. It cannot be doubted that those who traffic in drugs would make the most of it. . . .

It is no answer to say that in such cases the fact finder may infer positive knowledge. It is probable that many who performed the transportation function, essential to the drug traffic, can truthfully testify that they have no *positive* knowledge of the load they carry. Under appellant's interpretation of the statute, such persons will be convicted only if the fact finder errs in evaluating the credibility of the witness or deliberately disregards the law. . . .

It is worth emphasizing that the required state of mind differs from positive knowledge only so far as necessary to encompass a calculated effort to avoid the sanctions of the statute while violating its substance. "A court can properly find wilful blindness only where it can almost be said that the defendant actually knew." In the language of the instruction in this case, the government must prove, "beyond a reasonable doubt, that if the defendant was not actually aware . . . his ignorance in that regard was *solely* and *entirely* a result of . . . a conscious purpose to avoid learning the truth."

No legitimate interest of an accused is prejudiced by such a standard, and society's interest in a system of criminal law that is enforceable and that imposes sanctions upon all who are equally culpable requires it.

The conviction is affirmed.

KENNEDY, J., dissenting. The majority opinion justifies the conscious purpose jury instruction as an application of the wilful blindness doctrine recognized primarily by English authorities. . . .

The approach adopted in section 2.02(7) of the Model Penal Code clarifies, and, in important ways restricts, the English doctrine: . . This provision requires an awareness of a high probability that a fact exists, not merely a reckless disregard, or a suspicion followed by a failure to make further inquiry. It also establishes knowledge as a matter of subjective belief, an important safeguard against diluting the guilty state of mind required for conviction. It is important to note that section 2.02(7) is a *definition* of knowledge, not a substitute for it; as such, it has been cited with approval by the Supreme Court.

In light of the Model Penal Code's definition, the "conscious purpose" jury instruction is defective in three respects. First, it fails to mention the requirement that Jewell have been aware of a high probability that a controlled substance was in the car. It is not culpable to form "a conscious purpose to avoid learning the truth" unless one is aware of facts indicating a high probability of that truth. To illustrate, a child given a gift-wrapped package by his mother while on vacation in Mexico may form a conscious purpose to take it home without learning what is inside; yet his state of mind is totally innocent unless he is aware of a high probability that the package contains a controlled substance. Thus, a conscious purpose instruction is only proper when coupled with a requirement that one be aware of a high probability of the truth.

The second defect in the instruction as given is that it did not alert the jury that Jewell could not be convicted if he "actually believed" there was no controlled substance in the car. The failure to emphasize, as does the Model Penal Code, that subjective belief is the determinative factor, may allow a jury to convict on an objective theory of knowledge — that a reasonable man should have inspected the car and would have discovered what was hidden inside. . . .

Third, the jury instruction clearly states that Jewell could have been convicted even if found ignorant or "not actually aware" that the car contained a controlled substance. This is unacceptable because true ignorance, no matter how unreasonable, cannot provide a basis for criminal liability when the statute requires knowledge. A proper jury instruction based on the Model Penal Code would be presented as a way of defining knowledge, and not as an alterative to it. . . .

NOTES

1. Willful blindness instructions are commonly used to help the prosecution meet statutory requirements of "knowledge" not only in drug cases but in cases involving theft, securities fraud, environmental pollution, and a wide variety of other common law and regulatory offenses. See United States v. Pacific Hide & Fur Depot, Inc., 768 F.2d 1096 (9th Cir. 1985).

2. Does the *Jewell* court's approach to willful blindness in effect treat recklessness as sufficient to establish "knowledge"? Is a negligent failure to make inquiry sufficient to establish "knowledge"? For studies of these problems see Douglas Husak & Craig Callender, Wilful Ignorance, Knowledge, and the "Equal Culpability Thesis": A Study of the Deeper Significance of the Principle of Legality, [1994] Wis. L. Rev. 26; Note (Jonathan Marcus), Model Penal Code Section 2.02(7) and Willful Blindness, 102 Yale L.J. 2231 (1993); Robin Charlow, Wilful Ignorance and Criminal Culpability, 70 Tex. L. Rev. 1351 (1992); Ira Robbins, The Ostrich Instruction: Deliberate Ignorance as a Criminal Mens Rea, 81 J. Crim. L. & Criminology 191 (1990).

3. In order to avoid the risk that a jury may convict on the basis of mere negligence, some courts hold that willful blindness (or "ostrich") instructions, even if properly formulated, should not be given to the jury unless the evidence establishes both (1) that the defendant was subjectively aware of a high probability of illegal conduct, and (2) that the defendant purposefully contrived to avoid learning of the illegal conduct. See United States v. Farfan-Carreon, 935 F.2d 678, 680 (5th Cir. 1991). Thus, in a bank fraud prosecution, the court held it was error to give a willful blindness instruction, though a bank's owner failed to investigate certain questionable transactions, because the facts available to him "did not suggest that criminal activity was probably afoot." United States v. Barnhart, 979 F.2d 647, 652 (8th Cir. 1992).

With respect to the requirement that the defendant purposely *contrived* to avoid learning the truth, consider United States v. Giovannetti, 919 F.2d 1223 (7th Cir. 1990). Defendant Janis was convicted of aiding and abetting a gambling operation by renting his house to some gamblers, "knowing" that the lessees would use it as a wireroom. There was no direct evidence of Janis's knowledge, but he was a gambler himself, and knowing that his lessees were professional gamblers, he made no inquiries about their intended use of the house. The court (per Posner, J.) reversed the conviction, holding that it was error to give an "ostrich" instruction under these circumstances (id. at 1228-1229):

> [Notice] just what it is that real ostriches do (or at least are popularly supposed to do). They do not just fail to follow through on their suspicions of bad things. They are not merely *careless* birds. They bury their heads in the sand so that they will not see or hear bad things. They *deliberately* avoid acquiring unpleasant knowledge. The ostrich instruction is designed for cases in which there is evidence that the defendant, knowing or strongly suspecting that he is involved in shady dealings, takes steps to make sure that he does not acquire full or exact knowledge of the nature and extent of those dealings. . . .
>
> The government points out that the rented house . . . was a short way down a side street from the thoroughfare on which Janis commuted to work daily. It would have been easy for him to drive by the house from time to time to see what was doing, and if he had done so he might have discovered its use as a wireroom. He did not do so. But this is not the active avoidance with which the ostrich doctrine is concerned. . . . Janis failed to display curiosity, but he did nothing to prevent the truth from being communicated to him. He did not *act* to avoid learning the truth.
>
> [T]he deliberate effort to avoid guilty knowledge . . . can be a mental, as well as a physical, effort — a cutting off of one's normal curiosity by an effort of will. There is no evidence of either sort of effort here.

Questions: Is the decision analytically sound? If so, does the result suggest that defendants like Janis should not be convicted, or does it suggest that the statutory mens rea requirement should be relaxed? Why might it be sound to require actual knowledge rather than recklessness as a prerequisite to convicting a defendant like Janis? Cf. Alan C. Michael, Acceptance: The Missing State, 71 S. Cal.L.Rev. 953 (1998).

4. Consider the distinction drawn by David Luban between what he calls the ostrich and the fox. Contrived Ignorance, 87 Geo. L.J. 957, 962 (1999):

> The focus in a willful ignorance case is on whether the actor deliberately avoided guilty knowledge. The inquiry is about whatever steps the actor took toward off knowledge prior to the misdeed. [The fox.] The focus in the Model Penal Code, by contrast, is on how certain the actor is about a fact. The inquiry is about the actor's subjective state at the moment of the misdeed. [The ostrich.] These are completely different issues. An actor can be aware of the high probability of a fact whether or not she took steps to avoid knowing it, and an actor can screen herself from knowledge of facts regardless of whether their probability is high or low. . . . Douglas Husak and Craig Callender illustrate the latter with a nice pair of examples [Willful Ignorance, Knowledge, and the "Equal Culpability" Thesis, [1994] Wis. L. Rev. 29, 37-38]. Suppose that a dope distributor tells each of his three couriers never to look in the suitcase he gives to each one, adding that it isn't necessary for them to know what the suitcases contain. If the suitcases contain dope, the case is plainly one of willful ignorance. But now suppose that the distributor adds that two of the three suitcases contain nothing but clothing, that he is truthful, and that the distributors know he is truthful. If the couriers deliver the suitcases without looking inside and without asking any questions, the case seems indistinguishable from the first case. It is still willful ignorance. But in the second case, the courier with dope in his suitcase lacks awareness of the high probability that it contains dope. Indeed, he knows that the probability is one-third. He may even believe that his suitcase contains nothing but clothes. Thus, in the language of the Model Penal Code §2.02(7), he not only lacks awareness of a high probability of the fact's existence, "he actually believes that it does not exist."

b. Mistake of Fact

MODEL PENAL CODE

SECTION 2.04(1)-(2). IGNORANCE OR MISTAKE

[See Appendix.]

MODEL PENAL CODE AND COMMENTARIES, COMMENT TO §2.04 AT 269-271 (1985): Subsection (1) states the conventional position under which the significance of ignorance by the defendant of a matter of fact or law, or a mistake as to such matters, is determined by the mental state required for the commission of the offense involved. Thus ignorance or mistake is a defense when it negatives the existence of a state of mind that is essential to the commission of an offense, or when it establishes a state of mind that constitutes a defense under a rule of law relating to defenses. In other words, ignorance or mistake has only evidential import; it is significant whenever it is logically relevant, and it may be logically relevant to negate the required mode of culpability or to establish a special defense.

The critical legislative decisions, therefore, relate to the establishment of the culpability for specific offenses as they are defined in the criminal code. . . .

To put the matter as this subsection does is not to say anything that would not otherwise be true, even if no provision on the subject were made. As Glanville Williams has summarized the matter, the rule relating to mistake "is not a new rule; and the law could be stated equally well without reference to mistake. . . . It is impossible to assert that a crime requiring intention or recklessness can be committed although the accused laboured under a mistake negativing the requisite intention or recklessness. Such an assertion carries its own refutation." This obvious point has, however, sometimes been overlooked in general formulations purporting to require that mistake be reasonable if it is to exculpate, without regard to the mode of culpability required to commit the crime. This is unexceptionable in the case of mistake regarding an element of an offense as to which negligence is the culpability level. There is no justification, however, for requiring that ignorance or mistake be reasonable if the crime or the element of the crime involved requires acting purposely or knowingly for its commission.

It is true, of course, that whether recklessness or negligence suffices as a mode of culpability with respect to a given element of an offense is often raised for the first time in dealing with a question of mistake. That this may happen emphasizes the importance of perceiving that the question relates to the underlying rule as to the kind of culpability required with respect to the particular element of the offense involved. Generalizations about mistake of fact and mistake of law, or about honest and reasonable mistakes as relevant to general and specific intent crimes, tend to obscure rather than clarify that simple point.

NOTE

The Model Penal Code's mistake proposals have had a major influence on recent state penal code revisions. However, states have departed from the Model Penal Code in a number of ways. Consider, for example, the Pennsylvania provision (Pa. Cons. Stat. tit. 18, §304) that makes mistake of fact a defense when it negatives the "intent, knowledge, belief, recklessness, or negligence required" by the offense, but only if the mistake is one "for which there is a reasonable explanation or excuse."

Question: What is the effect of the qualifying clause?

REGINA v. PRINCE

Court of Crown Cases Reserved
L.R. 2 Cr. Cas. Res. 154 (1875)

[Defendant was convicted of taking an unmarried girl under 16 years of age out of the possession and against the will of her father in violation of 24 & 25 Vict., c. 100, §55, providing:

> Whosoever shall unlawfully take or cause to be taken any unmarried girl, being under the age of sixteen years, out of the possession and against the will of her father or mother, or of any person having the lawful care or charge of her, shall be guilty of a misdemeanor. . .

The jury found that though the girl, Annie Phillips, was 14 at the time, she had told the defendant that she was 18 before he took her away, that the defendant honestly believed that statement, and that his belief was reasonable. On a case stated by Denman, J., the Court for Crown Cases Reserved found that the prisoner was rightly convicted, Brett, J., dissenting.

BRAMWELL, B. [Finding that to sustain the defendant's position it was necessary to read into the statute language requiring that a person not believe the girl he takes is over the age of 16, the opinion continues:] These words are not there, and the question is, whether we are bound to construe the statute as though they were, on account of the rule that the mens rea is necessary to make an act a crime. I am of opinion that we are not, . . . and for the following reasons: The act forbidden is wrong in itself, if without lawful cause; I do not say illegal, but wrong. [W]hat the statute contemplates, and what I say is wrong, is the taking of a female of such tender years that she is properly called a *girl,* can be said to be in another's *possession,* and in that other's *care or charge.* No argument is necessary to prove this; it is enough to state the case. The legislature has enacted that if anyone does this wrong act, he does it at the risk of her turning out to be under sixteen. This opinion gives full scope to the doctrine of the mens rea. If the taker believed he had the father's consent, though wrongly, he would have no mens rea; so if he did not know she was in anyone's possession, nor in the care or charge of anyone. In those cases he would not know he was doing the *act* forbidden by the statute — an act which, if he knew she was in possession and in care or charge of anyone, he would know was a crime or not, according as she was under sixteen or not. He would not know he was doing an act wrong in itself, whatever was his intention, if done without lawful cause. The same principle applies in other cases. A man was held liable for assaulting a police officer in the execution of his duty, though he did not know he was a police officer. Why? Because the act was wrong in itself. So, also, in the case of burglary, could a person charged claim an acquittal on the ground that he believed it was past six when he entered, or in housebreaking, that he did not know the place broken into was a house? It seems to me impossible to say that where a person takes a girl out of her father's possession, not knowing whether she is or is not under sixteen, that he is not guilty; and equally impossible when he believes, but erroneously, that she is old enough for him to do a wrong act with safety. I think the conviction should be affirmed.

BRETT, J., [dissenting]. [I]f the facts had been as the prisoner, according to the findings of the jury, believed them to be, and had reasonable ground for believing them to be, he would have done no act which has ever been a criminal offence in England; he would have done no act in respect of which any civil action could have ever been maintained against him; he would have done no act for which, if done in the absence of the father, and done with the continuing consent of the girl, the father could have had any legal remedy. . . . Upon all the cases I think it is proved that there can be no conviction for crime in England in the absence of a criminal mind or mens rea. Then comes the question, what is the true meaning of the phrase. I do not doubt that it exists where the prisoner knowingly does acts which would constitute a crime if the result were as he anticipated, but in which the result may not improbably end by bringing the offence within a more serious class of crime. As if a man strikes with a dangerous weapon, with intent to do grievous bodily harm, and kills, the result makes the crime murder. The prisoner has run the risk. So, if a prisoner do the prohibited acts, without caring to consider what the truth is as to facts — as if a prisoner were to abduct a girl under sixteen without caring to consider whether she was in truth under sixteen — he runs the risk. So if he without abduction defiles a girl who is in fact under ten years old, with a belief that she is between ten and twelve. If the facts were as he believed he would be committing the lesser crime. Then he runs the risk of his crime resulting in the greater crime. It is clear that ignorance of the law does not excuse. It seems to me to follow that the maxim as to mens rea applies whenever the facts which are present in the prisoner's mind, and which he has reasonable ground to believe, and does believe to be the facts, would, if true, make his acts no criminal offence at all. I come to the conclusion that a mistake of facts, on reasonable grounds, to the extent that if the facts were as believed the acts of the prisoner would make him guilty of no criminal offence at all, is an excuse and that such excuse is implied in every criminal charge and every criminal enactment in England.

WHITE v. STATE, 44 Ohio App. 331, 185 N.E. 64 (1933). [Defendant was convicted of violating a statute providing that whoever, being the husband of a pregnant woman, leaves with intent to abandon such pregnant woman shall be imprisoned. The trial court had given an instruction to the effect that the defendant was no less guilty because he did not know his wife was pregnant. On appeal, held affirmed.] The sound doctrine underlying the rule that guilty knowledge is not required to accomplish the crime of rape with consent [statutory rape] is that the act of the accused is at best an immoral one, and that he cannot enter upon the accomplishment of an admittedly immoral act except at his peril, and if in law his act is in fact felony he must suffer the consequences thereof although so far as his actual knowledge was concerned he may not have known the enormity of the offense of which he is guilty. By like reasoning we take the view that a husband abandoning his wife is guilty of wrongdoing. It is a violation of his civil duty. He is charged with her support and protection. If he abandons her, he does so at his peril, and, if she be in fact at the time pregnant, though he may not have known it, he cannot plead that ignorance as a defense. He must make sure of his ground when he commits the simple wrong of leaving her at all.

NOTES AND QUESTIONS

1. The controversy over Prince: *The lesser-wrong principle of* Bramwell. In his book, An Inquiry into Criminal Guilt 149 (1963), Peter Brett states:

> [The opinion] of Bramwell, B. is to my mind clearly in accord with principle. It reflects the view that we learn our duties, not by studying the statute book, but by living in a community. A defense of mistake rests ultimately on the defendant's being able to say that he has observed the community ethic, and this Prince could not do.

But Professor Brett is an exception. Most of the academic commentary has been highly critical of *Prince.* See, e.g., Glanville Williams, Criminal Law — The General Part 189-190 (2d ed. 1961); George Fletcher, Rethinking Criminal Law 727 (1978). Consider Graham Hughes's response to Peter Brett in Criminal Responsibility, 16 Stan. L. Rev. 470, 480-481 (1964):

> [T]his appears as an appallingly dangerous position which comes close to giving the jury a discretion to create new crimes. In *Prince* what the accused was doing that he knew to be wrong was presumably to take away a young girl from the possession of her parents without their consent. Let us vary the position slightly and assume that the charge is one of unlawful sexual intercourse with a girl under sixteen. The accused reasonably believed that the girl was over sixteen. Should he be convicted because he knew that he was fornicating and because fornication is wrong according to the community ethic? In the first place this assumes that there is a clear community judgment about the wrongfulness of fornication, which is not so. . . . The truth is that there are many community ethics. . . . Even though ethical attitudes owe much to culture and environment, there is enough room for individual divergence to make Professor Brett's approach a slippery one.
>
> But the more serious objection is that there seems no reason why the community ethic concerning some conduct, even though clear, should be relevant to a determination of whether other conduct is criminal. The crime is that of fornicating with girls under sixteen, and it is not obvious that a general judgment about the morality of fornication should be determinative of guilt. Moral duties should not be identified with criminal duties. If fornication is not a crime in itself, as it is not in England, why should it become one when the defendant makes a reasonable mistake about the age of his partner?

Professor Meir Dan-Cohen disagrees, suggesting that "an interpretation of *Prince* is possible that both takes seriously Baron Bramwell's use of the concept of mens rea and withstands criticisms such as those of Professor Hughes." Decision Rules and Conduct Rules: On Acoustic Separation in Criminal Law, 97 Harv. L. Rev. 625, 655 (1984). He uses the *Prince* case as an example of how sometimes a single criminal statute may be taken as speaking to two audiences: to the general public, to which it directs a conduct rule, and to legal officials, to which it directs a decision rule. The age limitation in *Prince* was part of the decision rule addressed to the court, an arbitrary bright line to limit judicial discretion. The statute's conduct rule was an enactment of the moral norm against abducting girls from their parents. Therefore, the defendant's mistake as to the girl's age was irrelevant, since the precise age did not figure in the conduct rule addressed to him, and the court could not be accused of judicial law making. As Lord Bramwell observed, the statute said to the public: do not take "a female of such tender years that she is properly called a girl" from her parents. That is what the statute prohibited people from doing and that is what the defendant did. It is as though Parliament had enacted two statutes: one, addressed to the public, said don't take young girls from their parents; the other, addressed to officials, said don't prosecute or convict unless the girl is under sixteen. Professor Dan-Cohen defends the distinction between decision rules and conduct rules as follows:

> [C]oncerns other than reinforcement of community morality motivate decision rules. Primary among such concerns is the need to shape, control, and constrain the power wielded by decisionmakers. To attain this aim, the rules governing official decisionmaking must be characterized by a greater degree of precision and determinacy than can normally be expected of the community's moral precepts. Accordingly, whereas a conduct rule may be fully coextensive with the relevant moral precept, the corresponding decision rule need not be. Instead, the decision rule should define, as clearly and precisely as possible, a range of punishable conduct that is unquestionably within the bounds of the community's relevant moral norm.

More recently Professors Dan M. Kahan and Daniel Yeager have also come to the defense of Baron Bramwell's decision in *Prince.* Dan M. Kahan, Correspondence: Is Ignorance of Fact an Excuse Only for the Virtuous?, 96 Mich. L. Rev. 2123 (1998); Daniel Yeager, Kahan on Mistakes, 96 Mich. L. Rev. 2113 (1998). As Kahan wrote, "courts excuse a mistaken offender when, but only when, the offender's mistake negates the inference that he has failed to internalize society's moral norms." On this premise, they defend the decision of Baron Bramwell on the ground that the defendant was well aware of the then socially recognized possessory rights of a parent in a young unmarried girl whether below or not far above the age of sixteen.

2. *Questions on the controversy.*

(i) How well does Dan-Cohen's defense of Bramwell's decision withstand the criticism of Professor Hughes? Even if that decision does not amount to judicial lawmaking, why is it not still subject to the other criticism that Professor Hughes makes of it, that in light of the disagreement over changing moral and social norms it remits too much discretion to the judge and fails to give adequate guidance to the public?

(ii) Would Dan-Cohen's defense of Bramwell's opinion extend to *White?* One would think not. In *White,* the basic moral concern of the statute seems to be solicitude toward pregnant women and their needs. Far from being an arbitrary marker, pregnancy here is an essential part of the moral norm that is enacted by the statute. So when the court holds the defendant culpable just for deserting his wife, it goes beyond interpreting the statute. Instead it invokes a different and broader moral norm than the one the present statute can be plausibly said to enact and so engages in judicial lawmaking.

(iii) Would the defense of Bramwell's decision offered by Kahan/Yaeger extend to *White?* It would seem so, since their defense of Bramwell's lesser wrong analysis lacks the qualification developed by Professor Dan-Cohen. How could that be defended against Professor Hughes's criticism?

3. *The lesser-crime view of Brett J.* In reflecting on Brett J.'s approach to mens rea, consider this hypothetical. Suppose Prince had no interest in the girl but wanted only to steal her father's horse and carriage, which he drove away without any idea that the girl was napping in the back seat. Would he be guilty of abducting the girl under Brett J.'s lesser-crime principle? Note that this principle is alive and well today. It has figured prominently in recent drug-sentencing

cases. In United States v. Valencia-Gonzales, 172 F.3d 344 (5th Cir. 1999), for example, defendant was convicted of possessing a controlled substance, but was sentenced on the basis of his having carried heroin even though the government stipulated that he believed he was carrying cocaine, for which the law provided a lesser sentence. In a similar case, one federal judge, Judge Jack Weinstein, in a rare exception to the prevailing law, held such a sentence a violation of due process since it departed from the requirement that punishment be calibrated to culpability. United States v. Cordoba-Hincapie, 825 F. Supp. 485 (E.D.N.Y. 1993).

4. Prince *in perspective.* If the statute in *Prince* had explicitly required that the defendant know or have reason to know that the unmarried girl was under the age of sixteen, of course, these doctrines in the *Prince* case would not be applicable. These doctrines, it should be recognized, are used to import a mens rea requirement of some kind into a statute, which on its face imposed strict liability. The controversy just reviewed is over whether the sense of mens rea these doctrines provide is sufficient.

5. In a concurring opinion in *Prince,* Justice Blackburn makes the following observation:

> Section 50 enacts, that whosoever shall "unlawfully and carnally know and abuse any girl under the age of ten years," shall be guilty of felony. Section 51, whoever shall "unlawfully and carnally know and abuse any girl being above the age of ten years, and under the age of twelve years," shall be guilty of a misdemeanor.
>
> It seems impossible to suppose that the intention of the legislature in those two sections could have been to make the crime depend upon the knowledge of the prisoner of the girl's actual age. It would produce the monstrous result that a man who had carnal connection with a girl, in reality not quite ten years old, but whom he on reasonable grounds believed to be a little more than ten, was to escape altogether. He could not, in that view of the statute, be convicted of the felony, for he did not know her to be under ten. He could not be convicted of the misdemeanor, because she was in fact not above the age of ten.

Model Penal Code §2.04(2) is a response to this kind of situation. See the Comment on this section in Model Penal Code and Commentaries, Comment at 272-273 (1985).

PEOPLE v. OLSEN

Supreme Court of California
36 Cal. 3d 638, 685 P.2d 52 (1984)

BIRD, C. J. Is a reasonable mistake as to the victim's age a defense to a charge of lewd or lascivious conduct with a child under the age of 14 years (Pen. Code, §288, subd. (a)[1])?

1. Section 288, subdivision (a) provides in relevant part:

> Any person who shall willfully and lewdly commit any lewd or lascivious act . . . upon or with the body, or any part or member thereof, of a child under the age of 14 years, with the intent of arousing, appealing to, or gratifying the lust or passions or sexual desires of such person or of such child, shall be guilty of a felony and shall be imprisoned in the state prison for a term of three, six, or eight years. . . .

In early June 1981, Shawn M. was 13 years and 10 months old. At that time, her parents were entertaining out-of-town guests. Since one of the visitors was using Shawn's bedroom, Shawn suggested that she sleep in her family's camper trailer which was parked in the driveway in front of the house. Shawn's parents agreed to this arrangement on the condition that she keep the windows shut and door locked. . . .

At trial, Shawn testified to the following events. On her third night in the trailer, she locked the door as instructed by her parents. She then fell asleep, but was awakened by appellant Olsen who was knocking on the window and asking to be let in. Shawn said nothing and appellant left. Approximately a half-hour later, Garcia came up to the window and asked if he could enter. Shawn did not respond so he left. . . . After both appellant and Garcia left, Shawn went to sleep. Shawn was then awakened by the sound of barking dogs and by Garcia, who had a knife by her side and his hand over her mouth.[2] Garcia called to appellant to come in, and appellant entered the trailer.

Garcia told Shawn to let appellant "make love" to her, or he — Garcia — would stab her. . . .

Appellant proceeded to have sexual intercourse with Shawn. . . . While appellant was still [doing so], her father entered the trailer. Mr. M. grabbed appellant as he was trying to leave, and Garcia stabbed Mr. M. in order to free appellant.

Shawn testified that she knew Garcia "pretty well." . . . She also testified that she was very good friends "off and on" with appellant and that during one three-month period she spent almost every day at appellant's house. At the time of the incident, however, Shawn considered Garcia her boyfriend.[3]

Finally, Shawn admitted that she told both Garcia and appellant that she was over 16 years old. She also conceded that she looked as if she were over 16.[4]

Garcia testified to quite a different set of events. . . . On . . . the day before the offense Shawn invited him to spend the night in the trailer with her so that they could have sex. He and Shawn engaged in sexual intercourse about four times that evening. Shawn invited Garcia to come back the following night at midnight.

The next night, after two unsuccessful attempts to enter the trailer, Garcia and appellant were told by Shawn to return at midnight. . . . Shawn, wearing only a pair of panties, opened the door and invited them in. She told them . . . that she wanted "to make love" with appellant first. When Mr. M. entered the trailer, appellant was on top of Shawn. Garcia denied threatening Shawn with a knife, taking her nightgown off, breaking into the trailer or forcing her to have sex with them.[5]

2. Although Shawn testified she locked the trailer door, she failed to explain how Garcia entered the trailer. A subsequent examination of the trailer revealed that there were no signs of a forced entry.

3. Shawn admitted that she had engaged in intercourse before the night of June 3rd, but denied having any such prior experience with either Garcia or appellant. However, she did admit having had sexual relations, short of intercourse, with both of them in the past.

4. Patricia Alvarez, a police officer, testified that appellant told her that he thought Shawn was 17.

5. Appellant's sister corroborated Shawn's testimony that Shawn made daily visits to the Olsen home during a three-month period. She testified that during these visits Shawn and appellant would go into the latter's bedroom and close the door. On one occasion appellant's sister saw the two in bed together. [Four other witnesses described similar episodes involving Shawn and either appellant or other boys.]

At the conclusion of the trial, the court found Garcia and appellant guilty of violating section 288, subdivision (a).[7] In reaching its decision, the court rejected defense counsel's argument that a good faith belief as to the age of the victim was a defense to the section 288 charge. Appellant was sentenced to the lower term of three years in state prison. This appeal followed. . . .

The language of section 288 is silent as to whether a good faith, reasonable mistake as to the victim's age constitutes a defense to a charge under that statute. . . .

Twenty years ago, this court in People v. Hernandez [61 Cal. 2d 529, 393 P.2d 673 (1964)] overruled established precedent, and held that an accused's good faith, reasonable belief that a victim was 18 years or more of age was a defense to a charge of statutory rape.[10] . . .

One Court of Appeal has declined to apply *Hernandez* in an analogous context. In People v. Lopez (1969) 271 Cal. App. 2d 754, 77 Cal. Rptr. 59, the court refused to recognize a reasonable mistake of age defense to a charge of offering or furnishing marijuana to a minor. The court noted that the act of furnishing marijuana is criminal regardless of the age of the recipient and that furnishing marijuana to a minor simply yields a greater punishment than when the substance is furnished to an adult. "[A] mistake of fact relating only to the gravity of an offense will not shield a deliberate offender from the full consequences of the wrong actually committed." (Ibid.)

. . . There exists a strong public policy to protect children of tender years. [S]ection 288 was enacted for that very purpose. Furthermore, even the *Hernandez* court recognized this important policy when it made clear that it did not contemplate applying the mistake of age defense in cases where the victim is of "tender years." . . .

This conclusion is supported by the Legislature's enactment of section 1203.066. Subdivision (a)(3) of that statute renders certain individuals convicted of lewd or lascivious conduct who "honestly and reasonably believed the victim was 14 years old or older" eligible for probation. The Legislature's enactment of section 1203.066, subdivision (a)(3). . . . strongly indicates that the Legislature did not intend such a defense to a section 288 charge. To recognize such a defense would render section 1203.066, subdivision (a)(3) a nullity, since the question of probation for individuals who had entertained an honest and reasonable belief in the victim's age would never arise. . . .

Other legislative provisions also support the holding that a reasonable mistake of age is not a defense to a section 288 charge. Time and again, the Legislature has recognized that persons under 14 years of age are in need of special protection. . . .

The Legislature has also determined that persons who commit sexual offenses on children under the age of 14 should be punished more severely than those who commit such offenses on children under the age of 18. . . .

7. Garcia was also found guilty of assault with a deadly weapon with infliction of great bodily injury [in the assault on Mr. M.]. Both Garcia and appellant were found not guilty of burglary, forcible rape, and lewd or lascivious acts upon a child under the age of 14 by use of force. . . .

10. One commentator believes that *Hernandez* marked a clear break from the "universally accepted view of the courts in this country." (Annot., Mistake or Lack of Information as to Victim's Age as Defense to Statutory Rape (1966) 8 A.L.R.3d 1100, 1102-1105, and cases cited.) The view that mistake of age is not a defense to a charge of statutory rape still prevails in the overwhelming majority of jurisdictions.

It is significant that a violation of section 288 carries a much harsher penalty than does unlawful sexual intercourse (§261.5), the crime involved in *Hernandez.* Section 261.5 carries a maximum punishment of one year in the county jail or three years in state prison, while section 288 carries a maximum penalty of eight years in state prison. The different penalties for these two offenses further supports the view that there exists a strong public policy to protect children under 14. . . .

The legislative purpose of section 288 would not be served by recognizing a defense of reasonable mistake of age. . . . Accordingly, the judgment of conviction is affirmed.

GRODIN, J., concurring and dissenting. I agree that the enactment of Penal Code section 1203.066, which renders eligible for probation persons convicted of lewd or lascivious conduct who "honestly and reasonably believed the victim was 14 years old or older" is persuasive evidence that in the eyes of the Legislature such a belief is not a defense to the crime.[1] What troubles me is the notion that a person who acted with such belief, and is not otherwise shown to be guilty of any criminal conduct,[2] may not only be convicted but be sentenced to prison notwithstanding his eligibility for probation when it appears that his belief did not accord with reality. To me, that smacks of cruel or unusual punishment.

. . . I recognize . . . that our legal system includes certain "strict liability" crimes, but generally these are confined to the so-called "regulatory" or "public welfare" offenses. . . . (Morissette v. United States (1952) 342 U.S. 246). Moreover, with respect to such crimes, "*The accused, if he does not will the violation, usually is in a position to prevent it with no more care than society might reasonably expect . . . from one who assumed his responsibilities. Also, penalties commonly are relatively small, and conviction does no grave damage to an offender's reputation.*" (Id., at p. 256, emphasis added.)

Even in the regulatory context, "judicial and academic acceptance of liability without fault has not been enthusiastic." (Jeffries & Stephen, Defenses, Presumptions, and Burden of Proof in the Criminal Law (1979) 88 Yale L.J. 1325, 1373.) And "with respect to traditional crimes, it is a widely accepted normative principle that conviction should not be had without proof of fault. At least when the offense carries serious sanctions and the stigma of official condemnation, liability should be reserved for persons whose blameworthiness has been established" (Id., at pp. 1373-1374.)

. . . No doubt the standard of what is reasonable must be set relatively high in order to accomplish the legislative objective of protecting persons under 14 years of age against certain conduct. Perhaps it is not enough that a person "looks" to be more than 14; perhaps there is a duty of reasonable inquiry besides. At some

1. I do not agree that legislative intent to eliminate good faith mistake of fact as a defense can be inferred from the imposition of relatively higher penalties for that crime. On the contrary, as this court has stated in connection with the crime of bigamy: "The severe penalty imposed . . . the serious loss of reputation conviction entails, the infrequency of the offense, and the fact that it has been regarded . . . as a crime involving moral turpitude, make it extremely unlikely that the Legislature meant to include the morally innocent to make sure the guilty did not escape." (People v. Vogel (1956) 46 Cal. 2d 798, 804, 299 P.2d 850.)

2. The People suggest that defendant was at least guilty of "sexual intercourse accomplished with a female not the wife of the perpetrator, where the female is under the age of 18 years." Defendant was neither charged nor convicted of that offense, however, and it is by no means clear from the record that he had sexual intercourse with the victim.

point, however, the belief becomes reasonable by any legitimate standard, so that one would say the defendant is acting in a way which is no different from the way our society would expect a reasonable, careful, and law-abiding citizen to act.

At that point, it seems to me, the imposition of criminal sanctions, particularly imprisonment, simply cannot be tolerated in a civilized society. . . .

NOTE

The Model Penal Code also imposes strict liability as to the age of the victim under certain circumstances. Section 213.6(1) provides that where criminality turns on the child's being below the age of 10, the defense of reasonable mistake is not available; but where it turns on the child's being below a critical age other than 10, reasonable mistake is an affirmative defense. What is the theory behind this distinction? Can it be reconciled with §2.04(2) and its supporting commentary, page 225 supra? A defense of the Model Penal Code's position appears in Model Penal Code and Commentaries, Comment to §213.6 at 415-417 (1980).

In most jurisdictions a mistake as to age, even if reasonable, is not a defense to statutory rape. However, some states do allow the defense of reasonable mistake, either by statute or judicial ruling. The authorities are reviewed in Annotation, Mistake or Lack of Information as to Victim's Age as Defense to Statutory Rape, 46 A.L.R. 5th 499 (1997). The constitutionality of imposing strict liability in these cases is debated in the majority and dissenting opinions in Owens v. State, 72 A.2d 43 (Md. 1999).

NOTE ON MATERIAL AND JURISDICTIONAL ELEMENTS

It is widely accepted that a culpable mental state need not be proved as to those elements of a crime, such as jurisdiction or venue, that have no bearing on the harm that the offense seeks to prevent or on the existence of a justification or excuse. The Model Penal Code, for example, restricts the culpability requirements of §2.02 to what it defines in §1.13(10) as material elements. Because nonmaterial elements have no bearing on the person's culpability, it is logical to dispense with any requirement that the person be shown to have acted culpably with respect to them. A person, for example, charged in State *X* with shooting another in State *X* will hardly be heard to say in defense that he had every reason to believe he was in State *Y*. See Model Penal Code and Commentaries, Comment §1.13 at 211 (1985).

While state jurisdictional requirements are largely based on the locus of the crime, federal crimes often contain jurisdictional elements relating to the method used to commit the crime or the identity of the victim. A good example is 18 U.S.C. §1341, the federal mail fraud statute, which prohibits the use of the mails "for the purpose of executing [any scheme or artifice to defraud]." Section 1341 does not require the use of the mails to be a significant element of the fraudulent scheme; the statute merely requires a showing that the mails were used. Its purpose is to grant federal jurisdiction over what would otherwise be a state offense.

That jurisdictional elements do not require any culpable mental state is universally accepted, but controversies can arise over whether an element that serves jurisdictional purposes also serves purposes that require it to be treated as a "material" element. Consider 18 U.S.C. §111, which prohibits assaults upon federal officers who are engaged in the performance of their duties. In United States v. Feola, 420 U.S. 672 (1975), the defendants attempted to rob several men who had presented themselves as potential drug buyers. The men turned out to be undercover federal drug agents, and the defendants were therefore charged with assaulting federal officers. The United States Supreme Court held that the "federal officer" element of this offense is jurisdictional only, and thus a mistaken belief that the victim was a fellow criminal was no defense:

> [I]n order to effectuate the congressional purpose of according maximum protection to federal officers by making prosecutions for assaults upon them cognizable in the federal courts, §111 cannot be construed as embodying an unexpressed requirement that an assailant be aware that his victim is a federal officer. All the statute requires is an intent to assault, not an intent to assault a federal officer.

Justice Stewart, writing in dissent, noted that "[m]any states provide an aggravated penalty for assault upon state law enforcement officers; typically the victim-status element transforms the assault from a misdemeanor to a felony." He argued that §111 was intended to

> fil[l] the gap and suppl[y] analogous protection for federal officers. . . . [W]here the assailant reasonably thought his victim a common citizen . . . aggravation is simply out of place, and the case should be tried in the appropriate jurisdiction under the general law of assault, as are unknowing assaults on state officers.

Do you agree with the majority that the victim's status as a federal officer serves only as a way for the federal government to exert jurisdiction, or does it relate to "the harm or evil, incident to conduct, sought to be prevented by the law defining the offense" (Model Penal Code §1.13(10))? The penalty for violations of §111 (fine of up to $50,000 or imprisonment for not more than three years) is similar to that of the felony aggravated assault provisions described by Justice Stewart.

c. Strict Liability

INTRODUCTORY NOTE

In the treatment of mistake of fact in the preceding section we encountered cases of strict liability, that is, cases where liability was imposed without any demonstrated culpability, not even negligence. Here we consider the main problems presented by strict liability legislation — how and why it came to be relied on by legislators as a regulatory device; the role of courts in affecting the extent of strict liability through their authority to interpret statutes; what the virtues and vices of strict liability are; and how far it can be squared with the requirements of just punishment.

UNITED STATES v. BALINT, 258 U.S. 250 (1922). [Defendants were indicted for violating the Narcotic Act of 1914 by selling derivatives of opium and coca leaves without the order form required by the act.[a] The crime was punishable by up to five years in prison. Defendants demurred on the ground that the indictment failed to charge that they knew they were selling prohibited drugs. The Supreme Court held that proof of such knowledge was not required by the statute, stating:]

While the general rule at common law was that the scienter was a necessary element in the indictment and proof of every crime, and this was followed in regard to statutory crimes even where the statutory definition did not in terms include it, there has been a modification of this view in respect to prosecutions under statutes the purpose of which would be obstructed by such a requirement. It is a question of legislative intent to be construed by the court. [I]n the prohibition or punishment of particular acts, the State may in the maintenance of a public policy provide "that he who shall do them shall do them at his peril and will not be heard to plead in defense good faith or ignorance." Many instances of this are to be found in regulatory measures in the exercise of what is called the police power where the emphasis of the statute is evidently upon achievement of some social betterment rather than the punishment of the crimes as in cases of mala in se. . . . [The Act's] manifest purpose is to require every person dealing in drugs to ascertain at his peril whether that which he sells comes within the inhibition of the statute, and if he sells the inhibited drug in ignorance of its character, to penalize him. Congress weighed the possible injustice of subjecting an innocent seller to a penalty against the evil of exposing innocent purchasers to danger from the drug, and concluded that the latter was the result preferably to be avoided. Doubtless considerations as to the opportunity of the seller to find out the fact and the difficulty of proof of knowledge contributed to this conclusion.

UNITED STATES v. DOTTERWEICH, 320 U.S. 277 (1943). [Buffalo Pharmacal Company was a corporation that bought drugs from manufacturers, repackaged them, and shipped them to physicians and others under its own labels, which contained the manufacturer's description of the products. On two occasions the manufacturer's labels, and hence the corporation's labels, were in error, and as a consequence the corporation and Dotterweich, its president and general manager, were prosecuted for shipping misbranded or adulterated products in interstate commerce in violation of the Federal Food, Drug and Cosmetic Act.[b] The jury, remarkably, acquitted the corporation but convicted Dotterweich, who was sentenced to a fine and probation for 60 days, although under the statute he could have been sentenced to imprisonment for a year. The Supreme Court affirmed the conviction, holding that the statute required no mens rea at all with respect to whether those charged knew or should have known the shipment was mislabeled. Justice Frankfurter, writing for the Court, observed:]

a. "That it shall be unlawful for any person to sell, barter, exchange, or give away any of the aforesaid drugs except in pursuance of a written order of the person to whom such article is sold, bartered, exchanged, or given, on a form to be issued in blank for that purpose by the Commissioner of Internal Revenue. . . ."—Eds.

b. Section 301 of the Act prohibits the "Introduction or delivery for introduction into interstate commerce of any . . . drug . . . that is adulterated or misbranded."—Eds.

The Food and Drugs Act of 1906 was an exertion by Congress of its power to keep impure and adulterated food and drugs out of the channels of commerce. By the Act of 1938, Congress extended the range of its control over illicit and noxious articles and stiffened the penalties for disobedience. The purposes of this legislation thus touch phases of the lives and health of people which, in the circumstances of modern industrialism, are largely beyond self-protection. Regard for these purposes should infuse construction of the legislation if it is to be treated as a working instrument of government and not merely as a collection of English words. The prosecution to which Dotterweich was subjected is based on a now familiar type of legislation whereby penalties serve as effective means of regulation. Such legislation dispenses with the conventional requirement for criminal conduct — awareness of some wrongdoing. In the interest of the larger good it puts the burden of acting at hazard upon a person otherwise innocent but standing in responsible relation to a public danger. United States v. Balint, 258 U.S. 250. . . .

Hardship there doubtless may be under a statute which thus penalizes the transaction though consciousness of wrongdoing be totally wanting. Balancing relative hardships, Congress has preferred to place it upon those who have at least the opportunity of informing themselves of the existence of conditions imposed for the protection of consumers before sharing in illicit commerce, rather than to throw the hazard on the innocent public who are wholly helpless.

MORISSETTE v. UNITED STATES

Supreme Court of the United States
342 U.S. 246 (1952)

JUSTICE JACKSON delivered the opinion of the Court.

[Morissette, a junk dealer, openly entered an Air Force practice bombing range and took spent bomb casings that had been lying about for years exposed to the weather and rusting away. He flattened them out and sold them at a city junk market at a profit of $84. He was indicted and convicted of violating 18 U.S.C. §641, which made it a crime to "knowingly convert" government property.[a] There was no question that defendant knew that what he took and sold were Air Force bomb casings. His defense was that he honestly believed that they had been abandoned by the Air Force and that he was therefore violating no one's rights in taking them. The trial judge rejected Morissette's defense and instructed the jury that "[t]he question on intent is whether or not he intended to take the property." The court of appeals affirmed, ruling that the statute created several separate offenses, including stealing and knowing conversion. While the crime of stealing traditionally has required an intent to take another's property without claim of right, the court of appeals held that knowing conversion did not include an element of criminal intent because none was expressly required by the statute. In other words, the court of appeals assumed that Congress meant

a. "Whoever embezzles, steals, purloins, or knowingly converts to his use or the use of another, or without authority, sells, conveys or disposes of any record, voucher, money, or thing of value of the United States . . . shall be fined not more than $10,000 or imprisoned not more than ten years, or both; but if the value of such property does not exceed the sum of $100, he shall be fined not more than $1,000 or imprisoned not more than one year, or both." — EDS.

the term "knowingly convert" to carry its conventional tort law meaning—simply an intentional exercise of dominion over property that is not one's own. The Supreme Court reversed, concluding that the defendant must be proven to have had knowledge of the facts that made the conversion wrongful, that is, that the property had not been abandoned by its owner.]

The contention that an injury can amount to a crime only when inflicted by intention is no provincial or transient notion. It is as universal and persistent in mature systems of law as belief in freedom of the human will and a consequent ability and duty of the normal individual to choose between good and evil. A relation between some mental element and punishment for a harmful act is almost as instinctive as the child's familiar exculpatory "But I didn't mean to," and has afforded the rational basis for a tardy and unfinished substitution of deterrence and reformation in place of retaliation and vengeance as the motivation for public prosecution. . . .

Crime, as a compound concept, generally constituted only from concurrence of an evil-meaning mind with an evil-doing hand, was congenial to an intense individualism and took deep and early root in American soil. As the states codified the common law of crimes, even if their enactments were silent on the subject, their courts assumed that the omission did not signify disapproval of the principle but merely recognized that intent was so inherent in the idea of the offense that it required no statutory affirmation. . . .

However, the *Balint* and *Behrman*[b] offenses belong to a category of another character, with very different antecedents and origins. The crimes there involved depend on no mental element but consist only of forbidden acts or omissions. This, while not expressed by the Court, is made clear from examination of a century-old but accelerating tendency, discernible both here and in England, to call into existence new duties and crimes which disregard any ingredient of intent. The industrial revolution multiplied the number of workmen exposed to injury from increasingly powerful and complex mechanisms, driven by freshly discovered sources of energy, requiring higher precautions by employers. Traffic of velocities, volumes and varieties unheard of, came to subject the wayfarer to intolerable casualty risks if owners and drivers were not to observe new cares and uniformities of conduct. Congestion of cities and crowding of quarters called for health and welfare regulations undreamed of in simpler times. Wide distribution of goods became an instrument of wide distribution of harm when those who dispersed food, drink, drugs, and even securities, did not comply with reasonable standards of quality, integrity, disclosure and care. Such dangers have engendered increasingly numerous and detailed regulations which heighten the duties of those in control of particular industries, trades, properties or activities that affect public health, safety or welfare.[20]

While many of these duties are sanctioned by a more strict civil liability, lawmakers, whether wisely or not, have sought to make such regulations more ef-

b. United States v. Behrman, 258 U.S. 280 (1922), a companion case to *Balint.*—Eds.

20. Sayre, Public Welfare Offenses, 33 Col. L. Rev. 55, 73, 84 (1933), cites and classifies a large number of cases and concludes that they fall roughly into subdivisions of (1) illegal sales of intoxicating liquor, (2) sales of impure or adulterated food or drugs, (3) sales of misbranded articles, (4) violations of antinarcotic Acts, (5) criminal nuisances, (6) violations of traffic regulations, (7) violations of motor-vehicle laws, and (8) violations of general police regulations, passed for the safety, health or well-being of the community.

fective by invoking criminal sanctions to be applied by the familiar technique of criminal prosecutions and convictions. This has confronted the courts with a multitude of prosecutions, based on statutes or administrative regulations, for what have been aptly called "public welfare offenses." . . . Many of these offenses . . . are in the nature of neglect where the law requires care, or inaction where it imposes a duty. Many violations of such regulations result in no direct or immediate injury to person or property but merely create the danger or probability of it which the law seeks to minimize. [T]heir occurrence impairs the efficiency of controls deemed essential to the social order as presently constituted. In this respect, whatever the intent of the violator, the injury is the same, and the consequences are injurious or not according to fortuity. Hence, legislation applicable to such offenses, as a matter of policy, does not specify intent as a necessary element. The accused, if he does not will the violation, usually is in a position to prevent it with no more care than society might reasonably expect and no more exertion than it might reasonably exact from one who assumed his responsibilities. Also, penalties commonly are relatively small, and conviction does no grave damage to an offender's reputation. Under such considerations, courts have turned to construing statutes and regulations which make no mention of intent as dispensing with it and holding that the guilty act alone makes out the crime.[c] This has not, however, been without expressions of misgiving. . . .

After the turn of the Century . . . New York enacted numerous and novel regulations of tenement houses, sanctioned by money penalties. Landlords contended that a guilty intent was essential to establish a violation. Judge Cardozo wrote the answer:

> The defendant asks us to test the meaning of this statute by standards applicable to statutes that govern infamous crimes. The analogy, however, is deceptive. The element of conscious wrongdoing, the guilty mind accompanying the guilty act, is associated with a concept of crimes that are punished as infamous. Even there, it is not an invariable element. But in the prosecution of minor offenses there is a wider range of practice and of power. Prosecutions for petty penalties have always constituted in our law a class by themselves. That is true, though the prosecution is criminal in form.

Tenement House Dept. v. McDevitt, 215 N.Y. 160, 168, 109 N.E. 88, 90, (1915). . . .

Thus, for diverse but reconcilable reasons, state courts converged on the same result, discontinuing inquiry into intent in a limited class of offenses against such statutory regulations. . . .

Before long, similar questions growing out of federal legislation reached this Court. Its judgments were in harmony with this consensus of state judicial opin-

c. But see Henry M. Hart, The Aims of the Criminal Law, 23 L. & Contemp. Prob. 401, 431 n. 70 (1958): "In relation to offenses of a traditional type, the Court's opinion seems to be saying, we must be much slower to dispense with a basis for genuine blameworthiness in criminal intent than in relation to modern regulatory offenses. But it is precisely in the area of traditional crimes that the nature of the act itself commonly gives some warning that there may be a problem about its propriety and so affords, without more, at least some slight basis of condemnation for doing it. Thus, Morissette knew perfectly well that he was taking property which, at least up to the moment of caption, did not belong to him.

"In the area of regulatory crimes, on the other hand, the moral quality of the act is often neutral; and on occasion, the offense may consist not of any act at all, but simply of an intrinsically innocent omission, so that there is no basis for moral condemnation whatever." — Eds.

ion, the existence of which may have led the Court to overlook the need for full exposition of their rationale in the context of federal law. . . .

Neither this Court nor, so far as we are aware, any other has undertaken to delineate a precise line or set forth comprehensive criteria for distinguishing between crimes that require a mental element and crimes that do not. We attempt no closed definition, for the law on the subject is neither settled nor static. The conclusion reached in the *Balint* and *Behrman* Cases has our approval and adherence for the circumstances to which it was there applied. A quite different question here is whether we will expand the doctrine of crimes without intent to include those charged here.

Stealing, larceny, and its variants and equivalents, were among the earliest offenses known to the law that existed before legislation; they are invasions of rights of property which stir a sense of insecurity in the whole community and arouse public demand for retribution, the penalty is high and, when a sufficient amount is involved, the infamy is that of a felony, which, says Maitland, is ". . . as bad a word as you can give to man or thing." State courts of last resort, on whom fall the heaviest burden of interpreting criminal law in this country, have consistently retained the requirement of intent in larceny-type offenses. If any state has deviated, the exception has neither been called to our attention nor disclosed by our research.

Congress, therefore, omitted any express prescription of criminal intent from the enactment before us in the light of an unbroken course of judicial decision in all constituent states of the Union holding intent inherent in this class of offense, even when not expressed in a statute. Congressional silence as to mental elements in an Act merely adopting into federal statutory law a concept of crime already so well defined in common law and statutory interpretation by the states may warrant quite contrary inferences than the same silence in creating an offense new to general law, for whose definition the courts have no guidance except the Act. Because the offenses before this Court in the *Balint* and *Behrman* Cases were of this latter class, we cannot accept them as authority for eliminating intent from offenses incorporated from the common law. . . .

The Government asks us by a feat of construction radically to change the weights and balances in the scales of justice. The purpose and obvious effect of doing away with the requirement of a guilty intent is to ease the prosecution's path to conviction, to strip the defendant of such benefit as he derived at common law from innocence of evil purpose, and to circumscribe the freedom heretofore allowed juries. Such a manifest impairment of the immunities of the individual should not be extended to common-law crimes on judicial initiative. . . .

We hold that the mere omission from §641 of any mention of intent will not be construed as eliminating that element from the crimes denounced. . . .

Of course, the jury, considering Morissette's awareness that these casings were on government property, his failure to seek any permission for their removal and his self-interest as a witness, might have disbelieved his profession of innocent intent and concluded that his assertion of a belief that the casings were abandoned was an after-thought. Had the jury convicted on proper instructions it would be the end of the matter. But juries are not bound by what seems inescapable logic to judges. They might have concluded that the heaps of spent casings left in the hinterland to rust away presented an appearance of unwanted and abandoned junk, and that lack of any conscious deprivation of property or intentional injury was indicated by Morissette's good character, the openness of the taking, crushing and transporting of the casings, and the candor with which it was all admitted. They might have refused to brand Morissette as a thief. Had they done so, that too would have been the end of the matter.

Reversed.

STAPLES v. UNITED STATES

Supreme Court of the United States
511 U.S. 60 (1994)

JUSTICE THOMAS delivered the opinion of the Court.

[Defendant was charged with violating the National Firearms Act, which makes possession of an unregistered firearm punishable by up to 10 years in prison. The rifle found in his possession met the Act's definition of a firearm — a weapon capable of automatically firing more than one shot with a single pull of the trigger. It appears that the rifle originally had a metal piece that precluded automatic firing, but that it had at some time or other been filed down. Defendant testified that the rifle never fired automatically in his possession and that he didn't know it was capable of doing so. He sought an instruction that the government had to prove that he "knew that the gun would fire fully automatically." This was refused, and the jury convicted. On appeal, the Court of Appeals affirmed his conviction, and the Supreme Court granted certiorari.]

Whether or not §5861(d) requires proof that a defendant knew of the characteristics of his weapon that made it a "firearm" under the Act is a question of statutory construction. . . . Section 5861(d) is silent concerning the mens rea required for a violation. It states simply that "[i]t shall be unlawful for any person . . . to receive or possess a firearm which is not registered to him in the National Firearms Registration and Transfer Record." Nevertheless, silence on this point by itself does not necessarily suggest that Congress intended to dispense with a conventional mens rea element, which would require that the defendant know the facts that make his conduct illegal. . . On the contrary, we must construe the statute in light of the background rules of the common law, in which the requirement of some mens rea for a crime is firmly embedded. . . .

Relying on the strength of the traditional rule, we have stated that offenses that require no mens rea generally are disfavored, and have suggested that some indication of congressional intent, express or implied, is required to dispense with mens rea as an element of a crime.

. . . The Government argues that Congress intended the Act to regulate and restrict the circulation of dangerous weapons. Consequently, in the Government's view, this case fits in a line of precedent concerning what we have termed "public welfare" or "regulatory" offenses, in which we have understood Congress to impose a form of strict criminal liability through statutes that do not require the defendant to know the facts that make his conduct illegal. In construing such statutes, we have inferred from silence that Congress did not intend to require proof of mens rea to establish an offense. . . .

Typically, our cases recognizing such offenses involve statutes that regulate potentially harmful or injurious items. . . . In such situations, we have reasoned that as long as a defendant knows that he is dealing with a dangerous device of a character that places him "in responsible relation to a public danger," [United States v.] Dotterweich, [320 U.S. 277] at 281, he should be alerted to the probability of strict regulation, and we have assumed that in such cases Congress intended to place the burden on the defendant to "ascertain at his peril whether [his conduct] comes within the inhibition of the statute." [United States v.] Balint, [258 U.S. 250] at 254. . . .

[T]he Government argues that §5861(d) defines precisely the sort of regulatory offense described in *Balint.* In this view, all guns, whether or not they are statutory "firearms," are dangerous devices that put gun owners on notice that they must determine at their hazard whether their weapons come within the scope of the Act.

[T]he Government seeks support for its position from our decision in the United States v. Freed, 401 U.S. 601 (1971), which involved a prosecution for possession of unregistered grenades under §5861(d). The defendant knew that the items in his possession were grenades, and we concluded that §5861(d) did not require the Government to prove the defendant also knew that the grenades were unregistered.

[O]ur analysis in *Freed* likening the Act to the public welfare statute in *Balint* rested entirely on the assumption that the defendant knew that he was dealing with hand grenades — that is, that he knew he possessed a particularly dangerous type of weapon (one within the statutory definition of a "firearm"), possession of which was not entirely "innocent" in and of itself. . . .

In glossing over the distinction between grenades and guns, the Government ignores the particular care we have taken to avoid construing a statute to dispense with mens rea where doing so would "criminalize a broad range of apparently innocent conduct." Liparota [v. United States], 471 U.S. [419] at 426 (1985).

[T]here is a long tradition of widespread lawful gun ownership by private individuals in this country. Such a tradition did not apply to the possession of hand grenades in *Freed* or to the selling of dangerous drugs that we considered in *Balint*. . . . Roughly 50 per cent of American homes contain at least one firearm of some sort, and in the vast majority of States, buying a shotgun or rifle is a simple transaction that would not alert a person to regulation any more than would buying a car. . . .

We concur in the Fifth Circuit's conclusion on this point: "It is unthinkable to us that Congress intended to subject such law-abiding, well-intentioned citizens to a possible ten-year term of imprisonment if . . . what they genuinely and reasonably believed was a conventional semiautomatic [weapon] turns out to have worn down into or been secretly modified to be a fully automatic weapon." As we noted in *Morissette,* the "purpose and obvious effect of doing away with the requirement of a guilty intent is to ease the prosecution's path to conviction." We are reluctant to impute that purpose to Congress where, as here, it would mean easing the path to convicting persons whose conduct would not even alert them to the probability of strict regulation in the form of a statute such as §5861(d).

The potentially harsh penalty attached to violation of §5861(d) — up to 10 years' imprisonment — confirms our reading of the Act. . . . [P]unishing a violation as a felony is simply incompatible with the theory of the public welfare offense. In this view, absent a clear statement from Congress that mens rea is not required, we should not apply the public welfare offense rationale to interpret any statute defining a felony offense as dispensing with mens rea.

[Reversed and remanded.]

JUSTICE GINSBURG, with whom JUSTICE O'CONNOR joins, concurring in the judgment. . . .

The question before us is not whether knowledge of possession is required, but what level of knowledge suffices: (1) knowledge simply of possession of the object; (2) knowledge, in addition, that the object is a dangerous weapon; 3) knowledge, beyond dangerousness, of the characteristics that render the object subject to regulation, for example, awareness that the weapon is a machinegun. . . .

The Nation's legislators chose to place under a registration requirement only a very limited class of firearms, those they considered especially dangerous. The generally "dangerous" character of all guns, the Court therefore observes, did not suffice to give individuals in Staples' situation cause to inquire about the need for registration. Only the third reading . . . suits the purpose of the mens rea requirement — to shield people against punishment for apparently innocent activity. . . .

For these reasons, I conclude that conviction under §5861(d) requires proof that the defendant knew he possessed not simply a gun, but a machinegun. . . . I therefore concur in the Court's judgment.

PROBLEM

United States v. X-Citement Video, Inc., 513 U.S. 64 (1994), involved a conviction of defendant for violating the Protection of Children Against Sexual Exploitation Act of 1977, which provided:

> Any person who . . .
>
> (1) knowingly transports or ships in interstate or foreign commerce by any means including by computer or mails, any visual depiction, if . . .
>
> (A) the producing of such visual depiction involves the use of a minor engaging in sexually explicit conduct; and
>
> (B) such visual depiction is of such conduct;
>
> (2) knowingly receives, or distributes, any visual depiction that has been mailed, or has been shipped in interstate or foreign commerce, if . . .
>
> (A) the producing of such visual depiction involves the use of a minor engaging in sexually explicit conduct; and
>
> (B) such visual depiction is of such conduct; . . . shall be punished . . .

The Court of Appeals held that the statute's grammatical structure disallowed the conclusion that the defendant had to know the person depicted was a minor. The Supreme Court disagreed, concluding that "*Morissette,* reinforced by *Staples,* instructs that the presumption in favor of a scienter requirement should apply to each of the statutory elements that criminalize otherwise innocent conduct."

Questions: Do the precedents of *Morissette* and *Staples* justify finding a scienter requirement as to the age of the person depicted? Does the language of the statute support it? If the statute made it criminal to knowingly transport any visual depiction involving the use of a minor, the conclusion would be unmistakable. Should it matter that the statute makes it criminal to knowingly transport any visual depiction *if* it involves the use of a minor? Justice Scalia thought so, and dissented for this reason. He distinguished *Staples* on the ground that there the court applied the background common law rule of scienter to a statute that said nothing about the matter; and distinguished *Morissette* on the ground that the issue there was only the meaning of the term "knowingly converts." Justice Stevens, in his concurring opinion stated that "to give the statute its most grammatically correct reading, and merely require knowledge that a 'visual depiction' has been shipped in interstate commerce, would be ridiculous." Who has it right?

We've seen that statutory rape cases are usually not interpreted as requiring proof of knowledge that the girl was a minor. People v. Olsen, supra. Is there a good case for a different treatment of the age-scienter issue when the action involved is transmitting depictions rather than having sex?

NOTE ON STRICT LIABILITY AT COMMON LAW

The common law sometimes departed from its ordinary commitment to mens rea even before the regulatory era described by Justice Jackson. We have already examined one major departure — the view, still prevailing, that mistake of age is not a defense in sex offenses with minors. In addition, bigamy was interpreted as requiring no mens rea as to the death of the first husband. The lesser wrong and lesser crime principles at issue in the *Prince* case, supra page 226, may also be seen as imposing strict liability, at least in the sense that they dispense with a mens rea requirement (that is, knowledge, recklessness, or negligence) as to a material element of the crime charged. This is likewise true of the felony murder rule, which we will examine in detail in Chapter 5, Homicide, since it converts an accidental killing and a negligent or reckless killing that would otherwise be manslaughter into murder if the death occurs during a felony.

STATE v. GUMINGA

Supreme Court of Minnesota
395 N.W.2d 344 (1986)

YETKA, J. . . . On March 29, 1985, in the course of an undercover operation, two investigators for the City of Hopkins entered Lindee's Restaurant, Hopkins, Minnesota, with a 17-year-old woman. All three ordered alcoholic beverages. The minor had never been in Lindee's before, and the waitress did not ask the minor her age or request identification. When the waitress returned with their orders, the minor paid for all the drinks. After confirming that the drink contained alcohol, the officers arrested the waitress for serving intoxicating liquor to a minor in violation of Minn. Stat. §340.73 (1984). The owner of Lindee's, defendant George Joseph Guminga, was subsequently charged with violation of section 340.73 pursuant to Minn. Stat. §340.941 (1984), which imposes vicarious criminal liability on an employer whose employee serves intoxicating liquor to a minor. The state does not contend that Guminga was aware of or ratified the waitress's actions.

Guminga moved to dismiss the charges on the ground that section 340.941 violates the due process clauses of the federal and state constitutions. . . . After holding a hearing on August 28, 1985, the court denied the motion to dismiss. . . .

The certified question of law before this court is as follows:

> Whether Minn. Stat. §340.941, on its face, violates the defendant's right to due process of law under the Fourteenth Amendment to the United States Constitution and analogous provisions of the Constitution of the State of Minnesota.

We find that the statute in question does violate the due process clauses of the Minnesota and the United States Constitutions and thus answer the question in the affirmative. . . .

Minn. Stat. §340.73 (1984) provides criminal penalties [gross misdemeanor] for any person selling intoxicating liquor to a minor. . . . Minn. Stat. §340.941 (1984) imposes vicarious criminal liability on the employer for an employee's violation of section 340.73. . . . Under Minn. Stat. §609.03 (1984), a defendant who commits a gross misdemeanor may be sentenced to "imprisonment for not more than one year or to payment of a fine of not more than $3,000 or both." In addition, a defendant convicted under section 340.941 may, at the discretion of the licensing authority, have its license suspended, revoked or be unable to obtain a new license. . . .

Since this is not an appeal from a conviction, we do not yet know whether, if found guilty, Guminga would be subjected to imprisonment, a suspended sentence, or a fine. Even if there is no prison sentence imposed, under the new sentencing guidelines, a gross misdemeanor conviction will affect his criminal history score were he to be convicted of a felony in the future. . .

We find that criminal penalties based on vicarious liability under Minn. Stat. §340.941 are a violation of substantive due process and that only civil penalties would be constitutional. A due process analysis of a statute involves a balancing of the public interest protected against the intrusion on personal liberty while taking into account any alternative means by which to achieve the same end. . . . Section 340.941 serves the public interest by providing additional deterrence to violation of the liquor laws. The private interests affected, however, include liberty, damage to reputation and other future disabilities arising from criminal prosecution for an act which Guminga did not commit or ratify. Not only could Guminga be given a prison sentence or a suspended sentence, but, in the more likely event that he receives only a fine, his liberty could be affected by a longer presumptive sentence in a possible future felony conviction. Such an intrusion on personal liberty is not justified by the public interest protected, especially when there are alternative means by which to achieve the same end, such as civil fines or license suspension, which do not entail the legal and social ramifications of a criminal conviction. See Model Penal Code §1.04 comment (b) (1985).[3] . . .

3. We agree with the reasoning of the Georgia Supreme Court in Davis v. City of Peachtree City, 251 Ga. 219, 304 S.E.2d 701 (1983). *Davis* involved the criminal conviction of the president of a chain of convenience stores whose employee had sold liquor to a minor. The defendant was prosecuted under a city ordinance holding licensees responsible for the acts of their employees and received a $300 fine and a 60-day suspended sentence. The Georgia Supreme Court reversed the conviction: . . .

> Although some commentators and courts have found that vicarious criminal liability does not violate due process in misdemeanor cases which involve as punishment only a slight fine and not imprisonment, we decline to so hold. The damage done to an individual's good name and the peril imposed on an individual's future are sufficient reasons to shift the balance in favor of the individual. The imposition of such a burden on an employer "cannot rest on so frail a reed as whether his employee will commit a mistake in judgment," but instead can be justified only by the appropriate prosecuting officials proving some sort of culpability or knowledge by the employer.

The dissent argues that vicarious liability is necessary as a deterrent so that an owner will impress upon employees that they should not sell to minors. However, it does not distinguish between an employer who vigorously lectures his employees and one who does not. According to the dissent, each would be equally guilty. We believe it is a deterrent enough that the employee who sells to the minor can be charged under the statute and that the business is subject to fines or suspension or revocation of license. . . .

We find that, in Minnesota, no one can be convicted of a crime punishable by imprisonment for an act he did not commit, did not have knowledge of, or give expressed or implied consent to the commission thereof.

The certified question is thus answered in the affirmative. . . .

KELLEY, J. (dissenting): [I]mposition of vicarious liability and the threat of a short jail, not prison, sentence is reasonably related to the legislative purpose: enforcement of laws prohibiting liquor sales to minors. Without the deterrent of possible personal criminal responsibility and a sentence, the legislature could have rationally concluded that liquor establishment owners will be less likely to impress upon employees the need to require identification of age before serving liquor. Limiting punishment to a fine allows bar owners to view their liability for violations as nothing more than an expense of doing business. The gravity of the problems associated with minors who consume alcoholic beverages justifies the importance by the legislature of harsher punishment on those who help contribute to those problems. The state has the right to impose limited criminal vicarious liability on bar proprietors as a reasonable exchange for the state-granted privilege of a liquor license. . . .

NOTES ON VICARIOUS LIABILITY

1. Vicarious liability of employers. Courts generally uphold convictions of employers for the illegal conduct of their employees even in the absence of evidence of employer fault. See Annotation, 89 A.L.R.3d 1256 (1970). But, as reflected in the split opinions in the principal case, there is less agreement on conviction for offenses that carry a sanction of imprisonment as opposed to fines. Compare the principal case, *Guminga,* with State v. Beaudry, 123 Wis. 2d 40, 365 N.W.2d 593 (1985). The defendant and her husband were sole shareholders of a corporation with a license to sell alcohol at the Village Green Tavern. The defendant was the designated agent for the corporate licensee. It appeared that one night the tavern manager remained open past closing time, admittedly against the instructions of the absent owners, and for the sole purpose of entertaining his own friends. Nonetheless, the defendant was convicted on the basis of vicarious liability. The court upheld the conviction, even though the statute authorized a 90-day jail sentence, on the ground that the penalty imposed was solely a $200 fine. *Question:* Are the concerns over vicarious liability any different from those over strict liability?

2. Vicarious liability of parents. Should vicarious liability outside the employer-employee relationship be treated any differently? Consider State v. Akers, 400 A.2d 38 (N.H. 1979). A statute imposed criminal liability on parents of minor children who drive off-highway vehicles on public highways. No evidence of parental culpability (beyond the parental status) was required. The court struck down the statute, stating (id. at 40):

> Without passing upon the validity of statutes that might seek to impose vicarious criminal liability on the part of an employer for acts of his employees, we have no hesitancy in holding that any attempt to impose such liability on parents simply because they occupy the status of parents, without more, offends the due process clause of our State constitution.

In reaching its conclusion, the court appeared to invalidate all criminal liability, not just incarceration. On what principle can the court strike down vicarious parental liability "without passing upon" vicarious employer liability? What is the distinction between the two situations? See generally T. Weinstein, Visiting the Sins of the Child on the Parent: The Legality of Criminal Parental Liability Statutes, 64 So. Cal. L. Rev. 859 (1991).

STATE v. BAKER

Kansas Court of Appeal
571 P.2d 65 (1977)

SPENCER, J. Defendant has appealed his conviction of driving his motor vehicle at a speed of seventy-seven miles per hour in a fifty-five miles per hour zone in violation of K. S. A. 1976 Supp. 8-1336(a)(3).

Agreed upon facts are that prior to the trial of this matter to the court, the state moved to suppress evidence offered by the defendant that:

1. Defendant's cruise control stuck in the "accelerate" position causing the car to accelerate beyond the posted speed limit.
2. The defendant attempted to deactivate the cruise control by hitting the off button and the coast button and tapping the brakes.
3. These actions were not immediately successful in deactivating the cruise control.
4. Subsequent to the date of this incident, the defendant had the defective cruise control repaired.

The trial court sustained the motion, thus precluding the defendant from presenting the proffered evidence as a defense. . . . The result was that the defendant was found guilty of driving in excess of the posted speed limit, and, also, that defendant was the "driver" of the car as defined by K.S.A. 8-1416. The sentence of $10 and costs was suspended pending this appeal. . . .

[D]efendant readily concedes that a violation of the speeding statute (K.S.A. 1976 Supp. 8-1336) is an absolute liability offense when read in light of the absolute liability statute (K.S.A. 21-3204), which provides:

> A person may be guilty of an offense without having criminal intent if the crime is a misdemeanor and the statute defining the offense clearly indicates a legislative purpose to impose absolute liability for the conduct described. . . .

Defendant admits that this statute does away with the necessity of proving intent to commit the misdemeanor and, further, that any evidence of the defective cruise control would be inadmissible if introduced merely to negate an intent or culpable state of mind on the part of the motorist. His contention is that the evidence was offered to show that his speeding was not a voluntary act and, therefore, there was no criminal liability. He suggests that the evidence of a defective cruise control goes specifically to whether his speeding was a voluntary act on his part and has nothing to do "with the intent, or state of mind, of the defendant to do the crime to which his act amounted." In sum, the defendant suggests that even though the charge against him was an absolute liability offense per K.S.A. 21-3204, the state must prove that he acted voluntarily. . . .

We have no doubt that if defendant were able to establish that his act of speeding was the result of an unforeseen occurrence or circumstance, which was not caused by him and which he could not prevent, that such would constitute a valid defense to the charge. But, the evidence proffered suggests a malfunction of a device attached to the motor vehicle operated by the defendant over which he had or should have had absolute control. Defendant does not suggest that the operation of the motor vehicle on the day of his arrest was anything but a voluntary act on his part, nor that anyone other than himself activated the cruise control, which may have caused his excessive speed. . . .

In the New York case of People v. Shaughnessy, 66 Misc. 2d 19, 319 N.Y.S.2d 626 (1971), it was held that a defendant could not be found guilty of violating an ordinance prohibiting entry upon private property because the defendant was merely a passenger in the trespassing car and the state's evidence failed to show an overt voluntary act or omission by the defendant. In the case of State v. Kremer, 262 Minn. 190, 114 N.W.2d 88 (1962), the Minnesota Supreme Court held that a defendant could not be guilty of violating a city ordinance requiring all traffic to stop at a flashing red light when the evidence showed that defendant's brakes failed with no prior warning to the defendant. Again, the court found no overt voluntary act on the part of the defendant. . . .

In [State v.] Weller, [230 A.2d 242 (1967),] the Connecticut court stated that the defendant had a valid defense to the speeding charge because the spring which closes the throttle plate broke due to no fault of the defendant. The court reasoned that because "[t]here is not one scintilla of evidence of any intent on the part of the defendant to do the prohibited act . . ." the defendant's conviction should be overturned. . . .

In our view, unexpected brake failure and unexpected malfunction of the throttle on an automobile, both being essential components to the operation of the vehicle, differ significantly from the malfunction of a cruise control device to which the driver has voluntarily delegated partial control of that automobile. We believe it must be said that defendant assumed the full operation of his motor vehicle and when he did so and activated the cruise control attached to that automobile, he clearly was the agent in causing the act of speeding. . . .

NOTES AND QUESTIONS ON THE INVOLUNTARY ACT DEFENSE TO A STRICT LIABILITY OFFENSE

1. In *Baker* does the court satisfactorily distinguish the cases of the failed brakes and the sticky throttle? If these cases go only to the mens rea (irrelevant in a strict liability offense), why isn't it equally true of the cruise control? Is there any difference between the cruise control and these other cases other than in the degree of risk created?

How should the following hypotheticals be analyzed?

(a) The electric shoulder harness holding the driver suddenly malfunctions and grabs the driver's arms long enough to make the car spin widely back and forth in violation of the traffic laws.

(b) Suppose a child in the back seat lurches over and grabs the driver's arms in a strong show of affection, with the same consequence.

(c) Suppose a tornado picks up the car and deposits it the wrong way on a one-way street.

2. In State v. Miller, 309 Or. 362, 788 P.2d 974 (1990), the Oregon Supreme Court affirmed a driving-while-intoxicated conviction of a defendant who was not permitted to present evidence that unknown to him someone had laced his drink with alcohol. The court declared that the statute created strict liability with respect to the presence of alcohol in the driver's body.

Questions: Could he have successfully argued the defense of absence of a voluntary act? Why not? Suppose his conviction was for driving while in possession of an open container of drinking alcohol, which had been placed in his car without his knowledge. Would he then have a defense of no act? Compare the definition of voluntary act in Model Penal Code §2.01(4).

3. Question: Why should the absence of a voluntary act be a defense to a strict liability offense? See M. Budd & J. Lynch, Voluntariness, Causation and Strict Liability, [1978] Crim. L. Rev. 74, 75 n. 6:

> It is strange . . . that it is thought appropriate for the law to acquit those in a state of automatism of offences of strict liability but to convict those acting voluntarily. It seems to us that there is no sound basis for this difference in treatment. It must certainly be wrong for the law to treat differently those who are both equally free of moral blame and whose conviction would be equally relevant to advancing the purposes of strict liability.

For an exchange of views on this question in the context of the *Baker* case, see Douglas Husak & Brian P. McLaughlin, Time Frames, Voluntary Acts, and Strict Liability, 12 Law & Philosophy 95 (1993) and Larry Alexander, Reconsidering the Relationship Among Voluntary Acts, Strict Liability, and Negligence in Criminal Law, in Ellen Frankel Paul, Fred D. Miller Jr., and Jeffrey Paul, eds., Crime, Culpability, and Remedy 84 (1990).

REGINA v. CITY OF SAULT STE. MARIE

Supreme Court of Canada
85 D.L.R.3d 161 (1978)

DICKSON, J. . . . Various arguments are advanced in justification of absolute liability in public welfare offences. Two predominate. Firstly, it is argued that the protection of social interests requires a high standard of care and attention on the part of those who follow certain pursuits and such persons are more likely to be stimulated to maintain those standards if they know that ignorance or mistake will not excuse them. The removal of any possible loophole acts, it is said, is an incentive to take precautionary measures beyond what would otherwise be taken, in order that mistakes and mishaps be avoided. The second main argument is one based on administrative efficiency. Having regard to both the difficulty of proving mental culpability and the number of petty cases which daily come before the Courts, proof of fault is just too great a burden in time and money to place upon the prosecution. . . . In short, absolute liability, it is contended, is the most efficient and effective way of ensuring compliance with minor regulatory legislation and the social ends to be achieved are of such importance as to override the unfortunate by-product of punishing those who may be free of moral turpitude. In further justification, it is urged that slight penalties are usually imposed and that conviction for breach of a public welfare offence does not carry the stigma associated with conviction for a criminal offense.

Arguments of greater force are advanced against absolute liability. The most telling is that it violates fundamental principles of penal liability. It also rests upon assumptions which have not been, and cannot be, empirically established. There is no evidence that a higher standard of care results from absolute liability. If a person is already taking every reasonable precautionary measure, is he likely to take additional measures, knowing that however much care he takes, it will not serve as a defence in the event of breach? If he has exercised care and skill, will conviction have a deterrent effect upon him or others? Will the injustice of conviction lead to cynicism and disrespect for the law, on his part and on the part of others? These are among the questions asked. The argument that no stigma attaches does not withstand analysis, for the accused will have suffered loss of time, legal costs, exposure to the processes of the criminal law at trial and, however one may downplay it, the opprobrium of conviction. It is not sufficient to say that the public interest is engaged. . . . In serious crimes, the public interest is [also] involved and [nevertheless] mens rea must be proven. . . .

The unfortunate tendency in many past cases has been to see the choice as between two stark alternatives: (i) full mens rea; or (ii) absolute liability. . . . There has, however, been an attempt in Australia, in many Canadian Courts, and indeed in England, to seek a middle position, fulfilling the goals of public welfare offences while still not punishing the entirely blameless. There is an increasing and impressive stream of authority which holds that where an offence does not require full mens rea, it is nevertheless a good defence for the defendant to prove that he was not negligent. . . .

The doctrine proceeds on the assumption that the defendant could have avoided the prima facie offence through the exercise of reasonable care and he is given the opportunity of establishing, if he can, that he did in fact exercise such care. . . . This burden falls upon the defendant as he is the only one who will generally have the means of proof. This would not seem unfair as the alternative is absolute liability which denies an accused any defence whatsoever. While the prosecution must prove beyond a reasonable doubt that the defendant committed the prohibited act, the defendant must only establish on the balance of probabilities that he has a defence of reasonable care.

I conclude . . . that there are compelling grounds for the recognition of three categories of offences rather than the traditional two:

1. Offences in which mens rea, consisting of some positive state of mind such as intent, knowledge, or recklessness, must be proved by the prosecution. . . .
2. Offences in which there is no necessity for the prosecution to prove the

existence of mens rea; the doing of the prohibited act prima facie imports the offence, leaving it open to the accused to avoid liability by proving that he took all reasonable care. . . .

3. Offences of absolute liability where it is not open to the accused to exculpate himself by showing that he was free of fault.

Offences which are criminal in the true sense fall in the first category. Public welfare offences would, prima facie, be in the second category. . . . An offence of this type would fall in the first category only if such words as "wilfully," "with intent," "knowingly," or "intentionally" are contained in the statutory provision creating the offence. . . . Offences of absolute liability would be those in respect  of which the Legislature had made it clear that guilt would follow proof merely of the proscribed act. The over-all regulatory pattern adopted by the Legislature, the subject-matter of the legislation, the importance of the penalty, and the precision of the language used will be primary considerations in determining whether the offence falls into the third category.

NOTES

1. In an even more significant move against absolute liability than the *Sault Ste. Marie* case, the Supreme Court of Canada has done what the Supreme Court of the United States has consistently declined to do — it held absolute liabil-  ity unconstitutional. Specifically, it held that imprisonment for an absolute liability offense is a deprivation of liberty not "in accordance with the precepts of fundamental justice" guaranteed by Section 7 of the Canadian Charter of Rights and Freedoms. Reference Re Section 94(2) of the Motor Vehicle Act, 23 C.C.C.3d 289 (1985). The court's reasons were essentially those given in the *Sault Ste. Marie* case.

The Canadian Supreme Court was obliged to confront the qualification in Section 1 of the Charter that makes the protected rights and freedoms subject to "such reasonable limits prescribed by law as can be demonstrably justified in a free and democratic society." The Court held that administrative expediency could justify imprisonment for absolute liability "only in cases arising out of exceptional conditions, such as natural disasters, the outbreak of war, epidemics and the like." (Id. at 313.)

2. In Sweet v. Parsley, [1970] A.C. 132 (H.L. 1968), the defendant rented her farm house to some people who, unknown to her, smoked cannabis on the premises. She was convicted of violating §5(b) of the Dangerous Drugs Act of 1965. Section 5 provided:

If a person (a) being the occupier of any premises, permits those premises to be used for the purpose of smoking cannabis or cannabis resin or of dealing in cannabis or cannabis resin (whether by sale or otherwise); or (b) is concerned in the management of any premises used for any such purpose as aforesaid: he shall be guilty of an offence against this Act.

The House of Lords reversed the conviction, concluding that in the circumstances the defendant could not be said to be "concerned in the management" of premises used for the purpose of smoking cannabis. Lord Reid observed (id. at 150):

> When one comes to acts of a truly criminal character, it appears to me that there are at least two . . . factors which any reasonable legislator would have in mind. In the first place a stigma still attaches to any person convicted of a truly criminal offence, and the more serious or more disgraceful the offence the greater the stigma. So he would have to consider whether, in a case of this gravity, the public interest really requires that an innocent person should be prevented from proving his innocence in order that fewer guilty men may escape. And equally important is the fact that fortunately the Press in this country are vigilant to expose injustice and every manifestly unjust conviction made known to the public tends to injure the body politic by undermining public confidence in the justice of the law and of its administration. But I regret to observe that, in some recent cases where serious offences have been held to be absolute offences, the Court has taken into account no more than the wording of the Act and the character and seriousness of the mischief which constitutes the offence. . . .
>
> If this section means what the Court of Appeal have held that it means, then hundreds of thousands of people who sublet part of their premises or take in lodgers or are concerned in the management of residential premises or institutions are daily incurring a risk of being convicted of a serious offence in circumstances where they are in no way to blame. For the greatest vigilance cannot prevent tenants, lodgers or inmates or guests whom they bring in from smoking cannabis cigarettes in their own rooms.

3. The middle approach pioneered by the Australia and Canadian courts (discussed in the principal case) has been taken up by at least one American court. United States. v. United States District Court (Kantor), 858 F.2d 534 (9th Cir. 1988), involved a prosecution for producing pornographic films of a minor. Concluding from the statutory language and the legislative history that culpability as to the age of the minor was not an element of the offense,[a] the court nonetheless held that the defendant had an affirmative defense if he could show that he could not reasonably have learned that the minor was under 18. The court stated at 542:

> [T]he statute is silent on whether reasonable mistake of age may serve as an affirmative defense. Moreover, unlike the question whether scienter should be an element of the government's prima facie case, there is no evidence that Congress considered and rejected the possibility of providing for such a defense. . . . Moreover, the federal courts may, in limited circumstances, recognize an affirmative defense where a statute does not expressly provide it. For example, the . . . [Supreme] Court has . . . recognized entrapment as an affirmative defense, reasoning that, so long as Congress has not clearly indicated to the contrary, it "will always . . . be presumed that the legislature intended exceptions to its language which would avoid [injustice, oppression, or an absurd consequence.]" Sorrells v. United States, 287 U.S. 435 (1932).

See Laurie L. Levenson, Good Faith Defenses: Reshaping Strict Liability Crimes, 78 Cornell L. Rev. 401 (1993), for a proposal to generalize an affirmative defense of absence of blameworthy conduct to all strict liability crimes.

a. Of course, this decision long preceded the decision of the Supreme Court in United States v. X-Citement Video, Inc., 513 U.S. 64 (1994). See supra page 243.

NOTES ON THE ACADEMIC DEBATE

The great majority of academic writing has opposed absolute liability.[5] In recent years, however, some academics have to some degree defended the concept.[6] Some idea of the issues in dispute may be gleaned from the following excerpts.

Arthur Goodhart, Possession of Drugs and Absolute Liability, 84 L.Q. Rev. 382, 385-386 (1968): [T]here are certain offences that have a serious effect on the public interest but which it is difficult to prove under the usual procedure. It is then necessary to take other and more stringent steps to wipe out the evil, even at a minimal risk that an innocent man may be convicted. Lord Reid cites, although he does not entirely agree with it, the long-established saying that "it is better that ten guilty men should escape than that one innocent man should be convicted." . . . On the other hand it may be necessary in certain circumstances to alter the strict rules where an act, such as tempting young persons to buy drugs, is peculiarly harmful, and where it may be difficult to prove the existence of mens rea, although it is almost certain that it does exist. . . . The point here is that the future harm that the ten guilty men who have been acquitted may do, either by repeating their own offences or by encouraging others by showing how easy it is to avoid conviction, far exceeds any injury that the innocent man can suffer by his conviction. The question then becomes: Is it better that ten young persons should be tempted to become drug addicts than that one innocent man should be convicted of being in possession of unauthorized drugs?

Mark Kelman, Strict Liability: An Unorthodox View, in Encyclopedia of Crime and Justice 1512, 1516-1517 (1983): H. L. A. Hart's argument that the defendant convicted of a strict-liability offense "could not have helped" committing the crime depends on the use of a rationally indefensible narrow time frame in focusing on the defendant's conduct. . . . It may well be the case that if one looks only at the precise *moment* at which harm is consummated, the strictly liable actor may seem powerless to avoid criminality, but it is invariably the case that the actor could have avoided liability by taking earlier steps which were hardly impossible. . . .

It is significant to note that only by constructing the underlying material in the strict-liability situations with a very narrow time frame that the distinction between liability predicated on negligence, and strict liability, maintains its practical import in many critical situations.

An example is the familiar problem of "reasonable" (non-negligent) mistakes as to the victim's age in the statutory rape setting. Is one's view of a "reasonable" belief to be ascertained solely by reference to perceptions available to the defendant during the purportedly illegal seduction (she "*looked*" sixteen or "she told me she was sixteen"), or does one require that some checks prior to seduction be taken, such as checking birth certificates or asking parents? Of course, if one

5. For two frequently cited examples, see Herbert Packer, The Limits of the Criminal Sanction 121-131 (1968); Henry M. Hart, The Aims of the Criminal Law, 23 Law & Contemp. Prob. 401, 422-425 (1958).

6. See e.g., James Brady, Strict Liability Offenses: A Justification, 8 Crim. L. Bull. 217 (1972); Steven Nemerson, Criminal Liability Without Fault: A Philosophical Perspective, 75 Colum. L. Rev. 1517 (1975). Cf. Kenneth W. Simmons, When is Strict Criminal Liability Just? 87 J. Crim. L. and Cr. 1075 (1997).

is hostile to statutory rape laws in general, it is perfectly reasonable to negate them by defining negligent perceptions in terms of the girl's physical appearance — that is, in terms of judgments which can be made at the narrow time-framed moment of the allegedly criminal incident. But it is hardly conceivable that a defendant ought to attract serious sympathy as someone unable to avoid crime when he has certainly had the opportunity to check on the legal appropriateness of his companion as an object of sexual desire.[a]

Phillip Johnson, Strict Liability: The Prevalent View, in Encyclopedia of Crime and Justice 1518, 1520-1521 (1983): The objection to strict liability is not that it punishes people who are literally helpless to avoid committing the act, because it is obvious that they could have avoided any possibility of liability by not going into business in the first place. The point is that selling meat or managing a factory is a productive activity which the law means to encourage, not discourage, and we should not punish people who have taken all reasonable steps to comply with the law. Where strict liability is present in the traditional criminal law, as in the felony-murder doctrine or in the rule that mistake of age is no defense to statutory rape, the defendant's underlying conduct (robbery or fornication) is deemed wrongful or socially undesirable in itself. Unless we regard business activity as similarly inherently wrongful, holding business managers up to strict liability is unjustifiable even though they have voluntarily assumed their positions of employment.

Stephen J. Schulhofer, Harm and Punishment: A Critique of Emphasis on the Results of Conduct in the Criminal Law, 122 U. Pa. L. Rev. 1497, 1586-1587 (1974): [Some argue that strict liability can reduce the risk of injury because those who fear liability can avoid areas of activity subject to this stringent form of regulation. Although those] who continue to engage in the activity may be those who believe they can be careful enough, . . . there is no guarantee that these will be the ones who are in fact the most careful. Indeed, there is some reason to suspect that those who are most confident of their ability to avoid causing harm may be just the ones who are most likely to be especially careless.[290] Thus, the strict liability crime may exclude a few accident-prone people from the activity, but it may well fail to select out most of those about whom the law should be most concerned. At the same time, it may exclude from the activity many others who could play a valuable social role but are unwilling to face the risk of suffering criminal penalties for reasons beyond their control. Indeed, if the penalties are serious, those who are careful and make provision for risks may be the most likely to take the sensible precaution of not engaging in this activity at all.

. . . [Thus], the dynamic effect [of strict liability] could be to increase the total

a. Does this argument imply that there is no practical difference between a strict liability standard and a negligence standard with an expanded time frame? Will the precautions that an actor failed to take at earlier points in time necessarily involve "a gross deviation from the standard of care that a reasonable person would observe" (MPC §2.02(2)(d))? Note that by using a broad time frame, Professor Kelman is able to argue, in effect, that the defendant in his example *was* negligent. But will the defendant have the same opportunity to respond to such an argument if the applicable standard is strict liability rather than negligence? Will the jury's role be the same? — Eds.

290. This confidence may be one reason why such people are dangerous; if they were concerned about the danger, they would not be inadvertent so often. . . .

harm caused by increasing the proportion of those engaged in the activity who are relatively careless.

Model Penal Code and Commentaries, Comment to §2.05 at 282-283 (1985): This section makes a frontal attack on absolute or strict liability in the penal law, whenever the offense carries the possibility of criminal conviction, for which a sentence of probation or imprisonment may be imposed. The method used is not to abrogate strict liability completely, but to provide that when conviction rests upon that basis the grade of the offense is reduced to a violation, which is not a "crime" and under Sections 1.04(5) and 6.02(4) may result in no sentence other than a fine, or a fine and forfeiture or other authorized civil penalty.

This position is affirmed not only with respect to offenses defined by the penal code; it is superimposed on the entire corpus of the law so far as penal sanctions are involved. Since most strict liability offenses involve special regulatory legislation, normally found in titles of a code other than the criminal title, this superimposition is essential if the principle of no criminality, probation or imprisonment for strict liability offenses is to be made effective.

. . . It has been argued, and the argument undoubtedly will be repeated, that strict liability is necessary for enforcement in a number of the areas where it obtains. But if practical enforcement precludes litigation of the culpability of alleged deviation from legal requirements, the enforcers cannot rightly demand the use of penal sanctions for the purpose. Crime does and should mean condemnation and no court should have to pass that judgment unless it can declare that the defendant's act was culpable. This is too fundamental to be compromised. The law goes far enough if it permits the imposition of a monetary penalty in cases where strict liability has been imposed.

NOTE ON CULPABILITY AND EXCUSE

The principle of culpability, which we have thus far explored in the context of the mens rea elements of crimes, finds expression also in an important body of law having to do with excuses to criminal conduct — the defenses of intoxication, legal insanity, and duress all reflect that principle. These defenses are integrally related to the problems of actus reus and mens rea (in its special sense) with which we have so far been dealing; they all respond to fundamental principles in terms of which persons can be justly punished for their wrongful actions. For pedagogical reasons we explore these excuses below in Chapter 8, Section B.

d. Mistake of Law

PEOPLE v. MARRERO

New York Court of Appeals
69 N.Y.2d 382, 507 N.E.2d 1068 (1987)

[Defendant was arrested in a Manhattan social club for unlicensed possession of a loaded .38 caliber pistol, in violation of Penal Law §265.02. A provision of that statute (§265.02 (a)(1)(a)) expressly exempted "peace officers," a term defined in Criminal Procedure Law (CPL) §§1.20 and 2.10 to include "correction officers of any state correctional facility or of any penal correctional institution." At the time of the arrest the defendant protested that he was a federal corrections officer and therefore exempted from §265.02. He was nonetheless charged with violation of that provision. Thereafter, his pretrial motion to dismiss the indictment was granted on the ground that he was a peace officer within the meaning of the statutory exemption. The . . . Appellate Division reinstated the indictment, holding, by a 3-2 vote, that the defendant was not a "peace officer" within the meaning of CPL §§1.20, 2.10. The defendant was thereupon tried before a jury and convicted, the trial court rejecting his request for a jury instruction that it would be a good defense if he reasonably believed that the statutory exemption for peace officers applied to him as a federal correctional officer. The Appellate Division affirmed, and the defendant appealed.]

BELLACOSA, J. . . . The central issue is whether defendant's personal misreading or misunderstanding of a statute may excuse criminal conduct in the circumstances of this case.

The common-law rule on mistake of law was clearly articulated in Gardner v. People, (62 N.Y. 299). In *Gardner,* the defendants misread a statute and mistakenly believed that their conduct was legal. The court insisted, however, that the "mistake of law" did not relieve the defendants of criminal liability. . . . This is to be contrasted with People v. Weiss, 276 N.Y. 384, 12 N.E.2d 514 [1938,] where, in a kidnapping case, the trial court precluded testimony that the defendants acted with the honest belief that seizing and confining the [victim] was done with "authority of law." We held it was error to exclude such testimony since a good-faith belief in the legality of the conduct would negate an express and necessary element of the crime of kidnapping, i.e., intent, without authority of law, to confine or imprison another.[a] . . .

The desirability of the *Gardner*-type outcome . . . is underscored by Justice Holmes' statement: "It is no doubt true that there are many cases in which the criminal could not have known that he was breaking the law, but to admit the excuse at all would be to encourage ignorance where the lawmaker has determined to make men know and obey, and justice to the individual is rightly outweighed by the larger interests on the other side of the scales" (Holmes, The Common Law, at 48 [1881]).

The revisors of New York's Penal Law intended no fundamental departure from this common-law rule in Penal Law §15.20, which provides in pertinent part:

> 2. A person is not relieved of criminal liability for conduct because he engaged in such conduct under a mistaken belief that it does not, as a matter of law, constitute an offense, unless such mistaken belief is founded upon an official statement

a. In *Weiss,* the defendants were convicted of kidnapping a person suspected of the murder of the Lindbergh child. Kidnapping was defined as follows: "A person who wilfully: 1. Seizes, confines, inveigles, or kidnaps another, with intent to cause him, without authority of law, to be confined or imprisoned within this state, . . . against his will . . . is guilty of kidnapping." The defendants were denied the right to introduce testimony showing that they were led to believe that they had been authorized by a law enforcement officer to seize the victim. The Court of Appeals reversed, on the ground that such belief, if found by the jury to exist, would show that defendants lacked the intent to confine the victim, as the statute required, "without authority of law."—EDS.

> of the law contained in (a) a statute or other enactment . . . (d) an interpretation of the statute or law relating to the offense, officially made or issued by a public servant, agency, or body legally charged or empowered with the responsibility or privilege of administering, enforcing or interpreting such statute or law.

The defendant claims as a first prong of his defense that he is entitled to raise the defense of mistake of law under section 15.20(2)(a) because his mistaken belief that his conduct was legal was founded upon an official statement of the law contained in the statute itself. Defendant argues that his mistaken interpretation of the statute was reasonable in view of the alleged ambiguous wording of the peace officer exemption statute, and that his "reasonable" interpretation of an "official statement" is enough to satisfy the requirements of subdivision (2)(a). . . .

The prosecution . . . counters defendant's argument by asserting that one cannot claim the protection of mistake of law under section 15.20(2)(a) simply by misconstruing the meaning of a statute but must instead establish that the statute relied on actually permitted the conduct in question and was only later found to be erroneous. To buttress that argument, the People analogize New York's official statement defense to the approach taken by the Model Penal Code (MPC). Section 2.04 of the MPC provides:

> (3) A belief that conduct does not legally constitute an offense is a defense to a prosecution for that offense based upon such conduct when . . . (b) he acts in reasonable reliance upon an official statement of the law, *afterward determined to be invalid or erroneous,* contained in (i) a statute or other enactment (emphasis added).[b]

Although the drafters of the New York statute did not adopt the precise language of the Model Penal Code provision with the emphasized clause, it is evident and has long been believed that the Legislature intended the New York statute to be similarly construed. . . .

It was early recognized that the "official statement" mistake of law defense was a statutory protection against prosecution based on reliance on a statute that did *in fact* authorize certain conduct. . . . While providing a narrow escape hatch, the idea was simultaneously to encourage the public to read and rely on official statements of the law, not to have individuals conveniently and personally question the validity and interpretation of the law and act on that basis. If later the statute was invalidated, one who mistakenly acted in reliance on the authorizing statute would be relieved of criminal liability. That makes sense and is fair. To go further does not make sense and would create a legal chaos. . . .

Strong public policy reasons underlie the legislative mandate and intent which we perceive in rejecting defendant's construction of New York's mistake of law defense statute. If defendant's argument were accepted, the exception would swallow the rule. Mistakes about the law would be encouraged, rather than respect for and adherence to law. There would be an infinite number of

b. An example may help clarify the kind of situation that this provision contemplates. Suppose that a provision in a state anti-water pollution law exempts nonprofit corporations. Relying on that provision a nonprofit corporation dumps water in a way that would be a violation of the statute were it not for the exemption. In a prosecution of the corporation, the trial court finds this exemption invalid on some ground (perhaps because it conflicts with some federal legislation). The corporation would have a defense under this Model Penal Code provision. — Eds.

mistake of law defenses which could be devised from a good-faith, perhaps reasonable but mistaken, interpretation of criminal statutes, many of which are concededly complex. Even more troublesome are the opportunities for wrong-minded individuals to contrive in bad faith solely to get an exculpatory notion before the jury. These are . . . the realistic and practical consequences were the dissenters' views to prevail. Our . . . statutory scheme . . . was not designed to allow false and diversionary strategems. . . . This would not serve the ends of justice but rather would serve game playing and evasion from properly imposed criminal responsibility.

Accordingly, the order of the Appellate Division should be affirmed.

HANCOCK, J. (dissenting). . . . The basic difference which divides the court may be simply put. Suppose the case of a man who has committed an act which is criminal not because it is inherently wrong or immoral but solely because it violates a criminal statute. He has committed the act in complete good faith under the mistaken but entirely reasonable assumption that the act does not constitute an offense because it is permitted by the wording of the statute. Does the law require that this man be punished? The majority says that it does and holds that (1) Penal Law §15.02(2)(a) must be construed so that the man is precluded from offering a defense based on his mistake of law and (2) such construction is compelled by prevailing considerations of public policy and criminal jurisprudence. We take issue with the majority on both propositions.

There can be no question that under the view that the purpose of the criminal justice system is to punish blameworthiness or "choosing freely to do wrong"[1] our supposed man who has acted innocently and without any intent to do wrong should not be punished. . . . Since he has not knowingly committed a wrong there can be no reason for society to exact retribution. Because the man is law-abiding and would not have acted but for his mistaken assumption as to the law, there is no need for punishment to deter him from further unlawful conduct. Traditionally, however, under the ancient rule of Anglo-American common law that ignorance or mistake of law is no excuse, our supposed man would be punished.

The maxim "*ignorantia legis neminem excusat*" finds its roots in Medieval law. . . . Various justifications have been offered for the rule, but all are frankly pragmatic and utilitarian — preferring the interests of society (e.g., in deterring criminal conduct, fostering orderly judicial administration, and preserving the primacy of the rule of law) to the interest of the individual in being free from punishment except for intentionally engaging in conduct which he knows is criminal.

Today there is widespread criticism of the common-law rule mandating categorical preclusion of the mistake of law defense. The utilitarian arguments for retaining the rule have been drawn into serious question but the fundamental objection is that it is simply wrong to punish someone who, in good-faith reliance on the wording of a statute, believed that what he was doing was lawful. . . . This basic objection to the maxim "*ignorantia legis neminem excusat*" may have had less force in ancient times when most crimes consisted of acts which by their very nature were recognized as evil. In modern times, however, with the profusion of

1. "Historically, our substantive criminal law is based upon a theory of punishing the vicious will. It postulates a free agent confronted with a choice between doing right and doing wrong and choosing freely to do wrong" (Pound, Introduction to Sayre, Cases on Criminal Law [1927], quoted in Morissette v. United States, 342 U.S. 246, 250, n. 4).

legislation making otherwise lawful conduct criminal (*malum prohibitum*), the "common law fiction that every man is presumed to know the law has become indefensible in fact or logic."

With this background we proceed to a discussion of our disagreement with the majority's construction of Penal Law §15.20(2)(a). . . .

It is difficult to imagine a case more squarely within the wording of Penal Law §15.20(2)(a) or one more fitted to what appears clearly to be the intended purpose of the statute than the one before us. . . .

Defendant's mistaken belief that, as a Federal corrections officer, he could legally carry a loaded weapon without a license was based on the express exemption from criminal liability under Penal Law §265.02 accorded . . . to "peace officers" as defined in the Criminal Procedure Law and on his reading of the statutory definition for "peace officer" . . . as meaning a correction officer "of *any* penal correctional institution" (emphasis added), including an institution not operated by New York State. Thus, he concluded erroneously that, as a corrections officer in a Federal prison, he was a "peace officer" and, as such, exempt by the express terms of Penal Law §265.02(a)(1)(a). This mistaken belief, based in good faith on the statute defining "peace officer" is, defendant contends, the precise sort of "mistaken belief . . . founded upon an official statement of the law contained in . . . a statute or other enactment" which gives rise to a mistake of law defense under Penal Law §15.20(2)(a). He points out, of course, that when he acted in reliance on his belief he had no way of foreseeing that a court would eventually resolve the question of the statute's meaning against him and rule that his belief had been mistaken, as three of the five-member panel at the Appellate Division ultimately did in the first appeal.

The majority, however, has accepted the People's argument that to have a defense under Penal Law §15.20(2)(a) "a defendant must show that the statute *permitted his conduct,* not merely that he believed it did." . . .

Nothing in the statutory language suggests the interpretation urged by the People and adopted by the majority. . . . It is self-evident that in enacting Penal Law §15.20(2) as part of the revision and modernization of the Penal Law the Legislature intended to effect a needed reform by abolishing what had long been considered the unjust archaic common-law rule totally prohibiting mistake of law as a defense. . . .

The majority construes the statute, however, so as to rule out *any* defense based on mistake of law. In so doing, it defeats the only possible purpose for the statute's enactment and resurrects the very rule which the Legislature rejected in enacting Penal Law §15.20(2)(a) as part of its modernization and reform of the Penal Law. . . .

Instead, the majority bases its decision on an analogous provision in the Model Penal Code and concludes that despite its totally different wording and meaning Penal Law §15.20(2)(a) should be read as if it were Model Penal Code §2.04(3)(b)(i). But New York in revising the Penal Law did not adopt the Model Penal Code. As in New Jersey, which generally adopted the Model Penal Code but added one section which is substantially more liberal,[10] New York followed parts of the Model Penal Code provisions and rejected others. . . .

10. In addition to permitting defenses based on ignorance of the law and reasonable reliance on official statements afterward determined to be invalid or erroneous, the New Jersey statute provides a defense, under the following broad provision, when: "(3) The actor otherwise diligently

Thus, the precise phrase in the Model Penal Code limiting the defense under section 2.04(3)(b)(i) to reliance on a statute "afterward determined to be invalid or erroneous" which, if present, would support the majority's narrow construction of the New York statute, is omitted from Penal Law §15.20(2)(a). How the Legislature can be assumed to have enacted the very language which it has specifically rejected is not explained. . . .

NOTE ON THE RATIONALE OF IGNORANTIA LEGIS

The traditional explanation for the rule against allowing even reasonable mistakes of law to be a defense is that given by Justice Holmes, quoted in the *Marrero* decision: "to admit the excuse at all would be to encourage ignorance where the lawmaker has determined to make men know and obey." That explanation has been challenged by Professor Dan M. Kahan in a provocative article, Ignorance of Law *Is* an Excuse — But Only For the Virtuous, 96 Mich. L. Rev. 127 (1997). He argues that this can't be the explanation, because "if maximizing legal knowledge were really the objective . . . the law would apply a negligence standard. . . . Refusing to excuse even reasonable mistakes *discourages* investments in legal knowledge by making it hazardous for a citizen to rely on her private understanding of the law." Id. at 152. He finds the more convincing explanation in the view "that individuals are and should be aware of society's morality and that morality furnishes a better guide for action than does law itself. Thus, far from trying to maximize the incentive that presumptively bad men have to know the law, the doctrine seeks to obscure the law so that citizens are more likely to behave like good ones." Id. at 153. Therefore the courts need "to make contentious, context-specific judgments about which actors have characters good enough to be excused for their mistakes of law," id. at 152, in order to distinguish the loopholers who seek to exploit the uncertainties of the law, such as "designer drug manufacturers and other strategically inquisitive wrongdoers." As to the *Marrero* case, he observes (141):

> Marrero ignored the law's injunction to do what's right rather than what one thinks is legal. New York's restrictive gun possession law embodies its citizens' strong antipathy toward, and fear of, handguns. But rather than defer to those norms, Marrero decided to be strategic, availing himself of what must have appeared even to him to be a largely fortuitous gap in the law. That's the attitude that made the court see in Marrero's efforts to decode the law not an earnest and laudable attempt to obey but rather a "false and diversionary strategy," a form of "game playing and evasion." Other facts, not even mentioned by the court, also likely played a role: that the policy of the federal prison at which Marrero worked forbade guards to carry guns either on or off duty; that Marrero had supplied his girlfriend and another companion with guns, even though they clearly had no grounds for believing their possession to be lawful; and that Marrero menacingly reached for his weapon when the police approached him in the Manhattan club."[51]

pursues all means available to ascertain the meaning and application of the offense to his conduct and honestly and in good faith concludes his conduct is not an offense in circumstances in which a law-abiding[ch and prudent person would also so conclude" (N.J. Stat. Ann. §2C:2-4[c][3]).

51. See David De Gregorio, Comment, 54 Brook. L. Rev. 229, 231-232, 233 n.34 (1998).

Questions: (i) The argument that a negligence standard would achieve greater compliance than strict liability has been made and rejected in the context of the strict liability debate generally. See supra page 235. What could be the explanation of the persistence of strict liability generally other than the belief by legislators and courts, to some extent, that strict liability works? Is there nothing to the view that where no excuses are allowed people will have reason to be extra careful?

(ii) Should we be more concerned than Professor Kahan apparently is with giving prosecutors and courts the authority to determine whether the defendant in the particular case has a good enough character to deserve a mistake of law defense? Are we to understand that if Marrero had been an estimable citizen the court would (or should) have allowed the defense?

NOTE ON SCOPE OF THE IGNORANTIA LEGIS *DOCTRINE*

In Regina v. Smith (David), [1974] 2 Q.B. 354, defendant, in preparing to leave his rented apartment, damaged some wall panels and floor boards in order to retrieve stereo wiring he earlier had installed with the landlord's permission behind wall panels and floor boards of his own construction. He was charged with violating the Criminal Damage Act, which read: "A person who without lawful excuse destroys or damages any property belonging to another intending to destroy or damage any such property or being reckless as to whether any such property would be destroyed or damaged, shall be guilty of an offence." His defense, in his own words, was: "Look, how can I be done in for smashing my own property. I put the flooring and that in, so if I want to pull it down it's a matter for me." He was convicted under an instruction that told the jury that "belief by the defendant . . . that he had the right to do what he did is not a lawful excuse within the meaning of the Act . . . because in law he had no right to do what he did." On appeal, the prosecution argued that "the mental element in the offence relates only to causing damage or to destroying property, [so] that if in fact the property damaged or destroyed is shown to be another's property the offence is committed although the defendant did not intend or foresee damage to another person's property." The Court of Appeal reversed, finding the jury instruction erroneous and stating:

> Construing the language of section 1(1) we have no doubt that the actus reus is "destroying or damaging any property belonging to another." It is not possible to exclude the words "belonging to another" which describes the "property." Applying the ordinary principles of mens rea, the intention and recklessness and the absence of lawful excuse required to constitute the offence have reference to property belonging to another. It follows that in our judgment no offence is committed under this section if a person destroys or causes damage to property belonging to another if he does so in the honest though mistaken belief that the property is his own, and provided that the belief is honestly held it is irrelevant to consider whether or not it is a justifiable belief.

It is important to see why this case, as well as People v. Weiss discussed in the *Marrero* opinion, is not inconsistent with the basic doctrine that ignorance of the law is no excuse. The Model Penal Code's provisions develop the distinction. Section 2.04(1) provides:

> Ignorance or mistake as to a matter of fact or *law* is a defense if [it] negatives the purpose, belief, recklessness or negligence required to establish a material element of the offense. [Emphasis added.]

Section 2.02(9) provides:

> Neither knowledge nor recklessness or negligence as to whether conduct constitutes an offense or as to the existence, meaning or application of the law determining the elements of an offense is an element of such offense, unless the definition of the offense or the Code so provides.

The relationship between these two provisions is articulated in Model Penal Code and Commentaries, Comment to §2.02 at 250 (1985):

> Subsection (9) states the conventional position that knowledge of the existence, meaning or application of the law determining the elements of an offense is not an element of that offense, except in the unusual situations where the law defining the offense or the Code so provides.
>
> It should be noted that the general principle that ignorance or mistake of law is no excuse is greatly overstated; it has no application, for example, when the circumstances made material by the definition of the offense include a legal element. Thus it is immaterial in theft, when claim of right is adduced in defense, that the claim involves a legal judgment as to the right of property. Claim of right is a defense because the property must belong to someone else for the theft to occur and the defendant must have culpable awareness of that fact. Insofar as this point is involved, there is no need to state a special principle; the legal element involved is simply an aspect of the attendant circumstances, with respect to which knowledge, recklessness or negligence, as the case may be, is required for culpability. . . . The law involved is not the law defining the offense; it is some other legal rule that characterizes the attendant circumstances that are material to the offense.
>
> The proper arena for the principle that ignorance or mistake of law does not afford an excuse is thus with respect to the particular law that sets forth the definition of the crime in question. It is knowledge of *that* law that is normally not a part of the crime, and it is ignorance or mistake as to *that* law that is denied defensive significance by this subsection of the Code and by the traditional common law approach to the issue.

On the foregoing analysis, how should the following cases be decided?

(a) The defendant was a single woman who traveled with Leo Shuffelt from Vermont to Reno, Nevada, where Shuffelt instituted divorce proceedings against his wife, who was neither a Nevada resident nor present in Nevada. The Nevada judge entered a divorce decree, following which he married the defendant and Shuffelt. Upon return to Vermont, the defendant was prosecuted under a Vermont statute, commonly known as the *Blanket Act,* which provided: "A man with another man's wife, or a woman with another woman's husband, found in bed together, under circumstances affording presumption of an illicit intention, shall each be imprisoned in the state prison not more than three years or fined not more than $1,000." The defendant requested an instruction to the jury that

an honest belief in the validity of the Nevada divorce and of her subsequent marriage to Shuffelt would be a defense to the prosecution. Is she entitled to this instruction? Would she be if she had requested an instruction that a *reasonable* belief would be a defense? See State v. Woods, 107 Vt. 354, 179 A. 1 (1935).

(b) A physician, attending a patient whom he knows to be brain dead, takes steps to stop his heart, preliminary to removing it for a transplant. He believes the legislature in his jurisdiction has enacted a brain death statute. It hasn't, and the common law definition of death (cessation of heart functions) is in effect. Can the physician be convicted of *intentionally* killing his patient? On the one hand, ignorance of the law is no excuse. On the other hand, how can a person be found to have intentionally killed a person he believed already dead?

CHEEK v. UNITED STATES

Supreme Court of the United States
498 U.S. 192 (1991)

[Cheek, a professional pilot for American Airlines, was convicted of willfully failing to file a federal income tax return for a number of years in violation of 26 U.S.C. §7201, which provides that any person is guilty of a felony "who willfully attempts in any manner to evade or defeat any tax imposed by this title or the payment thereof." He was also convicted under §7203(1) for the misdemeanor offense of "willfully" failing to make a return required by law. His defense was that based on information he received from a group opposing the institution of taxation, he sincerely believed that under the tax laws he owed no taxes, including taxes on his wages, and that these laws were unconstitutional.

[After the trial judge gave his initial instructions, the jury sent out a note saying that it could not reach a verdict because "[w]e are divided on the issue as to if Mr. Cheek honestly & reasonably believed that he was not required to pay income tax." Thereupon the trial judge further instructed the jury that "[a]n honest but unreasonable belief is not a defense and does not negate willfulness," and that "[a]dvice or research resulting in the conclusion that wages of a privately employed person are not income or that the tax laws are unconstitutional is not objectively reasonable and cannot serve as the basis for a good faith misunderstanding of the law defense." The judge also instructed the jury that "[p]ersistent refusal to acknowledge the law does not constitute a good faith misunderstanding of the law."

[Cheek appealed his convictions, charging the trial judge with error in instructing that only an objectively reasonable misunderstanding of the law negates the statutory willfulness requirement. The Court of Appeals affirmed, and the Supreme Court granted certiorari.]

Justice White delivered the opinion of the Court.

The general rule that ignorance of the law or a mistake of law is no defense to criminal prosecution is deeply rooted in the American legal system. Based on the notion that the law is definite and knowable, the common law presumed that every person knew the law. . . .

The proliferation of statutes and regulations has sometimes made it difficult for the average citizen to know and comprehend the extent of the duties and obligations imposed by the tax laws. Congress has accordingly softened the impact of the common-law presumption by making specific intent to violate the law an element of certain federal criminal tax offenses. Thus, the Court almost 60 years ago interpreted the statutory term "willfully" as used in the federal criminal tax statutes as carving out an exception to the traditional rule. This special treatment of criminal tax offenses is largely due to the complexity of the tax laws. In United States v. Murdock, 290 U.S. 389 (1933), the Court recognized that:

> Congress did not intend that a person, by reason of a bona fide misunderstanding as to his liability for the tax, as to his duty to make a return, or as to the adequacy of the records he maintained, should become a criminal by his mere failure to measure up to the prescribed standard of conduct. . . .

Subsequent decisions . . . conclusively establish that the standard for the statutory willfulness requirement is the "voluntary, intentional violation of a known legal duty."

Cheek accepts [this] definition of willfulness, but . . . he challenges the ruling that a good-faith misunderstanding of the law or a good-faith belief that one is not violating the law, if it is to negate willfulness, must be objectively reasonable. We agree that the Court of Appeals and the District Court erred in this respect. Willfulness, as construed by our prior decisions in criminal tax cases, requires the Government to prove that the law imposed a duty on the defendant, that the defendant knew of this duty, and that he voluntarily and intentionally violated that duty. We deal first with the case where the issue is whether the defendant knew of the duty purportedly imposed by the provision of the statute or regulation he is accused of violating, a case in which there is no claim that the provision at issue is invalid. In such a case, if the Government proves actual knowledge of the pertinent legal duty, the prosecution, without more, has satisfied the knowledge component of the willfulness requirement. But carrying this burden requires negating a defendant's claim of ignorance of the law or a claim that because of a misunderstanding of the law, he had a good-faith belief that he was not violating any of the provisions of the tax laws. . . . In the end, the issue is whether, based on all the evidence, the Government has proved that the defendant was aware of the duty at issue, which cannot be true if the jury credits a good-faith misunderstanding and belief submission, whether or not the claimed belief or misunderstanding is objectively reasonable.

In this case, if Cheek asserted that he truly believed that the Internal Revenue Code did not purport to treat wages as income, and the jury believed him, the Government would not have carried its burden to prove willfulness, however unreasonable a court might deem such a belief. . . .

We thus disagree with the Court of Appeals' requirement that a claimed good-faith belief must be objectively reasonable if it is to be considered as possibly negating the Government's evidence purporting to show a defendant's awareness of the legal duty at issue. . . . Of course, the more unreasonable the asserted beliefs or misunderstandings are, the more likely the jury will consider them to be nothing more than simple disagreement with known legal duties . . . and will find that the Government has carried its burden of providing knowledge.

Cheek asserted in the trial court that he should be acquitted because he believed in good faith that the income tax law is unconstitutional as applied to him and thus could not legally impose any duty upon him of which he should have been aware. Such a submission is unsound, not because Cheek's constitutional arguments are not objectively reasonable or frivolous, which they surely are, but because [our] cases construed the willfulness requirement in the criminal provisions of the Internal Revenue Code to require proof of knowledge of the law. This was because in "our complex tax system, uncertainty often arises even among taxpayers who earnestly wish to follow the law" and "'it is not the purpose of the law to penalize frank difference of opinion or innocent errors made despite the exercise of reasonable care.'" United State v. Bishop, 412 US. 346, 360-361 (1973).

Claims that some of the provisions of the tax code are unconstitutional are submissions of a different order. They do not arise from innocent mistakes caused by the complexity of the Internal Revenue Code. Rather, they reveal full knowledge of the provisions at issue and a studied conclusion, however wrong, that those provisions are invalid and unenforceable. Thus in this case, Cheek paid his taxes for years, but after attending various seminars and based on his own study, he concluded that the income tax laws could not constitutionally require him to pay a tax.

We do not believe that Congress contemplated that such a taxpayer, without risking criminal prosecution, could ignore the duties imposed upon him by the Internal Revenue Code and refuse to utilize the mechanisms provided by Congress to present his claims of invalidity to the courts and to abide by their decisions. There is no doubt that Cheek, from year to year, was free to pay the tax that the law purported to require, file for a refund and, if denied, present his claims of invalidity, constitutional or otherwise, to the courts. Also, without paying the tax, he could have challenged claims of tax deficiencies in the Tax Court, with the right to appeal to a higher court if unsuccessful. Cheek took neither course in some years, and when he did was unwilling to accept the outcome. . . . Of course, Cheek was free in this very case to present his claims of invalidity and have them adjudicated, but like defendants in criminal cases in other contexts, who "willfully" refuse to comply with the duties placed upon them by the law, he must take the risk of being wrong.

We thus hold that [it] was therefore not error in this case for the District Judge to instruct the jury not to consider Cheek's claims that the tax laws were unconstitutional. However, it was error for the court to instruct the jury that petitioner's asserted beliefs that wages are not income and that he was not a taxpayer within the meaning of the Internal Revenue Code should not be considered by the jury in determining whether Cheek had acted willfully.

[On retrial defendant was convicted on an instruction allowing the jury to consider "whether the defendant's stated belief about the tax statute was reasonable as a factor in deciding whether he held that belief in good faith." United States v. Cheek, 3 F.3d 1057 (7th Cir. 1993).]

NOTE ON "WILLFULLY" AND "KNOWINGLY"

Consider this exchange between Judge Learned Hand and Professor Herbert Wechsler, Reporter for the Model Penal Code:

"JUDGE HAND: Do you use [wilfully] throughout? . . . It's a very dreadful word. MR. WECHSLER: We will never use it in the Code. . . . JUDGE HAND: . . . It's an awful word! It is one of the most troublesome words in the statute that I know. If I were to have the index purged, "wilful" would lead all the rest in spite of its being at the end of the alphabet. MR. WECHSLER: I agree with you Judge Hand, and I promise you unequivocally that the word will never be used in the definition of any offense in the code." (Quoted in United States v. Hayden, 64 F.3d 126, 129 n.5 (3rd Cir. 1994).)

The term "willfully" (and "knowingly") have continued to be used and they have given rise to much controversy over whether their use requires that the defendant be aware of the existence of the law he is charged with violating. Of course, ignorance of the law *is* a defense, obviously it must be, when the crime by its terms requires that a person know of the existence of the prohibition. See Model Penal Code §2.04(1)(b). Is that the case when statutes require that the defendant commit the prohibited action knowingly or willingly? The Supreme Court has followed a somewhat tortuous path in answering this question in a variety of statutory contexts. Consider the following line of cases.

United States v. International Minerals & Chemical Corp., 402 U.S. 558 (1971). Here the Court considered a statute making it a crime for a person to "knowingly violat[e]" a regulation of the Interstate Commerce Commission regarding the transportation of corrosive liquids. Did that mean the prosecution must prove that defendant knew of the existence and meaning of the regulation its actions violated, or was it sufficient to prove that the actions it knowingly committed violated those regulations? The Court held the latter.

Liparota v. United States, 471 U.S. 419 (1985). Here the Court reached the opposite conclusion. The Court had to interpret a statute governing food stamp fraud, which provided that "whoever knowingly uses, transfers, acquired, alters, or possesses coupons or authorization cards in any manner not authorized by [the statute] or the regulations [of the Department of Agriculture]" is subject to fine and imprisonment. Does this mean that the prosecution must prove the defendant knew of the existence and meaning of the regulation his actions violated, or only that he was aware of doing the actions that violated the regulation? This time the Court held for the former interpretation, influenced by the concern that "to interpret the statute otherwise would be to criminalize a broad range of apparently innocent conduct." The court continued:

> For instance, §2024(b)(1) declares . . . that "[c]oupons issued to eligible households shall be used by them only to purchase food in retail food stores which have been approved for participation in the food stamp program *at prices prevailing in such stores.*" (emphasis added). This seems to be the *only* authorized use. A strict reading of the statute with no knowledge-of-illegality requirement would thus render criminal a food stamp recipient who, for example, used stamps to purchase food from a store that, unknown to him, charged higher than normal prices to food stamp program participants.

[See Michael Vitiello, Does Culpability Matter?: Statutory Construction Under 42 U.S.C. §6928, 6 Tulane Env. L.J. 187, 235-246 (1993), for a helpful analysis of these two cases.]

Ratzlaf v. United States, 510 U.S. 135 (1994). Here once again the Court construed "willfully" to require proof that defendant knew of the existence and meaning of the criminal statute he was charged with violating; and once again the Court was confessedly influenced by wanting to avoid criminalizing otherwise innocent conduct. Ratzlaf sought to discharge a large gambling debt owed an importunate Reno casino by presenting it with $100,000 in cash. The casino's cashier explained to Ratzlaf that if it accepted the cash, the casino would have to report the transaction to state and federal authorities. However, he told Ratzlaf, the casino could accept a cashier's check for the full amount without triggering any reporting requirements. The casino then placed a limousine at Ratzlaf's disposal and assigned an employee to accompany him to banks in the vicinity. Informed that banks, too, are required to report cash transactions in excess of $10,000, Ratzlaf purchased cashier's checks, each for less than $10,000 and each from a different bank. The casino was satisfied, but the United States Attorney was not. The prosecutor obtained a conviction against Raztlaf under a federal law making it illegal to "structure" a transaction, that is, to break up a single transaction above the reporting threshold into two or more separate transactions for the purpose of evading a financial institution's reporting requirement. The statute subjected to criminal penalties "a person willfully violating" this antistructuring provision. The Supreme Court reversed the conviction, holding that the prosecution had to prove not only knowledge of the bank's reporting requirement, but also knowledge that the structuring he undertook to evade it constituted a criminal offense. The government argued that the defendant's structuring efforts were so obviously corrupt that the willfulness requirement is satisfied even without proof that the defendant was aware of a statute making such structuring a criminal offense. The Court rejected this argument, offering examples of "innocent" structuring, such as those designed to avoid an audit, to decrease the likelihood of burglary, or to keep a former spouse unaware of the depositor's wealth. More generally, it observed, quoting a lower court, "courts have noted many occasions on which persons, without violating any law, may structure transactions in order to avoid the impact of some regulation or tax."[7]

Bryan v. United States, 524 U.S. 184 (1998). The Firearms Owners' Protection Act made it a crime for anyone to "willfully" deal in firearms without a federal license. Defendant was convicted in the absence of proof that he knew a federal statute made it criminal to do so. Reviewing its prior decisions interpreting the "willfully" requirement, the Court held that the defendant has to be shown to act with knowledge that his conduct was unlawful, but not that he knew of the existence of the state with which he was charged. The Court found that there was ample evidence that he knew his conduct was unlawful. "Why else," the Court observed in footnote 8, "would he make use of straw purchasers and assure them he would shave the serial numbers off the guns?" Moreover, the Court thought his resales of the guns on street corners known for drug dealing was "not consistent with a good-faith belief in the legality of the enterprise." Therefore, reasoned the Court, in this case, unlike *Cheek* (supra page 263) and *Ratzlaff,* there was no danger of convicting the innocent, because even though there was

7. Congress soon amended the statute to undo the Court's interpretation. Money Laundering Suppression Act of 1994, Pub. L. 103-325, Tit. IV, §411, 108 Stat. 2253.

no evidence that he was aware of the law he was convicted of violating (i.e., the federal law that prohibits dealing in firearms without a federal license), there was adequate evidence that he knew he was dealing in firearms and that his conduct was unlawful. That was enough to show that he acted "with an evil-meaning mind," which is all the term "willfully" in this statute required.

For two helpful reviews of this line of cases see John S. Wiley, Not Guilty by Reason of Blamelessness: Culpability in Federal Criminal Interpretation, 85 Va. L. Rev. 1021 (1999), and Sharon Davies, The Jurisprudence of Willfulness: An Evolving Theory of Excusable Ignorance, 48 Duke L.J. 341 (1998).

UNITED STATES v. ALBERTINI

United States Court of Appeals, 9th Circuit
830 F.2d 985 (1987)

[Defendant engaged in a peace demonstration on a naval base in Hawaii after receiving from its commander a "bar letter" which prohibited him from entering the base. His entry constituted a violation of 18 U.S.C. §1832, and he was convicted under that provision. On appeal, the Ninth Circuit (*Albertini I*) reversed the conviction on the ground that the First Amendment protected his right to demonstrate at the base. Thereupon, after consulting with counsel, he demonstrated several more times, in defiance of another bar order, and was again prosecuted. The government petitioned for certiorari from *Albertini I* about this time, but the Supreme Court did not accept review until after the second group of demonstrations. The Supreme Court eventually reversed the Ninth Circuit's decision in *Albertini I* and held that the First Amendment did not preclude convicting him for demonstrating in defiance of a bar order. Thereupon the government pressed its prosecution for the second group of demonstrations (those which occurred after *Albertini I* but before the Supreme Court granted certiorari) and obtained a conviction. Albertini appealed, arguing that due process precluded the retroactive application of the Supreme Court's decision reversing *Albertini I* (which had upheld the legality of his conduct). In its second *Albertini* decision (*Albertini II*) the Ninth Circuit agreed and reversed his conviction for the second group of demonstrations, writing the following opinion:]

Goodwin, J. . . . The government claims that the litigation in which Albertini's claims were ultimately resolved against him by the Supreme Court was a unitary case or controversy and that this court could create no window of opportunity to engage in challenged conduct while Supreme Court review was still a possibility. Albertini says that after he received a favorable decision from this court, and at least before the petition for certiorari was granted, he was acting within his adjudicated legal rights and had a due process right to rely upon the judgment of this court.

The United States Constitution provides that neither Congress nor any state shall pass any ex post facto law. The prohibition against ex post facto enactments bans "[e]very law that makes an action done before the passing of the law, and which was innocent when done, criminal; and punishes such action."

Although the ex post facto clause applies to the legislature and not to the courts, "the principle on which the Clause is based — the notion that persons have a right to fair warning of that conduct which will give rise to criminal penalties — is fundamental to our concept of constitutional liberty." Marks v. United States, 430 U.S. 188, 191. . . .

In effect, Albertini obtained a declaratory judgment from this court that the actions in which he engaged were lawful. If the due process clause is to mean anything, it should mean that a person who holds the latest controlling court opinion declaring his activities constitutionally protected should be able to depend on that ruling to protect like activities from criminal conviction until that opinion is reversed, or at least until the Supreme Court has granted certiorari.[2] . . .

[T]he government argued that mistake of law is never a defense. There is an exception to the mistake of law doctrine, however, in circumstances where the mistake results from the defendant's reasonable reliance upon an official — but mistaken or later overruled — statement of the law. "It would be an act of 'intolerable injustice' to hold criminally liable a person who had engaged in certain conduct in reasonable reliance upon a judicial opinion instructing that such conduct is legal." Kratz [v. Kratz, 477 F. Supp. 468, 481 (E.D. Pa. 1979)]. As delineated by Section 2.04 of the Model Penal Code, the doctrine may in some circumstances protect a defendant's reasonable reliance on official advisory opinions. . . .

Albertini acted during a window of time when he reasonably believed his acts were protected under *Albertini [I]*. He cannot be convicted for acting in reliance on that opinion at least until the Supreme Court has granted certiorari. To hold otherwise would sanction a kind of "entrapment" by the government — convicting Albertini for acts that the government has told him are protected by the first amendment against prosecution. . . .

"When the 'entrapment' has been caused by a judicial opinion, the argument in favor of recognizing the reliance defense is even more compelling, since courts are the very entities charged with interpreting the law." *Kratz,* 477 F. Supp. at 482 n. 51. . . .

Reversed.

NOTES ON OFFICIAL RELIANCE

1. Questions: In footnote 2 the court of appeals left open the question of whether a conviction would have been proper for demonstrations that took place after the Supreme Court granted certiorari. Why should it matter whether the Supreme Court has granted certiorari or instead is still considering whether to grant it, so long as the time for review had not lapsed?

Suppose Albertini is president of a company that discharges toxic pollutants into a nearby river. His conviction of violating an environmental regulation is reversed by the court of appeals on the ground that the regulation was not promulgated by the regulatory agency in accordance with required procedures. Albertini thereupon resumes company operations and is prosecuted again, while at about the same time the government petitions for certiorari. If the Supreme Court then grants certiorari and subsequently holds that the regulations were properly promulgated, would the defendant have a good defense to the viola-

2. We do not . . . reach the issue whether Albertini would have been justified in relying upon *Albertini [I]* in the period after the Supreme Court granted certiorari and before it reversed.

tions committed after the court of appeals decision but before the grant of certiorari? Could *Albertini II* be distinguished?

2. In Hopkins v. State, 193 Md. 489, 69 A.2d 456 (1950), the defendant was convicted of violating a statute making it unlawful to erect or maintain any sign intended to aid in the solicitation of performance of marriages. He had erected signs that read: "Rev. W. F. Hopkins" and "W. F. Hopkins, Notary Public, Information." On appeal he argued that the trial judge erred in excluding testimony offered to show that the State's Attorney advised him before he erected the signs that they would not violate the law. The Maryland Supreme Court affirmed his conviction, stating:

> It is generally held that the advice of counsel, even though followed in good faith, furnishes no excuse to a person for violating the law and cannot be relied upon as a defense in a criminal action. . . . Moreover, advice given by a public official, even a State's Attorney, that a contemplated act is not criminal will not excuse an offender if, as a matter of law, the act performed did amount to a violation of the law. . . . These rules are founded upon the maxim that ignorance of the law will not excuse its violation. If an accused could be exempted from punishment for crime by reason of the advice of counsel, such advice would become paramount to the law. . . .
>
> In the case at bar defendant did not claim that the State's Attorney misled him regarding any facts of the case, but only that the State's Attorney advised him as to the law based upon the facts. Defendant was aware of the penal statute enacted by the Legislature. He knew what he wanted to do, and he did the thing he intended to do. He claims merely that he was given advice regarding his legal rights. . . . If the right of a person to erect a sign of a certain type and size depends upon the construction and application of a penal statute, and the right is somewhat doubtful, he erects the sign at his peril. In other words, a person who commits an act which the law declared to be criminal cannot be excused from punishment upon the theory that he misconstrued or misapplied the law.

3. The Model Penal Code proposed in §2.04(3) a limited defense based on a reasonable belief on the part of the defendant that the law is such that his conduct does not constitute an offense:

> (3) A belief that conduct does not legally constitute an offense is a defense to a prosecution for that offense based upon such conduct when:
>
> (a) the statute or other enactment defining the offense is not known to the actor and has not been published or otherwise reasonably made available prior to the conduct alleged; or
>
> (b) he acts in reasonable reliance upon an official statement of the law, afterward determined to be invalid or erroneous, contained in (i) a statute or other enactment; (ii) a judicial decision, opinion or judgment; (iii) an administrative order or grant of permission; or (iv) an official interpretation of the public officer or body charged by law with responsibility for the interpretation, administration or enforcement of the law defining the offense.

See Model Penal Code and Commentaries, Comment to §2.04 at 274-275 (1985):

> All of the categories dealt with in the formulation involve, for the most part, situations where the act charged in consistent with the entire law-abidingness of the

actor, where the possibility of collusion is minimal, and where a judicial determination of the reasonableness of the belief in legality should not present substantial difficulty. It is hard, therefore, to see how any purpose can be served by a conviction. It should be added that in the area of regulatory offenses, where the defense would normally apply, penal sanctions are appropriate in general only for deliberate evasion or defiance. When less than this is involved, lesser sanctions should suffice, for these typically are situations where a single violation works no major public or private injury; it is persistent violations that must be brought to book. And obviously the defense afforded by this section would normally be available to a defendant only once; after a warning he can hardly have a reasonable basis for belief in the legality of his behavior.

4. The defense of official reliance formulated by the Model Penal Code has achieved widespread acceptance. See, for example, United States v. Levin, 973 F.2d 463, 468 (6th Cir. 1992); Commonwealth v. Twitchell, 416 Mass. 114, 617 N.E.2d 609 (1993). A compilation of the cases may be found in the Annotation, "Official Statement" Mistake of Law Defense, 89 A.L.R.4th 1026 (1991).

Under the label, "entrapment by estoppel," the Supreme Court has held it to be a violation of due process to convict a defendant for conduct that governmental representatives had earlier in their official capacity stated was lawful. The doctrine was first asserted in Raley v. Ohio, 360 U.S. 423 (1959). Defendants invoked their privilege against self incrimination before an Ohio governmental commission investigating un-American activities after they were instructed by the commission that they were privileged to do so. This, apparently, was bad advice, however, since an Ohio statute granted automatic immunity in such situations thereby depriving them of any privilege to refuse to answer. They were then prosecuted and convicted for contempt for refusing to answer the commission's questions. The Supreme Court found this to violate due process, stating that to affirm the convictions in these circumstances "would be to sanction the most indefensible sort of entrapment by the State — convicting a citizen for exercising a privilege which the State clearly had told him was available to him" (438).

For discussions see John T. Parry, Culpability, Mistake, and Official Interpretations of Law, 25 Am. J. Crim. L. 1 (1997); Sean Connelly, Bad Advice: The Entrapment by Estoppel Doctrine in the Criminal Law, 48 U. Miami L. Rev. 627 (1994).

LAMBERT v. CALIFORNIA

Supreme Court of the United States
355 U.S. 225 (1957)

Justice Douglas delivered the opinion of the Court.

Section 52.38(a) of the Los Angeles Municipal Code defines "convicted person" as follows:

> Any person who, subsequent to January 1, 1921, has been or hereafter is convicted of an offense punishable as a felony in the State of California, or who has been or who is hereafter convicted of any offense in any place other than the State of California, which offense, if committed in the State of California, would have been punishable as a felony.

Section 52.39 provides that it shall be unlawful for "any convicted person" to be or remain in Los Angeles for a period of more than five days without registering; it requires any person having a place of abode outside the city to register if he comes into the city on five occasions or more during a 30-day period; and it prescribes the information to be furnished the Chief of Police on registering. Section 52.43(b) makes the failure to register a continuing offense, each day's failure constituting a separate offense.

Appellant, arrested on suspicion of another offense, was charged with a violation of this registration law. . . . The case was tried to a jury which found appellant guilty. The court fined her $250 and placed her on probation for three years. . . .

The registration provision, carrying criminal penalties, applies if a person has been convicted "of an offense punishable as a felony in the State of California" or, in case he has been convicted in another State if the offense "would have been punishable as a felony" had it been committed in California. No element of willfulness is by terms included in the ordinance nor read into it by the California court as a condition necessary for a conviction.

We must assume that appellant had no actual knowledge of the requirement that she register under this ordinance, as she offered proof of this defense which was refused. The question is whether a registration act of this character violates Due Process where it is applied to a person who has no actual knowledge of his duty to register, and where no showing is made of the probability of such knowledge.

. . . There is wide latitude on the lawmakers to declare an offense and to exclude elements of knowledge and diligence from its definition. . . But we deal here with conduct that is wholly passive — mere failure to register. It is unlike the commission of acts, or the failure to act under circumstances that should alert the doer to the consequences of his deed. Cf. . . . United States v. Balint, 258 U.S. 250; United States v. Dotterweich, 320 U.S. 277, 284. The rule that "ignorance of the law will not excuse" . . . is deep in our law, as is the principle that of all the powers of local government, the police power is "one of the least limitable." . . . On the other hand, Due Process places some limits on its exercise. Engrained in our concept of Due Process is the requirement of notice. Notice is sometimes essential so that the citizen has the chance to defend charges. Notice is required before property interests are disturbed, before assessments are made, before penalties are assessed. Notice is required in a myriad of situations where a penalty or forfeiture might be suffered for mere failure to act. Recent cases illustrating the point . . . involved only property interests in civil litigation. But the principle is equally appropriate where a person, wholly passive and unaware of any wrongdoing, is brought to the bar of justice for condemnation in a criminal case.

Registration laws are common and their range is wide. . . . Many such laws are akin to licensing statutes in that they pertain to the regulation of business activities. But the present ordinance is entirely different. Violation of its provisions is unaccompanied by any activity whatever, mere presence in the city being the test. Moreover, circumstances which might move one to inquire as to the necessity of registration are completely lacking. At most the ordinance is but a law enforcement technique designed for the convenience of law enforcement agencies through which a list of the names and addresses of felons then residing in a given community is compiled. The disclosure is merely a compilation of former convictions already publicly recorded in the jurisdiction where obtained. Nevertheless, this registrant on first becoming aware of her duty to register was given no opportunity to comply with the law and avoid its penalty, even though her default was entirely innocent. She could but suffer the consequences of the ordinance, namely, conviction with the imposition of heavy criminal penalties thereunder. We believe that actual knowledge of the duty to register or proof of the probability of such knowledge and subsequent failure to comply are necessary before a conviction under the ordinance can stand. . . . Its severity lies in the absence of an opportunity either to avoid the consequences of the law or to defend any prosecution brought under it. Where a person did not know of the duty to register and where there was no proof of the probability of such knowledge, he may not be convicted consistently with Due Process. Were it otherwise, the evil would be as great as it is when the law is written in print too fine to read or in a language foreign to the community.

Reversed. . . .

JUSTICE FRANKFURTER, whom JUSTICE HARLAN and JUSTICE WHITTAKER join, dissenting.

The present laws of the United States and of the forty-eight States are thick with provisions that command that some things not be done and others be done, although persons convicted under such provisions may have had no awareness of what the law required or that what they did was wrongdoing. The body of decisions sustaining such legislation, including innumerable registration laws, is almost as voluminous as the legislation itself. The matter is summarized in United States v. Balint, 258 U.S. 250, 252: "Many instances of this are to be found in regulatory measures in the exercise of what is called the police power where the emphasis of the statute is evidently upon achievement of some social betterment rather than the punishment of the crimes as in cases of mala in se."

Surely there can hardly be a difference as a matter of fairness, of hardship, or of justice, if one may invoke it, between the case of a person wholly innocent of wrongdoing, in the sense that he was not remotely conscious of violating any law, who is imprisoned for five years for conduct relating to narcotics, and the case of another person who is placed on probation for three years on condition that she pay $250, for failure, as a local resident, convicted under local law of a felony, to register under a law passed as an exercise of the State's "police power."

[W]hat the Court here does is to draw a constitutional line between a State's requirement of doing and not-doing. What is this but a return to Year Book distinctions between feasance and nonfeasance — a distinction that may have significance in the evolution of common law notions of liability, but is inadmissible as a line between constitutionality and unconstitutionality. . . .

If the generalization that underlies, and alone can justify, this decision were to be given its relevant scope, a whole volume of the United States Reports would be required to document in detail the legislation in this country that would fall or be impaired. I abstain from entering upon a consideration of such legislation, and adjudications upon it, because I feel confident that the present decision will turn out to be an isolated deviation from the strong current of precedents — a derelict on the waters of the law. Accordingly, I content myself with dissenting.

NOTES

1. Questions: What precisely, in Justice Frankfurter's view, is the "generalization that underlies, and alone can justify" the decision in *Lambert*? Would it invalidate all strict liability legislation, as he seems to imply? Would it invalidate the traditional rule that even reasonable mistake of law is not a defense? Could the generalization be confined to cases of omissions? Consider, for example, an ordinance that prohibited "convicted persons" from accepting employment as babysitters in the city of Los Angeles?

2. Problem. Cody Hutzell owned a gun. At some point, he was convicted of the misdemeanor of "domestic abuse assault," in the state court. Six months later, Congress enacted 18 U.S.C. §922(g)(9) making it a federal offense for any person who had been convicted of domestic violence to possess a firearm. Two years after that, Hutzell discharged his gun during an argument with his girlfriend and was prosecuted for violating §922(g)(9) by the continued possession of his gun. Is his conviction constitutional under *Lambert*? The court held yes, but a dissent argued to the contrary. Who had the stronger position? See United States v. Hutzell, 217 F.3d 966 (8th Cir. 2000).

3. Lambert's *background.* An account of the diplomatic maneuvering among the Justices that led to the final form of Justice Douglas's opinion is contained in Note (A. F. Brooke), When Ignorance of the Law Became an Excuse: *Lambert* and Its Progeny, 19 Am. J. Crim. L. 279 (1992). For an exchange of views on the majority opinion, see Steven B. Duke, Justice Douglas and the Criminal Law, in Stephen L. Wasby, ed., "He Shall Not Pass This Way Again": The Legacy of Justice William O. Douglas 133, 137 (1990), and Sanford H. Kadish, Justice Douglas and the Criminal Law: Another View, id. at 149, 150.

CALIFORNIA JOINT LEGISLATIVE COMMITTEE FOR REVISION OF THE PENAL CODE, PENAL CODE REVISION PROJECT

(Tent. Draft No. 2, 1968)

SECTION 500. IGNORANCE OR MISTAKE . . .

(2) A person's belief that his conduct does not constitute a crime is a defense only if it is reasonable and,

(a) if the person's mistaken belief is due to his ignorance of the existence of the law defining the crime, he exercised all the care which, in the circumstances, a law-abiding and prudent person would exercise to ascertain the law; or

(b) if the person's mistaken belief is due to his misconception of the meaning or application of the law defining the crime to his conduct,

(i) he acts in reasonable reliance upon an official statement of the law, afterward determined to be invalid or erroneous, contained in a statute, judicial decision, administrative order or grant of permission, or an official interpretation of the public officer or body charged by law with the responsibility for interpreting, administering or enforcing the law defining the crime; or,

[(ii) he otherwise diligently pursues all means available to ascertain the meaning and application of the crime to his conduct and honestly and in good faith concludes his conduct is not a crime in circumstances in which a law-abiding and prudent person would also so conclude].

Comments (64-67) . . . .

[We] think exculpation should be made out in all cases where a law-abiding and prudent person would not have learned of the law's existence. One such case is Lambert v. California, 355 U.S. 225 (1957). . . . Certainly there would not be many cases of this kind. Where the prohibition reaches plainly wrongful conduct, the conduct itself alerts the law-abiding and prudent person to the need for inquiry if there is any doubt. And even in the mala prohibita crimes the circumstances would normally suggest inquiry — engaging in such closely regulated activities as liquor selling, food merchandising, apartment renting, etc. But in the exceptional case, like *Lambert,* where this is not the case only a blind and brutal law would insist on punishment. Subsection (2)(b) is addressed to the situation where the defendant (still reasonably), although aware of the existence of the crime, was mistaken as to its meaning or its applicability to conduct. Subsection (i), dealing with situations of reliance on official and responsible interpretations . . . imports no innovation in present law. Subsection (ii), however, does, insofar as it generalized the essential quality of the unfairness in holding defendants who are misled by official reliance; i.e., they did all that could be done to learn the nature of the prohibition and in concluding that it was lawful reacted no differently than would any law-abiding and prudent person. The subsection is placed in brackets because some of the Reporters believe it may go too far for reasons that will be stated shortly. The case to be made in favor of this subsection is as follows:

The central point is that it is plainly unjust to hold a defendant criminally liable where a jury is prepared to conclude that the conditions of this subsection are met. A case which illustrates this is Long v. State, 44 Del. 262, 65 A.2d 489 (1949). The court reversed a conviction of bigamy because the court below excluded evidence offered by the defendant to show his reasonable belief that his Arkansas divorce legally severed his prior marriage relationship. [T]he court dealt with the defense as though it were a defense of misconception of the law defining the offense and allowed the defense on the ground that the defendant "before engaging in the conduct made a bona fide, diligent effort, adopting a course and resorting to sources and means at least as appropriate as any afforded under our legal system, to ascertain and abide by the law, and . . . acted in good faith reliance upon the results of such effort." We agree with the Delaware court that in such circumstances the practical difficulties commonly invoked to deny the defense of mistake of law are inapposite. It cannot be said to "encourage ignorance" of the law where the defense requires a showing of diligent and exhaustive effort to comprehend the law. And difficulties of proof are not here substantial since the defendant is required to show affirmative acts of inquiry addressed to an objective standard. We also agree with the conclusion of the Delaware court that punishing in the circumstances would be "unjust and arbitrary." . . .

On the other hand some feel that this provision is subject to abuse. It opens up a new and potentially time-consuming defense in many cases. Further, the defense can be too easily fabricated out of disingenuous advice obtained from lawyers ready to lend themselves to a scheme of evasion through venality or partisanship in their client's cause. Finally, it is believed that the potential injustice is adequately guarded against by the use of the prosecutor's discretion not to prosecute in cases in which the accused acted in good faith, and his conduct was not harmful.

NOTES

1. The California proposal, §2(b)(ii), was adopted in New Jersey. See N.J. Stat. Ann. tit. 2C, §2-4(c)(3). For arguments favoring substantial expansion of the mistake-of-law defense, see Douglas Husak & Andrew von Hirsch, Culpability and Mistake of Law, in Action and Value in Criminal Law 157-174 (John Gardner, Jeremy Horder, and Stephen Shute, eds., 1993); to the contrary, see Sharon Davies, The Jurisprudence of Willfullness, 48 Duke L.J. 341 (1998).

2. The German law treats the defense of mistake of law quite differently from English and American law. Since 1975, Section 17 of the German Penal Code has provided:

> If in doing the [criminal] act the actor fails to understand that he is acting wrongfully, he acts without culpability if he could not avoid making this mistake.

This statutory formulation derives from a famous 1952 decision of the Supreme Court of West Germany (2 BGH St. 194) in which the court . . . reasoned that blameworthiness is a necessary condition for guilt; hence, where mistake of law is inconsistent with moral blameworthiness, guilt should not be attached. The conscientious objector — one who is aware of the criminality of his conduct but rejects the moral judgment of the legislature — was excluded from the reach of this defense, because, "The culpability of the morally committed violator consists in his knowing that he substitutes his own system of values for that of the legal community." For discussion of the German approach, see George Fletcher, Rethinking Criminal Law 737-755 (1978); Raymond Youngs, Mistake of Law in Germany — Opening Up Pandora's Box, 64 J. Crim. L. 339 (2000). See also Vera Bolgar, The Present Function of the Maxim *Ignorantia Juris Neminem Excusat* — A Comparative Study, 52 Iowa L. Rev. 626 (1967).

PROBLEM: THE "CULTURAL DEFENSE"

Should the law afford an excuse for foreigners who violate the law by actions acceptable in their native cultures? An English court faced this issue in Rex. v. Esop, 7 C. & P. 456 (1836). A sailor who was a native of Bagdad was convicted for sodomy committed aboard an East India ship while it was docked in London harbor. The court sustained the conviction over the defendant's objection that sodomy was not a crime in his native land. A number of recent incidents reported in the press raise questions about the propriety of applying the traditional *ignorantia legis* rule in such situations. Here are examples of some of these incidents, as summarized in Doriane Lambelet Coleman, Individualizing Justice Through Multiculturalism: The Liberals' Dilemma, 96 Colum. L. Rev. 1093, 1093 (1996):

In California, a Japanese-American mother drowns her two young children in the ocean at Santa Monica and then attempts to kill herself; rescuers save her before she drowns. The children's recovered bodies bear deep bruises where they struggled as their mother held them under the water. The mother later explains that in Japan, where she is from, her actions would be understood as the time-honored, customary practice of parent-child suicide. She spends only one year in jail — the year she is on trial.

In New York, a Chinese-American woman is bludgeoned to death by her husband. Charged with murder, her husband explains that his conduct comports with a Chinese custom that allows husbands to dispel their shame in this way when their wives have been unfaithful. He is acquitted of murder charges.

Back in California, a young Laotian-American woman is abducted from her place of work at Fresno State University and forced to have sexual intercourse against her will. Her Hmong immigrant assailant explains that, among his tribe, such behavior is not only accepted, but expected — it is the customary way to choose a bride. He is sentenced to 120 days in jail, and his victim receives $900 in reparations.

A Somali immigrant living in Georgia allegedly cuts off her two-year old niece's clitoris, partially botching the job. The child was cut in accordance with the time-honored tradition of female circumcision; this custom attempts to ensure that girls and women remain chaste for their husbands. The State charges the woman with child abuse, but is unable to convict her.

The basic arguments in favor of some kind of defense in these cases is that it "will advance two desirable ends consistent with the broader goals of liberal society and the criminal law: (1) the achievement of individualized justice for the defendant; and (2) a commitment to cultural pluralism." James J. Sing, Culture as Sameness: Toward a Synthetic View of Provocation and Culture in the Criminal Law, 108 Yale L. J. 1845, 1847 (1999). Professor Coleman, however, in the article aforementioned, points to a clash of values within the liberal tradition (96 Colum. L. Rev. at 1094-1096):

Allowing sensitivity to a defendant's culture to inform the application of laws to that individual is good multiculturalism. It also is good progressive criminal defense philosophy, which has as a central tenet the idea that the defendant should get as much individualized (subjective) justice as possible. [But] these illustrations also raise an important question: What happens to the victims — almost always minority women and children — when multiculturalism and individualized justice are advanced by dispositive cultural evidence? The answer, both in theory and in practice, is stark: They are denied the protection of the criminal laws because their assailants generally go free, either immediately or within a relatively brief period of time. More importantly, victims and potential victims in such circumstances have no hope of relief in the future, either individually or as a group, because when cultural evidence is permitted to excuse otherwise criminal conduct, the system effectively is choosing to adopt a different, discriminatory standard of criminality for immigrant defendants, and hence, a different and discriminatory level of protection for victims who are members of the culture in question. This different standard may defeat the deterrent effect of the law, and it may become precedent, both for future cases with similar facts, and for the broader position that race- or national origin-based applications of the criminal law are appropriate. Thus, the use of cultural defenses is anathema to another fundamental goal of the progressive agenda, namely the expansion of legal protections for some of the least powerful members of American society: women and children. . . . The question of how to resolve the competing interests . . . I call the "Liberals' Dilemma.

There is a lively debate in the literature about these issues. Supporting a general defense, see Alison Dundes Renteln, A Justification of the Cultural Defense as Partial Excuse, 2 S. Cal. Rev. L. & Women's Stud. 437 (1993); Note, The Cultural Defense in the Criminal Law, 99 Harv. L. Rev. 1293 (1986). For a contrary view, see Julia Sams, The Availability of the "Cultural Defense" as an Excuse for Criminal Behavior, 16 G. J. Intl. & Comp. L. 335 (1986); Nancy Wanderer and Catherine Conners, Culture and Crime: Kargar and the Existing Framework for a Cultural Defense, 47 Buff. L. Rev. 829 (1999). The conflict between feminism and multiculturalism in this context is explored in Holly Maguigan, Cultural Evidence and Male Violence: Are Feminist and Multicultural Reformers on a Collision Course in Criminal Courts?, 70 N.Y.U. L. Rev. 36 (1995).

The cultural defense may also involve using the different culture of the defendant as evidence to rebut the existence of a particular mens rea required by the crime charged. See, e.g., People v. Wu, 286 Cal. Rptr. 869 (Cal. Ct. App. 1991) (premeditation, provocation); People v. Rhines, 182 Cal. Rptr. 478 (Cal. Ct. App. 1982) (mistake as to consent in rape prosecution). For further on this use of the cultural defense, see the article by Holly Maguigan, just cited, as well as Nancy S. Kim, The Cultural Defense and the Problem of Cultural Preemption: A Framework for Analysis, 27 N.M.L. Rev. 101 (1997); Note (F.S. Brelvi), "News of the Weird"; Special Normativity and the Problem of the Cultural Defense, 28 Colum. Hum. Rts. L. Rev. 657 (1997).

C. PROPORTIONALITY

INTRODUCTORY NOTE

The requirement that punishment be proportional to the seriousness of the offense has traditionally been a salient principle of punishment. It is manifested explicitly today in the statements of purpose contained in various criminal codes. The Model Penal Code (§1.02) includes among the purposes of the definition of crimes the aim "to differentiate on reasonable grounds between serious and minor offenses," and it includes among the purposes of sentencing provisions the aim "to safeguard offenders against excessive, disproportionate or arbitrary punishment." The New York Penal Law includes among the purposes of its provisions (§1.05): "To differentiate on reasonable grounds between serious and minor offenses and to prescribe proportionate penalties therefor." The California Penal Code, as amended in 1976, declares in §1170 that punishment is the purpose of imprisonment for crimes, which purpose is "best served by terms proportionate to the seriousness of the offense."

What is the justification for this concern with proportionality? If we believe excessive punishment, for whatever reason, is unjust, what constitutes excessive punishment? Is there a precise kind and degree of punishment appropriate to every criminal wrong, as Kant argued? How could it be determined? If this perspective is rejected, we may hold that some general proportion must be maintained between the crime and the amount of punishment in light of the seriousness of the crime. If so, is the point that certain crimes cannot be punished with more than a given quantum of punishment or rather that whatever the scale of punishment meted out in a particular society, whether high or low, less serious crime must be punished less than more serious crimes?

Perhaps the aim is not justice and fairness, whatever they might mean, but strictly utilitarian goals. If we hold this view, must we accept that any amount of punishment, no matter how severe, can be justifiable if, in the circumstances, it yields a desirable balance of utilities?

These are the principal issues addressed in the material that follows. See generally Alan H. Goldman, The Paradox of Punishment, 9 Phil. & Pub. Aff. 42 (1979), Alan Wertheimer, Should Punishment Fit the Crime?, 3 Soc. Theory & Prac. 403 (1975); Michael Clark, The Moral Gradation of Punishment, 21 Phil. Q. 132 (1971).

JEREMY BENTHAM, PRINCIPLES OF PENAL LAW

In 1 J. Bentham's Works, Pt. II, bk. 1 at 399-402 (J. Bowring ed. 1843)

Punishments may be too small or too great; and there are reasons for not making them too small, as well as not making them too great. The terms *minimum* and *maximum* may serve to mark the two extremes of this question, which require equal attention.

With a view of marking out the limits of punishment on the side of the first of these extremes, we may lay it down as a rule —

I. That the value of the punishment must not be less in any case than what is sufficient to outweigh that of the profit of the offence.

By the profit of the crime, must be understood not only pecuniary profit, but every advantage, real or apparent, which has operated as a motive to the commission of the crime.

The profit of the crime is the force which urges a man to delinquency — the pain of the punishment is the force employed to restrain him from it. If the first of these forces be the greater, the crime will be committed;[1] if the second, the crime will not be committed. If then a man, having reaped the profit of a crime, and undergone the punishment, finds the former more than equivalent to the latter, he will go on offending for ever; there is nothing to restrain him. If those, also, who behold him, reckon that the balance of gain is in favour of the delinquent, the punishment will be useless for the purposes of example. . . .

Rule III. *When two offences come in competition, the punishment for the greater offence must be sufficient to induce a man to prefer the less.*

Two offences may be said to be in competition, when it is in the power of an individual to commit both. When thieves break into a house, they may execute their purpose in different manners; by simply stealing, by theft accompanied with bodily injury, or murder, or incendiarism. If the punishment is the same for

1. That is to say, committed by those who are only restrained by the laws, and not by any other tutelary motives, such as benevolence, religion or honor.

simple theft, as for theft and murder, you give the thieves a motive for committing murder, because this crime adds to the facility of committing the former, and the chance of impunity when it is committed.

The great inconvenience resulting from the infliction of great punishments for small offences, is, that the power of increasing them in proportion to the magnitude of the offence is thereby lost.

Rule IV. *The punishment should be adjusted in such manner to each particular offence, that for every part of the mischief there may be a motive to restrain the offender from giving birth to it.*

Thus, for example, in adjusting the punishment for stealing a sum of money, let the magnitude of the punishment be determined by the amount of the sum stolen. If for stealing ten shillings an offender is punished no more than for stealing five, the stealing of the remaining five of those ten shillings is an offence for which there is no punishment at all.

Rule V. *The punishment ought in no case to be more than what is necessary to bring it into conformity with the rules here given.* . . .

Of the above rules of proportion, the four first may serve to mark the limits of the minimum side — the limits below which a punishment ought not to be diminished; the fifth will mark out the limits on the maximum side — the limits above which it ought not to be increased.

The minimum of punishment is more clearly marked than its maximum. What is *too little* is more clearly observed than what is *too much.* What is not sufficient is easily seen, but it is not possible so exactly to distinguish in excess: an approximation only can be attained. The irregularities in the force of temptations compel the legislator to increase his punishments, till they are not merely sufficient to restrain the ordinary desires of men, but also the violence of their desires when unusually excited.

The greatest danger lies in an error on the minimum side, because in this case the punishment is inefficacious; but this error is least likely to occur, a slight degree of attention sufficing for its escape; and when it does exist, it is at the same time clear and manifest, and easy to be remedied. An error on the maximum side, on the contrary, is that to which legislators and men in general are naturally inclined: antipathy, or a want of compassion for individuals who are represented as dangerous and vile, pushes them onward to an undue severity. It is on this side, therefore, that we should take the most precautions, as on this side there has been shown the greatest disposition to err.

By way of supplement and explanation to the first rule, and to make sure of giving to the punishment the superiority over the offence, the . . . following rules may be laid down: —

Rule VII. *That the value of the punishment may outweigh the profit of the offence, it must be increased in point of magnitude, in proportion as it falls short in point of certainty.*

Rule VIII. *Punishment must be further increased in point of magnitude, in proportion as it falls short in points of proximity.*

The profit of a crime is commonly more certain than its punishment; or, what amounts to the same thing, appears so to the offender. It is generally more immediate: the temptation to offend is present; the punishment is at a distance. Hence there are two circumstances which weaken the effect of punishment, its *uncertainty* and its *distance.*

HYMAN GROSS, A THEORY OF CRIMINAL JUSTICE 436 (1979): Th[e] general principle of proportion between crime and punishment is a principle of just desert that serves as the foundation of every criminal sentence that is justifiable. As a principle of criminal justice it is hardly less familiar or less important than the principle that only the guilty ought to be punished. Indeed, the requirement that punishment not be disproportionately great, which is a corollary of just desert, is dictated by the same principle that does not allow punishment of the innocent, for any punishment in excess of what is deserved for the criminal conduct is punishment without guilt.

H. L. A. HART & A. HONORÉ, CAUSATION IN THE LAW 395-396 (2d ed. 1985): On a deterrent theory the rationale of the differential severity of punishments is complex. First, one crime if unchecked may cause greater harm than another, and hence on general utilitarian grounds greater severity may be used in its repression than in the repression of the less harmful crime. Secondly, the temptation to commit one sort of crime may be greater than another and hence a more severe penalty is needed to deter. Thirdly, the commission of one crime may be a sign of a more dangerous character in the criminal needing longer sentence for incapacitation or reform.

A. C. EWING, A STUDY OF PUNISHMENT II: PUNISHMENT AS VIEWED BY THE PHILOSOPHER, 21 Canadian B. Rev. 102, 115-116 (1943): We are now in a position also to give a satisfactory reason why a graver offence should be punished more than a lighter one. To punish a lesser crime more severely than a greater would be either to suggest to men's minds that the former was worse when it was not, or, if they could not accept this, to bring the penal law in some degree into discredit or ridicule. One of the requirements of a good moral code is that there should be a right proportion between values, and, in so far as penal laws affect popular morality, they ought to help and not hinder right judgment in this matter. This is not to fall back on the old retributive conception that a certain amount of pain intrinsically fits a certain degree of moral badness. Granted that a certain degree of punishment is inflicted in a given society, for, e.g., thefts, and that certain other acts, e.g., murders, are morally worse, moral condemnation of the latter can only be suitably expressed by inflicting a severer punishment for them than for the former; but this would not be an objection to lowering the penalty for both, because there is no necessarily fixed scale that we can see by which so much guilt deserves so much pain. There is another bad effect of disproportionate punishments in so far as they involve excessive severity. It is this: if a man is very severely punished for a comparatively slight offence, people will be liable to forget about his crime and think only of his sufferings, so that he appears a victim of cruel laws, and the whole process, instead of reaffirming the law and intensifying men's consciousness that the kind of act punished is wrong, will have the opposite effect of casting discredit on the law and making the action of the lawbreaker appear excusable or even almost heroic. These punishments are specially liable to produce an effect of this sort on their victim. He will be likely to think the penalty excessive in any case, and the great danger of punishment is that this will lead to self-pity and despair, or anger and bitterness, instead of repentance, but if he has really good grounds for complaint, this danger will be doubled. The primary object of punishment is to lead both the offender and others to realize the badness of the act punished; but, if great severity is shown, they are much more likely to realize instead the cruelty of the punishment.

We may then regard punishment as a kind of language intended to express moral disapproval.

JAMES FITZJAMES STEPHEN, LAW, EQUALITY, FRATERNITY 152-154 (R. J. White ed. 1967): If vengeance affects, and ought to affect, the amount of punishment, every circumstance which aggravates or extenuates the wickedness of an act will operate in aggravation or diminution of punishment. If the object of legal punishment is simply the prevention of specific acts, this will not be the case. Circumstances which extenuate the wickedness of the crime will often operate in aggravation of punishment. If, as I maintain, both objects must be kept in view, such circumstances will operate in different ways according to the nature of the case.

A judge has before him two criminals, one of whom appears, from the circumstances of the case, to be ignorant and depraved, and to have given way to very strong temptation, under the influence of the other, who is a man of rank and education, and who committed the offence of which both are convicted under comparatively slight temptation. I will venture to say that if he made any difference between them at all every judge on the English bench would give the first man a lighter sentence than the second.

What should we think of such an address to the prisoners as this? You, *A*, are a most dangerous man. You are ignorant, you are depraved, and you are accordingly peculiarly liable to be led into crime by the solicitations or influence of people like your accomplice *B*. Such influences constitute to men like you a temptation practically all but irresistible. The class to which you belong is a large one, and is accessible only to the coarsest possible motives. For these reasons I must put into the opposite scale as heavy a weight as I can, and the sentence of the court upon you is that you be taken to the place from whence you came and from thence to a place of execution, and that there you be hanged by the neck till you are dead. As to you, *B*, you are undoubtedly an infamous wretch. Between you and your tool *A* there can, morally speaking, be no comparison at all. But I have nothing to do with that. You belong to a small and not a dangerous class. The temptation to which you gave way was slight, and the impression made upon me by your conduct is that you really did not care very much whether you committed this crime or not. From a moral point of view, this may perhaps increase your guilt; but it shows that the motive to be overcome is less powerful in your case than in *A*'s. You belong, moreover, to a class, and occupy a position in society, in which exposure and loss of character are much dreaded. This you will have to undergo. Your case is a very odd one, and it is not likely that you will wish to commit such a crime again, or that others will follow your example. Upon the whole, I think that what has passed will deter others from such conduct as much as actual punishment. It is, however, necessary to keep a hold over you. You will therefore be discharged on your own recognizances to come up and receive judgment when called upon, and unless you conduct yourself better for the future, you will assuredly be so called upon, and if you do not appear, your recognizances will be inexorably forfeited.

Caricature apart, the logic of such a view is surely unimpeachable. If all that you want of criminal law is the prevention of crime by the direct fear of punishment, the fact that a temptation is strong is a reason why punishment should be severe. In some instances this actually is the case. It shows the reason why political crimes and offences against military discipline are punished so severely. But in most cases the strength of the temptation operates in mitigation of punishment, and the reason of this is that criminal law operates not merely by producing fear, but also indirectly, but very powerfully, by giving distinct shape to the feeling of anger, and a distinct satisfaction to the desire of vengeance which crime excites in a healthy mind.

H. L. A. HART, LAW, LIBERTY AND MORALITY 36-37 (1963): [T]he questions "What sort of conduct may justifiably be punished?" and "How severely should we punish different offenses?" are distinct and independent questions. There are many reasons why we might wish the legal graduation of the seriousness of crimes, expressed in its scale of punishments, not to conflict with common estimates of their comparative wickedness. One reason is that such a conflict is undesirable on simple utilitarian grounds: it might either confuse moral judgments or bring the law into disrepute, or both. Another reason is that principles of justice or fairness between different offenders require morally distinguishable offences to be treated differently and morally similar offences to be treated alike. These principles are still widely respected, although it is also true that there is a growing disinclination to insist on their application where this conflicts with the forward-looking aims of punishment, such as prevention or reform. But those who concede that we should attempt to adjust the severity of punishment to the moral gravity of offences are not thereby committed to the view that punishment merely for immorality is justified. For they can in perfect consistency insist on the one hand that the only justification for having a system of punishment is to prevent harm and only harmful conduct should be punished, and, on the other, agree that when the question of the quantum of punishment for such conduct is raised, we should defer to principles which make relative moral wickedness of different offenders a partial determinant of the severity of punishment.

HARMELIN v. MICHIGAN

Supreme Court of the United States
501 U.S. 957 (1991)

JUSTICE SCALIA announced the judgment of the Court and delivered an opinion in which THE CHIEF JUSTICE joins.

Petitioner was convicted of possessing 672 grams of cocaine and sentenced to a mandatory term of life in prison without possibility of parole. . . .

Petitioner claims that his sentence is unconstitutionally "cruel and unusual" . . . because it is "significantly disproportionate" to the crime he committed. . . .

The Eighth Amendment, which applies against the States by virtue of the

Fourteenth Amendment, provides: "Excessive bail shall not be required, nor excessive fines imposed, nor cruel and unusual punishments inflicted." . . .

Solem v. Helm, 463 U.S. 277 (1983), set aside under the Eighth Amendment, because it was disproportionate, a sentence of life imprisonment without possibility of parole, imposed under a South Dakota recidivist statute for successive offenses that included three convictions of third-degree burglary, one of obtaining money by false pretenses, one of grand larceny, one of third-offense driving while intoxicated, and one of writing a "no account" check with intent to defraud. . . . [The Court held in favor of a] "general principle of proportionality," which was "deeply rooted and frequently repeated in common-law jurisprudence," had been embodied in the English Bill of Rights "in language that was later adopted in the Eighth Amendment," and had been "recognized explicitly in this Court for almost a century." . . .

[O]ur 5-to-4 decision eight years ago in *Solem* was scarcely the expression of clear and well accepted constitutional law. . . . Accordingly, we have addressed anew, and in greater detail, the question whether the Eighth Amendment contains a proportionality guarantee — with particular attention to the background of the Eighth Amendment . . . and to the understanding of the Eighth Amendment before the end of the 19th century. . . . We conclude from this examination that *Solem* was simply wrong; the Eighth Amendment contains no proportionality guarantee. . . .

[Justice Scalia discussed the history of the English Bill of Rights, and its influence on the Eighth Amendment. He concluded that the Amendment was adopted to outlaw certain modes of punishment (e.g., drawing and quartering) and to prevent judges from inventing and imposing "unusual" penalties not prescribed by law.]

We think it enough that those who framed and approved the Federal Constitution chose, for whatever reason, not to include within it the guarantee against disproportionate sentences that some State Constitutions contained. It is worth noting, however, that there was good reason for that choice — a reason that reinforces the necessity of overruling *Solem*. While there are relatively clear historical guidelines and accepted practices that enable judges to determine which *modes* of punishment are "cruel and unusual," *proportionality* does not lend itself to such analysis. . . . This is not to say that there are no absolutes; one can imagine extreme examples that no rational person, in no time or place, could accept. But for the same reason these examples are easy to decide, they are certain never to occur. The real function of a constitutional proportionality principle, if it exists, is to enable judges to evaluate a penalty that *some* assemblage of men and women *has* considered proportionate — and to say that it is not. For that real-world enterprise, the standards seem so inadequate that the proportionality principle becomes an invitation to imposition of subjective values.

This becomes clear, we think, from a consideration of the three factors that *Solem* found relevant to the proportionality determination: (1) the inherent gravity of the offense, (2) the sentences imposed for similarly grave offenses in the same jurisdiction, and (3) sentences imposed for the same crime in other jurisdictions. As to the first factor: . . . The difficulty of assessing gravity is demonstrated in the very context of the present case. Petitioner acknowledges that a mandatory life sentence might not be "grossly excessive" for possession of cocaine with intent to distribute. But surely whether it is a "grave" offense merely to possess a significant quantity of drugs — thereby facilitating distribution, subjecting the holder to the temptation of distribution, and raising the possibility of theft by others who might distribute — depends entirely upon how odious and socially threatening one believes drug use to be. Would it be "grossly excessive" to provide life imprisonment for "mere possession" of a certain quantity of heavy weaponry? If not, then the only issue is whether the possible dissemination of drugs can be as "grave" as the possible dissemination of heavy weapons. Who are we to say no? The Members of the Michigan Legislature, and not we, know the situation on the streets of Detroit.

The second factor suggested in *Solem* fails for the same reason. One cannot compare the sentences imposed by the jurisdiction for "similarly grave" offenses if there is no objective standard of gravity. Judges will be comparing what *they* consider comparable. . . . Moreover, even if "similarly grave" crimes could be identified, the penalties for them would not necessarily be comparable, since there are many other justifications for a difference. For example, since deterrent effect depends not only upon the amount of the penalty but upon its certainty, crimes that are less grave but significantly more difficult to detect may warrant substantially higher penalties. Grave crimes of the sort that will not be deterred by penalty may warrant substantially lower penalties, as may grave crimes of the sort that are normally committed once-in-a-lifetime by otherwise law-abiding citizens who will not profit from rehabilitation. Whether these differences will occur, and to what extent, depends, of course, upon the weight the society accords to deterrence and rehabilitation, rather than retribution, as the objective of criminal punishment. . . .

As for the third factor mentioned by *Solem*— the character of the sentences imposed by other States for the same crime — it must be acknowledged that that can be applied with clarity and ease. The only difficulty is that it has no conceivable relevance to the Eighth Amendment. That a State is entitled to treat with stern disapproval an act that other States punish with the mildest of sanctions follows a fortiori from the undoubted fact that a State may criminalize an act that other States do not criminalize *at all*. . . . What greater disproportion could there be than that? . . . Diversity not only in policy, but in the means of implementing policy, is the very *raison d'être* of our federal system. . . .

The first holding of this Court unqualifiedly applying a requirement of proportionality to criminal penalties was . . . Coker v. Georgia [,433 U.S. 584 (1977)], [where] the Court held that, because of the disproportionality, it was a violation of the Cruel and Unusual Punishments Clause to impose capital punishment for rape of an adult woman. . . . Proportionality review is one of several respects in which we have held that "death is different," and have imposed protections that the Constitution nowhere else provides. We would leave it there, but will not extend it further. . . .

The judgment of the Michigan Court of Appeals is affirmed.

JUSTICE KENNEDY, with whom JUSTICE O'CONNOR and JUSTICE SOUTER join, concurring in part and concurring in the judgment.

. . . I write this separate opinion because my approach to the Eighth Amendment proportionality analysis differs from Justice Scalia's. Regardless of whether Justice Scalia or the dissent has the best of the historical argument, stare decisis counsels our adherence to the narrow proportionality principle that has existed in our Eighth Amendment jurisprudence for 80 years. Although our proportionality decisions have not been clear or consistent in all respects, they can be reconciled, and they require us to uphold petitioner's sentence.

Our decisions recognize that the Cruel and Unusual Punishments Clause encompasses a narrow proportionality principle. We first interpreted the Eighth Amendment to prohibit "'greatly disproportioned'" sentences in Weems v. United States, 217 U.S. 349, 371 (1910). Since *Weems,* we have applied the principle in different Eighth Amendment contexts. Its most extensive application has been in death penalty cases. . . .

The Eighth Amendment proportionality principle also applies to noncapital sentences. In Rummel v. Estelle, 445 U.S. 263 (1980), we acknowledged the existence of the proportionality rule for both capital and noncapital cases, but we refused to strike down a sentence of life imprisonment, with possibility of parole, for recidivism based on three underlying felonies. In Hutto v. Davis, 454 U.S. 370 (1982), we recognized the possibility of proportionality review but held it inapplicable to a 40-year prison sentence for possession with intent to distribute nine ounces of marijuana. Our most recent decision discussing the subject is Solem v. Helm, 463 U.S. 277 (1983). There we held that a sentence of life imprisonment without possibility of parole violated the Eighth Amendment because it was "grossly disproportionate" to the crime of recidivism based on seven underlying nonviolent felonies. The dissent in *Solem* disagreed with the Court's application of the proportionality principle but observed that in extreme cases it could apply to invalidate a punishment for a term of years. . . .

[C]lose analysis of our decisions yields some common principles that give content to the uses and limits of proportionality review.

The first of these principles is that the fixing of prison terms for specific crimes involves a substantive penological judgment that, as a general matter, is "properly within the province of legislatures, not courts." . . . Thus, "reviewing courts . . . should grant substantial deference to the broad authority that legislatures necessarily possess in determining the types and limits of punishments for crimes." *Solem,* supra, at 290.

The second principle is that the Eighth Amendment does not mandate adoption of any one penological theory. . . . The federal and state criminal systems have accorded different weights at different times to the penological goals of retribution, deterrence, incapacitation, and rehabilitation. And competing theories of mandatory and discretionary sentencing have been in varying degrees of ascendancy or decline since the beginning of the Republic.

Third, marked divergences both in underlying theories of sentencing and in the length of prescribed prison terms are the inevitable, often beneficial, result of the federal structure. State sentencing schemes may embody different penological assumptions, making interstate comparison of sentences a difficult and imperfect enterprise. And even assuming identical philosophies, differing attitudes and perceptions of local conditions may yield different, yet rational, conclusions regarding the appropriate length of prison terms for particular crimes. Thus, the circumstance that a State has the most severe punishment for a particular crime does not by itself render the punishment grossly disproportionate. . . .

The fourth principle at work in our cases is that proportionality review by "federal courts should be informed by 'objective factors to the maximum possible extent.'" *Rummel,* supra, at 274-275. The most prominent objective factor is the type of punishment imposed. In *Weems,* "the Court could differentiate in an objective fashion between the highly unusual *cadena temporal*[a] and more traditional forms of imprisonment imposed under the Anglo-Saxon system." *Rummel,* 445 U.S., at 275. In a similar fashion, because "'the penalty of death differs from all other forms of criminal punishment,'" id., at 272, the objective line between capital punishment and imprisonment for a term of years finds frequent mention in our Eighth Amendment jurisprudence. By contrast, our decisions recognize that we lack clear objective standards to distinguish between sentences for different terms of years. Although "no penalty is per se constitutional," id., at 290, the relative lack of objective standards concerning terms of imprisonment has meant that "'outside the context of capital punishment, *successful* challenges to the proportionality of particular sentences [are] exceedingly rare.'" Id., at 289-290.

All of these principles — the primacy of the legislature, the variety of legitimate penological schemes, the nature of our federal system, and the requirement that proportionality review be guided by objective factors — inform the final one: the Eighth Amendment does not require strict proportionality between crime and sentence. Rather, it forbids only extreme sentences that are "grossly disproportionate" to the crime. . . .

Petitioner's life sentence without parole is the second most severe penalty permitted by law. It is the same sentence received by the petitioner in *Solem.* Petitioner's crime, however, was far more grave than the crime at issue in *Solem.*

The crime of uttering a no account check at issue in *Solem* was "'one of the most passive felonies a person could commit.'" *Solem,* 463 U.S., at 296. . . .

Petitioner was convicted of possession of more than 650 grams (over 1.5 pounds) of cocaine. This amount of pure cocaine has a potential yield of between 32,500 and 65,000 doses. From any standpoint, this crime falls in a different category from the relatively minor, nonviolent crime at issue in *Solem.* . . .

[F]acts and reports detailing the pernicious effects of the drug epidemic in this country do not establish that Michigan's penalty scheme is correct or the most just in any abstract sense. But they do demonstrate that the Michigan Legislature could with reason conclude that the threat posed to the individual and society by possession of this large an amount of cocaine — in terms of violence, crime, and social displacement — is momentous enough to warrant the deterrence and retribution of a life sentence without parole. . . . [I]ntra- and interjurisdictional analyses are appropriate only in the rare case in which a threshold comparison of the crime committed and the sentence imposed leads to an inference of gross disproportionality. . . .

JUSTICE WHITE, with whom JUSTICE BLACKMUN and JUSTICE STEVENS join, dissenting. . . .

The language of the [Eighth] Amendment does not refer to proportionality in so many words, but it does forbid "excessive" fines, a restraint that suggests that a determination of excessiveness should be based at least in part on whether the fine imposed is disproportionate to the crime committed. Nor would it be unreasonable to conclude that it would be both cruel and unusual to punish overtime parking by life imprisonment, or, more generally, to impose any pun-

a. *Cadena temporal* is a punishment based upon the Spanish Penal Code. It calls for incarceration at hard and painful labor with chains fastened to the wrists and ankles at all times. — EDS.

ishment that is grossly disproportionate to the offense for which the defendant has been convicted.

. . . Later in his opinion, Justice Scalia backtracks and appears to accept that the Amendment does indeed insist on proportional punishments in a particular class of cases, those that involve sentences of death. His fallback position is that outside the capital cases, proportionality review is not required by the Amendment. . . . This position . . . ignores the generality of the Court's several pronouncements about the Eighth Amendment's proportionality component. And it fails to explain why the words "cruel and unusual" include a proportionality requirement in some cases but not in others. . . .

The Court therefore has recognized that a punishment may violate the Eighth Amendment if it is contrary to the "evolving standards of decency that mark the progress of a maturing society." Trop [v. Dulles], [356 U.S. 86, 101 (1958)]. In evaluating a punishment under this test, "we have looked not to our own conceptions of decency, but to those of modern American society as a whole" in determining what standards have "evolved," and thus have focused not on "the subjective views of individual Justices," but on "objective factors to the maximum possible extent." It is this type of objective factor which forms the basis for the tripartite proportionality analysis set forth in *Solem*.

. . . Application of the *Solem* factors to the statutorily mandated punishment at issue here reveals that the punishment fails muster under *Solem* and, consequently, under the Eighth Amendment to the Constitution. . . .

The first *Solem* factor requires a reviewing court to assess the gravity of the offense and the harshness of the penalty. . . .

[I]n evaluating the gravity of the offense, it is appropriate to consider "the harm caused or threatened to the victim or society," based on such things as the degree of violence involved in the crime and "the absolute magnitude of the crime," and "the culpability of the offender," including the degree of requisite intent and the offender's motive in committing the crime, [*Solem,*] at 292-293.

Drugs are without doubt a serious societal problem. To justify such a harsh mandatory penalty as that imposed here, however, the offense should be one which will always warrant that punishment. Mere possession of drugs — even in such a large quantity — is not so serious an offense that it will always warrant, much less mandate, life imprisonment without possibility of parole. Unlike crimes directed against the persons and property of others, possession of drugs affects the criminal who uses the drugs most directly. . . .

The "absolute magnitude" of petitioner's crime is not exceptionally serious. . . . Indeed, the presence of a separate statute which reaches manufacture, delivery, or possession with intent to do either, undermines the State's position that the purpose of the *possession* statute was to reach drug dealers. . . . In addition, while there is usually a pecuniary motive when someone possesses a drug with intent to deliver it, such a motive need not exist in the case of mere possession. Finally, this statute applies equally to first-time offenders, such as petitioner, and recidivists. Consequently, the particular concerns reflected in recidivist statutes such as those in *Rummel* and *Solem* are not at issue here. . . .

The second prong of the *Solem* analysis is an examination of "the sentences imposed on other criminals in the same jurisdiction." [T]here is no death penalty in Michigan; consequently, life without parole, the punishment mandated here, is the harshest penalty available. It is reserved for three crimes: first-degree murder; manufacture, distribution, or possession with intent to manufacture or distribute 650 grams or more of narcotics; and possession of 650 grams or more of narcotics. Crimes directed against the persons and property of others — such as second-degree murder, rape, and armed robbery — do not carry such a harsh mandatory sentence, although they do provide for the possibility of a life sentence in the exercise of judicial discretion. It is clear that petitioner "has been treated in the same manner as, or more severely than, criminals who have committed far more serious crimes."

The third factor set forth in *Solem* examines "the sentences imposed for commission of the same crime in other jurisdictions." . . . Of the remaining 49 States, only Alabama provides for a mandatory sentence of life imprisonment without possibility of parole for a first-time drug offender, and then only when a defendant possesses *ten kilograms* or more of cocaine. . . . Thus, "it appears that [petitioner] was treated more severely than he would have been in any other State." *Solem,* supra, at 300. Indeed, the fact that no other jurisdiction provides such a severe, mandatory penalty for possession of this quantity of drugs is enough to establish "the degree of national consensus this Court has previously thought sufficient to label a particular punishment cruel and unusual."

Application of *Solem*'s proportionality analysis leaves no doubt that the Michigan statute . . . violates the Eighth Amendment's prohibition against cruel and unusual punishment. Consequently, I would reverse the decision of the Michigan Court of Appeals.

NOTES

1. *Interpretations of* Harmelin. State courts and lower federal courts have tended to interpret *Harmelin* as preserving the proportionality requirement advocated in Justice Kennedy's concurring opinion. See State v. Bartlett, 830 P.2d 823, 826 n.2 (Ariz. 1992). In Thomas v. State, 634 A.2d 1 (Md. 1993), defendant was sentenced to 20 years' imprisonment for slapping his wife. The Maryland Court of Appeals, applying Justice Kennedy's standard, overturned the sentence as "grossly disproportional" to a battery consisting of a single slap. But another court, also applying Justice Kennedy's standard, upheld a sentence totaling 100 years, with possibility of parole, for the rape and robbery of a woman by a nearly 14-year-old perpetrator. Hawkins v. Hargett, 200 F.3d 1279 (10th Cir. 1999). In *Bartlett,* supra, the Arizona Supreme Court, also applying the Kennedy test, found a mandatory 40-year term of imprisonment for two counts of statutory rape (consensual sex with minors) to violate the Eighth Amendment. A later court, however, overruled it insofar as it interpreted *Harmelin* to require an assessment of the circumstances surrounding the offense, rather than simply the offense as statutorily defined. State v. DePlano, 926 P.2d 494 (Ariz. 1996).

Obviously, then, the issue lends itself to subjective appraisals that produce very different results. A case involving a life sentence for a first offense delivery of $20 worth of crack cocaine drew a divided court in Henderson v. State, 322 Ark. 402, 910 S.W.2d 656 (1995). The majority concluded that the sentence was not "so wholly disproportionate as to the nature of the offense as to shock the moral sense of the community." How did they know? The dissenters thought otherwise. How did *they* know? What criteria should govern how such a question should be resolved?

2. *State constitutions.* Many state constitutions have their own prohibitions of cruel and unusual punishment. Their interpretations are not necessarily dependent on federal interpretation of the Eighth Amendment. In People v. Bullock, 485 N.W.2d 866 (1992), the Michigan Supreme Court overturned the law at issue in *Harmelin* on the ground that it violated the Michigan Constitution. The court emphasized the textual difference between the Eighth Amendment's prohibition of "cruel *and* unusual punishment" and the Michigan Constitution's prohibition of "cruel *or* unusual punishment" (italics added). It also emphasized that the Michigan provision was adopted in 1976 when sensibilities to the excesses of punishment were greater than they were in 1789 when the Eighth Amendment was adopted. The court held, therefore, that under the Michigan Constitution, the courts must apply a three-prong test, identical to that advanced in *Solem,* to determine whether a punishment is "cruel *or* unusual."

Question: Another Michigan law imposes the same punishment (life without possibility of parole) for possession *with intent to distribute.* Is this also unconstitutional under *Bullock?* The opinions leave the answer in doubt. See Mark Hansen, Michigan Drug Law Struck Down, A.B.A. J., Sept. 1992, at 25.

See also In re Lynch, 8 Cal. 3d 410, 503 P.2d 921 (1972), where the California Supreme Court heard a challenge to a sentence based on a state constitutional "cruel or unusual" provision similar to that of the Michigan Constitution. Defendant had been convicted of a second offense of indecent exposure and sentenced to imprisonment in the state prison for the indeterminate period of one year to life, at the discretion of the paroling authority. The court held that the sentence was "so disproportionate to the crime for which it is inflicted that it shocks the conscience and offends fundamental notions of human dignity."

A number of state constitutions expressly require that "[a]ll penalties shall be proportioned to the nature of the offense." Ind. Const. art. 1, §16; see also Me. Const. art. I, §9; Neb. Const. art. I, §15; N.H. Const. pt. 1, art. 18; Or. Const. art. I, §16; R.I. Const. art. I, §8; W. Va. Const. art. III, §5.

D. LEGALITY

SHAW v. DIRECTOR OF PUBLIC PROSECUTIONS

House of Lords
[1962] A.C. 220

[Appellant was convicted on an indictment containing three counts that alleged the following offenses: (1) conspiracy to corrupt public morals, (2) living on the earning of prostitution contrary to §30 of the Sexual Offences Act, 1956, and (3) publishing an obscene publication contrary to §2 of the Obscene Publications Act, 1959. The appeal on all three counts was dismissed, and the conviction upheld. Only discussion of the first count is included in the following extracts from several of the addresses.

[The essential facts, as stated by Viscount Simonds, are as follows: "When the Street Offences Act, 1959, came into operation it was no longer possible for prostitutes to ply their trade by soliciting in the streets, and it became necessary for them to find some other means of advertising the service that they were prepared to render. It occurred to the appellant that he could with advantage to himself assist them to this end. The device that he adopted was to publish . . . a magazine or booklet which was called 'Ladies' Directory.' It contained the names, addresses and telephone numbers of prostitutes with photographs of nude female figures, and in some cases details which conveyed to initiates willingness to indulge not only in ordinary sexual intercourse but also in various perverse practices."

[The first count charged the appellant in the following terms:

> State of offense: Conspiracy to corrupt public morals. Particulars of offence: Frederick Charles Shaw on divers days between the 1st day of October, 1959, and 23rd July, 1960, within the jurisdiction of the Central Criminal Court conspired with certain persons, who inserted advertisements in issues of a magazine entitled "Ladies' Directory" numbered 7, 7 revised, 8, 9, 10 and a supplement thereto, and with certain other persons whose names are unknown, by means of the said magazine and the said advertisements to induce readers thereof to resort to the said advertisers for the purposes of fornication and of taking part in or witnessing other disgusting and immoral acts and exhibitions with intent thereby to debauch and corrupt the morals as well of youth as of divers other liege subjects of Our Lady the Queen and to raise and create in their minds inordinate and lustful desires.]

VISCOUNT SIMONDS. . . . I am at a loss to understand how it can be said either that the law does not recognize a conspiracy to corrupt public morals or that, though there may not be an exact precedent for such a conspiracy as this case reveals, it does not fall fairly within the general words by which it is described. . . . In the sphere of criminal law I entertain no doubts that there remains in the courts of law a residual power to enforce the supreme and fundamental purpose of the law, to conserve not only the safety and order but also the moral welfare of the State, and that it is their duty to guard it against attacks which may be the more insidious because they are novel and unprepared for. . . . Such occasions will be rare, for Parliament has not been slow to legislate when attention has been sufficiently aroused. But gaps remain and will always remain since no one can foresee every way in which the wickedness of man may disrupt the order of society. Let me take a single instance. . . . Let it be supposed that at some future, perhaps early, date homosexual practices between adult consenting males are no longer a crime. Would it not be an offense if even without obscenity, such practices were publicly advocated and encouraged by pamphlet and advertisement? Or must we wait until Parliament finds time to deal with such conduct? I say, my Lords, that if the common law is powerless in such an event, then we should no longer do her reverence. . . .

The appeal on both counts should, in my opinion, be dismissed.

LORD MORRIS of Borth-y-Gest. . . . It is said that there is a measure of vagueness in a charge of conspiracy to corrupt public morals, and also that there might be peril of the launching of prosecutions in order to suppress unpopular or unorthodox views. My Lords, I entertain no anxiety on these lines. Even if accepted public standards may to some extent vary from generation to generation, current standards are in the keeping of juries, who can be trusted to maintain the corporate good sense of the community and to discern attacks upon values that must be preserved. If there were prosecutions which were not genuinely and fairly warranted juries would be quick to perceive this. There could be no conviction unless 12 jurors were unanimous in thinking that the accused person or persons had combined to do acts which were calculated to corrupt public morals. . . .

I would dismiss the appeal.

LORD REID. . . . In my opinion there is no such general offence known to the law as conspiracy to corrupt public morals. . . .

I agree with R. S. Wright, J., when he says . . . "There appear to be great theoretical objections to any general rule that agreement may make punishable that which ought not to be punished in the absence of agreement." And I think, or at least I hope, that it is now established, that the courts cannot create new offences by individuals. So far at least I have the authority of Lord Goddard, C. J., in delivering the opinion of the court in *Newland* [[1954] 1 Q.B. 158]: "[The power to create new offenses] would leave it to the judges to declare new crimes and enable them to hold anything which they considered prejudicial to the community to be a misdemeanor. However beneficial that might have been in days when Parliament met seldom or at least only at long intervals it surely is now the province of the legislature and not of the judiciary to create new criminal offenses." Every argument against creating new offences by an individual appears to me to be equally valid against creating new offences by a combination of individuals. . . . Notoriously, there are wide differences of opinion today as to how far the law ought to punish immoral acts which are not done in the face of the public. . . . Parliament is the proper place, and I am firmly of opinion the only proper place, to settle that. When there is sufficient support from public opinion, Parliament does not hesitate to intervene. Where Parliament fears to tread it is not for the courts to rush in. . . .

Finally I must advert to the consequences of holding that this very general offence exists. It has always been thought to be of primary importance that our law, and particularly our criminal law, should be certain: that a man should be able to know what conduct is and what is not criminal, particularly when heavy penalties are involved. Some suggestion was made that it does not matter if this offence is very wide: no one would ever prosecute and if they did no jury would ever convict if the breach was venial. Indeed, the suggestion goes even further: that the meaning and application of the words. . . . "debauch" and "corrupt" in this indictment ought to be entirely for the jury, so that any conduct of this kind is criminal if in the end a jury think it so. In other words, you cannot tell what is criminal except by guessing what view a jury will take, and juries' views may vary and may change with the passing of time. Normally the meaning of words is a question of law for the court. For example, it is not left to a jury to determine the meaning of negligence: they have to consider on evidence and on their own knowledge a much more specific question — Would a reasonable man have done what this man did? . . . If the trial judge's charge in the present case was right, if a jury is entitled to water down the strong words "deprave," "corrupt" or "debauch" so as merely to mean lead astray morally, then it seems to me that the court has transferred to the jury the whole of its functions as censor morum, the law will be whatever any jury may happen to think it ought to be, and this branch of the law will have lost all the certainty which we rightly prize in other branches of our law.

NOTES

1. There have been a number of critical commentaries on the *Shaw* case. See, e.g., H. L. A. Hart, Law, Liberty and Morality 7-12 (1963); Comment, 75 Harv.

L. Rev. 1652 (1962). For a favorable comment, see Arthur Goodhart, 77 Law Q. Rev. 560 (1961).

2. See A. T. Denning, Freedom under the Law 40-42 (1949):

> [T]he doctrine that acts done to the public mischief are punishable by law . . . is a doctrine quite unknown to France and the other freedom-loving countries of Western Europe where the law is contained in a written code. They take their stand on the principle that no one shall be punished for anything that is not expressly forbidden by law. *Nullum crimen, nulla poena, sine lege.* They regard that principle as their charter of liberty. In this country, however, the common law has not limited itself in that way. It is not contained in a code but in the breasts of the judges, who enunciate and develop the principles needed to deal with any new situations which arise.
>
> In recent years the judges have been faced with acts such as these: A man may call the fire brigade when there is no fire to attend to: or a woman may go to the police and tell them an invented story about being attacked: and thus these public servants may be diverted from their proper duties. In 1933 the judge declared such conduct to be criminal, even though it had not previously been expressly forbidden by law. No one will doubt that it was criminal, because it was a fraud affecting the public at large. But unfortunately the judges based their decision on a wider and much more questionable ground. They relied on an obiter dictum of a judge in 1801, who said that "all offences of a public nature, that is, such acts or attempts as tend to the prejudice of the community, are indictable."
>
> Now that mode of reasoning is dangerously similar to the reasoning by which the Russian jurists justify the punishment of any acts which are socially dangerous. Starting from the point of view that the interests of the State are paramount, their jurists say that the judges ought to punish any act which is dangerous to the State, even though it is not expressly forbidden. Article 16 of the Soviet Code says that "if the Code has not made provision for any act which is socially dangerous, it is to be dealt with on the basis, and as carrying the same degree of responsibility, as the offences which it most nearly resembles." So the only question for their judges is, Is the Act socially dangerous? That is precisely the same test as was stated by our judges in the public mischief case.

3. The doctrine of common law crimes, under which acts are made criminal if the court (or a court and a jury) regards them as directly tending to injure the public to such an extent as to require the state to punish the wrongdoer, even in the absence of an explicit statutory prohibition, was once recognized in many American jurisdictions. See Note, Common Law Crimes in the United States, 47 Colum. L. Rev. 1332 (1947). An example is Commonwealth v. Mochan, 177 Pa. Super. 454, 110 A.2d 788 (1955), in which this doctrine was successfully invoked to punish the maker of obscene telephone calls. The effect of extensive penal code revisions in the United States has been to eliminate common law crimes in the large majority of jurisdictions, but there are those that still retain it. See, e.g., Fla. Stat. §775.01 ("The common law of England in relation to crimes, except so far as the same relates to the modes and degrees of punishment, shall be of full force in this state where there is no existing provision by statute on the subject."); Mich. Comp. Laws, art. 3, §7; Va. Code §1-10; Wash. Rev. Code §9A.04.060. The cognate doctrine that criminalizes a conspiracy to commit acts against the public interest (page 680, infra) has also been rejected in many jurisdictions. At all events, the *Shaw* case represents an extreme instance of the abandonment of the principle of legality. Almost every precept associated with that principle is violated — that judges should not create new crimes, that the criminal law may operate only prospectively, that crimes must be defined with sufficient precision to serve as a guide to lawful conduct and to confine the discretion of police and prosecutors. In the cases that follow we will be concerned with more problematic issues concerning the reach of the principle of legality.

KEELER v. SUPERIOR COURT

Supreme Court of California
2 Cal. 3d 619, 470 P.2d 617 (1970)

[Five months after obtaining an interlocutory decree of divorce, a man intercepted his ex-wife on a mountain road. She was in an advanced state of pregnancy by another man; fetal movements had already been observed by her and by her obstetrician. Her ex-husband said to her, "I hear you're pregnant," glanced at her body and added, "You sure are. I'm going to stomp it out of you." He shoved his knee into her abdomen and struck her. The fetus was delivered stillborn, its head fractured.]

Mosk, J. . . . An information was filed charging petitioner, in count I, with committing the crime of murder (Pen. Code. §187) in that he did "unlawfully kill a human being, to wit Baby Girl Vogt, with malice aforethought." . . His motion to set aside the information for lack of probable cause (Pen. Code, §995) was denied, and he now seeks a writ of prohibition. . . .

Penal Code section 187 provides: "Murder is the unlawful killing of a human being, with malice aforethought." The dispositive question is whether the fetus which petitioner is accused of killing was, on February 23, 1969, a "human being" within the meaning of the statute. If it was not, petitioner cannot be charged with its "murder" and prohibition will lie.

Section 187 was enacted as part of the Penal Code of 1872. Inasmuch as the provision has not been amended since that date, we must determine the intent of the legislature at the time of its enactment. But section 187 was, in turn, taken verbatim from the first California statute defining murder, part of the Crimes and Punishments Act of 1850. . . . We begin, accordingly, by inquiring into the intent of the Legislature in 1850 when it first defined murder as the unlawful and malicious killing of a "human being." . . .

We conclude that in declaring murder to be the unlawful and malicious killing of a "human being" the Legislature of 1850 intended that term to have the settled common law meaning of a person who had been born alive, and did not intend the act of feticide — as distinguished from abortion — to be an offense under the laws of California. . . . We hold that in adopting the definition of murder in Penal Code section 187 the Legislature intended to exclude from its reach the act of killing an unborn fetus.

The People urge, however, that the sciences of obstetrics and pediatrics have greatly progressed since 1872, to the point where with proper medical care a normally developed fetus prematurely born at 28 weeks or more has an excellent chance of survival, i.e., is "viable"; that the common law requirement of live birth to prove the fetus had become a "human being" who may be the victim of murder is no longer in accord with scientific fact, since an unborn but viable fetus is now fully capable of independent life; and that one who unlawfully and maliciously terminates such a life should therefore be liable to prosecution for murder under section 187. We may grant the premises of this argument. . . . But we cannot join in the conclusion sought to be deduced. . . . To such a charge there are two insuperable obstacles, one "jurisdictional" and the other constitutional.

Penal Code section 6 declares in relevant part that "No act or omission" accomplished after the code has taken effect "is criminal or punishable, except as prescribed or authorized by this code, or by some of the statutes which it specifies as continuing in force and as not affected by its provisions, or by some ordinance, municipal, county, or township regulation. . . ." This section embodies a fundamental principle of our tripartite form of government, i.e., that subject to the constitutional prohibition against cruel and unusual punishment, the power to define crimes and fix penalties is vested exclusively in the legislative branch. . . . Stated differently, there are no common law crimes in California. . . .

We recognize that the killing of an unborn but viable fetus may be deemed by some to be an offense of similar nature and gravity; but as Chief Justice Marshall warned long ago, "It would be dangerous, indeed, to carry the principle, that a case which is within the reason or mischief of a statute, is within its provisions, so far as to punish a crime not enumerated in the statute, because it is of equal atrocity, or of kindred character, with those which are enumerated." United States v. Wiltberger (1820) 18 U.S. (5 Wheat.) 76, 96. Whether to thus extend liability for murder in California is a determination solely within the province of the Legislature. . . .

The second obstacle to the proposed judicial enlargement of section 187 is the guarantee of due process of law. Assuming arguendo that we have the power to adopt the new construction of this statute as the law of California, such a ruling, by constitutional command, could operate only prospectively, and thus could not in any event reach the conduct of petitioner on February 23, 1969.

The first essential of due process is fair warning of the act which is made punishable as a crime. "That the terms of a penal statute creating a new offense must be sufficiently explicit to inform those who are subject to it what conduct on their part will render them liable to its penalties, is a well-recognized requirement, consonant alike with ordinary notions of fair play and the settled rules of law." (Connally v. General Constr. Co. (1926) 269 U.S. 385, 391.) . . .

This requirement of fair warning is reflected in the constitutional prohibition against the enactment of ex post facto laws (U.S. Const., art. I, §§9, 10; Cal. Const. art. I, §16). When a new penal statute is applied retrospectively to make punishable an act which was not criminal at the time it was performed, the defendant has been given no advance notice consistent with due process. And precisely the same effect occurs when such an act is made punishable under a preexisting statute but by means of an unforeseeable *judicial* enlargement thereof. (Bouie v. City of Columbia (1964) 378 U.S. 347.)

In *Bouie* two Negroes took seats in the restaurant section of a South Carolina drugstore; no notices were posted restricting the area to whites only. When the defendants refused to leave upon demand, they were arrested and convicted of violating a criminal trespass statute which prohibited entry on the property of another "after notice" forbidding such conduct. Prior South Carolina decisions had emphasized the necessity of proving such notice to support a conviction under the statute. The South Carolina Supreme Court nevertheless affirmed the convictions, construing the statute to prohibit not only the act of entering after notice not to do so but also the wholly different act of remaining on the property after receiving notice to leave.

The United States Supreme Court reversed the convictions, holding that the South Carolina court's ruling was "unforeseeable" and when an "unforeseeable state-court construction of a criminal statute is applied retroactively to subject a person to criminal liability for past conduct, the effect is to deprive him of due process of law in the sense of fair warning that his contemplated conduct constitutes a crime." Analogizing to the prohibition against retrospective penal legislation, the high court reasoned:

> Indeed, an unforeseeable judicial enlargement of a criminal statute, applied retroactively, operates precisely like an ex post facto law, such as Art. I, §10, of the Constitution forbids. An ex post facto law has been defined by this Court as one "that makes an action done before the passing of the law, and which was *innocent* when done, criminal; and punishes such action," or "that *aggravates* a *crime,* or makes it *greater* than it was, when committed." Calder v. Bull, 3 Dall. 386, 390. If a state legislature is barred by the Ex Post Facto Clause from passing such a law, it must follow that a State Supreme Court is barred by the Due Process Clause from achieving precisely the same result by judicial construction. The fundamental principle that "the required criminal law must have existed when the conduct in issue occurred," Hall, General Principles of Criminal Law (2d ed. 1960), at 58-59, must apply to bar retroactive criminal prohibitions emanating from courts as well as from legislatures.

The court remarked in conclusion that "Application of this rule is particularly compelling where, as here, the petitioners' conduct cannot be deemed improper or immoral." In the case at bar the conduct with which petitioner is charged is certainly "improper" and "immoral," and it is not contended he was exercising a constitutionally favored right. But the matter is simply one of degree, and it cannot be denied that the guarantee of due process extends to violent as well as peaceful men. The issue remains, would the judicial enlargement of section 187 now proposed have been foreseeable to this petitioner? . . .

Turning to the case law, we find no reported decision of the California courts which should have given petitioner notice that the killing of an unborn but viable fetus was prohibited by section 187. . . .[a]

BURKE, J. The majority hold that "Baby Girl" Vogt, who, according to medical testimony, had reached the 35th week of development, had a 96 percent chance of survival, and was "definitely" alive and viable at the time of her death, nevertheless was not a "human being" under California's homicide statutes. In my view, in so holding, the majority ignore significant common law precedents, frustrate the express intent of the Legislature, and defy reason, logic and common sense. . . .

The majority opinion suggests that we are confined to common law concepts, and to the common law definition of murder or manslaughter. However, the Legislature, in Penal Code sections 187 and 192, has defined those offenses for us: homicide is the unlawful killing of a "human being." Those words need not be frozen in place as of any particular time, but must be fairly and reasonably interpreted by this court to promote justice and to carry out the evident purposes of the Legislature in adopting a homicide statute. . . .

a. Soon after the *Keeler* decision, the California legislature amended §187 of its Penal Code to include the killing of a "fetus" in the definition of murder. The Statute excepts voluntary abortion.—EDS.

We commonly conceive of human existence as a spectrum stretching from birth to death. However, if this court properly might expand the definition of "human being" at one end of that spectrum, we may do so at the other end. Consider the following example: All would agree that "Shooting or otherwise damaging a corpse is not homicide. . . ." However, it is readily apparent that our concepts of what constitutes a "corpse" have been and are being continually modified by advances in the field of medicine, including new techniques for life revival, restoration and resuscitation such as artificial respiration, open heart massage, transfusions, transplants and a variety of life-restoring stimulants, drugs and new surgical methods. Would this court ignore these developments and exonerate the killer of an apparently "drowned" child merely because that child would have been pronounced dead in 1648 and 1850? Obviously not. Whether a homicide occurred in that case would be determined by medical testimony regarding the capability of the child to have survived prior to the defendant's act. And that is precisely the test which this court should adopt in the instant case. . . .

The majority suggest that to do so would improperly create some new offense. However, the offense of murder is no new offense. Contrary to the majority opinion, the Legislature has not "defined the crime of murder in California to apply only to the unlawful and malicious killing of one who has been born alive." Instead, the Legislature simply used the broad term "human being" and directed the courts to construe that term according to its "fair import" with a view to effect the objects of the homicide statutes and promote justice. (Pen. Code, §4.) What justice will be promoted, what objects effectuated, by construing "human being" as excluding Baby Girl Vogt and her unfortunate successors? Was defendant's brutal act of stomping her to death any less an act of homicide than the murder of a newly born baby? No one doubts that the term "human being" would include the elderly or dying persons whose potential for life has nearly lapsed; their proximity to death is deemed immaterial. There is no sound reason for denying the viable fetus, with its unbounded potential for life, the same status.

The majority also suggest that such an interpretation of our homicide statutes would deny defendant "fair warning" that his act was punishable as a crime. Aside from the absurdity of the underlying premise that defendant consulted Coke, Blackstone or Hale before kicking Baby Girl Vogt to death, it is clear that defendant had adequate notice that his act could constitute homicide. Due process only precludes prosecution under a new statute insufficiently explicit regarding the specific conduct proscribed, or under a preexisting statute "by means of an unforeseeable *judicial* enlargement thereof."

Our homicide statutes have been in effect in this state since 1850. The fact that the California courts have not been called upon to determine the precise question before us does not render "unforeseeable" a decision which determines that a viable fetus is a "human being" under those statutes. Can defendant really claim surprise that a 5-pound, 18-inch, 34-week-old, living, viable child is considered to be a human being? . . .

NOTES

1. *Unexpected Interpretations.* Defendant was the live-in boy friend of a young woman with two small children. Though aware for some time that the four-month-old baby had been violently abused by its mother, he failed to take any steps to protect or seek medical or other help for the child. He was convicted of violating Conn. Gen. Stat. §53a-59(a), which provides: "A person is guilty of assault in the first degree when . . . (3) under circumstances evincing an extreme indifference to human life he recklessly engages in conduct which creates a risk of death to another person, and thereby causes serious physical injury to another person. . . ." A three-judge panel of the Appellate Court of Connecticut reversed, on the ground that the defendant, having no biological or legal relationship to the baby, had no duty and therefore could not be held to have violated the statute. However, a divided Supreme Court reversed (5 to 2), holding, in a case of first impression, that since the defendant had assumed a familial relationship with the mother and children he had a common law duty to protect the baby and to prevent further harm, and that by breaching that duty he could be found guilty of assault in violation of §53a-59(a). State v. Miranda, 245 Conn. 209, 715 A.2d 680 (1998). The case was remitted to the Appellate Court to consider the due process challenge to convicting the defendant of the Supreme Court's controversial interpretation of the statute. State v. Miranda, 56 Conn. App. 298, 742 A.2d 1276 (2000). That court stated, at 56 Conn. App. at 307, 742 A.2d at 1282:

> Using the test enunciated in Bouie v. Columbia, we conclude that no person of ordinary intelligence in the defendant's place would have had fair notice that §53a-59(a)(3) imposed a duty on him to protect the baby from abuse, to secure medical help for her or to report the abuse to the authorities. Three judges of this court and one justice of our Supreme Court agree that under the facts of this case, the defendant had no duty to act and could not be subject to conviction under that statute. Two other justices of the Supreme Court had serious doubts as to whether the new duty could be applied to the defendant without violating his constitutional right to due process. The defendant was, at the time the baby suffered serious, deplorable and life-threatening injuries, a twenty-one year old high school dropout, who had no biological or legal relationship to the baby. If the judges and justices of our Appellate and Supreme Courts cannot agree as to whether the statute put the defendant on notice that he had a duty to protect the baby, we cannot conclude that the defendant would have known that he was commiting assault in the first degree when he failed to protect the baby, to secure medical treatment for her or to report the situation to the authorities. We therefore reverse the trial court's judgment convicting the defendant of assault in the first degree in violation of §53a-59(a)(3).

2. Do these cases stand up? Are the decisions in the *Keeler, Bouie,* and *Miranda* compelled by the principle of legality? Was Keeler, when he "stomped" his pregnant ex-wife, acting under the view that his conduct was not homicidal because the common law did not treat a developed fetus as a "human being"? Were the civil rights protestors in *Bouie* surprised to discover that they were acting in violation of South Carolina law? Did Miranda actually believe that his shocking indifference to the fate of the infant was not a crime, if he thought about it at all? Or are these questions beside the point? See Dan M. Kahan, Some Realism About Retroactive Criminal Lawmaking, 3 Roger Wms. Univ. L. Rev. 95 (1997), for an attack on the standard liberal case against retroactivity in criminal matters. And see also Harold J. Kent, Should *Bouie* Be Buoyed: Judicial Retroactive Lawmaking and the Ex Post Facto Clause, 3 Roger Wms. Univ. L. Rev. 35, 51 (1997), for an analysis of the different concerns raised by legislative as contrasted with judicial retroactivity.

3. Vagueness and Degree. In Nash v. United States, 229 U.S. 373 (1912), the Supreme Court, in an opinion by Justice Holmes, upheld a conviction for unduly obstructing trade in violation of the Sherman Anti-Trust Act. Over the objection that the crime "contains in its definition an element of degree as to which estimates may differ, with the result that a man might find himself in prison because his honest judgment did not anticipate that of a jury of less competent men," Justice Holmes replied:

> [T]he law is full of instances where a man's fate depends on his estimating rightly, that is, as the jury subsequently estimates it, some matter of degree. If his judgment is wrong, not only may he incur a fine or a short imprisonment, as here; he may incur the penalty of death. "An act causing death may be murder, manslaughter, or misadventure, according to the degree of danger attending it" by common experience in the circumstances known to the actor. . . . "The criterion in such cases is to examine whether common social duty would, under the circumstances, have suggested a more circumspect conduct." 1 East, P.C. 262. If a man should kill another by driving an automobile furiously into a crowd, he might be convicted of murder, however little he expected the result. . . . If he did no more than drive negligently through a street, he might get off with manslaughter or less. . . . And in the last case he might be held although he himself thought that he was acting as a prudent man should. . . . We are of opinion that there is no constitutional difficulty in the way of enforcing the criminal part of the act. . . .

In United States v. Ragen, 314 U.S. 513, 523 (1941), the Court sustained a criminal conviction of a defendant for willfully taking a deduction of an unreasonable allowance for salaries on his income tax return, stating: "The mere fact that a penal statute is so framed as to require a jury upon occasion to determine a question of reasonableness is not sufficient to make it too vague to afford a practical guide to permissible conduct." See Ernst Freund, The Use of Indefinite Terms in Statutes, 30 Yale L.J. 437, 443-444 (1921).

Consider the following observations of Lord Simon on legal certainty in Knuller v. Director of Public Prosecutions, [1973] A.C. 435:

> Certainty is a desirable feature of any system of law. But there are some types of conduct desirably the subject matter of legal rule which cannot be satisfactorily regulated by specific statutory enactment, but are better left to the practice of juries and other tribunals of fact. They depend finally for their judicial classification not upon proof of the existence of some particular fact, but upon proof of the attainment of some degree. . . . Whether conduct causing death falls so far short of a proper duty of care as to amount to manslaughter cannot be known until the jury returns its verdict. . . . The driver of a motor vehicle may be accompanied by leading and junior counsel and by his solicitor as well; but he will still not know whether or not he has committed the offence of driving in a manner dangerous to the public or without due care and attention or without reasonable consideration for others or at an excessive speed until jury or justices so find. . . . Similarly with those many offenses which depend on whether admitted conduct was perpetrated dishonestly. Again, did the accused convene an assembly in such a manner as to cause reasonable people to fear a breach of the peace? . . . In none of these cases, which again could be greatly multiplied, can it in advance be said with certainty whether

an offence has been committed: and those who choose, in such situations, to sail as close as possible to the wind inevitably run some risk.

See generally John Jeffries, Legality, Vaugeness and the Construction of Penal Statutes, 71 Va. L. Rev. 189 (1985).

CITY OF CHICAGO v. MORALES

Supreme Court of the United States, 1999
527 U.S. 41

JUSTICE STEVENS announced the judgment of the Court. . . .

In 1992, the Chicago City Council enacted the Gang Congregation Ordinance, which prohibits "criminal street gang members" from "loitering" with one another or with other persons in any public place. The question presented is whether the Supreme Court of Illinois correctly held that the ordinance violates the Due Process Clause of the Fourteenth Amendment to the Federal Constitution. . .

The [city] council found that a continuing increase in criminal street gang activity was largely responsible for the city's rising murder rate, as well as an escalation of violent and drug related crimes. . . . Furthermore, the council stated that gang members "establish control over identifiable areas . . . by loitering in those areas and intimidating others from entering those areas; and . . . members of criminal street gangs avoid arrest by committing no offense punishable under existing laws when they know the police are present. . . ."

The ordinance creates a criminal offense punishable by a fine of up to $500, imprisonment for not more than six months, and a requirement to perform up to 120 hours of community service. Commission of the offense involves four predicates. First, the police officer must reasonably believe that at least one of the two or more persons present in a "public place" is a "criminal street gang member." Second, the persons must be "loitering," which the ordinance defines as "remaining in any one place with no apparent purpose." Third, the officer must then order "all" of the persons to disperse and remove themselves "from the area." Fourth, a person must disobey the officer's order. If any person, whether a gang member or not, disobeys the officer's order, that person is guilty of violating the ordinance.[1] . . .

1. (a) Whenever a police officer observes a person whom he reasonably believes to be a criminal street gang member loitering in any public place with one or more other persons, he shall order all such persons to disperse and remove themselves from the area. Any person who does not promptly obey such an order is in violation of this section.

(b) It shall be an affirmative defense to an alleged violation of this section that no person who was observed loitering was in fact a member of a criminal street gang.

(c) As used in this section:

(1) "Loiter" means to remain in any one place with no apparent purpose.

(2) "Criminal street gang" means any ongoing organization, association in fact or group of three or more persons, whether formal or informal, having as one of its substantial activities the commission of one or more of the criminal acts enumerated in paragraph (3), and whose members individually or collectively engage in or have engaged in a pattern of criminal gang activity. . . .

(5) "Public place" means the public way and any other location open to the public, whether publicly or privately owned.

(e) Any person who violates this Section is subject to a fine of not less than $100 and not more than $500 for each offense, or imprisonment for not more than six months, or both.

The Illinois Supreme Court . . . held "that the gang loitering ordinance violates due process of law in that it is impermissibly vague on its face and an arbitrary restriction on personal liberties." . . . We granted certiorari, and now affirm. Like the Illinois Supreme Court, we conclude that the ordinance enacted by the city of Chicago is unconstitutionally vague.

The basic factual predicate for the city's ordinance is not in dispute. As the city argues in its brief, "the very presence of a large collection of obviously brazen, insistent, and lawless gang members and hangers-on on the public ways intimidates residents, who become afraid even to leave their homes and go about their business. That, in turn, imperils community residents' sense of safety and security, detracts from property values, and can ultimately destabilize entire neighborhoods." The findings in the ordinance explain that it was motivated by these concerns. We have no doubt that a law that directly prohibited such intimidating conduct would be constitutional, but this ordinance broadly covers a significant amount of additional activity. Uncertainty about the scope of that additional coverage provides the basis for respondents' claim that the ordinance is too vague. . . .

Vagueness may invalidate a criminal law for either of two independent reasons. First, it may fail to provide the kind of notice that will enable ordinary people to understand what conduct it prohibits; second, it may authorize and even encourage arbitrary and discriminatory enforcement. See Kolender v. Lawson, 461 U.S. at 357. Accordingly, we first consider whether the ordinance provides fair notice to the citizen and then discuss its potential for arbitrary enforcement.

"It is established that a law fails to meet the requirements of the Due Process Clause if it is so vague and standardless that it leaves the publich uncertain as to the conduct it prohibits. . . ." Giaccio v. Pennsylvania, 382 U.S. 399, 402-403 (1966). The Illinois Supreme Court recognized that the term "loiter" may have a common and accepted meaning, but the definition of that term in this ordinance — "to remain in any one place with no apparent purpose" — does not. It is difficult to imagine how any citizen of the city of Chicago standing in a public place with a group of people would know if he or she had an "apparent purpose." If she were talking to another person, would she have an apparent purpose? If she were frequently checking her watch and looking expectantly down the street, would she have an apparent purpose?

Since the city cannot conceivably have meant to criminalize each instance a citizen stands in public with a gang member, the vagueness that dooms this ordinance is not the product of uncertainty about the normal meaning of "loitering," but rather about what loitering is covered by the ordinance and what is not. . . .[24] Its decision followed the precedent set by a number of state courts that have upheld ordinances that criminalize loitering combined with some other overt act or evidence of criminal intent. However, state courts have uniformly invalidated laws that do not join the term "loitering" with a second specific element of the crime.

The city's principal response to this concern about adequate notice is that loi-

24. One of the trial courts that invalidated the ordinance gave the following illustration: "suppose a group of gang members were playing basketball in the park, while waiting for a drug delivery. Their apparent purpose is that they are in the park to play ball. The actual purpose is that they are waiting for drugs. Under this definition of loitering, a group of people innocently sitting in a park discussing their futures would be arrested, while the 'basketball players' awaiting a drug delivery would be left alone."

terers are not subject to sanction until after they have failed to comply with an officer's order to disperse. . . . We find this response unpersuasive for at least two reasons.

First, the purpose of the fair notice requirement is to enable the ordinary citizen to conform his or her conduct to the law. "No one may be required at peril of life, liberty or property to speculate as to the meaning of penal statutes." Lanzetta v. New Jersey, 306 U.S. 451, 453 (1939). Although it is true that a loiterer is not subject to criminal sanctions unless he or she disobeys a dispersal order, the loitering is the conduct that the ordinance is designed to prohibit. If the loitering is in fact harmless and innocent, the dispersal order itself is an unjustified impairment of liberty. If the police are able to decide arbitrarily which members of the public they will order to disperse, then the Chicago ordinance becomes indistinguishable from the law we held invalid in Shuttlesworth v. Birmingham, 382 U.S. 87, 90 (1965).[29] Because an officer may issue an order only after prohibited conduct has already occurred, [the order] cannot provide the kind of advance notice that will protect the putative loiterer from being ordered to disperse. Such an order cannot retroactively give adequate warning of the boundary between the permissible and the impermissible applications of the law.

Second, the terms of the dispersal order compound the inadequacy of the notice afforded by the ordinance. It provides that the officer "shall order all such persons to disperse and remove themselves from the area." This vague phrasing raises a host of questions. After such an order issues, how long must the loiterers remain apart? How far must they move? If each loiterer walks around the block and they meet again at the same location, are they subject to arrest or merely to being ordered to disperse again? . . .

Lack of clarity in the description of the loiterer's duty to obey a dispersal order might not render the ordinance unconstitutionally vague if the definition of the forbidden conduct were clear, but it does buttress our conclusion that the entire ordinance fails to give the ordinary citizen adequate notice of what is forbidden and what is permitted. The Constitution does not permit a legislature to "set a net large enough to catch all possible offenders, and leave it to the courts to step inside and say who could be rightfully detained, and who should be set at large." United States v. Reese, 92 U.S. 214, 221 (1876). This ordinance is therefore vague "not in the sense that it requires a person to conform his conduct to an imprecise but comprehensible normative standard, but rather in the sense that no standard of conduct is specified at all." Coates v. Cincinnati, 402 U.S. 611, 614 (1971).

The broad sweep of the ordinance also violates "'the requirement that a legislature establish minimal guidelines to govern law enforcement.'" Kolender v. Lawson, 461 U.S. at 358. There are no such guidelines in the ordinance. In any public place in the city of Chicago, persons who stand or sit in the company of a gang member may be ordered to disperse unless their purpose is apparent. The mandatory language in the enactment directs the police to issue an order without first making any inquiry about their possible purposes. It matters not whether the reason that a gang member and his father, for example, might loiter

29. "Literally read . . . this ordinance says that a person may stand on a public sidewalk in Birmingham only at the whim of any police officer of the city. The constitutional vice of so broad a provision needs no demonstration." 382 U.S. 87 at 90.

near Wrigley Field is to rob an unsuspecting fan or just to get a glimpse of Sammy Sosa leaving the ballpark; in either event, if their purpose is not apparent to a nearby police officer, she may — indeed, she "shall" — order them to disperse.

Recognizing that the ordinance does reach a substantial amount of innocent conduct, we turn, then, to its language to determine if it "necesssarily entrusts lawmaking to the moment-to-moment judgment of the policeman on his beat." Kolender v. Lawson, 461 U.S. at 359. . . . The principal source of the vast discretion conferred on the police in this case is the definition of loitering as "to remain in any one place with no apparent purpose."

As the Illinois Supreme Court interprets that definition, it "provides absolute discretion to police officers to determine what activities constitute loitering." We have no authority to construe the language of a state statute more narrowly than the construction given by that State's highest court. . . .

Nevertheless, the city disputes the Illinois Supreme Court's interpretation, arguing that the text of the ordinance limits the officer's discretion in three ways. First, it does not permit the officer to issue a dispersal order to anyone who is moving along or who has an apparent purpose. Second, it does not permit an arrest if individuals obey a dispersal order. Third, no order can issue unless the officer reasonably believes that one of the loiterers is a member of a criminal street gang.

Even putting to one side our duty to defer to a state court's construction of the scope of a local enactment, we find each of these limitations insufficient. That the ordinance does not apply to people who are moving — that is, to activity that would not constitute loitering under any possible definition of the term — does not even address the question of how much discretion the police enjoy in deciding which stationary persons to disperse under the ordinance. Similarly, that the ordinance does not permit an arrest until after a dispersal order had been disobeyed does not provide any guidance to the officer deciding whether such an order should issue. The "no apparent purpose" standard for making that decision is inherently subjective because its application depends on whether some purpose is "apparent" to the officer on the scene.

Presumably an officer would have discretion to treat some purposes — perhaps a purpose to engage in idle conversation or simply to enjoy a cool breeze on a warm evening — as too frivolous to be apparent if he suspected a different ulterior motive. Moreover, an officer conscious of the city council's reasons for enacting the ordinance might well ignore its text and issue a dispersal order, even though an illicit purpose is actually apparent.

It is true, as the city argues, that the requirement that the officer reasonably believe that a group of loiterers contains a gang member does place a limit on the authority to order dispersal. That limitation would no doubt be sufficient if the ordinance only applied to loitering that had an apparently harmful purpose or effect, or possibly if it only applied to loitering by persons reasonably believed to be criminal gang members. But this ordinance . . . requires no harmful purpose and applies to non-gang members as well as suspected gang members. It applies to everyone in the city who may remain in one place with one suspected gang member as long as their purpose is not apparent to an officer observing them. Friends, relatives, teachers, counselors, or even total strangers might unwittingly engage in forbidden loitering if they happen to engage in idle conversation with a gang member.

Ironically, the definition of loitering in the Chicago ordinance not only extends its scope to encompass harmless conduct, but also has the perverse consequence of excluding from its coverage much of the intimidating conduct that motivated its enactment. As the city council's findings demonstrate, the most harmful gang loitering is motivated either by an apparent purpose to publicize the gang's dominance of certain territory, thereby intimidating nonmembers, or by an equally apparent purpose to conceal ongoing commerce in illegal drugs. As the Illinois Supreme Court has not placed any limiting construction on the language in the ordinance, we must assume that the ordinance means what it says and that it has no application to loiterers whose purpose is apparent. The relative importance of its application to harmless loitering is magnified by its inapplicability to loitering that has an obviously threatening or illicit purpose. . . .

In our judgment, the Illinois Supreme Court correctly concluded that the ordinance does not provide sufficiently specific limits on the enforcement discretion of the police. . . . We recognize the serious and difficult problems . . . that led to the enactment of this ordinance. "We are mindful that the preservation of liberty depends in part on the maintenance of social order." Houston v. Hill, 482 U.S. 451, 471-472 (1987). However, in this instance the city has enacted an ordinance that affords too much discretion to the police and too little notice to citizens who wish to use the public streets.

Accordingly, the judgment of the Supreme Court of Illinois is affirmed.

JUSTICE O'CONNOR, with whom JUSTICE BREYER joins, concurring. . . .

It is important to courts and legislatures alike that we characterize more clearly the narrow scope of today's holding. As the ordinance comes to this Court, it is unconstitutionally vague. Nevertheless, there remain open to Chicago reasonable alternatives to combat the very real threat posed by gang intimidation and violence. For example, the Court properly and expressly distinguishes the ordinance from laws the require loiterers to have a "harmful purpose," from laws that target only gang members, and from laws that incorporate limits on the area and manner in which the laws may be enforced. In addition, the ordinance here is unlike a law that "directly prohibits" the "presence of a large collection of obviously brazen, insistent, and lawless gang members and hangers-on on the public ways," . . .

In my view, the gang loitering ordinance could have been construed more narrowly. The term "loiter" might possibly be construed in a more limited fashion to mean "to remain in any one place with no apparent purpose other than to establish control over identifiable areas, to intimidate others from entering those areas, or to conceal illegal activities." Such a definition would be consistent with the Chicago City Council's findings and would avoid the vagueness problems of the ordinance as construed by the Illinois Supreme Court. As noted above, so would limitations that restricted the ordinance's criminal penalties to gang members or that more carefully delineated the circumstances in which those penalties would apply to nongang members.

JUSTICE THOMAS, with whom THE CHIEF JUSTICE and JUSTICE SCALIA join, dissenting. . . .

The Court concludes that the ordinance is . . . unconstitutionally vague because it fails to provide adequate standards to guide police discretion and because, in the plurality's view, it does not give residents adequate notice of how to conform their conduct to the confines of the law. I disagree on both counts.

At the outset, it is important to note that the ordinance does not criminalize loitering per se. Rather, it penalizes loiterer's failure to obey a police officer's order to move along. A majority of the Court believes that this scheme vests too much discretion in police officers. Nothing could be further from the truth. Far from according officers too much discretion, the ordinance merely enables police officers to fulfill one of their traditional functions. Police officers are not, and have never been, simply enforcers of the criminal law. They wear other hats — importantly, they have long been vested with the responsibility for preserving the public peace. . . . In their role as peace officers, the police long have had the authority and the duty to order groups of individuals who threaten the public peace to disperse. . . .

In order to perform their peace-keeping responsibilities satisfactorily, the police inevitably must exercise discretion. Indeed, by empowering them to act as peace officers, the law assumes that the police will exercise that discretion responsibly and with sound judgment. That is not to say that the law should not provide objective guidelines for the police, but simply that it cannot rigidly constrain their every action. By directing a police officer not to issue a dispersal order unless he "observes a person whom he reasonably believes to be a criminal street gang member loitering in any public place," Chicago's ordinance strikes an appropriate balance between those two extremes. Just as we trust officers to rely on their experience and expertise in order to make spur-of-the-moment determinations about amorphous legal standards such as "probable cause" and "reasonable suspicion," so we must trust them to determine whether a group of loiterers contains individuals (in this case members of criminal street gangs) whom the city has determined threaten the public peace. . . . In sum, the Court's conclusion that the ordinance is impermissibly vague because it "'necessarily entrusts lawmaking to the moment-to-moment judgment of the policeman on his beat,'" cannot be reconciled with common sense, longstanding police practice, or this Court's Fourth Amendment jurisprudence. . . .

I do not suggest that a police officer enforcing the Gang Congregation Ordinance will never make a mistake. Nor do I overlook the possibility that a police officer, acting in bad faith, might enforce the ordinance in an arbitrary or discriminatory way. But . . . instances of arbitrary or discriminatory enforcement of the ordinance, like any other law, are best addressed when (and if) they arise, . . .

The plurality's conclusion that the ordinance "fails to give the ordinary citizen adequate notice of what is forbidden and what is permitted," is similarly untenable. There is nothing "vague" about an order to disperse.[9] [I]t is safe to assume that the vast majority of people who are ordered by the police to "disperse and remove themselves from the area" will have little difficulty understanding how to comply.

[R]espondents in this facial challenge bear the weighty burden of establishing that the statute is vague in all its applications, "in the sense that no standard of conduct is specified at all." Coates v. Cincinnati, 402 U.S. 611, 614 (1971). I subscribe to the view of retired Justice White — "If any fool would know that a particular category of conduct would be within the reach of the statute, if there

9. . . . The logical implication of the plurality's assertion is that the police can never issue dispersal orders. For example, in the plurality's view, it is apparently unconstitutional for a police officer to ask a group of gawkers to move along in order to secure a crime scene.

is an unmistakable core that a reasonable person would know is forbidden by the law, the enactment is not unconstitutional on its face." Kolender, 461 U.S. at 370-371 (dissenting opinion). This is certainly such a case.

[T]he ordinance does not proscribe constitutionally protected conduct—there is no fundamental right to loiter. It is also anomalous to characterize loitering as "innocent" conduct when it has been disfavored throughout American history. [T]here is no risk of a trap for the unwary. The term "loiter" is no different from terms such as "fraud," "bribery," and "perjury." We expect people of ordinary intelligence to grasp the meaning of such legal terms despite the fact that they are arguably imprecise. . . .

The plurality also concludes that the definition of the term loiter — "to remain in any one place with no apparent purpose," — fails to provide adequate notice. "It is difficult to imagine," the plurality posits, "how any citizen of the city of Chicago standing in a public place . . . would know if he or she had an 'apparent purpose.'" The plurality underestimates the intellectual capacity of the citizens of Chicago. Persons of ordinary intelligence are perfectly capable of evaluating how outsiders perceive their conduct, and here "it is self-evident that there is a whole range of conduct that anyone with at least a semblance of common sense would know is [loitering] and that would be covered by the statute." See Smith v. Goguen, 415 U.S. 566, 584 (1974) (White, J., concurring in judgment). Members of a group standing on the corner staring blankly into space, for example, are likely well aware that passersby would conclude that they have "no apparent purpose." In any event, because this is a facial challenge, the plurality's ability to hypothesize that some individuals, in some circumstances, may be unable to ascertain how their actions appear to outsiders is irrelevant to our analysis. Here, we are asked to determine whether the ordinance is "vague in all of its applications." *Hoffman Estates,* 455 U.S. at 497. The answer is unquestionably no.

Today, the Court focuses extensively on the "rights" of gang members and their companions. It can safely do so — the people who will have to live with the consequences of today's opinion do not live in our neighborhoods. Rather, the people who will suffer from our lofty pronouncements are people like Ms. Susan Mary Jackson; people who have seen their neighborhoods literally destroyed by gangs and violence and drugs. They are good, decent people who must struggle to overcome their desperate situation, against all odds, in order to raise their families, earn a living, and remain good citizens. As one resident described, "There is only about maybe one or two percent of the people in the city causing these problems maybe, but it's keeping 98 percent of us in our houses and off the streets and afraid to shop." By focusing exclusively on the imagined "rights" of the two percent, the Court today has denied our most vulnerable citizens the very thing that JUSTICE STEVENS, elevates above all else — the "freedom of movement." And that is a shame. I respectfully dissent.

STEVE CHAPMAN, COURT UPHOLDS AMERICA'S RIGHT TO HANG OUT, Chicago Tribune, June 13, 1999, p. 19: The Chicago City Council is famous for many things, but legal scholarship has never been its strength. When it passed an anti-gang loitering ordinance seven years ago, aldermen were confident that no such expertise was needed. Told that the law might run afoul of the Constitution, one supporter snorted, "I don't believe when the Founding Fathers were drafting the Constitution that the Latin Kings were sitting in Philadelphia."

Last week, the Supreme Court convened in Washington, where street gangs are also common, and said that the presence of the Latin Kings or the Bloods or the Crips didn't warrant a suspension of the principles established in the Bill of Rights.

It would be interesting to transport James Madison to a street corner on Chicago's Southwest Side to engage a Latin King in a discussion of where a free society should draw the line between protecting liberties and upholding public safety. Under the city ordinance, though, Madison could have found himself ordered by a police officer to terminate the conversation and leave the vicinity, or else see how he liked talking law with fellow inmates of the Cook County Jail.

Madison was never affected by the ordinance, but plenty of Chicagoans were. In the three years the law was in force, before being invalidated by the courts, police [dispersed] some 89,000 [people at] public gatherings and arrested 42,000 people who didn't move fast enough or far enough to suit the cops. Not all were gang members, since the ordinance gives police the authority to disperse a group of 10, 20 or 100 if a single person present is even suspected of belonging to a gang. [T]hough most police are decent and well-intentioned, many are not, and giving them dictatorial powers over the streets inevitably means that many law-abiding people taking part in innocent activities will be coerced, inconvenienced or even hauled off to jail.

Justice Clarence Thomas, in a dissent, excoriated the six justices who voted to overturn the ordinance. "The people who will have to live with the consequences of today's opinion do not live in our neighborhoods," he snarled. True — and Clarence Thomas, ensconced in well-to-do Fairfax County, Va., will never be ordered to leave his front sidewalk for chatting with someone who, unknown to him, is a gang member.

Thomas failed to mention that the long-suffering people who do have to live with the consequences didn't all see the law as their friend. The ordinance had the support of most white aldermen, but only six of the council's 18 black members voted for it. They knew that some white cops enforcing the law would create a new crime of "standing around while black" to go with the old one of "driving while black." . . .

Part of life in a non-totalitarian country is the freedom of people to congregate in public for idle purposes without having to ask permission from the government. The City of Chicago can attack its gang problem without trampling that right.

NOTES

1. Papachristou v. City of Jacksonville, 405 U.S. 156 (1972), has long been regarded as the leading case on the constitutionality of vagrancy-type laws. The issue in that case was the constitutionality of the following ordinance:

> Rogues and vagabonds, or dissolute persons who go about begging, common gamblers, persons who use juggling or unlawful games or plays, common drunkards, common night thieves, pilferers or pickpockets, traders in stolen property, lewd, wanton and lascivious persons, keepers of gambling places, common railers and brawlers, persons wandering or strolling around from place to place without any

lawful purpose or object, habitual loafers, disorderly persons, persons neglecting all lawful business and habitually spending their time by frequenting houses of ill fame, gaming houses, or places where alcoholic beverages are sold or served, persons able to work but habitually living upon the earnings of their wives or minor children shall be deemed vagrants and, upon conviction in the Municipal Court shall be punished as provided for Class D offenses [punishable by 90 days' imprisonment, $500 fine, or both].

In an opinion by Justice Douglas the Court held the ordinance unconstitutional, stating:

> This ordinance is void-for-vagueness, both in the case that it "fails to give a person of ordinary intelligence fair notice that his contemplated conduct is forbidden by the statute," and because it encourages arbitrary and erratic arrests and conviction. . . . The poor among us, the minorities, the average householder are not in business and not alerted to the regulatory schemes of vagrancy laws; and we assume they would have no understanding of their meaning and impact if they read them. [The ordinance] makes criminal activities which by modern standards are normally innocent. "Nightwalking" is one. . . . Another aspect of the ordinance's vagueness [is] the effect of the unfettered discretion it places in the hands of the Jacksonville police. . . . Those generally implicated by the imprecise terms of the ordinance — poor people, nonconformists, dissenters, idlers — may be required to comport themselves according to the life-style deemed appropriate by the Jacksonville police and the courts. Where, as here, there are no standards governing the exercise of the discretion granted by the ordinance, the scheme permits and encourages an arbitrary and discriminatory enforcement of the law. . . . The implicit presumption in these generalized vagrancy standards — that crime is being nipped in the bud — is too extravagant to deserve extended treatment. Of course, vagrancy statutes are useful to the police. Of course they are nets making easy the round-up of so-called undesirables. But the rule of law implies equality and justice in its application."

Query: None of the opinions in *Morales* made any use of *Papachristou* one way or the other. Why not? Is it distinguishable from *Morales*? For an exploration of the issues raised by *Papachristou* and *Morales,* see Dorothy E. Roberts, Race, Vagueness, and the Social Meaning of Order-Maintenance Policing, 89 J. Crim. L. & Cr. 775 (1999).

2. The Chicago response. In February 2000, the Chicago City Council passed a new anti-gang ordinance to replace the one struck down in *Morales.* The new ordinance (Chi. Municipal Code §8-4-015) again directs police officers to disperse all persons engaged in "gang loitering" in a public place,[6] whenever they believe that one or more of those present are members of a criminal street gang. This time, the ordinance specifies that dispersal, in compliance with the order, means "remov[ing] themselves from within sight and hearing of the place at which the order was issued," and it defines gang loitering as

> remaining in any one place under circumstances that would warrant a reasonable person to believe that the purpose or effect of that behavior is to enable a criminal

6. The ordinance requires the Police Superintendent to designate particular areas within the city in which the ordinance will be enforced, and dispersal orders can be issued only when gang loitering occurs within such areas, but the location of the designated areas is not revealed to the public.

> street gang to establish control over identifiable areas, to intimidate others from entering those areas, or to conceal illegal activities.

Questions: Does the new ordinance meet the objections of Justices Stevens and O'Connor? Does it meet those of the *Papachristou* Court? Suppose that four teenagers hang out on a street corner on a hot night, talking loudly and playing their "boombox." An elderly resident of the neighborhood calls the police and asks them to disperse the group, stating that they are treating the corner as their private turf and that she feels intimidated from walking by in order to get to the corner store. If police reasonably believe that one of the youth is a gang member, are the teenagers subject to being dispersed under the ordinance? Should they be?

3. Other anti-gang and anti-loitering legislation. An Athens, Georgia, ordinance prohibits loitering, defined as being "in a place at a time or in a manner not usual for law-abiding individuals . . . under circumstances which cause a justifiable and reasonable alarm or immediate concern that such person is involved in unlawful drug activity." Relying on *Morales,* the Georgia Supreme Court held this ordinance unconstitutionally vague. The court explained that "[t]here are no overt acts necessary to trigger criminal liability under the statute, and no specific guidelines to inform law enforcement officers of what behavior might legitimately bring the officer to believe a person was 'involved in unlawful drug activity.'" Johnson v. Athens-Clarke County, 529 S.E.2d 613 (Ga. 2000).

The California Street Terrorism Enforcement and Prevention Act (STEP) declares that "any person who actively participates in any criminal street gang with knowledge that its members engage in or have engaged in a pattern of criminal gang activity, and who willfully promotes, furthers, or assists in any felonious criminal conduct by members of that gang" shall be guilty of a criminal offense. Calif. Pen. Code §186.22. Prior to *Morales* several state courts upheld this or similar legislation, stressing the requirement of specific intent and the exclusion of constitutionally protected activity. See, e.g., In re Alberto R., 235 Cal. App. 3d 1309, 1 Cal. Rptr. 2d 348 (1991); Jackson v. State, 634 N.E.2d 532 (Ind. 1994). Do these statutes survive *Morales*?

4. Consider Alfred Hill, Vagueness and Police Discretion: The Supreme Court in a Box, 51 Rutgers L. Rev. 1289 (1999). He writes at 1290:

> In the past it was assumed that a statute giving adequate notice to the offender gave adequate guidance to the police. If the police were arbitrary anyway, they could not justify their misconduct under the statute. If the statute itself must now contain additional guidelines to forestall such misconduct, what should such guidelines be? . . .
>
> Moreover, *Morales* reinforces certain earlier decisions that cast doubt on the validity of statutes vesting the police with discretion that is deemed excessive. . . . In this context, how much is too much? The exercise of discretion is indispensable to effective police work, especially in the case of minor offenses. Largely on the ground of excess police discretion, courts have already shown themselves inhospitable to unfamiliar types of statutes developed to meet the special needs of community policing. *Morales* bodes ill in this regard.

Professor Hill concludes, at 1318:

> The overruling of *Morales* would be a boon, especially in removing a cloud over the current practice known as community policing. The notion that police discre-

tion may be excessive, unaccompanied by objective standards for making that determination, is a dangerous one to bequeath to the inferior courts.

Questions: Consider a statute like the one described in footnote 29 of Justice Stevens' *Morales* opinion — one providing that a person may not stand on the sidewalk against orders of the police and that it is therefore an offense to remain on the sidewalk after being ordered to move on. Such a statute presumably gives the citizen clear notice of what he must do to avoid committing an offense. Would such a statute therefore be constitutional under Professor Hill's approach? Does clear notice to the offender obviate the need for constraints on the conditions in which an officer can issue such notice? Consider Cox v. Louisiana, 379 U.S. 536, 579 (1965) (opinion of Black, J.), noting that the Constitution requires "government by clearly defined laws, [rather than] government by the moment-to-moment opinions of a policeman on his beat."

For a thorough analysis largely endorsing Professor Hill's view that effective order-maintenance requires courts to accept a greater degree of police discretion, see Debra Livingston, Police Discretion and the Quality of Life in Public Places, 97 Colum. L. Rev. 551 (1997). For a more skeptical view, see Roberts, Note 1 supra; Bernard E. Harcourt, Reflecting on the Subject: A Critique of the Social Influence Conception of Deterrence, the Broken Windows Theory, and Order-Maintenance Policing New York Style, 97 Mich. L. Rev. 291 (1998).

MODEL PENAL CODE

Section 250.6. Loitering or Prowling

[See Appendix for text of this section.]

MODEL PENAL CODE AND COMMENTARIES, COMMENT TO §250.6 AT 388-389 (1980): This provision differs from prior legislation in that it is narrowly designed to reach only alarming loitering. Typical situations covered would be the following: a known professional pickpocket is seen loitering in a crowded railroad station; a person not recognized as a local resident is seen lurking in a doorway and furtively looking up and down the street to see if he is being watched; an unknown man is seen standing for some time in a dark alley where he has no apparent business. . . . None of these situations would be covered by the law of attempt, even under the expanded definition of that offense in Section 5.01 of the Model Code. In no case has there been a "substantial step in a course of conduct planned to culminate in [the] commission of the crime." Also, none of these situations involves possession of burglar's tools or other instruments of crime that would sustain a conviction under Section 5.06.

The major issue of policy is what response to make to such situations. At least five courses are open:

(i) Loitering or wandering "at unusual hours" or "without lawful business" may be punished as a completed offense. This is the approach characteristic of prior law.
(ii) The situation giving rise to alarm for persons or property may be treated as an occasion for police inquiry. Failure to explain oneself satisfactorily would constitute an offense.

(iii) The situation giving rise to alarm may be deemed a proper basis for detention and interrogation but not for criminal prosecution.
(iv) The situation might be dealt with only as a basis for police orders to "move on" and thus to remove the immediate alarm.
(v) Finally, the kind of situation described above might be viewed as giving rise to no legal consequence. An officer, of course, could make inquiry of suspicious persons, most of whom would answer voluntarily. Where the responses do not dissipate suspicion, the officer could make such observations as would facilitate later identification of the suspect if a crime did take place.

None of these alternatives is entirely satisfactory. The first authorizes criminal conviction without proof of anti-social behavior or inclination. Additionally, . . . it is difficult to imagine a statute of this sort that could pass constitutional muster under current standards. The second option is no doubt better, but it still imposes liability for failure to identify oneself or to give a credible account of one's behavior without further proof of anti-social purpose. . . . Finally, this kind of statute is also not free from constitutional doubt. The third approach involves a controversial and possibly unconstitutional change in the law of arrest rather than the definition of a substantive offense within the scope of the Model Code. The fourth solution, the police order to "move on," hardly solves the problem of the individual who is bent on crime and at the same time confers a disturbingly unbounded discretion on the police. The last option—authorizing no police action other than voluntary questioning and visual observation — is perhaps most consistent with the ideal of the role of police and with general normative principles governing the proper use of penal sanctions. Nonetheless, this total abandonment of the traditional vagrancy concept would lead to a significant loss in effective law enforcement and would encounter justifiably serious political resistance.

Section 250.6 of the Model seeks to provide the least objectionable form of the second alternative discussed above. . . .

As a matter of constitutional policy, abrogation of loitering statutes is arguably sound. There is irreducible indeterminacy in the definition of loitering, as there is necessarily discretion in the police to decide in the first instance what the "public safety demands" or whether the circumstances "justify suspicion" or "warrant alarm." . . . If even the Model Code provision is unconstitutionally vague, . . . then it seems likely that no general provision against loitering can be drafted to survive constitutional review. Of course, narrower proscriptions of loitering with specific purpose — e.g., to solicit deviate sexual relations — may continue to be valid, but there would be no provision to deal with the person who is obviously up to no good but whose precise intention cannot be ascertained. Most courts are willing to consider in a void-for-vagueness analysis the need for some provision and the impossibility of achieving greater precision. This factor cuts strongly in favor of the constitutionality of the Model Code provision.

NOTE

Courts have divided on whether the Model Penal Code formulation of the crime of loitering meets the constitutional requirements of *Papachristou* and now *Morales.* An Oregon court held a similar ordinance void for vagueness in City of Portland v. White, 9 Or. App. 239, 495 P.2d 778 (1972). See also Johnson v. Athens-Clarke County, 529 S.E.2d 613 (Ga. 2000). However, substantially similar statutes were upheld in State v. Ecker, 311 So. 2d 104 (Fla. 1975).

In Kolender v. Lawson, 461 U.S. 352 (1983), the Supreme Court held void for vagueness a California statute that required persons who loiter or wander on the streets to provide a "credible and reliable" identification and to account for their presence, when requested to do so by a police officer under circumstances that "indicate to a reasonable man that the public safety demands such identification." Speaking for the Court, Justice O'Connor wrote that the statute, as construed by the California courts, provided no standard for determining what a suspect must do to satisfy its requirements and therefore vested virtually complete discretion in the hands of the police.

Several courts have considered the effect of *Kolender* on loitering statutes closely patterned on the Model Penal Code formulation. In both Watts v. State, 463 So. 2d 205 (Fla. 1985), and Porta v. Mayor, City of Omaha, 593 F. Supp. 863 (D. Neb. 1984), courts distinguished the California provision involved in *Kolender* and upheld statutes comparable to Model Penal Code §250.6. In both cases, the loitering provisions at issue gave a suspected person the "opportunity" to justify his or her presence but did not require the person to do so and did not make the refusal to answer in itself an element of the offense; rather the refusal to identify was only one of several circumstances that the officer may consider in determining whether the circumstances warrant concern for the public safety. *Question:* Does this reasoning suggest that the Code provision is narrower than the statute involved in *Kolender,* or does the Code provision in effect vest the police officer with even broader discretion?

CHAPTER 4

RAPE

Few areas of criminal law have attracted as much attention and controversy over the past two decades as the law of rape. Widespread criticism that rape law was unfair to women led to extensive changes in the definition of rape, in the rules of evidence and procedure affecting rape trials, and in the processing of rape complaints.

Is rape law now in accord with prevailing attitudes about the expression of consent in sexual contacts? What are those attitudes (and are they the same for women as for men)? Are the currently prevailing attitudes unfair to women, and if so, should the criminal law move beyond them?

Issues analogous to these rarely present any difficulty in connection with crimes like homicide, burglary, robbery, and theft. But in connection with rape, these questions are both difficult to answer and acutely controversial. An understanding of the legal issues therefore requires attention to the nature of the targeted behavior, the kinds of harm it causes, and the social dynamics underlying it. We therefore begin by considering several contrasting perspectives on the social and behavioral aspects of rape. We then examine the relevant legal doctrines relevant to actus reus, mens rea, and problems of proof.

A. PERSPECTIVES

MARGARET T. GORDON & STEPHANIE RIGER, THE FEMALE FEAR: THE SOCIAL COST OF RAPE

2, 26-28, 32-36 (1991)

Most women experience fear of rape as a nagging, gnawing sense that something awful could happen, an angst that keeps them from doing things they want or need to do, or from doing them at the time or in the way they might otherwise do. Women's fear of rape is a sense that one must always be on guard, vigilant and alert, a feeling that causes a woman to tighten with anxiety if someone is walking too closely behind her, especially at night. . . . It is worse than fear of other crimes because women know they are held responsible for avoiding rape, and should they be victimized, they know they are likely to be blamed. . . .

[I]n 1986 there were 90,434 forcible rapes reported by police across the country to the FBI, representing an increase of 3.2 percent over 1985 and a rate of 73 per 100,000 women. . . .

Analyses of how UCR [Uniform Crime Reports] data are gathered and compiled [by the FBI] have indicated errors of omission and commission, most of which lead to the underrepresentation of the actual rate of rape. . . . Some police departments regularly conclude that as many as 50 percent of the charges of forcible rape received are not classifiable as offenses . . .

These findings and others gave rise to the National Crime Surveys (also often referred to as the victimization surveys) now regularly conducted in conjunction with the U.S. Census. [R]apes reported to surveyors in 1986 yield a rate of about 140 per 100,000 women. . . . Thus, the most current victimization surveys indicate a rate [double] that indicated by the UCR data. . . .

Perhaps the greatest source of error in the reported rate of rape is the nonreported incidents. This "doubly dark" figure of crime, which is reported *neither* to the police *nor* to a victimization survey interviewer, remains elusive. Research indicates that rapes by known assailants are particularly likely to go unreported, resulting in a serious underestimation of the extent of violence against women. . . .

When women living in [three] selected cities were asked in telephone interviews if they had ever been raped *or* sexually assaulted *at some time during their lives,* 2 percent said yes. That is a rate of 2,000 per 100,000, much higher than either yearly UCR or survey rates for these cities. But when women were asked the same question in person, the figures were even more startling. Eleven percent (or 11,000 in 100,000) said they had been raped or sexually assaulted. These rates are surprisingly high and help to underscore the problems with any of the figures now available. . . .

While stranger rapes may constitute people's image of what is typical, acquaintance rapes or nonstranger rapes, are an increasingly large proportion of actual rapes and now account for 55 to 60 percent of rapes reported to police. . . .

But the words "nonstranger" or "acquaintance" cover a wide range of types of relationships. [One] type of acquaintance rape is referred to as date rape; this occurs when the victim initially is willing to be in the company of a man who then becomes violent toward her. For several reasons, many of these rapes are not reported. . . . Although the victim may have resisted and been forced, she herself may not recognize it as rape *because* she was on a date. . . . Most important, date-rape victims often feel they won't be believed or will be perceived as having "asked for it"— by the police, the courts, and everyone else and, therefore, there is no point in reporting it. . . .

A special form of date rape is being increasingly reported on college campuses. In what may have become a typical campus rape, a young woman is assaulted by a young man she has met (often the same evening) at a party on campus. She may have danced with him, gone for a walk with him, gone to his room, or allowed him to walk her to her room. Many campus rapes seem to involve the use of excessive amounts of alcohol by one or both persons involved. One victim of campus rape blamed herself because she was drunk. When a faculty member reminded her that it is a crime to rape, but not a crime to get drunk, the coed decided to file charges. Experts in this field say, "Clearly, among college students, sexual aggression is rare among strangers and common among acquaintances." . . .

[R]esearchers argue that campus rape may be so prevalent because of norms in our society that condone sexual violence. People are conditioned to accept sexual roles in which male aggression is an acceptable part of our modern courtship culture. According to this line of reasoning, campus rapists are ordinary males operating in an ordinary social context, not even knowing they are doing something wrong, let alone against the law.

NOTES

1. Attempts to estimate the frequency of rape continue to produce widely divergent numbers. The 1986 NCS survey discussed by Gordon & Riger found an annual rape victimization rate of 140 per 100,000 women aged 12 or older. A more comprehensive Department of Justice study, the 1998 National Violence Against Women Survey (NVAW), found an annual rape victimization rate of 870 per 100,000 women aged 18 or older, equivalent to 876,000 completed and attempted rapes for this age group alone. Fifteen percent of the adult women had experienced one or more completed rapes in their lifetimes, and another 3 percent had been victims of attempted rape. For men, the NVAW survey found a lower but nonetheless substantial rate of victimization — 120 per 100,000 men aged 18 and older, or 111,000 rapes and attempted rapes for this age group per year; 3 percent of adult men had been victims of completed or attempted rape in their lifetimes.[1]

Among college women, victimization rates appear to be even higher. A 1999 national survey for the Department of Justice found that 2.8 percent of college women had experienced a completed or attempted rape during the preceding six months, suggesting an annual victimization rate of roughly 5600 per 100,000 college women.[2] Another major study, led by Professor Mary Koss,[3] found that 27 percent of college women had been victims of at least one rape or attempted rape since age 14.

Figures like these have stirred considerable controversy. One social scientist dismisses the Koss figures as unrealistic "[a]dvocacy numbers"; he notes that 73 percent of the women counted as rape victims did not label their own experience as "rape" and 42 percent of them subsequently dated and had sex again with their supposed attackers. See Neil Gilbert, The Phantom Epidemic of Sexual Assault, The Public Interest 54, 60, 63 (Spring 1991). Other researchers argue that such behavior on the part of victims — the tendency to blame themselves when their date turns violent and to deny that the experience was rape — is itself a confirmation of the seriousness and prevalence of sexual abuse. See Robin Warshaw, I Never Called It Rape (1988).

To keep this debate in perspective, it is important to stress that even the es-

1. Patricia Tjaden & Nancy Thoennes, Prevalence, Incidence, and Consequences of Violence Against Women: Findings From the National Violence Against Women Survey 3-4 (Natl. Institute of Justice 1998).

2. Bonnie S. Fisher, et al., Extent and Nature of the Sexual Victimization of College Women: A National-Level Analysis (Natl. Institute of Justice 1999).

3. Mary P. Koss, Christine A. Gidycz & Nadine Wisniewski, The Scope of Rape: Incidence and Prevalence of Sexual Aggression and Victimization in a National Sample of Higher Education Students, 55 J. Consulting & Clinical Psych. 162 (1987).

timates at the "low" end represent an enormous amount of abuse — at least 150,000 rapes per year. But the debate over the prevalence of rape remains important for understanding the nature of the task that criminal law confronts: Is the law addressing serious but infrequent, aberrational behavior? Or should the law condemn (and does it already condemn) a type of conduct that is commonplace among ordinary, otherwise law-abiding people?

The definitions of rape used in the studies become important here. In the NCS survey, rape is defined as "[c]arnal knowledge through the use of force or the threat of force, including attempts"; the survey does not include statutory rape (consensual sex involving a minor) or sex where the victim is incapacitated by drugs or alcohol.[4] In the Koss study, conduct was counted as rape under two circumstances: if the woman "had intercourse when [she] didn't want to because a man threatened or used some degree of physical force" and if she "had intercourse when [she] didn't want to because a man gave [her] alcohol or drugs."[5] Looking only at Koss's most serious category (intercourse because force was used or threatened), the victimization rate (9 percent since age 14) is still many times higher than that reported by NCS (0.14 percent per year, including attempts). What factors could account for this discrepancy?

Most statutes also treat intercourse as rape when the woman was *incapacitated* by drugs or alcohol. Is Koss's second category equivalent to the legal test? If not, should the legal test be expanded to cover all cases where a person "has intercourse when she doesn't want to because a man has given her drugs or alcohol"?

2. In another part of her study, Professor Koss examined cases of "sexual coercion" in which women submitted to sex because of pressures not included in most existing legal definitions of rape. Two percent of the women reported that they had had intercourse "because a man used his position of authority . . . to make [them]"; 25 percent of the women had "given in to sexual intercourse when [they] didn't want to, because [they] were overwhelmed by a man's continual arguments and pressure."[6] Should the law be modified to treat either or both of these situations as rape?

3. One element in the controversy concerns the prevalence of male sexual aggression. Consider this comment (Elizabeth A. Stanko, Intimate Intrusions 9 (1985)):

> To be a woman — in most societies, in most eras — is to experience physical and/or sexual terrorism at the hands of men. Our everyday behaviour reflects our precautions, the measures we take to protect ourselves. We are wary of going out at night, even in our own neighbourhoods. We are warned by men and other women not to trust strangers. But somehow they forget to warn us about men we know: our fathers, our acquaintances, our co-workers, our lovers, our teachers. Many men familiar to us also terrorize our everyday lives in our homes, our schools, our workplaces.
>
> Women's experiences of incest, battering, rape and sexual harassment become the sources for documenting all women's actual and potential experiences. . . . In each case, a woman endures an invasion of self, the intrusion of inner space, a violation of her sexual and physical autonomy.

4. U.S. Dept. of Justice Bureau of Justice Statistics, Criminal Victimization in the United States, 1992, at 156 (Mar. 1994).
5. Koss, et al., supra footnote 1, at 167.
6. Id.

Is this an accurate or widely shared perception? Many men clearly do not think so. As Professor Robin West writes (The Difference in Women's Hedonic Lives, 3 Wis. Women's L.J. 81, 95 (1987)), "[T]he claim that women's lives are ruled by fear is heard by these men as wildly implausible. They see no evidence in their own lives to support it." On the other hand, Professor Menachem Amir's study, Patterns in Forcible Rape (1971), reports (p. 130) "general assumptions . . . that there are constant pressures for sexual gratification and experience among all males and that some aggression is an expected part of the male role in sexual encounters." From this perspective, some male aggressiveness may be present, but not noticed as aberrant, in situations ranging from marriage through dates, jobs, and even encounters between strangers. Consider Professor West's comments on "street hassling" (supra, at 106-107):

> Street hassling is not trivial. . . . It is damaging to be pointed at, jeered at, laughed at for one's sexuality. This does not make [us] feel (primarily) "angry," "wronged" or even "assaulted." It makes [us] feel sexually ridiculous, exposed, dirty, vulgar, vulnerable and afraid.

Against this background, the controversy turns in part on what is understood as aggression, and it turns also on perceptions about the extent to which aggression is expected and acceptable (and to whom).

4. What precisely is the nature of the harm in rape? Many think of rape as a crime of violence. On this view the offense appears as a species of aggravated assault, and some would argue that the essential harm is similar to that experienced in any severe beating. Men who view rape in these terms often see the threat of rape as not fundamentally different from the threat of violent assault to which they are also exposed. In contrast, many feminists suggest that the important harm in rape is not violence but unwanted sexual intrusion. They argue that such unwanted sexual intimacy is for practical purposes rarely (outside the prison setting) experienced by men. Taking this view of the essential harm, feminists argue that men often have difficulty understanding when women feel raped and more generally what women fear about male behavior. Feminist law reformers assert that these "male" attitudes lead to inappropriate conceptions about the amount of force necessary to constitute rape. Consider Catharine A. MacKinnon, Feminism Unmodified 86-87 (1987):

> The point of view of men up to this time, called objective, has been to distinguish sharply between rape on the one hand and intercourse on the other; sexual harassment on the one hand and normal, ordinary sexual initiation on the other. . . . What women experience does not so clearly distinguish the normal, everyday things from those abuses from which they have been defined by distinction. . . . What we are saying is that sexuality in exactly these normal forms often *does* violate us. So long as we say that those things are abuses of violence, not sex, we fail to criticize what has been made of sex, what has been done to us *through* sex, because we leave the line between rape and intercourse, sexual harassment and sex roles . . . exactly where it is.

5. One reason that controversy about rape law continues is that underlying attitudes about sexual relationships have become highly controversial and are themselves in a state of flux. Criminal law always reflects, responds to, and acts upon the culture of the community. Nowhere have these interactions become more vivid, and more problematic, than in the law of rape. The nature of these interactions and their impact on the substantive law are among the themes of this chapter.

B. STATUTORY FRAMEWORKS

INTRODUCTORY NOTE

In the eighteenth century, Blackstone defined rape as "carnal knowledge of a woman forcibly and against her will."[7] Until the 1950s, most American statutes preserved Blackstone's definition, with only minor verbal differences. This uniformity began to erode in the 1960s with a wave of reforms initiated by the Model Penal Code. Further change occurred, beginning in the 1970s, with reforms prompted by the feminist movement. Along with new provisions altering procedures and rules of evidence (considered in Section E below), the reforms addressed in differing ways such substantive issues as the gender-specific character of the crime (traditionally, only a woman could be raped), the labeling of the offense as "rape," the degree of force and/or resistance required, the need to differentiate between degrees of the offense, and the traditional exemption for men who forcibly raped their wives.

The upshot is enormous diversity in state approaches today. Many states still adhere closely to traditional conceptions; in Maryland, for example, rape is defined, as in Blackstone's day, as "vaginal intercourse . . . by force or threat of force against the will and without the consent of the other person."[8] In other jurisdictions, statutory provisions combine new features with significant vestiges of the older concepts. And several state statutes make a sharp break with the past. To illustrate these variations, we present several representative statutes: the 1950 California provision, which was typical of the rape statutes of its time, the 1962 Model Penal Code proposal, and three contrasting regimes currently in effect — those of California, New York, and Wisconsin.

For an initial overview, we suggest that students note how statutory regimes have changed over time and how states now differ in their approach to four central issues: the gravity of the facts required to be proved, whether and in what way the crime is split into distinctly graded offenses, the level of punishment authorized, and whether or when spousal rape is punishable. We also suggest returning to these distinct regimes to consider which of them affords the best framework for resolving the concrete problems posed in the cases that follow.

CALIFORNIA PENAL CODE, TITLE 9 (1950)

SECTION 261. RAPE

Rape is an act of sexual intercourse accomplished with a female not the wife of the perpetrator, under either of the following circumstances:

(1) Where the female is under the age of eighteen years;

7. William Blackstone, 4 Commentaries on the Laws of England (1765) *210 (U. of Chicago Press 1979).

8. Md. Code, art. 27, §§462(a), 463(a)(1) (1999).

(2) Where she is incapable, through lunacy or other unsoundness of mind, whether temporary or permanent, of giving consent;

(3) Where she resists but her resistance is overcome by force or violence;

(4) Where she is prevented from resisting by threats of great and immediate bodily harm, accompanied by apparent power of execution, or by any intoxicating, narcotic, or anesthetic substance, or any controlled substance, administered by or with the privity of the accused.

(5) Where she is at the time unconscious of the nature of the act, and this is known to the accused. . . .

(6) Where she submits under the belief that the person committing the act is the victim's spouse, and this belief is induced by any artifice, pretense, or concealment practiced by the accused, with intent to induce such belief.

SECTION 264.

Rape is punishable by imprisonment in the State Prison [for] not more than fifty years. . . .

MODEL PENAL CODE (PROPOSED OFFICIAL DRAFT 1962)

SECTION 213.1. [SEE APPENDIX].

CALIFORNIA PENAL CODE, TITLE 9 (1999)

SECTION 261. RAPE; "DURESS"; "MENACE"

(a) Rape is an act of sexual intercourse accomplished with a person not the spouse of the perpetrator, under any of the following circumstances:

(1) Where a person is incapable, because of a mental disorder or developmental or physical disability, of giving legal consent, and this is known or reasonably should be known to the person committing the act. . . .

(2) Where it is accomplished against a person's will by means of force, violence, duress, menace, or fear of immediate and unlawful bodily injury on the person or another.

(3) Where a person is prevented from resisting by any intoxicating or anesthetic substance, or any controlled substance, and this condition was known, or reasonably should have been known by the accused.

(4) Where a person is at the time unconscious of the nature of the act, and this is known to the accused. . . .

(5) Where a person submits under the belief that the person committing the act is the victim's spouse, and this belief is induced by any artifice, pretense, or concealment practiced by the accused, with intent to induce the belief.

(6) Where the act is accomplished against the victim's will by threatening to retaliate in the future against the victim or any other person, and there is a reasonable possibility that the perpetrator will execute the threat. As used in this paragraph, "threatening to retaliate" means a threat to kidnap or falsely imprison, or to inflict extreme pain, serious bodily injury, or death. . . .

(b) As used in this section, "duress" means a direct or implied threat of force, violence, danger, or retribution sufficient to coerce a reasonable person of ordinary susceptibilities to perform an act which otherwise would not have been performed, or acquiesce in an act to which one otherwise would not have submitted. The total circumstances, including the age of the victim, and his or her relationship to the defendant, are factors to consider in appraising the existence of duress.

(c) As used in this section, "menace" means any threat, declaration, or act which shows an intention to inflict an injury upon another.

SECTION 261.5. UNLAWFUL SEXUAL INTERCOURSE WITH A MINOR . . .

(a) Unlawful sexual intercourse is an act of sexual intercourse accomplished with a person who is not the spouse of the perpetrator, if the person is a minor. For the purposes of this section, a "minor" is a person under the age of 18 years. . . .

SECTION 261.6. "CONSENT." . . .

In prosecutions under Section 261 [or] 262 . . . in which consent is at issue, "consent" shall be defined to mean positive cooperation in act or attitude pursuant to an exercise of free will. The person must act freely and voluntarily and have knowledge of the nature of the act or transaction involved. . . .

SECTION 262. SPOUSAL RAPE

(a) Rape of a person who is the spouse of the perpetrator is an act of sexual intercourse accomplished under any of the . . . circumstances [specified in §261(2), (3), (4), or (6)].

SECTION 264. PUNISHMENT FOR RAPE. . . .

(a) Rape, as defined in Section 261 or 262, is punishable by imprisonment in the state prison for three, six, or eight years. . . .[a]

[Unlawful sexual intercourse with a minor, as defined in Section 261.5, is punishable by imprisonment for a maximum of four years.]

a. California law provides for an additional five years imprisonment for each prior conviction of a similar offense and for life imprisonment in cases involving severe aggravating circumstances (e.g., kidnapping, torture, or use of a deadly weapon) or certain prior convictions for serious sex offenses. Cal. Penal Code §§667.6, 667.61. — EDS.

NEW YORK PENAL LAW (1999)

SECTION 130.00. SEX OFFENSES; DEFINITIONS OF TERMS. . . .

4. "Female" means any female person who is not married to the actor. . . .[b]
8. "Forcible compulsion" means to compel by either: (a) use of physical force; or (b) a threat, express or implied, which places a person in fear of immediate death or physical injury to himself, herself or another person, or in fear that he, she or another person will immediately be kidnapped.

SECTION 130.05. SEX OFFENSES; LACK OF CONSENT

1. Whether or not specifically stated, it is an element of every offense defined in this article, except the offense of consensual sodomy, that the sexual act was committed without consent of the victim.
2. Lack of consent results from: (a) Forcible compulsion; or (b) Incapacity to consent. . . .
3. A person is deemed incapable of consent when he or she is: (a) less than seventeen years old; or (b) mentally defective; or (c) mentally incapacitated [by "a narcotic or intoxicating substance administered to him without his consent"]; or (d) physically helpless. . . .

SECTION 130.20. SEXUAL MISCONDUCT

A person is guilty of sexual misconduct when:
1. Being a male, he engages in sexual intercourse with a female without her consent. . . . Sexual misconduct is a class A misdemeanor [one-year maximum]. . . .

SECTION 130.25. RAPE IN THE THIRD DEGREE

A person is guilty of rape in the third degree [four-year maximum] when:
1. He or she engages in sexual intercourse with another person to whom the actor is not married who is incapable of consent by reason of some factor other than being less than seventeen years old; or
2. Being twenty-one years old or more, he or she engages in sexual intercourse with another person to whom the actor is not married less than seventeen years old. . . .

SECTION 130.30. RAPE IN THE SECOND DEGREE

A person is guilty of rape in the second degree [seven-year maximum] when, being eighteen years old or more, he or she engages in sexual intercourse with another person to whom the actor is not married less than fourteen years old.

b. The statute specifies that "not married" includes spouses who are living apart under a court order of separation or a written separation agreement. — EDS.

Section 130.35. Rape in the First Degree

A male is guilty of rape in the first degree [25-year maximum] when he engages in sexual intercourse with a female:

1. By forcible compulsion; or
2. Who is incapable of consent by reason of being physically helpless; or
3. Who is less than eleven years old.

WISCONSIN STATUTES (1999)

Section 940.225. Sexual assault.

(1) First degree sexual assault. Whoever does any of the following is guilty of a Class B felony [40-year maximum]:

(a) Has sexual contact or sexual intercourse with another person without consent of that person and causes pregnancy or great bodily harm to that person.

(b) Has sexual contact or sexual intercourse with another person without consent of that person by use or threat of use of a dangerous weapon or any article used or fashioned in a manner to lead the victim reasonably to believe it to be a dangerous weapon. . . .

(2) Second degree sexual assault. Whoever does any of the following is guilty of a Class BC felony [25-year maximum]:

(a) Has sexual contact or sexual intercourse with another person without consent of that person by use or threat of force or violence.

(b) Has sexual contact or sexual intercourse with another person without consent of that person and causes injury, illness, disease or impairment of a sexual or reproductive organ, or mental anguish requiring psychiatric care for the victim.

(c) Has sexual contact or sexual intercourse with a person who suffers from a mental illness or deficiency which renders that person temporarily or permanently incapable of appraising the person's conduct, and the defendant knows of such condition.

(cm) Has sexual contact or sexual intercourse with a person who is under the influence of an intoxicant to a degree which renders that person incapable of appraising the person's conduct, and the defendant knows of such condition.

(d) Has sexual contact or sexual intercourse with a person who the defendant knows is unconscious. . . .

(3) Third degree sexual assault. Whoever has sexual intercourse with a person without the consent of that person is guilty of a Class D felony [five-year maximum]. . . .

(4) Consent. "Consent," as used in this section, means words or overt actions by a person who is competent to give informed consent indicating a freely given agreement to have sexual intercourse or sexual contact. . .

(6) Marriage not a bar to prosecution. A defendant shall not be presumed to be incapable of violating this section because of marriage to the complainant.

SECTION 948.02. SEXUAL ASSAULT OF A CHILD.

(1) First degree sexual assault. Whoever has sexual contact or sexual intercourse with a person who has not attained the age of 13 years is guilty of a Class B felony [40-year maximum].

(2) Second degree sexual assault. Whoever has sexual contact or sexual intercourse with a person who has not attained the age of 16 years is guilty of a Class BC felony [25-year maximum]. . . .

SECTION 948.09. SEXUAL INTERCOURSE WITH A CHILD AGE 16 OR OLDER.

Whoever has sexual intercourse with a child [under 18] who is not the defendant's spouse and who has attained the age of 16 years is guilty of a Class A misdemeanor [nine-month maximum].

C. ACTUS REUS

1. *Force, Nonconsent, and Resistance*

STATE v. RUSK

Court of Appeals of Maryland
289 Md. 230, 424 A.2d 720 (1981)

MURPHY, C.J. Edward Rusk was found guilty by a jury . . . of second degree rape in violation of Maryland Code Art. 27, §463(a)(1), which provides in pertinent part:

> A person is guilty of rape in the second degree if the person engages in vaginal intercourse with another person:
> (1) By force or threat of force against the will and without the consent of the other person. . . .[a]

On appeal, the Court of Special Appeals, sitting en banc, reversed the conviction; it concluded by an 8–5 majority that in view of the prevailing law as set forth in Hazel v. State, 221 Md. 464, 157 A.2d 922 (1960), insufficient evidence of Rusk's guilt had been adduced at the trial to permit the case to go to the jury. We granted certiorari to consider whether the Court of Special Appeals properly applied the principles of *Hazel*. . . .

At the trial, the 21-year-old prosecuting witness, Pat, testified that on the evening of September 21, 1977, she attended a high school alumnae meeting where she met a girl friend, Terry. After the meeting, Terry and Pat agreed to drive in

a. The Maryland statute provides that second-degree rape is punishable by imprisonment for a period not to exceed 20 years. First-degree rape is defined to include intercourse by force or threat of force where the defendant uses a deadly weapon, inflicts or threatens "suffocation, strangulation, disfigurement or serious physical injury," or is aided by one or more other persons. First-degree rape is punishable by a maximum of life imprisonment. — EDS.

their respective cars to Fells Point to have a few drinks. . . . They went to a bar where . . . Rusk approached and said "hello" to Terry. Terry, who was then conversing with another individual, momentarily interrupted her conversation and said "Hi, Eddie." Rusk then began talking with Pat and during their conversation both of them acknowledged being separated from their respective spouses and having a child. Pat told Rusk that she had to go home . . . [and] Rusk requested a ride to his apartment. Although Pat did not know Rusk, she thought that Terry knew him. She thereafter agreed to give him a ride. Pat cautioned Rusk on the way to the car that "I'm just giving a ride home, you know, as a friend, not anything to be, you know, thought of other than a ride." . . .

After a twenty-minute drive, they arrived at Rusk's apartment. . . . Pat testified that she was totally unfamiliar with the neighborhood. She parked the car at the curb . . . but left the engine running. Rusk asked Pat to come in, but she refused. . . . Pat said that Rusk was fully aware that she did not want to accompany him to his room. Notwithstanding her repeated refusals, Pat testified that Rusk reached over and turned off the ignition to her car and took her car keys. He got out of the car, walked over to her side, opened the door and said, "Now, will you come up?" Pat explained her subsequent actions:

> At that point, because I was scared, because he had my car keys. I didn't know what to do. I was someplace I didn't even know where I was. It was in the city. I didn't know whether to run. I really didn't think at that point, what to do.
>
> Now, I know that I should have blown the horn. I should have run. There were a million things I could have done. I was scared, at that point, and I didn't do any of them.

Pat testified that at this moment she feared that Rusk would rape her. She said: "[I]t was the way he looked at me, and said 'Come on up, come on up'; and when he took the keys, I knew that was wrong."

It was then about 1 A.M. Pat accompanied Rusk across the street into a totally dark house. . . . Rusk unlocked the door to his one-room apartment, and turned on the light. According to Pat, he told her to sit down. She sat in a chair beside the bed. Rusk sat on the bed. After Rusk talked for a few minutes, he left the room for about one to five minutes. Pat remained seated in the chair. She made no noise and did not attempt to leave. She said that she did not notice a telephone in the room. When Rusk returned, he turned off the light and sat down on the bed. Pat asked if she could leave; she told him that she wanted to go home and "didn't want to come up." She said, "Now, [that] I came up, can I go?" Rusk, who was still in possession of her car keys, said he wanted her to stay.

Rusk then asked Pat to get on the bed with him. He pulled her by the arms to the bed and began to undress her. . . . Pat removed the rest of her clothing, and then removed Rusk's pants because "he asked me to do it." After they were both undressed Rusk started kissing Pat as she was lying on her back. Pat explained what happened next:

> I was still begging him to please let, you know, let me leave. I said, "you can get a lot of other girls down there, for what you want," and he just kept saying, "no"; and then I was really scared, because I can't describe, you know, what was said. It was more the look in his eyes; and I said, at that point — I didn't know what to say; and I said, "If I do what you want, will you let me go without killing me?" Because

> I didn't know, at that point, what he was going to do; and I started to cry; and when I did, he put his hands on my throat, and started lightly to choke me; and I said, "If I do what you want, will you let me go?" And he said, yes, and at that time, I proceeded to do what he wanted me to.

Pat testified that Rusk made her perform oral sex and then vaginal intercourse.

Immediately after the intercourse, Pat asked if she could leave. She testified that Rusk said, "Yes," after which she got up and got dressed and Rusk returned her car keys. She said that Rusk then

> walked me to my car, and asked if he could see me again; and I said, "Yes"; and he asked me for my telephone number; and I said, "No, I'll see you down Fells Point sometime," just so I could leave.

Pat testified that she "had no intention of meeting him again." She asked him for directions out of the neighborhood and left.

. . . As she sat in her car reflecting on the incident, Pat said she began to

> wonder what would happen if I hadn't of done what he wanted me to do. So I thought the right thing to do was to go report it, and I went from there to Hillendale to find a police car.

She reported the incident to the police at about 3:15 A.M. . . .

Rusk and two of his friends, Michael Trimp and David Carroll, testified on his behalf. According to Trimp, they went in Carroll's car to Buggs' bar to dance, drink and "tr[y] to pick up some ladies." Rusk stayed at the bar, while the others went to get something to eat.

Trimp and Carroll next saw Rusk walking down the street arm-in-arm with a lady whom Trimp was unable to identify. . .

Carroll's testimony corroborated Trimp's. He saw Rusk walking down the street arm-in-arm with a woman. He said "[s]he was kind of like, you know, snuggling up to him like. . . . She was hanging all over him then." Carroll was fairly certain that Pat was the woman who was with Rusk. . . .

According to Rusk, when they arrived in front of his apartment Pat parked the car and turned the engine off. They sat for several minutes "petting each other." . . . Rusk testified that Pat came willingly to his room and that at no time did he make threatening facial expressions. . . . Rusk explained that after the intercourse, Pat "got uptight."

> Well, she started to cry. She said that — she said, "You guys are all alike," she says, "just out for," you know, "one thing." . . . And she said, that she just wanted to leave; and I said, "Well, okay"; and she walked out to the car. I walked out to the car. She got in the car and left.

Rusk denied placing his hands on Pat's throat or attempting to strangle her. He also denied using force or threats of force to get Pat to have intercourse with him.

In reversing Rusk's second degree rape conviction, the Court of Special Appeals quoting from *Hazel,* noted that:

> Force is an essential element of the crime [of rape] and to justify a conviction, the evidence must warrant a conclusion either that the victim resisted and her re-

> sistance was overcome by force or that she was prevented from resisting by threats to her safety.

Writing for the majority, Judge Thompson said:

> In all of the victim's testimony we have been unable to see any resistance on her part to the sex acts and certainly can we see no fear as would overcome her attempt to resist or escape as required by *Hazel.* Possession of the keys by the accused may have deterred her vehicular escape but hardly a departure seeking help in the rooming house or in the street. We must say that "the way he looked" fails utterly to support the fear required by *Hazel.*

. . . Of course, due process requirements mandate that a criminal conviction not be obtained if the evidence does not reasonably support a finding of guilt beyond a reasonable doubt. However, as the Supreme Court made clear in Jackson v. Virginia, 443 U.S. 307 (1979), the reviewing court does not ask itself whether *it* believes that the evidence established guilt beyond a reasonable doubt; rather, the applicable standard is "whether, after viewing the evidence in the light most favorable to the prosecution, *any* rational trier of fact could have found the essential elements of the crime beyond a reasonable doubt." (emphasis in original). . . .

The Court [in *Hazel*] noted that lack of consent is generally established through proof of resistance or by proof that the victim failed to resist because of fear. The degree of fear necessary to obviate the need to prove resistance, and thereby establish lack of consent, was defined in the following manner: "The kind of fear which would render resistance by a woman unnecessary to support a conviction of rape includes, but is not necessarily limited to, a fear of death or serious bodily harm, or a fear so extreme as to preclude resistance, or a fear which would well nigh render her mind incapable of continuing to resist, or a fear that so overpowers her that she does not dare resist."

. . . While *Hazel* made it clear that the victim's fear had to be genuine, it did not pass upon whether a real but unreasonable fear of imminent death or serious bodily harm would suffice. The vast majority of jurisdictions have required that the victim's fear be reasonably grounded in order to obviate the need for either proof of actual force on the part of the assailant or physical resistance on the part of the victim. We think that, generally, this is the correct standard. . . .

We think the reversal of Rusk's conviction by the Court of Special Appeals was in error for the fundamental reason so well expressed in the dissenting opinion by Judge Wilner when he observed that the majority had "trampled upon the first principle of appellate restraint [because it had] substituted [its] own view of the evidence (and the inferences that may fairly be drawn from it) for that of the judge and jury [and had thereby] improperly invaded the province allotted to those tribunals." In view of the evidence adduced at the trial, the reasonableness of Pat's apprehension of fear was plainly a question of fact for the jury to determine. . . . Quite obviously, the jury disbelieved Rusk and believed Pat's testimony. From her testimony, the jury could have reasonably concluded that the taking of her car keys was intended by Rusk to immobilize her alone, late at night, in a neighborhood with which she was not familiar; that after Pat had repeatedly refused to enter his apartment, Rusk commanded in firm tones that she do so; that Pat was badly frightened and feared that Rusk intended to rape her; . . . that Pat was afraid that Rusk would kill her unless she submitted; that she began to cry and Rusk then put his hands on her throat and began "lightly to choke" her; that Pat asked him if he would let her go without killing her if she complied with his demands; that Rusk gave an affirmative response, after which she finally submitted.

Just where persuasion ends and force begins in cases like the present is essentially a factual issue. . . . Considering all of the evidence in the case, with particular focus upon the actual force applied by Rusk to Pat's neck, we conclude that the jury could rationally find that the essential elements of second degree rape had been established and that Rusk was guilty of that offense beyond a reasonable doubt.[b] . . .

COLE, J., dissenting. [W]hen one of the essential elements of a crime is not sustained by the evidence, the conviction of the defendant cannot stand as a matter of law.

The majority, in applying this standard, concludes that "[i]n view of the evidence adduced at the trial, the reasonableness of Pat's apprehension of fear was plainly a question of fact for the jury to determine." In so concluding, the majority has skipped over the crucial issue. It seems to me that whether the prosecutrix's fear is reasonable becomes a question only after the court determines that the defendant's conduct under the circumstances was reasonably calculated to give rise to a fear on her part to the extent that she was unable to resist. . . .

While courts no longer require a female to resist to the utmost or to resist where resistance would be foolhardy, they do require her acquiescence in the act of intercourse to stem from fear generated by something of substance. She may not simply say, "I was really scared," and thereby transform consent or mere unwillingness into submission by force. These words do not transform a seducer into a rapist. She must follow the natural instinct of every proud female to resist, by more than mere words, the violation of her person by a stranger or an unwelcomed friend. She must make it plain that she regards such sexual acts as abhorrent and repugnant to her natural sense of pride. She must resist unless the defendant has objectively manifested his intent to use physical force to accomplish his purpose. The law regards rape as a crime of violence. The majority today attenuates this proposition. It declares the innocence of an at best distraught young woman. It does not demonstrate the defendant's guilt of the crime of rape.

. . . The majority suggests that "from her testimony the jury could have reasonably concluded that the taking of her keys was intended by Rusk to immobilize her alone, late at night, in a neighborhood with which she was unfamiliar. . . ." But on what facts does the majority so conclude? There is no evidence descriptive of the tone of his voice; her testimony indicates only the bare statement quoted above. . . .

She also testified that she was afraid of "the way he looked," and afraid of his statement, "come on up, come on up." But what can the majority conclude from this statement coupled with a "look" that remained undescribed? There is no evidence whatsoever to suggest that this was anything other than a pattern of conduct consistent with the ordinary seduction of a female acquaintance who at first suggests her disinclination. . . .

The majority relies on the trial court's statement that the defendant responded

b. Four judges joined the opinion sustaining the conviction. Three judges joined the dissent.—EDS.

affirmatively to her question "If I do what you want, will you let me go without killing me?" The majority further suggests that the jury could infer the defendant's affirmative response. The facts belie such inference since by the prosecutrix's own testimony the defendant made *no* response. *He said nothing!*

She then testified that she started to cry and he "started lightly to choke" her, whatever that means. Obviously, the choking was not of any persuasive significance. During this "choking" she was able to talk. She said "If I do what you want will you let me go?" It was at this point that the defendant said yes.

I find it incredible for the majority to conclude that on these facts, without more, a woman was *forced* to commit oral sex upon the defendant and then to engage in vaginal intercourse.

[T]here are no acts or conduct on the part of the defendant to suggest that these fears were created by the defendant or that he made any objective, identifiable threats to her which would give rise to this woman's failure to flee, summon help, scream, or make physical resistance. . . .

In my judgment the State failed to prove the essential element of force beyond a reasonable doubt and, therefore, the judgment of conviction should be reversed. . . .

ELIZABETH A. STANKO, INTIMATE INTRUSIONS, 9-11 (1985): [M]any characterise male physical and/or sexual aggression as linked to biological make-up, sparked by an innate, at times uncontrollable, sexual drive. After all, boys will be boys, we sigh. While we acknowledge that not all men publicly display this uncontrollable biological predisposition, we further believe its display is generally aroused by deserving, provoking women. . . . At the same time, though, we recognise that some male aggression is not sparked by provocative women. These, we reassure ourselves, are the rarest of situations. Above all, we retain traditional assumptions about women who experience sexual and/or physical assault; some women are alluring, masochistic and provoke the uncontrollable responses of some men, and some women are pure, proper but unfortunately come across some men who are uncontrollable. When we try to account for women's experience of male violence, explanations of it centre around the naturalness or unnaturalness of male aggression in relation to women's behaviour.

As a result, women's experiences of male violence are filtered through an understanding of *men's* behaviour which is characterised as either typical or aberrant. If it is considered typical, men's physical and sexual aggression toward women is left, to a large extent, unfettered. The sexual advance by a male professor toward a young female student, the 'rough sex,' the slapping of one's wife, the wolf whistle on the street, the comments about women's physicality, the man's brushing up against a female secretary's body in the xerox room (and on and on) are, most people accept, natural expressions of maleness. These expressions are assumed to be non-threatening to women, even, some would say, flattering. The vicious rape, the brutal murder of a woman, the cruel physical torture of a girlfriend are, we feel, the aberrant examples of maleness. These examples, most would agree, are threatening to women. In the abstract we easily draw lines between those aberrant (thus harmful) and those typical (thus unharmful) types of male behaviour. We even label the aberrant behaviour as potentially criminal behaviour.

What becomes lost, though, in this commonsensical separation between 'aberrant' and 'typical' male behaviour is a woman-defined understanding of what is threatening, of what women consider to be potentially violent. Often, women themselves are confused — sometimes defining male behaviour as typical, other times as aberrant — but none the less feel threatened by some displays of either. Women who feel violated or intimidated by typical male behaviour have no way of specifying how or why typical male behaviour feels like aberrant male behaviour. Essentially, the categories *typical* and *aberrant* are not useful for understanding women's feelings about, and thus women's experiences of male intimidation and violence. Confusing though they may be, women's experiences point to a potential for violence in many of women's ordinary encounters with men.

NOTES ON FORCE AND RESISTANCE

1. The force requirement. In the absence of force, nonconsensual intercourse traditionally was criminal only under special circumstances — when the victim was below a given age ("statutory" rape), unconscious, or mentally incompetent. See, e.g., Cal. Penal Code §261 (1950), pages 318-319 supra; Deborah W. Denno, Sexuality, Rape, and Mental Retardation, 1997 U. Ill. L. Rev. 315. A growing number of American jurisdictions now depart from this traditional approach by treating all instances of nonconsensual intercourse as a criminal offense (either rape or a lesser degree of sexual assault) even in the absence of force. Yet this emerging approach, which we explore infra, pages 338-346, remains very much the minority view. Most contemporary state statutes continue to specify that absent special circumstances, a conviction of rape requires proof of intercourse committed by "force" or "forcible compulsion." See e.g., New York Penal Law §§130.05(2); 130.20; 130.35 (1999), pages 320-321, supra.

2. The resistance requirement. (*a*) *Current law.* In some states, resistance is included among the formal statutory elements, but more often resistance has been read into the statutes as a requirement somehow implicit in the elements of force or nonconsent. Only one American state retains the old requirement that the victim resist "to the utmost,"[9] but several require "earnest resistance,"[10] and in roughly half the states, contemporary statutes or court decisions still require at least "reasonable resistance." See, e.g., Hull v. State, 687 So. 2d 708, 723 (Miss. 1996), holding that a rape victim must use "all reasonable physical resistance available to her under the circumstances." In the remaining states, resistance is no longer formally required, but courts continue to consider resistance (or its absence) as highly probative on the question whether the victim consented. The recent statutes and decisions are reviewed in Michelle Anderson, Reviving Resistance in Rape Law, 1998 U. Ill. L. Rev. 953 (1999).

(*b*) *Policy concerns.* California's statutory resistance requirement was repealed in 1980. Compare Cal. Penal Code §261(3) (1950) with Cal. Penal Code §261(2) (1999), pages 318-320 supra. The concerns that led to the repeal are summarized in People v. Barnes, 42 Cal. 3d 284, 295-302, 721 P. 2d 110, 117-120 (1986):

> The requirement that a woman resist her attacker appears to have been grounded in the basic distrust with which courts and commentators traditionally

9. La. Stat. Ann. §14:42.A(1) (West 1999), specifying that aggravated rape is committed "[w]hen the victim resists the act to the utmost, but whose resistance is overcome by force." In contrast, the Louisiana offense of "forcible rape" requires only reasonable resistance, §42:1, and there is no resistance requirement for the lesser offense of "simple rape." §43.

10. E.g., Ala. Code §13A-6-60 (1998); Or. Rev. Stat. §163.305 (1998); W. Va. Code §61-8B-1 (1998).

> viewed a woman's testimony regarding sexual assault. . . . [T]he requirement of resistance insured against wrongful conviction based solely on testimony the law considered to be inherently suspect. . . .
>
> Recently, however, the entire concept of resistance to sexual assault has been called into question. It has been suggested that while the presence of resistance may well be probative on the issue of force or nonconsent, its absence may not. For example, some studies have demonstrated that while some women respond to sexual assault with active resistance, others "freeze." . . . The "frozen fright" response resembles cooperative behavior. Indeed, as [one psychologist] notes, the "victim may smile, even initiate acts, and may appear relaxed and calm." Subjectively, however, she may be in a state of terror. . . . These findings . . . suggest that lack of physical resistance may reflect a "profound primal terror" rather than consent.
>
> Additionally, a growing body of authority holds that to resist in the face of sexual assault is to risk further injury. In a 1976 study . . . victims who resisted during coitus suffered increased violence as the assailant forced compliance. . . . On the other hand, other findings indicate that resistance has a direct correlation with deterring sexual assault. . . . Brownmiller argues that submissive behavior is not necessarily helpful to a rape victim and suggests that strong resistance on the part of women can thwart rape. (Brownmiller, [Against Our Will, Men, Women and Rape (1975)], at pp. 357, 360-361.) She suggests it would be well for women to undergo systematic training in self-defense in order to fight back against their attackers. [Thus,] physical resistance may increase the danger or may thwart the attack; the woman must therefore evaluate the threat she faces and decide how to react based on the kind of person she is. . . .
>
> [T]he law does not expect . . . that in defending oneself or one's property from [robbery, kidnapping and assault], a person must risk injury or death by displaying resistance in the face of attack. The amendment of §261(a)(2) acknowledges that previous [assumptions], which singled out the credibility of rape complaints as suspect, have no place in a modern system of jurisprudence.

Compare Michelle J. Anderson, Reviving Resistance in Rape Law, 1998 U. Ill. L. Rev. 953, 977-990. Professor Anderson agrees that victim resistance should not be an essential prerequisite to a rape conviction, but she notes that "[w]omen's fear that resisting rape risks serious injury or death is wildly exaggerated." She explains:

> Despite popular mythology, a woman's physical resistance to a sexual aggressor decreases her chance of being raped and does not increase her risk for serious bodily injury or death. The conclusion of the 1977 Department of Justice study of reported rapes — that women who resist are more likely to suffer serious injury — was flatly contradicted two years later by a 1979 Department of Justice study. . . . [O]f the women who fought back, more than 80 percent avoided being raped. Of the women who did not fight back, only 33 percent avoided being raped. [S]erious injury requiring medical attention and hospital treatment correlated positively with rape completion, and rape victims were injured more seriously than were victims of attempted rape. Therefore, according to the 1979 Department of Justice study, a . . . passive woman [would] increase both her risk that the rape would be completed and her risk of serious injury requiring medical attention. . . .
>
> More recent evidence shows that suffering additional injury . . . may prompt a woman's physical resistance. . . . Regression analysis determined that "there was, in fact, no association of victim resistance and the probability of *later* injury.". . .
>
> Resisting a rapist, [moreover], is associated with less self-blame, shorter recovery times, and obtaining treatment after the rape. One study concluded that "one of the most important functions of physical resistance is to keep women from feel-

ing depressed even if they have been raped." Resistance, then, appears to be potentially psychologically beneficial, even when ultimately unsuccessful in deterring the rapist.

Questions: Do statutes like California's solve the problem of resistance? What result if the *Rusk* case had been tried in California? What would be the result in *Rusk* under Model Penal Code §213.1?

(*c*) All courts recognize that resistance is unnecessary in at least some situations. That would be the case, for example, if the victim is jumped from behind and thrown to the ground by a stranger pointing a gun at her head. In such a situation the fear aroused by the defendant's conduct could overpower the victim and prevent her from resisting. Thus, the question whether the victim offered "reasonable" resistance is in effect displaced by the question whether the victim "reasonably" feared serious bodily harm — so that the "reasonable" amount of resistance, under the circumstances, was no resistance at all. See Merzbacher v. State, 697 A.2d 432, 442 (Md. 1997).

3. *The requirement of a "reasonable" apprehension.* In *Rusk* all the judges appeared to accept the rule that the victim's fear must be reasonably grounded; they divided only over the question whether a jury could properly find that it was, on the facts. Many courts seem to agree with that principle, even in the context of encounters between strangers under frightening circumstances. Consider People v. Warren, 113 Ill. App. 3d 1, 446 N.E.2d 591 (1983). The complainant was biking along an isolated reservoir when defendant approached and struck up a conversation. When she attempted to leave, the defendant placed his hand on her shoulder, saying, "This will only take a minute. My girlfriend doesn't meet my needs." He then lifted her off the ground and carried her into the woods, where he performed several sex acts. The complainant was 5′2″ tall and weighed about 100 pounds; the defendant was 6′3″ and weighed 185 pounds. Because the complainant did not scream, fight back or attempt to flee, the court reversed the conviction:

> Much of the State's case rests upon its contention that complainant's absence of effort in thwarting defendant's advances was motivated by her overwhelming fear. In support of this position, the State offers complainant's statement that she did not attempt to flee because, "it was in the middle of the woods and I didn't feel like I could get away from him and I thought he'd kill me." Moreover, complainant stated that she did not yell or scream because the people she had seen in the area were too far away and that under the circumstances she felt that screaming ". . . would be bad for me."
>
> Despite professing fear for her safety, complainant concedes that defendant did not strike her or threaten to strike her or use a weapon. . . . At no time did complainant tell defendant to leave her alone or put her down. . . . It is well settled that if complainant had the use of her faculties and physical powers, the evidence must show such resistance as will demonstrate that the act was against her will. If the circumstances show resistance to be futile or life endangering or if the complainant is overcome by superior strength or paralyzed by fear, useless or foolhardy acts of resistance are not required. We cannot say that any of the above factors are present here. Complainant's failure to resist when it was within her power to do so conveys the impression of consent regardless of her mental state, amounts to consent and removes from the act performed an essential element of the crime. We do not mean to suggest, however, that the complainant did in fact consent; however, she must communicate in some objective manner her lack of consent.

Why should the absence of resistance have to be explained by fears that are objectively "reasonable"? Why should the "reasonableness" of the victim ever be an issue, so long as the trier of fact is persuaded that her fears were genuine? One obvious concern is to assure that the defendant realizes the woman is submitting out of fear rather than desire. But suppose the defendant *knows* that the victim is genuinely afraid. Suppose that he subtly but deliberately reinforces those fears. (Reconsider the facts of *Rusk.*) Shouldn't a conviction be proper regardless of the "reasonableness" of the fears?[11] Conversely, suppose that the victim's fears are reasonable but that the defendant is totally unaware of them. Shouldn't a conviction be *improper,* regardless of whether the fears are "reasonable"? Or is it appropriate to require defendants to know when their conduct arouses fear of bodily harm and to make sure to dispel any apprehension on the part of their partners?

NOTES ON COERCION AND DURESS

1. Implicit threats. In State v. Alston, 310 N.C. 399, 312 S.E.2d 470 (1984), the defendant and his victim lived together for six months in an abusive relationship. After several episodes in which Alston had struck the victim, she moved out and ended their relationship. A month later, Alston encountered the victim at her school, said he was going to "fix" her face to show he "was not playing," and told her that he had a "right" to have sex with her one more time. He led her to the house of one of his friends, and when she told him she did not want to have sex, he pulled her up from a chair, took off her clothes, pushed her legs apart, and penetrated her. Alston was convicted of rape, but the North Carolina Supreme Court reversed. The court conceded that the evidence of nonconsent was "unequivocal," but it held that the evidence was insufficient to establish the element of "force." Do you agree? Consider these comments:

Susan Estrich, Real Rape 61-62, 65, 69 (1987): The victim's failure to resist, in the court's evaluation, was not a result of what the defendant did just before penetration. Therefore, there was no "force." . . . [Her] experience with him in the past . . . was deemed irrelevant. "Although [the victim's] general fear of the defendant may have been justified by his conduct on prior occasions, absent evidence that the defendant used force or threats to overcome the will of the victim to resist the sexual intercourse alleged to have been rape, such general fear was not sufficient to show that the defendant used the force required to support a conviction of rape." The undressing and the pushing of her legs apart — presumably the "incidental" force — were not even mentioned.

Alston reflects the adoption of the most traditional male notion of a fight as the working definition of "force." In a fight you hit your assailant with your fists or your elbows or your knees. In a fight the person attacked fights back. In these terms there was no fight in *Alston.* Therefore, there was no force.

. . . Apparently, [the judges] could not understand the woman's reaction. For me, it is not at all difficult to understand that a woman . . . who had sought to

11. Though most courts insist that the victim's fear must be objectively reasonable, at least one has held that a conviction can nonetheless be sustained, when "the victim's fear [is] unreasonable, [if] the perpetrator knew of the victim's subjective fear and took advantage of it." People v. Iniguez, 872 P.2d 1183, 1188 (Cal. 1994).

escape from the man, who is confronted and threatened by him, who summons the courage to tell him their relationship is over only to be answered by his assertion of a "right" to sex, would not fight his advances. She did not fight; she cried. It is the reaction of "sissies" in playground fights. It is the reaction of people who have already been beaten, or never had the power to fight in the first place. It is, from my reading, the most common reaction of women to rape.

To say that there is no "force" in this situation, as the North Carolina court did, is to create a gulf between power and force and to define the latter strictly in schoolboy terms. Alston did not beat his victim — at least not with his fists. He didn't have to. She had been beaten, physically and emotionally, long before. But that beating was one that the court simply refused to recognize.

[T]he "reasonable" woman under [this] view . . . is not a woman at all. [This] version of a reasonable person is one who does not scare easily, one who does not feel vulnerable, one who is not passive, one who fights back, not cries. The reasonable woman, it seems, is not a schoolboy "sissy"; she is a real man.

[Thus,] the force standard . . . ensures broad male freedom to "seduce" women who feel themselves to be powerless, vulnerable, and afraid. It effectively guarantees men freedom to intimidate women and exploit their weakness and passivity, so long as they don't "fight" with them. And it makes clear that the responsibility and blame for such seductions should be placed squarely on the woman.

Vivian Berger, Not So Simple Rape, 7 Crim. Justice Ethics 69, 75-76 (1988): I'm certain that Alston is a terrible person and that Cottie should be pitied rather than blamed. But did he *rape* her? I share the doubts of the appellate court that reversed his conviction. . . . I don't quarrel with [Estrich's] overall view that a "no" without an actual fight can turn intercourse into rape. Yet if she means, as the sentence on "beaten" people suggests, that Cottie's global "reaction" to a difficult situation, not just her tears and lack of resistance, is "common" *and* makes what occurred "rape," I find myself somewhat troubled.

. . . I worry that a *too* "understanding" attitude toward the Cotties of the world by the legal system may backfire and ultimately damage the cause of women in general. A good feminist, Estrich wants "to empower women in potentially consensual situations with the weapon of a rape charge." Well and good. But we don't want the law to patronize women; when it did, in a vast number of areas, we fought it and won significant victories. To treat as victims in a legal sense all of the female victims of life is at some point to cheapen, not celebrate, the rights to self-determination, sexual autonomy, and self- and societal respect of women. Naturally, no bright line exists to make the border separating justified use of rape law to safeguard female personhood and choice . . . from abuse of this law to "defend" women who abdicate self and will entirely. Because overprotection risks enfeebling instead of empowering women, the tension between reformist goals . . . seems to me to make cases like *Alston* a close call, not a springboard for moral outrage.

2. *Nonphysical threats.* Consider the following cases.

State v. Thompson, 792 P.2d 1103 (Mont. 1990): [Defendant, a high school principal, allegedly forced one of his students to submit to sexual intercourse by threatening to prevent her from graduating from high school. The court affirmed the dismissal of sexual assault charges.] Section 45-5-503, MCA, states the following:

> A person who knowingly has sexual intercourse without consent with a person of the opposite sex commits the offense of sexual intercourse without consent. . . .

The phrase "without consent"[,] . . . defined in §45-5-501, [means:]

> the victim is compelled to submit by force or by threat of imminent death, bodily injury, or kidnapping to be inflicted on anyone; . . .

The District Court in its order [dismissing the charges] defined force as follows:

> The word "force" is used in its ordinary and normal connotation: physical compulsion, the use or immediate threat of bodily harm, injury.

. . . [T]he State argues the District Court's definition of force is too limited. . . . [The State] contends that Thompson, in his position of authority as the principal, intimidated Jane Doe into the alleged acts. Furthermore, the State argues the fear and apprehension of Jane Doe show Thompson used force against her. We agree with the State that Thompson intimidated Jane Doe; however, we cannot stretch the definition of force to include intimidation, fear, or apprehension. Rather, we adopt the District Court's definition of force. . . .

The alleged facts, if true, show disgusting acts of taking advantage of a young person by an adult who occupied a position of authority over the young person. If we could rewrite the statutes to define the alleged acts here as sexual intercourse without consent, we would willingly do so. The business of courts, however, is to interpret statutes, not to rewrite them, nor to insert words not put there by the legislature. With a good deal of reluctance, and with strong condemnation of the alleged acts, we affirm the District Court.

Commonwealth v. Mlinarich, 498 A.2d 395 (Pa. Super. 1985), affirmed by an equally divided court, *542 A.2d 1335 (Pa. 1988):* [The victim was a 14-year-old girl who had been committed to a juvenile detention home after stealing from her brother. Subsequently defendant agreed to assume custody for her, and she was placed in defendant's home. The victim submitted to defendant's sexual advances after he threatened to send her back to the detention home if she refused his requests. He was convicted of corrupting the morals of a minor and of committing rape "by threat of forcible compulsion. . . ." 18 Pa. C.S. §3121(2). The Superior Court reversed the rape conviction:] Our task in this case is made more difficult because the victim of appellant's sexual advances was a fourteen year old child. The definition which we adopt, however, will know no age limitation. It is with a view to general application, therefore, that we attempt to define the parameters of the legislative proscription against sexual intercourse by forcible compulsion or threat of forcible compulsion.

The term "force" and its derivative, "forcible," when used to define the crime of rape, have historically been understood by the courts and legal scholars to mean physical force or violence. . . .

To define "forcible compulsion" so as to permit a conviction for rape whenever sexual intercourse is induced by "any threat" or by "physical, moral or intellectual means or by the exigencies of the circumstances" will undoubtedly have unfortunate consequences. If a man takes a destitute widow into his home and provides support for her and her family, such a definition of forcible compulsion will convict him of attempted rape if he threatens to withdraw his support and compel her to leave unless she engages in sexual intercourse. Similarly, a person may be guilty of rape if he or she extorts sexual favors from another person upon threat of discharging the other or his or her spouse from a position of employment, or upon threat of foreclosing the mortgage on the home of the other's parents, or upon threat of denying a loan application, or upon threat of disclosing the other's adultery or submission to an abortion. An interpretation of forcible compulsion which employs an ambiguous, generic definition of force will create the potential for a veritable parade of threats, express and implied, in support of accusations of rape and attempted rape. [S]uch an interpretation of forcible compulsion will place in the hands of jurors almost unlimited discretion to determine which acts, threats or promises will transform sexual intercourse into rape. Without intending to condone any of the foregoing, reprehensible acts, our use of them serves to illustrate the intolerable uncertainty which a wholly elastic definition of rape will create.

. . . We hold that rape, as defined by the legislature . . . requires actual physical compulsion or violence or a threat of physical compulsion or violence sufficient to prevent resistance by a person of reasonable resolution. . . .

[Judge Spaeth, dissenting, wrote:] It is frequently said that the words of a statute are to be "given their plain meaning," or are to be "understood according to their common and approved usage." These maxims, however, will not yield the meaning of the phrase, "threat of forcible compulsion," for "force" has more than one plain, or common and approved, meaning. Webster's Third New International Dictionary (1968) provides eleven definitions of "force," some of these being subdivided. . . .

As one considers the range and tone of these several definitions it becomes evident that appellant's threat . . . might, or might not, have been a "threat of forcible compulsion." It was *not* such a threat if "forcible" is to be considered as limited to meaning "to do violence to"; it *might* have been such a threat if "forcible" is to be construed as meaning "to constrain or compel by physical, moral, or intellectual means or by the exigencies of the circumstances," or as meaning "to press, impose, or thrust urgently, importunately, inexorably." . . .

Our problem, therefore, is not to choose *the* "plain meaning" of the phrase, "threat of forcible compulsion," but, rather, to decide *which of several* plain meanings the legislature had in mind when it used the phrase in enacting the Crimes Code. . . .

I have no hesitancy in concluding that the legislature did *not* mean force in the limited sense of "to do violence to," and *did* mean force in the more general sense of "to constrain or compel by physical, moral, or intellectual means or by the exigencies of the circumstances." Only this conclusion is consistent with the legislature's manifested agreement with the Model Penal Code that a "fresh approach" should be taken, and the focus of inquiry shifted away from the victim's consent to the actor's force.

. . . I believe that the jury was entitled to find that the complainant was compelled to submit to appellant's demands by the exigencies of her circumstances, and, further, that in submitting, she acted as a person of reasonable resolution.

3. Solutions to the problem of nonphysical threats. (*a*) Consider the following observations (Comment, Towards a Consent Standard in the Law of Rape, 43 U. Chi. L. Rev. 613, 644-645 (1976)):

> Although the force element has traditionally furthered the policy of physical protection, as well as serving an evidentiary function, . . . freedom of sexual choice rather than physical protection is the primary value served by criminalization of rape. Furthermore, a woman's decision to submit to physical force may be less agonizing than her decision to have intercourse with a person who holds economic or emotional power over her and her family. Although one can argue that a man who obtains intercourse through threats of nonphysical harm should be punished less severely than a violent rapist, the growing legal appreciation of the reality of mental injury and the power of economic duress suggests that he nonetheless should be punished. [T]he freedom of sexual choice which is to be protected by rape law can be as effectively negated by nonphysical as by physical coercion.

(*b*) Model Penal Code §213.1(2) permits a conviction for "gross sexual imposition" in cases where submission is compelled by threat of force or "by any threat that would prevent resistance by a woman of ordinary resolution." Reconsider State v. Thompson, Note 2 supra. Would the principal's threat in that case "prevent resistance by a woman of ordinary resolution"? Are the requirements for conviction under §213.1(2) too stringent?

How would MPC §213.1(2) apply in the hypothetical posed by the *Mlinarich* court: the destitute widow who submits to sexual intercourse with a man who will otherwise stop supporting her? Would the man be guilty of a crime under the MPC?

(*c*) Several states achieve a result similar to that of §213.1(2) by extending the offense of rape or sexual assault to situations in which consent is obtained by "duress" (Cal. Penal Code §261(a)(2), page 319 supra), "coercion,"[12] "extortion,"[13] or using a "position of authority."[14] Are these concepts broad enough to permit conviction in the *Thompson* case or in the case of the destitute widow? Are they *too* broad?

(*d*) In Commonwealth v. Rhodes, 510 A.2d 1217, 1225 (Pa. 1986), the court, relying on the broad dictionary meanings of force cited in the *Mlinarich* dissent, held: "[T]he phrase 'forcible compulsion' clearly connotes more than the exercise of sheer physical force or violence. . . . The phrase also connotes that act of using superior force — physical, moral, psychological, or intellectual — to compel a person to do a thing against that person's volition. . . ." In 1995, the Pennsylvania legislature, following *Rhodes*, adopted a statute defining the "forcible compulsion" required for a rape conviction as "[c]ompulsion by use of physical, intellectual, moral, emotional or psychological force, either express or implied." Pa. Stat. §3101.

Does a defendant commit rape in Pennsylvania if he uses *psychological* pressure, for example if "the victim had an adolescent crush on the Defendant and the Defendant was aware of her feelings for him" and obtained her consent by taking advantage of those feelings? See Commonwealth v. Meadows, 553 A.2d 1006, 1013 (Pa. Super. 1989) (upholding conviction on this basis). Do you agree? For discussion of *Meadows*, see Stephen J. Schulhofer, Unwanted Sex 91-93, 121-124 (1998).

12. E.g., N.J. Stat. §§2C:14-1 (j), 2 (c) (1), defining coercion to include threatening to "[a]ccuse anyone of an offense," "[e]xpose any secret which would tend to subject any person to hatred, contempt or ridicule"; or "[p]erform any other act which would not in itself substantially benefit the actor but which is calculated to substantially harm another person. . . ."

13. Del. Code, tit. 11, §776.

14. Wyo. Stat. §6-2-303(a)(vi).

4. *Problem.* How should the case of the destitute widow be decided under a standard like Pennsylvania's? In State v. Lovely, 480 A.2d 847 (N.H. 1984), the manager of a liquor store (Lovely), hired a drifter to work at the store, began paying the rent on the man's apartment, and eventually invited the man to move into Lovely's home, where they soon began a sexual relationship. When the drifter tried to break off the relationship, Lovely pressured the man to submit to further sexual acts by threatening to stop paying the man's rent, to kick him out of Lovely's home, and to get him fired from his liquor store job. The New Hampshire statute made it a felony to coerce submission to sexual penetration "by threatening to retaliate against the victim." Lovely's conviction was upheld; the court ruled that the trial judge had properly allowed the jury to consider, as impermissible retaliation, not only Lovely's threat to get the man fired but also his threats to stop paying the man's rent and to evict the man from Lovely's home.[15] Does this mean that a man who asks the destitute widow to move out of his apartment, because she is no longer willing to continue their affair, is guilty of a felony in New Hampshire or Pennsylvania? Should he be? Consider the following viewpoints.

(*a*) Schulhofer, supra Note 3(d), at 163-164:

> Sex is not a permissible condition of ordinary employment. But sexual fulfillment *is* a legitimate and valued goal of marriage and other ongoing, intimate relationships. [A wealthy man's] implicit "threat" ("I won't support you unless we have a sexual relationship") expresses one of the choices he is — and should be — entitled to make in shaping his personal relationships. And his "threat" takes from the woman nothing that she is — or should be — entitled to claim. . . .
>
> The coercion problem seems different when a man who is attracted to [a destitute] mother invites her to move into his apartment — on condition that she accept his sexual advances. Unlike [a wealthy fashion] model, the mother faces dire economic pressure that limits her freedom to refuse. The pressure may be even stronger if a man threatens to terminate a current relationship and throw the mother and her children out onto the street unless she meets his sexual needs. The mother may reasonably feel that she has no real choice but to submit to his demands.
>
> As always, however, conclusions about coercion [should] turn not on the degree of pressure but on the legitimacy of the proposal itself. When [a film] producer gives the fashion model a chance to star in a movie, on condition that she sleep with him, the pressure may be slight, but it is clearly illegitimate. When a man offers the desperate woman a chance to have food and a decent home, the pressure is intense, but it might *not* be illegitimate. We have to know whether the man's "threat" to withhold his assistance will violate the mother's rights. If . . . the relationship has been short-lived and without mutual commitments, existing laws would not obligate the man to support her.
>
> If we hope to safeguard sexual autonomy in a realistic way, we cannot ignore the impact of legal rules that leave the desperate mother vulnerable in this way. . . . An obligation of financial support could certainly be imposed upon [the man] even in the absence of marriage. . . .
>
> There are limits, however, to how far in this direction the law can sensibly develop, not just because of practical concerns but also because of the values associated with sexual autonomy itself. . . . A central component of the autonomy we now claim is the freedom to seek intimacy with persons of our own choosing and to seek sexual satisfaction as a legitimate dimension of an ongoing relationship. Equally important, in the case of relationships short of marriage or its equivalent, is the

15. Compare the narrow definition of "retaliate" in Cal. Penal Code §261(a)(6), page 319, supra.

freedom to move on — to live independently or to seek a new partner — when existing ties become a source of unacceptable emotional and sexual stress.

A legal system that obliged a man to support a former sexual partner, in the absence of the mutual commitments of a long-term relationship, would impose an enormous burden on these components of freedom. . . . Efforts to use financial leverage in personal relationships ("Do it tonight or pack your bags") surely deserve criticism under most circumstances. But they should not inevitably violate legal rights.

(*b*) Martha Chamallas, Consent, Equality, and the Legal Control of Sexual Conduct, 61 So. Cal. L. Rev. 777, 826 (1988):

The refusal to regard economically coerced sex as rape allows men to continue to use their economic superiority to gain sexual advantages, provided that they use only their own resources (not their employer's) and target only those women who show some willingness to tie sex to financial gain. From the target's standpoint, however, the economic pressure may feel the same regardless of whether it is her employer or her lover who threatens economic harm if sex is denied them.

(*c*) David P. Bryden, Redefining Rape, 3 Buffalo Crim. L. Rev. 317, 445 (2000):

Of course, men often "use their economic superiority to gain sexual advantages," but women often use their sexual superiority to gain economic advantages. So who is the extortionist?

5. For other efforts to distinguish between legitimate persuasion and illegitimate coercion, see Alan Wertheimer, Consent and Sexual Relations, 2 Legal Theory 89 (1996); Donald A. Dripps, Beyond Rape: An Essay on the Difference Between the Presence of Force and the Absence of Consent, 92 Colum. L. Rev. 1780 (1992); Robin L. West, Legitimating the Illegitimate: A Comment on *Beyond Rape,* 93 Colum. L. Rev. 1442 (1993); Lois Pineau, Date Rape: A Feminist Analysis, 8 Law & Phil. 217 (1989). See also the proposed Model Statute, §202(c), pages 364-365 infra.

NOTE ON ELIMINATING THE FORCE REQUIREMENT

Even in the absence of expressed or implied threats, the act of intercourse itself almost involves some degree of physical force. Should this kind of force meet the force requirement for a rape conviction? Why not simply eliminate the force requirement altogether? Consider the material that follows.

STATE IN THE INTEREST OF M.T.S.

New Jersey Supreme Court
129 N.J. 422, 609 A.2d 1266 (1992)

HANDLER, J. Under New Jersey law a person who commits an act of sexual penetration using physical force or coercion is guilty of second-degree sexual assault. The sexual assault statute does not define the words "physical force." The question posed by this appeal is whether the element of "physical force" is met simply by an act of non-consensual penetration involving no more force than necessary to accomplish that result.

That issue is presented in the context of what is often referred to as "acquaintance rape." The record in the case discloses that the juvenile, a seventeen-year-old boy, engaged in consensual kissing and heavy petting with a fifteen-year-old girl and thereafter engaged in actual sexual penetration of the girl to which she had not consented. There was no evidence or suggestion that the juvenile used any unusual or extra force or threats to accomplish the act of penetration.

The trial court determined that the juvenile was delinquent for committing a sexual assault. The Appellate Division reversed the disposition of delinquency, concluding that non-consensual penetration does not constitute sexual assault unless it is accompanied by some level of force more than that necessary to accomplish the penetration. We granted the State's petition for certification. . . .

[F]ifteen-year-old C.G. was living with her mother, her three siblings, and several other people, including M.T.S. and his girlfriend. . . . M.T.S., then age seventeen, was temporarily residing at the home with the permission of C.G.'s mother; he slept downstairs on a couch. C.G. had her own room on the second floor. . . . At trial, C.G. and M.T.S. offered very different accounts concerning the nature of their relationship. . . . The trial court did not credit fully either teenager's testimony.

C.G. stated that [on the day of May 21], M.T.S. had told her three or four times that he "was going to make a surprise visit up in [her] bedroom." [C.G. said she considered the comments a joke because M.T.S. frequently teased her. She testified that she had rejected all of his previous advances. C.G. testified that she awoke that night at approximately 1:30 A.M. and saw M.T.S., fully clothed, standing in her doorway. According to C.G., M.T.S. said "he was going to tease [her] a little bit." C.G. testified that she "didn't think anything of it"; she used the bathroom and returned to bed, falling into a "heavy" sleep within fifteen minutes. The next event C.G. claimed to recall was waking up with M.T.S. on top of her, her underpants and shorts removed.] She said "his penis was into [her] vagina." As soon as C.G. realized what had happened, she said, she immediately slapped M.T.S. once in the face, then "told him to get off [her], and get out." She did not scream or cry out. She testified that M.T.S. complied in less than one minute after being struck. . . .

C.G. said that after M.T.S. left the room, she "fell asleep crying." . . . She explained that she did not immediately tell her mother or anyone else in the house of the events of that morning because she was "scared and in shock." . . . By her own account, C.G. was not otherwise harmed by M.T.S.

[At about 7:00 A.M., C.G. went downstairs and told her mother about the encounter and said that they would have to "get [M.T.S.] out of the house." C.G. and her mother then filed a complaint with the police.]

According to M.T.S., he and C.G. had been good friends for a long time. [He] testified that during the three days preceding the incident they had been "kissing and necking" and had discussed having sexual intercourse. . . . He said C.G. repeatedly had encouraged him to "make a surprise visit up in her room."

M.T.S. testified that at exactly 1:15 A.M. on May 22, he entered C.G.'s bedroom as she was walking to the bathroom. He said C.G. soon returned from the bathroom, and the two began "kissing and all," eventually moving to the bed. Once they were in bed, he said, they undressed each other and . . . proceeded to engage in sexual intercourse. According to M.T.S., [he] "did it [thrust] three times, and then the fourth time . . . , that's when [she] pulled [him] off of her." M.T.S. said that as C.G. pushed him off, she said "stop, get off," and he "hopped off right away."

According to M.T.S., after about one minute, he asked C.G. what was wrong; she replied with a back-hand to his face. He recalled asking C.G. what was wrong a second time, and her replying, "how can you take advantage of me or something like that." M.T.S. said that he proceeded to get dressed and told C.G. to calm down, but that she then told him to get away from her and began to cry. Before leaving the room, he told C.G., "I'm leaving. . . . I'm going with my real girlfriend, . . . stay out of my life . . . don't tell anybody about this . . . it would just screw everything up." He then walked downstairs and went to sleep.

. . . M.T.S. was charged with conduct that if engaged in by an adult would constitute second-degree sexual assault. [T]he court concluded that the victim had consented to a session of kissing and heavy petting with M.T.S. The trial court did not find that C.G. had been sleeping at the time of penetration, but nevertheless found that she had not consented to the actual sexual act. Accordingly, the court concluded that the State had proven second-degree sexual assault beyond a reasonable doubt. On appeal, following the imposition of suspended sentences on the [sexual assault] charges,[a] the Appellate Division . . . reversed the juvenile's adjudication of delinquency for that offense.

. . . N.J.S.A. 2C:14-2c(1) defines "sexual assault" as the commission "of sexual penetration" "with another person" with the use of "physical force or coercion."[1] [B]oth the act of "sexual penetration" and the use of "physical force or coercion" are separate and distinct elements of the offense. . . .

a. In the case of an adult sexual assault offender, the New Jersey sentencing system ordinarily would not permit suspension of the minimum five-year term of imprisonment in the absence of "extraordinary and unanticipated" circumstances. See State v. Johnson, 118 N.J. 10, 570 A.2d 395, 396 (1990). — Eds.

1. The sexual assault statute, N.J.S.A.:2C:14-2c(1), reads as follows:

> c. An actor is guilty of sexual assault if he commits an act of sexual penetration with another person under any one of the following circumstances:
>
> (1) The actor *uses physical force or coercion,* but the victim does not sustain severe personal injury;
>
> (2) The victim is one whom the actor knew or should have known was physically helpless, mentally defective or mentally incapacitated;
>
> (3) The victim is on probation or parole, or is detained in a hospital, prison or other institution and the actor has supervisory or disciplinary power over the victim by virtue of the actor's legal, professional or occupational status;
>
> (4) The victim is at least 16 but less than 18 years old and:
>
> (a) The actor is related to the victim by blood or affinity to the third degree; or
>
> (b) The actor has supervisory or disciplinary power over the victim; or
>
> (c) The actor is a foster parent, a guardian, or stands in loco parentis within the household;
>
> (5) The victim is at least 13 but less than 16 years old and the actor is at least 4 years older than the victim.
>
> Sexual assault is a crime of the second degree [punishable by a minimum of 5 and a maximum of 10 years' imprisonment.]
>
> [When committed with a weapon or when "severe personal injury" is sustained, the offense is aggravated sexual assault, a crime of the first degree, punishable by a minimum of 10 and a maximum of 20 years' imprisonment. — Eds.]

The parties offer two alternative understandings of the concept of "physical force" as it is used in the statute. The State would read "physical force" to entail any amount of sexual touching brought about involuntarily. A showing of sexual penetration coupled with a lack of consent would satisfy the elements of the statute. The Public Defender urges an interpretation of "physical force" to mean force "used to overcome lack of consent." That definition equates force with violence and leads to the conclusion that sexual assault requires the application of some amount of force in addition to the act of penetration. . . .

Under traditional rape law, in order to prove that a rape had occurred, the State had to show both that force had been used and that the penetration had been against the woman's will. [A] woman who was above the age of consent had actively and affirmatively to withdraw that consent for the intercourse to be against her will. . . .

The judicial interpretation of the pre-reform rape law in New Jersey, with its insistence on resistance by the victim, greatly minimized the importance of the forcible and assaultive aspect of the defendant's conduct. . . . Critics of rape law agreed that the focus of the crime should be shifted from the victim's behavior to the defendant's conduct, and particularly to its forceful and assaultive, rather than sexual, character. [T]he reform goal was not so much to purge the entire concept of consent from the law as to eliminate the burden that had been placed on victims to prove they had not consented.

Similarly, [t]raditional interpretations of force were strongly criticized for failing to acknowledge that force may be understood simply as the invasion of "bodily integrity." Susan Estrich, Rape, 95 Yale L.J. 1087, 1105 (1986). In urging that the "resistance" requirement be abandoned, reformers sought to break the connection between force and resistance. . . .

[The] Model Penal Code (MPC) proposed provisions did not present a break from traditional rape law. They would have established two principal sexual offenses: aggravated rape . . . and [gross sexual imposition], defined as sexual intercourse . . . to which [the female] was compelled to submit by any threat that would prevent resistance by a woman of ordinary resolution. The comments to the MPC . . . state that "[c]ompulsion plainly implies non-consent," and that the words "compels to submit" require more than "a token initial resistance." A.L.I., MPC, §213.1, comments at 306 (revised commentary 1980).

The Legislature did not endorse the Model Penal Code approach to rape. Rather, it passed a fundamentally different proposal in 1978. . . . The new statutory provisions covering rape were formulated by a coalition of feminist groups assisted by the National Organization of Women (NOW) National Task Force on Rape. The stated intent of the drafters . . . had been to remove all features found to be contrary to the interests of rape victims. . . .

The reform statute defines sexual assault as penetration accomplished by the use of "physical force" or "coercion," but it does not define either "physical force" or "coercion." . . . The task of defining "physical force" therefore was left to the courts. . . .

The Legislature's concept of sexual assault and the role of force was significantly colored by its understanding of the law of assault and battery. . . . Any "unauthorized touching of another [is] a battery." Perna v. Pirozzi, 92 N.J. 446, 462, 457 A.2d 431 (1983). . . . Sexual contact is criminal under the same circumstances that render an act of sexual penetration a sexual assault, namely, when "physical force" or "coercion" demonstrates that it is unauthorized and offensive. N.J.S.A. 2C:14-3(b). Thus, just as any unauthorized touching is a crime under traditional laws of assault and battery, so is any unauthorized sexual contact a crime under the reformed law of criminal sexual contact, and so is any unauthorized sexual penetration a crime under the reformed law of sexual assault. . . . Under the new law, the victim no longer is required to resist and therefore need not have said or done anything in order for the sexual penetration to be unlawful. . . . [A]n interpretation of the statutory crime of sexual assault to require physical force in addition to that entailed in an act of involuntary or unwanted sexual penetration would be fundamentally inconsistent with the legislative purpose to eliminate any consideration of whether the victim resisted or expressed non-consent.

We note that the contrary interpretation of force — that the element of force need be extrinsic to the sexual act — would not only reintroduce a resistance requirement into the sexual assault law, but also would immunize many acts of criminal sexual contact short of penetration. . . . An actor is guilty of criminal sexual contact if he or she commits an act of sexual contact with another using "physical force" or "coercion." N.J.S.A. 2C:14-3(b). That the Legislature would have wanted to decriminalize unauthorized sexual intrusions on the bodily integrity of a victim by requiring a showing of force in addition to that entailed in the sexual contact itself is hardly possible.

. . . We conclude, therefore, that any act of sexual penetration engaged in by the defendant without the affirmative and freely-given permission of the victim to the specific act of penetration constitutes the offense of sexual assault. . . . The definition of "physical force" is satisfied under N.J.S.A. 2C:14-2c(1) if the defendant applies any amount of force against another person in the absence of what a reasonable person would believe to be affirmative and freely-given permission to the act of sexual penetration. . . . Although it is possible to imagine a set of rules in which persons must demonstrate affirmatively that sexual contact is unwanted or not permitted, such a regime would be inconsistent with modern principles of personal autonomy. The Legislature recast the law of rape as sexual assault to bring that area of law in line with the expectation of privacy and bodily control that long has characterized most of our private and public law. . . . Each person has the right not only to decide whether to engage in sexual contact with another, but also to control the circumstances and character of that contact. No one, neither a spouse, nor a friend, nor an acquaintance, nor a stranger, has the right or the privilege to force sexual contact.

[P]ermission to the specific act of sexual penetration . . . can be indicated either through words or through actions that, when viewed in the light of all the surrounding circumstances, would demonstrate to a reasonable person affirmative and freely-given authorization for the specific act of sexual penetration. [T]he law places no burden on the alleged victim to have expressed non-consent or to have denied permission, and no inquiry is made into what he or she thought or desired or why he or she did not resist or protest. . . . Under the reformed statute, a person's failure to protest or resist cannot be considered or used as justification for bodily invasion.

We acknowledge that cases such as this are inherently fact sensitive and depend on the reasoned judgment and common sense of judges and juries. The trial court concluded that the victim had not expressed consent to the act of intercourse, either through her words or actions. We conclude that the record provides reasonable support for the trial court's disposition. Accordingly, we reverse the judgment of the Appellate Division and reinstate the disposition of juvenile delinquency for the commission of second-degree sexual assault.

NOTES

1. Policy Concerns. Are there good reasons to require "extrinsic" force as a prerequisite to a criminal conviction? Is extrinsic force important in order to mark a bright line between rape and permissible seduction, or to corroborate other indications that the victim didn't consent and that the defendant had a culpable mens rea? For appraisal of these arguments, see David P. Bryden, Redefining Rape, 3 Buff. Crim. L. Rev. 317, 373-387 (2000).

2. Statutory reform. Although force or threat of force is a prerequisite to conviction in most jurisdictions, several states have made nonconsensual intercourse criminal in the absence of any force or threat.[16]

(*a*) Under Wis. Stat. §940.225 (pages 321-322 supra), first-degree and second-degree sexual assault include intercourse without consent by "use or threat of force or violence." Third-degree sexual assault is defined as "sexual intercourse with a person without the consent of that person," and consent is defined as "words or actions by a person who is competent to give informed consent indicating a freely given agreement to have sexual intercourse." The third-degree offense is punishable by up to five years' imprisonment.

(*b*) In Florida, nonconsensual penetration committed by a threat of force likely to cause serious injury is a first-degree felony punishable by up to 30 years' imprisonment. Nonconsensual penetration committed without using such force is a second-degree felony, punishable by up to fifteen years' imprisonment.[17] The preamble to the statute, enacted in 1992 (Fla. Ch. 92-135), states that conviction of the second-degree felony does not "require any force or violence beyond the force and violence that is inherent in the accomplishment of 'penetration.'"

(*c*) *Questions.* Do the Wisconsin and Florida statutes provide a satisfactory framework for resolving cases like *M.T.S.*? How do these statutes differ, in practice, from New Jersey's sexual assault statute, as interpreted in *M.T.S.*?

3. What is nonconsent? In states that have eliminated the force requirement, intercourse is criminal whenever consent is absent. But what circumstances establish an absence of consent? Traditionally, nonconsent could be proved only by physical resistance; verbal protests were considered insufficient because "a woman may desire sexual intercourse, [but] it is customary for her to say 'no, no, no' (although meaning 'yes, yes, yes') and to expect the male to be the aggressor. . . . It is always difficult in rape cases to determine whether the female really meant 'no.'"[18] This view has few defenders today. But if physical resistance is not

16. In addition to the Wisconsin and Florida examples discussed in text, see, e.g., Haw. Rev. Stat. §§707-700, 731, 732; Mo. Stat. Ann. §566.010; N.H. Rev. Stat. §632-A(2)(I)(m); Tenn. Code Ann. §39-13-503(a); Wash. Crim. Code §9A.44.060.

17. Fla. Stat. §794.011 (4) (b), (5). The statute states (§794.011 (1) (a)): "'Consent' means intelligent, knowing, and voluntary consent and does not include coerced submission."

18. Ralph Slovenko, A Panoramic View, in Sexual Behavior and the Law 5, 51 (R. Slovenko, ed. 1965).

necessary to signal nonconsent, what should the prosecution have to prove? Possible conceptions of nonconsent might include:

(1) verbal resistance (saying "no") *plus* other behavior that makes unwillingness clear (a totality of circumstances approach);
(2) verbal resistance alone ("no" always means no);
(3) verbal resistance *or* passivity, silence or ambivalence (anything other than affirmative permission by words or conduct); or
(4) the absence of verbal permission (not saying "yes").

The Wisconsin statute, Note 2(a) supra, and the *M.T.S.* court clearly opt for the third approach; only affirmative permission (by words or conduct) can count as consent. Should the law now be prepared to go further? Should it require explicit verbal permission ("the clearest and most unambiguous form of consent"),[19] in order to protect women from men whose wishful thinking leads them to misinterpret "body language"?

Alternatively, does the Wisconsin-*M.T.S.* approach already go too far? If a woman doesn't say no, does it make sense to treat her silence or failure to object as proof of *un*willingness? Does it violate contemporary mores, or patronize women, to treat intercourse as a felony when a woman *did not* say "no"? Compare People v. Warren, page 331, Note 3 supra ("Complainant's failure to resist when it was within her power to do so . . . amounts to consent"); Neb. Rev. Stat. §28-318(8) (1995): "Without consent means . . . the victim expressed a lack of consent through words [or conduct]. . . . The victim need only resist, either verbally or physically, so as to make the victim's refusal to consent genuine and real. . . ." Is this approach more realistic? Consider these views on the issue:

Douglas N. Husak & George C. Thomas III, Date Rape, Social Convention and Reasonable Mistakes, 11 Law & Phil. 95, 113-123 (1992): Consider the familiar claim that "no means no." [Presumably,] this claim is about the social conventions by which nonconsent is expressed. That is, when a woman says the word "no," she intends to express her lack of consent. . . . Yet those who repeat this phrase seldom provide any empirical support for it. [T]his common-sense notion turns out to be empirically questionable. [M]ost of the women in the Perper and Weis study described what the researchers called an "incomplete rejection" strategy . . . for example, permitting the man to hug and kiss her but not responding "in a really warm way."

[S]urely (common sense suggests that) under normal circumstances a woman who is faced with imminent sexual intercourse against her will should have no difficulty delivering an explicit, unambiguous "no." If so, virtually all incomplete rejection strategies would eventually escalate into blunt, explicit rejections. . . . Again, however, reality is more complex than ideology. . . . *F* [a woman] may escalate her incomplete rejection strategy but stop short of saying "no" or physically resisting. [This scenario] presents a series of problems that are too complex to permit a generalized judgment. . . . A single physical rejection (for example, *F* removes *M*'s hand from her leg) following hours of intense foreplay obviously

19. Lani Anne Remick, Comment, The Consent Standard in Rape, 141 U. Pa. L. Rev. 1103, 1133, 1137 (1993).

presents a very different picture of nonconsent than repeated physical and verbal rejections, delivered in an emotional and frightened manner. At some point along this spectrum, it is no longer reasonable for *M* to think that *F* has consented. The reason . . . is not that the word "no" has a magic, transcendental quality. Rather, [t]he social convention is that a certain pattern of linguistic and nonlinguistic behavior could not reasonably be understood to mean anything other than no.

Vivian Berger, Rape Law Reform at the Millennium, 3 Buff. Crim. L. Rev. 513, 522 (2000): [Professor Berger argues that a verbal "no" should suffice to establish nonconsent. But, she continues,] the jury has to believe that she *did* say "no.". . . Women should not be *over*protected. . . . [A] global portrayal, reflected in rape law, of females as weak, subordinate creatures, incapable of withstanding pressure of any sort, invites nullification and backlash and, on a philosophical level, cheapens rather than celebrates "the rights to self determination, sexual autonomy, and self- and societal respect of women."

Stephen J. Schulhofer, Taking Sexual Autonomy Seriously, 11 Law & Phil. 35, 74-75 (1992): Consider this parable. A hospitalized athlete, suffering from chronic knee problems, consults a surgeon, who recommends an operation. The athlete is not sure. If the operation is successful, he will enjoy a long, fulfilling career with his team. But there are imponderables. The operation carries a risk of a burdensome infection that can be hard to cure. The procedure may not produce the expected benefits. In any event, it is sure to be stressful in the short run. The athlete hesitates. There are clear advantages, clear disadvantages, and lots of uncertainties. What to do? Maybe he should postpone this big step for a while, see how things go without it. The surgeon is encouraging: "Try it. You'll like it." Still the athlete is unsure.

Now our surgeon becomes impatient. He has spent a lot of time with this case. The athlete's hesitation is becoming tiresome and annoying. So the surgeon signals an anesthesiologist to ready the drugs that will flow through an intravenous tube already in place. One last time the surgeon (a sensitive, modern male) reminds the athlete, "You don't have to go ahead with this. If you really want me to stop, just say so." But the athlete, his brain still clouded with doubts, fears, hopes, and uncertainties, says nothing. So the surgeon starts the anesthesia and just *does it.*

Consent? Of course not. But why not? The athlete was not compelled to submit. Nobody forced him. . . . Surely his silence proves that he was not unwilling. If he really objected, all he had to do was say so!

There are, to be sure, important contextual differences between surgery and sexual intimacy. But even allowing for those differences, it would not be implausible to find "consent" by the patient, provided we could get ourselves to think of illegal surgery as an offense requiring "forcible compulsion," and to think of "nonconsent" in this context as revulsion, aversion, or a clearly crystallized negative attitude.

We do not see matters this way because we are not thinking about a crime of violence. We are thinking about an offense against the patient's autonomy. . . . Nonconsent is simply anything that is not positive consent, anything that is not an affirmative, crystallized expression of willingness. To treat the athlete as a victim is not, of course, to patronize him. It is merely to recognize an obvious violation of the physical autonomy of his person.[a]

4. The meaning of affirmative consent. What constitutes "freely-given permission" within the meaning of *M.T.S.* or "voluntary consent" within the meaning of the Florida statute? (*a*) Suppose that a woman sleeps with her supervisor because he tells her he will help her get a promotion. Is this a case of voluntary consent or a case of criminal sexual assault? (*b*) Should the result be different if she sleeps with him because he promises, in return for sex, not to veto her promotion? (*c*) Recall the example of the destitute widow who submits to sexual intercourse with a man who will otherwise refuse to continue supporting her. In New Jersey and Florida is that a case of voluntary consent or a case of criminal sexual assault?

2. *Deception*

PEOPLE v. EVANS

Supreme Court, New York County, Trial Term
85 Misc. 2d 1088, 379 N.Y.S. 2d 912 (1975)

GREENFIELD, J. The question presented in this case is whether the sexual conquest by a predatory male of a resisting female constitutes rape or seduction. . . .

Since a jury has been waived, this Court is called upon to scrutinize the conduct involved and to draw the line between the legally permissible and the impermissible. . . .

[B]ased upon the testimony in this case, the Court first makes the following findings of fact:

The defendant, a bachelor of approximately thirty-seven years of age, aptly described in the testimony as "glib," on July 15, 1974, met an incoming plane at LaGuardia Airport, from which disembarked L.E.P., of Charlotte, North Carolina, a twenty-year-old petite, attractive second-year student at Wellesley College, an unworldly girl, evidently unacquainted with New York City and the sophisticated city ways, a girl who proved to be, as indicated by the testimony, incredibly gullible, trusting and naive. [The] defendant struck up a conversation with her, posing as a psychologist doing a magazine article and using a name that was not his, inducing Miss P. to answer questions for an interview.

The evidence further shows that the defendant invited Miss P. to accompany him by automobile to Manhattan, her destination being Grand Central Station. [Then the] defendant and a girl named Bridget took Miss P. to an establishment called Maxwell's Plum, which the defendant explained was for the purpose of conducting a sociological experiment in which he would observe her reactions and the reactions of males towards her in the setting of a singles bar. After several hours there, . . . she was induced to come up to an apartment . . . which the defendant explained was used as one of his five offices or apartments throughout the city. . . .

a. For criticism of the suggested parallels between consent to surgery and consent to sex, see David P. Bryden, Redefining Rape, 3 Buff. Crim. L. Rev. 317, 402-407 (2000). — EDS.

She had been there for one to two hours when the defendant made his move and pulled her on to the opened sofa-bed in the living room of that apartment and attempted to disrobe her. She resisted that . . . and ultimately she was able to ward off these advances and to get herself dressed again. At that point, the defendant's tactics, according to her testimony, appeared to have changed.

First, he informed her of his disappointment that she had failed the test, that this was all part of his psychological experiment, that, in fact, this was a way in which he was trying to reach her innermost consciousness. [Then,] he took steps to cause doubt and fear to arise in the mind of Miss P. He said, "Look where you are. You are in the apartment of a strange man. How do you know that I am really who I say I am? How do you know that I am really a psychologist?" Then, he went on and said, "I could kill you. I could rape you. I could hurt you physically."

Miss P. testified that at that point she became extremely frightened, that she realized, indeed, how vulnerable she was. . . . Then there was . . . an abrupt switch in which the defendant attempted to play on the sympathy of Miss P. by telling her a story about his lost love, how Miss P. had reminded him of her, and the hurt that he had sustained when she had driven her car off a cliff. Obviously, Miss P.'s sympathy was engaged, and at that time acting instinctively, she took a step forward and reached out for him and put her hand on his shoulders, and then he grabbed her and said, "You're mine, you are mine." There thereupon followed an act of sexual intercourse, an act of oral-genital contact; a half-hour later a second act of sexual intercourse, and then, before she left, about seven o'clock that morning, an additional act. . . .

The testimony indicates that during these various sexual acts Miss P., in fact, offered little resistance. She said that she was pinned down by the defendant's body weight, but in some manner all her clothing was removed, all his clothing was removed, and the acts took place. There was no torn clothing, there were no scratches, there were no bruises. Finally, at approximately seven A.M. Miss P. dressed and left the apartment. . . .

The question is whether having had sexual intercourse by the . . . means described constitutes rape in the first degree. The essential element of rape in the first degree is forcible compulsion. The prevailing view in this country is that there can be no rape which is achieved by fraud, or trick, or stratagem. Provided there is actual consent, the nature of the act being understood, it is not rape, absent a statute, no matter how despicable the fraud, even if a woman has intercourse with a man impersonating her husband or if a fraudulent ceremony leads her to believe she is legally married to a man (contra if an explicit statute to that effect exists) or even if a doctor persuades her that sexual intercourse is necessary for her treatment and return to good health. . . .

It should be noted that seduction, while not considered to be a criminal act at common law, has been made a criminal offense by statute in some jurisdictions. In seduction, unlike rape, the consent of the woman, implied or explicit, has been procured, by artifice, deception, flattery, fraud or promise. The declared public policy of this state looks with disfavor on actions for seduction since the civil action was abolished more than forty years ago[;] there are no presently existing penal sanctions against seduction. The law recognizes that there are some crimes where trickery and deceit do constitute the basis for a criminal charge. Since the common law, we have recognized the existence of larceny by trick. But of course, for a larceny there has to be a taking of property of value. I do not mean to imply that a woman's right to her body is not a thing of value, but it is not property in the sense which is defined by the law.

It is clear from the evidence in this case that . . . P. was intimidated; that she was confused; that she had been drowned in a torrent of words and perhaps was terrified. But it is likewise clear from the evidence that the defendant did not resort to actual physical force. . . .

So the question here is . . . whether threats uttered by the defendant had paralyzed her capacity to resist and had, in fact, undermined her will. . . . He said, ". . . I could kill you. I could rape you. I could hurt you physically." Those words, as uttered, are susceptible to two possible and diverse interpretations. The first would be in essence that — you had better do what I say, for you are helpless and I have the power to use ultimate force should you resist. That clearly would be a threat which would induce fear and overcome resistance. The second possible meaning of those words is, in effect, that — you are a foolish girl. You are in the apartment of a strange man. You put yourself in the hands of a stranger, and you are vulnerable and defenseless. The possibility would exist of physical harm to you were you being confronted by someone other than the person who uttered this statement.

Of course, it is entirely possible that Miss P., who heard the statements, construed that as a threat, even though it may not have been intended as such by the person who uttered those words. The question arises as to which is the controlling state of mind — that of a person who hears the words and interprets them as a threat, or the state of mind of the person who utters such words. It appears to the Court that the controlling state of mind must be that of the speaker. [T]his being a criminal trial, it is basic that the criminal intent of the defendant must be shown beyond a reasonable doubt. . . . And so, if he utters words which are taken as a threat by the person who hears them, but are not intended as a threat by the person who utters them, there would be no basis for finding the necessary criminal intent to establish culpability under the law. . . . Since the Court, therefore, can find neither forcible compulsion nor threat beyond a reasonable doubt, the defendant is found not guilty on the charges of rape, sodomy and unlawful imprisonment.

Now, acquittal on these charges does not imply that the Court condones the conduct of the defendant. The testimony in the case reveals that the defendant was a predator, and that naive and gullible girls like . . . P. were his natural prey. He posed. He lied. He pretended and he deceived. He used confidences which were innocently bestowed as leverage to effect his will. He used psychological techniques to achieve vulnerability and sympathy, and the erosion of resistance. A young and inexperienced girl like . . . P. was then unable to withstand the practiced onslaught of the defendant. . . . The Court finds his conduct, if not criminal, to be reprehensible. [Nevertheless,] the Court must conclude that the defendant's conduct towards Miss P. cannot be adjudged criminal so as to subject him to the penalty of imprisonment for up to twenty-five years. . . .

BORO v. SUPERIOR COURT, 163 Cal. App. 3d 1224, 210 Cal. Rptr. 122 (1985): Ms. R., the rape victim, . . . received a telephone call from a person who identified himself as "Dr. Stevens" and said that he worked at Peninsula Hospital.

"Dr. Stevens" told Ms. R. that he had the results of her blood test and that she had contracted a dangerous, highly infectious and perhaps fatal disease. . . .

"Dr. Stevens" further explained that there were only two ways to treat the disease. The first was a painful surgical procedure — graphically described — costing $9,000, and requiring her uninsured hospitalization for six weeks. A second alternative, "Dr. Stevens" explained, was to have sexual intercourse with an anonymous donor who had been injected with a serum which would cure the disease. The latter, nonsurgical procedure would only cost $4,500. When the victim replied that she lacked sufficient funds the "doctor" suggested that $1,000 would suffice as a down payment. The victim thereupon agreed to the nonsurgical alternative and consented to intercourse with the mysterious donor, believing "it was the only choice I had."

. . . Ms. R. . . . went to her bank, withdrew $1,000 and, as instructed, checked into [a] hotel. . . . About a half hour later the defendant "donor" arrived at her room [and] had sexual intercourse with her. At the time of penetration, it was Ms. R.'s belief that she would die unless she consented to sexual intercourse with the defendant: as she testified, "My life felt threatened, and for that reason and that reason alone did I do it."

[Defendant was charged with rape "accomplished by means of force or fear of immediate and unlawful bodily injury," Penal Code §261(2), and with rape "[w]here a person is at the time unconscious of the nature of the act and this is known to the accused," Penal Code §261(4). Conviction of either charge would carry a penalty of three, six, or eight years in prison. A pretrial motion to dismiss the former charge was granted by the lower court. Defendant challenged the lower court's failure to set aside the latter charge.[a]]

The People's position is [that] "at the time of the intercourse Ms. R., the victim, was 'unconscious of the nature of the act': because of [petitioner's] misrepresentation she believed it was in the nature of a medical treatment and not a simple, ordinary act of sexual intercourse." Petitioner, on the other hand, stresses that the victim was plainly aware of the *nature* of the act in which she voluntarily engaged, so that her motivation in doing so (since it did not fall within the proscription of section 261, subdivision (2)) is irrelevant.

[A]s a leading authority has written, "if deception causes a misunderstanding as to the fact itself (fraud in the factum) there is no legally-recognized consent because what happened is not that for which consent was given; whereas consent induced by fraud is as effective as any other consent, so far as direct and immediate legal consequences are concerned, if the deception relates not to the thing done but merely to some collateral matter (fraud in the inducement)." (Perkins & Boyce, Criminal Law (3d ed. 1982) p. 1079.) . . .

Another relatively common situation in the literature on this subject — discussed in detail by Perkins[,] is the fraudulent obtaining of intercourse by impersonating a spouse. . . . Some courts have taken the position that such a misdeed is fraud in the inducement on the theory that the woman consents to exactly what is done (sexual intercourse) and hence there is no rape; other courts, with better reason it would seem, hold such a misdeed to be rape on the theory that it involves fraud in the factum since the woman's consent is to an innocent act of marital intercourse while what is actually perpetrated upon her is an act of adultery. . . .

In California, of course, we have by statute adopted the majority view that such

a. The defendant was also charged with attempted grand theft and burglary (entry into the hotel room with intent to commit theft). These charges were not challenged on appeal. A fifth charge was dismissed with the consent of the prosecution. — Eds.

fraud is in the factum, not the inducement, and have thus held it to vitiate consent. [See Cal. Penal Code §261(a)(5), page 319, supra.]

[T]he Legislature well understood how to draft a statute to encompass fraud in the factum (§261, subd. (5)) and how to specify certain fraud in the inducement as vitiating consent.[4] [A] concurring opinion in Mathews [v. Superior Court, 119 Cal. App. 3d 309 (1981),] specifically decried the lack of a California statutory prohibition against fraudulently induced consent to sexual relations in circumstances other than those specified in section 261, subdivision (5) and then-section 268.

The People, however, direct our attention to Penal Code section 261.6, which in their opinion has changed the rule that fraud in the inducement does not vitiate consent. That provision reads as follows: "In prosecutions under sections 261, 286, 288a or 289, in which consent is at issue, 'consent' shall be defined to mean positive cooperation in act or attitude pursuant to an act of free will. The person must act freely and voluntarily and have knowledge of the nature of the act or transaction involved."

We find little legislative history for this section. . . . If the Legislature at that time had desired to correct the apparent oversight decried in *Mathews,* supra,[5] — it could certainly have done so. But the Attorney General's strained reading of section 261.6 would render section 261, subdivision (5) meaningless surplusage; and we are "exceedingly reluctant to attach an interpretation to a particular statute which renders other existing provisions unnecessary." . . .

To so conclude is not to vitiate the heartless cruelty of petitioner's scheme, but to say that it comprised crimes of a different order than a violation of section 261, subdivision (4).

Let a peremptory writ of prohibition issue. . . .

HOLMDAHL, J. . . . The case before us concerns a prosecution under section 261, subd. (4), and "consent is at issue." Consequently, section 261.6, defining "consent" applies in this case.[2] It is apparent from the abundance of appropriate adjectives and adverbs in the statute that the Legislature intended to the point of redundancy to limit "consent" to that which is found to have been truly free and voluntary, truly unrestricted and knowledgeable. . . . Recourse to the Oxford English Dictionary (1978) indicates that . . . "[v]oluntarily" is defined as "[o]f one's own free will or accord; without compulsion, constraint, or undue influence by others; freely, willingly. . . ." [W]hile the Legislature in section 261.6 did not expressly repeal the legalisms distinguishing "fraud in the factum" and "fraud in the inducement," its intention certainly was to restrict "consent" to cases of true, good faith consent, obtained without substantial fraud or deceit.

I believe there is a sufficient basis for prosecution of petitioner pursuant to section 261, subd. (4). . . .

4. Prior to its repeal [in] 1984, section 268 provided that: "Every person who, under promise of marriage, seduces and has sexual intercourse with an unmarried female of previous chaste character, is punishable by imprisonment in the state prison, or by a fine of not more than five thousand dollars [$5,000], or by both such fine and imprisonment."

5. It is not difficult to conceive of reasons why the Legislature may have consciously wished to leave the matter where it lies. Thus, as a matter of degree, where consent to intercourse is obtained by promises of travel, fame, celebrity and the like — ought the liar and seducer to be chargeable as a rapist? Where is the line to be drawn?

2. While the word "consent" appears only in section 261, subd. (1), all the subdivisions concern the victim's state of mind.

NOTES ON DECEPTION

1. In apparent response to the result in *Boro,* the California legislature enacted the following new provision (Penal Code §266c):

> Every person who induces any other person to engage in sexual intercourse, . . . when his or her consent is procured by false or fraudulent representation or pretense that is made with the intent to create fear, and which does induce fear, and that would cause a reasonable person in like circumstances to act contrary to the person's free will, and does cause the victim to so act, is punishable by imprisonment in either the county jail for not more than one year or in the state prison for two, three, or four years.
>
> As used in this section, "fear" means the fear of physical injury or death to the person or to any relative of the person or member of the person's family.

Question: Why did the legislature adopt such a narrow view of the circumstances under which it should be criminal to obtain consent to intercourse by misrepresentation?

2. How should *Evans* and *Boro* be decided under the *M.T.S.* standard, which permits a conviction for sexual assault any time there is intercourse in the absence of "affirmative and freely-given permission"? Should use of any deceptive inducement suffice to make the actor guilty of rape?

3. A person who knowingly uses false material representations to obtain tangible personal property is universally held guilty of a criminal offense, usually either theft or fraud. See, e.g., Model Penal Code §223.3, Appendix. Similarly, such a person would be universally held liable for damages in a civil suit. Yet there is generally neither civil nor criminal liability when the false representations are used to obtain sex. Why the distinction? For a detailed argument in favor of reinvigorating tort liability in such cases, see Jane E. Larson, "Women Understand So Little, They Call My Good Nature 'Deceit'": A Feminist Rethinking of Seduction, 93 Colum. L. Rev. 374 (1993). For a more skeptical view, see Martha Chamallas, Consent, Equality, and the Legal Control of Sexual Conduct, 61 S. Cal. L. Rev. 777, 834-835 (1988). A discussion of criminal liability in these situations appears in Stephen J. Schulhofer, Unwanted Sex 152-159 (1998); Patricia J. Falk, Rape by Fraud and Rape by Coercion, 64 Brook. L. Rev. 39 (1998).

D. MENS REA

COMMONWEALTH v. SHERRY

Supreme Judicial Court of Massachusetts
386 Mass. 682, 437 N.E. 2d 224 (1982)

[Three co-defendants were charged with rape and kidnapping. The jury acquitted on the kidnapping charge and convicted of rape. Each defendant was sentenced to a prison term of not less than three nor more than five years. The judge stipulated that only the first six months of the sentence was to be served, with the balance of the sentence suspended. Defendants appealed.]

Liacos, J. . . . The victim, a registered nurse, and the defendants, all doctors, were employed at the same hospital in Boston. The defendant Sherry, whom the victim knew professionally, with another doctor was a host at a party in Boston for some of the hospital staff on the evening of September 5, 1980. The victim was not acquainted with the defendants Hussain and Lefkowitz prior to this evening.

According to the victim's testimony, she had a conversation with Hussain at the party, during which he made sexual advances toward her. Later in the evening, Hussain and Sherry pushed her and Lefkowitz into a bathroom together, shut the door, and turned off the light. They did not open the door until Lefkowitz asked them to leave her in peace. At various times, the victim had danced with both Hussain and Sherry.

Some time later, as the victim was walking from one room to the next, Hussain and Sherry grabbed her by the arms and pulled her out of the apartment as Lefkowitz said, "We're going to go up to Rockport." The victim verbally protested but did not physically resist the men because she said she thought that they were just "horsing around" and that they would eventually leave her alone.[3] She further testified that once outside, Hussain carried her over his shoulder to Sherry's car and held her in the front seat as the four drove to Rockport. En route, she engaged in superficial conversation with the defendants. She testified that she was not in fear at this time. When they arrived at Lefkowitz's home in Rockport, she asked to be taken home. Instead, Hussain carried her into the house.

Once in the house, the victim and two of the men smoked some marihuana, and all of them toured the house. Lefkowitz invited them into a bedroom to view an antique bureau, and, once inside, the three men began to disrobe. The victim was frightened. She verbally protested, but the three men proceeded to undress her and . . . attempted intercourse. She told them to stop.[a] At the suggestion of one of the defendants, two of the defendants left the room temporarily. Each defendant separately had intercourse with the victim in the bedroom. The victim testified that she felt physically numbed and could not fight; she felt humiliated and disgusted. After this sequence of events, the victim claimed that she was further sexually harassed and forced to take a bath.

Some time later, Lefkowitz told the victim that they were returning to Boston because Hussain was on call at the hospital. On their way back, the group stopped to view a beach, to eat breakfast, and to get gasoline. The victim was taken back to where she had left her car the prior evening, and she then drove herself to an apartment that she was sharing with another woman.

The defendants testified to a similar sequence of events, although the details of the episode varied significantly. According to their testimony, Lefkowitz invited Sherry to accompany him from the party to a home that his parents owned in Rockport. The victim was present when this invitation was extended and inquired as to whether she could go along. As the three were leaving, Sherry extended an invitation to Hussain. At no time on the way out of the apartment, in

3. The victim testified that she was not physically restrained as they rode down an elevator with an unknown fifth person, or as they walked through the lobby of the apartment building where other persons were present.

a. The victim testified that when she asked the defendants why they were behaving in this manner, one of them replied, "Stop playing games." — Eds.

the elevator, lobby, or parking lot did the victim indicate her unwillingness to accompany the defendants.

Upon arrival in Rockport, the victim wandered into the bedroom where she inquired about the antique bureau. She sat down on the bed and kicked off her shoes, whereupon Sherry entered the room, dressed only in his underwear. Sherry helped the victim get undressed, and she proceeded to have intercourse with all three men separately and in turn. Each defendant testified that the victim consented to the acts of intercourse. . . .

The evidence was sufficient to permit the jury to find that the defendants had sexual intercourse with the victim by force and against her will. The victim is not required to use physical force to resist; any resistance is enough when it demonstrates that her lack of consent is "honest and real." The jury could well consider the entire sequence of events and acts of all three defendants as it affected the victim's ability to resist. . . .

The defendants . . . contend that because the judge failed to give two instructions exactly as requested, the judge's jury charge, considered as a whole, was inadequate and the cause of prejudicial error. The requested instructions in their entirety are set out in the margin.[8] . . .

[The trial judge refused to give the requested instructions. He stated that the jury "should look at the acts of the defendants, [the victim's] responses to [those] acts, whatever words were used, examining the entire atmosphere, and not look at [the case] from the point of view of the defendant's perceptions. . . . I don't think that's the law."]

To the extent the defendants, at least as to the first requested instruction, appear to have been seeking to raise a defense of good faith mistake on the issue of consent, the defendants' requested instruction would have required the jury to "find beyond a reasonable doubt that the accused had *actual knowledge* of [the victim's] lack of consent" (emphasis added). The defendants, on appeal, argue that mistake of fact negating criminal intent is a defense to the crime of rape. The defense of mistake of fact, however, requires that the accused act in good faith and with reasonableness. Whether a reasonable good faith mistake of fact as to the fact of consent is a defense to the crime of rape has never, to our knowledge, been decided in this Commonwealth. We need not reach the issue whether a reasonable and honest mistake to the fact of consent would be a defense, for even if we assume it to be so, the defendants did not request a jury instruction based on a reasonable good faith mistake of fact. We are aware of no American court of last resort that recognizes mistake of fact, without consideration of its reasonableness[,] as a defense; nor do the defendants cite such authority. There was no error.

[In a companion case arising out of the same facts,[b] Justice Brown of the Ap-

8. "Unless you find beyond a reasonable doubt that [the victim] clearly expressed her lack of consent, or was so overcome by force or threats of bodily injury that she was incapable of consenting, and unless you find beyond a reasonable doubt that the accused had actual knowledge of [the victim's] lack of consent, then you must find them not guilty."

"If you find that [the victim] had a reasonable opportunity to resist being taken to Rockport, Massachusetts, from the apartment . . . , and had a reasonable opportunity to avoid or resist the circumstances that took place in the bedroom at Rockport, but chose not to avail herself of those opportunities, then you must weigh her failure to take such reasonable opportunities on the credibility of her claim that she was kidnapped and raped."

b. Commonwealth v. Lefkowitz, 20 Mass. App. 513, 481 N.E.2d 277, 232 (1985). —Eds.

peals Court of Massachusetts commented as follows:] It is time to put to rest the societal myth that when a man is about to engage in sexual intercourse with a "nice" woman "a little force is always necessary." . . .

The essence of the offense of rape is lack of consent on the part of the victim. I am prepared to say that when a woman says "no" to someone[,] any implication other than a manifestation of non-consent that might arise in that person's psyche is legally irrelevant, and thus no defense. Any further action is unwarranted and the person proceeds at his peril. In effect, he assumes the risk. In 1985, I find no social utility in establishing a rule defining non-consensual intercourse on the basis of the subjective (and quite likely wishful) view of the more aggressive player in the sexual encounter.

COMMONWEALTH v. FISCHER

Superior Court of Pennsylvania
721 A.2d 1111 (1998)

BECK, J.: . . . Appellant, an eighteen-year-old college freshman, was charged with involuntary deviate sexual intercourse (IDSI), aggravated indecent assault and related offenses in connection with an incident that occurred in a Lafayette College campus dormitory. The victim was another freshman student appellant met at school.

At trial, both the victim and appellant testified that a couple of hours prior to the incident at issue, the two went to appellant's dorm room and engaged in intimate contact. The victim testified that the couple's conduct was limited to kissing and fondling. Appellant, on the other hand, testified that during this initial encounter, he and the victim engaged in "rough sex" which culminated in the victim performing fellatio on him. According to appellant, the victim acted aggressively at this first rendezvous by holding appellant's arms above his head, biting his chest, stating "You know you want me," and initiating oral sex.

After the encounter, the students separated and went to the dining hall with their respective friends. They met up again later and once more found themselves in appellant's dorm room. While their accounts of what occurred at the first meeting contained significant differences, their versions of events at the second meeting were grossly divergent. The victim testified that appellant locked the door, pushed her onto the bed, straddled her, held her wrists above her head and forced his penis into her mouth. She struggled with appellant throughout the entire encounter. . . . She also . . . repeatedly stated that she did not want to engage in sex, but her pleas went unheeded. According to the victim, appellant [said] "I know you want it," . . . and "Nobody will know where you are." When the victim attempted to leave, appellant blocked her path. Only after striking him in the groin with her knee was the victim able to escape.

Appellant characterized the second meeting in a far different light. He stated that as he led the victim into his room, she told him it would have to be "a quick one." . . . Thereafter, according to appellant, he began to engage in the same type of behavior the victim had exhibited in their previous encounter. Appellant admitted that he held the young woman's arms above her head, straddled her and placed his penis at her mouth. . . . When she [said] "no," appellant answered "No means yes." After another verbal exchange that included the victim's statement that she had to leave, appellant again insisted that "she wanted it." This time she answered "No, I honestly don't." Upon hearing this, appellant no longer sought to engage in oral sex and removed himself from her body. However, as the two lay side by side on the bed, they continued to kiss and fondle one another.

. . . According to appellant, the victim enjoyed the contact and responded positively to his actions. At some point, however, she stood up and informed appellant that she had to leave. When appellant again attempted to touch her, this time on the thigh, she told him she was "getting pissed." Before appellant could "rearrange himself," so that he could walk the victim to her class, she abruptly left the room.

At trial, . . . [m]edical personnel testified to treating the victim on the night in question. Many of the victim's friends and classmates described her as nervous, shaken and upset after the incident.

Defense counsel argued throughout the trial and in closing that appellant, relying on his previous encounter with the victim, did not believe his actions were taken without her consent. . . . In light of his limited experience and the victim's initially aggressive behavior, argued counsel, appellant's beliefs were reasonable. Further . . . as soon as appellant realized that the victim truly did not wish to engage in oral sex a second time, appellant stopped seeking same. As a result, appellant's actions could not be deemed forcible compulsion.

The jury returned a verdict of guilty on virtually all counts. Appellant was sentenced to two to five years in prison. On direct appeal, he retained new counsel who has raised a single issue [—] that trial counsel provided ineffective assistance in failing to request a jury charge on the defense of mistake of fact. Specifically, appellant claims that counsel should have asked the court to instruct the jurors that if they found appellant reasonably, though mistakenly, believed that the victim was consenting to his sexual advances, they could find him not guilty.

The standard of review for ineffectiveness challenges is clear. Appellant must establish: 1) an underlying issue of arguable merit; 2) the absence of a reasonable strategy on the part of counsel in acting or failing to act; and 3) prejudice as a result of counsel's action or inaction. . . .

Our initial inquiry is whether counsel would have been successful had he requested a mistake of fact instruction. Counsel cannot be deemed ineffective for failing to pursue a baseless claim. Further, the quality of counsel's stewardship is based on the state of the law as it existed at time of trial; counsel is not ineffective if he fails to predict future developments or changes in the law.

The Commonwealth relies . . . on an opinion by a panel of this court. Commonwealth v. Williams, 439 A.2d 765 (Pa. Super. 1982), concerned the rape and assault of a Temple University student. The facts established that the victim accepted a ride from the appellant on a snowy evening in Philadelphia. Instead of taking the young woman to the bus station, appellant drove her to a dark area, threatened to kill her and informed her that he wanted sex. The victim told Williams to "go ahead" because she did not wish to be hurt.

[Appellant there] argued, among other things, that the trial court erred in refusing to instruct the jury "that if the defendant reasonably believed that the prosecutrix had consented to his sexual advances that this would constitute a defense to the rape and involuntary deviate sexual intercourse charge." This court rejected Williams's claim and held:

> . . . When one individual uses force or the threat of force to have sexual relations with a person not his spouse and without the person's consent he has committed the crime of rape. *If the element of the defendant's belief as to the victim's state of mind is to be established as a defense to the crime of rape then it should be done by our legislature which has the power to define crimes and offenses. We refuse to create such a defense.*

Id. (emphasis supplied.) The Commonwealth insists that under *Williams,* appellant was not entitled to the instruction he now claims trial counsel should have requested.

In response, appellant makes two arguments. First, he argues that the "stranger rape" facts of *Williams* were far different from those of this case, making the case inapplicable. Second, he maintains that the law with respect to rape and sexual assault has changed significantly over the last decade, along with our understanding of the crime and its permutations, making a mistake of fact instruction in a date rape case a necessity for a fair trial. . . .

Although the rape and IDSI laws have always required the element of "forcible compulsion," that term was not initially defined. . . .[2] Not long after *Williams* was decided, our supreme court published Commonwealth v. Rhodes, 510 A.2d 1217 (1986). In that case, a twenty-year-old man was accused of raping an eight-year-old girl. The evidence established that the appellant took the victim, whom he knew, to an abandoned building and sexually assaulted her. The child complied with all of the appellant's instructions. . . . A panel of this court . . . held that while the crime of statutory rape clearly was established given the victim's age, there was no evidence of the forcible compulsion necessary for the rape conviction. Our supreme court disagreed. . . . Defining forcible compulsion as including "not only physical force or violence but also moral, psychological or intellectual force," the court held that forcible compulsion was established. . . .

The *Rhodes* court's inclusion of types of forcible compulsion other than physical was a significant change in the law. Of course, defining those new types was not an easy task. [In 1995,] the legislature amended the sexual assault law by adding a definition for forcible compulsion. The language of the amendment closely followed that used by the *Rhodes* court:

> "Forcible Compulsion." Compulsion by use of physical, intellectual, moral, emotional or psychological force, either express or implied. . . .

It is this broader definition, argues appellant in this case, that prompts the necessity for a mistake of fact jury instruction. . . . According to appellant: "The language of the present statute inextricably links the issues of consent with mens rea. To ask a jury to consider whether the defendant used 'intellectual or moral' force, while denying the instruction as to how to consider the defendant's mental state at the time of alleged encounter is patently unfair to the accused."

Appellant's argument is bolstered by the fact that the concept of "mistake of fact" has long been a fixture in the criminal law. The concept is codified in Pennsylvania and provides [18 Pa.C.S.A. §304]:

2. It is clear from a reading of the relevant statutes and accompanying case law that the rape and IDSI statutes rely on the same definitions. Therefore, despite the fact that this is an IDSI case, our discussion of rape laws and cases involving rape convictions is relevant to and probative of the issue before us.

> Ignorance or mistake as to a matter of fact, for which there is reasonable explanation or excuse, is a defense if . . . the ignorance or mistake negatives the intent, knowledge, belief, recklessness, or negligence required to establish a material element of the offense; or the law provides that the state of mind established by such ignorance or mistake constitutes a defense.

. . . Courts in other jurisdictions have likewise held that jury instructions regarding the defendant's reasonable belief as to consent are proper. See State v. Smith, 554 A.2d 713 (Conn. 1989).

Although the logic of these other cases is persuasive, we are unable to adopt the principles enunciated in them because of the binding precedent with which we are faced, namely, *Williams*. In an effort to avoid application of *Williams*, appellant directs our attention to the Subcommittee Notes of the Pennsylvania Criminal Suggested Standard Jury Instructions. The possible conflict between *Williams* and §304 (Mistake of Fact) was not lost on the Subcommittee. . . .

> In the opinion of the Subcommittee there may be cases, especially now that *Rhodes* has extended the definition of force to psychological, moral and intellectual force, where a defendant might non-recklessly or even reasonably, but wrongly, believe that his words and conduct do not constitute force or the threat of force and that a non-resisting female is consenting. An example might be "date rape" resulting from mutual misunderstanding. The boy does not intend or suspect the intimidating potential of his vigorous wooing. The girl, misjudging the boys' character, believes he will become violent if thwarted; she feigns willingness, even some pleasure. In our opinion the defendant in such a case ought not to be convicted of rape.

. . . We agree with the Subcommittee that the rule in *Williams* is inappropriate in the type of date rape case described above. Changing codes of sexual conduct, particularly those exhibited on college campuses, may require that we give greater weight to what is occurring beneath the overt actions of young men and women. Recognition of those changes, in the form of specified jury instructions, strikes us an appropriate course of action.

Despite appellant's excellent presentation of the issues, there remain two distinct problems precluding relief in this case. First . . . [t]his case . . . is not one of the "new" varieties of sexual assault contemplated by the amended statute. . . . This is a case of a young woman alleging physical force in a sexual assault and a young man claiming that he reasonably believed he had consent. In such circumstances, *Williams* controls.

We are keenly aware of the differences between *Williams* and this case. Most notable is the fact that Williams and his victim never met before the incident in question. Here, appellant and the victim not only knew one another, but had engaged in intimate contact just hours before the incident in question. It is clear, however, that the *Williams* court's basis for denying the jury instruction was its conclusion that the law did not require it and, further, that the judiciary had no authority to grant it. Even if we were to disagree with those conclusions, we are powerless to alter them.

In any event, distinguishing *Williams* on the basis of the parties' previous contacts . . . is not enough to allow appellant the relief he seeks. Even if we . . . are persuaded by appellant's arguments chronicling the history of sexual assault law . . . , we face a second barrier. Because this appeal raises ineffective assistance of counsel, we are required to find that appellant's trial lawyer made a mistake. That mistake is the failure to ask the trial court for an instruction that the *Williams* case held is unwarranted. In other words, we would have to find that counsel's failure to argue for a change in the law constituted ineffectiveness. This, of course, is not possible. We simply cannot announce a new rule of law and then find counsel ineffective for failing to predict same.

. . . The relief appellant seeks represents a significant departure from the current state of the law. Despite its compelling nature, it cannot be the basis for an ineffective assistance of counsel claim.

Judgment of sentence affirmed.

NOTES ON MISTAKE AS TO CONSENT

1. Strict liability? Note that the defendants in *Sherry* did not seek acquittal on the ground that their alleged mistake was both honest and reasonable. In Commonwealth v. Ascolillo, 405 Mass. 456, 541 N.E.2d 570 (1989), the defendant requested a jury instruction that a *reasonable* mistake as to consent would be a defense. The victim was an acquaintance, and the defendant claimed to have had consensual sexual relations with her numerous times in the past. She had come to his home and used cocaine with him just before the alleged rape. The trial judge refused to instruct on a defense of reasonable mistake, and the Supreme Judicial Court affirmed the rape conviction, holding that an honest and reasonable mistake as to consent was not a defense to rape in Massachusetts.

In a subsequent acquaintance rape case, Commonwealth v. Simcock, 31 Mass. App. 184, 575 N.E.2d 1137, 1142-1143 (1991), the trial judge not only refused a defense request for instructions on reasonable mistake but also gave the jury an instruction to the effect that "a belief that the victim consented would not be a defense even if reasonable." The appellate court affirmed the rape conviction, stating that the instruction was "nothing more than a statement of law consistent with Commonwealth v. Ascolillo." The court added (id. at 1142) that the result was "in harmony with the analogous rule that a defendant in a statutory rape case is not entitled to an instruction that a reasonable mistake as to the victim's age is a defense."

Questions: Is the analogy flawed? Or is the court right in suggesting that defendants should be held strictly accountable for the existence of consent by their sexual partners? The weight of American authority now runs strongly against the *Ascolillo* view, but a few states appear to have joined Massachusetts and Pennsylvania in opting for strict liability on the consent issue. See, e.g., State v. Reed, 479 A.2d 1291 (Me. 1984).

2. Recklessness or only negligence? Most of the recent American cases permit a mistake defense, but only when the defendant's error as to consent is honest and reasonable. See, e.g., State v. Oliver, 133 N.J. 141, 627 A.2d 144(1993); State v. Smith, 210 Conn. 132, 554 A.2d 713 (1989); People v. Mayberry, 15 Cal. 3d 143, 542 P.2d 1337 (1975). In England, in contrast, the House of Lords has held that the prosecution must prove that the defendant either knew consent was absent or was willing to proceed "willy-nilly, not caring whether the victim consents or no." See Regina v. Morgan, [1976] A.C. 182:

Once one has accepted, what seems to me abundantly clear, that the prohibited act in rape is non-consensual sexual intercourse, and that the guilty state of mind is an intention to commit it, it seems to me to follow as a matter of inexorable logic that there is no room either for a "defence" of honest belief or mistake, or of a defence of honest and reasonable belief or mistake. Either the prosecution proves that the accused had the requisite intent, or it does not. In the former case it succeeds, and in the latter it fails. Since honest belief clearly negatives intent, the reasonableness or otherwise of that belief can only be evidence for or against the view that the belief and therefore the intent was actually held. . . . Any other view . . . can only have the effect of saying that a man intends something which he does not. . . .

It matters not why [intent] is lacking if only it is not there, and in particular it matters not that the intention is lacking only because of a belief not based on reasonable grounds. . . .

In one of the few American decisions to require proof of recklessness, the court reasoned as follows (Reynolds v. State, 664 P.2d 621, 624-625 (Alaska App. 1983)):

[R]ecent cases have substantially diluted the requirement of "resistance to the utmost," increasing the risk that a jury might convict a defendant under circumstances where lack of consent was ambiguous. To counteract this risk, some courts . . . have held that the defendant is entitled to an instruction on reasonable mistake of fact. . . .

Alaska has dispensed with any requirement that the victim resist at all. . . . Thus, the legislature has substantially enhanced the risk of conviction in ambiguous circumstances. . . . We are satisfied, however, that the legislature counteracted this risk through its treatment of mens rea. It did this by shifting the focus of the jury's attention from the victim's resistance or actions to the defendant's understanding of the totality of the circumstances. Lack of consent is a "surrounding circumstance" which under the Revised Code, requires a complementary mental state as well as conduct to constitute a crime. No specific mental state is mentioned in AS 11.41.-410(a)(1) governing the surrounding circumstances of "consent." Therefore, the state must prove that the defendant acted "recklessly" regarding his putative victim's lack of consent.[a] This requirement serves to protect the defendant against conviction for first-degree sexual assault where the circumstances regarding consent are ambiguous at the time he has intercourse with the complaining witness.

3. The practical effect of a negligence standard. Does the mistake-of-fact standard matter? Consider Stephen J. Schulhofer, The Gender Question in Criminal Law, 7 Soc. Phil. & Pol. 105, 132-133 (1990):

Given the [*Sherry*] victim's isolation in an unfamiliar setting, her intimidation by three naked men, and her explicit protests, there could not possibly have been (from the feminist perspective) a reasonable mistake. For the same reasons, however, one would have to say that these defendants actually *knew* that the victim was not consenting. At the very least, they were all aware that she *might* not be consenting. . . . In other words, . . . these defendants were *subjectively* culpable and would be convicted whether or not we insist on a negligence standard.

a. The court based this conclusion on an Alaska statute providing, as does Model Penal Code §2.02(3), that when a penal prohibition is silent as to the required culpability, then the state must prove recklessness with respect to any specified circumstances or results. — EDS.

> [But there] is one perspective from which these defendants might have made an honest mistake. That is the perspective that "no" does not really mean "no," that women . . . just want to feign some initial reluctance. . . . But if you hold this view of consent (and of women) . . . you might even conclude that the victim really *did* consent — that the doctors made no mistake at all. Once one accepts this alternative (hopefully outmoded) conception of what consent means, the defendants could conceivably be acquitted even if they were tried under a strict liability standard.
>
> The point here is not that choice of the mens rea standard can never make a difference. Certainly, conviction becomes progressively easier as we move toward the strict liability approach. But we are working at the fringes of the problem. The [argument for a negligence standard] begs the most important question, or sweeps it under the rug of jury findings about reasonableness. This is really not a debate about mens rea standards. Rather, it is (or ought to be) a debate about what we mean by the construct that we call "consent." . . . The debate about mistake of fact standards diverts attention from the question of what it is that you have to be mistaken about. Rather than requiring that the mistake be reasonable, and then leaving the jurors to their own conceptions of what is "reasonable" and what is "consent," we need to spell out what the concept of consent means.

4. Limiting the reasonable mistake defense. Tyson v. State, 619 N.E.2d 276 (Ind. App. 1993), involved the prosecution of heavyweight boxing champion Mike Tyson for the rape of D.W., a woman who had agreed to accompany him to his hotel room at 2:00 A.M. Tyson testified that D.W. had responded positively to his kissing her in the limousine on the way to his hotel; that "we had both made it clear earlier that day what was going to happen"; and that D.W. cooperated in the act of intercourse. D.W. testified that when Tyson made sexual advances in the room, she was terrified, repeatedly objected and "tried to fight him" without success. The trial court refused to instruct the jury that a reasonable mistake as to consent would be a defense. Tyson was convicted of rape, and the court of appeals affirmed, upholding the refusal to instruct on reasonable mistake of fact (619 N.E.2d at 295):

> Tyson's description is a plain assertion of actual consent. . . . There is no recitation of equivocal conduct by D.W. which reasonably could have led Tyson to believe that D.W. only appeared to consent to the charged sexual conduct; no gray area exists from which Tyson can logically argue that he misunderstood D.W.'s actions. According to Tyson, he exerted no force and D.W. offered no resistance; instead, she was an active and equal participant in the conduct. While this testimony would negate an element of the crime — that Tyson forcibly engaged in sexual conduct with D.W. — and challenges D.W.'s credibility, it does not support the giving of a mistake of fact instruction.

Questions: Is this approach sound? In cases involving this type of "swearing contest," it seems obvious that once the jury finds one party to be telling the truth and the other party to be lying, there is no possibility for a reasonable mistake. But is it logically inevitable that one of the two competing stories must be completely true? What if the jury believes that *both* parties are exaggerating? See Rosanna Cavallaro, A Big Mistake: Eroding the Defense of Mistake of Fact About Consent in Rape, 86 J. Crim. L. & Criminology 815 (1996).

5. Victim consent in other crimes. Although victim consent is not a defense to homicide and other offenses involving the infliction of serious bodily injury, consent in many other situations can deprive conduct of its criminal character. See generally Model Penal Code §2.11, Appendix. Sexual contact is but one of these situations in which liability may turn on the consequences of a mistake about consent. Consider the following case.

State v. Kelly, 338 S.E.2d 405 (W. Va. 1985): [The defendant, a construction and demolition contractor, removed a number of valuable oak fireplace mantels from two unoccupied houses and sold the mantels to an antique dealer. Despite efforts to board up the houses, they had been frequently vandalized. Evidence suggested that the defendant had broken into the houses and torn locks off the front doors to gain access. He testified that a man named Bradley had called, met him at the houses and discussed tearing them down or salvaging their contents. After the defendant removed and sold the mantels, he paid the $140 proceeds to Bradley and received $40 for his efforts. He also testified that a neighbor told him that Bradley and his wife owned the houses. In fact, the houses were owned by Bradley's estranged wife and her business partner, neither of whom had consented to removal of the mantels. The defendant was convicted of larceny. The appellate court reversed.]

It is . . . fundamental to the definition of larceny that the personal property must be taken without the consent of the owner. [O]ne who takes property in good faith under fair color or claim of title, honestly believing he is the owner and has a right to take it, is not guilty of larceny, even though he is mistaken in such belief, since in such case the felonious intent is lacking. . . . This matter is summarized in W. LaFave & A. Scott, Handbook on Criminal Law 638 (1972), as follows:

> One may take the property of another honestly but mistakenly believing . . . that the owner has given him permission to take it as he did. In . . . such event, he lacks the intent to steal required for larceny, even though his mistaken but honest belief was unreasonable. . . .

In this case, we believe the evidence when viewed in the light most favorable to the prosecution . . . does not establish beyond a reasonable doubt that the defendant acted with criminal intent because he believed that he had proper authority to remove the mantels. . . . Consequently, we cannot assent to his conviction.

Questions: If actual knowledge of the owner's nonconsent is required for a larceny conviction, why shouldn't actual knowledge of the woman's nonconsent be required for a rape conviction? Does the requirement of some subjective awareness of wrongdoing flow from the essential character of conviction for any serious crime? Or does the need for that requirement depend on the particular kind of harm caused by failing to assure consent? Consider Susan Estrich, Real Rape 97-98 (1987):

> The man who has the inherent capacity to act reasonably but fails to has, through that failure, made a blameworthy choice for which he can justly be punished. The law has long punished unreasonable action which leads to loss of human life as manslaughter. . . . The injury of sexual violation is sufficiently great, the need to provide that additional incentive pressing enough, to justify negligence liability for rape as for killing.

6. Applying a reasonableness standard. What factors should determine whether a man's mistake about consent was "reasonable"? Consider the following comments.

Robin D. Weiner, Shifting the Communication Burden: A Meaningful Consent Standard in Rape, 6 Harv. Women's L.J. 143, 147-149 (1983): [A] gender gap in sexual communications exists. Men and women frequently misinterpret the intent of various dating behaviors and erotic play engaged in by their opposite-sexed partners. . . .

Because both men and women are socialized to accept coercive sexuality as the norm in sexual behavior, men often see extreme forms of this aggressive behavior as seduction, rather than rape. . . . Miscommunication of this sort may create a situation where submission would be reasonable behavior for a woman but would not indicate voluntary consent. A woman may believe she has communicated her unwillingness to have sex — and other women would agree, thus making it a "reasonable" female expression. Her male partner might still believe she is willing — and other men would agree with his interpretation, thus making it a "reasonable" male interpretation. The woman, who believes that she *has* conveyed her lack of consent, may interpret the man's persistence as an indication that he does not care if she objects and plans to have sex despite her lack of consent. She may then feel frightened by the man's persistence, and may submit against her will.

For an analysis of the cultural attitudes that influence conceptions of "consent" in sexual interaction, see Lynne Henderson, Getting to Know: Honoring Women in Law and in Fact, 2 Tex. J. Women & L. 41 (1993). The importance of nonverbal cues in communicating willingness or unwillingness in sexual encounters is discussed in Steven I. Friedland, Date Rape and the Culture of Acceptance, 43 Fla. L. Rev. 487 (1991).

7. Questions: How should law respond to the "gender gap"? Should notions of reasonableness be left to evolve in response to changing social mores? Or should legislatures and courts set specific standards, for example, by specifying that "no means no"? In one survey of women undergraduates, 39 percent reported that they had said "no" when they meant yes, and 61 percent of the sexually experienced women in the survey said that they had done so.[20] Ninety percent of these women said that fear of appearing promiscuous was an important reason for their behavior. Many said they wanted their dates to wait or "talk me into it," and some said that they told their dates "no" because they "want[ed] him to be more physically aggressive." The authors of the study pointed out that this pattern of communication, though rational for some women, can teach men to disregard women's refusals and thereby increase the incidence of rape.

Do findings of this sort imply that "no" often *doesn't* mean "no"? Or do such findings suggest an even greater need for legal standards to guarantee that "no" *will be treated as* "no"? Compare the following viewpoints.

20. Charlene L. Muehlenhard & Lisa C. Hollabaugh, Do Women Sometimes Say No When They Mean Yes?, 54 J. Personality & Soc. Psych. 872, 874-878 (1988). This study was confined to women at a single university in Texas, but more recent surveys at other colleges and universities across the United States report strikingly similar findings, with no regional differences. See Stephen J. Schulhofer, Unwanted Sex 260 (1998).

Douglas N. Husak & George C. Thomas III, Date Rape, Social Convention and Reasonable Mistakes, 11 Law & Phil. 95, 123, 125 (1992): The social convention wcs[a] provides the vehicle through which *M* [a man] interprets the words or actions of *F* [a woman]. [T]here is little empirical evidence that the social convention wcs is consistent with the view of men and women entailed by the [no-means-no] claims of some rape law reformers. Instead, the evidence suggests a convention wcs that might produce somewhat frequent mistakes of fact about a woman's consent. If so, and if the reformers succeed in restricting or eliminating the mistake-of-fact defense, some men will be convicted of rape even though they had reason to believe that consent had been given.

Some might welcome this result. As noted above, one might believe that it is more important to seek to change the social convention or to send a symbolic message than to do justice in an individual case. But if one believes that the criminal law should seek to apply the just result in particular cases, men whose belief in consent is consistent with the social convention seem unlikely candidates for convictions of a serious felony. For this reason, legislatures should proceed slowly when removing some of the common law barriers to rape convictions.

Catharine A. MacKinnon, Feminism, Marxism, Method, and the State: Toward a Feminist Jurisprudence, 8 Signs 635, 652-654 (1983): [M]en are systematically conditioned not even to notice what women want. They may have not a glimmer of women's indifference or revulsion. Rapists typically believe the woman loved it. . . .

Men's pervasive belief that women fabricate rape charges after consenting to sex makes sense in this light. To them, the accusations *are* false because, to them, the facts describe sex. To interpret such events as rapes distorts their experience. . . .

But the deeper problem is the rape law's assumption that a single, objective state of affairs existed, one which merely needs to be determined by evidence, when many (maybe even most) rapes involve honest men and violated women. When the reality is split — a woman is raped but not by a rapist? — the law tends to conclude that a rape *did not happen.* To attempt to solve this by adopting the standard of reasonable belief without asking, on a substantive social basis, to whom the belief is reasonable and why — meaning, what conditions make it reasonable — is one-sided: male-sided.

E. A STATUTORY SOLUTION?

Are the problems raised in the preceding sections best addressed by public discussion and education? Instead (or in addition), should we empower courts and juries to apply flexible standards of reasonableness in order to punish sexual overreaching? Or is it possible and desirable to adopt specific statutory criteria to mark the boundary between permissible and unlawful behavior? Consider the

a. The authors use the term "wcs" to designate the social conventions that women use to express consent to have sex. — Eds.

advantages and shortcomings of the following attempt to articulate specific statutory standards.

PROPOSED MODEL STATUTE[a]

SECTION 201. SEXUAL ASSAULT

(a) An actor is guilty of sexual assault, a felony of the second degree, if he uses physical force or a threat of physical force to compel another person to submit to an act of sexual penetration.

(b) An actor is guilty of sexual assault, a felony of the second degree, if he commits an act of sexual penetration with another person, when he knows that the victim is less than thirteen years old.

(c) An actor is guilty of aggravated sexual assault, a felony of the first degree, if he violates subsection (a) of this section while using a weapon or if he violates subsection (a) of this section and causes serious bodily harm to the victim.

SECTION 202. SEXUAL ABUSE

(a) An actor is guilty of sexual abuse, a felony of the third degree, if he commits an act of sexual penetration with another person, when he knows that he does not have the consent of the other person.

(b) Consent, for purposes of this section, means that at the time of the act of sexual penetration there are actual words or conduct indicating affirmative, freely given permission to the act of sexual penetration.

(c) Consent is not freely given, for purposes of this section, whenever:

(1) the victim is physically helpless, mentally defective, or mentally incapacitated; or

(2) the victim is at least thirteen years old but less than sixteen years old and the actor is at least four years older than the victim; or

(3) the victim is at least sixteen years old but less than eighteen years old and the actor is a parent, foster parent, guardian, or other person with supervisory or disciplinary authority over the victim; or

(4) the victim is on probation or parole, or is detained in a hospital, prison, or other custodial institution, and the actor has supervisory or disciplinary authority over the victim; or

(5) the actor obtains the victim's consent by threatening to:

(i) inflict bodily injury on a person other than the victim or commit any other criminal offense; or

(ii) accuse anyone of a criminal offense; or

(iii) expose any secret tending to subject any person to hatred, contempt, or ridicule, or to impair the credit or business repute of any person; or

(iv) take or withhold action as an official or cause an official to take or withhold action; or

(v) violate any other right of the victim or inflict any other harm that would not benefit the actor; or

a. Adapted from Stephen J. Schulhofer, Unwanted Sex 283-284 (1998).

(6) the actor is engaged in providing professional treatment, assessment, or counseling of a mental or emotional illness, symptom, or condition of the victim over a period concurrent with or substantially contemporaneous with the time when the act of sexual penetration occurs; or

(7) the actor obtains the victim's consent by representing that the act of sexual penetration is for purposes of medical treatment; or

(8) the actor obtains the victim's consent by leading the victim to believe that he is a person with whom the victim has been sexually intimate, or by representing that the victim is in danger of physical injury or illness.

SECTION 203. CULPABILITY

(a) Recklessness. Whenever knowledge of a fact is required to convict an actor of violating any provision of sections 201 or 202, the requirement of knowledge can be met by proof that, at the time of his conduct, the actor was consciously aware of a substantial and unjustifiable risk that the fact in question existed.

(b) Criminal Negligence. If the actor was not consciously aware of such a risk, he can nonetheless be convicted of violating the provision in question, provided that the prosecution proves that his failure to appreciate that risk involved a gross deviation from the standard of care that a reasonable person would observe in the actor's situation. If an actor is convicted of violating Article 201 on the basis of criminal negligence, the offense shall be graded as a felony of the third degree. If an actor is convicted of violating Article 202 on the basis of criminal negligence, the offense shall be graded as a felony of the fourth degree.

NOTE ON THE IMPACT OF REFORM

Most empirical studies find that reform efforts have had surprisingly little impact on rape reporting, processing of complaints, and conviction rates. A detailed study of one of the nation's most ambitious reforms, the 1975 Michigan statute, found the new law relatively unsuccessful in extending the criminal prohibition to conduct previously thought to be permissible or "borderline"; one law enforcement official dismissed the law's expanded coverage as "messing with the folkways."[21] A 1992 report analyzed data from six jurisdictions with widely differing approaches to reform, from the far-reaching Michigan effort to relatively minor reforms in Texas and Georgia.[22] The study found only small improvements in Michigan and virtually none in the other jurisdictions. Only Michigan had an increase in the reporting of rapes, and no jurisdiction experienced an increase in its conviction rate.[23] Researchers attributed these disappointing results to the wide discretion exercised by criminal justice officials, who "continue[d]

21. Jeanne C. Marsh, Alison Geist & Nathan Caplan, Rape and the Limits of Law Reform 25-26, 42-49, 107 (1982).

22. Cassia Spohn & Julia Horney, Rape Law Reform (1992).

23. Id. at 86, 160, 173. The finding that Michigan conviction rates (as a percentage of indictments) remained constant can nonetheless be viewed as a modest victory for the reform effort: Reporting rates had increased somewhat, more cases were coming into the system, and more were being indicted. The constant rate of conviction as a percentage of indictments suggests the possibility that the new law facilitated conviction in grey-area cases that might not have been prosecuted before. See id. at 104.

to use the informal norms developed in the courtroom work group to guide the processing of cases."[24]

Do these findings suggest that legislative reform is bound to prove futile? One researcher observes that "passage of the reforms sent an important symbolic message regarding the seriousness of rape cases," and that "[i]n the long run this symbolic message may be more important than the instrumental change that was anticipated."[25] But if cultural change is the key to improving case outcomes, what is the best way to achieve such change? When is it appropriate to use the criminal law to alter social norms that are prevalent in the community (or in substantial segments of it)?

F. THE MARITAL EXEMPTION

1 MATTHEW HALE, THE HISTORY OF THE PLEAS OF THE CROWN 629 (S. Emlyn ed. 1778): [T]he husband cannot be guilty of a rape committed by himself upon his lawful wife, for by their mutual matrimonial consent and contract the wife hath given up herself in this kind unto her husband, which she cannot retract.

PEOPLE v. LIBERTA

New York Court of Appeals
64 N.Y.2d 152, 474 N.E.2d 567 (1984)

WACHTLER, J. . . . Defendant Mario Liberta and Denise Liberta were married in 1978. Shortly after the birth of their son, in October of that year, Mario began to beat Denise. In early 1980 Denise brought a proceeding in the Family Court in Erie County seeking protection from the defendant. On April 30, 1980 a temporary order of protection was issued to her by the Family Court. Under this order, the defendant was to move out and remain away from the family home, and stay away from Denise. The order provided that the defendant could visit with his son once each weekend.

. . . On Tuesday, March 24, 1981 [defendant] called Denise to ask if he could visit his son on that day. Denise [allowed] him to pick up their son and her and take them both back to his motel after being assured that a friend of his would be with them at all times. . .

When they arrived at the motel the friend left. As soon as only Mario, Denise, and their son were alone in the motel room, Mario attacked Denise, threatened to kill her, and forced her to . . . engage in sexual intercourse with him. The son was in the room during the entire episode, and the defendant forced Denise to tell their son to watch what the defendant was doing to her.

The defendant allowed Denise and their son to leave shortly after the incident.

24. Id. at 173.
25. Cassia C. Spohn, The Rape Reform Movement: The Traditional Common Law and Rape Law Reforms, 39 Jurimetrics 119, 129-130 (1999).

Denise, after going to her parents' home, went to a hospital to be treated for scratches on her neck and bruises on her head and back, all inflicted by her husband. She also went to the police station, and on the next day she swore out a felony complaint. . . .

[The defendant was convicted of rape in the first degree, and the conviction was affirmed by the Appellate Division.]

Section 130.35 of the Penal Law provides in relevant part that "A male is guilty of rape in the first degree when he engages in sexual intercourse with a female . . . by forcible compulsion." "Female," for purposes of the rape statute, is defined as "any female person who is not married to the actor." [D]ue to the "not married" language in the [definition] of "female" . . . , there is a "marital exemption" for [forcible rape]. . . .

Until 1978, the marital exemption applied as long as the marriage still legally existed. In 1978, the Legislature expanded the definition of "not married" to include those cases where the husband and wife were living apart pursuant to either a court order "which by its terms or in its effect requires such living apart" or a decree, judgment, or written agreement of separation (Penal Law, §130.00, subd. 4). [T]he order of protection in the present case falls squarely within the first of these situations. . . . Accordingly, the defendant was properly found to have been statutorily "not married" to Denise at the time of the rape. . . . The defendant's claim is that [the statute violates] equal protection because [it burdens] him, but not others similarly situated. A litigant has standing to raise the claim even though he does not contend that under no circumstances could the burden of the statute be imposed upon him.

[T]he equal protection clause does not prohibit a State from making classifications, provided the statute does not arbitrarily burden a particular group of individuals. Where a statute draws a distinction based upon marital status, the classification must be reasonable and must be based upon "some ground of difference that rationally explains the different treatment" (Eisenstadt v. Baird, 405 U.S. 438, 447).

We find that there is no rational basis for distinguishing between marital rape and nonmarital rape. . . . Lord Hale's notion of an irrevocable implied consent by a married woman to sexual intercourse has been cited most frequently in support of the marital exemption. Any argument based on a supposed consent, however, is untenable. Rape is not simply a sexual act to which one party does not consent. Rather, it is a degrading, violent act which violates the bodily integrity of the victim and frequently causes severe, long-lasting physical and psychic harm. To ever imply consent to such an act is irrational and absurd. [A] marriage license should not be viewed as a license for a husband to forcibly rape his wife with impunity. . . . If a husband feels "aggrieved" by his wife's refusal to engage in sexual intercourse, he should seek relief in the courts governing domestic relations, not in "violent or forceful self-help."

The other traditional justifications for the marital exemption were the common-law doctrines that a woman was the property of her husband and that the legal existence of the woman was "incorporated and consolidated into that of the husband" (1 Blackstone's Commentaries (1966 ed.), p. 430). Both these doctrines, of course, have long been rejected in this State. Indeed, "[n]owhere in the common-law world — [or] in any modern society — is a woman regarded as chattel or demeaned by denial of a separate legal identity and the dignity associated with recognition as a whole human being" (Trammel v. United States, 445 U.S. 40, 52).

Because the traditional justifications for the marital exemption no longer have any validity, other arguments have been advanced in its defense. . . . While protecting marital privacy and encouraging reconciliation are legitimate State interests, there is no rational relation between allowing a husband to forcibly rape his wife and these interests. . . . Just as a husband cannot invoke a right of marital privacy to escape liability for beating his wife, he cannot justifiably rape his wife under the guise of a right to privacy.

Similarly, it is not tenable to argue that elimination of the marital exemption would disrupt marriages because it would discourage reconciliation. [I]f the marriage has already reached the point where intercourse is accomplished by violent assault it is doubtful that there is anything left to reconcile. This, of course, is particularly true if the wife is willing to bring criminal charges against her husband which could result in a lengthy jail sentence. . . .

The final argument in defense of the marital exemption is that marital rape is not as serious an offense as other rape and is thus adequately dealt with by the possibility of prosecution under criminal statutes, such as assault statutes, which provide for less severe punishment. The fact that rape statutes exist, however, is a recognition that the harm caused by a forcible rape is different, and more severe, than the harm caused by an ordinary assault. [Moreover,] numerous studies have shown that marital rape is frequently quite violent and generally has *more* severe, traumatic effects on the victim than other rape. . . . Justice Holmes wrote: "It is revolting to have no better reason for a rule of law than that so it was laid down in the time of Henry IV. It is still more revolting if the grounds upon which it was laid down have vanished long since, and the rule simply persists from blind imitation of the past" (Holmes, The Path of Law, 10 Harv. L. Rev. 457, 469). This statement is an apt characterization of the marital exemption; it lacks a rational basis, and therefore violates the equal protection clauses of both the Federal and State Constitutions.

[T]he remaining issue is the appropriate remedy for these equal protection violations. When a statute is constitutionally defective because of underinclusion, a court may either strike the statute, and thus make it applicable to nobody, or extend the coverage of the statute to those formerly excluded. . . .

This court's task is to discern what course the Legislature would have chosen to follow if it had foreseen our conclusions as to underinclusiveness. . . . Statutes prohibiting [forcible sexual assaults] are of the utmost importance, and to declare such statutes a nullity would have a disastrous effect on the public interest and safety. The inevitable conclusion is that the Legislature would prefer to eliminate the exemptions and thereby preserve the statutes. Accordingly we choose the remedy of striking the marital exemption . . . from section 130.35 of the Penal Law, so that it is now the law of this State that any person who engages in sexual intercourse . . . by forcible compulsion is guilty of . . . rape in the first degree. . . . Because [the statute] under which the defendant was convicted [is] not being struck down, his conviction is affirmed.

Though our decision does not "create a crime," it does, of course, enlarge the scope of [a criminal statute]. . . . The due process clause of the Fourteenth Amendment requires that an accused have had fair warning at the time of his conduct that such conduct was made criminal by the State. Defendant did not come within any of the exemptions which we have stricken, and thus his conduct was covered by the [statute] at the time of his attack on Denise. . . .

Accordingly, the order of the Appellate Division should be affirmed.

NOTES

1. The prevalence of marital rape. Although once assumed to be extremely rare, marital rape is now thought to occur with disturbing frequency. Reliable statistics concerning the percentage of women experiencing any form of rape are difficult to obtain, but one study based on interviews with a random sample of nearly 1000 women found that 14 percent of the women who had been married were the victims of at least one completed or attempted rape by their husbands. See Diana E. H. Russell, Rape in Marriage 57 (2d ed. 1990). The author added that since many of the marital rape victims might have been unwilling to disclose their experience, the 14 percent figure could underestimate the true incidence of marital rape. Another study (Irene Hanson Frieze, Investigating the Causes and Consequences of Marital Rape, 8 Signs 532 (1983)) found that marital rape had been experienced by up to 10 percent of all married women. Statistics on the incidence of nonmarital rape suggest that such rapes may affect 1 percent of women over a 12-month period and up to 20 percent of all women over their lifetime. With nonmarital rape at that general order of magnitude, Professor Frieze concludes (id. at 548) that "marital rape may be one of the most common forms of rape in our society."

2. The Model Penal Code view. The Model Penal Code, drafted in the 1950s, chose to preserve the marital exemption. Consider the following effort to justify the Model Penal Code position (Model Penal Code and Commentaries, Comment to §213.1, at 344-346 (1980)):

> First, marriage or equivalent relationship, while not amounting to a legal waiver of the woman's right to say "no," does imply a kind of generalized consent that distinguishes some versions of the crime of rape from parallel behavior by a husband. . . . At a minimum, therefore, husbands must be exempt from those categories of liability based not on force or coercion but on a presumed incapacity of the woman to consent. For example, a man who has intercourse with his unconscious wife should scarcely be condemned to felony liability on the ground that the woman in such circumstances is incapable of consenting to sex with her own husband, at least unless there are aggravating circumstances. . . . Plainly there must also be some form of spousal exclusion applicable to the crime of statutory rape. . . .
>
> The major context of which those who would abandon the spousal exclusion are thinking, however, is the situation of rape by force or threat. The problem with abandoning the immunity in many such situations is that the law of rape, if applied to spouses, would thrust the prospect of criminal sanctions into the ongoing process of adjustment in the marital relationship. . . . Retaining the spousal exclusion avoids this unwarranted intrusion of the penal law into the life of the family.
>
> Finally, there is the case of intercourse coerced by force or threat of physical harm. Here the law already authorizes a penalty for assault. . . . The issue is whether the still more drastic sanctions of rape should apply. The answer depends on whether the injury caused by forcible intercourse by a husband is equivalent to that inflicted by someone else. The gravity of the crime of forcible rape derives not merely from its violent character but also from its achievement of a particularly de-

grading kind of unwanted intimacy. Where the attacker stands in an ongoing relation of sexual intimacy, that evil, as distinct from the force used to compel submission, may well be thought qualitatively different. The character of the voluntary association of husband and wife, in other words, may be thought to affect the nature of the harm involved in unwanted intercourse. That, in any event, is the conclusion long endorsed by the law of rape and carried forward in the Model Code provision.

In accord with the Model Penal Code view that rape prosecutions can involve an "unseemly [intrusion upon] the intimacies of the marital relationship," see Michael G. Hilf, Marital Privacy and Spousal Rape, 16 New Eng. L. Rev. 31, 34 (1980). The author argues that the marital exemption remains sound for cohabiting spouses and should terminate only after divorce, legal separation, or a substantial period of living apart. The notion that the harm of marital rape is less serious than that of stranger rape is criticized in Diana E. H. Russell, Rape in Marriage 190-191, 198-199 (2d ed. 1990):

> [W]ife rape can be as terrifying and life-threatening to the victim as stranger rape. In addition, it often evokes a powerful sense of betrayal, deep disillusionment, and total isolation. Women often receive very poor treatment by friends, relatives, and professional services when they are raped by strangers. This isolation can be even more extreme for victims of wife rape. And just as they are more likely to be blamed, they are more likely to blame themselves.
>
> . . . When a woman has been raped by her husband she cannot seek comfort and safety at home. She can decide to leave the marriage or to live with what happened. Either choice can be devastating. [S]taying usually means being raped again, often repeatedly. . . . Since the victim of wife rape "accepted" it the first time, why not the second, and the third, and so on? . . . Being raped or beaten by a husband is likely to progressively lower a wife's sense of self-worth as the abuse continues. And the lower the self-esteem, the more difficult it is to stop the abuse or leave the marriage. A vicious cycle is set in motion that can lead a wife to suicide or madness.

3. Legislative developments. Recent statutory reforms have substantially eroded the marital rape exemption. Though two states still preserve a broad exemption,[26] roughly half the states have abolished the exemption entirely[27] or retained it only to the extent of exempting husbands from prosecution for statutory rape (i.e., the situation in which intercourse is consensual but the wife is under the legally prescribed age of consent).[28] Nonetheless, nearly half the states retain qualified versions of the marital rape exemption — for example, by prescribing lower punishment for marital rape,[29] or by permitting prosecution only when the husband has used the most serious forms of force.[30] See Kelly C. Connerton, The Resurgence of the Marital Rape Exemption, 61 Alb. L. Rev. 237 (1997); Developments in the Law — Domestic Violence, 106 Harv. L. Rev. 1498, 1533-1534 (1993).

4. Judicial approaches. When state statutes do not explicitly require that the rape victim be "a female not his wife," courts have some flexibility in determin-

26. Okla. Stat. Ann., tit. 21, §1111 (1999); Ky. Rev. Stat. Ann. §510.035 (1999).
27. E.g., Fla. Stat. Ann. §39.902 (1999).
28. E.g., 18 Pa. Cons. Stat. Ann. §§3121, 3122.1 (1998).
29. E.g., S.C. Code Ann. §§16-3-615, 652 (1998) (maximum punishment of 10 years, versus 30 years for nonmarital rape).
30. E.g., Ohio Rev. Code Ann. §§2907.02-.06 (1999).

ing whether the common law marital exemption should remain a part of contemporary law. Although defendants have argued that such a change in previously settled understandings should come only from the legislature, several courts have held that a marital exemption should no longer be read into their statutes. See, e.g., Warren v. State, 336 S.E.2d 221 (Ga. 1985) (parties were living together at the time of the incident); State v. Smith, 85 N.J. 193, 426 A.2d 38 (1981) (parties had been living apart for one year). In England the House of Lords has likewise abolished the marital exemption by judicial decision. See R. v. R., [1991] 4 All E.R. 481.

A narrower approach is taken in Weishaupt v. Commonwealth, 227 Va. 389, 315 S.E.2d 847 (1984). The court there held that a husband charged with rape cannot invoke the marital exemption when the wife has "conduct[ed] herself in a manner that establishes a de facto end to the marriage." (In *Weishaupt* the wife had moved out of the common home, and the parties had been separated for 11 months at the time of the offense). But in Kizer v. Commonwealth, 321 S.E.2d 291 (Va. 1984), a rape conviction based on a violent sexual assault was nonetheless reversed. In that case the husband had moved to separate quarters, the parties had not engaged in sexual intercourse for more than six months, and the husband had filed for custody of the child. However, because the wife had at various points made attempts to make the marriage "work" and because she had hesitated to file for divorce, the court found that her "vacillating" conduct was too equivocal to establish that the husband knew or should have known that she considered the marriage at an end.

Does *Weishaupt* provide a workable compromise approach? If not, is a simple "living apart" test preferable? Or is preservation of the marital exemption under any conditions fundamentally unsound?

G. PROBLEMS OF PROOF

The preceding sections suggest some of the ways in which concerns about unfounded accusations of rape influenced the law relating to the required actus reus and mens rea. The same concerns have also influenced the law of evidence. Their influence has been felt in three important areas: requirements of corroboration, jury instructions relating to the complainant's credibility, and rules relating to cross-examination. The present section examines these three areas, the first two briefly (their interest is now largely historical) and the third, which presents problems of continuing difficulty and importance, in some detail.

1. *Corroboration and Jury Instructions*

UNITED STATES v. WILEY

United States Court of Appeals, D.C. Circuit
492 F.2d 547 (1974)

[The court held that a complainant's testimony had not been adequately corroborated by independent evidence, as the District of Columbia cases then required. Judge Bazelon's concurring opinion, excerpted here, gives voice to the basic dilemma presented not only by the corroboration issue but by all of the problems of proof examined in this section.]

BAZELON, J. (concurring). The notion that the testimony of a single witness is inadequate to prove a crime is an ancient one. The Code of the Emperor Justinian provided that on any important issue the testimony of one witness was insufficient. Ecclesiastical law refined this approach by requiring, for example, that against the word of a Cardinal, forty-four witnesses were required. But the common law gradually moved toward other modes of inquiry into the truth. Ultimately the common law rejected the requirement of corroboration for all crimes except perjury. Thus there was no common law requirement of corroboration for any sex offense.

Today thirty-five states have similarly rejected the corroboration requirement for rape. Of those jurisdictions that retain the requirement, about half, including the District of Columbia, do so in the absence of legislation. The substance of corroboration requirements varies enormously from state to state, ranging from a requirement of corroboration for force, penetration and identity, to minimal corroboration of any part of the complainant's testimony.

Numerous justifications have been advanced for the requirement of corroboration in sex cases. An examination of these rationales reveals a tangled web of legitimate concerns, out-dated beliefs, and deep-seated prejudices.

The most common basis advanced for the requirement is that false charges of rape are more prevalent than false charges of other crimes. . . . It is contended that a woman may fabricate a rape accusation because, having consented to intercourse she is ashamed and bitter, or because she is pregnant and feels pressured to create a false explanation, or because she hates the man she accuses or wishes to blackmail him. . . .

There are, however, countervailing reasons not to report a rape. One said to be a victim of rape may be stigmatized by society, there may be humiliating publicity, and the necessity of facing the insinuations of defense counsel may be a deterrent. Moreover, those claiming to have been raped may be treated harshly by the police and by hospitals. One result of all of these obstacles is that rape is one of the most under-reported of all crimes. . . .

In addition to the problem of false charges, the corroboration requirement is justified on the theory that rape is a charge unusually difficult to defend against. In 1680 Lord Chief Justice Hale wrote, in one of the most oft-quoted passages in our jurisprudence, that rape "is an accusation easily to be made and hard to be proved, and harder to be defended by the party accused, tho never so innocent." The same theme has been echoed by modern commentators and courts. . . . Juries are said to be unusually sympathetic to a woman wronged, thus weakening the presumption of innocence.

Again, there is little hard evidence with which to test this theory. What studies are available suggest that . . . juries may be more skeptical of rape accusations than is often supposed. . . .

Still another basis for the corroboration requirement lies in "the sorry history of racism in America." There has been an enormous danger of injustice when a black man accused of raping a white woman is tried before a white jury. Of the 455 men executed for rape since 1930, 405 (89 percent) were black. In the vast majority of these cases the complainant was white.

All of the safeguards that developed in this context should not be automatically applied today. Juries are more integrated than in the past and racial prejudice may be at a somewhat lower level. Numerous rape victims are black and their interests, as well as those of white women, may have been slighted by the concern for black defendants.

A final theory of the corroboration requirement is that it stems from discrimination against women. It is said that traditional sex stereotypes have resulted in rape laws that protect men rather than women. Penalties are high because a "good" woman is a valued possession of a man. Corroboration is required because to a "good" woman rape is "a fate worse than death" and she should fight to the death to resist it. If no such fight is put up, the woman must have consented or at least enticed the rapist, who is therefore blameless. In sum it is said to be the "male desire to 'protect' his 'possession' which results in laws designed to protect the male — both the 'owner' and the assailant — rather than protecting the physical well-being and freedom of movement of women." . . .

Analyzing all of these justifications in order to separate the valid from the invalid is no easy task. . . . But at least for the immediate present, I find that the flexible corroboration rule developed by this Court provides the best accommodation of numerous conflicting considerations. . . . To guard against [the] possible dangers [of fabrication] we retain a corroboration rule which provides that "independent corroborative evidence will be regarded as sufficient when it would permit the jury to conclude beyond a reasonable doubt that the victim's account of the crime was not a fabrication." . . . In cases such as this one where that evidence is lacking the dangers to the defendant outweigh the difficulties created for the prosecution. . . .

Thus I concur in the court's opinion reversing defendant's conviction.

NOTES

1. The concern about false charges. Although the treatment of rape victims in the criminal justice system has improved since the time of the *Wiley* decision, rape remains the most underreported of the major crimes. In one recent survey, the Justice Department found that victims report 61 percent of robberies, 44 percent of other violent crimes (like assault), but only 28 percent of rapes. See N.Y. Times, Aug. 28, 2000, at A10. For this and other reasons, many scholars believe that concerns about false charges are wildly exaggerated. They argue that there is no more reason to impose heightened requirements of proof in prosecutions for rape than in prosecutions for any other offense. See Susan Brownmiller, Against Our Will: Men, Women and Rape 386-387 (1975).

Some scholars, however, suggest (contrary to Judge Bazelon's argument in *Wiley*) that the pressures against reporting a rape may not counterbalance the reasons to make a false charge: rape might be underreported by some groups of potential complainants *and* overreported by others. Professor Alan Dershowitz points to FBI statistics indicating that police classify 8.4 percent of reported rapes as "unfounded," and he argues that the "[number of] false rape reports each year . . . is dramatically higher than the number of false reports of other serious crimes," namely 3.8 percent for burglary, 3.5 percent for robbery, and 1.6 percent for assault.[31] (Does the 8.4 percent figure show that false reports are

31. Alan Dershowitz, The Abuse Excuse 275 (1994).

more common for rape or that undue police skepticism is more common for rape?) Another scholar found a high rate of false reports on the basis of data that in one city, 41 percent of rape complainants later told the police that no rape had occurred.[32] (Which was false — the initial report or the subsequent recantation?). Other data sometimes suggest disturbingly high risks of false reports, but the studies again are subject to many varying interpretations. For review of the issues and the empirical evidence, see David P. Bryden & Sonja Lengnick, Rape in the Criminal Justice System, 87 J. Crim. L. & Criminology 1194, 1295-1315 (1997).

2. *Current law.* (*a*) *The corroboration requirement.* By the time of the *Wiley* decision, most American jurisdictions had already abandoned a specific corroboration requirement for rape prosecutions. See Note, The Rape Corroboration Requirement: Repeal Not Reform, 81 Yale L.J. 1365, 1367-1370 (1972). Since then, the remaining jurisdictions have moved in the same direction. See Annot., 31 A.L.R.4th 120 (1982). No American state now requires corroboration in all forcible rape cases.[33]

Three years after the *Wiley* decision, the United States Court of Appeals for the District of Columbia Circuit also decided to abandon the corroboration requirement. In United States v. Sheppard, 569 F.2d 114, 118-119 (D.C. Cir. 1977), Judge J. Skelley Wright wrote for the court:[34]

> The corroboration requirement poses a potentially severe obstacle to legitimate convictions for sex offenses. Operation of the rule serves to foreclose jury consideration of cases in which a highly credible complainant prosecutes charges, on the basis of her testimony alone, against a defendant whose account of the events is clearly less credible. . . . Elimination of the corroboration requirement, however, hardly leaves defendants unprotected against unjust convictions. . . . Where the motivation of the complainant in bringing the charge is an issue, as in a case where the defendant contends that she consented to the intercourse, the defense attorney is free to emphasize to the jury the dangers of falsification, and the judge should instruct the jury as to those dangers and the difficulty of establishing consent. Finally, protection against unjust convictions on a case-by-case basis is afforded by the general rule that judgments of acquittal or reversals of convictions must be granted where substantial evidence does not exist to support a guilty verdict, whether or not independent corroboration is technically present.

Questions: Does Judge Wright's emphasis on the "substantial evidence" requirement suggest that appellate courts should not defer heavily to the trier of fact? Or that they should not do so when corroboration is absent? How would Judge Wright have decided the *Rusk* case (page 323 supra) and the *M.T.S.* case (page 338 supra)?

(*b*) *Special jury instructions.* Many American jurisdictions have long required that in a rape prosecution the jury must be given an instruction like the following (from Cal. Jury Instructions — Criminal No. 10.22 (3d ed. 1970)):

32. Eugene Kanin, False Rape Allegations, 23 Archives Sexual Behav. 81 (1994).

33. Texas, one of the few states to preserve some form of the old rule, still requires corroboration in cases involving an adult victim who reports the offense more than a year after it occurred. See Carmell v. Texas, 120 S. Ct. 1620 (2000); Tex. Code Crim. Proc. §38.07 (1998).

34. Judge Bazelon, who was also a member of the three-judge panel, joined in the opinion and did not write separately.

> A charge such as that made against the defendant in this case is one which is easily made and, once made, difficult to defend against, even if the person accused is innocent. Therefore, the law requires that you examine the testimony of the female person named in the information with caution.

The instruction, based on the remarks of Sir Matthew Hale previously quoted (page 366 supra), has fallen into disfavor for essentially the same reasons that have brought the corroboration requirement under attack. In recent years several jurisdictions have barred the instruction, either by statute (e.g., Pa. Stat. Ann. tit. 18, §3106) or by judicial decision (e.g., People v. Rincon-Pineda, 14 Cal. 3d 864, 538 P.2d 247 (1975)).

3. The Model Penal Code. In sex offense prosecutions, the MPC requires both corroboration and a special jury instruction warning the jury to evaluate the complainant's testimony "with special care." See Model Penal Code §213.6(5), Appendix. These proposals, drafted in the 1950s and approved by the American Law Institute in 1962, have largely been superseded by the more recent developments described in Note 2 above.

2. *Cross Examination and Shield Laws*

SUSAN ESTRICH, PALM BEACH STORIES, 11 Law & Phil. 5, 14 (1992): Precisely because it is all but impossible these days to argue successfully that no means yes, or that men are privileged to have sex with crying women, or even that stupidity as to consent should serve as a defense, men charged with rape, and those who defend them, have few options but to argue the incredibility of the woman victim. And the argument has appeal, I think, because many people, including many prosecutors and judges, remain ambivalent about the expansion of rape liability: unwilling to continue to afford men the privilege of aggression, but also chary with their sympathy for women who should know better. So the old myths of the lying woman are reasserted, now that the rules of liability will no longer protect male defendants.

Thus, we face a new stage in the changing realities of rape law — a final battle, one hopes, in the effort to expand liability to include date rape and acquaintance rape. The debate is less and less about what counts as force, or what is required to prove nonconsent. Today's debate, on the radio, in the newspaper, and in the courtroom, is about when women should be believed — and about what we need to know about the woman before we can decide whether to believe her.

STATE ex rel. POPE v. SUPERIOR COURT

Supreme Court of Arizona
113 Ariz. 22, 545 P.2d 946 (1976)

GORDON, J. The County Attorney of Mohave County acting on behalf of the State of Arizona brings this special action requesting that this Court reconsider existing law on the admissibility of evidence concerning the unchaste character of a complaining witness in a prosecution for first degree rape. . . .

Almost every jurisdiction [once permitted] the substantive use of evidence concerning the unchastity of a prosecutrix where the defense of consent is raised in a forcible rape prosecution. . . . The leading case in Arizona is State v. Wood, 59 Ariz. 48, 122 P.2d 416 (1942), where we [reasoned]: ". . . [C]ommon experience teaches us that the woman who has once departed from the paths of virtue is far more apt to consent to another lapse than is the one who has never stepped aside from that path." . . .

The "logic" and "common experience of mankind" upon which we rested our holding in State v. Wood, supra, now clearly dictate that the case be overturned. It is no longer satisfactory to argue that we should "more readily infer assent in the practised [sic] Messalina, in loose attire, than in the reserved and virtuous Lucretia." People v. Abbot, 19 Wend. 192 (N.Y. 1838). The reasoning consistently advanced by this Court to bar most prior bad acts of a witness applies with even greater force in a rape prosecution. Reference to prior unchaste acts of the complaining witness "injects collateral issues into the case which . . . divert the jury's attention from the real issue, the guilt or innocence of the accused." A prosecutrix in a forcible rape prosecution "should not be expected to come prepared to defend every incident of [her] past life." . . .

We recognize there are certain limited situations where evidence of prior unchaste acts has sufficient probative value to outweigh its inflammatory effect and require admission. These would include evidence of prior consensual sexual intercourse with the defendant or testimony which directly refutes physical or scientific evidence, such as the victim's alleged loss of virginity, the origin of semen, disease or pregnancy. . . . [Where] the defendant alleges the prosecutrix actually consented to an act of prostitution, the accused should be permitted to present evidence of her reputation as a prostitute and her prior acts of prostitution to support such a defense. In addition, evidence concerning unchastity would be admissible in conjunction with an effort by the defense to show that the complaining witness has made unsubstantiated charges of rape in the past.

In these and other instances in which the evidence concerning unchastity is alleged to be sufficiently probative to compel its admission despite its inflammatory effect, a hearing should be held by the court outside the presence of the jury prior to the presentation of the evidence. . . . If the defendant alleges that proffered evidence falls into one of the above exceptions, the trial court should allow its admission if it is not too remote and appears credible. . . .

Hays, J. (specially concurring). I concur with the result reached by the majority opinion, but I cannot approve a procedure which permits evidence of the prosecutrix' reputation as a prostitute even on the limited issue of consent. In advancing to a more reasonable and logical position by overruling State v. Wood, 59 Ariz. 48, 122 P.2d 416 (1942), we should take a full step rather than mincing toward the final goal. . . .

I am also unable to concur with the majority's position which rather vaguely states that the defense may show that "the complaining witness has made unsubstantiated charges of rape in the past." The reason or logic in carving out such an exception to the rule excluding evidence of the unchastity of the complaining witness in a rape case escapes me. . . .

NOTES

1. Did the court go far enough in *Pope*? If the court's assumptions about sexual mores are sound, how can one justify its willingness to admit evidence of prior acts of prostitution? On what basis can one justify an exception even for evidence of prior consensual intercourse with defendant?

2. Did the court go too far in *Pope*? Recall that the general test for the probative value of evidence does not require that the evidence make some fact likely to be true; rather probative value requires only that the fact be somewhat more likely to be true given the evidence than it would be without the evidence. See pages 20-21 supra. By this standard, doesn't evidence of prior sexual activity have at least some probative value? For example, if the complaining witness has often consented to sexual intercourse with men shortly after meeting them in a bar, wouldn't that fact make it at least a little bit more likely that she consented to intercourse with the defendant shortly after meeting him in a bar?

The rationale for excluding evidence of a complainant's prior sexual history presumably is not that such evidence completely lacks probative value. Rather, the principal justification for exclusion is that any probative value is outweighed by the prejudicial effect. (At pages 22-32 supra we discuss this all-important principle of evidence law.) In the present context two kinds of prejudicial effect are especially important. First, such evidence can impair the truth-finding function at trial because its value may be overestimated or because it may lead to confusion of the issues. Second, the very process of airing such evidence can be painful or embarrassing to the victim, aggravating the psychological injury of the original offense and deterring other victims from seeking prosecution. Many rape victims once reported feeling that they had been raped twice — first by their assailant and then a second time in the courtroom. See Vivian D. Berger, Man's Trial, Woman's Tribulation: Rape Cases in the Courtroom, 77 Colum. L. Rev. 1 (1977).

3. Are there situations where evidence of a complainant's prior sexual activity should be admissible despite its prejudicial effect? Nearly all American jurisdictions have enacted "rape shield laws" to limit the admissibility of evidence bearing on a rape complainant's prior sexual behavior. For discussion of the issues posed by these statutes, see J. Alexander Tanford & Anthony Bocchino, Rape Victim Shield Laws and the Sixth Amendment, 128 U. Pa. L. Rev. 544 (1980); Berger, supra Note 2. Some of the statutes are extremely restrictive, admitting evidence of sexual history only when it involves prior incidents with the defendant. Another approach provides a detailed list of exceptions to the rule of exclusion. Some states combine a list of specific exceptions with a catch-all exception for any other evidence that has probative value greater than its prejudicial effect. Finally, a few states simply provide a procedure for pretrial hearings while leaving the ultimate decision entirely to the trial judge's discretion. See Harriett R. Galvin, Shielding Rape Victims in the State and Federal Courts: A Proposal for the Second Decade, 70 Minn. L. Rev. 763 (1986).

"Rape shield" statutes are motivated primarily by the need to protect victim-witnesses from serious abuses in the trial process. But to what extent do these statutes interfere with the defendant's right to a fair trial? Consider the cases that follow.

STATE v. DeLAWDER

Maryland Court of Special Appeals
28 Md. App. 212, 344 A.2d 446 (1975)

ORTH, C.J. . . . Lee Franklin DeLawder was found guilty by a jury in the Circuit Court for Montgomery County of carnal knowledge of a female under the age of 14 years. A 15 year sentence was imposed. The judgment was affirmed on direct appeal. [DeLawder then sought postconviction relief.] . . .

In affirming the judgment on direct appeal, we held that the trial court did not err in sustaining objections made to questions attempting to show that the prosecuting witness had sexual intercourse with other men on other occasions. The general rule is that because consent is not an issue in a carnal knowledge prosecution, evidence that the prosecutrix had prior intercourse with men other than the accused, or that her reputation for chastity was bad is immaterial when offered as an excuse or justification, and so is inadmissible for that reason. . . . The trial judge correctly applied these rules. . . .

As *Davis* [v. Alaska, 415 U.S. 308 (1974)] was decided subsequent to our decision, we must determine whether it affects the validity of DeLawder's conviction. In *Davis,* the Supreme Court of the United States reviewed the reach of the Confrontation Clause of the Sixth Amendment to the federal Constitution. . . . "Confrontation means more than being allowed to confront the witness physically. 'Our cases construing the [confrontation] clause hold that a primary interest secured by it is the right of cross-examination.'" "Cross-examination," the Court observed, "is the principal means by which the believability of a witness and the truth of his testimony are tested. . . ." A witness may be discredited by a general attack on his credibility by introducing evidence of a prior criminal conviction of that witness. . . . A witness may also be discredited . . . by means of cross-examination directed toward revealing possible biases, prejudices, or ulterior motives of the witness. . . . The Supreme Court has recognized "that the exposure of a witness's motivation in testifying is a proper and important function of the constitutionally protected right of cross-examination." . . .

Davis was convicted of burglary and grand larceny . . . at a trial in which the court [prohibited] the questioning of Richard Green, a key prosecution witness, concerning Green's adjudication as a juvenile delinquent relating to a burglary and his probation status at the time of the events as to which he was to testify. The motion was granted in reliance on a state rule and statute which preserved the confidentiality of juvenile adjudications of delinquency. . . . The defense made clear that it did not intend to use Green's juvenile record to impeach his credibility generally, but only as necessary to examine him for any possible bias and prejudice. "Not only might Green have made a hasty and faulty identification of [Davis] to shift suspicion away from himself as one who robbed the Polar Bar, but Green might have been subject to undue pressure from the police and made his identification under fear of possible probation revocation." The trial court rejected even this limited use of Green's adjudication, but defense counsel did his best to expose Green's state of mind at the time he discovered the safe. Green, however, made a flat denial to questions whether he was upset by the fact that the [stolen] safe was found on his property, whether he felt the authorities might suspect him, and whether he felt uncomfortable about it. . . .

The Alaska Supreme Court . . . affirmed the conviction on the grounds that the scope of cross-examination allowed was adequate to develop the issue of bias and convey it to the jury. The Supreme Court did not accept this. It said: "On the basis of the limited cross-examination that was permitted, the jury might well have thought that defense counsel was engaged in a speculative and baseless line of attack on the credibility of an apparently blameless witness. . . . [T]o make any such inquiry effective, defense counsel should have been permitted to expose to the jury the facts from which jurors, as the sole triers of fact and credibility, could appropriately draw inferences relating to the reliability of the witness." It held that disallowance of the defense's attempt to show bias . . . by cross-examination concerning the witness's juvenile record violated Davis's Sixth and Fourteenth Amendment rights.[2] . . .

DeLawder's counsel made clear from the onset of the case that the defense strategy would be to discredit the prosecuting witness [by] proving that at the time of the alleged incident, she thought she was pregnant by someone else and claimed that DeLawder raped her because she was afraid to tell her mother she voluntarily had sexual intercourse with others. To show that she thought she was pregnant at the time of the alleged encounter with DeLawder, it would be necessary to establish that she had engaged in prior acts of sexual intercourse. . . .

We cannot speculate . . . as to whether the jury . . . would have accepted this line of reasoning had counsel been permitted to present it fully. But [it] seems clear to us, in the light of *Davis,* that defense counsel should have been permitted to expose to the jury the facts from which jurors, as the sole triers of fact and credibility, could appropriately draw inferences relating to the reliability of the witness. By being prevented from so doing DeLawder was denied the right of effective cross-examination. . . . We conclude, as the Court concluded in *Davis,* that the desirability that the prosecutrix fulfill her public duty to testify free from embarrassment and with her reputation unblemished must fall before the right of an accused to seek out the truth in the process of defending himself. . . .

NOTES

1. A number of courts have held that restrictive rape shield statutes are unconstitutional when they bar use of relevant sexual history evidence. E.g., Commonwealth v. Spiewak, 617 A.2d 696 (Pa. Super. 1992). Some courts have avoided striking down their rape shield statutes by reading in a "catch-all" exception for any evidence needed to preserve the defendant's right to a fair trial. E.g., Neeley v. Commonwealth, 437 S.E.2d 721 (Va. App. 1993).

2. Though "rape shield" statutes have proved much more porous than reformers initially expected, they have nonetheless had a major impact on the administration of rape trials. Empirical studies uniformly report that victims are

2. The Court did not challenge the State's interest as a matter of its own policy in the administration of criminal justice to seek to preserve the anonymity of a juvenile offender.

> . . . Whatever temporary embarrassment might result to Green or his family by disclosure of his juvenile record — if the prosecution insisted on using him to make its case — is outweighed by petitioner's right to probe into the influence of possible bias in the testimony of a crucial identification witness. . . .

much better treated in the judicial process and that efforts to limit the admissibility of sexual history evidence are largely successful.[35]

3. Determining the balance between probative value and prejudicial effect can be especially difficult when an incident implicates powerful social prejudices. In Neeley v. Commonwealth, 437 N.E.2d 721 (Va. App. 1993), the facts touched both racial and sexual nerves. The complainant, a 14-year-old white female, alleged that defendant, a young African-American male who lived nearby, climbed through her bedroom window in the middle of the night and forcibly raped her. Defendant denied entering the house that evening. The prosecution introduced expert testimony that a hair fragment found in the complainant's cervix, though not positively identifiable as defendant's, was "characteristic of hair from a person of African-American descent." The defendant offered to prove that shortly before the alleged rape, the complainant had had sexual intercourse with her boyfriend and that the boyfriend was also African-American. A provision of the state's rape shield law permitted the use of sexual history evidence when "offered to provide an alternative explanation for physical evidence of the offense charged which is introduced by the prosecution, limited to evidence designed to explain the presence of semen, pregnancy, disease, or physical injury to the complaining witness's intimate parts. . . ." Because the defendant's evidence was not offered to explain the presence of "semen, pregnancy, disease, or physical injury . . . ," it did not meet the terms of this or any other statutory exception, and the trial court excluded it. On appeal, should the ruling be upheld? Or, as applied to these facts, is the statutory exclusion unconstitutional?

4. "Public" behavior. Should prior sexual history evidence be excluded under a rape shield law even when the conduct in question occurred in public? Consider State v. Colbath, 130 N.H. 316, 540 A.2d 1212 (1988). Defendant met the complainant at a tavern and later went with her to his trailer, where they had intercourse — forcible according to her testimony, consensual according to his. At trial the tavern owner's daughter described the complainant's behavior at the tavern as "hanging all over everyone and making out with Richard Colbath and a few others." The trial judge instructed the jury to disregard the testimony concerning the complainant's behavior with anyone other than defendant. Defendant argued that the testimony was properly admissible and that the instruction was therefore erroneous. He argued, in particular, that the rape shield law (which excluded evidence of prior sexual conduct with others) was inapplicable because the conduct occurred in public. The court (per Souter, J.) found it unnecessary to decide whether public sexual conduct was, per se, outside the reach of the rape shield law, but held for the defendant on narrower grounds (540 A.2d at 1216-1217):

> [D]escribing a complainant's open, sexually suggestive conduct in the presence of patrons of a public bar obviously has far less potential for damaging the sensibilities than revealing what the same person may have done in the company of another behind a closed door. On the other hand, evidence of public displays of general interest in sexual activity can be taken to indicate a contemporaneous receptiveness to sexual advances that cannot be inferred from evidence of private behavior with chosen sex partners.

35. See Cassia Spohn & Julia Horney, Rape Law Reform: Grassroots Revolution and Its Impact 129 (1992).

. . . It would, in fact, understate the importance of such evidence in this case to speak of it merely as relevant. We should recall that the fact of intercourse was not denied, and that the evidence of assault was subject to the explanation that the defendant's jealous [live-in] companion [who had discovered him with the complainant in the trailer] had inflicted the visible injuries. The companion's furious behavior had a further bearing on the case, as well, for the jury could have regarded her attack as a reason for the complainant to regret a voluntary liaison with the defendant, and as a motive for the complainant to allege rape as a way to explain her injuries and excuse her undignified predicament. . . . [T]he outcome of the prosecution could well have turned on a very close judgment about the complainant's attitude of resistance or consent.

Because little significance can be assigned here either to the privacy interest or to a fear of misleading the jury, the trial court was bound to recognize the defendant's interest in presenting probably crucial evidence of the complainant's behavior closely preceding the alleged rape. . . . Because the jury instruction effectively excluded the evidence in question, the conviction must be reversed . . . .

Compare Wood v. Alaska, 957 F.2d 1544 (9th Cir. 1992). Defendant and complainant had been close friends. As in *Colbath,* intercourse was admitted; the defense was consent. Defendant alleged that on occasions prior to the incident, complainant told him that she had posed for *Penthouse,* a sexually explicit men's magazine, had acted in pornographic movies, and had been paid to have sex while people took pictures of her. He also offered to prove that she had shown him her *Penthouse* photographs and that he perceived that "in some respects [her conduct] seemed to be a sexual come-on." The trial judge excluded the evidence under Alaska's rape-shield law, and defendant was convicted of sexual assault. In habeas corpus proceedings asserting the denial of his constitutional rights, the U.S. Court of Appeals (per Rymer, J.) first held that the excluded evidence was relevant on the issue of consent. Nonetheless, the court said, the prejudicial effect outweighed the probative value, even though the behavior had occurred in nationally distributed magazines and films (957 F.2d at 1552-1554):

[U]nlike *Davis* [v. Alaska, page 378 supra], the interests in this case go beyond that of protecting the witness. Of significantly more import are the concerns, intrinsic to the truth-finding process itself, that introducing the evidence would confuse the issues and unduly prejudice the jury. . . . The proffered evidence in this case is particularly prejudicial because it indicates not only that M.G. had extramarital sex, but also that she posed nude and had sex both for money and for the purpose of making pornography. Because many people consider prostitution and pornography to be particularly offensive, there is a significant possibility that jurors would be influenced by their impression of M.G. as an immoral woman. They could also conclude, contrary to the rape law, that a woman with her sexual past cannot be raped, or that she somehow deserved to be raped after engaging in these sexual activities. . . .

Because [the evidence] is not highly probative and the risk of confusion and prejudice is substantial, we conclude that the trial court acted within its discretion when it excluded the evidence.

5. Prior behavior of the defendant. In Chapter 1, we considered the principle that evidence of prior misconduct by a defendant is not admissible for purposes of proving a propensity to engage in conduct of a similar nature. See pages 22-32 supra. As we saw there, most jurisdictions apply the prior-misconduct rule just as strictly in rape trials as in other kinds of prosecutions. See especially page 30, Note 2(b) supra.

Is the willingness of courts to admit evidence of some prior sexual acts by a rape complainant inconsistent with the rule that precludes reference to prior misconduct by the defendant? In one highly publicized prosecution, William Kennedy Smith was charged with committing a sexual assault upon a woman who had accompanied him back to his family's vacation home, after drinking and dancing with him at a bar. The case turned on the credibility of the woman's testimony that Smith ignored her protests and forced her to submit. Prior to trial, three other women came forward to allege that Smith had sexually assaulted them. The trial judge excluded this evidence, and Smith was acquitted. See N.Y. Times, Dec. 13, 1992, at B14. Was the ruling correct? If not, should the judge admit evidence of the prior sexual conduct of *both* Smith and his accuser? Consider Susan Estrich, Teaching Rape Law, 102 Yale L.J. 509, 519 (1992):

> One [approach] is to say that we need symmetry: exclude all the evidence about both of them. That's the approach the judge followed in the William Kennedy Smith case. On the surface, it is neat and appealing. The only problem is that it's a false symmetry. . . . [E]vidence that a man has abused other women is much more probative of rape than evidence that a woman has had consensual sex with other men is probative of consent. [T]he mere fact that a woman has had lovers tells us almost nothing about whether she consented on the particular occasion that she is charging as rape. But won't we all look at a defendant differently if three other women have also come forward to say they were abused? The danger with such evidence is not that it proves so little, but that it may prove too much. Symmetry won't get you out of this hole. . . .
>
> Thus even if most students can agree these days that no means no, and that force can be established if you push a woman down, there's very little agreement about what we need to know about her or him before deciding whether she in fact said yes or no, and whether he actually pushed her down or just lay down with her. The consensus on what counts as rape is more apparent than real.

GOVERNMENT OF THE VIRGIN ISLANDS v. SCUITO

United States Court of Appeals, 3d Circuit
623 F.2d 869 (1980)

ADAMS, J. In this appeal from a conviction for forcible rape, the defendant Louis Scuito asserts . . . [that the] trial judge abused or failed to exercise his discretion in denying the defendant's motion for a psychiatric examination of the complainant. . . .

The complainant worked as a waitress at the Drunken Shrimp restaurant, where the defendant was a frequent patron. When the complainant worked late on the night of July 9, 1978, the owner of the restaurant arranged for Scuito to give the complainant a ride to her apartment. It is undisputed that Scuito took a detour down a beach road, where the two had sexual intercourse, after which he took the complainant home. The crucial issue at trial was solely whether she consented.

According to the complainant, Scuito turned down the beach road to relieve himself, and then continued to a turnaround, stopped the jeep, and began kissing her. She expressed lack of interest, but the defendant then told her he had a knife and would throw her into the ocean if she did not cooperate. She testified that she did not actually see the knife in the dark, but felt "something metal" cut into her neck, after which she ceased resistance and attempted to calm him and avoid harm by cooperating. At trial there was medical and other testimony of a cut on the side of the complainant's neck where she said the knife was held. After taking off her clothes, the defendant raped and sodomized her. During the course of the assault she prayed and recited her "mantra."[2] Upon being dropped off at home, she kissed the defendant on the forehead because, she testified, "I was praying for him" and "it was just kind of like an end to the prayer."

Scuito testified that he casually knew the complainant and her sister and had previously driven them home from the restaurant. He said that on the night of July 9, when he gave the complainant a ride to her apartment, she seemed "a little spaced, not all there." While riding home, she offered him marijuana and he drove off the main road to smoke it with her. He later "came on to her," he said. Although initially she protested, he eventually changed her mind without using or threatening any physical force.

Prior to the first trial there had been a discussion between counsel and the court regarding the admissibility of evidence that Scuito previously had raped another young woman after threatening to shoot her with a flare gun. . . . The prosecutor agreed not to mention the other alleged rape in the opening statement to the jury, but reserved the right to seek admission of the evidence . . . if the testimony that was adduced created the opportunity. . . .

[The first trial ended in a mistrial after the prosecutor indirectly referred to the previous flare-gun rape by the defendant.]

. . . Scuito moved before the second trial for a psychiatric examination of the complainant. In a supporting affidavit, his attorney made the following specific representations:

> [1] I have been informed by any number of persons in the community that the said complainant appears to be often, if not almost constantly, in a "spaced out" or trancelike state; I have personally observed this; I have been further informed by persons in the community that the said complainant is addicted to, and does continually use, controlled substances, and that she is frequently in altered states of consciousness therefrom; and I have further observed and been told of the said complainant's habit of dressing and being seen publicly in see-through top garments which seem indicative of socially aberrant behavior;
>
> [2] Further, my observation of the said complainant at the first trial herein showed, in my opinion, a rather strange and mysterious countenance on her part, and her testimony appeared strange, not only from the standpoint of her account of not reporting the alleged crimes until the next day, but particularly from her admitted interest and devotion to a certain book, written by a guru devotee of Timothy Leary which contains passages of religious-like worship of LSD and other mind-altering drugs; [and]
>
> [3] That the foregoing observations are highly indicative of a personality which fantasizes to extremes and which indulges in and seeks altered states of consciousness. . . .

2. A mantra has been defined as "[a] sound aid used while meditating. Each meditator has his own personal mantra which is never to be revealed to any other person." Malnak v. Yogi, 592 F.2d 197, 198 (3d Cir. 1979). . . .

Defendant does not press the extreme position, espoused by Wigmore, that a psychiatric examination of a complainant should be required in all sexual offense prosecutions.[14] Rather, defendant agrees with the Government that the decision to order an examination is "entrusted to the sound discretion of the trial judge in light of the particular facts." . . .

This discretion is not, of course, unbounded, for there are countervailing considerations weighing heavily against ordering a psychiatric examination of a complainant. As set out by the Court of Appeals for the District of Columbia Circuit, they are that "a psychiatric examination may seriously impinge on a witness' right to privacy; the trauma that attends the role of complainant to sex offense charges is sharply increased by the indignity of a psychiatric examination; the examination itself could serve as a tool of harassment; and the impact of all these considerations may well deter the victim of such a crime from lodging any complaint at all." United States v. Benn, 476 F.2d at 1131. . .

Fed. R. Evid. 412 is specifically addressed to evidence of a rape victim's prior sexual conduct,[16] whereas defendant's motion was not an attempt to introduce such evidence, but an effort to obtain an expert opinion regarding the complainant's general ability to perceive reality and separate fact from fantasy. Because the rule does not directly apply to his motion, the defendant argues that the court either abused or did not exercise its discretion in denying the motion. The judge's ruling, however, was not based on the letter but on the spirit of Rule 412. The principal purpose of that rule is, as its legislative history demonstrates, quite similar to the countervailing considerations quoted above: "to protect rape victims from the degrading and embarrassing disclosure of intimate details about their private lives." The rationale, according to one commentator, "is to prevent the victim, rather than the defendant, from being put on trial."

We hold that in relying on the *spirit* of Rule 412 the trial judge exercised discretion, and that nothing alleged in defense counsel's affidavit indicates that he abused his discretion. To the extent admissible, and we express no opinion on that matter, evidence that the complainant was thought by members of the community to indulge in drugs leading to "altered states of consciousness" or to dress in a manner "indicative of socially aberrant behavior" could be introduced by direct rather than expert testimony. If, however, such matters are not relevant or otherwise admissible, there is no justification for letting them into the trial by allowing an expert to give his opinion regarding them. . . .

The judgment of the trial court will be affirmed.

NOTES AND QUESTIONS

1. Suppose that the defendant had sought to present the evidence about the complainant's state of mind through ordinary witnesses rather than through ex-

14. See 3A Wigmore on Evidence §924a, at 737 (Chadbourne rev. 1970) ("No judge should let a sex offense charge go to the jury unless the female complainant's social history and mental makeup have been examined and testified to by a qualified physician.") (italics deleted). The Wigmore position does not seem to be accepted in any jurisdiction.

16. [Rule 412 excludes "(1) evidence offered to prove that any alleged victim engaged in other sexual behavior; and (2) evidence offered to prove any alleged victim's sexual predisposition." Rule 412 would not literally apply to the kind of "mental stability" evidence at issue in *Scuito.* — Eds.]

pert testimony. Should such evidence be admissible under the circumstances? If so, is it really preferable for the matter to be explored through testimony about haphazard observations and "general reputation," rather than through the testimony of experts? Is the disfavoring of expert testimony justified in terms of the truth-seeking function of the trial or only in terms of the desire to protect the complainant from degrading psychological tests? If the latter explanation is the more satisfactory, is the result in *Scuito* consistent with Davis v. Alaska?

2. Compare *Scuito* with United States v. Lindstrom, 698 F.2d 1154 (11th Cir. 1983). *Lindstrom* was a mail fraud prosecution in which the defendants sought to show that the allegations against them were the product of a vendetta resulting from the mental illness of the prosecution's principal witness. The trial judge, fearing that "the defense would attempt to put the witness herself on trial," permitted only a few narrowly framed questions designed to show that the witness had had mental and emotional problems in the past. The appellate court held that the defendants should have been allowed to cross-examine more extensively and should have been allowed access to the witness's psychiatric records in order to test her perception, credibility, and motivation.

Questions: Should *Lindstrom* have been decided differently if the witness had accused the defendants of rape? If cases of this kind cannot be distinguished in terms of the crime that the complainant charges, should cross-examination about mental problems and access to psychiatric records be barred in both types of cases?

3. In *Scuito* the defendant was denied the right to compel a psychiatric examination of the complainant. Should the result be different if the defendant seeks access to records of psychiatric treatment already provided to the complainant on her initiative, or are the complainant's privacy interests even stronger in the latter situation?

Consider Commonwealth v. Stockhammer, 409 Mass. 867, 570 N.E.2d 992 (1991). The defendant and the complainant were college classmates who had become close friends. Prior to April 1988 there was no sexual dimension to their relationship, and the complainant had a boyfriend in another city. The alleged rape occurred in 1988, and the complainant promptly described the incident to a friend but asked the friend not to tell anyone about it. The complainant continued to see the defendant and invited him to visit her at her parents' home later that Spring. In December 1988 the complainant broke up with her boyfriend, and in January 1989 she was hospitalized after an apparent suicide attempt. She reported having a minor problem with her boyfriend but made no mention of having been raped. Shortly thereafter, an anonymous caller told her father that the complainant had been telling others about a sexual assault, and when confronted by her father, she told him that the defendant had raped her. She then reported the incident to the police. She also received extended psychiatric treatment, first as a hospital inpatient and subsequently during four months of counseling from a social worker. Defendant admitted the sexual encounter of April 1988 and claimed that it was consensual. He was convicted of rape, but on appeal the court reversed, holding that defense counsel was entitled to inspect records of the complainant's psychiatric treatment in order to search for evidence to buttress the defendant's claim that the rape charge was fabricated.

Compare Susan Estrich, Palm Beach Stories, 11 Law & Phil. 5, 17-18 (1992):

Stockhammer is precisely the sort of case that probably would not even have been prosecuted ten years ago; it is the sort of conviction that might well have been reversed by an appeals court on the grounds of absence of force as recently as five years ago. In 1991, however, when the Massachusetts Supreme Judicial Court reversed the defendant's conviction (some things don't change), they did so not on culpability grounds such as force or consent, but by holding that the defendant was entitled under the state constitution to review the woman's psychiatric treatment records. . . .

What is striking about *Stockhammer* is that the records in question related to treatment the woman sought after the rape — when many women need psychological help, as the court itself recognized. . . . The bitter irony, of course, is that I can think of few greater deterrents to getting help than the knowledge that one's records may later be viewed not just by a judge, but by defense counsel, the defendant, a jury of strangers, and a bevy of curious newspaper readers.

CHAPTER 5

HOMICIDE

A. INTRODUCTION

There are two principal questions one may ask in considering a particular category of crime. The first is a question of criminality: What distinguishes criminal behavior from noncriminal behavior? The second is a question of punishment grading: What factors warrant greater or lesser punishment within the area of behavior defined as criminal? In the preceding chapter on rape, we dealt primarily with questions of the first kind. In this chapter, we will deal primarily with questions of the latter kind.

The distinction between criminal and noncriminal homicide usually raises such issues as causation, necessity, self-defense, defense of another, insanity, duress, etc. We will deal separately with such general issues later.

The questions of homicide grading will constitute the principal focus of the materials in this section. Following the introductory historical and statutory materials, we deal in Section B with the factors that influence the categorization of intended killings into homicidal crimes of greater or lesser punishment — murder in the several degrees and voluntary manslaughter. In Section C, a similar inquiry is pursued with respect to killings that are unintentional. It will be helpful to bear in mind, that apart from certain unintended killings that are not considered criminal, virtually all the varieties of behavior dealt with are crimes of some sort, the only question being what crime is involved, which is to say, what punishment is authorized.

REPORT OF THE ROYAL COMMISSION ON CAPITAL PUNISHMENT, 1945-1953

25-28 (1953)

Basic Principles of the Law of Murder in England

72. Homicide is the killing of a human being by a human being. Unlawful homicide may be murder, manslaughter, suicide or infanticide. Murder and man-

slaughter are felonies at common law and are not defined by statute. The traditional definition or description of murder . . . is in common practice often . . . briefly defined as "unlawful killing with 'malice aforethought'"; while manslaughter is defined as "unlawful killing without 'malice aforethought.'" . . .

74. The meaning of "malice aforethought," which is the distinguishing criterion of murder, is certainly not beyond the range of controversy. The first thing that must be said about it is that neither of the two words is used in its ordinary sense: the phrase "malice aforethought" is now a highly technical term of art. "It is now only an arbitrary symbol. For the 'malice' may have in it nothing really malicious; and need never be really 'aforethought,' except in the sense that every desire must necessarily come before — though perhaps only an instant before — the act which is desired. The word 'aforethought,' in the definition, has thus become either false or else superfluous. The word 'malice' is neither; but it is apt to be misleading, for it is not employed in its original (and its popular) meaning." "Malice aforethought" is simply a comprehensive name for a number of different mental attitudes which have been variously defined at different stages in the development of the law, the presence of any one of which in the accused has been held by the courts to render a homicide particularly heinous and therefore to make it murder. These states of mind have been variously expressed by various authorities, but the statement of the modern law most commonly cited as authoritative is that given in 1877 by Sir James Stephen in his Digest of the Criminal Law:

> Malice aforethought means any one or more of the following states of mind preceding or co-existing with the act or omission by which death is caused, and it may exist where that act is unpremeditated.
>
> (a) An intention to cause the death of, or grievous bodily harm to, any person, whether such person is the person actually killed or not;
> (b) knowledge that the act which causes death will probably cause the death of, or grievous bodily harm to, some person, whether such person is the person actually killed or not, although such knowledge is accompanied by indifference whether death or grievous bodily harm is caused or not, or by a wish that it may not be caused;
> (c) an intent to commit any felony whatever;
> (d) an intent to oppose by force any officer of justice on his way to, in, or returning from the execution of the duty of arresting, keeping in custody, or imprisoning any person whom he is lawfully entitled to arrest, keep in custody, or imprison, or the duty of keeping the peace or dispersing an unlawful assembly, provided that the offender has notice that the person killed is such an officer so employed. . . .

75. We must now consider how "malice aforethought" came to be the distinctive element of murder and to bear such a meaning as is given to it at the present time. . . . It is sufficient to say here that "murder" originally meant a "secret killing" and only gradually, from the fourteenth century onwards, came to be the name of the worst form of homicide characterised by "malice prepense" or "malice aforethought." The next stage is marked by a series of statutes in the reigns of Henry VII and VIII which largely took away the benefit of clergy from murders "of malice prepensed." It seems clear that at this period and for some-

time afterwards "malice prepense" or "malice aforethought" was understood to mean a deliberate, premeditated intent to kill formed some time beforehand, and that no killing "on a sudden," even without provocation or on slight provocation, was considered to be murder. In effect the law regarded unlawful killings as being of only two kinds — killing with malice aforethought and killing on a sudden quarrel. Experience showed, however, that this view was much too simple and the definitions founded upon it inadequate. There were many kinds of killing which should clearly be considered unlawful but which did not fall into either of these categories, and many such cases seemed to deserve the extreme penalty although the offender had no premeditated desire to kill his victim. During the last four centuries the meaning to be given to the term "malice aforethought" has been affected by the changes in the conception of mens rea as a necessary ingredient in criminal liability at common law for all crimes. The courts and the writers of legal textbooks have responded to this change by giving to "malice aforethought" a wider and more technical meaning. As Stephen put it, "the loose term 'malice' was used, and then when a particular state of mind came under their notice, the Judges called it 'malice' or not, according to their view of the propriety of hanging particular people. That is, in two words, the history of the definition of murder." There can be no doubt that the term now covers, and has for long covered, all the most heinous forms of homicide, as well as some cases — those of "constructive murder" — whose inclusion in the category of murder has often been criticised.

76. Thus the following propositions are commonly accepted:

(i) It is murder if one person kills another with intent to do so, without provocation or on slight provocation, although there is no premeditation in the ordinary sense of the word.
(ii) It is murder if one person is killed by an act intended to kill another.
(iii) It is murder if a person is killed by an act intended to kill, although not intended to kill any particular individual, as if a man throws a bomb into a crowd of people.
(iv) It is murder if death results from an act which is intended to do no more than cause grievous bodily harm. An early example may be found in the case of Grey, where a blacksmith, who had had words with an apprentice, struck him on the head with an iron bar and killed him. It was held that it "is all one as if he had run him through with a sword" and he was found guilty of murder.
(v) It is murder if one person kills another by an intentional act which he knows to be likely to kill or to cause grievous bodily harm, although he may not intend to kill or to cause grievous bodily harm and may either be recklessly indifferent as to the results of his act or may even desire that no harm should be caused by it.

CALIFORNIA PENAL CODE

Section 187. Murder Defined

(a) Murder is the unlawful killing of a human being, or a fetus,[a] with malice aforethought.[b] . . .

Section 188. Malice Defined: Express and Implied Malice

Such malice may be express or implied. It is expressed when there is manifested a deliberate intention unlawfully to take away the life of a fellow creature. It is implied, when no considerable provocation appears, or when the circumstances attending the killing show an abandoned and malignant heart.

When it is shown that the killing resulted from the intentional doing of an act with express or implied malice as defined above, no other mental state need be shown to establish the mental state of malice aforethought. Neither an awareness of the obligation to act within the general body of laws regulating society nor acting despite such awareness is included within the definition of malice.

Section 189. Degrees of Murder

All murder which is perpetrated by means of a destructive device or explosive, knowing use of ammunition designed primarily to penetrate metal or armor, poison, lying in wait, torture, or by any other kind of willful, deliberate, and premeditated killing, or which is committed in the perpetration or attempt to perpetrate arson, rape, robbery, burglary, mayhem, kidnapping, train wrecking, or any act punishable under Section 286, 288, 288a, or 289 [prohibiting various forcible sexual acts and certain sexual acts with minors], is murder of the first degree [punishable by death or imprisonment for life without possibility of parole, where special enumerated circumstances exist, or imprisonment for 25 years to life]; and all other kinds of murders are of the second degree [punishable by imprisonment for 15 years to life]. . . .

To prove the killing was "deliberate and premeditated," it shall not be necessary to prove the defendant maturely and meaningfully reflected upon the gravity of his or her act.

a. Except where done in the course of a legal abortion or by a physician pursuant to a medical judgment or where consented to by the mother. Section 187(b). The language was added following Keeler v. Superior Court, page 294 supra, 1970 Cal. Laws ch. 1311, §1. In People v. Davis, 872 P.2d 591 (Cal. 1994), the court held that viability is not an element of the offense of fetal murder; the killing of a fetus can constitute murder, within the meaning of §187(a), as long as the state can show that the fetus has progressed beyond the embryonic stage of seven to eight weeks. — Eds.

b. For a study of the evolving interpretation of this term in California, see Suzanne Mounts, Malice Aforethought in California: A History of Legislative Abdication and Judicial Vacillation, 33 U.S.F. L. Rev. 313 (1999). — Eds.

SECTION 192. MANSLAUGHTER . . .

Manslaughter is the unlawful killing of a human being without malice. It is of three kinds:

(a) VOLUNTARY — upon a sudden quarrel or heat of passion. [Punishable by imprisonment for three, six, or eleven years.]

(b) INVOLUNTARY — in the commission of an unlawful act, not amounting to felony; or in the commission of a lawful act which might produce death, in an unlawful manner, or without due caution and circumspection. This subdivision shall not apply to acts committed in the driving of a vehicle. [Punishable by imprisonment for two, three, or four years.]

(c) VEHICULAR —

(1) . . . driving a vehicle in the commission of an unlawful act, not amounting to felony, and with gross negligence; or driving a vehicle in the commission of a lawful act which might produce death, in an unlawful manner, and with gross negligence. [Punishable by up to one year in county jail or imprisonment for two, four, or six years.]

(2) . . . driving a vehicle in the commission of an unlawful act, not amounting to felony, but without gross negligence; or driving a vehicle in the commission of a lawful act which might produce death, in an unlawful manner, but without gross negligence. [Punishable by a county jail term not to exceed one year.] . . .

This section shall not be construed as making any homicide in the driving of a vehicle punishable which is not a proximate result of the commission of an unlawful act, not amounting to a felony, or the commission of a lawful act which might produce death, in an unlawful manner.

"Gross negligence," as used in this section, shall not be construed as prohibiting or precluding a charge of murder under Section 188 upon facts exhibiting wantonness and a conscious disregard for life to support a finding of implied malice, or upon facts showing malice. . . .

PENNSYLVANIA CONSOLIDATED STATUTES, TITLE 18

SECTION 2501. CRIMINAL HOMICIDE

(a) OFFENSE DEFINED. — A person is guilty of criminal homicide if he intentionally, knowingly, recklessly or negligently causes the death of another human being.

(b) CLASSIFICATION. — Criminal homicide shall be classified as murder, voluntary manslaughter, or involuntary manslaughter.

SECTION 2502. MURDER

(a) MURDER OF THE FIRST DEGREE. — A criminal homicide constitutes murder of the first degree when it is committed by an intentional killing. [Punishable by death or life imprisonment.]

(b) MURDER OF THE SECOND DEGREE.—A criminal homicide constitutes murder of the second degree when it is committed while defendant was engaged as a principal or an accomplice in the perpetration of a felony. [Punishable by life imprisonment.]

(c) MURDER OF THE THIRD DEGREE.—All other kinds of murder shall be murder of the third degree. Murder of the third degree is a felony of the first degree. [Punishable by maximum of 20 years.]

(d) DEFINITIONS.—As used in this section the following words and phrases shall have the meanings given to them in this subsection: . . .

"Intentional killing." Killing by means of poison, or by lying in wait, or by any other kind of willful, deliberate and premeditated killing.

"Perpetration of a felony." The act of the defendant in engaging in or being an accomplice in the commission of, or an attempt to commit, or flight after committing, or attempting to commit robbery, rape, or deviate sexual intercourse by force or threat of force, arson, burglary or kidnapping. . . .

SECTION 2503. VOLUNTARY MANSLAUGHTER

(a) GENERAL RULE.—A person who kills an individual without lawful justification commits voluntary manslaughter if at the time of the killing he is acting under a sudden and intense passion resulting from serious provocation by:

(1) the individual killed; or

(2) another whom the actor endeavors to kill, but he negligently or accidentally causes the death of the individual killed.

(b) UNREASONABLE BELIEF KILLING JUSTIFIABLE.—A person who intentionally or knowingly kills an individual commits voluntary manslaughter if at the time of the killing he believes the circumstances to be such that, if they existed, would justify the killing under Chapter 5 of this title, but his belief is unreasonable.

(c) GRADING.—Voluntary manslaughter is a felony of the first degree. [Twenty-year maximum.]

SECTION 2504. INVOLUNTARY MANSLAUGHTER

(a) GENERAL RULE.—A person is guilty of involuntary manslaughter when as a direct result of the doing of an unlawful act in a reckless or grossly negligent manner, or the doing of a lawful act in a reckless or grossly negligent manner, he causes the death of another person.

(b) GRADING.—Involuntary manslaughter is a misdemeanor of the first degree. [Five-year maximum.]

SECTION 2505. CAUSING OR AIDING SUICIDE

(a) CAUSING SUICIDE AS CRIMINAL HOMICIDE.—A person may be convicted of criminal homicide for causing another to commit suicide only if he intentionally causes such suicide by force, duress, or deception.

(b) AIDING OR SOLICITING SUICIDE AS AN INDEPENDENT OFFENSE.—A person who intentionally aids or solicits another to commit suicide is guilty of a felony of the second degree if his conduct causes such suicide or an attempted suicide, and otherwise of a misdemeanor of the second degree. [Two-year maximum.]

NEW YORK PENAL LAW

SECTION 125.00. HOMICIDE DEFINED

Homicide means conduct which causes the death of a person . . . under circumstances constituting murder, manslaughter in the first degree, manslaughter in the second degree, [or] criminally negligent homicide. . . .

SECTION 125.10. CRIMINALLY NEGLIGENT HOMICIDE

A person is guilty of criminally negligent homicide when, with criminal negligence,[a] he causes the death of another person.

Criminally negligent homicide is a class E felony. [Four-year maximum.]

SECTION 125.15. MANSLAUGHTER IN THE SECOND DEGREE

A person is guilty of manslaughter in the second degree when:

1. He recklessly[b] causes the death of another person; or . . .
3. He intentionally[c] causes or aids another person to commit suicide.

Manslaughter in the second degree is a class C felony. [15-year maximum.]

SECTION 125.20. MANSLAUGHTER IN THE FIRST DEGREE

A person is guilty of manslaughter in the first degree when:

1. With intent to cause serious physical injury to another person, he causes the death of such person or of a third person; or

2. With intent to cause the death of another person, he causes the death of such person or of a third person under circumstances which do not constitute murder because he acts under the influence of extreme emotional disturbance, as defined in paragraph (a) of subdivision one of section 125.25. . .

Manslaughter in the first degree is a class B felony. [25-year maximum.]

SECTION 125.25. MURDER IN THE SECOND DEGREE

A person is guilty of murder in the second degree when:

1. With intent to cause the death of another person, he causes the death of

a. Defined similarly to Model Penal Code §2.02(2)(d), Appendix. See N.Y. Penal Law §15.05(4). —EDS.

b. Defined similarly to Model Penal Code §2.02(2)(c), Appendix. See N.Y. Penal Law §15.05(3). —EDS.

c. Defined similarly to "purposely" in Model Penal Code §2.02(2)(a), Appendix. See N.Y. Penal Law §15.05(1). —EDS.

M²

such person or of a third person; except that in any prosecution under this subdivision, it is an affirmative defense that:

(a) The defendant acted under the influence of extreme emotional disturbance for which there was a reasonable explanation or excuse, the reasonableness of which is to be determined from the viewpoint of a person in the defendant's situation under the circumstances as the defendant believed them to be. . . . ; or

(b) The defendant's conduct consisted of causing or aiding, without the use of duress or deception, another person to commit suicide. . . . ; or

2. Under circumstances evincing a depraved indifference to human life, he recklessly engages in conduct which creates a grave risk of death to another person, and thereby causes the death of another person; or

3. Acting either alone or with one or more other persons, he commits or attempts to commit robbery, burglary, kidnapping, arson, rape in the first degree, sodomy in the first degree, sexual abuse in the first degree, aggravated sexual abuse, escape in the first degree, or escape in the second degree, and, in the course of and in furtherance of such crime or of immediate flight therefrom, he, or another participant, if there be any, causes the death of a person other than one of the participants; except that in any prosecution under this subdivision, in which the defendant was not the only participant in the underlying crime, it is an affirmative defense that the defendant:

(a) Did not commit the homicidal act or in any way solicit, request, command, importune, cause or aid the commission thereof; and

(b) Was not armed with a deadly weapon, or any instrument, article or substance readily capable of causing death or serious physical injury and of a sort not ordinarily carried in public places by law-abiding persons; and

(c) Had no reasonable ground to believe that any other participant was armed with such a weapon, instrument, article or substance; and

(d) Had no reasonable ground to believe that any other participant intended to engage in conduct likely to result in death or serious physical injury. . . .

Murder in the second degree is a class A-I felony. [Punishable by from 15 years to life imprisonment.]

Section 125.27. Murder in the First Degree

[Under this section, those intentional killings that would be second-degree murder under §125.25(1) are raised to first-degree murder in a variety of special circumstances, such as when the victim is a police officer or an employee of a state or local correctional institution, or when the crime is committed while a defendant is either in custody under a life sentence or is at large after having escaped from such custody. The statute classifies first-degree murder as a class A-I felony punishable by death.]

MODEL PENAL CODE

SECTION 210.1 TO 210.4

[See Appendix for text of this section.]

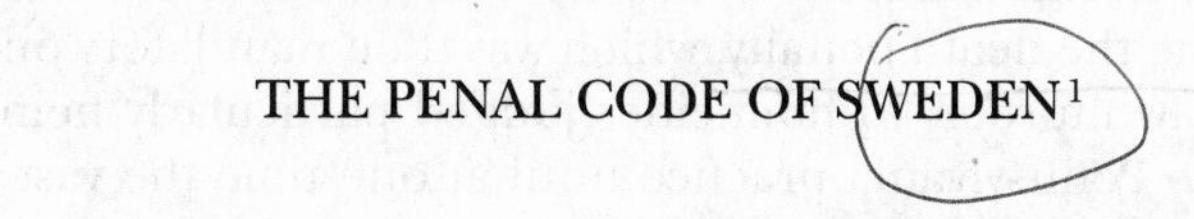

THE PENAL CODE OF SWEDEN[1]

SECTION 1

A person who takes the life of another shall be sentenced for *murder* to imprisonment for ten years or for life.

SECTION 2

If, in view of the circumstances that led to the act or for other reasons, the crime mentioned in Section 1 is considered to be less grave, imprisonment for *manslaughter* shall be imposed for at least six and at most ten years. . . .

SECTION 7

A person who through carelessness causes the death of another shall be sentenced for *causing another's death* to imprisonment for at most two years or, if the crime is less grave, to pay a fine.

If the crime is grave, imprisonment shall be imposed for at least six months and at most four years.

If the offender commits the crime while in charge of a motor vehicle and under the influence of alcoholic beverages, it is a grave offense and the option of a fine is not available.

B. LEGISLATIVE GRADING OF INTENDED KILLINGS

1. *The Premeditation-Deliberation Formula*

INTRODUCTORY NOTE

Model Penal Code and Commentaries, Comment to §210.2 at 16 (1980): Prior to the recodification effort begun by the Model Penal Code, most American jurisdictions maintained a law of murder built around [the] common-law [concepts]. The most significant departure was the division of murder into degrees, a change

1. National Council for Crime Prevention (Sweden), The Swedish Penal Code 1990, ch. 3, §§1-7 (1990).

initiated by the Pennsylvania legislation of 1794. That statute provided that "all murder, which shall be perpetrated by means of poison, or by lying in wait, or by any other kind of willful, deliberate and premeditated killing, or which shall be committed in the perpetration, or attempt to perpetrate any arson, rape, robbery or burglary shall be deemed murder in the first degree; and all other kinds of murder shall be deemed murder in the second degree." The thrust of this reform was to confine the death penalty, which was then mandatory on conviction of any common-law murder, to homicides judged particularly heinous. Other states followed the Pennsylvania practice until at one time the vast majority of American jurisdictions differentiated degrees of murder and the term "first-degree murder" passed into common parlance.

COMMONWEALTH v. CARROLL

Supreme Court of Pennsylvania
412 Pa. 525, 194 A.2d 911 (1963)

Bell, C.J. The defendant, Carroll, pleaded guilty generally to an indictment charging him with the murder of his wife, and was tried by a judge without a jury in the Court of Oyer and Terminer of Allegheny County. The Court found him guilty of first degree murder and sentenced him to life imprisonment. Following argument and denial of motions in arrest of judgment and for a new trial, defendant took this appeal. The only questions involved are thus stated by the appellant:

> [1] Does not the evidence sustain a conviction no higher than murder in the second degree?
>
> [2] Does not the evidence of defendant's good character, together with the testimony of medical experts, including the psychiatrist for the Behavior Clinic of Allegheny County, that the homicide was not premeditated or intentional, *require* the Court below to fix the degree of guilt of defendant no higher than murder in the second degree?

The defendant married the deceased in 1955, when he was serving in the Army in California. Subsequently he was stationed in Alabama, and later in Greenland. During the latter tour of duty, defendant's wife and two children lived with his parents in New Jersey. Because this arrangement proved incompatible, defendant returned to the United States on emergency leave in order to move his family to their own quarters. On his wife's insistence, defendant was forced first to secure a "compassionate transfer" back to the States, and subsequently to resign from the Army in July of 1960, by which time he had attained the rank of Chief Warrant Officer. Defendant was a hard worker, earned a substantial salary and bore a very good reputation among his neighbors.

In 1958, decedent-wife suffered a fractured skull while attempting to leave defendant's car in the course of an argument. Allegedly this contributed to her mental disorder which was later diagnosed as a schizoid personality type. In 1959 she underwent psychiatric treatment at the Mental Hygiene Clinic in Aberdeen, Maryland. She complained of nervousness and told the examining doctor "I feel like hurting my children." This sentiment sometimes took the form of sadistic "discipline" toward their very young children. Nevertheless, upon her discharge from the Clinic, the doctors considered her much improved. With this background we come to the immediate events of the crime.

In January, 1962, defendant was selected to attend an electronics school in Winston-Salem, North Carolina, for nine days. His wife greeted this news with violent argument. Immediately prior to his departure for Winston-Salem, at the suggestion and request of his wife, he put a *loaded* .22 calibre pistol on the window sill at the head of their common bed, so that she would feel safe. On the evening of January 16, 1962, defendant returned home and told his wife that he had been temporarily assigned to teach at a school in Chambersburg, which would necessitate his absence from home four nights out of seven for a ten week period. A violent and protracted argument ensued at the dinner table and continued until four o'clock in the morning.

Defendant's own statement after his arrest details the final moments before the crime:

> We went into the bedroom a little before 3 o'clock on Wednesday morning where we continued to argue in short bursts. Generally she laid with her back to me facing the wall in bed and would just talk over her shoulder to me. I became angry and more angry especially what she was saying about my kids and myself, and sometime between 3 and 4 o'clock in the morning I remembered the gun on the window sill over my head. I think she had dozed off. *I reached up and grabbed the pistol and brought it down and shot her twice in the back of the head.*[2]

Defendant's testimony at the trial elaborated this theme. He started to think about the children:

> seeing my older son's feet what happened to them. I could see the bruises on him and Michael's chin was split open, four stitches. I didn't know what to do. I wanted to help my boys. Sometime in there she said something in there, she called me some kind of name. I kept thinking of this. *During this time I either thought or felt — I thought of the gun, just thought of the gun.* I am not sure whether I felt my hand move toward the gun — I saw my hand move, the next thing — the only thing I can recollect after that is right after the shots or right during the shots. I saw the gun in my hand just pointed at my wife's head. She was still lying on her back — I mean her side. I could smell the gunpowder and I could hear something — it sounded like running water. I didn't know what it was at first, didn't realize what I'd done at first. Then I smelled it. I smelled blood before. . . .

Q. At the time you shot her, Donald, were you fully aware and intend to do what you did?
A. I don't know positively. All I remember hearing was two shots and feeling myself go cold all of a sudden.

Shortly thereafter defendant wrapped his wife's body in a blanket, spread and sheets, tied them on with a piece of plastic clothesline and took her down to the cellar. He tried to clean up as well as he could. That night he took his wife's body, wrapped in a blanket with a rug over it to a desolate place near a trash dump. He

2. When pressed on cross-examination defendant approximated that five minutes elapsed between his wife's last remark and the shooting.

then took the children to his parents' home in Magnolia, New Jersey. He was arrested the next Monday in Chambersburg where he had gone to his teaching assignment.

Although defendant's brief is voluminous, the narrow and only questions which he raises on this appeal are as hereinbefore quoted. Both are embodied in his contention that the crime amounted only to second degree murder and that his conviction should therefore be reduced to second degree or that a new trial should be granted. . . .

[The court then reviewed the Pennsylvania murder statute, which at the time divided murder into two degrees, in accordance with the formula adopted in 1794. That formula, still in effect for Pennsylvania in 1963 and followed in many states to this day, is quoted above in the excerpt immediately preceding *Carroll.*[a] Then, as now, first-degree murder included killings by poison, lying in wait "or any other kind of willful, deliberate and premeditated killing."]

The specific intent to kill which is necessary to constitute in a nonfelony murder, murder in the first degree, may be found from a defendant's words or conduct or from the attendant circumstances together with all reasonable inferences therefrom, and may be inferred from the intentional use of a deadly weapon on a vital part of the body of another human being. . . .

If we consider only the evidence which is favorable to the Commonwealth, it is without the slightest doubt sufficient in law to prove first degree. However, even if we believe all of defendant's statements and testimony, there is no doubt that this killing constituted murder in the first degree. Defendant first urges that there was insufficient time for premeditation in the light of his good reputation. This is based on an isolated and oft repeated statement in Commonwealth v. Drum, 58 Pa. 9, 16, that "'no time is too short for a wicked man to frame in his mind the scheme of murder.'" Defendant argues that, conversely, a long time is necessary to find premeditation in a "good man." We find no merit in defendant's analogy or contention. As Chief Justice Maxey appropriately and correctly said in Commonwealth v. Earnest, 342 Pa. 544, 549-550, 21 A.2d 38, 40: "Whether the intention to kill and the killing, that is, the premeditation and the fatal act, were within a brief space of time or a long space of time is immaterial if the killing was in fact intentional, wilful, deliberate and premeditated." . . .

Defendant further contends that the time and place of the crime, the enormous difficulty of removing and concealing the body, and the obvious lack of an escape plan, militate against and make a finding of premeditation legally impossible. This is a "jury argument"; it is clear as crystal that such circumstances do not negate premeditation. This contention of defendant is likewise clearly devoid of merit.

Defendant's most earnestly pressed contention is that the *psychiatrist's opinion of* what *defendant's state of mind must have been and was at the time of the crime,* clearly establishes not only the lack but also the legal impossibility of premeditation. Dr. Davis, a psychiatrist of the Allegheny County Behavior Clinic, testified that defendant was

> for a number of years . . . passively going along with a situation which he [was] not controlling and he [was] not making any decisions, and finally a decision [was]

a. A further refinement adopted by Pennsylvania in 1976 produced three degrees of murder; see the current statute set out at pages 391-392 supra. — Eds.

> forced on him. . . . He had left the military to take this assignment, and he was averaging about nine thousand a year; he had a good job. He knew that if he didn't accept this teaching assignment in all probability he would be dismissed from the Government service, and at his age and his special training he didn't know whether he would be able to find employment. More critical to that was the fact that at this point, as we understand it, his wife issued an ultimatum that if he went and gave this training course she would leave him. . . . He was so dependent upon her he didn't want her to leave. He couldn't make up his mind what to do. He was trapped. . . .

The doctor then gave *his opinion* that "rage," "desperation," and "panic" produced

> an impulsive automatic reflex type of homicide, . . . as opposed to an intentional premeditated type of homicide, . . . Our feeling was that if this gun had fallen to the floor he wouldn't have been able to pick it up and consummate that homicide. And I think if he had to load the gun he wouldn't have done it. This is a matter of opinion, but this is our opinion about it.

There are three answers to this contention. First, as we have hereinbefore stated, neither a judge nor a jury has to believe all or any part of the testimony of the defendant or of any witness. Secondly, the opinion of the psychiatrists was based to a large extent upon statements made to them by the defendant, which need not be believed and which are in some instances opposed by the facts themselves. Thirdly, a psychiatrist's opinion of a defendant's impulse or lack of intent or state of mind is, in this class of case, entitled to very little weight, and this is especially so when defendant's own actions, or his testimony or confession, or the facts themselves, belie the opinion. . . .

Defendant's *own statement* after his arrest, upon which his counsel so strongly relies, *as well as his testimony at his trial*, clearly convict him of first degree murder and justify the finding and sentence of the Court below. Defendant himself described his actions at the time he killed his wife. From his own statements and from his own testimony, it is clear that, terribly provoked by his allegedly nagging, belligerent and sadistic wife, *defendant remembered the gun, deliberately took it down, and deliberately fired two shots into the head of his sleeping wife*. There is no doubt that this was a willful, deliberate and premeditated murder.

While defendant makes no contention that he was insane at the commission of the murder or at any time, what this Court said in Commonwealth v. Tyrrell, 405 Pa. 210, 220-221, 174 A.2d 852, 856-57, is equally appropriate here:

> Defendant's psychiatrist did not testify that the defendant was insane. What he did say was that because defendant's wife frequently picked on him and just before the killing insulted or goaded him, defendant had an emotional impulse to kill her which he could not resist. . . . [*S*]*ociety would be almost completely unprotected from criminals if the law permitted a blind or irresistible impulse or inability to control one's self, to excuse or justify a murder or to reduce it from first degree to second degree.* In the times in which we are living, nearly every normal adult human being has moments or hours or days or longer periods when he or she is depressed and disturbed with resultant emotional upset feelings and so-called blind impulses; and the young especially have many uncontrolled emotions every day which are euphemistically called irresistible impulses. *The Courts of Justice should not abdicate their function and duty of determining criminal responsibility to the psychiatrist.* In such event, the test will differ

not only with each psychiatrist but also with the prevailing psychiatric winds of the moment. . . .

Just as the Courts cannot abdicate to the psychiatrists the task of determining criminal responsibility in law, so also they cannot remit to psychiatrists the right to determine the intent or the state of mind of an accused at the time of the commission of a homicide. . . .

Judgment and sentence affirmed.

NOTES

1. Many courts follow the *Carroll* approach by suggesting that some premeditation is required, and simultaneously holding that "no time is too short" for the necessary premeditation to occur. Consider Young v. State, 428 So. 2d 155, 158 (Ala. Crim. App. 1982). Defendant and his brother were playing cards with several friends when an argument and then a scuffle broke out. Defendant fired several shots, and two of the men were hit; each died from a single .22 caliber shot to the chest. The court upheld defendant's conviction on two counts of first-degree murder. Stressing that "[no] appreciable space of time between the formation of the intention to kill and the act of killing" was required, the court said (428 So. 2d at 158) that "[p]remeditation and deliberation may be formed while the killer is 'pressing the trigger that fired the fatal shot.'"

Question: Given decisions like *Carroll* and *Young,* what is the difference between a premeditated intention to kill and an intention to kill without premeditation?

2. Later Pennsylvania decisions go even further than *Carroll,* by holding that "the requirement of premeditation and deliberation is met whenever there is a conscious purpose to bring about death. . . . We can find no reason where there is a conscious intent to bring about death to differentiate between the degree of culpability on the basis of the elaborateness of the design to kill." Commonwealth v. O'Searo, 352 A.2d 30, 37-38 (1976).

STATE v. GUTHRIE

Supreme Court of Appeals of West Virginia
194 W.Va. 657, 461 S.E.2d 163 (1995)

CLECKLEY, Justice:

The defendant, Dale Edward Guthrie, appeals the . . . jury verdict finding him guilty of first degree murder. [He] was sentenced to serve a life sentence with a recommendation of mercy. . . .

It is . . . undisputed that on the evening of February 12, 1993, the defendant removed a knife from his pocket and stabbed his co-worker, Steven Todd Farley, in the neck and killed him. The two men worked together as dishwashers at Danny's Rib House in Nitro and got along well together before this incident. On the night of the killing, the victim, his brother, Tracy Farley, and James Gibson were joking around while working in the kitchen of the restaurant. The victim was poking fun at the defendant who appeared to be in a bad mood. He told the defendant to "lighten up" and snapped him with a dishtowel several times. Apparently, the victim had no idea he was upsetting the defendant very much. The dishtowel flipped the defendant on the nose and he became enraged.

The defendant removed his gloves and started toward the victim. Mr. Farley, still teasing, said: "Ooo, he's taking his gloves off." The defendant then pulled a knife from his pocket and stabbed the victim in the neck. He also stabbed Mr. Farley in the arm as he fell to the floor. Mr. Farley looked up and cried: "Man, I was just kidding around." The defendant responded: "Well, man, you should have never hit me in my face." . . .

It is . . . undisputed that the defendant suffers from a host of psychiatric problems. He experiences up to two panic attacks daily and had received treatment for them at the Veterans Administration Hospital in Huntington for more than a year preceding the killing. He suffers from chronic depression (dysthymic disorder), an obsession with his nose (body dysmorphic disorder), and borderline personality disorder. The defendant's father shed some light on his nose fixation. He stated that dozens of times a day the defendant stared in the mirror and turned his head back and forth to look at his nose. His father estimated that 50 percent of the time he observed his son he was looking at his nose. The defendant repeatedly asked for assurances that his nose was not too big. This obsession began when he was approximately seventeen years old. The defendant was twenty-nine years old at the time of trial.

The defendant testified he suffered a panic attack immediately preceding the stabbing. He described the attack as "intense"; he felt a lot of pressure and his heart beat rapidly. In contrast to the boisterous atmosphere in the kitchen that evening, the defendant was quiet and kept to himself. He stated that Mr. Farley kept irritating him that night. The defendant could not understand why Mr. Farley was picking on him because he had never done that before. Even at trial, the defendant did not comprehend his utter overreaction to the situation. In hindsight, the defendant believed the better decision would have been to punch out on his time card and quit over the incident. However, all the witnesses related that the defendant was in no way attacked, as he perceived it, but that Mr. Farley was playing around. The defendant could not bring himself to tell the other workers to leave him alone or inform them about his panic attacks. . . .

The principal question before us under this assignment of error is whether our instructions on murder when given together [are] wrong and confusing. . . . [T]he defendant argues [that] the instructions were . . . improper because the terms wilful, deliberate, and premeditated were equated with a mere intent to kill. . . .

State's Instruction No. 8, . . . stated:

> The Court instructs the jury that to constitute a willful, deliberate and premeditated killing, it is not necessary that the intention to kill should exist for any particular length of time prior to the actual killing; it is only necessary that such intention should have come into existence for the first time at the time of such killing, or at any time previously.

State's Instruction No. 10 stated: ". . . in order to constitute a 'premeditated' murder an intent to kill need exist only for an instant." State's Instruction No. 12 stated: . . . "[W]hat is meant by the language willful, deliberate and premeditated is that the killing be intentional." State's Instruction Nos. 10 and 12 are commonly referred to as *Schrader* instructions.

The linchpin of the problems that flow from these instructions is the failure adequately to inform the jury of the difference between first and second degree murder. Of particular concern is the lack of guidance to the jury as to what constitutes premeditation and the manner in which the instructions confuse premeditation with the intent to kill. . . .

While many jurisdictions do not favor the distinction between first and second degree murder, . . . we do not have the judicial prerogative to abolish the distinction between first and second degree murder and rewrite the law of homicide for West Virginia. . . . On the other hand, we believe within the parameters of our current homicide statutes the *Schrader* definition of premeditation and deliberation is confusing, if not meaningless. To allow the State to prove premeditation and deliberation by only showing that the intention came "into existence for the first time at the time of such killing" completely eliminates the distinction between the two degrees of murder. Hence, we feel compelled in this case to attempt to make the dichotomy meaningful by making some modifications to our homicide common law.

Premeditation and deliberation should be defined in a more careful, but still general way to give juries both guidance and reasonable discretion. Although premeditation and deliberation are not measured by any particular period of time, there must be some period between the formation of the intent to kill and the actual killing, which indicates the killing is by prior calculation and design. . . . This means there must be an opportunity for some reflection on the intention to kill after it is formed. The accused must kill purposely after contemplating the intent to kill. Although an elaborate plan or scheme to take life is not required, our *Schrader* instruction's notion of instantaneous premeditation and momentary deliberation is not satisfactory for proof of first degree murder. In Bullock v. United States, 122 F.2d 213, 214 (1941), the court discussed the need to have some appreciable time elapse between the intent to kill and the killing:

> To speak of premeditation and deliberation which are instantaneous or which take no appreciable time, is a contradiction in terms. . . . Statutes like ours, which distinguish deliberate and premeditated murder from other murder, reflect a belief that one who meditates an intent to kill and then deliberately executes it is more dangerous, more culpable or less capable of reformation than one who kills on sudden impulse; or that the prospect of the death penalty is more likely to deter men from deliberate than from impulsive murder. The deliberate killer is guilty of first degree murder; the impulsive killer is not.

Thus, there must be some evidence that the defendant considered and weighed his decision to kill in order for the State to establish premeditation and deliberation under our first degree murder statute. This is what is meant by a ruthless, cold-blooded, calculating killing. Any other intentional killing, by its spontaneous and nonreflective nature, is second degree murder. . . .

[W]e agree with the defendant that the language in our opinion in *Schrader* virtually eliminates the distinction in this State between first and second degree murder, equating as it does premeditation with the formation of the intent to kill. . . .

[Reversed and remanded for a new trial.]

NOTES ON PREMEDITATION

The *Carroll* and *Guthrie* approaches exemplify the split in American jurisdictions on the meaning of premeditation. The *Carroll* approach largely erases the distinction between first-degree murder and second-degree murder. But while the *Guthrie* approach gives meaning to the distinction, it raises two troublesome issues: What kinds of proof of premeditation suffice to permit a jury to find premeditation, and how reliable is the premeditation as a test for distinguishing the very worst form of murder?

1. Proof of premeditation. Jurisdictions that require proof of actual reflection on the decision to kill have had to consider what kinds of evidence are sufficient to support a first-degree murder conviction. The court in the *Guthrie* case addressed this question in footnotes 23 and 24 of its opinion, where it observed:

> In the absence of statements by the accused which indicate the killing was by prior calculation and design, a jury must consider the circumstances in which the killing occurred to determine whether it fits into the first degree category. Relevant factors include the relationship of the accused and the victim and its condition at the time of the homicide; whether plan or preparation existed either in terms of the type of weapon utilized or the place where the killing occurred; and presence of reason or motive to deliberately take life. No one factor is controlling. Any one or all taken together may indicate actual reflection on the decision to kill.
>
> As examples of what type of evidence supports a finding of first degree murder, we identify three categories: (1) "planning activity — facts regarding the defendant's behavior prior to the killing which might indicate a design to take life; (2) facts about the defendant's prior relationship or behavior with the victim which might indicate a motive to kill; and (3) evidence regarding the nature or manner of the killing which indicate a deliberate intention to kill according to a preconceived design. See People v. Anderson, 70 Cal.2d 15, 447 P.2d 942 (1968).

In the *Guthrie* case the court reversed and remanded because of the erroneous instruction, but it found the evidence adequate to permit a jury to conclude beyond a reasonable doubt that the defendant was guilty of premeditated murder. Do you agree? Are the evidentiary tests stated in the *Anderson* case met? Are they met on the facts of the *Carroll* case?

2. Distinguishing the worst murders. The *Anderson* case referred to in the previous note was a particularly grisly and ugly murder of a 10-year-old daughter of the woman the defendant was living with. As the California Supreme Court reviewed the facts, the victim's older brother and mother returned home in the late afternoon to find the defendant just in his slacks and blood on the kitchen floor and the living room couch. Defendant's explanations first that he had cut himself and later that the victim had cut herself proved false when they found her nude body under some boxes and blankets on the floor. Police later found the defendant's blood-spotted clothing and a knife; the victim's bloodstained clothes throughout the house; and blood in almost every room except the kitchen, which appeared to have been mopped. Over 60 wounds, extending over the victim's entire body, were found. Several of the wounds were post-mortem. The court found this evidence insufficient to support a first-degree murder conviction on the theory of premeditation and deliberation: there was no evidence that defendant planned the killing; nothing in the prior relationships between the defendant and the victim revealed a motive for killing her; and the manner of killing by multiple random knife wounds suggested an explosion of violence rather than a preconceived design to kill.

Questions: How do you explain the court's conclusion in the *Anderson* case? Was the court wrong in finding insufficient evidence of premeditation? Did the court get the concept of premeditation all wrong, or was it something else that makes the result problematic? Consider Samuel H. Pillsbury, Judging Evil: Rethinking the Law of Murder and Manslaughter 104-105 (1998):

> As a matter of statutory interpretation, the *Anderson* decision is defensible. Premeditation does seem to involve coolness and calculation, and proof of those was weak at trial. . . . [But] even if we assume the killing was unplanned and impassioned, there were significant aggravating circumstances. . . . The butchering of a child for reasons of sexual frustration and rage represents an extreme challenge to the value of human life. It ranks high on any intuitive scale of wrongdoing, and may explain why many appellate courts have been so reluctant to take premeditation seriously — it leads to decisions like *Anderson.* In particular, the case leads us to doubt whether an impassioned decision to kill is necessarily less culpable than a dispassionate one. In *Anderson* the source of the rage represents a major aggravating factor. Nor does the lack of planning constitute a reliable sign of lesser culpability. As in *Anderson,* depending on motivation, an unplanned killing may present a more culpable offense than a reflective killing by a brooding, self-doubting, self-reflective offender. *Anderson* suggests that what premeditation misses is the moral importance of the motive for the homicide.

Consider also State v. Forrest, 321 N.C. 186, 362 S.E.2d 252 (N.C. 1987). The defendant took a pistol with him on a visit to his hospitalized, terminally ill father and, sobbing with emotion, killed his father with a single shot to the head. He was convicted of first-degree murder and sentenced to life imprisonment. The North Carolina Supreme Court upheld the conviction. Wouldn't these facts meet even the tests of premeditation announced by the *Guthrie* and *Anderson* cases?

Following the lead of the Model Penal Code, some states have rejected premeditation and deliberation as the basis for identifying murders that deserve the greatest punishment. See, e.g., the New York provisions, page 393 supra. The rationale of this approach is set out in Model Penal Code and Commentaries, Comment to §210.6, at 127-128 (1980):

> [T]he case for a mitigated sentence on conviction of murder does not depend on a distinction between impulse and deliberation. Prior reflection may reveal the uncertainties of a tortured conscience rather than exceptional depravity. The very fact of a long internal struggle may be evidence that the homicidal impulse was deeply aberrational and far more the product of extraordinary circumstances than a true reflection of the actor's normal character. Thus, for example, one suspects that most mercy killings are the consequence of long and careful deliberation, but they are not especially appropriate cases for imposition of capital punishment. . . . It also seems clear, moreover, that some purely impulsive murders will present no extenuating circumstances. The suddenness of the killing may simply reveal callousness so complete and depravity so extreme that no hesitation is required.

2. *Provocation*

GIROUARD v. STATE

Court of Appeals of Maryland
321 Md. 532, 583 A.2d 718 (1991)

COLE, Judge. In this case we are asked to reconsider whether the types of provocation sufficient to mitigate the crime of murder to manslaughter should be limited to the categories we have heretofore recognized, or whether the sufficiency of the provocation should be decided by the factfinder on a case-by-case basis. Specifically, we must determine whether words alone are provocation adequate to justify a conviction of manslaughter rather than one of second degree murder.

The Petitioner, Steven S. Girouard, and the deceased, Joyce M. Girouard, had been married for about two months on October 28, 1987, the night of Joyce's death. Both parties . . . were in the army. The . . . marriage was often tense and strained, and there was some evidence that after marrying Steven, Joyce had resumed a relationship with her old boyfriend, Wayne.

On the night of Joyce's death [an angry argument developed during which she] continued to taunt him by saying, "I never did want to marry you and you are a lousy fuck and you remind me of my dad" [who had apparently abused her as a child]. The barrage of insults continued with her telling Steven that she wanted a divorce, that the marriage had been a mistake and that she had never wanted to marry him. She also told him she had seen his commanding officer and filed charges against him for abuse. She then asked Steven, "What are you going to do?" Receiving no response, she continued her verbal attack. She added that she had filed charges against him in the Judge Advocate General's Office (JAG) and that he would probably be court martialed. . . .

After pausing for a moment, Joyce [again] asked what Steven was going to do. What he did was lunge at her with the kitchen knife he had hidden behind the pillow and stab her 19 times. Realizing what he had done, he dropped the knife and went to the bathroom to shower off Joyce's blood. Feeling like he wanted to die, Steven . . . slit his own wrists, . . . but when he realized that he would not die from his self-inflicted wounds, he . . . called the police, telling the dispatcher that he had just murdered his wife.

When the police arrived they found Steven wandering around outside his apartment building. Steven was despondent and tearful and seemed detached, according to police officers who had been at the scene. He was unconcerned about his own wounds, talking only about how much he loved his wife and how he could not believe what he had done. Joyce Girouard was pronounced dead at the scene.

Steven Girouard was convicted, at a court trial . . . of second degree murder and was sentenced to 22 years of incarceration, 10 of which were suspended. . . .

Petitioner relies primarily on out of state cases to provide support for his argument that the provocation to mitigate murder to manslaughter should not be limited only to the traditional circumstances of: extreme assault or battery upon the defendant; mutual combat; defendant's illegal arrest; injury or serious abuse of a close relative of the defendant's; or the sudden discovery of a spouse's adultery.[a] Petitioner argues that manslaughter is a catchall for homicides which are criminal but that lack the malice essential for a conviction of murder. [He] argues that the trial judge did find provocation (although he held it inadequate to mitigate murder) and that the categories of provocation adequate to mitigate should be broadened to include factual situations such as this one.

The State counters by stating that [w]ords spoken by the victim, no matter how abusive or taunting, fall into a category society should not accept as adequate provocation.... Thus, the State argues that the courts below were correct in holding that the taunting words by Joyce Girouard were not provocation adequate to reduce Steven's second degree murder charge to voluntary manslaughter....

We focus our attention on an examination of the ultimate issue in this case, that is, whether the provocation of Steven by Joyce was enough in the eyes of the law so that the murder charge against Steven should have been mitigated to voluntary manslaughter. For provocation to be "adequate," it must be "calculated to inflame the passion of a reasonable man and tend to cause him to act for the moment from passion rather than reason." The issue we must resolve, then, is whether the taunting words uttered by Joyce were enough to inflame the passion of a reasonable man so that that man would be sufficiently infuriated so as to strike out in hot-blooded blind passion to kill her. Although we agree with the trial judge that there was needless provocation by Joyce, we also agree with him that the provocation was not adequate to mitigate second degree murder to voluntary manslaughter.

Although there are few Maryland cases discussing the issue at bar, those that do hold that words alone are not adequate provocation.... Other jurisdictions overwhelmingly agree with our cases and hold that words alone are not adequate provocation.... Perkins on Criminal Law, at p. 62, states that it is "with remarkable uniformity that even words generally regarded as 'fighting words' in the community have no recognition as adequate provocation in the eyes of the law."...

Thus, with no reservation, we hold that the provocation in this case was not enough to cause a reasonable man to stab his provoker 19 times. Although a psychologist testified to Steven's mental problems and his need for acceptance and love, we agree . . . that "there must be not simply provocation in psychological fact, but one of certain fairly well-defined classes of provocation recognized as being adequate as a matter of law." The standard is one of reasonableness; it does not and should not focus on the peculiar frailties of mind of the Petitioner. That standard of reasonableness has not been met here. We cannot in good conscience countenance holding that a verbal domestic argument ending in the death of one spouse can result in a conviction of manslaughter. We agree with the trial judge that social necessity dictates our holding. Domestic arguments easily escalate into furious fights. We perceive no reason for a holding in favor of those who find the easiest way to end a domestic dispute is by killing the offending spouse....

Affirmed.

a. Maryland law was amended in 1997 to provide:

> The discovery of one's spouse engaged in sexual intercourse with another person does not constitute legally adequate provocation for the purpose of mitigating a killing from the crime of murder to voluntary manslaughter when the killing was provoked by that discovery. Md. Code, 1997, Art. 27, §387A.—Eds.

MAHER v. PEOPLE

Supreme Court of Michigan
10 Mich. 212, 81 Am. Dec. 781 (1862)

CHRISTIANCY, J. The prisoner was charged with an assault with intent to kill and murder one Patrick Hunt. [The prosecution's evidence was that defendant entered a saloon in a much agitated manner, approached Hunt, said something unintelligible to him, and shot him, inflicting a non-fatal wound "in and through the left ear." Maher offered evidence to show an adulterous intercourse between his wife and Hunt less than an hour before the assault. His evidence was that he followed his wife and Hunt as they entered the woods together, that when they left a half hour later he followed Hunt to the saloon, that just before he entered the saloon a friend told him that Hunt and his wife had had intercourse in the woods the day before. The trial court ruled this evidence inadmissible and convicted Maher of assault with intent to murder.]

Was the evidence properly rejected? This is the main question in the case, and its decision must depend upon the question whether the proposed evidence would have tended to reduce the killing — had death ensued — from murder to manslaughter. . . . If the homicide — in case death had ensued — would have been but manslaughter, then defendant could not be guilty of the assault with intent to murder, but only of a simple assault and battery. The question therefore involves essentially the same principles as where evidence is offered for a similar purpose in a prosecution for murder. . . .

[W]ithin the principle of all the recognized definitions [of malice aforethought], the homicide must, in all ordinary cases, have been committed with some degree of coolness and deliberation or, at least, under circumstances in which ordinary men . . . would not be liable to have their reason clouded or obscured by passion; and the act must be prompted by, or the circumstances indicate that it sprung from, a wicked, depraved or malignant mind. . . .

But if the act of killing, though intentional, be committed under the influence of passion or in heat of blood, produced by an adequate or reasonable provocation, and before a reasonable time has elapsed for the blood to cool and reason to resume its habitual control, and is the result of the temporary excitement, by which the control of reason was disturbed, rather than of any wickedness of heart or cruelty or recklessness of disposition: then the law, out of indulgence to the frailty of human nature, or rather, in recognition of the laws upon which human nature is constituted, very properly regards the offense as of a less heinous character than murder, and gives it the designation of manslaughter.

To what extent the passions must be aroused and the dominion of reason disturbed to reduce the offense from murder to manslaughter, the cases are by no means agreed. . . .

The principle involved . . . would seem to suggest as the true general rule that reason should, at the time of the act, be disturbed or obscured by passion to an extent which *might render* ordinary men, of fair average disposition, *liable* to act rashly or without due deliberation or reflection, and from passion, rather than judgment.

To the question, what shall be considered in law a reasonable or adequate provocation for such state of mind, so as to give to a homicide, committed under its influence, the character of manslaughter? On principle, the answer, as a general rule, must be, anything the natural tendency of which would be to produce such a state of mind in ordinary men, and which the jury are satisfied did produce it in the case before them — not such a provocation as must, by the laws of the human mind, produce such an effect with the *certainty that physical effects follow from physical causes;* for then the individual could hardly be held morally accountable. Nor, on the other hand, must the provocation, in every case, be held sufficient or reasonable, because such a state of excitement has followed from it; for then, by habitual and long continued indulgence of evil passions, a bad man might acquire a claim to mitigation which would not be available to better men, and on account of that very wickedness of heart which, in itself, constitutes an aggravation both in morals and in law.

In determining whether the provocation is sufficient or reasonable, *ordinary human nature,* or the average of men recognized as men of fair average mind and disposition, should be taken as the standard — unless, indeed, the person whose guilt is in question be shown to have some peculiar weakness of mind or infirmity of temper, not arising from wickedness of heart or cruelty of disposition.[a]

It is doubtless, in one sense, the province of the court to define what, in law, will constitute a reasonable or adequate provocation, but not, I think, in ordinary cases, to determine whether the provocation proved in the particular case is sufficient or reasonable. This is essentially a question of fact, and to be decided with reference to the peculiar facts of each particular case. . . . [J]urors from the mode of their selection, coming from the various classes and occupations of society, and conversant with the practical affairs of life, are, in my opinion, much better qualified to judge of the sufficiency and tendency of a given provocation and much more likely to fix, with some degree of accuracy, the standard of what constitutes the average of ordinary human nature, than the judge whose habits and course of life give him much less experience of the workings of passion in the actual conflicts of life.

The judge, it is true, must, to some extent, assume to decide upon the sufficiency of the alleged provocation, when the question arises upon the admission of testimony, and when it is so clear as to admit of no reasonable doubt upon any theory, that the alleged provocation could not have had any tendency to produce such state of mind, in ordinary men, he may properly exclude the evidence; but, if the alleged provocation be such as to admit of any reasonable doubt, whether it might not have had such tendency, it is much safer, I think, and more in accordance with principle, to let the evidence go to the jury under the proper instructions. . . . The law can not with justice assume by the light of past decision, to catalogue all the various facts and combinations of facts which shall be held to constitute reasonable or adequate provocation. Scarcely two past cases can be found which are identical in all their circumstances; and there is no reason to hope for greater uniformity in future. Provocations will be given without reference to any previous model, and the passions they excite will not consult the precedents.

The same principles which govern, as to the extent to which the passions must

a. This qualification for persons "of peculiar weakness of mind or infirmity of temper" was later rejected in Michigan. People v. Sullivan, 231 Mich. App. 510, 520, 586 N.W.2d 578, 583 n.1 (1998). — Eds.

be excited and reason disturbed, apply with equal force . . . to the question of cooling time. This, like the provocation itself, must depend upon the nature of man and the laws of the human mind, as well as upon the nature and circumstances of the provocation. . . . I am aware there are many cases in which it has been held a question of law, but I can see no principle on which such a rule can rest. The court should, I think, define to the jury the principles upon which the question is to be decided, and leave them to determine whether the time was reasonable under all the circumstances of the particular case. . . .

It remains only to apply these principles to the present case. The proposed evidence, in connection with what had already been given, would have tended strongly to show the commission of adultery by Hunt with the prisoner's wife, within half an hour before the assault; that the prisoner saw them going to the woods together, under circumstances calculated strongly to impress upon his mind the belief of the adulterous purpose; that he followed after them to the woods; that Hunt and the prisoner's wife were, not long after, seen coming from the woods, and that the prisoner followed them, and went in hot pursuit after Hunt to the saloon, and was informed by a friend on the way that they had committed adultery the day before in the woods. I can not resist the conviction that this would have been sufficient evidence of provocation to go to the jury, and from which, when taken in connection with the excitement and "great perspiration" exhibited on entering the saloon, the hasty manner in which he approached and fired the pistol at Hunt, it would have been competent for the jury to find that the act was committed in consequence of the passion excited by the provocation, and in a state of mind which, within the principle already explained, would have given to the homicide had death ensued, the character of manslaughter only. . . .

The judgment should be reversed and a new trial granted.

MANNING, J. I differ from my brethren in this case. I think the evidence was properly excluded. To make that manslaughter which would otherwise be murder, the provocation — I am not speaking of its sufficiency, but of the provocation itself — must be given in the presence of the person committing the homicide. The cause of the provocation must occur in his presence. . . . Any other rule in an offense so grave as taking the life of a fellow-being, in the heat of passion, I fear would be more humane to the perpetrator than wise in its effects on society. More especially since the abolition of the death penalty for murder, and the division of the crime into murder in the first and second degree there is not now the same reason, namely, the severity of the punishment, for relaxing the rules of law in favor of a party committing homicide as before. It would, it seems to me, be extremely mischievous to let passion engendered by suspicion, or by something one has heard, enter into and determine the nature of a crime committed while under its influence. The innocent as well as the guilty, or those who had not as well as those who had given provocation, might be the sufferers. If it be said that in such cases the giving of the provocation must be proved or it would go for nothing; the answer is, that the law will not, and should not permit the lives of the innocent to be exposed with the guilty in this way, as it would do did it not require the cause of the provocation to occur in the presence of the person committing the homicide.

NOTES

1. The *Girouard* and *Maher* cases represent contrasting approaches to provocation. For a review of the law in various American jurisdictions today, see Victoria Nourse, Passion's Progress: Modern Law Reform and the Provocation Defense, 106 Yale L.J. 1331 (1999).

2. *Rationale of the Provocation Defense.* (a) *Provocation as Partial Excuse:* The *Maher* opinion states the classic case for the provocation doctrine — a concession to the frailty of human nature. See also the observations of Boochever, J., concurring in United States v. Roston, 986 F.2d 1287, 1294 (9th Cir. 1993):

> [Our cases require] that the provocation must be such as would "arouse a reasonable and ordinary person to kill someone." I cannot envision such a provocation that would not constitute justification for the crime. "[A] reasonable person does not kill even when provoked. . . ." Model Penal Code §210.3 cmt. 5(a), at 56 (1980). The Model Criminal Jury Instructions for the Ninth Circuit set forth what appears to me to be a more appropriate standard: "Provocation, in order to be adequate, must be such as might naturally cause a reasonable person in the passion of the moment to lose self-control and act on impulse and without reflection." This standard does not imply that reasonable people kill, but rather focuses on the degree of passion sufficient to reduce the actor's ability to control his actions.

For a justification of the doctrine in these terms, see Jerome Michael & Herbert Wechsler, A Rationale of the Law of Homicide, 37 Colum. L. Rev. 1261, 1281-1282 (1937):

> Provocation . . . must be estimated by the probability that [the provocative] circumstances would affect most men in like fashion. . . . Other things being equal, the greater the provocation, measured in that way, the more ground there is for attributing the intensity of the actor's passions and his lack of self-control on the homicidal occasion to the extraordinary character of the situation in which he was placed rather than to any extraordinary deficiency in his own character. While it is true, it is also beside the point, that most men do not kill on even the gravest provocation; the point is that the more strongly they would be moved to kill by circumstances of the sort which provoked the actor to the homicidal act, and the more difficulty they would experience in resisting the impulse to which he yielded, the less does his succumbing serve to differentiate his character from theirs. But the slighter the provocation, the more basis there is for ascribing the actor's act to an extraordinary susceptibility to intense passion, to an unusual deficiency in those other desires which counteract in most men the desires which impel them to homicidal acts, or to an extraordinary weakness of reason, and consequent inability to bring such desires into play.

But compare Stephen J. Morse, Undiminished Confusion in Diminished Capacity, 75 J. Crim. L. & Criminology 1, 33-34 (1984):

> I would abolish [the provocation defense] and convict all intentional killers of murder. Reasonable people do not kill no matter how much they are provoked, and even enraged people generally retain the capacity to control homicidal or any other kind of aggressive or antisocial desires. We cheapen both life and our conception of responsibility by maintaining the provocation/passion mitigation. This may seem harsh and contrary to the supposedly humanitarian reforms of the evolv-

> ing criminal law. But this . . . interpretation of criminal law history is morally mistaken. It is humanitarian only if one focuses sympathetically on perpetrators and not on their victims, and views the former as mostly helpless objects of their overwhelming emotions and irrationality. This sympathy is misplaced, however, and is disrespectful to the perpetrator. As virtually every human being knows because we all have been enraged, it is easy not to kill, even when one is enraged.

(b) *Provocation as Partial Justification:* A different account of the provocation defense is that it rests at least in part on notions of justification. Consider A. J. Ashworth, The Doctrine of Provocation, 35 Camb. L.J. 292, 307-308 (1976):

> The term partial justification [is closely related to] the moral notion that the punishment of wrongdoers is justifiable. This is not to argue that it is ever morally right to kill a person who does wrong. Rather, the claim implicit in partial justification is that an individual is *to some extent* morally justified in making a punitive return against someone who intentionally causes him serious offence, and that this serves to differentiate someone who is provoked to lose his self-control and kill from the unprovoked killer. Whereas the paradigmatic case of murder might be an attack on an innocent victim, the paradigm of provocation generally involves moral wrongs by both parties. [T]he complicity of the victim cannot and should not be ignored, for the blameworthiness of his conduct has a strong bearing on the court's judgment of the seriousness of the provocation and the reasonableness of the accused's failure to control himself.

A contrary view is expressed in Joshua Dressler, Rethinking Heat of Passion: A Defense in Search of a Rationale, 73 J. Crim. L. & Criminology 421, 456-458 (1982):

> [A] substantial moral problem exists with this approach. It is morally questionable to suggest that there is less societal harm in Victim's death merely because he acted immorally. One must remember that Victim's immoral conduct in no way jeopardized the life of the defendant or anyone else. [H]is immoral conduct should not make his life less deserving of protection by society. [A] justification rule would also have anomalous results in many cases. For example, suppose Actor walks in and finds his wife in bed with Victim, under circumstances in which it is unclear to the observer whether the intercourse is consensual or not. Actor kills Victim. As a matter of excuse, it may be easy to partially excuse Defendant in either case. But if the issue is Victim's moral right to life, the proper answer might depend on whether Victim's conduct in fact constituted rape, adultery or fornication, and perhaps on whether Victim was, or should have been, aware of the woman's marital status. It is not plausible to speak of the heat of passion doctrine, at least as we now know it, as being affected by these subtleties.

3. Sexual infidelity as provocation. (a) Why has the law traditionally regarded sexual infidelity as adequate provocation? What does it share with the few other categories that the common law deemed legally sufficient provocation — serious physical injury or assault, mutual quarrel or combat, illegal arrest? For discussion of the cultural presuppositions of voluntary manslaughter doctrine, see Donna K. Coker, Heat of Passion and Wife Killing: Men Who Batter/Men Who Kill, 2 So. Cal. Rev. L. & Women's Stud. 71 (1992). Note that women seldom kill their unfaithful male partners. Should this fact have a bearing on the reasonableness of a husband's lethal response to unfaithfulness by his wife?

The law of provocation has been severely criticized from a feminist perspective. See, e.g., Jeremy Horder, Provocation and Responsibility 193-194 (1992):

> The use of the provocation defence is dominated by men, for whom the use of violence [to secure] a woman's "unconditional, unjudgmental attentive acceptance" is all too commonly regarded as natural or understandable — perhaps even appropriate. It is thus largely from a male-centered perspective that the reduction of an intentional killing from murder to manslaughter is capable of being regarded as a compassion to human infirmity. From a feminist perspective the existence of such mitigation simply reinforces in the law that which public institutions ought in fact to be seeking to eradicate, namely, the acceptance that there is something natural, inevitable, and hence in some (legal) sense . . . forgivable about men's violence against women, and their violence in general.

Questions: If Horder's point is valid, what are its implications? Should the provocation defense be abolished entirely? If not, should the courts hold as a matter of law that adultery or sexual infidelity can never constitute sufficient provocation? See Deborah E. Milgate, Note, The Flame Flickers, But Burns On: Modern Judicial Applications of the Ancient Heat of Passion Defense, 51 Rutgers L. Rev. 193, 194-195 (1998).

(b) Courts that permit sudden discovery of sexual infidelity to qualify as a potential basis for a heat-of-passion claim nonetheless interpret the boundaries of this category narrowly. In Dennis v. State, 661 A.2d 175 (Md. App. 1995), the defendant, after observing his wife, her dress raised, in a sexual embrace with another man, burst into the room and fatally shot the other man. The court held it proper to instruct the jury that the circumstances could qualify as legally adequate provocation only if the defendant had suddenly discovered sexual intercourse taking place, not other sorts of sexual intimacy or sexual contact. State v. Turner, 708 So. 2d 232 (Ala. Crim. App. 1997), was an unusual case in which an enraged woman shot and killed a sexually unfaithful man. But the court held that voluntary manslaughter instructions were not required because the defendant and her victim, though they had lived together for many years, were not legally married. *Question:* Does the fact of marriage have any emotional significance where the parties have long lived together?

4. *Homosexual advances as provocative acts.* Trial judges have allowed defendants to raise a provocation defense in a number of recent cases in which a man killed in response to an unwelcome, though nonviolent, homosexual advance. Several appellate courts, however, have ruled provocation claims of this sort to be insufficient as a matter of law, e.g., People v. Garcia, 651 N.E.2d 100, 109 (1995); Commonwealth v. Pierce, 642 N.E.2d 579 (Mass. 1994). *Question:* Why should such proposals to engage in consensual sexual activity, whether from a member of the same or the opposite sex, ever be sufficient provocation to reduce an intentional killing from murder to manslaughter? See Robert B. Mison, Comment, Homophobia in Manslaughter: The Homosexual Advance as Insufficient Provocation, 80 Cal. L. Rev. 133 (1992) (opposing permitting provocation in these cases). Compare Joshua Dressler, When "Heterosexual" Men Kill "Homosexual" Men: Reflections on Provocation Law, Sexual Advances, and the "Reasonable Man" Standard, 85 J. Crim. Law & Criminol. 726 (1995), arguing that "an unwanted sexual advance is a basis for justifiable indignation," that "ordinary, fallible human beings might become so upset that their out of control reaction de-

serves mitigated punishment," and therefore that there are sometimes valid, non-homophobic reasons to permit a provocation defense in such cases.

5. Cooling time. The common law view is that too long a lapse of time between the provocation and the act of killing will render the provocation inadequate "as a matter of law" and therefore deprive the defendant of the right to an instruction on voluntary manslaughter. For example, in United States v. Bordeaux, 980 F.2d 534 (8th Cir. 1992), defendant was told, during the course of an all-day drinking party, that Shelby White Bear, also at the party, had raped defendant's mother 20 years earlier. Later, about mid-day, defendant's mother confirmed the report. Sometime during the early evening, defendant and some friends severely beat White Bear and left him lying in a bedroom. Defendant returned to the bedroom shortly afterward, saw White Bear lying on the floor bleeding, and slashed his throat. He then told a friend that he had killed White Bear because of the rape and said he would do it again because "[h]e deserved it." The court of appeals upheld the trial judge's refusal to instruct the jury on voluntary manslaughter and affirmed the conviction of murder. The court said that evidence of a prior argument or continuing dispute was insufficient to warrant a voluntary manslaughter instruction in the absence of "some sort of instant incitement." Because the revelation of the rape had occurred much earlier in the day, and because the fatal act was committed "well after" the beating of White Bear had ended, the court found that there would be "no rational basis for the jury to find that Bordeaux killed White Bear in the heat of passion. . . ."

The cooling-time limitation can sometimes be surmounted by the argument that an event immediately preceding the homicide had rekindled the earlier provocation. But many courts refuse to take note of "rekindling." Consider, for example, State v. Gounagias, 88 Wash. 304, 153 P. 9 (1915). The deceased had committed an act of sodomy upon the defendant and then bragged to others about it. Those who heard of the episode repeatedly ridiculed the defendant, and after two weeks he finally lost control and killed the man who had assaulted him. The defendant argued that the cumulative effect of the taunts, reminding him of the previous provocation, led to a sudden heat of passion. But the court held that the legally sufficient provoking event had occurred two weeks before the killing and that the interval constituted adequate cooling time as a matter of law. Many modern courts are similarly unwilling to allow "rekindling" of prior provocation. In Commonwealth v. LeClair, 708 N.E.2d 107 (Mass. 1999), a man had for several weeks suspected his wife of infidelity and upon suddenly confirming his suspicions, he strangled her in a rage. The court held that his prior suspicions provided adequate cooling time, and therefore no manslaughter instructions were required. Some courts, however, permit the jury to make the judgment whether sufficient cooling time has elapsed. Thus, in People v. Berry, 556 P.2d 777 (Cal. 1976), the provoked defendant waited for his victim in her apartment for 20 hours before killing her. The court held that the defendant was nevertheless entitled to a manslaughter instruction, because the jury could find that the defendant's heat of passion resulted from a long-smoldering prior course of provocative conduct by the victim, the passage of time serving to aggravate rather than cool defendant's agitation.

6. Victims other than the provoker. Should the provocation defense be available when the person killed was not the source of the provocation? The problem arises in several ways.

(a) Consider this hypothetical. Three friends, Chandra, John, and Maria, are having a drink at the local bar when suddenly the conversation becomes acrimonious. Chandra sics her little dog, Layka, on John, and while John is struggling with the dog and screaming with fear and anger, cruelly tells him the lie that the dog has never had a rabies inoculation. Maria is amused by the whole incident and laughs uproariously. John, thoroughly enraged, shoots both Chandra and Maria dead. Assuming John is entitled to a voluntary manslaughter instruction in a prosecution for the murder of Chandra, is he entitled to such an instruction in a prosecution for the murder of Maria?

(b) In State v. Mauricio, 117 N.J. 402, 568 A.2d 879 (1990), a bouncer forcefully ejected the defendant from a bar. He slammed defendant against a wall and then kicked and pushed him down the stairs, making him hit his head sharply on the floor. Expecting the bar to close shortly (it was 2:30 A.M.), defendant waited outside for the bouncer to emerge. About five minutes later, a patron who had not been involved in the fight left the bar. Defendant mistook the patron for the bouncer, followed him, and shot him dead. The New Jersey Supreme Court reversed a murder conviction, holding that the trial judge had erred in refusing to give voluntary manslaughter instructions. Several states would reach the same result by statute. See, e.g., Pa. Stat. §2503(a)(2), page 392 supra. Are these results sound if the provocation defense is designed to afford mitigation for partially *justified* killings? Or do these results suggest that provocation must be viewed as a partial *excuse*? Compare Tex. Pen. Code §19.04 requiring the provocation be given "by the individual killed or another acting with the person killed."

(c) Suppose that the person killed is not associated with the provoker and is not the accidental victim of rage directed against the provoker. Should a justifiably enraged defendant be able to claim mitigation to manslaughter when the person he intends to kill is an innocent bystander? In Rex. v. Scriva, [1951] Vict. L. R. 298, a father observed an automobile driver knock down and severely injure his daughter. When the father, brandishing a knife, went after the driver, a bystander attempted to restrain him, and the father then fatally stabbed the bystander. In People v. Spurlin, 156 Cal. App. 3d 119, 202 Cal. Rptr. 663 (1984), the defendant killed his wife after an intense argument over their respective sexual escapades, and he then killed his sleeping nine-year-old son.

In cases like *Scriva* and *Spurlin,* are the assaults against the nonprovokers unreasonable as a matter of law? Or does the very fact that the defendant attacked an innocent party reinforce the claim of a total loss of control? In both of the above cases, the courts held that no provocation defense was available with respect to the charges of murdering the nonprovoking relatives or bystanders. On what principle can such results be justified? Compare R. S. O'Regan, Indirect Provocation and Misdirected Retaliation, [1968] Crim. L. Rev. 319, 323: "Once an accused loses his self-control it is unreal to insist that his retaliatory acts be directed only against his provoker. When his reason has been dethroned a man cannot be expected . . . 'to guide his anger with judgment.'"

7. *Defendants who elicit provocation.* In Regina v. Johnson, [1989] 2 All E.R. 839, the defendant had made threatening and insulting remarks to Roberts and his female friend. Roberts and the woman attacked defendant, poured beer over his head, and then pinned him to a wall and punched him. Defendant pulled out a knife and fatally stabbed Roberts. The trial judge refused to instruct the jury on provocation, ruling that "[i]t is rather difficult to see how a man who excites

provocative conduct can in turn rely on it as provocation in the criminal law." The appellate court reversed, stating, "[W]e find it impossible to accept that the mere fact that a defendant caused a reaction in others, which in turn led him to lose his self-control, should result in the issue of provocation being kept outside a jury's consideration." Do you agree? Some American statutes explicitly disallow the provocation defense where the defendant induced the provocative action. N.D. Century code §12.1-16-01; Or. Rev. Stat. §163.135(1) (1995).

8. The Model Penal Code approach. The Model Penal Code (§210.3(1)(b)) rejects the common law provocation formula and adopts a standard that is even more flexible than that of the *Maher* case. The operation of the MPC approach is illustrated in the case that follows.

PEOPLE v. CASASSA

New York Court of Appeals
49 N.Y.2d 668, 404 N.E.2d 1310 (1980)

JASEN, J. . . . On February 28, 1977, Victoria Lo Consolo was brutally murdered. Defendant Victor Casassa and Miss Lo Consolo . . . met in August, 1976 as a result of their residence in the same apartment complex. Shortly thereafter, defendant asked Miss Lo Consolo to accompany him to a social function and she agreed. The two apparently dated casually on other occasions until November, 1976 when Miss Lo Consolo informed defendant that she was not "falling in love" with him. Defendant claims that Miss Lo Consolo's candid statement of her feelings "devastated him."

Miss Lo Consolo's rejection of defendant's advances also precipitated a bizarre series of actions on the part of defendant which, he asserts, demonstrate the existence of extreme emotional disturbance upon which he predicates his affirmative defense. Defendant, aware that Miss Lo Consolo maintained social relationships with others, broke into the apartment below Miss Lo Consolo's on several occasions to eavesdrop. These eavesdropping sessions allegedly caused him to be under great emotional stress. Thereafter, on one occasion, he broke into Miss Lo Consolo's apartment while she was out. Defendant took nothing, but, instead, observed the apartment, disrobed and lay for a time in Miss Lo Consolo's bed. During this break-in, defendant was armed with a knife which, he later told police, he carried "because he knew that he was either going to hurt Victoria or Victoria was going to cause him to commit suicide."

Defendant's final visit to his victim's apartment occurred on February 28, 1977. Defendant brought several bottles of wine and liquor with him to offer as a gift. Upon Miss Lo Consolo's rejection of this offering, defendant produced a steak knife which he had brought with him, stabbed Miss Lo Consolo several times in the throat, dragged her body to the bathroom and submerged it in a bathtub full of water to "make sure she was dead." . . .

Defendant [was charged with second-degree murder. He] waived a jury and proceeded to trial before the County Court. . . . The defendant did not contest the underlying facts of the crime. Instead, the sole issue presented to the trial court was whether the defendant, at the time of the killing, had acted under the influence of "extreme emotional disturbance." The defense presented only one witness, a psychiatrist, who testified, in essence, that the defendant had become obsessed with Miss Lo Consolo and that the course which their relationship had taken, combined with several personality attributes peculiar to defendant, caused him to be under the influence of extreme emotional disturbance at the time of the killing.

In rebuttal, the People produced several witnesses. Among these witnesses was a psychiatrist who testified that although the defendant was emotionally disturbed, he was not under the influence of "extreme emotional disturbance" within the meaning . . . of the Penal Law, because his disturbed state was not the product of external factors but rather was "a stress he created from within himself, dealing mostly with a fantasy, a refusal to accept the reality of the situation."

The trial court . . . considered the appropriate test to be whether in the totality of the circumstances the finder of fact could understand how a person might have his reason overcome. Concluding that the test was not to be applied solely from the viewpoint of defendant, the court found that defendant's emotional reaction at the time of the commission of the crime was so peculiar to him that it could not be considered reasonable so as to reduce the conviction to manslaughter in the first degree. Accordingly, the trial court found defendant guilty of the crime of murder in the second degree. . . .

On this appeal defendant contends that the trial court erred in failing to afford him the benefit of the affirmative defense of "extreme emotional disturbance". . . .

Section 125.25 (subd. 1, par. [a]) of the Penal Law provides that it is an affirmative defense to the crime of murder in the second degree where "[t]he defendant acted under the influence of extreme emotional disturbance for which there was a reasonable explanation or excuse." . . .

In enacting [this provision], the Legislature adopted the language of the manslaughter provisions of the Model Penal Code. The only substantial distinction between the New York statute and the Model Penal Code is the designation by the Legislature of "extreme emotional disturbance" as an "affirmative defense," thus placing the burden of proof on this issue upon defendant. . . .

The "extreme emotional disturbance" defense is an outgrowth of the "heat of passion" doctrine [but] the new formulation is significantly broader in scope than the "heat of passion" doctrine which it replaced.

For example, the "heat of passion" doctrine required that a defendant's action be undertaken as a response to some provocation which prevented him from reflecting upon his actions. Moreover, such reaction had to be immediate. The existence of a "cooling off" period completely negated any mitigating effect which the provocation might otherwise have had. In *Patterson* [39 N.Y.2d 288], however, this court recognized that "[a]n action influenced by an extreme emotional disturbance is not one that is necessarily so spontaneously undertaken. Rather, it may be that a significant mental trauma has affected a defendant's mind for a substantial period of time, simmering in the unknowing subconscious and then inexplicably coming to the fore." This distinction between the past and present law of mitigation, enunciated in *Patterson,* was expressly adopted by the trial court and properly applied in this case.

The thrust of defendant's claim, however, concerns a question arising out of another perceived distinction between "heat of passion" and "extreme emotional disturbance" which was not directly addressed in *Patterson,* to wit: whether, assuming that the defense is applicable to a broader range of circumstances, the standard by which the reasonableness of defendant's emotional reaction is to be tested must be an entirely subjective one. Defendant relies principally upon our decision in *Patterson* and upon the language of the statute to support his claim that the reasonableness of his "explanation or excuse" should be determined solely with reference to his own subjective viewpoint. Such reliance is misplaced.

In *Patterson,* . . . we noted that "[t]he purpose of the extreme emotional disturbance defense is to permit the defendant to show that his actions were caused by a mental infirmity not arising to the level of insanity, and that he is less culpable for having committed them." [But we] did not hold that all mental infirmities not arising to the level of insanity constitute "extreme emotional disturbance" within the meaning of the statute. This . . . is a question that has never been decided by this court. . . .

Consideration of the Comments to the Model Penal Code, from which the New York statute was drawn, are instructive. The defense of "extreme emotional disturbance" has two principal components — (1) the particular defendant must have "acted under the influence of extreme emotional disturbance," and (2) there must have been "a reasonable explanation or excuse" for such extreme emotional disturbance, "the reasonableness of which is to be determined from the viewpoint of a person in the defendant's situation under the circumstances as the defendant believed them to be." The first requirement is wholly subjective — i.e., it involves a determination that the particular defendant did in fact act under extreme emotional disturbance, that the claimed explanation as to the cause of his action is not contrived or sham.

The second component is more difficult to describe — i.e., whether there was a reasonable explanation or excuse for the emotional disturbance. It was designed to sweep away "the rigid rules that have developed with respect to the sufficiency of particular types of provocation, such as the rule that words alone can never be enough. . . . The ultimate test, however, is objective; there must be 'reasonable' explanation or excuse for the actor's disturbance." In light of these comments and the necessity of articulating the defense in terms comprehensible to jurors, we conclude that the determination whether there was reasonable explanation or excuse for a particular emotional disturbance should be made by viewing the subjective, internal situation in which the defendant found himself and the external circumstances as he perceived them at the time, however inaccurate that perception may have been, and assessing from that standpoint whether the explanation or excuse for his emotional disturbance was reasonable, so as to entitle him to a reduction of the crime charged from murder in the second degree to manslaughter in the first degree.[2] We recognize that even such a description of the defense provides no precise guidelines and necessarily leaves room for the exercise of judgmental evaluation by the jury. This, however, appears to have been the intent of the draftsmen. "The purpose was explicitly to give full scope to what amounts to a plea in mitigation based upon a mental or emotional trauma of significant dimensions, with the jury asked to show whatever empathy it can." (Wechsler, Codification of Criminal Law in the United States: The Model Penal Code, 68 Col. L. Rev. 1425, 1446.)

By suggesting a standard of evaluation which contains both subjective and ob-

2. We emphasize that this test is to be applied to determine whether defendant's emotional disturbance, and not the act of killing, was supported by a reasonable explanation or excuse.

jective elements, we believe that the drafters of the code adequately achieved their dual goals of broadening the "heat of passion" doctrine to apply to a wider range of circumstances while retaining some element of objectivity in the process. The result of their draftsmanship is a statute which offers the defendant a fair opportunity to seek mitigation without requiring that the trier of fact find mitigation in each case where an emotional disturbance is shown — or as the drafters put it, to offer "room for argument as to the reasonableness of the explanations or excuses offered." . . .

We conclude that the trial court, in this case, properly applied the statute. The court apparently accepted, as a factual matter, that defendant killed Miss Lo Consolo while under the influence of "extreme emotional disturbance," a threshold question which must be answered in the affirmative before any test of reasonableness is required. The court, however, also recognized that in exercising its function as trier of fact, it must make a further inquiry into the reasonableness of that disturbance. In this regard, the court considered each of the mitigating factors put forward by defendant, including his claimed mental disability, but found that the excuse offered by defendant was so peculiar to him that it was unworthy of mitigation. The court obviously made a sincere effort to understand defendant's "situation" and "the circumstances as defendant believed them to be," but concluded that the murder in this case was the result of defendant's malevolence rather than an understandable human response deserving of mercy. We cannot say, as a matter of law, that the court erred in so concluding. . . .

In our opinion, this statute would not require that the jury or the court as trier of fact find mitigation on any particular set of facts, but, rather, allows the finder of fact the opportunity to do so, such opportunity being conditional only upon a finding of extreme emotional disturbance in the first instance. . . .

[Affirmed.]

NOTES ON THE MODEL PENAL CODE

1. *Influence of the Model Penal Code formulation.* At least 14 states have adopted, in whole or in part, the Model Penal Code's "extreme emotional disturbance" formula for reducing murder to manslaughter. See, e.g., Rainey v. State, 310 Ark. 419, 837 S.W.2d 453 (1992). However, in four of these states (Maine, Ohio, Washington, and Wisconsin) courts or legislatures returned to common law formulations after a brief experience with the Model Penal Code. See Richard Singer, The Resurgence of Mens Rea: I — Provocation, Emotional Disturbance, and the Model Penal Code, 27 B.C.L. Rev. 243, 292-294 (1986). What features of the Model Penal Code approach might account for these reactions?

2. *Distinctive features of the Model Penal Code formulation.* What was the "provocation" in the *Casassa* case? Under the Model Penal Code standard, does emotional disturbance require manslaughter instructions even when the disturbance is not attributable to any provocative behavior at all? In State v. Elliot, 177 Conn. 1, 411 A.2d 3 (1979), the defendant had for years suffered from an overwhelming fear of his brother. One day, for no apparent reason, he appeared at his brother's house and killed him. The defendant was convicted of murder, but the Connecticut Supreme Court reversed, holding that instructions on extreme emotional disturbance were required. The Court said:

> [T]he defense does not require a provoking or triggering event. [T]o establish the "heat of passion" defense a defendant had to prove that the "hot blood" had not had time to "cool off" at the time of the killing. A homicide influenced by an extreme emotional disturbance, in contrast, is not one which is necessarily committed in the "hot blood" stage, but rather one that was brought about by a significant mental trauma that caused the defendant to brood for a long period of time and then react violently, seemingly without provocation.

Question: If the traditional provocation formula and the Model Penal Code approach produce different results in a case like *Elliot,* which approach is preferable? For a study of the developments in Model Penal Code jurisdictions, see Victoria Nourse, Passion's Progress: Modern Law Reform and the Provocation Defense, 106 Yale L.J. 1331 (1997). She concludes that the Model Penal Code's formulation has aggravated the unfairness to women of the provocation defense by expanding greatly the kinds of frictions in intimate settings that may suffice to establish manslaughter.

3. *Roles of Judge and Jury.* In People v. Walker, 100 A.D.2d 220, 473 N.Y.S.2d 460 (1984), the defendant, a drug dealer, received a $4,500 consignment of marijuana from his supplier, William Edmunds. He failed to pay Edmunds and claimed that he had been robbed of the marijuana. In spite of the defendant's plea for additional consignments, Edmunds refused to supply him. One evening, the defendant encountered Edmunds in a restaurant frequented by drug dealers. A witness heard an angry argument between the two. Edmunds demanded his money, the defendant responded that he did not have any money, and Edmunds then asked how he could afford to eat in the restaurant. The defendant replied that Edmunds should give him money, to which Edmunds responded, "The only dough you're going to get is the dough in that bread." The defendant was then heard to say, "Take your damn hand out of my plate," after which he rose, gun in hand, and fired several shots in rapid succession, killing Edmunds.

At Walker's trial on murder charges, the judge refused to instruct the jury on an extreme emotional disturbance defense. Was this error? The appellate court affirmed, but a dissenting judge commented:

> [The Model Penal Code] explicitly intended to discard the general rule at common law "that words alone, no matter how insulting, could not amount to adequate provocation." In declining to charge the affirmative defense in this case the trial court may well have applied correctly the traditional rule that had prevailed in the courts of this country. [T]he court failed to appreciate that the rule it was attempting to follow was one of those [the Model Penal Code] intended to be discarded. . . .
>
> [T]he threshold issue clearly is whether there is evidence that the defendant "acted under the influence of extreme emotional disturbance." As we have been instructed by the Court of Appeals in *Casassa,* this requirement "is wholly subjective." From the evidence presented at the trial the jury could reasonably have found that the defendant killed the deceased in a burst of anger, that a smoldering sense of grievance had been ignited by insulting and contemptuous words and actions. . . .
>
> Once it is determined that there was "evidence of extreme emotional disturbance," the controlling rule is clear. . . : "it is for the trier of fact to decide, in light of all the circumstances of the case, whether there exists a reasonable explanation or excuse for the actor's mental condition." (Model Penal Code and Commentaries, §210.3, p. 61.) . . .
>
> This is not a sympathetic case. The plight of a narcotics dealer cut off from his

source of supply, and then subjected to insulting and contemptuous words and actions by his former supplier, is not likely to evoke widespread feelings of acute compassion. Nevertheless, it is clear that the controlling statutory sections were carefully designed to permit the essential judgment on the kind of issue presented here to be made by jurors on the basis of all the circumstances, and not by the trial judge as a matter of law.

NOTES ON THE REASONABLE PERSON REQUIREMENT

Both the common law formulations and the Model Penal Code require an objective element — not every defendant who flies off the handle and kills is a candidate for the provocation defense. His loss of self-control must in some sense meet some objective standard of "reasonableness." What should that mean? Consider the following:

1. The Model Penal Code Solution: As the *Casassa* opinion points out, the Model Penal Code solution makes the test whether the defendant acted "under the influence of extreme emotional disturbance for which there is reasonable explanation or excuse," and then directs that the determination of the reasonableness of the explanation or excuse shall be made "from the viewpoint of a person in the actor's situation under the circumstances as he believes them to be." In explaining this formulation, the Reporter's Comments state (Model Penal Code and Commentaries, Comment to §210.3, at 62-63 (1980)):

> The word "situation" is designedly ambiguous. On the one hand, it is clear that personal handicaps and some external circumstances must be taken into account. Thus, blindness, shock from traumatic injury, and extreme grief are all easily read into the term "situation." This result is sound, for it would be morally obtuse to appraise a crime for mitigation of punishment without reference to these factors. On the other hand, it is equally plain that idiosyncratic moral values are not part of the actor's situation. An assassin who kills a political leader because he believes it is right to do so cannot ask that he be judged by the standard of a reasonable extremist. Any other result would undermine the normative message of the criminal law. In between these two extremes, however, there are matters neither as clearly distinct from individual blameworthiness as blindness or handicap nor as integral a part of moral depravity as a belief in the rightness of killing. Perhaps the classic illustration is the unusual sensitivity to the epithet "bastard" of a person born illegitimate. An exceptionally punctilious sense of personal honor or an abnormally fearful temperament may also serve to differentiate an individual actor from the hypothetical reasonable man, yet none of these factors is wholly irrelevant to the ultimate issue of culpability. The proper role of such factors cannot be resolved satisfactorily by abstract definition of what may constitute adequate provocation. The Model Code endorses a formulation that affords sufficient flexibility to differentiate in particular cases between those special aspects of the actor's situation that should be deemed material for purpose of grading and those that should be ignored. There thus will be room for interpretation of the word "situation," and that is precisely the flexibility desired. . . . In the end, the question is whether the actor's loss of self-control can be understood in terms that arouse sympathy in the ordinary citizen. Section 210.3 faces this issue squarely and leaves the ultimate judgment to the ordinary citizen in the function of a juror assigned to resolve the specific case.

2. Problems. Consider how the Model Penal Code would deal with each of the following special circumstances of the defendant:

(a) Age and Gender. In D.P.P.V. Camplin, [1978] A.C. 705, the defendant, a boy of fifteen, was sodomized against his will and then mocked by deceased. The defendant then broke the deceased's skull with a heavy frying pan. The court held that the jury should be instructed that the standard of self-control to be demanded of a person (the "reasonable man") is that of a person of the sex and age of the defendant. The court gave as a reason for the age qualification that "to require old heads on young shoulders is inconsistent with the law's compassion of human infirmity." What is the reason for the gender qualification? That one gender has more self-control than the other? Which one? That men and women are provoked in different ways by different things? See Abbe Smith, Criminal Responsibility, Social Responsibility, and Angry Young Men, 21 N.Y.U. Rev. L. & Soc. Change 433, 470 (1994-1995); Robin West, Jurisprudence, and Gender, 55 U. Chi. L. Rev. 1 (1988).

(b) Culture. Should the defendant's nationality and cultural background be taken into account? Suppose that the defendant recently immigrated from a country where the provoking circumstances (e.g., marital infidelity or a particular insult) are regarded as far more serious than they are in the United States. Suppose that ordinary people in the immigrant's country are far more likely to respond violently to such circumstances. Should the defendant's response be assessed from the perspective of the reasonable person of his cultural background? Or is it more appropriate to hold such a defendant to the standards of self-control that our society expects Americans to exercise? Consider the views of an Australian Justice on this question in Masciantonio v. R., 129 Austr. L.R. 575 (High Court Australia, 1995) (dissenting):

> Without incorporating [the general characteristics of an ordinary person of the same age, race, culture and background as the accused on the self-control issue] the law of provocation is likely to result in discrimination and injustice. In a multicultural society such as Australia, invocation [of the reasonable man standard] in cases heard by juries of predominately Anglo-Saxon-Celtic origin almost certainly results in the accused being judged by the standard of self-control attributed to a middle class Australian of Anglo-Saxon-Celtic heritage. . . . If it is objected that this will result in one law of provocation for one class of persons and another law for a different class, I would answer that that must be the natural consequence of true equality before the law in a multicultural society when the criterion of criminal liability is made to depend upon objective standards of personhood.

Question: Would this argument have equal force where the issue is guilt or innocence rather than degree of punishment? Compare the issue of the cultural defense discussed supra page 276.

(c) Battered Women. In State v. McClain, 248 N.J. Super. 409, 591 A.2d 652 (1991), defendant shot and killed the man with whom she had lived for nine years in a troubled relationship. Though the man had not physically assaulted the defendant for several years (there had been two beating incidents, several years apart, earlier in the relationship), a psychologist testified that the defendant suffered from battered woman syndrome because a series of psychological humiliations had triggered a mental "breakdown" and led to the killing. The court held that evidence relating to defendant's status as a battered woman was "irrelevant on the question of whether the victim's conduct was adequately provocative because that inquiry requires application of the 'reasonable person' test." For a criticism, see Lawrence S. Lustberg & John V. Jacobi, The Battered

Woman as a Reasonable Person: A Critique of the Appellate Division Decision in *State v. McClain,* 22 Seton Hall L. Rev. 365 (1992). See also State v. Felton, 110 Wis. 2d 485, 329 N.W.2d 161, 172-173 (1983): "It is proper in applying the objective test . . . to consider how other persons similarly situated with respect to that type, or that history, of provocation would react. [T]he objective test may be satisfied by considering the situation of the ordinary person who is a battered spouse." Compare J.C.S., Comment on R. v. Thornton [1996] Crim. L. R. 597, 598:

> The concept of an ordinary person suffering from a personality disorder and battered woman syndrome is a difficult one. It could be . . . put to the jury in some such form as: "If you think that she may in fact have lost her self-control, you must not convict of murder unless you are sure that a woman, suffering from this personality disorder and from battered woman syndrome but otherwise an ordinary woman, exercising such restraint as could reasonably be expected of a woman in that condition, would not have lost her self-control and done what the accused did." But this seems substantially to abandon the notion of the reasonable or ordinary person.

Question: Consider how the Model Penal Code formulation would affect the defense of provocation in a battered woman case. The problem of battered spouse syndrome is explored at greater length in Chapter 8, infra.

(d) Mental Disorder. What of evidence of mental or personality disorder generally? May such evidence be permitted to enter into a judgment of whether defendant was reasonably provoked? In State v. Klimas, 94 Wis. 2d 288, 288 N.W.2d 157 (Wis. Ct. App., 1979), the defendant, after many months of intense conflict with his wife, shot and killed her. He claimed to be distraught over the disintegration of his marriage, his wife's relationship with another man, and her efforts to obtain a divorce. He sought to introduce psychiatric testimony to the effect that he had been suffering a severe depression, that events on the day preceding the killing had "overwhelmed" him, and that although not legally insane, he was "a desperate man overwhelmed by a psychotic depressive illness." The defendant apparently sought to have his conduct assessed from the perspective of a person in that emotional situation. The trial judge ruled the psychiatric evidence irrelevant and therefore inadmissible. Was this error?

3. A view from abroad. The development of the English law of provocation is instructive:

(a) The modern development begins with the enactment of the English Homicide Act of 1957, which provided:

> Where on a charge of murder there is evidence on which the jury can find that the person charged was provoked (whether by things done or by things said or by both together) to lose his self-control, the question whether the provocation was enough to make a reasonable man do as he did shall be left to be determined by the jury; and in determining that question the jury shall take into account everything both done and said according to the effect which, in their opinion, it would have on a reasonable man.

This made two changes in common law doctrine. First, it made the jury the sole judge of whether a provocation that led to defendant's loss of self-control was enough to make a reasonable person do as he did; second, it eliminated any restriction on the kind of acts that could amount to provocation, authorizing the jury to take account of things said as well as things done.

(b) This left open whether the statute called for a third change in common law doctrine, namely the rule that the proper standard was the reasonable man devoid of any particular characteristics of the accused. This doctrine was famously exemplified in Bedder v. D.P.P., [1954] 2 All E.R. 801, in which the House of Lords affirmed a murder conviction of an impotent 18-year-old male for killing a prostitute. She had taunted him for his impotence and he responded with a knife. The jury had been instructed to consider whether a reasonable man who was not impotent would have reacted in the same way. This was held to be correct on the ground that:

> It would be plainly illogical not to recognize an unusually excitable or pugnacious temperament in the accused as a matter to be taken into account but yet to recognise for that purpose some unusual physical characteristic, be it impotence or another.

(c) That doctrine prevailed until the House of Lords chose to take a different view in D.P.P. v. Camplin, [1978] A.C. 705. The case involved a 15-year-old boy who killed an older man in response to sexual abuse and taunting. The trial judge had instructed the jury that in applying the reasonable man standard, they had to consider whether,

> the provocation was sufficient to make a reasonable man in like circumstances act as the defendant did. Not a reasonable boy, as [counsel for Camplin] would have it, or a reasonable lad; it is an objective test — a reasonable man.

The House of Lords concluded that this instruction was in error and that the standard should have been individualized by requiring the jury to consider whether the provocation would have been sufficient to cause a reasonable person *of the defendant's age* to lose his self control. In considering to what extent the standard should be individualized, the House of Lords reasoned that since provocation by words was often aimed at some characteristic of the defendant, such as some disability or race, the change in the law allowing words and taunts to constitute adequate provocation would be ineffectual if the defendant had to be assumed to lack such a characteristic. So it held that in considering the gravity of the provocation, the reasonable man should be assumed to share the characteristics of the defendant relevant to the words or taunt. However, in considering the self-control to be exercised, the jury was to apply the standard of the person of reasonable self-control, without regard to any special characteristics of the person.

Note, however, that by its own newly announced standard, the trial judge's instruction would have been correct — the defendant had not been taunted for his age. And with respect to the degree of self-control to be exercised, the standard — by its own reasoning — should have been entirely objective. But as one of the Law Lords noted, "to require old heads on young shoulders is inconsistent with the law's compassion [for] human infirmity." The House of Lords therefore held that,

> The reasonable man referred to in the [test] is a person having the power of self-control to be expected of an ordinary person of the sex and age of the accused, but

> in other respects sharing such of the accused's characteristics as they think would affect the gravity of the provocation to him.

This distinction was applied in a later case involving a glue sniffing addict who killed a person for taunting him about his addiction. Regina v. Morhall, [1995] 1 A.C. 90. The House held that the jury should have been instructed to consider the defendant's glue sniff addiction in judging the seriousness of the provocation, but then ask whether a person with ordinary powers of self-control would have reacted to the provocation as the defendant did.

(d) The *Camplin* approach, which was followed as well in Australia, New Zealand, and Canada, has now been abandoned in England. In Regina v. Smith (Morgan), [2000] Weekly Law Reports 654, involving a clinically depressed alcoholic who stabbed and killed his friend for stealing from him, the House, in a 3-2 decision, rejected the distinction between gravity of the provocation and powers of self-control. Lord Hoffman, who delivered the lead majority opinion, concluded that the distinction was practically unworkable, tending to produce "glazed looks" in jurors' eyes when told to consider such oddities as "the reasonable glue sniffer" or "the reasonable depressed person." The jury was no longer to be instructed in terms of the "formula of the reasonable man equipped with an array of unreasonable eligible characteristics." They were to be free to conclude that "there was some characteristic of the accused, whether temporary or permanent, which affected the degree of control which society could reasonably have expected of *him* and which it would be unjust not to take into account." He concluded (678-679):

> [J]udges should not be required to describe the objective element in the provocation defence by reference to a reasonable man, with or without attribution of personal characteristics. [They should explain that to find provocation] the jury must think that the circumstances were such as to make the loss of self-control sufficiently *excusable* to reduce the gravity of the offence from murder to manslaughter. . . . In deciding what should count as a sufficient excuse, they have to apply what they consider to be appropriate standards of behavior; on the one hand making allowance for human nature and the power of the emotions, but, on the other hand, not allowing someone to rely upon his own violent disposition.

(e) Questions: Is the distinction between gravity of the provocation and power of self-control theoretically justifiable, even if juries find it difficult to apply? Can the gravity of the provocation to the accused be assessed without some standard of reasonableness? How is taunting an impotent man for his impotence to be distinguished from taunting a baseball fanatic for the poor performance of his team?

Compare the formulations of the House of Lords in *Smith* (Morgan) with the formulation of the Model Penal Code. Have they arrived at the same place? How would *Camplin* be decided under the Model Penal Code? Does the Model Penal Code approach or the House of Lords position in *Smith (Morgan)* give sufficient guidance to the jury to assure uniform application of the law?

Is there a lesson in the English experience? It may be that once you start down the road to individualizing the characteristics of the defendant there is no satisfactory stopping pace short of remitting the matter to the jury with a frank statement of the dilemma. At least that seems to be what the English law and the Model Penal Code come to.

C. LEGISLATIVE GRADING OF UNINTENDED KILLINGS

1. *The Creation of Homicidal Risk*

The material in this section is organized around the following issues:

Subsection a deals with the criteria for establishing criminal, as opposed to solely civil, liability for unintended homicide.

Subsection b raises the issue whether criminal liability for unintended homicide should rest on a subjective or objective standard.

Subsection c considers the special circumstances that may make an unintended killing murder.

a. Distinguishing Civil and Criminal Liability

COMMONWEALTH v. WELANSKY

Massachusetts Supreme Judicial Court
316 Mass. 383, 55 N.E.2d 902 (1944)

LUMMUS, J. On November 28, 1942, and for about nine years before that day, a corporation named New Cocoanut Grove, Inc., maintained and operated a "night club" in Boston. . . . The corporation, its officers and employees, and its business, were completely dominated by the defendant Barnett Welansky. . . . The defendant was accustomed to spend his evenings at the night club, inspecting the premises and superintending the business. On November 16, 1942, he became suddenly ill, and was carried to a hospital, where he was in bed for three weeks and remained until discharged on December 11, 1942. . . . There is no evidence of any act, omission or condition at the night club on November 28, 1942 (apart from the lighting of a match hereinafter described), that was not within the usual and regular practice during the time before the defendant was taken ill when he was at the night club nearly every evening. . . .

The physical arrangement of the night club on November 28, 1942, as well as on November 16, 1942, when the defendant last had personal knowledge of it, was as follows. [The only entrance to the club was through a single revolving door. Various rooms were connected by narrow passageways and corridors to one another and to a small number of exits. Three of the emergency exits were in obscure locations, poorly marked and accessible only to knowledgeable employees. The court observed that an emergency escape "would be difficult for a patron not thoroughly familiar with parts of the premises not ordinarily open to him." Two other emergency exits were marked by "Exit" lights and equipped with panic bars, but one of the two was blocked by a screen and dining tables; the other was regularly kept locked and the court noted that "if that door should be left so that it could be opened by means of the panic bar, a patron might leave through that door without paying his bill."]

A little after ten o'clock on the evening of Saturday, November 28, 1942, the night club was well filled with a crowd of patrons. It was during the busiest season of the year. An important football game in the afternoon had attracted many visitors to Boston. [T]here were from two hundred fifty to four hundred persons in the Melody Lounge, from four hundred to five hundred in the main dining room and the Caricature Bar, and two hundred fifty in the Cocktail Lounge. . . .

A bartender in the Melody Lounge noticed that an electric light bulb which was in or near the cocoanut husks of an artificial palm tree in the corner had been turned off and that the corner was dark. He directed a sixteen year old bar boy who was waiting on customers at the tables to cause the bulb to be lighted. [The bar boy lit a match to see the bulb, turned the bulb in its socket to light it, and blew out the match. The flame of the match ignited a palm tree, which in turn ignited a low cloth ceiling nearby.] The fire spread with great rapidity. . . . The crowd were panic stricken, and rushed and pushed in every direction through the night club, screaming, and overturning tables and chairs in their attempts to escape.

The door at the head of the Melody Lounge stairway was not opened until firemen broke it down from outside with an axe and found it locked by a key lock, so that the panic bar could not operate. . . . The head waiter and another waiter tried to get open the panic doors from the main dining room to Shawmut Street, and succeeded after some difficulty. The other two doors to Shawmut Street were locked, and were opened by force from outside by firemen and others. . . . A considerable number of patrons escaped through the Broadway door, but many died just inside that door. Some employees, and a great number of patrons, died in the fire.

[Defendant was charged with numerous counts of involuntary manslaughter based on overcrowding, installation of flammable decorations, absence of fire doors, and failure to maintain proper means of egress.]

The defendant was found guilty [and sentenced] upon each count for a term of not less than twelve years and not more than fifteen years, the first day of said term to be in solitary confinement and the residue at hard labor, the sentences to run concurrently. . . .

The Commonwealth disclaimed any contention that the defendant intentionally killed or injured the persons named in the indictments as victims. It based its case on involuntary manslaughter through wanton or reckless conduct. The judge instructed the jury correctly with respect to the nature of such conduct.

Usually wanton or reckless conduct consists of an affirmative act, like driving an automobile or discharging a firearm, in disregard of probable harmful consequences to another. But where as in the present case there is a duty of care for the safety of business visitors invited to premises which the defendant controls, wanton or reckless conduct may consist of intentional failure to take such care in disregard of the probable harmful consequences to them or of their right to care.

To define wanton or reckless conduct so as to distinguish it clearly from negligence and gross negligence is not easy. Sometimes the word "wilful" is prefaced to the words "wanton" and "reckless" in expressing the concept. That only blurs it. Wilful means intentional. In the phrase "wilful, wanton or reckless conduct," if "wilful" modifies "conduct" it introduces something different from wanton or reckless conduct, even though the legal result is the same. Wilfully causing harm is a wrong, but a different wrong from wantonly or recklessly causing harm. If "wilful" modifies "wanton or reckless conduct" its use is accurate. What must be intended is the conduct, not the resulting harm. The words "wanton" and "reckless" are practically synonymous in this connection, although the word "wanton" may contain a suggestion of arrogance or insolence or heartlessness that is lacking in the word "reckless." But intentional conduct to which either word applies is followed by the same legal consequences as though both words applied.

The standard of wanton or reckless conduct is at once subjective and objective, as has been recognized ever since Commonwealth v. Pierce, 138 Mass. 165, 52 Am. Rep. 264. Knowing facts that would cause a reasonable man to know the danger is equivalent to knowing the danger. . . . The judge charged the jury correctly when he said, "To constitute wanton or reckless conduct, as distinguished from mere negligence, grave danger to others must have been apparent and the defendant must have chosen to run the risk rather than alter his conduct so as to avoid the act or omission which caused the harm. If the grave danger was in fact realized by the defendant, his subsequent voluntary act or omission which caused the harm amounts to wanton or reckless conduct, no matter whether the ordinary man would have realized the gravity of the danger or not. But even if a particular defendant is so stupid (or) so heedless . . . that in fact he did not realize the grave danger, he cannot escape the imputation of wanton or reckless conduct in his dangerous act or omission, if an ordinary normal man under the same circumstances would have realized the gravity of the danger. A man may be reckless within the meaning of the law although he himself thought he was careful."

Jury Inst

The essence of wanton or reckless conduct is intentional conduct, by way either of commission or of omission where there is a duty to act, which conduct involves a high degree of likelihood that substantial harm will result to another. Wanton or reckless conduct amounts to what has been variously described as indifference to or disregard of probable consequences to that other. . . .

The words "wanton" and "reckless" are thus not merely rhetorical, vituperative expressions used instead of negligent or grossly negligent. They express a difference in the degree of risk and in the voluntary taking of risk so marked, as compared with negligence, as to amount substantially and in the eyes of the law to a difference in kind. . . .

Notwithstanding language used commonly in earlier cases, and occasionally in later ones, it is now clear in this Commonwealth that at common law conduct does not become criminal until it passes the borders of negligence and gross negligence and enters into the domain of wanton or reckless conduct. There is in Massachusetts at common law no such thing as "criminal negligence." . . .

To convict the defendant of manslaughter, the Commonwealth was not required to prove that he caused the fire by some wanton or reckless conduct. Fire in a place of public resort is an ever present danger. It was enough to prove that death resulted from his wanton or reckless disregard of the safety of patrons in the event of fire from any cause.

[A]ffirmed.

NOTES AND QUESTIONS

1. *Questions on* Welansky. Was the defendant aware of the risk to which his conduct had exposed his patrons and employees? Does the fact that the defendant himself spent most of his evenings at the club support or undercut the claim that he was aware of the risk?

Did the trial judge's instructions make actual awareness of the risk a prerequisite to conviction? Does the appellate court's opinion do so? What are the distinctive features of conduct that "passes the borders of negligence and gross negligence and enters into the domain of wanton and reckless conduct"? How is "wanton and reckless conduct" in Massachusetts different from ordinary civil negligence?

The court states that wanton and reckless conduct requires "a high degree of likelihood" of injury to another. Was that true in this case? What was the statistical likelihood that a raging fire would break out in this restaurant at a time when it was filled to capacity? What does "likelihood" mean?

2. *Defining unintended criminal homicide: Traditional formulations.* A persistent problem faced by the courts and legislatures has been the formulation of the "extra" or "plus" qualities that differentiate unintended homicides that give rise to criminal liability from those that, at most, produce civil liability for negligence. Consider the following:

State v. Barnett, 218 S.C. 415, 63 S.E.2d 57, 58-59 (1951): The degree of negligence necessary to establish criminal liability has perplexed the courts of England and America for centuries. The subject has at times been the source of much confusion. In the early development of the criminal law in England it was held that ordinary negligence, that is, the failure to exercise due care, was sufficient. Later it was found that this rule was too harsh. A noted English authority observed that an accident brought about by an act of ordinary negligence "may be the lot of even the wisest and the best of mankind." The English courts finally concluded that more carelessness was required to create criminal liability than civil but they found it difficult to determine "how much more." They use such words as "gross," "reckless" and "culpable," and hold that it is for the jury to decide, in view of all the circumstances, whether the act was of such character as to be worthy of punishment. . . . There was a tendency in the early American decisions to follow the rule first adopted in England to the effect that ordinary negligence was sufficient. That standard was soon repudiated, however, by the great majority of the courts in this country and it is now generally held that the negligence of the accused must be "culpable," "gross," or "reckless," that is, the conduct of the accused must be such a departure from what would be the conduct of an ordinarily prudent or careful man under the same circumstances as to be incompatible with a proper regard for human life, or conduct amounting to an indifference to consequences. Of course, under all the authorities the conduct of the accused must be judged in the light of the potential danger involved in the lawful act being performed. In perhaps a majority of the states, the offense of involuntary manslaughter is now defined by statute. Although variously worded, these statutes, with a few exceptions, have been construed as requiring gross negligence or recklessness.

Andrews v. Director of Public Prosecutions, [1937] A.C. 576, 581-583: My Lords, of all crimes manslaughter appears to afford more difficulties of definition, for it concerns homicide in so many and so varying conditions. . . . Expressions will be found which indicate that to cause death by any lack of due care will amount to manslaughter; but as manners softened and the law became more humane a narrower criterion appeared. . . . So . . . in Rex v. Bateman [19 Crim. App. 8] a charge of manslaughter was made against a qualified medical practitioner. [T]he

Lord Chief Justice, after pointing out that in a civil case once negligence is proved the degree of negligence is irrelevant, said, "In a criminal Court, on the contrary, the amount and degree of negligence are the determining question. There must be mens rea. . . . In explaining to juries the test which they should apply to determine whether the negligence, in the particular case, amounted or did not amount to a crime, judges have used many epithets such as 'culpable,' 'gross,' 'wicked,' 'clear,' 'complete.' But whatever epithet be used and whether an epithet be used or not, in order to establish criminal liability the facts must be such that, in the opinion of the jury, the negligence of the accused went beyond a mere matter of compensation between subjects and showed such disregard for the life and safety of others as to amount to a crime against the State and conduct deserving punishment."

Model Penal Code and Commentaries, Comment to §2.02 at 240 (1980): [Under traditional] statutes, as at common law, the concept of criminal negligence has been left to judicial definition, and the definitions vary greatly in their terms. As Jerome Hall has put it, the judicial "opinions run in terms of 'wanton and wilful negligence,' 'gross negligence,' and more illuminating yet, 'that degree of negligence that is more than the negligence required to impose tort liability.' The apex of this infelicity is 'wilful, wanton negligence,' which suggests a triple contradiction — 'negligence' implying inadvertence; 'wilful,' intention; and 'wanton,' recklessness."

3. *The Model Penal Code formulation.* Under the Model Penal Code, homicide is manslaughter when it is committed "recklessly." §210.3(1)(a). Under §2.02(2)(c), a person acts recklessly with respect to the death of another when he consciously disregards a substantial and unjustifiable risk that his conduct will cause that result. Additionally, the nature and degree of risk must be such that, considering all the circumstances, its disregard "involves a gross deviation from the standard of conduct that a law-abiding person would observe in the actor's situation." The Model Penal Code also creates a lesser offense of "negligent homicide" where the defendant acts without awareness of such a risk. §210.4. Many modern statutory revisions have followed the Model Penal Code. See Model Penal Code and Commentaries, Comment to §210.4 at 87-88 (1980). For a careful exposition and systematic application of the Model Penal Code formulations in an unusual reckless manslaughter prosecution of an out-of-control ski instructor who collided with and killed another skier, see People v. Hall, 999 P.2d 207 (2000). The court in that decision sustained the sufficiency of the prosecution, and on the subsequent trial a jury returned a verdict of negligent homicide. New York Times, Saturday, November 18, 2000, p. A9, col. 5.

NOTES

1. *Contributory Negligence.* In civil cases, the deceased's contributory negligence was once a complete defense, although that has changed in many jurisdictions with the adoption of comparative negligence. In criminal cases, however, the deceased's contributory negligence or other misconduct has never afforded a defense. Consider Dickerson v. State, 441 So. 2d 536 (Miss. 1983). In the early morning hours, the defendant was driving slightly in excess of the speed limit

when he suddenly became aware of a vehicle blocking his lane. The defendant applied his brakes, but not in time to avoid a collision that killed the driver of the other car. There was evidence that the deceased was himself quite intoxicated and guilty of gross negligence in parking his vehicle in the middle of the highway with its lights off. The court upheld defendant's manslaughter conviction for manslaughter, finding no error in excluding this evidence (id. at 538):

> Contributory negligence is not a defense to manslaughter. All that the state must prove with respect to the victim is that he was prior to the incident a live human being. The homicide laws of this State protect all living beings within the jurisdiction, sinners as well as saints, drunks as well as deacons.

Note, however, that although contributory negligence does not automatically afford a defense, as it would in a civil case, it may have a bearing on the question of whether the defendant's conduct was a proximate cause of the death. Consider, for example, a person driving with more than the permitted alcohol in his blood who strikes and kills a pedestrian who staggers into his car in a drunken stupor. See the material on causation in Chapter 6, page 517 infra.

2. Justification of the risk. Some risks may not be negligent or reckless in view of the object for which they are taken. See J. W. Salmond, Jurisprudence 416 (8th ed. 1930):

> [F]or the proper determination of [lack of reasonable care] there are two chief matters of consideration. The first is the magnitude of the risk to which other persons are exposed, while the second is the importance of the object to be attained by the dangerous form of activity. The reasonableness of any conduct will depend upon the proportion between these two elements. To expose others to danger for a disproportionate object is unreasonable, whereas an equal risk for a better cause may lawfully be run without negligence. By driving trains at the rate of fifty miles an hour, railway companies have caused many fatal accidents which could quite easily have been avoided by reducing the speed to ten miles, but this additional safety would be attained at too great a cost of public convenience, and therefore in neglecting this precaution the companies do not fall below the standard of reasonable care and are not guilty of negligence.

Question: What determines whether a risk is justified? Consider these situations:

(a) In Parrish v. State, 97 So. 2d 356 (Fla. Dist. App. 1957), the defendant, in a car with companions, pursued his ex-wife through the city streets of Jacksonville in the early hours of the morning. He was armed with a bayonet and was apparently endeavoring to carry out his threat to kill her. He caught up with her at one point and broke her car window with his bayonet, but she maneuvered her car and eluded him. Continuing her escape she disregarded a stop sign and drove at a high rate of speed into a through street. In so doing, she struck another car and subsequently died of the injuries. The defendant was convicted of second-degree murder for having killed the deceased by an act "imminently dangerous to another, and evidencing a depraved mind regardless of human life." *Questions:* Suppose the deceased had survived but the driver of the car she struck had been killed. Could *she* be held for manslaughter? Can the creation of risk of death or injury to other innocent persons be justified where it is employed as a means to save oneself from like injury? Would her conduct be noncriminal if she drove directly into a group of people blocking the street and killed several? See Anno-

tation, Unintentional killing of or injury to third person during attempted self-defense, 55 A.L.R.3d 620 (1974).

(b) A federal panel estimated that raising the speed limit from 55 MPH to 65 MPH would cause an additional 500 deaths per year but save 850,000 hours of travel time for every life lost. N.Y. Times, Nov. 28, 1984, at A16. *Question:* Is enactment of the higher speed limit justifiable? At what point does the saving in driving time justify the additional loss of life?

b. Objective versus Subjective Standards of Liability

STATE v. WILLIAMS

Washington Court of Appeals
4 Wash. App. 908, 484 P.2d 1167 (1971)

HOROWITZ, C.J. Defendants, husband and wife, were charged by information filed October 3, 1968, with the crime of manslaughter for negligently failing to supply their 17-month child with necessary medical attention, as a result of which he died on September 12, 1968. Upon entry of findings, conclusions and judgment of guilty, sentences were imposed on April 22, 1969.[a] Defendants appeal.

The defendant husband, Walter Williams, is a 24-year-old full-blooded Shoshon[e] Indian with a sixth-grade education. His sole occupation is that of laborer. The defendant wife, Bernice Williams, is a 20-year-old part Indian with an 11th grade education. At the time of the marriage, the wife had two children, the younger of whom was a 14-month-old son. Both parents worked and the children were cared for by the 85-year-old mother of the defendant husband. The defendant husband assumed parental responsibility with the defendant wife to provide clothing, care and medical attention for the child. Both defendants possessed a great deal of love and affection for the defendant wife's young son.

The court expressly found:

> That both defendants were aware that William Joseph Tabafunda was ill during the period September 1, 1968 to September 12, 1968. The defendants were ignorant. They did not realize how sick the baby was. They thought that the baby had a toothache and no layman regards a toothache as dangerous to life. They loved the baby and gave it aspirin in hopes of improving its condition. They did not take the baby to a doctor because of fear that the Welfare Department would take the baby away from them. They knew that medical help was available because of previous experience. They had no excuse that the law will recognize for not taking the baby to a doctor.
>
> The defendants Walter L. Williams and Bernice J. Williams were negligent in not seeking medical attention for William Joseph Tabafunda.
>
> That as a proximate result of this negligence, William Joseph Tabafunda died.

From these and other findings, the [trial] court concluded that the defendants were each guilty of the crime of manslaughter as charged. . . .

[The court of appeals held that both defendants were under a legal duty to

a. The judge imposed a sentence of three years, indefinitely deferred subject to specified conditions being met. See Paul H. Robinson, Teacher's Manual, Criminal Law Case Studies 18 (2000). —EDS.

obtain medical assistance for the child.] On the question of the quality or seriousness of breach of the duty, at common law, in the case of involuntary manslaughter, the breach had to amount to more than mere ordinary or simple negligence — gross negligence was essential. . . . Under [Washington] statutes [however] the crime is deemed committed even though the death of the victim is the proximate result of only simple or ordinary negligence. . . .

The concept of simple or ordinary negligence describes a failure to exercise the "ordinary caution" necessary to make out the defense of excusable homicide. Ordinary caution is the kind of caution that a man of reasonable prudence would exercise under the same or similar conditions. If, therefore, the conduct of a defendant, regardless of his ignorance, good intentions and good faith, fails to measure up to the conduct required of a man of reasonable prudence, he is guilty of ordinary negligence because of his failure to use "ordinary caution." . . . If such negligence proximately causes the death of the victim, the defendant, as pointed out above, is guilty of statutory manslaughter. . . .

The remaining issue of proximate cause requires consideration of the question of when the duty to furnish medical care became activated. If the duty to furnish such care was not activated until after it was too late to save the life of the child, failure to furnish medical care could not be said to have proximately caused the child's death. Timeliness in the furnishing of medical care also must be considered in terms of "ordinary caution." [T]he duty as formulated in People v. Pierson, 176 N.Y. 201, 68 N.E. 243 (1903) . . . properly defines the duty contemplated by our manslaughter statutes. . . . The court there said: "We quite agree that the Code does not contemplate the necessity of calling a physician for every trifling complaint with which the child may be afflicted, which in most instances may be overcome by the ordinary household nursing by members of the family; that a reasonable amount of discretion is vested in parents, charged with the duty of maintaining and bringing up infant children; and that the standard is at what time would an ordinarily prudent person, solicitous for the welfare of his child and anxious to promote its recovery, deem it necessary to call in the services of a physician."

It remains to apply the law discussed to the facts of the instant case.

Defendants . . . contended below and on appeal that they are not guilty of the crime charged. Because of the serious nature of the charge against the parent and step-parent of a well-loved child, and out of our concern for the protection of the constitutional rights of the defendants, we have made an independent examination of the evidence to determine whether it substantially supports the court's express finding on proximate cause and its implied finding that the duty to furnish medical care became activated in time to prevent death of the child. . . .

Dr. Gale Wilson, the autopsy surgeon and chief pathologist for the King County Coroner, testified that the child died because an abscessed tooth had been allowed to develop into an infection of the mouth and cheeks, eventually becoming gangrenous. This condition, accompanied by the child's inability to eat, brought about malnutrition, lowering the child's resistance and eventually producing pneumonia, causing the death. Dr. Wilson testified that in his opinion the infection had lasted for approximately 2 weeks, and that the odor generally associated with gangrene would have been present for approximately 10 days before death. He also expressed the opinion that had medical care been first obtained in the last week before the baby's death, such care would have been obtained too late to have saved the baby's life. Accordingly, the baby's apparent condition between September 1 and September 5, 1968 became the critical period for the purpose of determining whether in the exercise of ordinary caution defendants should have provided medical care for the minor child.

The testimony concerning the child's apparent condition during the critical period is not crystal clear, but is sufficient to warrant the following statement of the matter. The defendant husband testified that he noticed the baby was sick about 2 weeks before the baby died. The defendant wife testified that she noticed the baby was ill about a week and a half or 2 weeks before the baby died. The evidence showed that in the critical period the baby was fussy; that he could not keep his food down; and that a cheek started swelling up. The swelling went up and down, but did not disappear. In that same period, the cheek turned "a bluish color like." The defendants, not realizing that the baby was as ill as it was or that the baby was in danger of dying, attempted to provide some relief to the baby by giving the baby aspirin during the critical period and continued to do so until the night before the baby died. The defendants thought the swelling would go down and were waiting for it to do so; and defendant husband testified, that from what he had heard, neither doctors nor dentists pull out a tooth "when it's all swollen up like that." There was an additional explanation for not calling a doctor given by each defendant. Defendant husband testified that "the way the cheek looked, . . . and that stuff on his hair, they would think we were neglecting him and take him away from us and not give him back." Defendant wife testified that the defendants were "waiting for the swelling to go down," and also that they were afraid to take the child to a doctor for fear that the doctor would report them to the welfare department, who, in turn, would take the child away. "It's just that I was so scared of losing him." They testified that they had heard that the defendant husband's cousin lost a child that way. The evidence showed that the defendants did not understand the significance or seriousness of the baby's symptoms. However, there is no evidence that the defendants were physically or financially unable to obtain a doctor, or that they did not know an available doctor, or that the symptoms did not continue to be a matter of concern during the critical period. Indeed, the evidence shows that in April 1968 defendant husband had taken the child to a doctor for medical attention.

In our opinion, there is sufficient evidence from which the court could find, as it necessarily did, that applying the standard of ordinary caution, i.e., the caution exercisable by a man of reasonable prudence under the same or similar conditions, defendants were sufficiently put on notice concerning the symptoms of the baby's illness and lack of improvement in the baby's apparent condition in the period from September 1 to September 5, 1968 to have required them to have obtained medical care for the child. The failure so to do in this case is ordinary or simple negligence, and such negligence is sufficient to support a conviction of statutory manslaughter.

The judgment is affirmed.

NOTES AND QUESTIONS

1. The manslaughter statutes involved in *Williams* were repealed in 1975. The current statutes create two degrees of manslaughter: recklessly causing death and causing death by criminal negligence. See Wash. Rev. Code §9A.32.060;

Wash. Rev. Code §9A.32.070 (1997). In accord with generally prevailing law, Washington no longer imposes manslaughter liability in cases involving ordinary negligence. See State v. Norman, 808 P.2d 1159, 1162 (1991).

Questions: Would the *Williams* court have reached a different result under the statute in effect today? On the court's view of the facts, wouldn't the behavior of the Williams couple also involve "criminal" negligence?

2. Many will find the conviction of the Williams couple unjust and, perhaps, pointless. Why were the defendants punished?

(a) Note that the court calls attention to the race of the defendants. In what respect, if any, did their race have a bearing on the issues in the case? Was it relevant at all?

(b) Were the defendants punished only because of their ignorance? If the conviction seems unjust, is this because they were unaware of the degree of danger to their child? If so, does it follow that punishment for negligence (where there is no awareness of the risk) is always unjust? Consider the materials in the following Note in thinking about these questions.

NOTES ON STANDARDS OF LIABILITY

1. *Objective and subjective liability defined.* The concepts of objective and subjective standards are subject to a variety of interpretations. See G. Fletcher, Rethinking Criminal Law 504 et seq. (1978). In general, objective or external standards determine liability on the basis of *general norms* of proper and reasonable behavior. Thus, the provocation standard imports an objective standard insofar as the law requires that what provoked the defendant to kill would have severely tested the self-control of a reasonable person. Negligence is an objective standard insofar as liability turns on whether the action of defendant created a risk of a kind and degree which, in the circumstances, a reasonable person would not have taken. Subjective or internal standards of liability, on the other hand, look to the *individual* characteristics of the actor, and, insofar as they are thoroughgoing in their subjectivity, take "account of the infinite varieties of temperament, intellect and education which make the internal character of a given act so different." O. W. Holmes, The Common Law 108 (1881). Premeditation and deliberation are subjective standards, since they look to what the particular defendant experienced. The same is true of the diminished-capacity defense, see infra page 919. Tension between these two kinds of standards runs through the whole of the criminal law.

A standard of negligence is, as we have indicated, substantially objective. Should its objectivity be qualified by requiring that defendant have been aware of the risk entailed (or, in the Model Penal Code's terminology, by requiring recklessness rather than negligence) before criminal liability may be imposed?

2. *In defense of an objective standard.* Justice Holmes applied and defended an objective standard in Commonwealth v. Pierce, 138 Mass. 165, 171-176 (1884). In this case defendant was convicted of manslaughter

> on evidence that he publicly practised as a physician, and, being called to attend a sick woman, caused her, with her consent, to be kept in flannels saturated with kerosene for three days, more or less, by reason of which she died. There was evidence that he had made similar applications with favorable results in other cases,

but that in one the effect had been to blister and burn the flesh as in the present case.

The alleged errors in the trial court's instructions to the jury turned on its refusal to charge that a finding of recklessness was required for conviction. Holmes formulated the issue as follows (id. at 175-176):

> But recklessness in a moral sense means a certain state of consciousness with reference to the consequences of one's acts. No matter whether defined as indifference to what those consequences may be, or as a failure to consider their nature or probability as fully as the party might and ought to have done, it is understood to depend on the actual condition of the individual's mind with regard to consequences, as distinguished from mere knowledge of present or past facts or circumstances from which some one or everybody else might be led to anticipate or apprehend them if the supposed act were done. We have to determine whether recklessness in this sense was necessary to make the defendant guilty of felonious homicide, or whether his acts are to be judged by the external standard of what would be morally reckless, under the circumstances known to him, in a man of reasonable prudence.
>
> More specifically, the questions raised by the foregoing requests and rulings are whether an actual good intent and the expectation of good results are an absolute justification of acts, however foolhardy they may be if judged by the external standard supposed, and whether the defendant's ignorance of the tendencies of kerosene administered as it was will excuse the administration of it.

After reviewing the objective standards applicable in civil cases, Holmes concluded:

> If this is the rule adopted in regard to the redistribution of losses, which sound policy allows to rest where they fall in the absence of a clear reason to the contrary, there would seem to be at least equal reason for adopting it in the criminal law, which has for its immediate object and task to establish a general standard, or at least general negative limits, of conduct for the community, in the interest of the safety of all.[a]

3. Criticism of the objective standard. Summarizing the arguments against negligence liability, Professor Glanville Williams wrote (Criminal Law: The General Part 122-123 (2d ed. 1961)):

> The retributive theory of punishment is open to many objections, which are of even greater force when applied to inadvertent negligence than in crimes requiring mens rea. Some people are born feckless, clumsy, thoughtless, inattentive, irresponsible, with a bad memory and a slow "reaction time." With the best will in the world, we all of us at some times in our lives make negligent mistakes. It is hard to see how justice (as distinct from some utilitarian reason) requires mistakes to be punished.
>
> Again, the deterrent theory, which is normally accepted as a justification for criminal punishment, finds itself in some difficulty when applied to negligence. At best the deterrent effect of the legal sanction is a matter of faith rather than of proved scientific fact; but there is no department in which this faith is less firmly

a. For a defense of liability for inadvertent negligence, see A. D. Woozley, Negligence and Ignorance, 53 Phil. 293 (1978). — Eds.

grounded than that of negligence. Hardly any motorist but does not firmly believe that if he is involved in an accident it will be the other fellow's fault. It may seem, therefore, that the threat of punishment for negligence must pass him by, because he does not realize that it is addressed to him. Even if a person admits that he occasionally makes a negligent mistake, how, in the nature of things, can punishment for inadvertence serve to deter?

4. The Model Penal Code position on liability without awareness. The Model Penal Code takes the position that awareness of the risk (recklessness) is required for manslaughter, but a person who is unaware of the risk may be punished for the crime of negligent homicide. Compare §§210.3(1)(a) and 210.4, Appendix. In support of retaining negligence as a basis of criminal liability, Model Penal Code and Commentaries, Comment to §2.02 at 243-244 (1980), states:

> When people have knowledge that conviction and sentence, not to speak of punishment, may follow conduct that inadvertently creates improper risk, they are supplied with an additional motive to take care before acting, to use their faculties and draw on their experience in gauging the potentialities of contemplated conduct. To some extent, at least, this motive may promote awareness and thus be effective as a measure of control. Moreover, moral defect can properly be imputed to instances where the defendant acts out of insensitivity to the interests of other people, and not merely out of an intellectual failure to grasp them.

5. A dissenting view on awareness. In Samuel H. Pillsbury, Crimes of Indifference, 49 Rutgers L. Rev. 105, 106, 150-151 (1996) Professor Pillsbury disagrees that awareness of the risk is required to show culpability. He summarizes his argument as follows:

> [T]he modern trend to require that the defendant have actual awareness of fatal risks [to be guilty of murder or manslaughter] is a mistake, based on a misconception of responsible choice. . . .
>
> We may blame persons for failing to perceive risks to others when we can trace their lack of awareness to bad perception priorities. In such a case, we judge the person guilty of a bad choice. In setting his or her perception priorities, the individual assigned too low a priority to the value of other human beings. The key to culpability for failure to perceive is why the person failed to perceive. Assume two cases in which a driver runs a red light and fatally injures a pedestrian in the crosswalk. One case involves a father rushing his severely injured child to the hospital. Another involves a teenager showing off for his friends. Assume that in both cases the driver saw neither the light nor the pedestrian. Culpability should depend on the drivers' reasons for perceptive failure, not on the failure itself. The father's lack of perception may be attributed to his overriding and morally worthy desire to help his child. The teenager's failure to perceive may be attributed to morally blameworthy perception priorities. The teenager placed a higher value on winning the admiration of friends than on attending to the risks of fast driving. The teenager's conduct demonstrates an attitude of indifference toward others, a morally culpable state to which society should forcefully respond by conviction and punishment. Meanwhile, the father's conduct demonstrates a tragic conflict between valuing his child and valuing others.
>
> Individuals deserve punishment for all acts displaying serious disregard for the moral worth of other human beings. Such acts involve many different levels of awareness. . . . In all cases we should judge the actor's choices: what she has cho-

sen to care about and perceive, and what she has chosen not to care about and perceive. These choices give the individual's conduct a distinct moral meaning.

6. The defendant's ability to conform. Professor Hart has argued that the difficulty with punishing for negligence does not arise from punishing a person who is unaware of the risk he or she is creating. Rather, the difficulty arises from punishing the person for departing from an external or invariant standard that he or she might have been *unable* to meet. H. L. A. Hart, Punishment and Responsibility, 153-154 (1968):

> The expression "objective" and its partner "subjective" are unhappy because, as far as negligence is concerned, they obscure the real issue. . . . For, when negligence is made criminally punishable, this itself leaves open the question: whether, before we punish, both or only the first of the following two questions must be answered affirmatively:
>
> (i) Did the accused fail to take those precautions which any reasonable man with normal capacities would in the circumstances have taken?
> (ii) Could the accused, given his mental and physical capacities, have taken those precautions?
>
> One use of the dangerous expressions "objective" and "subjective" is to make the distinction between these two questions: given the ambiguities of those expressions, the distinction would have been more happily expressed by the expressions "invariant" standard of care, and "individualized conditions of liability." It may well be that, even if the "standard of care" is pitched very low so that individuals are held liable only if they fail to take very elementary precautions against harm, there will still be some unfortunate individuals who, through lack of intelligence, powers of concentration or memory, or through clumsiness, could not attain even this low standard. If our conditions of liability are invariant and not flexible, i.e., if they are not adjusted to the capacities of the accused, then some individuals will be held liable for negligence though they could not have helped their failure to comply with the standard. In *such* cases, indeed, criminal responsibility will be made independent of any "subjective element," since the accused could not have conformed to the required standard. But this result [has] nothing to do with negligence being taken as a basis for criminal liability. . . . "Absolute liability" results, not from the admission of the principle that one who has been grossly negligent is criminally responsible for the consequent harm even if "he had no idea in his mind of harm to anyone," but from the refusal in the application of this principle to consider the capacities of an individual who has fallen below the standard of care.

The present German law adopts an approach similar to Hart's. As expressed in a leading 1922 case, The Case of the Gable-Wall (Giebelmauer), 56 RGSt 343, 349 (1922), negligence for criminal law purposes is as follows: "A harm caused by defendants can be said to be caused by negligence only when it is established that they disregarded the care which they were obliged to exercise and of which they were capable under the circumstances and according to their personal knowledge and abilities. . . ." For discussion of this approach, see George Fletcher, The Theory of Criminal Negligence: A Comparative Analysis, 119 U. Pa. L. Rev. 401 (1971).

Questions: This approach would seem to make legal guilt and moral blameworthiness more nearly the same, but is it workable? How could we know whether a defendant lacked the capacity to be aware of a danger, except in cases of demonstrable mental abnormality? And must the incapacity be total, or is it enough that his capacity is unduly limited? And if the latter, then what does unduly mean? Just how difficult must it be for the defendant to have known? Consider the Williams couple. Were they unable to be aware of the degree of danger, or was it just that they were in fact unaware this time? One should consider these kinds of questions again when confronting the defense of diminished capacity generally, infra page 919.

7. The Model Penal Code on individualization. In contrast to the German approach, the Model Penal Code's definition of negligence (see §2.02(2)(d), Appendix) rejects a fully individualized standard. However, some elements of an individualized standard are invited by its reference to "the care that would be exercised by a reasonable person in his [the actor's] situation." Model Penal Code and Commentaries, Comment to §2.02 at 242 (1985) states:

> There is an inevitable ambiguity in "situation." If the actor were blind or if he had just suffered a blow or experienced a heart attack, these would certainly be facts to be considered in a judgment involving criminal liability, as they would be under traditional law. But the heredity, intelligence or temperament of the actor would not be held material in judging negligence, and could not be without depriving the criterion of all its objectivity. The Code is not intended to displace discriminations of this kind, but rather to leave the issue to the courts.

Recall that the Model Penal Code took a similar approach in its formulation of provocation, where the objectivity of the standard is qualified by the sentence (§210.3): "The reasonableness of such explanation or excuse shall be determined from the viewpoint of a person *in the actor's situation* under the circumstances as he believes them to be." [Italics added.]

Question: How would the *Williams* case be decided under the Code?

8. The case law on individualization. Although the Model Penal Code leaves to the courts the problem of determining the appropriate degree of individualization, the courts remain ambivalent or in conflict. In State v. Everhart, 291 N.C. 700, 231 S.E.2d 604 (1977), the defendant, a young girl with an IQ of 72, gave birth in her own bedroom and, thinking that the baby had been born dead, wrapped it from head to foot in a blanket. The baby smothered to death. The court reversed a conviction for involuntary manslaughter, holding that because of the defendant's low IQ and the admittedly accidental nature of the death, the state had not proved culpable negligence. Compare Edgmon v. State, 702 P.2d 643, 645 (Alaska App. 1985). The court there held that individual capabilities would have to be considered in assessing recklessness (necessary in Alaska for a manslaughter conviction) but that "[i]n contrast, peculiarities of a given individual — his or her intelligence, experience, and physical capabilities — are irrelevant in determining criminal negligence [necessary for the lesser negligent homicide offense] since the standard is one of a reasonably prudent person."

PROBLEM

In Walker v. Superior Court, 47 Cal. 3d 112, 763 P.2d 852 (1988), defendant's four-year-old daughter fell ill with flu-like symptoms, and four days later she developed a stiff neck. In accord with the tenets of her religion, defendant, a member of the Church of Christ Scientist, elected to treat her daughter with prayer rather than medicine.[1] An "accredited Christian Scientist prayer practitioner" was summoned to supervise the child's treatment. Over a 17-day period, the child's condition worsened. She lost weight, grew disoriented, and eventually died of meningitis.

Questions: Is the mother guilty of involuntary manslaughter? In what respects are the arguments for conviction stronger or weaker than those in the *Williams* case? Prevailing interpretations of the First Amendment right to free exercise of religion make clear that there is no constitutional defense in such cases.[2] But how should the parents' religious beliefs be treated in considering whether, in a case like *Walker,* their conduct is criminally negligent? Should those beliefs, and the special deference owed to religious conviction in our society, count among the justifications that can be weighed against the degree of the risk? Are the parents' religious beliefs part of their "situation," so that the proper standard would be to consider the actions expected of a reasonable person of the defendant's religion? In *Walker,* the court sustained the manslaughter indictment, holding (763 P.2d at 868) that "criminal negligence must be evaluated objectively" and that the controlling question was whether "a reasonable person in defendant's position would have been aware of the risk involved." Would this be the proper approach under the Model Penal Code? For discussion of the issues, see Edward Smith, Note, The Criminalization of Belief: When Free Exercise Isn't, 42 Hastings L.J. 1491 (1991).

c. The Line Between Murder and Manslaughter

COMMONWEALTH v. MALONE

Supreme Court of Pennsylvania
354 Pa. 180, 47 A.2d 445 (1946)

MAXEY, C.J. This is an appeal from the judgment and sentence under a conviction of murder in the second degree.[a] William H. Long, age 13 years, was

1. The court explained (763 P.2d at 855 n. 1):

> Members of the Church "believe that disease is a physical manifestation of errors of the mind." (Comment, Religious Beliefs and the Criminal Justice System: Some Problems of the Faith Healer, (1975) 8 Loyola L.A.L. Rev. 396, 397, fn. 7.) The use of medicine is believed to perpetuate such error and is therefore discouraged. Nonetheless, "the Church sets up no abstract criteria for determining what diseases or injuries should be treated by prayer or other methods but, rather, leaves such questions to individual decision in concrete instances. . . . If some turn in what they think is an urgent time of need to medical treatment for themselves or their children, they are *not*— contrary to some recent charges — stigmatized by their church." (Talbot, The Position of the Christian Science Church, (1983) 26 N.E. Med. J. 1641, 1642, italics in original.)

2. In Commonwealth v. Barnhart, 497 A.2d 616, 624-625 (Pa. Super. 1985), the court upheld a manslaughter conviction on facts comparable to those in the *Walker* case. On the First Amendment issue, the court cited Prince v. Massachusetts, 321 U.S. 158, 170 (1944): "Parents may be free to become martyrs themselves. But it does not follow they are free, in identical circumstances, to make martyrs of their children before they (the children) have reached the age of full and legal discretion when they can make that choice for themselves".

a. The Pennsylvania homicide statute in effect at the time divided murder into two degrees, in accordance with the formula adopted in 1794. After classifying certain especially heinous murders killed by a shot from a 32-caliber revolver held against his right side by the defendant, then aged 17 years. These youths were on friendly terms at the time of the homicide. The defendant and his mother while his father and brother were in the U.S. Armed Forces, were residing in Lancaster, Pa., with the family of William H. Long, whose son was the victim of the shooting.

On the evening of February 26th, 1945, when the defendant went to a moving picture theater, he carried in the pocket of his raincoat a revolver which he had obtained at the home of his uncle on the preceding day. In the afternoon preceding the shooting, the decedent procured a cartridge from his father's room and he and the defendant placed it in the revolver.

After leaving the theater, the defendant went to a dairy store and there met the decedent. Both youths sat in the rear of the store ten minutes, during which period the defendant took the gun out of his pocket and loaded the chamber to the right of the firing pin and then closed the gun. A few minutes later, both youths sat on stools in front of the lunch counter and ate some food. The defendant suggested to the decedent that they play "Russian Poker."[1] Long replied, "I don't care; go ahead." The defendant then placed the revolver against the right side of Long and pulled the trigger three times. The third pull resulted in a fatal wound to Long. The latter jumped off the stool and cried: "Oh! Oh! Oh!" and Malone said: "Did I hit you, Billy? Gee, Kid, I'm sorry." Long died from the wounds two days later.

The defendant testified that the gun chamber he loaded was the first one to the right of the firing chamber and that when he pulled the trigger he did not "expect to have the gun go off." He declared he had no intention of harming Long, who was his friend and companion. The defendant was indicted for murder, tried and found guilty of murder in the second degree and sentenced to a term in the penitentiary for a period not less than five years and not exceeding ten years. A new trial was refused and after sentence was imposed, an appeal was taken.

Appellant alleges certain errors in the charge of the court and also contends that the facts did not justify a conviction for any form of homicide except involuntary manslaughter. This contention we overrule. A specific intent to take life is, under our law, an essential ingredient of murder in the first degree. At common law, the "grand criterion" which "distinguished murder from other killing" was malice on the part of the killer and this malice was not necessarily "malevolent to the deceased particularly" but "any evil design in general; the dictate of a wicked, depraved and malignant heart"; 4 Blackstone 199. . . .

When an individual commits an act of gross recklessness for which he must reasonably anticipate that death to another is likely to result, he exhibits that "wickedness of disposition, hardness of heart, cruelty, recklessness of consequences, and a mind regardless of social duty" which proved that there was at that time in him "the state or frame of mind termed malice." This court has de-

as murders of the first degree, the statute provided simply that "[a]ll other kinds of murder shall be murder in the second degree." Comparable statutory language continues to define second-degree murder in many jurisdictions and what is now called "third-degree murder" in Pennsylvania. See 18 Pa. Stat. Ann. §2502 (c), reproduced at page 391 supra. — Eds.

1. It has been explained that "Russian Poker" is a game in which the participants, in turn, place a single cartridge in one of the five chambers of a revolver cylinder, give the latter a quick twirl, place the muzzle of the gun against the temple and pull the trigger, leaving it to chance whether or not death results to the trigger puller.

clared that if a driver "wantonly, recklessly, and in disregard of consequences" hurls "his car against another, or into a crowd" and death results from that act "he ought . . . to face the same consequences that would be meted out to him if he had accomplished death by wantonly and wickedly firing a gun": Com. v. Mayberry, 290 Pa. 195, 199, 138 A. 686, 688, citing cases from four jurisdictions. . . .

The killing of William H. Long by this defendant resulted from an act intentionally done by the latter, in reckless and wanton disregard of the consequences which were at least sixty percent certain from his thrice attempted discharge of a gun known to contain one bullet and aimed at a vital part of Long's body. This killing was, therefore, murder, for malice in the sense of a wicked disposition is evidenced by the intentional doing of an uncalled-for act in callous disregard of its likely harmful effects on others. The fact that there was no motive for this homicide does not exculpate the accused. In a trial for murder proof of motive is always relevant but never necessary.

All the assignments of error are overruled and the judgment is affirmed.

NOTES

1. The facts in Malone. In concluding that there was a 60 percent chance of the gun's discharging, the court apparently assumed that the defendant twirled the revolver cylinder once before beginning to pull the trigger (see footnote 1 of the opinion), contrary to the implication of the defendant's testimony that he loaded the chamber to the right of the firing pin and fired without spinning the cylinder. On the court's assumption, pulling the trigger of a five-chambered gun three consecutive times creates, as the court said, a three-out-of-five chance of the gun's discharging. Some, however, might want to argue that the relevant risk is that of the gun's discharging on the third pull, which is one out of three. Which is the appropriate way to characterize the defendant's course of conduct? Would it make any difference to the defendant's liability? Suppose the gun discharged at the very first pull, when the chance of that happening would have been one out of five? Would that have made a difference?

If, in fact, the defendant did just what he testified he did — loaded the chamber to the right of the firing pin and then fired without twirling the chamber — how is it that the gun discharged? There are several possibilities. Conceivably the gun misfired in some fashion. Or conceivably there was *more than one* bullet in the gun. (Recall the testimony about how the gun was handled during the afternoon preceding the shooting.) If the court had accepted the defendant's version of the facts, would the result have been different? If a defendant pulls the trigger of a gun believed to be empty, forgetting that it had been loaded the previous day, and death results, should he or she be guilty of murder rather than manslaughter?

2. Definitions of unintentional murder. The common law formulations of the circumstances under which an unintentional killing constituted murder rather than manslaughter have been incorporated into many American statutes either directly or by reference to such common law terms as *malice*. The formulas have tended to carry more flavor than meaning — "the dictate of a wicked, depraved and malignant heart"; "an abandoned and malignant heart"; "a depraved heart regardless of human life." The *Malone* case is an example of circumstances in which the criteria have been held to have been met. Many states continue to adhere to these formulations, although others have altered them in ways suggested by the Model Penal Code. The Code treats an unintended killing as murder when it is committed recklessly (as defined in §2.02(2)(c)) and "under circumstances manifesting extreme indifference to the value of human life." (§210.2, Appendix.) The Comment supporting §210.2 explains (Model Penal Code and Commentaries, Comment to §210.2 at 21-22 (1980)):

> Under the Model Code, [the first] judgment must be made in terms of whether the actor's conscious disregard of the risk, given the circumstances of the case, so far departs from acceptable behavior that it constitutes a "gross deviation from the standard of conduct that a law-abiding person would observe in the actor's situation." Ordinary recklessness in this sense is made sufficient for a conviction of manslaughter under Section 210.3(1)(a). In a prosecution for murder, however, the Code calls for the further judgment whether the actor's conscious disregard of the risk, under the circumstances, manifests extreme indifference to the value of human life. The significance of purpose or knowledge as a standard of culpability is that, cases of provocation or other mitigation apart, purposeful or knowing homicide demonstrates precisely such indifference to the value of human life. Whether recklessness is so extreme that it demonstrates similar indifference is not a question, it is submitted, that can be further clarified. It must be left directly to the trier of fact under instructions which make it clear that recklessness that can fairly be assimilated to purpose or knowledge should be treated as murder and that less extreme recklessness should be punished as manslaughter.
>
> Insofar as Subsection (1)(b) includes within the murder category cases of homicide caused by extreme recklessness, though without purpose to kill, it reflects both the common law and much pre-existing statutory treatment usually cast in terms of conduct evidencing a "depraved heart regardless of human life" or some similar words.

3. Problem. Would Malone have been guilty of murder under the Model Penal Code? Consider People v. Roe, 74 N.Y.2d 20, 542 N.E.2d 610 (1989), another juvenile Russian Roulette accidental killing. The New York homicide statute, patterned closely on the Model Penal Code formula, makes a killing murder when it is committed recklessly "[u]nder circumstances evincing a depraved indifference to human life." The court upheld a murder conviction of the 15-year-old defendant. But Judge Bellacosa dissented, emphasizing that defendant and deceased were young teenagers, that defendant reacted with spontaneous despair and anguish when the gun fired, screaming, "Don't die. I killed my best friend's brother." He concluded: "This is not evidence beyond a reasonable doubt of that hardness of heart or that malignancy of attitude qualifying as 'depraved indifference.' Frankly, the evidence proves the opposite."

Query: Does the dissent make a persuasive case? What kind of a case, by contrast, would the dissent believe deserved to be treated as depraved murder? Consider State v. Davidson, 987 P.2d 335 (Sup. Ct. Kans. 1999). Defendant's two Rottweiler dogs escaped their fenced-in area, as they had several times before, and as before they attacked people, this time attacking and killing an eleven-year-old child waiting for a bus. The court affirmed a conviction of reckless second-degree murder, defined substantially like the Model Penal Code. The court stated:

> Here, defendant argues that all she did was let the dogs into the fenced area, take a pill, and go to sleep. This argument conveniently ignores significant aspects of

> her conduct that contributed to the tragic death of Chris. The State presented evidence that she selected powerful dogs with a potential for aggressive behavior and that she owned a number of these dogs in which she fostered aggressive behavior by failing to properly train the dogs. She ignored the advice from experts on how to properly train her dogs and their warnings of the dire results which could occur from improper training. She was told to socialize her dogs and chose not to do so. She ignored the evidence of the dogs getting out on numerous occasions and her failure to properly secure the gate. She ignored the aggressive behavior her dogs displayed toward her neighbors and their children. . . . Here, the evidence, viewed in a light most favorable to the State, showed that defendant created an unreasonable risk and then consciously disregarded it in a manner and to the extent that it reasonably could be inferred that she was extremely indifferent to the value of human life.

4. *Murder by omission.* We have seen that the death of an infant through its parents' neglect may constitute manslaughter. State v. Williams, page 431 supra. May such neglect constitute murder? A California court upheld a second-degree murder conviction of a father for his conscious and callous failure to feed his child resulting in death through malnutrition and dehydration. The evidence showed that the father was aware during the last two weeks of the baby's life that it was starving to death, that he did not remember anyone's having fed the baby in that period, and that he did nothing himself to feed the baby, although he could have if he had really wanted to, because he "just didn't care." The court stated: "The omission of a duty is in law the equivalent of an act and when death results, the standard for determination of the degree of homicide is identical." People v. Burden, 72 Cal. App. 3d 603, 616 (Dist. App. 1977). In accord, see Simpkins v. State, 88 Md. App. 607, 596 A.2d 655 (1991).

UNITED STATES v. FLEMING

United States Court of Appeals, 4th Circuit
739 F.2d 945 (1984)

WINTER, C.J.: . . . Defendant David Earl Fleming was convicted of second-degree murder, in violation of 18 U.S.C. §1111,[1] in the death of Margaret Jacobsen Haley. . . .

Fleming's car was observed at about 3:00 P.M. on June 15, 1983, traveling southbound on the George Washington Memorial Parkway in northern Virginia [a park within federal jurisdiction] at speeds variously estimated by witnesses as between 70 and 100 miles per hour. The speed limit on the Parkway is, at most points, 45 miles per hour. Fleming several times directed his southbound car into the northbound lanes of the Parkway in order to avoid traffic congestion in the southbound lanes. Northbound traffic had to move out of his way in order

1. 18 U.S.C. §1111(a) provides:

> Murder is the unlawful killing of a human being with malice aforethought. Every murder perpetrated by poison, lying in wait, or any other kind of willful, deliberate, malicious, and premeditated killing; or committed in the perpetration of [designated felonies] is murder in the first degree.
> Any other murder is murder in the second degree.

to avoid a head-on collision. At one point, a pursuing police officer observed Fleming steer his car into the northbound lanes, which were separated from the southbound lanes at that point and for a distance of three-tenths of a mile by a raised concrete median, and drive in the northbound lanes, still at a high rate of speed, for the entire length of the median. At two other points, Fleming traveled in northbound lanes that were separated from the southbound lanes by medians.

Approximately six miles from where his car was first observed traveling at excessive speed, Fleming lost control of it on a sharp curve. The car slid across the northbound lanes, striking the curb on the opposite side of the highway. After striking the curb, Fleming's car straightened out and at that moment struck the car driven by Mrs. Haley that was coming in the opposite direction. Fleming's car at the moment of impact was estimated by witnesses to have been traveling 70 to 80 miles per hour; the speed limit at that point on the Parkway was 30 miles per hour. Mrs. Haley received multiple severe injuries and died before she could be extricated from her car.

Fleming was pulled from the wreckage of his car and transported to a Washington hospital for treatment. His blood alcohol level was there tested at .315 percent.

Fleming was indicted by a grand jury on a charge of second-degree murder. . . . He was tried before a jury and convicted.

Defendant maintains that the facts of the case cannot support a verdict of murder. Particularly, defendant contends that the facts are inadequate to establish the existence of malice aforethought, and thus that he should have been convicted of manslaughter at most.

Malice aforethought, as provided in 18 U.S.C. §1111(a), is the distinguishing characteristic which, when present, makes a homicide murder rather than manslaughter. . . . Proof of the existence of malice does not require a showing that the accused harbored hatred or ill will against the victim or others. Neither does it require proof of an intent to kill or injure. Malice may be established by evidence of conduct which is "reckless and wanton and a gross deviation from a reasonable standard of care, of such a nature that a jury is warranted in inferring that defendant was aware of a serious risk of death or serious bodily harm." To support a conviction for murder, the government need only have proved that defendant intended to operate his car in the manner in which he did with a heart that was without regard for the life and safety of others.[3]

We conclude that the evidence regarding defendant's conduct was adequate to sustain a finding by the jury that defendant acted with malice aforethought. . . .

The difference between malice, which will support conviction for murder, and gross negligence, which will permit of conviction only for manslaughter, is one of degree rather than kind. In the present case, . . . the facts show a devi-

3. We note that, even assuming that subjective awareness of the risk is required to establish murder where the killing resulted from reckless conduct, an exception to the requirement of subjective awareness of risk is made where lack of such awareness is attributable solely to voluntary drunkenness. See, e.g., Model Penal Code §2.08(2) ("When recklessness establishes an element of the offense, if the actor, due to self-induced intoxication, is unaware of a risk of which he would have been aware had he been sober, such unawareness is immaterial.") Defendant's state of voluntary intoxication thus would not have been relevant to whether the jury could have inferred from the circumstances of the crime that he was aware of the risk created by his conduct.

ation from established standards of regard for life and the safety of others that is markedly different in degree from that found in most vehicular homicides. In the average drunk driving homicide, there is no proof that the driver has acted while intoxicated with the purpose of wantonly and intentionally putting the lives of others in danger. Rather, his driving abilities were so impaired that he recklessly put others in danger simply by being on the road and attempting to do the things that any driver would do. In the present case, however, danger did not arise only by defendant's determining to drive while drunk. Rather, in addition to being intoxicated while driving, defendant drove in a manner that could be taken to indicate depraved disregard of human life, *particularly* in light of the fact that *because he was drunk* his reckless behavior was all the more dangerous. . . .

Affirmed.

NOTES AND QUESTIONS

1. The murder/manslaughter distinction. What is the difference between dangerous conduct that should lead to a murder conviction and dangerous conduct that should lead to conviction for manslaughter only? In *Fleming,* the court says that the difference is "one of degree," but a degree of what? Is the crucial factor the probability of harm, the defendant's awareness of that probability, both of these factors, or neither one? What distinguishing factor was the jury required to find in *Fleming?*

2. Murder by drunk driving. In accord with *Fleming,* the great majority of American courts have held, usually in drunk driving cases, that egregiously dangerous driving can support a conviction of murder. See David Luria, Death on the Highway: Reckless Driving as Murder, 67 Or. L. Rev. 799 (1988). Usually the theory is that the defendant had an actual awareness of a great risk of fatal harm. See, e.g., Pears v. State, 672 P.2d 903 (Alaska App. 1983): Despite warnings by two police officers and by a companion that he was too drunk to drive, the defendant returned to his truck and drove at high speed through several stop signs and red lights until he collided with a car at an intersection. Two people in the car were killed. The appellate court affirmed a murder conviction, holding that the statutory requirement of "extreme indifference to the value of human life" was satisfied because the warnings Pears had received made him "abundantly aware of the dangerous nature of his driving. . . ." (672 P.2d at 910), and his actions therefore were not merely inadvertent.

Compare People v. Watson, 30 Cal. 3d 290, 637 P.2d 279 (1981), another case of a drunk driver being convicted of murder. Here the court found sufficient evidence of an actual awareness of the danger merely because the defendant "had driven his car to the establishment where he had been drinking, and he must have known that he would have to drive it later. It also may be presumed that defendant was aware of the hazards of driving while intoxicated." 637 P.2d at 285-286. In dissent, Chief Justice Bird observed (id. at 288):

> [I]t cannot be found that respondent committed an act likely to kill. The act of speeding through a green light at 55 or 60 miles per hour in a 35-mile-per-hour zone was dangerous, but was not an act likely to result in the death of another. It was 1 o'clock in the morning. The person whose car respondent nearly collided with testified that he saw no other cars around. . . .

> The fact that respondent was under the influence of alcohol made his driving more dangerous. . . . No one holds a brief for this type of activity. However, [d]eath or injury is not the probable result of driving while under the influence of alcohol. "Thousands, perhaps hundreds of thousands, of Californians each week reach home without accident despite their driving intoxicated." . . . I submit that the majority's reasoning that such an inference may be drawn to support a finding of implied malice will be used to establish second degree murder in every case in which a person drives a car to a bar, a friend's home, or a party, drinks alcohol so that he is under its influence, drives away and is involved in a fatal accident.

3. Questions: What is there about the drunken driver that makes her deserving of more punishment than the sober driver? Compare two cases. Driver *A* drives at 80 m.p.h. in a zone posted for 40 m.p.h., swerving in and out to pass with undiminished speed, passing in distinctly marked no passing areas, broadsiding other cars and finally colliding head on with an oncoming vehicle and killing its driver. Driver *B* drives precisely the same way and with the same consequence, the only difference being that Driver *A* is sober but Driver *B* is very drunk. Is it clear that Driver *B* is more culpable than Driver *A*? Might that be so because *B* voluntarily handicapped her driving abilities by drink? On the other hand, perhaps *A* is more culpable because she chose to drive in this maniacal way, while *B*'s bad judgment and lack of skill were the result of her drinking (her choice, to be sure, but a choice to get drunk, not to drive in this egregious way)? Or should intoxication neither aggravate nor mitigate, the culpability judgment rather turning solely on whether the specific driving behavior constituted recklessness of such egregiousness as to warrant a murder conviction? See James Jacobs, Drunk Driving: An American Dilemma 87-88 (1989).

4. The Model Penal Code. What is the Model Penal Code position on the issue of liability for inadvertent murder? Note that under §210.2(1)(b), murder requires proof that the defendant acted "recklessly under circumstances manifesting extreme indifference to the value of human life." According to the official Comment (Model Penal Code and Commentaries, Comment to §210.2 at 27-28 (1980)):

> The Model Code provision makes clear that inadvertent risk creation, however extravagant and unjustified, cannot be punished as murder. . . . This result is consistent with the general conception of the Model Code that serious felony sanctions should be grounded securely in the subjective culpability of the actor. To the extent that inadvertent risk creation, or negligence, should be recognized as a form of criminal homicide, that question should be faced separately from the offense of murder. . . . At the least it seems clear that negligent homicide should not be assimilated to the most serious forms of criminal homicide catalogued under the offense of murder.

Questions: Does the Commentary accurately describe the standard mandated by the Code's text? Note that the choice between a subjective and an objective standard seldom has much practical bite, because defendants cannot easily persuade a jury that they honestly failed to perceive a risk that the reasonable person would perceive. Such a claim can be quite plausible, however, if the defendant was intoxicated. Situations involving intoxication (for example, drunk driving) are therefore the primary ones in which the choice between a subjective and an objective standard is likely to make a difference. How are such situations treated under the Code? Reconsider Model Penal Code §2.08(2) and the *Fleming* case, especially page 461, footnote 3 supra. Is the Model Penal Code Commentary accurate in asserting that "inadvertent risk creation . . . cannot be punished as murder"?

These issues confronted the Supreme Court of New Hampshire under a statute, derived from the Model Penal Code, which makes a killing murder when the defendant acted "recklessly under circumstances manifesting an extreme indifference to the value of human life." N.H. Rev. Stat. Ann. §630:1-b, I(b). In State v. Dufield, 549 A.2d 1205 (N.H. 1988), the trial court refused to allow expert testimony offered to prove that the defendant, who was intoxicated, could not have formed the requisite conscious indifference to human life. A unanimous court upheld the murder conviction. Relying on the approach of Model Penal Code §2.08(2), Justice Souter (then a judge of the state supreme court) said (549 A.2d at 1208):

> [T]he statutory definition of reckless conduct . . . precludes the recognition of voluntary intoxication as an excuse, and thus "postulate[s] a general equivalence between the risks created by the conduct of the drunken actor and the risks created . . . in becoming drunk." [C]onsistent policy demands the same treatment of socially deviant conduct [with regard to the additional statutory requirement of] circumstances manifesting an extreme indifference to the value of human life. The law in each case invests an adult defendant with responsibility to know what sort of person he is, and to stay sober if his intoxication will jeopardize the lives and safety of others.

5. *Intent to inflict great bodily harm.* In a case of unintended killing what legal effect should be given to evidence that the defendant intended to inflict serious injury short of death? Obviously, such facts have evidentiary significance on the question whether the defendant recklessly or negligently created a risk of death. But the common law went further, by giving such facts independent substantive significance. The malice required for murder was established by the intent of the defendant to do great bodily harm to the victim. See G. Williams, Textbook of Criminal Law 210 (1978). The intent-to-inflict-grievous-harm formula is followed in many American jurisdictions. See Wayne R. LaFave & Austin W. Scott, Jr., Criminal Law 616-617 (2d ed. 1986). In some states, the doctrine survives as a consequence of statutes retaining the common law definition of murder (that is, "malice aforethought"). In a few states, homicide statutes adopt the "great bodily harm" formula explicitly, e.g., Ill. Ann. Stat. ch. 720, §5/9-1(a).

What is the justification for treating an intent to inflict grievous harm as independently sufficient to support a murder conviction whenever death happens to result? Is there, in practice, any significant difference between this standard and the normal mens rea requirement (an intention, or recklessness, with respect to the risk of *death*)?

2. *The Felony-Murder Rule*

a. The Basic Doctrine

REGINA v. SERNÉ

Central Criminal Court
16 Cox Crim. Cas. 311 (1887)

The prisoners Leon Serné and John Henry Goldfinch were indicted for the murder of a boy, Sjaak Serné, the son of the prisoner Leon Serné, it being alleged that they wilfully set on fire a house and shop, No. 274 Strand, London, by which act the death of the boy had been caused.

It appeared that the prisoner Serné with his wife, two daughters, and two sons were living at the house in question; and that Serné, at the time he was living there, in Midsummer, 1887, was in a state of pecuniary embarrassment, and had put into the premises furniture and other goods of but very little value, which at the time of the fire were not of greater value than £30. It also appeared that previously to the fire the prisoner Serné had insured the life of the boy Sjaak Serné, who was imbecile, and on the first day of September, 1887, had insured his stock at 274 Strand, for £500, his furniture for £100, and his rent for another £100; and that on the 17th of the same month the premises were burnt down.

Evidence was given on behalf of the prosecution that fires were seen breaking out in several parts of the premises at the same time, soon after the prisoners had been seen in the shop together, two fires being in the lower part of the house and two above, on the floor whence escape could be made on the roof of the adjoining house, and in which part were the prisoners, and the wife, and two daughters of Serné, who escaped. That on the premises were a quantity of tissue transparencies for advertising purposes, which were of a most inflammable character; and that on the site of one of the fires was found a great quantity of these transparencies close to other inflammable materials. That the prisoner Serné, his wife and daughters, were rescued from the roof of the adjoining house, the other prisoner being rescued from a window in the front of the house, but that the boys were burnt to death, the body of the one being found on the floor near the window from which the prisoner Serné, his wife, and daughters had escaped, the body of the other being found at the basement of the premises.

STEPHEN, J. Gentlemen, it is now my duty to direct your attention to the law and the facts into which you have to inquire. The two prisoners are indicted for the wilful murder of the boy Sjaak Serné, a lad of about fourteen years of age; . . . The definition of murder is unlawful homicide with malice aforethought, and the words malice aforethought are technical. You must not, therefore, construe them or suppose that they can be construed by ordinary rules of language. The words have to be construed according to a long series of decided cases, which have given them meanings different from those which might be supposed. One of those meanings is, the killing of another person by an act done with an intent to commit a felony. Another meaning is, an act done with the knowledge that the act will probably cause the death of some person. Now it is such an act as the last which is alleged to have been done in this case; and if you think that either or both of these men in the dock killed this boy, either by an act done with intent to commit a felony, that is to say, the setting of the house on fire in order to cheat the insurance company, or by conduct which to their knowledge was likely to cause death and was therefore eminently dangerous in itself — in either of these cases the prisoners are guilty of wilful murder in the plain meaning of the word.

I will say a word or two upon one part of this definition, because it is capable of being applied very harshly in certain cases, and also because, though I take the law as I find it, I very much doubt whether the definition which I have given, although it is the common definition, is not somewhat too wide. Now when it is said that murder means killing a man by an act done in the commission of a felony, the mere words cover a case like this, that is to say, a case where a man gives another a push with an intention of stealing his watch, and the person so pushed, having a weak heart or some other internal disorder, dies. To take another very old illustration, it was said that if a man shot a fowl with intent to steal it and accidentally killed a man, he was to be accounted guilty of murder, because the act was done in the commission of a felony.[a] I very much doubt, however, whether that is really the law, or whether the Court for the Consideration of Crown Cases Reserved would hold it to be so.

The present case, however, is not such as I have cited, nor anything like them. In my opinion the definition of the law which makes it murder to kill by an act done in the commission of a felony might and ought to be narrowed, while that part of the law under which the Crown in this case claim to have proved a case of murder is maintained. I think that, instead of saying that any act done with intent to commit a felony and which causes death amounts to murder, it would be reasonable to say that any act known to be dangerous to life and likely in itself to cause death, done for the purpose of committing a felony which causes death, should be murder. As an illustration of this, suppose that a man, intending to commit a rape upon a woman, but without the least wish to kill her, squeezed her by the throat to overpower her, and in so doing killed her, that would be murder. I think that every one would say in a case like that, that when a person began doing wicked acts for his own base purposes, he risked his own life as well as that of others. That kind of crime does not differ in any serious degree from one committed by using a deadly weapon, such as a bludgeon, a pistol, or a knife. If a man once begins attacking the human body in such a way, he must take the consequences if he goes further than he intended when he began. That I take to be the true meaning of the law in the subject.

In the present case, gentlemen, you have a man sleeping in a house with his wife, his two daughters, his two sons, and a servant, and you are asked to believe that this man, with all these people under his protection, deliberately set fire to the house in three or four different places and thereby burnt two of them

a. Coke, 3d Institute 56 (1644): "If the act be unlawful it is murder. As if *A* meaning to steale a deer in the park of *B,* shooteth at the deer, and by the glance of the arrow killeth a boy that is hidden in a bush; this is murder, for that the act was unlawful, although *A* had no intent to hurt the boy, nor knew not of him. But if *B* the owner of the park had shot at his own deer, and without any ill intent had killed the boy by the glance of his arrow, this had been homicide by misadventure, and no felony.

"So if one shoot at any wild fowle upon a tree, and the arrow killeth any reasonable creature afar off, without any evill intent in him, this is per infortunium: for it was not unlawful to shoot at the wilde fowle: but if he had shot at a cock or hen, or any tame fowle of another mans, and the arrow by mischance had killed a man, this had been murder, for the act was unlawfull." — Eds.

to death. It is alleged that he arranged matters in such a way that any person of the most common intelligence must have known perfectly well that he was placing all those people in deadly risk. It appears to me that if that were really done, it matters very little indeed whether the prisoners hoped the people would escape or whether they did not. If a person chose, for some wicked purpose of his own to sink a boat at sea, and thereby caused the deaths of the occupants, it matters nothing whether at the time of committing the act he hoped that the people would be picked up by a passing vessel. He is as much guilty of murder if the people are drowned, as if he had flung every person into the water with his own hand. Therefore, gentlemen, if Serné and Goldfinch set fire to this house when the family were in it, and if the boys were by that act stifled or burnt to death, then the prisoners are as much guilty of murder as if they had stabbed the children. I will also add, for my own part, that I think, in so saying, the law of England lays down a rule of broad, plain common-sense. . . .

There was a case tried in this court which you will no doubt remember, and which will illustrate my meaning. It was the Clerkenwell explosion case in 1868, when a man named Barrett was charged with causing the death of several persons by an explosion which was intended to release one or two men from custody; and I am sure that no one can say truly that Barrett was not justly hanged. With regard to the facts in the present case, the very horror of the crime, if crime it was, the abomination of it, is a reason for your taking the most extreme care in the case, and for not imputing to the prisoners anything which is not clearly proved. God forbid that I should, by what I say, produce on your minds, even in the smallest degree any feeling against the prisoners. You must see, gentlemen, that the evidence leaves no reasonable doubt upon your minds; but you will fail in the performance of your duty if, being satisfied with the evidence, you do not convict one or both the prisoners of wilful murder, and it is wilful murder of which they are accused.

[Verdict, not guilty.]

PEOPLE v. STAMP, 2 Cal. App. 3d 203, 82 Cal. Rptr. 598 (1969): [Defendant burglarized the business premises of one Carl Honeyman and robbed him at gunpoint. During the robbery, Honeyman had been led from his office by the elbow and required to lie on the floor for about ten minutes, until the defendant had fled. Shortly thereafter, Honeyman began suffering chest pains, collapsed and died of a heart attack. He was described as "an obese 60-year-old man, with a history of heart disease, who was under a great deal of pressure due to the intensely competitive nature of his business. Additionally, he did not take good care of his heart." Doctors testified that "[t]he fright induced by the robbery was too much of a shock to Honeyman's system." Defendant's conviction of first-degree murder was upheld. The court stated:] The [felony-murder] doctrine is not limited to those deaths which are foreseeable. Rather a felon is held strictly liable for *all* killings committed by him or his accomplices in the course of the felony. As long as the homicide is the direct causal result of the robbery the felony-murder rule applies whether or not the death was a natural or probable consequence of the robbery. So long as a victim's predisposing physical condition, regardless of its cause, is not the *only* substantial factor bringing about his death, that condition and the robber's ignorance of it, in no way destroys the robber's criminal responsibility for the death. So long as life is shortened as a re-

sult of the felonious act it does not matter that the victim might have died soon anyway. In this respect, the robber takes his victim as he finds him. [See also Minor v. State, 264 Ga. 195, 442 S.E.2d 754 (1994); Thomas v. State, 436 N.E.2d 1109 (Ind. 1982)]

NOTE ON THE CAUSATION REQUIREMENT

Although a defendant can be held liable under the felony-murder rule in the absence of fault (i.e., mens rea) with respect to the death, the prosecution still must establish that the defendant's conduct "caused" the death, under the normal standards of causation. As we shall see in Chapter 6, these standards require the defendant's criminal acts to be both the "but for" cause of the harm and the "proximate" cause of the harm. "Proximity" is usually said to mean that the harm was the natural and probable consequence, or the foreseeable consequence, of the criminal act. For example, in King v. Commonwealth, 6 Va. App. 351, 368 S.E.2d 704 (1988), defendant King and his co-pilot were transporting 500 pounds of marijuana in a light plane when they became lost in fog and crashed into a mountainside. King survived the crash, but his co-pilot did not, and as a result King was charged and convicted of felony-murder. The appellate court reversed, holding that the drug-distribution crime was not the proximate cause of the death. Although the "but for" requirement was met, the crash was not a foreseeable result of the felony since it was not made more likely by the fact that the plane's cargo was contraband. The court noted that, in contrast, a finding of proximate causation might have been possible if the crash had resulted from flying the plane at low altitude to avoid detection.[3]

One does occasionally find incautious statements to the effect that no causal relation between the felony and the death is required.[4] But on examination these appear to be one of two kinds of cases. One is where the death, though not foreseeable, nevertheless satisfies the proximate cause requirement, as in *Stamp*, supra, under the special causation rule that the defendant must "take his victim as he finds him." See Chapter 6, especially the Note on vulnerability of the victim, page 525 infra. The other kind of case is where the foreseeability requirement is satisfied by a finding that the defendant directly killed the deceased in the course of a felony found to be inherently dangerous so that the death *was* readily foreseeable.

NOTES ON THE RATIONALE OF THE FELONY-MURDER RULE

We have previously examined the proposition sometimes asserted that the mens rea of a lesser offense may substitute for the mens rea of a greater offense. Reconsider Regina v. Prince, page 226 supra. Precisely that proposition serves as the basis of liability in felony-murder. Does it have any greater justification in

3. Note that the result in *King* contrasts with the broader application of the felony-murder rule implied by several of Coke's hypotheticals, page 449 n.a, supra. The *King* case, however, is representative of contemporary law.

4. See People v. Pulido, 936 P.2d 1235 (Cal. 1997); State v. Terry, 447 S.E.2d 720 (1994).

homicidal crimes than in other crimes? If the law is sound in requiring a particular mens rea to establish murder, is it, by definition, unsound to require less solely because the actor is guilty of another crime? The offense accompanying the killing has its own punishment. In what sense does the offense also add to the criminality of the killing (as by making an otherwise noncriminal killing criminal) or to the grade of the criminal killing (as by making murder what otherwise would be manslaughter)?

Consider the following comments on the felony-murder rule.

1. People v. Washington, 62 Cal. 2d 777, 402 P.2d 130, 133 (1965): The purpose of the felony-murder rule is to deter felons from killing negligently or accidentally by holding them strictly responsible for killings they commit.

2. T. B. Macaulay, A Penal Code Prepared by the Indian Law Commissioners, Note M, 64-65 (1837): It will be admitted that, when an act is in itself innocent, to punish the person who does it because bad consequences which no human wisdom could have foreseen have followed from it would be in the highest degree barbarous and absurd. [T]o pronounce [that person] guilty of one offence because a misfortune befell him while he was committing another offence . . . is surely to confound all the boundaries of crime. . . .

To punish as a murderer every man who, while committing a heinous offence, causes death by pure misadventure, is a course which evidently adds nothing to the security of human life. No man can so conduct himself as to make it absolutely certain that he shall not be so unfortunate as to cause the death of a fellow creature. The utmost that he can do is to abstain from everything which is at all likely to cause death. No fear of punishment can make him do more than this: and therefore to punish a man who has done this can add nothing to the security of human life. The only good effect which such punishment can produce will be to deter people from committing any of those offences which turn into murders what are in themselves mere accidents. It is in fact an addition to the punishment of those offences, and it is an addition in the very worst way. For example, hundreds of persons in some great cities are in the habit of picking pockets. They know that they are guilty of a great offence. But it has never occurred to one of them, nor would it occur to any rational man, that they are guilty of an offence which endangers life. Unhappily one of these hundreds attempts to take the purse of a gentleman who has a loaded pistol in his pocket. The thief touches the trigger: the pistol goes off: the gentleman is shot dead. To treat the case of this pick-pocket differently from that of the numerous pickpockets who steal under exactly the same circumstances, with exactly the same intentions, with no less risk of causing death, with no greater care to avoid causing death, — to send them to the house of correction as thieves, and him to the gallows as a murderer, — appears to us an unreasonable course. If the punishment for stealing from a person be too light, let it be increased, and let the increase fall alike on all the offenders. Surely the worst mode of increasing the punishment of an offence is to provide that, besides the ordinary punishment, every offender shall run an exceedingly small risk of being hanged. The more nearly the amount of punishment can be reduced to a certainty the better. But if chance is to be admitted there are better ways of admitting it. It would be a less capricious, and therefore a more salutary course, to provide that every fiftieth or every hundredth thief selected by lot should be hanged, than to provide that every thief should be hanged who, while engaged in stealing, should meet with an unforeseen misfortune such as might have befallen the most virtuous man while performing the most virtuous action.

3. *George P. Fletcher, Reflections on Felony-Murder, 12 Sw. U. L. Rev. 413, 427-429 (1981):* [One] unrefined mode of thought behind the [felony-murder] rule begins not with the deadly outcome, but with the felonious background. That someone engages in a felony lowers the threshold of moral responsibility for the resulting death. If there is a principle behind this way of thinking, it is that a wrongdoer must run the risk that things will turn out worse than she expects. The same principle has motivated common law courts and legislatures to reject the claim of mistake in cases of abducting infants, statutory rape, and assaulting a police officer. If the act is wrong, even as the defendant conceives the facts to be, then she presumably has no grounds for complaining if the facts turn out to be worse than she expects. . . .

[This mode of thought violates] a basic principle of just punishment. Punishment must be proportional to wrongdoing. When the felony-murder rule converts an accidental death into first-degree murder, then punishment is rendered disproportionate to the wrong for which the offender is personally responsible. [T]he principle that the wrongdoer must run the risk explicitly obscures the question of actual responsibility for the harmful result.

There may be an apology for the felony-murder rule, but it is one that could easily excuse too much injustice in our substantive criminal law. If we compare our combined system of substantive law and procedural rights with the total system that prevails in a Continental jurisdiction, say, in West Germany, we could hazard the following generalization. American law achieves a balance of advantage between defense and prosecution by bestowing extraordinary procedural protections on the accused and yet compensating the prosecution with rules of strict liability, felony-murder, conspiracy, and vicarious liability. German law, in contrast, offers fewer procedural protections — no jury, no exclusionary rule in our sense, fewer restrictions on hearsay evidence — yet the German substantive law is more refined and more consistent with principles of individual responsibility. . . . What the [American] law of procedure grants the accused, the law of substance takes away.

4. *James J. Tomkovicz, The Endurance of the Felony-Murder Rule, 51 Wash. & Lee L. Rev. 1429, 1448-1449 (1994):* The primary justification offered for the contemporary felony-murder rule is deterrence. The doctrine is allegedly designed to save lives by threatening potential killers with the serious sanction for first or second degree murder. One deterrent argument holds that the threat of a murder conviction for any killing in furtherance of a felony, even an accidental killing, might well induce a felon to forego committing the felony itself. . . . Another argument, the more prevalent of the two main deterrent explanations of felony-murder, maintains that the rule is aimed at discouraging certain conduct during the felony, not the felony itself. The goal is to encourage greater care in the performance of felonious acts. . . . Still another view suggests that felons who might kill intentionally in order to complete their felonies successfully will be discouraged . . . because of their awareness that the chance of constructing a de-

fense that would eliminate or mitigate liability is virtually nonexistent and that, therefore, their likely fate is a murder conviction. . . .

The problem with the modern felony-murder doctrine is not only that it seeks practical goals by prescribing severe punishments without proof of fault, but that it does so on the basis of unproven and highly questionable assumptions. While the felony-murder rule must save some lives, the odds are that the number is small indeed. The number of killings during felonies is relatively low.[5] The subset of such killings that are nonculpable — thus not already subject to the threat of a substantial sanction — is undoubtedly considerably smaller. Further, the addition of a small risk of a murder sanction for an unlikely event is probably not a major influence on some prospective felons' behavior, and a good number of those who are affected in some way probably would not have killed in any event. Moreover, some who are aware of and even sensitive to the threatened sanction will probably still kill negligently or accidentally.

Admittedly, it would be difficult, if not impossible, to prove that the felony-murder rule does not annually save a considerable number of lives. Nonetheless, in a world in which the evidence is uncertain (or nonexistent) and in which it seems unlikely that felons actually hear the rule's deterrent message in the ways that courts presume that they do, common sense would suggest putting the burden of proof upon those who contend that deterrent gains are sufficient to outweigh the infringement of our fundamental philosophy of fault and punishment. . . .

Assertions that the doctrine exists to prevent killings that occur in the course of felonies and that it actually achieves its goals are rooted in blind faith or self-delusion. More should be required. . . . Without a credible foundation in established facts, deterrence is not a real justification, but is instead a poor excuse for our infidelity [to fundamental principles of culpability].

5. Model Penal Code and Commentaries, Comment to §210.2 at 37-39 (1980): [The American Law Institute recommended eliminating the felony-murder rule. However, it provided that for the purpose of establishing murder by an act "committed recklessly under circumstances manifesting extreme indifference to the value of human life," the fact that the actor is "engaged, or is an accomplice in the commission of, or an attempt to commit, or flight after committing or attempting to commit robbery, rape or deviate sexual intercourse by force or threat of force, arson, burglary, kidnapping or felonious escape" creates a re-

5. Compare the following as reported in Model Penal Code and Commentaries, Comment to §210.2 at 38 n.96: "One study indicates that out of 1.5 million robberies and robbery attempts annually, there are roughly 2,090 robbery-related homicides, a fatality rate of .14 percent. See Phillip J. Cook, Robbery Violence, 78 J. Crim. L. & Criminology 357, 358-359, 362-363 (1987). But in response to data of this sort, Professor Cole observes (Killings During Crime, 28 Am. Crim. L. Rev. 73, 105 (1990):

> The statistics have struck some as indicating that felonies are not particularly dangerous to life. For example, only about .6 percent of all armed robberies end in death. But just because this rate is lower than we might have thought does not mean that robberies are safe relative to the normal range of human activities governed by the laws relating to simple killings. If the average robbery takes an hour (probably a high estimate), that means one homicide occurs every 166 hours of robbery. If everyday activities were as dangerous as robbery, and if the average person is awake 16 hours a day, then the average person would kill one person every eleven days.

buttable presumption (defined in §1.12(5)) that the required indifference and recklessness existed.

[In support of this proposal, the Comment states:] Principled argument in favor of the felony-murder doctrine is hard to find. The defense reduces to the explanation that Holmes gave for finding the law "intelligible as it stands":

> [I]f experience shows, or is deemed by the law-maker to show, that somehow or other deaths which the evidence makes accidental happen disproportionately often in connection with other felonies, or with resistance to officers, or if on any other ground of policy it is deemed desirable to make special efforts for the prevention of such deaths, the law-maker may consistently treat acts which, under the known circumstances, are felonious, or constitute resistance to officers, as having a sufficiently dangerous tendency to be put under a special ban. The law may, therefore, throw on the actor the peril, not only of the consequences foreseen by him, but also of consequences which, although not predicted by common experience, the legislator apprehends.[95]

The answer to such arguments is twofold. First, there is no basis in experience for thinking that homicides *which the evidence makes accidental* occur with disproportionate frequency in connection with specified felonies. Second, it remains indefensible in principle to use the sanctions that the law employs to deal with murder unless there is at least a finding that the actor's conduct manifested an extreme indifference to the value of human life. The fact that the actor was engaged in a crime of the kind that is included in the usual first-degree felony-murder enumeration or was an accomplice in such crime, as has been observed, will frequently justify such a finding. Indeed, the probability that such a finding will be justified seems high enough to warrant the presumption of extreme indifference that Subsection (1)(b) creates. But liability depends, as plainly it should, upon the crucial finding. The result may not differ often under such a formulation from that which would be reached under some form of the felony-murder rule. But what is more important is that a conviction on this basis rests solidly upon principle.

NOTES ON THE MISDEMEANOR-MANSLAUGHTER RULE

1. The basic doctrine. Just as a felony resulting in death can provide a basis for a murder conviction without proof of malice, in many states a misdemeanor resulting in death can provide a basis for an involuntary manslaughter conviction without proof of recklessness or negligence. The misdemeanor-manslaughter rule, also known as the "unlawful-act doctrine," was reflected in the traditional common law definition of involuntary manslaughter. The language of Cal. Penal Code §192(b), drawn from Blackstone's formulation, is typical: Involuntary manslaughter is a killing "in the commission of an unlawful act, not amounting to a felony; or in the commission of a lawful act which might produce death, in an unlawful manner, or without due caution and circumspection."

In states that retain the traditional common law formula, the prosecution thus

95. O. Holmes, The Common Law 49 (1881).

has two distinct theories available to establish involuntary manslaughter. If a defendant, after driving through a red light, has killed a pedestrian, the prosecution can argue for involuntary manslaughter on the basis that the defendant's conduct amounted to criminal negligence under the circumstances. See page 425 supra. In the alternative, however, in states that recognize the unlawful-act doctrine, the prosecution need only show that the defendant's unlawful act caused the death; proof of criminal negligence becomes unnecessary. See State v. Hupf, 48 Del. 254, 101 A.2d 355 (1953)).

2. *Limitations on the unlawful-act doctrine.* In states that retain the unlawful-act doctrine, some of its harshest effects have been moderated by a variety of limitations. Most of these limitations are similar to the ones that apply to the felony-murder rule.

(a) Proximate cause. As indicated in the Note on the Causation Requirement, page 451 supra, the felony-murder rule applies only when the crime committed is the proximate cause of the death. Nearly all jurisdictions impose a similar limitation on the misdemeanor-manslaughter rule. Thus, in Commonwealth v. Williams, 133 Pa. Super. 104, 1 A.2d 812 (1938), the defendant had been convicted of manslaughter by vehicle on the basis of his unlawful act of failing to renew his driver's license. The court reversed, holding that the expiration of the license had no causal connection to the accident, which had resulted from the carelessness of another driver.

(b) Regulatory offenses. Some courts restrict the unlawful-act doctrine to malum in se as opposed to malum prohibitum misdemeanors. E.g., Mills v. State, 13 Md. App. 196, 282 A.2d 147 (1971). Many other courts, however, have explicitly rejected that limitation. See, e.g., State v. Hose, 187 W. Va. 429, 419 S.E.2d 690 (1992) (truck driver convicted of involuntary manslaughter for fatal accident that occurred after he violated federal and state laws by remaining on duty for more than 15 hours).

(c) Dangerousness. Another approach is to limit the doctrine to misdemeanors that rise to the level of criminal negligence (State v. Stanislaw, 153 Vt. 517, 573 A.2d 286 (1990); State v. Burrell, 699 P.2d 499 (Kan. 1985)) or to violations that "evince a marked disregard for the safety of others" (State v. Lingman, 97 Utah 180, 91 P.2d 457 (1939)). Another approach to limiting the rule is illustrated by People v. Cox, 2 P.3d 1189 (Cal. 2000). The court held that even though the California involuntary manslaughter provision applies to any death caused by "an unlawful act . . . *or* [a lawful act committed] without due caution and circumspection;" a conviction under the unlawful-act branch of the statute requires proof that the underlying conduct was dangerous to human life under the circumstances of its commission.

A related strategy is to limit the unlawful-act doctrine to misdemeanors designed to protect human safety, e.g., State v. Powell, 426 S.E.2d 91 (N.C. App. 1993). But this approach leaves considerable room for unlawful-act manslaughter in cases that might not involve criminal negligence. In *Powell,* a jogger was killed by two Rottweiler dogs that had escaped from the defendant's fenced yard. A local ordinance required that dogs be restrained by a secure fence or leash at all times. The court ruled that the ordinance was a "safety" ordinance, designed to protect persons as well as property, and therefore that the defendant was guilty of involuntary manslaughter under the unlawful-act doctrine, *regardless* of whether he had been reckless or negligent in allowing the dogs to escape. Is this a justified result? What should be the range of penalties applicable to non-negligent dog owners who violate a local leash law?

NOTES ON STATUTORY REFORM OF THE FELONY-MURDER RULE

England, whose judges created the felony-murder rule through the common law process, abolished it by statute in 1957 (Homicide Act of 1957, 5 & 6 Eliz. 2, ch. 11, §1):

> Where a person kills another in the course or furtherance of some other offence, the killing shall not amount to murder unless done with the same malice aforethought (express or implied) as is required for a killing to amount to murder when not done in the course or furtherance of another offence.

In this country, the felony-murder rule has proven of greater durability. See James J. Tomkovicz, The Endurance of the Felony-Murder Rule, 51 Wash. & Lee L. Rev. 1429, 1431 (1994). Despite the substantial influence of the Model Penal Code in other areas, it has had small success in moving the states away from the felony-murder rule. However, statutes over the years have qualified the severity of the common law rule in a variety of ways.

1. When common law murder was divided into two degrees by the Pennsylvania statute of 1794 (see page 395 above), certain particularly dangerous felonies — arson, rape, robbery, and burglary — were designated as the only felonies on which a first-degree felony-murder conviction could be obtained. Where this approach is followed (see, e.g., 18 U.S.C. §1111; Cal. Penal Code §189, page 390 supra), a killing in the course of a nondesignated felony still triggers the felony-murder rule, but (in the absence of deliberation and premeditation) the offense will only be murder in the second degree.

2. Some states have designated particular felonies (such as rape, arson, burglary, kidnapping, and robbery) as the only felonies on which a felony-murder conviction may be obtained; other felonies serve only as the possible basis of a manslaughter conviction (Ind. Code §35-42-1-4; La. Rev. Stat. tit. 14, §31) or cannot by themselves serve as the basis for conviction of any form of culpable homicide (N.Y. Pen. Law §125.25(3), page 394 supra).

3. Another approach is to require that a killing in the course of the felony be otherwise culpable before it may constitute murder — for example, that the defendant has "recklessly" caused the death of another (Del. Code Ann. tit. 11, §636) or that the defendant has caused another's death by "an act clearly dangerous to human life" (Tex. Pen. Code §19.02).

Question: To what extent do these various qualifications meet the criticisms of the felony-murder rule made by Macaulay, Tomcovicz, and the Model Penal Code, supra.

NOTES ON JUDICIAL REFORM

1. Abolition. One state Supreme Court has abolished the felony-murder rule. In People v. Aaron, 409 Mich. 672, 299 N.W.2d 304 (1980). Defendants in several unrelated cases were convicted of first-degree murder for deaths that occurred in the course of robbery or arson. In each case the jury instructions permitted conviction on the basis of the felony, without other evidence of malice. The Michigan Supreme Court reversed the convictions, stating:

> Michigan does not have a statutory felony-murder doctrine which designates as murder any *death* occurring in the course of a felony without regard to whether it was the result of accident, negligence, recklessness or willfulness. Rather, Michigan has a statute which makes a *murder* occurring in the course of one of the enumerated felonies a first-degree murder:
>
> > Murder which is perpetrated by means of poison, lying in wait, or other willful, deliberate, and premeditated killing, or which is committed in the perpetration, or attempt to perpetrate [designated felonies] is murder of the first degree, and shall be punished by imprisonment for life. M.S.A. §28.548.
>
> The Michigan Legislature adopted verbatim the first-degree murder statute of Pennsylvania, the statute we have today. . . . In Commonwealth ex rel. Smith v. Myers, 438 Pa. 224, 261, A.2d 550, the Pennsylvania Supreme Court stated: "Clearly this statutory felony-murder rule merely serves to raise the degree of certain murders to first degree; it gives no aid to the determination of what constitutes murder in the first place." . . . This Court has not been faced previously with a decision as to whether it should abolish the felony-murder doctrine. Thus, the common-law doctrine remains the law in Michigan. . . .
>
> We believe that it is no longer acceptable to equate the intent to commit a felony with the intent to kill, intent to do great bodily harm, or wanton and willful disregard of the likelihood that the natural tendency of a person's behavior is to cause death or great bodily harm. Today we exercise our role in the development of the common law by abrogating the common-law felony-murder rule. We hold that in order to convict a defendant of murder, as that term is defined by Michigan case law, it must be shown that he acted with intent to kill or to inflict great bodily harm or with a wanton and willful disregard of the likelihood that the natural tendency of his behavior is to cause death or great bodily harm. We further hold that the issue of malice must always be submitted to the jury.
>
> The first-degree murder statute will continue to operate in that all *murder* committed in the perpetration or attempted perpetration of the enumerated felonies will be elevated to first-degree murder.

2. *Statutory interpretations.* In People v. Dillon, 34 Cal. 3d 441, 668 P.2d 697 (1983), the California Supreme Court considered following *Aaron* but decided not to, even though the wording of California's statute is identical to Michigan's and even though both statutes were explicitly based on the 1794 Pennsylvania model. The court concluded that subsequent reenactments by the California legislature demonstrated an intent to codify the felony-murder rule in that state. But *Aaron* has influenced judicial interpretation of homicide statutes in several other states. In State v. Ortega, 112 N.M. 554, 817 P.2d 1196 (1991), a case of homicide in the course of a kidnapping and robbery, the court read into New Mexico's first-degree felony-murder statute a requirement that the state prove intent to kill or conscious disregard for life. Similarly, in Commonwealth v. Matchett, 386 Mass. 492, 436 N.E.2d 400 (1982), the court held that before prosecutors can invoke that state's second-degree felony-murder rule for nonenumerated felonies, the jury must find that the defendant demonstrated a conscious disregard for the risk to human life.

3. Constitutional issues. If the felony-murder rule is required by statute, then to what extent is its application to nonintentional killings unconstitutional? In *Dillon,* supra Note 1, the court read California's felony-murder statute as imposing first-degree murder liability for a wide range of robbery killings — from accidental to premeditated homicides — and held that in order to comply with the constitutional prohibition on cruel and unusual punishment (see page 287 supra), the sentencing court would have to consider whether the first-degree penalty, life imprisonment, was disproportionate to the culpability of the defendant in the particular case.

A related approach is developed in Nelson E. Roth & Scott E. Sundby, The Felony-Murder Rule: A Doctrine at Constitutional Crossroads, 70 Cornell L. Rev. 446 (1985). The authors argue that courts should hold the felony-murder rule unconstitutional because its effect is either to conclusively presume malice (thus violating the requirement of proof beyond a reasonable doubt) or to eliminate malice (thus violating the Eighth Amendment requirement that severe punishments be proportional to culpability). Although no United States court has, to our knowledge, adopted this position to date, the Roth and Sundby arguments played a large role in influencing the New Mexico Supreme Court to read an intent requirement into that state's felony-murder statute, in order to avoid serious constitutional questions. See *Ortega,* supra Note 1. And in The Queen v. Vaillancourt, [1987] S.C.R. 636, the Canadian Supreme Court held that the felony-murder rule provisions of that country's Criminal Code, by permitting conviction in the absence of mens rea, violate the Canadian Charter of Rights and Freedoms, in particular §7 (requiring respect for "principles of fundamental justice") and §11(d) (guaranteeing the presumption of innocence).

NOTE ON JUDICIAL LIMITATIONS

Aside from the developments canvassed in the preceding Note, the major judicial involvement with the felony-murder rule has been in formulating and applying limitations to its reach. Three of the most important are presented in the following material: the "inherently dangerous-felony" limitation, the merger doctrine, and the "killings-not-in-furtherance" limitation.

b. The "Inherently Dangerous-Felony" Limitation

PEOPLE v. PHILLIPS

Supreme Court of California
64 Cal. 2d 574, 414 P.2d 353 (1966)

Tobriner, J. Defendant, a doctor of chiropractic, appeals from a judgment of the Superior Court of Los Angeles County convicting him of second degree murder in connection with the death from cancer of one of his patients. We reverse solely on the ground that the trial court erred in giving a felony-murder instruction. . . .

[Deceased was an eight-year-old child with a fast-growing cancer of the eye. Her parents were advised at a medical center to consent to immediate removal of the eye as the only means of saving or prolonging her life. However, defendant induced them not to do so by representing that he could cure her without surgery by treatment designed "to build up her resistance." Defendant charged the parents $700 for his treatment and medicine. The child died in about six months.]

Defendant challenges the propriety of the trial court's instructions to the jury. The court gave the following tripartite instruction on murder in the second degree:[4]

> [T]he unlawful killing of a human being with malice aforethought, but without a deliberately formed and premeditated intent to kill, is murder of the second degree:
>
> (1) If the killing proximately results from an unlawful act, . . . performed by a person who knows that his conduct endangers the life of another, or . . .
>
> (3) If the killing is done in the perpetration or attempt to perpetrate a felony such as Grand Theft. If a death occurs in the perpetration of a course of conduct amounting to Grand Theft, which course of conduct is a proximate cause of the unlawful killing of a human being, such course of conduct constitutes murder in the second degree, even though the death was not intended.

The third part of this instruction rests upon the felony-murder rule and reflects the prosecution's theory that defendant's conduct amounted to grand theft by false pretenses in violation of Penal Code section 484. . . .

Despite defendant's contention that the Penal Code does not expressly set forth any provision for second degree felony murder and that, therefore, we should not follow any such doctrine here, the concept lies imbedded in our law. [T]he perpetration of some felonies, exclusive of those enumerated in Penal Code section 189, may provide the basis for a murder conviction under the felony-murder rule.

We have held, however, that only such felonies as are in themselves "inherently dangerous to human life" can support the application of the felony-murder rule. We have ruled that in assessing such peril to human life inherent in any given felony "we look to the elements of the felony in the abstract, not the particular 'facts' of the case." (People v. Williams, 63 Cal. 2d 452, 458, fn. 5).

We have thus recognized that the felony-murder doctrine expresses a highly artificial concept that deserves no extension beyond its required application. Indeed, the rule itself has been abandoned by the courts of England, where it had its inception. It has been subjected to severe and sweeping criticism. No case to our knowledge in any jurisdiction has held that because death results from a course of conduct involving a felonious perpetration of a fraud, the felony-murder doctrine can be invoked.

4. The record suggests that the evidence would have supported a finding of involuntary manslaughter. The jury might, for example, have found that defendant sincerely, though *unreasonably,* believed that the removal of Linda from the hospital and treatment according to the principles of chiropractic would be in her best interests. Having so found, the jury could have concluded that in causing Linda's removal from the hospital and so endangering her life defendant acted "without due caution and circumspection." (Pen. Code, §192, subd. 2.) Accordingly, the trial court should have given a manslaughter instruction. The record reveals, however, that defendant's counsel strongly opposed the manslaughter instruction and indicated to the trial court that he considered it "tactically" to defendant's advantage to confront the jury with the limited choice between murder and acquittal. Thus the failure of the trial court to instruct on manslaughter, though erroneous, was invited error; defendant may not properly complain of such error on appeal.

Admitting that grand theft is not inherently dangerous to life, the prosecution asks us to encompass the entire course of defendant's conduct so that we may incorporate such elements as would make his crime inherently dangerous. In so framing the definition of a given felony for the purpose of assessing its inherent peril to life the prosecution would abandon the statutory definition of the felony as such and substitute the factual elements of defendant's actual conduct. In the present case the Attorney General would characterize that conduct as "grand theft medical fraud," and this newly created "felony," he urges, clearly involves danger to human life and supports an application of the felony-murder rule.

To fragmentize the "course of conduct" of defendant so that the felony-murder rule applies if any segment of that conduct may be considered dangerous to life would widen the rule beyond calculation. It would then apply not only to the commission of specific felonies, which are themselves dangerous to life, but to the perpetration of *any* felony during which defendant may have acted in such a manner as to endanger life.

The proposed approach would entail the rejection of our holding in *Williams.* That case limited the felony-murder doctrine to such felonies as were themselves inherently dangerous to life. That decision eschews the prosecution's present sweeping concept because, once the Legislature's own definition is discarded, the number or nature of the contextual elements which could be incorporated into an expanded felony terminology would be limitless. We have been, and remain, unwilling to embark on such an uncharted sea of felony murder.

The felony-murder instruction should not, then, have been given; its rendition, further, worked prejudice upon defendant. It withdrew from the jury the issue of malice, permitting a conviction upon the bare showing that Linda's death proximately resulted from conduct of defendant amounting to grand theft. The instruction as rendered did not require the jury to find either express malice or the implied malice which is manifested in an "intent with conscious disregard for life to commit acts likely to kill." (People v. Washington, 62 Cal. 2d 777, 780.) . . .

The prosecution does not deny that the giving of a felony-murder instruction engendered the possibility of a conviction of murder in the absence of a finding of malice. It contends, however, that even if the jury acted on the erroneous instruction it must necessarily have found facts which establish, as a matter of law, that defendant acted with conscious disregard for life and hence with malice. . . . The prosecution urges that the jury could not have convicted defendant under the felony-murder instruction without having found that he made representations to the [parents] which he knew to be false or which he recklessly rendered without information which would justify a reasonable belief in their truth. Such a finding does not, however, establish as a matter of law the existence of an "intent with conscious disregard for life to commit acts likely to kill." (People v. Washington, supra.) In the absence of a finding that defendant subjectively appreciated the peril to which his conduct exposed the girl, we cannot determine that he acted with conscious disregard for life. The record contains evidence from which a trier of fact could reasonably have concluded that although defendant made false representations concerning his ability to cure, he nevertheless believed that the treatment which he proposed to give would be as efficacious in relieving pain and prolonging life as the scheduled surgery.

Of course the jury could have concluded from some of the evidence that defendant did *not* entertain any such belief in the relative efficacy of his proposed treatment. We cannot, however, undertake to resolve this evidentiary conflict without invading the province of the trier of fact. We cannot predicate a finding of conscious disregard of life upon a record that would as conclusively afford a basis for the opposite conclusion. . . .

The judgment is reversed.[a]

PEOPLE v. SATCHELL, 6 Cal. 3d 28, 489 P.2d 1361 (1972): [Defendant, an ex-felon with four prior felony convictions, was convicted of second-degree murder arising out of a street fight. Defendant shot and killed the deceased with a sawed-off shotgun he obtained from his car. Section 12021 of the Penal Code made it a felony for an ex-felon to possess such a weapon. The trial judge gave the following second-degree felony-murder instruction:

> The unlawful killing of a human being, whether intentional, unintentional or accidental, which occurs as a direct causal result of the commission of or attempt to commit a felony inherently dangerous to human life, namely, the crime of possession of a concealable firearm by a felon, and where there was in the mind of the perpetrator the specific intent to commit such crime, is murder of the second degree.

The supreme court held this instruction erroneous and reversed the conviction, concluding that the felony of possession of a concealable weapon by an ex-felon was not a "felony inherently dangerous to human life." The court started by recalling the approach to felony murder established by several recent California decisions; namely that, "Although it is the law in this state, it should not be extended beyond any rational function that it is designed to serve," and that the "highly artificial concept of strict criminal liability incorporated in the felony-murder doctrine [must] be given the narrowest possible application consistent with its ostensible purpose — which is to deter those engaged in felonies from killing negligently or accidentally." The court then continued:]

It bears emphasis that, in determining whether a felony is inherently dangerous for purposes of the felony-murder rule we assess that felony *in the abstract.* The felony here in question is possession of a concealable firearm by one who has previously been convicted of a (i.e., another) felony. We do *not* look to the specific facts of the case before us in order to determine whether, in light of the nature of the particular felony of which defendant was previously convicted, his possession of a concealable firearm was inherently dangerous. Rather, we direct our attention to the genus of crimes known as felonies and determine whether the possession of a concealable firearm by one who has been convicted of *any crime within that genus* is an act inherently dangerous to human life which, as such, justifies the extreme consequence (i.e., imputed malice) which the felony-murder doctrine demands.

. . . [T]he range of antisocial activities which are criminally punishable as felonies in this state is very wide indeed. Some of these felonies . . . distinctly manifest a propensity for acts dangerous to human life on the part of the perpetrator.

a. On retrial Phillips was convicted of second-degree murder. The theory of the prosecution this time was that defendant had exhibited actual malice by causing the deceased to terminate a surgical treatment that would have prolonged her life. The court of appeal affirmed the conviction. People v. Phillips, 270 Cal. App. 2d 381, 75 Cal. Rptr. 720 (1969). — Eds.

Others, of which a random sampling is set forth in the margin,[19] just as distinctly fail to manifest such a propensity. Surely it cannot be said that a person who has committed a crime in this latter category, when he arms himself with a concealable weapon, presents a danger to human life so significantly more extreme than that presented by a nonfelon similarly armed as to justify the imputation of malice to him if a homicide should result. Accordingly, because we can conceive of such a vast number of situations wherein it would be grossly illogical to impute malice, we must conclude that the violation of section 12021 by one previously convicted of a felony is not itself a felony *inherently* dangerous to human life which will support a second-degree felony-murder instruction.

NOTES AND QUESTIONS

1. Question. What would be the result if §12021 had made it a felony for a person who had been convicted of a felony of personal violence to possess a concealable firearm?

2. In *People v. Henderson, 19 Cal. 3d 86, 560 P.2d 1180 (1977),* the California Supreme Court reversed a second-degree felony-murder conviction based on the felony of "false imprisonment . . . effected by violence, menace, fraud or deceit." Defendant held the victim hostage by holding a gun to his head. When the hostage ducked and attempted to deflect the barrel of the gun from his head, the gun went off and killed a bystander. The court found that unlawful restraint of another does not necessarily involve the requisite danger to human life for a felony-murder conviction and that the statutory factors elevating the offense to a felony — violence, menace, fraud, or deceit — do not all involve conduct that is life endangering. While the factors of violence or menace may involve such danger, the others do not. Therefore, viewing the offense as a whole and in the abstract, it is not an offense inherently dangerous to human life. The prosecution argued that the matter would not differ in substance if the legislature had created two separate false imprisonment felonies, one by violence or menace, the other by fraud or deceit. The court disagreed, finding this difference to be crucial (19 Cal. 3d at 95):

> The Legislature has not evinced a particular concern for violent as opposed to nonviolent acts of false imprisonment by separate statutory treatment, proscription, or punishment. Accordingly, we cannot conclude that the cause of deterring homicide during the commission of false imprisonment is better served by imputing malice to one who kills in the course of committing false imprisonment rather than allowing the jury to determine directly the question of the presence of malice aforethought.

Query: Should the formalities of how the statute is written be given the import the court gives them?

19. See, for example, Corporations Code (fraudulent and deceptive acts relating to corporations); Elections Code, (elections offenses); Financial Code, (unauthorized sale of investment certificates); Government Code, (interference with the legislative process); Insurance Code, (false or fraudulent insurance claim). . . .

The Penal Code, of course, renders felonious many activities which do not indicate a propensity for dangerous acts.

PEOPLE v. STEWART

Supreme Court of Rhode Island, 1995
663 A.2d 912

WEISBERGER, Chief Justice. [Tracy Stewart, mother of an infant under two months of age, went on a crack binge for two to three days, during which she neither fed nor cared for the infant, which died from dehydration. She was charged with second degree felony-murder.]

The prosecution did not allege that defendant intentionally killed her son but rather that he had been killed during the commission of an inherently dangerous felony, specifically, wrongfully permitting a child to be a habitual sufferer.[a] Moreover, the prosecution did not allege that defendant intentionally withheld food or care from her son. Rather the state alleged that because of defendant's chronic state of cocaine intoxication, she may have realized what her responsibilities were but simply could not remember whether she had fed her son, when in fact she had not. . . . The defendant was found guilty of both second-degree murder and wrongfully permitting a child to be a habitual sufferer. . . .

The defendant contends that wrongfully permitting a child to be a habitual sufferer is not an inherently dangerous felony and cannot therefore serve as the predicate felony to a charge of second-degree murder. In advancing her argument, defendant urges this court to adopt the approach used by California courts to determine if a felony is inherently dangerous. This approach requires that the court consider the elements of the felony "in the abstract" rather than look at the particular facts of the case under consideration. With such an approach, if a statute can be violated in a manner that does not endanger human life, then the felony is not inherently dangerous to human life. ; . . .

In People v. Caffero, 201 Cal. App. 3d 678 (1989), a two-and-one-half-week-old baby died of a massive bacterial infection caused by lack of proper hygiene that was due to parental neglect. The parents were charged with second-degree felony murder and felony-child-abuse, with the felony-child-abuse charge serving as the predicate felony to the second-degree-murder charge. Examining California's felony-child abuse statute in the abstract, instead of looking at the particular facts of the case, the court held that because the statute could be violated in ways that did not endanger human life, felony-child abuse was not inherently dangerous to human life. By way of example, the court noted that a fractured limb, which comes within the ambit of the felony-child abuse statute, is unlikely to endanger the life of an infant, much less of a seventeen-year-old. Id. (the statute applied to all minors below the age of eighteen years, not only to young children). Because felony-child-abuse was not inherently dangerous to human life, it could not properly serve as a predicate felony to a charge of second-degree felony murder. . . .

We decline defendant's invitation to adopt the California approach in determining whether a felony is dangerous to life. . . . We believe that the better approach is for the trier of fact to consider the facts and circumstances of the particular case to determine if such felony was inherently dangerous in the manner

a. The reference is to R.I. Gen. L. §11-9-5, the child neglect statute, which makes it a felony to wrongfully cause or permit a child under the age of 18 to be a habitual sufferer for want of food and proper care.—EDS.

and the circumstances in which it was committed. . . . We now join a number of states that have adopted this approach. See, e.g., Commonwealth v. Ortiz, 560 N.E.2d 698 (Mass. 1990).

A number of felonies at first glance would not appear to present an inherent danger to human life but may in fact be committed in such a manner as to be inherently dangerous to life. The crime of escape from a penal facility is an example of such a crime. On its face, the crime of escape is not inherently dangerous to human life. But escape may be committed or attempted to be committed in a manner wherein human life is put in danger. Indeed in State v. Miller, 52 R.I. 440, 410 A.2d 121 (1980), this court upheld the defendant's conviction of second-degree murder on the basis of the underlying felony of escape when a prison guard was killed by an accomplice of the defendant during an attempted escape from the Rhode Island State prison. By way of contrast, the California Supreme Court has held that the crime of escape, viewed in the abstract, is an offense that is not inherently dangerous to human life and thus cannot support a second-degree felony-murder conviction. People v. Lopez, 6 Cal.3d 45, 51, 489 P.2d 1372 (1971).

[T]he proper procedure [to determine whether a felony is inherently dangerous] is to present the facts and circumstances of the particular case to the trier of fact and for the trier of fact to determine if a felony is inherently dangerous in the manner and the circumstances in which it was committed. This is exactly what happened in the case at bar. The trial justice instructed the jury that before it could find defendant guilty of second-degree murder, it must first find that wrongfully causing or permitting a child to be a habitual sufferer for want of food or proper care was inherently dangerous to human life "in its manner of commission." This was a proper charge. By its guilty verdict on the charge of second-degree murder, the jury obviously found that wrongfully permitting a child to be a habitual sufferer for want of food or proper care was indeed a felony inherently dangerous to human life in the circumstances of this particular case.

. . . The defendant's motions for judgment of acquittal on the felony-murder charge on the ground that wrongfully permitting a child to be a habitual sufferer is not an inherently dangerous felony were properly denied.

NOTE ON DRUG DISTRIBUTION AS A DANGEROUS FELONY

In Heacock v. Commonwealth, 323 S.E.2d 90 (Va. 1984), the court held that felony distribution of cocaine met the inherent dangerousness requirement and noted that cocaine had been classified as a controlled substance because of its "high potential for abuse." For contrary conclusions, see State v. Wesson, 802 P.2d 574 (Kan. 1990); State v. Aarsvold, 376 N.W.2d 518, 522 (Minn. 1985) ("use of cocaine, even when injected, does not generally cause death"). Distribution of heroin was held insufficient to trigger the felony-murder rule in Commonwealth v. Bowden, 456 Pa. 278, 309 A.2d 714 (1973), and State v. Randolph, 676 S.W.2d 943 (Tenn. 1984). In *Randolph,* the court said:

> [D]eath is neither the inevitable nor necessarily the most probable result of the injection of a controlled substance. . . . However, when all the circumstances shown

> in this record are taken into account [defendant had been warned that the heroin was dangerous and should not be sold until it had been "cut"], we are of the opinion that, if competently established beyond a reasonable doubt, they could justify a conclusion by the trier of fact that appellant and his co-defendants acted with such conscious indifference to the consequences . . . as to evince malice.

The question arose in somewhat different form in State v. Amaro, 436 So. 2d 1056 (Fla. App. 1983). In this case, the drug dealers were surprised by police. After Amaro had been placed under arrest, one of his co-felons (who was hiding in a bedroom) shot and killed an officer. Rejecting the argument that the arrest had terminated Amaro's responsibility (see page 476 infra), the court held that Amaro could be convicted of felony-murder on the basis of the underlying felony, which in this case was the possession and distribution of marijuana. The court never considered whether this underlying felony meets the inherent dangerousness requirement. Does it?

c. The Merger Doctrine

PEOPLE v. SMITH

California Supreme Court
35 Cal. 3d 798, 678 P.2d 886 (1984)

Mosk, J. Defendant appeals from a judgment convicting her of second degree murder (Pen. Code §187), felony child abuse (§273a, subd. (1)), and child beating (§273d). The court sentenced her to imprisonment for 15 years to life on the murder count and stayed service of sentence on the 2 remaining counts to avoid double punishment. The principal issue on appeal is whether felony child abuse may serve as the underlying felony to support a conviction of second degree murder on a felony-murder theory. . . .

Defendant and her two daughters, three-and-a-half-year-old Bethany (Beth) and two-year-old Amy, lived with David Foster. On the day Amy died, she refused to sit on the couch instead of the floor to eat a snack. Defendant became angry [and she and Foster beat the child cruelly]. Amy stiffened and went into respiratory arrest. Defendant and Foster took her to the hospital, where defendant admitted that she "beat her too hard." . . . Amy died that evening. Her injuries were consistent with compressive force caused by numerous blows by hands, fists, and a paddle. The severe head injury that was the direct cause of death occurred within an hour before the child was brought to the hospital. . . .

The court gave the jury the standard instructions defining murder, malice aforethought, second degree murder, second degree felony murder, and manslaughter. The second degree felony-murder instruction informed the jury that an unlawful killing, whether intentional, unintentional, or accidental, is second degree murder if it occurs during the commission of a felony inherently dangerous to human life, and that felony child abuse is such a crime. Defendant contends that on the facts of this case the crime of felony child abuse was an integral part of and included in fact within the homicide, and hence that it merged into the latter under the rule of People v. Ireland (1969) 70 Cal. 2d 522, 538-540. We agree.

Our opinions have repeatedly emphasized that felony murder, although the law of this state, is a disfavored doctrine. . . . because 'in almost all cases in which it is applied it is unnecessary' and 'it erodes the relation between criminal liability and moral culpability.'" In accord with this policy, we restricted the scope of the felony-murder rule in *Ireland* by holding it inapplicable to felonies that are an integral part of and included in fact within the homicide. In that case the defendant and his wife were experiencing serious marital difficulties which eventually culminated in defendant's drawing a gun and killing his wife. The jury was instructed that it could find the defendant guilty of second degree felony murder if it determined that the homicide occurred during the commission of the underlying felony of assault with a deadly weapon. Like all felony-murder instructions, this instruction had the "effect of 'reliev[ing] the jury of the necessity of finding one of the elements of the crime of murder' to wit, malice aforethought." (People v. Ireland, supra, 70 Cal. 2d at p. 538.) We reasoned that "the utilization of the felony-murder rule in circumstances such as those before us extends the operation of that rule 'beyond any rational function that it is designed to serve.' To allow such use of the felony-murder rule would effectively preclude the jury from considering the issue of malice aforethought in all cases wherein homicide has been committed as a result of a felonious assault — a category which includes the great majority of all homicides. This kind of bootstrapping finds support neither in logic nor in law. We therefore hold that *a second degree felony-murder instruction may not properly be given when it is based upon a felony which is an integral part of the homicide and which the evidence produced by the prosecution shows to be an offense included in fact within the offense charged.*" (Italics added.)

Very soon after *Ireland* we again had occasion to consider the question of merger in People v. Wilson (1969) 1 Cal. 3d 431. There the defendant forcibly entered his estranged wife's apartment carrying a shotgun. Once inside the apartment, he fatally shot a man in the living room and proceeded to break into the bathroom where he killed his wife. The jury was instructed on second degree felony murder based on the underlying felony of assault with a deadly weapon, and convicted the defendant of second degree murder of the man. We determined that the predicate felony was a "necessary ingredient of the homicide" and reversed under *Ireland,* which explicitly prohibited use of the felony-murder rule in such circumstances.

The defendant was also convicted of the first degree murder of his wife, and we reversed that conviction on similar grounds. The jury was instructed on first degree murder on the theory that the homicide was committed in the course of a burglary because the defendant had entered the premises with intent to commit a felony, i.e., assault with a deadly weapon.[a] We held that the felony-murder rule cannot apply to burglary-murder cases in which "the entry would be nonfelonious but for the intent to commit the assault, and the assault is an integral part of the homicide and is included in fact in the offense charged. . . ." We reasoned that "Where a person enters a building with an intent to assault his vic-

a. *Wilson* involved two separate entries, one into the apartment through the front door and one into the bathroom. However, the crucial entry, for purposes of the first degree felony-murder instruction, was the defendant's entry into the bathroom for the purpose of inflicting violent injury upon his wife. Section 459 of the Cal. Penal Code provides that "Every person who enters any house, room, apartment [and other defined structures] . . . with intent to commit . . . any felony is guilty of burglary." — Eds.

tim with a deadly weapon, he is not deterred by the felony-murder rule. That doctrine can serve its purpose only when applied to a felony independent of the homicide." We concluded that an instruction telling the jury that "the intent to assault makes the entry burglary and that the burglary raises the homicide resulting from the assault to first degree murder without proof of malice aforethought and premeditation" used the same bootstrap reasoning we condemned in *Ireland*. . . .

Cases in which the second degree felony-murder doctrine has withstood an *Ireland* attack include those in which the underlying felony was furnishing narcotics; driving under the influence of narcotics; poisoning food, drink or medicine (People v. Mattison (1971) 4 Cal. 3d 177); armed robbery (People v. Burton (1971) 6 Cal. 3d 375); kidnapping; and finally, felony child abuse by malnutrition and dehydration (§273a, subd. (1); People v. Shockley (1978) 79 Cal. App. 3d 669). . . .

In People v. Burton, supra, we refined the *Ireland* rule. [In *Burton* the defendant was charged with felony-murder on the basis of a killing in the course of an armed robbery. He argued that the armed robbery was not independent of the homicide, within the meaning of *Ireland*. Because robbery is defined as the felonious taking of property "accomplished by force or fear" (Penal Code §211), the defendant noted that robbery necessarily includes an assault and that armed robbery necessarily includes an assault with a deadly weapon. Thus, he claimed, armed robbery met the *Ireland* test, in that the underlying offense was "an integral part of the homicide and . . . an offense included in fact within the [homicide] charged." The *Burton* court rejected this reasoning and held that armed robbery was sufficiently independent to support a felony-murder conviction.]

[We held in *Burton* that even] if the felony was included within the facts of the homicide and was integral thereto, a further inquiry is required to determine if the homicide resulted "from conduct for an independent felonious purpose" as opposed to a "single course of conduct with a single purpose." In cases like *Ireland*, the "purpose of the conduct was the very assault which resulted in death"; on the other hand, "in the case of armed robbery, as well as the other felonies enumerated in section 189 of the Penal Code, there is an independent felonious purpose, namely in the case of robbery to acquire money or property belonging to another."[b]

Our task is to apply the foregoing rules to the offense at issue here — felony child abuse defined by section 273a, subdivision (1).[4] We recognize that a violation of its terms can occur in a wide variety of situations: the definition broadly

b. In *Burton*, the court elaborated as follows (6 Cal. 3d at 387): "[T]here is a very significant difference between deaths resulting from assaults with a deadly weapon, when the purpose of the conduct was the very assault which resulted in death, and deaths resulting from conduct for an independent felonious purpose, such as robbery or rape, which happened to be accomplished by a deadly weapon and technically includes assault with a deadly weapon. Our inquiry cannot stop with the fact that death resulted from the use of a deadly weapon and, therefore, technically included an assault with a deadly weapon, but must extend to an investigation of the purpose of the conduct." — Eds.

4. Section 273a, subdivision (1), provided: "Any person who, under circumstances or conditions likely to produce great bodily harm or death, willfully causes or permits any child to suffer, or inflicts thereon unjustifiable physical pain or mental suffering, . . . is punishable by imprisonment in the county jail not exceeding 1 year, or in the state prison for not less than 1 year nor more than 10."

includes both active and passive conduct, i.e., child abuse by direct assault and child endangering by extreme neglect. Two threshold considerations, however, govern all types of conduct prohibited by this law: first, the conduct must be willful; second, it must be committed "under circumstances or conditions likely to produce great bodily harm or death." Absent either of these elements, there can be no violation of the statute.

The language of *Ireland, Wilson* and *Burton* bars the application of the felony-murder rule "where the purpose of the conduct was the very assault which resulted in death." In cases in which the violation of section 273a, subdivision (1), is a direct assault on a child that results in death (i.e., causing or permitting a child to suffer or inflicting thereon unjustifiable physical pain), it is plain that the purpose of the child abuse was the "very assault which resulted in death." It would be wholly illogical to allow this kind of assaultive child abuse to be bootstrapped into felony murder merely because the victim was a child rather than an adult, as in *Ireland*.

In the present case the homicide was the result of child abuse of the assaultive variety. Thus, the underlying felony was unquestionably an "integral part of" and "included in fact" in the homicide within the meaning of *Ireland*. . . . Accordingly, despite our deep abhorrence of the crime of child abuse, we see no escape from our duty to apply the merger doctrine we carefully enunciated in *Ireland* and its progeny. . . .

The People argue that the present case is controlled by People v. Shockley, supra, but that decision is distinguishable on its facts. In *Shockley*, the death followed from malnutrition and dehydration; by contrast, the cause of death here was unquestionably a severe beating. The *Shockley* court envisaged this very distinction when it stated that "Where the underlying felony is based on an independent felony *not related to the assault causing the murder*, a different result follows." (Italics added.) Here the death of the child was directly caused by an assault that in turn was the basis of the charge of felony child abuse; on these facts, *Ireland* compels application of the merger rule.[7]

It was therefore error to give a felony-murder instruction in this case. [Reversed.]

NOTES AND QUESTIONS

1. *Burglary and merger.* Many courts have followed New York in holding, unlike California, that burglary based on an intent to assault will support a felony-murder conviction (usually first-degree murder), even though a similar assault will not support a felony-murder charge in the absence of an entry into a building or room. People v. Miller, 297 N.E.2d 85 (N.Y. 1973); United States v. Loonsfoot, 950 F.2d 116 (6th Cir. 1990); Smith v. State, 499 So.2d 750 (Miss. 1986). Does the distinction have merit? Why should the punishment be so much greater

7. Because of this factual distinction we need not address the question whether the merger doctrine applies when the defendant is guilty of felony child abuse of the nonassaultive variety, e.g., by extreme neglect — as in *Shockley* — or by failure to intervene when a child in his care or custody is placed in a life-endangering situation.

when the assault is indoors rather than outdoors? The New York court explained its holding in the *Miller* case as follows (297 N.E.2d at 87-88):

> Where, as here, the criminal act underlying the burglary is an assault with a dangerous weapon, the likelihood that the assault will culminate in a homicide is significantly increased by the situs of the assault. When the assault takes place within the domicile, the victim may be more likely to resist the assault; the victim is also less likely to be able to avoid the consequences of the assault, since his paths of retreat and escape may be barred or severely restricted by furniture, walls and other obstructions incidental to buildings. Further, it is also more likely that when the assault occurs in the victim's domicile, there will be present family or close friends who will come to the victim's aid and be killed.

Questions: Do these considerations persuade you that indoor assaults are more likely to result in deaths than outdoor assaults? Even if that is so, why should differences in dangerousness be the basis for determining when the merger doctrine applies? Is an outdoor robbery (which clearly does trigger the felony-murder rule in nearly all jurisdictions) more dangerous than an outdoor assault with intent to kill (which clearly does not)?

2. The unraveling of the doctrine in California. In People v. Hansen, 9 Cal. 4th 300, 885 P.2d 1022 (1994), the California Supreme Court took still another turn in its treatment of the merger doctrine. In this case, defendant gave Echaves money to buy methamphetamine for him. When Echaves did not return with the drugs, defendant obtained a gun in order either to get back his money or beat up Echaves. He then drove past Echaves' apartment, firing repeatedly into the building. A 13-year-old child living in Echaves' apartment was killed by the shots. Defendant was convicted of second-degree felony murder on the basis of the felony of discharge of a firearm at an inhabited building (Cal. Penal Code §246). After concluding that the felony was inherently dangerous to human life, the Court addressed the defendant's contention that the felony merged with the resulting homicide and could not therefore serve as the predicate for a felony murder charge.

The court rejected the *Ireland* "integral part of the homicide test" because it would preclude the felony-murder rule for those felonies most likely to result in death. It also rejected the "independent purpose" of *Burton* because under it, "a felon who acts with a purpose other than specifically to inflict injury upon someone — for example, with the intent to sell narcotics for financial gain, or to discharge a firearm at a building solely to intimidate the occupants — is subject to greater criminal liability for an act resulting in death than a person who actually intends to injure the person of the victim."[a] Instead the court preferred an ad hoc approach, which would allow all inherently dangerous felonies to serve as a predicate for felony — murder so long as doing so would "not elevate all felonious assaults to murder or otherwise subvert the legislative intent." The court concluded (315):

> Most homicides do not result from violations of section 246, and thus, unlike the situation in People v. Ireland, application of the felony-murder doctrine in the present context will not have the effect of "preclud[ing] the jury from consider-

a. Other jurisdictions continue to follow the independent purpose test. See, e.g., People v. Morgan, 718 N.E.2d 206 (Ill. App. Ct. 1999), *appeal pending*, 724 N.E.2d 1273 (Sup. Ct. Ill. 2000).

ing the issue of malice aforethought . . . [in] the great majority of all homicides." Similarly, application of the felony-murder doctrine in the case before us would not frustrate the Legislature's deliberate calibration of punishment for assaultive conduct resulting in death, based upon the presence or absence of malice aforethought. . . . Indeed, . . . application of the felony-murder rule, when a violation of section 246 results in the death of a person, clearly is consistent with the traditionally recognized purpose of the second degree felony-murder doctrine — namely the deterrence of negligent or accidental killings that occur in the course of the commission of dangerous felonies.

Question: What is left of the merger doctrine in California? Why has the court experienced such difficulty in dealing with the merger problem? Assuming a felony-murder rule, is there a rational line that can be drawn between dangerous felonies that may and may not serve as the predicate felony for the felony murder doctrine? Does the *Hansen* case draw such a line?

d. Killings Not "in Furtherance" of the Felony

STATE v. CANOLA

Supreme Court of New Jersey
73 N.J. 206, 374 A.2d 20 (1977)

CONFORD, J. Defendant, along with three confederates, was in the process of robbing a store when a victim of the robbery, attempting to resist the perpetration of the crime, fatally shot one of the co-felons. The sole issue for our resolution is whether, under N.J.S.A. 2A:113-1, defendant may be held liable for felony murder. . . .

The facts of this case . . . may be summarized as follows. The owner of a jewelry store and his employee, in an attempt to resist an armed robbery, engaged in a physical skirmish with one of the four robbers. A second conspirator, called upon for assistance, began shooting, and the store owner returned the gunfire. Both the owner and the felon, one Lloredo, were fatally shot in the exchange, the latter by the firearm of the owner.

Defendant and two others were indicted on two counts of murder, one count of robbery and one count of having been armed during the robbery. The murder counts were based on the deaths, respectively, of the robbery victim and the co-felon. After trial on the murder counts defendant was found guilty on both and was sentenced to concurrent terms of life imprisonment. The Appellate Division unanimously affirmed the conviction for the murder of the robbery victim, [and] . . . upheld the trial court's denial of a motion to dismiss the count addressed to the homicide of the co-felon. [We granted a petition for certification addressed to this count.]

Conventional formulations of the felony murder rule would not seem to encompass liability in this case. [T]he early formulations of the felony murder rule by such authorities as Lord Coke, Foster and Blackstone and of later ones by Judge Stephen and Justice Holmes . . . were concerned solely with situations where the felon or a confederate did the actual killing. [T]he English courts never applied the felony murder rule to hold a felon guilty of the death of his co-felon at the hands of the intended victim. . . .

It is clearly the majority view throughout the country that, at least in theory, the doctrine of felony murder does not extend to a killing, although growing out of the commission of the felony, if directly attributable to the act of one other than the defendant or those associated with him in the unlawful enterprise. . . . This rule is sometimes rationalized on the "agency" theory of felony murder.[2] [The] contrary view, . . . would attach liability under the felony murder rule for *any* death proximately resulting from the unlawful activity — even the death of a co-felon — notwithstanding the killing was by one resisting the crime. . . .

At one time the proximate cause theory was espoused by the Pennsylvania Supreme Court. . . . Commonwealth v. Almeida, 362 Pa. 596, 68 A.2d 595 (1949). The reasoning of the *Almeida* decision, involving the killing of a policeman shot by other police attempting to apprehend robbers, was distinctly circumvented when the question later arose whether it should be applied to an effort to inculpate a defendant for the killing of his co-felon at the hands of the victim of the crime. Commonwealth v. Redline, 391 Pa. 486, 137 A.2d 472 (1958). The court there held against liability. Examining the common-law authorities relied upon by the *Almeida* majority, the *Redline* court concluded: "As already indicated, *Almeida* was, itself, an extension of the felony-murder doctrine by judicial decision and is not to be extended in its application beyond facts such as those to which it was applied." The court then held that "in order to convict for felony-murder, *the killing must have been done by the defendant or by an accomplice or confederate or by one acting in furtherance of the felonious undertaking.*" The court refused, however, actually to overrule the *Almeida* decision, thereby creating a distinction . . . between the situation in which the victim was an innocent party and the killing therefore merely "excusable" and that in which the deceased was a felon and the killing thus "justifiable." Twelve years later the Pennsylvania court did overrule *Almeida* in a case involving Almeida's companion, Smith. (Commonwealth ex rel. Smith v. Myers, 438 Pa. 218, 261 A.2d 550 (1970).) The court noted, inter alia, the harsh criticism leveled against the common-law felony rule, its doubtful deterrent effect, the failure of the cases cited in *Almeida* to support the conclusions reached therein, the inappropriateness of tort proximate-cause principles to homicide prosecution, and the "will-of-the-wisp" distinction drawn by the *Almeida* court between justifiable and excusable homicides. . . .

The course of the decisions in Michigan illustrates the influence of the Pennsylvania cases in the development of the felony murder rule in other jurisdictions. In People v. Podolski, 332 Mich. 508, 52 N.W.2d 201 (1952), the bullet killing the deceased officer came from the revolver of a fellow officer attempting to stop defendant's armed robbery of a bank. In affirming the murder conviction, the court adopted both the language and reasoning of the Pennsylvania court . . . , to the effect that if a robber sets in motion a chain of events which should have been within his contemplation, he is liable for any death which results.

After the Pennsylvania court changed course in *Redline,* supra, the Michigan court followed suit in People v. Austin, 370 Mich. 12, 129 N.W.2d 766 (1963), where defendants' indictments for the slaying of their accomplice by the robbery victim were quashed. Relying heavily on Pennsylvania's curtailment of the

2. The classic statement of the theory is found in an early case applying it in a context pertinent to the case at bar, Commonwealth v. Campbell, 89 Mass. (7 Allen) 541, 544 (Sup. Jud. Ct. 1863), as follows: "No person can be held guilty of homicide unless the act is either actually or constructively his, and it cannot be his act in either sense unless committed by his own hand or by someone acting in concert with him or in furtherance of a common object or purpose."

expansion of the felony murder rule, the court, while not overruling *Podolski,* nonetheless refused to extend liability to instances where the deceased was a co-felon. . . .

To be distinguished from the situation before us here, and from the generality of the cases discussed above, are the so-called "shield" cases. The first of these were the companion cases of Taylor v. State, 55 S.W. 961 (Tex. Cr. App. 1900), and Keaton v. State, 57 S.W. 1125 (Tex. Cr. App. 1900). In attempting to escape after robbing a train, defendants thrust the brakeman in front of them as a shield, as a result of which he was fatally shot by law officers. The court had no difficulty in finding defendants guilty of murder. The court in *Taylor* noted the correctness of the *Campbell* case doctrine that a person could not be held liable for homicide unless the act is either actually or constructively committed by him, but indicated it was inapplicable to a case where defendants forced deceased to occupy a place of danger in order that they might carry out the crime. In *Keaton,* the court said defendant would be responsible for the "reasonable, natural and probable result of his act" of placing deceased in danger of his life. The conduct of the defendants in cases such as these is said to reflect "express malice," justifying a murder conviction.

This review of the development in this country of the felony murder rule in relation to culpability for lethal acts of non-felons shows that, despite its early limitation to deadly acts of the felons themselves or their accomplices, the rule has undergone several transformations and can no longer be stated in terms of universal application. . . .

Reverting to our immediate task here, it is to determine whether our own statute necessarily mandates the proximate cause concept of felony murder, as thought by the Appellate Division majority. . . . [T]he view of the Appellate Division was that the "ensues clause" of N.J.S.A. 2A:113-1[a] must be deemed to have expanded the culpability of the felon to killings by others not confederated with him, if proximately related to the felonious enterprise, else the clause would be meaningless surplusage in the act. . . .

[A]ssuming the statute is facially susceptible to the interpretation here advocated by the State, it is appropriate to consider the public policy implications of the proposed doctrine as an extension of prior assumptions in this State as to the proper limitations of the felony murder rule.

Most modern progressive thought in criminal jurisprudence favors restriction rather than expansion of the felony murder rule. . . . It has frequently been observed that although the rule was logical at its inception, when all felonies were punishable by death, its survival to modern times when other felonies are not thought to be as blameworthy as premeditated killings is discordant with rational and enlightened views of criminal culpability and liability. . . .

In view of all of the foregoing, it appears to us regressive to extend the application of the felony murder rule beyond its classic common-law limitation to acts by the felon and his accomplices, to lethal acts of third persons not in fur-

a. That statute, the felony-murder provision in effect at the time of the *Canola* decision, provided as follows: "If any person, in committing or attempting to commit arson, burglary, kidnapping, rape, robbery, sodomy or any unlawful act against the peace of this state, of which the probable consequences may be bloodshed, kills another, *or if the death of anyone ensues from the committing or attempting to commit any such crime or act; . . . then such person so killing is guilty of murder.*" (Emphasis added.) — Eds.

therance of the felonious scheme. The language of the statute does not compel it, and, as indicated above, is entirely compatible with the traditional limitations of the rule. Tort concepts of foreseeability and proximate cause have shallow relevance to culpability for murder in the first degree. Gradations of criminal liability should accord with [the] degree of moral culpability for the actor's conduct. . . .

The judgment of the Appellate Division is modified so as to strike the conviction and sentencing of defendant for murder of the co-felon Lloredo.

SULLIVAN, J. (concurring in result only). The practical result of the majority holding is that even though some innocent person or a police officer be killed during the commission of an armed robbery, the felon would bear no criminal responsibility of any kind for that killing as long as it was not at the hand of the felon or a confederate. The legislative intent, as I see it, is otherwise.

The thrust of our felony murder statute, N.J.S.A. 2A:113-1, is to hold the criminal liable for any killing which ensues during the commission of a felony, even though the felon, or a confederate, did not commit the actual killing. The only exception I would recognize would be the death of a co-felon, which could be classified as a justifiable homicide and not within the purview of the statute. . . .

NOTES

As *Canola* indicates, courts have often drawn distinctions that depend on who does the killing and who is killed. Consider to what extent liability for felony-murder does and should depend on the identity of the actual killer or victim.

1. Who does the killing? Under the agency theory, the identity of the actual killer becomes a central issue; only if the act of killing is done by a co-felon or someone acting in concert with a co-felon will the felony-murder rule be applicable. Thus, when the act of killing is committed by a police officer or bystander, the felony-murder rule is not applicable. Under the proximate-cause theory, in contrast, the central issue is whether the killing, no matter by whose hand, is within the foreseeable risk of the commission of the felony.

For a while, the agency theory was favored,[6] but more recently an increasing number of states have adopted the proximate cause theory.[7] Complicating the picture are statutory revisions that use language that arguably introduces proximate-cause concepts. For example, New York law (Penal Law §125.25, page 394 supra) provides that a person is guilty of murder if, "in the course of and in furtherance of [designated felonies,] he, or another participant . . . causes the death of a person other than one of the participants." Several other states follow the New York model. See, e.g., Conn. Gen. Stat. §53A-54(c); Or. Rev. Stat. §163.115.

Questions: Does the New York statute's "in furtherance" requirement imply adoption of the agency approach, or does its "he . . . causes" language require

6. See State v. Branson, 487 N.W.2d 880 (Minn. 1992); State v. Bonner, 330 N.C. 536, 411 S.E.2d 598 (1992); State v. Hoang, 243 Kan. 40, 755 P.2d 7 (1988); Annot., 89 A.L.R.4th 683 (1991).

7. See People v. Dekens, 695 N.E.2d 474 (Ill. 1998); Palmer v. State, 704 N.E.2d 124 (Ind. 1999). A survey of these aspects of felony-murder law in all the states may be found in the appendix to Michelle S. Simon, Whose Crime Is it Anyway?: Liability for the Lethal Acts of Nonparticipants in the Felony, 72 Univ. Det. Mercy L. Rev. 223, 260 (1994).

adoption of the proximate-cause theory? The New York Court of Appeals chose the latter interpretation and upheld a felony-murder conviction where a policeman was fatally shot by a fellow officer in the course of a gun battle with several armed robbers. See People v. Hernandez, 82 N.Y. 309, 624 N.E.2d 661 (1993). Do you agree with that reading of the statute?

The Wisconsin statute is among the broadest; it imposes felony-murder liability upon any person who "causes the death of another human being while committing or attempting to commit [designated felonies]." Wis. Stat. §940.03. In State v. Oimen, 516 N.W.2d 399 (Wis. 1994), a robbery victim had fired upon his assailants and killed one of them. The Wisconsin Supreme Court held that the surviving felon could be convicted of felony murder. The court interpreted the statute as rejecting any limitation based on the identity of either the person shooting or the person killed.

In New Jersey, the legislature responded to *Canola* by adopting a new statute modeled closely on that of New York. Under N.J. Stat. §2C:11-3a(3), a person is now guilty of murder whenever he commits or attempts to commit a designated felony, and "in the course of and in furtherance of [the crime] . . . *any person causes* the death of any person other than one of the participants" (emphasis added). The New Jersey statute, like that of New York, affords an affirmative defense for felons who can show that they had no reason to anticipate the use of deadly force. N.J. Stat. §2C:11-3a(3)(a)-(d). The New Jersey Supreme Court held that this statute was intended to adopt the position that Justice Sullivan had advanced, concurring in *Canola:* a proximate-cause approach, coupled with an exception precluding liability when the victim is a cofelon. See State v. Martin, 119 N.J. 2, 573 A.2d 1359 (1990). Thus, although the *Canola* decision remains influential in guiding judicial interpretation of the felony-murder rule outside New Jersey, the decision has been superseded by legislation in its home state.

What accounts for the tendency of some legislatures to expand the felony-murder rule by adopting the proximate-cause approach? Consider People v. Hernandez, supra, 624 N.E.2d at 665-666:

> [W]e believe New York's . . . proximate cause theory to be consistent with fundamental principles of criminal law. Advocates of the agency theory suggest that no culpable party has the requisite mens rea when a nonparticipant is the shooter. We disagree. The basic tenet of felony murder liability is that the mens rea of the underlying felony is imputed to the participant responsible for the killing. . . . Whether the death is an immediate result or an attenuated one, the necessary mens rea is present if the causal act is part of the felonious conduct.
>
> No more persuasive is the argument that the proximate cause view will extend criminal liability unreasonably. First, New York law is clear that felony murder does not embrace any killing that is coincidental with the felony but instead is limited to those deaths caused by one of the felons in furtherance of their crime. More than civil tort liability must be established; criminal liability will adhere only when the felons' acts are a sufficiently direct cause of the death.
>
> When the intervening acts of another party are supervening or unforeseeable, the necessary causal chain is broken, and there is no liability for the felons. . . . Second, the New York felony murder statute spells out the affirmative defense available to the accomplice who does not cause the death. . . .
>
> In short, our established common-law rules governing determinations of causality and the availability of the statutory defense provide adequate boundaries to felony murder liability.

2. Killings not in furtherance of the felony. We have been considering killings committed by persons other than the felons. If one of the felons commits the killing, does it always follow that the other felons are guilty of felony murder? In United States v. Heinlein, 490 F.2d 725 (D.C. Cir. 1973), three defendants participated in a rape. In defending herself, the woman slapped Heinlein, who, enraged at the blow, stabbed and killed her. On these facts Heinlein could, of course, be held for felony murder. But what of the other two? Is it enough that Heinlein killed in the course of a felony they were helping him commit? Or is the killing by Heinlein outside their common purpose, unplanned and unexpected by them, and therefore not attributable to them? Insofar as a jurisdiction adopts an agency theory in dealing with the liability of a felon for killings committed by another, as the court did in *Canola,* it would appear that the unanticipated actions of a felon not in furtherance of the common purpose could no more be attributed to other felons than the actions of a policeman or victim could be attributed to them. The court so held in the *Heinlein* case.

Consider the following problems in applying the "in furtherance" requirement when one of the felons is the actual killer.

(a) In People v. Cabaltero, 31 Cal. App. 2d 52, 87 P.2d 364 (1939), a look-out during a robbery panicked at the approach of a car and fired shots at the occupants. The leader of the group, angered by his cofelon's stupidity, shot and killed him. The leader could, of course, be convicted of first-degree murder. Could the other members of the group be convicted of murder as well?

(b) Police officers enter a house to arrest marijuana dealers making a sale. After the principals are arrested, a police officer searching the house is shot and killed by a cofelon attempting to evade arrest. Are the dealers who had already been arrested responsible for the killing on a felony-murder theory, or are they relieved of liability on the ground that the arrest terminated their participation? In State v. Amaro, 436 So. 2d 1056 (Fla. App. 1983), the court upheld the convictions, finding that the cofelon's act was foreseeable and in furtherance of the common design. What should be the result if some of the felons had been taken to jail before the shooting took place?

3. Who is killed? The *Canola* case discusses a number of decisions that exclude the death of one of the felons as a basis for felony murder regardless of who actually does the killing. A number of recent statutes specifically exclude killings of participants in the felony. E.g., Alaska Stat. §11.41.110; Colo. Rev. Stat. §18-3-101; N.J. Stat. Ann. §2C:11-3. What is the appeal of this distinction?

(a) Agency and proximate cause theories. Under the proximate cause theory, it would seem logical to hold a surviving felon liable no matter whose death, the co-felon's or an innocent person's, was proximately caused by the felony. See Palmer v. State, 704 N.E.2d 124 (Ind. 1999); People v. Dekens, 695 N.E.2d 474 (Ill. 1998). But what should be the result under the agency theory? It is essential that one of the felons do the killing, but as long as that requirement is met and the killing is committed in furtherance of the felony, why does it matter who the victim is? A case in which a felon kills another felon in furtherance of the felony is readily conceivable. Suppose, for example, that one robber accidentally shoots and kills a co-felon while firing at a policeman. Does the act of shooting cease to be "in furtherance of the felony" when we discover whom the bullet strikes?

(b) Justifiable homicide? Suppose the felon is killed by a policeman. Is that a reason for not applying the felony murder rule to the surviving felon? The following argument was advanced in the *Redline* case, discussed in *Canola:*

> The victim of the homicide was one of the robbers who, while resisting apprehension in his effort to escape was shot and killed by a policeman in the performance of his duty. Thus, the homicide was justifiable and, obviously, could not be availed of, on any rational legal theory, to support a charge of murder. How can anyone, no matter how much of an outlaw he may be, have a criminal charge lodged against him for the consequences of the lawful conduct of another person?

How cogent is the reasoning? Suppose two felons are holed up in a house and engaged in a gun battle with police officers surrounding the house. Felon *A* tells felon *B* to run out the back door where, he says, the coast is clear. He says this because he wants felon *B* dead and he knows that the police have the back door well covered. As felon *B* dashes out, gun in hand, he is shot dead by police. Is it self-evident that felon *A* is not criminally liable for the police officer's killing of felon *B?*

(c) Protecting the innocent? Another argument for the exemption of the death of felons was stated as follows in State v. Williams, 254 So. 2d 548, 550-551 (Fla. Dist. App. 1971):

> [T]he statute is primarily designed to protect the *innocent public;* and it would be incongruous to reach a conclusion having the effect of placing the perpetrators themselves beneath its mantle. . . . This does not mean to say however, that co-conspirators acting in furtherance of their conspiracy . . . can kill or murder each other with impunity. . . . Certainly, one conspirator may be guilty of the murder of a co-conspirator if the facts support premeditated murder or a lesser degree of unlawful homicide. But this is quite apart from the felony-murder concept with which we are here concerned.

Compare United States v. Martinez, 16 F.3d 202 (7th Cir. 1994). In this case, Martinez, along with Mahn and Mares, planned to bomb several of Chicago's adult bookstores whose owners had refused to pay them "protection" money. Mares built six pipe bombs that could be detonated by remote-control electronic devices. He and Mahn then drove through downtown Chicago, placed one of the bombs and headed for a second destination along one of Chicago's main streets, "traversing an area dense with electro-magnetic signals" (id. at 208). One of their bombs exploded, killing Mares. The court held that Martinez and Mahn could be sentenced for felony murder, on the basis of the death of their co-felon. Judge Posner wrote for the Court (16 F.3d at 207):

> The lives of criminals are not completely worthless, so their deaths should not be considered nonevents for sentencing purposes. [W]e add that liability for felony murder in a case such as the present serves the practical function of deterring felons from using lethal weaponry, more broadly from committing the kind of felony in which someone is likely to be shot or run down or otherwise injured (and hence possibly killed), by punishing them severely should death result — to anyone.

TAYLOR v. SUPERIOR COURT

Supreme Court of California
3 Cal. 3d 578, 477 P.2d 131 (1970)

BURKE, J. Petitioner and his codefendant Daniels were charged by information with the murder of John H. Smith, robbery, assault with a deadly weapon against Linda West, and assault with a deadly weapon against Jack West. The superior court denied petitioner's motion to set aside the information as to the murder count, and we issued an alternative writ of prohibition.

At the preliminary hearing, the following facts were adduced regarding the murder count: On the evening of January 12, 1969, two men attempted to rob Jax Liquor Store which was operated by Mrs. Linda Lee West and her husband Jack. Mrs. West testified that James Daniels entered the store first and asked Mr. West, who was behind the counter, for a package of cigarettes. While Mr. West was getting the cigarettes, John Smith entered the store and approached the counter. Mrs. West, who was on a ladder at the time the two men entered the store, then heard her husband say something about money. Turning her attention to the counter, she heard Daniels repeatedly saying, "Put the money in the bag," and observed her husband complying with the order.

While Mr. West was putting the money from the register in the bag, Daniels repeatedly referred to the fact that he and Smith were armed. According to Mrs. West, Daniels "chattered insanely" during this time, telling Mr. West "Put the money in the bag. Put the money in the bag. Put the money in the bag. Don't move or I'll blow your head off. He's got a gun. He's got a gun. Don't move or we'll have an execution right here. Get down on the floor. I said on your stomach, on your stomach." Throughout this period, Smith's gun was pointed at Mr. West. Mrs. West testified that Smith looked "intent" and "apprehensive" as if "waiting for something big to happen." She indicated that Smith's apparent apprehension and nervousness was manifested by the way he was staring at Mr. West.

While Daniels was forcing Mr. West to the floor, Mrs. West drew a pistol from under her clothing and fired at Smith, who was standing closest to her. Smith was struck on the right side of the chest. Mrs. West fired four more shots in rapid succession, and observed "sparks" coming from Smith's gun, which was pointed in her direction. A bullet hole was subsequently discovered in the wall behind the place Mrs. West had been standing, approximately eight or nine feet above the floor. During this period, Mr. West had seized a pistol and fired two shots at Smith. Mrs. West's last shot was fired at Daniels as he was going out of the door. He "lurched violently and almost went down, [but] picked himself up and kept going." Smith died as the result of multiple gunshot wounds.

The evidence at the preliminary examination indicated that petitioner [Taylor] was waiting outside the liquor store in a getaway car. He was apprehended later and connected with the crime through bills in his possession and through the automobile which was seen by a witness leaving the scene of the robbery.

Under Penal Code section 995, an information must be set aside if the defendant has been committed without "reasonable or probable cause." Of course, the probable cause test is not identical with the test which controls a jury in a murder case. The jury must be convinced to a moral certainty and beyond a reasonable doubt of the existence of . . . every essential element of that crime. But a magistrate conducting a preliminary examination must be convinced of only such a state of facts as would lead a man of ordinary caution or prudence to believe, and conscientiously entertain a strong suspicion of the guilt of the accused. . . .

Petitioner correctly contends that he cannot be convicted under the felony-murder doctrine, since

> When a killing is not committed by a robber or his accomplice but by his victim, malice aforethought is not attributable to the robber, for the killing is not committed

> by him in the perpetration or attempt to perpetrate robbery. [It is not enough that the killing was a risk reasonably to be foreseen and that the robbery might therefore be regarded as a proximate cause of the killing. Section 189 requires that the felon or his accomplice commit the killing, for if he does not, the killing is not committed to perpetrate the felony. Indeed, in the present case the killing was committed to thwart a felony.]

People v. Washington, 62 Cal. 2d 777, 781, 402 P.2d 130, 133 (1965) [where the victim of an armed robbery shot and killed the defendant's cofelon]. However, apart from the felony-murder doctrine, petitioner could be found guilty of murder on a theory of vicarious liability.

As stated in People v. Gilbert, 63 Cal. 2d 690, 704, 408 P.2d 365, 373,

> When the defendant or his accomplice, with a conscious disregard for life, intentionally commits an act that is likely to cause death, and his victim or a police officer kills in reasonable response to such act, the defendant is guilty of murder. In such a case, the killing is attributable, not merely to the commission of a felony, but to the intentional act of the defendant or his accomplice committed with conscious disregard for life. Thus, the victim's self-defensive killing or the police officer's killing in the performance of his duty cannot be considered an independent intervening cause for which the defendant is not liable, for it is a reasonable response to the dilemma thrust upon the victim or the policeman by the intentional act of the defendant or his accomplice.

Therefore, if petitioner were an accomplice to the robbery, he would be vicariously responsible[1] for any killing attributable to the intentional acts of his associates committed with conscious disregard for life, and likely to result in death. We must determine whether the committing magistrate had any rational ground for believing that Smith's death was attributable to intentional acts of Smith and Daniels meeting those criteria.

Petitioner relies upon the following language in *Washington,* wherein defendant's accomplice merely pointed a gun at the robbery victim who, without further provocation, shot and killed him: "In every robbery there is a possibility that the victim will resist and kill. The robber has little control over such a killing once the robbery is undertaken as this case demonstrates. To impose an additional penalty for the killing would discriminate between robbers, *not on the basis of any difference in their own conduct,* but solely on the basis of the response by others that the robber's conduct happened to induce."

As indicated by the italicized words in the foregoing quotation, the central inquiry in determining criminal liability for a killing committed by a resisting victim or police officer is whether the *conduct* of a defendant or his accomplices was sufficiently provocative of lethal resistance to support a finding of implied malice. If the trier of fact concludes that under the particular circumstances of the instant case Smith's death proximately resulted from acts of petitioner's accomplices done with conscious disregard for human life, the natural consequences

1. "Under the rules defining principals and criminal conspiracies, the defendant may be guilty of murder for a killing attributable to the act of his accomplice. To be so guilty, however, the accomplice must cause the death of another human being by an act committed in furtherance of the common design." (People v. Gilbert, supra.) Petitioner does not dispute that the conduct of his confederates set forth above was in furtherance of the robbery.

of which were dangerous to life, then petitioner may be convicted of first degree murder.[2]

For example, we pointed out in *Washington* that "Defendants who initiate gun battles may also be found guilty of murder if their victims resist and kill. Under such circumstances, 'the defendant for a base, anti-social motive and with wanton disregard for human life, does an act that involves a high degree of probability that it will result in death,' and it is unnecessary to imply malice by invoking the felony-murder doctrine."

Petitioner contends that since neither Daniels nor Smith fired the first shot, they did not "initiate" the gun battle which led to Smith's death. However, depending upon the circumstances, a gun battle can be initiated by acts of provocation falling short of firing the first shot. Thus, in People v. Reed, 270 Cal. App. 2d 37, defendant resisted the officers' commands to "put up your hands," and pointed his gun toward the officers and toward the kidnap-robbery victim. The officers commenced firing, wounding defendant and killing the victim. Although defendant did not fire a single shot, his murder conviction was upheld on the theory that his "aggressive actions" were sufficient evidence of implied malice, and that "under these circumstances it may be said that defendant initiated the gunplay. . . ." . . .

In the instant case, the evidence at the preliminary hearing set forth above discloses acts of provocation on the part of Daniels and Smith from which the trier of fact could infer malice, including Daniels' coercive conduct toward Mr. West and his repeated threats of "execution," and Smith's intent and nervous apprehension as he held Mr. West at gunpoint. The foregoing conduct was sufficiently provocative of lethal resistance to lead a man of ordinary caution and prudence to conclude that Daniels and Smith "initiated" the gun battle, or that such conduct was done with conscious disregard for human life and with natural consequences dangerous to life.[3] Accordingly, we conclude that the evidence supported the magistrate's finding that reasonable and probable cause existed to charge petitioner with first degree murder. . . .

PETERS, J. (dissenting). . . . In *Washington,* two robbers held up a service station. The owner, Carpenter, was in the office totaling up the receipts and disbursements while an employee was depositing the money in a vault in an adjoining room. Upon hearing someone yell "robbery," Carpenter opened his desk and took out a revolver. A few moments later one of the robbers, Ball, entered the office and pointed a revolver at Carpenter. Carpenter fired immediately, mortally wounding Ball. Washington, the accomplice, was convicted of the murder of Ball. We reversed the murder conviction. We held that the felony-murder doc-

2. . . . When murder has been established pursuant to the foregoing principles, Penal Code section 189 may be invoked to determine its degree. (People v. Gilbert, supra.)

3. Petitioner contends that we should ignore evidence regarding Smith's conduct, on the theory that Smith could not have been held responsible for his own death. We rejected a similar contention in *Washington,* stating that "A distinction based on the person killed, however, would make the defendant's criminal liability turn upon the marksmanship of victims and policemen. A rule of law cannot reasonably be based on such a fortuitous circumstance. . . ." Therefore, the trier of fact may find that Smith set into motion, through the intentional commission of acts constituting implied malice and in furtherance of the robbery, a gun battle resulting in his own death. Since petitioner may be held vicariously responsible for *any* killing legally attributable to his accomplices, he may be charged with Smith's death. . . .

trine could not be invoked to convict Washington of murder because the killing was not committed by Washington or his accomplice. . . .

In *Washington* the decedent-accomplice pointed a gun directly at the victim. If this court was of the opinion that a defendant in such a situation could properly be convicted of murder for the killing committed by the victim, it would have so stated and would have held that Washington could be so convicted of murder. Instead, it held that Washington could not be convicted of murder and mentioned only one case where defendants could properly be convicted of murder for a killing committed by the victim: the case where the defendants initiate the gun battle. Therefore, *Washington* stands for the proposition that the act of pointing a gun at the victim, unlike the act of initiating a gun battle, is *not* an act done "with wanton disregard for human life," involving "a high degree of probability that it will result in death" from which malice can be implied. . . .

The majority . . . purport to distinguish [*Washington*] simply by characterizing it as a case "wherein defendant's accomplice *merely* pointed a gun at the robbery victim who, *without further provocation,* shot and killed him." (Italics added.) . . . The majority are making the incredible statement that because the robber in *Washington* did not articulate his obvious threat — because, in the majority's words, he "merely" pointed a gun at the victim — it cannot be said that he committed an act with conscious disregard for life and likely to result in death, whereas if he articulated his threat — as did the robbers in the instant case — his act could be found to have met such criteria.

To me, it is too obvious to dispute that inherent in the brandishing of a gun in a robbery is the conditional threat of the robber that he will use the gun if his demands are not complied with. . . . It is unreasonable to assume that, just because the robber in *Washington* did not articulate his threat, the victim in that case had less reason to fear for his safety or, as the majority assert, less "provocation" for shooting the robber than did the victims in the instant case. It is absurd to suggest that the robber's acts in *Washington* were, as a matter of law, not "sufficiently provocative of lethal resistance to support a finding of implied malice," whereas the robbers' acts in the instant case could be so considered. . . . The difference between an implied and an express threat furnishes no significant basis for discrimination between robbers. . . .

[T]he majority's purported distinction of *Washington* . . . simply demonstrates a desire on the part of the majority to overrule *Washington* sub silento. . . .

NOTES

1. Developments in other jurisdictions. Courts in at least two other states have expressed agreement with the principle adopted in *Taylor* — namely that, apart from the felony-murder rule, the doctrine of malice based on recklessness can be invoked to hold a felon responsible for a killing committed by a victim in response to provocative behavior by one of the felons. See Dowden v. State, 758 S.W.2d 264, 272-273 (Tex. Crim. App. 1988); People v. Guraj, 431 N.Y.S.2d 925 (Sup. Ct. 1980).

Of course, as the *Canola* case indicates, all jurisdictions will hold a felon for murder, under a theory of malice based on recklessness, in a "shield" situation

— that is, where a hostage is shot by someone acting in opposition to the felony. Is there some reason why this result should be less controversial than the result in *Taylor?* On what basis can the two situations be distinguished?

2. *Recklessness of the person killed.* In *Taylor* the finding of recklessness was based on the behavior of cofelons Smith and Daniels. This presented a potential problem because it was Smith himself who was killed, but the court rejected the argument that Taylor should not be held liable for Smith's recklessness in provoking his own death. See footnote 3 of the opinion.

That aspect of the *Taylor* holding was subsequently modified by People v. Antick, 15 Cal. 3d 79, 539 P.2d 43 (1975). Following a residential burglary, during which a variety of household goods was stolen, police observed a moving car, packed with household goods, occupied by a driver and one passenger. Shortly, they came upon the car, parked beside the road. Only the driver, Bose, was in it. As Bose was being frisked, he pulled a gun from his waist and fired at one of the officers, who returned the fire. Bose then broke away and sought to escape, but another officer brought him down with gunfire. Bose died from the wounds. Subsequently, the police uncovered evidence that the defendant was the other man in the car when it was first spotted and that he had participated with Bose in the burglary. Defendant was charged with murder under both the felony-murder and vicarious-liability theories, and the jury convicted. The court ruled that the conviction could not be upheld under either theory. The felony-murder theory was inapplicable inasmuch as the killing was not committed by a felon or a confederate acting in furtherance of the felony. Turning to the vicarious-liability theory, the court said:

> In order to predicate defendant's guilt upon the theory [of vicarious liability], it is necessary to prove that Bose committed a murder, in other words, that he caused the death of another human being and that he acted with malice.
>
> It is well settled that Bose's conduct in initiating a shootout with police officers may establish the requisite malice. . . . However, Bose's malicious conduct did not result in the unlawful killing of *another* human being, but rather in Bose's own death. The only homicide which occurred was the justifiable killing of Bose by the police officer. Defendant's criminal liability certainly cannot be predicated upon the actions of the officer. As Bose could not be found guilty of murder in connection with his own death, it is impossible to base defendant's liability for this offense upon his vicarious responsibility for the crime of his accomplice. . . .
>
> [D]efendant in the instant case may not be held vicariously liable for a crime which his accomplice did not commit.

Question: Suppose a case with identical facts except that the police officer's bullet struck and killed someone other than the confederate who initiated the gun battle — another confederate, say, or a bystander. Presumably, in this event, the defendant could have been held for murder, but would there be any difference in the defendant's culpability?

3. *Problem.* In United States v. Martinez, 16 F.3d 202 (7th Cir. 1994), Martinez, Mahn, and Mares planned to bomb several adult bookstores with bombs built by Mares. While Mahn was driving himself and Mares to one of their targets a bomb exploded, killing Mares. Are Mahn and Martinez guilty of felony-murder? Under *Antick,* is Mares' death a homicide or a suicide?

D. THE DEATH PENALTY

The preceding materials suggest the variety of homicidal behavior and the importance of classifying such behavior in degrees of seriousness, by reference to the dangerousness of the conduct and the moral turpitude of the offender. What penalty should be authorized for the most serious homicidal offenses? Are there situations in which capital punishment is an appropriate or even a necessary response to a criminal offense? In this section we explore the case for and against the death penalty, in terms of principles applicable to criminal punishments generally and in terms of the special requirements of constitutional law flowing from the Eighth Amendment prohibition of "cruel and unusual punishments." Of course, the two perspectives are closely intertwined. We believe it preferable to put constitutional problems to one side, for a moment, and to consider first the factors that might motivate a state legislator or a concerned citizen in supporting or opposing capital punishment as a policy matter.

1. *The Current Context*[8]

In 1977, capital punishment resumed in the United States under the modern death-penalty regime, and by the end of 1998, 500 executions had taken place. The pace of executions, moreover, has accelerated significantly in recent years. There were a total of 11 executions during the first seven years, but 68 inmates were executed in 1998 and in 1999 there were 98 executions, an average of two per week.

At the end of 1998 (the most recent year for which comprehensive data are available), 3,452 prisoners were on death row awaiting execution. Seventy-two of the inmates (2 percent) were age 17 or younger at the time of their arrest; the youngest death-row inmate was 18, and the oldest was 83. Women were a small but growing minority — 48 inmates or 1.4 percent of the total. In terms of race and ethnicity, 55 percent were white, 43 percent were black, and 10 percent (including all races) were of Hispanic origin. Thirty-five percent had no prior felony convictions, and only 9 percent had a prior homicide conviction.

Despite significant recent fluctuations, public support for the death penalty remains high. In a 1994 Gallup Poll, 80 percent of Americans favored capital punishment for murder, and in 1999 the figure was 71 percent.[9] The following year, support for the death penalty dropped to 66 percent in the wake of media attention to innocent men who had been erroneously convicted and sentenced to death[10] (see page 490 infra). Support for the death penalty also declines when people are asked to compare it to a sentence of life imprisonment without pos-

8. Except as otherwise noted, all statistics in this section are drawn from U.S. Dept. of Justice, Bureau of Justice Statistics, Capital Punishment 1998 (December 1999).

9. Mark Gillespie, Public Opinion Supports the Death Penalty, Gallup News Service, Feb. 24, 1999. See also Samuel R. Gross, Update: American Public Opinion on the Death Penalty, 83 Cornell L. Rev. 1448 (1998).

10. N.Y. Times, March 26, 2000, §6, p. 19.

sibility of parole. When people are asked specifically to consider this alternative, only 50-60 percent still prefer the death penalty.[11]

Nationwide figures, moreover, mask substantial state-to-state variation in death-penalty practice. Although opinion polls find almost no significant regional variation in public support for capital punishment,[12] states differ in the extent to which that support is translated into criminal justice policy. Michigan and Wisconsin ban capital punishment, while neighboring Illinois, with broadly similar demographics, permits it and has imposed almost 300 death sentences since 1973. All told, twelve states do not authorize the death penalty under any circumstances,[13] many others almost never impose it in practice, and nine death-penalty states have had no executions in the modern era. In contrast, just five states — Florida, Louisiana, Missouri, Texas, and Virginia — accounted for two-thirds of all executions during the 1977-1998 period, and a single state, Texas, carried out one-third of the executions. The pattern continued in 1999; Texas executed 35 inmates (36 percent of the American total), and Texas and Virginia together accounted for half of all executions.

These variations underscore the controversy that persists even in an era of widespread public support for capital punishment. What factors shape (and should shape) a citizen's views on this fundamental question? And when, in a democracy, is it appropriate for elected officials and criminal justice professionals to support conceptions of appropriate punishment different from those preferred by the public at large?

2. *Policy Considerations*

Suppose that a bill pending in the legislature of your state proposes to abolish the death penalty. Would you support or oppose such a bill? Or would you support it only with certain amendments or exceptions? (Which ones?) What reasons would you advance in support of your position?

In the familiar public debate about capital punishment, principles that traditionally are central to the study of criminal law seldom inform the discussion. In Chapter 2 we examined a variety of materials bearing on the justification for criminal punishments. One concern throughout that chapter was to identify the extent to which punishment serves various utilitarian goals. Another was to consider whether utilitarian benefits are necessary to justify punishment. In other words, is there an *obligation* to punish wrongdoers in proportion to their desert, regardless of the social utility (or disutility) of doing so? These issues, which

11. See Gross, supra at 1455-1457. In the February 2000 survey, 52 percent preferred the death penalty to life without parole. N.Y. Times, March 26, 2000, §6, p. 19. When asked to choose between the death penalty and a sentence of life without parole plus restitution, 44% in a national survey preferred the latter and only 41 percent preferred the death penalty. See Richard C. Dieter, Sentencing for Life: Americans Embrace Alternatives to the Death Penalty, in The Death Penalty in America: Current Controversies 116, 117 (H. Bedau ed., 1997).

12. Gross, supra, at 1451; U.S. Dept. of Justice, Bureau of Justice Statistics, Sourcebook of Criminal Justice Statistics 1996, p. 159 (1997).

13. Likewise, the death penalty is banned throughout Western Europe and in most other industrialized nations. See Hugo A. Bedau, The Status of the Death Penalty Worldwide, in The Death Penalty in America: Current Controversies 344, 345, 78-83 (H. Bedau ed., 1997).

Chapter 2 explores with reference to the justification of punishments in general, can provide a framework for examining the justification of the ultimate punishment. Consider the following materials as they bear on these questions.

a. Deterrence

For many years, debate about the death penalty focused intensely on the question whether the death penalty deters (or — more precisely — whether the death penalty deters more effectively than life imprisonment). More recently, that issue has receded to some extent. Many of those opposed to the death penalty say they would reject it as immoral or unfair even if it were known to deter. Conversely, many proponents of the death penalty consider it a morally appropriate response to certain crimes, whether or not it deters.

Is it justified to set aside the deterrence issue in this way? If the death penalty really does deter, wouldn't it be wrong to forgo the opportunity to use capital punishment and thereby save innocent lives? Conversely, if there is no reason to conclude that the death penalty has a net deterrent effect (and if it actually encourages some murders), wouldn't it be wrong to inflict capital punishment without any prospect of a crime-control benefit?

If the deterrence question ultimately must play some role in judgments about the death penalty, what should we conclude about its actual deterrent effect? Consider the material that follows.

THORSTEN SELLIN, THE DEATH PENALTY

A Report for the Model Penal Code Project of the American Law Institute
21-22, 34, 63 (1959)

It seems reasonable to assume that if the death penalty exercises a deterrent or preventive effect, [m]urders should be less frequent in states that have the death penalty than in those that have abolished it, other factors being equal. [Likewise, m]urders should increase when the death penalty is abolished and should decline when it is restored. . . .

The data examined reveal that [the] *level* of the homicide death rates varies in different groups of states. It is lowest in the New England areas and in the northern states of the middle west and lies somewhat higher in Michigan, Indiana and Ohio. [But w]ithin each group of states having similar social and economic conditions and populations, it is impossible to distinguish the abolition state from the others. . . .

Anyone who carefully examines the above data is bound to arrive at the conclusion that the death penalty, as we use it, exercises no influence on the extent or fluctuating rates of capital crimes. It has failed as a deterrent.

ERNEST VAN DEN HAAG, ON DETERRENCE AND THE DEATH PENALTY, 60 J. Crim. L., Criminology & Pol. Sci. 141, 145-146 (1969): Prof. Sellin seems to think that [the] lack of evidence for deterrence is evidence for the lack of deterrence. It is not. It means that deterrence has not been demonstrated statistically

— not that non-deterrence has been. . . . I doubt that offenders are aware of the absence or presence of the death penalty state by state or period by period. Such unawareness . . . does not argue against the death penalty if by deterrence we mean a preconscious, general response to a severe, but not necessarily specifically and explicitly apprehended, or calculated threat . . . .

I do not argue for a version of deterrence which would require me to believe that an individual shuns murder while in North Dakota, because of the death penalty, and merrily goes to it in South Dakota since it has been abolished there; or that he will start the murderous career from which he had hitherto refrained, after abolition. I hold that the generalized threat of the death penalty may be a deterrent, and the more so, the more generally applied. Deterrence will not cease in the particular areas of abolition or at the particular times of abolition. Rather, general deterrence will be somewhat weakened, through local (partial) abolition. Even such weakening will be hard to detect owing to changes in many offsetting, or reinforcing, factors.

HUGO BEDAU, THE COURTS, THE CONSTITUTION, AND CAPITAL PUNISHMENT 55-57 (1957): Van den Haag has not given any reason why, in the quest for deterrent efficacy, one should fasten (as he does) on the severity of the punishments in question, rather than, as Bentham long ago counseled, on all the relevant factors, notably the facility, celerity, and reliability with which the punishment can be inflicted. Van den Haag cannot hope to convince anyone who has studied the matter that the death penalty and "life" imprisonment differ only in their severity, and that in all other respects affecting deterrent efficacy they are equivalent. . . .

NOTE ON THE EHRLICH STUDY

Whatever the weakness of studies suggesting the absence of a deterrent effect, those who would abolish the death penalty long drew comfort from the fact that no empirical study had ever succeeded in detecting the *presence* of a deterrent effect. The abolitionist position was dealt a significant blow, therefore, when economist Isaac Ehrlich, using complex techniques pioneered in econometric analysis, did find a significant correlation between capital punishment and the deterrence of homicide. See Isaac Ehrlich, The Deterrent Effect of Capital Punishment: A Question of Life and Death, 65 Am. Econ. Rev. 397 (1975). Ehrlich examined the relationship over time between the national homicide rate and the national "execution risk" (actual executions as a percentage of total murder convictions). Controlling for other variables that presumably have an impact on the homicide rate, he found that increases in execution risk were associated with decreases in the homicide rate. His much-publicized conclusion was that for the period 1933 to 1967 each additional execution might have saved eight lives.

Ehrlich's research prompted an enormous outpouring of commentary, most of it critical.[14] The next excerpt discusses some of the more important issues that have been raised.

14. E.g., David C. Baldus & James W. L. Cole, A Comparison of the Work of Thorsten Sellin & Isaac Ehrlich on the Deterrent Effect of Capital Punishment, 85 Yale L.J. 170 (1975); William J. Bowers & Glenn L. Pierce, The Illusion of Deterrence in Isaac Ehrlich's Research on Capital Pun-

RICHARD O. LEMPERT, DETERRENCE AND DESERT: AN ASSESSMENT OF THE MORAL BASES FOR CAPITAL PUNISHMENT, 79 Mich. L. Rev. 1177, 1210-1212, 1222-1224 (1981): In Ehrlich's model, the deterrent effects of the probability of execution given conviction are dwarfed by the deterrent effects of the probability of conviction given arrest. It is commonly thought that the possibility of capital punishment makes it more difficult to convict, and there is evidence that supports this view. If the presence of the death penalty were to reduce the conviction rate for homicide by seventeen percent, Ehrlich's own findings indicate that executing would be counterproductive. My intuition is that the presence of the death penalty would not reduce convictions this far, but it might well reduce them to the point where the tradeoff between executions and lives saved would have vitally different policy implications. . . .

A second difficulty with Ehrlich's study, which he himself recognizes, is its failure to include any measure of the length of prison sentences in general and the probability of life sentences in particular. This is not a mere technical deficiency; it is fundamental. Without some measure of the probability of life sentences, Ehrlich's research does not address the fundamental issue in the debate. That issue is not whether executions deter, but *whether they deter more than prison sentences for life*. . . .

[Third,] replication of Ehrlich's research consistently reveals that when data from the years 1965 through 1969 are eliminated from the analysis the impact of the conditional probability of execution on the homicide rate is no longer statistically significant.

[N]othing about the theory of economic man suggests that people ought to respond to incentives one way during the period 1933-1962 or 1935-1964, and another way during the period 1933-1969 or 1941-1969. Thus, the sensitivity of Ehrlich's results to time destroys the theoretical underpinnings of his approach.

[Professor Lempert then summarizes the results of statistical studies subsequent to Ehrlich's. He concludes:] As it is, the body of econometric research overwhelmingly favors the conclusion that executions do not deter. . . . It may never be possible for social scientists to be certain that the death penalty does not deter homicide, but there is now enough research that fails to reveal deterrence that for purposes of moral argument one must proceed as if the death penalty does not deter. At some point possibilities become so mere that they cannot serve as a moral basis for action.

NOTE

A recent comprehensive review of the empirical literature on deterrence appears in William C. Bailey & Ruth D. Peterson, Murder, Capital Punishment, and Deterrence, in The Death Penalty in America: Current Controversies 135-161 (H. Bedau ed., 1997). Referring to claims that the death penalty deters homicide (because of its severity) and claims that, to the contrary, it encourages homicide (because it brutalizes society), the authors conclude (id. at 153-154):

---

ishment, 85 Yale L.J. 187 (1975); Peter Passell & John B. Taylor, The Deterrent Effect of Capital Punishment: Another View, 67 Am. Econ. Rev. 445 (1977). For responses to these critics, see Isaac Ehrlich, Deterrence: Evidence and Inference, 85 Yale L.J. 209 (1975); Isaac Ehrlich, The Deterrent Effect of Capital Punishment: A Reply, 67 Am. Econ. Rev. 452 (1977).

> [T]he evidence . . . is overwhelmingly contrary to deterrence theory. The bulk of evidence does not support the brutalization thesis either. . . . The findings of the early comparative studies [by Sellin] are especially important because they demonstrate that even during a period when the death penalty was in greater use in the United States, and when the delay between capital offenses and executions was considerably shorter, the provision for capital punishment did not appear to discourage murder. . . .
>
> It is true that Isaac Ehrlich [was] the first investigator to report evidence of deterrence. . . . However, analyses by a number of other economists have failed to confirm Ehrlich's findings. . . . Thus, it appears that neither economists nor sociologists, nor persons from any other discipline (law, psychology, engineering, etc.) have produced credible evidence of a significant deterrent effect for capital punishment.

These conclusions have recently been confirmed by a study of homicide rates in the last 20 years reported in the New York Times, September 22, 2000, at A-1. The study showed that the 12 states without a death penalty have not had higher homicide rates than the states with it, and that 10 of the 12 had rates below the national average. It also showed that homicide rates over the period showed strikingly similar ups and downs in the states with and without the death penalty.

b. Error, Irrevocability and Inequality

HUGO A. BEDAU, INNOCENCE AND THE DEATH PENALTY

in The Death Penalty in America: Current Controversies 344, 345, 350-359 (H. Bedau ed., 1997).

The most conclusive evidence that innocent people are condemned to death under modern death sentencing procedures comes from the surprisingly large number of people whose convictions have been overturned and who have been freed from death row. [In the period 1973-1993, a]t least 48 people have been released from prison after serving time on death row . . . with significant evidence of their innocence. In 43 of these cases, the defendant was subsequently acquitted, pardoned, or charges were dropped. [O]ne defendant was released when the parole board became convinced of his innocence.

[Professor Bedau describes the circumstances for each of the 48 cases. Many involved complete factual innocence — definitive proof that the defendant was in no way involved in the offense. Some involved what might be termed "legal innocence" — the defendant was not definitively exonerated but there was prosecutorial misconduct and/or incompetent defense, together with insufficient evidence of actual guilt. In the latter cases, he notes, there may have been "a lingering doubt" about complete innocence, but the evidence fell far short of proving guilt beyond a reasonable doubt. Bedau then summarizes the factors that led to conviction and a death sentence in these cases.]

Some of these men were convicted on the basis of perjured testimony or because the prosecutor withheld exculpatory evidence. In other cases, racial prejudice was a determining factor. In others, defense counsel failed to conduct the necessary investigation that would have disclosed exculpatory evidence.

. . . The cases outlined above might convey a reassuring impression that, although mistakes are made, the system of appeals and reviews will ferret out such cases prior to execution. In one sense that is occasionally true: the system of appeals sometimes allows for correction of factual errors. But there is another sense in which these cases illustrate the inadequacies of the system. [Many of t]hese men were found innocent *despite the system* and only as a result of [unusual media attention or other] extraordinary efforts not generally available to death row defendants.

Indeed, in some cases, these men were found innocent as a result of sheer luck. In the case of Walter McMillian, his volunteer outside counsel had obtained from the prosecutors an audio tape of one of the key witnesses' statements incriminating Mr. McMillian. After listening to the statement, the attorney flipped the tape over to see if anything was on the other side. It was only then that he heard the same witness complaining that he was being pressured to frame Mr. McMillian. With that fortuitous break, the whole case against McMillian began to fall apart. . . .

Most of the releases from death row over the past twenty years came only after many years and many failed appeals. . . . Too often, the reviews afforded death row inmates on appeal and habeas corpus do not offer a meaningful opportunity to present claims of innocence. . . . After trial, the legal system becomes locked in a battle over procedural issues rather than a reexamination of guilt. . . . Accounts which report that a particular case has been appealed numerous times before many judges may be misleading. [W]hen Roger Keith Coleman was executed in Virginia [in 1992,] it was reported that his last appeal to the Supreme Court "was Coleman's 16th round in court." However, the Supreme Court had earlier declared that Coleman's constitutional claims were barred because his prior attorneys had filed an appeal too late in 1986. His evidence was similarly excluded from review in state court as well. Instead, Coleman's innocence was debated only in the news media and considerable doubt concerning his guilt went with him to his execution. . . .

Investigation of innocence ends after execution. . . . Judging by past experience, a substantial number of death row inmates are innocent and there is a high risk that some of them will be executed. The danger is enhanced by the failure to provide adequate counsel and the narrowing of the opportunities to raise the issue of innocence on appeal. Once an execution occurs, the error is final.

ERNEST VAN DEN HAAG, PUNISHING CRIMINALS 219-220 (1975): Errors would not justify the abolition of the death penalty for retributionists. Many social policies have unintended effects that are statistically certain, irrevocable, unjust, and deadly. Automobile traffic unintentionally kills innocent victims; so does surgery (and most medicines); so does the death penalty. These activities are justified, nevertheless, because benefits (including justice) are felt to outweigh the statistical certainty of unintentionally killing innocents. The certain death of innocents argues for abolishing the death penalty no more than for abolishing surgery or automobiles. Injustice justifies abolition only if the losses to justice outweigh the gains — if more innocents are lost than saved by imposing the penalty compared to whatever net result alternatives (such as no punishment or life imprisonment) would produce. If innocent victims of future murderers are saved by virtue of the death penalty imposed on convicted murderers, it must be retained, just as surgery is, even though some innocents will be lost through miscarriages of justice — as long as more innocent lives are saved than lost. More justice is done with than without the death penalty. . . .

NOTES

1. *The paradox of close scrutiny.* The errors discussed by Professor Bedau, and the fact that the normal trial and appellate process failed to detect them, seem to contradict the common assumption that capital cases receive particularly close judicial scrutiny. For discussion of countervailing forces that press criminal justice officials to quickly solve brutal, potentially capital crimes, see Samuel R. Gross, Lost Lives: Miscarriages of Justice in Capital Cases, 61 L. & Contemp. Prob. 125 (1998).

2. *Recent developments.* With the advent of DNA testing and other sophisticated forensic techniques, claims of factual innocence can sometimes be verified or refuted scientifically, at least when traces of the killer's blood, semen, or hair fibers are found at the scene. Nonetheless, many states allow only a brief period for presenting newly discovered evidence; as of the end of 1999, New York and Illinois were the only states that afforded a right to conduct post-conviction DNA testing in cases concluded before this technology became available.

Despite this barrier, new cases of factual innocence have come to light in recent years, and scientific testing has provided a means to establish factual innocence with a certainty unavailable before. In addition to the cases of innocence identified by Professor Bedau, DNA testing since 1996 has definitively exonerated 63 other convicted prisoners, including eight inmates under sentence of death. See Jim Dwyer, Peter Neufeld & Barry Scheck, Actual Innocence 261-267 (2000). Another influential factor in recent years has been the use of journalism students to re-investigate the cases of prisoners nearing their execution dates. As a result of these and factors, Illinois, which carried out twelve executions from 1977 through 1999, had thirteen of its death-row inmates definitively exonerated and released in the same period.

Observers draw conflicting lessons from these developments. Some conclude that these exonerations show that our justice system lavishes great care on death-penalty cases and that it succeeds in identifying errors before a capital sentence is carried out. They also suggest that as DNA testing is now available before trial, we can have even greater confidence that false accusations in future cases will be identified *prior* to conviction. Other observers are pessimistic. They suggest that forensic evidence is not available in most cases and that the outcome of these cases will still be affected by the factors that led to false convictions before the availability of DNA testing — faulty eyewitness identifications, perjured testimony, planted evidence, jailhouse informants who falsely claim that their cellmate confessed to them, and so on. See Dwyer et al., supra at 263-265. For these observers, DNA exonerations simply confirm the presence in a few cases of dangers that are likely to be present, but undetectable, in many others.

Against the background of the thirteen death-row exonerations in Illinois, these latter concerns prompted its governor, a committed death-penalty supporter, to impose a moratorium on executions in that state, until the flaws in its death-penalty system could be identified and corrected. See N.Y. Times, Feb. 1, 2000, at A1.

3. Counsel. An important factor contributing to erroneous convictions is the quality of defense counsel and the adequacy of the system for selecting them. Although big-city public defenders are often dedicated and experienced, there remains great concern that many lawyers appointed to handle capital trials, especially those selected by judges in small rural counties, are often insufficiently competent or committed.[15] See Stephen B. Bright, Counsel for the Poor: The Death Sentence Not for the Worst Crime but for the Worst Lawyer, 103 Yale L.J. 1835 (1994). The author concludes:

> Inadequate legal representation . . . is pervasive in those jurisdictions which account for most of the death sentences. [In] numerous cases . . . the poor were defended by lawyers who lacked even the most rudimentary knowledge, resources, and capabilities needed for the defense of a capital case. Death sentences have been imposed in cases in which defense lawyers had not even read the state's death penalty statute . . . , slept through part of the trial, or [were] intoxicated during trial. . . .
>
> There are several interrelated reasons for the poor quality of representation in those important cases. Most fundamental is the wholly inadequate funding for the defense of indigents. As a result, there is simply no functioning adversary system in many states.

A related problem is whether the system of post-conviction review, including federal habeas corpus proceedings, is adequate to identify miscarriages of justice that occur through poor lawyering at the original trial. See Welsh S. White, Capital Punishment's Future, 91 Mich. L. Rev. 1429, 1435-1438 (1993).

4. Racial Discrimination. Concerns about possible unfairness in prosecuting the poor intersect with concerns about possible race bias in administrating the death penalty. Detailed empirical studies of possible racial discrimination have been the basis for litigation that we consider at pages 506-513 infra, in connection with the constitutional limits on capital punishment.

c. The Sanctity of Human Life

RAMSEY CLARK, STATEMENT, Hearings on S. 1760 ("To Abolish the Death Penalty") before the Subcommittee on Criminal Laws and Procedures, Senate Judiciary Committee, 90th Cong. 2d Sess. (July 2, 1968): Life is an end in itself. A humane and generous concern for every individual, for his safety, his health and his fulfillment, will do more to soothe the savage heart than the fear of state-inflicted death which chiefly serves to remind us how close we remain to the jungle.

"Murder and capital punishment are not opposites that cancel one another,

15. See Paul Duggan, In Texas, Defense Lapses Fail to Halt Executions, Wash. Post, May 12, 2000, at A1; ABA Criminal Justice Section, Task Force on Death Penalty Habeas Corpus, Toward a More Just and Effective System of Review in State Death Penalty Cases 55 (Ira P. Robbins, reporter, 1990). In Texas, for example, elected local judges allegedly often appoint as defense lawyers weak attorneys who are known for not rocking the boat or who have contributed to the judge's election campaign; a bill that would have ended this appointment system unanimously passed the state legislature but was vetoed by the governor in 1999. See Duggan, supra; Bob Herbert, In America: Criminal Justice, N.Y. Times, June 24, 1999.

but similars that breed their kind," Shaw advises. When the state itself kills, the mandate "thou shalt not kill" loses the force of the absolute.

Surely the abolition of the death penalty is a major milestone in the long road up from barbarism. There was a time when self preservation necessitated its imposition. . . . Our civilization has no such excuse. . . .

Our emotions may cry vengeance in the wake of a horrible crime. But reason and experience tell us that killing the criminal will not undo the crime, prevent other crimes, or bring justice to the victim, the criminal, or society. Executions cheapen life. We must cherish life. . . .

ERNEST VAN DEN HAAG, PUNISHING CRIMINALS 213 (1975): No matter what can be said for abolition of the death penalty, it will be perceived symbolically as a loss of nerve: social authority no longer is willing to pass an irrevocable judgment on anyone. Murder is no longer thought grave enough to take the murderer's life, no longer horrendous enough to deserve so fearfully irrevocable a punishment. . . . Life becomes cheaper as we become kinder to those who wantonly take it. The responsibility we avoid is indeed hard to bear. Can we sit in judgment and find that anyone is so irredeemably wicked that he does not deserve to live? Many of us no longer believe in evil, only in error or accident. How can one execute a murderer if one believes that he became one only by error or accident and is not to blame? Yet if life is to be valued and secured, it must be known that anyone who takes the life of another forfeits his own.

NOTES AND QUESTIONS

1. Consider Professor van den Haag's argument that respect for life requires that "anyone who takes the life of another forfeits his own." Does this principle mean that all reckless and negligent homicides must be punished by the death penalty? Does it imply that even accidental killings must be punished by the death penalty? Why shouldn't they be?

If culpability requirements rule out the death penalty for accidental and negligent killings, does the respect-for-life argument nonetheless require that the death penalty be mandatory for all intentional killings? Does respect for the value of innocent life preclude sentence reductions on the basis of provocation, diminished mental capacity, temporary emotional disturbance and the like?

2. For further development of the argument that respect for the sanctity of life *requires* the death penalty, see Walter Berns, For Capital Punishment 153-176 (1979). Ethical arguments based on the sanctity of life are closely related to concepts derived from specifically religious sources. Although we cannot present here an adequate sampling of arguments advanced from the viewpoint of the principal religious faiths, that perspective is of considerable importance for this aspect of the capital punishment debate. In Punishing Criminals, Professor van den Haag comments (id. at 225):

> [I]t is not easy to see what "sanctity" [of life] could mean outside of its religious context other than the assertion, disguised as proof, that it is wrong to put criminals to death. . . . Unless one resorts to a religiously or, in some other way, revealed source, one cannot show that society, unlike the murderer, must hold life unconditionally

inviolate; and the fact that the nonreligious urge it so religiously cannot commend this precept to believers. The death penalty has been part of all major religious traditions: Graeco-Roman, Judaic, Islamic, and Christian.

Note, however, that many American religious denominations have officially condemned capital punishment on religious grounds. For discussion of the religious issues by several leading theologians, see The Death Penalty in America 123-130, 171-182 (H. Bedau ed. 1964).

3. Constitutional Limitations

INTRODUCTORY NOTE

Until the 1950s, opponents of the death penalty had largely devoted their efforts to legislative reform, but thereafter abolitionists began a concentrated assault on the constitutionality of capital punishment.[16] Recall that at common law all murder had been punishable by death. Gradually, the scope of capital punishment had been narrowed, first by the division of murder into two degrees, so that only the more serious was subject to mandatory capital punishment, and then by the introduction of discretion in sentencing even for the highest category of criminal homicides. By the beginning of the twentieth century, 23 American jurisdictions made capital punishment discretionary in first-degree murder cases, and by 1962 all the remaining jurisdictions had adopted this approach.[17]

Litigation challenging this punishment scheme focused on two issues:

(1) Procedural due process. All the states committed the death penalty decision to the discretion of judge or jury, but none provided any standards to guide the exercise of that discretion. The reliance on unguided discretion was prevalent in sentencing decisions generally, but many thought that when a choice between life and death was to be made, due process required some explicit criteria of decision. The Court rejected that view in McGautha v. California, 402 U.S. 183, 207-208 (1971), holding that "committing to the untrammelled discretion of the jury the power to pronounce life or death is [not] offensive to anything in the Constitution." The Court reasoned that

> [an] attempt to catalog the appropriate factors in this elusive area could inhibit rather than expand the scope of consideration. . . . The infinite variety of cases . . . would make general standards either meaningless "boiler plate" or a statement of the obvious that no jury would need.

McGautha proved to be less significant than it seemed, however, because the same concerns about unguided discretion soon surfaced in attacks based on the cruel-and-unusual-punishment clause.

(2) Cruel and unusual punishment. Only a year after *McGautha,* a 5-4 majority

16. The development of a detailed strategy for litigation against the death penalty is recounted in Michael Meltsner, Cruel and Unusual: The Supreme Court and Capital Punishment (1973).

17. The history is detailed in Model Penal Code and Commentaries, Comment to §210.6 at 120-132 (1980).

of the Court held in Furman v. Georgia, 408 U.S. 238 (1972), that capital punishment, as then administered, violated the Eighth Amendment's prohibition of "cruel and unusual punishments." The Court's holding was stated in a brief per curiam opinion that made no attempt to set forth the majority's reasoning. Each of the justices filed a separate concurring or dissenting opinion explaining his own approach to the Eighth Amendment issue.

Justices Brennan and Marshall concluded that all capital punishment was unconstitutional. The other three concurring justices put their objections to capital punishment on narrower grounds. Justice Douglas stressed the potential for discriminatory administration of the death penalty. Justice Stewart said (id. at 309-310), in a passage that reflects Justice White's position as well:

> These death sentences are cruel and unusual in the same way that being struck by lightning is cruel and unusual. [I]f any basis can be discerned for the selection of these few to be sentenced to die, it is the constitutionally impermissible basis of race. But racial discrimination has not been proved, and I put it to one side. I simply conclude that the Eighth and Fourteenth Amendments cannot tolerate the infliction of a sentence of death under legal systems that permit this unique penalty to be so wantonly and so freakishly imposed.

The Chief Justice and Justices Blackmun, Powell and Rehnquist dissented. The dissenters stressed the long tradition and continued acceptance of capital punishment and argued that the majority's position involved an unwarranted intrusion into the legislative process.

Because a clear majority of the justices had neither rejected capital punishment outright nor indicated under what conditions it might be preserved, *Furman* created considerable confusion for states that desired to retain the death penalty. Two alternatives appeared viable: (1) enacting legislation to make capital punishment mandatory in certain cases and (2) establishing guidelines to determine who would be subjected to capital punishment. By 1976, at least 35 states and the United States Congress had enacted new capital punishment legislation; half of these jurisdictions had adopted provisions for a mandatory death penalty, while the remainder opted for schemes under which the sentencing authority would be required to consider specified aggravating and mitigating circumstances.[18] The Court soon confronted challenges to the new legislation.

GREGG v. GEORGIA

Supreme Court of the United States
428 U.S. 153 (1976)

[Gregg was convicted by a jury on two counts of armed robbery and two counts of murder. After the guilty verdicts, a penalty hearing was held before the same jury, under guidelines enacted in response to the *Furman* decision. The jury imposed the death sentence on each count. The Georgia Supreme Court set aside

18. For details concerning these enactments, see Samuel R. Gross, The Romance of Revenge: Capital Punishment in America, 13 Stud. L., Pol. & Socy. 71, 84-92 (1993); Model Penal Code and Commentaries, Comment to §210.6 at 156-157 & nn. 144-148 (1980).

the death sentences for armed robbery, on the ground that capital punishment had rarely been imposed for that crime, but the court affirmed the convictions on all counts and upheld the death sentences on the murder counts. The United States Supreme Court granted certiorari.]

JUSTICE STEWART, JUSTICE POWELL, and JUSTICE STEVENS announced the judgment of the Court and filed an opinion delivered by JUSTICE STEWART. . . .

We address initially the basic contention that the punishment of death for the crime of murder is, under all circumstances, "cruel and unusual" in violation of the Eighth and Fourteenth Amendments of the Constitution. . . . We now hold that the punishment of death does not invariably violate the Constitution. . . .

It is clear from the . . . precedents that the Eighth Amendment has not been regarded as a static concept. As Chief Justice Warren said, in an oft-quoted phrase, "[t]he Amendment must draw its meaning from the evolving standards of decency that mark the progress of a maturing society." Trop v. Dulles, 356 U.S. 86, 101 (1958). Thus, an assessment of contemporary values concerning the infliction of a challenged sanction is relevant to the application of the Eighth Amendment. . . .

But our cases also make clear that public perceptions of standards of decency with respect to criminal sanctions are not conclusive. A penalty also must accord with "the dignity of man," which is the "basic concept underlying the Eighth Amendment." Trop v. Dulles, supra, 356 U.S., at 100. This means, at least, that the punishment not be "excessive." [T]he inquiry into "excessiveness" has two aspects. First, the punishment must not involve the unnecessary and wanton infliction of pain. Second, the punishment must not be grossly out of proportion to the severity of the crime.

Of course, the requirements of the Eighth Amendment must be applied with an awareness of the limited role to be played by the courts. [W]hile we have an obligation to insure that constitutional bounds are not overreached, we may not act as judges as we might as legislators. . . .

Therefore, in assessing a punishment selected by a democratically elected legislature against the constitutional measure, we presume its validity. We may not require the legislature to select the least severe penalty possible so long as the penalty selected is not cruelly inhumane or disproportionate to the crime involved. And a heavy burden rests on those who would attack the judgment of the representatives of the people.

. . . We now consider specifically whether the sentence of death for the crime of murder is a per se violation of the Eighth and Fourteenth Amendments to the Constitution. We note first that history and precedent strongly support a negative answer to this question. It is apparent from the text of the Constitution itself that the existence of capital punishment was accepted by the Framers. . . . For nearly two centuries, this Court, repeatedly and often expressly, has recognized that capital punishment is not invalid per se. . . .

Four years ago, the petitioners in *Furman* and its companion cases predicated their argument primarily upon the asserted proposition that standards of decency had evolved to the point where capital punishment no longer could be tolerated. . . . The petitioners in the capital cases before the Court today renew the "standards of decency" argument, but developments during the four years since *Furman* have undercut substantially the assumptions upon which their argument rested. Despite the continuing debate, dating back to the 19th century, over the morality and utility of capital punishment, it is now evident that a large proportion of American society continues to regard it as an appropriate and necessary criminal sanction. . . . The legislatures of at least 35 States have enacted new statutes that provide for the death penalty for at least some crimes that result in the death of another person. [T]he relative infrequency of jury verdicts imposing the death sentence does not indicate rejection of capital punishment per se. Rather, the reluctance of juries in many cases to impose the sentence may well reflect the humane feeling that this most irrevocable of sanctions should be reserved for a small number of extreme cases. . . .

As we have seen, however, the Eighth Amendment demands more than that a challenged punishment be acceptable to contemporary society. The Court also must ask whether it comports with the basic concept of human dignity at the core of the Amendment. Although we cannot "invalidate a category of penalties because we deem less severe penalties adequate to serve the ends of penology," the sanction imposed cannot be so totally without penological justification that it results in the gratuitous infliction of suffering.

The death penalty is said to serve two principal social purposes: retribution and deterrence of capital crimes by prospective offenders.

In part, capital punishment is an expression of society's moral outrage at particularly offensive conduct. This function may be unappealing to many, but it is essential in an ordered society that asks its citizens to rely on legal processes rather than self-help to vindicate their wrongs. "The instinct for retribution is part of the nature of man, and channeling that instinct in the administration of criminal justice serves an important purpose in promoting the stability of a society governed by law. When people begin to believe that organized society is unwilling or unable to impose upon criminal offenders the punishment they 'deserve,' then there are sown the seeds of anarchy — of self-help, vigilante justice, and lynch law." Furman v. Georgia, 408 U.S., at 308 (Stewart, J., concurring). . . .

Statistical attempts to evaluate the worth of the death penalty as a deterrent to crimes by potential offenders have occasioned a great deal of debate. The results simply have been inconclusive. . . . The value of capital punishment as a deterrent of crime is a complex factual issue the resolution of which properly rests with the legislatures, which can evaluate the results of statistical studies in terms of their own local conditions and with a flexibility of approach that is not available to the courts. . . .

Finally, we must consider whether the punishment of death is disproportionate in relation to the crime for which it is imposed. There is no question that death as a punishment is unique in its severity and irrevocability. . . . But we are concerned here only with the imposition of capital punishment for the crime of murder, and when a life has been taken deliberately by the offender, we cannot say that the punishment is invariably disproportionate to the crime. It is an extreme sanction, suitable to the most extreme of crimes.

We hold that the death penalty is not a form of punishment that may never be imposed, . . . regardless of the procedure followed in reaching the decision to impose it. . . . Because of the uniqueness of the death penalty, *Furman* held that it could not be imposed under sentencing procedures that created a substantial risk that it would be inflicted in an arbitrary and capricious manner. . . .

Jury sentencing has been considered desirable in capital cases in order "to maintain a link between contemporary community values and the penal system

— a link without which the determination of punishment could hardly reflect 'the evolving standards of decency that mark the progress of a maturing society.'" But it creates special problems. Much of the information that is relevant to the sentencing decision may have no relevance to the question of guilt, or may even be extremely prejudicial to a fair determination of that question. This problem, however, is scarcely insurmountable. Those who have studied the question suggest that a bifurcated procedure — one in which the question of sentence is not considered until the determination of guilt has been made — is . . . likely to ensure elimination of the constitutional deficiencies in *Furman*.

But the provision of relevant information under fair procedural rules is not alone sufficient to guarantee that the information will be properly used. . . . Since the members of a jury will have had little, if any, previous experience in sentencing, they are unlikely to be skilled in dealing with the information they are given. . . . It seems clear, however, that the problem will be alleviated if the jury is given guidance regarding the factors about the crime and the defendant that the State, representing organized society, deems particularly relevant to the sentencing decision. . . .

While some have suggested that standards to guide a capital jury's sentencing deliberations are impossible to formulate, the fact is that such standards have been developed. [The Court here referred to the Model Penal Code proposals. See §210.6, Appendix.] While such standards are by necessity somewhat general, they do provide guidance to the sentencing authority and thereby reduce the likelihood that it will impose a sentence that fairly can be called capricious or arbitrary. . . .

In summary, the concerns expressed in *Furman* that the penalty of death not be imposed in an arbitrary or capricious manner can be met by a carefully drafted statute that ensures that the sentencing authority is given adequate information and guidance. As a general proposition these concerns are best met by a system that provides for a bifurcated proceeding at which the sentencing authority is apprised of the information relevant to the imposition of sentence and provided with standards to guide its use of the information. . . .

We now turn to consideration of the constitutionality of Georgia's capital-sentencing procedures. In the wake of *Furman,* Georgia amended its capital punishment statute, but chose not to narrow the scope of its murder provisions. Thus, now as before *Furman,* in Georgia "[a] person commits murder when he unlawfully and with malice aforethought, either express or implied, causes the death of another human being." Ga. Code Ann. §26-1101(a) (1972). All persons convicted of murder "shall be punished by death or by imprisonment for life." §26-1101(c) (1972).

Georgia did act, however, to narrow the class of murderers subject to capital punishment by specifying 10 statutory aggravating circumstances, one of which must be found by the jury to exist beyond a reasonable doubt before a death sentence can ever be imposed.[48] In addition, the jury is authorized to consider

48. The text of the statute enumerating the various aggravating circumstances is [as follows:

(1) The offense of murder, rape, armed robbery, or kidnapping was committed by a person with a prior record of conviction for a capital felony, or the offense of murder was committed by a person who has a substantial history of serious assaultive criminal convictions.

(2) The offense of murder, rape, armed robbery, or kidnapping was committed while the

any other appropriate aggravating or mitigating circumstances. The jury is not required to find any mitigating circumstance in order to make a recommendation of mercy that is binding on the trial court, but it must find a *statutory* aggravating circumstance before recommending a sentence of death. . . .

On their face these procedures seem to satisfy the concerns of *Furman*. No longer should there be "no meaningful basis for distinguishing the few cases in which [the death penalty] is imposed from the many cases in which it is not."

The petitioner contends, however, that the changes in the Georgia sentencing procedures are only cosmetic, that the arbitrariness and capriciousness condemned by *Furman* continue to exist. . . . First, the petitioner focuses on the opportunities for discretionary action that are inherent in the processing of any murder case under Georgia law. He notes that the state prosecutor has unfettered authority to select those persons whom he wishes to prosecute for a capital offense and to plea bargain with them. Further, at the trial the jury may choose to convict a defendant of a lesser included offense rather than find him guilty of a crime punishable by death, even if the evidence would support a capital verdict. And finally, a defendant who is convicted and sentenced to die may have his sentence commuted by the Governor of the State and the Georgia Board of Pardons and Paroles.

The existence of these discretionary stages is not determinative of the issues before us. At each of these stages an actor in the criminal justice system makes a decision which may remove a defendant from consideration as a candidate for the death penalty. *Furman,* in contrast, dealt with the decision to impose the death sentence on a specific individual who had been convicted of a capital offense. Nothing in any of our cases suggests that the decision to afford an individual defendant mercy violates the Constitution. *Furman* held only that, in order to minimize the risk that the death penalty would be imposed on a capriciously selected group of offenders, the decision to impose it had to be guided by standards so that the sentencing authority would focus on the particularized circumstances of the crime and the defendant. . . .

For the reasons expressed in this opinion, we hold that the statutory system

---

offender was engaged in the commission of another capital felony, or aggravated battery, or the offense of murder was committed while the offender was engaged in the commission of burglary or arson in the first degree.

(3) The offender by his act of murder, armed robbery, or kidnapping knowingly created a great risk of death to more than one person in a public place by means of a weapon or device which would normally be hazardous to the lives of more than one person.

(4) The offender committed the offense of murder for himself or another, for the purpose of receiving money or any other thing of monetary value.

(5) The murder of a judicial officer, former judicial officer, district attorney or solicitor or former district attorney or solicitor during or because of the exercise of his official duty.

(6) The offender caused or directed another to commit murder or committed murder as an agent or employee of another person.

(7) The offense of murder, rape, armed robbery, or kidnapping was outrageously or wantonly vile, horrible or inhuman in that it involved torture, depravity of mind, or an aggravated battery to the victim.

(8) The offense of murder was committed against any peace officer, corrections employee or fireman while engaged in the performance of his official duties.

(9) The offense of murder was committed by a person in, or who has escaped from, the lawful custody of a peace officer or place of lawful confinement.

(10) The murder was committed for the purpose of avoiding, interfering with, or preventing a lawful arrest or custody in a place of lawful confinement, of himself or another.]

under which Gregg was sentenced to death does not violate the Constitution. Accordingly, the judgment of the Georgia Supreme Court is affirmed. . . .

[The concurring opinion of Justice White, joined by the Chief Justice and Justice Rehnquist, the concurring opinion of Justice Blackmun, and the dissenting opinion of Justice Brennan are omitted.]

JUSTICE MARSHALL, dissenting. . . .

I would be less than candid if I did not acknowledge that [legislative] developments [since *Furman*] have a significant bearing on a realistic assessment of the moral acceptability of the death penalty to the American people. But if the constitutionality of the death penalty turns, as I have urged, on the opinion of an *informed* citizenry, then even the enactment of new death statutes cannot be viewed as conclusive. In *Furman,* I observed that the American people are largely unaware of the information critical to a judgment on the morality of the death penalty, and concluded that if they were better informed they would consider it shocking, unjust, and unacceptable. . . .

The two purposes that sustain the death penalty as nonexcessive in the Court's view are general deterrence and retribution. . . . The evidence I reviewed in *Furman* remains convincing, in my view, that "capital punishment is not necessary as a deterrent to crime in our society." . . .

The other principal purpose said to be served by the death penalty is retribution. . . . As my Brother Brennan stated in *Furman,* "[t]here is no evidence whatever that utilization of imprisonment rather than death encourages private blood feuds and other disorders." It simply defies belief to suggest that the death penalty is necessary to prevent the American people from taking the law into their own hands. . . .

NOTES

1. Mandatory death penalty statutes. (a) In Woodson v. North Carolina, 428 U.S. 280 (1976), the Court held that a mandatory death sentence for any first-degree murder violates the Eighth Amendment. Justice Stewart, joined by Justices Powell and Stevens, gave three reasons for this conclusion:

(i) Mandatory capital punishment is inconsistent with contemporary standards of decency. He noted that the recent enactment of mandatory-sentence statutes was not a reversal of the historical trend of popular rejection of mandatory sentences but was only an effort to retain the death penalty in light of *Furman.*

(ii) Mandatory sentences fail to provide standards that will effectively guide the jury. Justice Stewart noted experience with earlier mandatory schemes, under which "[j]uries continued to find the death penalty inappropriate in a significant number of first-degree murder cases and refused to return guilty verdicts for that crime." Id. at 291. He therefore concluded that "mandatory statutes enacted in response to *Furman* have simply papered over the problem of unguided and unchecked jury discretion." Id. at 302. (Do you find this point convincing? If so, does it not apply with virtually equal force to the statute upheld in *Gregg?*)

(iii) Most important, Justice Stewart reasoned that the fundamental respect for individual dignity underlying the Eighth Amendment requires (id. at 303-304)

> the particularized consideration of relevant aspects of the character and record of each convicted defendant [and the circumstances of the offense] before the imposition upon him of a sentence of death. . . . A process that [fails to provide such consideration] . . . treats all persons convicted of a designated offense not as uniquely individual human beings, but as members of a faceless, undifferentiated mass to be subjected to the blind infliction of the penalty of death.

(b) Shuman killed a fellow prisoner while serving a sentence of life imprisonment without possibility of parole. He was convicted of murder, and under the applicable Nevada statute the offense carried a mandatory penalty of death. Despite intimations in the earlier cases that mandatory capital punishment might be permissible in these narrow circumstances, the Court held Shuman's death sentence unconstitutional. Sumner v. Shuman, 483 U.S. 66 (1987). Writing for the Court, Justice Blackmun stressed that "the fundamental respect for humanity underlying the Eighth Amendment . . . requires consideration of the character and record of the offender and the circumstances of the particular offense" (id. at 75). The Court noted that prior conviction of an offense carrying a life sentence provided insufficient information about the seriousness of the present killing, the defendant's leadership role in its commission, or mitigating circumstances that might fall short of a complete defense. The Court also noted that a mandatory capital sentence was not essential for deterrence because life prisoners who kill would still face the death penalty under a regime of guided discretion.

2. *Other guided-discretion statutes. (a)* In Jurek v. Texas, 428 U.S. 262 (1976), the Court considered a post-*Furman* statute that limits capital punishment to five categories of intentional homicide[19] and then provides the following procedure for determining whether to impose the death penalty in any such case. The jury is directed to answer three questions: (1) whether the conduct was done deliberately and with a reasonable expectation of causing death; (2) whether "there is a probability that the defendant would commit criminal acts of violence that would constitute a continuing threat to society" (id. at 269); and (3) if raised by the evidence, whether the defendant's conduct was an unreasonable response to provocation by the deceased. If the jury gives a negative answer to any question, life imprisonment is imposed, but if the jury finds beyond a reasonable doubt that the answer to all three questions is affirmative, then the death sentence must be imposed. Although this approach is quasi-mandatory in directing capital punishment under specified conditions, the Court treated the case as closer to *Gregg* than to *Woodson* and sustained the statutory scheme. The plurality opinion (by Justices Stewart, Powell, and Stevens) reasoned that the five categories of capital murder were equivalent to aggravating circumstances and noted that Texas courts had read the second question put to the jury, the probability of future violence, as permitting the defense to place before the jury whatever mitigating circumstances might exist. The plurality did not, however, clarify how

19. The categories are murder of a peace officer or firefighter, intentional murder in the course of specified felonies, murder committed for remuneration, murder committed while escaping from prison, or murder of a prison employee by an inmate.

a jury, unaided by further guidelines, could make a rational response to the broad and ambiguously worded second question. The plurality simply concluded that "[b]ecause this system serves to assure that sentences of death will not be 'wantonly' or 'freakishly' imposed, it does not violate the Constitution." Id. at 276.

(b) Lockett v. Ohio, 438 U.S. 586 (1978), involved a post-*Furman* statute that specified that once any of seven aggravating circumstances was found, the death penalty must be imposed unless it is found that (1) the victim had induced or facilitated the offense, (2) it was unlikely that the defendant would have committed the offense but for the fact that he or she was under duress, coercion, or strong provocation, or (3) the offense was primarily the product of the defendant's psychosis or mental deficiency. The Court struck down this statute by a 7-1 vote, but the Court was widely split in its reasoning. Chief Justice Burger, writing for himself and Justices Stewart, Powell, and Stevens, found the narrow range of permissible mitigating circumstances to be a fatal flaw. "[T]he sentencer, in all but the rarest kind of capital case, [must] not be precluded from considering *as a mitigating factor,* any aspect of a defendant's character or record and any of the circumstances of the offense that the defendant proffers as a basis for a sentence less than death." Id. at 604.

Questions: Chief Justice Burger's view seems to flow naturally from *Woodson,* but is it compatible with the goals of confining and structuring the jury's decision? Is it consistent with the principles implicit in *Furman* and *Gregg?*

(c) Cases subsequent to *Lockett* reaffirmed and extended the principle espoused by the plurality in that case. In Eddings v. Oklahoma, 455 U.S. 104 (1982), the defense offered in mitigation the fact that the defendant, who was 16 years old at the time of the offense, had a history of beatings by a harsh father and serious emotional disturbance. The state statute permitted consideration of "any mitigating circumstances," but the sentencing judge ruled that while the defendant's youth was relevant in mitigation, the troubled family background and emotional disturbance were not relevant as a matter of law. The Court held that the evidence of Eddings' background could not be ruled irrelevant and that the sentencer must give some consideration to it. The Court said that "a consistency produced by ignoring individual differences is a false consistency." (455 U.S. at 112.)

In Skipper v. South Carolina, 476 U.S. 1 (1986), the Court held it impermissible to exclude evidence regarding the defendant's good behavior in jail *while awaiting trial.* Three dissenters argued that such evidence had little probative value given the special incentives for good behavior under the circumstances.

A different aspect of the *Lockett* principle was considered in Penry v. Lynaugh, 492 U.S. 302 (1989). In *Penry* there was evidence that the defendant suffered from organic brain damage and significant mental retardation that left him with the mental age of a 6½-year-old; there was also evidence that, in his childhood, he had suffered serious beatings and other abuse. This potentially mitigating evidence was admitted at his trial, as *Lockett* clearly requires, but under the Texas death penalty scheme (see page 500 supra), the judge was in effect required to impose the death penalty if the jury answered affirmatively to the question whether "there is a probability that the defendant would commit criminal acts of violence that would constitute a continuing threat to society." The Supreme Court held (5-4) that the narrow focus of the jury's inquiry under the Texas scheme violated *Lockett* by preventing the jury from considering the defendant's mental retardation and abused background as *mitigating* factors and by precluding a "reasoned moral response" to the mitigating evidence. (Id. at 328.)

The scope of *Penry* was limited by Graham v. Collins, 506 U.S. 461 (1993). In *Graham* the defendant relied for mitigation on evidence of his youth (he was 17 at the time of the offense), unstable family background, and positive character traits. The evidence was admitted at trial, but, as in *Penry,* the jury was able to consider the evidence only within the narrow framework of the question whether he would pose a "continuing threat to society." This time the Court held (5-4) that *Lockett* was *not* violated, reasoning that the defendant had been permitted to place his mitigating evidence before the jury and that his evidence, unlike Penry's, did have some mitigating relevance on the "continuing threat" issue. *Penry,* the Court said, "does *not* broadly suggest the invalidity of the [Texas] special issues framework." (Id. at 474, emphasis in original.) In *Graham* Justice White, who had dissented in *Penry,* wrote the majority opinion, and Justice O'Connor, who had written the majority opinion in *Penry,* was now one of the four dissenters.

3. Crimes other than intentional murder. (a) In Coker v. Georgia, 433 U.S. 584, 592 (1977), the Court held that the death penalty "is grossly disproportionate and excessive punishment for the crime of rape and is therefore forbidden by the Eighth Amendment. . . ." Justice White, in the principal opinion, said (id. at 597-598):

> We do not discount the seriousness of rape as a crime. It is highly reprehensible, both in a moral sense and in its almost total contempt for the personal integrity and autonomy of the female victim. . . . Short of homicide, it is "the ultimate violation of self."
>
> Rape is without doubt deserving of serious punishment; but in terms of moral depravity and of the injury to the person and to the public, it does not compare with murder. . . . Although it may be accompanied by another crime, rape by definition does not include the death of or even the serious injury to another person. . . . We have the abiding conviction that the death penalty, which "is unique in its severity and revocability," . . . is an excessive penalty for the rapist who, as such, does not take human life.

(b) The Court has not yet considered the constitutionality of capital punishment for such crimes as espionage or aircraft hijacking. Of course, these crimes may create a risk of death, perhaps to many persons, but given *Coker,* should the death penalty be permissible when death does not actually occur?

(c) When is it constitutional to impose capital punishment on someone guilty of murder who did not actually intend to take life? Consider the situations of this kind that we have explored in previous sections of this chapter: an offender who causes death accidentally or even recklessly in the course of committing rape; an accomplice, not intending to kill, who is held for a homicide perpetrated accidentally, recklessly, or even intentionally by his cofelon. For Eighth Amendment purposes, should the proportionality analysis focus on the injury caused or on the injury intended?

In Enmund v. Florida, 458 U.S. 782 (1982), the evidence suggested that the defendant had waited in a getaway car while two accomplices approached a rural farmhouse and then robbed and murdered the elderly couple who lived there.

The defendant was convicted of murder and sentenced to death, on the theory that the felony-murder rule made Enmund responsible for the lethal acts of his cofelons. The Supreme Court held that the Eighth Amendment prohibits imposition of the death penalty on a defendant "who does not himself kill, attempt to kill, or intend that a killing take place or that lethal force will be employed." Id. at 797. The Court stressed that Enmund's culpability was "plainly different from that of the robbers who killed" and that it is "fundamental that 'causing harm intentionally must be punished more severely than causing the same harm unintentionally.'" Id. at 798, quoting H. L. A. Hart, Punishment and Responsibility 162 (1968).

Tison v. Arizona, 481 U.S. 137 (1987), involved two brothers, Raymond and Ricky Tison, who helped their father Gary escape from prison, where he was serving time on a murder conviction for killing a guard in a prior prison escape attempt. The Arizona court found that Raymond and Ricky supplied weapons and a getaway car to their father, knowing his willingness to use lethal force to effect his escape. They helped him lock up the guards and fled with him into the desert. During the course of the escape, the Tisons decided to flag down a passing motorist in order to steal another car. After they had succeeded in stopping a car carrying a family of four, Gary Tison guarded the group and sent his two sons away to get water; while Raymond and Ricky were some distance away, their father murdered all four of the captives (including a two-year-old child). Gary Tison subsequently escaped into the desert but died there of exposure. Raymond and Ricky were apprehended, convicted of murder for the four killings committed by their father, and sentenced to death.

Do the death sentences in *Tison* violate the Eighth Amendment proportionality requirement as developed in *Enmund?* A 5-4 majority of the Supreme Court did not think so. Recognizing that the defendants neither committed the killing nor had an actual intent to kill, the Court held that "major participation in the felony committed, combined with reckless indifference to human life, is sufficient to satisfy the *Enmund* culpability requirement" (id. at 158). Justice O'Connor, writing for the majority, explained (id. at 157):

> [S]ome nonintentional murderers may be among the most dangerous and inhumane of all — the person who tortures another not caring whether the victim lives or dies, or the robber who shoots someone in the course of the robbery. . . . This reckless indifference to the value of human life may be every bit as shocking to the moral sense as an "intent to kill." Indeed it is for this very reason that the common law and modern criminal codes alike have classified behavior such as occurred in this case along with intentional murders. See, e.g., G. Fletcher, Rethinking Criminal Law §6.5, pp. 447-448 (1978) (". . . [T]he Model Penal Code treats reckless killing, 'manifesting extreme indifference to the value of human life,' as equivalent to purposeful and knowing killing.")

What should be the result if the killing is neither intentional nor reckless? Suppose, for example, that a robber inflicts no violent injuries but that a robbery victim dies of a heart attack induced by fright. (Reconsider the facts of People v. Stamp, page 450 supra). Or suppose that a robber pushes the victim away and that the latter trips, falls and suffers a fatal cranial injury. Does the *Enmund-Tison* requirement — that reckless indifference to human life is a prerequisite to capital punishment — apply only when the defendant is not the actual killer? In *Tison,* Justice O'Connor implied that a felony murderer who "actually killed" could be executed even when the killing was purely accidental (481 U.S. at 150), and the California Supreme Court has so held, People v. Anderson, 742 P.2d 1306 (Cal. 1987). Is this defensible? How does a defendant's role as the "actual" killer substitute for the *culpability* requirement of a murderous mens rea? The issue is examined in Welsh S. White, Life in the Balance 92-96 (1984). For a critique of *Tison,* see Richard A. Rosen, Felony Murder and the Eighth Amendment Jurisprudence of Death, 31 B.C.L. Rev. 1103, 1146-1163 (1990).

4. In Callins v. Collins, 510 U.S. 1141 (1994), Justice Blackmun, dissenting from the Supreme Court's refusal to review Callins's death sentence, offered the following comments on the law of capital punishment (id. at 1144-1153):

> Experience has taught us that the constitutional goal of eliminating arbitrariness and discrimination from the administration of death can never be achieved without compromising an equally essential component of fundamental fairness — individualized sentencing. It is tempting, when faced with conflicting constitutional commands, to sacrifice one for the other or to assume that an acceptable balance between them already has been struck. In the context of the death penalty, however, such jurisprudential maneuvers are wholly inappropriate. The death penalty must be imposed "fairly, and with reasonable consistency, or not at all." Eddings v. Oklahoma, 455 U.S. 104, 112 (1982). . . .
>
> From this day forward, I no longer shall tinker with the machinery of death. For more than 20 years I have endeavored — indeed, I have struggled — along with a majority of this Court, to develop procedural and substantive rules that would lend more than the mere appearance of fairness to the death penalty endeavor. Rather than continue to coddle the Court's delusion that the desired level of fairness has been achieved, . . . I feel morally and intellectually obligated simply to concede that the death penalty experiment has failed. It is virtually self-evident to me now that no combination of procedural rules or substantive regulations ever can save the death penalty from its inherent constitutional deficiencies. . . . The problem is that the inevitability of factual, legal, and moral error gives us a system that we know must wrongly kill some defendants, a system that fails to deliver the fair, consistent, and reliable sentences of death required by the Constitution. . . .
>
> This unique level of fairness is born of the appreciation that death truly is different from all other punishments. . . . Because of the qualitative difference of the death penalty, "there is a corresponding difference in the need for reliability in the determination that death is the appropriate punishment in a specific case." [*Woodson,* 428 U.S. at 305.] . . . [A]lthough individualized sentencing in capital cases was not considered essential at the time the Constitution was adopted, *Woodson* recognized that American standards of decency could no longer tolerate a capital sentencing process that failed to afford a defendant individualized consideration in the determination whether he or she should live or die. . . . The notion of prohibiting a sentencer from exercising its discretion "to dispense mercy on the basis of factors too intangible to write into a statute," *Gregg,* 428 U.S., at 222 (White, J., concurring), is offensive to our sense of fundamental fairness and respect for the uniqueness of the individual. . . .
>
> Yet, as several Members of the Court have recognized, there is real "tension" between the need for fairness to the individual and the consistency promised in *Furman.* On the one hand, discretion in capital sentencing must be "'controlled by clear and objective standards so as to produce non-discriminatory [and reasoned]

application.'" *Gregg,* 428 U.S. at 198 (opinion of Stewart, Powell, and Stevens, JJ.). On the other hand, the Constitution also requires that the sentencer be able to consider "any relevant mitigating evidence regarding the defendant's character or background, and the circumstances of the particular offense." . . . Thus, the Constitution, by requiring a heightened degree of fairness to the individual, and also a greater degree of equality and rationality in the administration of death, demands sentencer discretion that is at once generously expanded and severely restricted.

The theory underlying . . . *Lockett* is that an appropriate balance can be struck between the *Furman* promise of consistency and the *Lockett* requirement of individualized sentencing. . . . While one might hope that providing the sentencer with as much relevant mitigating evidence as possible will lead to more rational and consistent sentences, experience has taught otherwise. It seems that the decision whether a human being should live or die is so inherently subjective — rife with all of life's understandings, experiences, prejudices, and passions — that it inevitably defies the rationality and consistency required by the Constitution.

Justice Scalia, concurring in the Court's denial of review, responded to Justice Blackmun as follows (id. at 1141-1142):

The Fifth Amendment provides that "[n]o person shall be held to answer for a capital . . . crime, unless on a presentment or indictment of a Grand Jury, . . . nor be deprived of life . . . without due process of law." This clearly permits the death penalty to be imposed, and establishes beyond doubt that the death penalty is not one of the "cruel and unusual punishments" prohibited by the Eighth Amendment. . . .

Though Justice Blackmun joins those of us who have acknowledged the incompatibility of the Court's *Furman* and *Lockett-Eddings* lines of jurisprudence, he unfortunately draws the wrong conclusion. . . . Surely . . . at least one of these judicially announced irreconcilable commands which cause the Constitution to prohibit what its text explicitly permits must be wrong.

5. Questions. (a) Interpreting the constitutional text. A clause of the Fifth Amendment omitted from Justice Scalia's quotation provides: "[N]or shall any person be subject for the same offense to be twice put in jeopardy of life or limb." Does this provision of the Constitution permit imposition of severe corporal punishment and "establish beyond doubt that [such a] penalty is not one of the 'cruel and unusual punishments' prohibited by the Eighth Amendment" (*Callins,* supra at 1127)? If not, then is it plausible to read the Constitution's "due process," "equal protection," and "cruel and unusual punishments" clauses as limiting the circumstances in which government is permitted to subject offenders to loss of life or limb?

(b) Reconciling the requirements of consistency and individualization. For a close examination of the tension between *Furman* and *Lockett,* see Scott E. Sunby, The *Lockett* Paradox: Reconciling Guided Discretion and Unguided Mitigation in Capital Sentencing, 38 U.C.L.A. L. Rev. 1147 (1991). Professor Sunby argues (id. at 1207) that death penalty administration does not pose an "all-or-nothing [choice] between discretion or no discretion," and that the Court can continue to seek a middle ground between the position of Justice Scalia (which entails overruling *Lockett*) and that of Justice Blackmun (which entails overruling *Gregg*).

McCLESKEY v. KEMP

Supreme Court of the United States
481 U.S. 279 (1987)

JUSTICE POWELL delivered the opinion of the Court.

This case presents the question whether a complex statistical study that indicates a risk that racial considerations enter into capital sentencing determinations proves that petitioner McCleskey's capital sentence is unconstitutional under the Eighth or Fourteenth Amendment.

I

McCleskey, a black man, was convicted of two counts of armed robbery and one count of murder in the Superior Court of Fulton County, Georgia, on October 12, 1978. McCleskey's convictions arose out of the robbery of a furniture store and the killing of a white police officer during the course of the robbery. The evidence at trial indicated that McCleskey and three accomplices planned and carried out the robbery. All four were armed. . . . During the course of the robbery, a police officer, answering a silent alarm, entered the store through the front door. [Two shots] struck the officer. One hit him in the face and killed him. At trial, the State introduced evidence that at least one of the bullets that struck the officer was fired [by McCleskey].

The jury convicted McCleskey of murder [and] found two aggravating circumstances to exist beyond a reasonable doubt: the murder was commited during the course of an armed robbery, and the murder was committed upon a peace officer engaged in the performance of his duties. . . . McCleskey offered no mitigating evidence. The jury recommended that he be sentenced to death. . . . The court followed the jury's recommendation and sentenced McCleskey to death. [T]he Supreme Court of Georgia affirmed. . . .

[After state court challenges, McCleskey filed a petition for a writ of habeas corpus.] His petition raised 18 claims, one of which was that the Georgia capital sentencing process is administered in a racially discriminatory manner in violation of the Eighth and Fourteenth Amendments to the United States Constitution. In support of his claim, McCleskey proffered a statistical study performed by Professors David C. Baldus, George Woodworth, and Charles Pulaski (the Baldus study) that purports to show a disparity in the imposition of the death sentence in Georgia based on the race of the murder victim and, to a lesser extent, the race of the defendant. The Baldus study is actually two sophisticated statistical studies that examine over 2,000 murder cases that occurred in Georgia during the 1970s. The raw numbers collected by Professor Baldus indicate that defendants charged with killing white persons received the death penalty in 11% of the cases, but defendants charged with killing blacks received the death penalty in only 1% of the cases. The raw numbers also indicate a reverse racial disparity according to the race of the defendant: 4% of the black defendants received the death penalty, as opposed to 7% of the white defendants.

Baldus also divided the cases according to the combination of the race of the defendant and the race of the victim. He found that the death penalty was assessed in 22% of the cases involving black defendants and white victims; 8% of the cases involving white defendants and white victims; 1% of the cases involving black defendants and black victims; and 3% of the cases involving white defendants and black victims. . . .

Baldus subjected his data to an extensive analysis, taking account of 230 variables that could have explained the disparities on nonracial grounds. One of his models concludes that, even after taking account of 39 nonracial variables, defendants charged with killing white victims were 4.3 times as likely to receive a death sentence as defendants charged with killing blacks. [T]he Baldus study indicates that black defendants, such as McCleskey, who kill white victims have the greatest likelihood of receiving the death penalty.[5]

The District Court . . . found that the methodology of the Baldus study was flawed in several respects. . . . Accordingly, the Court dismissed the petition. The Court of Appeals affirmed. . . .

II

McCleskey's first claim is that the Georgia capital punishment statute violates the Equal Protection Clause of the Fourteenth Amendment.[7] . . . As a black defendant who killed a white victim, McCleskey claims that the Baldus study demonstrates that he was discriminated against because of his race and because of the race of his victim. . . .

Our analysis begins with the basic principle that a defendant who alleges an equal protection violation has the burden of proving "the existence of purposeful discrimination." [T]o prevail under the Equal Protection Clause, McCleskey must prove that the decision-makers in *his* case acted with discriminatory purpose. He offers no evidence specific to his own case that would support an inference that racial considerations played a part in his sentence. Instead, he relies solely on the Baldus study. . . . McCleskey's claim that these statistics are sufficient proof of discrimination, without regard to the facts of a particular case, would extend to all capital cases in Georgia, at least where the victim was white and the defendant is black.

. . . McCleskey challenges decisions at the heart of the State's criminal justice system. . . . Because discretion is essential to the criminal justice process, we would demand exceptionally clear proof before we would infer that the discretion had been abused. . . . Accordingly, we hold that the Baldus study is clearly

5. Baldus's 230-variable model divided cases into eight different ranges, according to the estimated aggravation level of the offense. Baldus argued in his testimony to the District Court that the effects of racial bias were most striking in the mid-range cases. "[W]hen the cases become tremendously aggravated so that everybody would agree that if we're going to have a death sentence, these are the cases that should get it, the race effects go away. It's only in the mid-range of cases where the decision makers have a real choice as to what to do. If there's room for the exercise of discretion, then the [racial] factors begin to play a role." Under this model, Baldus found that 14.4% of the black-victim mid-range cases received the death penalty, and 34.4% of the white-victim cases received the death penalty. According to Baldus, the facts of McCleskey's case placed it within the mid-range.

7. Although the District Court rejected the findings of the Baldus study as flawed, the Court of Appeals assumed that the study is valid and reached the constitutional issues. Accordingly, those issues are before us. As did the Court of Appeals, we assume the study is valid statistically without reviewing the factual findings of the District Court. . . .

insufficient to support an inference that any of the decisionmakers in McCleskey's case acted with discriminatory purpose.

McCleskey also suggests that the Baldus study proves that the State as a whole has acted with a discriminatory purpose. He appears to argue that the State has violated the Equal Protection Clause by adopting the capital punishment statute and allowing it to remain in force despite its allegedly discriminatory application. But "'[d]iscriminatory purpose' . . . implies more than intent as volition or intent as awareness of consequences. It implies that the decisionmaker, in this case a state legislature, selected or reaffirmed a particular course of action at least in part 'because of,' not merely 'in spite of,' its adverse effects upon an identifiable group." For this claim to prevail, McCleskey would have to prove that the Georgia Legislature enacted or maintained the death penalty statute *because of* an anticipated racially discriminatory effect. In Gregg v. Georgia, 428 U.S. 153 (1976), this Court found that the Georgia capital sentencing system could operate in a fair and neutral manner. There was no evidence then, and there is none now, that the Georgia Legislature enacted the capital punishment statute to further a racially discriminatory purpose. . . .

[IV]

McCleskey also argues that the Baldus study demonstrates that the Georgia capital sentencing system violates the Eighth Amendment. . . .

To evaluate McCleskey's challenge, we must examine exactly what the Baldus study may show. Even Professor Baldus does not contend that his statistics *prove* that race enters into any capital sentencing decisions or that race was a factor in McCleskey's particular case.[29] . . . There is, of course, some risk of racial prejudice influencing a jury's decision in a criminal case. . . . The question "is at what point that risk becomes constitutionally unacceptable."

McCleskey's argument that the Constitution condemns the discretion allowed decisionmakers in the Georgia capital sentencing system is antithetical to the fundamental role of discretion in our criminal justice system. Discretion in the criminal justice system offers substantial benefits to the criminal defendant. Not only can a jury decline to impose the death sentence, it can decline to convict, or choose to convict of a lesser offense. . . . Similarly, . . . a prosecutor can decline to charge, offer a plea bargain,[34] or decline to seek a death sentence in any particular case. Of course, "the power to be lenient [also] is the power to discriminate," K. Davis, Discretionary Justice 170 (1973), but a capital-punishment

29. According to Professor Baldus: "McCleskey's case falls in [a] grey area where . . . you would find the greatest likelihood that some inappropriate consideration may have come to bear on the decision. In an analysis of this type, obviously one cannot say that we can say to a moral certainty what it was that influenced the decision. We can't do that."

[*Questions:* Is the Court saying that in order to "prove" a proposition for purposes of constitutional litigation, a party must establish that proposition "to a moral certainty"? Is this the proper burden of persuasion? — Eds.]

34. In this case, for example, McCleskey declined to enter a guilty plea. According to his trial attorney: "[T]he Prosecutor was indicating that we might be able to work out a life sentence if he were willing to enter a plea. But we never reached any concrete stage on that because Mr. McCleskey's attitude was that he didn't want to enter a plea. So it never got any further than just talking about it."

system that did not allow for discretionary acts of leniency "would be totally alien to our notions of criminal justice." Gregg v. Georgia, 428 U.S., at 200, n. 50.

. . . The discrepancy indicated by the Baldus study is "a far cry from the major systemic defects identified in *Furman*."[36] Where the discretion that is fundamental to our criminal process is involved, we decline to assume that what is unexplained is invidious.[b] In light of the safeguards designed to minimize racial bias in the process, the fundamental value of jury trial in our criminal justice system, and the benefits that discretion provides to criminal defendants, we hold that the Baldus study does not demonstrate a constitutionally significant risk of racial bias affecting the Georgia capital-sentencing process.[37]

V

Two additional concerns inform our decision in this case. First, McCleskey's claim, taken to its logical conclusion, throws into serious question the principles that underlie our entire criminal justice system. The Eighth Amendment is not limited in application to capital punishment, but applies to all penalties. Thus, if we accepted McCleskey's claim that racial bias has impermissibly tainted the capital sentencing decision, we could soon be faced with similar claims as to other types of penalty. Moreover, the claim that his sentence rests on the irrelevant factor of race easily could be extended to apply to claims based on unexplained discrepancies that correlate to membership in other minority groups, and even to gender. . . . Also, there is no logical reason that such a claim need be limited to racial or sexual bias. If arbitrary and capricious punishment is the touchstone under the Eighth Amendment, such a claim could — at least in theory — be based upon any arbitrary variable, such as the defendant's facial characteristics, or the physical attractiveness of the defendant or the victim,[44] that some statistical study indicates may be influential in jury decisionmaking. As these examples illustrate, there is no limiting principle to the type of challenge brought by McCleskey. . . .

Second, McCleskey's arguments are best presented to the legislative bodies. . . . Legislatures also are better qualified to weigh and "evaluate the results of statistical studies in terms of their own local conditions and with a flexibility of approach that is not available to the courts," Gregg v. Georgia, supra. . . . Despite McCleskey's wide ranging arguments that basically challenge the validity of

36. The Baldus study in fact confirms that the Georgia system results in a reasonable level of proportionality among the class of murderers eligible for the death penalty. As Professor Baldus confirmed, the system sorts out cases where the sentence of death is highly likely and highly unlikely, leaving a mid-range of cases where the imposition of the death penalty in any particular case is less predictable.

b. Is the pattern in this case "unexplained"? — Eds.

37. . . . The dissent repeatedly emphasizes the need for "a uniquely high degree of rationality in imposing the death penalty." [Yet,] no suggestion is made as to how greater "rationality" could be achieved under any type of statute that authorizes capital punishment. [T]he dissent's call for greater rationality is no less than a claim that a capital-punishment system cannot be administered in accord with the Constitution. . . .

44. Some studies indicate that physically attractive defendants receive greater leniency in sentencing than unattractive defendants, and that offenders whose victims are physically attractive receive harsher sentences than defendants with less attractive victims.

capital punishment in our multi-racial society, the only question before us is whether in his case the law of Georgia was properly applied. We agree with the District Court and the Court of Appeals for the Eleventh Circuit that this was carefully and correctly done in this case.

Accordingly, we affirm. . . .

JUSTICE BRENNAN, [with whom JUSTICES MARSHALL, BLACKMUN, and STEVENS join], dissenting. . . .

It is important to emphasize at the outset that the Court's observation that McCleskey cannot prove the influence of race on any particular sentencing decision is irrelevant in evaluating his Eighth Amendment claim. Since Furman v. Georgia, 408 U.S. 238 (1972), the Court has been concerned with the *risk* of the imposition of an arbitrary sentence, rather than the proven fact of one. . . . As Justice O'Connor observed in Caldwell v. Mississippi, 472 U.S. 320, 343 (1985), a death sentence must be struck down when the circumstances under which it has been imposed "creat[e] an unacceptable *risk* that 'the death penalty [may have been] meted out arbitrarily or capriciously' or through 'whim or mistake'" (emphasis added). This emphasis on risk . . . reflects the fact that concern for arbitrariness focuses on the rationality of the system as a whole, and that a system that features a significant probability that sentencing decisions are influenced by impermissible considerations cannot be regarded as rational. . . . McCleskey's claim does differ, however, in one respect from these earlier cases: it is the first to base a challenge not on speculation about how a system *might* operate, but on empirical documentation on how it *does* operate. . . .

The Baldus study . . . distinguishes between those cases in which (1) the jury exercises virtually no discretion because the strength or weakness of aggravating factors usually suggests that only one outcome is appropriate; and (2) cases reflecting an "intermediate" level of aggravation, in which the jury has considerable discretion in choosing a sentence. McCleskey's case falls into the intermediate range. In such cases, . . . just under 59% — almost 6 in 10 — defendants comparable to McCleskey would not have received the death penalty if their victims had been black. . . .

The statistical evidence in this case . . . relentlessly documents the risk that McCleskey's sentence was influenced by racial considerations. This evidence shows that there is a better than even chance in Georgia that race will influence the decision to impose the death penalty: a majority of defendants in white-victim crimes would not have been sentenced to die if their victims had been black. . . . In determining the guilt of a defendant, a state must prove its case beyond a reasonable doubt. . . . Surely, we should not be willing to take a person's life if the chance that his death sentence was irrationally imposed is *more* likely than not. . .

McCleskey's claim is not a fanciful product of mere statistical artifice. For many years, Georgia operated openly and formally precisely the type of dual system the evidence shows is still effectively in place. . . . By the time of the Civil War, a dual system of crime and punishment was well established in Georgia. The state criminal code contained separate sections for "Slaves and Free Persons of Color" and for all other persons. [Justice Brennan here cited numerous instances in which the Georgia Penal Code had provided more severe punishments for crimes committed by blacks and for crimes (especially rape) committed against white victims.]

. . . Citation of past practices does not justify the automatic condemnation of current ones. But it would be unrealistic to ignore the influence of history in assessing the plausible implications of McCleskey's evidence. "[A]mericans share a historical experience that has resulted in individuals within the culture ubiquitously attaching a significance to race that is irrational and often outside their awareness." Lawrence, The Id, The Ego, and Equal Protection: Reckoning With Unconscious Racism, 39 Stan. L. Rev. 327 (1987). As we said in Rose v. Mitchell:

> [W]e . . . cannot deny that, 114 years after the close of the War Between the States and nearly 100 years after *Strauder,* racial and other forms of discrimination still remain a fact of life, in the administration of justice as in our society as a whole. Perhaps today that discrimination takes a form more subtle than before. But it is not less real or pernicious. 443 U.S. 545, 558-559 (1979).

. . . The Court . . . declines to find McCleskey's evidence sufficient in view of "the safeguards designed to minimize racial bias in the [capital sentencing] process." In Gregg v. Georgia, 428 U.S., at 226, the Court rejected a facial challenge to the Georgia capital sentencing statute, describing such a challenge as based on "simply an assertion of lack of faith" that the system could operate in a fair manner. Justice White observed that the claim that prosecutors might act in an arbitrary fashion was "unsupported by any facts." . . . *Gregg* bestowed no permanent approval on the Georgia system. It simply held that the State's statutory safeguards were assumed sufficient to channel discretion without evidence otherwise. . . .

The Court next states [its] fear that recognition of McCleskey's claim would open the door to widespread challenges to all aspects of criminal sentencing. [T]o reject McCleskey's powerful evidence on this basis is to ignore both the qualitatively different character of the death penalty and the particular repugnance of racial discrimination. . . .

Finally, the Court justifies its rejection of McCleskey's claim by cautioning against usurpation of the legislatures' role in devising and monitoring criminal punishment. . . . Those whom we would banish from society or from the human community itself often speak in too faint a voice to be heard above society's demand for punishment. It is the particular role of courts to hear these voices, for the Constitution declares that the majoritarian chorus may not alone dictate the conditions of social life.

[I]t has been scarcely a generation since this Court's first decision striking down racial segregation, and barely two decades since the legislative prohibition of racial discrimination in major domains of national life. These have been honorable steps, but we cannot pretend that in three decades we have completely escaped the grip of an historical legacy spanning centuries. Warren McCleskey's evidence confronts us with the subtle and persistent influence of the past. His message is a disturbing one to a society that has formally repudiated racism, and a frustrating one to a Nation accustomed to regarding its destiny as the product of its own will. Nonetheless, we ignore him at our peril, for we remain imprisoned by the past as long as we deny its influence in the present. . . .

JUSTICE BLACKMUN, [with whom JUSTICES MARSHALL, BRENNAN, and STEVENS join], dissenting. . . .

The Court today seems to give a new meaning to our recognition that death is different. Rather than requiring "a correspondingly greater degree of scrutiny of the capital sentencing determination," California v. Ramos, 463 U.S. 992, 998-999 (1983), the Court relies on the very fact that this is a case involving capital punishment to apply a *lesser* standard of scrutiny under the Equal Protection Clause. . . .

A criminal defendant alleging an equal protection violation must prove the existence of purposeful discrimination. He may establish a prima facie case of purposeful discrimination "by showing that the totality of the relevant facts gives rise to an inference of discriminatory purpose." Batson v. Kentucky, 106 S. Ct., at 1721. Once the defendant establishes a prima facie case, the burden shifts to the prosecution to rebut that case. "The State cannot meet his burden on mere general assertions that its officials did not discriminate or that they properly performed their official duties." Ibid. The State must demonstrate that the challenged effect was due to "'permissible racially neutral selection criteria.'" Ibid. . . .

McCleskey . . . demonstrated that it was more likely than not that the fact that the victim he was charged with killing was white determined that he received a sentence of death — 20 out of every 34 defendants in McCleskey's midrange category would not have been sentenced to be executed if their victims had been black. [T]he race of the victim is more important in explaining the imposition of a death sentence than is the factor whether the defendant was a prime mover in the homicide.[9] Similarly, the race-of-victim factor is nearly as crucial as the statutory aggravating circumstance whether the defendant had a prior record of a conviction for a capital crime.[10] . . . In sum, McCleskey has demonstrated a clear pattern of differential treatment according to race that is "unexplainable on grounds other than race."

The Court's explanations for its failure to apply this well-established equal protection analysis to this case are not persuasive. . . . I do not believe acceptance of McCleskey's claim would eliminate capital punishment in Georgia. [I]n extremely aggravated murders the risk of discriminatory enforcement of the death penalty is minimized. . . . Moreover, the establishment of guidelines for Assistant District Attorneys as to the appropriate basis for exercising their discretion at the various steps in the prosecution of a case would provide at least a measure of consistency. The Court's emphasis on the procedural safeguards in the system ignores the fact that there are none whatsoever during the crucial process leading up to trial. As Justice White stated for the plurality in Turner v. Murray, I find "the risk that racial prejudice may have infected petitioner's capital sentencing unacceptable in light of the ease with which that risk could have been minimized." 106 S. Ct., at 1688. I dissent.

JUSTICE STEVENS, with whom JUSTICE BLACKMUN joins, dissenting.

. . . This sort of disparity is constitutionally intolerable. It flagrantly violates the Court's prior "insistence that capital punishment be imposed fairly, and with reasonable consistency, or not at all." Eddings v. Oklahoma, 455 U.S. 104, 112 (1982).

The Court's decision appears to be based on a fear that the acceptance of

9. A defendant's chances of receiving a death sentence increase by a factor of 4.3 if the victim is white, but only by 2.3 if the defendant was the prime mover behind the homicide.

10. A prior record of a conviction for murder, armed robbery, rape, or kidnapping with bodily injury increases the chances of a defendant's receiving a death sentence by a factor of 4.9.

McCleskey's claim would sound the death knell for capital punishment in Georgia. If society were indeed forced to choose between a racially discriminatory death penalty (one that provides heightened protection against murder "for whites only") and no death penalty at all, the choice mandated by the Constitution would be plain. But the Court's fear is unfounded. One of the lessons of the Baldus study is that there exist certain categories of extremely serious crimes for which prosecutors consistently seek, and juries consistently impose, the death penalty without regard to the race of the victim or the race of the offender. If Georgia were to narrow the class of death-eligible defendants to those categories, the danger of arbitrary and discriminatory imposition of the death penalty would be significantly decreased, if not eradicated. . . . [S]uch a restructuring of the sentencing scheme is surely not too high a price to pay. . . .

NOTES

1. *Racial discrimination.* For helpful discussions of the issues posed by the *McCleskey* case, see David C. Baldus, George G. Woodworth & Charles A. Pulaski, Equal Justice and the Death Penalty (1990); Welsh S. White, The Death Penalty in the Eighties, 113-139 (1987); Randall Kennedy, *McCleskey v. Kemp:* Race, Capital Punishment, and the Supreme Court, 101 Harv. L. Rev. 1388 (1988); Samuel R. Gross, Race and Death: The Judicial Evaluation of Evidence of Discrimination in Capital Sentencing, 18 U.C. Davis L. Rev. 1275 (1985).

For several years, critics of the result in *McCleskey* have sought to overturn the decision by enacting national legislation requiring states to demonstrate that their enforcement of the death penalty is racially neutral. A provision to this effect was passed by the United States House of Representatives as part of the Crime Control Act of 1994, but the House-Senate conference committee deleted it from the bill. See N.Y. Times, July 29, 1994, at A1, A9.

2. *Gender discrimination with respect to defendants?* Consider Elizabeth Rapaport, The Death Penalty and Gender Discrimination, 25 Law & Socy. Rev. 367, 367-368 (1991):

> A gross comparison of the death-sentencing rates for men and women suggests that women convicted of murder are underrepresented on death row. Two percent of men but only one tenth of 1 percent of women convicted of murder are condemned to die.
>
> For a feminist to raise the issue of gender discrimination and capital punishment is not an altogether comfortable undertaking. At worst, it suggests a campaign to exterminate a few more wretched sisters. In my view, however, the issue is worth confronting. The reputed leniency that women receive with respect to death sentencing supports the view widely held in our society that women are incapable of achieving, nor are they in fact held to, the same standards of personal responsibility as are men. Although there may well be fields of endeavor in which the most profound forms of equality call for recognition of difference, equal democratic citizenship can proceed from no other premise than that of equal personal responsibility for decisions and actions. The chivalry from which women supposedly benefit is too costly: In ideological coin it is supposed to be repaid with tacit recognition of the moral inferiority of females and our lack of aptitude for full citizenship. As

a matter of both logic and political necessity, then, feminists must embrace either gender-neutral evenhandedness or abolitionism.

Professor Rapaport goes on to examine data on the characteristics of male and female murderers. She concludes that a woman offender's low likelihood of receiving a death sentence is primarily the result of legitimate sentencing variables (less serious crimes or less serious prior records), but that women's "underrepresentation" on death row may also be due in part to the continued hold of the "chivalry" notion. (Id. at 374.)

3. Gender discrimination with respect to victims? The types of murder classified as "aggravated," and therefore eligible for the death penalty, typically include felony murders and other "stranger" homicides. See, for example, the Georgia statute quoted at page 497 n. 48 supra. Conversely, killings of spouses or acquaintances, which are often killings of a woman by a man, are much less likely to be punished by the death penalty. Does this mean that there is a "*McCleskey*" problem of inadequate protection for one class of potential victims? Consider Rapaport, supra Note 2, at 377-382:

> Domestic crimes may . . . become capital cases if they are regarded as especially brutal crimes or if they are also pecuniary crimes. But the paradigmatic domestic killing, arising out of hot anger at someone who is capable, as it were by definition, of calling out painful and sudden emotion in his or her killer, is virtually the antithesis of a capital murder. Yet there are features of domestic homicides that could plausibly be regarded as among the most reprehensible crimes: They involve the betrayal of familial trust and responsibility. . . . They also have characteristics that could be read as inherent extreme brutality. The victims of family murders are typically especially vulnerable to their killers because of physical weakness and psychological dependency. Often the victims have been the objects of prior and habitual violence by their killers.
>
> . . . [T]here is, from a feminist point of view, an invidious subordination of the interests of women involved in the failure of the statutes to attach our society's most profound condemnation to crimes that destroy the domestic peace. . . . The supposition that predatory violence is more reprehensible than domestic violence is a symptom or effect of the ancient family privacy doctrine that has supported male domestic authority, and the parental authority of both sexes, at the price of tolerating if not encouraging a culture of domestic violence.
>
> One piece of evidence that on the surface suggests social valuing of female victims is the finding that murderers of women are more likely to be death sentenced than murderers of men. We cannot, however, infer from this finding that the higher likelihood of a death sentence reflects a societal judgment that murders of female victims are in all circumstances more serious than murders of male victims. . . . It is congruent with patriarchal values, and offensive to feminist values, that violence against women belonging to others be more heavily sanctioned than violence against your own women.
>
> . . . [T]he criminal law is not being mobilized to sufficiently discredit, discourage, and sanction crimes of domestic oppression from which women and children suffer disproportionately.

Compare Phyllis L. Crocker, Feminism and Defending Men on Death Row, 29 St. Mary's L. J. 981, 1007 (1998). Having worked in a battered woman's shelter and having later represented men facing capital punishment, Professor Crocker describes "the conflict between being a feminist and representing a man on death row who killed a woman he had physically abused." She concludes (id.):

> Mario Marquez . . . brutally killed his wife and niece, because his own life was so wretched, and because nothing in our legal or social systems intervened, at any point, to stop the collision between his disastrous impairments and his wife's life. . . . We should not isolate our anger at the violence against a woman by thinking it impossible to represent, or understand, a man on death row who killed that woman. The tragedy of the woman's death and the tragedy of the defendant's life together reflect the devastating toll we take when, as a society, we fail to protect our children and we fail to protect each other.

4. Assessing the constitutional doctrines. Consider Carol S. Steiker & Jordan M. Steiker, Sober Second Thoughts: Reflections on Two Decades of Constitutional Regulation of Capital Punishment, 109 Harv. L. Rev. 355, 357-360, 433-436 (1995):

> Virtually no one thinks that the constitutional regulation of capital punishment has been a success. [S]ome critics claim that the Court's work has burdened the administration of capital punishment with an overly complex, absurdly arcane, and minutely detailed body of constitutional law that . . . "obstructs, delays, and defeats" the administration of capital punishment. [A] different set of critics claims that the Supreme Court has in fact turned its back on regulating the death penalty and no longer even attempts to meet the concerns about the arbitrary and discriminatory imposition of death that animated . . . *Furman.* These critics note that the Court's intervention has done little or nothing to remedy the vast overrepresentation on death row of the young, poor, and mentally retarded or the continuing influence of race on the capital sentencing decision. Under this view, in the anguished words of Justice Blackmun, . . . the Court has done no more than "tinker with the machinery of death."
>
> [W]e conclude that both sets of criticisms of the Court's work are substantially correct: the death penalty is, perversely, both over- and under-regulated.
>
> [There is] a substantial hidden cost of the Court's chosen path . . . , which creates an impression of enormous regulatory effort but achieves negligible regulatory effects. [P]owerful evidence suggests that death penalty law makes actors within the criminal justice system more comfortable with their roles by inducing an exaggerated belief in the essential rationality and fairness of the system. [T]he Court's focus on controlling the discretion of capital sentencers creates a false aura of rationality, even science, around the necessarily moral task of deciding life or death [and] has diluted judges' and jurors' sense of ultimate responsibility for imposing the death penalty.
>
> [Although] members of the general public do not know much about the intricacies of the Court's death penalty doctrine, our guess is that they *think* they know a great deal. [T]he public's impression [is] that any death sentences that are imposed and finally upheld are the product of a rigorous — indeed, *too* rigorous — system of constraints. . . . The Supreme Court's death penalty law, by creating an impression of enormous regulatory effort while achieving negligible regulatory effects, effectively obscures the true nature of our capital sentencing system, in which the pre-*Furman* world of unreviewable sentencer discretion lives on, with much the same consequences in terms of arbitrary and discriminatory sentencing patterns.

CHAPTER 6

THE SIGNIFICANCE OF RESULTING HARM

A. CAUSATION

Where a crime is defined without regard to any result of the defendant's conduct (for example, attempt, conspiracy, burglary), there is no need to face the issue of causation. But where a particular result of a defendant's conduct is a necessary element of the crime charged, a perplexing problem sometimes arises as to whether the defendant's act caused the result. Homicide cases are the most fertile source of causation problems. When the actor kills the very person he meant to kill (or knew he would kill), in precisely the way he intended, no causation difficulty arises. Nor is there difficulty in the case of unintended killings when the death occurs in precisely the way that the defendant's risky conduct made likely. But when the intended death occurs in a way not intended or the unintended death occurs in an unlikely way, the law must distinguish variations (between the actual result and the result intended or risked) that preclude liability from variations that do not preclude liability. The following hypotheticals will suggest the scope of the problem.

(1) Accused places poison by the bedside of his sick wife intending that she drink it. During the night she dies of a heart attack without having consumed the drink.
(2) Same as above, except that the wife sips the poison and is repelled by the taste; to wash it away, she goes to the bathroom for water, slips and injures herself fatally.
(3) Accused attempts to shoot her husband, but she misses. He thereupon boards a train for his mother's home and is killed in a train wreck.
(4) Accused shoots at deceased intending to kill him. The bullet misses but deceased dies of fright.
(5) While thoroughly intoxicated, accused No. 1 drives his car containing sleeping children at a speed greatly in excess of the speed limit. He crashes into the rear of a truck stalled in the middle of the road around a bend, the truck's driver, accused No. 2, having failed to leave his lights on or otherwise give warning to approaching cars. The children of accused No. 1 are killed in the crash.

(6) Accused administers a vicious blow to victim's head with a black-jack. The victim is taken to a hospital for treatment where (a) due to negligent medical treatment of the wound he dies of meningitis, (b) he dies of scarlet fever communicated by a nurse, (c) he is mortally wounded by a knife-wielding maniac, (d) he is decapitated by a maniac, (e) he deliberately takes a fatal dose of sleeping pills to end his misery, or (f) he is seized with an attack of appendicitis from which he dies.
(7) Accused No. 1 throws a live hand grenade into the room of accused No. 2 intending to kill him. The latter seizes it and throws it out his window where it falls to the crowded street below, exploding and killing several persons.
(8) Accused and deceased engage in an armed robbery. Deceased is killed in an exchange of bullets with the police.

1. *Foreseeability and Coincidence*

PEOPLE v. ACOSTA

Court of Appeal of California, 4th Appellate District
284 Cal. Rptr. 117 (1991)

WALLIN, J. Vincent William Acosta appeals his conviction on three counts of second degree murder . . . contending: (1) there was insufficient evidence his conduct was the proximate cause of the deaths; (2) there was insufficient evidence of malice. . . .

At 10 P.M. on March 10, 1987, Officers Salceda and Francis of the Santa Ana Police Department's automobile theft detail saw Acosta in Elvira Salazar's stolen Nissan Pulsar parked on the street. The officers approached Acosta and identified themselves. Acosta inched the Pulsar forward, then accelerated rapidly. He led Salceda, Francis and officers from other agencies on a 48-mile chase along numerous surface streets and freeways throughout Orange County. The chase ended near Acosta's residence in Anaheim.

During the chase, Acosta engaged in some of the most egregious driving tactics imaginable. He ran stop signs and red lights, and drove on the wrong side of streets, causing oncoming traffic to scatter or swerve to avoid colliding with him. . . .

Police helicopters from Anaheim, Costa Mesa, Huntington Beach, and Newport Beach assisted in the chase by tracking Acosta. During the early part of the pursuit, the Costa Mesa and Newport Beach craft were used, pinpointing Acosta's location with their high beam spotlights. The Costa Mesa helicopter was leading the pursuit, in front of and below the Newport Beach helicopter. As they flew into Newport Beach, the pilots agreed the Newport Beach craft should take the lead. . . .

At the direction of the Costa Mesa pilot, the Newport Beach helicopter moved forward and descended while the Costa Mesa helicopter banked to the right. Shortly after commencing this procedure, the Costa Mesa helicopter, having terminated radio communication, came up under the Newport Beach helicopter from the right rear and collided with it. Both helicopters fell to the ground. Three occupants in the Costa Mesa helicopter died as a result of the crash.

Menzies Turner, a retired Federal Aviation Administration (FAA) investigator, testified as an expert and concluded the accident occurred because the Costa Mesa helicopter, the faster of the two aircraft, made a 360-degree turn and closed too rapidly on the Newport Beach helicopter. He opined the Costa Mesa helicopter's pilot violated an FAA regulation prohibiting careless and reckless operation of an aircraft by failing to properly clear the area, not maintaining communication with the Newport Beach helicopter, failing to keep the other aircraft in view at all times, and not changing his altitude. He also testified the Costa Mesa pilot violated another FAA regulation prohibiting operation of one aircraft so close to another as to create a collision hazard.

Turner could not think of any reason for the Costa Mesa helicopter's erratic movement. The maneuver was not a difficult one, and was not affected by the ground activity at the time. He had never heard of a midair collision between two police helicopters involved in tracking a ground pursuit, and had never investigated a midair collision involving helicopters.[3] . . .

Acosta claims there was insufficient evidence . . . that he proximately caused the deaths of the victims. . . .

Acosta argues that although a collision between ground vehicles was a foreseeable result of his conduct, one between airborne helicopters was not, noting his expert had never heard of a similar incident. He also contends the Costa Mesa helicopter pilot's violation of FAA regulations was a superseding cause. Because the deaths here were unusual, to say the least, the issue deserves special scrutiny. . . .

"Proximate cause" is the term historically used[6] to separate those results for which an actor will be held responsible from those not carrying such responsibility. The term is, in a sense, artificial, serving matters of policy surrounding tort and criminal law and based partly on expediency and partly on concerns of fairness and justice. Because such concerns are sometimes more a matter of "common sense" than pure logic, the line of demarcation is flexible, and attempts to lay down uniform tests which apply evenly in all situations have failed. That does not mean general guidelines and approaches to analysis cannot be constructed.

The threshold question in examining causation is whether the defendant's act was an "actual cause" of the victim's injury. It is a sine qua non test: But for the defendant's act would the injury have occurred? Unless an act is an actual cause of the injury, it will not be considered a proximate cause.

[The court then reviewed the various verbal tests used by courts and concluded that in this case the issue was whether the death of the helicopter pilots was foreseeable.]

Prosser and Keeton, in an in-depth discussion of the dynamics of foresight, conclude that although it is desirable to exclude extremely remarkable and unusual results from the purview of proximate cause, it is virtually impossible to express a logical verbal formula which will produce uniform results. (Prosser & Keeton, [Torts] 300 [(5th ed. 1984)].) I agree. The standard should be simply stated, exclude extraordinary results, and allow the trier of fact to determine the

3. Our research yielded no published civil or criminal case nationwide which involved a two-helicopter collision.

6. The American Law Institute has urged the use of "legal cause" instead. Although there is some merit to its arguments, I abide with the traditional term, "proximate cause."

issue on the particular facts of the case using "the common sense of the common man as to common things." As with other ultimate issues, appellate courts must review that determination, giving due deference to the trier of fact.

The "highly extraordinary result" standard serves that purpose. It is consistent with the definition of foreseeability used in California. It does not involve the defendant's state of mind, but focuses upon the objective conditions present when he acts.[19] . . .

Here, but for Acosta's conduct of fleeing the police, the helicopters would never have been in position for the crash. . . .

The result was not highly extraordinary. Although a two-helicopter collision was unknown to expert witness Turner and no reported cases describe one, it was "a possible consequence which reasonably might have been contemplated." Given the emotional dynamics of any police pursuit, there is an "appreciable probability" that one of the pursuers, in the heat of the chase, may act negligently or recklessly to catch the quarry. That no pursuits have ever before resulted in a helicopter crash or midair collision is more a comment on police flying skill and technology than upon the innate probabilities involved. . . . Given these circumstances, a finding of proximate cause is appropriate. . . .

[On the other issue in the case, whether there was sufficient evidence of malice, the court found in the negative because there was not enough evidence to show that Acosta consciously disregarded the risk to the helicopter pilots: "In the absence of more evidence, no reasonable juror could find a conscious disregard for a risk which is barely objectively cognizable."]

The judgment is reversed. . . .

CROSBY, J., . . . Whether the defendant may be held criminally culpable for the tragic deaths in this case is the key issue before us. Justice Wallin says yes, but not for murder. . . . I disagree . . . because the law does not assign blame to an otherwise blameworthy actor when neither the intervening negligent conduct nor the risk of harm was foreseeable.

Or, as Justice Cardozo put it,

> We are told that one who drives at reckless speed through a crowded city street is guilty of a negligent act and, therefore, of a wrongful one irrespective of the consequences. Negligent the act is, and wrongful in the sense that it is unsocial, but wrongful and unsocial in relation to other travelers, only because the eye of vigilance perceives the risk of damage. . . . [R]isk imports relation; it is risk to another or to others within the range of apprehension.

(Palsgraf v. Long Island R. Co. (1928) 248 N.Y. 339.) The occupants of these helicopters were surely not "within the range of apprehension" of a fleeing criminal on the ground.

To be sure, defendant represented a threat to everyone traveling the same roads and would have been responsible for any injury directly or indirectly caused by his actions in those environs; but to extend that responsibility to persons in the air, whose role was merely to observe his movements, a simple enough task in

19. The Model Penal Code takes a similar approach, focusing on whether the result is "too remote or accidental in its occurrence to have a [just] bearing on the actor's liability or on the gravity of his offense." (Model Pen. Code, §2.03(2)(b).) . . .

far speedier helicopters, defies common sense. . . . They were not in the zone of danger in this case by any stretch of the imagination, and the manner and circumstances of the collision could hardly have reasonably been foreseen. . . . Although less remote than a dispatcher suffering a coronary, perhaps, this was a "highly extraordinary result" by any measure and, properly viewed, beyond the long arm of the criminal law. . . .

QUESTIONS

1. Acosta was not guilty of murder, the court holds, because he didn't have a murderous mens rea; it couldn't be found that he "consciously disregarded a risk which was barely objectively cognizable." Would the court have reached the same conclusion if Acosta had collided with and killed another driver on the ground? If not, what practical difference is there between the conclusions reached by the majority and the dissent?

2. If Acosta was not guilty of murder, what crime *did* he commit? Is the "barely objectively cognizable" risk to the helicopter pilots sufficient to make Acosta guilty of criminally negligent homicide? Why should the low likelihood of the harm that actually occurred be relevant in determining whether Acosta acted with a culpable mens rea?

PEOPLE v. ARZON

Supreme Court, New York County
92 Misc. 2d 739, 401 N.Y.S.2d 156 (1978)

MILONAS, J. The defendant was indicted on September 28, 1977 for two counts of murder in the second degree and arson in the third degree after he allegedly intentionally set fire to a couch, thus causing a serious fire on the fifth floor of an abandoned building at 358 East 8th Street in New York County. The New York City Fire Department, in responding to the conflagration, arrived to find the rear portion of the fifth and sixth floors burning. The firemen attempted to bring the situation under control, but making no progress and there being no additional assistance available, they decided to withdraw from the building. At that point, they were suddenly enveloped by a dense smoke, which was later discovered to have arisen from another independent fire that had broken out on the second floor.

Although this fire was also determined to have originated in arson, there is virtually no evidence implicating the defendant in its responsibility. However, the combination of the thick smoke and the fifth floor fire made evacuation from the premises extremely hazardous, and, in the process, Fireman Martin Celic sustained injuries from which he subsequently died. Accordingly, the defendant was accused of murder in the second degree for having, "Under circumstances evincing a depraved indifference to human life, recklessly engaged in conduct which created a grave risk of death to another person," thereby causing the death of Martin Celic, and with felony murder. The third charge of the indictment, arson, is not at issue for purposes of the instant application.

It is the defendant's contention that the evidence before the grand jury is insufficient to support the first two counts. He argues that . . . murder requires a causal link between the underlying crime and the death, a connection which, in the defendant's view, is here lacking.

There is remarkably little authority on precisely what sort of behavior constitutes "depraved indifference to human life." In the leading case on the subject, People v. Kibbe, 35 N.Y.2d 407, 321 N.E.2d 773 (1974), the Court of Appeals affirmed the [murder] conviction of defendants who had abandoned their helplessly intoxicated robbery victim by the side of a dark road in subfreezing temperature, one-half mile from the nearest structure, without shoes or eyeglasses, with his trousers at his ankles, his shirt pulled up and his outer clothing removed. The court held that while the deceased was actually killed by a passing truck, the defendants' conduct was a sufficiently direct cause of the ensuing death to warrant criminal liability and that "it is not necessary that the ultimate harm be intended by the actor. It will suffice if it can be said beyond a reasonable doubt, as indeed it can here be said, that the ultimate harm is something which should have been foreseen as being reasonably related to the acts of the accused."

Clearly, an obscure or merely probable connection between the defendant's conduct and another person's death is not enough to support a charge of homicide. People v. Stewart, [40 N.Y.2d 692, 358 N.E.2d 487 (1976)]. In *Stewart,* the victim had been operated upon for a stab wound in the stomach inflicted by the defendant. Afterwards, the surgeon performed an entirely unrelated hernia procedure on him, and he died. According to the court, "the prosecutor must, at least, prove that the defendant's conduct was an actual cause of death, in the sense that it forged a link in the chain of causes which actually brought about the death. . . ." In this instance, the possibility that death resulted from a factor not attributable to the defendant could not be ruled out beyond a reasonable doubt, since the patient would, in all likelihood, have survived except for the hernia operation. . . .

[T]he defendant's conduct need not be the sole and exclusive factor in the victim's death. In the standard established by People v. Kibbe, supra, and People v. Stewart, supra, an individual is criminally liable if his conduct was a sufficiently direct cause of the death, and the ultimate harm is something which should have been foreseen as being reasonably related to his acts. It is irrelevant that, in this instance the fire which had erupted on the second floor intervened, thus contributing to the conditions that culminated in the death of Fireman Celic. In *Kibbe,* the victim was killed when he was struck by a truck. This did not relieve the defendants in that case from criminal responsibility for his murder, as it does not absolve the defendant here. Certainly, it was foreseeable that firemen would respond to the situation, thus exposing them, along with the persons already present in the vicinity, to a life-threatening danger. The fire set by the defendant was an indispensable link in the chain of events that resulted in the death. It continued to burn out of control, greatly adding to the problem of evacuating the building by blocking off one of the access routes. At the very least, the defendant's act, as was the case in *Kibbe,* placed the deceased in a position where he was particularly vulnerable to the separate and independent force, in this instance, the fire on the second floor.

Consequently, the defendant's motion to dismiss the [murder counts] of the indictment is denied.

PEOPLE v. WARNER-LAMBERT CO., 51 N.Y.2d 295, 414 N.E.2d 660 (1980): [Defendant corporation and several of its officers and employees were indicted for second-degree manslaughter (N.Y. Penal Law §125.15, page 393 supra) and criminally negligent homicide (N.Y. Penal Law §125.10, page 393 supra). Several of the corporation's employees were killed (and many more injured) in a massive explosion at one of its chewing-gum factories. Evidence before the grand jury showed that the corporation used two potentially explosive substances in its manufacturing process, magnesium stearate (MS) and liquid nitrogen; that defendants had earlier been warned by their insurance carrier that the high concentrations of MS dust, combined with other conditions, created an explosion hazard; and that these hazards were not eliminated by the time of the accident. On the issue of what triggered the explosion there was apparently no hard proof, only speculations by experts that it could have been caused by mechanical sparking in the machines or by the liquid nitrogen dripping onto a concentration of MS and igniting under the impact of a moving metal part. The court held that the evidence before the grand jury was not legally sufficient to establish the foreseeability of the immediate, triggering cause of the explosion and therefore dismissed the indictment. The court stated:]

It has been the position of the People that but-for causation is all that is required for the imposition of criminal liability. Thus, it is their submission, reduced to its simplest form, that there was evidence of a foreseeable and indeed foreseen risk of explosion of MS dust and that in consequence of defendants' failure to remove the dust a fatal explosion occurred. The chain of physical events by which the explosion was set off, i.e., its particular cause, is to them a matter of total indifference. On oral argument the People contended that liability could be imposed if the cause of the explosion were the lighting of a match by an uninvited intruder or the striking of a bolt of lightning. In effect they would hold defendants to the status of guarantors until the ambient dust was removed. It thus appears that the People would invoke an expanded application of proximate cause principles lifted from the civil law of torts.

We have rejected the application of any such sweeping theory of culpability under our criminal law, however. . . . [In People v. Kibbe (discussed in the *Arzon* case, supra)] the critical issue was whether the defendants should be held criminally liable for murder when the particular cause of death was vehicular impact rather than freezing. Under the theory now advanced by the People it would have been irrelevant that death had been the consequence of one particular chain of causation rather than another; it would have been enough that the defendants exposed their victim to the risk of death and that he died. That, of course, was not the analysis of culpability that we adopted. [W]e held that . . . "We subscribe to the requirement that the defendants' actions must be a *sufficiently direct cause* of the ensuing death before there can be any imposition of criminal liability, and recognize, of course, that this standard is greater than that required to serve as a basis for tort liability." Thus, we were concerned for the nature of the chain of particularized events which in fact led to the victim's death; it was not enough that death had occurred as the result of the defendants' abandonment of their helpless victim. To analogize the factual situation in the case now before us to that in *Kibbe* it might be hypothesized that the abandoned victim in *Kibbe* instead of being either frozen to death or killed when struck by a passing motor vehicle was killed when struck by an airplane making an emergency landing on the highway or when hit by a stray bullet from a hunter's rifle — occasions of death not reasonably to have been foreseen when the defendants abandoned their victim.

NOTES ON FORESEEABILITY

1. *The specific causal mechanism.* Is *Warner-Lambert* correct in requiring that the defendant foresee the specific triggering cause of an explosion? Or should it be sufficient that a defendant foresee enhanced danger *in the event* of a spark or other precipitating cause? Consider the following variations.

(a) In Commonwealth v. Welansky, page 425 supra, several hundred night-club patrons died in a fire caused when a busboy carelessly struck a match; the defendant, who was responsible for the lack of adequate safety exits in the club, was held liable for involuntary manslaughter. Is the result consistent with *Warner-Lambert?* Suppose there had been no evidence of how the fire in *Welansky* had started?

(b) People v. Deitsch, 97 A.D.2d 327, 470 N.Y.S.2d 158 (1983), involved a warehouse fire that killed an employee who was trapped on the sixth floor when the flames broke out. Evidence before the grand jury suggested that bales of material stored in the building blocked the fire escape and that signs indicating the escape route might have been inadequate. However, the cause of the fire was never determined. The defendants controlled the building, and there was evidence that they were aware of its conditions. Can they properly be charged with manslaughter? The court upheld the indictment. Distinguishing *Warner-Lambert,* the court said (470 N.Y.S.2d at 164):

> In the instant case the theory of the prosecution is not that the defendants caused the fire which resulted in Logan's death. Rather, the prosecution is predicated upon the theory that defendants created conditions in the warehouse which they should have foreseen could result in death in the event of a fire. This case bears more of a resemblance to People v. Kibbe than it does to *Warner-Lambert.* In *Kibbe* . . . the court held that by creating the circumstances that led to death by a foreseeable intervening event, the defendants caused death in a sufficiently direct manner to warrant imposing criminal liability. Similarly, in the instant case, the Grand Jury might well have concluded that defendants created unsafe conditions in the warehouse which led to Logan's death by a foreseeable intervening cause — the fire.

Question: Why can't the same be said of *Warner-Lambert?*

(c) In support of a foreseeability standard, Professor Lawrence Crocker argues that "the key concept [in proximate cause analysis] is probability — probability as it would be understood by ordinary persons antecedent to the event, with no special access to information about the facts of the event."[1] Applying this test, what should be the result in *Deitsch?* In *Warner-Lambert?*

If we can't determine how a fire started, should the person responsible for a hazardous condition be held liable, because it is plausible to assume that the fa-

1. Crocker, A Retributive Theory of Causation, [1994] J. Contemp. Legal Issues 65, 100.

tal spark was produced in some ordinary way? Or should that person escape liability, because the prosecution has not proved beyond a reasonable doubt that the fatal spark was *not* produced in some bizarre, unforeseeable way? Criticizing the foreseeability test, Professor Michael Moore argues that the concept of foreseeability is inherently arbitrary and manipulable, because of what he calls "the multiple-description problem," namely that "there are many equally accurate ways to describe any particular [harm-causing event]," and thus conclusions about foreseeability inevitably depend on the level of generality at which we choose to describe what occurred.[2]

2. Vulnerability of the victim. In People v. Stamp, page 450 supra, a robbery victim who suffered from severe coronary disease died of a heart attack triggered by fright experienced during the offense. The court held the defendant guilty of felony-murder, stating that liability was "not limited to those deaths which are foreseeable. [T]he robber takes his victim as he finds him."

Questions: If death results from an unusual disease unforeseeably contracted by the victim after an assault, the defendant presumably is relieved of liability. This remains true even when the victim would not have contracted the disease, but for the situation created by the injuries. Why should the result be different when the disease producing death was contracted by the victim *before* the defendant's assault? Why should it be the case that the defendant always "takes his victim as he finds him"?

Consider State v. Lane, 444 S.E.2d 233 (N.C. App. 1994). Lane argued with Linton and punched him once in the face. Linton, who was extremely drunk, fell to the street. A city rescue squad arrived on the scene but concluded that Linton had not suffered any serious injury. He died two days later from brain swelling caused by the punch. A medical examiner testified that because Linton was a chronic alcoholic, he was especially susceptible to incurring such an injury from any blow to the head. At trial, Lane was convicted of misdemeanor-manslaughter under the unlawful-act doctrine. What result on appeal? Is it unfair to apply the vulnerable-victim rule against Lane when the victim himself is responsible for his preexisting condition? Or is it inappropriate to permit conclusions about causation to turn on the perceived blameworthiness of the victim?

3. Is medical malpractice foreseeable? (a) Consider the following efforts to summarize the applicable principle:

1 M. Hale, Pleas of the Crown 428: [If a] wound or hurt be not mortal, but with ill applications by the party, or those about him, of unwholesome salves or medicines the party dies, if it can clearly appear, that this medicine, and not the wound, was the cause of his death, it seems it is not homicide, but then that must appear clearly and certainly to be so.

But if a man receives a wound, which is not in itself mortal, but either for want of helpful applications, or neglect thereof, it turns to a gangrene, or a fever, and that gangrene or fever be the immediate cause of his death, yet, this is murder or manslaughter in him that gave the stroke or wound, for that wound, tho it were not the immediate cause of his death, yet, if it were the mediate cause thereof, and the fever or gangrene was the immediate cause of his death, yet the

2. Moore, Foreseeing Harm Opaquely, In Action and Value in Criminal Law 125, 126-127 (S. Shute, et al., eds. 1993).

wound was the cause of the gangrene or fever, and so consequently is causa causati.

Regina v. Cheshire, [1991] 3 All E.R. 670: [I]f at the time of death the original wound is still an operating cause and a substantial cause, then the death can properly be said to be the result of the wound, albeit that some other cause of death is also operating. Only if it can be said that the original wounding is merely the setting in which another cause operates can it be said that the death does not result from the wound.

(b) Many courts find the initial assailant liable for the victim's death even when significant medical error contributes to the result. But courts disagree about the extent to which subsequent medical mistakes may bear on the initial assailant's liability. Consider the following cases:

Hall v. State, 159 N.E. 420, 426 (1927): [During the course of a robbery, defendant struck several blows to the victim's head, fracturing the victim's skull. The victim died 10 days later, as a result of blood poisoning attributable to the skull fracture. At trial, the judge barred the defendant from asking the coroner questions designed to show that the victim's wound received incompetent medical treatment and that "the cause of his death was the doctor's treatment, or a disease brought on by the wound or by the treatment, and not the act of the [defendant]." A conviction of first-degree murder was sustained, with the appellate court holding that even favorable answers to the questions put would not have authorized the jury to return a different verdict:] It is not indispensable to a conviction that a wound be necessarily fatal and the direct cause of death. If the wound caused death indirectly through a chain of natural effects and causes unchanged by human action, such as the consequential development of septicaemia or blood poisoning, he who inflicted the wound or injury is responsible. A person who inflicts a serious wound upon another, calculated to destroy or endanger his life, will not be relieved of responsibility, even though unskilled or improper medical treatment aggravates the wound and contributes to the death. Every person is held to contemplate and be responsible for the natural consequences of his own acts, and the criminality of an act is not altered or diminished by the fact that other causes cooperated in producing the fatal result.

State v. Shabazz, 719 A.2d 40, 444-445 (1998): [The defendant allegedly stabbed the victim in the abdomen, lung and liver. The victim was taken to Yale–New Haven Hospital, where he underwent surgery, followed by a period in the post-operative recovery room. Thereafter he was placed in a regular hospital room. He died the following morning, due to heavy bleeding that resulted from the liver surgery. The trial judge barred the defense from introducing the testimony of two medical experts who would have testified that the hospital had been grossly negligent (1) by giving the victim an anticoagulant drug after surgery, when the medical objective at that point was to encourage rather than prevent clotting of the blood; and (2) by transferring the victim to a regular room, rather than placing him in the intensive care unit, where his vital signs could have been closely monitored. The appellate court held that the defense testimony was properly excluded:] [T]here was no evidence from which the jury rationally could have inferred that the hospital's gross negligence was the sole cause of the victim's death. Both [defense experts] acknowledged that the stab wounds . . .

would have been fatal in the absence of any medical treatment. At the most, the purported gross negligence would have been a contributing factor, not the sole cause. . . . We see no sound reason of policy why a defendant who has committed a homicidal act should escape criminal liability simply because the hospital . . . contributed to the death. [G]ross negligence may permit the defendant to escape liability [only] when it was the sole cause of the death. . . .

United States v. Main, 113 F.3d 1046 (9th Cir. 1997): [Fleeing a traffic stop at high speed, defendant's truck veered off the road and collided with an obstacle. Defendant was thrown clear, but his passenger was trapped inside the wreckage. The pursuing officer reached the scene and noticed that the passenger, lying down in a fetal position, was still breathing. The officer decided not to move him, because of fear that head or neck injuries might be aggravated by movement. When another officer arrived seven minutes later, the passenger was dead, apparently because he had been left in a position in which he could not breathe properly. Defendant argued that the first officer's failure to move the victim or summon assistance more promptly was an intervening cause. The trial judge refused to instruct the jury that it could find that the defendant's actions were not the proximate cause of death, and defendant was convicted of involuntary manslaughter. The court of appeals (per Noonan, J.) reversed:] It will be said that a failure to get prompt medical attention is not an unlikely hazard for the victim of an automobile accident. Agreed. But that judgment remains a judgment . . . that is in the province of the jury. When the jury is not told that it must find that the victim's death was within the risk created by the defendant's conduct, an element of the crime has been erroneously withdrawn from the jury.

(c) Is the result in *Main* reconcilable with the results in *Hall* and *Shabazz*? When *should* subsequent treatment errors relieve the initial wrongdoer of liability for the ultimate harm?

NOTE ON OMISSIONS AS CAUSES

An intruder pushes a small child into a pool. Suppose that the child's baby sitter deliberately refuses to come to its aid and that the child then drowns. It is clear that the baby sitter had a duty to save the child, but can we say that the baby sitter *caused* the child to drown? It is sometimes argued that only the intruder, not the baby sitter, can plausibly be considered the cause of the child's death. See discussion in Michael Moore, Act and Crime 78 et seq. (1993); Alison McIntyre, Guilty Bystanders? On the Legitimacy of Duty to Rescue Statutes, 23 Phil. & Pub. Affairs 157 (1994).

Is the argument convincing? There is rarely only one but-for cause of a result. A number of conditions may be necessary for an event to occur (in the case of a fire — wood, paper, a breeze, the striking of a match). The baby sitter's omission is a necessary condition in the same sense: But for the sitter's failure to aid, the child would not have died. But when we make this claim with respect to an omission, does it follow that every passer-by who failed to rescue the baby must be considered the cause of its death? One solution is to say that omissions by the passers-by are indeed necessary conditions, and thus causes — but nonculpable causes — of the result. Whatever we may think of these verbal and conceptual difficulties, courts are uniformly willing to treat an omission as the legal cause of a result in situations where there is a duty to act. See, e.g., Jones v. United States, page 190 supra, and Notes following.

MODEL PENAL CODE

SECTION 2.03. CAUSAL RELATIONSHIP BETWEEN CONDUCT AND RESULT; DIVERGENCE BETWEEN RESULT DESIGNED OR CONTEMPLATED AND ACTUAL RESULT OR BETWEEN PROBABLE AND ACTUAL RESULT

[See Appendix for text of this section.]

NOTES ON STATUTORY STANDARDS

1. Most state codes include no explicit rules for determining causation. In these jurisdictions, the courts are left to resolve causation issues on the basis of evolving common law principles. Roughly a dozen states have adopted causation provisions based in whole or in part on the Model Penal Code formulation. See Model Penal Code and Commentaries, Comment to §2.03, at 264-265 (1985).

2. In evaluating any of the causation standards that might be proposed, consider two questions. First, *what difference will it make,* in terms of whether the defendant's conduct is punishable at all or in terms of the severity of the punishment, if the defendant's conduct is held to be the "cause" of the result. This question should be asked with respect to each of the cases and hypotheticals in this chapter. Second, what is the *reason* for that difference in liability or in the severity of punishment. In other words, why should the result of conduct ever make a difference? Consider Meir Dan-Cohen, Causation, in 1 Encyclopedia of Crime and Justice 165-166 (1983):

> The functional analysis of causation is . . . greatly impeded by discovering that there is considerable difficulty in establishing the relevance of the occurrence of actual harm to criminal liability or severity of punishment. . . . The rational and moral grounds for punishment, it has been argued, should lead one to focus on the defendant's conduct and state of mind or degree of culpability, not on whether some harmful result actually followed from that conduct. . . .
>
> That the actual death of the victim is somehow relevant to determining the accused's criminal liability is nonetheless a widely shared and deeply entrenched intuition. . . . The legal concept of causation may accordingly be seen as a corollary of this intuition. Although the intuition itself resists rationalization by reference to the goals of the criminal law, . . . it is hard to deny both the pervasiveness of that underlying sentiment and the influence it actually exerts on the criminal law, even in the absence of compelling rational arguments to support it. . . . Posed in connection with the retributive goal of punishment, the question of causation (namely, "Is there a causal relation between *A*'s conduct and *B*'s death?") amounts to asking whether punishing *A* is necessary to satisfy the retributive urge aroused by the fact of *B*'s death.
>
> [T]o the extent that causation plays a role in serving the retributive goal of punishment, ... the concept of causation is inextricably bound up, in ordinary usage,

> with the entire complex of blaming. [T]he statement that *A* caused *B*'s death may, in ordinary speech, be as much a conclusory statement, based on the prior tacit judgment that *A* deserves to be punished for *B*'s death, as it is an independent statement of fact which leads to that conclusion. Put differently, in ordinary usage the concepts of causation and blame or deserts often reverse the idealized roles usually assigned to them in moral and legal theory. [O]ne would expect the conclusion that *A* should be punished for *B*'s death to be based, in part, on the judgment that *A* caused *B*'s death. In fact, the conclusion that *A* deserves to be punished may be directly and intuitively generated by the retributive urge, preceding and merely rationalized by the finding of a sufficient causal relationship between *A*'s acts and *B*'s death.

Compare Michael S. Moore, Causation and Responsibility, 16 Soc. Philos. & Policy 1, 4-5 (Summer 1999). Putting aside as inadequate any policy-based approach defining "cause" for legal purposes, he writes:

> [L]egal liability tracks moral responsibility . . . and moral responsibility is for those harms we *cause.* "Cause" has to mean what we mean when we assign moral responsibility *for* some harm, and what we mean in morality is to name a causal relation that is natural and *not* of the law's creation. . . . If the point of criminal law were [the] utilitarian point of deterring crime, then a constructed idea of legal cause perhaps could be justified; such a functional definition would take into account the incentive effects of various liability rules. But the function of criminal law is not utilitarian; it is retributive. . . . This requires that its liability rules track closely the moral criteria for blameworthiness. One of those criteria is causation of morally prohibited states of affairs. Thus, again, "cause" as used in criminal law must mean what it means in morality, and what it means in morality is to name a relation that is natural and *not* of the law's creation.

NOTES ON TRANSFERRED INTENT

1. Defendant shoots at Lucky, intending to kill him. The bullet misses but strikes and kills Unlucky, perhaps because the bullet ricocheted in an odd way. Is Defendant guilty of murdering Unlucky, regardless of how unforeseeable that killing may have been? The law is clear in all jurisdiction — the answer is yes. The conceptual justification is the doctrine of transferred intent, according to which Defendant's intent to kill Lucky is "transferred" to his action that killed Unlucky.

Does this approach make sense? Isn't it a pure fiction to say that Defendant intended to kill Unlucky, when in fact he killed Unlucky by accident? Absent the notion of "transferring" his intent, we might say that Defendant is guilty of the attempted murder of Lucky and (perhaps) the involuntary manslaughter of Unlucky — if the required level of criminal negligence could be shown. Why should we punish Defendant much more severely than other would-be murderers whose attempts miscarry?

Consider Justice Mosk, concurring in People v. Scott, 14 Cal. 4th 544, 556 (1996): "[O]ne cannot reasonably distinguish between *A,* who unlawfully kills *B* unlawfully intending to kill *B,* and *X,* who unlawfully kills *Y* unlawfully intending to kill *Z.* Both *A* and *X* harbor the same blameworthy mental state, an unlawful intent to kill. Both *A* and *X* cause the same blameworthy result, an unlawful killing."[3] The Model Penal Code would likewise convict the defendant of murder in these scenarios; §2.03(2)(a) provides that where the crime requires that a defendant intentionally cause a particular result (e.g., killing someone), that element of the crime is satisfied if the defendant accidentally causes that result to one person while intentionally trying to cause it to another.

Is there a principled justification for this approach? Consider these situations:

(a) Doris shoots at her enemy, intending to kill him, then hops in her car and speeds away. Her enemy recovers from his wounds, but a pedestrian hit by Doris's speeding car is accidentally killed. Did Doris *murder* the pedestrian? Is there a logically relevant difference between this situation and the case above in which Defendant's shot accidentally killed Unlucky?

(b) Suppose that when Doris shoots at her enemy, intending to kill him, the bullet hits him, passes through his body, goes through the floor and kills a tenant in the apartment below. If Doris's enemy dies, is the doctrine of transferred intent still available, so that Doris is guilty of murdering her enemy *and* the tenant? Or is her intent "used up," so that in the case of the tenant she is guilty only of involuntary manslaughter? The cases are divided.[4] Which is the better view? Is there any good reason to hold Doris responsible for *two* murders? But if Doris has *not* intentionally killed the tenant, why should that conclusion change in the event that her enemy luckily recovers from his wounds?

For useful criticism of the transferred-intent doctrine, see Douglas Husak, Transferred Intent, 10 Notre Dame J.L., Ethics & Pub. Policy 65 (1996).

2. The problem of transferred intent is not confined to homicidal crimes. See, e.g., State v. Contua-Ramirez, 718 P.2d 1030 (1986), where the defendant, attempting to strike his wife, accidentally hit their baby, whom she was holding in her arms. The court upheld a conviction for intentionally injuring the child. Intentional assault upon an adult was a class 1 misdemeanor, but intentional injury of a child was a class 4 felony. The court held that the defendant could be convicted of the more serious offense. Is this sound?

2. *Subsequent Human Actions*

a. Subsequent Actions Intended to Produce the Result

PEOPLE v. CAMPBELL

Court of Appeals of Michigan
124 Mich. App. 333, 335 N.W.2d 27 (1983)

HOEHN, J. [Campbell and Basnaw were drinking heavily. Campbell, who was angry with Basnaw for having had sex with Campbell's wife, encouraged Basnaw

3. But Justice Mosk goes on to write that the transferred-intent doctrine, "a peculiarly mischievous legal fiction" (id. at 554), should nonetheless be abolished. He argues that the transferred-intent doctrine is unnecessary to produce a murder conviction in situations like his hypothetical; because *X*'s actions, maliciously endangering human life, caused the death of *Y*, *X* is arguably guilty of murder in any event.

4. Compare State v. Rodrigues-Gonzales, 790 P.2d 287 (Ariz. App. 1990) (finding defendant guilty of multiple murders), with People v. Birreuta, 208 Cal. Rptr. 635 (Ct. App. 1984) (only one murder).

to kill himself. When Basnaw said he had no weapon, Campbell offered to sell Basnaw his own gun, for any price. Eventually, he gave Basnaw his gun with five shells and left. Shortly thereafter, Basnaw shot and killed himself. Charged with murder, Campbell moved to dismiss the information, on the ground that a homicide charge cannot be based on the act of providing a weapon to a person who subsequently uses it to commit suicide. The circuit court denied the motion and the court of appeals granted leave to appeal.]

The prosecutor argues that inciting to suicide, coupled with the overt act of furnishing a gun to an intoxicated person, in a state of depression, falls within the prohibition, "or other wilful, deliberate and premeditated killing." There exists no statutory definition of the term "murder." That crime is defined in the common law. "Homicide is the killing of one human being by another." . . . The term suicide excludes by definition a homicide. Simply put, the defendant here did not kill another person.

A second ground militates against requiring the defendant to stand trial for murder. Defendant had no present intention to kill. He provided the weapon and departed. Defendant hoped Basnaw would kill himself but hope alone is not the degree of intention requisite to a charge of murder. . . .

While we find the conduct of the defendant morally reprehensible, we do not find it to be criminal under the present state of the law. The remedy for this situation is in the Legislature.

The trial court is reversed and the case is remanded with instructions to quash the information and warrant and discharge the defendant.

PEOPLE v. KEVORKIAN

Supreme Court of Michigan
447 Mich. 436, 527 N.W.2d 714 (1994)

CAVANAGH, C.J., and BRICKLEY and GRIFFIN, J.J. [Defendant Kevorkian allegedly assisted in the deaths of Sherry Miller and Marjorie Wantz on October 23, 1991, roughly a year before Michigan enacted a statute that prohibited giving assistance in a suicide. He was indicted on two counts of murder. The circuit judge dismissed the charges, concluding that assisting in suicide does not fall within the crime of murder. On appeal, the court of appeals concluded that the circuit court erred in quashing the information. Kevorkian appealed that ruling to the Michigan Supreme Court.]

Each woman was said to be suffering from a condition that caused her great pain or was severely disabling. Each separately had sought defendant Kevorkian's assistance in ending her life. The women and several friends and relatives met the defendant at a cabin in Oakland County on October 23, 1991.

According to the testimony presented at the defendant's preliminary examination, the plan was to use his "suicide machine." The device consisted of a board to which one's arm is strapped to prevent movement, a needle to be inserted into a blood vessel and attached to IV tubing, and containers of various chemicals that are to be released through the needle into the bloodstream. Strings are tied to two of the fingers of the person who intends to die. The strings are attached to clips on the IV tubing that control the flow of the chemicals. As explained by one witness, the person raises that hand, releasing . . . a fast-acting barbiturate [used] to administer anesthesia rapidly. When the person falls asleep, the hand drops, pulling the other string, which [allows] potassium chloride to flow into the body in concentrations sufficient to cause death.

The defendant tried several times, without success, to insert the suicide-machine needle into Ms. Miller's arm and hand. He then left the cabin, returning several hours later with a cylinder of carbon monoxide gas and a mask apparatus. He attached a screw driver to the cylinder, and showed Ms. Miller how to use the tool as a lever to open the gas valve. The defendant then turned his attention to Ms. Wantz. He was successful in inserting the suicide-machine needle into her arm. The defendant explained to Ms. Wantz how to activate the device. . . . The device was activated, and Ms. Wantz died.

The defendant then placed the mask apparatus on Ms. Miller. The only witness at the preliminary examination who was present at the time said that Ms. Miller opened the gas valve by pulling on the screw driver. The cause of her death was determined to be carbon-monoxide poisoning. . . .

The Court of Appeals majority [in reinstating the murder charges] relied principally on People v. Roberts, 178 N.W. 690 (1920). . . . In *Roberts,* the defendant's wife was suffering from advanced multiple sclerosis and in great pain. She previously had attempted suicide and, according to the defendant's statements at the plea proceeding, requested that he provide her with poison. He agreed, and placed a glass of poison within her reach. She drank the mixture and died. The defendant was charged with murder. He pleaded guilty, and the trial court determined the crime to be murder in the first degree.

The defendant [argued on appeal] that because suicide is not a crime in Michigan, and his wife thus committed no offense, he committed none in acting as an accessory before the fact. The Court rejected that argument, explaining:

> [D]efendant is not charged with [being an accessory to the offense of suicide]. He is charged with murder and the theory of the people was that he committed the crime by means of poison. [W]hen defendant mixed the paris green with water and placed it within reach of his wife to enable her to put an end. . . . to her life, he was guilty of murder by means of poison within the meaning of the statute, even though she requested him to do so. By this act he deliberately placed within her reach the means of taking her own life, which she could have obtained in no other way by reason of her helpless condition.

[D]efendant Kevorkian [argues] that the discussion of this issue in *Roberts* was dicta because the defendant in that case had pleaded guilty of murder, and thus the controlling authority was People v. Campbell, 335 N.W.2d 27 (1983). . . . We must [therefore] determine whether *Roberts* remains viable.

. . . To convict a defendant of criminal homicide, it must be proven that death occurred as a direct and natural result of the defendant's act. [F]ew jurisdictions, if any, have retained the early common-law view that assisting in a suicide is murder. The modern statutory scheme in the majority of states treats assisted suicide as a separate crime, with penalties less onerous than those for murder.

Recent decisions draw a distinction between active participation in a suicide and involvement in the events leading up to the suicide, such as providing the means. [I]n State v. Sexson, 869 P.2d 301 (N.M. App. 1994), the defendant was charged with first-degree murder in connection with the fatal shooting of his wife. . . . It was not disputed that there was a suicide agreement between the two. . . . The defendant claimed simply to have held the rifle in position while the decedent pulled the trigger, and that he had failed to then kill himself because he "freaked out." . . . The appellate court rejected the defendant's argument that he could not be prosecuted under the more general murder statute because of the specific assisted suicide statute . . . :

> The wrongful act triggering criminal liability for . . . assisting suicide is "aiding another" in the taking of his or her own life. It is well accepted that "aiding," in the context of determining whether one is criminally liable for their involvement in the suicide of another, is intended to mean providing the means to commit suicide, not actively performing the act which results in death. . . . [Sexson's] action transcends merely providing Victim a means to kill herself and becomes active participation in the death of another.

[This] distinction [is] consistent with the overwhelming trend of modern authority. [In *In re* Joseph G, 34 Cal. 3d 429, 436 (1983)], the California Supreme Court explained that a conviction of murder is proper if a defendant participates in the final overt act that causes death, such as firing a gun or pushing the plunger on a hypodermic needle [but not] where a defendant is involved merely "in the events leading up to the commission of the final overt act, such as furnishing the means. . . ."

[W]e would overrule *Roberts* to the extent that it can be read to support the view that the common-law definition of murder encompasses the act of intentionally providing the means by which a person commits suicide. Only where there is probable cause to believe that death was the direct and natural result of a defendant's act can the defendant be properly bound over on a charge of murder.[70]

[T]he lower courts did not have the benefit of the analysis set forth in this opinion for evaluating the degree of participation by defendant Kevorkian in the events leading to the deaths of Ms. Wantz and Ms. Miller. Accordingly, we remand this matter to the circuit court for reconsideration of the defendant's motion to quash in light of the principles discussed in this opinion.

BOYLE, J. (concurring in part and dissenting in part). . . . I disagree with the conclusion that one who provides the means for suicides and participates in the acts leading up to death may not be charged with murder as long as the final act is that of the decedent. . . . Absent standards established to distinguish between those who are in fact terminally ill or suffering in agony and rationally wish to die and those who are not, there is no principled vehicle in the judicial arsenal to protect against abuse. . . .

The lead opinion [distinguishes] between acts of participation that are merely "the events leading up to" the deaths of the decedents and "the final overt act that causes death." . . . Such a "test" [is] an invitation to [let results turn on whether] the defendant intended to kill [for] impure reasons. . . . To the extent that this Court reduces culpability for those who actively participate in acts that produce death, we do so at the risk of the most vulnerable members of our society — the

70. However, there may be circumstances where one who recklessly or negligently provides the means by which another commits suicide could be found guilty of a lesser offense, such as involuntary manslaughter. There are a number of cases in which providing a gun to person known to the defendant to be intoxicated and despondent or agitated has constituted sufficient recklessness to support such a conviction. . . .

elderly, the ill, the chronically depressed, those suffering from a panoply of stressful situations: adolescence, loss of employment, the death of a child or spouse, divorce, alcoholism, the abuse of other mind-altering substances, and the burden of social stigmatization.

[T]he cases cited [by the lead opinion] do not support [its] conclusion that if the defendant did not participate "in the act that . . . directly cause[s] death," he cannot be bound over on a charge of murder. Sexson did not pull the trigger, he held up the gun. . . . Likewise, defendant Kevorkian did not pull the trigger for Ms. Miller, but he assisted Ms. Miller in completing the act. In Ms. Wantz's case, his involvement was even more direct. . . . There is no principled method by which the Court can amend the common-law definition of murder, included in the statutes of this state.

NOTES ON ASSISTED SUICIDE

1. *Subsequent Kevorkian cases.* Kevorkian allegedly continued to help others commit suicide after the enactment of Michigan's assisted-suicide statute, and accordingly he was charged under the new statute as well. A trial judge dismissed those charges, but the Michigan Supreme Court, in another portion of its opinion, reinstated them and remanded the assisted-suicide prosecutions for trial. Meanwhile, Kevorkian, in an effort to help another patient, personally injected lethal drugs into a 52-year-old man suffering from Lou Gehrig's disease. He also made a videotape of his actions, gave the tape to CBS News (which aired it on prime-time television), and dared prosecutors to file charges against him. They did so, and in March 1999 Kevorkian was convicted of murder, not assisted suicide, because he himself had administered the fatal injection. He was sentenced to a minimum of 10 to 25 years in prison.[5]

2. *Current law.* The *Campbell* and *Kevorkian* cases reflect generally prevailing American law: One who successfully urges or assists another to commit suicide is not guilty of murder, at least so long as the deceased was mentally responsible and was not forced, deceived, or otherwise subject to pressures that rendered his action partly involuntary. Most states also reject the possibility of a manslaughter or negligent homicide conviction, provided again that the deceased's actions were fully voluntary.[6] In accord, §210.5(1) of the Model Penal Code permits convicting a person of criminal homicide for causing another to take his life, but "only if he purposely causes such suicide by force, duress or deception."

New York Penal Law §125.15 departs from this restrictive approach by making it manslaughter (punishable by a 15-year-maximum sentence) when a person "intentionally causes or aids another person to commit suicide"; the statute apparently applies regardless of whether the suicide victim was acting under deception or duress.

Most states that follow the more restrictive approach do not permit defen-

5. See N.Y., Times, March 27, 1999, at A1.

6. E.g., City of Akron v. Head, 657 N.E.2d 1389 (Ohio Mun. 1995). State v. Bier, 591 P.2d 1115 (Mont. 1979), is one of the rare modern decisions to the contrary. When defendant's wife said she wanted to commit suicide, he placed a loaded, cocked pistol within her reach, and she used it to kill herself. On the theory that defendant's act was a gross deviation from a reasonable standard of care, the court upheld a conviction for negligent homicide.

dants like Campbell and Kevorkian to act with impunity, however. A majority of the states now have statutes that define a separate offense for assisting a suicide. Many are similar to Model Penal Code §210.5(2), which makes it a felony (punishable at the same level as manslaughter) to purposely aid or solicit another to commit suicide.

Such statutes have become highly controversial. There are hotly contested questions concerning whether there should be a constitutional right, statutory right, or criminal-law justification defense for doctors who help terminally ill patients or others in extreme pain to commit suicide. In Washington v. Glucksberg, 521 U.S. 702 (1997), the Supreme Court held that individuals who wish to commit suicide have no constitutional right to obtain assistance in doing so. But jurisdictions remain free to permit such assistance by statute; the Netherlands and at least one American state (Oregon) have done so. That aspect of the subject is explored in detail in the material on justifications, Chapter 8A, infra.

3. An exception for reckless or negligent aid? In footnote 70 of its opinion, the *Kevorkian* court draws an important distinction: One who intentionally provides another person with the means to commit suicide cannot be convicted of murder, but under the court's holding, one who *recklessly or negligently* makes such means available to a person who is "intoxicated and despondent or agitated" can sometimes be convicted of a lesser degree of homicide, such as involuntary manslaughter. What is the logic of this position? If the decedent's actions are not fully rational, and therefore do not break the causal chain, why can't a defendant who provides lethal means, and does so intentionally, be convicted of murder? Conversely, if the decedent is sufficiently rational for his actions to constitute a superceding cause, how can the defendant be convicted of causing any homicide at all? The court gave this example of a situation in which homicide charges would be appropriate (527 N.W.2d, at 739 n.70):

> [I]n People v Duffy, 595 N.E.2d 814 (1992), the defendant provided a gun to the intoxicated and despondent decedent, who had said he wanted to kill himself, and urged him to "blow his head off." The decedent proceeded to shoot himself. Duffy was [convicted] of manslaughter in the second degree [on the theory] that he had recklessly caused the death. . . . The New York Court of Appeals concluded:
>
> > [A] person who, knowing that another is contemplating immediate suicide, deliberately prods that person to go forward and furnishes the means of bringing about death may certainly be said to have "consciously disregard[ed] a substantial and unjustifiable risk" that his actions would result in the death of that person.

As Judge Boyle noted in dissent (id. at 744 n.7), the majority's approach produces a paradox: "[O]ne who is only criminally careless and does not participate at all may be found guilty of a fifteen-year felony, while one who [participates] with the intent to cause death can only be charged with assisted suicide, punishable by a maximum penalty of five years. . . ."

What is the right approach to a case like *Duffy*? If the defendant *"deliberately"* prodded the decedent to go forward, should the defendant be guilty of murder, manslaughter, or no offense at all? If Duffy can be convicted of homicide because he knew his actions made a suicidal act more likely, why shouldn't Kevorkian be guilty of homicide in the cases where he provided Ms. Miller and Ms. Wantz with the means to take their own lives?

Reconsider the *Campbell* case. Basnaw, heavily intoxicated, was contemplating suicide, and the defendant, knowing this, gave him a gun and encouraged him to use it. Given the *Kevorkian* court's apparent willingness to uphold manslaughter charges in a case like *Duffy,* is *Campbell* still good law in Michigan? Or is there a significant difference between the two cases? At what point does a suicide victim's intoxication or despondency become sufficient to render the person who helps him guilty of homicide?

NOTES ON INTERVENING HUMAN ACTION

1. *Foreseeability vs. autonomy.* It is plain that Brasnow's suicide was a readily foreseeable result of Campbell's actions. Likewise, the death of Kevorkian's patients was readily foreseeable. Indeed, both Campbell and Kevorkian wanted their actions to have precisely the effects that they did have. If the doctrines studied in the preceding section were applicable, Campbell and Kevorkian would surely be found to have caused the death of others. Why doesn't the foreseeability test of causation apply in cases like these?

A leading explanation points to a powerful strain in our culture that treats human action as differing from physical events.[7] We tend to regard a person's acts as the product of his or her choice, not as inevitable results of a chain of events governed by physical laws. This view (roughly, the assumption of free will and the rejection of determinism) is of course hotly contested in philosophical literature. But whether accurate or not, the assumption of free will reflects the way most people in Western cultures respond to human action, and it reflects, most importantly, the premise on which notions of blame in the criminal law ultimately rest. Naturally, the rules of causation in the law tend to embody the same premise.

As a result, the law of causation treats *physical events* that follow from a person's actions as caused by him or her (subject to the requirements of proximity, foreseeability, and so forth), but it ordinarily does not treat *human* action that follows from an initial actor's conduct as caused by that actor, even when the subsequent human action is entirely foreseeable.[8] The results that follow from the second person's actions are caused by him or her alone. As it is sometimes put, there has been a *novus actus interveniens,* a later action by another person that displaces the relevance of prior conduct by others and provides a new foundation for causal responsibility. As Glanville Williams explains:[9]

> The legal attitude, in general, rests on what is known to philosophers as the principle of autonomy, which enters deeply into our traditional moral perceptions, reinforced by language. . . . The autonomy doctrine, expressing itself through its

7. See Sanford H. Kadish, Blame and Punishment: Essays in the Criminal Law 140-145 (1987).

8. The Model Penal Code's terminology partly reflects and partly departs from this causal conception. It provides that one who assists a voluntary suicide ordinarily cannot be convicted of homicide (§210.5(1)), but it also creates a separate offense for a person who aids or encourages a suicide, with felony penalties applicable when "his conduct *causes* such suicide" to occur. (§210.5(2)). The latter provision appears to presuppose that one can "cause" the entirely voluntary suicide of another person. (When a suicide is not fully voluntary, a person who causes it can be prosecuted for homicide under §210.5(1)).

9. *Finis* for *Novus Actus?,* 48 Camb. L. J. 391, 392 (1989).

corollary, the doctrine of *novus actus interveniens,* teaches that the individual's will is the autonomous (self-regulating) prime cause of behavior.

This conception of human action creates the need for special rules to govern the responsibility of one person for the acts of another. The law of causation is not available to ground the responsibility of the first actor, so other doctrines must be created to hold responsible those who instigate or help another to commit a crime. (These other doctrines, principally those of complicity and conspiracy, are explored in Chapter 7, infra.)

2. Qualifications and exceptions. Not all subsequent human actions are treated as outside of causal law — only those that have been chosen freely, what Hart and Honoré call "voluntary" or "free, deliberate and informed" human actions.[10] Actions that are involuntary in the traditional sense (e.g., a spasm produced in person *B* by drugs that person *A* administered) are of course caused by the prior actor *A,* as are actions by *B* taken without full knowledge of the circumstances. Other kinds of action that may be caused by a prior actor are those "constrained" by compulsion of duty, by duress, or by a momentary emergency precipitated by the prior actor. Examples would include the firefighter who enters a burning building (*Arzon,* supra page 521), or the helicopter pilot who participates in a police chase (*Acosta,* supra page 518). Similarly, when a defendant perpetrates a robbery, "the victim's self-defensive killing or the police officer's killing in the performance of his duty cannot be considered an independent intervening cause . . . for it is a reasonable response to the dilemma thrust upon the victim or the policeman by the intentional act of the defendant."[11]

One other factor seems to influence conclusions about when human action will be considered an independent intervening cause. Subsequent actions that are freely chosen and *intended* to produce a harmful result (as in the *Campbell* and *Kevorkian* cases) are typically treated as intervening to "break" the causal chain. Subsequent actions that unintentionally *risk* harm sometimes insulate the prior actor from liability, but sometimes they do not. (We consider these less predictable cases in Section b below) Given the lack of uniformity in the decisions, it is probably accurate to think of the *novus actus* doctrine less as a hard rule than as a principle that tends to pull the law in a certain direction, without always having enough force to pull it all the way.

STEPHENSON v. STATE

Supreme Court of Indiana
205 Ind. 141, 179 N.E. 633 (1932)

[Defendant, with the aid of several of his associates, abducted the deceased, a woman he had known socially for several months, and in the ensuing days subjected her to various forms of sexual perversion, including the infliction of bite wounds on her body. Deceased seized an opportunity secretly to buy and take six tablets of bichloride of mercury in an effort to commit suicide. She became

10. H. L. A. Hart and Tony Honoré, Causation in the Law (2d ed. 1985).
11. People v. Gilbert, 408 P.2d 365, 374 (Cal. 1965).

violently ill. Defendant had her drink a bottle of milk and suggested that he take her to a hospital; she refused. Defendant thereupon proceeded to drive her to her home. On the way deceased's pain grew worse, and she screamed for a doctor. Defendant, however, did not stop until he reached his home. Soon thereafter she was taken to her parents. They summoned a doctor who treated her for poisoning. In the ensuing 10 days, all her wounds healed normally except one which became infected. She grew worse and died, although the infected wound had healed at the time of her death. The medical cause of death was apparently a combination of shock, loss of food and rest, action of the poison and the infection, and lack of early treatment, probably none of which, taken singly, would have been sufficient to result in death.

[The indictment against defendant was in four counts. The first count charged him with murder arising from the following: that on March 16 he kidnapped the deceased from his home in Indianapolis, where she had been visiting, detained her on a railroad train en route to Chicago, struck, beat, bit, and grievously wounded her with intent to rape in a drawing room on the train, and forced her to get off at Hammond and to occupy a hotel bed with him; that on March 17 deceased, "distracted with the pain and shame so inflicted upon her," swallowed poison; that defendant neither administered an antidote nor called for medical help although able to do so; that the same day he forced her into a car and drove her back to Indianapolis where he kept her in his garage without administering an antidote or calling for medical help until March 18; and that finally she died on April 14 "from the effects of her wounds inflicted as aforesaid and said poison taken as aforesaid."

[The jury found defendant guilty of second-degree murder under this first count of the indictment, and the supreme court affirmed.]

PER CURIAM. . . . Appellant very earnestly argues that the evidence does not show appellant guilty of murder. He points out in his brief that, after they reached the hotel, Madge Oberholtzer left the hotel and purchased a hat and the poison, and voluntarily returned to his room, and at the time she took the poison she was in an adjoining room to him, and that she swallowed the poison without his knowledge, and at a time when he was not present. From these facts he contends that she took her life by committing suicide; that her own act in taking poison was [the act of] an intervening responsible agent which broke the causal connection between his acts and the death; that his acts were not the proximate cause of her death, but the taking of the poison was the proximate cause of death. . . .

In the case of State v. Preslar, [48 N.C. 421 (1856)], the defendant in the nighttime fought with his wife, and she left to go in the house of her father. When she reached a point about two hundred yards from her father's home, she, for some reason, did not want to go in the house till morning, laid down on a bed cover, which she had wrapped around her, till daylight. The weather was cold and the next morning she could not walk, but made herself known. She afterwards died. The court held that the wife without necessity exposed herself, and the defendant was not guilty. . . . But we do not believe that the rule stated in the above case is controlling here. . . .

In Rex v. Valade (Que.) 22 Rev. de Jur. 524, 26 Can. Cr. Cas. 233, where the accused induced a young girl under the age of consent to go along with him to a secluded apartment, and there had criminal sexual intercourse with her, following which she jumped from a window to the street to get away from him, and was killed by the fall, the accused was held guilty of murder. Bishop in his work on Criminal Law, vol. 2 (9th Ed.), page 484, says: "When suicide follows a wound inflicted by the defendant his act is homicidal, if deceased was rendered irresponsible by the wound and as a natural result of it."

We do not understand that by the rule laid down by Bishop, supra, that the wound which renders the deceased mentally irresponsible is necessarily limited to a physical wound. We should think the same rule would apply if a defendant engaged in the commission of a felony such as rape or attempted rape, and inflicts upon his victim both physical and mental injuries, the natural and probable result of which would render the deceased mentally irresponsible and suicide followed, we think he would be guilty of murder. In the case at bar, appellant is charged with having caused the death of Madge Oberholtzer while engaged in the crime of attempted rape. The evidence shows that appellant, together with Earl Gentry and the deceased, left their compartment on the train and went to a hotel about a block from the depot, and there appellant registered as husband and wife, and immediately went to the room assigned to them. This change from their room on the train to a room in the hotel is of no consequence, for appellant's control and dominion over the deceased was absolute and complete in both cases. The evidence further shows that the deceased asked for money with which to purchase a hat, and it was supplied her by "Shorty," at the direction of appellant, and that she did leave the room and was taken by Shorty to a shop and purchased a hat and then, at her request, to a drug store where she purchased the bichloride of mercury tablets, and then she was taken back to the room in the hotel, where about 10 o'clock A.M. she swallowed the poison. Appellant argues that the deceased was a free agent on this trip to purchase a hat, etc., and that she voluntarily returned to the room in the hotel. This was a question for the jury, and the evidence would justify them in reaching a contrary conclusion. Appellant's chauffeur accompanied her on this trip, and the deceased had, before she left appellant's home in Indianapolis, attempted to get away, and also made two unsuccessful attempts to use the telephone to call help. She was justified in concluding that any attempt she might make, while purchasing a hat or while in the drug store to escape or secure assistance, would be no more successful in Hammond than it was in Indianapolis. We think the evidence shows that the deceased was at all times from the time she was entrapped by the appellant at his home on the evening of March 15th till she returned to her home two days later, in the custody and absolute control of appellant. Neither do we think the fact that the deceased took the poison some four hours after they left the drawing-room on the train or after the crime of attempted rape had been committed necessarily prevents it from being a part of the attempted rape. . . . At the very moment Madge Oberholtzer swallowed the poison she was subject to the passion, desire, and will of appellant. She knew not what moment she would be subjected to the same demands that she was while in the drawing-room on the train. What would have prevented appellant from compelling her to submit to him at any moment? The same forces, the same impulses, that would impel her to shoot herself during the actual attack or throw herself out of the car window after the attack had ceased, [were] pressing and overwhelming her at the time she swallowed the poison. The evidence shows that she was so weak that she staggered as she left the elevator to go to the room in the hotel, and was assisted by appellant and Gentry; that she was very ill, so much that she could not eat, all of which was the direct and proximate result of the treatment accorded to her by appellant.

We think the situation no different here than we find in . . . the *Valade* Case, supra. To say that there is no causal connection between the acts of appellant and the death of Madge Oberholtzer, and that the treatment accorded her by appellant had no causal connection with the death of Madge Oberholtzer would be a travesty on justice. The whole criminal program was so closely connected that we think it should be treated as one transaction, and should be governed by the same principles of law as was applied in the case of . . . Rex v. Valade, supra. We therefore conclude that the evidence was sufficient and justified the jury in finding that appellant by his acts and conduct rendered the deceased distracted and mentally irresponsible, and that such was the natural and probable consequence of such unlawful and criminal treatment, and that the appellant was guilty of murder in the second degree as charged in the first count of the indictment.

COMMENT ON *STEPHENSON,* 31 Mich. L. Rev. 659, 668-674 (1933): At the outset it is clear that homicide cannot be committed by the defendant unless the intervening actor who strikes the fatal blow has been rendered irresponsible by defendant's unlawful act. This act may provide another with the opportunity, the instrument, or the motive for striking, but if it leaves him sane, the courts will not look behind the last responsible, self-determining actor. . . . Suppose a man commits suicide after losing all his money to a criminal swindler; is the swindler guilty of homicide? . . . Our common law, whatever may be said of divine law, does not hold him responsible for the death.

A new element enters the situation when the intervening actor is insane. . . . Where a policeman was grappling with a lunatic to arrest him, and defendant by freeing his hand enabled the lunatic to shoot the policeman, defendant was held guilty of homicide. From this case we may derive the principle that an insane intervening actor will not break the causal connection between defendant's act and the death.

We have been assuming, however, that the intervening actor is already insane at the time of defendant's act. The facts of Stephenson v. State put a further strain on the causal connection. To convict of homicide there, it was necessary to prove, not only that deceased was irresponsible when she took the poison, but also that defendant's unlawful acts caused her irresponsibility. For such a conviction no square precedent is to be found. Indeed the cases reveal, if anything, a marked reluctance to permit proof of any purely mental link in the causal chain. . . .

It is true that certain psychological phenomena have been admitted to proof when they have been induced by physical violence. The mentally paralyzing effect of fear and the mentally unbalancing effect of pain and fever are sufficiently familiar to the average man so that he can pass a sound judgment upon their causal relation. . . . Where a dangerous wound has been inflicted, which unseats the mind of deceased through pain or fever and so causes him to kill himself, the courts are . . . ready to hold defendant for homicide.

These last cases come nearest to supporting the majority opinion in Stephenson v. State, but they are not squarely in point. The prosecution did not seriously contend, nor did the court think, that deceased was rendered irresponsible by the physical injuries, the bruises and bites, inflicted by defendant. It was rather the shame and humiliation of having been raped. . . .

We have noted above that all prior unlawful actors in the causal chain are insulated from liability if the person who strikes the fatal blow is a responsible, self-determining actor. The law recognizes a number of situations, however, in which a man who takes his own life or another's is not responsible. Insanity destroys his responsibility, as we have seen, and criminal liability for the death may then be cast on the next previous actor. So also the actual killer's responsibility will be destroyed if he acts innocently in ignorance of fact, or in necessary self-defense, or instinctively as a result of fear, or in pursuance of public duty. Here, human nature being what it is, the law excuses the homicidal act because it represents the average man's natural and instinctive reaction to a situation in which he finds himself; and conversely because the reaction is natural and instinctive, the law holds for homicide the previous actor who unlawfully created the situation. . . .

Such liability of an antecedent actor is best illustrated where he has created a situation in which another's mortal blow is motivated by the powerful instinct of self-preservation. At the point of a gun *A* commands *B* to jump from a moving train, and *B* is killed in the jump; by violence and threats of death *A* drives his wife poorly-clad from the house, and she dies of exposure; *A* shoots at a boat to frighten its occupants, *B* jumps overboard upsetting the boat, and *C* is drowned. In these cases desperate measures of escape are warranted; the imminence of deadly peril prompts *B* to act first and think afterwards. . . .

When a situation arises in which the law makes the performance of a homicidal act a duty, and prescribes penalties for disobedience, we feel without hesitation that the unlawful creator of that situation is criminally guilty of the death. Where *A* obtains *C*'s conviction of a capital offense by perjured testimony, and executioner *B* hangs *C*, the proximity of causation between *A*'s unlawful act and the death seems amply clear. So the master of a vessel is guilty of homicide if he sends a sailor into the rigging, knowing or chargeable with knowledge that he is not fit to go aloft, and the sailor falls to his death. . . .

It is difficult to fit Stephenson v. State into this picture of liability. True, the law justifies the taking of life when necessary to prevent the commission of rape. And had deceased been helpless in the manual grasp of defendant at the time of her suicidal act, or had a third-party defender, bursting upon the scene, shot her to death through faulty aim, then defendant might have been liable for her death within the principles developed above. But one can scarcely overlook the fact that deceased was alone and unmolested, and in a position to summon help, at the time she took the poison. The predominant motive for her suicide, clearly, was not to escape further assault but to escape the shame of what had already been done to her. The case represents a new and doubtful departure in so far as it suggests that the unlawful infliction of shame and disgrace may lead so naturally to suicide as to amount to a killing by him who inflicted it.

NOTES ON SUBSEQUENT VICTIM BEHAVIOR

1. Variations on Stephenson. To support its finding that Stephenson caused the victim's death, the court emphasizes that until she returned to her home in Indianapolis, she "was at all times . . . in the custody and absolute control of the appellant." Is the court implying that the result would be different if (as defendant claimed) Madge Oberholtzer had been a "free agent" at the time she bought and consumed the poison? Would the court reach a different result if she had taken the poison after she returned home to Indianapolis? Why should the last situation be treated differently from *Stephenson* itself?

One possible answer might be that the victim's suicidal act would no longer be foreseeable. But isn't such an act at least as foreseeable as the collision of the helicopters in *Acosta?* Another possible answer is that the two situations are not significantly different — that Stephenson should be held liable in both. With respect to that possibility, consider the case that follows.

2. In February 1993, Jose Alonso Garcia was indicted for sexually assaulting a 79-year-old woman. When the woman died of congestive heart failure a month after the attack, he was also indicted for first-degree felony murder. Prosecutors argued that the woman died because Garcia "destroyed her will to live," and pointed to testimony that the deceased cried daily after the incident and ceased talking about her future. Prosecutors analogized this case to one where a victim collapses of a heart attack during or shortly after the crime. A rape prosecutor from New York expressed doubts about this theory: "I think they'll have a huge causation problem. I mean, how many of my victims, down the road, either commit suicide or die of drug or alcohol abuse because of rape?" Wall St. J., Aug. 23, 1993, at B4.

3. Problem. According to newspaper reports,[12] Shirley Eagan, 69, shot her daughter, 42-year-old Georgette Smith, upon learning that her daughter planned to place her in a nursing home. The bullet struck Smith in the neck and paralyzed her from the neck down. She was kept alive only by life support systems at a local hospital. When the hospital refused to disconnect her life support, she brought suit to compel the hospital to permit her die. In her petition Smith pleaded with the court not to leave her the way she was, hardly able to speak, unable to swallow, fed through a tube, with no control over her bodily functions. "All I can do is wink my eyes, wiggle my nose and wiggle my tongue. I can't move any other part of my body. I want to die because I can't live this way." Doctors stated that her condition was irreversible, and psychiatrists concluded that she was mentally competent. The judge ordered that she should be permitted to die: "Mrs. Smith has made a difficult choice, a choice which she has the right to make. This court has found that she is competent to make that choice." The hospital then withdrew life support, and Smith died within minutes. Reflecting on the case, a local editorial observed:[13]

> One school of thought held that the shooting, which caused injuries that resulted in Ms. Smith's decision to have the life support turned off, warranted a murder charge. The other view held that, because Ms. Smith made her own decision to withdraw life support, the situation called for a charge of attempted murder.

In the end, the district attorney chose to prosecute Eagan only for attempted murder, perhaps because her severely deteriorating health and mental instability made a greater charge inappropriate. And the jury acquitted Eagan of the lesser offense as well.

12. See, e.g., N.Y. Times, May 19, 1999, p. 1; May 20, 1999, p. 18; May 26, 1999, p. 26.
13. Orlando Sentinel, Aug. 23, 1999, p. A12.

Questions: If the prosecutor had filed homicide charges and the jury had convicted Eagan of murder or manslaughter, would it be proper to sustain such a conviction on appeal? Suppose that Smith's initial injury had been inflicted by a robber during the course of a holdup and that she then chose to end her life by having her life support removed. Could the robber be convicted of murdering her?

4. In Regina v. Blaue, [1975] 3 All E.R. 446, defendant had stabbed a girl. With proper treatment and a blood transfusion, her wounds would not have proved fatal. But as a Jehovah's Witness, she refused a transfusion and died. Is this a preexisting-condition case (thus liability for homicide) or an intervening-actor case (thus no liability for homicide)?

One answer might be to say that the subsequent victim behavior in *Blaue* was an omission, not an act. But why should a life-endangering omission be treated differently from a life-endangering act? If her wounds were readily treatable, but a brother who had a duty to help refused to do so because he hoped to inherit her share of an estate, would we say that his "mere omission" could not break the causal chain and that the initial assailant was liable for homicide? Can we distinguish such a case from *Blaue?*

NOTES ON SUBSEQUENT ACTS OF THIRD PARTIES

1. Consider the story of Uriah the Hittite, as told in the Bible, 2 Samuel 11, 12. Uriah was a captain in King David's army. David ordered his General to place Uriah in the "forefront of the hardest fighting, and then draw back from him, that he may be struck down and die." David's motive was to be rid of Uriah so he could then marry Uriah's wife, Bath-sheba. David's plan worked: Uriah was killed in the battle with the Ammonites, and David married Bath-sheba. The judgment of the Lord upon King David as reported by Nathan the Prophet was: "You have struck down Uriah the Hittite with a sword, the man himself you murdered by the sword of the Ammonites." Would it be proper for a court to so hold under American law? Is the decision in *Campbell* consistent with the Biblical judgment?

Consider Glanville Williams, *Finis* for *Novus Actus?* 48 Camb. L.J. 391 (1989):

> A distinguished writer recently raised the question whether a general who orders his troops to battle intentionally kills those of his men who fall in action. He was considering this as a problem on intention. There may be some argument on intentionality, but none on the subject of killing. Obviously, it is the enemy, not the general, who kills the men. The reason why the general cannot be said to kill them is not because he does not want to kill them; not because he does not expect the deaths of many of them to follow from obedience to his command; and not because he is justified in issuing the command; it is simply that he has not committed or helped the act of killing, or influenced anybody to do the deed.
>
> A person is primarily responsible for what he himself does. He is not responsible, not blameworthy, for what other people do. The fact that his own conduct, rightful or wrongful, provided the background for a subsequent voluntary and wrong act by another does not make him responsible for it. What he does may be a but-for cause of the injurious act, but he did not do it. His conduct is not an imputable cause of it. Only the later actor, the doer of the act that intervenes between the first act and the result, the final wielder of human autonomy in the matter, bears responsibility (along with his accomplices) for the result that ensues.

Questions: How cogent is Professor Williams' analysis? Recall an analogous problem considered in connection with felony murder, page 477 supra: Felons *A* and *B*, holed up in a house, are fighting off the police. Felon *A* tells felon *B* to run out the back door where, he says, the coast is clear. He says that, though he knows police have the door well covered, because he wants *B* dead. Felon *B* dashes out the back door and is shot dead by police. The police, of course, are duty-bound to shoot, so their actions are not fully "voluntary." But the same must be said of the enemy soldiers who killed the opposing troops in Williams' example. Is it "[obvious that] it is the enemy, not the general, who kills the men"?

2. In Bailey v. Commonwealth, 229 Va. 258, 329 S.E.2d 37 (1985), an appeal from a conviction of involuntary manslaughter, the court summarized the facts as follows:

> Bailey and Murdock lived about two miles apart in the Roanoke area. On the evening in question, each was intoxicated. . . . Murdock was also "legally blind," with vision of only 3/200 in the right eye and 2/200 in the left. Bailey knew that Murdock had "a problem with vision" and that he was intoxicated on the night in question.
>
> Bailey also knew that Murdock owned a handgun and had boasted "about how he would use it and shoot it and scare people off with it." Bailey knew further that Murdock was easily agitated and that he became especially angry if anyone disparaged his war hero, General George S. Patton. During [an extended and vituperative conversation] Bailey implied that General Patton and Murdock himself were homosexuals.
>
> Also during the conversation, Bailey persistently demanded that Murdock arm himself with his handgun and wait on his front porch for Bailey to come and injure or kill him. Murdock responded by saying he would be waiting on his front porch, and he told Bailey to "kiss [his] mother or [his] wife and children good-bye because [he would] never go back home."
>
> Bailey then made two anonymous telephone calls to the Roanoke City Police Department. In the first, Bailey reported "a man . . . out on the porch [at Murdock's address] waving a gun around." A police car was dispatched to the address, but the officers reported they did not "see anything."
>
> Bailey called Murdock back on the radio and chided him for not "going out on the porch." More epithets and threats were exchanged. Bailey told Murdock he was "going to come up there in a blue and white car" [the court here notes that both Bailey and the police drove blue and white cars] and demanded that Murdock "step out there on the . . . porch" with his gun "in [his] hands" because he, Bailey, would "be there in just a minute."
>
> Bailey telephoned the police again. This time, Bailey identified Murdock by name and told the dispatcher that Murdock had "a gun on the porch," had "threatened to shoot up the neighborhood," and was "talking about shooting anything that moves." Bailey insisted that the police "come out here and straighten this man out." . . .
>
> Three uniformed police officers, Chambers, Beavers, and Turner, were dispatched to Murdock's home. None of the officers knew that Murdock was intoxicated or that he was in an agitated state of mind. Only Officer Beavers knew that Murdock's eyesight was bad, and he did not know "exactly how bad it was."
>
> When the officers arrived on the scene, they . . . observed Murdock come out of his house with "something shiny in his hand." . . .
>
> Officer Chambers approached Murdock . . . and told him to "[l]eave the gun alone and walk down the stairs away from it." Murdock "just sat there." When Cham-

bers repeated his command, Murdock cursed him. Murdock then reached for the gun, stood up, advanced in Chambers' direction, and opened fire. Chambers retreated and was not struck.

All three officers returned fire, and Murdock was struck. Lying wounded on the porch, he said several times, "I didn't know you was the police." He died from "a gunshot wound of the left side of the chest." In the investigation which followed, Bailey stated that he was "the hoss that caused the loss."

Questions: Was he? How would you analyze the liability of Bailey? Did he kill Murdock?

3. Can the actor ever be an intervening and superseding cause of a result initiated by the actor's original conduct? For example, in Thabo Meli v. Regina, [1954] 1 All E.R. 373 (P.C.), the defendants attacked the deceased with the intent to kill him. Believing he was dead, when in fact he was alive, they rolled him over a cliff where he subsequently died from exposure rather than from the original attack. Presumably the defendants might be found guilty of manslaughter in their reckless treatment of a body that might have been alive. Could they have been found guilty of murder on the basis of their initial assault? Another example is Regina v. Church, [1965] 49 Crim. App. 206, where the defendant, after assaulting and injuring the deceased, threw her body into the Thames in panic, believing he had killed her. In fact, she was then alive and died from drowning. Was this murder? See Geoffrey Marston, Contemporaneity of Act and Intention in Crimes, 86 L.Q. Rev. 208 (1970).

b. Subsequent Actions that Recklessly Risk the Result

COMMONWEALTH v. ROOT

Supreme Court of Pennsylvania
403 Pa. 571, 170 A.2d 310 (1961)

JONES, C.J. The appellant was found guilty of involuntary manslaughter for the death of his competitor in the course of an automobile race between them on a highway. . . .

The testimony, which is uncontradicted in material part, discloses that, on the night of the fatal accident, the defendant accepted the deceased's challenge to engage in an automobile race; that the racing took place on a rural 3-lane highway; that the night was clear and dry, and traffic light; that the speed limit on the highway was 50 miles per hour; that, immediately prior to the accident, the two automobiles were being operated at varying speeds of from 70 to 90 miles per hour; that the accident occurred in a no-passing zone on the approach to a bridge where the highway narrowed to two directionally-opposite lanes; that, at the time of the accident, the defendant was in the lead and was proceeding in his right hand lane of travel; that the deceased, in an attempt to pass the defendant's automobile, when a truck was closely approaching from the opposite direction, swerved his car to the left, crossed the highway's white dividing line and drove his automobile on the wrong side of the highway head-on into the oncoming truck with resultant fatal effect to himself.

This evidence would of course amply support a conviction of the defendant for speeding, reckless driving and, perhaps, other violations of The Vehicle Code. [But] unlawful or reckless conduct is only one ingredient of the crime of involuntary manslaughter. Another essential and distinctly separate element of the crime is that the unlawful or reckless conduct charged to the defendant was the *direct* cause of the death in issue. The first ingredient is obviously present in this case but, just as plainly, the second is not.

While precedent is to be found for application of the tort law concept of "proximate cause" in fixing responsibility for criminal homicide, the want of any rational basis for its use in determining criminal liability can no longer be properly disregarded. When proximate cause was first borrowed from the field of tort law and applied to homicide prosecutions in Pennsylvania, the concept connoted a much more direct causal relation in producing the alleged culpable result than it does today. Proximate cause, as an essential element of a tort founded in negligence, has undergone in recent times, and is still undergoing, a marked extension. More specifically, this area of civil law has been progressively liberalized in favor of claims for damages for personal injuries to which careless conduct of others can in some way be associated. To persist in applying the tort liability concept of proximate cause to prosecutions for criminal homicide after the marked expansion of *civil* liability of defendants in tort actions for negligence would be to extend possible *criminal* liability to persons chargeable with unlawful or reckless conduct in circumstances not generally considered to present the likelihood of a resultant death. . . .

Here, the action of the deceased driver in recklessly and suicidally swerving his car to the left lane of a 2-lane highway into the path of an oncoming truck was not forced upon him by any act of the defendant; it was done by the deceased and by him alone, who thus directly brought about his own demise. . . .

Legal theory which makes guilt or innocence of criminal homicide depend upon such accidental and fortuitous circumstances as are now embraced by modern tort law's encompassing concept of proximate cause is too harsh to be just. . . .

In the case now before us, the deceased was aware of the dangerous condition created by the defendant's reckless conduct in driving his automobile at an excessive rate of speed along the highway but, despite such knowledge, he recklessly chose to swerve his car to the left and into the path of an oncoming truck, thereby bringing about the head-on collision which caused his own death. [T]he defendant's reckless conduct was not a sufficiently direct cause of the competing driver's death to make him criminally liable therefor.

[Reversed.]

EAGEN, J., dissenting. . . . If the defendant did not engage in the unlawful race and so operate his automobile in such a reckless manner, this accident would never have occurred. He helped create the dangerous event. He was a vital part of it. The victim's acts were a natural reaction to the stimulus of the situation. The race, the attempt to pass the other car and forge ahead, the reckless speed, all of these factors the defendant himself helped create. He was part and parcel of them. That the victim's response was normal under the circumstances, that his reaction should have been expected and was clearly foreseeable, is to me beyond argument. That the defendant's recklessness was a substantial factor is obvious. All of this, in my opinion, makes his unlawful conduct a direct cause of the resulting collision. . . .

PEOPLE v. KERN, 545 N.Y.S.2d 4 (App. Div. 1989): [This case arose from the infamous "Howard Beach incident," in which a group of white youths assaulted several black men who were walking in the neighborhood after their car had broken down. The teenagers chased the men, while wielding bats, screaming racial epithets, and threatening to kill them. One of the men, Griffith, tried to escape by running across a highway; he was struck by a car and killed. The defendants were convicted of second-degree manslaughter and appealed, arguing that there was insufficient evidence of causation, and furthermore that the driver (Blum) who struck Griffith had been negligent, and therefore his actions constituted an intervening act that broke the chain of causation. Upholding the convictions the court stated:] [U]nder these circumstances, the defendants' actions were a "sufficiently direct cause" of Griffith's ensuing death so as to warrant the imposition of criminal liability. . . . [T]he only reasonable alternative left open to Griffith while being persistently chased and threatened by the defendants and their friends, several of whom were carrying weapons, was to seek safety by crossing the parkway where he unfortunately met his death. Clearly, on the basis of these facts, it cannot be said that the defendants' despicable conduct was not a sufficiently direct cause of Griffith's death. The defendants will not be heard to complain that, in desperately fleeing their murderous assault, Griffith chose the wrong escape route.

The defendants' further assertion that Blum's alleged negligent operation of his vehicle was an intervening proximate cause of Griffith's death is also without merit. Based on the circumstances surrounding the incident, including the dark early morning hour, it cannot be said that an intervening wrongful act occurred to relieve the defendants from the directly foreseeable consequences of their actions. Moreover, even if we assume that Blum was less than cautious in the operation of his vehicle, the facts demonstrate that his actions were not the sole cause of Griffith's ensuing death since it was the defendants' wrongful conduct which forced Griffith to seek refuge from his assailants by crossing the highway.

QUESTIONS

1. Is *Kern* inconsistent with *Root* or is it distinguishable?

2. In People v. Matos, 83 N.Y.2d 509 (1994), the defendant, running from the scene of an armed robbery he had just committed, climbed a ladder to the roof of a building and fled in the dark across the Manhattan rooftops. The police officer pursuing him fell down an air shaft and plunged 25 feet to his death. The New York Court of Appeals upheld a conviction for felony murder on the ground that the officer's death was a foreseeable result of the defendant's burglary and his flight therefrom.

Is *Matos* inconsistent with *Root* or is it distinguishable?

3. In a highly publicized auto accident, Princess Diana and a friend were killed, along with the driver of their car, when he crashed into the pillar of a tunnel in Paris. See N.Y. Times, Sept. 6, 1997, at A1. Evidence suggested that "paparazzi" were pursuing her car at high speed in order to take pictures of her with her companion. Her driver, who was heavily intoxicated, apparently accelerated to evade the paparazzi and then lost control of the car. The attempt to take her picture in public was not illegal, but in the course of their chase, the paparazzi apparently reached speeds that were dangerous and possibly unlawful. French authorities considered holding some of the photographers responsible for the crash, but ultimately decided not to charge any of them.[14] What would be the result under American law? If the accident had occurred in an American city, could the paparazzi be convicted of manslaughter for the deaths of Diana and her companion? For the death of her driver? Is this situation controlled by *Root* or by *Kern* and *Matos?*

4. Defendant stabbed Thomas in the back and side. Thomas was treated at a hospital and released in stable condition. After his release, he resumed his prior consumption of cocaine. The drug raised his blood pressure and caused his internal wounds to bleed again; within a week he died from internal bleeding. Defendant was charged with murder. Is the defendant responsible for Thomas' death, because he takes his victim as he finds him? Or is he not responsible, because Thomas' act of taking cocaine constitutes an intervening cause? Should the answer depend on whether Thomas was addicted and therefore could not act "voluntarily"? See State v. Perez-Cervantez, 952 P.2d 204 (Wash. App. 1998).

Should the result in *Perez-Cervantez* be different from the result in State v. Lane, page 525, Note 2(b), where the defendant punched a drunk, who then died from brain swelling attributable to the impact of the punch on a brain affected by chronic alcoholism? Arguably, the upshot of the vulnerable-victim and intervening-actor doctrines would be that Lane is liable, because his victim's substance abuse occurred before the illegal blow, but that Perez-Cervantez is not liable because his victim's substance abuse occurred, in part, after the illegal blow. Does this difference in results make sense? Is there any sound policy reason for treating the two cases differently?

STATE v. McFADDEN

Supreme Court of Iowa
320 N.W.2d 608 (1982)

Allbee, J. This case stems from a drag race between defendant Michael Dwayne McFadden and another driver, Matthew Sulgrove, which occurred on a Des Moines city street in April 1980. . . . Sulgrove lost control of his automobile and swerved into a lane of oncoming traffic, where he struck a lawfully operated northbound vehicle. This third vehicle contained a six-year-old passenger, Faith Ellis, who was killed in the collision along with Sulgrove. Defendant's automobile did not physically contact either of the two colliding vehicles.

Defendant was charged with two counts of involuntary manslaughter, a violation of section 707.5(1), The Code 1979. Having waived a jury, defendant was tried to the court and convicted and sentenced on both counts. In this appeal, he challenged the validity of his convictions and the sentences imposed. . . . [D]efendant does not argue that the evidence was insufficient for trial court to find that both he and Sulgrove recklessly committed those public offenses prior to the accident. Rather, defendant's main contention is that proof of the causation element . . . was lacking.

Trial court found that defendant was guilty of involuntary manslaughter un-

14. Washington Post, Aug. 18, 1999, at C1.

der each of three separate theories: (1) that defendant aided and abetted Sulgrove in Sulgrove's commission of involuntary manslaughter; (2) that defendant was vicariously responsible for Sulgrove's commission of involuntary manslaughter by reason of their joint participation in the public offense of drag racing; and (3) that defendant himself committed the crime of involuntary manslaughter by recklessly engaging in a drag race so as to proximately cause the Sulgrove-Ellis collision.

We note that aiding and abetting and joint criminal conduct are theories of vicarious liability, based on Sulgrove's commission of involuntary manslaughter. Although a vicarious liability theory may be sufficient to convict defendant for the death of Faith Ellis,[a] the same is not true with regard to the death of Sulgrove. This is because the involuntary manslaughter statute requires proof that the perpetrator caused the death of "another person." Obviously, Sulgrove could not have committed involuntary manslaughter with respect to his own death. Therefore, a theory under which defendant is only vicariously liable for Sulgrove's crime would be inadequate to convict defendant for Sulgrove's death. We turn, then, to consideration of the third theory of liability, i.e., that defendant's reckless commission of the public offense of drag racing was a proximate cause of the Sulgrove and Ellis deaths. . . .

Defendant asserts that because Sulgrove was a competitor in the drag race, he assumed the risk of his own death, and therefore defendant could not be convicted or sentenced for that death. . . . We quote with approval the following discussion from [Commonwealth v. Peak, 12 Pa. D. & C. 379, 382 (1961)] which is pertinent to the issue at hand:

> Defendants by participating in the unlawful racing initiated a series of events resulting in the death of Young. Under these circumstances, decedent's own unlawful conduct does not absolve defendants from their guilt. The acts of defendants were contributing and substantial factors in bringing about the death of Young. The acts and omissions of two or more persons may work concurrently as the efficient cause of an injury and in such case each of the participating acts or omissions is regarded in law as a proximate cause.

We hold that the fact of Sulgrove's voluntary and reckless participation in the drag race does not of itself bar defendant from being convicted of involuntary manslaughter for Sulgrove's death.

Next, defendant contends trial court erred in applying the civil standard of proximate cause in a criminal prosecution, rather than adopting the more stringent standard of "direct causal connection" used by the Pennsylvania court in Commonwealth v. Root, 403 Pa. 571, 580, 170 A.2d 310, 314 (1961). In *Root,* the court held that "the tort liability concept of proximate cause has no proper place in prosecutions for criminal homicide and more direct causal connection is required for conviction." . . . We had occasion to consider a similar standard-of-causation issue in State v. Marti, 290 N.W.2d 570, 584-585 (Iowa 1980), which upheld the involuntary manslaughter conviction of a man who provided an obviously intoxicated, suicidal woman with the means to shoot herself by loading a gun for her and placing it within her reach. As here, the defendant in *Marti* ar-

a. The possibility of an aiding-and-abetting theory in cases of this kind is considered infra page 624.

gued that the trial court "inappropriately adopted the standards of proximate cause applied in civil cases." Unlike the Pennsylvania court in *Root,* however, we said in *Marti* that we were "unwilling to hold as a blanket rule of law that instructions used in civil trials regarding proximate cause are inappropriate for criminal trials." Id. We explained: "One reason for this is the similar functions that the requirement of proximate cause plays in both sorts of trials." The element of proximate cause in criminal prosecutions serves as a requirement that there be a sufficient causal relationship between the defendant's conduct and a proscribed harm to hold him criminally responsible. Similarly, in the law of torts it is the element that requires there to be a sufficient causal relationship between the defendant's conduct and the plaintiff's damage to hold the defendant civilly liable. . . .

[D]efendant has suggested no specific policy differences, nor can we think of any, that would justify a different standard of proximate causation under our involuntary manslaughter statute than under our tort law. The *Root* court opined that "[l]egal theory which makes guilt or innocence of criminal homicide depend upon such accidental and fortuitous circumstances as are now embraced by modern tort law's encompassing concept of proximate cause is too harsh to be just." We do not agree. Proximate cause is based on the concept of foreseeability. We believe the foreseeability requirement, coupled with the requirement of recklessness . . . will prevent the possibility of harsh or unjust results in involuntary manslaughter cases. . . .

Accordingly, we hold that trial court did not err in applying ordinary proximate cause principles to determine whether the causation element . . . had been met, and in declining to adopt the more stringent "direct causal connection" standard of *Root.*

[Convictions affirmed.]

COMMONWEALTH v. ATENCIO

Supreme Judicial Court of Massachusetts
345 Mass. 627, 189 N.E.2d 323 (1963)

Wilkins, C.J. Each defendant has been convicted upon an indictment for manslaughter in the death of Stewart E. Britch. . . . The defendants argue assignments of error in the denial of motions for directed verdicts. . . .

Facts which the jury could have found are these. On Sunday, October 22, 1961, the deceased, his brother Ronald, and the defendants spent the day drinking wine in the deceased's room in a rooming house in Boston. At some time in the afternoon, with reference to nothing specific so far as the record discloses, Marshall said, "I will settle this," went out, and in a few minutes returned clicking a gun, from which he removed one bullet. Early in the evening Ronald left, and the conversation turned to "Russian roulette."

[T]he "game" was played. The deceased and Atencio were seated on a bed, and Marshall was seated on a couch. First, Marshall examined the gun, saw that it contained one cartridge, and after spinning it on his arm, pointed it at his head, and pulled the trigger. Nothing happened. He handed the gun to Atencio, who repeated the process, again without result. Atencio passed the gun to the deceased, who spun it, put it to his head, then pulled the trigger. The cartridge exploded, and he fell over dead. . . .

We are of opinion that the defendants could properly have been found guilty of manslaughter. This is not a civil action against the defendants by the personal representatives of Stewart Britch. In such a case his voluntary act, we assume, would be a bar. Here the Commonwealth had an interest that the deceased should not be killed by the wanton or reckless conduct of himself and others. . . . Such conduct could be found in the concerted action and cooperation of the defendants in helping to bring about the deceased's foolish act. . . .

The defendants argue as if it should have been ruled, as matter of law, that there were three "games" of solitaire and not one "game" of "Russian roulette." That the defendants participated could be found to be a cause and not a mere condition of Stewart Britch's death. It is not correct to say that his act could not be found to have been caused by anything which Marshall and Atencio did, nor that he would have died when the gun went off in his hand no matter whether they had done the same. The testimony does not require a ruling that when the deceased took the gun from Atencio it was an independent or intervening act not standing in any relation to the defendants' acts which would render what he did imputable to them. It is an oversimplification to contend that each participated in something that only one could do at a time. There could be found to be mutual encouragement in a joint enterprise. In the abstract, there may have been no duty on the defendants to prevent the deceased from playing. But there was a duty on their part not to cooperate or join with him in the "game." Nor, if the facts presented such a case, would we have to agree that if the deceased, and not the defendants, had played first that they could not have been found guilty of manslaughter. The defendants were much more than merely present at a crime. It would not be necessary that the defendants force the deceased to play or suggest that he play.

We are referred in both briefs to cases of manslaughter arising out of automobiles racing upon the public highway. . . .

Whatever may be thought of those . . . decisions, there is a very real distinction between drag racing and "Russian roulette." In the former much is left to the skill, or lack of it, on the competitor. In "Russian roulette" it is a matter of luck as to the location of the one bullet, and except for a misfire (of which there was evidence in the case at bar) the outcome is a certainty if the chamber under the hammer happens to be the one containing the bullet. . . .

The judgments on the indictments for manslaughter are affirmed. . . .

NOTES AND QUESTIONS

1. In Lewis v. State, 474 So. 2d 766 (Ala. Crim. App. 1985), the defendant introduced Damon Sanders (a 15-year-old boy) to the game of Russian roulette and played it with him on several occasions without incident. (It was unclear whether the gun had been loaded on those occasions.) After one such game the defendant put the gun away and went into the next room to make a phone call. While he was on the phone, other witnesses outside the house observed Sanders spin the chamber, point the gun at his head and pull the trigger; the gun fired, killing Sanders instantly. The court accepted the state's premise that Sanders would not have died if the defendant had not "directed, instructed and influenced" Sanders to play the game, and that the defendant would have been liable if he had been in the room or otherwise playing the game at the time. The court nonetheless held that liability was precluded because "the free will of the victim is seen as an intervening cause which . . . breaks the chain of causation." Id. at 771, quoting Susan W. Brenner, Undue Influence in the Criminal Law: A Proposed Analysis of "Causing Suicide," 47 Alb. L. Rev. 62, 83 (1982).

Question: Is this situation distinguishable from that in *Atencio?* For criticism of decisions like *McFadden* and *Atencio,* see Daniel B. Yeager, Dangerous Games and the Criminal Law, Crim. J. Ethics 3-12 (Winter/Spring 1997).

2. In Commonwealth v. Feinberg, 433 Pa. 558, 253 A.2d 636 (1969), the defendant was a proprietor of a cigar store in a skid-row area of Philadelphia. One of the items he had regularly stocked and sold was sterno, a canned heat containing methanol. Late in 1963 he received a single shipment of a new kind of sterno called "industrial" sterno, which contained a much higher percentage of methanol. This made it far more dangerous for persons to consume internally. Imprinted on the lids of the new sterno was the legend: "Institutional sterno. Danger. Poison. For use only as a fuel. Not for consumer use. For industrial and commercial use." The defendant sold approximately 400 cans of the new industrial sterno before returning the remainder of the shipment to the manufacturer. About 32 persons in the skid-row area died as a result of methanol poisoning caused by drinking the cans of industrial sterno sold by defendant. Defendant was subsequently tried and convicted of manslaughter. The record showed that the defendant was aware of the proclivity of some of his customers to consume the sterno for its intoxicating effect. There was also sufficient evidence that the defendant was aware or should have been aware that the sterno was toxic if consumed. On appeal the Supreme Court of Pennsylvania affirmed the conviction. In explaining why *Root* was inapplicable, the court said:

> Defendant contends that the drinking of liquor by deceased was his voluntary act and served as an intervening cause, breaking the causal connection between the giving of the liquor by defendant and the resulting death. The drinking of the liquor, in consequence of defendant's act, was, however, what the defendant contemplated. Deceased, it is true, may have been negligent in drinking, but, where the defendant was negligent, then the contributory negligence of the deceased will be no defense in a criminal action.

3. The drug provider. Suppose that Lydia gives Gus a gun at Gus' request, knowing or even hoping that he will kill himself. As we have seen, if Gus uses the gun to kill himself, Lydia cannot be held for killing him; at most she might be guilty of assisting a suicide. See People v. Campbell, page 530 supra. But suppose that Lydia provides Gus with cocaine or heroin, not expecting or hoping that he will kill himself with it, but just to indulge his desire to get high. If Gus dies of a drug overdose, shouldn't the intervening-act doctrine preclude finding that Lydia killed Gus — just as it does when she gives him a gun?

Some courts avoid that result by finding that the drug user's act was not fully voluntary. In State v. Wassil, 658 A.2d 548, 556 (1995), for example, the court said that "because [the decedent] already was inebriated at the time the defendant delivered the drugs to him, he did not voluntarily, consciously disregard a known risk to himself when he injected the drugs." When the drug user's actions are fully voluntary, it is sometimes argued the seller should not be liable for his death.[15] But courts often ignore or reject the intervening-act doctrine and hold the drug supplier responsible for the foreseeable, though freely chosen, acts of his purchaser. E.g., People v. Galle, 573 N.E.2d 569 (N.Y. 1991); Regina v. Kennedy, [1999] Crim. L. Rev. 65.[16] See also Ramirez, Homicide Liability for the Furnishing of Dangerous Narcotics, 6 St. Louis U. Pub. L. Rev. 161 (1987).

Which is the better view? Recall that in *Feinberg,* Note 2, supra, the court held the supplier liable, despite the subsequent reckless acts of his customers, where the intoxicant he had supplied was not in itself illegal. If Feinberg's homicide liability was properly based on his sales of sterno, doesn't homicide liability follow a fortiori in the case of a supplier of cocaine or heroin? In *Wassil,* supra, the court stated (658 A.2d, at 556) that this approach, rejecting the intervening-actor doctrine in drug-supplier cases, is followed by "courts in the majority, if not the entirety, of the jurisdictions that have considered the question." How can we account for the apparent paradox that if Lydia only intends to help Gus enjoy the drug, she can be held liable for killing him, but if she intends for Gus to die, she cannot be?

4. Statutory formulations. §2.03 of the Model Penal Code holds an actor responsible for a result when his action is a but-for antecedent, if it involves the same kind of harm he intended or risked, so long as it is "not too remote or accidental in its occurrence to have a [just] bearing on the actor's liability or on the gravity of his offense." This formulation has been criticized; H. L. A. Hart and Tony Honoré object (Causation in the Law 398 (2d ed. 1985)) that this provision

> does not provide *specifically* for those cases where causal problems arise because, although the accused did not intend it, another human action besides accused's is involved in the production of the proscribed harm. These are treated merely as one kind of case where harm may or may not be "too accidental" in its manner or occurrence. This is surely a weakness in a scheme which is designed to reproduce, and to allow the jury to express, the convictions of common sense that, even if harm would not have occurred without the act of accused, it is still necessary to distinguish, for purposes of punishment, one manner of upshot from another. For whatever else may be vague or disputable about common sense in regard to causation and responsibility, it is surely clear that the primary case where it is reluctant to treat a person as having caused harm which would not have occurred without his act is that where another voluntary human action has intervened.

Are the points well taken? Would it be an improvement to provide, as several states have, that the result must be "not too dependent on the another's volitional act" to have a [just] bearing, etc.? See Haw. Rev. Stat. §§702-215(2) & 702-216(2); N.J. Stat. Ann. tit. 2C, §2C2-3. The Model Penal Code drafters did not think so. The commentary (Comment to §2.03 at 262) states that the language of §2.03

> does not accept the view that volitional human intervention should be treated differently from other intervening causes, but neither does it mandate a contrary po-

15. Cf. State v. Mauldin, 529 P.2d 124 (Kan. 1974), where the court held against liability *for felony murder,* resting its conclusion not on a lack of causation but rather on the ground that the act of injecting the drug took place after the felony (drug distribution) had terminated.

16. For pointed criticism of the result in *Kennedy,* see J. C. Smith, Commentary, [1999] Crim. L. Rev. 67.

sition. It is up to the trier of fact to give weight to such variables if it is persuaded that these considerations are significant.

B. ATTEMPT

1. *Introduction*

Statutory definitions of the crime of attempt are usually minimal. Consider some representative examples: "A person is guilty of an attempt to commit a crime when, with intent to commit a crime, he engages in conduct which tends to effect the commission of such crime" (N.Y. Penal Law §110.00); "Every person who attempts to commit any crime, but fails, or is prevented or intercepted in its perpetration shall be punished . . ." (Cal. Penal Code §664); "A person commits an attempt when, with intent to commit a specific offense, he does any act which constitutes a substantial step toward the commission of that offense" (Ill. Stat. Ch. 720, §5/8-4(a)).

At common law attempts were misdemeanors. Today the usual punishment for attempt is a reduced factor of the punishment for the completed crime. In California (Cal. Penal Code §664) attempt carries a maximum term of not more than one-half of the highest maximum term authorized for the completed offense. Under the New York Penal Law, which uses punishment classification of offenses, the sentence for an attempt is one classification below that for the completed crime (§110.05), except for certain offenses, notably drug offenses, where the punishment is the same. Since the Model Penal Code proposals, however, a substantial minority of states have departed from the predominant scheme by making the punishment the same for the attempt as for the crime attempted, except for crimes punishable by death or life imprisonment. See, e.g., Conn. Gen. Stat. Ann. §53a-51; Del. Code Ann. tit. 11, §531; Ill. Ann. Stat. Ch. 720, §5/8-4(c); Pa. Stat. Ann. tit. 18, §905.

What is the justification for the traditional approach to the punishment grading of attempt? The relationship of harm to the proper degree of punishment is a pervasive problem in criminal law. The issue is implicit in several topics we have already considered. Thus, all the cases on causation in effect require us to consider the reasons why conduct that causes harm should ever be treated differently from identical conduct that does not. A similar issue is implicit in the Chapter 5 materials dealing with homicidal risk creation. An actor whose recklessness or criminal negligence creates a substantial risk of death can be convicted of manslaughter and sometimes even of murder, provided that death actually results. But what crime has the actor committed if the person he endangers suffers only nonlethal injuries or escapes with no injuries at all? Because such an actor is not "attempting" to kill anyone, he normally cannot be convicted of any form of attempted homicide. (We explore this point in connection with the mens rea of attempt at page 556 infra.) Absent some statutory risk-creation offense (such as Model Penal Code §211.2), such an actor may have committed no crime at all. But even if there is a criminal offense that applies to his conduct, its penalties will be far lower than those applicable under homicide statutes when a death occurs. The law of attempts poses the same issue in its starkest form. The actor who intentionally seeks to cause a harm (the death of another person, for example) is traditionally punished much less severely if his attempt proves unsuccessful. Is it justified to attribute importance in punishment to the actual result of a defendant's conduct? Consider the following comments.

JAMES FITZJAMES STEPHEN, A HISTORY OF THE CRIMINAL LAW (VOL. 3) 311 (1883): If two persons are guilty of the very same act of negligence, and if one of them causes thereby a railway accident, involving the death and mutilation of many persons, whereas the other does no injury to anyone, it seems to me that it would be rather pedantic than rational to say that each had committed the same offence, and should be subjected to the same punishment. In one sense, each has committed an offence, but the one has had the *bad luck* to cause a horrible misfortune, and to attract public attention to it, and the other the good *fortune* to do no harm. Both certainly deserve punishment, but it gratifies a natural public feeling to choose out for punishment the one who actually has caused great harm, and the effect in the way of preventing a repetition of the offence is much the same as if both were punished.

H. L. A. HART, THE MORALITY OF THE CRIMINAL LAW 52-53 (1965): [Professor Hart, after quoting the above extract from Stephen, observes:] This doctrine allocating to "public feeling" so important a place in the determination of punishment reflects the element of populism which, as we have seen, is often prominent in English judicial conceptions of the morality of punishment. But it conflicts with important principles of justice as between different offenders which would prima facie preclude treating two persons, guilty of "the very same act" of negligence, differently because of a fortuitous difference in the outcome of these acts. No doubt there is often an inclination to treat punishment like compensation and measure it by the outcome alone. There may even be at times a public demand that this should be done. And no doubt if the machinery of justice were nullified or could not proceed unless the demand were gratified we might have to gratify it and hope to educate people out of this misassimilation of the principles of punishment to those of compensation. But there seems no good reason for adopting this misassimilation as a principle or to stigmatise as pedantic the refusal to recognise that the difference made by "bad fortune" and "good luck" to the outcome of the very same acts justifies punishing the one and not the other.

STEPHEN J. SCHULHOFER, ATTEMPT, in 1 Encyclopedia of Crime and Justice 97 (1983): [T]he most plausible explanation for more lenient treatment of attempts is that the community's resentment and demand for punishment are not aroused to the same degree when serious harm has been averted. This explanation, however, raises further questions. Can severe punishment (in the case of completed crime, for example) be justified simply by reference to the fact that society "demands" or at least desires this? To what extent should the structure of penalties serve to express intuitive societal judgments that cannot be rationalized in terms of such instrumental goals as deterrence, isolation, rehabilitation, and even retribution — that is, condemnation reflecting the moral culpability of the act? Conversely, to what extent should the criminal justice system see its mission as one not of expressing the intuitive social demand for punishment, but rather as one of restraining that demand and of protecting *from* punishment the offender who, rationally speaking, deserves a less severe penalty?

MODEL PENAL CODE: *Section 5.05(1)*. Except as otherwise provided in this Section, attempt, solicitation and conspiracy are crimes of the same grade and degree as the most serious offense which is attempted or solicited or is an object of the conspiracy. An attempt, solicitation or conspiracy to commit a [capital crime or a] felony of the first degree is a felony of the second degree. [Under §6.06, a felony of the first degree is punishable by imprisonment for a term whose minimum is between 1 and 10 years and whose maximum is life. A felony of the second degree is punishable by imprisonment for a term whose minimum is between one and three years and whose maximum is 10 years.]

MODEL PENAL CODE AND COMMENTARIES, Comment to §5.05 at 490 (1985): The theory of this grading system may be stated simply. To the extent that sentencing depends upon the antisocial disposition of the actor and the demonstrated need for a corrective sanction, there is likely to be little difference in the gravity of the required measures depending on the consummation or the failure of the plan. It is only when and insofar as the severity of sentence is designed for general deterrent purposes that a distinction on this ground is likely to have reasonable force. It is doubtful, however, that the threat of punishment for the inchoate crime can add significantly to the net deterrent efficacy of the sanction threatened for the substantive offense that is the actor's object, which he, by hypothesis, ignores. Hence, there is a basis for economizing in use of the heaviest and most afflictive sanctions by removing them from the inchoate crimes.

NOTE

For further exploration of these issues, see H. L. A. Hart, Punishment and Responsibility 129-131 (1968); Sanford H. Kadish, The Criminal Law and the Luck of the Draw, 84 J. Crim. L. & Criminology 679 (1994); Stephen J. Schulhofer, Harm and Punishment: A Critique of Emphasis on the Results of Conduct in the Criminal Law, 122 U. Pa. L. Rev. 1497 (1974). For a defense of lesser punishment when the harm does not occur, see Michael Moore, The Independent Moral Significance of Wrongdoing, 1 J. Contemp. Leg. Issues 1 (1994), and for a critique of Professor Moore's argument, see Kimberly D. Kessler, The Role of Luck in the Criminal Law, 142 U. Pa. L. Rev. 2183 (1994). For an economist's analysis of the issues see Steven Shavell, Deterrence and the Punishment of Attempts, 19 J. Legal Stud. 435 (1990).

2. *Mens Rea*

SMALLWOOD v. STATE

Court of Appeals, Maryland
343 Md. 97, 680 A.2d 512, 1996

Murphy, Chief Judge. [Smallwood was convicted in a non-jury trial of three counts of assault with intent to murder his rape victims, based on evidence that despite his awareness that he was HIV positive and that he had been warned by social worker of the need to practice "safe sex" to avoid contaminating his partners, he did not use a condom in any of his attacks.]

Smallwood argues that the fact that he engaged in unprotected sexual intercourse, even though he knew that he carried HIV, is insufficient to infer an intent to kill. The most that can reasonably be inferred, Smallwood contends, is that he is guilty of recklessly endangering his victims by exposing them to the risk that they would become infected themselves. The State disagrees, arguing that the facts of this case are sufficient to infer an intent to kill. The State likens Smallwood's HIV-positive status to a deadly weapon and argues that engaging in unprotected sex when one is knowingly infected with HIV is equivalent to firing a loaded firearm at that person.

In Faya v. Almaraz, 329 Md. 435, 438-440, 620 A.2d 327 (1993), . . . we described HIV as a retrovirus that attacks the human immune system, weakening it, and ultimately destroying the body's capacity to ward off disease. We also noted that:

> [t]he virus may reside latently in the body for periods as long as ten years or more, during which time the infected person will manifest no symptoms of illness and function normally. . . . Medical studies have indicated that most people who carry the virus will progress to AIDS. . . .

In this case, we must determine what legal inferences may be drawn when an individual infected with the HIV virus knowingly exposes another to the risk of HIV-infection, and the resulting risk of death by AIDS.

As we have previously stated, "[t]he required intent in the crimes of assault with intent to murder and attempted murder is the specific intent to murder, i.e., the specific intent to kill under circumstances that would not legally justify or excuse the killing or mitigate it to manslaughter." State v. Earp, 319 Md. 156, 167, 571 A.2d 1227 (1990). [Smallwood] was properly found guilty of attempted murder and assault with intent to murder only if there was sufficient evidence from which the trier of fact could reasonably have concluded that Smallwood possessed a specific intent to kill at the time he assaulted each of the three women. . . .

An intent to kill may be proved by circumstantial evidence. "[S]ince intent is subjective and, without the cooperation of the accused, cannot be directly and objectively proven, its presence must be shown by established facts which permit a proper inference of its existence." Davis v. State, 204 Md. 44, 51, 102 A.2d 816 (1954). Therefore, the trier of fact may infer the existence of the required intent from surrounding circumstances such as "the accused's acts, conduct and words." State v. Raines, 326 Md. 582, 591, 606 A.2d 265 (1992). As we have repeatedly stated, "under the proper circumstances, an intent to kill may be inferred from the use of a deadly weapon directed at a vital part of the human body." Raines, supra, 326 Md. at 591; . . . [T]here we upheld the use of such an inference. In that case, Raines and a friend were traveling on a highway when the defendant fired a pistol into the driver's side window of a tractor trailer in an adjacent lane. The shot killed the driver of the tractor trailer, and Raines was convicted of first degree murder. The evidence in the case showed that Raines shot at the driver's window of the truck, knowing that the truck driver was immediately behind the window. We concluded that "Raines's actions in directing the gun at the window, and therefore at the driver's head on the other side of the window, permitted an inference that Raines shot the gun with the intent to kill."

The State argues that our analysis in *Raines* rested upon two elements: (1) Raines knew that his weapon was deadly, and (2) Raines knew that he was firing it at someone's head. The State argues that Smallwood similarly knew that HIV infection ultimately leads to death, and that he knew that he would be exposing his victims to the risk of HIV transmission by engaging in unprotected sex with them. Therefore, the State argues, a permissible inference can be drawn that Smallwood intended to kill each of his three victims. The State's analysis, however, ignores several factors.

First, we must consider the magnitude of the risk to which the victim is knowingly exposed. The inference drawn in *Raines,* supra, rests upon the rule that "[i]t is permissible to infer that 'one intends the natural and probable consequences of his act.'" Davis v. State, supra. Before an intent to kill may be inferred based solely upon the defendant's exposure of a victim to a risk of death, it must be shown that the victim's death would have been a natural and probable result of the defendant's conduct. . . . When a deadly weapon has been fired at a vital part of a victim's body, the risk of killing the victim is so high that it becomes reasonable to assume that the defendant intended the victim to die as a natural and probable consequence of the defendant's actions.

. . . While the risk to which Smallwood exposed his victims when he forced them to engage in unprotected sexual activity must not be minimized, the State has presented no evidence from which it can reasonably be concluded that death by AIDS is a probable result of Smallwood's actions to the same extent that death is the probable result of firing a deadly weapon at a vital part of someone's body. Without such evidence, it cannot fairly be concluded that death by AIDS was sufficiently probable to support an inference that Smallwood intended to kill his victims in the absence of other evidence indicative of an intent to kill.

In this case, we find no additional evidence from which to infer an intent to kill. Smallwood's actions are wholly explained by an intent to commit rape and armed robbery, the crimes for which he has already pled guilty. . . .

The cases cited by the State demonstrate the sort of additional evidence needed to support an inference that Smallwood intended to kill his victims. The defendants in these cases have either made explicit statements demonstrating an intent to infect their victims or have taken specific actions demonstrating such an intent and tending to exclude other possible intents. In State v. Hinkhouse, 139 Or. App. 446, 912 P.2d 921 (1996), for example, the defendant engaged in unprotected sex with a number of women while knowing that he was HIV positive. The defendant had also actively concealed his HIV-positive status from these women, had lied to several of them by stating that he was not HIV-positive, and had refused the women's requests that he wear condoms. Id. 912 P.2d at 923-24. There was also evidence that he had told at least one of his sexual partners that "if he were [HIV-]positive, he would spread the virus to other people." Id. at 924. The Oregon Court of Appeals found this evidence to be sufficient to demonstrate an intent to kill, and upheld the defendant's convictions for attempted murder.

In State v. Caine, 652 So. 2d 611 (La. App. 1995), a conviction for attempted second degree murder was upheld where the defendant had jabbed a used syringe into a victim's arm while shouting "I'll give you AIDS." The defendant in Weeks v. State, 834 S.W.2d 559 (Tex. App. 1992), made similar statements, and was convicted of attempted murder after he spat on a prison guard. In that case, the defendant knew that he was HIV-positive, and the appellate court found that "the record reflects that [Weeks] thought he could kill the guard by spitting his HIV-infected saliva at him." There was also evidence that at the time of the spitting incident, Weeks had stated that he was "going to take someone with him when he went, that he was 'medical now,' and that he was 'HIV-4.'" . . .

In contrast with these cases, the State in this case would allow the trier of fact to infer an intent to kill based solely upon the fact that Smallwood exposed his victims to the risk that they might contract HIV. Without evidence showing that such a result is sufficiently probable to support this inference, we conclude that Smallwood's convictions for attempted murder and assault with intent to murder must be reversed.[a]

NOTES AND QUESTIONS

1. The Intent Requirement. Both the common law and most American statutory formulations agree with the holding in the principal case that an attempt requires a purpose (or "specific intent") to produce the proscribed result, even when recklessness or some lesser mens rea would suffice for conviction of the completed offense. See, e.g., People v. Campbell, 72 N.Y.2d 602, 532 N.E.2d 86 (1988); Keys v. State, 766 P.2d 270 (Nev. 1988); Model Penal Code §5.01(1)(b). For example, in Illinois murder is the unlawful killing of another either with intent to kill or greatly injure, or with knowledge that one's acts will cause death or will create a strong probability of doing so. Ill. Rev. St. ch.38, par.9-1(a). A person commits an attempt when, "with the intention to commit a specific offense" he does a substantial act toward committing that offense. Ill. Rev. Stat. ch.38, par.8-4. Therefore, a person who acts knowing that his acts create strong probability of killing another commits the crime of murder if the victim dies. But is he guilty of attempted murder if the victim survives? The Illinois courts have held no, consistent with the requirement of a specific intent for the crime of attempt. People v. Kraft, 133 Ill. App. 3d 294, 478 N.E.2d 1154 (1985). This is a well accepted position. A recent example is Jones v. State, 689 N.E.2d 722 (Ind. 1997), where defendant shot at a house full of people wounding several and killing one. He was convicted of murder of the person he killed but acquitted of attempted murder of those he wounded. The court rejected defendant's claim that this was an inconsistent verdict. Attempted murder requires a specific intent to kill, but it is sufficient for murder that defendant engages in conduct knowing of a high probability that in doing so he will kill someone.

2. Strict liability. Is specific intent required where the object crime imposes strict liability? In principle it would seem not, though there are few cases. See Wayne R. LaFave, Criminal Law 545 (3d ed. 2000). A recent case that presented

a. A review of the law of attempt in the context of the intentional transmission of the AIDS virus appears in Comment, (Linda Bell), 2 Thurgood Marshall L. Rev. 243 (1995). See also Amy L. McGuire (Comment), AIDS as a Weapon: Criminal Prosecution of HIV Exposure, 36 Hous. L. Rev. 1787 (1999).—Eds.

the issue is United States v. Gracidas-Ulibarry, 192 F.3d 926 (9th Cir. 1999). A federal statute made it criminal for a deported person to reenter, attempt to enter, or to be found in the country. Defendant, who was riding in the back seat of the car as it was about to cross into the United States, was convicted of attempting to reenter under an instruction that failed to require the jury to find that he intended to do so. The government argued this was correct, reasoning that since the statute made entering or being found in the country strict liability offenses, the same must be true of the attempt to reenter. The court agreed, but a dissenting opinion on this point observed: "It is an axiom of American criminal law that an attempt includes an element of specific intent even if the crime attempted does not." Question: Who was right? Cf. John Smith, Two Problems of Criminal Attempts, 70 Harv. L. Rev. 422, 143 (1957): If "crimes of . . . strict liability are necessary and valid instruments of policy, then there is no reason for not applying this same policy in the case of attempts."

3. Why Specific Intent? Why should the law require a "specific intent" or "purpose" in the law of attempt? How can it be unsound to convict for an attempted crime if the defendant, though he lacked "purpose," had the mental state sufficient for conviction of the substantive offense? Consider three possible explanations. One is linguistic: To attempt something is to try to accomplish it and one cannot be said to try if one does not intend to succeed. Another explanation is moral: One who intends to commit a criminal harm does a greater moral wrong than one who does so recklessly or negligently. The third is utilitarian: As Justice Holmes put it in The Common Law 68 (1881): "The importance of the intent is not to show that the act was wicked but that it was likely to be followed by hurtful consequences."

What would Justice Holmes say about a case like Thacker v. Commonwealth, 134 Va. 767, 114 S.E. 504 (1922)? A drunk, angered by the refusal of a woman who was camping in a tent with her child to admit him, walked down the road a way, turned, and shot at the light shining through the canvas. If the bullet had accidentally killed the woman, the defendant could be convicted of murder. But in *Thacker,* the bullet fortunately missed the woman. The court held that defendant, lacking intent to kill, could not be convicted of attempted murder. Why do we need the bullet to hit the woman to be assured that the action "was likely to be followed by hurtful consequences"? Moreover, if the defendant is not guilty of attempt, for what crime (if any) could he be convicted? Do the penalties provided for an offense such as Model Penal Code §211.2 (reckless endangerment) afford adequate punishment for a case of this kind? Consider another observation of Justice Holmes in The Common Law at 66:

> It may be true in the region of attempts, as elsewhere, the law began with cases of actual intent, as those cases are the most obvious ones. But it cannot stop with them, unless it attaches more importance to the etymological meaning of the word attempt than to the general principles of punishment. Accordingly there is at least color of authority for the proposition that an act is punishable as an attempt, if, supposing it to have produced its natural and probable effect, it would have amounted to a substantive crime.

Consider People v. Thomas, 729 P.2d 972 (Colo. 1986), which has added to the color of authority of which Justice Holmes spoke. The defendant fired three shots at a man he believed to be a fleeing rapist. Two of the shots struck the man.

The defendant claimed that one of the shots had been fired accidentally and that the other two were warning shots. At trial, he was convicted of attempted reckless manslaughter under Colo. Rev. Stat. §18-2-101(1), which provides:

> A person commits criminal attempt if, acting with the kind of culpability otherwise required for commission of an offense, he engages in conduct constituting a substantial step toward the commission of the offense.

Noting that the statute differed from Model Penal Code §5.01, the Colorado Supreme Court read the statute literally as dispensing with the requirement of specific intent and upheld a conviction for attempted reckless manslaughter. The court reasoned that the traditional requirement of intent served to identify cases where conduct was likely to produce harmful consequences. The court found that the necessary potential for future harm is present not only in cases of intentional conduct but also when the defendant knows that the prohibited result is practically certain to occur or when he recklessly disregards a substantial risk. *Question:* Under the court's interpretation of the statute why wouldn't every armed robbery in which the victim is not killed amount to an attempted felony-murder?

4. *Attempted Felony-Murder?* Suppose that two felons fire at a bank guard in the course of their escape from a bank holdup. The guard is wounded but survives. The evidence suggests that the felons intended to frighten the guard but did not intend to kill him. Can the robbers be convicted of attempted felony-murder on the ground that they had a specific intent to commit the felony? Most states that have considered the issue have rejected the concept of attempted felony murder. See the collection of cases in Note (Brian Roark), State v. Lea: Attempt Plus Felony-Murder Does Not Equal Attempted Felony-Murder, 76 N.C. L. Rev. 2361, 2381 n. 146 (1998). Arkansas is a rare exception. See White v. Stale, 166 Ark. 499, 585 S.W.2d 952 (1979). Why this virtual unanimity? If the mens rea for the felony may fictitiously supply the mens rea for murder, can't it supply the mens rea for attempted murder as well? After all, if defendant could be held for felony-murder if the victim died, why should he not be held for the attempt if the victim survives? On the other hand, if that view were accepted, would a robber whose victim suffers a *nonfatal* heart attack be guilty of attempted felony-murder? Would every robber and burglar be guilty of attempted felony murder, even if shots are never fired and none of the victims suffered any physical injury? In State v. Gray 654 So. 2d 552 (1995), the Florida Supreme Court overruled a prior decision supporting the crime of attempted felony-murder, observing that this view "has proven more troublesome than beneficial," and noting the difficulty experienced by a bar committee in drafting an appropriate jury instruction on the attempted felony-murder doctrine. *Questions:* Why troublesome, why the difficulty?

5. *Attempted Manslaughter?* In State v. Holbron, 80 Hawaii 27, 904 P.2 912 (1995), the court held that the requirement of specific intent means that there can be no crime of attempted (involuntary) manslaughter, although it is widely accepted that there is a crime of attempted (voluntary) manslaughter. As representing "virtually the entire universe of American case law" the court quoted the following from J. C. Smith, Two Problems in Criminal Attempts, 70 Harv. L. Rev. 422, 429, 434 (1957):

> [T]here can be no attempt to commit involuntary manslaughter. The consequence involved in that crime is the death of the victim and an act done with intent to achieve this, if an attempt at all, is attempted murder. It is of the essence of involuntary manslaughter that the consequence be produced. . . . recklessly. . . . but not intentionally.
>
> An attempt to commit voluntary manslaughter, on the other hand, may theoretically be possible. *D*, acting under such provocation as would reduce murder to manslaughter, strikes at *P* with a hatchet with intent to kill him but misses. Assuming that the doctrine of provocation applies on a charge of attempted murder, *D* would appear to be guilty of attempted manslaughter. This variety of manslaughter may be committed when the consequence involved in the complete crime is intended.

6. *Meaning of Specific Intent.* While the specific intent requirement is broadly accepted, what it means and how it is to apply can be problematical.

(a) *Intent and Knowledge.* How much additional evidence would have been required to support an inference that Smallwood intended to kill? The court's opinion discusses several cases as examples. In *Hinkhouse,* the defendant, like Smallwood, knew he had AIDS and failed to use condoms. But unlike Smallwood, Hinkhouse concealed his infection from his otherwise consenting partners. Why is that enough to establish intent to kill? Consider the Model Penal Code's distinction between purpose and knowledge. §2.02(a) and (b).

(b) *Probabilities.* Consider the emphasis the opinion in *Smallwood* places on probability of death when it compares infecting another with AIDS and shooting with a firearm. How do the probabilities of the action causing death bear on the presence of intent? If the effect of AIDS was certain death within a matter of months, would the result be otherwise in *Smallwood?* Would that fact be sufficient even if the defendant were not aware of that fact? Consider this hypothetical: Defendant, in order to destroy a competitor's experimental aircraft, plants a bomb on the plane and sets it to explode in midair, knowing that the test pilot will be killed, though having no particular wish that that should happen. The bomb fails to explode. May the defendant be convicted of attempted murder? Does she have a "purpose" or "specific intent" to kill? (Note the solution to this problem in Model Penal Code §5.01(1)(b): The required mens rea is satisfied if the defendant acts "with the purpose of causing or with the belief that [his conduct] will cause" the prohibited result.

(c) *Conditional Intent.* We've discussed conditional intent earlier in connection with Holloway v. United States, supra page 218, which followed the prevailing view that a conditional intent qualifies as an intent. Consider the implication of this position for the crime of attempt. If a defendant holds a gun to the head of his victim and tells her that he will shoot her dead then and there if she doesn't hand over her wallet (and meaning it), he commits attempted robbery (taking property from the person of another by force or threat) — his intent to steal her wallet was not even conditional. But does he also commit attempted murder?

7. *Attendant Circumstances.* Does the specific intent requirement extend to the attendant circumstances that may be necessary elements of the crime attempted? Consider the following.

(a) In Regina v. Khan, [1990] 1 W.L.R. 813, the defendant was charged with attempted rape. The judge instructed the jury that the completed offense of rape requires proof that the defendant had intercourse and either knew that the

Refer to p. 623

woman did not consent or "was reckless as to whether [she] was consenting or not." The judge then explained the law applicable to attempts and added, "As in the case of rape the principles relevant to consent apply in exactly the same way in attempted rape. I do not suppose you need me to go through it again. Apply the same principles as to rape." Defendant was convicted of attempted rape. The Court of Appeal affirmed, stating:

> The only difference between the two offences is that in rape sexual intercourse takes place whereas in attempted rape it does not, although there has to be some act which is more than preparatory to sexual intercourse. Considered in that way, the intent of the defendant is precisely the same in rape and in attempted rape and the mens rea is identical, namely, an intention to have intercourse plus a knowledge of or recklessness as to the woman's absence of consent. . . .
>
> If this is the true analysis, as we believe it is, the attempt does not require any different intention on the part of the accused from that for the full offence of rape. We believe this to be a desirable result which in the instant case did not require the jury to be burdened with different directions as to the accused's state of mind, dependent upon whether the individual achieved or failed to achieve sexual intercourse.

(b) In Commonwealth v. Dunne, 394 Mass. 10, 474 N.E.2d 538 (1985), the defendant was convicted of assault with intent to commit statutory rape, an offense that the court referred to as "attempted statutory rape." The statutory age of consent was sixteen, and the victim was fifteen years and four months old on the date of the offense. There was no allegation that the defendant knew (or should have known) that the victim was underage. Affirming the conviction, the court said:

> [In] Commonwealth v. Miller, 385 Mass. 521, 522, 432 N.E.2d 463 (1982) . . . we held that in a prosecution for statutory rape "it is immaterial that the defendant reasonably believed that the victim was sixteen years of age or older." This is the rule in most jurisdictions. Similarly, in a prosecution for an assault with intent to commit statutory rape, this court has held that whether or not the defendant is aware of the victim's age is irrelevant. . . . Indeed, it would be incongruous for us to posit one rule for the completed act and another for the attempt.

Are these cases sound? How can a person be convicted of attempting (trying) to do what he is unaware of doing?

(c) How the text of the Model Penal Code (§5.01) would handle these cases is less than clear, but the commentary states explicitly that §5.01(1)(c) is meant to reach the same conclusion as these cases. Model Penal Code and Commentaries, Comments to §5.01 at 301-304 (1985):

> Under the formulation in Subsection (1)(c), the proffered defense would not succeed in either case. In the statutory rape example, the actor must have a purpose to engage in sexual intercourse with a female in order to be charged with the attempt, and must engage in a substantial step in a course of conduct planned to culminate in his commission of that act. With respect to the age of the victim, however, it is sufficient if he acts "with the kind of culpability otherwise required for the commission of the crime," which in the case supposed is none at all. Since, therefore,

mistake as to age is irrelevant with respect to the substantive offense, it is likewise irrelevant with respect to the attempt.

Question: Is this a persuasive reading of Subsection (1)(c)? That section says a person is guilty of an attempt if he purposely does something "which, under the circumstances as he believes them to be" is a substantial step in commission of the crime. But under the circumstances as the defendants believed them to be in these cases their actions were not a step in the commission of the crime, but only a step toward having consensual sex with an adult woman. How else might this subsection be read?

(d) For a probing analysis of the issues involved in considering the mens rea as to attendant circumstances required for attempt, see Larry Alexander & Kimberley D. Kessler, Mens Rea and Inchoate Crimes, 87 J. Crim. L. & Cr. 1139, 1157 (1997). Concerning the difficulties of distinguishing circumstances from conduct or consequences, see R. A. Duff, The Circumstances of an Attempt, 50 Camb. L.J. 104-111 (1991), and Recklessness in Attempts (Again), 15 Oxford J. Leg. Stud. 309 (1995); Richard Buxton, Circumstances, Consequences and Attempted Rape, [1984] Crim. L. Rev. 25.

3. *Preparation versus Attempt*

KING v. BARKER [1924] N.Z.L.R. 865: That the common law has recognized the distinction between acts of attempt and acts of preparation — between acts which are, and acts which are not, too remote to constitute a criminal attempt — is undoubted. . . . If, however, we proceed to inquire as to the precise nature of the distinction thus recognised and indicated, we find that the common law authorities are almost as silent as the Crimes Act itself. . . . The rule . . . suggested [by Baron Parke] in R. v. Eagleton [169 E.R. 826 (1855)] was that in order to constitute a criminal attempt, as opposed to mere preparation, the accused must have taken the last step which he was able to take along the road of his criminal intent. He must have done all that he intended to do and was able to do for the purpose of effectuating his criminal purpose. When he has stopped short of this, whether because he has repented, or because he has been prevented, or because the time or occasion for going further has not arrived, or for any other reason, he still has a locus penitentiae[17] and still remains within the region of innocent preparation. . . . On this principle the act of firing a pistol at a man would be attempted murder, although the bullet missed him. So would the act of pulling the trigger, although the pistol missed fire. But the prior and preliminary acts of procuring and loading the pistol, and of going with it to look for his enemy, and of lying in wait for him, and even of presenting the pistol at him, would not constitute criminal attempts, none of these being the proximate and final step towards the fulfillment of his criminal purpose. . . .

Subsequent authorities make it clear that the [*Eagleton*] test is not the true one. [I]n R. v. White, [1910] 2 K.B. 124 it was held that the first administration of poison in a case of intended slow poisoning by repeated doses amounted in itself to attempted murder. It is said by the Court: "The completion [or attempted

17. An opportunity to repent, change one's mind. — Eds.

completion] of one of a series of acts intended by a man to result in killing is an attempt to murder, even though the completed act would not, unless followed by other acts, result in killing. It might be the beginning of an attempt but would none the less be an attempt.

Although the [*Eagleton*] test has been rejected, no definite substitute for it has been formulated. All that can be definitely gathered from the authorities is that to constitute a criminal attempt, the first step along the way of criminal intent is not necessarily sufficient and the final step is not necessarily required. The dividing line between preparation and attempt is to be found somewhere between these two extremes; but as to the method by which it is to be determined the authorities give no clear guidance.

PEOPLE v. RIZZO

Court of Appeals of New York
246 N.Y. 334, 158 N.E. 888, 1927

CRANE, J. The police of the city of New York did excellent work in this case by preventing the commission of a serious crime. It is a great satisfaction to realize that we have such wide-awake guardians of our peace. Whether or not the steps which the defendant had taken up to the time of his arrest amounted to the commission of a crime, as defined by our law, is, however, another matter. He has been convicted of an attempt to commit the crime of robbery in the first degree, and sentenced to state's prison. There is no doubt that he had the intention to commit robbery, if he got the chance. An examination, however, of the facts is necessary to determine whether his acts were in preparation to commit the crime if the opportunity offered, or constituted a crime in itself, known to our law as an attempt to commit robbery in the first degree. Charles Rizzo, the defendant, appellant, with three others, Anthony J. Dorio, Thomas Milo, and John Thomasello, on January 14th planned to rob one Charles Rao of a pay roll valued at about $1,200 which he was to carry from the bank for the United Lathing Company. These defendants, two of whom had firearms, started out in an automobile, looking for Rao or the man who had the pay roll on that day. Rizzo claimed to be able to identify the man, and was to point him out to the others, who were to do the actual holding up. The four rode about in their car looking for Rao. They went to the bank from which he was supposed to get the money and to various buildings being constructed by the United Lathing Company. At last they came to One Hundred and Eightieth street and Morris Park avenue. By this time they were watched and followed by two police officers. As Rizzo jumped out of the car and ran into the building, all four were arrested. The defendant was taken out from the building in which he was hiding. Neither Rao nor a man named Previti, who was also supposed to carry a pay roll, were at the place at the time of the arrest. The defendants had not found or seen the man they intended to rob. No person with a pay roll was at any of the places where they had stopped, and no one had been pointed out or identified by Rizzo. The four men intended to rob the pay roll man, whoever he was. They were looking for him, but they had not seen or discovered him up to the time they were arrested.

Does this constitute the crime of an attempt to commit robbery in the first degree? The Penal Law, §2, prescribes: "An act, done with intent to commit a crime, and tending but failing to effect its commission, is an attempt to commit that crime."

The word "tending" is very indefinite. It is perfectly evident that there will arise differences of opinion as to whether an act in a given case is one tending to commit a crime. "Tending" means to exert activity in a particular direction. Any act in preparation to commit a crime may be said to have a tendency towards its accomplishment. The procuring of the automobile, searching the streets looking for the desired victim, were in reality acts tending toward the commission of the proposed crime. The law, however, had recognized that many acts in the way of preparation are too remote to constitute the crime of attempt. The line has been drawn between those acts which are remote and those which are proximate and near to the consummation. The law must be practical, and therefore considers those acts only as tending to the commission of the crime which are so near to its accomplishment that in all reasonable probability the crime itself would have been committed, but for timely interference. The cases which have been before the courts express this idea in different language, but the idea remains the same. The act or acts must come or advance very near to the accomplishment of the intended crime. [As said by Justice Holmes, dissenting in Hyde v. United States, 225 U.S. 347, 387 (1912):] "There must be dangerous proximity to success." . . .

How shall we apply this rule of immediate nearness to this case? The defendants were looking for the pay roll man to rob him of his money. This is the charge in the indictment. . . . To constitute the crime of robbery, the money must have been taken from Rao by means of force or violence, or through fear. The crime of attempt to commit robbery was committed, if these defendants did an act tending to the commission of this robbery. Did the acts above described come dangerously near to the taking of Rao's property? Did the acts come so near the commission of robbery that there was reasonable likelihood of its accomplishment but for the interference? Rao was not found; the defendants were still looking for him; no attempt to rob him could be made, at least until he came in sight; he was not in the building at One Hundred and Eightieth street and Morris Park avenue. There was no man there with the pay roll for the United Lathing Company whom these defendants could rob. Apparently no money had been drawn from the bank for the pay roll by anybody at the time of the arrest. In a word, these defendants had planned to commit a crime, and were looking around the city for an opportunity to commit it, but the opportunity fortunately never came. Men would not be guilty of an attempt at burglary if they had planned to break into a building and were arrested while they were hunting about the streets for the building not knowing where it was. Neither would a man be guilty of an attempt to commit murder if he armed himself and started out to find the person whom he had planned to kill but could not find him. So here these defendants were not guilty of an attempt to commit robbery in the first degree when they had not found or reached the presence of the person they intended to rob.

NOTES

1. *The Dangerous Proximity Test.* The New York attempt statute has been amended to require that the defendant engage in conduct "which tends to ef-

fect the commission" of the crime. N.Y. Pen. Law §110. The Court of Appeal has held that this made no change in the law, which continues to be as stated in *Rizzo*. People v. Acosta, 609 N.E.2d 518, 521 (N.Y. 1993).

Compare State v. Duke, 700 So. 2d 580 (Fla. App. 1998). A detective in the county sex unit was surfing the Internet chat rooms looking for persons attempting to solicit children for sexual acts. He found the defendant and, posing as a 12-year old girl, "Niki," had several conversations about defendant engaging in sex with "Niki." They arranged to meet at a certain night at a parking lot where defendant would signal by flashing his lights and then take "Niki" to his home to engage in various sex acts. But when defendant flashed his lights he was immediately arrested. He was convicted of attempted sexual battery on these facts, but the appellate court reversed on the ground that the overt acts of defendant were all planning and did not go far enough toward their consummation to constitute an attempt at a sexual battery. Somewhat apologetically, the court concluded: "We note the difficulty in policing the internet, and the challenges the cyber world poses to preventing criminal acts against children. This may be an area the Legislature needs to address specifically."

2. *Proximity evaluated.* Are the results in *Rizzo* and *Duke* justifiable? Consider the following observations of Professor Glanville Williams, Police Control of Intending Criminals, [1955] Crim. L. Rev. 66, 69:

> In a rational system of justice the police would be given every encouragement to intervene early where a suspect is clearly bent on crime. Yet in England, if the police come on the scene too early they may find that they can do nothing with the intending offender except admonish him. This is largely because of the rule that an attempt, to be indictable, must be sufficiently "proximate" to the crime intended. . . . One is led to ask whether there is any real need for the requirement of proximity in the law of attempt. Quite apart from this requirement, it must be proved beyond reasonable doubt that the accused intended to commit the crime . . . and that he did some act towards committing it. If only a remote act of preparation is alleged against him, that will weigh with the court in deciding whether he had the firm criminal intention alleged against him. If, however, the court finds that this intention existed, is there any reason why the would-be criminal should not be dealt with by the police and by the criminal courts?

Compare by the same author Criminal Law: The General Part 631 (2d ed. 1961):

> [John] Austin put forward the interesting view that in attempt the party is really punished for his intention, the act being required as evidence of a *firm* intention. There is much to be said for this. Admitting that intention in general can be proved by a confession a confession is not sufficient proof in attempt because, standing alone, it gives no assurance that the accused would have had the constancy of purpose to put his plan into execution. The commission of the proximate act proves not merely the purpose but (in considerable degree) the firmness of the purpose.

NOTE ON THE INTERACTION BETWEEN PROXIMITY AND ABANDONMENT

One reason for judicial reluctance to move the threshold of criminality to an earlier point in time has been the desire to preserve for the defendant a "locus penitentiae"— an opportunity to repent, to change one's mind. It is important to see how that opportunity is lost once the defendant crosses the threshold of criminality. First, a defendant may be arrested before she has the chance to take the steps remaining to complete the crime. Such a defendant will be liable for attempt even though we can never be sure that she would have taken those steps. Second, a defendant may not be arrested until after she has "repented" and fully abandoned the criminal plan. Here the appearance of unfairness is even more striking: The defendant could be held liable for committing an attempt (by crossing the threshold of criminality), even though she later did everything in her power to turn back and even though she successfully prevented any actual harm.

Should defendant's abandoning her criminal purpose defeat liability for the attempt? If inchoate crimes are to be treated like other offenses, the answer would have to be negative: Remorse and restitution may affect the sentence, but they cannot erase liability once the elements necessary for conviction are complete. Applying this reasoning, the law traditionally denied any defense of abandonment, and many courts continue to adhere to that view. See, e.g., State v. Stewart, 143 Wis. 2d 28, 420 N.W.2d 44 (1988); People v. Dillon, 34 Cal. 3d 441, 668 P.2d 697 (1983). To minimize the resulting potential for unfairness, courts may therefore insist that the threshold of criminality be placed very close to the last act, even when this approach means freeing some defendants who almost certainly would *not* have repented. Recall the facts of *Rizzo* and *Duke.*

A way to avoid this dilemma is to recognize abandonment (sometimes called renunciation) as a complete defense. A number of states have done so, either by statute or judicial decision. A typical requirement is that the abandonment occur "under circumstances manifesting a voluntary and complete renunciation of [the] criminal purpose." N.Y. Penal Code §4.10. Model Penal Code §5.01(4), upon which the New York provision is based, is similar. For the definition of when the renunciation is considered "voluntary" and "complete," see Model Penal Code §5.01(4). Most of the recently revised codes adopt a renunciation defense substantially similar to that of the Model Penal Code. For a canvas of the recent cases and statutes, see Daniel G. Moriarty, Extending the Defense of Renunciation, 62 Temple L. Rev. 1, 7-11 (1989). For a critical view of the defense, see Evan Tsen Lee (Note), Cancelling Crime, 30 Conn. L. Rev. 117 (1997).

Consider these cases: *(a)* In People v. Johnston, 448 N.Y.S.2d 902, 902-903 (App. Div. 1982), defendant entered a gas station, pulled a gun, and demanded money. When the station attendant produced only $50 and said that this was all the cash available, defendant departed, stating, "I was just kidding, forget it ever happened." The court denied a renunciation defense, but several commentators favor a defense in these circumstances. See George P. Fletcher, Rethinking Criminal Law 191-192 (1978); Paul R. Hoeber, The Abandonment Defense to Criminal Attempt and Other Problems of Temporary Individuation, 74 Cal. L. Rev. 377, 411-412 (1986). Which is the better view?

(b) In People v. McNeal, 393 N.W.2d 907 (Mich. App. 1986), defendant accosted a girl who had been waiting at a bus stop and forced her at knife point to accompany him to a house, with the intent to rape her. After an extended conversation in which the girl pleaded with him to let her go, defendant released the girl, saying that he was sorry and would never engage in such behavior again. The court affirmed a conviction for attempted sexual assault, upholding a finding that because of the victim's "unexpected resistance," the defendant's renun-

ciation was not voluntary. On similar facts, the court in Ross v. State, 601 So. 2d 872, 875 (Miss. 1992), found abandonment as a matter of law and reversed a conviction for attempted rape, stating: "[Defendant] did not fail in his attack. No one prevented him from completing it. [The victim] did not sound an alarm. She successfully persuaded Ross, of his own free will, to abandon his attempt."

McQUIRTER v. STATE

Alabama Court of Appeals
36 Ala. App. 707, 63 So. 2d 388 (1953)

PRICE J. Appellant, a Negro man, was found guilty of an attempt to commit an assault with intent to rape, under an indictment charging an assault with intent to rape. The jury assessed a fine of $500.

About 8:00 o'clock on the night of June 29, 1951, Mrs. Ted Allen, a white woman, with her two children and a neighbor's little girl, were drinking Coca-Cola at the "Tiny Diner" in Atmore. When they started in the direction of Mrs. Allen's home she noticed appellant sitting in the cab of a parked truck. As she passed the truck appellant said something unintelligible, opened the truck door and placed his foot on the running board.

Mrs. Allen testified appellant followed her down the street and when she reached Suell Lufkin's house she stopped. As she turned into the Lufkin house appellant was within two or three feet of her. She waited ten minutes for appellant to pass. When she proceeded on her way, appellant came toward her from behind a telephone pole. She told the children to run to Mr. Simmons' house and tell him to come and meet her. When appellant saw Mr. Simmons he turned and went back down the street to the intersection and leaned on a stop sign just across the street from Mrs. Allen's home. Mrs. Allen watched him at the sign from Mr. Simmons' porch for about thirty minutes, after which time he came back down the street and appellant went on home. . . .

Mr. W. E. Strickland, Chief of Police of Atmore, testified that appellant stated in the Atmore jail he didn't know what was the matter with him; that he was drinking a little; that he and his partner had been to Pensacola; that his partner went to the "Front" to see a colored woman; that he didn't have any money and he sat in the truck and made up his mind he was going to get the first woman that came by and that this was the first woman that came by. He said he got out of the truck, came around the gas tank and watched the lady and when she started off he started off behind her; that he was going to carry her in the cotton patch and if she hollered he was going to kill her. He testified appellant made the same statement in the Brewton jail. . . .

Appellant, as a witness in his own behalf, testified he and Bill Page, another Negro, carried a load of junk-iron from Monroeville to Pensacola; on their way back to Monroeville they stopped in Atmore. They parked the truck near the "Tiny Diner" and rode to the "Front," the colored section, in a cab. Appellant came back to the truck around 8:00 o'clock and sat in the truck cab for about thirty minutes. He decided to go back to the "Front" to look for Bill Page. As he started up the street he saw prosecutrix and her children. He turned around and waited until he decided they had gone, then he walked up the street toward the "Front." When he reached the intersection at the street telegraph pole he decided he didn't want to go to the "Front" and sat around there a few minutes, then went on to the "Front" and stayed about 25 to 30 minutes, and came back to the truck.

He denied that he followed Mrs. Allen or made any gesture toward molesting her or the children. He denied making the statements testified to by the officers. . . . Appellant insists the trial court erred in refusing the general affirmative charge and in denying the motion for a new trial on the ground the verdict was contrary to the evidence. . . .

Under the authorities in this state, to justify a conviction for an attempt to commit an assault with intent to rape the jury must be satisfied beyond a reasonable doubt that defendant intended to have sexual intercourse with prosecutrix against her will, by force or by putting her in fear. Intent is a question to be determined by the jury from the facts and circumstances adduced on the trial, and if there is evidence from which it may be inferred that at the time of the attempt defendant intended to gratify his lustful desires against the resistance of the female a jury question is presented. In determining the question of intention the jury may consider social conditions and customs founded upon racial differences, such as that the prosecutrix was a white woman and defendant was a Negro man.

After considering the evidence in this case we are of the opinion it was sufficient to warrant the submission of the question of defendant's guilt to the jury, and was ample to sustain the judgment of conviction. . . .

Affirmed.

NOTES AND QUESTIONS

1. McQuirter. What is troublesome about the conviction in this case? The context of racial bigotry certainly is — black man, white woman, small town of the South in the 1950s. So also is the evidence of intent, which came solely from the sheriff's testimony about what the defendant said in jail. But even if the context involved no racial element and there had been no evidence of defendant's admission, wouldn't the result still have been troublesome? Why should that be? Recall the earlier criticism of the dangerous proximity test. Does a case like this redeem that test?

2. The Equivocality Test. Another approach that would have foreclosed a case like *McQuirter* is the equivocality test. It is an alternative to the dangerous proximity test for determining what acts suffice for attempt (once intent is proven), looking not to how far the defendant has gone but how clearly his acts bespeak his intent. The principle was formulated as follows by one of the first courts to adopt it, The King v. Barker, [1924] N.Z.L.R. 865, 874-875:

> An act done with intent to commit a crime is not a criminal attempt unless it is of such a nature as to be in itself sufficient evidence of the criminal intent with which it is done. A criminal attempt is an act which shows criminal intent on the face of it. The case must be one in which *Res ipsa loquitur.* An act, on the other hand, which is in its own nature and on the face of it innocent is not a criminal attempt. It cannot be brought within the scope of criminal attempt by evidence aliunde [e.g., admission or confession] as to the criminal purpose with which it is done. . . . The law does not punish men for their guilty intentions or resolutions in themselves. Nor

does it commonly punish them even for the expression, declaration, or confession of such intentions or resolutions. That a man's unfulfilled criminal purposes should be punishable they must be manifested not by his words merely, or by acts which are in themselves of innocent or ambiguous significance, but by overt acts which are sufficient in themselves to declare and proclaim the guilty purpose with which they are done. . . . The reason for thus holding a man innocent who does an act with intent to commit a crime is the danger involved in the admission of evidence upon which he may be punished for acts which in themselves and in appearance are perfectly innocent.

. . . To buy a box of matches with intent to use them in burning a haystack is not an attempt to commit arson, for it is in itself and in appearance an innocent act, there being many other reasons than arson for buying matches. The act does not speak for itself of any guilty design. . . . But he who takes matches to a haystack and there lights one of them and blows it out on finding that he is observed, has done an act which speaks for itself, and he is guilty of criminal attempt accordingly. . . . The purchaser of matches would not be guilty of attempted arson even if he declared to the vendor or to any other person the guilty purpose with which he bought them. Such evidence is relevant for the purpose of satisfying the jury that the requisite criminal intent existed, but it is not relevant in determining the prior question of law whether the act charged amounts in law to an attempt or is too remote for that purpose. . . .

That strictly formulated, the test has few adherents, but it has influenced the widely adopted Model Penal Code proposal, as we shall see, and several American jurisdictions have formulations that resemble it. In People v. Miller, 2 Cal. 2d 527, 531-532, 42 P.2d 308 (1935), defendant, who had threatened to kill Jeans, entered a field where Jeans and the local constable were planting hops. Defendant was carrying a rifle, and he walked straight toward them. He stopped once to load his rifle, but at no time did he lift it to take aim. Jeans fled, and the constable disarmed the defendant. A conviction of attempted murder was reversed. The court stated:

The reason for requiring evidence of a direct act, however slight, toward consummation of the intended crime, is . . . that in the majority of cases up to that time the conduct of the defendant, consisting merely of acts of preparation, has never ceased to be equivocal; and this is necessarily so, irrespective of his declared intent. It is that quality of being equivocal that must be lacking before the act becomes one which may be said to be a commencement of the commission of the crime, or an overt act, or before any fragment of the crime itself has been committed, and this is so for the reason that, so long as the equivocal quality remains, no one can say with certainty what the intent of the defendant is. . . . In the present case, up to the moment the gun was taken from defendant, no one could say with certainty whether defendant had come into the field to carry out his threat to kill Jeans or merely to demand his arrest by the constable.

See also Wis. Stat. Ann. tit. 45, §939.32(3):

An attempt to commit a crime requires that the actor have an intent to perform acts and attain a result which, if accomplished, would constitute such crime and that he does acts toward the commission of the crime which demonstrate unequivocally, under all the circumstances, that he formed that intent and would commit the crime except for the intervention of another person or some other extraneous factor.

The test has been criticized by Professor Williams. See Glanville Williams, Criminal Law: The General Part 630 (2d ed. 1961):

> *D* goes up to a haystack, fills his pipe, and lights a match. The act of lighting the match, even to a suspicious-minded person, is ambiguous. It may indicate only that *D* is going to light his pipe; but perhaps, on the other hand, the pipe is only a "blind" and *D* is really bent on setting fire to the stack. We do not know. Therefore, on the equivocality test, the act is not proximate. But suppose that as a matter of actual fact *D*, after his arrest, confesses to the guilty intent, and suppose that that confession is believed. We are now certain of the intent and the only question is as to proximity. It becomes clear that the act satisfies all the requirements for a criminal attempt. Since it is practically the last act that *D* intended to do in order to commit the crime (the very last being setting the match to the stack), it is almost necessarily proximate. That the act is ambiguous, which in itself might have created a doubt as to the mens rea, no longer matters, for the mens rea has been proved by the confession.

NOTE ON SUBSTANTIVE CRIMES OF PREPARATION

There are many inchoate substantive crimes in our law that do not require resort to the law of attempt with its various restrictions. Several come from the common law. These include the crimes of solicitation (or incitement) and conspiracy, both of which we deal with later in this book. In addition, there are two other important substantive common law crimes which consist of preparatory behavior: burglary and assault.

1. Burglary. Common law burglary was defined as breaking and entering a dwelling of another at night with the intent to commit some felony inside. Under the common law of attempt, a person apprehended while breaking into a dwelling with intent to commit a felony would not be guilty of attempt because he would not have arrived at the scene of his projected felony. The development of the offense of burglary provided a partial solution to this problem. Today, cases and statutes have gradually enlarged the offense. Under some statutes an entry is all that is required, in day as well as at night, into any structure, with intent to commit any crime. For example, in People v. Salemme, 3 Cal. App. 4th 775, 3 Cal. Rptr. 2d 398 (1992), the court held that the defendant had committed burglary when he entered a person's home with the intent to perpetrate a fraudulent sale of securities.

2. Assault. Assault is another inchoate substantive crime, sometimes defined as the infliction of harm upon another (a battery), see Model Penal Code §2.11(1)(a), but more often as an attempt to commit a battery. See, e.g., Cal. Penal Code §240: "An assault is an unlawful attempt, coupled with a present ability, to commit a violent injury on the person of another." Note that the crime of assault is typically defined more narrowly than the tort of assault. A person who deliberately places another in fear of a battery, but does not actually intend to carry out the attack, normally would not be guilty of assault under traditional criminal law definitions, although she might be liable for damages in tort. Some modern statutes extend the definition of assault to cover such conduct under some circumstances. See Model Penal Code §211.1(1)(c).

3. Modern statutes. The law today contains many instances of merely preparatory behavior defined as substantive crimes. As the court in State v. Young, 57 N.J. 240, 271 A.2d 569 (1970), observed, in holding within the police power of the state a law forbidding entry into school buildings with the intent to disrupt classes:

> There are a host of statutes, federal and State, which condemn acts, themselves innocent, if done with a forbidden intent. . . . The possession of certain counterfeit obligations is made criminal but only if the obligation is possessed "with intent to defraud," 18 U.S.C.A. §480. There is nothing necessarily wrong in teaching or demonstrating the use, application or making of a firearm or explosive or incendiary device or a technique capable of causing injury or death, but 18 U.S.C.A. §231(a)(1) makes it a crime to do so "intending that the same will be unlawfully employed for use in, or in furtherance of, a civil disorder which may in any way or degree obstruct, delay, or adversely affect commerce" or the performance of any federally protected function. . . . There are a number of statutes which make possession criminal if there is an intent to do some hostile act. [For example, laws] relating to possession of burglar tools; relating to possession of counterfeits, [and] to weapons and explosives. [T]he many statutes we recounted above have the common feature of punishing an act only because of the evil purpose it pursues, without regard to whether the act would constitute an attempt to commit the offense the statutes seek to head off, and even though the act, absent such purpose, may be one protected by the Constitution.

4. Policing measures. Other approaches that avoid the restrictions of the law of attempt include measures for dealing with persons who engage in suspicious activity not amounting to an attempt to commit a crime. One approach is procedural, allowing police to stop and detain a suspect in circumstances short of those justifying an arrest on probable cause under the Fourth Amendment. See Terry v. Ohio, 392 U.S. 1 (1968). The other approach is substantive, making it a crime to loiter or prowl or gather in circumstances giving rise to danger to others, or to apprehension that a crime will be attempted. See City of Chicago v. Morales, supra page 300.

5. Stalking. To these must be added so-called antistalking statutes, which criminalize harassing conduct that serves to terrorize and torment another, or which may serve as a prelude to a violent attack. These statutes were the product of a wave of widely reported incidents in the press of persons, primarily women, suffering continued harassment and sometimes violent injury, perpetrated by their victimizers, who might include "obsessed fans, divorced or separated spouses, ex-lovers, rejected suitors, neighbors, coworkers, classmates, gang members, former employees, [or] disgruntled defendants, as well as complete strangers."[18] One recent news report[19] notes, for example:

> For more than a month, a young woman in Stratford, N.J., was hounded by a man she had briefly dated. He followed her to work and to the hairdresser. He left repeated messages on her answering machine. She talked to the police several times and filed a harassment complaint, but there was little the police could do except

18. Kathleen G. McAnaney, Laura A. Curliss, C. Elizabeth Abeyta-Price, Note, From Imprudence to Crime: Anti-Stalking Laws, 68 Notre Dame L. Rev. 819, 821-823 (1993).
19. Tamar Lewin, New Laws Address Old Problem, N.Y. Times, Feb. 8, 1993, at A1.

ask the man to stop. "Our hands were tied," said Jay Wilkins, a detective in the Stratford Police Department. "We were in the position of waiting for a crime to happen."

California was the first to enact an antistalking law, in 1990; since then virtually all states have followed.[20] There is much agreement that legislation of this kind is desirable. The chief difficulty has been drafting a law that criminalizes the targeted activity without sweeping in constitutionally protected activity, like speech, and without using terms of excessive vagueness. The California law, Cal. Penal Code §646.9, makes stalking a crime subject to a maximum of one year in prison and defines stalking as:

> [a]ny person who willfully, maliciously, and repeatedly follows or harasses another person and who makes a credible threat with the intent to place that person in reasonable fear for his or her safety, or the safety of his or her immediate family, . . .

The term "harasses" is defined as:

> a knowing and willful course of conduct directed at a specific person which seriously alarms, annoys, torments, or terrorizes the person, and which serves no legitimate purpose. This course of conduct must be such as would cause a reasonable person to suffer substantial emotional distress, and must actually cause substantial emotional distress to the person.

"Credible threat" is defined to mean:

> a verbal or written threat or a threat implied by a pattern of conduct . . . made with the intent to place the person that is the target of the threat in reasonable fear for his or her safety . . . and made with the apparent ability to carry out the threat. . . . It is not necessary to prove that the defendant had the intent to actually carry out the threat.

Questions: Does the California statute represent an adequate response to the problem of "stalking"? Does it pose a danger of criminalizing conduct that should not be subject to punishment? Are its terms too vague to give notice to ordinary citizens of what is prohibited or to confine the discretion of prosecutors and judges? The California Courts of Appeal have rejected several vagueness challenges to the California statute, most recently in People v. Ewing, 76 Cal. App. 4th 199 (1999). The court found the words "annoy," "torment," and "terrorize" not to be so subjective as to be unconstitutionally vague. The Kansas Supreme Court, on the other hand, found similar words in its own antistalking statute to be unconstitutionally vague. The problem was that the Kansas statute, unlike its California model, failed to define those terms in relation to an objective standard, so that the liability of the defendant would depend on the particular sensibilities of the particular victim. State v. Bryan, 910 P.2d 212 (1996).

For arguments in support of antistalking statutes, see Gilligan, supra footnote 20; Marion Buckley, Stalking Laws — Problem or Solution? 9 Wis. Wom. L.J. 23 (1994). For a more critical view, suggesting that statutes like that of Cali-

20. See Matthew J. Gilligan, Note, Stalking the Stalker: Developing New Laws to Thwart Those Who Terrorize Others, 27 Ga. L. Rev. 285 (1992).

fornia violate constitutional prohibitions against vagueness and overbreadth, see Robert P. Faulkner & Douglas H. Hsiao, And Where You Go I'll Follow: The Constitutionality of Antistalking Laws and Proposed Model Legislation, 31 Harv. J. Legis. 1 (1994).

UNITED STATES v. JACKSON

United States Court of Appeals, 2d Circuit
560 F.2d 112 (1977)

FREDERICK VAN PELT BRYAN, J.: Robert Jackson, William Scott, and Martin Allen appeal from judgments of conviction entered . . . after a trial before Chief Judge Jacob Mishler without a jury.

Count one of the indictment alleged that between June 11 and June 21, 1976 the appellants conspired to commit an armed robbery of the Manufacturers Hanover Trust. . . . Counts two and three each charged appellants with an attempted robbery of the branch on June 14 and on June 21, 1976, respectively. . . . Chief Judge Mishler filed a memorandum of decision finding each defendant guilty on all . . . counts.

Appellants' principal contention is that the court below erred in finding them guilty on counts two and three. While they concede that the evidence supported the conspiracy convictions on count one, they assert that, as a matter of law, their conduct never crossed the elusive line which separates "mere preparation" from "attempt."[a] . . . The Government's evidence at trial consisted largely of the testimony of Vanessa Hodges, an unindicted co-conspirator, and of various FBI agents who surveilled the Manufacturers Hanover branch on June 21, 1976. . . .

[On June 11, 1976, Vanessa Hodges recruited Martin Allen to rob the Manufacturers Hanover branch in Flushing, Queens. Allen agreed, proposed the date of June 14 and told her he had guns and a car. On June 14 Allen arrived with a confederate, Jackson, in a car containing a sawed-off shotgun, shells, materials intended as masks and handcuffs to bind the bank manager. After picking up another confederate, Scott, they drove to the bank, where Allen entered to check the surveillance cameras, while Jackson installed a false cardboard license plate on the car. Scott then also entered the bank, but returned with the news that the tellers were separating the weekend deposits and many patrons were still there. They then rescheduled the robbery for June 21.

[On June 18 Hodges was arrested on an unrelated offense and decided to cooperate with the police. She told FBI agents of the robbery planned for June 21, and early on that date FBI agents took surveillance positions around the bank. They saw a brown Lincoln with a New York license on the front and a cardboard facsimile of a license plate on the rear. It came to a stop near the bank and was

a. Since the defendants conceded the validity of their conspiracy convictions, why did it matter whether they could also be convicted of attempt? Note that the federal conspiracy statute, 18 U.S.C. §371, carries a maximum sentence of five years' imprisonment, while 18 U.S.C. §2113(a) provides that attempted bank robbery is punishable by a maximum of twenty years' imprisonment. In the present case, the defendant Jackson received a two-year sentence on the conspiracy count and a suspended sentence on the other counts; Scott received a five-year sentence on the conspiracy count and concurrent seven-year terms on the attempt counts; Allen received a five-year sentence on the conspiracy count and concurrent ten-year terms on the attempt counts. — EDS.

occupied by three men fitting the description Hodges had provided. One of the men got out, stood for a while on a corner in front of the bank and then returned to the car. The Lincoln drove up and down the streets near the bank, then stopped for several minutes a few blocks away. When it returned and parked near the bank, agents noticed that its front license plate was now missing. After parking for thirty minutes, the car began moving in the direction of the bank.]

At some point near the bank as they passed down Flushing Avenue, the appellants detected the presence of the surveillance agents. The Lincoln . . . was overtaken by FBI agents who ordered the appellants out of the car and arrested them. The agents then observed a black and red plaid suitcase in the rear of the car. The zipper of the suitcase was partially open and exposed two loaded sawed-off shotguns, a toy nickel-plated revolver, a pair of handcuffs, and masks. A New York license plate was seen lying on the front floor of the car. All of these items were seized.

In his memorandum of decision, Chief Judge Mishler concluded that the evidence against Jackson, Scott, and Allen was "overwhelming" on [the conspiracy count]. In contrast, he characterized the question of whether the defendants had attempted a bank robbery as charged in counts two and three or were merely engaged in preparations as "a close one." After canvassing the authorities . . . Chief Judge Mishler applied the following two-tiered inquiry formulated in United States v. Mandujano, 499 F.2d 370, 376 (5th Cir. 1974):

> First, the defendant must have been acting with the kind of culpability otherwise required for the commission of the crime which he is charged with attempting. . . . Second, the defendant must have engaged in conduct which constitutes a substantial step toward commission of the crime. A substantial step must be conduct strongly corroborative of the firmness of the defendant's criminal intent.

He concluded that on June 14 and again on June 21, the defendants took substantial steps, strongly corroborative of the firmness of their criminal intent, toward commission of the crime of bank robbery and found the defendants guilty on each of the two attempt counts. These appeals followed.

[T]here is no comprehensive statutory definition of attempt in federal law. . . .

Chief Judge Kaufman, writing for [this court in United States v. Stallworth, 543 F.2d 1038 (2d Cir. 1976),] selected the two-tiered inquiry of United States v. Mandujano, supra, as stating the proper test for determining whether . . . conduct constituted an attempt. He observed that this analysis "conforms closely to the sensible definition of an attempt proffered by the American Law Institute's Model Penal Code [§5.01]."

The draftsmen of the Model Penal Code recognized the difficulty of arriving at a general standard for distinguishing acts of preparation from acts constituting an attempt. . . .

The formulation upon which the draftsmen ultimately agreed required, in addition to criminal purpose, that an act be a substantial step in a course of conduct designed to accomplish a criminal result, and that it be strongly corroborative of criminal purpose in order for it to constitute such a substantial step. The following differences between this test and previous approaches to the preparation-attempt problem were noted:

MPC test

> First, this formulation shifts the emphasis from what remains to be done — the chief concern of the proximity tests — to what the actor *has already done.* The fact that further major steps must be taken before the crime can be completed does not preclude a finding that the steps already undertaken are substantial. It is expected, in the normal case, that this approach will broaden the scope of attempt liability.
>
> Second, although it is intended that the requirement of a substantial step will result in the imposition of attempt liability only in those instances in which some firmness of criminal purpose is shown, no finding is required as to whether the actor would probably have desisted prior to completing the crime. . . .
>
> Finally, the requirement of proving a substantial step generally will prove less of a hurdle for the prosecution than the *res ipsa loquitur* approach, which requires that the actor's conduct must itself manifest the criminal purpose. . . .

Model Penal Code §5.01, Comment at 47 (Tent. Draft No. 10, 1960).

The draftsmen concluded that, in addition to assuring firmness of criminal design, the requirement of a substantial step would preclude attempt liability, with its accompanying harsh penalties, for relatively remote preparatory acts. At the same time, however, by not requiring a "last proximate act" or one of its various analogues it would permit the apprehension of dangerous persons at an earlier stage than the other approaches without immunizing them from attempt liability. . . .

In the case at bar, Chief Judge Mishler [concluded that on both June 14 and June 21] these men were seriously dedicated to the commission of a crime, had passed beyond the stage of preparation, and would have assaulted the bank had they not been dissuaded by certain external factors, *viz.*, the breaking up of the weekend deposits and crowd of patrons in the bank on June 14 and the detection of the FBI surveillance on June 21.

We cannot say that these conclusions . . . were erroneous. On two separate occasions, appellants reconnoitered the place contemplated for the commission of the crime and possessed the paraphernalia to be employed in the commission of the crime — loaded sawed-off shotguns, extra shells, a toy revolver, handcuffs, and masks — which was specially designed for such unlawful use and which could serve no lawful purpose under the circumstances. Under the Model Penal Code formulation, either type of conduct, standing alone, was sufficient as a matter of law to constitute a "substantial step" if it strongly corroborated their criminal purpose. Here both types of conduct coincided on both June 14 and June 21, along with numerous other elements strongly corroborative of the firmness of appellants' criminal intent. [We] thus affirm the convictions for attempted bank robbery on counts two and three.

NOTE ON STATUTORY REFORM

The Model Penal Code draws on elements of both the proximity and the equivocality tests. As *Jackson* indicates, the Model Penal Code approach has proved influential with many courts. In a number of jurisdictions, statutory provisions reflect the Model Penal Code. Altogether, roughly half the states and two-thirds of the federal circuits now use a "substantial step" test comparable to that of the Model Penal Code. See Young v. State, 439 A.2d 352, 361 (Md. 1985);

for a current survey, see Robert Batey, Book Review (Paul Robinson's Criminal Law), 73 Notre Dame L. Rev. 781, 794 (1998). Only Connecticut, however includes the situations specified in §5.01(2) as prima facie substantial steps. Conn. Gen. Stat. Ann. §53(a)-49. Some states have adopted the Model Penal Code's substantial step formulation without the requirement that the actor's conduct strongly corroborate the intent. E.g., Ga. Code §16-4-1; Ill. Stat. ch. 720, §5/8-4; 18 Pa. Stat. Ann §901.

Several of the statutory formulations include significant variations on the Model Penal Code approach:

(a) Colo Rev. Stat., §18-2-101 defines a "substantial step" as one which is "strongly corroborative of the firmness of the actor's purpose." *Question:* What is the intention behind this change in wording?

(b) 11 Del. Code Ann. §532 defines a substantial step as "an act or omission which leaves no reasonable doubt as to the defendant's intention to commit the crime. . . ." *Question:* How does this language alter the effect of the normal requirement of proof beyond a reasonable doubt? Is the change a desirable one?

PROBLEMS

1. In *United States v. Harper, 33 F.3d 1143 (9th Cir. 1994),* defendants were found in a car parked in a parking lot adjacent to a branch of the Bank of America. Under a bush six feet from their car the police found two handguns, and in the car the police found a stun gun and surgical gloves, as well as ammunition for the two hand guns. An ATM camera showed that one of the defendants, Harper, had used a stolen ATM card to withdraw $20 from the ATM, but had not removed the cash. As known to Harper, who had once worked for the bank and one of its ATM service companies, this created a "bill trap," causing the ATM to shut down and summon the ATM technicians to repair it, their response time being between 45 and 90 minutes. The prosecution obtained a conviction for conspiracy and attempted bank robbery, the latter on the theory that Harper had deliberately set the "bill trap" in order to rob the technicians of the money in the machine when they arrived to repair it. The Court of Appeals affirmed the conspiracy conviction but reversed the attempt conviction, stating:

> True, Harper had left money in the ATM, causing a bill trap that would eventually bring service personnel to the ATM. That act, however, is equivocal in itself. The robbery was in the future and . . . the defendants never made a move toward the victims or the Bank to accomplish the criminal portion of their intended mission. They had not taken a step of "such substantiality that, unless frustrated, the crime would have occurred." United States v. Buffington, 815 F.2d 1292 (9th Cir. 1987). Their situation is therefore distinguishable from that of the defendant in United States v. Moore, 921 F.2d 207 (9th Cir. 1990), upon which the government relies. In *Moore,* the defendant was apprehended "walking toward the bank, wearing a ski mask, and carrying gloves, pillowcases and a concealed, loaded gun." These actions were a true commitment toward the robbery, which would be in progress the moment the would-be robber entered the bank thus attired and equipped. That stage of the crime had not been reached by [the defendants]; their actual embarkation on the robbery lay as much as 90 minutes away from the time when Harper left money in the ATM, and that time had not expired when they were apprehended. . . .

When criminal intent is clear, identifying the point at which the defendants' activities ripen into an attempt is not an analytically satisfying enterprise. There is, however, a substantial difference between causing a bill trap, which will result in the appearance of potential victims, and moving toward such victims with gun and mask, as in United States v. Moore, 921 F.2d 207 (9th Cir. 1990). Making an appointment with a potential victim is not of itself such a commitment to an intended crime as to constitute an attempt, even though it may make a later attempt possible. Little more happened here. . . . Accordingly, we reverse the appellants' convictions for attempted bank robbery.

Question: Would the Model Penal Code produce the same result? Consider especially the circumstances specified in §5.01(2) as sufficiently substantial if strongly corroborative, especially "lying in wait" and "seeking to entice the contemplated victim of the crime to go to the place contemplated for its commission."

2. *United States v. Mandujano, 499 F.2d 370, (5th Cir. 1974):*

Alfonso H. Cavalier, Jr., [was] a San Antonio police officer assigned to the Office of Drug Abuse Law Enforcement. Agent Cavalier testified that, at the time the case arose, he was working in an undercover capacity and represented himself as a narcotics trafficker. [P]ursuant to information Cavalier had received, he and a government informer went to the Tally-Ho Lounge. . . . Once inside the bar, the informant introduced Cavalier to Roy Mandujano. After some general conversation Mandujano asked the informant if he was looking for "stuff." Cavalier said, "Yes" . . . and told Mandujano he was looking for an ounce sample of heroin to determine the quality of the material. Mandujano replied that he had good brown Mexican heroin for $650.00 an ounce, but that if Cavalier wanted any of it he would have to wait until later in the afternoon when the regular man made his deliveries. Cavalier said that he was from out of town and did not want to wait that long. Mandujano offered to locate another source, and made four telephone calls in an apparent effort to do so. The phone calls appeared to be unsuccessful, for Mandujano told Cavalier he wasn't having any luck contacting anybody. Cavalier stated that he could not wait any longer. Then Mandujano said he had a good contact, a man who kept narcotics around his home, but that if he went to see this man, he would need the money "out front." . . . Cavalier counted out $650.00 to Mandujano, and Mandujano left the premises of the Tally-Ho Lounge at about 3:30 P.M. About an hour later, he returned and explained that he had been unable to locate his contact. He gave back the $650.00 and told Cavalier he could still wait until the regular man came around. Cavalier left, but arranged to call back at 6:00 P.M. When Cavalier called at 6:00 and again at 6:30, he was told that Mandujano was not available. Cavalier testified that he did not later attempt to contact Mandujano because, "based on the information that I had received, it would be unsafe for either my informant or myself to return to this area."

Question: On these facts, defendant Mandujano was convicted of attempting to distribute heroin. The Fifth Circuit affirmed. Is the result proper under the Model Penal Code test?

3. *United States v. Joyce, 693 F.2d 838 (8th Cir. 1982):*

[Government informant James Gebbie called Joyce and informed him that cocaine] was available for purchase in St. Louis. Joyce indicated that he had twenty-two thousand dollars and would be in St. Louis the following day, October 21, 1980. Gebbie and Joyce agreed that twenty-two thousand dollars would be more than sufficient to purchase a pound of cocaine.

On October 21, 1980, Joyce flew from Oklahoma City, Oklahoma to St. Louis, Missouri, where he met Gebbie and undercover officer Robert Jones, who was posing as a cocaine seller. Jones and Gebbie took Joyce to a room in a local St. Louis hotel, where Joyce immediately asked to see the cocaine. Jones told Joyce that the cocaine was not in the hotel room, but could be easily obtained by Jones if Joyce was interested in dealing rather than merely talking. After Joyce professed his interest in dealing, Jones recited prices for various quantities of cocaine and Joyce said that he could "handle" a pound of cocaine for twenty thousand dollars. Officer Jones then went to his office and obtained the cocaine.

When officer Jones returned to the hotel room, he handed Joyce a duct-tape wrapped plastic package said to contain a kilogram of cocaine. Without unwrapping the tape, Joyce immediately returned the package, stating that he could not see the cocaine. Jones then unwrapped about half of the tape covering the plastic package and handed the package back to Joyce. Joyce again returned the package to Jones and asked Jones to open up the package so that Joyce could examine the cocaine more closely. Jones answered that he would only open the plastic package if and when Joyce showed the money that he intended to use to purchase the cocaine.[a] Joyce then replied that he would not produce his money until Jones first opened up the plastic package. After Jones persisted in asking Joyce to produce his money, Joyce again refused, stating that he would not deal with officer Jones no matter how good the cocaine was. Realizing that Joyce was not going to show his money or purchase the cocaine, Jones told Joyce to leave and Joyce left, with no apparent intention of returning at a later time to purchase any cocaine.

As Joyce left the hotel, he was arrested by DEA agents. A search warrant was thereafter obtained and used to search Joyce's luggage revealing twenty-two thousand dollars in cash.

[Joyce was convicted of attempting to purchase cocaine with intent to distribute, but the Eighth Circuit, applying the Model Penal Code formulation, reversed. The court explained:]

. . . Whatever intention Joyce had to procure cocaine was abandoned prior to the commission of a necessary and substantial step to effectuate the purchase of cocaine. . . . While Joyce professed a desire to purchase cocaine during his preliminary discussions with Jones, Joyce never attempted to carry through with that desire by producing the money necessary to purchase and hence ultimately possess the cocaine. And, although Jones gave Joyce the sealed and wrapped package said to contain a kilogram of cocaine, Joyce did not open the package but immediately returned the package to Jones who in turn refused to open the package because Joyce refused to produce the money necessary to effectuate the purchase of a pound of cocaine. Thus, all we have here is a preliminary discussion regarding the purchase of cocaine which broke down. . . .

We also find unpersuasive the government's claim that Joyce would have purchased the cocaine had it not been for Jones's refusal to open the package of cocaine. We simply fail to see why Joyce's motive for refusing to commit a "substantial step" toward possession of the cocaine is particularly relevant. Joyce's motive for refusing to purchase the cocaine here is no different than had he refused to purchase because he disagreed with Jones as to the price for which the cocaine was offered. And, while we may agree with the government's suggestion that Joyce, who was presumably "street-wise," may have been tipped off that Jones was a DEA undercover agent when Jones refused to open the package, we fail to see how an in-

a. Elsewhere in its opinion, the court stated that "Jones was acting in compliance with DEA guidelines which prohibit illegal drugs from going into the physical possession of persons under investigation."—Eds.

creased awareness of the risk of apprehension converts what would otherwise be "mere preparation" into an attempt.

Question: Is the result sound? Compare People v. Acosta, 80 N.Y.2d 665, 671, 609 N.E.2d 518, 521 (1993):

> A person who orders illegal narcotics from a supplier, admits a courier into his or her home and examines the quality of the goods has unquestionably passed beyond mere preparation and come "very near" to possessing those drugs. Indeed, the only remaining step between the attempt and the completed crime is the person's acceptance of the proffered merchandise, an act entirely within his or her control.

STATE v. DAVIS

Supreme Court of Missouri
319 Mo. 1222, 6 S.W.2d 609 (1928)

DAVIS, C. [Defendant was convicted of attempted murder in the first degree on the following facts. He and Alberdina Lourie planned to have the latter's husband, Edmon Lourie, killed in order to collect the insurance and live together. He sought the help of Earl Leverton in obtaining an ex-convict to do the job, but Leverton disclosed the plot to Dill, a police officer, who decided to pose as the ex-convict. Defendant paid Dill $600 to carry out plans he had devised for killing Lourie. After several conferences and one aborted plan, a scheme was arranged whereby Dill was to appear at the Lourie home, kill Edmon, and feign a robbery by "mussing up" Alberdina and taking her jewels. At the appointed hour Dill appeared at the Lourie home but at this point revealed his identity. He then proceeded to defendant's home where he made an arrest.]

The sufficiency of the evidence to sustain the conviction is raised. . . .

[T]he great weight of authority warrants the assertion that mere solicitation, unaccompanied by an act moving directly toward the commission of the intended crime, is not an overt act constituting an element of the crime of attempt. [T]he state contends that the arrangement of a plan for the accomplishment of the murder of Lourie and the selecting and hiring of the means or instrumentality by which the murder was to be consummated were demonstrated. We take it that the state means by the foregoing declarations that overt acts were shown. To that we do not agree. The evidence goes no further than developing a verbal arrangement with Dill, the selection of Dill as the one to kill Lourie, the delivery of a certain drawing and two photographs of Lourie to Dill, and the payment of a portion of the agreed consideration. These things were mere acts of preparation, failing to lead directly or proximately to the consummation of the intended crime. . . .

The employment of Dill as agent to murder Lourie was not tantamount to an attempt. Dill not only had no intention of carrying out the expressed purpose of defendant, but was guilty of no act directly or indirectly moving toward the consummation of the intended crime. He did nothing more than listen to the plans and solicitations of defendant without intending to act upon them. It was not shown that Dill committed an act that could be construed as an attempt. . . .

It follows from what we have said that the judgment must be reversed, and the defendant discharged. It is so ordered.

UNITED STATES v. CHURCH, 29 Mil. J. Rptr. 679 (Ct. Milit. Rev. 1989): [Appellant] was found guilty of the attempted premeditated murder of his wife. . . . His sentence, as adjudged and approved, extends to a dishonorable discharge, confinement for ten years, [and] forfeiture of all pay and allowances. . . . [On appeal] defense counsel conceded that the appellant is guilty of soliciting another to commit murder, but argued forcefully that he was not guilty of attempted murder because no act beyond mere preparation was proven.[3] To resolve this matter, it will be necessary to review the evidence of record in some detail.

[Appellant, an airman stationed in North Dakota, had separated from his wife after two years of marriage. The wife won custody of their son and moved with the child to Michigan. Appellant hoped to regain custody of his son but realized that he was unlikely to succeed in doing so through the courts. At that point he began talking about finding a "hit man" to kill his wife. Eventually some of appellant's associates began to take him seriously, and they reported the matter to the Office of Special Investigations (OSI). Shortly thereafter, an undercover OSI agent was presented as a "hit man."

[In a motel room meeting, appellant provided the agent with a partial payment; expense money for the round trip flight to Michigan; street maps of Mrs. Church's neighborhood; photographs of Mrs. Church and their son; and descriptions of all the people in the house, including where they slept and what their work schedules were. Appellant also approved use of the weapon the agent presented, a .22-caliber pistol with silencer, and he expressed a preference for where on the victim he wanted the shots placed. The job was to be done while appellant was conspicuously on duty in North Dakota. Unbeknownst to appellant, the entire conversation was videotaped. Several days later appellant was notified through command channels that his wife had been murdered. Appellant put on "a Class A act" of grief. That same day, he was notified by the undercover agent to meet him at the North Dakota motel. Appellant arrived, expressed satisfaction with the job done, paid the agent, and identified his wife's "body" from a staged photograph. This meeting also was videotaped. Appellant was then arrested.]

In various factual situations involving "contracting out" for crimes, [many courts have] held that the evidence only established mere acts of preparation not leading directly or proximately to consummation of the intended crime. . . . Typical, and perhaps closest factually to the present appellant's case, [is State v. Davis, supra]. . . .

Not all authority favors the defense position. A few state courts have upheld attempt convictions in cases involving crimes for hire. . . . Appellate defense counsel urge that it would be inappropriate to adopt this minority view under military law. . . . We are not convinced, however, that military law should extend so far as to hold that a factual situation such as that present in the *Davis* [case] will not constitute an attempt to commit a crime. . . . The appellant's conduct in obtaining the services of Nicholas Karnezis to murder his wife, his detailed participation in planning the intended crime, up to advising the agent exactly how

3. Among other punishments, confinement for 20 years is authorized for attempted murder, whereas the period of confinement authorized for soliciting another to commit murder is 5 years. . . .

he wanted his wife shot, and his payment of the agreed upon consideration, . . . constitutes "a substantial step toward commission of the crime," and establishes the requisite overt act amounting to more than mere preparation. We can envision nothing else the appellant could possibly have done to effect what he believed would be his wife's murder, short of committing the act himself (which is precisely what he did not want to do). As characterized by appellate government counsel during oral argument, the appellant armed a missile (Nick) and fired it off, fully believing it was aimed directly at his intended victim.

NOTE

On review of the decision in *Church,* the U.S. Court of Military Appeals noted (32 Mil. J. Rptr. 70, 70-71 n. 1, 74 n. 7 (1991)):

> The real stake in this appeal is the sentence. If, as appellant contends, he is merely guilty of soliciting murder, the most he can be confined is 5 years. If, however, he is guilty of attempted murder, the maximum confinement is 20 years, with the result that his approved sentence would stand.
>
> Of course, if the facts stood as appellant believed and hoped them to be, he would be guilty as a principal to premeditated murder — and conspiracy as well. Under those circumstances, the *minimum* term he could have received would have been confinement for life. Fortuitously for all concerned, appellant's efforts were frustrated by law enforcement personnel. Thus, murder is not applicable because the intended victim is not dead. Conspiracy is also arguably not available because the *agent* did not actually agree to kill Mrs. Church. . . .
>
> These vast distinctions in punishment ceilings among solicitations, attempts, and completed offenses — at least when the crimes are very serious — reflect the traditional view that the punishment should be commensurate with the *resulting harm,* irrespective of the badness of the actor or the seriousness of the threat. The modern approach, on the other hand, . . . is to make the punishment levels generally the same or nearly the same for solicitations, attempts, and completed offenses — based upon the badness of the actor, not upon the fortuitousness of the results. *See, e.g.,* §5.05, Model Penal Code; §2X1.1, Federal Sentencing Guidelines; §§12.-32(a) and 15.03(d), Vernon's Code of Texas Annotated, Penal Code. Narrowing these vast discrepancies in punishment ceilings would lessen the premium put on factfinder hair-splitting as the evidence proceeds down the continuum of solicitation, conspiratorial agreement, overt act in furtherance of the conspiracy, act beyond mere preparation tending to effect commission of a crime, etc. It would also remove the illogical consequence that the punishment for soliciting premeditated murder can be no greater than that for soliciting the making of a check of $101 without sufficient funds.

Affirming the conviction, the court held:

> It is clear that appellant did everything he thought not only necessary but possible to make the enterprise successful — before, during, and after the supposed crime. Looking to his conduct only, we agree the evidence was sufficient for a rational factfinder to find, beyond a reasonable doubt, that his actions exceeded mere preparation.

NOTES ON SOLICITATION

1. *Solicitation as an attempt.* Near the end of its opinion in the *Davis* case, the court states: "It was not shown that Dill committed an act that could be construed as an attempt." What difference would it have made if Dill *had* gone further than he had? Would the prosecution's difficulties have been resolved if Dill had been instructed by the district attorney to play the scene to the hilt, as, for example, by leveling his pistol at the husband's chest? Could this feigned overt act of attempt be attributed to the defendant as his, the defendant's, genuine overt act of attempt? Since Dill was only a feigned participant, can the defendant's guilt be made to rest in any way on the acts of Dill? See State v. Hayes, page 633 infra.

Courts differ over the question whether solicitation constitutes an attempt. In accord with *Church,* recent federal cases hold that a solicitation can constitute a punishable attempt if it represents a "substantial step" under the circumstances. See United States v. American Airlines, Inc., 743 F.2d 1114, 1121 (5th Cir. 1984); United States v. May, 625 F.2d 186, 194 (8th Cir. 1980). But many states adhere to the view that "no matter what acts the solicitor commits, he cannot be guilty of an attempt because it is not his purpose to commit the offense personally." Model Penal Code and Commentaries, Comment to §5.02 at 369 (1985).

2. *Solicitation as an independent crime.* At common law, inciting or soliciting another to commit a crime was a crime itself, independent of any other offense that either party might commit. For a long time, American codes by and large did not contain provisions incorporating this offense, but rather made criminal the solicitation of particular crimes. However, a substantial number of states now have general solicitation statutes. They are usually patterned after Model Penal Code §5.02. The commentary defends that formulation as follows (Model Penal Code and Commentaries, Comment to §5.02 at 365-366, 375-378 (1985)):

> It has been argued [that the solicitor's] conduct is not dangerous because the resisting will of an independent moral agent is interposed between the solicitor and the commission of the crime that is his object. By the same token it is urged that the solicitor, manifesting his reluctance to commit the crime himself, is not a significant menace. The opposing view is that a solicitation is, if anything, more dangerous than a direct attempt, because it may give rise to the special hazard of cooperation among criminals. Solicitation may, indeed, be thought of as an attempt to conspire. . . .
>
> There should be no doubt on this issue. Purposeful solicitation presents dangers calling for preventive intervention and is sufficiently indicative of a disposition towards criminal activity to call for liability. Moreover, the fortuity that the person solicited does not agree to commit or attempt to commit the incited crime plainly should not relieve the solicitor of liability, when otherwise he would be a conspirator or an accomplice. . . .

3. *Free Speech.* Solicitation of crime may in some circumstances be protected speech under the First Amendment. For a sustained discussion of this and related issues see Kent Greenawalt, Speech, Crime, and the Uses of Language (1989). See also the learned opinion of the court on the line between punishable and protected speech: Rice v. Paladin Enterprises, 128 F.3d 233 (4th Cir. 1997) (upholding the civil liability of a publisher of a how-to-do-it murder manual for a user's murder of three people).

4. *Impossibility*

PEOPLE v. JAFFE

New York Court of Appeals
185 N.Y. 497, 78 N.E. 169 (1906)

BARTLETT, J. The indictment charged that the defendant on the 6th day of October, 1902, in the county of New York, feloniously received 20 yards of cloth, of the value of 25 cents a yard, belonging to the copartnership of J. W. Goddard & Son, knowing that the said property had been feloniously stolen, taken, and carried away from the owners. It was found under section 550 of the Penal Code, which provides that a person who buys or receives any stolen property knowing the same to have been stolen is guilty of criminally receiving such property. The defendant was convicted of an attempt to commit the crime charged in the indictment. The proof clearly showed, and the district attorney conceded upon the trial, that the goods which the defendant attempted to purchase on October 6, 1902, had lost their character as stolen goods at the time when they were offered to the defendant and when he sought to buy them. In fact the property had been restored to the owners and was wholly within their control and was offered to the defendant by their authority and through their agency. The question presented by this appeal, therefore, is whether upon an indictment for receiving goods, knowing them to have been stolen, the defendant may be convicted of an attempt to commit the crime where it appears without dispute that the property which he sought to receive was not in fact stolen property.

The conviction was sustained by the Appellate Division chiefly upon the authority of the numerous cases in which it has been held that one may be convicted of an attempt to commit a crime notwithstanding the existence of facts unknown to him which would have rendered the complete perpetration of the crime itself impossible. Notably among these are what may be called the "Pickpocket Cases," where, in prosecutions for attempts to commit larceny from the person by pocketpicking, it is held not to be necessary to allege or prove that there was anything in the pocket which could be the subject of larceny. Much reliance was also placed in the opinion of the learned Appellate Division upon the case of People v. Gardner, 144 N.Y. 119, 38 N.E. 1003, where a conviction of an attempt to commit the crime of extortion was upheld, although the woman from whom the defendant sought to obtain money by a threat to accuse her of a crime was not induced to pay the money by fear, but was acting at the time as a decoy for the police, and hence could not have been subjected to the influence of fear.

In passing upon the question here presented for our determination, it is important to bear in mind precisely what it was that the defendant attempted to do. He simply made an effort to purchase certain specific pieces of cloth. He believed the cloth to be stolen property, but it was not such in fact. The purchase, therefore, if it had been completely effected, could not constitute the crime of receiving stolen property, knowing it to be stolen, since there could be no such thing as knowledge on the part of the defendant of a nonexistent fact, although there might be a belief on his part that the fact existed. As Mr. Bishop well says, it is a mere truism *that there can be no receiving of stolen goods which have not been stolen.* 2. Bishop's New Crim. Law, §1140. It is equally difficult to perceive how there can be an attempt to receive stolen goods, knowing them to have been stolen, when they have not been stolen in fact.

The crucial distinction between the case before us and the pickpocket cases, and others involving the same principle, lies not in the possibility or impossibility of the commission of the crime, but in the fact that, in the present case, the act, which it was doubtless the intent of the defendant to commit, would not have been a crime if it had been consummated. If he had actually paid for the goods which he desired to buy and received them into his possession, he would have committed no offense under section 550 of the Penal Code, because the very definition in that section of the offense of criminally receiving property makes it an essential element of the crime that the accused shall have known the property to have been stolen or wrongfully appropriated in such a manner as to constitute larceny. . . . No man can know that to be so which is not so in truth and in fact. He may believe it to be so but belief is not enough under this statute. In the present case . . . the goods which the defendant intended to purchase had lost their character as stolen goods at the time of the proposed transaction. Hence, no matter what was the motive of the defendant, and no matter what he supposed, he could do no act which was intrinsically adapted to the then present successful perpetration of the crime denounced by this section of the Penal Code, because neither he nor any one in the world could know that the property was stolen property inasmuch as it was not, in fact, stolen property. In the pickpocket cases the immediate act which the defendant had in contemplation was an act which, if it could have been carried out, would have been criminal, whereas in the present case the immediate act which the defendant had in contemplation (to wit, the purchase of the goods which were brought to his place for sale) could not have been criminal under the statute even if the purchase had been completed. . . .

If all which an accused person intends to do would, if done, constitute no crime, it cannot be a crime to attempt to do with the same purpose a part of the thing intended. The crime of which the defendant was convicted necessarily consists of three elements: First, the act; second, the intent; and third, the knowledge of an existing condition. There was proof tending to establish two of these elements, the first and second, but none to establish the existence of the third. This was knowledge of the stolen character of the property sought to be acquired. There could be no such knowledge. The defendant could not know that the property possessed the character of stolen property when it had not in fact been acquired by theft. . . . A particular belief cannot make that a crime which is not so in the absence of such belief. Take, for example, the case of a young man who attempts to vote, and succeeds in casting his vote under the belief that he is but 20 years of age, when he is in fact over 21 and a qualified voter. His intent to commit a crime, and his belief that he was committing a crime, would not make him guilty of any offense under these circumstances, although the moral turpitude of the transaction, on his part, would be just as great as it would if he were in fact under age. So also, in the case of a prosecution under the statute of this state, which makes it rape in the second degree for a man to perpetrate an act of sexual intercourse with a female not his wife under the age of 18 years. There could be no conviction if it was established upon the trial that the female was in fact over the age of 18 years, although the defendant believed her to be younger and intended to commit the crime. No matter how reprehensible would be his act in morals, it would not be the act forbidden by this particular statute. "If what a man contemplates doing would not be in law a crime, he could not be said, in point of law, to intend to commit the crime. If he thinks his act will be a crime, this is a mere mistake of his understanding where the law holds it not to be such, his real intent being to do a particular thing. If the thing is not a crime, he does not intend to commit one whatever he may erroneously suppose." 1 Bishop's Crim. Law (7th Ed.) §742.

The judgment of the Appellate Division and of the Court of General Sessions must be reversed, and the defendant discharged upon this indictment. . . .

PEOPLE v. DLUGASH

New York Court of Appeals
41 N.Y.2d 725, 363 N.E.2d 1155 (1977)

JASEN, J. . . . For years, serious studies have been made on the subject in an effort to resolve the continuing controversy when, if at all, the impossibility of successfully completing the criminal act should preclude liability for even making the futile attempt. The 1967 revision of the Penal Law approached the impossibility defense to the inchoate crime of attempt in a novel fashion. The statute provides that, if a person engaged in conduct which would otherwise constitute an attempt to commit a crime,

> it is no defense to a prosecution for such attempt that the crime charged to have been attempted was, under the attendant circumstances, factually or legally impossible of commission, if such crime could have been committed had the attendant circumstances been as such person believed them to be.

(Penal Law, §110.10.) This appeal presents to us, for the first time, a case involving the application of the modern statute. We hold that, under the proof presented by the People at trial, defendant Melvin Dlugash may be held for attempted murder [of Michael Geller], though the target of the attempt may have already been slain, by the hand of another [Bush], when Dlugash made his felonious attempt. . . .

Defendant stated [to police] that, on the night of December 21, 1973, he, Bush and Geller had been out drinking. Bush had been staying at Geller's apartment and, during the course of the evening, Geller several times demanded that Bush pay $100 towards the rent on the apartment. According to defendant, Bush rejected these demands, telling Geller that "you better shut up or you're going to get a bullet." All three returned to Geller's apartment at approximately midnight, took seats in the bedroom, and continued to drink until sometime between 3:00 and 3:30 in the morning. When Geller again pressed his demand for rent money, Bush drew his .38 caliber pistol, aimed it at Geller and fired three times. Geller fell to the floor. After the passage of a few minutes, perhaps two, perhaps as much as five, defendant walked over to the fallen Geller, drew his .25 caliber pistol, and fired approximately five shots in the victim's head and face. Defendant contended that, by the time he fired the shots, "it looked like Mike Geller was already dead." . . .

After [Officer] Carrasquillo had taken the bulk of the statement, he asked the defendant why he would do such a thing. According to Carrasquillo, the defendant said, "gee, I really don't know." Carrasquillo repeated the question 10 minutes later, but received the same response. After a while, Carrasquillo asked the question for a third time and defendant replied, "well, gee, I guess it must have been because I was afraid of Joe Bush."

[A]t the trial . . . the prosecution sought to establish that Geller was still alive at the time defendant shot at him. Both physicians testified that each of the two chest wounds, for which defendant alleged Bush to be responsible, would have caused death without prompt medical attention. Moreover, the victim would have remained alive until such time as his chest cavity became fully filled with blood. Depending on the circumstances, it might take 5 to 10 minutes for the chest cavity to fill. Neither prosecution witness could state, with medical certainty, that the victim was still alive when, perhaps five minutes after the initial chest wounds were inflicted, the defendant fired at the victim's head.

The defense produced but a single witness, the former Chief Medical Examiner of New York City. This expert said that, in his view, Geller might have died of the chest wounds "very rapidly" since, in addition to the bleeding, a large bullet going through a lung and the heart would have other adverse medical effects. . . .

The trial court declined to charge the jury, as requested by the prosecution, that defendant could be guilty of murder on the theory that he had aided and abetted the killing of Geller by Bush. Instead, the court submitted only two theories to the jury: that defendant had either intentionally murdered Geller or had attempted to murder Geller.

The jury found the defendant guilty of murder. . . .

On appeal, the Appellate Division reversed the judgment of conviction on the law and dismissed the indictment. The court ruled that "the People failed to prove beyond a reasonable doubt that Geller had been alive at the time he was shot by defendant; defendant's conviction of murder thus cannot stand." . . .

Further, the court held that the judgment could not be modified to reflect a conviction for attempted murder because "the uncontradicted evidence is that the defendant, at the time that he fired the five shots into the body of the decedent, believed him to be dead, and . . . there is not a scintilla of evidence to contradict his assertion in that regard." . . .

Preliminarily, we state our agreement with the Appellate Division that the evidence did not establish, beyond a reasonable doubt, that Geller was alive at the time defendant fired into his body. To sustain a homicide conviction, it must be established, beyond a reasonable doubt, that the defendant caused the death of another person. . . . While the defendant admitted firing five shots at the victim approximately two to five minutes after Bush had fired three times, all three medical expert witnesses testified that they could not, with any degree of medical certainty, state whether the victim had been alive at the time the latter shots were fired by the defendant. Thus, the People failed to prove beyond a reasonable doubt that the victim had been alive at the time he was shot by the defendant. Whatever else it may be, it is not murder to shoot a dead body. . . .

[W]e must now decide whether, under the evidence presented, the defendant may be held for attempted murder, though someone else perhaps succeeded in killing the victim. . . .

The most intriguing attempt cases are those where the attempt to commit a crime was unsuccessful due to mistakes of fact or law on the part of the would-be criminal. A general rule developed in most American jurisdictions that legal impossibility is a good defense but factual impossibility is not. . . . Thus, for example, it was held that defendants who shot at a stuffed deer did not attempt to take a deer out of season, even though they believed the dummy to be a live animal. The court stated that there was no criminal attempt because it was no crime to "take" a stuffed deer, and it is no crime to attempt to do that which is legal. (State v. Guffey, 262 S.W.2d 152 [Mo. App.]; see, also, State v. Taylor, 345 Mo. 325, 133 S.W.2d 336 [no liability for attempt to bribe a juror where person bribed was not, in fact, a juror].) These cases are illustrative of legal impossibility. . . .

On the other hand, factual impossibility was no defense. For example, a man was held liable for attempted murder when he shot into the room in which his target usually slept and, fortuitously, the target was sleeping elsewhere in the house that night. (State v. Mitchell, 170 Mo. 633, 71 S.W. 175.) Although one bullet struck the target's customary pillow, attainment of the criminal objective was factually impossible. . . . On the same view, it was held that men who had sexual intercourse with a woman, with the belief that she was alive and did not consent to the intercourse, could be charged for attempted rape when the woman had, in fact, died from an unrelated ailment prior to the acts of intercourse. (United States v. Thomas, 13 U.S.C.M.A. 278.)

The New York cases can be parsed out along similar lines. One of the leading cases on legal impossibility is People v. Jaffe, 185 N.Y. 497, 78 N.E. 169, in which we held that there was no liability for the attempted receipt of stolen property when the property received by the defendant in the belief that it was stolen was, in fact under the control of the true owner. . . . Similarly, in People v. Teal, 196 N.Y. 372, 89 N.E. 1086, a conviction for attempted subornation of perjury was overturned on the theory that the testimony attempted to be suborned was irrelevant to the merits of the case. Since it was not subornation of perjury to solicit false, but irrelevant, testimony, "the person through whose procuration the testimony is given cannot be guilty of subornation of perjury and, by the same rule, an unsuccessful attempt to that which is not a crime when effectuated, cannot be held to be an attempt to commit the crime specified." Factual impossibility, however, was no defense. Thus, a man could be held for attempted grand larceny when he picked an empty pocket. (People v. Moran, 123 N.Y. 254, 25 N.E. 412.) . . .

As can be seen from even this abbreviated discussion, the distinction between "factual" and "legal" impossibility was a nice one indeed and the courts tended to place a greater value on legal form than on any substantive danger the defendant's actions posed for society. The approach of the draftsmen of the Model Penal Code was to eliminate the defense of impossibility in virtually all situations. [See §5.01(1), Appendix.] Under the code provision, to constitute an attempt, it is still necessary that the result intended or desired by the actor constitute a crime. However, the code suggested a fundamental change to shift the locus of analysis to the actor's mental frame of reference and away from undue dependence upon external considerations. The basic premise of the code provision is that what was in the actor's own mind should be the standard for determining his dangerousness to society and, hence, his liability for attempted criminal conduct. . . . In the belief that neither of the two branches of the traditional impossibility arguments detracts from the offender's moral culpability . . . the

Legislature substantially carried the [Model Penal] code's treatment of impossibility into the 1967 revision of the Penal Law. . . . Thus, a person is guilty of an attempt when, with intent to commit a crime, he engages in conduct which tends to effect the commission of such crime. (Penal Law, §110.00.) It is no defense that, under the attendant circumstances, the crime was factually or legally impossible of commission, "if such crime could have been committed had the attendant circumstances been as such person believed them to be." (Penal Law, §110.10). Thus, if defendant believed the victim to be alive at the time of the shooting, it is no defense to the charge of attempted murder that the victim may have been dead. . . .

Turning to the facts of the case before us, we believe that there is sufficient evidence in the record from which the jury could conclude that the defendant believed Geller to be alive at the time defendant fired shots into Geller's head. . . . The jury convicted the defendant of murder. Necessarily, they found that defendant intended to kill a live human being. Subsumed within this finding is the conclusion that defendant acted in the belief that Geller was alive. Thus, there is no need for additional fact findings by a jury. Although it was not established beyond a reasonable doubt that Geller was, in fact, alive, such is no defense to attempted murder since a murder would have been committed "had the attendant circumstances been as [defendant] believed them to be." The jury necessarily found that defendant believed Geller to be alive when defendant shot at him.

The Appellate Division erred in not modifying the judgment to reflect a conviction for the lesser included offense of attempted murder. . . .

NOTES ON IMPOSSIBILITY

1. *Factual impossibility.* When attempts misfire because of poor aim or the use of a defective or inadequate weapon, such as an unloaded gun, courts have traditionally classified the situation as one of mere factual impossibility and denied a defense. In State v. Smith, 262 N.J. Super. 487, 621 A.2d 493 (1993), defendant was a county jail inmate who had tested positive for HIV, the virus that causes AIDS. During an altercation with several guards, defendant spat in one officer's face, bit his hand and said, "[N]ow die you pig, die from what I have." At his trial for attempted murder of the officer, defendant offered evidence that it was medically impossible to transmit HIV by spitting or biting, but the court held, affirming the conviction, that such evidence was irrelevant so long as the defendant himself had believed it possible to infect the officer and had intended to kill him.

2. *Legal impossibility.* Prior to the enactment of statutes addressed to the issue of impossibility, courts had taken a variety of positions. All courts agreed that there is a defense of legal impossibility when, unknown to the actor, what the actor planned to do had not been made criminal. There was dispute, however, over whether "legal impossibility" could be a defense in other situations, and if so, how was it distinguished from "factual impossibility," which was not a defense.

The California Supreme Court, in a case virtually identical to *Jaffe,* reached the opposite result. People v. Rojas, 55 Cal. 2d 252, 358 P.2d 921 (1961). As in New York at the time *Jaffe* was decided, the California cases had upheld convictions of attempted larceny where a pickpocket picked an empty pocket, and of attempted theft by deception where the intended victim had not been deceived. The California court saw no distinction in principle between such cases and a case of attempted receipt of stolen property. It rejected the precedent of the Jaffe case, quoting approvingly the following criticism of that decision in Jerome Hall, General Principles of Criminal Law 127 (1947):

> The confusion between what the defendant actually did and his intent is apparent. Intent is in the mind; it is not the external realities to which intention refers. The fact that defendant was mistaken regarding the external realities did not alter his intention, but simply made it impossible to effectuate it.

The Model Penal Code has had a major influence on this debate. About two-thirds of the states have revised their codes since the Model Penal Code proposals were formulated. Nearly all of them have rejected the impossibility defense entirely. See Model Penal Code and Commentaries, Comment to §5.01 at 317 (1985). A few cases, however, continue to reflect the *Jaffe* view or variations on it. Thus, in State v. Collins, 54 Ohio App. 3d 134, 561 N.E.2d 954 (1988), defendant was convicted of attempting to receive stolen goods, on facts similar to those in *Jaffe*. The relevant Ohio statute, Rev. Code §2923.02(B), provided "It is no defense to a charge under this section that, in retrospect, commission of the offense which was the object of the attempt was impossible under the circumstances." The court nonetheless reversed the conviction. The court held that the Ohio provision precluded a defense of factual impossibility but that the defense of *legal* impossibility should remain available in the absence of unambiguous statutory language to the contrary.

The situation in the federal courts was summed up as follows in United States v. Duran, 884 F. Supp. 577, 581 (D.D.C.1995):

> The Circuit cases dealing with legal impossibility fall into three categories. While the Third Circuit held in *Berrigan* that, regardless of criminal intent, legal impossibility is a valid defense, [every Circuit that considered it has rejected it, and] the Second Circuit's view is that, consistent with the Model Penal Code, "attempt is established when the defendants' actions would have constituted the completed crime if the surrounding circumstances were as they believed them to be." The Fifth Circuit takes a middle ground, requiring "that the objective acts of the defendant taken as a whole, strongly corroborate the required culpability for criminal attempt." The Ninth and Eleventh Circuits have specifically adopted the Fifth Circuit view.

The *Duran* case involved a prosecution for attempting to assassinate the President of the United States. The government's proof purported to show that the defendant, fired at a person he believed was the President of the United States. The person resembled the President and was standing on the White House grounds. The court, adopting the Fifth Circuit's approach, denied a motion of acquittal at the conclusion of the government's case, stating (at 583):

> Based on the evidence proffered by the Government in this case, a reasonable jury could find that this crime of attempt was complete long before the Defendant even pulled the trigger of his firearm — when, for example, having left a trail of written threats on the President and other governmental officials from Colorado to Washington, D.C., he arrived at the White House on the morning of October 29, 1994,

> concealing a rifle under his trench coat. The fact that [the person he shot] was standing in front of the White House at the time of the shooting, while President Clinton was elsewhere, is irrelevant. [T]he evidence was sufficient to show that the Defendant had the specific intent to kill the President and that his intent was corroborated by the steps he took in preparation for the actual shooting.

The approach of the Third and Fifth Circuits was developed in the following cases:

UNITED STATES v. BERRIGAN, 482 F.2d 171 (3d Cir. 1973): [Father Berrigan, an imprisoned Vietnam War resister, was convicted of an attempt to violate a federal statute making it criminal to take anything into or out of a federal prison contrary to regulations of the Attorney General. The latter had promulgated a regulation prohibiting such traffic "without the knowledge and consent" of the prison warden. The conviction was based on evidence that Berrigan had smuggled letters into and out of a prison through a courier, believing that the warden was ignorant of what was going on. In fact the warden had prior knowledge of the arrangement and had agreed to let the courier pretend cooperation in the plan. The court reversed the conviction:] Generally speaking factual impossibility is said to occur when extraneous circumstances unknown to the actor or beyond his control prevent consummation of the intended crime. The classic example is the man who puts his hand in the coat pocket of another with the intent to steal his wallet and finds the pocket empty. . . . Legal impossibility is said to occur where the intended acts, even if completed, would not amount to a crime. Thus, legal impossibility would apply to those circumstances where (1) the motive, desire and expectation is to perform an act in violation of the law; (2) there is intention to perform a physical act; (3) there is a performance of the intended physical act; and (4) the consequence resulting from the intended act does not amount to a crime.[35]

Were intent to break the law the sole criterion to be considered in determining criminal responsibility . . . we could sustain the conviction. . . . Clearly, it can be said that Father Berrigan intended to send letters to Sister McAlister. . . . Normally, of course, the exchange of letters is not a federal offense. Where one of the senders is in prison, however, the sending may or may not be a criminal offense. If the letter is sent within normal channels with the consent and knowledge of the warden it is not a criminal offense. Therefore, an attempt to send a letter through normal channels cannot be considered an attempt to violate the law because none of the intended consequences is in fact criminal. If the letter is sent without the knowledge and consent of the warden, it is a criminal offense and so is the attempt because both the intended consequence and the ac-

35. Intent as used in this connection must be distinguished from motive, desire, and expectation. If *C* by reason of his hatred of *A* plans to kill him, but mistaking *B* for *A* shoots *B,* his motive desire and expectation are to kill *A* but his intent is to kill *B* . . . If *A* takes an umbrella which he believes to belong to *B,* but which in fact is his own, he does not have the intent to steal, his intent being to take the umbrella he grasps in his hand, which is his own umbrella. . . . If a man mistakes a stump for his enemy and shoots at it, notwithstanding his desire and expectation to shoot his enemy, his intent is to shoot the object aimed at, which is the stump. Keedy, Criminal Attempts at Common Law, 102 U. of Pa. L. Rev. 464, 466-467 (1954). . . .

tual consequence are in fact criminal. Here, we are faced with a third situation where there is a motivation, desire and expectation of sending a letter without the knowledge and consent, and the intended act is performed, but unknown to the sender, the transmittal is accomplished with the knowledge and consent of the warden.

Applying the principles of the law of attempt to the instant case, the writing of the letters, and their copying and transmittal by the courier . . . constituted the *Act.* This much the government proved. What the government did not prove — and could not prove because it was a legal impossibility — was the "external, objective situation which the substantive law may require to be present," to-wit, absence of knowledge and consent of the warden. Thus, the government failed to prove the "*Circumstances or attendant circumstances*" vital to the offense. Without such proof, the *Consequence* or *Result* did not constitute an offense that violated the federal statute. . . . Simply stated, attempting to do that which is not a crime is not attempting to commit a crime.

UNITED STATES v. OVIEDO, 525 F.2d 881 (5th Cir. 1976): [An undercover agent contacted defendant and asked to buy heroin. Defendant agreed and appeared at an arranged time and place with what he claimed was heroin. The agent then performed a field test with positive result and arrested defendant. However, a later laboratory test of the substance revealed it was not in fact heroin but procaine hydrochloride (not a controlled substance), which happens to give a positive reaction to the usual field test. The prosecution therefore charged defendant with attempted distribution of heroin, and a jury convicted, apparently rejecting defendant's testimony that he knew the substance was not heroin and was only trying to "rip off" the agent. On appeal, the Fifth Circuit reversed the conviction.

[The court rejected the traditional distinction between legal and factual impossibility, saying:] These definitions are not particularly helpful here, for they do nothing more than provide a different focus for the analysis. In one sense, the impossibility involved here might be deemed legal, for those *acts* which Oviedo set in motion, the transfer of the substance in his possession, were not a crime. In another sense, the impossibility is factual, for the *objective* of Oviedo, the sale of heroin, was proscribed by law, and failed only because of a circumstance unknown to Oviedo.

[However, the court also rejected an approach that would find an attempt because the objective of defendant was criminal, since "It would allow us to punish one's thoughts, desires, or motives, through indirect evidence, without reference to any objective fact." The court concluded:] We reject the notion . . . , adopted by the district court, that the conviction in the present case can be sustained since there is sufficient proof of intent, not because of any doubt as to the sufficiency of the evidence in that regard, but because of the inherent dangers such a precedent would pose in the future. . . .

When the defendant sells a substance which is actually heroin, it is reasonable to infer that he knew the physical nature of the substance, and to place on him the burden of dispelling that inference. . . . However, if we convict the defendant of attempting to sell heroin for the sale of a non-narcotic substance, we eliminate an objective element that has major evidentiary significance and we increase the risk of mistaken conclusions that the defendant believed the goods were narcotics.

Thus, we demand that in order for a defendant to be guilty of a criminal attempt, the objective acts performed, without any reliance on the accompanying mens rea, mark the defendant's conduct as criminal in nature. . . .

. . . We cannot conclude that the objective acts of Oviedo apart from any indirect evidence of intent mark his conduct as criminal in nature. Rather, those acts are consistent with a noncriminal enterprise. Therefore, we will not allow the jury's determination of Oviedo's intent to form the sole basis of a criminal offense.

THE CASE OF LADY ELDON'S FRENCH LACE

A hypothetical decision on a hypothetical state of facts, by the editors

A perennial in the crop of attempt hypotheticals was suggested by Dr. Wharton.[1] "Lady Eldon, when traveling with her husband on the Continent, bought what she supposed to be a quantity of French lace, which she hid, concealing it from Lord Eldon in one of the pockets of the coach. The package was brought to light by a customs officer at Dover. The lace turned out to be an English manufactured article, of little value, and of course, not subject to duty. Lady Eldon had bought it at a price vastly above its value, believing it to be genuine, intending to smuggle it into England." Dr. Wharton, supra, and Professor Sayre[2] conclude that she could be found guilty of an attempt since she intended to smuggle dutiable lace into England. Professor Keedy disagrees, finding the fallacy of the argument in the failure to recognize "that the particular lace which Lady Eldon intended to bring into England was not subject to duty and therefore, although there was the wish to smuggle, there was not the intent to do so."[3]

Keedy was employing the distinction he has advanced between intent, on the one hand, and motive, desire, and expectation, on the other,[4] a distinction that served as the linchpin of the decision in People v. Jaffe, supra, and United States v. Berrigan, supra. As he sees it, what people intend to do on a particular occasion is to be determined by what they do in fact, rather than by what they thought they were doing. The lace was in fact not dutiable; thus, there was no intent on the part of Lady Eldon to smuggle dutiable French lace into the country, and there could be no conviction of the crime of attempt to do so, since what she intended to do on this view was not a crime — a straightforward case of legal impossibility. Professor Perkins has not, so far as we can tell, addressed himself to this particular case. But from what he has written it is clear that he would concur with Keedy. Presumably his analysis would rest on his distinction between primary and secondary intent.[5] Only the former may be considered in determining the existence of the necessary intent to establish an attempt. It, like Keedy's

1. 1 Criminal Law 304 n. 9 (12th ed. 1932).
2. Criminal Attempts, 41 Harv. L. Rev. 821, 852 (1928).
3. Criminal Attempts at Common Law, 102 U. Pa. L. Rev. 464, 477 n. 85 (1954).
4. Id. at 466-468.
5. Rollin M. Perkins, Criminal Attempt and Related Problems, 2 U.C.L.A.L. Rev. 319, 330-332 (1955).

term *intent,* is determined by what the actor objectively and in fact did. What the actor believed he was doing, on the level of the facts as the actor took them to be, constitutes secondary intent. Apparently the latter is basically the same in description and function as what Keedy refers to as the motive, desire, or expectation.

We concur with Wharton and Sayre.

We submit, with respect, that Keedy and Perkins, and the courts that follow their reasoning, have been guilty of some plain silliness in supporting their position. Their conclusion that Lady Eldon must be acquitted rests on the premise that what a person intends to do is what he actually does, even if that was the furthest thing from the person's mind:

"You're eating my salad."

"Sorry, I didn't mean to; I thought it was mine."

"You might have *thought* it was yours. But in fact it was mine. So it was my salad you intended to eat. You should be ashamed!"

Surely this is an extraordinary way of regarding what a person intended, quite at odds with common sense and common language. Where a circumstance is not known to the actor, there is no way consistent with straight thought that his act can be regarded as intentional as to that circumstance.

Of course, it is hardly unknown for courts to adopt strained and artificial reasoning to support a sound result. Is that the case here? Is it sound to conclude that the type of conduct engaged in by Lady Eldon should not be made criminal? Let us consider if it is.

Suppose Lady Eldon believed she had purchased an inexpensive English lace but in fact had purchased an expensive French lace. Certainly she could not be found guilty of smuggling if she got past the customs inspector or of an attempt if she failed. The reason is that the intent to smuggle French lace, necessary to establish either offense, does not exist. (We are assuming this is not a crime of absolute liability). And it does not exist because her intent is judged by what she believed she was doing and not by what she in fact did. Now why should it make any more difference in Wharton's hypothetical that her act was objectively lawful than it does in our variation that her act was objectively unlawful? Why in both cases should not the intent be judged by the same standard, what she believed she was doing, rather than what she did in fact?

It may be answered that while an innocent mind can exculpate, a criminal mind simpliciter cannot inculpate. The reasoning might be as follows: There is no legitimate purpose to be served by punishing those who mean to act blamelessly; and while a purpose could be served by punishing a person who decides to commit a crime (to the extent that all must first decide to commit an intentional crime before actually committing it, some will thereby be prevented from committing it, at this or another occasion) other considerations make it inexpedient and undesirable to do so. What are those considerations? They are those, presumably, which underlie the principle which forbids punishing people for their thoughts alone, i.e., that thinking evil is not a reliable indication that a person will do evil and the criminal law may properly concern itself only with acts. See page 181 supra.

But can this be said of Lady Eldon? Has she merely *thought* to smuggle French lace? No. She has *done* everything in her power and all she thought necessary to smuggle French lace. Has she shown herself to be less eligible for the imposition of criminal sanctions because, through no fault of her own, she failed? Surely not.

From the basic postulate that the law concerns itself with acts and not thoughts, it may be argued that the law is concerned not with what a person *may* do but with what he in fact *does*. But the conclusion is erroneous. There are many crimes that may be established without proof that acts have occurred that actually invade the interest sought to be protected. The law of attempts and conspiracy are prime examples. The reason for punishing in such cases is based not on what the actor has already done but rather on what is apprehended he is likely to do subsequently. As Holmes has pointed out, even larceny may be viewed in this way, since there is no requirement that the possessor be permanently deprived of his property, only that the actor intend to deprive him of it.[6] Looked at objectively, apart from intent, the acts done may be wholly innocuous — like striking a match or having a quiet conversation. The innocuous acts are made criminal because, combined with the requisite intent of that actor, they demonstrate him to be likely to commit the injury that the law seeks to prevent.

Perhaps it may be argued that there is a different policy supporting exculpation in cases like Lady Eldon's — namely, that in real cases, as opposed to hypotheticals, intention must be proved rather than supposed, and it is too dangerous to the innocent to permit juries to speculate on a defendant's intent in the absence of actions that strongly evidence that intent. One may fully agree with this, however, without concluding that Lady Eldon should be acquitted. Of course it would be evidentiary of Lady Eldon's intent to smuggle if she had been found with dutiable French lace at the border. (But only evidentiary — after all, she might have thought it was English lace, or it might have been put with her things by her maid without her knowledge.) But why should it be held, as it was in United States v. Oviedo, supra, that, since the lace was nondutiable in fact, a finding of intent will necessarily be suspect, regardless of the strength of the evidence? Suppose, for example, that the lace were carefully secreted in a specially tailored, concealed pocket of the coach; that the coachman testified to incriminating statements Lady Eldon made to Lord Eldon; that a letter from her to her sister, which described her newly bought "French lace" in exquisite and appreciative detail, had been introduced; that her receipt showed she paid a price appropriate for French lace rather than for the vastly less expensive English lace. There would seem little danger to the innocent in allowing a jury to find an attempt to smuggle French lace on these facts. Indeed, in cases like *Jaffe* and *Berrigan,* "attempt" is charged only because of the involvement of an undercover agent, whose participation prevents completion of the intended crime. Whatever else one may say about such investigatory tactics, they do not necessarily render suspect the evidence of the defendant's intent; indeed, in practice, they usually render that evidence far *less* speculative than it otherwise would be. The proper remedy for speculative and unreliable jury findings of intent is a court alert to preclude such findings in particular cases where the evidence is insufficient.

In the end, then, the arguments in favor of Lady Eldon (and those which have been used to reverse convictions in cases like *Jaffe, Oviedo,* and *Berrigan*) are founded on unpersuasive policy considerations rationalized by a peculiar and Pickwickian interpretation of what it means to intend to do an act, one that is

6. The Common Law 72 (1881).

utterly at odds both with the common usage of our language and its usage elsewhere in the criminal law.[7] *We conclude that the innocuous character of the action actually done (innocuous in the sense that it could not constitute a crime under the actual circumstances) will not save her from an attempt conviction if she believed that the circumstances were otherwise, and, had her belief been correct, what she set out to do would constitute a crime.* This is the principle that has found favor in virtually every serious statutory effort to deal with the problem, and in numerous decisions reached without benefit of a specific statute to tell the court that a person intends to do what he thinks he intends to do. Indeed, it is worth noting that not only has *Jaffe* been undone by the New York Penal Code, see *Dluglash,* supra, but so has *Berrigan,* which was narrowly confined to its facts, if not tacitly overruled, in a later Third Circuit decision, United States v. Kai-Lo Hsu, 155 F.3d 189 (3d Cir. 1998).

We must say a few words more about the final qualification to the principle just asserted; namely, that "had her belief (in the circumstances) been correct, what she set out to do would constitute a crime." The point can best be made by altering the hypothetical. Suppose the lace that Lady Eldon had purchased was in fact the expensive French lace she meant to buy. The customs officer at Dover brings it to light. He then says to Lady Eldon: "Lucky you returned to England today rather than yesterday. I just received word this morning that the government has removed French lace from the duty list." Could Lady Eldon be held for attempt to smuggle French Lace in these circumstances? Certainly what she did and what she intended to do were not different simply because she acted one day later, when French lace was removed from the duty list. But there is this important difference: that at the time she acted, *what* she intended to do (always judged, of course, from her own perspective) was not a violation of the criminal law, even though she thought it was.[8]

It is true that under the Canon Law of the Medieval Church, a person who committed a permissible action in the belief it was forbidden was considered guilty and subject to the same penance as that required of one who had actually done a forbidden action. Stephan Kuttner, Kanonistische Schuldlehre 209-213 (1935). But that was a reflection of the Church's concern with the state of a person's soul, a concern that is foreign to secular law.

Of course, in the case of Lady Eldon, her action showed her to be a person who would break some law under some circumstances. But what law? The law against smuggling French lace? There no longer was such a law. The criminal laws gen-

7. Consider the Missouri court's reason for reversing the conviction of a hunter for attempting to take a deer out of season where the evidence showed that the defendant, believing that he had a live deer in his sights, shot at a stuffed deer placed in the woods by a game warden: "If the state's evidence showed an attempt to take the dummy, it fell far short of proving an attempt to take a deer." State v. Guffey, 262 S.W.2d 152 (Mo. App. 1953). In a Styrofoam dummy case, the Washington Supreme court held to the contrary. State v. Walsh, 123 Wash.2d 741, 870 P.2d 974 (1994).

8. See R. v. Taaffee [1983] 2 All E.R. 625, affirmed [1984] A.C. 539 (House of Lords). A truck driver, caught at the border carrying packages containing a quantity of cannabis, claimed that he thought he was smuggling in money. In fact, there was no law prohibiting the importation of money. The court concluded that if the jury believed his story he could not be convicted of the offense of fraudulent evasion (essentially attempted smuggling), stating:

> Does it make any difference that the appellant thought wrongly that by clandestinely importing currency he was committing an offence? . . . We think . . . his actions morally reprehensible. [That] did not . . . turn what he . . . believed to be the importation of currency into the commission of a criminal offence. His views on the law as to the importation of currency were to that extent, in our judgment, irrelevant.

erally? Fortunately our law has not gone so far in accepting that *any* antisocial attitude is sufficient to justify criminal punishment. That a person has violated what she thought was a law raises the odds of her violating an actual law in the future. But the principle of legality stands against condemning people for what they may be expected to do, even in a case like this variation of Lady Eldon where the odds are very much raised. As Professor Williams has pointed out, "if the legislature has not seen fit to prohibit the consummated act, a mere approach to consummation should a fortiori be guiltless. Any other view would offend against the principle of legality; in effect the law of attempt would be used to manufacture a new crime, when the legislature has left the situation outside the ambit of the law." Glanville Williams, Criminal Law: The General Part 633-634 (2d ed. 1961). Had the criminal law been changed as supposed in our variation of the Lady Eldon hypothetical, therefore, it would be just as wrong to convict her as to convict an abortionist of attempted abortion where the abortion was committed, unknown to the defendant, after the abortion law was repealed or held invalid. These are the true cases of legal impossibility.

But, it should be noted, these situations are totally different from cases like *Jaffe* and *Berrigan,* even though the courts in each case made it seem otherwise, by asserting that what the defendants intended to do could not have constituted a crime. What the abortionist intended to do (and did) could not constitute a crime because there was no such crime. What Jaffe and Berrigan intended to do (and thought they did) was indeed a crime. It is only through a perverse use of intent that we can say that Jaffe intended to receive honestly obtained property or that Berrigan intended to send out a letter the warden knew about, and that therefore they intended to do what was no crime at all.

Lady Eldon, in the actual hypothetical, in contrast to the modified hypothetical, presents no more a case of genuine legal impossibility than do *Jaffe* and *Berrigan.* She will be convicted of attempt to smuggle French lace.

COMMENT, 7 Hypothetical L. Rev. 1, 3-4 (1962-2001): The hypothetical *Lady Eldon* decision is a good effort, but it doesn't quite work.

First: Consider a safecracker who tries to open a safe with magic incantations. Under the *Lady Eldon* analysis, the safecracker would merely have made a mistake of fact, and he could be convicted of attempt. Or consider the case of Leroy Ivy and John Henry Ivy, two brothers who tried to use voodoo to kill a judge who had sentenced one of them to prison for robbery.[9] The brothers paid the judge's housekeeper $100 for his photo and a lock of his hair, which they planned to mail to a voodoo practitioner in Jamaica. Police officers in Tupelo, Mississippi, foiled the plot by arresting Leroy Ivy before he could send off the items needed to cast the spell. Charged with attempting to kill the judge, the brothers pleaded guilty and were sentenced to five and ten years respectively. But these defendants, like the safecracker, are more pathetic than dangerous. As early as 1863 Baron Park observed in Attorney General v. Sillem, 159 Eng. Rep 178, 221 (1863):

> If a statute simply made it a felony to attempt to kill any human being, . . . an attempt by means of witchcraft . . . would not be an offence within such a statute. The

9. For accounts of the case, see Fred Grimm, Man Charged in Plot to Kill Judge By Hex, Miami Herald, Mar. 31, 1989, at 1, 10; R. J. Smith, Conspiracy to Commit Voodoo, Village Voice, Sept. 26, 1989, at 37-41.

> poverty of language compels one to say "an attempt to kill by means of witchcraft," but such an attempt is really no attempt at all to kill. It is true the sin or wickedness may be as great as an attempt . . . by competent means; but human laws are made, not to punish sin, but to prevent crime and mischief.

The Model Penal Code, in recognition of this problem, gives a court the power to dismiss a prosecution or decrease the penalty if "the particular conduct charged to constitute a criminal attempt . . . is so inherently unlikely to result or culminate in the commission of a crime that neither such conduct nor the actor presents a public danger." Section 5.05(2). But this is to commend the matter to the discretion of the judge; it is not a statement of a rule of law. A better approach is that taken by the revised Minnesota Criminal Code which states an exception to its rule that impossibility is no defense where the "impossibility would have been clearly evident to a person of normal understanding." Minn. Stat. Ann. §609.17.2. A similar solution has been developed by Professor Robbins, who proposes that a person be guilty of attempt only when "he purposely does or omits to do anything that, *under the circumstances as a reasonable person would believe them to be,*" is a substantial step in a course of conduct planned to culminate in commission of the crime.[10]

Second: The effort to deal with the so-called true legal impossibility problem comes off more smoothly than convincingly. Consider the following case. Two friends, Mr. Fact and Mr. Law, go hunting in the morning of October 15 in the fields of the state of Dakota, whose law makes it a misdemeanor to hunt any time other than from October 1 to November 30. Both kill deer on the first day out, October 15. Mr. Fact, however, was under the erroneous belief that the date was September 15, and Mr. Law was under the erroneous belief that the hunting season was confined to the month of November, as it was the previous year. Under the *Lady Eldon* formulation, Mr. Fact could be convicted of an attempt to hunt out of season, but Mr. Law could not be. We fail to see how any rational system of criminal law could justify convicting one and acquitting the other on the fragile and unpersuasive distinction that one was suffering under a mistake of fact, and the other under a mistake of law. Certainly if the ultimate test is the dangerousness of the actor (i.e., readiness to violate the law), as *Lady Eldon* would have it, no distinction is warranted — Mr. Law has indicated himself to be no less "dangerous" than Mr. Fact.[11]

10. Ira P. Robbins, Attempting the Impossible: The Emerging Consensus, 23 Harv. J. Legisl. 377, 441 (1986) (emphasis added). See also N.J. Stat. Ann. §2C:5-la(1). A recent case, however, makes one question the adequacy of these formulations. In Weeks v. Scott, 55 F.3d 1059 (1st Cir. 1995), an HIV-infected defendant was convicted of attempted murder by spitting in his victim's face. The conviction was upheld because there was evidence that the chances of infecting the victim in this way, while low, were greater than zero. Suppose the scientific evidence showed that the chances of his succeeding were no greater than those of the voodoo practitioner. Would the defendant then have as much claim to be acquitted as the voodoo practitioner? Why should it matter that his misconception about how the HIV virus is spread is widely shared, which is to say reasonable, so long as HIV transmission in that manner is in fact impossible? Would the HIV defendant have to be acquitted if the statute requires the defendant to do an act that "tends to effect the commission" of the intended crime, for example N.Y. Pen. Law §110.00; Texas Pen. Code §15.01(a)?

11. For discussion of the problems posed by this hypothetical, see Kenneth W. Simons, Mistake and Impossibility, Law and Fact, and Culpability: A Speculative Essay, 81 J. Crim. L. & Criminology 447, 467-469 (1990) and Fernand N. Dutile & Harold F. Moore, Mistake and Impossibility: Arranging a Marriage Between Two Difficult Partners, 74 Nw. U.L. Rev. 166, 166-167 (1979). The latter article disagrees with the reasoning of the Hypothetical Law Review comment on this point: "[We argue] that Mr. Law in the Kadish and [Schulhofer] example would be acquitted, since the trans-

The same point can be made with the very example that the Editors use to support their *Lady Eldon* opinion — the case in which, unbeknownst to Lady Eldon, French lace has just been removed from the duty list. The Editors ask, in effect, *What law* did she show her readiness to break? Not smuggling French lace, they say, because there's no longer such a law. Correct. Not criminal laws generally, they say, because that would rest criminality on a mere speculation based on the defendant's proclivity. Correct again. But how about the law against smuggling? Has she shown herself to be less a smuggler, just because she arrived right after French lace had been removed from the duty list? The Editors err in treating the case as if duties had been repealed on all goods, whereas only one item had been removed from the duty list.

Third: In formulating a rule that would eliminate the defense of factual impossibility in all cases, the opinion overlooks the strong case for retaining the defense in one class of cases. These are the cases in which the acts done by the defendant are as consistent with an innocent as with a culpable state of mind. Take for example the old saw about the professor who takes his own umbrella thinking it belongs to his colleague. The act is utterly neutral. A man taking his own umbrella conveys no evidence of guilt. Of course the matter changes if it can be proved that he believed it was his colleague's umbrella. But proof of state of mind is inherently unreliable where there are only ambiguous acts to support the inference.

Consider how the Model Penal Code deals with this very concern when it addresses itself to a different problem, i.e., drawing the line between preparation and attempt. This is typically the situation in which the actor has not yet completed all he set out to do. In Section 5.01, the Model Penal Code requires that his acts be "strongly corroborative of the actor's criminal purpose." The primary function of this requirement is to avoid the risk of false convictions. Where the evidence of intent falls below a certain level we are not willing to allow the jury to speculate.

Now both the *Lady Eldon* opinion and the Model Penal Code are short-sighted for not seeing that the same concern may exist in the class of impossibility cases under discussion. In this respect the court in *Oviedo*, page 593 supra, and cases that have followed its lead, are on very solid ground. If concern about false convictions calls for the requirement that the acts strongly corroborate the intent when the actor had further acts to do to achieve his objective, then the same concern calls for the same requirement where the actor believed he had done all he needed to. If it is answered that in the latter cases the completed conduct carries the criminal intent on its face, the response must be that while this is generally so, it need not be so. The professor taking his own umbrella surely is such a case.

To put the suggestion in statutory form, we propose the following amendment to Model Penal Code's Section 5.01:

---

action, even as he contemplated it, was not within the statute, while Mr. Fact would not [be acquitted]. From the standpoint of symmetry, or the dangerous propensities of the defendant, there is no way to justify the result. From a 'moral' standpoint they are equally culpable.[But] it is totally unclear how any system based on liability for intending to violate the law, as opposed to intending *conduct* that *is* in violation of the law, could function as a properly justified system of criminal law. Such a system provides neither appropriate deterrence to crime nor proper retribution for crime." —Eds.

> A person is guilty of an attempt to commit a crime if, acting with the kind of culpability otherwise required for commission of the crime, he: (a) purposely engages in conduct that *strongly corroborates the required culpability and* would constitute the crime if the attendant circumstances were as he believes them to be. . . ."[12]

NOTE

For a rewarding effort to untangle the variety of knots presented by the *Lady Eldon* case, see Larry Alexander, Inculpatory and Exculpatory Mistakes and the Fact/Law Distinction, 12 Law & Philosophy 33, 43-70 (1993).

12. On the issues raised by this statutory proposal, see Robbins, supra at 400-12; Thomas Weigend, Why Lady Eldon Should Be Acquitted: The Social Harm in Attempting the Impossible, 27 De Paul L. Rev. 231 (1979). A related proposal has been developed by Professor Fletcher, who suggests that attempts be punishable only when two conditions are satisfied: "the actor must attempt an act punishable under the law, and, further, this attempt must be dangerous on its face." George P. Fletcher, Constructing a Theory of Impossible Attempts, 5 Crim. J. Ethics 53, 67 (1986) (emphasis added).

CHAPTER 7

GROUP CRIMINALITY

A. ACCOUNTABILITY FOR THE ACTS OF OTHERS

INTRODUCTORY NOTES

1. *From common law to statute.* At the common law there were distinct categories of circumstances that rendered a person a participant in a course of criminal conduct. These distinctions had consequences for both procedure and punishment. The following excerpts from 4 Blackstone, Commentaries, ch. 3, *34-39, broadly describe those categories:

> A man may be *principal* in an offence in two degrees. A principal, in the first degree, is he that is the actor, or absolute perpetrator of the crime; and, in the second degree, he is who is present, aiding, and abetting the fact to be done. Which presence need not always be an actual immediate standing by, within sight or hearing of the fact; but there may be also a constructive presence, as when one commits a robbery or murder, and another keeps watch or guard at some convenient distance. . . .
>
> An *accessory* is he who is not the chief actor in the offence, nor present at its performance, but is some way concerned therein, either before or after the fact committed. . . .
>
> As to . . . who may be an accessory *before* the fact, Sir Matthew Hale defines him to be one, who being absent at the time of the crime committed, doth yet procure, counsel, or command another to commit a crime. Herein absence is necessary to make him an accessory; for if such procurer, or the like, be present, he is guilty of the crime as principal. . . .
>
> An accessory *after* the fact may be, where a person, knowing a felony to have been committed, receives, relieves, comforts, or assists the felon. . . .

Modern statutes have largely eliminated the significance of these discrete modes of criminal participation: (1) Apart from the accessory after the fact, who is still generally subject to a lesser punishment, the punishment is the same for the three main modes of complicity. (2) It is no longer the case that accessories to crime cannot be convicted until their principal is convicted (although, of course, it must be proved that a crime was committed). (3) It is no longer necessary in most states for a defendant to be charged with a particular form of complicity. The defendant may simply be charged with the substantive crime committed by the person the defendant aided or encouraged.

These changes are the result of statutes antedating the wave of legislative reform initiated by the Model Penal Code. These older statutes abolish all distinctions between principals and accessories before the fact, requiring that all be treated as principals. The California Penal Code is representative:

SECTION 31

All persons concerned in the commission of a crime, whether it be felony or misdemeanor, and whether they directly commit the act constituting the offense, or aid and abet in its commission, or, not being present, have advised and encouraged its commission, and all persons counseling, advising or encouraging children under the age of fourteen years, lunatics or idiots to commit any crime, or who, by fraud, contrivance, or force, occasion the drunkenness of another for the purpose of causing him to commit any crime, or who, by threats, menaces, command, or coercion, compel another to commit any crime, are principals in any crime so committed.

SECTION 32

Every person who, after a felony has been committed, harbors, conceals or aids a principal in such felony, with the intent that said principal may avoid or escape from arrest, trial, conviction or punishment, having knowledge that said principal has committed such felony or has been charged with such felony or convicted thereof, is an accessory to such felony.

SECTION 33

Except in cases where a different punishment is prescribed, an accessory is punishable by a fine not exceeding five thousand dollars, or by imprisonment in the state prison, or in county jail not exceeding one year, or by both such fine and imprisonment.

SECTION 971

The distinction between an accessory before the fact and a principal, and between principals in the first and second degree is abrogated; and all persons concerned in the commission of a crime, who by the operation of other provisions of this code are principals therein, shall hereafter be prosecuted, tried, and punished as principals, and no other facts need be alleged in any accusatory pleading against any such person than are required in an accusatory pleading against a principal.

See also the federal complicity statute, 18 U.S.C. §2:

(a) Whoever commits an offense against the United States or aids, abets, counsels, commands, induces or procures its commission, is punishable as a principal.
(b) Whoever willfully causes an act to be done which if directly performed by him or another would be an offense against the United States, is punishable as a principal.

The statutes of more recent vintage, influenced by the Model Penal Code proposals (see §2.06, Appendix), typically make people who are accomplices of another person accountable for that person's conduct and define people as accomplices in the other person's offense if they solicit that person to commit such an offense or aid that person in planning or committing it. See, e.g., N.J. Stat. Ann. tit. 2C, §2C:2-6.

2. Conspiracy as a doctrine of complicity. An additional basis for holding one person liable for the crimes of another derives from the doctrine of conspiracy. In general terms, a criminal conspiracy is an agreement or combination by two or more persons to commit a crime. Conspiracy is a substantive crime in itself, but it has the further consequence of making each of the coconspirators criminally responsible for the criminal acts of fellow conspirators committed in furtherance of the planned criminal enterprise, whether or not those particular criminal acts were planned, so long as they were reasonably foreseeable. A coconspirator, therefore, may be liable for the criminal acts of fellow conspirators even though strictly under the law of principals and accessories (requiring aiding, abetting, encouraging, etc.) the person might not be liable. This problem is explored in the conspiracy section, in connection with Pinkerton v. United States, page 671 infra and the materials following.

3. Punishment. American law punishes accomplices the same as principals. This is in contrast to the approach in other legal systems. For example, the German Penal Code (§25) provides different punishments for the perpetrator, the instigator and the aider, and the law is rich in doctrine for distinguishing between these classifications of participants. See C. Roxin, Täterschaft und Tatherrschaft (1984). Judge Posner comments on the American approach in United States v. Ambrose, 740 F.2d 505, 508-509 (7th Cir. 1985):

> [Although the language of] 18 U.S.C. §2(a), [supra] makes clear that an aider and abettor can be punished as severely as the principal, it does not make clear that he must always be punished so severely. History is against such an interpretation. The distinction between "principal" and "aider and abettor" goes back to the time when all felonies carried the same sanction — death. By enabling the courts to punish a class of less culpable offenders — aiders and abettors as distinct from principals — less severely, the distinction introduced a welcome element of gradation into the sentencing of felons. But as judges acquired more and more sentencing discretion, the need to distinguish between principals and aiders and abettors diminished, and since it was sometimes a difficult decision to make there was a movement to abolish it with regard to determining criminal liability. This movement culminated in 18 U.S.C. §2(a). But the purpose was not to make sure that aiders and abettors were always punished as severely as principals. Indeed, in passing the statute Congress must have realized that judges would use their sentencing discretion to proportion the severity of the sentence to the aider and abettor's fault. The history suggests that, rather than being intended to limit sentencing discretion, the abolition of the distinction between principals and aiders and abettors presupposed such discretion.

Guidelines for mitigating the sentence depending on the defendant's role in the offense may be found in U.S. Sentencing Comm., Federal Sentencing Guidelines Manual Sections 3B.1.1-3B1.3 (1999).

4. The theory of complicity. The relationship between the doctrine of complicity and other doctrines of criminal liability is explored in the following excerpt.

Sanford H. Kadish, A Theory of Complicity, in Issues in Contemporary Legal Philosophy: The Influence of H. L. A. Hart 288 (Ruth Gavison ed. 1987):[1] [We] regard a person's acts as the products of his choice, not of regularities of nature which require that certain happenings will occur whenever certain conditions are present. Therefore, antecedent events do not cause a person to act in the same way they cause things to happen, and neither do the antecedent acts of others. To treat the acts of others as causing a person's actions would be inconsistent with the premise on which we hold a person responsible. . . .[a]

The . . . implication [of this] is that when we seek to determine the responsibility of one person for the volitional actions of another the concept of physical cause is not available to determine the answer, for whatever the relation of one person's acts to those of another, it cannot be described in terms of that sense of cause and effect appropriate to the occurrence of natural events without doing violence to our concept of a human action as freely chosen. . . .

How, then, can the law reach those whose conduct makes it appropriate to punish for the criminal actions of others — a person, for example, who persuades or helps another to commit a crime? . . . If it were not for the very special way in which we conceive of human actions, causation doctrine might serve this purpose, on the view that one who intentionally causes another to commit certain actions falls under the prohibition against committing those actions. But our conception of human actions as controlled by choice will not allow that to work. . . . Some alternative doctrine is needed, therefore, which imposes liability on the actor who is to blame for the conduct of another, but which does so upon principles that comport with our perception of human actions. This is the office of the doctrine of complicity.

1. *Mens Rea*

INTRODUCTORY NOTE

The problem of the mens rea for complicity is complicated by the presence of two levels of mens rea: that required of the accomplice (the helper or encourager) and that required of the principal (the actual perpetrator). As we shall shortly see, a true purpose, often called a specific intent, is generally required to hold a person liable as an accomplice; that is, he must actually intend his action to further the criminal action of the principal. We explore the meaning of this requirement and qualifications to it in subsection a: Actions of the Principal.

But then we have a further problem. Suppose the crime committed by the principal does not require that the perpetrator have knowledge of some attendant circumstance (strict liability), or makes it sufficient that the perpetrator was negligent in not being aware of that circumstance. Does the general requirement of purpose mean that an accomplice must have this knowledge even though the principal need not? We will deal with this problem in Subsection b, Attendant Circumstances.

1. For further discussion of the theoretical issues see Joshua Dressler, Reassessing the Theoretical Underpinnings of Accomplice Liability: New Solutions to an Old Problem, 37 Hastings L. Rev. 91 (1985).

a. See the material in the Causation chapter, page 536 supra. — Eds.

And we have one final problem, that of the result caused by the principal's action. Sometimes a principal is liable for causing some result, the death of another, for example, when he was reckless or negligent, even though he didn't intend it. Under what circumstances is the accomplice liable when he did not intend for anyone to be killed? This is the subject of Subsection c, Results.

a. Actions of the Principal

HICKS v. UNITED STATES

Supreme Court of the United States

150 U.S. 442 (1893)

JUSTICE SHIRAS delivered the opinion of the Court.

John Hicks, an Indian, was jointly indicted with Stand Rowe, also an Indian, for the murder of Andrew J. Colvard, a white man, by shooting him with a gun on the 13th of February, 1892. Rowe was killed by the officers in the attempt to arrest him, and Hicks was tried separately and found guilty in March, 1893. We adopt the statement of the facts in the case made in the brief for the government as correct and as sufficient for our purposes:

> It appears that on the night of the 12th of February, 1892, there was a dance at the house of Jim Rowe, in the Cherokee Nation; that Jim Rowe was a brother to Stand Rowe, who was indicted jointly with the defendant; . . . that Stand Rowe and the defendant were engaged in what was called "scouting," viz., eluding the United States marshals who were in search of them with warrants for their arrest, and were armed for the purpose of resisting arrest; they appeared at the dance, each armed with a Winchester rifle; they were both Cherokee Indians. The deceased, Andrew J. Colvard, was a white man who had married a Cherokee woman; he [was also at] the dance on . . . on the evening of the 12th. A good deal of whiskey was drank [sic] during the night by the persons present, and Colvard appears to have been drunk at some time during the night. Colvard spoke Cherokee fluently, and appears to have been very friendly with Stand Rowe and the defendant Hicks. . . .
>
> Some time after sunrise on the morning of the 13th, about 7 o'clock, [four witnesses] saw Stand Rowe, coming on horseback in a moderate walk, with his Winchester rifle lying down in front of him. . . . Stand Rowe halted within five or six feet of the main road, and the men on the porch saw Mr. Colvard and the defendant Hicks riding together down the main road from the direction of Jim Rowe's house.
>
> As Colvard and Hicks approached the point where Stand Rowe was sitting on his horse, Stand Rowe rode out into the road and halted. Colvard then rode up to him in a lope or canter, leaving Hicks, the defendant, some 30 or 40 feet in his rear. The point where the three men were together on their horses was about 100 yards from where the four witnesses stood on the porch. The conversation between the three men on horseback was not fully heard by the four men on the porch, and all that was heard was not understood, because part of it was carried on in the Cherokee tongue; but some part of this conversation was distinctly heard and clearly understood by these witnesses; they saw Stand Rowe twice raise his rifle and aim it at Colvard, and twice he lowered it; they heard Colvard say, "I am a friend to both of you"; they saw and heard the defendant Hicks laugh aloud when Rowe directed his rifle toward Colvard; they saw Hicks take off his hat and hit his horse on the neck or shoulder with it; they heard Hicks say to Colvard, "Take off your hat and die like

> a man"; they saw Stand Rowe raise his rifle for the third time, point it at Colvard, fire it; . . . they saw Colvard fall from his horse; they went to where he was lying in the road and found him dead; they saw Stand Rowe and John Hicks ride off together after the shooting.

Hicks testified in his own behalf, denying that he had encouraged Rowe to shoot Colvard, and alleging that he had endeavored to persuade Rowe not to shoot. . . .

The language attributed to Hicks, and which he denied having used, cannot be said to have been entirely free from ambiguity. It was addressed not to Rowe, but to Colvard. Hicks testified that Rowe was in a dangerous mood, and that he did not know whether he would shoot Colvard or Hicks. The remark made — if made — accompanied with the gesture of taking off his own hat, may have been an utterance of desperation, occasioned by his belief that Rowe would shoot one or both of them. That Hicks and Rowe rode off together after seeing Colvard fall was used as a fact against Hicks, pointing to a conspiracy between them. Hicks testified that he did it in fear of his life; that Rowe had demanded that he should show him the road which he wished to travel. Hicks further testified, and in this he was not contradicted, that he separated from Rowe a few minutes afterwards, on the first opportunity, and that he never afterwards had any intercourse with him, nor had he been in the company of Rowe for several weeks before the night of the fatal occurrence.

Two of the assignments of error are especially relied on by the counsel of the accused. One arises out of that portion of the charge wherein the judge sought to instruct the jury as to the evidence relied on as showing that Hicks aided and abetted Rowe in the commission of the crime. . . .

We agree with the counsel for the plaintiff in error in thinking that this instruction was erroneous in two particulars. It omitted to instruct the jury that the acts or words of encouragement and abetting must have been used by the accused with the intention of encouraging and abetting Rowe. So far as the instruction goes, the words may have been used for a different purpose, and yet have had the actual effect of inciting Rowe to commit the murderous act. Hicks, indeed, testified that the expressions used by him were intended to dissuade Rowe from shooting. But the jury were left to find Hicks guilty as a principal because the effect of his words may have had the result of encouraging Rowe to shoot, regardless of Hicks' intention. In another part of the charge the learned judge did make an observation as to the question of intention in the use of the words, saying:

> If the deliberate and intentional use of words has the effect to encourage one man to kill another, he who uttered these words is presumed by the law to have intended that effect, and is responsible therefor.

This statement is itself defective in confounding the intentional use of the words with the intention as respects the effect to be produced. Hicks no doubt, *intended* to use the words he did use, but did he thereby *intend* that they were to be understood by Rowe as an encouragement to act? However this may be, we do not think this expression of the learned judge availed to cure the defect already noticed in his charge, that the mere use of certain words would suffice to warrant the jury in finding Hicks guilty, regardless of the intention with which they were used.

Another error is contained in that portion of the charge now under review, and that is the statement:

> that if Hicks was actually present at that place at the time of the firing by Stand Rowe, and he was there for the purpose of either aiding, abetting, advising, or encouraging the shooting of Andrew J. Colvard by Stand Rowe, and that, as a matter of fact, he did not do it, but was present for the purpose of aiding or abetting or advising or encouraging his shooting, but he did not do it because it was not necessary, it was done without his assistance, the law says there is a third condition where guilt is fastened to his act in that regard.

We understand this language to mean that where an accomplice is present for the purpose of aiding and abetting in a murder, but refrains from so aiding and abetting because it turned out not to be necessary for the accomplishment of the common purpose, he is equally guilty as if he had actively participated by words or acts of encouragement. Thus understood, the statement might, in some instances, be a correct instruction. Thus, if there had been evidence sufficient to show that there had been a previous conspiracy between Rowe and Hicks to waylay and kill Colvard, Hicks, if present at the time of the killing, would be guilty, even if it was found unnecessary for him to act. But the error of such an instruction, in the present case, is in the fact that there was no evidence on which to base it. The evidence, so far as we are permitted to notice it, as contained in the bills of exception, and set forth in the charge, shows no facts from which the jury could have properly found that the encounter was the result of any previous conspiracy or arrangement. The jury might well, therefore, have thought that they were following the court's instructions, in finding the accused guilty because he was present at the time and place of the murder, although he contributed neither by word or action to the crime, and although there was no substantial evidence of any conspiracy or prior arrangement between him and Rowe. . . .

The judgment of the court below is reversed and the cause remanded, with directions to set aside the verdict and award a new trial.

NOTES

1. Variations on Hicks. Consider the responsibility of Hicks for the killing by Rowe in the following hypothetical situations.

(i) Hicks hears that Rowe has set out to kill his old enemy, Colvard, and goes along to enjoy the spectacle.

(ii) Same situation as in (i), except that while watching Rowe's assault on Colvard with satisfaction, Hicks shouts such words of encouragement to Rowe as "Go get him!" and "Attaboy!"

(iii) Same situation as in (i), except that Hicks resolves to make certain Rowe succeeds — by helping him if necessary.

(iv) Same situation as in (iii), except that Hicks tells Rowe on the way that he will help him if it seems necessary.

2. Problem of the agent provocateur. Wilson and Pierce spent an evening drinking together. At one point Wilson discovered his watch missing and accused Pierce of stealing it. Pierce adamantly denied the accusation. The subject of their conversation turned to feats of crime. They decided to burglarize a drugstore. Later that evening Wilson boosted Pierce through a transom. While Pierce was inside, Wilson telephoned the police and returned to receive bottles of whiskey that Pierce handed to him through the transom. When the police arrived Wilson told them that Pierce was inside the store. Pierce escaped through the back door, and Wilson led police to Pierce's hotel room, where he identified Pierce as the burglar. Shortly after Pierce's arrest Wilson told the police that his connection with the burglary was for the purpose of getting even with Pierce for taking his watch, which he hoped in this way to recover. Nevertheless, Wilson was convicted of aiding in the commission of the burglary. On appeal, the defendant contended the trial court committed error in charging:

> One may not participate in the commission of a felony and then obtain immunity from punishment on the ground that he was a mere detective or spy. One who attempts to detect the commission of crime in others must himself stop short of lending assistance, or participation in the commission of the crime.

The Colorado Supreme Court reversed. Wilson v. People, 103 Colo. 441, 87 P.2d 5 (1939). Agreeing that the instruction was erroneous, the court quoted 1 F. Wharton, Criminal Law §271 (12th ed. 1932):

> A detective entering apparently into a criminal conspiracy already formed for the purpose of exploding it is not an accessory before the fact. For it should be remembered that while detectives, when acting as decoys, may apparently provoke the crime, the essential element of dolus, or malicious determination to violate the law, is wanting in their case. And it is only the formal, and not the substantive, part of the crime that they provoke. They provoke, for instance, in larceny, the asportation of the goods, but not the ultimate loss by the owner. They may be actuated by the most unworthy of motives, but the animus furandi in larceny is not imputable to them; and it is in larcenous cases or cheats that they are chiefly employed.

Questions: Can the result in the *Wilson* case be explained on the ground that Wilson lacked the mens rea of burglary (breaking and entry with intent to steal) because he did not intend that Pierce should succeed in stealing the bottles of whiskey? The problem with this reasoning is that even though Wilson did not intend that Pierce should succeed in stealing, he did intend for Pierce to commit the crime of burglary and, in fact, intentionally helped him to do so.

Then how can we account for the result that Wilson is not guilty of the crime he intentionally helped Pierce to commit? Perhaps the following hypothetical will help: Suppose Wilson, in order to secure the conviction of Pierce of attempted murder, gives Pierce a gun with which to kill *X*. Though he assures Pierce the gun is loaded, in fact he deliberately unloaded it before giving it to Pierce. Pierce shoots *X* with the intention of killing him. Pierce is surely guilty of attempted murder. But would Wilson also be guilty of attempted murder, on the ground that he intentionally helped Pierce to commit that crime? How could he be, since he had no intention that *X* should be killed?

3. A variation on these scenarios is where the provocateur induces the defendant to help him, the provocateur, commit the crime. For example, suppose the same facts as in the *Wilson* case, except that Pierce hoisted Wilson through the transom. Wilson would, of course, have the same defense. But how about Pierce? Could he be convicted of being an accomplice to Wilson's "burglary"? These situations are further explored in State v. Hayes and the notes following, infra page 633.

STATE v. GLADSTONE

Supreme Court of Washington
78 Wash. 2d 306, 474 P.2d 274 (1980)

HALE, J. A jury found defendant Bruce Gladstone guilty of aiding and abetting one Robert Kent in the unlawful sale of marijuana. . . .

Gladstone's guilt as an aider and abettor in this case rests solely on evidence of a conversation between him and one Douglas MacArthur Thompson concerning the possible purchase of marijuana from one Robert Kent. There is no other evidence to connect the accused with Kent who ultimately sold some marijuana to Thompson. . . .

[Thompson, Kent, and defendant, Gladstone, were all students at the University of Puget Sound. Thompson was hired by the Tacoma Police Department to attempt a purchase of marijuana from Gladstone. Thompson visited defendant at his home and asked to buy marijuana. Defendant replied that he did not have enough to sell him any but volunteered the name of Kent as someone who did have enough and who was willing to sell. He then gave Thompson Kent's address and, at Thompson's request, drew a map to direct him to Kent's residence. Thompson went there and bought marijuana from Kent. There was no evidence of any communication between defendant and Kent concerning marijuana, but only, the court said, of "a possible accommodation to someone who said he wanted to buy marijuana."]

If all reasonable inferences favorable to the state are accorded the evidence, it does not, in our opinion, establish the commission of the crime charged. That vital element — a nexus between the accused and the party whom he is charged with aiding and abetting in the commission of a crime — is missing. The record contains no evidence whatever that Gladstone had any communication by word, gesture or sign, before or after he drew the map, from which it could be inferred that he counseled, encouraged, hired, commanded, induced or procured Kent to sell marijuana to Douglas Thompson as charged, or took any steps to further the commission of the crime charged. He was not charged with aiding and abetting Thompson in the purchase of marijuana, but with Kent's sale of it. . . .

[E]ven without prior agreement, arrangement or understanding, a bystander to a robbery could be guilty of aiding and abetting its commission if he came to the aid of a robber and knowingly assisted him in perpetrating the crime. But . . . there is no aiding and abetting unless one "'in some sort associate himself with the venture, that he participate in it as in something that he wishes to bring about, that he seek by his action to make it succeed.'" Nye & Nissen v. United States, 336 U.S. 613, 619 (1949).

Gladstone's culpability, if at all, must be brought within R.C.W. 9.01.030, which makes a principal of one who aids and abets another in the commission of the crime. Although an aider and abettor need not be physically present at the commission of the crime to be held guilty as a principal, his conviction depends on proof that he did something in association or connection with the principal to accomplish the crime. Learned Hand, J., we think, hit the nail squarely when, in United States v. Peoni, 100 F.2d 401, 402 (2d Cir. 1938), he wrote that, in order to aid and abet another to commit a crime, it is necessary that a defendant "in some sort associate himself with the venture, that he participate in it as in something that he wishes to bring about, that he seek by his action to make it succeed. All the words used — even the most colorless, "abet" — carry an implication of purposive attitude towards it." . . .

It would be a dangerous precedent indeed to hold that mere communications to the effect that another might or probably would commit a criminal offense amount to an aiding and abetting of the offense should it ultimately be committed.

There being no evidence whatever that the defendant ever communicated to Kent the idea that he would in any way aid him in the sale of any marijuana, or said anything to Kent to encourage or induce him or direct him to do so, or counseled Kent in the sale of marijuana, or did anything more than describe Kent to another person as an individual who might sell some marijuana, or would derive any benefit, consideration or reward from such a sale, there was no proof of an aiding and abetting, and the conviction should, therefore, be reversed as a matter of law. Remanded with directions to dismiss.

HAMILTON, J. (dissenting). . . . I am satisfied that the jury was fully warranted in concluding that appellant, when he affirmatively recommended Kent as a source and purveyor of marijuana, entertained the requisite conscious design and intent that his action would instigate, induce, procure or encourage perpetration of Kent's subsequent crime of selling marijuana to Thompson. . . .

NOTES AND QUESTIONS

1. Questions on Gladstone. The court emphasizes that defendant was "not charged with aiding and abetting Thompson in the purchase of marijuana, but with Kent's sale of it." Could he have been charged and convicted of aiding and abetting Thompson's purchase? What difficulties would be presented? Cf. Model Penal Code §§2.06(3) and 5.01(3). Would the reasoning of the majority, finding the defendant not liable as an aider and abettor of Kent's sale, be equally applicable to preclude his liability as an aider and abettor (or an attempted aider and abettor) of Thompson's purchase? Why should it not? Why should it matter that Thompson asked for and received the aid? Would the defendant's state of mind as to the purchase by Thompson be any different than it was as to the sale by Kent?

2. Model Penal Code and Commentaries, Comment to §2.06 at 315-316 (1985), states the issue as follows:

> [Should] knowingly facilitating the commission of a crime . . . be sufficient for complicity, absent a true purpose to advance the criminal end[?] The problem, to be sure, is narrow in its focus: often, if not usually, aid rendered with guilty knowledge implies purpose since it has no other motivation. But there are many and important cases where this is the central question in determining liability. A lessor rents with knowledge that the premises will be used to establish a bordello. A vendor sells with knowledge that the subject of the sale will be used in the commission

of a crime. A doctor counsels against an abortion during the third trimester but, at the patient's insistence, refers her to a competent abortionist. A utility provides telephone or telegraph service, knowing it is used for bookmaking. An employee puts through a shipment in the course of his employment though he knows the shipment is illegal. A farm boy clears the ground for setting up a still, knowing that the venture is illicit. Such cases can be multiplied indefinitely; they have given courts much difficulty when they have been brought, whether as prosecutions for conspiracy or for the substantive offense involved.

The solution originally proposed by the Model Penal Code was contained in §2.04(3)(b) (Tent. Draft No. 1 1953):

A person is an accomplice of another person in the commission of a crime if . . . acting with knowledge that such other person was committing or had the purpose of committing the crime, he knowingly, substantially facilitated its commission.

In defense of this proposal the Commentary observed (id., Comment at 27-32):

The draft, it is submitted, should not embrace the *Peoni* limitation [referring to Judge Hand's dictum in United States v. Peoni, quoted in *Gladstone,* supra]. Conduct which knowingly facilitates the commission of crimes is by hypothesis a proper object of preventive effort by the penal law, unless, of course, it is affirmatively justifiable. It is important in that effort to safeguard the innocent but the requirement of guilty knowledge adequately serves this end — knowledge both that there is a purpose to commit a crime and that one's own behavior renders aid. There are, however, infinite degrees of aid to be considered. This is the point, we think, at which distinctions should be drawn. Accordingly, when a true purpose to further the crime is lacking, the draft requires that the accessorial behavior substantially facilitate commission of the crime and that it do so to the knowledge of the actor. This qualification provides a basis for discrimination that should satisfy the common sense of justice. A vendor who supplies materials readily available upon the market arguably does not make substantial contribution to commission of the crime since the materials could have as easily been gotten elsewhere.

[W]hen the only interest of the actor is his wish for freedom to forego concern about the criminal purposes of others, though he knowingly facilitates in a substantial measure the achievement of such purposes, it is an interest that, we think, is properly subordinated generally to the larger interest of preventing crime.

The Model Penal Code's 1953 proposals were rejected by the American Law Institute. The Code now requires that the actor have "the purpose of promoting or facilitating" the commission of the crime. Section 2.06(3)(a).

Question: What are the inadequacies, if any, in the reporter's arguments that led to its rejection? Consider Glanville Williams, Criminal Law: The General Part 369-370 (2d ed. 1961):

From the point of view of policy the question is one of some complexity. On the one side are the policy of repressing crime, and the difficulty of distinguishing between the merchant who knowingly assists a crime and the ordinary accessory before the fact. On the other side stand the undesirability of giving too great an extension to the criminal law, and the inconvenience to legitimate trade of requiring a merchant to concern himself with the affairs of his customers. The difficulty is increased by the number of different modes in which the question may arise. The merchant may desire the crime, or he may foresee it as certain if he sells the com-

> modity, or he may foresee it as belonging to one of many degrees of probability. The sale may be completely in the ordinary course of business, or the order may in some way be a special one — as when a tailor makes a suit with secret pockets for poaching or smuggling. The merchant may charge the usual price or an extra price on account of the legal risk. The commodity may be appropriate only to a single crime (as with poison that is consumed only once), or may enable the purchaser to engage in a life of crime. The crime in contemplation may be a serious or a trivial one.

See also George Fletcher, Rethinking Criminal Law 676 (1978):

> From the standpoint of the supplier, the problem of refusing services to known criminals closely resembles the problem of intervening to prevent impending harm. The grocery store, the gas station, the physician, the answering service all provide routine services. Does the business-person have a duty to make an exception just because he or she knows that the purchaser is engaged in illegal activity? That question of duty corresponds to the problem of the motorist who must decide whether to stop his car and render aid to an accident victim. The assumption underlying both fields is that people are entitled to carry on their lives without deviating every time doing so might help a person in distress or hamper the execution of a criminal plan.

The case against imposing liability for knowing aid is made in R. A. Duff, "Can I Help You?" Accessorial Liability and the Intention to Assist, 10 Legal Stud. 167 (1990). See generally Candace Couteau (Comment), The Mental Element for Accomplice Liability, 59 La. L. Rev. 325 (1998).

3. Criminal facilitation. One response to these contending considerations is compromise: Make aid without a true purpose a separate crime with a lesser penalty than the crime aided. New York has pioneered this approach with a new crime called "criminal facilitation."[2] N.Y. Penal Code §115 provides:

> A person is guilty of criminal facilitation in the second degree when, believing it probable that he is rendering aid to a person who intends to commit a crime, he engages in conduct which provides such person with means or opportunity for the commission thereof and which in fact aids such person to commit a felony. Criminal facilitation in the second degree is a class A misdemeanor.[3]

Note that the formula of liability is wider than that originally proposed by the Model Penal Code, which would have required "knowing" aid as a basis of accomplice liability. It is enough under the New York formulation that the aider believes it "probable" that the person aided will commit a crime.

Question: Would the defendant in the *Gladstone* case be guilty of criminal facilitation under the New York statute? See People v. Gordon, 32 N.Y.2d 62, 295 N.E.2d 777 (1973), holding in the negative. Do you agree?

4. In United States v. Fountain, 768 F.2d 790 (7th Cir. 1985), a prison inmate (Gometz) was convicted of aiding and abetting another inmate (Silverstein) to

2. Several jurisdictions have followed New York's lead. Ariz. Rev. Stat. Ann. tit. 13, §13-1004; Ky. Rev. Stat. Ann. §506.080; N.D. Cent. Code §12.1-06-02.

3. Section 115.05 makes such conduct first-degree criminal facilitation when the crime committed is a class A felony (such crimes as murder, for example) and subjects it to punishment as a class C felony (maximum 15 years of imprisonment).

murder a guard. The evidence disclosed that Silverstein, in handcuffs, was being led down the corridor by some guards. When he reached Gometz's cell he thrust his manacled hands through the bars. Gometz came close and pulled up his shirt to reveal a knife in his waistband. Somehow Silverstein got free of the handcuffs, seized the knife, and stabbed the guard with it. Judge Posner held that to convict Gometz it was not necessary to prove that it was Gometz's purpose that Silverstein should kill the guard; it was enough that he knew when he helped Silverstein obtain the knife that Silverstein would use it to attack the guards. In holding that knowledge was enough, the court borrowed the approach of a California conspiracy case (People v. Lauria, reported page 704 infra) that held that *purpose* was required to convict of lesser offenses, but that *knowledge* sufficed to convict of major crimes. Judge Posner stated (id. at 798):

> In People v. Lauria, — not a federal case, but illustrative of the general point — the court, en route to holding that knowledge of the principal's purpose would not suffice for aiding and abetting of just any crime, said it would suffice for "the seller of gasoline who knew the buyer was using his product to make Molotov cocktails for terroristic use." Compare the following hypothetical cases. In the first, a shopkeeper sells dresses to a woman whom he knows to be a prostitute. The shopkeeper would not be guilty of aiding and abetting prostitution unless the prosecution could establish the elements of Judge Hand's test. Little would be gained by imposing criminal liability in such a case. Prostitution, anyway a minor crime, would be but trivially deterred, since the prostitute could easily get her clothes from a shopkeeper ignorant of her occupation. In the second case, a man buys a gun from a gun dealer after telling the dealer that he wants it in order to kill his mother-in-law, and he does kill her. The dealer would be guilty of aiding and abetting the murder. This liability would help to deter — and perhaps not trivially given public regulation of the sale of guns — a most serious crime. We hold that aiding and abetting murder is established by proof beyond a reasonable doubt that the supplier of the murder weapon knew the purpose for which it would be used.

5. The material presented up to this point on the required mens rea of the accomplice as to the principal's criminal action rests on the premise that an actual intention of some kind must exist. This is the Model Penal Code view and represents one strand of authority. There are, however, many cases and statutes that depart from that strict requirement. They are the subject of the material that follows.

PEOPLE v. LUPARELLO

California Court of Appeal, 4th District
187 Cal. App. 3d 410, 231 Cal. Rptr. 832 (1987)

KREMER, J. [Defendant Luparello wanted to locate Terri, his former lover who had deserted him to marry another. He thought he could discover her whereabouts from Mark Martin, a good friend of her current husband. To that end he enlisted the help of several friends, telling them that he wanted the information at any cost. His friends visited Martin but failed to get the information they sought. They returned the next evening armed with gun and sword, but without

Luparello apparently, and lured Martin outside. Thereupon one of their group, waiting in a car, shot and killed Martin. Luparello was charged and convicted of murder.

The trial court charged the jury with several different theories by which Luparello's guilt for first degree murder could be affixed; among these were . . . aiding and abetting. On appeal . . . Luparello . . . attacks the theoretical underpinnings of . . . aiding-and-abetting liability, and specifically argues the murder here was the unplanned and unintended act of a coconspirator and therefore not chargeable to Luparello under complicity theory.

Luparello first faults [the] theor[y] for "imposing" the mens rea of the perpetrator upon him. As Luparello views it, [the] theor[y] work[s] to presume conclusively the accomplice shares the perpetrator's intent. . . . Luparello errs when he concludes the perpetrator and accomplice must "share" an identical intent to be found criminally responsible for the same crime. Technically, only the perpetrator can (and must) manifest the mens rea of the crime committed. Accomplice liability is premised on a different or, more appropriately, an equivalent mens rea. This equivalence is found in intentionally encouraging or assisting or influencing the nefarious act. . . . Thus, to be a principal to a crime . . . the aider and abettor must intend to commit the offense or to encourage or facilitate its commission. Liability is extended to reach the actual crime committed, rather than the planned or "intended" crime, on the policy [that] aiders and abettors should be responsible for the criminal harms they have naturally, probably and foreseeably put in motion. And it is precisely this policy which Luparello next challenges. . . .

The California Supreme Court [stated] in the recent case of People v. Croy, 41 Cal. 3d 1, 710 P.2d 392:

> The requirement that the jury determine the intent with which a person tried as an aider and abettor has acted is not designed to ensure that his conduct constitutes the offense with which he is charged. His liability is vicarious. . . . [H]e is guilty not only of the offense he intended to facilitate or encourage, but also of any reasonably foreseeable offense committed by the person he aids and abets. . . .

Adopting the reasoning of the Supreme Court, we find the . . . aiding and abetting theor[y] proffered here do[es] not suffer the theoretical infirmities of which Luparello complains. In the circumstances of this case, [it] provides a sound basis to derive Luparello's criminal responsibility for first degree murder. . . .

Judgments affirmed.

WIENER, J., concurring:

I concur . . . in the result reached by the majority under the compulsion of . . . People v. Croy (1985) 41 Cal. 3d 1, 12, footnote 5, 710 P.2d 392. [That case] require[s] a holding that an aider and abettor or co-conspirator is liable not only for those crimes committed by a co-felon which he intended or agreed to facilitate but also for any additional crimes which are "reasonably foreseeable."[2] . . .

2. Henceforth I refer to this principle as the "foreseeable consequence" doctrine because that is the terminology used in *Croy.* I am concerned, however, about how a principle which was originally phrased in terms of "probable and natural consequences" was slightly modified to become the "natural and reasonable consequences" and has now been saddled with a monicker traditionally associated with theories of expanding tort liability. If we were to return to strict interpretation of the "natural and probable" standard, I would argue that liability could not be imposed here on Lu-

The fact that the Supreme Court has announced a principle of law certainly requires that as an intermediate appellate court we follow it. This does not mean, however, that the announced principle is either logically consistent or theoretically sound.

. . . The major fallacy I see in the "foreseeable consequence" doctrine is not so much that it attributes an unintended act to the accomplice/co-conspirator but rather that it assesses the degree of his culpability for that act not by his own mental state but rather by the mental state of the perpetrator and/or the circumstances of the crime. The present case provides an appropriate example. The assault on Mark Martin contemplated by the conspiracy involved a foreseeable risk of death or serious injury. We can assume (although there was no jury finding on the issue) that Luparello was criminally negligent in failing to appreciate the degree of risk. Under usual circumstances, a person negligently causing the death of another is guilty, at most, of involuntary manslaughter. Here, however, Luparello's liability is not based on his individual mental state but instead turns on the jury's finding that the unidentified shooter intentionally killed Martin while lying in wait. Thus, Luparello is guilty of first degree murder. If the circumstances of Luparello's participation were exactly the same but the shooter did not "lie in wait," Luparello could only be convicted of second degree murder. I am intrigued by the notion that if unknown to Luparello, the shooter ingested drugs and/or alcohol to the point where he did not in fact harbor the requisite malice, Luparello would presumably be guilty only of voluntary manslaughter. . . . I find such fortuity of result irrational. So too, apparently, do Professors LaFave and Scott in their treatise [Handbook on Criminal Law (1972) p. 516:]

> The "natural and probable consequence" rule of accomplice liability, if viewed as a broad generalization, is inconsistent with more fundamental principles of our system of criminal law. It would permit liability to be predicated upon negligence even when the crime involved requires a different state of mind. Such is not possible as to one who has personally committed a crime, and should likewise not be the case as to those who have given aid or counsel.

[T]he "foreseeable consequence" doctrine [and] the . . . felony-murder rule [are] . . . both founded on the same outmoded and logically indefensible proposition that if a person exhibits some intent to violate the law, we need not be terribly concerned that the contemplated crime was far less serious than the crime which actually took place. . . .

The artificial imputation of stepped-up intent, inherent in both the felony-murder rule and the "foreseeable consequence" doctrine, is inconsistent with the "universal and persistent" notion that criminal punishment must be proportional to the defendant's culpable mental state. Justice Mosk's dissent in Taylor v. Superior Court (1970) 3 Cal. 3d 578, 593, 477 P.2d 131 expressed it well: "Fundamental principles of criminal responsibility dictate that the defendant be subject to a greater penalty only when he has demonstrated a greater degree of culpability." The fact that the accomplice or co-conspirator intended to facilitate

---

parello because in no sense can it be said that Mark Martin's death was the "probable" result of a conspiracy to assault him in order to obtain information.

some less serious criminal act does not render these fundamental principles inapplicable.

ROY v. UNITED STATES, 652 A.2d 1098 (D.C. Ct. App. 1995). [Peppi Miller was a paid police informant who approached defendant Roy in an attempt to make an undercover buy of a hand gun. Roy told him to return later with $400, and when he did so was referred to Ross, who took him to another area. There Ross gave Miller the gun while Miller counted out the $400, but then Ross asked for the gun back, said he changed his mind, and robbed Miller of the $600 in his possession. To Miller's request for an explanation, he replied that he was avenging Miller's earlier stickup of one of his own group. Roy was convicted as an accomplice to Ross's armed robbery. The trial court included an instruction that it would suffice to find defendant liable if the robbery was the natural and probable consequence of the illegal attempt to sell a hand gun, even if he did not intend Ross to rob Miller. At the same time, however, the judge invited a reexamination of the natural and probable consequence rule, stating:] The criminal law is trying . . . in these cases . . . to draw a line to serve two different policies that are . . . inconsistent with each other. On the one hand, there's clearly a policy in the criminal law not to hold people responsible for things that they did not intend to do. . . . On the other hand, there is a competing policy that says, if you put criminal conduct in motion, or you intentionally assist in the commission of a crime, then you are held responsible for the natural and probable consequences of that crime, even if they go beyond what you put in motion. . . . Somewhere between those two things, the law draws a line in what you can be held liable for, and what you can't.

The natural and probable consequence doctrine of aiding and abetting . . . ought to be examined again by our Court of Appeals. . . . An early court borrowed a doctrine that was really an exception applicable in the case of the felony murder doctrine and then grafted it onto the law of aiding and abetting generally, actually borrowed it [also] from the law of conspiracy, and then grafted it onto the law of aiding and abetting as it applies to [any] offense and then repeated it so often that it became self-fulfilling without much analysis in the later cases.

In my opinion this case represents the outer reaches of the permissible use of the doctrine that a person can be criminally liable for an offense which he himself did not intend but which is arguably a natural and probable consequence of an offense which he did intend. . . .

[The Court of Appeals reversed, finding the evidence insufficient to support a conviction on this theory, stating:] By invoking the "natural and probable consequences" theory, the government insists that we sustain Roy's convictions of armed robbery . . . without requiring a showing that Roy intended to participate in the robbery of Miller or in any other crime of violence. Armed robbery is a felony punishable by life imprisonment; selling a handgun, on the other hand, constitutes . . . a misdemeanor of which Roy has been independently convicted. The government's application of the "natural and probable consequences" doctrine would thus dramatically expand Roy's exposure even where . . . he did not intend that a crime of violence be committed.

This court has stated that "an accessory is liable for any criminal act which in the ordinary course of things was the natural and probable consequence of the crime that he advised or commanded, although such consequence may not have been intended by him." . . . The phrase "in the ordinary course of things" refers to what may reasonably ensue from the planned events, not to what might conceivably happen, and in particular suggests the absence of intervening factors. . . . It is not enough for the prosecution to show that the accomplice knew or should have known that the principal might conceivably commit the offense which the accomplice is charged with aiding and abetting. Without inserting additional phrases or adjectives into the calculus, we think that our precedents require the government to prove a good deal more than that. A "natural and probable" consequence in the "ordinary course of things" presupposes an outcome within a reasonably predictable range. . . .

The government contends that the armed robbery of Miller was in furtherance of the common purpose because it resulted in the defendants' obtaining Miller's money — an achievement which, according to the government, was the defendant's prime design and plan in the first place. In our view, however, an exchange of a handgun for $400 is qualitatively different from an armed robbery in which Ross stole $600 and retained for himself the object which, in Roy's contemplation, was supposed to be sold. . . . The government [also] argues that Peppi Miller was a logical target of a robbery because, "given the illegal nature of the activity in which he was involved, [he] was unlikely to file a complaint with the police about the robbery." This reasoning, however, recognizes no apparent limiting principle. If we were to accept the government's position, then the robbery of any buyer or seller in a drug or unlicensed pistol sale would be viewed as the "natural and probable consequence" of that transaction, for a participant in any illegal project may well be reluctant to invoke the aid of the constabulary. . . .

No impartial jury could rationally conclude, beyond a reasonable doubt, that Roy "cross[ed] a moral divide by setting out on a project involving either the certain or contingent" commission of a robbery. Viewed in the light most favorable to the prosecution, the evidence would perhaps support a finding that Roy should have known that it was conceivable that Ross might rob Miller. The evidence was insufficient, however, to show that a robbery would follow in the "ordinary course of events," or that it was a "natural and probable consequence" of the activities in which Roy was shown to have engaged. We must therefore reverse for evidentiary insufficiency Roy's conviction for armed robbery.

PROBLEM

Where defendant's partner in an illegal drug sale is found to possess a firearm while making the sale (thereby raising the punishment for the drug sale) may defendant be held liable as an accomplice under the natural and probable consequences doctrine? Some courts have held that to be held as an accomplice for the possession charge the defendant must know at the outset of the crime, at least to "a practical certainty," that his confederate was carrying a gun. United States v. Powell, 929 F.2d 724 (D.C. Cir. 1991); United States v. Morrow, 923 F.2d 427 (6th Cir. 1991). Other courts have disagreed. In United States v. Johnson, 886 F.2d 1120 (9th Cir. 1989) the court justified liability on the common understanding that the "drug industry . . . is a dangerous, violent business" making the defendant guilty as an accomplice so long as he "could have reasonably foreseen" that the principal would carry a weapon. Which view is more persuasive?

NOTES AND QUESTIONS

1. State of the law: The natural and probable consequences test used in the *Luparello* case is widely applied, but it is controversial, as may be inferred from the opinions in the *Roy* case. Some courts reject it. For example, in State v. Marr, 342 N.C. 607, 467 S.E.2d 236 (1996), defendant arranged for two others to break into the victim's trailer and steal tools. The others did so but in the course of their burglary they shot the victim and burned down his trailer. The defendant was convicted of several crimes, including arson and armed robbery, under an instruction that an accomplice "is responsible for all of the incidental consequences which might be reasonably expected to result, from the intended wrong." The court reversed these convictions and upheld only those convictions that "were within the area which the defendant procured, counseled, commanded, or encouraged." Id. at 239-240. For a description of the various approaches in American jurisdictions, see Note (Grace Muller), The Mens Rea of Accomplice Liability, 61 So. Cal. L. Rev. 2169 (1988); Robert Batey, Book Review, 73 Notre Dame L. Rev. 781, 790 (1998).

2. Model Penal Code: The Model Penal Code lent its support to the view that purpose is a requirement for accomplice liability. Model Penal Code and Commentaries, Comment to §2.06 at 310-313 (1985) state:

> Subsection (3)(a) requires that the actor have the purpose of promoting or facilitating the commission of the offense. . . . This does not mean, of course, that the precise means used in the commission of the crime must have been fixed or contemplated or, when they have been, that liability is limited to their employment. One who solicits an end, or aids or agrees to aid in its achievement, is an accomplice in whatever means may be employed, insofar as they constitute an offense fairly envisaged in the purposes of the association. But when a wholly different crime has been committed, thus involving conduct not within the conscious objectives of the accomplice, he is not liable for it. . . . Whatever may have been the law on the point, . . . it is submitted that the liability of an accomplice ought not to be extended beyond the purposes that he shares. Probabilities have an important evidential bearing on these issues; to make them independently sufficient is to predicate the liability on negligence when, for good reason, more is normally required before liability is found.

3. In Regina v. Hyde, [1991] 1 Q.B. 134, three defendants beat and kicked the victim, but one of them, who it could not be established, crushed his skull with a heavy stick. The Court of Appeal upheld a conviction of all three of murder, approving a jury instruction that any of the three who foresaw as a real possibility that one of the others would murder the victim could be found guilty of murder. This represents what has come to be called the "joint enterprise" theory of accomplice liability, an English version of the American natural and probable consequence test. See Regina v. Powell, [1997] 4 All E.R. (H.L. 1997). Professor John C. Smith has defended this theory. Commentary, [1991] Crim. L. Rev. 134. Though recognizing that the secondary party is made liable to conviction for murder despite the fact that he is only reckless, he argues:

> there is a difference between (i) recklessness whether death be caused (which is sufficient for manslaughter but not for murder) and (ii) recklessness whether

> murder be committed. The accessory's recklessness must extend to the principal's mens rea of murder. The person who embarks on a joint enterprise knowing that his confederate may intentionally kill is taking a deliberate risk of assisting or encouraging not merely killing but murder.

Questions: How convincing is the distinction in culpability between the person who recklessly risks killing another and the person who recklessly risks that another will kill intentionally? They both risk the same result (the death of another) and assuming the degree of risk to be the same, why isn't their culpability the same? One might argue that because it is a worse thing that a person is murdered than killed recklessly, it is worse to risk the former than the latter, even when the risk to life is identical. Even so, is the person who risks that another will kill just as bad as the person who intentionally kills? After all, the fault of the accomplice is recklessness. This is sufficient for manslaughter, but what makes it sufficient for murder? Is it that he and the principal are already engaged in some criminal action? Compare the felony murder doctrine. See the discussion in C. M. V. Clarkson, Complicity, Powell and Manslaughter, [1998] Crim. L. Rev. 556.

b. Attendant Circumstances

UNITED STATES v. XAVIER

United States Court of Appeals, Third Circuit
2 F.3d 1281 (1993)

Scirica, Circuit Judge. [Franklin and Clement Xavier, two brothers, discovered one of their enemies, Alton Pennyfeather, seated in a car outside a grocery store. Clement instructed his brother to wait inside the store until he returned. He left in his truck and returned a few minutes later with an unidentified man who handed Franklin a .38 caliber pistol. Franklin then shot at the car in which Pennyfeather was sitting. This appeal involved the conviction of Clement of several crimes, including, as Count VI, aiding and abetting an ex-felon's (that is, Franklin's) possession of a firearm.]

Defendant contends he was wrongfully convicted for aiding and abetting possession of a firearm by a convicted felon. 18 U.S.C. §§2(a), 922(g)(1). He claims the government never proved his knowledge of Franklin Xavier's conviction, which, he asserts, is an essential element of the crime. The government concedes "proof of knowledge (or reasonable cause to believe) of an ex-felon's status is a required element for conviction, as an aider and abettor, under Section 922(g)(1)." We agree.

Section 922(g) proscribes possession of a firearm by anyone "(1) who has been convicted in any court of a crime punishable by imprisonment for a term exceeding one year. . . ." We have recognized §922(g) is not a specific intent statute. But criminal liability for aiding and abetting a §922(g) violation stands on a different footing because it depends on the status of the person possessing the firearm. Congress addressed this exact situation in §922(d). That statute provides: "It shall be unlawful for any person to sell or otherwise dispose of any firearm to any person knowing or having cause to believe that such person — (1) is under indictment for, or has been convicted in any court of, a crime punishable by imprisonment for a term exceeding one year. . . ." As the text of the statute indicates, one cannot be criminally liable under §922(d) without knowledge or reason to know of the transferee's status. See United States v. Murray, 988 F.2d 518, 522 (5th Cir. 1993) ("[I]t is the purchaser's status as a felon which makes the activity criminal. If the aider and abettor does not know this fact, it is difficult to say he shared in the criminal intent of the principal.").

Defendant was convicted as an aider and abettor under §922(g) for precisely the activity proscribed in §922(d) — providing a firearm to a convicted felon. Allowing aider and abettor liability under §922(g)(1), without requiring proof of knowledge or reason to know of the possessor's status, would effectively circumvent the knowledge element in §922(d)(1) and, as the government concedes in its brief, "would abrogate congressional intent." Therefore, we hold there can be no criminal liability for aiding and abetting a violation of §922(g)(1) without knowledge or having cause to believe the possessor's status as a felon. Unless there is evidence a defendant knew or had cause to believe he was aiding and abetting possession by a convicted felon, it has not shown a "guilty mind" under 18 U.S.C. §2(a).

[Conviction on Count VI reversed.]

NOTES

1. *Question.* Should the *Xavier* case have come out the same way even if Congress had not addressed the exact situation in §922(d)? Should a court need explicit legislative instruction not to convict a person who innocently assists another to commit a strict liability offense? Some courts have thought not. Compare Giorgianni v. The Queen, 156 C.L.R. 473 (High Ct. Austr. 1985) ("[N]o one may be convicted of aiding, abetting, counseling or procuring the commission of an offense unless, knowing all the essential facts which made what was done a crime, he intentionally aided, abetted, counseled or procured the acts of the principal offender."); Johnson v. Youden, [1950] 1 K.B. 544 (reversing conviction for aiding and abetting a strict liability offense the court held that: "Before a person can be convicted of aiding and abetting the commission of an offence, he must at least know the essential matters which constitute that offence.").

2. *The Model Penal Code's waffle.* As we saw, the Model Penal Code takes the position that for complicity liability, purpose (as distinguished from mere knowledge) is required as to the "commission of the offense." §2.06(3)(a). But does this mens rea requirement apply to the *attendant-circumstance* elements of the contemplated offense? The Comment states (Model Penal Code and Commentaries, Comment to §2.06 at page 311 n. 37 (1985)):

> There is deliberate ambiguity as to whether the purpose requirement extends to circumstance elements of the contemplated offense or whether, as in the case of attempts, the policy of the substantive offense on this point should control. The result, therefore, is that the actor must have a purpose with respect to the proscribed conduct, with his attitude towards the circumstances to be left to resolution by the courts. . . .

How should the courts resolve this issue? Consider this hypothetical: *A* encourages *B* to have sexual relations with a female who is underage. If the crime of statutory rape only requires that the primary actor be negligent as to her age, is the secondary actor liable as an accomplice if he too was negligent as to her age, or must he have *known* she was underage? If the state imposes strict liability as to the age of the female for the principal, should that suffice for the accomplice?

Recall that where a defendant is charged with an *attempt* to commit some crime the Model Penal Code holds that the mens rea of the substantive crime governs the liability of the defendant. So, in the hypothetical given, supra page 563, the person who tries but fails to have sex with an underage female would be guilty of attempted statutory rape even if the defendant had no grounds to suspect she might be underage. Why doesn't the Model Penal Code take the same position in the case of complicity? What might have led to their greater caution in this case?

c. Results

STATE v. McVAY

Supreme Court of Rhode Island
47 R.I. 292, 132 A. 436 (1926)

BARROWS, J. Heard on a certification of a question of law before trial. Three indictments for manslaughter, each containing four counts, were brought against the captain and engineer of the steamer Mackinac, as principals, and against Kelley, as accessory before the fact. The steamer carried several hundred passengers from Pawtucket to Newport via Narragansett Bay. The boiler producing the steam by which the vessel was propelled burst near Newport and many lives were lost. The present indictments are for causing the deaths of three persons killed by escaping steam after the explosion of the boiler. . . .

The same question is raised upon each indictment. That question is:

> May a defendant be indicted and convicted of being an accessory before the fact to the crime of manslaughter arising through criminal negligence as set forth in the indictment?

. . . The charge against Kelley as accessory is that "before said felony and manslaughter was committed," he did, at Pawtucket, "feloniously and maliciously aid, assist, abet, counsel, hire, command and procure the said George W. McVay and John A. Grant [the captain and engineer, respectively], the said felony and manslaughter in manner and form aforesaid to do and commit." . . .

Kelley

Because the manslaughter charge is "without malice" and "involuntary," Kelley contends that he cannot be indicted legally as an accessory before the fact. The argument is that manslaughter, being a sudden and unpremeditated crime, inadvertent and unintentional by its very nature, cannot be "maliciously" incited before the crime is committed. . . .

While every one must agree that there can be no accessory before the fact when a killing results from a sudden and unpremeditated blow, we do not think it can be broadly stated that premeditation is inconsistent with every charge of manslaughter. Manslaughter may consist, among other things, of doing an unlawful act resulting in unintentional killing, such as violation of motor vehicle laws or administration of drugs to procure an abortion. Manslaughter is likewise committed if an unintentional killing is occasioned by gross negligence in the doing of an act lawful in itself. There is no inherent reason why, prior to the commission of such a crime, one may not aid, abet, counsel, command, or procure the doing of the unlawful act or of the lawful act in a negligent manner. A premeditated act may be involved in such unlawful homicides.

[T]he present indictment for involuntary manslaughter is not self-contradictory when it charges Kelley to be an accessory before the fact. It was possible for him at Pawtucket to intentionally direct and counsel the grossly negligent act which the indictment charges resulted in the crime. Involuntary manslaughter, as set forth in this indictment, means that defendants exercised no conscious volition to take life, but their negligence was of such a character that criminal intention can be presumed. The crime was consummated when the explosion occurred. The volition of the principals was exercised when they chose negligently to create steam which the boiler could not carry. The doing of the act charged or failure to perform the duty charged was voluntary and intentional in the sense that defendants exercised a choice among courses of conduct. It is obvious that Kelley could participate and is charged with participating in procuring defendants to act in a grossly negligent manner prior to the explosion. . . . Specific duties are stated to have been laid upon the captain and engineer. Defendant is charged with full knowledge of those duties and of the fact that the boiler was unsafe. He is charged with counseling and procuring the principals at Pawtucket to disregard their duties and negligently create steam. . . . The facts set forth in these indictments, if existent, are such that a jury might find that defendant Kelley, with full knowledge of the possible danger to human life, recklessly and willfully advised, counseled, and commanded the captain and engineer to take a chance by negligent action or failure to act.

We therefore answer the question certified on each indictment in the affirmative. . . .

PEOPLE v. RUSSELL

91 N.Y.2d 280, 693 N.E.2d 193 (1998)
Court of Appeals of New York

Chief Judge Kaye. Shortly before noon on December 17, 1992 [the three defendants] engaged in a gun battle . . . on Centre Mall of the Red Hook Housing Project in Brooklyn. During the course of the battle, Patrick Daly, a public school principal looking for a child who had left school, was fatally wounded by a single stray nine millimeter bullet that struck him in the chest. [Defendants] were all charged with second degree murder. . . . Although ballistics tests were inconclusive in determining which defendant actually fired the bullet that killed Daly, the theory of the prosecution was that each of [the defendants] acted with the mental culpability required for commission of the crime, and that each "intentionally aided" the defendant who fired the fatal shot (Penal Law §20.00). [The jury] convicted defendants of second degree, depraved indifference murder (Penal Law §125.25 [2]).

On appeal, each defendant challenges the sufficiency of the evidence. Because the evidence, viewed in the light most favorable to the prosecution, could have led a rational trier of fact to find, beyond a reasonable doubt, that each defendant was guilty of depraved indifference murder as charged, we affirm the order of the Appellate Division sustaining all three convictions.

A depraved indifference murder conviction requires proof that defendant, under circumstances evincing a depraved indifference to human life, recklessly engaged in conduct creating a grave risk of death to another person, and thereby caused the death of another person (Penal Law §125.25 [2]). . . .

Although defendants underscore that only one bullet killed Patrick Daly and it is uncertain which of them fired that bullet, the prosecution was not required to prove which defendant fired the fatal shot when the evidence was sufficient to establish that each defendant acted with the mental culpability required for the commission of depraved indifference murder, and each defendant "intentionally aided" the defendant who fired the fatal shot. Defendants urge, however, that the evidence adduced at trial did not support a finding that they — as adversaries in a deadly gun battle — shared the "community of purpose" necessary for accomplice liability. We disagree. The fact that defendants set out to injure or kill one another does not rationally preclude a finding that they intentionally aided each other to engage in the mutual combat that caused Daly's death.

People v. Abbott (84 A.D.2d 11, 445 N.Y.S.2d 344 [1981]) provides an apt illustration. That case involved two defendants — Abbott and Moon — who were engaged in a "drag race" on a residential street when Abbott lost control and smashed into another automobile, killing the driver and two passengers. Both defendants were convicted of criminally negligent homicide, but Moon asserted that he was not responsible for Abbott's actions and that his conviction should be set aside. Rejecting this argument, the court found that, although Moon did not strike the victim's car and was Abbott's adversary in a competitive race, he intentionally participated with Abbott in an inherently dangerous and unlawful activity and therefore shared Abbott's culpability. Moon's "conduct made the race possible" in the first place, as there would not have been a race had Moon not "accepted Abbott's challenge."

In the present case, the jurors were instructed: "If you find that the People have proven beyond a reasonable doubt that defendants took up each other's challenge, shared in the venture and unjustifiably, voluntarily and jointly created a zone of danger, then each is responsible for his own acts and the acts of the others . . . [and] it makes no difference [whose bullet] penetrated Mr. Daly and caused his death."

[T]here was adequate proof to justify the finding that the three defendants tacitly agreed to engage in the gun battle that placed the life of any innocent bystander at grave risk and ultimately killed Daly. Indeed, unlike an unanticipated ambush or spontaneous attack that might have taken defendants by surprise, the gunfight in this case only began after defendants acknowledged and accepted each other's challenge to engage in a deadly battle on a public concourse. . . .

The evidence adduced at trial was also sufficient for the jury to determine that all three defendants acted with the mental culpability required for depraved indifference murder, and that they intentionally aided and encouraged each other to create the lethal crossfire that caused the death of Patrick Daly.

[A]ffirmed.

NOTES

1. Model Penal Code. §2.06(3) provides that one who aids or solicits another person to commit an offense is an accomplice of that person only if he or she acts "with the purpose of promoting or facilitating the commission of the offense." Subsection 4, however, provides:

> When causing a particular result is an element of an offense, an accomplice in the conduct causing such result is an accomplice in the commission of the offense, if he acts with the kind of culpability, if any, with respect to that result that is sufficient for the commission of the offense.

Questions: What does it mean to be "an accomplice in the conduct" causing the result? The concept is not explicitly defined. How would this provision resolve the issues in the *McVay, Abbott,* and *Russell* cases? In *McVay* it seems that Kelley should be regarded as an accomplice in the conduct of the captain and the engineer because, knowing the dangerous condition of the boiler, he intentionally ordered them to fire the boilers, the very reckless act that directly caused the explosion and the deaths. Is it equally clear in *Abbott* that the concept would apply? Did participating in the race make Moon an accomplice in Abbott's conduct of crashing into the victim's car? Did Moon intend that Abbott should drive through the intersection in the manner he did? Or rather was he reckless as to the possibility that he would drive in that manner? And how about *Russell?* Did participating in the public shootout make Russell an accomplice in the conduct of whoever it was whose shot killed the victim?

2. Russell and *Abbott* revisit the drag race problem, which we considered in the Causation section in connection with Commonwealth v. Root, supra page 545, and State v. McFadden, supra page 548. While those cases dealt with the liability of the defendants in terms of causation, *Russell* and *Abbott* deal with it in terms of complicity; that is, not whether the defendants personally caused the deaths, but whether they are accomplices of those who did. Which of these doctrinal approaches is the more satisfactory? In Daniel B. Yeager, Dangerous Games and the Criminal Law, 16 Crim. Just. Ethics 3 (Winter/Spring 1997), Professor Yeager makes a case for the inapplicability of either of these doctrines to game-playing situations like *Abbott* (the drag race case) where the conduct of two persons is analytically required by the definition of the crime.

PROBLEM

In State v. Ayers, 478 N.W.2d 606 (Iowa 1991), the Iowa Supreme Court reversed an involuntary manslaughter conviction arising out of the defendant's sale of a hand gun to a 16-year-old who did not possess a hand gun permit. Shortly after purchasing the gun, the minor showed it off at a party with some friends, one of whom pushed his arm, resulting in the discharge of the gun and the death of one of his friends. Defendant was not present and not involved with the party. Reversing his conviction, the court stated:

> It is not enough that Ayers' conduct was outrageous and criminal. [W]here the criminal liability arises from the act of another, it must appear that the act was done

in furtherance of the common design, or in prosecution of the common purpose for which the parties were assembled or combined together.

Two years later, in State v. Travis, 497 N.W.2d 905 (Iowa App. 1993), the Iowa Court of Appeals reviewed an involuntary manslaughter conviction arising out of the following situation. Travis, though aware that his motorcycle was defective and that there were children playing in the area, drove the motorcycle around in a reckless manner, with his 15-year-old friend, Engler, on the back pillion. Thereafter, though aware that Engler had no experience driving motorcycles, Travis offered to permit him to drive. He gave Engler some basic instructions — where the brakes and accelerator were, how to shift gears — and then sat on the pillion behind his young friend while the latter drove. Although it was almost dark, the headlights were not on. They did not see the victim, a 6-year-old child, until they were 4 feet away from her. "Engler did not attempt to swerve or brake and testified Travis did not instruct him likewise. The motorcycle hit [the child], sending her approximately seventy feet and killing her." Engler pleaded guilty to involuntary manslaughter, and Travis was convicted by a jury as an aider and abettor in involuntary manslaughter. The court affirmed, stating (id. at 909):

> To support a conviction on a theory of aiding and abetting, the record must contain substantial evidence to show the defendant assented to or lent countenance and approval to the criminal act either by an act of participation in it or in some manner encouraging it prior to or at the time of commission.
>
> Although the defendant's mere presence is insufficient to support a conviction on a theory of aiding and abetting, the requisite participation can be inferred from circumstantial evidence including presence, companionship and conduct before and after the offense is committed.
>
> Travis did not merely assent to Engler's driving his motorcycle, he initiated it. While riding as passenger, he failed to provide sufficient instruction; nor did he tell Engler to slow down or drive with caution. In addition, while Travis was earlier driving the vehicle and Engler accompanied him as a passenger, he role-modeled driving the vehicle in a reckless manner. We find the evidence of Travis's conduct sufficient to support the charge of aiding and abetting.

The court distinguished *Ayers* on the grounds that Ayers was nowhere near the accident at the time it occurred (absence of "proximity to harm," the court stated) and that Ayers had no subsequent involvement with the the principal after he sold him the gun.

QUESTIONS

1. Is *Travis* governed by the same principle that governed the conviction of Kelley in State v. McVay, supra page 623? Could it be said of Travis, as it was of Kelley, that he "intentionally direct[ed] and counsel[ed] the grossly negligent act which the indictment charges resulted in the crime"?

2. Is *Ayers* properly distinguishable from *Travis*? Why should it make any difference that Ayers was not present at the party when the gun went off? Should the case have been decided differently if he had been present? Should *Travis* have come out differently if, instead of riding on the back pillion of the motorcycle, he went off somewhere? In State v. McVay should the court have held that

Kelley was not liable as an aider and abettor because he was in port at Pawtucket when the ship's boiler exploded at sea en route to Newport?

2. *Actus Reus*

WILCOX v. JEFFERY

King's Bench Division
[1951] 1 All E.R. 464

LORD GODDARD, C.J. This is a Case stated by the metropolitan magistrate at Bow Street Magistrate's Court before whom the appellant, Herbert William Wilcox, the proprietor of a periodical called "Jazz Illustrated," was charged on an information that

> on Dec. 11, 1949, he did unlawfully aid and abet one Coleman Hawkins in contravening art. 1(4) of the Aliens Order, 1920, by failing to comply with a condition attached to a grant of leave to land, to wit, that the said Coleman Hawkins should take no employment paid or unpaid while in the United Kingdom, contrary to art. 18(2) of the Aliens Order, 1920. . . .

The case is concerned with the visit of a celebrated professor of the saxophone, a gentleman by the name of Hawkins who was a citizen of the United States. He came here at the invitation of two gentlemen of the name of Curtis and Hughes, connected with a jazz club which enlivens the neighborhood of Willesden. . . . Mr. Hawkins . . . arrived with four French musicians. When they came to the airport, among the people who were there to greet them was the appellant. He had not arranged their visit, but he knew they were coming and he was there to report the arrival of these important musicians for his magazine. So, evidently, he was regarding the visit of Mr. Hawkins as a matter which would be of interest to himself and the magazine which he was editing and selling for profit. Messrs. Curtis and Hughes arranged a concert at the Princes Theatre, London. The appellant attended that concert as a spectator. He paid for his ticket. Mr. Hawkins went on the stage and delighted the audience by playing the saxophone. The appellant did not get up and protest in the name of the musicians of England that Mr. Hawkins ought not to be here competing with them and taking the bread out of their mouths or the wind out of their instruments. It is not found that he actually applauded, but he was there having paid to go in, and, no doubt, enjoying the performance, and then, lo and behold out comes his magazine with a most laudatory description, fully illustrated, of this concert. On those facts the magistrate has found that he aided and abetted.

Reliance is placed by the prosecution on R. v. Coney ((1882), 8 Q.B.D. 534) which dealt with a prize fight. This case relates to a jazz band concert, but the particular nature of the entertainment provided, whether by fighting with bare fists or playing on saxophones, does not seem to me to make any difference to the question which we have to decide. The fact is that a man is charged with aiding and abetting an illegal act, and I can find no authority for saying that it matters what that illegal act is, provided that the aider and abettor knows the facts sufficiently well to know that they would constitute an offence in the principal. In R. v. Coney the prize fight took place in the neighborhood of Ascot, and four or five men were convicted of aiding and abetting the fight. The conviction was quashed on the ground that the chairman had not given a correct direction to the jury when he told them that, as the prisoners were physically present at the fight, they must be held to have aided and abetted. That direction, the court held, was wrong, it being too wide. The matter was very concisely put by Cave, J., whose judgment was fully concurred in by that great master of the criminal law, Stephen, J. Cave, J., said (8 Q.B.D. 540): "Where presence may be entirely accidental, it is not even evidence of aiding and abetting. Where presence is prima facie not accidental it is evidence, but no more than evidence, for the jury."

There was not accidental presence in this case. The appellant paid to go to the concert and he went there because he wanted to report it. He must, therefore, be held to have been present, taking part, concurring, or encouraging, whichever word you like to use for expressing this conception. It was an illegal act on the part of Hawkins to play the saxophone or any other instrument at this concert. The appellant clearly knew that it was an unlawful act for him to play. He had gone there to hear him, and his presence and his payment to go there was an encouragement. He went there to make use of the performance, because he went there, as the magistrate finds and was justified in finding, to get "copy" for his newspaper. It might have been entirely different, as I say, if he had gone there and protested, saying: "The musicians' union do not like you foreigners coming here and playing and you ought to get off the stage." If he had booed, it might have been some evidence that he was not aiding and abetting. If he had gone as a member of a claque to try to drown the noise of the saxophone, he might very likely be found not guilty of aiding and abetting. In this case it seems clear that he was there, not only to approve and encourage what was done, but to take advantage of it by getting "copy" for his paper. In those circumstances there was evidence on which the magistrate could find that the appellant aided and abetted, and for these reasons I am of opinion that the appeal fails. . . .

Appeal dismissed with costs.

STATE ex rel. ATTORNEY GENERAL v. TALLY, JUDGE, 102 Ala. 25, 69, 15 So. 722, 739 (1894): [On an impeachment proceeding against Judge Tally, it was established as follows: Ross had seduced Judge Tally's sister-in-law. Her brothers, the Skeltons, followed Ross to the nearby town of Stevenson, in order to kill him. Judge Tally went to the local telegraph office at Scottsboro and while there learned that one of Ross's relatives had sent Ross a telegram warning, "Four men on horseback with guns following. Look out." Judge Tally then sent his own telegram to the telegraph operator at Stevenson (whom he knew), telling him not to deliver the warning telegram to Ross. The operator received both telegrams and failed to deliver the message to Ross. The Skelton brothers caught up with Ross and killed him. On these facts, the court held that the judge was an accomplice of the Skelton brothers in the killing:]

We are therefore clear to the conclusion that before Judge Tally can be found guilty of aiding and abetting the Skeltons to kill Ross, it must appear that his vigil at Scottsboro to prevent Ross from being warned of his danger was by preconcert with them, or at least known to them, whereby they would naturally be incited, encouraged and emboldened, "given confidence" to the deed, or that he aided them to kill Ross, contributed to Ross's death in point of physical fact by means of the telegram he sent to Huddleston [the telegraph operator.] . . .

The assistance given, however, need not contribute to the criminal result in the sense that but for it the result would not have ensued. It is quite sufficient if it facilitated a result that would have transpired without it. It is quite enough if the aid merely renders it easier for the principal actor to accomplish the end intended by him and the aider and abettor, though in all human probability the end would have been attained without it. If the aid in homicide can be shown to have put the deceased at a disadvantage, to have deprived him of a single chance of life, which but for it he would have had, he who furnishes such aid is guilty though it can not be known or shown that the dead man, in the absence thereof, would have availed himself of that chance. As where one counsels murder he is guilty as an accessory before the fact, though it appears to be probable that murder would have been done without his counsel, and as where one being present by concert to aid if necessary is guilty as a principal in the second degree, though had he been absent murder would have been committed, so where he who facilitates murder, even by so much as destroying a single chance of life the assailed might otherwise have had, he thereby supplements the efforts of the perpetrator, and he is guilty as principal in the second degree at common law, and is principal in the first degree under our statute, notwithstanding it may be found that in all human probability the chance would not have been availed of, and death would have resulted anyway.

PROBLEMS ON THE MATERIALITY OF THE AID OR ENCOURAGEMENT GIVEN

1. Causation and complicity. Consider the contrast between causation and accessorial liability. In both kinds of liability, the issue is whether the defendant is liable for an event that takes place through intermediate occurrences. For the defendant to be held to have caused the event, the prosecution must establish — as a minimum — that, but for the defendant's action, the event would not have occurred. On the other hand, for the defendant to be held accessorially liable for an event through the intermediate action of another person, as the *Tally* case and Wilcox v. Jeffery make clear, it is not necessary to establish a but-for relation between the defendant's action and the criminal conduct of another. Even if the same result might have occurred without the defendant's contribution, he can be liable as an accomplice if he acted with the required mens rea.

How should we account for this difference between causation and accessorial liability? For a possible explanation, see Sanford H. Kadish, A Theory of Complicity, excerpted supra page 606.

2. Attempted complicity? We just noted that even a minimal possibility of actual aid or encouragement suffices for accessorial liability. *Question:* Need there be any actual aid or encouragement at all? Consider these variations on cases we have just read.

In *Hicks,* suppose the defendant deliberately shouted encouragement to Rowe to spur him on to kill Colvard, but it is shown at the trial that Rowe was completely deaf and was, moreover, totally unaware of Hicks's presence.

In *Tally,* what would have been the result:

(a) if the telegraph operator had disregarded the judge's instructions and had tried, though in vain, to deliver the warning telegram?

(b) if the telegraph operator followed the judge's instructions and did not deliver the warning, but the pursuers never succeeded in catching up with their intended victim?
(c) if the pursuers did catch up, but were effectively resisted by their victim?

In the *Hicks* and the first *Tally* hypothetical, there is attempted encouragement or aid to the person who commits the crime, but none in fact rendered. What should be the liability of the defendants? Under the law before the Model Penal Code, there would be no liability. See J. C. Smith, Aid, Abet, Counsel or Procure, in Reshaping the Criminal Law 132-133 (P. R. Glazebrook ed. 1978): "An attempt to counsel . . . does not amount to counselling. Advice or encouragement proffered at the scene of the crime but not communicated to the mind of the principal offender does not amount to aiding and abetting."

These difficulties are avoided by the Model Penal Code, §2.06(3), and the jurisdictions that follow its lead.[4] Defendants in the first and third of the above *Tally* hypotheticals would be accomplices because a person acting with the required mens rea is an accomplice whether the person aids or "attempts to aid" another person in planning or committing the offense. Moreover, §2.06(3)(a)(i) makes solicitation the basis for accomplice liability, and §5.02(2) provides that solicitation is established even if the actor fails to communicate with the person he solicits to commit the crime. In support of its position the Comment to the Model Penal Code observes (Model Penal Code and Commentaries, Comment to §2.06 at 314 (1985)):

> The inclusion of attempts to aid may go in part beyond present law, but attempted complicity ought to be criminal, and to distinguish it from effective complicity appears unnecessary where the crime has been committed. Where complicity is based upon agreement or solicitation, one does not ask for evidence that they were actually operative psychologically on the person who committed the offense; there ought to be no difference in the case of aid.

Note the difficulty introduced in the second *Tally* hypothetical. Here the crime the defendant tried to aid is not committed. Does §2.06(3) cover the situation? How should it be dealt with? As an attempt to be an accomplice (by attempting to aid in the commission of a crime)? The Model Penal Code solution to this problem is sketched in the Comment to §2.06 supra, at 314 n. 46:

> Section 2.06(3) of the Model Code is predicated . . . on the actual commission of an offense by the person aided. Assuming the requisite culpability, one who aids, or attempts to aid, or agrees to aid, is thus liable under this section only if the principal actor actually commits an offense. If the principal actor completes the offense, then a charge for the substantive crime can be made against both him and the accomplice; if the principal actor attempts to commit the offense, then again both may be charged with the attempt.
>
> Where the principal actor commits neither the completed offense nor an attempt, however, a different situation is presented. The purported accomplice in that situation would not be liable under Section 2.06 because he did not aid in the

4. See, e.g., Ky. Rev. Stat. Ann. ch. 500, §502.020; N.J. Stat. Ann. §2C:2-6(c); 18 Pa. Cons. Stat. Ann. §306(c); Tex. Pen. Code Ann. §7.02.

commission of a crime. His conduct designed to render aid may be criminal, however, either as an attempt (Section 5.01(3)) or, in the case of preconcert, as criminal conspiracy (Section 5.03(1)(b)). In both situations liability for the abortive effort plainly seems appropriate.

3. Complicity by omission. Can a person become an accomplice by failing to act to prevent another from committing a crime? Consistent with the general approach to determining criminal liability for omissions, the Model Penal Code provides that a person can be an accomplice if he has a legal duty to prevent the offense and he fails to do so with the purpose of promoting or facilitating the crime. §2.06(3)(a)(iii). In support of its position the commentary states (p. 320):

> The policeman or the watchman who closes his eyes to a burglary fails to present an obstacle to its commission that he is obliged to interpose. If his purpose is to promote or facilitate its perpetration, a fact that normally can be proved only by preconcert with the criminals, no reason can be offered for denying his complicity. But if the dereliction is not purposeful in that respect, as when it rests upon timidity or inefficiency, it is unduly harsh to view it as participation in the crime.

In what kinds of situations might complicity by omission be found in the absence of preconcert? Consider State v. Davis, 182 W. Va. 482, 388 S.E.2d 506 (1989). The victim, a friend of the Davis family, went to defendant's home to pick up her laundry. When defendant's son attempted to drag her into his bedroom, the victim pleaded with defendant to help her. Defendant told her that he could not help and then stepped out of the way while his son dragged her into the bedroom. Defendant followed and lay down next to her on the bed while his son raped her. The court found that defendant was not a mere bystander: the attack occurred in his home, the perpetrator was his son, and the victim was a family friend. The court held that in these circumstances the defendant's refusal to help, and his presence during the rape, "facilitated and encouraged" the perpetrator's actions. 388 S.E.2d at 512.

Questions: Would the result be the same under the Model Penal Code formulation? Did the father have a legal duty to prevent the rape? Is this a case where silence gives encouragement, as well as consent? For a discussion of these issues in another context, see David Lanham, Drivers, Control and Accomplices, [1982] Crim. L. Rev. 419.

Consider also People v. Stanciel, 606 N.E.2d 1201 (Ill. 1992). Violetta Burgos was charged as an accomplice to murder when her boyfriend, Stanciel, beat her three-year-old daughter to death. Burgos had violated a court order to keep Stanciel away from the child and had authorized Stanciel to discipline the child despite his past and ongoing abusive behavior. Though Burgos did not perform any of the acts that led to her daughter's death, the court ruled that her failure to protect her child from Stanciel rendered Burgos an accomplice to her daughter's murder.

Questions: Would the result be the same under the Model Penal Code? Plainly the mother was here under a legal duty, but is there enough evidence on these facts to support a finding that she acted with the purpose that Stanciel should beat the child to death? Suppose she had not authorized him to discipline the child and had stood by out of fear?

Many cases have held, in accord with *Stanciel,* that a mother can be convicted as an aider and abettor of child abuse for failing to protect a child from abuse by a third party. See State v. Walden, 293 S.E.2d 780 (N.C. 1982); Dorothy E. Roberts, Motherhood and Crime, 79 Iowa L. Rev. 95 (1993). But the view is not unanimous. In State v. Rundle, 176 Wis. 2d 985, 500 N.W.2d 916 (1993), the Wisconsin Supreme Court reversed a conviction of a father for aiding and abetting his wife in the intentional and reckless physical abuse of their child (a statutory offense). The court found that his knowing failure to intervene alone did not constitute actual aid to his wife in her abuse of the child. A dissent, however, observed:

> I fail to see the difference between a lookout during a burglary, who objectively aids the principal burglar by merely watching for possible danger, and Kurt's conduct in this case, which objectively aided his wife's abuse by effectively guarding against intervention by others. . . . The [lookout's] conduct is no more affirmative than Kurt's conduct, yet the majority concludes that Kurt is not an aider and abetter.

Question: Are the lookout's and parent's cases comparable or distinguishable?

In cases where the failure to intervene by one with a duty to act does satisfy the actus reus requirement, should she become liable as an accomplice regardless of what her mens rea was? In *Walden,* supra, the court adverted to the mens rea issue, but resolved it as follows (293 S.E.2d at 787):

> [There must be] something showing [her] consent to the criminal purpose and contribution to its execution. But [we] hold that the failure of a parent who is present to take all steps reasonably possible to protect the parent's child from an attack by another person constitutes an act of omission by the parent showing the parent's consent and contribution to the crime being committed.

Question: Is this an adequate resolution of the mens rea problem?

3. *The Relationship Between the Liability of the Parties*

STATE v. HAYES

Supreme Court of Missouri
105 Mo. 76, 16 S.W. 514 (1891)

THOMAS, J. The defendant appeals from a sentence of five years' imprisonment in the penitentiary for burglary and larceny. [Defendant proposed to one Hill that he join him in the burglary of a general store. Hill, actually a relative of the store owners, feigned acquiescence in order to obtain the arrest of defendant and advised the store owners of the plan. On the night of the planned burglary, defendant and Hill arrived at the store together. Defendant raised the window and assisted Hill in climbing through into the building. Hill handed out a side of bacon. Shortly thereafter they were apprehended.] It will be seen the trial court told the jury in [its] instruction that defendant was guilty of burglary if he, with a felonious intent, assisted and aided Hill to enter the building, notwithstanding Hill himself may have had no such intent. In this we think the court erred. One cannot read this record without being convinced beyond a reasonable doubt that Hill did not enter the warehouse with intent to steal. . . . We may assume, then, for the sake of the argument, that Hill committed no crime in entering the wareroom. The act of Hill, however, was by the instruction of the court imputed to defendant. This act, according to the theory of the instructions, so far as Hill was concerned, was not a criminal act, but when it was imputed to defendant it became criminal because of the latter's felonious intent. This would probably be true if Hill had acted under the control and compulsion of defendant, and as his passive and submissive agent. But he was not a passive agent in this transaction. He was an active one. He acted of his own volition. He did not raise the window and enter the building with intent to commit crime, but simply to entrap defendant in the commission of crime, and have him captured.

Judge Brewer sets this idea in a very clear light in State v. Jansen, 22 Kan. 498. He says: "The act of a detective may perhaps be not imputable to the defendant, as there is a want of community of motive. The one has a criminal intent, while the other is seeking the discovery and punishment of crime." Where the owner learns that his property is to be stolen, he may employ detectives and decoys to catch the thief. And we can do no better than to quote again from Judge Brewer in the case above cited, as to the relation of the acts of detectives and the thief when a crime is alleged to have been committed by the two. He says: "Where each of the overt acts going to make up the crime charged is personally done by the defendant, and with criminal intent, his guilt is complete, no matter what motives may prompt or what acts be done by the party who is with him, and apparently assisting him. Counsel have cited and commented upon several cases in which detectives figured, and in which defendants were adjudged guiltless of the crimes charged. But this feature distinguishes them: that some act essential to the crime charged was in fact done by the detective, and not by the defendant, and, this act not being imputable to the defendant, the latter's guilt was not made out. The intent and act must combine, and all the elements of the act must exist and be imputable to the defendant."

Applying the principle here announced to the case at bar, we find that defendant did not commit every overt act that went to make up the crime. He did not enter the warehouse, either actually or constructively, and hence he did not commit the crime of burglary, no matter what his intent was, it clearly appearing that Hill was guilty of no crime. To make defendant responsible for the acts of Hill, they must have had a common motive and common design. The design and the motives of the two men were not only distinct, but dissimilar, even antagonistic. . . . The court should instruct the jury that if Hill broke into and entered the wareroom with a felonious intent, and defendant was present, aiding him with the same intent, then he is guilty; but if Hill entered the room with no design to steal, but simply to entrap defendant, and capture him in the commission of crime, and defendant did not enter the room himself, then he is not guilty of burglary and larceny as charged. He may be found guilty, however, of petit larceny, in taking and removing the bacon after it was handed to him. This overt act he did in fact commit. . . . The judgment is reversed, and the cause remanded for new trial.[a]

VADEN v. STATE, 768 P.2d 1102 (Alaska 1989): [Fish and Wildlife Protection officers received a tip that Vaden, a local guide, was promoting illegal hunting

a. Compare Wilson v. People, supra page 610, a comparable fact situation except that the roles of principal and accomplice are reversed. — Eds.

practices by his customers. They assigned one of their undercover agents, John Snell, to pose as a hunter and to commission Vaden's services. On the hunt, Vaden piloted the aircraft and maneuvered it to facilitate Snell's shooting game from the plane with a shotgun Vaden had lent him for the purpose. Snell shot and killed four foxes. Vaden was convicted, as Snell's accomplice, of taking foxes from an aircraft and hunting during closed season, in violation of Alaskan law. On appeal, the Supreme Court of Alaska affirmed the convictions, rejecting Vaden's argument that because Snell's action was justified in light of the needs of law enforcement (the "public authority justification defense"), no criminal action occurred for which he could be convicted of being an accomplice. The court reasoned that the action of Snell was not justified, but that even if it were, it would not avail Vaden, because the justification would be personal to the agent.[b] The majority also found that no entrapment had been shown and that the actions of Snell, while unlawful, were not so outrageous as to constitute a denial of due process. The dissenting opinion reasoned:] The accomplice liability charges should fail on [the] ground [of] the long-standing common law rule that the act of a feigned accomplice may never be imputed to the targeted defendant for purposes of obtaining a conviction. In State v. Neely, 90 Mont. 199, 300 P. 561 (1931), the Montana Supreme Court applied this principle under circumstances akin to those in the case at bar. In *Neely,* a cattle owner employed a detective, Harrington, to "get in" with suspected cattle thieves during an act of cattle rustling. Harrington associated himself with the criminal enterprise, and the crime was carried out. Harrington himself, however, committed the principal offense of purloining the cattle, while the targeted suspect merely stood watch outside the premises and offered various other forms of assistance before and after commission of the offense. The court reversed Neely's conviction as an accomplice to the crime. . . .[5] The principle enunciated in *Neely,* which has been repeated by numerous courts under a variety of factual circumstances . . . is based in sound reason. It is the general rule that one who aids and abets another in criminal activity is liable for all of the "natural and probable consequences" of his accomplice's criminal acts. Thus, the potential for abuse inherent in law enforcement methods such as those employed in the case at bar is substantial. Once an agent has succeeded in persuading an individual to take some substantial act in furtherance of his general criminal scheme, the ultimate liability of the targeted defendant, if any, will depend upon which foreseeable crimes the agent chooses to commit in order to secure convictions against his criminal "accomplice." In this case, Officer Snell shot four foxes. Vaden, as pilot of the plane from which they were shot, was charged with four separate criminal counts of taking foxes from the air out of season. Had Snell opted to shoot a fifth fox, one more count could have been added to Vaden's indictment. In my view, it is clearly inconsistent with due process principles, and manifestly unjust, that the ultimate

Dissent

b. The justification referred to is that of law enforcement representatives who sometimes may break the law (not involving personal violence) in the course of enforcing it against others; for example, according to the New York Penal Law §35.05, when the conduct "is performed by a public servant in the reasonable exercise of his official powers, duties or functions." Compare the materials on Choice of the Lesser Evil, page 809, infra. — EDS.

5. Notably, this was not a case in which the court found that the owner's consent to Harrington's taking vitiated the unlawfulness of his acts. Like the majority today, the court in *Neely* concluded that Harrington had exceeded his rightful authority in taking and butchering the cattle. Id. 300 P. at 565. Nonetheless, the court concluded that Harrington's acts, as a feigned accomplice, could not be imputed to Neely.

criminal liability of a defendant should be made to depend upon the good aim and/or the good intentions of the police officer charged with securing his arrest.

NOTES AND QUESTIONS

1. *Questions.* The dissent invokes the rule that acts of a feigned accomplice may not be imputed to the targeted defendant for purpose of obtaining a conviction against him. This appears to be what underlay the decision to reverse the conviction of the *Hayes* case. But is the situation in the *Vaden* case distinguishable? Snell did shoot the foxes in violation of law, and Vaden did help him do so. How can it be that Snell's motive in violating the hunting laws (to secure a conviction against Vaden) could render Vaden not guilty? In the *Vaden* case there are plausible answers, turning on the public policy of discouraging unacceptable law enforcement practices. But the dissent in *Vaden* relies on a principle that is not confined to law enforcement personnel. If Snell were a private individual with a grudge against Vaden, would the dissent's argument hold up? Was Snell a "feigned" principal at all?

2. *Entrapment.* The requirements of the defense of entrapment by a law enforcement person vary in different jurisdictions. The Model Penal Code's proposed formulation represents the law in many. See §2.13. Essentially it provides a defense if law enforcement representatives induce another to commit an offense using methods "which create a substantial risk that such an offense will be committed by persons other than those who are ready to commit it." For discussion see Model Penal Code and Commentaries, Comment to §2.13 at 405-413 (1985).

TAYLOR v. COMMONWEALTH

Court of Appeals of Virginia
31 Va. App. 54, 521 S.E.2d 293, 1999

ANNUNZIATA, JUDGE. Tomika T. Taylor ("appellant") appeals her conviction as a principal in the second degree for abduction in violation of Code §18.2-47. She contends the evidence was legally insufficient to support her conviction because the person she aided in committing the abduction was the natural father of the child abducted. She argues that the father's legal justification in taking the child precludes her conviction. A panel of this Court reversed appellant's conviction on that ground. [W]e affirm appellant's conviction.

[A]ppellant and her fiance, Avery Moore, arrived at the home of Meshia Powell, ostensibly to see the ten-month-old son of Powell and Moore. Powell and Moore had never been married and had not lived together. The child had been in Powell's care since his birth. Moore was not present for the birth, had seen the child only once, and had never paid child support. No custody order was in effect and no proceeding was pending. . . . [Moore, with the assistance of appellant, overcame the resistance of the mother and removed the child from her possession.]

Code §18.2-47 provides in pertinent part:

> Any person who, by force, intimidation or deception, and without legal justification or excuse, seizes, takes, transports, detains or secretes the person of another, with the intent to deprive such other person of his personal liberty or to withhold or conceal him from any person, authority or institution lawfully entitled to his charge, shall be deemed guilty of "abduction." . . . Abduction for which no punishment is otherwise prescribed shall be punished as a Class 5 felony.

Appellant argues that, in the absence of a court order which curtailed Moore's custodial rights as a natural parent, Moore's taking of his child did not violate Code §18.2-47 because his conduct was legally justified. Appellant further argues that, because Moore's actions did not constitute abduction, she cannot be convicted as a principal in the second degree. We disagree and affirm the conviction.

[U]nder Virginia law, an accomplice is "a person who knowingly, voluntarily, and with common intent with the principal offender unites in the commission of a crime." A principal in the second degree is an accomplice who is "present, aiding and abetting, and intend[s] his or her words, gestures, signals, or actions to in some way encourage, advise, urge, or in some way help the person committing the crime to commit it." . . .

Proceeding from the premise that her criminal liability as a principal in the second degree derives from Moore's liability as a principal in the first degree, appellant raises the following specific issues on appeal: (1) whether a natural parent acting under the circumstances of this case is justified or excused from liability for the crime of abduction and (2) whether a person charged as an accomplice is shielded from criminal liability based derivatively on the parent's excuse or justification.

A number of jurisdictions have recognized that, in the absence of a court order awarding custody to another, a parent cannot be convicted of abduction and other similar crimes by taking exclusive custody of his or her child. See, e.g., State v. Stocksdale, 138 N.J. Super. 312, 350 A.2d 539, 541 (1975) (recognizing that, because "each parent has an equal right to custody of a child in the absence of a court order, a parent does not commit the crime of kidnapping by taking exclusive possession of the child where no such order exists."). [T]his reasoning has been adopted by a majority of courts considering the issue. . . .

Code §18.2-47 exempts three persons from liability: (1) individuals who are legally justified, (2) individuals who are legally excused, and (3) any law-enforcement officer acting in the performance of his or her duty. Only the second exemption, "legal excuse," is raised by the contentions in this case.

While the terms, "legal justification," and "excuse" are often used interchangeably, they are distinct legal concepts. [A]s to the concept of excuse, there appears to be general agreement with the proposition that "[e]xcuses, in contrast [to justifications], are always personal to the actor."[1] Excuses rest on the presence within the actor of a condition or status that exculpates him or her from culpability for otherwise criminal conduct.[2] Because excuses relate to a condition that is peculiar to the actor, such defenses are generally considered to

1. George P. Fletcher, Rethinking Criminal Law 762 (1978).
2. See Robert F. Schopp, Justification Defenses and Just Convictions, 24 Pac. L.J. 1233, 1238 (1993) ("Excuses are specific to defendants because they exculpate these individuals for their criminal conduct due to disabilities, such as infancy or psychological disorder, that undermine the attribution of culpability for this particular conduct to these defendants.")

be non-delegable and, thus, unavailable to an accomplice.[4] Based on the foregoing principles, even were we to conclude that Moore's abduction of the child was excused by his parental relationship to the child, appellant's "accessorial liability would not be undercut by [Moore's] personal excuse."[5] In short, the defense of "legal excuse," is personal to Moore and unavailable to appellant.

Having concluded that the evidence does not support the finding that appellant's conduct was legally excused, it remains only to determine whether the evidence adduced at trial was sufficient to establish appellant's culpability as a principal in the second degree to abduction under Code §18.2-47. [The court held that it was and affirmed appellant's conviction.]

ELDER, JUDGE, with whom BENTON, J., joins, dissenting. [A]ppellant's conviction for abduction under the facts of this case depended on whether Moore's actions were legally justified or excused. The majority rejects this approach, holding that appellant is not entitled to rely upon Moore's defense of excuse, if he has such a defense. It also holds implicitly that the facts do not support a defense of justification. A split of authority exists regarding whether an agent or other person present with and assisting a parent to gain exclusive custody of a child may be found guilty of kidnapping when the parent himself has committed no illegal act. . . . I would hold that the approach adopted by a majority of jurisdictions — and rejected by the majority of this Court — is the better reasoned. As explained in *Stocksdale,*

> . . . An aider or abettor . . . may generally be convicted where the principal has a defense personal to himself which exonerates him from criminal responsibility. There are, however, exceptions to this general rule of accessorial liability. Accomplice liability, for example, is not sustained where the defense of one party not only exonerates himself but also changes the character of the act so that it can no longer be viewed as criminal in nature. 350 A.2d at 543-44.

In a parental abduction case such as this one, appellant's liability as a principal in the second degree is wholly derivative of Moore's liability. The existence of legal justification or excuse for Moore's actions does not simply immunize him from criminal liability; rather, it so "changes the character of the act . . . that it can no longer be viewed as criminal in nature." Id. at 544. Therefore, I would hold that appellant's acts in aiding and abetting Moore, like Moore's acts, did not violate Code §18.2-47.

For the foregoing reasons, I would hold (1) that a parent does not commit abduction in violation of Code §18.2-47 when the parent takes his child from the custody of the child's other natural parent "with the intent [only] to withhold or conceal him from [the other natural parent] lawfully entitled to his charge" as long as no custody order is then pending or in effect, and (2) that one who aids that parent in taking the child does not commit abduction. Therefore, I would

4. Justification defenses, on the other hand, "appeal to the special circumstances in which the ordinarily criminal conduct was performed, and they exonerate the defendant because the conduct was socially acceptable under these conditions." Schopp, supra, at 1238. The defense of justification, unlike that of excuse, generally provides a right to persons other than the primary actor to assist, or to directly defend the interests of, the primary actor because a third party is in the same position as the primary actor to evaluate the circumstances warranting the conduct in question. See Fletcher, supra, at 761-762. . . .

5. Fletcher, supra, at 762.

reverse and dismiss appellant's abduction conviction without reaching the question of the factual sufficiency of the evidence.

NOTES AND QUESTIONS

1. Questions on the concepts. The majority concluded without argument that the concept of legal justification was not an issue in the case. The dissent thought otherwise, that Moore was justified in taking the child. Which is the more persuasive position? Was this a case where Moore committed a wrong in taking his child but deserved to be forgiven, or is it closer to the case of someone who asserts his right over jointly owned property?

2. Questions on the policy. Many cases agree with the dissent that the parent is justified and therefore so is the accomplice. In these jurisdictions is there any basis for a distinction depending on whether the parent is the principal or the accomplice? Suppose a parent hires another person to remove the child while he himself stays away. One court thought the situations were distinguishable. In Wilborn v. Superior Ct., 51 Cal. 2d 828, 337 P.2d 65, 66 (1959), the court stated that,

> whatever may be the right of one parent . . . to invade the possession of the other to take or entice away their mutual offspring, such right may not be delegated to an agent. To hold otherwise would result in untold confusion and provoke many possible breaches of the peace in that the parent having possession of the child would be at the mercy of persons acting as alleged agents of the other parent.

3. For a review of the cases, see Annotation, 20 A.L.R.4th 823 §4 (1997). And see generally Douglas Husak, Justifications and the Criminal Liability of Accessories, 80 J. Crim. L. & Criminology 491 (1989).

NOTES AND PROBLEMS ON THE DERIVATIVE NATURE OF ACCOMPLICE LIABILITY

The derivative nature of accomplice liability is an axiom in the doctrine of complicity: "It is hornbook law that a defendant charged with aiding and abetting the commission of a crime by another cannot be convicted in the absence of proof that the crime was actually committed." United States v. Ruffin, 613 F.2d 408, 412 (2d Cir. 1979); "There must be a guilty principal before there can be an aider and abettor." United States v. Jones, 425 F.2d 1048, 1056 (9th Cir. 1970).

It is important, however, not to confuse derivative liability with vicarious liability. Accomplice liability does not involve imposing liability on one party for the wrongs of another solely because of the relationship between the parties. Liability requires *culpability* and *conduct* by the secondary actor — intentional conduct designed to persuade or help — that makes it appropriate to blame him for what the primary actor does. The term "derivative" merely means that his liability is dependent on the principal's violating the law. What is at issue is the responsibility of the secondary actor for the principal actor's violation of law. Unless the latter occurs, there can be no accomplice liability.

This axiom of accessorial liability gives rise to many problems, one kind of which we have just examined in connection with the principal case, Taylor v. Commonwealth. To a large extent these problems can be solved by making an attempt to aid a sufficient basis of complicity liability. See Model Penal Code §2.06(3)(ii). But traditionally (and under the present law of many, if not most jurisdictions) this option has not been available, so that the problems persist.

1. Assisting suicide. One problem that would not be solved by making it a crime to attempt to aid and abet is that involved in assisting a suicide. We saw in the chapter on causation, supra page 530, that the *novus actus interveniens* doctrine precludes convicting the aider or encourager for murder or manslaughter, because under that doctrine it is the suicide who kills him or herself. But the doctrines of complicity turn out to be no more hospitable to convicting the helper, since the concept of derivative liability requires a guilty principal and suicide is no longer a crime anywhere. At all events, the problem has been rendered largely academic by the widespread enactment of statutes making it criminal to assist a suicide.

2. The nonculpable principal as innocent agent. In State v. Hayes, supra page 633, suppose that the absence of a "common motive and common design" on the part of Hill was not due to his motive to catch Hayes but to the fact that he was being coerced at gunpoint by Hayes, so that Hill would have a complete defense. In this case, Hayes would be held guilty of burglary through the use of Hill, his innocent agent. This standard doctrine, the so-called *innocent agent* doctrine, is expressed in §2.06(2)(a) of the Model Penal Code as follows: "A person is legally accountable for the conduct of another person when . . . acting with the kind of culpability that is sufficient for the commission of the offense, he causes an innocent or irresponsible person to engage in such conduct." The drafter's comment states (Model Penal Code and Commentaries, Comment to §206 at 300 (1985)):

> Subsection (2)(a) is based upon the universally acknowledged principle that one is no less guilty of the commission of a crime because he uses the overt conduct of an innocent or irresponsible agent. He is accountable in such cases as if the conduct were his own. At common law, he was considered a principal for such behavior.

3. Limits of the innocent agent doctrine. There may be difficulties in employing an innocent agent doctrine even where the mens rea of the defendant and the innocence of the agent are established.

(a) One such case is where the statute defines the crime so that it can only be committed by designated classes of persons of which the defendant is not a member. For example, if a statute prohibits an officer or employee of a bank from entering false records of transactions, then one who is not an officer or an employee cannot commit the offense. If the latter person helps or encourages a culpable officer or employee to do so, he can be held as an accomplice. As such, his liability is derived from that of the culpable officer or employee. If, however, he dupes an innocent officer or employee into doing so unknowingly, the absence of a guilty principal precludes accomplice liability. The usual recourse, therefore, is to apply the innocent-agency doctrine on the theory that the instigator has done the prohibited act, using the officer or employee as his instrument. But because the instigator is not an officer or employee, he cannot violate the statute. Thus, in this case, the innocent-agency doctrine would not make him liable.

Federal courts have solved the difficulty by interpreting the federal aiding and abetting statute to mean that one is criminally liable as a principal for causing another to commit criminal acts where the other, even though innocent, has the capacity to do so and the defendant does not. See United States v. Ruffin, 613 F.2d 408 (2d Cir. 1979). The federal statute, 18 U.S.C. §2(b) reads: "Whoever willfully causes an act to be done which if directly performed by him *or another* would be an offense against the United States, is punishable as a principal." (Emphasis added.)

(b) A second situation where this difficulty can arise is rarer: It is where the nature of the action prohibited is such that it can be done only by the body of the person him or herself and not through the instrumentality of another. For example, a sober defendant may cause an insensate and disorderly drunk to appear in a public place by physically depositing him there. But we could hardly say that the sober person has, through the instrumentality of the drunk, himself committed the criminal action of being drunk and disorderly in a public place. *Question:* How would 18 U.S.C. §2(b) handle this case? For a discussion of these situations, see Sanford H. Kadish, Blame and Punishment 172 (1987).

4. The culpable-but-unconvictable principal. Another class of cases raising questions for the traditional derivative liability doctrine are those in which the principal would be guilty except for a policy-based defense that makes him unconvictable. Consider, for example, Farnsworth v. Zerbst, 98 F.2d 541 (5th Cir. 1938), where the defendant conspired with and aided another in the commission of espionage, but the latter could not be convicted because of diplomatic immunity; or United States v. Azadian, 436 F.2d 81 (9th Cir. 1971), where the defendant aided a principal who had been acquitted on grounds of entrapment. As the courts held in these cases, there is no reason to grant the accomplice a defense simply because the principal has a defense — the grounds of granting the principal a defense are reasons of policy that are inapplicable to the accomplice. Yet how can convicting the accomplice be squared with the rule that makes the liability of the accomplice turn on the liability of the principal?

Consider People v. Eberhardt, 169 Cal. App. 3d 292, 215 Cal. Rptr. 161 (1985). The defendant was convicted of conspiring with his Native American wife to violate the California Fish and Game Code, which prohibited the sale of fish taken from the Klamath River and of salmon taken in California waters by gill net. The defendant's wife was immune from prosecution by the state because federal law preempted the state from enforcing these laws against Native Americans. Over the objection that it takes two guilty persons to conspire, the court upheld the conviction, stating (at 300): "Mrs. Eberhardt['s . . .] immunity from prosecution by the state is not inconsistent with her culpability as a coconspirator, and the fact that she cannot be prosecuted by the state does not amount to a declaration of her innocence." *Question:* Could it be well argued that Mrs. Eberhardt enjoyed a privilege to fish by force of federal law rather than simply a personal immunity from prosecution under state law?

5. The acquitted principal. We have seen that in general there can be no guilty aider and abettor without a guilty principal; the situations in the above Notes are distinguishable or are exceptions to that rule. What happens when the principal has been acquitted? May the accomplice who is subsequently tried raise that acquittal as a defense? In a situation of this kind where the principal had been acquitted of federal bribery charges, the United States Supreme Court affirmed a conviction of the accomplice, stating, United States v. Standefer, 447 U.S. 10, 25-26 (1980):

> This case does no more than manifest the simple, if discomforting, reality that "different juries may reach different results under any criminal statute. That is one of the consequences we accept under our jury system." Roth v. United States, 354 U.S. 476, 492 (1957). While symmetry of results may be intellectually satisfying, it is not required. Here, [defendant] received a fair trial at which the Government bore the burden of proving beyond reasonable doubt that [the principal] violated 26 U.S.C. §7214(a)(2) and that petitioner aided and abetted him in that venture. He was entitled to no less — and to no more.

6. Defenses limited to the accomplice. May an accomplice have a defense even though she acts with the required mens rea? Consider the following:

(a) In The Queen v. Tyrell, [1894] 1 Q.B. 710, the court reversed a conviction of a minor for aiding, abetting and encouraging statutory rape upon her by an adult, stating:

> [I]t is impossible to say that the Act, which is absolutely silent about aiding or abetting, or soliciting or inciting, can have intended that the girls for whose protection it was passed should be punishable under it for the offences committed upon themselves.

The same reasoning has been applied to victims charged with conspiracy to commit an offense. See Gebardi v. United States, page 724 infra. For further discussion of the victim rule, see Glanville Williams, Victims and Other Exempt Parties in Crime, 10 Legal Stud. 245 (1990); Brian Hogan, Victims as Parties to Crime, [1962] Crim. L. Rev. 683.

(b) The Model Penal Code contains a provision, followed in a number of states, that a person is not an accomplice in an offense committed by another either if he is victim of that offense or if the offense is so defined that his conduct is inevitably incident to its commission. §2.06(6)(a), (b). The Comment on this provision states (Model Penal Code and Commentaries, Comment to §2.06 at 324-325 (1985)):

> Exclusion of the victim does not wholly meet the problems that arise. Should a woman be deemed an accomplice when a criminal abortion is performed upon her? Should the man who has intercourse with a prostitute be viewed as an accomplice in the act of prostitution, the purchaser an accomplice in the unlawful sale, the unmarried party to a bigamous marriage an accomplice of the bigamist, the bribe-giver an accomplice of the taker? . . . What is common to these cases, . . . is that the question is before the legislature when it defines the individual offense involved. No one can draft a prohibition of adultery without awareness that two parties to the conduct necessarily will be involved. The provision, therefore, is that the general section on complicity is inapplicable, leaving to the definition of the crime itself the selective judgment that must be made.

NOTES ON DIFFERENCES IN THE DEGREE OF CULPABILITY

1. Does it follow from the derivative nature of accomplice liability that the secondary party cannot be convicted of a more serious crime than that committed by the principal actor? Consider the following situations.

(a) Regina v. Richards, [1974] Q.B. 776. The defendant, Isabelle Richards,

hired two men to beat up her husband. She told them she "wanted them to beat him up bad enough to put him in the hospital for a month." The men accosted Mr. Richards and struggled with him, but he escaped without suffering any serious injuries. Mrs. Richards and the two men were tried together on charges of felonious assault, requiring proof of wounding with intent to cause grievous bodily harm, and misdemeanor assault, requiring proof of intent to cause harm, but not necessarily serious harm. The two men were acquitted on the felony charges and convicted on the misdemeanor count. Mrs. Richards, tried as their accomplice, was convicted of felonious assault. On appeal, the court reversed her felony conviction, stating:

> [The prosecution] says that here one can properly look at the actus reus, that is the physical blows struck upon Mr. Richards, and separately the intention with which the blows were struck. . . . We do not take that view. . . . There is proved on the evidence in this case one offence and one offence only, namely, the offence of unlawful wounding without the element of specific intent. . . . That is the short point in the case as we see it. If there is only one offence committed, and that is the offence of unlawful wounding, then the person who has requested that offence to be committed, or advised that that offence be committed, cannot be guilty of a graver offence than that in fact which was committed.

Question: Was the decision correct? Commentators have disagreed. See Sanford H. Kadish, Blame and Punishment 181-186 (1987); J. C. Smith, Comment, [1987] Crim. L. Rev. 480, 484; J. C. Smith & B. Hogan, Criminal Law 154 (8th ed. 1996). The argument against the decision is that the blows struck by Mrs. Richards hirelings should be treated as her own actions on the ground that she "caused" them. The contrary argument is that this would be true only if the hirelings were innocent agents, her unwitting instrument not knowing fully what they were doing. But since that apparently was not the case, their actions are their own and could not be said to be "caused" by Mrs. Richards, any more than any accomplice "causes" the actions of the principal. See Sanford H. Kadish, A Theory of Complicity, supra page 606, and compare the result and reasoning in State v. Hayes, supra page 633.

(*b*) Consider Shakespeare's *Othello:* Iago calmly and maliciously drives Othello into a blind rage and incites him to kill his wife Desdemona, by getting Othello to believe (falsely) that Desdemona has been unfaithful to him. Othello might be guilty of no more than manslaughter. Should it follow that Iago cannot be convicted of first-degree murder? Or consider this case: "*D* hands a gun to *E* informing him that it is loaded with blank ammunition only and telling him to go and scare *P* by discharging it. The ammunition is in fact live (as *D* knows) and *P* is killed. *E* is convicted only of manslaughter."[a] Could it be that *D* could not be held for more than manslaughter?

Professor Glanville Williams has offered the following argument for permitting the accessory to be held liable for a greater offense than the principal's in cases like these: "In effect the primary party is an innocent agent in respect of part of the responsibility of the secondary party."[b] He also stated: "If a person can act through a completely innocent agent, there is no reason why he should

a. J. C. Smith, Smith & Hogan Criminal Law 154 (8th ed. 1996).
b. Criminal Law: The General Part 391 (2d ed. 1961).

not act through a semi-innocent agent. It is wholly unreasonable that the partial guilt of the agent should operate as a defence to the instigator."[c]

An alternative argument is that the actions of the principal perpetrator (Othello or *E* in our example) are not fully volitional. As a result, those actions cannot pose a barrier to our treating the actions of an instigator (such as Iago or *E*) as the *cause* of the resulting death. See the material on causation supra page 536. When that is so, there is no difficulty in making the crime each party commits dependent on his own mens rea, because each is treated as a principal who has caused the death.[d] This rests on the non-controversial premise that the action of an intervening actor (like Othello) can be insufficiently volitional to break the causal chain, but sufficiently volitional to hold him responsible for his actions.

2. Does it follow from the theory of derivative liability that the instigator can be held for no lesser crime than that committed by the perpetrator? For example, suppose that an enraged Othello had hired someone else to kill Desdemona. The hired killer, presumably, would be guilty of murder. Does it follow that Othello is also guilty of murder? In Moore v. Lowe, 116 W. Va. 165, 168, 180 S.E. 1, 2 (1935), a hired killer murdered the defendant's husband at her instigation. The court held that, as an accessory to the murder, the defendant could be convicted of manslaughter. In support of its position, the court quoted 1 Wharton, Criminal Law 363-364 (12th ed. 1932):

> [T]he offense of the instigator is not necessarily of the same grade as that of the perpetrator. The instigator may act in hot blood, in which case he will be guilty only of manslaughter, while the perpetrator may act coolly, and thus be guilty of murder.

B. LIABILITY WITHIN THE CORPORATE FRAMEWORK

The two main problems of corporate criminality with which these materials deal are: (1) For whose acts is the corporation responsible? (2) On what ground may corporate officials be held liable for acts of lesser employees?

The first problem involves the rationale of corporate punishment as a supplement or substitute for punishment of the individual actors; it also involves the legal criteria for determining which actions, of which employees and officials, render the corporation criminally liable.

The second problem deals with the *personal* criminal liability of individual employees and officials who act for the corporation. The lesser employees present no special issue; the normal legal doctrines of personal and accomplice liability suffice. The major issue is the individual liability of high officials of corporations who may be accountable for the actions of lower-echelon employees even though they would not be liable under the rigorous requirements of purpose or knowledge imposed by the usual doctrines of accomplice liability.

c. Textbook on Criminal Law 374 (2d ed. 1983).
d. Sanford H. Kadish, Blame and Punishment 183 (1987).

A useful overview of these subjects is John Coffee, Corporate Criminal Responsibility, in Encyclopedia of Crime and Justice 253-264 (1983). There is now a comprehensive, three-volume treatment of the subject by Kathleen Brickey, Corporate Criminal Liability: A Treatise on the Criminal Liability of Corporations, Their Officers and Agents (2d ed. 1992).

1. *Liability of the Corporate Entity*

NEW YORK CENTRAL & HUDSON RIVER RAILROAD CO. v. UNITED STATES

United States Supreme Court
212 U.S. 481 (1909)

JUSTICE DAY delivered the opinion of the court.

This is a writ of error to the Circuit Court of the United States for the Southern District of New York, sued out by the New York Central and Hudson River Railroad Company, plaintiff in error. In the Circuit Court the railroad company and Fred L. Pomeroy, its assistant traffic manager, were convicted for the payment of rebates to the American Sugar Refining Company and others, upon shipments of sugar from the city of New York to the city of Detroit, Michigan. . . .

The principal attack in this court is upon the constitutional validity of certain features of the Elkins act. 32 Stat. 847. That act, among other things, provides:

> (1) That anything done or omitted to be done by a corporation common carrier subject to the act to regulate commerce, and the acts amendatory thereof, which, if done or omitted to be done by any director or officer thereof, or any receiver, trustee, lessee, agent or person acting for or employed by such corporation, would constitute a misdemeanor under said acts, or under this act, shall also be held to be a misdemeanor committed by such corporation, and upon conviction thereof it shall be subject to like penalties as are prescribed in said acts, or by this act, with reference to such persons, except as such penalties are herein changed. . . . In construing and enforcing the provisions of this section, the act, omission or failure of any officer, agent or other person acting for or employed by any common carrier, acting within the scope of his employment, shall in every case be also deemed to be the act, omission or failure of such carrier, as well as of that person.

It is contended that these provisions of the law are unconstitutional because Congress has no authority to impute to a corporation the commission of criminal offenses, or to subject a corporation to a criminal prosecution by reason of the things charged. The argument is that to thus punish the corporation is in reality to punish the innocent stockholders, and to deprive them of their property without opportunity to be heard, consequently without due process of law. . . . As no action of the board of directors could legally authorize a crime, and as indeed the stockholders could not do so, the arguments come to this: that owing to the nature and character of its organization and the extent of its power and authority, a corporation cannot commit a crime of the nature charged in this case.

Some of the earlier writers on common law held the law to be that a corporation could not commit a crime. . . . In Blackstone's Commentaries, chapter 18, §12, we find it stated: "A corporation cannot commit treason, or felony, or other crime in its corporate capacity, though its members may in their distinct individual capacities." The modern authority, universally, so far as we know, is the other way. In considering the subject, Bishop's New Criminal Law, §417, devotes a chapter to the capacity of corporations to commit crime, and states the law to be: "Since a corporation acts by its officers and agents their purposes, motives, and intent are just as much those of the corporation as are the things done. If, for example, the invisible, intangible essence of air, which we term a corporation, can level mountains, fill up valleys, lay down iron tracks, and run railroad cars on them, it can intend to do it, and can act therein as well viciously as virtuously." . . .

It is now well established that in actions for tort the corporation may be held responsible for damages for the acts of its agent within the scope of his employment. And this is the rule when the act is done by the agent in the course of his employment, although done wantonly or recklessly or against the express orders of the principal. In such cases the liability is not imputed because the principal actually participates in the malice or fraud, but because the act is done for the benefit of the principal, while the agent is acting within the scope of his employment in the business of the principal, and justice requires that the latter shall be held responsible for damages to the individual who has suffered by such conduct. . . .

It is true that there are some crimes, which in their nature cannot be committed by corporations. But there is a large class of offenses, of which rebating under the Federal statutes is one, wherein the crime consists in purposely doing the things prohibited by statute. In that class of crimes we see no good reason why corporations may not be held responsible for and charged with the knowledge and purposes of their agents, acting within the authority conferred upon them. . . .

It is a part of the public history of the times that statutes against rebates could not be effectually enforced so long as individuals only were subject to punishment for violation of the law, when the giving of rebates or concessions inured to the benefit of the corporations of which the individuals were but the instruments. This situation, developed in more than one report of the Interstate Commerce Commission, was no doubt influential in bringing about the enactment of the Elkins Law, making corporations criminally liable. . . .

We see no valid objection in law, and every reason in public policy, why the corporation, which profits by the transaction, and can only act through its agents and officers, shall be held punishable by fine because of the knowledge and intent of its agents to whom it has intrusted authority to act in the subject-matter of making and fixing rates of transportation, and whose knowledge and purposes may well be attributed to the corporation for which the agents act. [T]he law . . . cannot shut its eyes to the fact that the great majority of business transactions in modern times are conducted through [corporations], and particularly that interstate commerce is almost entirely in their hands, and to give them immunity from all punishment because of the old and exploded doctrine that a corporation cannot commit a crime would virtually take away the only means of effectually controlling the subject-matter and correcting the abuses aimed at. . . .

UNITED STATES v. HILTON HOTELS CORP.

United States Court of Appeals, 9th Circuit
467 F.2d 1000 (1972)

BROWNING, J. This is an appeal from a conviction under an indictment charging a violation of section 1 of the Sherman Act, 15 U.S.C. §1.

Operators of hotels, restaurants, hotel and restaurant supply companies, and other businesses in Portland, Oregon, organized an association to attract conventions to their city. To finance the association, members were asked to make contributions in predetermined amounts. Companies selling supplies to hotels were asked to contribute an amount equal to one per cent of their sales to hotel members. To aid collections, hotel members, including appellant, agreed to give preferential treatment to suppliers who paid their assessments, and to curtail purchases from those who did not.

The jury was instructed that such an agreement by the hotel members, if proven, would be a per se violation of the Sherman Act. Appellant argues that this was error.

We need not explore the outer limits of the doctrine that joint refusals to deal constitute per se violations of the Act, for the conduct involved here was of the kind long held to be forbidden without more. . . . [The court's discussion of substantive antitrust law under the Sherman Act is omitted.]

Appellant's president testified that it would be contrary to the policy of the corporation for the manager of one of its hotels to condition purchases upon payment of a contribution to a local association by the supplier. The manager of appellant's Portland hotel and his assistant testified that it was the hotel's policy to purchase supplies solely on the basis of price, quality, and service. They also testified that on two occasions they told the hotel's purchasing agent that he was to take no part in the boycott. The purchasing agent confirmed the receipt of these instructions, but admitted that, despite them, he had threatened a supplier with loss of the hotel's business unless the supplier paid the association assessment. He testified that he violated his instructions because of anger and personal pique toward the individual representing the supplier.

Based upon this testimony, appellant requested certain instructions bearing upon the criminal liability of a corporation for the unauthorized acts of its agents. These requests were rejected by the trial court. The court instructed the jury that a corporation is liable for the acts and statements of its agents "within the scope of their employment," defined to mean "in the corporation's behalf in performance of the agent's general line of work," including "not only that which has been authorized by the corporation, but also that which outsiders could reasonably assume the agent would have authority to do." The court added:

> A corporation is responsible for acts and statements of its agents, done or made within the scope of their employment, even though their conduct may be contrary to their actual instructions or contrary to the corporation's stated policies.

Appellant objects only to the court's concluding statement.

Congress may constitutionally impose criminal liability upon a business entity for acts or omissions of its agents within the scope of their employment. Such liability may attach without proof that the conduct was within the agent's actual authority, and even though it may have been contrary to express instructions.

The intention to impose such liability is sometimes express, New York Central & Hudson R.R. Co. v. United States, 212 U.S. 481, but it may also be implied. The text of the Sherman Act does not expressly resolve the issue. For the reasons that follow, however, we think the construction of the Act that best achieves its purpose is that a corporation is liable for acts of its agents within the scope of their authority even when done against company orders. . . .

Legal commentators have argued forcefully that it is inappropriate and ineffective to impose criminal liability upon a corporation, as distinguished from the human agents who actually perform the unlawful acts. . . . But it is the legislative judgment that controls, and "the great mass of legislation calling for corporate criminal liability suggests a widespread belief on the part of legislators that such liability is necessary to effectuate regulatory policy." ALI Model Penal Code, Comment on §2.07, Tentative Draft No. 4, p. 149 (1956). Moreover, the strenuous efforts of corporate defendants to avoid conviction, particularly under the Sherman Act, strongly suggest that Congress is justified in its judgment that exposure of the corporate entity to potential conviction may provide a substantial spur to corporate action to prevent violations by employees.

Because of the nature of Sherman Act offenses and the context in which they normally occur, the factors that militate against allowing a corporation to disown the criminal acts of its agents apply with special force to Sherman Act violations.

Sherman Act violations are commercial offenses. They are usually motivated by a desire to enhance profits.[4] They commonly involve large, complex, and highly decentralized corporate business enterprises, and intricate business processes, practices, and arrangements. More often than not they also involve basic policy decisions, and must be implemented over an extended period of time.

Complex business structures, characterized by decentralization and delegation of authority, commonly adopted by corporations for business purposes, make it difficult to identify the particular corporate agents responsible for Sherman Act violations. At the same time, it is generally true that high management officials, for whose conduct the corporate directors and stockholders are the most clearly responsible, are likely to have participated in the policy decisions underlying Sherman Act violations, or at least to have become aware of them.

Violations of the Sherman Act are a likely consequence of the pressure to maximize profits that is commonly imposed by corporate owners upon managing agents and, in turn, upon lesser employees. In the face of that pressure, generalized directions to obey the Sherman Act, with the probable effect of foregoing profits, are the least likely to be taken seriously. And if a violation of the Sherman Act occurs, the corporation, and not the individual agents, will have realized the profits from the illegal activity.

In sum, identification of the particular agents responsible for a Sherman Act violation is especially difficult, and their conviction and punishment is peculiarly ineffective as a deterrent. At the same time, conviction and punishment of the business entity itself is likely to be both appropriate and effective.

4. A purpose to benefit the corporation is necessary to bring the agent's acts within the scope of his employment. Standard Oil Co. v. United States, 307 F.2d 120, 128-129 (5th Cir. 1962).

For these reasons we conclude that as a general rule a corporation is liable under the Sherman Act for the acts of its agents in the scope of their employment, even though contrary to general corporate policy and express instructions to the agent.

Thus the general policy statements of appellant's president were no defense. Nor was it enough that appellant's manager told the purchasing agent that he was not to participate in the boycott. The purchasing agent was authorized to buy all of appellant's supplies. Purchases were made on the basis of specifications, but the purchasing agent exercised complete authority as to source. He was in a unique position to add the corporation's buying power to the force of the boycott. Appellant could not gain exculpation by issuing general instructions without undertaking to enforce those instructions by means commensurate with the obvious risks. . . . Affirmed.

NOTES

1. *The case for corporate liability.* Is corporate criminal liability fair, in view of the fact that the loss (that is, the fine and other adverse consequences of conviction) is suffered by shareholders? Is corporate criminal liability useful? Can punishing the corporation add to the deterrent effect of punishing the individual corporate actors? Consider the following observations in Model Penal Code and Commentaries, Comment to §2.07 at 335-339 (1985):

> [Imposing] criminal penalties on corporate bodies results in a species of vicarious liability. . . . In most cases, the shareholders have not participated in the criminal conduct and lack the practical means of supervision of corporate management to prevent misconduct by corporate agents. [T]he fact that the direct impact of corporate fines is felt by a group ordinarily innocent of criminal conduct underscores the point that such fines ought not to be authorized except where they clearly may be expected to accomplish desirable social purposes.
>
> [T]he ultimate justification of corporate criminal responsibility must rest in large measure on an evaluation of the deterrent effects of corporate fines on the conduct of corporate agents. Is there a reason for anticipating a substantially higher degree of deterrence from fines levied on corporate bodies than . . . from proceeding directly against the guilty officer or agent or from other feasible sanctions of a noncriminal character?
>
> . . . If the agent cannot be prevented from committing an offense by the prospect of personal liability, he ordinarily will not be prevented by the prospect of corporate liability. [Yet] there are probably cases in which the economic pressures within the corporate body are sufficiently potent to tempt individuals to hazard personal liability for the sake of company gain, especially where the penalties threatened are moderate and where the offense does not involve behavior condemned as highly immoral by the individual's associates. This tendency may be particularly strong where the individual knows that his guilt may be difficult to prove or where a favorable reaction to his position by a jury may be anticipated even where proof of guilt is strong. A number of . . . juries have held the corporate defendant criminally liable while acquitting the obviously guilty agents who committed the criminal acts.
>
> This may reflect more than faulty or capricious judgment on the part of the ju-

ries. It may represent a recognition that the social consequences of a criminal conviction may fall with a disproportionately heavy impact on the individual defendants where the conduct involved is not of a highly immoral character. It may also reflect a shrewd belief that the violation may have been produced by pressures on the subordinates created by corporate managerial officials even though the latter may not have intended or desired the criminal behavior and even though the pressures can only be sensed rather than demonstrated. . . .

The case so made out, however, does not demonstrate the wisdom of corporate fines generally. Rather, it tends to suggest that such liability can best be justified in cases in which penalties directed to the individual are moderate and where the criminal conviction is least likely to be interpreted as a form of social moral condemnation. This indicates a general line of distinction between the "malum prohibitum" regulatory offenses, on the one hand, and more serious offenses on the other.

For some skeptical views on corporate liability, see Daniel R. Fiscel & Alan O. Skyes, Corporate Crime, 25 J. Legal Stud. 319 (1996) (corporate criminal liability spurs excessive monitoring and litigation costs and should be discarded in favor of civil liability); Jennifer Arlen, The Potentially Perverse Effects of Corporate Criminal Liability, 23 J. Legal Stud. 833 (1994) (strict corporate liability may deter corporate monitoring by making criminal exposure more likely, so that its imposition may increase the likelihood of crime); Jennifer Arlen, *Corporate Crime and Its Control,* in THE NEW PALGRAVE DICTIONARY OF ECONOMICS AND THE LAW 492-97 (Peter Newman, ed., 1998) (government-imposed civil penalties more effective at deterring wrongdoing at lower costs, due to lower procedural hurdles and sanctioning costs). For other discussions pro and con, see Lawrence Friedman, In Defense of Corporate Criminal Liability, 23 Harv. J. L. & Pub. Policy 833 (2000); Brent Fisse, Reconstructing Corporate Criminal Law: Deterrence, Retribution, Fault, and Sanctions, 56 S. Cal. L. Rev. 1141 (1983); John Coffee, "No Soul to Damn: No Body to Kick": An Unscandalized Inquiry into the Problem of Corporate Punishment, 79 Mich. L. Rev. 386 (1981).

2. *The respondeat superior approach.* The use of the tort doctrine of respondeat superior announced in the *New York Central* case and developed in the *Hilton Hotels* case is one of the two main approaches to corporate liability in the United States. (The other is the more restrictive doctrine of the Model Penal Code, which is discussed infra page 657.) The requirements of liability under the respondeat superior approach have been summarized as follows in Note, Developments in the Law — Corporate Crime: Regulating Corporate Behavior through Criminal Sanctions, 92 Harv. L. Rev. 1227, 1247-1251 (1979):

Under the doctrine of respondeat superior, a corporation may be held criminally liable for the acts of any of its agents if an agent (1) commits a crime (2) within the scope of employment (3) with the intent to benefit the corporation.

First, it must be proved that an illegal act was committed by an agent of the corporation, and that the agent acted with the specific intent required by the governing statute. [I]t is not necessary to prove that a specific person acted illegally, only that *some* agent of the corporation committed the crime. Thus, proving that a corporate defendant committed the illegal act is in practice substantially easier than an individual prosecution. . . .

Second, to establish corporate liability under the doctrine of respondeat superior, the prosecution must show that the illegal act was committed within the agent's scope of employment. The traditional agency definition limits scope of employment to conduct that is authorized, explicitly or implicitly, by the principal or that is similar or incidental to authorized conduct. However, courts generally find conduct to fall within the scope of employment even if it was specifically forbidden by a superior and occurred despite good faith efforts on the part of the corporation to prevent the crime. Thus, scope of employment in practice means little more than that the act occurred while the offending employee was carrying out a job-related activity. . . .

Third, it must be proved that the agent committed the crime with the intent to benefit the corporation. The corporation may be held criminally liable even if it received no actual benefit from the offense, although the existence or absence of benefit is relevant as evidence of an intent to benefit.

The requirements of scope of employment and intent to benefit the corporation can also be met through ratification. When an employee commits a crime with no intent to benefit the corporation, or while acting outside the scope of his employment, subsequent approval of the act by his supervisor will be sufficient to hold the corporation liable for the employee's criminal act. In a sense, under the doctrine of ratification, a corporation is culpable for approving the criminal act, rather than committing it.

The reach of the respondeat superior doctrine is exhibited in United States v. Sun-Diamond Growers of California, 138 F.3d 961 (D.C. Cir., 1997). Defendant Sun-Diamond (an agricultural cooperative entity) was charged with wire fraud and illegal campaign contributions. Douglas, an officer of the defendant with some responsibility for lobbying, devised a fraudulent scheme to conceal his misappropriation of defendant's funds to support the congressional campaign of the brother of the Secretary of Agriculture, Mike Espy. The court upheld a conviction of Douglas's employer, stating at 970:

Sun-Diamond says Douglas's scheme was designed to — and did in fact — defraud his employer, not benefit it. In this circumstance, it strenuously argues, there can be no imputation: "[T]o establish precedent holding a principal criminally liable for the acts of an agent who defrauds and deceives the principal while pursuing matters within his self-interest merely because the agent's conduct may provide some incidental benefit to the principal serves to punish innocent principals with no countervailing policy justifications.

This argument has considerable intuitive appeal — Sun-Diamond does look more like a victim than a perpetrator, at least on the fraud charges. The facts in the record, however — that Douglas hid the illegal contribution scheme from others at the company and used company funds to accomplish it — do not preclude a valid finding that he undertook the scheme to benefit Sun-Diamond. Part of Douglas's job was to cultivate his, and Sun-Diamond's, relationship with Secretary Espy. By responding to the Secretary's request to help his brother, Douglas may have been acting out of pure friendship, but the jury was entitled to conclude that he was instead, or also, with an intent (however befuddled) to further the interests of his employer. The scheme came at some cost to Sun-Diamond but it also promised some benefit. . . . Where there is adequate evidence for imputation (as here), the only thing that keeps deceived corporations from being indicted for the acts of their employee-deceivers is not some fixed rule of law or logic but simply the sound exercise of prosecutorial discretion.

And the answer to Sun-Diamond's claim of the absence of any "countervailing policy justification" is simply the justification usually offered in support of holding corporate principals liable for the illegal acts of their agents: to increase incentives for corporations to monitor and prevent illegal employee conduct.

3. Respondeat superior evaluated. In Corporate Culpability Under the Federal Sentencing Guidelines, 34 Ariz. L. Rev. 743 (1992), Jennifer Moore criticizes the doctrine as being overinclusive:

> Under a theory of imputed culpability, what makes a corporation "culpable" is not (primarily) any feature of the corporation as such, but the mere fact that an agent committed a crime. Thus the theory will frequently label a corporation culpable . . . even when the corporation's policies or procedures suggest that it is not "justly to blame" for the crime.

She also finds that it can be underinclusive as well:

> There are some situations in which corporate policies or procedures do cause a crime, yet the doctrine of respondeat superior is unable to find the corporation culpable because there is no individual culpability to impute.
>
> A . . . way in which courts have coped with the problem of underinclusiveness is the development of the "collective knowledge" doctrine. This doctrine enables courts to find liability in cases in which the corporation seems "justly to blame" for the crime, but no single individual has the required mens rea. It permits a finding of corporate mens rea to be derived from the collective knowledge of the corporation's members. In United States v. Bank of New England, N.A., for example, the bank was found guilty of "willfully" violating the Currency Transaction Reporting Act even though no one of its agents was found to have had the required "willfulness." . . . The fact that some employees were aware of the Act's reporting requirements, while other employees were aware of the transactions, was enough to constitute willfulness on the part of the Bank.

COMMONWEALTH v. BENEFICIAL FINANCE CO.

Supreme Judicial Court of Massachusetts
360 Mass. 188, 275 N.E.2d 33 (1971)

SPIEGEL, J. [Individual and corporate defendants, including Beneficial Finance Co., were convicted of bribing, and conspiring to bribe, state banking officials in order to obtain favorable treatment from the state Small Loans Regulatory Board. The corporate convictions were based on acts committed by employees of the corporation who were neither officers nor directors of the corporation. One of the employees, Farrell, was an officer and director of Beneficial Management Co., a wholly owned subsidiary of BFC. Another, Glynn, reported to Farrell but was on the payroll of Industrial Bankers, another wholly owned BFC subsidiary. Glynn had direct contact with the state officials who were bribed. Farrell supervised Glynn's activities and also chaired an intercorporate meeting at which the bribery plan was adopted.]

The defendants and the Commonwealth have proposed differing standards upon which the criminal responsibility of a corporation should be predicated. The defendants argue that a corporation should not be held criminally liable for the conduct of its servants or agents unless such conduct was performed, authorized, ratified, adopted or tolerated by the corporations' directors, officers or other "high managerial agents" who are sufficiently high in the corporate hierarchy to warrant the assumption that their acts in some substantial sense reflect corporate policy. This standard is that adopted by the American Law Institute Model Penal Code. . . . Section 2.07 of the Code provides that, except in the case of regulatory offences and offences consisting of the omission of a duty imposed on corporations by law, a corporation may be convicted of a crime if "the commission of the offence was authorized, requested, commanded, performed or recklessly tolerated by the board of directors or by a high managerial agent acting in behalf of the corporation within the scope of his office or employment." The section proceeds to define "high managerial agent" as "an officer of a corporation . . . or any other agent . . . having duties of such responsibility that his conduct may fairly be assumed to represent the policy of the corporation."

The Commonwealth, on the other hand, argues that the standard applied by the judge in his instructions to the jury was correct. These instructions, which prescribe a somewhat more flexible standard than that delineated in the Model Penal Code, state in part, as follows:

> [T]he Commonwealth does not have to prove that the individual who acted criminally was expressly requested or authorized in advance by the corporation to do so, nor must the Commonwealth prove that the corporation expressly ratified or adopted that criminal conduct on the part of that individual or those individuals. It does not mean that the Commonwealth must prove that the individual who acted criminally was a member of the corporation's board of directors, or that he was a high officer in the corporation, or that he held any office at all. If the Commonwealth did prove that an individual for whose act it seeks to hold a corporation criminally liable was an officer of the corporation, the jury should consider that. But more important than that, it should consider what the authority of that person was as such officer in relation to the corporation. The mere fact that he has a title is not enough to make the corporation liable for his criminal conduct. The Commonwealth must prove that the individual for whose conduct it seeks to charge the corporation criminally was placed in a position by the corporation where he had enough power, duty, responsibility and authority to act for and in behalf of the corporation to handle the particular business or operation or project of the corporation in which he was engaged at the time that he committed the criminal act, with power of decision as to what he would or would not do while acting for the corporation, and that he was acting for and in behalf of the corporation in the accomplishment of that particular business or operation or project, and that he committed a criminal act while so acting. . . .

The difference between the judge's instructions to the jury and the Model Penal Code lies largely in the latter's reference to a "high managerial agent" and in the Code requirement that to impose corporate criminal liability, it at least must appear that its directors or high managerial agent "authorized . . . or recklessly tolerated" the allegedly criminal acts. The judge's instructions focus on the authority of the corporate agent in relation to the particular corporate business in which the agent was engaged. The Code seems to require that there be authorization or reckless inaction by a corporate representative having some relation to framing corporate policy, or one "having duties of such responsibility that his conduct may fairly be assumed to represent the policy of the corporation." Close examination of the judge's instructions reveals that they preserve the underlying "corporate policy" rationale of the Code by allowing the jury to infer "corporate policy" from the position in which the corporation placed the agent in commissioning him to handle the particular corporate affairs in which he was engaged at the time of the criminal act.

[The court then analyzed prior Massachusetts cases concerning vicarious criminal liability and found "a long line of decisions in this Commonwealth holding that before criminal responsibility can be imposed on the master, based on a master-servant relationship under the doctrine of respondeat superior, actual participation in, or approval of, the servant's criminal act must be shown." The court also noted that this rule was applied in both mala in se and mala prohibita offenses.]

The thrust of each of the cases cited above involving a human principal is that it is fundamental to our criminal jurisprudence that for more serious offences guilt is personal and not vicarious. . . . [But] the very nature of a corporation as a "person" before the law renders it impossible to equate the imposition of vicarious liability on a human principal with the imposition of vicarious liability on a corporate principal. "A corporation can act only through its agents. . . . [C]orporate criminal liability is necessarily vicarious." Note, Criminal Liability of Corporations for Acts of Their Agents, 60 Harv. L. Rev. 283. . . . Thus, the issue is not whether vicarious liability should be imposed on a corporation under the "direct participation and assent rule" of the master-servant cases cited above, but rather, whether the acts and intent of natural persons, be they officers, directors or employees, can be treated as the acts and intent of the corporation itself. For the foregoing reasons, despite the strenuous urging of the defendants, we are unconvinced that the standard for imposing criminal responsibility on a human principal adequately deals with the evidentiary problems which are inherent in ascribing the acts of individuals to a corporate entity. . . .

[The court examined several federal cases, including *New York Central,* 212 U.S. 481, supra page 645, where corporations were held criminally liable for the acts of their employees. Defendants had argued that all the federal cases imposing criminal liability on corporations either involved regulatory crimes in which intent was not an element or, when the crimes charged did require intent, presented situations in which someone high in the corporate heirarchy had directed, approved or acquiesced in the agent's criminal act. The court concluded that the precedents supported corporate liability for intentional crimes even when a minor employee, such as a salesman, had performed the critical acts. The court then addressed one defendant's objection that applying such a rule imposes criminal liability based upon a civil law standard.]

It may be that the theoretical principles underlying this standard are, in general, the same as embodied in the rule of respondeat superior. Nevertheless, as we observed at the outset, the judge's instructions, as a whole and in context, required a greater quantum of proof in the practical application of this standard than is required in a civil case. In focusing on the "kinship" between the authority of an individual and the act he committed, the judge emphasized that the jury must be satisfied "beyond a reasonable doubt" that the act of the individual "*constituted*" the act of the corporation. Juxtaposition of the traditional criminal law requirement of ascertaining guilt beyond a reasonable doubt (as opposed to the civil law standard of the preponderance of the evidence), with the rule of respondeat superior, fully justifies application of the standard enunciated by the judge to a criminal prosecution against a corporation for a crime requiring specific intent.

The foregoing is especially true in view of the particular circumstances of this case. In order to commit the crimes charged in these indictments, the defendant corporations either had to offer to pay money to a public official or conspire to do so. The disbursal of funds is an act peculiarly within the ambit of corporate activity. These corporations by the very nature of their business are constantly dealing with the expenditure and collection of moneys. It could hardly be expected that any of the individual defendants would conspire to pay, or would pay, the substantial amount of money here involved, namely $25,000, out of his own pocket. The jury would be warranted in finding that the disbursal of such an amount of money would come from the corporate treasury. A reasonable inference could therefore be drawn that the payment of such money by the corporations was done as a matter of corporate policy and as a reflection of corporate intent, thus comporting with the underlying rationale of the Model Penal Code, and probably with its specific requirements.

Moreover, we do not think that the Model Penal Code standard really purports to deal with the evidentiary problems which are inherent in establishing the quantum of proof necessary to show that the directors or officers of a corporation authorize, ratify, tolerate, or participate in the criminal acts of an agent when such acts are apparently performed on behalf of the corporation. Evidence of such authorization or ratification is too easily susceptible of concealment. As is so trenchantly stated by the judge: "Criminal acts are not usually made the subject of votes of authorization or ratification by corporate Boards of Directors; and the lack of such votes does not prevent the act from being the act of the corporation." . . .

Additional factors of importance are the size and complexity of many large modern corporations which necessitate the delegation of more authority to lesser corporate agents and employees. As the judge pointed out: "There are not enough seats on the Board of Directors, nor enough offices in a corporation, to permit the corporation engaged in widespread operations to give such a title or office to every person in whom it places the power, authority, and responsibility for decision and action." This latter consideration lends credence to the view that the title or position of an individual in a corporation should not be conclusively determinative in ascribing criminal responsibility. In a large corporation, with many numerous and distinct departments, a high ranking corporate officer or agent may have no authority or involvement in a particular sphere of corporate activity, whereas a lower ranking corporate executive might have much broader power in dealing with a matter peculiarly within the scope of his authority. Employees who are in the lower echelon of the corporate hierarchy often exercise more responsibility in the *everyday operations* of the corporation than the directors or officers. Assuredly, the title or office that the person holds may be considered, but it should not be the decisive criterion upon which to predicate corporate responsibility. . . .

Considering everything we have said above, we are of opinion that the quantum of proof necessary to sustain the conviction of a corporation for the acts of its agents is sufficiently met if it is shown that the corporation has placed the agent in a position where he has enough authority and responsibility to act for and in behalf of the corporation in handling the *particular* corporate business, operation or project in which he was engaged at the time he committed the criminal act. The judge properly instructed the jury to this effect and correctly stated that this standard does not depend upon the responsibility or authority which the agent has with respect to the entire corporate business, but only to his position with relation to the particular business in which he was serving the corporation.

[The court then considered whether, under the legal standards it enunciated, the conduct of Farrell and Glynn and their relationship to Beneficial sufficed to support the conviction of Beneficial. The conduct of these two individuals presented a problem because neither was formally an employee of Beneficial. The court, after examining the interlocking relationships and the functional identity of the corporate operations (Beneficial and its subsidiaries were all part of the "Beneficial Finance System," a term used by Beneficial to describe its overall operations) concluded that there was "sufficient evidence to support a finding that there existed between defendants Farrell and Glynn and the corporation Beneficial Management a relationship of agency with the corporation Beneficial which empowered Farrell and Glynn to act on behalf of Beneficial in dealing with" the state officials who were bribed.]

STATE v. CHRISTY PONTIAC-GMC, 354 N.W.2d 17 (1984): [The Supreme Court of Minnesota upheld the conviction of a corporation for theft and forgery based on the fraudulent activities of its employees in retaining for the corporation rebates intended for the purchaser. Stating that it was not "troubled by any anthropomorphic implications in assigning specific intent to a corporation for theft or forgery," it dealt with the evidentiary basis for corporate criminal responsibility as follows (id. at 19-20):] Criminal liability, especially for more serious crimes, is thought of as a matter of personal, not vicarious, guilt. One should not be convicted for something one does not do. In what sense, then, does a corporation "do" something for which it can be convicted of a crime? . . . If a corporation is to be criminally liable, it is clear that the crime must not be a personal aberration of an employee acting on his own; the criminal activity must, in some sense, reflect corporate policy so that it is fair to say that the activity was the activity of the corporation.

[W]e hold that a corporation may be guilty of a specific intent crime committed by its agent if: (1) the agent was acting within the course and scope of his or her employment, having the authority to act for the corporation with respect to the particular corporate business which was conducted criminally; (2) the agent was acting, at least in part, in furtherance of the corporation's business interests; and (3) the criminal acts were authorized, tolerated, or ratified by corporate management.

This test is not quite the same as the test for corporate vicarious liability for a civil tort of an agent. The burden of proof is different, and, unlike civil liability, criminal guilt requires that the agent be acting at least in part in furtherance of the corporation's business interests. Moreover, it must be shown that corporate management authorized, tolerated, or ratified the criminal activity. Ordinarily, this will be shown by circumstantial evidence, for it is not to be expected that management authorization of illegality would be expressly or openly stated. Indeed, there may be instances where the corporation is criminally liable even though the criminal activity has been expressly forbidden. What must be shown is that from all the facts and circumstances, those in positions of managerial authority or responsibility acted or failed to act in such a manner that the criminal activity reflects corporate policy, and it can be said, therefore, that the criminal act was authorized or tolerated or ratified by the corporation.

NOTES

1. The Model Penal Code approach. The Model Penal Code provisions represent an attempt to cut back on the traditional scope of corporate liability based on respondeat superior. Their influence may be seen in a number of state revisions. See Model Penal Code and Commentaries, Comment to §2.07 at 340 n. 18 (1985). Professor Brickey summarizes the Model Penal Code proposals as follows (Kathleen F. Brickey, Rethinking Corporate Liability Under the Model Penal Code, 19 Rutgers L.J. 593, 596-598 (1988)):

> The Code adopts a trifurcated scheme of corporate liability that draws intersecting lines between acts and omissions, between true crimes and regulatory offenses, and between the operatives who are the "hands" of the corporation and the policy makers who constitute its "mind."
>
> Among the most expansive of the three rules is section 2.07(1)(a), which adopts a broad respondeat superior theory of liability. Under this rule, a corporation may incur liability for minor infractions and for non-Code penal offenses when a legislative purpose to impose liability on corporations "plainly appears," provided that the conduct constituting the offense is performed by a corporate agent acting within the scope of his employment and on behalf of the corporation.
>
> The potential reach of the (1)(a) liability rule is limited, however, by the availability of a due diligence defense. Proof that "the high managerial agent having supervisory responsibility over the subject matter of the offense employed due diligence to prevent its commission" exonerates the corporation from criminal liability.
>
> The second rule of corporate liability pertains to omissions as opposed to acts. Subsection (1)(b) provides that a corporation is accountable for failure to discharge specific duties imposed on corporations by law. Neither the text of this provision nor the comments address the question of whose omission may lead to liability.
>
> The third rule of liability is by far the most restrictive. Under subsection (1)(c), a corporation will incur liability for true crimes — that is, for an offense defined in the Penal Code — only if the conduct constituting the offense is authorized, commanded, solicited, performed, or recklessly tolerated by the board of directors or a "high managerial agent" whose acquiescence to the wrongdoing — by virtue of his position of authority — may fairly be regarded as reflecting corporate policy.

Question: Consider whether the *Hilton Hotels* case, supra, would be decided the same way under the Model Penal Code.

For criticism of the Model Penal Code proposals, see Kathleen Brickey's article, supra, and Jennifer Moore, Corporate Culpability Under the Federal Sentencing Guidelines, 34 Ariz. L. Rev. 743 (1992).

2. Other alternatives. Commentators have floated a number of alternatives to the Model Penal Code and respondeat superior approaches for dealing with corporate criminality. One kind of alternative involves strategies to influence the internal functioning of the corporation. See, e.g., Christopher Stone, Where the Law Ends 124 (1975) (proposing legally mandated requirements on the way the corporation does its business); John Coffee, "No Soul to Damn: No Body to Kick": An Unscandalized Inquiry into the Problem of Corporate Punishment, 79 Mich. L. Rev. 386 (1981) (proposing that judges impose internal controls on convicted corporations as a condition of probation). A related group of proposals bases corporate fault on systemic conditions of corporate operation that encourage criminal actions by employees. See, e.g., Pamela H. Bucy, Corporate

Ethos: A Standard for Imposing Corporate Criminal Liability, 75 Minn. L. Rev. 1095, 1099-1101, 1145 (1991):

> [E]ach corporate entity has a distinct and identifiable personality or "ethos." The government can convict a corporation under this standard only if it proves that the corporate ethos encouraged agents of the corporation to commit the criminal act. Central to this approach is the assumption that organizations possess an identity that is independent of specific individuals who control or work for the organization.
>
> [In determining] whether there existed a corporate ethos that encouraged the criminal conduct. . . . factfinders should examine the corporation's internal structure. . . . Beginning with the corporate hierarchy, the factfinders should determine whether the directors' supervision of officers, or management's supervision of employees was dilatory. Next, factfinders should examine the corporate goals, as communicated to the employees, to determine whether these goals could be achieved only by disregarding the law. The third and fourth factors focus on the corporation's affirmative steps to educate and monitor employees and are more relevant in some fields than others. . . . The factfinders should [also] assess . . . how the corporation has reacted to past violations, to further evaluate whether the corporation encourages or discourages illegal behavior. . . .
>
> The . . . corporate ethos standard . . . rewards those corporations that make efforts to educate and motivate their employees to follow the letter and spirit of the law. This encourages responsible corporate behavior. This advantage is in sharp contrast to the Model Penal Code's standard of liability that discourages higher echelon employees from properly supervising lower echelon employees. This advantage also contrasts with the minimal deterrence achieved by imposing criminal liability on individuals within the corporation. Convicting individual agents and employees of a corporation does not stop other corporate employees from committing future criminal acts if sufficient internal corporate pressure to violate the law continues to exist. In such an environment, the agents are cogs in a wheel. Those convicted are simply replaced by others whose original propensity to obey the law is similarly overcome by a corporate ethos that encourages illegal acts. Unless inside or outside forces change the lawless ethos, it will corrupt each generation of corporate agents. The proposed standard of liability addresses this problem by punishing any corporation that establishes a lawless ethos which overcomes its employees' propensity to obey the law.

2. *Liability of Corporate Agents*

INTRODUCTORY NOTE

Personal liability of corporate officers and agents has not been much affected by the conceptual concerns that hindered development of criminal liability of the corporate entity. One argument against criminal liability was that corporate agents should not be criminally liable for their actions when they acted for the corporation in a representative capacity. But this argument never drew much support in the case law. See 3A W. Fletcher, Encyclopedia of the Law of Private Corporations §1348, at 630 (1975); Note, Individual Liability of Agents for Corporate Crime under the Proposed Federal Criminal Code, 31 Vand. L. Rev. 965, 971 (1978). The prevailing view is reflected in §2.07(6) of the Model Penal Code:

(a) A person is legally accountable for any conduct he performs or causes to be performed in the name of the corporation or an unincorporated association or in its behalf to the same extent as if it were performed in his own name or behalf.

(b) Whenever a duty to act is imposed by law upon a corporation or an unincorporated association, any agent of the corporation or association having primary responsibility for the discharge of the duty is legally accountable for reckless omission to perform the required act to the same extent as if the duty were imposed by law directly upon himself.

A major problem in seeking to impose criminal liability on individual corporate actors derives from the bureaucratic arrangement of corporate activities, with lower employees responsible to higher-level employees in a hierarchy leading up to the highest officers. This arrangement often makes it difficult to fasten liability upon the upper-echelon employees and officers under the prevailing standards of accomplice liability requiring intentional aiding or encouraging criminal conduct of another, for these doctrines are designed for personal rather than bureaucratic relationships. The doctrine of vicarious liability would be one solution, but its use entails potential unfairness and injustice. The materials that follow explore these problems.

GORDON v. UNITED STATES

United States Court of Appeals, 10th Circuit
203 F.2d 248 (1953), rev'd, *347 U.S. 909 (1954)*

[Defendant partners in a sewing-machine and appliance business were convicted of violating the Defense Production Act by selling sewing machines on credit terms prohibited by that act and regulations issued thereunder. Section 601 provided that any person who "willfully" violated its provisions or any regulation or order issued thereunder should upon conviction be punished as therein specified. The case was not submitted to the jury on the question whether the partners had actual notice of the transactions. Instead, it was tried and submitted on the theory that knowledge of one partner regarding the transactions was "imputable, attributable and chargeable" to the other and that the knowledge and acts of the salespeople who made the sales and kept the records while acting in the course of their employment were imputable and chargeable to the employing partners. On the "very perplexing question whether the partners can be held criminally responsible for the knowledge and acts of their agents and employees, who the evidence shows, while acting in the course of their employment, actually made the sales without having collected the required down payment," the court, per MURRAH, J., answered in the affirmative, stating:]

Deeply rooted in our criminal jurisprudence is the notion that criminal guilt is personal to the accused; that wilfulness or a guilty mind is an essential ingredient of a punishable offense, and that one cannot intend an act in which he did not consciously participate, acquiesce, or have guilty knowledge. Morissette v. United States, 342 U.S. 246.

Amenable to this notion, the courts have been reluctant to hold the master or the employer criminally responsible for the acts of his agent or employee which he did not authorize, counsel, advise, approve or ratify.

It is only in the so-called public welfare offenses usually involving police regulation of food, drink and drugs that the courts have relaxed the necessity for proof of a wilful intent.

In our case wilfulness is specifically made a prerequisite to guilt. Indeed it is the gist of the offenses charged in all of the counts in the information. And the trial court instructed the jury that in every crime or public offense there must be a "union or joint operation of act and intent" but "that the intent or intention is manifest by the circumstances connected with the offense as well as by direct testimony."

What the court did in effect was to make wilfulness an essential element of the offenses charged in the information, and to charge the employers with the guilty knowledge and acts of the employees in determining the question of wilfulness. . . .

The effect of this is not to dispense with wilfulness or guilty knowledge as an element of the offense. It is to charge the employer with knowledge of records he is required to keep and acts he is required or forbidden to do, and which he necessarily keeps, does or omits to do by and through his agents and employees. To be sure, the knowledge with which he is charged is not direct; it is constructive. If it be called vicarious responsibility, it is nevertheless a responsibility of him on whom the law places the duty. It is permissible proof of a wilfulness which in its proper context denotes more than mere negligence but less than bad purpose or evil motive. It connotes a course of conduct which may be construed by the triers of facts as deliberate and voluntary, hence intentional; or it may be construed as negligent, inadvertent and excusable. The act or omission itself is not inexorably penalized. The ultimate question of guilt is left to the ameliorating influence of those who sit in judgment. Considered in this light, we do not think the instructions of the court fall short of the traditional standards for guilt.

HUXMAN, J. dissenting: . . . The partners denied intent to violate the law or any knowledge that their employees were violating it. They were entitled to have their testimony weighed and evaluated under proper instructions by the court together with all other relevant evidence. They were entitled to have the jury told that they were not criminally liable for the acts of their employees, although committed within the scope of their employment, unless they directed such activities or had guilty knowledge thereof. It is a principle embedded in the English law from time immemorial that the sins of the father shall not be visited upon the son merely because the father is the agent of the son and his unlawful acts were committed within the scope of his employment, under a criminal statute making wilfulness an element of the offense when the son had no knowledge of or part in such violations.

Strong reliance is placed upon Inland Freight Lines v. United States, 191 F.2d 313, by this court. But that case is clearly distinguishable. There the sole defendant was the corporation charged with keeping false records and it was held that the knowledge of its agents was the knowledge of the corporation. That is the well established principle of criminal law as applied in the case of a corporation. It is, as the law recognizes, the only way a corporation can be held criminally responsible for violations of penal statutes. While a corporation is recognized as a separate legal entity, such separate entity is a pure fiction of the law. As a separate entity and aside from its agents and employees a corporation can do nothing. It has no conscience, will, or power of thought. It acts only through its agents. Their acts are the only acts it can commit and their knowledge of necessity is the only knowledge it can have.

The only cases in which a principal without actual intent or knowledge of criminal acts of wrong-doing by his employees has been held criminally responsible for such acts arose under welfare statutes such as the Pure Food and Drug Laws, Liquor Laws and Weight and Measure Acts. But under all of these acts where a principal was held guilty because of the acts of his agents without knowledge or intent on his part wilfulness was not an element of the offense and the statute made the doing of the act the offense.

NOTE

The United States Supreme Court granted certiorari and reversed the Tenth Circuit's decision in *Gordon* in the following per curiam opinion (347 U.S. 909, 909 (1954)):

> Petitioners are business partners in the sale of appliances. They were convicted under Section 603 of the Defense Production Act of 1950 . . . which provides that "Any person who willfully violates" regulations promulgated under the Act shall be guilty of crime. The jury was instructed that the knowledge of petitioners' employees was chargeable to petitioners in determining petitioners' willfulness. Because of the instruction, the government has confessed error. We agree, and accordingly reverse the judgment and remand the case to the district court for retrial.

Four years later, the Supreme Court held a partnership liable for the "knowing and willful" violation of the Motor Carrier Act, 18 U.S.C. §835, 49 U.S.C. §332(a), based on the conduct of an employee, and distinguished *Gordon* by explaining, "here the government does not seek to hold the individual partners, but only the partnership as an entity." United States v. A & P Trucking Co., 358 U.S. 121, 126 (1958).

UNITED STATES v. PARK

Supreme Court of the United States
421 U.S. 658 (1975)

CHIEF JUSTICE BURGER delivered the opinion of the Court. . . .

Acme Markets, Inc., is a national retail food chain with approximately 36,000 employees, 874 retail outlets, 12 general warehouses, and four special warehouses. Its headquarters, including the office of the president, respondent Park, who is chief executive officer of the corporation, are located in Philadelphia, Pa. In a five-count information filed in the United States District Court for the District of Maryland, the Government charged Acme and respondent with violations of the Federal Food, Drug, and Cosmetic Act. Each count of the information alleged that the defendants had received food that had been shipped in interstate commerce and that, while the food was being held for sale in Acme's Baltimore warehouse following shipment in interstate commerce, they caused it to be held in a building accessible to rodents and to be exposed to contamination by rodents. These acts were alleged to have resulted in the food's being adulterated within the meaning of 21 U.S.C. §§342(a)(3) and (4),[1] in violation of 21 U.S.C. §331(k).[2]

Acme pleaded guilty to each count of the information. Respondent pleaded not guilty. The evidence at trial demonstrated that in April 1970 the Food and Drug Administration (FDA) advised respondent by letter of insanitary conditions in Acme's Philadelphia warehouse. In 1971 the FDA found that similar conditions existed in the firm's Baltimore warehouse. An FDA consumer safety officer testified concerning evidence of rodent infestation and other insanitary conditions discovered during a 12-day inspection of the Baltimore warehouse in November and December 1971. He also related that a second inspection of the warehouse had been conducted in March 1972. On that occasion the inspectors found that there had been improvement in the sanitary conditions, but that "there was still evidence of rodent activity in the building and in the warehouses and we found some rodent-contaminated lots of food items."

The Government also presented testimony by the Chief of Compliance of the FDA's Baltimore office, who informed respondent by letter of the conditions at the Baltimore warehouse after the first inspection.[6] There was testimony by Acme's Baltimore division vice president, who had responded to the letter on behalf of Acme and respondent and who described the steps taken to remedy the insanitary conditions discovered by both inspections. The Government's final witness, Acme's vice president for legal affairs and assistant secretary, identified respondent as the president and chief executive officer of the company and read a bylaw prescribing the duties of the chief executive officer.[7] He testified

1. Section 402 of the Act, 21 U.S.C. §342, provides in pertinent part:

> A food shall be deemed to be adulterated —
> (a) . . . (3) if it consists in whole or in part of any filthy, putrid, or decomposed substance, or if it is otherwise unfit for food; or (4) if it has been prepared, packed, or held under insanitary conditions whereby it may have become contaminated with filth, or whereby it may have been rendered injurious to health. . . .

2. Section 301 of the Act, 21 U.S.C. §331, provides in pertinent part:

> The following acts and the causing thereof are prohibited: . . .
> (k) The alteration, mutilation, destruction, obliteration, or removal of the whole or any part of the labeling of, or the doing of any other act with respect to, a food, drug, device, or cosmetic, if such act is done while such article is held for sale (whether or not the first sale) after shipment in interstate commerce and results in such article being adulterated or misbranded.

6. The letter, dated January 27, 1972, included the following:

> We note with much concern that the old and new warehouse areas used for food storage were actively and extensively inhabited by live rodents. Of even more concern was the observation that such reprehensible conditions obviously existed for a prolonged period of time without any detection, or were completely ignored. . . .
> We trust this letter will serve to direct your attention to the seriousness of the problem and formally advise you of the urgent need to initiate whatever measures are necessary to prevent recurrence and ensure compliance with the law.

7. The bylaw provided in pertinent part:

> The Chairman of the board of directors or the president shall be the chief executive officer of the company as the board of directors may from time to time determine. He shall, subject to the board of directors, have general and active supervision of the affairs, business, offices and employees of the company. . . .
> He shall, from time to time, in his discretion or at the order of the board, report the op-

that respondent functioned by delegating "normal operating duties," including sanitation, but that he retained "certain things, which are the big, broad, principles of the operation of the company," and had "the responsibility of seeing that they all work together." . . .

Respondent was the only defense witness. He testified that, although all of Acme's employees were in a sense under his general direction, the company had an "organizational structure for responsibilities for certain functions" according to which different phases of its operation were "assigned to individuals who, in turn, have staff and departments under them." He identified those individuals responsible for sanitation, and related that upon receipt of the January 1972 FDA letter, he had conferred with the vice president for legal affairs, who informed him that the Baltimore division vice president "was investigating the situation immediately and would be taking corrective action and would be preparing a summary of the corrective action to reply to the letter." Respondent stated that he did not "believe there was anything [he] could have done more constructively than what [he] found was being done."

On cross-examination, respondent conceded that providing sanitary conditions for food offered for sale to the public was something that he was "responsible for in the entire operation of the company," and he stated that it was one of many phases of the company that he assigned to "dependable subordinates." Respondent was asked about and, over the objections of his counsel, admitted receiving, the April 1970 letter addressed to him from the FDA regarding insanitary conditions at Acme's Philadelphia warehouse. He acknowledged that, with the exception of the division vice president, the same individuals had responsibility for sanitation in both Baltimore and Philadelphia. Finally, in response to questions concerning the Philadelphia and Baltimore incidents, respondent admitted that the Baltimore problem indicated the system for handling sanitation "wasn't working perfectly" and that as Acme's chief executive officer he was responsible for "any result which occurs in our company."

At the close of the evidence, respondent's renewed motion for a judgment of acquittal was denied. The relevant portion of the trial judge's instructions to the jury challenged by respondent is set out in the margin.[9] Respondent's counsel objected to the instructions on the ground that they failed fairly to reflect our decision in United States v. Dotterweich, [320 U.S. 277 (1943)], and to define "'responsible relationship.'" The trial judge overruled the objection. The jury

---

erations and affairs of the company. He shall also perform such other duties and have such other powers as may be assigned to him from time to time by the board of directors.

9. . . . "The main issue for your determination is . . . whether the Defendant held a position of authority and responsibility in the business of Acme Markets. . . .

"The statute makes individuals, as well as corporations, liable for violations. An individual is liable if it is clear, beyond a reasonable doubt, that the elements of the adulteration of the food as to travel in interstate commerce are present. As I have instructed you in this case, they are, and that the individual had a responsible relation to the situation, even though he may not have participated personally.

"The individual is or could be liable under the statute, even if he did not consciously do wrong. However, the fact that the Defendant is pres[id]ent and is a chief executive officer of the Acme Markets does not require a finding of guilt. Though, he need not have personally participated in the situation, he must have had a responsible relationship to the issue. The issue is, in this case, whether the Defendant, John R. Park, by virtue of his position in the company, had a position of authority and responsibility in the situation out of which these charges arose."

found respondent guilty on all counts of the information, and he was subsequently sentenced to pay a fine of $50 on each count.[10]

The Court of Appeals reversed the conviction and remanded for a new trial. That court viewed the Government as arguing "that the conviction may be predicated solely upon a showing that [respondent] was the President of the offending corporation," and it stated that as "a general proposition, some act of commission or omission is an essential element of every crime." It reasoned that, although our decision in United States v. Dotterweich had construed the statutory provisions under which respondent was tried to dispense with the traditional element of "'awareness of some wrongdoing,'" the Court had not construed them as dispensing with the element of "wrongful action." The Court of Appeals concluded that the trial judge's instructions "might well have left the jury with the erroneous impression that Park could be found guilty in the absence of 'wrongful action' on his part," and that proof of this element was required by due process. It . . . directed that on retrial the jury be instructed as to "wrongful action," which might be "gross negligence and inattention in discharging . . . corporate duties and obligations or any of a host of other acts of commission or omission which would 'cause' the contamination of food." . . .

The question presented by the Government's petition for certiorari in United States v. Dotterweich, [supra, page 236 this casebook], and the focus of this Court's opinion, was whether "the manager of a corporation, as well as the corporation itself, may be prosecuted under the Federal Food, Drug, and Cosmetic Act of 1938 for the introduction of misbranded and adulterated articles into interstate commerce." In Dotterweich, a jury had disagreed as to the corporation, a jobber purchasing drugs from manufacturers and shipping them in interstate commerce under its own label, but had convicted Dotterweich, the corporation's president and general manager. The Court of Appeals reversed the conviction on the ground that only the drug dealer, whether corporation or individual, was subject to the criminal provisions of the Act, and that where the dealer was a corporation, an individual connected therewith might be held personally only if he was operating the corporation "as his 'alter ego.'"

In reversing the judgment of the Court of Appeals and reinstating Dotterweich's conviction, this Court looked to the purposes of the Act and noted that they "touch phases of the lives and health of people which, in the circumstances of modern industrialism, are largely beyond self-protection." It observed that the Act is of "a now familiar type" which "dispenses with the conventional requirement for criminal conduct — awareness of some wrongdoing. In the interest of the larger good it puts the burden of acting as hazard upon a person otherwise innocent but standing in responsible relation to a public danger."

Central to the Court's conclusion that individuals other than proprietors are subject to the criminal provisions of the Act was the reality that "the only way in which a corporation can act is through the individuals who act on its behalf." . . .

At the same time, however, the Court was aware of the concern which was the motivating factor in the Court of Appeals' decision, that literal enforcement

10. Sections 303(a) and (b) of the Act, 21 U.S.C. §§333(a) and (b), provide:

> (a) Any person who violates a provision of section 331 of this title shall be imprisoned for not more than one year or fined not more than $1,000, or both. . .

"might operate too harshly by sweeping within its condemnation any person however remotely entangled in the proscribed shipment." A limiting principle, in the form of "settled doctrines of criminal law" defining those who "are responsible for the commission of a misdemeanor," was available. In this context, the Court concluded, those doctrines dictated that the offense was committed "by all who . . . have . . . a responsible share in the furtherance of the transaction which the statute outlaws."

The Court recognized that, because the Act dispenses with the need to prove "consciousness of wrongdoing," it may result in hardship even as applied to those who share "responsibility in the business process resulting in" a violation. It regarded as "too treacherous" an attempt "to define or even to indicate by way of illustration the class of employees which stands in such a responsible relation." The question of responsibility, the Court said, depends "on the evidence produced at the trial and its submission — assuming the evidence warrants it — to the jury under appropriate guidance." The Court added: "In such matters the good sense of prosecutors, the wise guidance of trial judges, and the ultimate judgment must be trusted." . . .

Dotterweich and the cases which have followed reveal that in providing sanctions which reach and touch the individuals who execute the corporate mission — and this is by no means necessarily confined to a single corporate agent or employee — the Act imposes not only a positive duty to seek out and remedy violations when they occur but also, and primarily, a duty to implement measures that will insure that violations will not occur. The requirements of foresight and vigilance imposed on responsible corporate agents are beyond question demanding, and perhaps onerous, but they are no more stringent than the public has a right to expect of those who voluntarily assume positions of authority in business enterprises whose services and products affect the health and well-being of the public that supports them. Cf. Wasserstrom, Strict Liability in the Criminal Law, 12 Stan. L. Rev. 731, 741-745 (1960).

The Act does not, as we observed in *Dotterweich,* make criminal liability turn on "awareness of some wrongdoing" or "conscious fraud." The duty imposed by Congress on responsible corporate agents is, we emphasize, one that requires the highest standard of foresight and vigilance, but the Act, in its criminal aspect, does not require that which is objectively impossible. The theory upon which responsible corporate agents are held criminally accountable for "causing" violations of the Act permits a claim that a defendant was "powerless" to prevent or correct the violation to "be raised defensively at a trial on the merits." United States v. Wiesenfeld Warehouse Co., 376 U.S. 86, 91 (1964). If such a claim is made, the defendant has the burden of coming forward with evidence, but this does not alter the Government's ultimate burden of proving beyond a reasonable doubt the defendant's guilt, including his power, in light of the duty imposed by the Act, to prevent or correct the prohibited condition. Congress has seen fit to enforce the accountability of responsible corporate agents dealing with products which may affect the health of consumers by penal sanctions cast in rigorous terms, and the obligation of the courts is to give them effect so long as they do not violate the Constitution.

We cannot agree with the Court of Appeals that it was incumbent upon the District court to instruct the jury that the Government had the burden of establishing "wrongful action" in the sense in which the Court of Appeals used that phrase. The concept of a "reasonable relationship" to, or a "reasonable share" in, a violation of the Act indeed imports some measure of blameworthiness; but it is equally clear that the Government establishes a prima facie case when it introduces evidence sufficient to warrant a finding by the trier of the facts that the defendant had, by reason of his position in the corporation, responsibility and authority either to prevent in the first instance, or promptly to correct, the violation complained of, and that he failed to do so. . . .

Reading the entire charge satisfies us that the jury's attention was adequately focused on the issue of respondent's authority with respect to the conditions that formed the basis of the alleged violations. Viewed as a whole, the charge did not permit the jury to find guilt solely on the basis of respondent's position in the corporation. . . .

Reversed.

JUSTICE STEWART, with whom JUSTICE MARSHALL and JUSTICE POWELL join, dissenting.

Although agreeing with much of what is said in the Court's opinion, I dissent from the opinion and judgment, because the jury instructions in this case were not consistent with the law as the Court today expounds it.

As I understand the Court's opinion, it holds that in order to sustain a conviction under §301(k) of the Federal Food, Drug, and Cosmetic Act the prosecution must at least show that by reason of an individual's corporate position and responsibilities, he had a duty to use care to maintain the physical integrity of the corporation's food products. A jury may then draw the inference that when the food is found to be in such condition as to violate the statute's prohibitions, that condition was "caused" by a breach of the standard of care imposed upon the responsible official. This is the language of negligence, and I agree with it.

To affirm this conviction, however, the Court must approve the instructions given to the members of the jury who were entrusted with determining whether the respondent was innocent or guilty. Those instructions did not conform to the standards that the Court itself sets out today.

The trial judge instructed the jury to find Park guilty if it found beyond a reasonable doubt that Park "had a responsible relation to the situation. . . . The issue is, in this case, whether the Defendant, John R. Park, by virtue of his position in the company, had a position of authority and responsibility in the situation out of which these charges arose." Requiring, as it did, a verdict of guilty upon a finding of "responsibility," this instruction standing alone could have been construed as a direction to convict if the jury found Park "responsible" for the condition in the sense that his position as chief executive officer gave him formal responsibility within the structure of the corporation. But the trial judge went on specifically to caution the jury not to attach such a meaning to his instruction, saying that "the fact that the Defendant is pres[id]ent and is a chief executive officer of the Acme Markets does not require a finding of guilt." "Responsibility" as used by the trial judge therefore had whatever meaning the jury in its unguided discretion chose to give it.

The instructions, therefore, expressed nothing more than a tautology. They told the jury: "You must find the defendant guilty if you find that he is to be held accountable for this adulterated food." In other words: "You must find the defendant guilty if you conclude that he is guilty." . . .

To be sure, "the day [is] long past when [courts] . . . parsed instructions and engaged in nice semantic distinctions," Cool v. United States, 409 U.S. 100, 107 (Rehnquist, J., dissenting). But this Court has never before abandoned the view that jury instructions must contain a statement of the applicable law sufficiently precise to enable the jury to be guided by something other than its rough notions of social justice. And while it might be argued that the issue before the jury in this case was a "mixed" question of both law and fact, this has never meant that a jury is to be left wholly at sea, without any guidance as to the standard of conduct the law requires. . . .

The *Dotterweich* case stands for two propositions, and I accept them both. First, "any person" within the meaning of 21 U.S.C. §333 may include any corporate officer or employee "standing in responsible relation" to a condition or transaction forbidden by the Act. 320 U.S., at 281. Second, a person may be convicted of a criminal offense under the Act even in the absence of "the conventional requirement for criminal conduct — awareness of some wrongdoing." Ibid.

But before a person can be convicted of a criminal violation of this Act, a jury must find — and must be clearly instructed that it must find — evidence beyond a reasonable doubt that he engaged in wrongful conduct amounting at least to common-law negligence. There were no such instructions, and clearly, therefore, no such finding in this case. . . .

NOTES

1. The Responsible Corporate Officer Doctrine. The theory of liability established in *Dotterweich* and *Park* has become known as the "responsible corporate officer" doctrine. Under the doctrine, the prosecutor must present sufficient evidence "to warrant a finding by the trier of the facts that the defendant had, by reason of his position in the corporation, responsibility and authority either to prevent in the first instance, or promptly to correct, the violation complained of, and that he failed to do so." United States v. Park, 421 U.S. 658, 673-674 (1975). Although a defendant can raise as a defense that the "defendant was 'powerless' to prevent or correct the violation," federal courts have been slow to recognize situations in which it was "objectively impossible" to avoid the harm. See United States v. Gel Spice Co., 773 F2d. 427 (2d Cir. 1985). The court in United States v. New England Grocers Supply Co. 488 F. Supp. 230 (D. Mass. 1980), addressed the difficulty in "ascertain[ing] from [*Park*] the exact nature and scope of the impossibility defense":

> One interpretation . . . is that it relates only to the power of the corporate officer, by virtue of his position in the corporation, to correct or prevent violations of the Act. Under this interpretation, the evidence introduced by the defendant at trial to sustain his impossibility defense would serve only to rebut the evidence introduced by the government in establishing its prima facie case. [T]he impossibility defense would not serve as an affirmative defense, but would merely provide corporate officers a defense open to all who are criminally accused, that is, rebuttal of the government's proof.
>
> An alternative interpretation of the impossibility defense is that it is satisfied by evidence that the corporate officer exercised "extraordinary care" and was still unable to prevent violations. Under this interpretation, the impossibility defense

would serve as an affirmative defense, incorporating an objective element — use of extraordinary care — into a strict liability offense.

In light of the severe penalties which may be imposed for a second violation under the Act, I am inclined to adopt [the latter] more lenient position of the impossibility defense. Id. at 235-36.

New England Grocers makes clear that the impossibility defense is available only to individuals and not to corporations.

2. *Vicarious liability?* Reconsider the *Guminga* case, supra page 244. Guminga's objection was to the kind of vicarious liability exemplified in the tort doctrine of respondeat superior; namely, where the liability of *A* for the acts of *B* is based solely on some relationship between them rather than on any culpable conduct of *A*. Is the liability of Park (and Dotterweich) objectionable in the same way? Consider Note, Developments in the Law — Corporate Crime: Regulating Corporate Behavior through Criminal Sanctions, 92 Harv. L. Rev. 1227, 1262 n. 102 (1979):

> It should be stressed that holding corporate officials criminally responsible for causing strict liability violations is not imposing vicarious liability. In *Park* and *Dotterweich,* corporate executives were culpable for their own failure to exercise the quality of care needed to prevent violations within the realms of their own authority; their guilt was not vicariously imputed from the guilt of their subordinates.

UNITED STATES v. MacDONALD & WATSON WASTE OIL CO.

United States Court of Appeals, 1st Circuit
933 F.2d 35 (1991)

CAMPBELL, C.J. [MacDonald & Watson Waste Oil Co., a corporation engaged in the business of transporting and disposing of contaminated wastes, operated a disposal facility at the Poe Street Lot, a facility leased from the Narragansett Improvement Company (NIC). Neither MacDonald nor NIC held a permit authorizing them to dispose of solid hazardous wastes in that site, although NIC did have a permit to dispose of *liquid* wastes there.

[MacDonald was hired to remove solid waste (toluene-contaminated soil) from the grounds of the Master Chemical Company. An employee of MacDonald supervised the transportation of the contaminated soil from Master Chemical to the Poe Street Lot. Subsequently Eugene K. D'Allesandro, president of MacDonald, was convicted of knowingly transporting and causing the transportation of hazardous waste to a facility that did not have a permit, in violation of the Resource Conservation and Recovery Act (RCRA), §3008(d)(1). The company was also convicted, but discussion of its liability is omitted.]

D'Allesandro . . . contends that his conviction . . . must be vacated because the district court incorrectly charged the jury regarding the element of knowledge in the case of a corporate officer. Section 3008(d)(1) penalizes "Any person who . . . (1) knowingly transports or causes to be transported any hazardous waste identified or listed under this subchapter . . . to a facility which does not have a permit. . . ." In his closing, the prosecutor conceded that the government had "no direct evidence that Eugene D'Allesandro actually knew that the Master Chemical shipments were coming in," i.e., were being transported to the Poe Street Lot under contract with his company. The prosecution did present evidence, however, that D'Allesandro was not only the President and owner of MacDonald & Watson but was a "hands-on" manager of that relatively small firm. There was also proof that . . . D'Allesandro's subordinates had contracted for and transported the Master Chemical waste for disposal at [the Poe Street] site. The government argued that D'Allesandro was guilty of violating §3008(d)(1) because, as the responsible corporate officer, he was in a position to ensure compliance with RCRA and had failed to do so even after being warned by a consultant on two earlier occasions that other shipments of toluene-contaminated soil had been received from other customers, and that such material violated NIC's permit. In the government's view, any failure to prove D'Allesandro's actual knowledge of the Master Chemical contract and shipments was irrelevant to his criminal responsibility under §3008(d)(1) for those shipments.

The court apparently accepted the government's theory. It instructed the jury as follows:

> When an individual Defendant is also a corporate officer, the Government may prove that individual's knowledge in either of two ways. The first way is to demonstrate that the defendant had actual knowledge of the act in question. The second way is to establish that the defendant was what is called a responsible officer of the corporation committing the act. In order to prove that a person is a responsible corporate officer three things must be shown.
>
> First, it must be shown that the person is an officer of the corporation, not merely an employee.
>
> Second, it must be shown that the officer had direct responsibility for the activities that are alleged to be illegal. Simply being an officer or even the president of a corporation is not enough. The Government must prove that the person had a responsibility to supervise the activities in question.
>
> And the third requirement is that the officer must have known or believed that the illegal activity of the type alleged occurred. . . .

. . . We agree with D'Allesandro that the jury instructions improperly allowed the jury to find him guilty without finding he had actual knowledge of the alleged transportation of hazardous waste on July 30 and 31, 1986, from Master Chemical Company, Boston, Massachusetts, to NIC's site, knowledge being an element the statute requires. We must, therefore, reverse his conviction.

The seminal cases regarding the responsible corporate officer doctrine are United States v. Dotterweich, 320 U.S. 277 (1943), and United States v. Park, 421 U.S. 658 (1975). These cases concerned misdemeanor charges . . . [that] dispensed with a scienter requirement. . . . But while *Dotterweich* and *Park* thus reflect what is now . . . well-established law in respect to public welfare statutes and regulations lacking an express knowledge or other *scienter* requirement, we know of no precedent for failing to give effect to a knowledge requirement that Congress has expressly included in a criminal statute. Especially is that so where, as here, the crime is a felony carrying possible imprisonment of five years and, for a second offense, ten. . . .

[T]he district court charged, in effect, that proof that D'Allesandro was a responsible corporate officer would conclusively prove the element of his knowledge of the Master Chemical shipments. . . . In a crime having knowledge as an express element, a mere showing of official responsibility under *Dotterweich* and *Park* is not an adequate substitute for direct or circumstantial proof of knowledge. . . .

We vacate the conviction of Eugene D'Allesandro . . . and remand for a new trial or such other action as may be consistent herewith.

NOTES

1. For commentary, see Comment (Jeremy D. Heep), Adapting the Responsible Corporate Officer Doctrine in Light of *United States v. MacDonald & Watson Waste Oil Co.,* 78 Minn. L. Rev. 699 (1994); Barry M. Hartman & Charles A. De Monaco, The Present Use of the Responsible Officer Doctrine in the Criminal Enforcement of Environmental Laws, 23 Envtl. L. Rep. 10145 (1993).

2. A critical view of the increasing practice of seeking convictions of corporate officers for the crimes of their corporations is taken in Margaret Graham Tebo, Guilty By Reason of Title, 86 ABA J. 44 (May 2000). She notes at 45:

> [A] number of former U.S. attorneys say [the] Justice [Department] subscribes to the view that holding high-level executives criminally liable will often bring changes in the behavior of their companies. Prosecutors and regulators at the state and local levels seem to agree. Apparently, so do legislators, who have incorporated criminal penalties into an increasing number of regulatory statutes, such as the federal clean air and water acts, aimed at carrying out public policy priorities. Typically, those provisions make the highest-ranking official involved in a particular company activity the ultimately responsible party, even where that person's direct participation in the violation cannot be shown.
>
> Many federal environmental, antitrust and health care statutes have been interpreted by courts to be public welfare legislation, meaning that no showing of direct personal involvement is necessary to convict a manager for company violations. Courts have consistently held that these public welfare statutes do not require findings of intent, or even negligence, to support convictions. The courts have repeatedly denied attempts to challenge such laws as unconstitutional due process violations.
>
> Such was the case with Edward Hanousek, a project manager for the White Pass & Yukon Railroad in Alaska. One day in 1994, an employee of a subcontractor on the project struck an oil pipeline with his backhoe, spilling several thousand gallons of oil into the Skagway River. Hanousek, who was off duty and at home when the spill occurred, was convicted under the Clean Water Act of negligently discharging oil into a navigable waterway. He was sentenced consecutively to six months in jail, six months in a halfway house and six months of supervised release, plus a $5,000 fine.
>
> The U.S. Supreme Court rejected Hanousek's petition for certiorari [letting] stand a decision that Hanousek suffered no due process violation.

The decision the author is referring to is United States v. Hanousek, 176 F.3d 1116 (9th Cir. 1999). In this case, the court held that since the criminal provisions of the Clean Water Act constitute public welfare legislation they did not violate due process in imposing liability for ordinary as opposed to gross negligence. It further rejected defendant's argument that he was being held vicariously liable for the negligence of the backhoe operators, pointing out that the trial court did in fact instruct the jury that the discharge must have been "caused by the negligence of the particular defendant," presumably in failing to adequately protect the pipeline. *Question:* Is the author's criticism of the decision well grounded?

Question: Since the Clean Water Act is seen as public welfare legislation, was the instruction necessary to preserve the conviction against a due process challenge?

C. CONSPIRACY

CLARENCE DARROW, THE STORY OF MY LIFE 64 (1932): If there are still any citizens interested in protecting human liberty, let them study the conspiracy laws of the United States.

MODEL PENAL CODE AND COMMENTARIES, Comment to §5.03 at 387 (1985): [C]onspiracy as an offense has two different aspects, reflecting the different functions it serves in the legal system. In the first place, conspiracy is an inchoate crime, complementing the provisions dealing with attempt and solicitation in reaching preparatory conduct before it has matured into commission of a substantive offense. Second, it is a means of striking against the special danger incident to group activity, facilitating prosecution of the group, and yielding a basis for imposing added penalties when combination is involved.

INTRODUCTORY NOTE

Conspiracy is an offense carrying its own penalty, and a conspiracy charge also has collateral effects on the rules of procedure, evidence, and criminal liability for other offenses. Before considering the elements of conspiracy as a substantive crime, we examine the most important of these collateral consequences. The collateral effects are crucial for understanding the implications of a prosecution for conspiracy.

1. An Overview: The Consequences of a Conspiracy Charge

KRULEWITCH v. UNITED STATES

Supreme Court of the United States
336 U.S. 440 (1949)

JUSTICE BLACK delivered the opinion of the Court.

A federal district court indictment charged in three counts that petitioner and a woman defendant had (1) induced and persuaded another woman to go on October 20, 1941, from New York City to Miami, Florida for the purpose of prostitution, in violation of 18 U.S.C.A. §399 [now §2422]; (2) transported or caused her to be transported from New York to Miami for that purpose, in violation of 18 U.S.C.A. §398 [now §2421]; and (3) conspired to commit those offenses in violation of 18 U.S.C.A. §88 [now §371]. Tried alone, the petitioner was convicted on all three counts of the indictment. The Court of Appeals affirmed. We granted certiorari limiting our review to consideration of alleged error in admission of certain hearsay testimony against petitioner over his timely and repeated objections.

The challenged testimony was elicited by the Government from its complaining witness, the person whom petitioner and the woman defendant allegedly induced to go from New York to Florida for the purpose of prostitution. The testimony narrated the following purported conversation between the complaining witness and petitioner's alleged co-conspirator, the woman defendant.

> She asked me, she says, "You didn't talk yet?" And I says, "No." And she says, "Well, don't," she says, "until we get you a lawyer." And then she says, "Be very careful what you say." And I can't put it in exact words. But she said, "It would be better for us two girls to take the blame than Kay (the defendant) because he couldn't stand it, he couldn't stand to take it."

The time of the alleged conversation was more than a month and a half after October 20, 1941, the date the complaining witness had gone to Miami. Whatever original conspiracy may have existed between petitioner and his alleged co-conspirator to cause the complaining witness to go to Florida in October, 1941, no longer existed when the reported conversation took place in December, 1941. For on this latter date the trip to Florida had not only been made — the complaining witness had left Florida, had returned to New York, and had resumed her residence there. Furthermore, at the time the conversation took place, the complaining witness, the alleged co-conspirator, and the petitioner had been arrested. They apparently were charged in a United States District Court of Florida with the offense of which petitioner was here convicted.

It is beyond doubt that the central aim of the alleged conspiracy — transportation of the complaining witness to Florida for prostitution — had either never existed or had long since ended in success or failure when and if the alleged co-conspirator made the statement attributed to her. The statement plainly implied that petitioner was guilty of the crime for which he was on trial. It was made in petitioner's absence and the Government made no effort whatever to show that it was made with his authority. The testimony thus stands as an unsworn, out-of-court declaration of petitioner's guilt. This hearsay declaration, attributed to a co-conspirator, was not made pursuant to and in furtherance of objectives of the conspiracy charged in the indictment, because if made, it was after those objectives either had failed or had been achieved. . . .

Although the Government recognizes that the chief objective of the conspiracy — transportation for prostitution purposes — had ended in success or failure before the reported conversation took place, it nevertheless argues for admissibility of the hearsay declaration as one in furtherance of a continuing subsidiary objective of the conspiracy. Its argument runs this way. Conspirators about to commit crimes always expressly or implicitly agree to collaborate with each other to conceal facts in order to prevent detection, conviction and punishment. Thus the argument is that even after the central criminal objectives of a conspiracy have succeeded or failed, an implicit subsidiary phase of the conspiracy always survives, the phase which has concealment as its sole objective. The Court of Appeals adopted this view. It viewed the alleged hearsay declaration as one in furtherance of this continuing subsidiary phase of the conspiracy, as part of "the implied agreement to conceal." It consequently held the declaration properly admitted.

We cannot accept the Government's contention. There are many logical and practical reasons that could be advanced against a special evidentiary rule that permits out-of-court statements of one conspirator to be used against another. But however cogent these reasons, it is firmly established that where made in furtherance of the objectives of a going conspiracy, such statements are admissible as exceptions to the hearsay rule. . . . The Government now asks us to expand this narrow exception to the hearsay rule and hold admissible a declaration, not made in furtherance of the alleged criminal transportation conspiracy charged, but made in furtherance of an alleged implied but uncharged conspiracy aimed at preventing detection and punishment. [U]nder this rule plausible arguments could generally be made in conspiracy cases that most out-of-court statements offered in evidence tended to shield co-conspirators. We are not persuaded to adopt the Government's implicit conspiracy theory which in all criminal conspiracy cases would create automatically a further breach of the general rule against the admission of hearsay evidence. . . .

Reversed.

JUSTICE JACKSON, concurring in the judgment and opinion of the Court.

This case illustrates a present drift in the federal law of conspiracy which warrants some further comment because it is characteristic of the long evolution of that elastic, sprawling and pervasive offense. Its history exemplifies the "tendency of a principle to expand itself to the limit of its logic."[1] The unavailing protest of courts against the growing habit to indict for conspiracy in lieu of prosecuting for the substantive offense itself, or in addition thereto, suggests that loose practice as to this offense constitutes a serious threat to fairness in our administration of justice.

The modern crime of conspiracy is so vague that it almost defies definition. Despite certain elementary and essential elements,[4] it also, chameleon-like, takes on a special coloration from each of the many independent offenses on which it may be overlaid. It is always "predominantly mental in composition" because it consists primarily of a meeting of minds and an intent.

. . . It is not intended to question that the basic conspiracy principle has some place in modern criminal law, because to unite, back of a criminal purpose, the strength, opportunities and resources of many is obviously more dangerous and more difficult to police than the efforts of a lone wrongdoer. It also may be trivialized, as here, where the conspiracy consists of the concert of a loathsome panderer and a prostitute to go from New York to Florida to ply their trade and it would appear that a simple Mann Act prosecution would vindicate the majesty

1. The phrase is Judge Cardozo's — Nature of Judicial Process, p. 51. [See Justice Holmes in Hudson County Water Co. v. McCarter, 209 U.S. 349, 355 (1908): "All rights tend to declare themselves absolute to their logical extreme. Yet all in fact are limited by the neighborhood of principles of policy which are other than those on which the particular right is founded, and which become strong enough to hold their own when a certain point is reached." — EDS.

4. Justice Holmes supplied an oversimplified working definition in United States v. Kissel, 218 U.S. 601, 608: "A conspiracy is a partnership in criminal purposes." This was recently restated "A conspiracy is a partnership in crime." Pinkerton v. United States, 328 U.S. 640, 644. The latter is inaccurate, since concert in criminal purposes, rather than concert in crime, establishes the conspiracy. . . .

of federal law. However, even when appropriately invoked, the looseness and pliability of the doctrine present inherent dangers which should be in the background of judicial thought wherever it is sought to extend the doctrine to meet the exigencies of a particular case.

Conspiracy in federal law aggravates the degree of crime over that of unconcerted offending. The act of confederating to commit a misdemeanor, followed by even an innocent overt act in its execution, is a felony and is such even if the misdemeanor is never consummated. The more radical proposition also is well-established that at common law and under some statutes a combination may be a criminal conspiracy even if it contemplates only acts which are not crimes at all when perpetrated by an individual or by many acting severally.

Thus, the conspiracy doctrine will incriminate persons on the fringe of offending who would not be guilty of aiding and abetting or of becoming an accessory, for those charges only lie when an act which is a crime has actually been committed.

Attribution of criminality to a confederation which contemplates no act that would be criminal if carried out by any one of the conspirators is a practice peculiar to Anglo-American law. . . . Most other countries have devised what they consider more discriminating principles upon which to prosecute criminal gangs, secret associations, and subversive syndicates. . . .

The interchangeable use of conspiracy doctrine in civil as well as penal proceedings opens it to the danger, absent in the case of many crimes, that a court having in mind only the civil sanctions will approve lax practices which later are imported into criminal proceedings. In civil proceedings this Court frankly has made the end a test of the means, saying, "To require a greater showing would cripple the Act," United States v. Griffith, 334 U.S. 100. . . . Further, the Court has dispensed with even the necessity to infer any definite agreement, although that is the gist of the offense. . . .

Of course, it is for prosecutors rather than courts to determine when to use a scatter gun to bring down the defendant, but there are procedural advantages from using it which add to the danger of unguarded extension of the concept.

An accused, under the Sixth Amendment, has the right to trial "by an impartial jury of the state and district wherein the crime shall have been committed." The leverage of a conspiracy charge lifts this limitation from the prosecution and reduces its protection to a phantom, for the crime is considered so vagrant as to have been committed in any district where any one of the conspirators did any one of the acts, however innocent, intended to accomplish its object. The Government may, and often does, compel one to defend at a great distance from any place he ever did any act because some accused confederate did some trivial and by itself innocent act in the chosen district. . . .

When the trial starts, the accused feels the full impact of the conspiracy strategy. Strictly, the prosecution should first establish prima facie the conspiracy and identify the conspirators, after which evidence of acts and declarations of each in the course of its execution are admissible against all. But the order of proof of so sprawling a charge is difficult for a judge to control. As a practical matter, the accused often is confronted with a hodgepodge of acts and statements by others which he may never have authorized or intended or even known about, but which help to persuade the jury of existence of the conspiracy itself. In other words, a conspiracy often is proved by evidence that is admissible only upon assumption that conspiracy existed. The naive assumption that prejudicial effects can be overcome by instructions to the jury all practicing lawyers know to be unmitigated fiction.

The trial of a conspiracy charge doubtless imposes a heavy burden on the prosecution, but it is an especially difficult situation for the defendant. . . .

A co-defendant in a conspiracy trial occupies an uneasy seat. There generally will be evidence of wrongdoing by somebody. It is difficult for the individual to make his own case stand on its own merits in the minds of jurors who are ready to believe that birds of a feather are flocked together. If he is silent, he is taken to admit it and if, as often happens, co-defendants can be prodded into accusing or contradicting each other, they convict each other. . . .

Against this inadequately sketched background, I think the decision of this case in the court below introduced an ominous expansion of the accepted law of conspiracy. . . .

It is difficult to see any logical limit to the [Government's theory of] "implied conspiracy," either as to duration or means. . . . On the theory that the law will impute to the confederates a continuing conspiracy to defeat justice, one conceivably could be bound by another's unauthorized and unknown commission of perjury, bribery of a juror or witness, or even putting an incorrigible witness with damaging information out of the way.

Moreover, the assumption of an indefinitely continuing offense would result in an indeterminate extension of the statute of limitations. If the law implies an agreement to cooperate in defeating prosecution, it must imply that it continues as long as prosecution is a possibility, and prosecution is a possibility as long as the conspiracy to defeat it is implied to continue. . . .

There is, of course, strong temptation to relax rigid standards when it seems the only way to sustain convictions of evildoers. But statutes authorize prosecution for substantive crimes for most evil-doing without the dangers to the liberty of the individual and the integrity of the judicial process that are inherent in conspiracy charges. We should disapprove the doctrine of implied or constructive crime in its entirety and in every manifestation. And I think there should be no straining to uphold any conspiracy conviction where prosecution for the substantive offense is adequate and the purpose served by adding the conspiracy charge seems chiefly to get procedural advantages to ease the way to conviction. . . .

PAUL MARCUS, CRIMINAL CONSPIRACY LAW: TIME TO TURN BACK FROM AN EVER EXPANDING, EVER MORE TROUBLING AREA, 1 Wm. & Mary Bill of Rights J. 1, 8-11 (1992): Perhaps the most striking change in the conspiracy area during the past two decades has been the enormous number of cases involving many defendants, complex evidentiary issues, and dozens and dozens of complicated charges. While it was not highly unusual twenty years ago to see such big and cumbersome cases, today it is absolutely commonplace. Consider, for instance, this handful of recent and somewhat typical cases:

- United States v. Casamento,[42] with twenty-one defendants, 275 witnesses, thousands of exhibits, and 40,000 pages of transcripts; the trial lasted seventeen months.

42. 887 F.2d 1141 (2d Cir. 1989).

- United States v. Ianniello,[43] lasted more than thirteen months at the trial level; involved eleven defendants.
- United States v. Accetturo,[44] twenty-six-defendant trial; lasted fifteen months.
- United States v. Kopituk,[45] involved a seven-month trial with twelve defendants, seventy counts, 130 witnesses, and more than 22,000 pages of transcript.
- United States v. Martino,[46] with twenty defendants and thirty-five counts; produced a record of almost 100 volumes holding more than 11,000 pages of the testimony of over 200 witnesses, along with five boxes of exhibits.

It is difficult to imagine how a jury goes about sorting the testimony of hundreds of witnesses, or considering evidence it heard more than a year earlier. Indeed, how does a jury begin to apply the reasonable doubt standard when there are more than fifty counts charging more than a dozen different individuals? In today's world of conspiracy prosecution, however, such a situation — while perhaps not the norm — occurs with great frequency.

NOTES ON THE CO-CONSPIRATOR EXCEPTION TO THE HEARSAY RULE

1. *What is hearsay?* Rule 801 of the Federal Rules of Evidence defines hearsay as "a statement, other than one made by the declarant while testifying at the trial or hearing, offered in evidence to prove the truth of the matter asserted." Thus, in *Krulewitch,* if witness *A* had testified at trial, "Kay was the brains behind all this, the guy who arranged it," *A*'s statement would not be hearsay. But if witness *B* testified at trial that *A* had told her out of court, "Kay was the brains behind all this, the guy who arranged it," then *A*'s statement would be hearsay.

What out-of-court statement was recounted at the *Krulewitch* trial? Why was it relevant at all? And why was it hearsay?

2. *The hearsay rule and its exceptions.* Because hearsay assertions are not subject to cross-examination, they are normally inadmissible. But there are many exceptions to this rule. Typically, the exceptions come into play when the person making the statement is unavailable as a witness and circumstances surrounding the statement afford some assurance of its reliability. Illustrative are "dying declarations" and "admissions against penal interest." Both kinds of statements are usually admissible as exceptions to the hearsay rule. But the Sixth Amendment guarantees the accused the right to confront and cross-examine the witnesses against him, and when a hearsay statement is admitted at trial, the accused has no opportunity to confront or cross-examine the person who made it. As a result, the Supreme Court has held, hearsay statements are admissible only when they fall within a "firmly rooted hearsay exception," or when they contain "particularized guarantees of trustworthiness." Lilly v. Virginia, 527 U.S. 116, 125 (1999).

43. 866 F.2d 540 (2d Cir. 1989).
44. 842 F.2d 1408 (3d Cir. 1988).
45. 690 F.2d 1289 (11th Cir. 1982).
46. 648 F.2d 367 (5th Cir. 1981).

The application of these rules is illustrated by the treatment of "admissions against penal interest." It is not unusual, when two defendants are implicated in an offense, that one will give police a statement admitting some involvement but claiming that the other defendant was the primary instigator. Such a statement is an admission against the penal interest of the person making it, because it confesses some involvement. Nonetheless, in *Lilly,* supra, the Supreme Court noted that an accomplice may have a strong motive to lie when he attempts to place blame on others. Thus, the Court held, a blame-shifting statement lacks "particularized guarantees of trustworthiness" and therefore cannot be admitted under the penal-interest exception to the hearsay rule.

The catch, for present purposes, is that *Lilly* allows two alternative ways to avoid cross-examination: hearsay statements falling with a "firmly rooted" exception are admissible even when they *do not* have "particularized guarantees of trustworthiness." And the Court has held that the coconspirator exception, unlike the penal-interest exception, qualifies as "firmly rooted." See Bourjaily v. United States, 483 U.S. 171, 183 (1987). As the law currently stands, therefore, a blame-shifting statement — if made during a conspiracy and in furtherance of it — is admissible under the coconspirator exception, despite the declarant's motivation to lie and the defendant's inability to cross-examine him.

3. The co-conspirator exception. The doctrine permitting introduction against one co-conspirator of out-of-court statements made by another applies whether or not the parties have been formally indicted or convicted of conspiracy, provided that the statement is in furtherance of a conspiratorial agreement between them. This doctrine is widely followed in state courts. For federal prosecutions it is now codified in Rule 801(d)(2)(E) of the Federal Rules of Evidence. What is the rationale of this doctrine? Consider United States v. Trowery, 542 F.2d 623 (3d Cir. 1976):

> The co-conspirator exception to the hearsay rule [is] a rule of evidence founded, to some extent, on concepts of agency law. It may be applied in both civil and criminal cases. . . . Its rationale is the common sense appreciation that a person who has authorized another to speak or to act to some joint end will be held responsible for what is later said or done by his agent, whether in his presence or not. . . .

See also United States v. Gil, 604 F.2d 546, 549 (7th Cir. 1979):

> The evidentiary principle . . . is a limited application of agency principles, viewing a conspiracy as a "partnership in crime." It is justified in part because of the assurances of accuracy traditionally associated with statements against interest and the community of interest among the conspirators. It has also been candidly proposed by commentators . . . that the exception is largely a result of necessity, since it is most often invoked in conspiracy cases in which the proof would otherwise be very difficult and the evidence largely circumstantial.

Compare Phillip Johnson, The Unnecessary Crime of Conspiracy, 61 Cal. L. Rev. 1137, 1183 (1973):

> The justification for admitting these "vicarious admissions" is not altogether easy to grasp. Some authorities have found the analogy to the substantive liability of the principal for his agent's acts compelling. Because the employer is liable for the

> torts of his servant committed within the scope of the employment, and the conspirator for the crimes of his co-conspirator committed in furtherance of the common objective, these authorities have reasoned that the principal should bear the risk of what his agents say as well as the risk of what they do. It does not seem that hearsay statements of agents are admitted because they are regarded as carrying some particular guarantee of trustworthiness. Although there are some suggestions in the literature that an agent is not likely to make statements against his principal's interest unless they are true, the authorities agree that admissions of the agent, like those of the principal himself, are admissible whether or not he thought the statements to be against his or his principal's interest at the time he made them.

For further discussion, see Stephen Whitzman, Proof of Conspiracy: The Co-Conspirator's Exception to the Hearsay Rule, 28 Crim. L.Q. 203 (1986).

4. *Bootstrapping?* In United States v. Glasser, 315 U.S. 60 (1942), the Court held that the hearsay declarations of an alleged co-conspirator become admissible only if there is independent proof that the conspiracy exists and that the defendant was connected with it. "Otherwise," the Court said, "hearsay would lift itself by its own bootstraps to the level of competent evidence." But this limit on the co-conspirator exception was later discarded. In Bourjaily v. United States, 483 U.S. 171 (1987), the Court held that co-conspirator hearsay becomes admissible under the Federal Rules of Evidence whenever the judge determines by a preponderance of the evidence that the defendant was a member of the conspiracy. The Court also held that the judge may consider the hearsay statement itself, along with other evidence, in making this determination. This usually means, of course, that the jury hears this evidence before its admissibility is determined. If the evidence is later held inadmissible, the jury is told to disregard it.[5] A few state courts have rejected the *Bourjaily* approach and insisted that the conspiracy be proved by evidence independent of the conspiracy. See, e.g., People v. Hardy, 5 Cal. Rptr. 796, 824 (Cal. 1992); Romani v. State, 542 So. 2d 984 (Fla. 1989). In the latter case, the court noted (542 So. 2d at 986): "We are apprehensive that adopting the *Bourjaily* rule would frequently lead to the admission of statements which are not reliable. Our present rule of disallowing the statement itself in determining its admissibility helps assure that a defendant is convicted only on credible evidence."

NOTES ON THE DURATION OF A CONSPIRACY

Conspiracy traditionally has been viewed as a continuing offense. The basic rule is that once formed, a conspiracy remains in effect until its objectives have either been achieved or abandoned. See United States v. Kissel, 218 U.S. 601 (1910). Thus, unlike most criminal offenses, the statute of limitations for conspiracy begins to run not when the offense is committed (that is, when the agreement is made), but when the conspiracy terminates. One effect of this concept is that a conspiracy often can remain subject to prosecution long after the initial

5. One court has said that this is a bit like throwing a skunk into the jury box and telling the jury not to smell it. See United States v. Dunn, 307 F.2d 883, 886 (5th Cir. 1962). The effectiveness of cautionary jury instructions is a problem that pervades criminal law and procedure. We examine it in detail starting at page 32 supra.

agreement was made and long after some of its members have ceased any active participation in the activities. In addition, because the various collateral consequences of conspiracy come into play only with respect to the period when the conspiracy is in existence, it may be crucial for defendants to try to shorten that period or for prosecutors to try to extend it. Consider the following problems.

1. The breadth of the conspiratorial objectives. In accord with *Krulewitch,* most of the recent decisions have refused to infer that an implicit agreement to cover up the crime is inherent in every conspiracy. See State v. Rivenbark, 533 A.2d 271 (Md. Ct. App. 1987). And in Grunewald v. United States, 353 U.S. 391, 404 (1957), the Court held that a particular conspiracy cannot be treated as including a cover-up agreement unless there is "direct evidence [of] an express original agreement among the conspirators to continue to act in concert in order to cover up . . . traces of the crime. . . ." Thus, the Court explained (id. at 402):

> [A] subsidiary conspiracy to conceal may not be implied from circumstantial evidence showing merely that the conspiracy was kept a secret and that the conspirators took care to cover up their crime. . . . Acts of covering up, even though done in the context of a mutually understood need for secrecy, cannot themselves constitute proof that concealment of the crime after its commission was part of the initial agreement. . . .

What would be the result in a case like *Krulewitch,* if the prosecution alleges that the conspirators did agree to help each other cover up the crime? When would the objective of such a conspiracy be achieved? When would the statute of limitations begin to run?

2. Abandonment. A conspiracy is generally considered to be abandoned when none of the conspirators is engaging in any action to further the conspiratorial objectives. If such inactivity continues for a period equal to the statute of limitations, prosecution will be barred. See Model Penal Code §5.03(7)(b). But what if a particular defendant "wants out" of an ongoing conspiracy? Can a conspirator cut off his responsibility for later acts and statements of his co-conspirators by terminating his own participation? When should withdrawal by a particular defendant start the statute of limitations running as to him? Courts traditionally have required that a defendant take "affirmative action" to announce his withdrawal to all the other conspirators. Hyde v. United States, 225 U.S. 347, 369 (1912); United States v. Dabbs, 134 F.3d 1071, 1083 (11th Cir. 1998). Some courts have gone even further, requiring that a defendant not only announce his withdrawal but thwart the success of the conspiracy. These courts compare an ongoing conspiracy to a ticking time bomb. On this view, a defendant should not be able to disassociate himself merely by walking away while the bomb continues to tick; he must prove that he "defused the bomb" by reporting the conspirators to police or otherwise thwarting the plot. See Eldredge v. United States, 62 F.2d 449, 451-452 (10th Cir. 1932). But this stringent requirement no longer applies in the federal courts. See United States v. United States Gypsum Co., 438 U.S. 422, 464-465 (1978):

> Affirmative acts inconsistent with the object of the conspiracy and communicated in a manner reasonably calculated to reach co-conspirators have generally been regarded as sufficient to establish withdrawal or abandonment.

The Model Penal Code approach is in accord with the flexible *U.S. Gypsum* standard. See Model Penal Code §5.03(7)(c), Appendix. The recent authorities are discussed in Roger C. Spaeder & Gary D. Weinfeld, Effective Withdrawal from a Business Conspiracy, 9 Crim. Just. 8 (ABA), (Spring 1994).

3. Renunciation as a complete defense. Should a defendant's change of heart and withdrawal from the conspiracy afford a defense to the conspiracy charge itself? As in the case of abandoned attempts, the common law answer was no. See page 568 supra. The theory was that once the crime was committed, it could not be "uncommitted." Post-offense conduct was considered relevant only to sentencing. Today most states, following the lead of the Model Penal Code, allow a complete defense for renunciation under some circumstances. See Note, 75 Colum. L. Rev. 1122, 1169 (1975). The Code allows the defense only if the circumstances manifest renunciation of the actor's criminal purpose *and* the actor succeeds in preventing commission of the criminal objectives. Model Penal Code §5.03(6). Some states consider this latter requirement too severe and therefore require only that the actor make a substantial effort to prevent the crime. See, e.g., Ark. Code Ann. §5-3-405(2)(B) (Michie 1987).

NOTES ON OTHER CONSEQUENCES OF A CONSPIRACY CHARGE

1. Criminalizing noncriminal objectives. As Justice Jackson indicates, concurring in *Krulewitch,* "at common law and under some statutes a combination may be a criminal conspiracy even if it contemplates only acts which are not crimes at all when perpetrated by an individual." Traditionally, an agreement became punishable as a conspiracy if the objectives were criminal or "unlawful," or if the agreement contemplated pursuing a lawful objective by criminal or "unlawful" means. See Commonwealth v. Hunt, 45 Mass. 111 (1842). The broadest and most troublesome reach of this common law rule occurs when conspiracy doctrine is invoked to punish conduct deemed offensive to "public morals." The common law rule can also be troublesome when it is applied to criminalize conduct that may be inconsistent with civil law regulations or precedents.

(a) Public morals. In Shaw v. Director of Public Prosecutions, [1962] A.C. 220, page 290 supra, the House of Lords upheld a conviction for "conspiracy to corrupt public morals," on the basis of a defendant's agreement to publish a directory listing prostitutes and their services. In the United States, most of the recently enacted Codes reject this doctrine and confine criminal conspiracy to those agreements whose objectives are otherwise criminal. See Note, Conspiracy: Statutory Reform Since the Model Penal Code, 75 Colum. L. Rev. 1122, 1129 (1975). But in some states an agreement to pursue noncriminal objectives can be a criminal conspiracy. For example, Cal. Penal Code §182(a) makes it a punishable conspiracy for two or more persons to agree:

> (1) To commit any crime.
> (2) Falsely and maliciously to indict another for any crime, or to procure another to be charged or arrested for any crime.
> (3) Falsely to move or maintain any suit, action or proceeding.
> (4) To cheat and defraud any person of any property, by any means which are in themselves criminal, or to obtain money or property by false pretenses or by false promises with fraudulent intent not to perform such promises.

(5) To commit any act injurious to the public health, to public morals, or to pervert or obstruct justice, or the due administration of the laws. . . .

Question: Can a prosecution under §182(a)(5) survive a challenge for unconstitutional vagueness? Reconsider City of Chicago v. Morales, page 300 supra. In Musser v. Utah, 333 U.S. 95 (1948), the Court held that a statute punishing conspiracy to commit acts injurious to public morals would be unconstitutionally vague unless narrowed by the state supreme court. On remand the state court held the provision unconstitutional in the context of a prosecution for preaching and practicing polygamy. State v. Musser, 118 Utah 537, 223 P.2d 193 (1950).

(b) Other noncriminal objectives. Even where the "public morals" doctrine is not invoked, statutes may use the conspiracy concept to punish those who agree to pursue objectives that are improper or unlawful but not criminal. Consider Cal. Penal Code §182(a)(2)-(3) supra. Similarly, the federal conspiracy statute, 18 U.S.C. §371, provides:

> If two or more persons conspire either to commit any offense against the United States, or to defraud the United States, or any agency thereof in any manner or for any purpose, and one or more of such persons do any act to effect the object of the conspiracy, each shall be fined under this title or imprisoned not more than five years, or both. If, however, the offense, the commission of which is the object of the conspiracy, is a misdemeanor only, the punishment for such conspiracy shall not exceed the maximum punishment provided for such misdemeanor.

The term "defraud the United States" has been construed to reach not only conduct that subjects the Government to monetary loss, but any act that interferes with a governmental interest. Consider United States v. Hay, 527 F.2d 990 (10th Cir. 1975): Defendant was employed by a private firm that contracted with the South Vietnamese government to build a water system for the city of Saigon, a project partially financed by the U.S. Agency for International Development. Defendant helped a French subcontractor obtain reimbursement for fraudulent cost-overrun claims submitted to the South Vietnamese. Because the U.S. loan funds had been exhausted before the claims were submitted, the financial loss fell entirely on the government of South Vietnam. Was defendant properly convicted of conspiracy to defraud the United States? The court held in the affirmative, stating (527 F.2d at 998): "[The U.S.] interest is not limited strictly to accounting for United States Government funds . . . but extends to seeing that the entire project is administered honestly and efficiently. . . ."

Question: Does this approach avoid the vagueness problems raised by prosecutions for conspiracy to corrupt "public morals"?

(c) Problem. The so-called Boland Amendment, a rider to an appropriations statute, provided that no federal funds were to be used by the Defense Department or the Central Intelligence Agency to support the "Contra" rebels who were then opposing the Nicaraguan government. No criminal or civil penalties were specified for failure to adhere to this proviso. Defendant, a staff member at the National Security Counsel, allegedly agreed with other government officials on a plan to divert federal funds to the CIA for use in supporting the Contras. On such facts would the defendant be subject to criminal punishment under 18 U.S.C. §371? Cf. United States v. North, 920 F.2d 940 (D.C. Cir. 1990) (reversing conviction on other grounds).

2. *The level of punishment.* The traditional approach to grading is to treat conspiracy as a generic offense and to prescribe a punishment range unrelated to those authorized for the object crimes. Thus, 18 U.S.C. §371 provides that the punishment for conspiracy is up to five years' imprisonment, regardless of the seriousness of the object offense. One perverse result of this approach, described by Justice Jackson, has now been eliminated: The current federal statute specifies that when the object crime is a misdemeanor, punishment for the conspiracy shall not exceed that authorized for the misdemeanor. Nonetheless, there are surviving traces of the common law doctrine that made it a felony to conspire to commit a misdemeanor. Under Cal. Penal Code §182, a conspiracy to commit a crime against certain federal or state officials is a felony punishable by imprisonment for five, seven, or nine years; an agreement to throw a tomato at such an official would call for a *minimum* sentence of five years, though actually throwing the tomato, without a prior agreement, would be a misdemeanor assault carrying a *maximum* sentence of one year. Under 18 U.S.C. §371 an agreement to commit murder carries the same five-year maximum sentence as an agreement to commit a minor theft or embezzlement, and an agreement to commit a felony carrying a two-year maximum subjects the conspirators to a five-year sentence, while an individual who commits the object offense by himself faces only the two-year maximum.

Though this approach to grading survives in a number of jurisdictions, the majority of states now reject it. Most fix the punishment for conspiracy at some term less than that provided for the object crime. See Note, 75 Colum. L. Rev. 1122, 1183-1188 (1975). Roughly a third of the states, following the lead of the Model Penal Code, make the punishment for conspiracy the same as that authorized for the object crime, except in the case of the most serious felonies. See Model Penal Code §5.05(1), Appendix. Recall that this is the same approach that the Model Penal Code uses in the case of attempts. But are the two offenses really comparable for grading purposes? Note that an attempt is not punishable under the Code until the defendant has taken a "substantial step" that is "strongly corroborative" of the criminal purpose. In such a case, punishment is permitted up to the level authorized for the object crime. But a conspiracy may be punishable from the moment that an agreement is made. (We will explore this problem in detail when we take up the actus reus of conspiracy. See page 694 infra.) When defendants have not taken significant steps to put their plan into action, is it appropriate to impose the same punishment authorized for successful commission of the object crime?

What should be the appropriate level of punishment in the opposite situation, when the conspirators have actually committed the object crimes? Inchoate offenses such as attempt and solicitation are said to "merge" with their object crimes, so that a defendant charged with both the completed crime and an attempt cannot be punished for both. But the same approach is not always followed in the case of conspiracy. Instead, the traditional view permits separate punishments, with consecutive sentences, for the object crime and the conspiracy to commit it. In Callanan v. United States, 364 U.S. 587 (1961), the defendant was convicted of obstructing interstate commerce by extortion and of conspiring to obstruct commerce by that same extortion. The maximum punishment for obstructing commerce was 20 years. The trial court imposed a sentence of 12 years on the obstruction count and another 12 years to run consecutively on the conspiracy count. The defendant alleged that Congress did not intend to authorize punishment for both the conspiracy and the obstruction itself. The Court rejected the claim, stating (id. at 593-594):

> "It has been long and consistently recognized by the Court that the commission of the substantive offense and a conspiracy to commit it are separate and distinct offenses." Pinkerton v. United States, 328 U.S. 640, 643. . . .
>
> This settled principle derives from the reason of things in dealing with socially reprehensible conduct: . . . Concerted action both increases the likelihood that the criminal object will be successfully attained and decreases the probability that the individuals involved will depart from their path of criminality. Group association for criminal purposes often, if not normally, makes possible the attainment of ends more complex than those which one criminal could accomplish. Nor is the danger of a conspiratorial group limited to the particular end toward which it has embarked. Combination in crime makes more likely the commission of crimes unrelated to the original purpose for which the group was formed. In sum, the danger which a conspiracy generates is not confined to the substantive offense which is the immediate aim of the enterprise.

The Model Penal Code takes a different position. Section 1.07(1)(b) provides that a defendant may not be convicted of more than one offfense if "one offense consists only of a conspiracy or other form of preparation to commit the other." See Model Penal Code and Commentaries, Comment to §5.03, at 390 (1985):

> When a conspiracy is declared criminal because its object is a crime, it is entirely meaningless to say that the preliminary combination is more dangerous than the forbidden consummation; the measure of its danger is the risk of such a culmination.[a] On the other hand, the combination may and often does have criminal objectives that transcend any particular offenses that have been committed in pursuance of its goals. In the latter case, cumulative sentences for conspiracy and substantive offenses ought to be permissible, subject to the general limits on cumulation that the Code prescribes. In the former case, when the preliminary agreement does not go beyond the consummation, double conviction and sentence are barred.

For analysis of the practice of stacking conspiracy charges and substantive counts, and the resulting "compound liability" in which a single act can sustain liability for multiple offenses, see Susan W. Brenner, RICO, CCE, and Other Complex Crimes: The Transformation of American Criminal Law, 2 Wm. & Mary Bill of Rights J. 239 (1993).

3. Liability for substantive offenses. One of the most important collateral consequences of conspiracy is that in many jurisdictions a party can sometimes be held liable for crimes committed by co-conspirators during the course of the conspiracy, even when he could not be held accountable for those crimes under traditional principles of accomplice liability. We examine this doctrine in detail in connection with Pinkerton v. United States, infra Section C2.

4. Assessing the collateral consequences of conspiracy. Consider the observations of

a. See also Note, Feasibility and Admissibility of Mob Mentality Defenses, 108 Harv. L. Rev. 1111 (1995), arguing that because of the psychology of mob behavior, certain criminal acts of a group, such as rioting and looting, are less blameworthy than similar behavior undertaken by an individual acting alone. — Eds.

Professor Phillip Johnson in The Unnecessary Crime of Conspiracy, 61 Cal. L. Rev. 1137, 1139-1140 (1973):

> The law of criminal conspiracy is not basically sound. It should be abolished, not reformed.
>
> The central fault of conspiracy law and the reason why any limited reform is bound to be inadequate can be briefly stated. What conspiracy adds to the law is simply confusion, and the confusion is inherent in the nature of the doctrine. The confusion stems from the fact that conspiracy is not only a substantive inchoate crime in itself, but the touchstone for invoking several independent procedural and substantive doctrines. We ask whether a defendant agreed with another person to commit a crime initially for the purpose of determining whether he may be convicted of the offense of conspiracy even when the crime itself has not yet been committed. If the answer to that question is in the affirmative, however, we find that we have also answered a number of other questions that would otherwise have to be considered independently. Where there is evidence of conspiracy, the defendant may be tried jointly with his criminal partners and possibly with many other persons whom he has never met or seen, the joint trial may be held in a place he may never have visited, and hearsay statements of other alleged members of the conspiracy may be used to prove his guilt. Furthermore, a defendant who is found guilty of conspiracy is subject to enhanced punishment and may also be found guilty of any crime committed in furtherance of the conspiracy, whether or not he knew about the crime or aided in its commission.
>
> Each of these issues involves a separate substantive or procedural area of the criminal law of considerable importance and complexity. The essential vice of conspiracy is that it inevitably distracts the courts from the policy questions or balancing of interests that ought to govern the decision of specific legal issues and leads them instead to decide those issues by reference to the conceptual framework of conspiracy. Instead of asking whether public policy or the interests of the parties require a particular holding, the courts are led instead to consider whether the theory of conspiracy is broad enough to permit it. What is wrong with conspiracy, in other words, is much more basic than the overbreadth of a few rules. The problem is not with particular results, but with the use of a single abstract concept to decide numerous questions that deserve separate consideration in light of the various interests and policies they involve.

2. *Conspiracy as a Form of Accessorial Liability*

PINKERTON v. UNITED STATES

Supreme Court of the United States
328 U.S. 640 (1946)

JUSTICE DOUGLAS delivered the opinion of the Court.

Walter and Daniel Pinkerton are brothers who live a short distance from each other on Daniel's farm. They were indicted for violations of the Internal Revenue Code. The indictment contained ten substantive counts and one conspiracy count. The jury found Walter guilty on nine of the substantive counts and on the conspiracy count. It found Daniel guilty on six of the substantive counts and on the conspiracy count. Walter was fined $500 and sentenced generally on the substantive counts to imprisonment for thirty months. On the conspiracy count he was given a two year sentence to run concurrently with the other sentence. Daniel was fined $1,000 and sentenced generally on the substantive counts to imprisonment for thirty months. On the conspiracy count he was fined $500 and given a two year sentence to run concurrently with the other sentence. The judgments of conviction were affirmed by the Circuit Court of Appeals. . . .

It is contended that there was insufficient evidence to implicate Daniel in the conspiracy. But we think there was enough evidence for submission of the issue to the jury.

There is, however, no evidence to show that Daniel participated directly in the commission of the substantive offenses on which his conviction has been sustained, although there was evidence to show that these substantive offenses were in fact committed by Walter in furtherance of the unlawful agreement or conspiracy existing between the brothers. The question was submitted to the jury on the theory that each petitioner could be found guilty of the substantive offenses, if it was found at the time those offenses were committed petitioners were parties to an unlawful conspiracy and the substantive offenses charged were in fact committed in furtherance of it.[6]

Daniel relies on United States v. Sall (C.C.A. 3d) 116 F.2d 745. That case held that participation in the conspiracy was not itself enough to sustain a conviction for the substantive offense even though it was committed in furtherance of the conspiracy. The court held that, in addition to evidence that the offense was in fact committed in furtherance of the conspiracy, evidence of direct participation in the commission of the substantive offense or other evidence from which participation might fairly be inferred was necessary.

We take a different view. We have here a continuous conspiracy. There is here no evidence of the affirmative action on the part of Daniel which is necessary to establish his withdrawal from it. Hyde v. United States, 225 U.S. 347, 369. As stated in that case, "Having joined in an unlawful scheme, having constituted agents for its performance, scheme and agency to be continuous until full fruition be secured, until he does some act to disavow or defeat the purpose he is in no situation to claim the delay of the law. As the offense has not been terminated or accomplished, he is still offending. And we think, consciously offending, offending as certainly, as we have said, as at the first moment of his confederation, and consciously through every moment of its existence." And so long as the partnership in crime continues the partners act for each other in carrying it forward. It is settled that "an overt act of one partner may be the act of all without any new agreement specifically directed to that act." Motive or intent may be proved by the acts or declarations of some of the conspirators in furtherance of the common objective. The governing principle is the same when the substantive offense is committed by one of the conspirators in furtherance of the unlawful project. The criminal intent to do the act is established by the formation of the conspiracy. Each conspirator instigated the commission of the crime. The unlawful agreement contemplated precisely what was done. It was formed for the purpose. The act done was in execution of the enterprise. The rule which holds responsible one who counsels, procures, or commands another to com-

6. . . . Daniel was not indicted as an aider or abetter (see Criminal Code, §332, 18 U.S.C.A. 550), nor was his case submitted to the jury on that theory.

mit a crime is founded on the same principle. That principle is recognized in the law of conspiracy when the overt act of one partner in crime is attributable to all. An overt act is an essential ingredient of the crime of conspiracy under §37 of the Criminal Code, 18 U.S.C.A. §88 [now §371]. If that can be supplied by the act of one conspirator, we fail to see why the same or other acts in furtherance of the conspiracy are likewise not attributable to the others for the purpose of holding them responsible for the substantive offense.

A different case would arise if the substantive offense committed by one of the conspirators was not in fact done in furtherance of the conspiracy, did not fall within the scope of the unlawful project, or was merely a part of the ramifications of the plan which could not be reasonably foreseen as a necessary or natural consequence of the unlawful agreement. But as we read this record, that is not this case.

Affirmed.

JUSTICE RUTLEDGE, dissenting in part.

The judgment concerning Daniel Pinkerton should be reversed. In my opinion it is without precedent here and is a dangerous precedent to establish.

Daniel and Walter, who were brothers living near each other, were charged in several counts with substantive offenses, and then a conspiracy count was added naming those offenses as overt acts. The proof showed that Walter alone committed the substantive crimes. There was none to establish that Daniel participated in them, aided and abetted Walter in committing them, or knew that he had done so. Daniel in fact was in the penitentiary, under sentence for other crimes, when some of Walter's crimes were done.

There was evidence, however, to show that over several years Daniel and Walter had confederated to commit similar crimes concerned with unlawful possession, transportation, and dealing in whiskey, in fraud of the federal revenues. On this evidence both were convicted of conspiracy. Walter also was convicted on the substantive counts on the proof of his committing the crimes charged. Then, on that evidence without more than the proof of Daniel's criminal agreement with Walter and the latter's overt acts, which were also the substantive offenses charged, the court told the jury they could find Daniel guilty of those substantive offenses. They did so. . . .

Daniel has been held guilty of the substantive crimes committed only by Walter on proof that he did no more than conspire with him to commit offenses of the same general character. There was no evidence that he counseled, advised or had knowledge of those particular acts or offenses. There was, therefore, none that he aided, abetted or took part in them. There was only evidence sufficient to show that he had agreed with Walter at some past time to engage in such transactions generally. As to Daniel this was only evidence of conspiracy, not of substantive crime.

The Court's theory seems to be that Daniel and Walter became general partners in crime by virtue of their agreement and because of that agreement without more on his part Daniel became criminally responsible as a principal for everything Walter did thereafter in the nature of a criminal offense of the general sort the agreement contemplated, so long as there was not clear evidence that Daniel had withdrawn from or revoked the agreement. Whether or not his commitment to the penitentiary had that effect, the result is a vicarious criminal responsibility as broad as, or broader than, the vicarious civil liability of a partner for acts done by a co-partner in the course of the firm's business. . . .

STATE v. BRIDGES, 133 N.J. 447, 628 A.2d 270 (1993) (Handler, J.): [At a birthday party for a 16-year-old friend, defendant got into a heated argument with another guest, Andy Strickland. Defendant left, yelling that he would return with help. He recruited two acquaintances, Bing and Rolle, to accompany him back to the party, where he expected a confrontation. On the way back, they stopped at Bing's house and picked up guns, to be used to hold Strickland's supporters at bay while defendant fought it out with him. When they returned to the party, defendant began fighting with a friend of Strickland's, while Bing and Rolle stood by. A member of the crowd hit Bing in the face, whereupon Bing and Rolle drew their guns and began firing—first into the air and then into the crowd, as onlookers tried to flee. One of the onlookers was fatally wounded. At trial defendant was convicted of conspiracy to commit aggravated assault and of several substantive crimes including murder. On the murder count defendant was sentenced to life imprisonment, with parole ineligibility for a minimum of 30 years. The intermediate appellate court held that defendant was not responsible for the murder committed by Rolle and Bing in the course of the conspiracy. The prosecution appealed to the New Jersey Supreme Court.]

The Appellate Division majority determined that the Code of Criminal Justice, which provides that the involvement in a conspiracy can be the basis for criminal liability for the commission of substantive crimes, N.J.S.A. 2C:2-6b(4), requires a level of culpability and state of mind that is identical to that required of accomplice liability. The Appellate Division therefore ruled that a conspirator is vicariously liable for the substantive crimes committed by co-conspirators only when the conspirator had the same intent and purpose as the co-conspirator who committed the crimes.

The provision of the New Jersey Code of Criminal Justice . . . that posits criminal liability on the basis of participation in a conspiracy is silent with respect to its culpability requirement. It provides:

> A person is legally accountable for the conduct of another person when: . . . He is engaged in a conspiracy with such other person.

The majority below concluded that the Code contemplated "complete congruity" between accomplice and vicarious conspirator liability. . . . The Appellate Division majority reasoned that *Pinkerton* . . . mandates that a crime "must have been within [a co-conspirator's] contemplation when he entered into the agreement and reasonably comprehended by his purpose and intention in entering into the agreement."

. . . That understanding of *Pinkerton* is not supported. . . . [I]t has not been disputed that [*Pinkerton*] purported to impose vicarious liability on each conspirator for the acts of others based on an objective standard of reasonable foreseeability. . . . [I]t was understood that the liability of a co-conspirator under the objective standard of reasonable foreseeability would be broader than that of an accomplice, where the defendant must actually foresee and intend the result of his or her acts.

That understanding of *Pinkerton* is also widely accepted by commentators and treatises, whether they are critical of its rule, or only expounding the existing law. . . .

We appreciate the concern of the concurring opinion that such a standard of vicarious liability for conspirators differs from that of accomplices. Although conspirator liability is circumscribed by the requirement of a close causal connection between the conspiracy and the substantive crime, that standard concededly is less strict than that defining accomplice accountability. It is, however, evident that the Legislature chose to address the special dangers inherent in group activity and therefore intended to include the crime of conspiracy as a distinctive basis for vicarious criminal liability.[a] . . .

Accordingly, we conclude, and now hold, that a co-conspirator may be liable for the commission of substantive criminal acts that are not within the scope of the conspiracy if they are reasonably foreseeable as the necessary or natural consequences of the conspiracy. . . .

The conspiracy [here] did not have as its objective the purposeful killing of another person. Nevertheless, the evidence discloses that the conspiratorial plan contemplated bringing loaded guns to keep a large contingent of young hostile partygoers back from a beating of one of their friends, and that it could be anticipated that the weapon might be fired at the crowd. . . .

From that evidence a jury could conclude that a reasonably foreseeable risk and a probable and natural consequence of carrying out a plan to intimidate the crowd by using loaded guns would be that one of the gunslingers would intentionally fire at somebody, and, under the circumstances, that act would be sufficiently connected to the original conspirational plan to provide a just basis for a determination of guilt for that substantive crime.

[Reversed.]

O'Hern, J., concurring in part and dissenting in part. An interpretation of the provisions of the Code of Criminal Justice that would allow a sentence of life imprisonment to be imposed on the basis of the negligent appraisal of a risk that another would commit a homicide, conflicts with the internal structure of the Code. . . . If we assume, as the majority does, that Bridges did not intend that Shawn Lockley be killed, he could not have been convicted of attempted murder.

Nor could defendant have been convicted as an accomplice to the murder. . . .

And finally, defendant could not even have been found guilty of conspiracy to commit murder. A person is guilty of a conspiracy to commit an offense only if "*with the purpose* of promoting or facilitating its commission he" or she agrees

a. N.J. Stat. §2C:2-6 provides as follows:

> b. A person is legally accountable for the conduct of another person when: . . .
> (3) He is an accomplice of such other person in the commission of an offense; or
> (4) He is engaged in a conspiracy with such other person.
> c. A person is an accomplice of another person in the commission of an offense if:
> (1) With the purpose of promoting or facilitating the commission of the offense; he
> (a) Solicits such other person to commit it;
> (b) Aids or agrees or attempts to aid such other person in planning or committing it; or
> (c) Having a legal duty to prevent the commission of the offense, fails to make proper effort so to do; or
> (2) His conduct is expressly declared by law to establish his complicity. — Eds.

with another person that they will "engage in conduct which constitutes such crime" or agrees to aid such person "in the planning or commission of such crime." N.J.S.A. 2C:5-2a (emphasis added).

The Code establishes a carefully-measured grid of criminal responsibility. . . . Thus, one who causes the death of another with the knowledge or purpose to kill will be guilty of murder and can be sentenced to death in certain circumstances or to life imprisonment with a minimum of thirty years without parole. . . .

The manslaughter offenses require a finding that an actor causing death has exhibited a reckless disregard for human life. When that recklessness is in disregard of a *probability* that death may occur, the offense is aggravated manslaughter and carries a penalty of up to thirty years in prison. When the proof shows reckless disregard of a possibility of causing death, the offense is reckless manslaughter and carries the penalty of a first-degree crime, up to twenty years in prison. Except for one form of vehicular homicide, N.J.S.A. 2C:11-4b(3), *no negligent homicide* exists under New Jersey law, much less a crime of negligent murder.

. . . This case is an example of the most extreme sort — life imprisonment with no possibility of parole for thirty years on the basis of a negligent mental state. . . . The most reasonable construction of N.J.S.A. 2C:2-6b(4) is that the Legislature intended that the conspirator to the commission of an offense, like an accomplice to the commission of an offense, be punished as a principal. . . . No liability is foreseen [under the statute] other than for the crime or crimes that were the object of the conspiracy.

NOTES AND PROBLEMS

1. *Liability of a new conspirator for prior acts of co-conspirators.* It is often said that upon joining an ongoing conspiracy, a person becomes liable for all acts committed by co-conspirators in furtherance of the conspiracy, including acts committed prior to his joining. See, e.g., 16 Am. Jur. 2d Conspiracy §20 (1979). Such statements are sometimes misinterpreted to suggest that a defendant is liable under *Pinkerton* for *substantive crimes* that co-conspirators committed before he joined the conspiracy. But *Pinkerton* liability is not retroactive. As explained in United States v. Blackmon, 839 F.2d 900, 908-909 (2d Cir. 1988):

> The confusion here is that with regard to liability for *conspiracy,* a defendant may be legally responsible for acts of co-conspirators prior to that defendant's entry into the conspiracy [in the sense that such acts may be used as evidence against him in the prosecution for the crime of conspiracy], whereas, with regard to *substantive offenses,* a defendant cannot be retroactively liable for offenses committed prior to his joining the conspiracy.

2. *Conspiracy and complicity compared.* As we saw in the section on complicity, pages 615-621 supra, many jurisdictions now use an objective foreseeability test to determine the liability of an accomplice for originally unintended crimes committed by the principal in the course of the criminal endeavor. In these jurisdictions, the *Pinkerton* theory of conspiratorial liability and the objective theory of accomplice liability produce similar results. Under the more traditional view,

illustrated by the *Bridges* case, liability as an *accomplice* requires proof that the secondary party intended to promote or facilitate the specific offense for which the prosecution seeks to hold him accountable. In jurisdictions adhering to this view, liability as a co-conspirator under a *Pinkerton* theory represents a considerable expansion of the liability that the co-conspirator would face under the normal rules of accomplice liability. See, e.g., United States v. Shea, 150 F.3d 44, 49-51 (1st Cir. 1998).

3. Problems. (a) In the following hypothetical case, consider the liability of each of the parties for the crimes committed by the others under (1) the normal doctrines of complicity and (2) the doctrine of vicarious conspiratorial accessorial liability (Note, Developments in the Law — Criminal Conspiracy, 72 Harv. L. Rev. 920, 996 (1959)):

> *A* is the organizer and ringleader of a conspiracy to rob banks. He hires *B* and *C* to rob banks *1* and *2* respectively. Although *B* and *C* do not meet face-to-face, both know that they are members of a large conspiracy and each knows of the other's assignment. At *A*'s instigation, *D,* knowing of the conspiracy, steals a car for use in the robberies. *B* and *C* perform their robberies, the former using *D*'s car.

(b) In People v. Luparello, 187 Cal. App. 3d 410, 231 Cal. Rptr. 832 (1987), supra page 615, defendant, who was attempting to locate his former girlfriend Terri, agreed with several friends to beat up a man named Martin, in order to force Martin to disclose Terri's whereabouts. When one of the conspirators lured Martin outside of his house, another conspirator, who was waiting in a parked car, fired six shots at Martin and killed him. Luparello, who was not present at the scene, was convicted of first-degree murder. Is the conviction proper under the *Pinkerton* doctrine? Under any other doctrine?

(c) In People v. Brigham, 216 Cal. App. 3d 1039, 265 Cal. Rptr. 486 (1989), defendant and one Bluitt set out to kill a man named "Chuckie." They saw a teenager on the street, defendant said, "That is Chuckie," and the two men walked toward the teenager, carrying their weapons. When they got closer, defendant said to Bluitt, "[T]hat is not Chuckie. . . . Don't do it. . . . That's not the dude." Bluitt rejected defendant's advice, saying that he wanted to let people "know we [are] serious." Bluitt fired twice, killing the teenager. Because of Bluitt's "hardheaded and erratic nature," the prosecution argued and the jury found that defendant could "reasonably foresee" that Bluitt, once set in motion, might knowingly kill someone other than his assigned target. On this basis defendant was convicted of first-degree murder. Is the conviction proper under the *Pinkerton* doctrine? Under any other doctrine?

(d) Defendant was charged with violating 18 U.S.C. §922(g)(1), which made it a felony for a person with a previous felony conviction to possess a gun that had traveled in interstate commerce. The government sought to establish possession under a vicarious liability theory premised on *Pinkerton.* It argued that since defendant's coconspirator possessed a gun, its possession could also be attributed to her, even though the coconspirator's possession of the gun was not a crime. United States v. Walls, 2000 WL 1146610 (7th Cir. 2000). Is this a legitimate application of *Pinkerton?* The court thought not, concluding:

> [T]he government uses a cut-and-paste approach, taking the firearm possession by one conspirator, adding it to the felon status of another conspirator, and thereby

creating a substantive offense for that second conspirator. It is a significant expansion of the *Pinkerton* doctrine that appears to be difficult to limit.

Do you agree?

UNITED STATES v. ALVAREZ, 755 F.2d 830 (11th Cir. 1985) (Kravitch, J.): [A run-down motel in Miami, Florida was the scene of a drug "buy" that had been arranged after long negotiation. Undercover agents from the Bureau of Alcohol, Tobacco, and Firearms (BATF) were in the motel room with the drug dealers, waiting for another dealer to return with a quantity of cocaine that the agents had agreed to buy for $147,000. On the arrival of the cocaine other agents outside began to converge on the motel and a shoot-out started in the motel room. One of the BATF agents was killed and the other agent, along with two of the cocaine dealers, was seriously wounded. All the dealers were convicted of conspiracy to commit and commission of various drug offenses. Two of them, Alvarez and Simon, who shot the agents, were also convicted of first-degree murder of a federal agent. Three of the dealers, Portal, Concepcion, and Hernandez, were convicted of second-degree murder, though they played no part in the shooting.] Appellants Portal, Concepcion, and Hernandez contend that their murder convictions . . . were based on an unprecedented and improper extension of Pinkerton v. United States, 328 U.S. 640 (1946). . . . The[y] argue that murder is not a reasonably foreseeable consequence of a drug conspiracy, and that their murder convictions therefore should be reversed. We conclude that, although the murder convictions of the three appellants may represent an unprecedented application of *Pinkerton,* such an application is not improper. . . .

Upon reviewing the record, we find ample evidence to support the jury's conclusion that the murder was a reasonably foreseeable consequence of the drug conspiracy alleged in the indictment. In making this determination, we rely on two critical factors. First, the evidence clearly established that the drug conspiracy was designed to effectuate the sale of a large quantity of cocaine. . . .

Second, based on the amount of drugs and money involved, the jury was entitled to infer that, at the time the cocaine sale was arranged, the conspirators must have been aware of the likelihood (1) that at least some of their number would be carrying weapons, and (2) that deadly force would be used, if necessary, to protect the conspirators' interests. . . . In our opinion, these two critical factors provided ample support for the jury's conclusion that the murder was a reasonably foreseeable consequence of the drug conspiracy alleged in the indictment. . . .

The three appellants also contend that, even if the murder was reasonably foreseeable, their murder convictions nevertheless should be reversed. The appellants argue that the murder was sufficiently distinct from the intended purposes of the drug conspiracy, and that their individual roles in the conspiracy were sufficiently minor, that they should not be held responsible for the murder. We are not persuaded. . . .

We acknowledge that the instant case is not a typical *Pinkerton* case. Here, the murder of Agent Rios was not within the originally intended scope of the conspiracy, but instead occurred as a result of an unintended turn of events. We have not found, nor has the government cited, any authority for the proposition that all conspirators, regardless of individual culpability, may be held responsible under *Pinkerton* for reasonably foreseeable but originally unintended substantive crimes.[25] Furthermore, we are mindful of the potential due process limitations on the *Pinkerton* doctrine in cases involving attenuated relationships between the conspirator and the substantive crime.

Nevertheless, these considerations do not require us to reverse the murder convictions of Portal, Concepcion, and Hernandez. . . . All three were more than "minor" participants in the drug conspiracy. Portal served as a lookout in front of the Hurricane Motel during part of the negotiations that led to the shoot-out, and the evidence indicated that he was armed. Concepcion introduced the agents to Alvarez, the apparent leader of the conspiracy, and was present when the shoot-out started. Finally, Hernandez, the manager of the motel, allowed the drug transactions to take place on the premises and acted as a translator during part of the negotiations that led to the shoot-out.

In addition, all three appellants had actual knowledge of at least some of the circumstances and events leading up to the murder. The evidence that Portal was carrying a weapon demonstrated that he anticipated the possible use of deadly force to protect the conspirators' interests. Moreover, both Concepcion and Hernandez were present when Alvarez stated that he would rather be dead than go back to prison, indicating that they, too, were aware that deadly force might be used to prevent apprehension by Federal agents.

. . . We therefore hold that *Pinkerton* liability for the murder of Agent Rios properly was imposed on the three appellants. . . .[27]

NOTE ON THE MERITS OF PINKERTON

1. In support of the *Pinkerton* rule, see the statement of Deputy Assistant Attorney General Kenney to a Senate subcommittee considering this issue in the context of a revision of the federal criminal law (quoted in Note, 75 Colum. L. Rev. 1122, 1152 (1975)):

> The ever-increasing sophistication of organized crime presents a compelling reason against abandonment of *Pinkerton.* Complicated and highly refined stock frauds . . . and narcotics conspiracies represent a substantial and ever-increasing threat

25. The imposition of *Pinkerton* liability for such crimes is not wholly unprecedented. See, e.g., Government of Virgin Islands v. Dowling, 633 F.2d 660, 666 (3d Cir.) (1980) (conspiracy to commit bank robbery; substantive crime of assault with deadly weapons against police officers, committed during escape attempt); Park v. Huff, 506 F.2d 849, 859 (5th Cir.) (1975) (liquor conspiracy; substantive crime of first degree murder of local district attorney, committed in attempt to stop investigation of illegal liquor sales). In each of the aforementioned cases, however, vicarious liability was imposed only on "major" participants in the conspiracy.

At trial in the instant case, the government's attorney argued that *Pinkerton* liability for Agent Rios's murder properly could be imposed on all of the conspirators, and expressed the view that prosecutorial discretion would protect truly "minor" participants, such as appellants Rios and Raymond, from liability for the far more serious crimes committed by their coconspirators. We do not find this argument persuasive. In our view, the liability of such "minor" participants must rest on a more substantial foundation than the mere whim of the prosecutor.

27. Although our decision today extends the *Pinkerton* doctrine to cases involving reasonably foreseeable but originally unintended substantive crimes, we emphasize that we do so only within narrow confines. Our holding is limited to conspirators who played more than a "minor" role in the conspiracy, or who had actual knowledge of at least some of the circumstances and events culminating in the reasonably foreseeable but originally unintended substantive crime.

to society justifying retention of the *Pinkerton* doctrine. Empirical evidence has repeatedly demonstrated that those who form and control illegal enterprises are generally well insulated from prosecutions, with the exception of prosecutions predicated upon the theory of conspiracy. To preclude uniformly their exposure to additional sanctions, regardless of the circumstances, for the very crimes which sustain their illegal ventures, would have the most unfortunate and inequitable consequences.

2. Compare People v. McGee, 49 N.Y.2d 48, 399 N.E.2d 1177, 1181-1182 (1979), where the court observed, in rejecting the *Pinkerton* doctrine:

> The crime of conspiracy is an offense separate from the crime that is the object of the conspiracy. Once an illicit agreement is shown, the overt act of any conspirator may be attributed to other conspirators to establish the offense of conspiracy. . . . It is not offensive to permit a conviction of conspiracy to stand on the overt act committed by another, for the act merely provides corroboration of the existence of the agreement and indicates that the agreement has reached a point where it poses a sufficient threat to society to impose sanctions. . . . But it is repugnant to our system of jurisprudence, where guilt is generally personal to the defendant, . . . to impose punishment, not for the socially harmful agreement to which the defendant is a party, but for substantive offenses in which he did not participate. . . .

3. Although the federal courts and several state courts continue to subject coconspirators to vicarious liability under *Pinkerton*,[6] it appears that a majority of the states now reject the *Pinkerton* doctrine. In accord with the Model Penal Code, most jurisdictions currently hold, either by statute or by judicial decision, that conspirators are liable for substantive crimes of their coconspirators only when the strict conditions for accomplice liability are met.[7] Supporting that position, the drafters of the Model Penal Code explain (Model Penal Code and Commentaries, Comment to 2.06(3) at 307 (1985)):

> [T]here appears to be no better way to confine within reasonable limits the scope of liability to which conspiracy may theoretically give rise. In People v. Luciano [277 N.Y. 348, 14 N.E.2d 433 (1938)], for example, Luciano and others were convicted of sixty-two counts of compulsory prostitution, each count involving a specific instance of placing a girl in a house of prostitution, receiving money for so doing or receiving money from the earnings of a prostitute — acts proved to have been committed pursuant to a combination to control commercialized vice in New York City.
>
> Liability was properly imposed with respect to these defendants, who directed and controlled the combination. They solicited and aided the commission of numberless specific crimes. . . . But would so extensive a liability be just for each of the prostitutes or runners involved in the plan? They have, of course, committed their own crimes; they may actually have assisted in others but they exerted no substantial influence on the behavior of a hundred other prostitutes or runners, each pur-

6. E.g., United States v. Diaz, 176 F.3d 52 (2d Cir. 1999); People v. Grant, 565 N.W.2d 389 (Mich. 1997); People v. Solis, 25 Cal. Rptr. 184 (App. 1993).

7. E.g., State ex rel. Woods v. Cohen, 844 P.2d 1147 (Ariz. 1992); People v. McGee, supra Note 2; Commonwealth v. Stasiun, 206 N.E.2d 672 (Mass. 1965); Ala. Code §13A-2-23 & Commentary (1999); Ill. Comp. Stat., ch. 720 §5/5-2 (West 1999); N.D. Code §12.1-03-01(1)(c) (1999); Note, 75 Colum. L. Rev. 1122, 1151 (1975).

suing his own ends within the shelter of the combination. A court would and should hold that they are parties to a conspiracy. . . . And they should also be held for those crimes they actually committed, or . . . for those to which they were accomplices. However, law would lose all sense of just proportion if simply because of the conspiracy itself each were held accountable for thousands of additional offenses of which he was completely unaware and which he did not influence at all. . . .

Conspiracy may prove solicitation, aid or agreement to aid, etc.; it is evidentially important and may be sufficient for that purpose. But whether it suffices ought to be decided by the jurors; they should not be told that it establishes complicity as a matter of law. . . .

3. *The Actus Reus of Conspiracy*

INTRODUCTORY NOTE

As we have seen, conspiracy is typically defined as an agreement by two or more persons to commit a crime. The actus reus of the offense, therefore, is the agreement itself. As the Supreme Court stated in Ianelli v. United States, 420 U.S. 770, 777 n. 10 (1975), "agreement remains the essential element of the crime." But agreements to commit crime are rarely reduced to writing and even oral agreements are unlikely to make clear or explicit all the terms and conditions of the joint undertaking. How then can the necessary agreement be described and proved? For a representative statement of the applicable standard, consider United States v. James, 528 F.2d 999, 1011 (5th Cir. 1976):

> To establish the common plan element of a conspiracy, it is not necessary for the government to prove an express agreement between the alleged conspirators to go forth and violate law. . . . "A conspiracy is seldom born of open covenants openly arrived at. The proof, by the very nature of the crime, must be circumstantial and therefore inferential to an extent varying with the conditions under which the crime may be consummated." Direct Sales Co. v. United States, 319 U.S. 703, 714. Knowledge by a defendant of all details or phases of a conspiracy is not required. It is enough that he knows the essential nature of it. "And, it is black letter law that all participants in a conspiracy need not know each other; all that is necessary is that each know that it has a scope and that for its success it requires an organization wider than may be disclosed by his personal participation."

INTERSTATE CIRCUIT, INC. v. UNITED STATES

Supreme Court of the United States
306 U.S. 208 (1939)

JUSTICE STONE delivered the opinion of the Court.

. . . This case is here on appeal . . . from a final decree of the District Court for northern Texas restraining appellants from continuing in a combination and conspiracy condemned by the court as a violation of Section 1 of the Sherman Anti-Trust Act. . . .

[The case involved two related movie theater chains, Interstate Circuit and Texas Consolidated Theaters, which together dominated the market for exhibiting films in the cities where their theaters were located. The other members of the alleged conspiracy were eight independent corporations that distributed films to theaters; together the eight distributed 75 percent of all first-run films exhibited in the United States. Interstate and Consolidated admittedly had entered contractual agreements with each of the eight distributors, specifying the terms on which the theaters would exhibit their films, but each individual contract between the exhibitor and a distributor could not by itself constitute an unlawful conspiracy. In order to prove the Sherman Act violation, the Government had to establish that the eight distributors had an agreement with one another.

[The centerpiece of the Government's case was a letter written by O'Donnell, Interstate's manager, to each distributor, in which he asked compliance with two demands as a condition of Interstate's continued exhibition of that distributor's films. One demand was that the distributor agree that on subsequent runs it would not permit its films to be shown in theaters charging an admission price of less than 25 cents. (At the time, 1934-1935, admission tickets to see second-run films in Texas theaters sold for as little as 10 or 15 cents!) Interstate's second demand was that the distributor agree not to permit its first-run motion pictures to be shown on a double-bill with another feature film.

[The letter addressed to each distributor identified all eight distributors as addressees of the proposal, and subsequently each distributor agreed with Interstate to accept the proposed restrictions. On this basis the trial court found that the distributors had agreed and conspired *with one another* to take uniform action on the Interstate proposals and to impose the demanded restrictions, in violation of the Sherman Act.]

As is usual in cases of alleged unlawful agreements to restrain commerce, the Government is without the aid of direct testimony that the distributors entered into any agreement with each other to impose the restrictions upon subsequent-run exhibitors. In order to establish agreement it is compelled to rely on inferences drawn from the course of conduct of the alleged conspirators.

The trial court drew the inference of agreement from the nature of the proposals made on behalf of Interstate and Consolidated; from the manner in which they were made; from the substantial unanimity of action taken upon them by the distributors; and from the fact that appellants did not call as witnesses any of the superior officials who negotiated the contracts with Interstate or any official who, in the normal course of business, would have had knowledge of the existence or non-existence of such an agreement among the distributors. This conclusion is challenged by appellants because not supported by subsidiary findings or by the evidence. We think this inference of the trial court was rightly drawn from the evidence. . . .

The O'Donnell letter named on its face as addressees the eight local representatives of the distributors, and so from the beginning each of the distributors knew that the proposals were under consideration by the others. Each was aware that all were in active competition and that without substantially unanimous action with respect to the restrictions for any given territory there was risk of a substantial loss of the business and good will of the subsequent-run and independent exhibitors, but that with it there was the prospect of increased profits. There was, therefore, strong motive for concerted action, full advantage of which was taken by Interstate and Consolidated in presenting their demands to all in a single document.

There was risk, too, that without agreement diversity of action would follow.

Compliance with the proposals involved a radical departure from the previous business practices of the industry and a drastic increase in admission prices of most of the subsequent-run theatres. . . .

It taxes credulity to believe that the several distributors would, in the circumstances, have accepted and put into operation with substantial unanimity such far-reaching changes in their business methods without some understanding that all were to join, and we reject as beyond the range of probability that it was the result of mere chance. . . .

While the District Court's finding of an agreement of the distributors among themselves is supported by the evidence, we think that in the circumstances of this case such agreement for the imposition of the restrictions upon subsequent-run exhibitors was not a prerequisite to an unlawful conspiracy. It was enough that, knowing that concerted action was contemplated and invited, the distributors gave their adherence to the scheme and participated in it. Each distributor was advised that the others were asked to participate; each knew that cooperation was essential to successful operation of the plan. They knew that the plan, if carried out, would result in a restraint of commerce, which, we will presently point out, was unreasonable within the meaning of the Sherman Act, and knowing it, all participated in the plan. The evidence is persuasive that each distributor early became aware that the others had joined. With that knowledge they renewed the arrangement and carried it into effect for the two successive years.

It is elementary that an unlawful conspiracy may be and often is formed without simultaneous action or agreement on the part of the conspirators. . . .

We think the conclusion is unavoidable that the conspiracy and each contract between Interstate and the distributors by which those consequences were effected are violations of the Sherman Act and that the District Court rightly enjoined the conspiracy among the distributors. Affirmed.

NOTES ON THE REQUIRED AGREEMENT

1. *Parallel action or common action? Interstate Circuit* is a landmark in the law of conspiracy, not only for antitrust cases but for the general problem of establishing the existence of a conspiratorial relationship. Consider the Court's statement that "in the circumstances of this case [an] agreement for the imposition of the restrictions . . . was not a prerequisite to an unlawful conspiracy. . . . It is elementary that an unlawful conspiracy may be and often is formed without simultaneous action or agreement on the part of the conspirators." How can this "elementary" proposition be reconciled with the definition of conspiracy? Without an agreement, what would the "conspiracy" be? Note that the evidence in *Interstate Circuit* could support an inference that the distributors actually spoke to one another and agreed to act in common. In other words, there might have been an express agreement, but its existence must be inferred from circumstantial evidence. Presumably, the Court meant that it was not necessary to establish *this kind* of agreement. Even if one were convinced that the distributors never communicated with one another at all, there would be a conspiracy because "each knew that cooperation was essential" and acted accordingly. In other words, a conspiracy may exist if there is no communication and no *express* agreement, provided that there is a tacit agreement reached without communication. But then what is the difference between parallel action that occurs because of a tacit agreement (that is, a conspiracy) and parallel action that occurs without any agreement at all?

2. *The Coleridge instruction.* In Rex v. Murphy, 173 Eng. Rep. 502, 508 (1837), Coleridge, J., directed the jury as follows:

> You have been properly told that this being a charge of conspiracy, if you are of opinion that the acts, though done, were done without common concert and design between these two parties, the present charge cannot be supported. On the other hand, I am bound to tell you, that although the common design is the root of the charge, it is not necessary to prove that these two parties came together and actually agreed in terms to have this common design, and to pursue it by common means, and so to carry it into execution. This is not necessary, because in many cases of the most clearly-established conspiracies there are no means of proving any such thing, and neither law nor common sense requires that it should be proved. If you find that these two persons pursued by their acts the same object, often by the same means, one performing one part of an act and the other another part of the same act, so as to complete it, with a view to the attainment of the object which they were pursuing, you will be at liberty to draw the conclusion that they have been engaged in a conspiracy to effect that object. The question you have to ask yourselves is, "Had they this common design, and did they pursue it by these common means — the design being unlawful."

See Theodore W. Cousens, Agreement as an Element of Conspiracy, 23 Va. L. Rev. 898 (1937), describing the importation of the Coleridge instruction into the United States and its widespread acceptance by American courts. Commenting on this instruction, Glanville Williams observed (Criminal Law: The General Part 667 (2d ed. 1961)):

> Properly read, this direction is a valuable statement of a principle of the law of evidence; but it is capable of dangerous misinterpretation. . . . A conspiracy is not merely a concurrence of wills but a concurrence resulting from agreement. Of course, if . . . two burglars actually executed their respective plans and were both caught in the house, they would be under a heavy suspicion of having acted in concert, and would be fortunate to convince a jury that they had not. . . . Nevertheless, if the jury are satisfied that the concurrence of the defendants' acts was accidental, the conspiracy charge must fail, for the concurrence of acts is only evidence of conspiracy, not equivalent to conspiracy. It is submitted that Coleridge, J., did not mean anything other than this; his direction meant only that agreement could be implied from acts in the absence of evidence that the concurrence was accidental.

3. *Problems. (a)* During an urban riot, one teenager shouts to three of his friends, "There's great stuff in that store, and the owner's a cheat. Let's go get it!" All four run into the store and start grabbing goods. Seeing the looting, two passersby, strangers to each other, enter the store and join in the looting. Are the four teenagers guilty of conspiracy? Are the two passersby guilty of conspiracy with each other? Are they guilty of conspiracy with the four teenagers?

Note that the answer can be important for several reasons. A conspiracy charge could permit a substantial increase in punishment. And if looter *X* assaults or kills the store owner while making his escape, his co-conspirator *Y* could be held liable for the assault or homicide. Has any of the looters conspired with any of the others? Are all of them guilty of conspiring with all the others?

(b) Motorist *M* loudly protests the action of an officer who stops him for a traffic violation, and a croud gathers. When the officer attempts to make an arrest, *M* pushes the officer to the ground and various members of the crowd then assault the officer. Is *M* guilty of conspiracy? Griffin v. State, 455 S.W.2d 882 (Ala. 1970), finds a conspiracy on similar facts. Is this a correct result under the *Interstate Circuit* principle?

(c) During a party attended by members of the rival Crips and Bloods gangs, Garcia, one of the Bloods, began "talking smack" (deliberately insulting) Crips members who were present, and several of his fellow Bloods did likewise. At some point, the confrontation escalated. Garcia and others drew weapons, and shooting broke out. Several Crips were seriously injured, presumably by gunfire from the rival gang. Garcia was seen shooting, but there was no evidence that any of the wounded were shot by him. He was convicted of conspiracy to commit aggravated assault, on the theory that he was vicariously liable under *Pinkerton* for acts of assault committed by other Bloods. Can common gang membership, together with parallel action (insulting their rivals, drawing their weapons) prove a conspiratorial agreement under the *Interstate Circuit* principle? The Ninth Circuit didn't think so. Do you agree? Reversing Garcia's conviction, the court said (United States v. Garcia. 151 F.3d 1243, 1245-1246 (9th Cir. 1998):

> An inference of an agreement is permissible only when the nature of the acts would logically require coordination and planning. [There was] nothing to suggest that the violence began in accordance with some prearrangement. The facts establish only that . . . an ongoing gang-related dispute erupted into shooting. . . . Such evidence does not establish that parties to a conspiracy "work[ed] together understandingly, with a single design for the accomplishment of a common purpose."
>
> [W]e are left only with gang membership as proof that Garcia conspired with fellow Bloods to shoot the [victims]. The government points to expert testimony . . . [stating] that generally gang members have a "basic agreement" to back one another up in fights, an agreement which requires no advance planning or coordination. This testimony . . . at most establishes one of the characteristics of gangs but not a specific objective of a particular gang — let alone a specific agreement on the part of its members to accomplish an illegal objective.
>
> [A]llowing a conviction on this basis would "smack[] of guilt by association." . . . Acts of provocation such as "talking smack" or bumping into rival gang members [at most] indicates that members of a particular gang may be looking for trouble, or ready to fight. . . . The fact that gang members attend a function armed with weapons may prove that they are prepared for violence, but without other evidence it does not establish that they have made plans to initiate it. And the fact that more than one member of the Bloods was shooting at rival[s] does not prove a prearrangement — the Crips, too, were able to pull out their guns almost immediately, suggesting that readiness for a gunfight requires no prior agreement. Such readiness may be a sad commentary on the state of mind of many of the nation's youth, but it is not indicative of a criminal conspiracy. [Otherwise, any] gang member could be held liable for any other gang member's act at any time so long as the act was predicated on "the common purpose of 'fighting the enemy.'" [A] general prac-

tice of supporting one another in fights . . . does not constitute the type of illegal objective that can form the predicate for a conspiracy charge.

UNITED STATES v. ALVAREZ

United States Court of Appeals, 5th Circuit
625 F.2d 1196 (1981)

[An indictment named Alvarez, Cifarelli, Cruz, and Peterson as co-conspirators in a plan to import 110,000 pounds of marijuana from Colombia by air. According to the government's evidence, an undercover DEA agent (Martinez) met Cifarelli at the Opa-Locka airport. Alvarez drove a pickup truck in which Cruz and Cifarelli were riding. The truck was loaded with some household appliances, including a washer and dryer; the DEA agent asked Cifarelli who Alvarez was and Cifarelli said Alvarez "would be at the off-loading site in the United States." The agent then spoke to Alvarez in Spanish and asked him if he planned to be at the unloading site. Alvarez nodded his head, signifying "yes," smiled, and asked the DEA agent if he was going on the plane. The agent said he was. After the conversation, Alvarez unloaded the household appliances from the truck. The agent then spoke with Cruz, and, after Cruz outlined his plans for arrival of the plane and its unloading, all were arrested.

[On appeal, a three-judge panel reversed Alvarez's conviction. The panel stated:

> A defendant does not join a conspiracy merely by participating in a substantive offense, or by associating with persons who are members of a conspiracy. . . . Therefore, even if a conspiracy between two parties is established, not every act of a third person that assists in the accomplishment of the objective of the conspiracy is a sufficient basis to demonstrate his concurrence in that agreement. . . .
>
> When we consider all the evidence in the case, we find that, at most, the government proved that Alvarez was a menial who intended to lend his pickup truck and his strong back to a plot confected by the mind of others. . . . Whatever his subjective transgressions, he was not shown to have been a conspirator or to have adopted or joined in the scheme contrived by others.

[The Fifth Circuit granted a rehearing en banc.]

Reavley, J. . . . A panel of this court . . . concluded that the government had failed to produce sufficient evidence that Alvarez had joined in the agreement to engage in illegal activity. Sitting en banc we now reach a different conclusion; the evidence was sufficient to convict.

The government was not required to prove that Alvarez had knowledge of all the details of the conspiracy or each of its members, provided that [the] prosecution established his knowledge of the essential of the conspiracy. Nor can a defendant escape criminal responsibility on the grounds that he did not join the conspiracy until well after its inception, or because he plays only a minor role in the total scheme.

We agree with the panel that the aggregate of the evidence is sufficient to infer that Alvarez knew that criminal activity was afoot. It must also have been obvious to him that there was conspiracy to import the contraband because prior planning and concerted action would be required to load the marijuana in Colombia, fly it into this country, and unload it upon its arrival. Alvarez' joinder in the illicit compact is inferable on two fronts. First, there is direct evidence that Alvarez intended to be at the off-loading site. A jury may well conclude that his intended presence manifested a prior agreement to assist in the unloading. Alternatively, the nodded head may be viewed as assurance to Martinez, then thought to be one in confederacy with Cifarelli and Cruz, that Alvarez would be at the unloading site to insure that the aircraft was unloaded rapidly. That such assurances to assuage jittery accomplices can constitute conduct in furtherance of the conspiracy, indicating joinder, [has also been] recognized. . . .

The evidence would have been insufficient to support the conviction without the proof that Cifarelli and Alvarez assured agent Martinez that Alvarez would be on hand at the place and time of the airplane's return to Florida. That proof, combined with all of the other evidence, clearly warranted the verdict of guilt. A reasonable jury could very well conclude that only one with knowledge of the marijuana, and who had agreed to participate in the scheme to accomplish its importation, would promise to be on hand at a remote and unlikely area for the unloading of cargo. . . .

[J]udgment of conviction is affirmed.

VANCE, J., with whom FAY, RUBIN, KRAVITCH, HENDERSON, POLITZ, HATCHETT, TATE, and THOMAS A. CLARK, JJ., join, dissenting. Alvarez nodded his head and smiled. For this he will go to the penitentiary.

In another case a smile and the nod of the head may be sufficient to establish guilt. Here it clearly was not.

This is not a case where an alleged conspirator was engaged in an illegal act or in the presence of a large quantity of contraband so that it reasonably may be inferred that he knew what was afoot. . . . Alvarez was engaged in a completely legal act. He was loading a washing machine onto an airplane. He was asked whether he was going to be there at the unloading site when the plane got back. It was in response to this innocuous inquiry that he smiled and nodded his head. This is all the admissible evidence to which we are cited to show that Alvarez knew of the unlawful conspiracy and agreed to join in it. . . .

Alvarez may have been a guilty co-conspirator or he may have been a humble workman performing a lawful act totally unrelated to any conspiracy, who simply indicated that he would report back to work as instructed. To my mind the majority opinion suggests no way that a jury reasonably could accept one hypothesis to the exclusion of the other.

The conspiracy statutes are vitally important to the protection of society. Yet the potential for injustice in conspiracy cases is enormous. The prosecutor's net may well ensnare the innocent as well as the guilty. The presentation of evidence in such cases is sometimes almost chaotic. We should use particular care to ensure that the prosecution actually proved that the defendant was a participant in the conspiracy before he is sent to prison. Our concept of justice rests on the basic notion that it is only for personal guilt that punishment is justified. . . . I would reverse.

PROBLEM

The COWBOY, a large shrimping boat fully equipped with shrimping gear, left a Florida port with its captain and a crew of four, including Freeman, who was the cook. After several hours of sailing, the captain diverted the ship from its original course and proceeded to a point off the coast of Nicaragua, where the crew of another vessel loaded 20 tons of marijuana into the shrimping boat's ice hold while the COWBOY's crew looked on. The COWBOY then sailed toward the United States, but it was intercepted by the U.S. Coast Guard. The captain and his four crew members were convicted of conspiracy to import marijuana. Did the crew members join in the conspiratorial agreement? Does the reasoning of the majority in *Alvarez* support a finding of conspiracy here? In United States v. Freeman, 660 F.2d 1030, 1036 (5th Cir. 1981), the court, upholding the convictions of all four crew members, stated:

> Appellants contend that mere presence and association is insufficient to convict them of conspiracy. The simple response to this argument is that a ten day voyage on a vessel that was bulging with 41,000 pounds of marijuana constitutes much more than "mere presence" or "mere association." . . . [T]he probable length of the voyage, . . . the large quantity of marijuana on board, which made it indisputable that [defendants] had knowledge of the marijuana, and the necessarily close relationship between the captain of the trawler and his . . . crew were factors from which the jury could reasonably find guilt beyond a reasonable doubt.

Judge Godbold, dissenting on this point, commented (id. at 1038-1040):

> [Under the majority's approach,] every officer and every crewman on every fishing and shrimping boat that makes a "long voyage" . . . is now prima facie a conspirator if a large quantity of contraband is found aboard. . . . [T]here is evidence from which it can be inferred that [the crew] had knowledge of a conspiracy in progress on the vessel. But knowledge is not participation in the conspiracy. . . . [Nor is] the crew's usual performance of duty and their failure to mutiny, take to lifeboats, or radio the Coast Guard.

NOTES ON THE OVERT ACT REQUIREMENT

Both at common law and under statutory formulations, conduct can be punishable as a conspiracy at points much farther back in the stages of preparation than the point where liability begins to attach for attempt. In some instances conspiracy is punishable without any overt act at all. In other situations an overt act must be proved, but the act may fall well short of the kind of conduct sufficient to constitute an attempt.

1. *Liability without an overt act.* At common law, the sole actus reus of conspiracy was the agreement itself; no "overt act" was required in addition. Does this mean that the offense becomes purely mental? Consider Mulcahy v. The Queen, L.R. 3 E. & I. App. 306, 316-317 (H.L. Ire. 1868). Defendants were indicted for conspiracy to foment the Irish rebellion. They argued that the indictment was defective for failing to charge some overt act, such as publishing writings or procuring arms. The court rejected the argument, stating:

> A conspiracy consists not merely in the intention of two or more, but in the agreement of two or more to do an unlawful act, or to do a lawful act by unlawful means. So long as such a design rests in intention only, it is not indictable. When two agree to carry it into effect, the very plot is an act in itself, and the act of each of the parties, promise against promise, actus contra actum, capable of being enforced, if lawful, punishable if for a criminal object or for the use of criminal means. And so far as proof goes, conspiracy . . . is generally a matter of inference deduced from certain criminal acts of the parties accused, done in pursuance of an apparent criminal purpose in common between them. The number and the compact give weight and cause danger, and this is more especially the case in a conspiracy like those charged in this indictment. Indeed, it seems a reduction to absurdity, that procuring a single stand of arms should be a sufficient overt act to make the disloyal design indictable, and that conspiring with a thousand men to enlist should not.

2. *Statutes requiring an overt act.* American conspiracy statutes have typically added an overt-act requirement. Note, for example, the wording of 18 U.S.C. §371, quoted in Note 1(b), page 681 supra. But it is not unusual for statutes to dispense with this overt-act requirement in the case of conspiracies to commit the most serious offenses. See, e.g., Model Penal Code §5.03(5), Appendix. Many statutes are silent on the subject. In the case of 21 U.S.C. §846, which makes no mention of an overt-act requirement for conspiracies to distribute illegal drugs, the Supreme Court has allowed conviction without proof of an overt act.[8] In the case of 18 U.S.C. §1951, punishing conspiracies to commit robbery or extortion, courts are currently split on whether an overt-act requirement should be read into the statute.[9]

The usual reason for requiring proof of an overt act is explained in Yates v. United States, 354 U.S. 298, 334 (1957): "The function of the overt act in a conspiracy prosecution is simply to manifest 'that the conspiracy is at work' . . . and is neither a project still resting solely in the minds of the conspirators nor a fully completed operation no longer in existence." Thus, even when an overt-act requirement applies, it generally can be satisfied by acts that would be considered equivocal or merely preparatory in the law of attempts. See Holmes, J., dissenting in Hyde v. United States, 225 U.S. 347, 387-388 (1912):

> An attempt, in the strictest sense, is an act expected to bring about a substantive wrong by the forces of nature. With it is classed the kindred offence where the act and the natural conditions present or supposed to be present are not enough to do the harm without a further act, but where it is so near to the result that if coupled with an intent to produce that result, the danger is very great. But combination, intention and overt act may all be present without amounting to a criminal attempt — as if all that were done should be an agreement to murder a man fifty miles away and the purchase of a pistol for the purpose. There must be dangerous proximity to success. . . . On the other hand, the essence of the conspiracy is being combined for an unlawful purpose — and if an overt act is required, it does not matter how remote the act may be from accomplishing the purpose, if done to effect it; that is, I suppose, in furtherance of it in any degree.

8. United States v. Shabani, 513 U.S. 10 (1994).

9. Compare United States v. Pistone, 177 F.3d 957 (11th Cir. 1999) (proof of overt act unnecessary), with United States v. Stephens, 964 F.2d 424 (5th Cir. 1992) (opposite).

By contrast, some states have required a more substantial overt act. Ohio, for example, provides that an overt act is sufficient only "when it is of a character that manifests a purpose on the part of the actor that the object of the conspiracy should be completed." Ohio Rev. Code Ann. tit. 29, §2923.01(B). Maine goes further toward bringing together the points at which liability begins for attempt and for conspiracy: The statute requires a "substantial step," which it defines as "conduct which, under the circumstances in which it occurs, is strongly corroborative of the firmness of the actor's intent to complete commission of the crime"; it further provides that "speech alone may not constitute a substantial step." Maine Rev. Stat. Ann. tit. 17-A, §151(4).

3. *Justifications for the traditional approach.* Unlike the Maine and Ohio statutes just mentioned, the traditional view is that any "overt act" (or sometimes the act of agreement alone) suffices to render conduct punishable as a conspiracy. But what is there about an agreement to commit a crime that justifies dispensing with the normal requirement of substantial preparatory conduct? Consider Note, 14 U. Toronto Fac. L. Rev. 56, 61-62 (1956):

> Since we are fettered by an unrealistic law of criminal attempts, overbalanced in favour of external acts, awaiting the lit match or the cocked and aimed pistol, the law of criminal conspiracy has been employed to fill the gap. If there are two persons involved, legal sanctions can be applied to the actor's intentions; this can seldom be done if only one person is involved and if he is wise in the ways of the law but acts unsuccessfully alone.

Does this argument remain valid under modern codes that eliminate unrealistically rigid requirements from the law of attempt? For another defense of the traditional position, consider Model Penal Code and Commentaries, Comment to §5.03 at 388 (1985):

> *First:* The act of agreeing with another to commit a crime, like the act of soliciting, is concrete and unambiguous; it does not present the infinite degrees and variations possible in the general category of attempts. The danger that truly equivocal behavior may be misinterpreted as preparation to commit a crime is minimized; purpose must be relatively firm before the commitment involved in agreement is assumed.
>
> *Second:* If the agreement was to aid another to commit a crime or if it otherwise encouraged the crime's commission, complicity would be established in the commission of the substantive offense. It would be anomalous to hold that conduct that would suffice to establish criminality, if something else is done by someone else, is insufficient if the crime is never consummated. . . .
>
> *Third:* [T]he the act of combining with another is significant both psychologically and practically, the former because it crosses a clear threshold in arousing expectations, the latter because it increases the likelihood that the offense will be committed.

4. *Questions.* In *Alvarez,* page 699 supra, would the defendant's actions be punishable as an attempt? If not, what does the fact of agreement (even if there was one) add to his actions? In light of the policies against treating mere preparatory conduct as criminal, how does Alvarez's expressed willingness to help unload a future shipment suffice to justify treating his conduct as criminal?

4. *The Mens Rea of Conspiracy*

PEOPLE v. LAURIA

California District Court of Appeal
251 Cal. App. 2d 471, 59 Cal. Rptr. 628 (1967)

FLEMING, J. In an investigation of call-girl activity the police focused their attention on three prostitutes actively plying their trade on call, each of whom was using Lauria's telephone answering service, presumably for business purposes.

On January 8, 1965, Stella Weeks, a policewoman, signed up for telephone service with Lauria's answering service. Mrs. Weeks, in the course of her conversation with Lauria's officer manager, hinted broadly that she was a prostitute concerned with the secrecy of her activities and their concealment from the police. She was assured that the operation of the service was discreet and "about as safe as you can get." It was arranged that Mrs. Weeks need not leave her address with the answering service, but could pick up her calls and pay her bills in person.

On February 11, Mrs. Weeks talked to Lauria on the telephone and told him her business was modeling and she had been referred to the answering service by Terry, one of the three prostitutes under investigation. She complained that because of the operation of the service she had lost two valuable customers, referred to as tricks. Lauria defended his service and said that her friends had probably lied to her about having left calls for her. But he did not respond to Mrs. Weeks' hints that she needed customers in order to make money, other than to invite her to his house for a personal visit in order to get better acquainted. In the course of his talk he said "his business was taking messages."

On February 15, Mrs. Weeks talked on the telephone to Lauria's office manager and again complained of two lost calls, which she described as a $50 and a $100 trick. On investigation the office manager could find nothing wrong, but she said she would alert the switchboard operators about slip-ups on calls.

On April 1, Lauria and the three prostitutes were arrested. Lauria complained to the police that this attention was undeserved, stating that Hollywood Call Board had 60 to 70 prostitutes on its board while his own service had only 9 or 10, that he kept separate records for known or suspected prostitutes for the convenience of himself and the police. When asked if his records were available to police who might come to the office to investigate call girls, Lauria replied that they were whenever the police had a specific name. However, his service didn't "arbitrarily tell the police about prostitutes on our board. As long as they pay their bills we tolerate them." In a subsequent voluntary appearance before the Grand Jury Lauria testified he had always cooperated with the police. But he admitted he knew some of his customers were prostitutes, and he knew Terry was a prostitute because he had personally used her services, and he knew she was paying for 500 calls a month.

Lauria and the three prostitutes were indicted for conspiracy to commit prostitution, and nine overt acts were specified. Subsequently the trial court set aside the indictment as having been brought without reasonable or probable cause. The People have appealed. . . .

To establish agreement, the People need show no more than a tacit, mutual understanding between co-conspirators to accomplish an unlawful act. . . . Here the People attempted to establish a conspiracy by showing that Lauria, well aware that his codefendants were prostitutes who received business calls from customers through his telephone answering service, continued to furnish them with such service. This approach attempts to equate knowledge of another's criminal activity with conspiracy to further such criminal activity, and poses the question of the criminal responsibility of a furnisher of goods or services who knows his product is being used to assist the operation of an illegal business. Under what circumstances does a supplier become a part of a conspiracy to further an illegal enterprise by furnishing goods or services which he knows are to be used by the buyer for criminal purposes?

The two leading cases on this point face in opposite directions. In United States v. Falcone, 311 U.S. 205, the sellers of large quantities of sugar, yeast, and cans were absolved from participation in a moonshining conspiracy among distillers who bought from them, while in Direct Sales Co. v. United States, 319 U.S. 703, a wholesaler of drugs was convicted of conspiracy to violate the federal narcotic laws by selling drugs in quantity to a codefendant physician who was supplying them to addicts. The distinction between these two cases appears primarily based on the proposition that distributors of such dangerous products as drugs are required to exercise greater discrimination in the conduct of their business than are distributors of innocuous substances like sugar and yeast.

In the earlier case, *Falcone,* the sellers' knowledge of the illegal use of the goods was insufficient by itself to make the sellers participants in a conspiracy with the distillers who bought from them. Such knowledge fell short of proof of a conspiracy, and evidence on the volume of sales was too vague to support a jury finding that respondents knew of the conspiracy [with others] from the size of the sales alone.

In the later case of *Direct Sales,* the conviction of a drug wholesaler for conspiracy to violate federal narcotic laws was affirmed on a showing that it had actively promoted the sale of morphine sulphate in quantity and had sold codefendant physician, who practiced in a small town in South Carolina, more than 300 times his normal requirements of the drug, even though it had been repeatedly warned of the dangers of unrestricted sales of the drug. The court contrasted the restricted goods involved in *Direct Sales* with the articles of free commerce involved in *Falcone:* "All articles of commerce may be put to illegal ends," said the court. "But all do not have inherently the same susceptibility to harmful and illegal use. . . . This difference is important for two purposes. One is for making certain that the seller knows the buyer's intended illegal use. The other is to show that by the sale he intends to further, promote and cooperate in it. This intent, when given effect by overt act, is the gist of conspiracy. While it is not identical with mere knowledge that another proposes unlawful action, it is not unrelated to such knowledge. . . . The step from knowledge to intent and agreement may be taken. There is more than suspicion, more than knowledge, acquiescence, carelessness, indifference, lack of concern. There is informed and interested cooperation, stimulation, instigation. And there is also a 'stake in the venture' which, even if it may not be essential, is not irrelevant to the question of conspiracy." (319 U.S. at 710-713.)

While *Falcone* and *Direct Sales* may not be entirely consistent with each other in their full implications, they do provide us with a framework for the criminal liability of a supplier of lawful goods or services put to unlawful use. Both the element of *knowledge* of the illegal use of the goods or services and the element of *intent* to further that use must be present in order to make the supplier a participant in a criminal conspiracy.

Proof of *knowledge* is ordinarily a question of fact and requires no extended discussion in the present case. . . . Because Lauria knew in fact that some of his customers were prostitutes, it is a legitimate inference he knew they were subscribing to his answering service for illegal business purposes and were using his service to make assignations for prostitution. . . .

The more perplexing issue in the case is the sufficiency of proof of *intent* to further the criminal enterprise. . . . Direct evidence of participation, such as advice from the supplier of legal goods or services to the user of those goods or services on their use for illegal purpose, such evidence as appeared in a companion case we decide today, People v. Roy, 59 Cal. Rptr. 636, provides the simplest case.[a] . . . But in cases where direct proof of complicity is lacking, intent to further the conspiracy must be derived from the sale itself and its surrounding circumstances in order to establish the supplier's express or tacit agreement to join the conspiracy.

In the case at bench the prosecution argues that since Lauria knew his customers were using his service for illegal purposes but nevertheless continued to furnish it to them, he must have intended to assist them in carrying out their illegal activities. . . .

1. Intent may be inferred from knowledge, when the purveyor of legal goods for illegal use has acquired a stake in the venture. (United States v. Falcone, 2 Cir. 109 F.2d 579, 581.)[b] For example, in Regina v. Thomas, (1957), 2 All E.R. 181, 342, a prosecution for living off the earnings of prostitution, the evidence showed that the accused, knowing the woman to be a convicted prostitute, agreed to let her have the use of his room between the hours of 9 P.M. and 2 A.M. for a charge of £3 a night. The Court of Criminal Appeal refused an appeal from the conviction, holding that when the accused rented a room at a grossly inflated rent to a prostitute for the purpose of carrying on her trade, a jury could find he was living on the earnings of prostitution.

In the present case, no proof was offered of inflated charges for the telephone answering services furnished the codefendants.

a. In this case the court upheld liability. The facts were similar, but the answering service operator actively participated in the business of prostitution by making arrangements for the sharing of customers between two supposed prostitutes who used the service. The court said, speaking of the operator, "Perhaps she was motivated solely by a desire to further the welfare and serve the interests of her customers and acted without thought of added profit for herself. But disinterested loyalty and devotion to the patrons of her service provide no excuse for the promotion of a criminal enterprise." 59 Cal. Rptr. at 641. — EDS.

b. In United States v. Falcone, Judge Learned Hand wrote the opinion of the Second Circuit Court of Appeals. He stated: "Civilly, a man's liability extends to any injuries which he should have apprehended to be likely to follow from his acts. . . . There are indeed instances of criminal liability of the same kind, where the law imposes punishment merely because the accused did not forbear to do that from which the wrong was likely to follow; but in prosecutions for conspiracy or abetting, his attitude towards the forbidden undertaking must be more positive. It is not enough that he does not forego a normally lawful activity, of the fruits of which he knows that others will make an unlawful use; he must in some sense promote their venture himself, make it his own, have a stake in its outcome. The distinction is especially important today when so many prosecutors seek to sweep within the drag-net of conspiracy all those who have been associated in any degree whatever with the main offenders. We may agree that morally the defendants at bar should have refused to sell to illicit distillers; but, both morally and legally, to do so was toto coelo different from joining with them in running the stills." — EDS.

2. Intent may be inferred from knowledge, when no legitimate use for the goods or services exists. The leading California case is People v. McLaughlin, 111 Cal. App. 2d 781, 245 P.2d 1076, in which the court upheld a conviction of the suppliers of horse-racing information by wire for conspiracy to promote bookmaking, when it had been established that wire service information had no other use than to supply information needed by bookmakers to conduct illegal gambling operations. . . .

In Shaw v. Director of Public Prosecutions, [1962] A.C. 220, the defendant was convicted of conspiracy to corrupt public morals and of living on the earnings of prostitution, when he published a directory consisting almost entirely of advertisements of the names, addresses, and specialized talents of prostitutes. Publication of such a directory, said the court, could have no legitimate use and serve no other purpose than to advertise the professional services of the prostitutes whose advertisements appeared in the directory. The publisher could be deemed a participant in the profits from the business activities of his principal advertisers. . . .

However, there is nothing in the furnishing of telephone answering service which would necessarily imply assistance in the performance of illegal activities. Nor is any inference to be derived from the use of an answering service by women, either in any particular volume of calls, or outside normal working hours. Nightclub entertainers, registered nurses, faith healers, public stenographers, photographic models, and free lance substitute employees, provide examples of women in legitimate occupations whose employment might cause them to receive a volume of telephone calls at irregular hours.

3. Intent may be inferred from knowledge, when the volume of business with the buyer is grossly disproportionate to any legitimate demand, or when sales for illegal use amount to a high proportion of the seller's total business. In such cases an intent to participate in the illegal enterprise may be inferred from the quantity of the business done. For example, in *Direct Sales,* supra, the sale of narcotics to a rural physician in quantities 300 times greater than he would have normal use for provided potent evidence of an intent to further the illegal activity.[c] In the same case the court also found significant the fact that the wholesaler had attracted as customers a disproportionately large group of physicians who had been convicted of violating the Harrison Act. In Shaw v. Director of Public Prosecutions, [1962] A.C. 220, almost the entire business of the directory came from prostitutes.

No evidence of any unusual volume of business with prostitutes was presented by the prosecution against Lauria.

Inflated charges, the sale of goods with no legitimate use, sales in inflated amounts, each may provide a fact of sufficient moment from which the intent of the seller to participate in the criminal enterprise may be inferred. . . . because in one way or another the supplier has acquired a special interest in the operation of the illegal enterprise. His intent to participate in the crime of which he has knowledge may be inferred from the existence of his special interest.

Yet there are cases in which it cannot reasonably be said that the supplier has a stake in the venture or has acquired a special interest in the enterprise, but

c. The court in *Direct Sales* also emphasized the quantity discounts the defendant offered to the physician. — Eds.

in which he has been held liable as a participant on the basis of knowledge alone. . . . In Regina v. Bainbridge (1959), 3 W.L.R. 656 (CCA 6), a supplier of oxygen-cutting equipment to one known to intend to use it to break into a bank was convicted as an accessory to the crime. . . . It seems apparent from these cases that a supplier who furnishes equipment which he *knows* will be used to commit a serious crime may be deemed from that knowledge alone to have intended to produce the result. . . . For instance, we think the operator of a telephone answering service with positive knowledge that his service was being used to facilitate the extortion of ransom, the distribution of heroin, or the passing of counterfeit money who continued to furnish the service with knowledge of its use, might be chargeable on knowledge alone with participation in a scheme to extort money, to distribute narcotics, or to pass counterfeit money. The same result would follow the seller of gasoline who knew the buyer was using his product to make Molotov cocktails for terroristic use.

Logically, the same reasoning could be extended to crimes of every description. Yet we do not believe an inference of intent drawn from knowledge of criminal use properly applies to the less serious crimes classified as misdemeanors. The duty to take positive action to dissociate oneself from activities helpful to violations of the criminal law is far stronger and more compelling for felonies than it is for misdemeanors or petty offenses. . . . We believe the distinction between the obligations arising from knowledge of a felony and those arising from knowledge of a misdemeanor continues to reflect basic human feelings about the duties owed by individuals to society. Heinous crime must be stamped out, and its suppression is the responsibility of all. Venial crime and crime not evil in itself present less of a danger to society, and perhaps the benefits of their suppression through the modern equivalent of the posse, the hue and cry, the informant, and the citizen's arrest, are outweighed by the disruption to everyday life brought about by amateur law enforcement and private officiousness in relatively inconsequential delicts which do not threaten our basic security. . . .

With respect to misdemeanors, we conclude that positive knowledge of the supplier that his products or services are being used for criminal purposes does not, without more, establish an intent of the supplier to participate in the misdemeanors. With respect to felonies, we do not decide the converse, viz. that in all cases of felony knowledge of criminal use alone may justify an inference of the supplier's intent to participate in the crime. The implications of *Falcone* make the matter uncertain with respect to those felonies which are merely prohibited wrongs. . . . But decision on this point is not compelled, and we leave the matter open.

From this analysis of precedent we deduce the following rule: the intent of a supplier who knows of the criminal use to which his supplies are put to participate in the criminal activity connected with the use of his supplies may be established by (1) direct evidence that he intends to participate, or (2) through an inference that he intends to participate based on, (a) his special interest in the activity, or (b) the aggravated nature of the crime itself.

When we review Lauria's activities in the light of this analysis, we find no proof that Lauria took any direct action to further, encourage, or direct the call-girl activities of his codefendants and we find an absence of circumstances from which his special interest in their activities could be inferred. Neither excessive charges for standardized services, nor the furnishing of services without a legitimate use, nor an unusual quantity of business with call girls, are present. The offense which he is charged with furthering is a misdemeanor, a category of crime which has never been made a required subject of positive disclosure to public authority. Under these circumstances, although proof of Lauria's knowledge of the criminal activities of his patrons was sufficient to charge him with that fact, there was insufficient evidence that he intended to further their criminal activities, and hence insufficient proof of his participation in a criminal conspiracy with his codefendants to further prostitution. Since the conspiracy centered around the activities of Lauria's telephone answering service, the charges against his codefendants likewise fail for want of proof.

In absolving Lauria of complicity in a criminal conspiracy we do not wish to imply that the public authorities are without remedies to combat modern manifestations of the world's oldest profession. Licensing of telephone answering services under the police power, together with the revocation of licenses for the toleration of prostitution, is a possible civil remedy. The furnishing of telephone answering service in aid of prostitution could be made a crime. (Cf. Pen. Code, §316, which makes it a misdemeanor to let an apartment with knowledge of its use for prostitution.) Other solutions will doubtless occur to vigilant public authorities if the problem of call-girl activity needs further suppression.

The order is affirmed.

NOTES ON MENS REA

1. *Purpose or knowledge in felony cases.* Does the *Lauria* court's analysis imply that knowledge alone is a sufficient mens rea for conspiracy when the object crime is a felony? If there was no "agreement" between Lauria and the prostitutes in California, in what sense would such an "agreement" exist, on identical facts, in a state that declared prostitution a felony?

What should be the result when the object offense is a very serious crime? Recall that in United States v. Fountain, page 614 supra, the court held (relying on *Lauria*) that Gometz, who supplied a knife knowing that it would be used to kill, could be an accomplice in the murder. Should the same facts be sufficient to hold Gometz for conspiracy to commit murder? Even if knowledge alone is considered sufficient for aiding and abetting liability, might it make sense to hold that more is required to make the supplier and his customer "partners in crime"? In this regard, consider how accomplice liability differs from conspiracy liability. What is Supplier's liability, under each theory, if he provides a stolen car for use in a bank robbery but Customer never attempts the crime? What is Supplier's liability if Customer kidnaps a teller and holds her hostage in order to facilitate his escape?

The Model Penal Code solution to these problems is to require purpose for *both* conspiracy and accomplice liability. See §§2.06(3)(a); 5.03(1). For the commentary relevant to these provisions, see the Model Penal Code discussion of accomplice mens rea, set out at pages 612-613 supra. Most states likewise require purpose in conspiracy cases, even when the object crime is a serious felony. Thus, in Commonwealth v. Camerano, 677 N.E.2d 678 (Mass. App. 1997), defendant rented land to Howell and permitted him to erect a garden enclosure in which, as Camerano surely knew, Howell was growing a large amount of marijuana.

Though Camerano could have evicted Howell at any time, he allowed Howell to remain and collected $200 per month in rent, money that Howell allegedly could not have obtained from any legal source. Camerano's conviction for conspiracy to possess and distribute marijuana was nonetheless reversed, with the court noting (id. at 681) that "[i]ntent is a requisite mental state for conspiracy, not mere knowledge or acquiescence." In United States v. Scotti, 47 F.3d 1237 (2d Cir. 1995), Scotti threatened to "break Egnat's legs and burn down [his] house" unless he came up with $50,000 to pay an extortionate debt. Scotti then asked Rodriguez, a mortgage broker, to help Egnat arrange a mortgage to obtain the cash. Rodriguez did so, knowing that Egnat had been threatened and was reluctantly agreeing to the transaction. Rodriguez's assistance, with full knowledge of the circumstances, was held insufficient to make him guilty of conspiracy to commit extortion.

2. Problems. (a) Zahm wanted to use Lawrence's house trailer as a site for manufacturing methamphetamine. The chemicals used to "cook" methamphetamine can soil or damage the work area, and there is a risk of explosion when the volatile ingredients are heated to high temperatures. Lawrence agreed to accept $1,000 for leasing the trailer to Zahm for one day. Zahm was unable to find all the necessary equipment, and the "cook" was never carried out. Is Lawrence guilty of conspiracy to manufacture methamphetamine? United States v. Blankenship, 970 F.2d 283 (7th Cir. 1992), holds that he is not. Do you agree? What arguments can be made in support of the court's conclusion?

(b) Morse owned a Beechcraft light plane that had no passenger seats, leaving more room for cargo. Though witnesses testified that the plane was worth $50,000 to $70,000, he asked two young buyers to pay $80,000 for it and then raised his price to $115,000, to be paid in cash installments. The buyers agreed, took possession of the plane, and used it to smuggle marijuana from Mexico to Texas. Is Morse guilty of conspiracy to import marijuana? In United States v. Morse, 851 F.2d 1317, 1319-1320 (11th Cir. 1988), the court held:

> The circumstantial evidence in this case adequately supports Morse's conspiracy convictions. First, the plane in Florida that Morse sold to Colding was particularly suited for smuggling: there were no passenger seats in the plane, leaving more room for hauling marijuana; one witness — a customs agent — testified that "a Beechcraft Queen Aire happens to be one of the profile aircraft that is involved in narcotic smuggling." Second, Morse sold the plane for $115,000, almost twice its market value; he had raised the price from $80,000 after meeting with Cauthen and Colding. Third, all payments were made in cash of low denominations. Fourth, Morse sold the plane to Colding, a twenty-three year old, without any contract or receipt to evidence the transaction. Fifth, Morse, who never had registered *his* purchase of the plane with the Federal Aviation Administration (FAA), sold the plane without providing the FAA with an aircraft registration application or bill of sale as required by law. Sixth, Morse was informed that the plane had been used to smuggle marijuana; yet he made no attempt to contact law enforcement officials. Seventh, when Colding failed to pay the balance of the agreed purchase price, Morse did not threaten to file suit to recover the money.

Question: Is this analysis consistent with the reasoning of *Lauria, Direct Sales,* and *Falcone?*

3. Corrupt motive. In a leading common law precedent, People v. Powell, 63 N.Y. 88 (1875), the court held that to be criminal, a conspiracy must be animated by a "corrupt" motive or an intention to engage in conduct known to be wrongful. The effect of the *Powell* doctrine is illustrated by Commonwealth v. Gormley, 77 Pa. Super. 298, 301-303 (1921). The defendant, an election officer, was indicted for conspiracy to violate the election law by entering the votes cast in the official tally sheets before the time set by law and for the substantive offense of entering false figures on the sheets. The jury acquitted him on the substantive charge but found him guilty of the conspiracy. The court reversed on appeal, finding error in the trial judge's refusal to allow testimony of the defendant's good faith (there was apparently no opposition candidate) and ignorance of the criminality of his act. The court said:

> The reason for the court's refusal . . . was that a defendant having violated the plain provisions of a statute, he cannot give his reasons why he did so. That a violation of the act subjects the defendant to the penalties prescribed whether he is conscious that he is violating the law or not. This view is no doubt correct as applied to the second count of the indictment charging a violation of the election laws. The legislature can declare an act a crime regardless of intent. As to the charge of conspiracy, we think the testimony was admissible. . . .
>
> [In] People v. Powell, 63 N.Y. 88, . . . it was said, "To make an agreement between two or more persons to do an act innocent in itself a criminal conspiracy, it is not enough that it appears that the act which was the object of the agreement was prohibited. The confederation must be corrupt. The agreement must have been entered into with an evil purpose, as distinguished from a purpose simply to do the act prohibited, in ignorance of the prohibition. This is implied in the meaning of the word conspiracy." . . .
>
> It follows that if a material part of the crime is the intention, the defendant may introduce any testimony that throws light on it. On the charge of making fraudulent entries on the tally sheet, the defendants had no right to show their intention and ignorance of the law was no answer to the charge, but the trial being had upon two counts, one charging conspiracy, the testimony should not have been excluded and defendants should have been allowed to explain their action and their motives.

Question: Doesn't this approach in effect make mistake of law a defense in a conspiracy prosecution? The *Powell* doctrine has been widely criticized. See Model Penal Code and Commentaries, Comment to §503, at 417-418 (1985):

> The *Powell* rule, and many of the decisions that rely on it, may be viewed as a judicial endeavor to import fair mens rea requirements into statutes creating regulatory offenses that do not rest on traditional concepts of personal fault and culpability. This should, however, be the function of the statutes defining such offenses. Section 2.04(3) specifies the limited situations when ignorance of the criminality of one's conduct is a defense in general. There is no good reason why the fortuity of concert should be used as a device for limiting criminality in this area. . . .

The *Powell* doctrine has been rejected in England, see Churchill v. Walton, [1967] 2 A.C. 224, and in most of the state codifications enacted in the wake of the Model Penal Code. See Note, Conspiracy: State Statutory Reform Since the Model Penal Code, 75 Colum. L. Rev. 1122, 1131 n. 48 (1975).

4. *Attendant circumstances.* In cases like Commonwealth v. Gormley and People v. Powell (see Note 3 supra), the "corrupt motive" defense amounts to a claim of ignorance of the law. As the preceding Note indicates, the current trend is

toward parity between the requirements for conspiracy and the substantive offense on this issue: If ignorance of the law is no defense with respect to the substantive offense, it is likewise no defense to a conspiracy charge. Should the result be different where the defendant claims a mistake of *fact* as to some attendant circumstance; that is, should mistake of fact be a defense to a conspiracy charge even if it would not be a defense in a prosecution for the substantive offense? Consider the following situations.

(a) Jurisdictional facts. In United States v. Feola, 420 U.S. 672 (1975), defendants, planning to steal substantial sums from a group they believed to be prospective drug buyers, drew guns on their victims, who were in fact undercover federal agents. The defendants were then charged with assaulting, and conspiring to assault, federal officers. The Supreme Court held that defendants' ignorance that their victims were federal officers was not a defense to the substantive charge of assaulting a federal officer; it was enough that they knew they were assaulting someone. Should ignorance of the status of the victims nonetheless be a defense to the conspiracy charge? How can it be said that defendants conspired (that is, "agreed") to assault a federal officer? The Court upheld the conspiracy convictions, but on narrow grounds. The Court took care to distinguish Judge Learned Hand's "traffic light analogy," a famous argument *against* parity between the mens rea requirements for conspiracy and the object crime. Judge Hand wrote in United States v. Cummins, 123 F.2d 271, 273:

> While one may, for instance, be guilty of running past a traffic light of whose existence one is ignorant, one cannot be guilty of conspiring to run past such a light, for one cannot agree to run past a light unless one supposes that there is a light to run past.

In *Feola,* the Court noted that "[t]he problem posed by the traffic light analogy is not before us," and said it would "save for another day" the question whether a party can be punished for conspiracy on the basis of an agreement to engage in apparently innocent conduct where the unintended result of engaging in that conduct is the violation of a criminal statute. The Court ruled the "traffic light analogy" inapt because in *Feola* the defendants' mistake concerned a fact that was not relevant to guilt or innocence but was "jurisdictional only" (420 U.S. at 677 n. 9). The Court explained (id at 694):

> [W]e fail to see how the agreement is any less blameworthy or constitutes less of a danger to society solely because the participants are unaware of which body of law they intend to violate. . . . [I]mposition of a requirement of knowledge of those facts that serve only to establish federal jurisdiction would render it more difficult to serve the policy behind the law of conspiracy without serving any other apparent social policy. . . .

(b) Facts that increase the gravity of the offense. Suppose that Supplier and Dealer meet with Buyer and negotiate terms for a large purchase of drugs. At Buyer's request, they agree to deliver the drugs to him at Seedy's Bar, at the corner of Fourth and Elm. Before the delivery is made, Supplier and Dealer are arrested. Buyer turns out to be an undercover agent, and (unknown to Dealer and Supplier) Seedy's Bar turns out to be directly across the street from a public school. State law imposes much higher penalties for drug sales that occur within 1,000

feet of a school. Can Dealer and Suppler be convicted of conspiracy to distribute drugs within 1,000 feet of a school? Consider United States v. Freed, 401 U.S. 601 (1971). In that case, the Supreme Court upheld an indictment charging both possession and conspiracy to possess unregistered hand grenades, despite its failure to allege that the defendant knew the grenades were unregistered. The Court treated the substantive offense of possessing unregistered hand grenades as imposing strict liability so far as the fact of registration was concerned. The Court disposed of the conspiracy charge as follows (id. at n. 14):

> We need not decide whether a criminal conspiracy to do an act "innocent in itself" and not known by the alleged conspirators to be prohibited must be actuated by some corrupt motive other than the intention to do the act which is prohibited and which is the object of the conspiracy. An agreement to acquire hand grenades is hardly an agreement innocent in itself. Therefore what we have said of the substantive offense satisfies on these special facts the requirements for a conspiracy.

Questions: Is this holding sound? So far as the conspiracy count was concerned, was the defendant arguing only that he did not know it was a crime to possess grenades or that he did not agree to possess unregistered grenades? Did the Court confuse two separate defenses, namely, the defense of ignorance of the criminality of the agreement and the defense of lack of agreement to do the prohibited act?

(c) Facts essential to criminality. Suppose that, in contrast to United States v. Freed, supra, the alleged conspiracy involves an act "innocent in itself." For example, suppose that Alan and Mary, after spending an evening together, decide to go to a motel where they will have consensual sexual relations. Bill agrees to drive them there, knowing their intentions, but just before they leave, Mary's parents arrive on the scene and foil the plan. Though neither Alan nor Bill could have known it, Mary is underage. Can Alan and Bill be convicted of conspiracy to commit statutory rape?

We considered variations on this hypothetical at two earlier points above. With respect to attempt liability, the Model Penal Code Commentary states that a person in Alan's position would be guilty of attempted statutory rape. See page 563 supra. With respect to Bill's liability as an accomplice, §2.06(3)(a) appears to preclude conviction, but in this instance the Commentary argues that the Code is ambiguous and states that the issue was left for the courts to decide. See page 622 supra. The Code and its Commentary reflect a similar ambivalence with respect to the mens rea for conspiracy. The Commentary states that the Code is ambiguous and that the issue was left to the courts. See Model Penal Code and Commentaries, Comment to §5.03 at 413 (1985). Yet §5.03(1) provides that a person is guilty of conspiracy to commit a crime only if he acts "with the purpose of promoting or facilitating its commission." How can it be said that either Alan or Bill has "the purpose of promoting or facilitating [the] commission" of the crime of statutory rape?

Apart from the question of textual interpretation, what is the sensible way to resolve this problem? Should the policies that determine the mens rea for the object crime logically govern the matter on the conspiracy charge as well? Or, given the very early point at which conspiracy liability can attach, is it important to require subjective culpability? Whatever may be the right solution to this problem for complicity and attempts, how can a mens rea that is less than purpose or knowledge ever suffice for conspiracy, which — by definition — consists of an *agreement* to engage in the prohibited conduct?

The English approach acknowledges these concerns. The English Criminal Law Act, 1977, ch. 45, §1(2) states:

> Where liability for any offence may be incurred without knowledge on the part of the person committing it of any particular fact or circumstance necessary for the commission of the offence, a person shall nevertheless not be guilty of conspiracy to commit that offence by virtue of subsection (1) above unless he and at least one other party to the agreement intend or know that that fact or circumstance shall or will exist at the time when the conduct constituting the offence is to take place.

5. *Scope of the Agreement — Single or Multiple Conspiracies*

MODEL PENAL CODE AND COMMENTARIES, Comment to §5.03 at 422-423 (1985): Much of the most perplexing litigation in conspiracy has been concerned less with the essential elements of the offense than with the scope to be accorded to a combination, i.e., the singleness or multiplicity of the conspiratorial relationships typical in a large, complex and sprawling network of crime. . . . [I]n most of these cases it is clear that each defendant has committed or conspired to commit one or more crimes; the question now is, to what extent is he a conspirator with each of the persons involved in the larger criminal network to commit the crimes that are its objects. . .

The inquiry may be crucial for a number of purposes. These include not only defining each defendant's liability but also the propriety of joint prosecution, admissibility against a defendant of the hearsay acts and declarations of others, questions of multiple prosecution or conviction and double jeopardy, satisfaction of the overt act requirement or statutes of limitation or rules of jurisdiction and venue, and possibly liability for substantive crimes executed pursuant to the conspiracy. The scope problem is thus central to the present concern of courts and commentators about the use of conspiracy, a concern based on the conflict between the need for effective means of prosecuting large criminal organizations, and the dangers of prejudice to individual defendants.

KOTTEAKOS v. UNITED STATES

Supreme Court of the United States
328 U.S. 750 (1946)

JUSTICE RUTLEDGE delivered the opinion of the Court.

The only question is whether petitioners have suffered substantial prejudice from being convicted of a single general conspiracy by evidence which the Government admits proved not one conspiracy but some eight or more different ones of the same sort executed through a common key figure, Simon Brown. Petitioners were convicted under the general conspiracy section of the Criminal Code, 18 U.S.C.A. §88 [now §371], of conspiring to violate the provisions of the National Housing Act. The judgments were affirmed by the Circuit Court of Appeals. . . .

The indictment named thirty-two defendants, including the petitioners. The gist of the conspiracy, as alleged, was that the defendants had sought to induce various financial institutions to grant credit, with the intent that the loans for advances would then be offered to the Federal Housing Administration for insurance upon applications containing false and fraudulent information.

Of the thirty-two persons named in the indictment nineteen were brought to trial and the names of thirteen were submitted to the jury. Two were acquitted; the jury disagreed as to four; and the remaining seven, including petitioners, were found guilty.

The government's evidence may be summarized briefly, for the petitioners have not contended that it was insufficient, if considered apart from the alleged errors relating to the proof and the instructions at the trial.

Simon Brown, who pleaded guilty, was the common and key figure in all of the transactions proven. He was president of the Brownie Lumber Company. Having had experience in obtaining loans under the National Housing Act, he undertook to act as broker in placing for others loans for modernization and renovation, charging a five per cent commission for his services. Brown knew, when he obtained the loans, that the proceeds were not to be used for the purposes stated in the applications. [The Court then summarized the evidence against several defendants.]

The evidence against the other defendants whose cases were submitted to the jury was similar in character. They too had transacted business with Brown relating to National Housing Act loans. But no connection was shown between them and petitioners, other than that Brown had been the instrument in each instance for obtaining the loans. In many cases the other defendants did not have any relationship with one another, other than Brown's connection with each transaction. As the Circuit Court of Appeals said, there were "at least eight, and perhaps more, separate and independent groups, none of which had any connection with any other, though all dealt independently with Brown as their agent." As the Government puts it, the pattern was "that of separate spokes meeting at a common center," though we may add without the rim of the wheel to enclose the spokes.

The proof therefore admittedly made out a case, not of a single conspiracy, but of several, notwithstanding only one was charged in the indictment. The Court of Appeals aptly drew analogy in the comment, "Thieves who dispose of their loot to a single receiver — a single 'fence' — do not by that fact alone become confederates; they may, but it takes more than knowledge that he is a 'fence' to make them such." It stated that the trial judge "was plainly wrong in supposing that upon the evidence there could be a single conspiracy; and in the view which he took of the law, he should have dismissed the indictment."[a] Nevertheless the

a. Judge Learned Hand wrote the opinion for the court of appeals. The sentences quoted are part of the following paragraph in which he stated, in reference to the view of the trial judge (151 F.2d at 172): "He was apparently misled by an erroneous understanding of the rule that, when anyone joins an existing conspiracy, he takes it over as it is, and becomes a party to it in its earlier phases, and that the declarations of other conspirators, even though made before he has entered, are competent against him. What he failed to remember was that to bring this rule into operation it is not enough that, when one joins with another in a criminal venture, he knows that his confederate is engaged in other criminal undertakings with other persons, even though they may be of the same general nature. The acts and declarations of confederates, past or future, are never competent against a party except in so far as they are steps in furtherance of a purpose common to him appellate court held the error not prejudicial, saying among other things that "especially since guilt was so manifest, it was 'proper' to join the conspiracies," and "to reverse the conviction would be a miscarriage of justice." This is indeed the Government's entire position. . . .

[T]he trial court itself was confused in the charge which it gave to guide the jury in deliberation. The court instructed:

> The indictment charges but one conspiracy, and to convict each of the defendants of a conspiracy the Government would have to prove, and you would have to find, that each of the defendants was a member of that conspiracy. You cannot divide it up. It is one conspiracy, and the question is whether or not each of the defendants or which of the defendants, are members of that conspiracy.

On its face, as the Court of Appeals said, this portion of the charge was plainly wrong in application to the proof made; and the error pervaded the entire charge, not merely the portion quoted. The jury could not possibly have found, upon the evidence, that there was only one conspiracy. The trial court was of the view that one conspiracy was made out by showing that each defendant was linked to Brown in one or more transactions, and that it was possible on the evidence for the jury to conclude that all were in a common adventure because of this fact and the similarity of purpose presented in the various applications for loans.

The view, specifically embodied throughout the instructions, obviously confuses the common purpose of a single enterprise with the several, though similar purposes of numerous separate adventures of like character. It may be that, notwithstanding the misdirection, the jury actually understood correctly the purport of the evidence, as the Government now concedes it to have been, and came to the conclusion that the petitioners were guilty only of the separate conspiracies in which the proof shows they respectively participated. But, in the face of the misdirection and in the circumstances of this case, we cannot assume that the lay triers of fact were so well informed upon the law or that they disregarded the permission expressly given to ignore that vital difference.

As we have said, the error permeated the entire charge, indeed the entire trial. Not only did it permit the jury to find each defendant guilty of conspiring with thirty-five other potential co-conspirators, . . . when none of the evidence would support such a conviction. . . . It had other effects. . . . Carrying forward his premise that the jury could find one conspiracy on the evidence, the trial judge further charged that, if the jury found a conspiracy,

> then the acts or the statements of *any* of those whom you so find to be conspirators between the two dates that I have mentioned, may be considered by you in evi-

---

and them. . . . In the case at bar, we assume that Lekacos and Kotteakos and Regenbogen knew that Brown was for the time being acting as a broker for a number of other persons, who were getting loans in fraud of the Act, and who were making false representations to the bank like those which they themselves were making. But that was not enough to make them confederates with the other applicants; it did not give them any interest in the success of any loans but their own; there was no interest, no venture, common to them and anyone else but Brown himself. Thieves who dispose of their loot to a single receiver — a single 'fence' — do not by that fact alone become confederates: they may, but it takes more than knowledge that he is a 'fence' to make them such. United States v. Falcone, 311 U.S. 205; United States v. Peoni, 2 Cir., 10 F.2d 401." — Eds.

dence as against *all* of the defendants whom you so find to be members of *the* conspiracy.

(Emphasis added.) . . .

On those instructions it was competent not only for the jury to find that all of the defendants were parties to a single common plan, design and scheme, where none was shown by the proof, but also for them to impute to each defendant the acts and statements of the others without reference to whether they related to one of the schemes proven or another, and to find an overt act affecting all in conduct which admittedly could only have affected some. . . .

Here toleration went too far. . . .

Reversed.

BLUMENTHAL v. UNITED STATES, 332 U.S. 539, 557-559 (1947): [Defendants Weiss and Goldsmith were, respectively, owner and sales manager of the Francisco Distributing Company, a licensed wholesale liquor dealing agency. Defendants Feigenbaum, Blumenthal, and Abel were local businesspeople with no connection with the company except as hereafter stated. Weiss and Goldsmith, acting in the name of Francisco, received shipment of two carloads of whiskey from an unidentified person or persons with whom they agreed to distribute the shipment under the Francisco name in such a way as to conceal the fact that they were selling the whiskey at prices above those legally permitted at the time. Weiss and Goldsmith arranged with Feigenbaum, Blumenthal, and Abel, all unknown to one another, for them to sell portions of the shipment to various taverns at prices above the maximum permitted. There was no evidence that the salesmen knew of the unknown owner's existence or part in the plan. Defendants were convicted of a single conspiracy in a single count holding they had conspired together and with the unidentified owner to sell the shipment of whiskey at prices over the ceiling set by law. On appeal it was contended that there was not one but two conspiracies — one between the unidentified owner and Weiss and Goldsmith; the other between Weiss and Goldsmith, on the one hand, and Feigenbaum and Blumenthal, on the other. The Supreme Court affirmed, upholding the finding of one large conspiracy:]

We think that in the special circumstances of this case the two agreements were merely steps in the formation of the larger and ultimately more general conspiracy. In that view it would be perversion of justice to regard the salesmen's ignorance of the unknown owner's participation as furnishing adequate ground for reversal of their convictions. Nor does anything in the *Kotteakos* decision require this. The scheme was in fact the same scheme; the salesmen knew or must have known that others unknown to them were sharing in so large a project; and it hardly can be sufficient to relieve them that they did not know, when they joined the scheme, who those people were or exactly the parts they were playing in carrying out the common design and object of all. By their separate agreements, if such they were, they became parties to the larger common plan, joined together by their knowledge of its essential features and broad scope, though not of its exact limits, and by their common single goal.

The case therefore is very different from the facts admitted to exist in the *Kotteakos* case. Apart from the much larger number of agreements there involved, no two of those agreements were tied together as stages in the formation of a larger all-inclusive combination, all directed to achieving a single unlawful end or result. On the contrary each separate agreement had its own distinct, illegal end. Each loan was an end in itself, separate from all others, although all were alike in having similar illegal objects. Except for Brown, the common figure, no conspirator was interested in whether any loan except his own went through. And none aided in any way, by agreement or otherwise, in procuring another's loan. The conspiracies therefore were distinct and disconnected, not parts of a larger general scheme, both in the phase of agreement with Brown and also in the absence of any aid given to others as well as in specific object and result. There was no drawing of all together in a single, over-all, comprehensive plan.

Here the contrary is true. All knew of and joined in the overriding scheme. All intended to aid the owner, whether Francisco or another, to sell the whiskey unlawfully, though the two groups of defendants differed on the proof in knowledge and belief concerning the owner's identity. All by reason of their knowledge of the plan's general scope, if not its exact limits, sought a common end, to aid in disposing of the whiskey. True, each salesman aided in selling only his part. But he knew the lot to be sold was larger and thus that he was aiding in a larger plan. He thus became a party to it and not merely to the integrating agreement with Weiss and Goldsmith.

ANDERSON v. SUPERIOR COURT, 78 Cal. App. 2d 22, 24-25, 177 P.2d 315, 317 (1947): [Petitioner sought a writ of prohibition to prevent her prosecution under an indictment returned by the grand jury. Evidence before the grand jury revealed that Stern had made arrangements with many persons for them to refer to him women desiring abortions. Such persons were paid a fee for this service. Petitioner was one of the people who had referred women to Stern. She was indicted for conspiring to commit abortions, the conspiracy embracing not only Stern and herself but the greater enterprise among Stern and the others who referred women to him. She was also indicted for the substantive offenses of abortions performed on women she had referred to Stern and abortions committed by Stern upon women referred by others. Denying the writ, the court stated:] The inference is almost compelled, if the evidence is believed, that this petitioner knew that Stern was engaged in the commission of abortions not casually but as a regular business and that others, like herself, had conspired with him to further his operations. If the grand jury concluded that, with this knowledge, she saw fit to join with him and those others, even though unknown to her, in furthering the unlawful activities of the group we cannot say that the grand jury did not have substantial evidence upon which to find the indictment.

If she did join the conspiracy she is responsible for the substantive offenses later committed as a part of the conspiracy.

UNITED STATES v. BRUNO

United States Court of Appeals, 2d Circuit
105 F.2d 921, rev'd on other grounds, *308 U.S. 287 (1939)*

Per Curiam. Bruno and Iacono were indicted along with 86 others for a conspiracy to import, sell and possess narcotics; some were acquitted; others, besides these two, were convicted, but they alone appealed. They complain . . . that if the evidence proved anything, it proved a series of separate conspiracies, and not a single one, as alleged in the indictment. . . .

The evidence allowed the jury to find that there had existed over a substantial period of time a conspiracy embracing a great number of persons, whose object was to smuggle narcotics into the Port of New York and distribute them to addicts both in this city and in Texas and Louisiana. This required the cooperation of four groups of persons: the smugglers who imported the drugs; the middlemen who paid the smugglers and distributed to retailers; and two groups of retailers — one in New York and one in Texas and Louisiana — who supplied the addicts. The defendants assert that there were, therefore, at least three separate conspiracies: one between the smugglers and the middlemen, and one between the middlemen and each group of retailers. The evidence did not disclose any cooperation or communication between the smugglers and either group of retailers, or between the two groups of retailers themselves; however, the smugglers knew that the middlemen must sell to retailers, and the retailers knew that the middlemen must buy from importers of one sort or another. Thus the conspirators at one end of the chain knew that the unlawful business would not, and could not, stop with their buyers; and those at the other end knew that it had not begun with their sellers. That being true, a jury might have found that all the accused were embarked upon a venture, in all parts of which each was a participant, and an abettor in the sense that the success of that part with which he was immediately concerned, was dependent upon the success of the whole. . . . It might still be argued that there were two conspiracies; one including the smugglers, the middlemen and the New York group, and the other, the smugglers, the middlemen and the Texas & Louisiana group, for there was apparently no privity between the two groups of retailers. That too would be fallacious. Clearly, quoad the smugglers, there was but one conspiracy, for it was of no moment to them whether the middlemen sold to one or more groups of retailers, provided they had a market somewhere. So too of any retailer; he knew that he was a necessary link in a scheme of distribution, and the others, whom he knew to be convenient to its execution, were as much parts of a single undertaking or enterprise as two salesmen in the same shop. We think therefore that there was only one conspiracy.

UNITED STATES v. BORELLI, 336 F.2d 376 (2d Cir. 1964): [In this case, dealing with an elaborate heroin importing and distributing operation, Judge Friendly wrote:] As applied to the long term operation of an illegal business, the common pictorial distinction between "chain" and "spoke" conspiracies can obscure as much as it clarifies. The chain metaphor is indeed apt in that the links of a narcotics conspiracy are inextricably related to one another, from grower, through exporter and importer, to wholesaler, middleman, and retailer, each depending for his own success on the performance of all the others. But this simple picture tends to obscure that the links at either end are likely to consist of a number of persons who may have no reason to know that others are performing a role similar to theirs — in other words the extreme links of a chain conspiracy may have elements of the spoke conspiracy.[2] Moreover, whatever the value of the chain

2. Thus, in the oft-cited *Bruno* case, although it is clear enough that "quoad the smugglers, there was but one conspiracy . . . ," it is not so clear why the New York and Texas groups of retailers were

concept where the problem is to trace a single operation from the start through its various phases to its successful conclusion, it becomes confusing when, over a long period of time, certain links continue to play the same role but with new counterparts, as where importers who regard their partnership as a single continuing one, having successfully distributed one cargo through *X* distributing organization, turn, years later, to moving another cargo obtained from a different source through *Y*. . . .

The basic difficulty arises in applying the seventeenth century notion of conspiracy, where the gravamen of the offense was the making of an *agreement* to commit a readily identifiable crime or series of crimes, such as murder or robbery, to what in substance is the conduct of an illegal business over a period of years. . . . Although it is usual and often necessary in conspiracy cases for the agreement to be proved by inference from acts, the gist of the offense remains the agreement, and it is therefore essential to determine what kind of agreement or understanding existed as to each defendant. It is a great deal harder to tell just *what* agreement can reasonably be inferred from the purchase, even the repeated purchase, of contraband, than from the furnishing of dynamite to prospective bank robbers or the exchange of worthless property for securities to be subsequently distributed. . . . A seller of narcotics in bulk surely knows that the purchasers will undertake to resell the goods over an uncertain period of time, and the circumstances may also warrant the inference that a supplier or a purchaser indicated a willingness to repeat. But a sale or a purchase scarcely constitutes a sufficient basis for inferring agreement to cooperate with the opposite parties for whatever period they continue to deal in this type of contraband, unless some such understanding is evidenced by other conduct. . . .

PROBLEM

What degree of interdependence between parties should be necessary to show that they are part of the same "agreement"? When should antagonism or indifference between two parties be considered inconsistent with their membership in a single "conspiracy"? Suppose that a shoe store owner hires two salespeople to work on commission, and that the salespeople compete for the attention of customers entering the store, because each one wants to serve as many customers as possible. Are the owner and salespeople parties to a single agreement, or are there separate agreements between the owner and each salesperson? The issue has proved especially troublesome in drug conspiracy prosecutions. In United States v. Morris, 46 F.3d 410, 416 (5th Cir. 1995), various suppliers had sold cocaine to Costa, who in turn distributed it to dealers. The participants, some 23 individuals, were convicted of being members of a single conspiracy. One of the suppliers challenged that finding on appeal. The court wrote:

> The success of this conspiracy depended on the continued willingness of each member to perform his function. If the [suppliers] discontinued selling, there

---

not in a "spoke" relation with the smugglers and the middleman, so that there would be two conspiracies unless the evidence permitted the inference that each group of retailers must have known the operation to be so large as to require the other as an outlet.

would be no cocaine for Costa and the [dealers] to buy. . . . If [the dealers] ceased to buy, there would be no reason for Costa to buy from the [suppliers].

. . . Munoz, [however], argues that his organization could not have been in the same conspiracy as the other suppliers, such as the Laredo Organization, which were [his] competitors. [Costa] stated that he initially approached the Laredo Organization for cocaine after becoming unhappy with Munoz. . . . We are not persuaded by this argument. [T]he larger, common plan was the purchase and sale of drugs through Costa for profit. Munoz is no less a part of this larger, common plan because Costa also purchased from others. . . . Indeed such purchases may in fact be necessary from time to time to keep the larger, common plan in existence.

Question: Is this analysis consistent with *Kotteakos* and *Bruno*? Compare the court's approach in *Morris* to United States v. Torres-Ramirez, 213 F.3d 978, 981-982 (7th Cir. 2000). In the latter case, Torres-Ramirez, "a big-time drug dealer" in California, sold two kilos of cocaine to Hardin in Los Angeles. He invited Hardin to make future purchases when he was in California but would not commit to specific terms. Hardin returned to Indiana and sold the cocaine there. Torres-Ramirez was convicted of conspiracy to distribute cocaine in the latter state, but the court of appeals reversed, explaining:

The district court told the jury. . . . : "To establish [that] the seller has joined a conspiracy . . . , the government must [prove] an enduring relationship that directly or indirectly shows the seller has knowledge of the conspiracy to distribute drugs." This sentence is . . . false. . . . *Knowing* of a conspiracy differs from *joining* a conspiracy. Every seller of large quantities knows that his buyer intends to resell, and thus knows that his buyer is involved in a criminal conspiracy. No one distributes two kilograms on the street by himself. [But the] district judge needed to tell the jury to look for an agreement to join the Indiana distribution network, not just for knowledge of its existence.

[W]e conclude [moreover] that the evidence would not have supported a conviction under the proper legal standard. [T]his is a one-sale case. . . . Torres-Ramirez did not care whether the [Indiana] redistribution venture succeeded; he had his money already.

NOTE ON MULTIPLE OBJECTIVES

In all of the foregoing cases, prosecutors sought to establish a single, inclusive conspiracy, while defendants attempted to break up the alleged relationship into smaller conspiracies. In United States v. Braverman, 317 U.S. 49 (1942), the positions were reversed: The Government indicted a group of defendants on seven counts, each charging a conspiracy to violate a separate provision of the internal revenue laws. The applicable statute carried a maximum penalty of two years on each count. Defendants were convicted on all seven counts and each defendant was sentenced to eight years' imprisonment. The Supreme Court reversed:

The gist of the crime of conspiracy as defined by the statute is the agreement to commit one or more unlawful acts. . . . Whether the object of a single agreement is to commit one or many crimes, it is in either case that agreement which constitutes the conspiracy which the statute punishes. The one agreement cannot be taken to be several agreements and hence several conspiracies because it envisages the violation of several statutes rather than one. . . . For such a violation, only the single penalty prescribed by the statute can be imposed.[a]

Question: If conspiracy is regarded as an inchoate offense, punishing combinations that threaten a substantive harm, does it make sense to treat an agreement to commit seven different crimes as only a single offense?

NOTE ON THE MODEL PENAL CODE APPROACH

The Model Penal Code proposes an innovative solution to the problems of defining the scope of a conspiratorial relationship:

Model Penal Code and Commentaries, Comment to §5.03 at 425-431 (1985): The combined operation of Subsections (1), (2) and (3) is relied upon to delineate the identity and scope of a conspiracy. All three provisions focus on the culpability of the individual actor. Subsections (1) and (2) limit the scope of his conspiracy both in terms of its criminal objectives, to those crimes that he had the purpose of promoting or facilitating, and in terms of parties, to those with whom he agreed, except when the same crime that he conspired to commit is, to his knowledge, also the object of a conspiracy between one of his co-conspirators and another person or persons. Subsection (3) provides that his conspiracy is a single one despite a multiplicity of criminal objectives, as long as such crimes are the object of the same agreement or continuous conspiratorial relationship. . . .

The Model Code provision would require a different approach to a case such as *Bruno* and might produce different results. Since the overall operation involved the separate crimes of importing by the smugglers and possession and sale by each group [smugglers, distributors, and retailers], the question as to each defendant would be whether and with whom he conspired to commit *each* of these crimes, under the criteria set forth in Subsections (1) and (2). The conspiratorial objective for the purpose of this inquiry could not be characterized in the manner of the *Bruno* court, as "to smuggle narcotics into the Port of New York and distribute them to addicts both in [New York] and in Texas and Louisiana." This is indeed the overall objective of the entire operation. It also may be true that *some* of the participants conspired to commit all of the crimes involved in the operation; under Subsection (3), as under prevailing law, they would be guilty of only one conspiracy if all these crimes were the object of the same agreement or continuing conspiratorial relationship, and the objective of *that* conspiracy or relationship could fairly be phrased in terms of the overall operation. But this multiplicity of criminal objectives affords a poor referent for test-

a. Albernaz v. United States, 450 U.S. 333 (1981), sharply limited the *Braverman* rule. In *Albernaz,* the defendant had conspired with others to import and distribute marijuana. He was convicted on two counts, one charging conspiracy to import and the other conspiracy to distribute. Accepting the premise that there was only a single agreement, the Court nonetheless upheld the two convictions, emphasizing that separate statutes proscribed conspiracy to import and conspiracy to distribute. The Court held that by enacting two statutes, each with its own penalties, Congress had manifested its intention to authorize separate convictions and punishments. The Court distinguished *Braverman* on the ground that "the conspiratorial agreement in *Braverman,* although it had many objectives, violated but a single statute." Id. at 339. — Eds.

ing the culpability of each individual who is in any manner involved in the operation.

With the conspiratorial objectives characterized as the particular crimes and the culpability of each participant tested separately, it would be possible to find in a case such as *Bruno,* considering for the moment only each separate chain of distribution, that the smugglers conspired to commit the illegal sales of the retailers, but that the retailers did not conspire to commit the importing of the smugglers. Factual situations warranting such a finding may easily be conceived. For example, the smugglers might depend upon and seek to foster their retail markets, while the retailers might have many suppliers and be indifferent to the success of any single source. The court's approach in *Bruno* does not admit of such a finding, for treating the conspiratorial objective as the entire series of crimes involved in smuggling, distributing, and retailing requires a finding either of no conspiracy or of a single conspiracy in which all three links in the chain conspired to commit all of each other's crimes.

It also would be possible to find, with the inquiry focused on each individual's culpability as to each criminal objective, that some of the parties in a chain conspired to commit the entire series of crimes while others conspired to commit only some of these crimes. Thus the smugglers and the middlemen in *Bruno* may have conspired to commit, promote, or facilitate the importing and the possession and sales of all of the parties down to the final retail sale; the retailers might have conspired with them as to their own possession and sales, but might be indifferent to all the steps prior to their receipt of the narcotics. In this situation, a smuggler or a middleman might have conspired with all three groups to commit the entire series of crimes, while a retailer might have conspired with the same parties but to achieve fewer criminal objectives. Such results are conceptually difficult to reach under existing doctrine not only because of the frequent failure to focus separately on the different criminal objectives, but also because of the traditional view of the agreement as a bilateral relationship between each of the parties, congruent in scope both as to its party and its objective dimensions.

6. *Parties*

INTRODUCTORY NOTE

Because conspiracy liability shares with accomplice liability the need for the participation of another party, both doctrines pose similar issues concerning the nature of the required relationship. We considered in the section on accomplices whether, for example, a secondary party *S* can be liable for aiding the principal when *S* is in effect a victim of the principal's conduct. We also considered whether a secondary party may be liable even when the party who commits the proscribed act is not liable — for example, when the principal party was a feigned participant, had a personal immunity, or was acquitted of the charge. Here we consider similar issues in connection with conspiracy. Consider the parallels and differences in the legal treatment of these issues in the two kinds of liability.

GEBARDI v. UNITED STATES

Supreme Court of the United States
287 U.S. 112 (1932)

JUSTICE STONE delivered the opinion of the Court.

This case is here on certiorari to review a judgment of conviction for conspiracy to violate the Mann Act. Petitioners, a man and a woman, not then husband and wife, were indicted in the District Court for Northern Illinois, for conspiring together, and with others not named, to transport the woman from one state to another for the purpose of engaging in sexual intercourse with the man. At the trial without a jury there was evidence from which the court could have found that the petitioners had engaged in illicit sexual relations in the course of each of the journeys alleged; that the man purchased the railway tickets for both petitioners for at least one journey, and that in each instance the woman, in advance of the purchase of the tickets, consented to go on the journey and did go on it voluntarily for the specified immoral purpose. There was no evidence supporting the allegation that any other person had conspired. The trial court . . . gave judgment of conviction, which the Court of Appeals . . . affirmed.

Congress set out in the Mann Act to deal with cases which frequently, if not normally, involve consent and agreement on the part of the woman to the forbidden transportation. In every case in which she is not intimidated or forced into the transportation, the statute necessarily contemplates her acquiescence. Yet this acquiescence, though an incident of a type of transportation specifically dealt with by the statute, was not made a crime under the Mann Act itself. Of this class of cases we say that the substantive offense contemplated by the statute itself involves the same combination or community of purpose of two persons only which is prosecuted here as conspiracy. If this were the only case covered by the Act, it would be within those decisions which hold, consistently with the theory upon which conspiracies are punished, that where it is impossible under any circumstances to commit the substantive offense without cooperative action, the preliminary agreement between the same parties to commit the offense is not an indictable conspiracy either at common law or under the federal statute. . . . But criminal transportation under the Mann Act may be effected without the woman's consent as in cases of intimidation or force (with which we are not now concerned). We assume, therefore, . . . that the decisions last mentioned do not in all strictness apply. We do not rest our decision upon the theory of those cases. . . . We place it rather upon the ground that we perceive in the failure of the Mann Act to condemn the woman's participation in those transportations which are effected with her mere consent, evidence of an affirmative legislative policy to leave her acquiescence unpunished. . . . It would contravene that policy to hold that the very passage of the Mann Act effected a withdrawal by the conspiracy statute of that immunity which the Mann Act itself confers.

It is not to be supposed that the consent of an unmarried person to adultery with a married person, where the latter alone is guilty of the substantive offense, would render the former an abettor or a conspirator, or that the acquiescence of a woman under the age of consent would make her a co-conspirator with the man to commit statutory rape upon herself. The principle, determinative of this case, is the same.

On the evidence before us the woman petitioner has not violated the Mann Act and, we hold, is not guilty of a conspiracy to do so. . . .

As there is no proof that the man conspired with anyone else to bring about the transportation, the convictions of both petitioners must be reversed.

NOTES

1. *The* Gebardi *rule.* The general principle reflected in *Gebardi* is widely accepted. See Glanville Williams, Criminal Law: The General Part 673 (2d ed. 1961): "One may submit with some confidence that a person cannot be convicted of conspiracy when there is a recognized rule of justice or policy exempting him from prosecution from the substantive crime." For a statutory statement of a similar principle, see Model Penal Code §5.04(2), Appendix. See also Ill. Ann. Stat. ch. 720, §5/8-3 (1993): "It is a defense to a charge of solicitation or conspiracy that if the criminal object were achieved the accused would not be guilty of an offense."

2. *The Wharton rule.* Justice Stone notes that the *Gebardi* case was not governed by the line of precedent holding that "where it is impossible under any circumstances to commit the substantive offense without cooperative action, the preliminary agreement between the same parties to commit the offense is not an indictable conspiracy." That line of precedent exemplifies what has become known as the "Wharton rule." It was explained as follows (2 F. Wharton, Criminal Law §1604 at 1862 (12th ed. 1932)):

> [When] plurality of agents is logically necessary, conspiracy, which assumes the voluntary accession of a person to a crime of such a character that it is aggravated by a plurality of agents, cannot be maintained. . . . In other words, . . . when the law says, such an offense — e.g., adultery — shall have a certain punishment, it is not lawful for the prosecution to evade this limitation by indicting the offense as conspiracy.

Compare Model Penal Code and Commentaries, Comment to §5.04 at 482-483 (1985):

> The classic Wharton's rule cases involve crimes such as dueling, bigamy, adultery, and incest, but it has also been said to apply to gambling, the giving and receiving of bribes, and the buying and selling of contraband goods. The rule has been unevenly applied and has been subject to a number of exceptions and limitations.
>
> It seems clear that Wharton's rule as generally stated and the rationale that conspiracy "assumes . . . a crime of such a nature that it is aggravated by a plurality of agents" completely overlook the functions of conspiracy as an inchoate crime. That an offense inevitably requires concert is no reason to immunize criminal preparation to commit it. Further, the rule operates to immunize from a conspiracy prosecution *both* parties to *any* offense that inevitably requires concert, thus disregarding the legislative judgment that at least one should be punishable and taking no account of the varying policies that ought to determine whether the other should be. The rule is supportable only insofar as it avoids cumulative punishment for conspiracy and the completed substantive crime, for it is clear that the legislature would have taken the factor of concert into account in grading a crime that inevitably requires concert. This consideration is of course irrelevant under the Model

Code, which precludes cumulative punishment in any case for a conspiracy with a single criminal objective and the completed substantive crime.

In Ianelli v. United States, 420 U.S. 770 (1975), eight defendants were convicted and punished for violating 18 U.S.C. §1955, which makes it a crime for five or more persons to conduct a gambling business in violation of state law. They were also convicted and punished for conspiring to violate §1955 by conducting that same gambling business. The Supreme Court rejected a Wharton rule challenge to that latter conviction. The Court held that the ultimate issue was whether the legislature intended separate punishments for conspiracy and for the substantive offense, and that when the substantive offense requires concert, Wharton's rule creates only a presumption against separate punishments, in the absence of legislative intent to the contrary. With respect to §1955, the Court concluded that the statute's requirement of concerted activity by five or more people reflected only a concern to avoid federal jurisdiction over small-scale gambling operations that pose a limited threat to federal interests and that Congress did not intend to bar separate punishments. Thus, the Court sustained the convictions for both conspiracy and the substantive §1955 offense, even though the only way that the latter crime could be committed was by concerted activity. See Note, An Analysis of Wharton's Rule, 71 Nw. U.L. Rev. 547 (1976).

3. Problems. (a) 21 U.S.C. §861 makes it a crime "for any person at least 18 years of age to knowingly and intentionally [employ] a person under 18 years of age" to sell or distribute drugs. Palmer and Harris organized a group of juveniles to sell cocaine. They both knew that the youngsters working for them were under 18. The prosecution proved that Palmer was over 18, and he was therefore liable under §861. But because the prosecution did not prove Harris's age, Harris could not be convicted of violating §861 personally. Can Harris be convicted of conspiring with Palmer to violate §861? Cf. United States v. Harris, 959 F.2d 246, 262-264 (D.C. Cir. 1992).

(b) The Foreign Corrupt Practices Act makes it a crime for any U.S. citizen to bribe a foreign government official, but it does not make it an offense for such an official to accept the bribe. Can Canadian officials who took bribes from U.S. citizens be convicted of conspiracy to violate the FCPA? See United States v. Castle, 925 F.2d 831 (5th Cir. 1991).

GARCIA v. STATE

Supreme Court of Indiana
71 Ind. 366, 394 N.E.2d 106 (1979)

PRENTICE, J. Defendant was convicted in a trial by jury of conspiracy to commit murder, a class A felony. . . . On appeal she raises the . . . issue . . . whether the defendant can be convicted of conspiracy when the only person with whom the defendant conspired was a police informant who only feigned his acquiescence in the scheme. . . .

The evidence introduced at trial consisted of the following: On September 30, 1977, State's witness, Allen Young, was first contacted by the defendant with regard to certain marital problems that she was having. She stated that her husband constantly beat her and her children and that she "couldn't take it any longer"— that she wanted her husband killed. [After several subsequent conversations with defendant] Young went to the Whiting Police Department and discussed the matter with two detectives. He offered to call the defendant and let them listen and record the conversation, which they did. During the conversation, Young again asked the defendant if she wanted him to help her find someone to kill her husband, and she responded affirmatively. Young replied that he would try to find someone. Several more conversations took place. . . . At their final meeting, Young, accompanied by a plain-clothed detective, introduced the defendant to the detective, stating that here was a man who might be willing to do the job. The defendant then produced $200, a picture of her husband, and a record of his daily habits and gave them to the detective. She agreed to pay the balance of the contract price when the "job" was completed. Defendant was subsequently arrested.

At trial, Young testified that he only feigned his acquiescence in the plan and at no time did he intend to actually carry it out.

The issue is whether the conspiracy section of our new penal code adopts the Model Penal Code's "unilateral" concept or whether it retains the traditional "bilateral" concept.

The bilateral concept is the traditional view of conspiracy as derived from common law. It is formulated in terms of two or more persons agreeing to commit a crime, each with intent to do so. In cases where the person or persons with whom the defendant conspired only feigned his acquiescence in the plan, the courts have generally held that neither person could be convicted of conspiracy because there was no "conspiratorial agreement." . . .

Reacting to criticism of this viewpoint, the drafters of the Model Penal Code, though not without internal disagreement, adopted a "unilateral" concept, as follows: [The court then quoted Model Penal Code §§5.03(1) and 5.04(1). See Appendix.]

In explanation of their new approach, the Drafters of the Model Penal Code commented:

> . . . The definition of the Draft departs from the traditional view of conspiracy as an entirely bilateral or multilateral relationship. . . . Attention is directed instead to each individual's culpability by framing the definition in terms of the conduct which suffices to establish the liability of any given actor, rather than the conduct of a group of which he is charged to be a part — an approach which in this comment we have designated "unilateral."
>
> One consequence of this approach is to make it immaterial to the guilt of a conspirator whose culpability has been established that the person or all of the persons with whom he conspired have not been or cannot be convicted. . . . Under the unilateral approach of the Draft, the culpable party's guilt would not be affected by the fact that the other party's agreement was feigned. . . . True enough, the project's chances of success have not been increased by the agreement; indeed, its doom may have been sealed by this turn of events. But the major basis of conspiratorial liability — the unequivocal evidence of a firm purpose to commit a crime — remains the same. . . .

M.P.C. §5.03 [Tent. Draft No. 10,] Comments at pp. 104-105. . . .

This concept has been adopted, in whole or in part, in at least 26 states and is under consideration in most of the remaining states. See Note, Conspiracy: Statutory Reform Since the Model Penal Code, 75 Col. L. R. 1122, 1125 (1975).

In 1976, our Indiana Legislature repealed the existing conspiracy statute[2] and adopted Ind. Code §35-41-5-2 . . . which reads as follows:

> [Sec. 2.] (a) A person conspires to commit a felony when, with intent to commit the felony, he agrees with another person to commit the felony. . . .
>
> (c) It is no defense that the person with whom the accused person is alleged to have conspired:
>
> (1) has not been prosecuted;
> (2) has not been convicted;
> (3) has been acquitted;
> (4) has been convicted of a different crime;
> (5) cannot be prosecuted for any reason; or
> (6) lacked the capacity to commit the crime.

. . . [I]t is clear upon the face of the act that defenses available under the multilateral concept were to be eliminated. The inclusion of the "catch-all" subproviso (5) can leave no doubt. Clearly "any reason," as recited therein, includes the absence of criminal culpability on the part of a co-conspirator — including a sole co-conspirator. The words "agrees" and "agreement" have not been used as words of art denoting a "meeting of the minds" and "contract." Rather, the former is descriptive of the defendant's state of mind at the time he communicated with another in furtherance of the felony; and the latter refers to the defendant's understanding.

Defendant has cited us to numerous cases supporting the bilateral concept requiring "concurrence of sentiment and cooperative conduct in the unlawful and criminal enterprise"; however, those cases were not decided under statutes remotely similar to our own. . . . Her argument that, by definition, an agreement requires the concurrence of sentiment of at least two individuals . . . is not persuasive in the light of the express wording of the entire enactment. . . .

The judgment of the trial court is affirmed.

NOTES

1. *The traditional offense of conspiracy.* In jurisdictions that have not reformulated their definition of conspiracy, the requirement of bilateral agreement remains, and conspiracy charges will not lie when the defendant's only collaborators are undercover informants or other feigned participants. See, e.g., United States v. Andrades, 169 F.3d 131, 135 (2d Cir. 1999); McDougle v. State, 721 So. 2d 660, 662 (Miss. App. 1998).

2. The repealed conspiracy statute read as follows:

> 35-1-111-1 [10-1101]. Conspiracy to commit a felony. — Any person or persons who shall unite or combine with any other person or persons for the purpose of committing a felony, within or without this state . . . shall, on conviction, be [punished.]"

2. Modern conspiracy statutes. In jurisdictions that have adopted definitions of conspiracy similar to that proposed by the Model Penal Code, many courts have held, in accord with *Garcia,* that a defendant can be guilty of conspiracy if he agrees to commit a crime with a feigned accomplice. E.g., State v. Roldan, 714 A.2d 351, 355 (N.J. Super. 1998). But in Connecticut and Illinois, two states with conspiracy statutes patterned on the Model Penal Code, courts have held that the requirement of bilateral agreement survives. See State v. Grullon, 212 Conn. 195, 562 A.2d 481 (1989); People v. Foster, 99 Ill. 2d 48, 457 N.E.2d 405, 407 (1983). The Illinois statute states that a "person commits conspiracy when, with intent that an offense be committed, he agrees with another to the commission of that offense." Ill. Rev. Stat. ch. 720, §5/8-2(a). In *Foster,* the Illinois Supreme Court held that the required "agree[ment]" could not exist unless at least two parties genuinely intended to carry out the plan. Rejecting the reasoning of the *Garcia* case, the court said (457 N.E.2d at 407): "We doubt . . . that the drafters could have intended what represents a rather profound change in the law of conspiracy without mentioning it in the comments to section 8-2." The court noted, however, that the Illinois solicitation statute would (like the corresponding Model Penal Code provision) "embrace virtually every situation in which one could be convicted of conspiracy under the unilateral theory." Id., at 408.

3. The case in favor of the traditional view is stated as follows in United States v. Escobar De Bright, 742 F.2d 1196, 1198-1200 (9th Cir. 1984):

> Criminal conspiracy is an offense separate from the actual criminal act because of the perception "that collective action toward an antisocial end involves a greater risk to society than individual action toward the same end." In part, this view is based on the perception that group activity increases the likelihood of success of the criminal act and of future criminal activity by members of the group, and is difficult for law enforcement officers to detect. . . .
>
> Such dangers, however, are non-existent when a person "conspires" only with a government agent. There is no continuing criminal enterprise and ordinarily no inculcation of criminal knowledge and practices. Preventive intervention by law enforcement officers also is not a significant problem in such circumstances. The agent, as part of the "conspiracy," is quite capable of monitoring the situation in order to prevent the completion of the contemplated criminal plan; in short, no cloak of secrecy surrounds any agreement to commit the criminal acts.
>
> Finally, the [traditional] rule responds to the same concern that underlies the entrapment defense: the legitimate law enforcement function of crime prevention "does not include the manufacturing of crime." Allowing a government agent to form a conspiracy with only one other party would create the potential for law enforcement officers to "manufacture" conspiracies when none would exist absent the government's presence.

See also Dierdre A. Burgman, Unilateral Conspiracy: Three Critical Perspectives, 29 DePaul L. Rev. 75 (1979); Paul Marcus, Conspiracy: The Criminal Agreement in Theory and Practice, 65 Geo. L.J. 925, 927 (1977).

4. Attempted conspiracy? In states that adhere to the bilateral approach, can a defendant who "agrees" to commit a crime with an undercover agent or pretended "hit man" be convicted of attempted conspiracy? In State v. Kihnel, 488 So. 2d 1238, 1241 (La. App. 1986), the court held in the negative:

> Attempt and conspiracy are both inchoate crimes. Just as there can be no attempt to commit an attempt, such as "attempted assault" . . . we conclude that under the bilateral formulation of conspiracy there can be no "attempted conspiracy."
>
> As part of the very foundation of criminal law, crimes include both a criminal act (or omission) and a criminal intent. "Attempted conspiracy" suggests a crime formed only of criminal intent, as it is the agreement which constitutes the act. We are not prepared to judicially legislate such a crime.

For thorough discussion of the problem, see Ira Robbins, Double Inchoate Crimes, 26 Harv. J. Legis. 1, 54-58, 80-83, 91-94 (1989).

7. *Criminal Enterprises and RICO*

INTRODUCTORY NOTE

The preceding materials illustrate some of the difficulties of prosecuting complex, ongoing criminal organizations and some of the dangers that conspiracy doctrines pose to innocent individuals and petty offenders who find themselves in contact with the activities of such organizations. In response to a perception that traditional conspiracy law provided inadequate tools for combatting sophisticated criminal enterprises, Congress in 1970 passed the Racketeer Influenced and Corrupt Organizations Act, popularly known as RICO. The growing body of RICO law and its importance in modern law enforcement have made RICO a distinctive branch of conspiracy law that is worth careful study in its own right. In examining the RICO statute, reprinted below, consider to what extent its provisions reach activities that could not be punished under traditional conspiracy doctrines, and to what extent its provisions change the treatment of activities that remain punishable under the traditional doctrines. Note also the broad list of criminal conduct that qualifies as "racketeering activity" within the meaning of RICO and the tendency for that list to expand over time. Crimes that have been added to the definition of "racketeering activity" since 1988 and the date they were added are shown in italics in §1961(1)(B) below.

RACKETEER INFLUENCED AND CORRUPT ORGANIZATIONS ACT

18 U.S.C. ch. 96

§1961. Definitions

As used in this chapter —

(1) "racketeering activity" means (A) any act or threat involving murder, kidnapping, gambling, arson, robbery, bribery, extortion, dealing in obscene matter, or dealing in a controlled substance . . . , which is chargeable under State law and punishable by imprisonment for more than one year; (B) any act which is indictable under any of the following provisions of title 18, United States Code: [References are to sections relating to bribery, counterfeiting, theft from interstate shipment, embezzlement from pension and welfare funds, extortionate credit transactions, the transmission of gambling information, fraud, *fraud in connection with identification documents [April 1996], unlawful procurement of passports*

[April 1996], unlawful procurement of citizenship or citizenship papers [Sept. 1996], obscenity, obstruction of justice, *misuse of passports, visas and other documents [April 1996], peonage and slavery [April 1996],* interference with commerce by robbery or extortion, racketeering, interstate transportation of wagering paraphernalia, unlawful welfare fund payments, prohibition of illegal gambling businesses, money laundering, *sexual exploitation of children [1988],* interstate transportation of stolen property, *trafficking in counterfeit labels for computer programs, recordings or audiovisual works [July 1996], criminal copyright infringement [July 1996],* trafficking in motor vehicles or their parts, and trafficking in contraband cigarettes]; (C) any act which is indictable under title 29, United States Code, section 186 (dealing with restrictions on payments and loans to labor organizations) or section 501(c) (relating to embezzlement from union funds), [or] (D) any offense involving [bankruptcy fraud], fraud in the sale of securities, or the felonious manufacture, importation, receiving, concealment, buying, selling, or otherwise dealing in a controlled substance . . . punishable under any law of the United States. . . .

(4) "enterprise" includes any individual, partnership, corporation, association, or other legal entity, and any union or group of individuals associated in fact although not a legal entity;

(5) "pattern of racketeering activity" requires at least two acts of racketeering activity, one of which occurred after the effective date of this chapter [Oct. 15, 1970] and the last of which occurred within ten years (excluding any period of imprisonment) after the commission of a prior act of racketeering activity. . . .

§1962. Prohibited Activities

(a) It shall be unlawful for any person who has received any income derived, directly or indirectly, from a pattern of racketeering activity or through collection of an unlawful debt . . . to use or invest [any part of such income in acquisition of] any enterprise . . . the activities of which affect interstate or foreign commerce. . . .

(b) It shall be unlawful for any person through a pattern of racketeering activity or through collection of an unlawful debt to acquire or maintain [any interest in any enterprise the activities of which affect] interstate or foreign commerce.

(c) It shall be unlawful for any person employed by or associated with any enterprise engaged in, or the activities of which affect, interstate or foreign commerce, to conduct or participate, directly or indirectly, in the conduct of such enterprise's affairs through a pattern of racketeering activity or collection of unlawful debt.

(d) It shall be unlawful for any person to conspire to violate any of the provisions of subsection (a), (b), or (c) of this section.

§1963. Criminal Penalties

(a) Whoever violates any provision of section 1962 of this chapter shall be fined under this title or imprisoned not more than 20 years (or for life if the violation is based on a racketeering activity for which the maximum penalty includes life imprisonment), or both. . . .

NOTES

The RICO statute has become one of the most controversial provisions in the federal criminal code. RICO bases criminal liability on new, potentially elastic concepts such as the "enterprise" and "racketeering activity." The penalties imposed for a violation of RICO can be far higher than those that would apply when the underlying criminal acts are not part of a "pattern" of "racketeering activity," and the statute provides powerful prosecutorial tools to compel forfeiture of assets derived from racketeering. In addition, RICO permits individuals harmed by racketeering to bring civil suits, and it awards treble damages for injuries resulting from RICO violations. By including a provision for treble damage lawsuits, the statute creates a fertile field for civil litigation, and expansive interpretations of RICO in civil suits open the door in turn to wider criminal liability. This note sets out the most important decisions governing the elements of a RICO violation.

1. The "enterprise." Because much of RICO's original focus was on preventing organized crime from infiltrating and capturing control of legitimate businesses, some courts held that the "enterprise" must be an organization engaged in some legal activities. In contrast, these courts reasoned, an ordinary criminal conspiracy, in which individuals associate for the sole and specific purpose of committing criminal acts, could not by itself constitute the kind of "enterprise" with which RICO was concerned. But in United States v. Turkette, 452 U.S. 576 (1981), the Supreme Court held that an "enterprise" for RICO purposes can include an exclusively criminal organization. In response to the argument that this approach would make the required "enterprise" synonymous with the required "pattern of racketeering activity," the court said (452 U.S. at 583):

> The enterprise is an entity, for present purposes a group of persons associated together for a common purpose of engaging in a course of conduct. The pattern of racketeering activity is, on the other hand, a series of criminal acts as defined by the statute. The former is proved by evidence of an ongoing organization, formal or informal, and by evidence that the various associates function as a continuing unit. The latter is proved by evidence of the requisite number of acts of racketeering committed by the participants in the enterprise. While the proof used to establish these separate elements may in particular cases coalesce, proof of one does not necessarily establish the other. The "enterprise" is not the "pattern of racketeering activity"; it is an entity separate and apart from the pattern of activity in which it engages. The existence of an enterprise at all times remains a separate element which must be proved by the Government.

Elaborating on *Turkette,* the court in United States v. Bledsoe, 674 F.2d 647, 665 (8th Cir. 1982), held that a RICO "enterprise" must have "continuity of both structure and personality" and "an 'ascertainable structure' distinct from that inherent in the conduct of a pattern of racketeering activity."

2. The "pattern." In H.J. Inc. v. Northwestern Bell Telephone Co., 492 U.S. 229 (1989), phone company customers sued for treble damages, alleging that Northwestern and several of its employees had violated RICO by bribing members of the Minnesota Public Utilities Commission (MPUC) to approve excessive rates. The court of appeals upheld the dismissal of the case, on the ground that the acts of alleged bribery did not constitute a "pattern" because they were all part of a "single scheme" to influence the MPUC. The Supreme Court reversed. the Court held that a RICO "pattern" must involve something more than just two predicate acts, but that a pattern need not involve separate illegal schemes and need not involve conduct indicative of organized crime activity in the traditional sense. Drawing on RICO's legislative history, the Court interpreted the "pattern" element to require proof "that the racketeering predicates are related, *and* that they . . . pose a threat of continued criminal activity." 492 U.S. at 239. The Court also held that Congress intended courts to define "relatedness" by referring to 18 U.S.C. §3575(e), which specifies that criminal conduct is related

> if it embraces criminal acts that have the same or similar purposes, results, participants, victims, or methods of commission, or otherwise are interrelated by distinguishing characteristics and are not isolated events.

In an opinion concurring only in the judgment, Justice Scalia, joined by the Chief Justice and Justices O'Connor and Kennedy, commented (492 U.S. at 252-256):

> Elevating to the level of statutory text a phrase taken from the legislative history, the Court counsels the lower courts: "continuity plus relationship." This seems to me about as helpful to the conduct of their affairs as "life is a fountain." . . . It hardly closes in on the target to know that "relatedness" refers to acts that are related by "purposes, results, participants, victims, . . . methods of commission, *or* [just in case that is not vague enough] *otherwise.*" Is the fact that the victims of both predicate acts were women enough? Or that both acts had the purpose of enriching the defendant? Or that the different coparticipants of the defendant in both acts were his co-employees? I doubt that the lower courts will find the Court's instructions much more helpful than telling them to look for a "pattern"—which is what the statute already says.
>
> The Court finds "continuity" more difficult to define precisely. "Continuity," it says, "is both a closed- and open-ended concept, referring either to a closed period of repeated conduct, or to past conduct that by its nature projects into the future with a threat of repetition." I have no idea what this concept of a "closed period of repeated conduct" means. Virtually all allegations of racketeering activity, in both civil and criminal suits, will relate to past periods that are "closed" (unless one expects plaintiff or the prosecutor to establish that the defendant not only committed the crimes he did, but is still committing them), and all of them *must* relate to conduct that is "repeated," because of RICO's multiple-act requirement. . . .
>
> It is clear to me . . . that the word "pattern" in the phrase "pattern of racketeering activity" was meant to import some requirement beyond the mere existence of multiple predicate acts. . . . But what that something more is, is beyond me. As I have suggested, it is also beyond the Court. Today's opinion has added nothing to improve our prior guidance, which has created a kaleidoscope of circuit positions, except to clarify that RICO may in addition be violated when there is a "threat of continuity." It seems to me this increases rather than removes the vagueness. . . .
>
> No constitutional challenge to this law has been raised in the present case, and so that issue is not before us. That the highest Court in the land has been unable

to derive from this statute anything more than today's meager guidance bodes ill for the day when that challenge is presented.

3. "Conduct" and "participation." Reves v. Ernst & Young, 113 S. Ct. 1163 (1993), involved a civil suit growing out of the insolvency of an Arkansas farmers' cooperative. In auditing the co-op's books, the Arthur Young accounting firm (which later merged into Ernst & Young) permitted one of the co-op's major assets to be carried at its original cost of $4.5 million rather than its market value of $1.5 million, and failed to disclose the problematic nature of the $4.5 million valuation. When the co-op became insolvent in 1984, the trustee in bankruptcy sued Arthur Young and several individual accountants, alleging that the co-op's noteholders had been defrauded by misrepresentations that violated various securities laws and RICO. The Supreme Court held that Arthur Young and its accountants had not violated §1962(c) because, in order to "conduct or participate directly or indirectly in the conduct of [an] enterprise's affairs," an individual must have some role in directing or managing the business of the enterprise (which in this case was the co-op). Justice Blackmun wrote for the Court (113 S. Ct. at 1170, 1173):

> In order to "participate, directly or indirectly, in the conduct of such enterprise's affairs," one must have some part in directing those affairs. Of course, the word "participate" makes clear that RICO liability is not limited to those with primary responsibility for the enterprise's affairs, . . . but *some* part in directing the enterprise's affairs is required. The "operation or management" test expresses this requirement in a formulation that is easy to apply.
>
> . . . We agree that liability under §1962(c) is not limited to upper management, but we disagree that the "operation or management" test is inconsistent with this proposition. An enterprise is "operated" not just by upper management but also by lower-rung participants in the enterprise who are under the direction of upper management. An enterprise also might be "operated" or "managed" by others "associated with" the enterprise who exert control over it as, for example, by bribery.

Question: Does the "operation or management" test protect low-level employees and outside professionals from conviction of racketeering offenses under RICO? Consider Daniel R. Fischel & Alan O. Sykes, Civil RICO After *Reves:* An Economic Commentary, [1993] Sup. Ct. Rev. 157, 190-194:

> On first reading, the [*Reves*] opinion provides considerable comfort to professionals. . . . Only those who have "some part in directing the enterprise's affairs" can be liable. . . . [But] there is sufficient contradictory language in *Reves* to make the issue murky at best. . . . The Court [stated] that: "An enterprise is 'operated' not just by upper management but also by lower-rung participants in the enterprise who are under the direction of upper management." With this one sentence, the Court undercut much of its earlier emphasis on the importance of "directing" an enterprise's affairs. Now the "direction" requirement includes both those who direct, as well as those who take direction. For a Court that prides itself on the importance of the plain language of its statute, this contorted interpretation of the words "operated" and "direction" is, at the very least, paradoxical. . . .
>
> Why was it "clear" that Arthur Young was not acting "under the direction" of the Co-op's management? Presumably the Court was referring to the absence of any direct evidence [that] Co-op management instruct[ed] Arthur Young to use fraudulent numbers. For Arthur Young's liability to turn on this point, however, is to ex-

alt form over substance. The sale of the Co-op notes at inflated prices benefited the Co-op, not Arthur Young. Why else would Arthur Young knowingly participate and assist in the Co-op's fraud except at the behest of management? And even if Arthur Young somehow decided to participate in the fraud independently as opposed to being directed to do so by management, why should this be exonerating? The more the fraud can be attributed to Arthur Young and management as opposed to just management, the stronger the case for imposing liability on both. . . .

To determine whether a defendant played a role in directing an enterprise's affairs also requires a definition of "enterprise." In *Reves,* the enterprise was the Co-op but this is not the only possibility. . . . What if the plaintiff in *Reves* had alleged that an association in fact consisting of Arthur Young, Jack White [Co-op's general manager], and the Co-op constituted the racketeering enterprise and that Arthur Young directed the affairs of this "enterprise"?

Such an allegation might be sufficient if the plaintiff could demonstrate that the alleged association in fact was, as *Turkette* requires, "ongoing" and functioned "as a continuing unit." . . . In future cases, courts' attitude toward association in fact enterprises will be critical in light of the obvious incentives of plaintiffs to allege such associations in fact to satisfy *Reves*'s "operation or management" test.

4. RICO conspiracies. Section 1962(c) can be viewed as a kind of conspiracy statute: by imposing criminal liability on those who "participate . . . in the conduct of [an] enterprise's affairs through a pattern of racketeering activity," §1962(c) reaches what is inherently a type of group crime. But the RICO statute also includes a provision, §1962(d), that punishes conspiracies to violate §1962(c). See page 731 supra. Does this provision in effect prohibit conspiring to engage in a conspiracy? What are the effects of §1962(d), and how does it change the traditional law of conspiracy? Consider the case that follows.

UNITED STATES v. ELLIOTT

United States Court of Appeals, 5th Circuit
571 F.2d 880 (1978)

SIMPSON, J. In this case we deal with the question of whether and, if so, how a free society can protect itself when groups of people, through division of labor, specialization, diversification, complexity of organization, and the accumulation of capital, turn crime into an ongoing business. . . .

Today we review the convictions of six persons accused of conspiring to violate the RICO statute, two of whom were also accused and convicted of substantive RICO violations. . . . Predictably, the government and the defendants differ as to what this case is about. According to the defendants, what we are dealing with is a leg, a tail, a trunk, an ear — separate entities unaffected by RICO proscriptions. The government, on the other hand, asserts that we have come eyeball to eyeball with a single creature of behemoth proportions, securely within RICO's grasp. After a careful, if laborious study of the facts and the law, we accept, with minor exceptions, the government's view. . . .

[All six defendants were indicted and convicted of conspiracy to violate 18 U.S.C. §1962(c), in violation of 18 U.S.C. §1962(d). The essence of the conspiracy charge was that the defendants agreed to participate in the conduct of the affairs of an enterprise whose purposes were to commit thefts, fence stolen property, illegally traffic in narcotics, obstruct justice, and engage in other criminal activities. Thirty-seven unindicted co-conspirators were named, and 25 overt acts were listed. The Court of Appeals described the facts as falling into ten specific episodes. Each defendant was involved in one or several of these episodes, but never in concert with more than two other defendants. Only J. C. Hawkins was involved in every episode.

[In 1970 defendant Foster defrauded a group of investors in a nursing home, built by his construction company and leased to the investor group by a corporation set up by Foster. The day before the nursing home was to open Foster paid J. C. Hawkins and Recea Hawkins to burn it down.

[Between 1971 and 1974 defendants J. C. Hawkins, Delph, and Taylor furnished counterfeit titles to and sold cars stolen by a major car theft ring.

[In 1972 and 1973 defendant J. C. Hawkins masterminded several thefts. In 1972 he and defendants Elliott and Recea Hawkins stole and fenced a truckload of Hormel meat. When a friend of J. C. Hawkins who had stored the stolen meat in his grocery store was indicted for possession of stolen goods, J. C. influenced the outcome of the trial by tampering with a juror.

[In 1973 J. C. Hawkins stole two trucks and attempted to sell them to another man, Jimmy Reeves. Suspecting that Reeves was informing to the police, J. C. had Reeves killed by Recea Hawkins.

[Later in 1973, defendants J. C. Hawkins and Foster were involved in two thefts, J. C. committing the thefts and Foster providing storage for the stolen goods. A third theft in late 1973 involved defendant Recea Hawkins as well. Defendants Delph and Taylor were not involved in any of the thefts committed in 1972 and 1973.

[Between 1971 and 1976 a number of drug transactions took place. One involved defendant Taylor alone, another defendant Elliott alone, and another, defendant J. C. Hawkins alone. Another transaction involved defendants Delph and Taylor together, and another J. C. Hawkins and Recea Hawkins.

[Finally, in 1976, defendant J. C. Hawkins planned to steal fungicide from a chemical company. None of the other defendants was involved.

[Following conviction, the trial court imposed these sentences: J. C. Hawkins, 80 years' imprisonment; Recea Hawkins, 50 years' imprisonment; Delph and Taylor, each 10 years' imprisonment; Foster, 1 year in prison and 5 years of probation; Elliott, 5 years' probation.]

. . . In this appeal, all defendants, with the exception of Foster, argue that while the indictment alleged but one conspiracy, the government's evidence at trial proved the existence of several conspiracies, resulting in a variance which substantially prejudiced their rights and requires reversal, citing Kotteakos v. United States, 328 U.S. 750 (1946). Prior to the enactment of the RICO statute, this argument would have been more persuasive. However, as we explain below, RICO has displaced many of the legal precepts traditionally applied to concerted criminal activity. Its effect in this case is to free the government from the strictures of the multiple conspiracy doctrine and to allow the joint trial of many persons accused of diversified crimes.

A. Prior Law: Wheels and Chains

1. *Kotteakos* and the Wheel Conspiracy Rationale: The Court in *Kotteakos* held that proof of multiple conspiracies under an indictment alleging a single con-

spiracy constituted a material variance requiring reversal where a defendant's substantial rights had been affected. At issue was "the right not to be tried en masse for the conglomeration of distinct and separate offenses committed by others." 328 U.S. at 775. *Kotteakos* thus protects against the "spill-over effect," the transference of guilt from members of one conspiracy to members of another. . . .

2. *Blumenthal* and the Chain Conspiracy Rationale: The impact of *Kotteakos* was soon limited by the Court in Blumenthal v. United States, 332 U.S. 539 (1947), where the indictment charged a single conspiracy to sell whiskey at prices above the ceiling set by the Office of Price Administration. The owner of the whiskey, through a series of middlemen, had devised an intricate scheme to conceal the true amount he was charging for the whiskey. Although some of the middlemen had no contact with each other and did not know the identity of the owner, they had to have realized that they were indispensable cogs in the machinery through which this illegal scheme was effectuated. The Court concluded that "in every practical sense the unique facts of this case reveal a single conspiracy of which the several agreements were essential and integral steps." Thus the "chain conspiracy" rationale evolved. . . .

3. Limits of the Chain Conspiracy Rationale: The rationale of *Blumenthal* applies only insofar as the alleged agreement has "a common end or single unified purpose." . . . Generally, where the government has shown that a number of otherwise diverse activities were performed to achieve a simple goal, courts have been willing to find a single conspiracy. This "common objective" test has most often been used to connect the many facets of drug importation and distribution schemes. The rationale falls apart, however, where the remote members of the alleged conspiracy are not truly interdependent or where the various activities sought to be tied together cannot reasonably be said to constitute a unified scheme. . . .

Applying pre-RICO conspiracy concepts to the facts of this case, we doubt that a single conspiracy could be demonstrated. Foster had no contact with Delph and Taylor during the life of the alleged conspiracy. Delph and Taylor, so far as the evidence revealed, had no contact with Recea Hawkins. The activities allegedly embraced by the illegal agreement in this case are simply too diverse to be tied together on the theory that participation in one activity necessarily implied awareness of others. Even viewing the "common objective" of the conspiracy as the raising of revenue through criminal activity, we could not say, for example, that Foster, when he helped to conceal stolen meat, had to know that J. C. was selling drugs to persons unknown to Foster, or that Delph and Taylor, when they furnished counterfeit titles to a car theft ring, had to know that the man supplying the titles was also stealing goods out of interstate commerce. The enterprise involved in this case probably could not have been successfully prosecuted as a single conspiracy under the general federal conspiracy statute, 18 U.S.C. §371.

B. RICO to the Rescue: The Enterprise Conspiracy

In enacting RICO, Congress found that "organized crime continues to grow" in part "because the sanctions and remedies available to the Government are unnecessarily limited in scope and impact." [W]e are convinced that, through RICO, Congress intended to authorize the single prosecution of a multi-faceted, diversified conspiracy by replacing the inadequate "wheel" and "chain" rationales with a new statutory concept: the enterprise.

. . . Under the general federal conspiracy statute, "the precise nature and extent of the conspiracy must be determined by reference to the agreement which embraces and defines its objects. Whether the object of a single agreement is to commit one or many crimes, it is in either case that agreement which constitutes the conspiracy which the statute punishes." Braverman v. United States, 317 U.S. 49, 53. In the context of organized crime, this principle inhibited mass prosecutions because a single agreement or "common objective" cannot be inferred from the commission of highly diverse crimes by apparently unrelated individuals. RICO helps to eliminate this problem by creating a substantive offense which ties together these diverse parties and crimes. . . . The gravamen of the conspiracy charge in this case is not that each defendant agreed to commit arson, to steal goods from interstate commerce, to obstruct justice, and to sell narcotics; rather, it is that each agreed to participate, directly and indirectly, in the affairs of the enterprise by committing two or more predicate crimes. Under the statute, it is irrelevant that each defendant participated in the enterprise's affairs through different, even unrelated crimes, so long as we may reasonably infer that each crime was intended to further the enterprise's affairs. To find a single conspiracy, we still must look for agreement on an overall objective. What Congress did was to define that objective through the substantive provisions of the Act.

C. Constitutional Considerations

The "enterprise conspiracy" is a legislative innovation in the realm of individual liability for group crime. We need to consider whether this innovation comports with the fundamental demand of due process that guilt remain "individual and personal." *Kotteakos,* supra, 328 U.S. at 772.

The substantive proscriptions of the RICO statute apply to insiders *and outsiders*— those merely "associated with" an enterprise — who participate directly *and indirectly* in the enterprise's affairs through a pattern of racketeering activity. Thus, the RICO net is woven tightly to trap even the smallest fish, those peripherally involved with the enterprise. This effect is enhanced by principles of conspiracy law also developed to facilitate prosecution of conspirators at all levels. Direct evidence of agreement is unnecessary: "proof of such an agreement may rest upon inferences drawn from relevant and competent circumstantial evidence — ordinarily the acts and conduct of the alleged conspirators themselves." United States v. Morado, 454 F.2d at 174. . . .

Undeniably, then, under the RICO conspiracy provision, remote associates of an enterprise may be convicted as conspirators on the basis of purely circumstantial evidence. We cannot say, however, that this section of the statute . . . offends the rule that guilt be individual and personal. The Act does not authorize that individuals "be tried en masse for the conglomeration of distinct and separate offenses committed by others." *Kotteakos,* supra. Nor does it punish mere association with conspirators or knowledge of illegal activity; its proscriptions are directed against conduct, not status. To be convicted as a member of an enterprise conspiracy, an individual, by his words or actions, must have objectively manifested an agreement to participate, directly or indirectly, in the affairs of an enterprise *through the commission of two or more predicate crimes.* One whose agreement with the members of an enterprise did not include this vital element cannot be convicted under the Act. Where, as here, the evidence establishes that each defendant, over a period of years, committed several acts of racketeering activity in furtherance of the enterprise's affairs, the inference of an agreement to do so is unmistakable. . . .

In the instant case, it is clear that "the essential nature of the plan" was to associate for the purpose of making money from repeated criminal activity. Defendant Foster, for example, hired J. C. Hawkins to commit arson, helped him to conceal large quantities of meat and shirts stolen from interstate commerce, and bought a stolen forklift from him. . . . Foster knew he was directly involved in an enterprise whose purpose was to profit from crime. . . . Foster also had to know that the enterprise was bigger than his role in it, and that others unknown to him were participating in its affairs. He may have been unaware that others who had agreed to participate in the enterprise's affairs did so by selling drugs and murdering a key witness. That, however, is irrelevant to his own liability, for he is charged with agreeing *to participate* in the enterprise through his own crimes, not with agreeing *to commit* each of the crimes through which the overall affairs of the enterprise were conducted. We perceive in this no significant extension of a co-conspirator's liability. When a person "embarks upon a criminal venture of indefinite outline, he takes his chances as to its content and membership, so be it that they fall within the common purposes as he understands them." United States v. Andolschek, 142 F.2d [503, 507 (2d Cir. 1944)].[31]

Our society disdains mass prosecutions because we abhor the totalitarian doctrine of mass guilt. We nevertheless punish conspiracy as a distinct offense because we recognize that collective action toward an illegal end involves a greater risk to society than individual action toward the same end. That risk is greatly compounded when the conspirators contemplate not a single crime but a career of crime. "There are times when of necessity, because of the nature and scope of the particular federation, large numbers of persons taking part must be tried to-

31. . . . A close look at the modus operandi of the enterprise reveals a pattern of interdependence which bolsters our conclusion that the functions of each "department" directly contributed to the success of the overall operation. Many of the enterprise's practices were analogous to those common in legitimate businesses:

— *Investment Capital:* Most of the enterprise's activities depended upon the ready availability of investment capital, or "front money," to finance the purchase of stolen goods and narcotics for eventual resale at a profit. In this sense, money brought in from one project could be used to purchase goods in another unrelated project.

— *"Good Will":* Part of the value of a business is the reputation it has established in the community, its "good will." The enterprise here benefited from a negative form of "good will." For example, Foster and J. C. exploited their cooperation in the Sparta nursing home arson to gain the confidence of James Gunnells when they needed his help in concealing stolen meat; that earlier endeavor furnished proof that Foster and J. C. could be trusted in criminal pursuits. Similarly, J. C.'s threats of physical harm to many of those involved with the enterprise helped to build a fear in the community which deterred potential witnesses from going to the police. In this way, each successful criminal act and each threat contributed to the success of the enterprise as a whole.

— *Arrangements to Limit Liability:* Like most large business organizations, this enterprise conducted its affairs in a manner calculated to limit its liability for the acts of its agents. J. C. erroneously believed that he could limit each person's liability by keeping him as isolated from the others as possible — in other words, that it would be safer to have the affairs of the enterprise conducted through chains composed of many persons playing limited roles than through a small circle of individuals performing many functions. Where overlap was unavoidable, the enterprise's ongoing operations depended upon each member's confidence that the others would remain silent. . . .

gether or perhaps not at all. . . . When many conspire, they invite mass trial by their conduct." *Kotteakos,* supra, 328 U.S. at 773.

We do not lightly dismiss the fact that under this statute four defendants who did not commit murder have been forced to stand trial jointly with, and as confederates of, two others who did. Prejudice inheres in such a trial; . . . But the Constitution does not guarantee a trial free from the prejudice that inevitably accompanies any charge of heinous group crime; it demands only that the potential for transference of guilt be minimized to the extent possible under the circumstances. . . . The RICO statute does not offend this principle. Congress, in a proper exercise of its legislative power, has decided that murder, like thefts from interstate commerce and the counterfeiting of securities, qualifies as racketeering activity. This, of course, ups the ante for RICO violators who personally would not contemplate taking a human life. Whether there is a moral imbalance in the equation of thieves and counterfeiters with murderers is a question whose answer lies in the halls of Congress, not in the judicial conscience. . . .

[The court affirmed all the conspiracy convictions except Elliott's. The court found the evidence insufficient to support a reasonable inference of his guilt:]

Viewed in a light most favorable to the government, the evidence against Elliott proved the following:

(1) Early in the spring of 1971, Joe Fuchs gave Elliott a bottle of 500 amphetamine capsules without a prescription.
(2) Shortly thereafter, Elliott negotiated a deal with Fuchs for Joe Breland to build an enclosed porch and for Fuchs to repay Elliott and Breland with amphetamine pills. During the next year, Fuchs delivered the pills in installments of 400.
(3) In April, 1972, Elliott, apparently as a favor for J. C., either sold or gave to Fuchs a 50 pound piece of stolen Hormel meat.
(4) In May, 1973, Elliott, serving as a juror in the trial of Rudolph Flanders for possession of meat from the same stolen shipment, held out for acquittal, causing a mistrial. No evidence was presented that Elliott had been contacted in advance about how he would vote in the Flanders case, although J. C. had told others that he felt Elliott would cooperate.
(5) In January, 1976, Elliott encouraged Fuchs to lie to a federal grand jury about how he acquired the stolen meat given to him by Elliott in 1972.

This evidence could not be taken to support, to the exclusion of all other reasonable hypotheses, a conclusion by the jury that Elliott agreed to participate, directly or indirectly, in the affairs of an enterprise through a pattern of racketeering activity. At best, this evidence discloses that Elliott used a close friend, Joe Fuchs, as a personal source of amphetamines and that he became peripherally involved in a stolen meat deal, an involvement he later attempted to conceal. The government failed to prove that Elliott's amphetamine transactions with Fuchs were in any way connected with the affairs of the enterprise. The Hormel meat, on the other hand, undeniably was acquired as a result of enterprise activity, but Elliott's cooperation with J. C. Hawkins in disposing of a small portion of the meat is insufficient to prove beyond a reasonable doubt that Elliott knowingly and intentionally joined the broad conspiracy to violate RICO. Elliott's acts are equally consistent with the hypothesis that he conspired with J. C. and Fuchs for the limited purpose of aiding in the distribution of stolen meat, an offense with which he was not charged in this case. Under this hypothesis, Elliott agreed to participate in the affairs of the enterprise, but not through a *pattern* of racketeering activity, hence, not in violation of the Act. Similarly, Elliott's two subsequent attempts to cover up the facts in the Hormel meat case are subject to two interpretations: (1) as possible overt acts in furtherance of an agreement to participate in the enterprise's affairs through a pattern of racketeering activity, or (2) as efforts at concealment undertaken after the object of his more limited conspiracy with J. C. and Fuchs had been accomplished, on the theory that "every conspiracy will inevitably be followed by actions taken to cover the conspirators' traces." Grunewald v. United States, 353 U.S. 391 (1957). To allow these predictable acts of concealment to be construed as independent evidence that Elliott agreed to conduct a pattern of racketeering activity would unjustifiably broaden the already pervasive scope of the RICO statute. We hold, then, that the more reasonable conclusion dictated by these facts is that, while Elliott may have conspired to distribute stolen meat, the jury could not reasonably conclude that he conspired to violate RICO.

NOTES

1. Comparing RICO conspiracy with ordinary conspiracy. If under pre-RICO law there would be insufficient proof in *Elliott* to tie Foster, Delph, and Taylor together with J. C. Hawkins in a single agreement, how does passage of the RICO statute create a single agreement between them? Conversely, if — as the *Elliott* court holds — these conspirators agreed "to associate for the purpose of making money from repeated criminal activity," then why would pre-RICO law pose any barrier to finding a single agreement? Consider Michael Goldsmith, RICO and Enterprise Criminality: A Response to Gerard E. Lynch, 88 Colum. L. Rev. 774, 798 (1988):

> The answer [to this question] is that the enterprise itself is an important link in the evidentiary chain: a defendant's knowledge of the enterprise's existence is probative of a central purpose. Thus, upon proof that such an enterprise exists, the enterprise itself provides the basis for inferring one large conspiracy instead of many smaller ones. The objective of this conspiracy, which potentially encompasses many crimes, is to conduct enterprise affairs through a pattern of racketeering activity. In contrast, because ordinary conspiracy cases do not involve proof of enterprise, this unifying function is absent.

2. The "enterprise." One of the many criticisms of the *Elliott* case was expressed as follows in Barry Tarlow, RICO: The New Darling of the Prosecutor's Nursery, 49 Ford. L. Rev. 165, 243, 251-252 (1980):

> The primary flaw in the *Elliott* view is the court's assumption that the scope of a RICO substantive offense or a RICO conspiracy is defined by the enterprise. The court believed that, although the defendants must agree to commit a pattern of racketeering activity, they need not agree to commit the same pattern as long as the defendants' patterns involve the same enterprise. Applying *Elliott* to a legitimate enterprise, however, it is apparent that the enterprise does not always supply a substantial connection between the activities of the defendants.

The following hypothetical illustrates this defect in *Elliott.* Assume that five police officers are charged with operating the same police department through the following patterns: (1) Officer A makes illegal payments in 1971 to a legislator to obtain a salary increase; (2) Officer B receives bribes in 1973 in exchange for protecting prostitution; (3) Officer C murders two minority citizens while arresting them in 1975; (4) Officer D removes cocaine from the evidence locker in 1977 and sells it with the aid of individuals he is supposedly investigating; and (5) Officer E embezzles money from the police pension benefit plan in 1979. All of the police officers know of, but are not involved in, the activities of the other officers.

Under a literal application of *Elliott,* these parties would be part of a single chargeable 1962(c) or 1962(d) RICO offense solely because their acts occurred in the conduct of the same enterprise.

3. Interdependence. In United States v. Sutherland, 656 F.2d 1181 (5th Cir. 1981), one defendant was a traffic court judge, and each of the other two (Walker and Maynard) was a person allegedly involved with the judge in a scheme to fix traffic tickets. The government conceded that neither Walker nor Maynard knew of the other's activities; under pre-RICO law there would have been two separate conspiracies — a "wheel" without a "rim." But the government claimed that the affairs of the traffic court constituted the RICO "enterprise" and that the three defendants could be charged with a single "enterprise conspiracy" under RICO. In essence, the government argued that "so long as the object of each conspiracy is participation in the same enterprise in violation of RICO, it matters not that the different conspiracies are otherwise unrelated." Id. at 1191. The Fifth Circuit conceded that some of the language in *Elliott* lent support to this argument, but noted that *Elliott* was addressed primarily to the problem that under prior law, it was difficult to infer a single agreement from the commission of highly diverse crimes. *Elliott* explained that "RICO helps to eliminate this problem by creating a substantive offense which ties together these diverse parties and crimes." The court then clarified the holding in *Elliott* (id. at 1192-1194):

> *Elliott* does indeed hold that on the facts of that case a series of agreements that under pre-RICO law would constitute multiple conspiracies could under RICO be tried as a single "enterprise" conspiracy. But the language of *Elliott* explains that what ties these conspiracies together is not the mere fact that they involve the same enterprise, but is instead — as in any other conspiracy — an "agreement on an overall objective." What RICO does is to provide a new criminal objective by defining a new substantive crime. . . .
>
> *Elliott* does not stand for the proposition that multiple conspiracies may be tried on a single "enterprise conspiracy" count under RICO merely because the various conspiracies involve the same enterprise. What *Elliott* does state is two-fold: (1) a pattern of agreements that absent RICO would constitute multiple conspiracies may be joined under a single RICO conspiracy count if the defendants have agreed to commit a substantive RICO offense; and (2) such an agreement to violate RICO may, as in the case of a traditional "chain" or "wheel" conspiracy, be established on circumstantial evidence, i.e., evidence that the nature of the conspiracy is such that each defendant must necessarily have known that others were also conspiring to violate RICO.
>
> In this case the government has not attempted to prove that Walker and Maynard agreed with each other to participate in a bribery scheme with Sutherland, nor has it contended that the nature of each defendant's agreement with Sutherland

> was such that he or she must necessarily have known that others were also conspiring to commit racketeering offenses in the conduct of the Municipal Court. We must conclude, therefore, that the multiple conspiracy doctrine precluded the joint trial of the two multiple conspiracies involved in this case on a single RICO conspiracy count. . . .

Compare United States v. Malony, 71 F.3d 645 (7th Cir. 1995). Here, lawyers who had bribed Cook County (Illinois) Judge Thomas Malony to "fix" four individual cases (including three murder cases) were found to be members of a single RICO conspiracy, on the basis of evidence that one of the lawyers alerted another to the impending federal investigation. In United States v. Castro, 89 F.3d 1443 (11th Cir. 1996), another judicial bribery case, three lawyers, Boehme, Lechtner, and Luongo, were charged with paying kickbacks to judges in exchange for receiving appointments as public defenders in a Florida Circuit Court. Despite the absence of evidence that the lawyers cooperated or benefited from appointments obtained by any of the others, the court held that the lawyers and judges were properly convicted of engaging in a single RICO conspiracy involving a single enterprise (the Circuit Court). Disagreeing on this point, Judge Barkett noted (id. at 1458-1459):

> To prove the existence of a single overarching conspiracy, rather than multiple independent conspiracies, the government must show that the conspirators agreed to an overall objective. . . . *Sutherland* warns, however, that it is not enough that the defendants were simply participating in the conduct of the same enterprise or had knowledge of other criminal activity; the gravamen of a RICO conspiracy, like any other conspiracy, is that the defendant not only knows about the conspiracy, but also *agrees to participate* in it to accomplish an overall objective.
>
> . . . With respect to Luongo, the government did not present any evidence to suggest he was even aware that there was any other criminal activity afoot in the Circuit Court. [The evidence,] while possibly establishing knowledge [by Boehme and Lechtner] of other criminal activity within the Circuit Court, [is] insufficient to establish . . . that [they] agreed to accomplish anything more than the receipt of court appointments for their own monetary gain. Nothing suggests . . . that they would be interested in or benefit from the similar activities of others.

NOTE ON THE CONTROVERSY OVER RICO

The RICO statute has remained extremely controversial. Some of the principal issues concern its potential for distorting civil litigation; also prominent in the debate are concerns about RICO's provisions for pretrial seizure of a defendant's assets, forfeiture of assets connected to the "enterprise," and related procedural matters. These strands in the RICO debate cannot be pursued in depth here, but many of the most important themes in the debate raise problems of substantive criminal law — the breadth and potential vagueness of the RICO offense, the risk of guilt by association, and the possibility for criminal liability greatly disproportionate to personal fault. These issues are central to conspiracy law in general and to other topics that pervade the subject of criminal law. Consider the comments that follow.

DAVID SENTELLE,[11] RICO: THE MONSTER THAT ATE JURISPRUDENCE

Lecture to the CATO Institute, Oct. 18, 1989, pp. 5-13

The [RICO] monster is . . . hungrily devouring traditional concepts of American jurisprudence. Among the traditional concepts the monster is eating, I would include federalism, the separation of powers, . . . repose of actions and perhaps even the basic concept of government of laws, not of men.

As to federalism: . . . look back to the language of section 1961(1) defining "racketeering activity." Within the incredible compass of that definition, Section (1)(A) adopts wholesale great areas of State criminal law encompassing "any act or threat involving murder, kidnapping, gambling, arson, robbery, bribery, extortion, dealing in obscene matter, or dealing in narcotic or other dangerous drugs, which is chargeable under *State* law and punishable by imprisonment for more than one year." (Emphasis added.)

. . . The almost boundless breadth of RICO, invites, perhaps requires, the Article II Executive in the form of the prosecutor and the Judiciary in the form of Article III Judges to undertake the Article I Legislative role of defining federal crimes. . . .

[D]efenders of RICO . . . tell us that we should rely on prosecutorial discretion to protect against the overbreadth of RICO. Even some of those who seek to reform RICO by the repeal of its civil remedy would retain criminal RICO because they are willing to rely on the discretion of prosecutors despite their distrust of civil plaintiff's attorneys. But we are not given angels in the form of men to make prosecutorial decisions. If we can rely on the discretion of Executive Branch officials to protect our liberties, why did we need a Constitution creating a limited government and a Bill of Rights protecting our liberties in the first place? . . .

Finally, we see the RICO monster violently attacking traditional principles of repose of actions. . . . The definition of "pattern of racketeering activity" permits the use of "at least two acts of racketeering activity, one of which occurred after the effective date of this chapter and the last of which occurred within ten years (excluding any period of imprisonment) after the commission of a prior act of racketeering activity." . . .

In other words, RICO creates an essentially perpetual cause of action alien to our traditional jurisprudence. . . . Congress, of course, has the power to make determinations as to the period of limitations. Nonetheless, one must wonder if Congress in the RICO statute really made a conscious decision to create a perpetual cause of action or simply unwittingly unleashed a monster. . . .

GERARD E. LYNCH, RICO: THE CRIME OF BEING A CRIMINAL

87 Colum. L. Rev. 661, 920, 932-955, 967-970 (1987)

Fundamental to our traditional law of crimes, criminal procedure and evidence is a conception of crime that is transaction-bound. [T]he core of any defi-

11. David Sentelle is a U.S. Circuit Judge on the U.S. Court of Appeals for the D.C. Circuit.

nition of crime is a particular act or omission. That act or omission is conceived as taking place in an instant of time so precise that it can be associated with a particular mental state of intention, awareness of risk, or neglect of due care. . . . Even the crime of conspiracy, which in practice may permit an examination of an extended course of conduct by one or more individuals, does so in the guise of using that course of conduct as evidence from which to infer that a particular act of "agreement" occurred, presumably at a specific, if not precisely ascertainable, moment in time. . . .

. . . The requirement that criminal punishment be based on a specific act has deep roots. The very nature of criminal punishment, as distinct from other uses of the compulsive power of the state (such as mandatory treatment for physical or mental illness), requires that a person not be punished for bad character, tendency to commit crime, or even a specifically formulated intention to commit some particular prohibited act. Before the state can deprive a citizen of liberty in a *punitive* way, the individual must manifest that character or tendency by the commission of some concrete prohibited act.

In significant part, the purpose of this limitation is the protection of an individual from punishment for thoughts or traits not yet exemplified by actual harmful conduct. But the moral basis of the focus on particular acts extends beyond this problem. Even for those accused of committing what is unquestionably a concrete, particular offense, we are careful to guard against the possibility that a defendant may be convicted and punished for bad character rather than for the particular act charged. The insistence on incident-based liability thus has important consequences for our rules of procedure and evidence. . . .

RICO prosecutions of criminal enterprises present a serious challenge to . . . this transaction-based model of crime. . . . The very words of the statute reveal an intent to prohibit not any particular, time-bound action, but a course of conduct extending over a potentially lengthy period of time. [T]he defining characteristic of the "pattern of racketeering" is the relationship of certain conduct to other conduct and to the "enterprise," which itself is an abstract construct of certain interpersonal relationships.

[T]he fact that RICO define[s] a crime entails some of its most dramatic procedural and evidentiary consequences. . . . Suppose, for example, the authorities develop evidence that the same defendant from whom they have recently made an undercover purchase of narcotics is a member of an organized crime family who committed a contract killing three years earlier. Under our ordinary, transaction-bound rules of procedure and evidence, the defendant would have to be tried separately for each offense. . . . In a trial on the narcotics charge alone, moreover, the evidence of a prior homicide committed by the defendant would likely be excluded as irrelevant and highly prejudicial. . . . And the prosecutor presumably would not even think about trying to elicit evidence of crimes that some *other* member of the same crime family had committed, in which this particular defendant was not personally involved. Evidence of the defendant's involvement in organized crime or of the murder he may have committed might finally surface after the defendant's conviction, as part of an argument for a severe sentence.

If the case could be indicted and tried under RICO, however, all of the evidence regarding this defendant's activities could easily be presented in the same trial. Since the government would have to allege and prove a pattern of racketeering activity, the murder and the narcotics offense could be alleged as elements of the same crime, the violation of section 1962(c). The rules precluding admission of evidence of other crimes, consequently, would simply have no application — evidence of the homicide would not be evidence of a *prior* crime, but evidence of the very offense charged in the indictment. . . .

One value served by the transaction model of crime is its preclusion of punishment in the absence of behavior manifesting a concrete threat of harm. . . . "Character" or "predicted danger" are flexible and unpredictable standards of decision, too easily used as tools of oppression.

These substantive concerns, however, are not directly violated by RICO. Although the distinguishing features of RICO are its somewhat amorphous associational and course of conduct elements, a fundamental prerequisite of a substantive RICO violation is the commission of particular criminal acts. These predicate racketeering acts are themselves conventional, transactionally defined crimes. . . .

Recognizing the importance of context to the gravity of individual criminal acts, increasing the possibility of convicting racketeers who might otherwise slip through the cracks in a transaction-based model of procedure, and utilizing the dramatic context of the criminal trial to educate the public to models of criminal activity more significant than the isolated derelictions of particular individuals are important and appropriate goals for criminal law. . . .

Such arguments are tenable, however, only if the RICO trial affords due process. . . . [I]s it within the physical and mental capacity of a jury to recall accurately the separate evidence relating to so many different individuals and so many separate incidents? What is the effect on a jury pool of the elimination of all potential jurors who cannot serve in a trial that may last over a year? . . . The threat of substantive injustice in RICO cases may come far more from such practical concerns than from the conceptual issues discussed above.

NOTES ON ENTERPRISE LIABILITY UNDER STATE LAW

1. State RICO. At least 33 states have enacted antiracketeering statutes closely tracking the structure and terminology of federal RICO. See Susan W. Brenner, RICO, CCE, and Other Complex Crimes: The Transformation of American Criminal Law?, 2 Wm. & Mary Bill of Rights J. 239, 273 (1992). Because these statutes are similar to the federal model, state courts often look to federal RICO precedent in interpreting them. In some jurisdictions, however, state statutes have been interpreted to reach even more broadly than federal RICO. An example is State v. Schlosser, 681 N.E.2d 911 (Ohio 1997). The defendant operated a telemarketing company that collected a fee in return for promising to provide a Visa or Master Card to individuals his employees called; the individuals never received their cards. The defendant was convicted of eleven counts of doing business as a credit services company without registering with the state's Division of Consumer Finance, and based on those eleven offenses he was convicted of engaging in a pattern of racketeering in violation of Ohio RICO. The record contained evidence that the defendant may have knowingly misrepresented to his clients their chances of obtaining credit cards. But the trial court found it unnecessary to determine whether the defendant had knowingly defrauded the clients, because it ruled that the predicate regulatory offense (a misdemeanor) and

Ohio RICO (a felony offense) both imposed strict liability. The Ohio Supreme Court affirmed (id. at 914):

> Offenses under [Ohio] RICO are *mala prohibita,* i.e., the acts are made unlawful for the good of the public welfare regardless of the state of mind. . . . "Whether a defendant knowingly, recklessly or otherwise engages in a pattern of corrupt activity, the effect of his activities on the local and national economy is the same. Requiring the finding of a specific culpable mental state for a RICO violation obstructs the purpose of the statute. . . ."

Questions: Is the expansive interpretation of Ohio RICO an appropriate response to the dangers posed by racketeering and organized crime? Or does it exacerbate the problems of substantive and procedural fairness that arise under federal RICO?

2. *State antigang statutes.* Nearly a dozen states have recently enacted statutes that make it an offense to aid or conspire to aid crimes intended to further the activities of a "criminal street gang." See Brenner, supra Note 1, at 275-276; Peter J. Henning, Individual Liability for Conduct by Criminal Organizations in the United States, 44 Wayne L. Rev. 1305, 1345-1349 (1998). In Lanzetta v. New Jersey, 306 U.S. 451 (1939), the Supreme Court held void for vagueness a New Jersey statute that made it a crime for any person with a criminal record, not engaged in a lawful occupation, "to be a member of any gang consisting of two or more persons." "Gang" was not defined in the statute, and the Court held that it was impossible to derive concrete meaning for it from history, sociology, or the common law. The new antigang statutes are more specific, but their definitions of "street gang" and "gang participation" can be broad. Their grading provisions can make felony sanctions applicable to acts that would otherwise be classified as simple misdemeanors or even minor violations like petty vandalism. In addition, because young urban gang members often organize themselves along explicit ethnic or racial lines, antigang prosecutions and penalty enhancements can be used to target particular minority groups. Consider Iowa Code Ann. §723A (1993):

> 723A.1. Definitions . . .
>
> 2. "Criminal street gang" means any ongoing organization, association, or group of three or more persons, whether formal or informal, having as one of its primary activities the commission of one or more criminal acts, which has an identifiable name or identifying sign or symbol, and whose members individually or collectively engage in or have engaged in a pattern of criminal gang activity.
>
> 3. "Pattern of criminal gang activity" means the commission, attempt to commit, conspiring to commit, or solicitation of two or more criminal acts, provided the criminal acts were committed on separate dates or by two or more persons who are members of, or belong to, the same criminal street gang.
>
> 723A.2. Criminal Gang Participation
>
> A person who actively participates in or is a member of a criminal street gang and who willfully aids and abets any criminal act committed for the benefit of, at the direction of, or in association with any criminal street gang, commits a class "D" felony.

Questions: Do the modern antigang statutes fill an important gap in existing criminal law? Do they adequately respond to the concerns that underlie *Lanzetta?*

PROBLEM

Indiana's "criminal gang activity" statute makes it a Class D felony to actively participate in any "group with at least five (5) members that specifically . . . promotes, sponsors or assists in [or] requires as a condition of membership . . . the commission of a felony . . . or the offense of battery." Although consent is generally a defense to simple battery in Indiana, its courts have ruled that "intra-group fighting and specifically the beatings given to other members as part of initiation or punishment" qualify as "battery" within the meaning of the gang-activity statute, even when such batteries are entirely consensual. Jackson v. State, 634 N.E.2d 532, 534 (Ind. App. 1994).

Members of a Marion, Indiana, gang called the "G's" burglarized a store and stole several guns. Jackson, a member of the G's, was suspected of involvement in the burglary, but his participation was never proved. Instead, he was charged with violating the gang-activity statute. As part of their initiation into the G's, new members were punched or burned on the right side of their chest, and members had to submit to beatings as punishment for violating group rules. But there was no evidence that members of the G's were required to commit felonies as a condition of membership. And there was no evidence that Jackson himself had committed any felonies or participated in any beatings of other group members. On the basis of the group's membership and initiation policies, and the fact that he was an active participant, Jackson's gang-activity conviction was upheld. See *Jackson,* supra.

Is the result sound? If so, are members of a boxing club and the members of the University of Indiana football team also guilty of criminal gang activity in Indiana? Are Indianapolis police officers guilty of criminal gang activity when they go through hand-to-hand combat training at the police academy? On what principle (if any) can we distinguish Jackson's culpability from that of people who participate in these other groups?

CHAPTER 8

EXCULPATION

A. INTRODUCTION: THE CONCEPTS OF JUSTIFICATION AND EXCUSE

There are three distinct sorts of defenses that can be invoked to bar conviction for an alleged crime. The first asserts that the prosecution has failed to establish one or more required elements of the offense. The defendant may, for example, deny that he was anywhere near the scene of the crime, or he may concede that he fired the fatal shot but deny that he acted intentionally. We have considered defenses of this sort throughout the first seven chapters of this book. They are simply efforts to refute (or raise a reasonable doubt about) whatever the prosecution must prove. Of course, the prosecution always retains the burden of proving its own case — and disproving any such rebuttal efforts — beyond a reasonable doubt.

In the present chapter, we deal with two sorts of defenses that have a quite different character. Justifications and excuses do not seek to refute any required element of the prosecution's case; rather they suggest further considerations that negate culpability even when all elements of the offense are clearly present.[1] Thus, claims of self-defense and insanity both suggest reasons to bar conviction even when it has been clearly proved that the defendant killed someone intentionally. It is customary, moreover, to distinguish sharply between these two groups of defenses (justifications and excuses). Self-defense, for example, is traditionally considered a justification, while insanity is considered an excuse. Pragmatists sometimes argue that this distinction is not very important — whether labeled a justification or an excuse, the defense, once proved, requires acquittal. But as J. L. Austin explains in the excerpt below, the distinction is important to clear thinking because it points to a fundamental difference in the reasons *why* culpability is lacking.

1. Justifications and excuses are sometimes treated differently from other defenses for purposes of assigning the burden of proof. See Patterson v. New York, Chapter 1, supra.

J. L. AUSTIN, A PLEA FOR EXCUSES

57 Proceedings Aristotelian Socy. 1, 2-3 (1956-1957)

One way of [defending conduct] is to admit flatly that he, *X*, did do that very thing, *A*, but to argue that it was a good thing, or the right or sensible thing, or a permissible thing to do, either in general or at least in the special circumstances of the occasion. To take this line is to *justify* the action, to give reasons for doing it . . .

A different way of going about it is to admit that it wasn't a good thing to have done, but to argue that it is not quite fair or correct to say *baldly* "*X* did *A*." We may say it isn't fair just to say *X* did it; perhaps he was under somebody's influence, or was nudged. Or, it isn't fair to say baldly he *did A;* it may have been partly accidental or an unintentional slip. Or, it isn't fair to say he did simply *A* — he was really doing something quite different and *A* was only incidental, or he was looking at the whole thing quite differently. Naturally these arguments can be combined or overlap or run into each other.

In the one defence, briefly, we accept responsibility but deny that it was bad: in the other, we admit that it was bad but don't accept full, or even any, responsibility.

By and large, justifications can be kept distinct from excuses. . . . But the two certainly can be confused, and can *seem* to go very near to each other, even if they do not perhaps actually do so. [W]hen we plead, say, provocation, there is genuine uncertainty or ambiguity as to what we mean — is *he* partly responsible, because he roused a violent impulse or passion in me, so that it wasn't truly or merely me acting "of my own accord" (excuse)? Or is it rather that, he having done me such injury, I was entitled to retaliate (justification)? . . . But that the defences I have for convenience labelled "justification" and "excuse" are in principle distinct can scarcely be doubted.

B. PRINCIPLES OF JUSTIFICATION

1. *Protection of Life and Person*

UNITED STATES v. PETERSON

United States Court of Appeals, District of Columbia Circuit
483 F.2d 1222 (1973)

Robinson, J. . . . Self-defense, as a doctrine legally exonerating the taking of human life, is as viable now as it was in Blackstone's time, . . . But "[t]he law of self-defense is a law of necessity"; the right of self-defense arises only when the necessity begins, and equally ends with the necessity; and never must the necessity be greater than when the force employed defensively is deadly. The "necessity must bear all semblance of reality, and appear to admit of no other alternative, before taking life will be justifiable as excusable." Hinged on the exigencies of self-preservation, the doctrine of homicidal self-defense emerges from the body of the criminal law as a limited though important exception to legal outlawry of the arena of self-help in the settlement of potentially fatal personal conflicts.

So it is that necessity is the pervasive theme of the well defined conditions which the law imposes on the right to kill or maim in self-defense. There must have been a threat, actual or apparent, of the use of deadly force against the defender. The threat must have been unlawful and immediate. The defender must have believed that he was in imminent peril of death or serious bodily harm, and that his response was necessary to save himself therefrom. These beliefs must not only have been honestly entertained, but also objectively reasonable in light of the surrounding circumstances. It is clear that no less than a concurrence of these elements will suffice.

PEOPLE v. GOETZ

New York Court of Appeals
68 N.Y.2d 96, 497 N.E.2d 41 (1986)

WACHTLER, C.J. A Grand Jury has indicted defendant on attempted murder, assault, and other charges for having shot and wounded four youths on a New York City subway train after one or two of the youths approached him and asked for $5. The lower courts, concluding that the prosecutor's charge to the Grand Jury on the defense of justification was erroneous, have dismissed the attempted murder, assault and weapons possession charges. We now reverse and reinstate all counts of the indictment.

The precise circumstances of the incident giving rise to the charges against defendant are disputed, and ultimately it will be for a trial jury to determine what occurred. We feel it necessary, however, to provide some factual background to properly frame the legal issues before us. Accordingly, we have summarized the facts as they appear from the evidence before the Grand Jury. We stress, however, that we do not purport to reach any conclusions or holding as to exactly what transpired or whether defendant is blameworthy. The credibility of witnesses and the reasonableness of defendant's conduct are to be resolved by the trial jury.

On Saturday afternoon, December 22, 1984, Troy Canty, Darryl Cabey, James Ramseur, and Barry Allen boarded an IRT express subway train in The Bronx and headed south toward lower Manhattan. The four youths rode together in the rear portion of the seventh car of the train. Two of the four, Ramseur and Cabey, had screwdrivers inside their coats, which they said were to be used to break into the coin boxes of video machines.

Defendant Bernhard Goetz boarded this subway train at 14th Street in Manhattan and sat down on a bench towards the rear section of the same car occupied by the four youths. Goetz was carrying an unlicensed .38 caliber pistol loaded with five rounds of ammunition in a waistband holster. The train left the 14th Street station and headed towards Chambers Street.

It appears from the evidence before the Grand Jury that Canty approached Goetz, possibly with Allen beside him, and stated "give me five dollars." Neither Canty nor any of the other youths displayed a weapon. Goetz responded by standing up, pulling out his handgun and firing four shots in rapid succession. The first shot hit Canty in the chest; the second struck Allen in the back; the third went through Ramseur's arm and into his left side; the fourth was fired at Cabey, who apparently was then standing in the corner of the car, but missed, deflecting instead off of a wall of the conductor's cab. After Goetz briefly surveyed the scene around him, he fired another shot at Cabey, who then was sitting on the end bench of the car. The bullet entered the rear of Cabey's side and severed his spinal cord.

All but two of the other passengers fled the car when, or immediately after, the shots were fired. The conductor, who had been in the next car, heard the shots and instructed the motorman to radio for emergency assistance. The conductor then went into the car where the shooting occurred and saw Goetz sitting on a bench, the injured youths lying on the floor or slumped against a seat, and two women who had apparently taken cover, also lying on the floor. Goetz told the conductor that the four youths had tried to rob him.

While the conductor was aiding the youths, Goetz headed towards the front of the car. The train had stopped just before the Chambers Street station and Goetz went between two of the cars, jumped onto the tracks and fled. Police and ambulance crews arrived at the scene shortly thereafter. Ramseur and Canty, initially listed in critical condition, have fully recovered. Cabey remains paralyzed, and has suffered some degree of brain damage.

On December 31, 1984, Goetz surrendered to police in Concord, New Hampshire. . . . [A]fter receiving *Miranda* warnings, he made two lengthy statements, both of which were tape recorded with his permission. In the statements . . . Goetz admitted that he had been illegally carrying a handgun in New York City for three years. He stated that he had first purchased a gun in 1981 after he had been injured in a mugging. Goetz also revealed that twice between 1981 and 1984 he had successfully warded off assailants simply by displaying the pistol.

According to Goetz's statement, the first contact he had with the four youths came when Canty, sitting or lying on the bench across from him, asked "how are you," to which he replied "fine." Shortly thereafter, Canty, followed by one of the other youths, walked over to the defendant and stood to his left, while the other two youths remained to his right, in the corner of the subway car. Canty then said "give me five dollars." Goetz stated that he knew from the smile on Canty's face that they wanted to "play with me." Although he was certain that none of the youths had a gun, he had a fear, based on prior experiences, of being "maimed."

Goetz then established "a pattern of fire," deciding specifically to fire from left to right. His stated intention at that point was to "murder [the four youths], to hurt them, to make them suffer as much as possible." When Canty again requested money, Goetz stood up, drew his weapon, and began firing, aiming for the center of the body of each of the four. Goetz recalled that the first two he shot "tried to run through the crowd [but] they had nowhere to run." Goetz then turned to his right to "go after the other two." One of these two "tried to run through the wall of the train, but . . . he had nowhere to go." The other youth (Cabey) "tried pretending that he wasn't with [the others]" by standing still, holding on to one of the subway hand straps, and not looking at Goetz. Goetz nonetheless fired his fourth shot at him. He then ran back to the first two youths to make sure they had been "taken care of." Seeing that they had both been shot, he spun back to check on the latter two. Goetz noticed that the youth who had been standing still was now sitting on a bench and seemed unhurt. As Goetz told the police, "I said '[y]ou seem to be all right, here's another,'" and he then fired the shot which severed Cabey's spinal cord. Goetz added that "if I was a little more under self-control . . . I would have put the barrel against his forehead and fired." He also admitted that "if I had had more [bullets], I would have shot them again, and again, and again." . . .

Penal Law article 35 recognizes the defense of justification, which "permits the use of force under certain circumstances." One such set of circumstances pertains to the use of force in defense of a person, encompassing both self-defense and defense of a third person. Penal Law §35.15 (1) sets forth the general principles governing all such uses of force: "[a] person may . . . use physical force upon another person when and to the extent he *reasonably believes* such to be necessary to defend himself or a third person from what he *reasonably believes* to be the use or imminent use of unlawful physical force by such other person" (emphasis added).

Section 35.15 (2) sets forth further limitations on these general principles with respect to the use of "deadly physical force": "A person may not use deadly physical force upon another person under circumstances specified in subdivision one unless (a) He *reasonably believes* that such other person is using or about to use deadly physical force . . . or (b) He *reasonably believes* that such other person is committing or attempting to commit a kidnapping, forcible rape, forcible sodomy or robbery" (emphasis added). . . .

Because the evidence before the second Grand Jury included statements by Goetz that he acted to protect himself from being maimed or to avert a robbery, the prosecutor correctly chose to charge the justification defense in section 35.15 to the Grand Jury. The prosecutor properly instructed the grand jurors to consider whether the use of deadly physical force was justified to prevent either serious physical injury or a robbery, and, in doing so, to separately analyze the defense with respect to each of the charges. He elaborated upon the prerequisites for the use of deadly physical force essentially by reading or paraphrasing the language in Penal Law §35.15. The defense does not contend that he committed any error in this portion of the charge.

When the prosecutor had completed his charge, one of the grand jurors asked for clarification of the term "reasonably believes." The prosecutor responded by instructing the grand jurors that they were to consider the circumstances of the incident and determine "whether the defendant's conduct was that of a reasonable man in the defendant's situation." It is this response by the prosecutor — and specifically his use of "a reasonable man" — which is the basis for the dismissal of the charges by the lower courts. As expressed repeatedly in the Appellate Division's plurality opinion, because section 35.15 uses the term "*he* reasonably believes," the appropriate test, according to that court, is whether a defendant's beliefs and reactions were "reasonable to *him.*" Under that reading of the statute, a jury which believed a defendant's testimony that he felt that his own actions were warranted and were reasonable would have to acquit him, regardless of what anyone else in defendant's situation might have concluded. Such an interpretation defies the ordinary meaning and significance of the term "reasonably" in a statute, and misconstrues the clear intent of the Legislature, in enacting section 35.15, to retain an objective element as part of any provision authorizing the use of deadly physical force.

Penal statutes in New York have long codified the right recognized at common law to use deadly physical force, under appropriate circumstances, in self-defense. These provisions have never required that an actor's belief as to the intention of another person to inflict serious injury be correct in order for the use of deadly force to be justified, but they have uniformly required that the belief comport with an objective notion of reasonableness. . . .

In 1961 the Legislature established a Commission to undertake a complete revision of the Penal Law and the Criminal Code. The impetus for the decision to update the Penal Law came in part from the drafting of the Model Penal Code by the American Law Institute, as well as from the fact that the existing law was poorly organized and in many aspects antiquated. . . . While using the Model Penal Code provisions on justification as general guidelines . . . the drafters of the new Penal Law did not simply adopt them verbatim.

The provisions of the Model Penal Code with respect to the use of deadly force in self-defense reflect the position of its drafters that any culpability which arises from a mistaken belief in the need to use such force should be no greater than the culpability such a mistake would give rise to if it were made with respect to an element of a crime. Accordingly, under Model Penal Code §3.04 (2) (b), a defendant charged with murder (or attempted murder) need only show that he "*believe[d]* that [the use of deadly force] was necessary to protect himself against death, serious bodily injury, kidnapping or [forcible] sexual intercourse" to prevail on a self-defense claim (emphasis added). If the defendant's belief was wrong, and was recklessly, or negligently formed, however, he may be convicted of the type of homicide charge requiring only a reckless or negligent, as the case may be, criminal intent (see, Model Penal Code §3.09 . . .).

New York did not follow the Model Penal Code's equation of a mistake as to the need to use deadly force with a mistake negating an element of a crime, choosing instead to use a single statutory section which would provide either a complete defense or no defense at all to a defendant charged with any crime involving the use of deadly force. The drafters of the new Penal Law adopted in large part the structure and content of Model Penal Code §3.04, but, crucially, inserted the word "reasonably" before "believes."

The plurality below agreed with defendant's argument that the change in the statutory language from "reasonable ground," used prior to 1965, to "he reasonably believes" in Penal Law §35.15 evinced a legislative intent to conform to the subjective standard contained in Model Penal Code §3.04. This argument, however, ignores the plain significance of the insertion of "reasonably." Had the drafters of section 35.15 wanted to adopt a subjective standard, they could have simply used the language of section 3.04. "Believes" by itself requires an honest or genuine belief by a defendant as to the need to use deadly force. Interpreting the statute to require only that the defendant's belief was "reasonable to *him,*" as done by the plurality below, would hardly be different from requiring only a genuine belief; in either case, the defendant's own perceptions could completely exonerate him from any criminal liability.

We cannot lightly impute to the Legislature an intent to fundamentally alter the principles of justification to allow the perpetrator of a serious crime to go free simply because that person believed his actions were reasonable and necessary to prevent some perceived harm. To completely exonerate such an individual, no matter how aberrational or bizarre his thought patterns, would allow citizens to set their own standards for the permissible use of force. . . .

We can only conclude that the Legislature retained a reasonableness requirement to avoid giving license for such actions. . . .

Goetz also argues that the introduction of an objective element will preclude a jury from considering factors such as the prior experiences of a given actor and thus, require it to make a determination of "reasonableness" without regard to the actual circumstances of a particular incident. This argument, however, falsely presupposes that an objective standard means that the background and other relevant characteristics of a particular actor must be ignored. To the contrary, we have frequently noted that a determination of reasonableness must be based on the "circumstances" facing a defendant or his "situation." Such terms encompass more than the physical movements of the potential assailant. [T]hese terms include any relevant knowledge the defendant had about that person. They also necessarily bring in the physical attributes of all persons involved, including the defendant. Furthermore, the defendant's circumstances encompass any prior experiences he had which could provide a reasonable basis for a belief that another person's intentions were to injure or rob him or that the use of deadly force was necessary under the circumstances. . . .

The prosecutor's instruction to the second Grand Jury that it had to determine whether, under the circumstances, Goetz's conduct was that of a reasonable man in his situation was thus essentially an accurate charge. . . .

Accordingly, the order of the Appellate Division should be reversed, and the dismissed counts of the indictment reinstated.

NOTES ON THE GOETZ *CASE*

The jury subsequently convicted Goetz on the charge of carrying an unlicensed concealed weapon, but acquitted him on all other counts. N.Y. Times, June 18, 1987, at B6. He was sentenced on the weapons count to one year in jail, with the possibility of release after 60 days. N.Y. Times, Jan. 14, 1989, at 1.

The *Goetz* case became a cause célèbre. Two book-length studies appeared. George Fletcher, A Crime of Self-Defense: Bernhard Goetz and the Law on Trial (1988); Lilian Rubin, Quiet Rage: Bernie Goetz in a Time of Madness (1988). Consider the following reactions.

Joseph Berger, Goetz Case: *Commentary on Nature of Urban Life, N.Y. Times, June 18, 1987, at B6:* The jury's decision in the Bernhard Goetz case seemed to be a verdict on the nature of contemporary urban life, churning up issues of vulnerability, rage and racial tensions that lie just beneath the surface.

The acquittal of Mr. Goetz on charges of attempted murder broke no dramatic new legal ground, in the opinion of legal experts. But in the context of the national debate on the balance between self-defense and social order, it appeared to widen the circumstances that justify the use of deadly force. . . .

There was almost no evidence presented that any of the four youths who approached Mr. Goetz had actually tried to rob him before he shot them. Thus the jury, by rejecting the charge of attempted murder, seemed to be saying that in the nervousness that courses through much of urban experience, from riding the subway at night to walking a darkened street, such evidence may not matter all that much. Perceptions, the jury suggested, can attain the power of facts.

"The jury decided that no man is reasonable when he's surrounded by four thugs," said Alan Dershowitz, professor of law at Harvard Law School. "It's hard to pay attention to lines drawn by academics in a classroom."

Mr. Dershowitz, noting that jurors often nullify self-defense standards set by the law, said he believed that what Mr. Goetz did was by definition illegal in New York State and every other state. It is illegal, he said, to shoot a person after the immediate danger has passed. "It doesn't change the law," he said of the verdict. "It may show the law is somewhat out of line with people's passions today."

The jury's decision also seemed to be a back-handed commentary on the effectiveness of the police and the courts. Burt Neuborne, a professor at New York University Law School, said, "The jurors had so little faith in the criminal justice system, both to protect us and to bring the guilty to justice, that they were willing to tolerate a degree of vigilante behavior that I think rationally cannot be justified." . . .

Crime has become such a daily feature of urban life that several of the jurors had themselves been victims. It is often on people's minds, determining where they live, how and when they travel, and how they spend their time.

The jury seemed to be saying that the fear of crime, in someone who has been a previous mugging victim like Mr. Goetz, can weigh so heavily on one's emotions that it can lead to conduct that might normally be considered wrongful. The jury in the Goetz case apparently believed there was not enough evidence to show that Mr. Goetz acted out of any motive other than fear. . . .

Underlying the issue of crime in this case was the issue of race. Scholars such as Dr. Kenneth B. Clark, professor emeritus of psychology at the City University of New York, have expressed doubt that Mr. Goetz would have shot four white youths asking him for money.

However, Marvin E. Wolfgang, a criminologist at the University of Pennsylvania, said that perceptions about who is more likely to commit a crime have some statistical basis. The rates of crime for four violent offenses — homicide, rape, robbery and aggravated assault — are at least ten times as high for blacks as they are for whites, he said.

"The expectation that four young black males are going to do you harm is indeed greater than four young whites," he said. "I can understand the black position that this is a racist attitude, but it's not unrealistic."

It is possible that jurors have absorbed such racially based perceptions about who is going to commit a crime. Elijah Anderson, a black sociologist at the University of Pennsylvania who spent three years studying street-corner life in a tough, black neighborhood in Philadelphia, said law-abiding people, black and white, have a distinctive way of relating "to people they assume to be members of the black underclass."

People, he said, "can be very intimidated by young black males or people who seem to represent this so-called underclass by their dress or comportment, very intimidated." . . .

Because it raises such issues, the jury verdict may pose some hard questions for the American public to deal with. Will some New Yorkers come to feel that they can now make hair-trigger assumptions about the character of people who somehow threaten them, and if they have a gun, use it in self-defense? Will blacks have to fear that if they look at someone the wrong way or dress too casually they may be mistaken for criminals? . . .

Stephen L. Carter, When Victims Happen to be Black, 97 Yale L.J. 420, 425-26 (1988): Shortly after a New York jury acquitted Bernhard Goetz [a cartoon appeared of a] post-Goetz subway car: two elderly women seated side-by-side in a car empty of other passengers, a screwdriver lying nearby, and outside, a crowd of people, eyes widened with fear, running away from the car. One of the women says to the other: 'Heavens! . . . I was just reaching for my lipstick.'

[T]he artist managed . . . to capture the shuddering tensions apparent in public reactions to the Goetz incident and the verdict in his trial, and much more besides. Mr. Goetz's public — those who declared him a hero from the first — can find in this cartoon a portrait of salvation of a sort. The people fleeing are thugs and toughs, the anonymous yet ubiquitous individuals who frequent New York's subway trains and cast terror with a glance. . . .

[T]he story of the subway car as perceived by Mr. Goetz's public — the choice of transgressor, the choice of victim — might have been starkly different had Mr. Goetz been black and the others white, and had Mr. Goetz cried 'self-defense' while the others insisted that when he pulled the gun, they had been minding their own business. For in that event, a public with no real knowledge of the facts other than the stories told by the participants and the skin colors of the shooter and his victims would not have raced at once to Mr. Goetz's defense. . . .

Against this background, consider once more the cartoon [just described], this time from the point of view of Mr. Goetz's critics, the ones who have condemned the verdict as opening the hunting season on young black men. Now the people fleeing the car are frightened innocents, victims themselves, probably black or brown, who can no longer be certain which gesture of impatience or annoyance someone else will take as a threat, who are now loathe to ask directions or change of a dollar for fear of a fatal misinterpretation. The elderly women left alone in the car are . . . aging, they are women, they are white. . . . And because in society's eyes they are the archetypal victims, were they to shoot and to testify to their fear, their story would be readily believed; the tale told by their tormenters would surely be doubted. . . .

These law-abiding people of color who might feel obliged to flee the subway car are not victims in the [traditional] sense, for there are no transgressors angrily forcing them out of the subway car. Yet if they nevertheless choose flight, it does no good to tell them that they are not victims because there are no transgressors who might be punished for causing their fear. The dominant culture is unable to rationalize that fear within its vision of victimhood, but for the frightened, fear is itself a truth. Because the dominant culture constructs victimhood in a way that denies this truth, those who see in the lionization of Bernhard Goetz a reason for terror, rather than a cause for celebration, might offer another perspective on what should count as victimhood.

Jody D. Armour, Race Ipsa Loquitur: Of Reasonable Racists, Intelligent Beyesians, and Involuntary Negrophobes, 46 Stan. L. Rev. 781, 787-788, 790, 792, 794, 795 (1994): The Reasonable Racist asserts that, even if his belief that blacks are "prone to violence" stems from pure prejudice, he should be excused for considering the victim's race before using force because most similarly situated Americans would have done so as well. For inasmuch as the criminal justice system operates on the assumption that "blame is reserved for the (statistically) deviant,"[18] an individual racist in a racist society cannot be condemned for an expression of human frailty as ubiquitous as racism. . . .

The flaw in the Reasonable Racist's self-defense claim lies in his primary assumption that the sole objective of criminal law is to punish those who deviate from statistically defined norms. For even if the "typical" American believes that blacks' "propensity" toward violence justifies a quicker and more forceful response when a suspected assailant is black, this fact is legally significant only if the law defines *reasonable* beliefs as *typical* beliefs. The reasonableness inquiry, however, extends beyond typicality to consider the social interests implicated in a given situation. Hence not all "typical" beliefs are per se reasonable. . . . If we accept that racial discrimination violates contemporary social morality, then an actor's failure to overcome his racism for the sake of another's health, safety, and personal dignity is blameworthy and thus unreasonable, independent of whether or not it is "typical." . . .

A second argument which a defendant may advance to justify acting on race-based assumptions is that, given statistics demonstrating blacks' disproportionate involvement in crime, it is reasonable to perceive a greater threat from a black person than a white person. . . .

Although biases in the criminal justice system exaggerate the differences in rates of violent crime by race, it may, tragically, still be true that blacks commit a disproportionate number of crimes. Given that the blight of institutional racism continues to disproportionately limit the life chances of African-Americans, and that desperate circumstances increase the likelihood that individuals caught in this web may turn to desperate undertakings, such a disparity, if it exists, should sadden but not surprise us. . . .

To the extent that socioeconomic status explains the overinvolvement of blacks in robbery and assault (assuming that there is, in fact, such overinvolvement), race serves merely as a proxy for socioeconomic status. But if race is a proxy for socioeconomic factors, then race loses its predictive value when one controls for those factors. . . .

The use of race-based generalizations in the self-defense context has an especially grievous effect: . . . Ultimately, race-based evidence of reasonableness impairs the capacity of jurors to rationally and fairly strike a balance between the costs of waiting (increased risk for the person who perceives imminent attack) and the costs of not waiting (injury or death to the immediate victim, exclusion of blacks from core community activities, and, ultimately, reduction of individuals to predictable objects). In fact, such evidence may be so effective at tapping the racism — conscious or unconscious — which has been proven to infect jury deliberations, that it should arguably be excluded under the "more prejudicial than probative" standard of most states' evidence codes, of which the provisions in section 403 of the Federal Rules of Evidence are illustrative.[55]

18. Mark Kelman, Reasonable Evidence of Reasonableness, 17 Critical Inquiry 798, 801 (1991).

55. See Fed. R. Evid. 403. Rule 403 reads, in relevant part: "Although relevant, evidence may be excluded if its probative value is substantially outweighed by the danger of unfair prejudice, confusion of the issues, or misleading the jury. . . ."

For exploration of the juror impact of stereotypes about African-Americans, as well as widely held stereotypes about Asian-Americans and Latinos, see Cynthia Kwei Yung Lee, Race and Self-Defense: Toward a Normative Conception of Reasonableness, 81 Minn. L. Rev. 367, 402-452 (1996).

NOTES ON REASONABLENESS

1. *A subjective test?* Is the conventional position requiring that the defendant's defensive action must be reasonable preferable to a wholly subjective rule? Professor Glanville Williams advanced the following argument in behalf of a subjective view (quoted in Model Penal Code and Commentaries, Comment to §3.09 at 152, n. 10 (1985)):

> The criminal law of negligence works best when it gives effect to the large number of rules of prudence which are commonly observed though not directly incorporated into the law. Such rules include the rule against pulling out on a blind corner, the rule against carrying a gun in such a way that it is pointing at another person, the rule against deliberately pointing a gun at another person, even in play, and so on. These rules are not part either of enacted or of common law, but as customary standards of behavior they become binding via the law of negligence. Are there any similar rules of behavior applicable when a person acts in self-defense or in making an arrest? It must be recollected that the injury he inflicts on the other is in itself intentional, so that the usual rules of prudence in respect to the handling of weapons are not in question. The only question is whether the defendant was negligent in arriving at the conclusion that the use of the force in question was called for. It is hard to imagine what rules of prudence could normally serve in this situation. Either the defendant is capable of drawing the inferences that a reasonable man would draw or he is not. If he is not, and he is a peace officer, his tendency to make miscalculations would certainly justify his dismissal from the police force. But there is no obvious case for the intervention of the criminal courts.
>
> The only common situation in which a person makes an unreasonable mistake in what he believes to be self-defense is when he is drunk or otherwise in an abnormal mental state. For example, a drunken person may misconstrue a gesture as an attempt to kill, and, acting under this misconception, he may take a knife and kill or nearly kill the person whom he mistakenly supposes to be an assailant. It is submitted that the solution of this problem lies in provisions directed specifically to it. There should be a specific offense of being drunk and dangerous. . . . Where the defendant is insane or feeble-minded, the problem of treatment belongs to the wider problem of insanity and feeblemindedness in the criminal law.

Consider the following critique of the reasonableness requirement. R. Restak, The Fiction of the "Reasonable Man," The Washington Post, Sunday, May 17, 1987, at C3:

> As a neurologist and neuropsychiatrist with over a decade of experience in conducting pretrial interviews of individuals who have acted violently, the "reasonable person" argument seems an illogical and outdated approach to fully understanding events such as occurred on the New York subway in December of 1984 when Bernhard Goetz shot and injured four teenagers.
>
> On the basis of what I know about the human brain I'm convinced that there are

no reasonable people under conditions in which death or severe bodily harm are believed imminent.

Deep within the brain of every reasonable person resides the limbic system: an ancient interconnected network of structures that anatomically and chemically haven't changed much over hundreds of thousands of years. We share these structures with jungle animals as well as animals that many reasonable people keep as pets. Moreover, the limbic system is capable under conditions of extreme duress of overwhelming the cerebral cortex wherein are formulated many of the reasonable person's most reasonable attributes, like interpretation, judgment and restraint. . . . Emotions are not incidental and subsidiary to rational processes. Instead, the reasonable person, even at his or her most reasonable moments, is influenced by emotional processes. . . .

In view of what we now know of such cases, the logic of the "reasonable man" standard — in the Bernhard Goetz case or similar cases in the future — may be inherently flawed.

"We don't contend that the defendant had no cause for apprehension" said Assistant District Attorney Gregory Waples on the first day of the trial. He went on to argue that Goetz, once aroused, should have been capable of stopping himself at some point. The firing of a second shot into Darrell Cabey — after, as the prosecution has contended, the immediate threat was over — is crucial to the state's argument. "When he fired that last shot," Waples said, "beyond the slightest doubt, Cabey was seated helpless doing nothing to threaten or menace Bernhard Goetz." . . .

The prosecutor's logic is this: Once Goetz coolly discerned that he was out of danger, he should have calmed down, put away his gun and awaited the arrival of the police.

[S]uch expectations are neurologically unrealistic. Once aroused, the limbic system can become a directive force for hours, sometimes days, and can rarely be shut off like flipping a switch. The heart keeps pounding, the breathing — harsh and labored — burns in the throat; the thoughts keep churning as fear is replaced by anger and finally, murderous rage. . . .

Consider Goetz' response to the question "Did you just shoot each one of these people just once?"

Goetz: "Well, you see that's why I, that's, that's one of the things that puzzles me. . . . Because you know what you're doing, you cannot do something and not know it. I mean, how could I do it and not know it? But if you can accept this, I was out of control, and that's, you know, but that's, that's, it's true, maybe you should always be in control, but if you, if you put people in a situation where they're threatened with mayhem, several times, and then if, then if something happens, and if a person acts, turns into a vicious animal. . . . That's not the end of the shooting. That's what. . . . It's not the end. I ran back to the first two, to make sure."

Is that what a reasonable person would do under such circumstances?

Although lawyers and judges love to explore such questions, . . . I'm convinced that they're . . . products of an outmoded mentality that places an overemphasis on empty intellectualization to the exclusion of those deep and powerful emotional currents of fear, self-preservation or territoriality that can surface in any one of us and overpower the cogitations of reason.

Granted that this isn't a pretty or elegant arrangement. But as long as our brain is put together the way it is, no one should be too confident that he or she would remain completely reasonable under conditions where their life is perceived to be in imminent danger. Moreover, this critical perception of threat isn't based on rationality. It's fueled by those limbic derived emotions that have promoted the survival of our species.

Isn't it preferable therefore to face up courageously to these sometimes frightening and unpleasant realities instead of pretending that questions such as those being asked about Bernhard Goetz can be answered by courtroom speculations about how a reasonable person would have responded in his place?

To expect reasonable behavior in the face of perceived threat, terror and rage is itself a most unreasonable expectation.

Questions: (1) What would it mean for the law "to face up courageously to these . . . realities"? Is it Restak's point that the law should allow a complete defense whenever the defendant subjectively fears for his life, regardless of the circumstances?

(2) Consider Justice Holmes' oft-quoted epigram: "Detached reflection cannot be demanded in the presence of an uplifted knife." Brown v. United States, 256 U.S. 335, 343 (1921). Does the evidence of the operation of the limbic system say something different from that? Reconsider the arguments for and against criminal liability for negligence, page 434 supra.

2. *Qualifications to the objective rule.* As in other instances in which the law employs an objective standard, there is always the question of just how objective the standard is to be — that is, how far should features of defendant's particular situation be taken into account in determining whether the choice of defensive force was reasonable? Compare the discussion of the reasonable-provocation standard, page 420 supra, and the discussion of the definition of negligence and recklessness, page 434 supra. Recall the Model Penal Code standards (§2.02), calling for a judgment (in the case of recklessness) whether the risk is of a nature and degree that "its disregard involves a gross deviation from the standard of conduct that a law-abiding person would observe *in the actor's situation*" and (in the case of negligence) whether that risk "involves a gross deviation from the standard of care that a reasonable person would observe *in the actor's situation.*" (Italics added.) The Model Penal Code's position represents a partial individualizing of the objective standard of the reasonable person. See page 438 supra, where this issue is discussed in connection with the definition of criminal negligence. Was the jury's verdict in the *Goetz* case defensible under the Model Penal Code approach?

3. *Beliefs and actions.* What is it, precisely, that must be reasonable? In the *Goetz* case, for example, should the result turn exclusively on whether Goetz's *belief* in an impending danger was reasonable, or should it be necessary for the defendant to show, in addition, that the *actions* he took were reasonable?

In principle, there should be no doubt that reasonableness must extend to actions as well as beliefs. Indeed in theory, there may be little difference between saying that a belief in the need to shoot was reasonable, and saying that the act of shooting was reasonable. But in many states, model jury instructions emphasize that beliefs and fears must be reasonable, without making explicit that the defendant's actions must be reasonable as well. See Lee, supra, 81 Minn. L. Rev. at 469-471.[2] The result, Professor Lee finds, is that jurors may too readily accept

2. The Model Penal Code suffers from a similar ambiguity. Section 2.02(2)(d) defines negligence as a "failure to perceive," and it is this failure to perceive, rather than the defendant's conduct itself, that must involve "a gross departure from [a reasonable] standard of care." Similarly in connection with self-defense, §3.04 provides that the use of force "is justifiable when the actor believes" that certain facts exist; §3.09(2) withdraws this defense for under certain conditions if "the actor is reckless or negligent *in having such belief.* . . ."

self-defense claims in cases like *Goetz,* where a fear might arguably seem reasonable, but the actions taken in response to that fear are not.

4. A grading problem. Where reasonableness is required for total exculpation, how should the law deal with a person who holds an honest but unreasonable belief in the need to use lethal force? Assume such a person kills because she genuinely believes it is the only way to save her life, but she comes to her conclusion on grossly unreasonable grounds. She has killed intentionally and, under the prevailing objective test, she has no defense of self-defense. Thus, she would be guilty of murder, just like the person who kills for revenge or gain. This appears to be the generally prevailing view.[3] But several states avoid this result through various doctrines of mitigation. One, known as the doctrine of "imperfect self-defense," classifies the crime as voluntary manslaughter, on the theory that "malice" is lacking and that the lesser culpability in a killing of this sort is similar to that in a killing in a heat of passion.[4] The other approach, even less common, is to classify the killing as involuntary manslaughter.[5] A problem for this theory is that involuntary manslaughter presupposes an unintentional killing, while a killing in self-defense is ordinarily intentional. The justification, nonetheless, is that actor's culpability most closely approximates that of a person whose criminal negligence causes an unintentional death.

The Model Penal Code is similar to this last approach: a person who kills in the honest but unreasonable belief in the need to kill would be guilty of negligent homicide. The drafting device through which the Model Penal Code achieves this result is to specify in the various justification provisions the circumstances that the actor must believe to exist in order for his or her action to be justified and to employ the following general provision (§3.09(2)) to deal with mistaken belief in those circumstances:

> When the actor believes that the use of force upon or toward the person of another is necessary for any of the purposes for which such belief would establish a justification under §§3.03 to 3.08 but the actor is reckless or negligent in having such belief or acquiring or failing to acquire any knowledge or belief which is material to the justifiability of his use of force, the justification afforded by those Sections is unavailable in a prosecution for an offense for which recklessness or negligence, as the case may be, suffices to establish culpability.

The approach has not been influential in state statutory reform. See Note, Justification: The Impact of the Model Penal Code on State Law Reform, 75 Colum. L. Rev. 914, 920 (1975).

5. Problem. As we have seen, the Model Penal Code and the New York self-defense formulations differ in the way they deal with the reasonableness requirement. Consider how the following hypothetical should be analyzed under each formulation: The defendant shoots to kill *Z* in the honest but unreasonable belief that it is necessary to do so to save the defendant's life. He misses, and *Z* es-

3. E.g., State v. Abdalaziz, 725 N.E.2d 799 (1999); State v. Beeler, 1999 WL 506234 (Mo. App. 1999); State v. Shaw, 721 A.2d 486 (Vt. 1998).

4. See, e.g., Faulkner v. State, 458 A.2d 81 (Md. App. 1983). Some state statutes also take this approach, e.g., Pa. Cons. Stat. tit. 18, §2503(b), supra page 392.

5. E.g., Shannon v. Commonwealth, 767 S.W.2d 548 (Ky. 1988).

capes unharmed. Is the defendant guilty of attempted murder? Of attempt to commit manslaughter?

STATE v. KELLY

Supreme Court of New Jersey
91 N.J. 178, 478 A.2d 364 (1984)

WILENTZ, C.J. . . . On May 24, 1980, defendant, Gladys Kelly, stabbed her husband, Ernest, with a pair of scissors. He died shortly thereafter at a nearby hospital. . . .

Ms. Kelly was indicted for murder. At trial, she did not deny stabbing her husband, but asserted that her action was in self-defense. To establish the requisite state of mind for her self-defense claim, Ms. Kelly called Dr. Lois Veronen as an expert witness to testify about the battered-woman's syndrome. After hearing a lengthy voir dire examination of Dr. Veronen, the trial court ruled that expert testimony concerning the syndrome was inadmissible on the self-defense issue. . . .

Ms. Kelly was convicted of reckless manslaughter. [We] reverse.

The Kellys had a stormy marriage. Some of the details of their relationship, especially the stabbing, are disputed. The following is Ms. Kelly's version of what happened — a version that the jury could have accepted and, if they had, a version that would make the proffered expert testimony not only relevant, but critical.

The day after the marriage, Mr. Kelly got drunk and knocked Ms. Kelly down. Although a period of calm followed the initial attack, the next seven years were accompanied by periodic and frequent beatings, sometimes as often as once a week. During the attacks, which generally occurred when Mr. Kelly was drunk, he threatened to kill Ms. Kelly and to cut off parts of her body if she tried to leave him. Mr. Kelly often moved out of the house after an attack, later returning with a promise that he would change his ways. Until the day of the homicide, only one of the attacks had taken place in public.

The day before the stabbing, Gladys and Ernest went shopping. They did not have enough money to buy food for the entire week, so Ernest said he would give his wife more money the next day.

The following morning he left for work. Ms. Kelly next saw her husband late that afternoon at a friend's house. She had gone there with her daughter, Annette, to ask Ernest for money to buy food. He told her to wait until they got home, and shortly thereafter the Kellys left. After walking past several houses, Mr. Kelly, who was drunk, angrily asked "What the hell did you come around here for?" He then grabbed the collar of her dress, and the two fell to the ground. He choked her by pushing his fingers against her throat, punched or hit her face, and bit her leg.

A crowd gathered on the street. Two men from the crowd separated them, just as Gladys felt that she was "passing out" from being choked. Fearing that Annette had been pushed around in the crowd, Gladys then left to look for her. . . .

After finding her daughter, Ms. Kelly then observed Mr. Kelly running toward her with his hands raised. Within seconds he was right next to her. Unsure of whether he had armed himself while she was looking for their daughter, and thinking that he had come back to kill her, she grabbed a pair of scissors from her pocketbook. She tried to scare him away, but instead stabbed him.[1]

The central question in this case is whether the trial court erred in its exclusion of expert testimony on the battered-woman's syndrome. That testimony was intended to explain defendant's state of mind and bolster her claim of self-defense. We shall first examine the nature of the battered-woman's syndrome and then consider the expert testimony proffered in this case and its relevance. . . .

As the problem of battered women has begun to receive more attention, sociologists and psychologists have begun to focus on the effects a sustained pattern of physical and psychological abuse can have on a woman. The effects of such abuse are what some scientific observers have termed "the battered-woman's syndrome," a series of common characteristics that appear in women who are abused physically and psychologically over an extended period of time by the dominant male figure in their lives. Dr. Lenore Walker, a prominent writer on the battered-woman's syndrome, defines the battered woman as one

> who is repeatedly subjected to any forceful physical or psychological behavior by a man in order to coerce her to do something he wants her to do without concern for her rights. Battered women include wives or women in any form of intimate relationships with men. Furthermore, in order to be classified as a battered woman, the couple must go through the battering cycle at least twice. Any woman may find herself in an abusive relationship with a man once. If it occurs a second time, and she remains in the situation, she is defined as a battered woman. [L. Walker, The Battered Woman (1979) at xv.]

According to Dr. Walker, relationships characterized by physical abuse tend to develop battering cycles. Violent behavior directed at the woman occurs in three distinct and repetitive stages that vary both in duration and intensity depending on the individuals involved.

Phase one of the battering cycle is referred to as the "tension-building stage," during which the battering male engages in minor battering incidents and verbal abuse while the woman, beset by fear and tension, attempts to be as placating and passive as possible in order to stave off more serious violence.

Phase two of the battering cycle is the "acute battering incident." At some point during phase one, the tension between the battered woman and the batterer becomes intolerable and more serious violence inevitable. The triggering event that initiates phase two is most often an internal or external event in the life of the battering male, but provocation for more severe violence is sometimes provided by the woman who can no longer tolerate or control her phase-one anger and anxiety.

Phase three of the battering cycle is characterized by extreme contrition and loving behavior on the part of the battering male. During this period the man will often mix his pleas for forgiveness and protestations of devotion with prom-

1. This version of the homicide — with a drunk Mr. Kelly as the aggressor both in pushing Ms. Kelly to the ground and again in rushing at her with his hands in a threatening position after the two had been separated — is sharply disputed by the State. The prosecution presented testimony intended to show that the initial scuffle was started by Gladys; that upon disentanglement, while she was restrained by bystanders, she stated that she intended to kill Ernest; that she then chased after him, and upon catching up with him stabbed him with a pair of scissors taken from her pocketbook.

ises to seek professional help, to stop drinking, and to refrain from further violence. For some couples, this period of relative calm may last as long as several months, but in a battering relationship the affection and contrition of the man will eventually fade and phase one of the cycle will start anew.

The cyclical nature of battering behavior helps explain why more women simply do not leave their abusers. The loving behavior demonstrated by the batterer during phase three reinforces whatever hopes these women might have for their mate's reform and keeps them bound to the relationship. R. Langley & R. Levy, Wife Beating: The Silent Crisis 112-114 (1977).

Some women may even perceive the battering cycle as normal, especially if they grew up in a violent household. . . . Other women, however, become so demoralized and degraded by the fact that they cannot predict or control the violence that they sink into a state of psychological paralysis and become unable to take any action at all to improve or alter the situation. There is a tendency in battered women to believe in the omnipotence or strength of their battering husbands and thus to feel that any attempt to resist them is hopeless.

In addition to these psychological impacts, external social and economic factors often make it difficult for some women to extricate themselves from battering relationships. A woman without independent financial resources who wishes to leave her husband often finds it difficult to do so because of a lack of material and social resources. . . . Thus, in a violent confrontation where the first reaction might be to flee, women realize soon that there may be no place to go. Moreover, the stigma that attaches to a woman who leaves the family unit without her children undoubtedly acts as a further deterrent to moving out.

In addition, battered women, when they want to leave the relationship, are typically unwilling to reach out and confide in their friends, family, or the police, either out of shame and humiliation, fear of reprisal by their husband, or the feeling they will not be believed.

Dr. Walker and other commentators have identified several common personality traits of the battered woman: low self-esteem, traditional beliefs about the home, the family, and the female sex role, tremendous feelings of guilt that their marriages are failing, and the tendency to accept responsibility for the batterer's actions.

Finally, battered women are often hesitant to leave a battering relationship because, in addition to their hope of reform on the part of their spouse, they harbor a deep concern about the possible response leaving might provoke in their mates. They literally become trapped by their own fear. Case histories are replete with instances in which a battered wife left her husband only to have him pursue her and subject her to an even more brutal attack.

The combination of all these symptoms — resulting from sustained psychological and physical trauma compounded by aggravating social and economic factors — constitutes the battered-woman's syndrome. Only by understanding these unique pressures that force battered women to remain with their mates, despite their long-standing and reasonable fear of severe bodily harm and the isolation that being a battered woman creates, can a battered woman's state of mind be accurately and fairly understood.

The voir dire testimony of Dr. Veronen, sought to be introduced by defendant Gladys Kelly, conformed essentially to this outline of the battered-woman's syndrome. . . .

In addition, Dr. Veronen was prepared to testify as to how, as a battered woman, Gladys Kelly perceived her situation at the time of the stabbing, and why, in her opinion, defendant did not leave her husband despite the constant beatings she endured.

Whether expert testimony on the battered-woman's syndrome should be admitted in this case depends on whether it is relevant to defendant's claim of self-defense, and, in any event, on whether the proffer meets the standards for admission of expert testimony in this state. We examine first the law of self-defense and consider whether the expert testimony is relevant.

. . . The use of force against another in self-defense is justifiable "when the actor reasonably believes that such force is immediately necessary for the purpose of protecting himself against the use of unlawful force by such other person on the present occasion." N.J.S.A. 2C:3-4(a). Further limitations exist when deadly force is used in self-defense. The use of such deadly force is not justifiable

> unless the actor reasonably believes that such force is necessary to protect himself against death or serious bodily harm. . . . [N.J.S.A. 2C:3-4(b)(2).]

Gladys Kelly claims that she stabbed her husband in self-defense, believing he was about to kill her. The gist of the State's case was that Gladys Kelly was the aggressor, that she consciously intended to kill her husband, and that she certainly was not acting in self-defense.

The credibility of Gladys Kelly is a critical issue in this case. If the jury does not believe Gladys Kelly's account, it cannot find she acted in self-defense. The expert testimony offered was directly relevant to one of the critical elements of that account, namely, what Gladys Kelly believed at the time of the stabbing, and was thus material to establish the honesty of her stated belief that she was in imminent danger of death. . . .

As can be seen from our discussion of the expert testimony, Dr. Veronen would have bolstered Gladys Kelly's credibility. Specifically, by showing that her experience, although concededly difficult to comprehend, was common to that of other women who had been in similarly abusive relationships, Dr. Veronen would have helped the jury understand that Gladys Kelly could have honestly feared that she would suffer serious bodily harm from her husband's attacks, yet still remain with him. This, in turn, would support Ms. Kelly's testimony about her state of mind (that is, that she honestly feared serious bodily harm) at the time of the stabbing.

On the facts of this case, we find that the expert testimony was relevant to Gladys Kelly's state of mind, namely, it was admissible to show she *honestly* believed she was in imminent danger of death. . . .

We also find the expert testimony relevant to the reasonableness of defendant's belief that she was in imminent danger of death or serious injury. We do not mean that the expert's testimony could be used to show that it was understandable that a battered woman might believe that her life was in danger when indeed it was not and when a reasonable person would not have so believed. . . . Expert testimony in that direction would be relevant solely to the honesty of defendant's belief, not its objective reasonableness. Rather, our conclusion is that the expert's testimony, if accepted by the jury, would have aided it in determining whether, under the circumstances, a reasonable person would have believed there was imminent danger to her life.

At the heart of the claim of self-defense was defendant's story that she had been repeatedly subjected to "beatings" over the course of her marriage. . . . When that regular pattern of serious physical abuse is combined with defendant's claim that the decedent sometimes threatened to kill her, defendant's statement that on this occasion she thought she might be killed when she saw Mr. Kelly running toward her could be found to reflect a reasonable fear; that is, it could so be found if the jury believed Gladys Kelly's story of the prior beatings, if it believed her story of the prior threats, and, of course, if it believed her story of the events of that particular day.

The crucial issue of fact on which this expert's testimony would bear is why, given such allegedly severe and constant beatings, combined with threats to kill, defendant had not long ago left decedent. Whether raised by the prosecutor as a factual issue or not, our own common knowledge tells us that most of us, including the ordinary juror, would ask himself or herself just such a question. [O]ne of the common myths, apparently believed by most people, is that battered wives are free to leave. To some, this misconception is followed by the observation that the battered wife is masochistic, proven by her refusal to leave despite the severe beatings; to others, however, the fact that the battered wife stays on unquestionably suggests that the "beatings" could not have been too bad for if they had been, she certainly would have left. The expert could clear up these myths, by explaining that one of the common characteristics of a battered wife is her *inability* to leave despite such constant beatings; her "learned helplessness"; her lack of anywhere to go; her feeling that if she tried to leave, she would be subjected to even more merciless treatment; her belief in the omnipotence of her battering husband; and sometimes her hope that her husband will change his ways. . . .

The difficulty with the expert's testimony is that it *sounds* as if an expert is giving knowledge to a jury about something the jury knows as well as anyone else, namely, the reasonableness of a person's fear of imminent serious danger. That is not at all, however, what this testimony is *directly* aimed at. It is aimed at an area where the purported common knowledge of the jury may be very much mistaken, an area where jurors' logic, drawn from their own experience, may lead to a wholly incorrect conclusion. . . . After hearing the expert, instead of saying Gladys Kelly could not have been beaten up so badly for if she had, she certainly would have left, the jury could conclude that her failure to leave was very much part and parcel of her life as a battered wife. The jury could conclude that instead of casting doubt on the accuracy of her testimony about the severity and frequency of prior beatings, her failure to leave actually reinforced her credibility.

Since a retrial is necessary, we think it advisable to indicate the limit of the expert's testimony on this issue of reasonableness. It would not be proper for the expert to express the opinion that defendant's belief on that day was reasonable, not because this is the ultimate issue, but because the area of *expert* knowledge relates, in this regard, to the reasons for defendant's failure to leave her husband. Either the jury accepts or rejects that explanation and, based on that, credits defendant's stories about the beatings she suffered. No expert is needed, however, once the jury has made up its mind on those issues, to tell the jury the logical conclusion, namely, that a person who has in fact been severely and continuously beaten might very well reasonably fear that the imminent beating she was about to suffer could be either life-threatening or pose a risk of serious injury. What the expert could state was that defendant had the battered-woman's syndrome, and could explain that syndrome in detail, relating its characteristics to defendant, but only to enable the jury better to determine the honesty and reasonableness of defendant's belief. Depending on its content, the expert's testimony might also enable the jury to find that the battered wife, because of the prior beatings, numerous beatings, as often as once a week, for seven years, from the day they were married to the day he died, is particularly able to predict accurately the likely extent of violence in any attack on her. That conclusion could significantly affect the jury's evaluation of the reasonableness of defendant's fear for her life.

Having determined that testimony about the battered-woman's syndrome is relevant, we now consider whether Dr. Veronen's testimony satisfies the limitations placed on expert testimony by Evidence Rule 56(2) and by applicable case law. . . . In effect, this Rule imposes three basic requirements for the admission of expert testimony: (1) the intended testimony must concern a subject matter that is beyond the ken of the average juror; (2) the field testified to must be at a state of the art such that an expert's testimony could be sufficiently reliable; and (3) the witness must have sufficient expertise to offer the intended testimony. [The court remanded for a hearing on these issues.[a]]

NOTES ON THE BATTERED WOMAN'S SYNDROME

1. *The problem of domestic violence.* Justice Department surveys indicate that in a single recent year, almost one million women were severely beaten by their spouse or other domestic partner. Men too are frequently slapped, kicked or beaten by their spouse or girlfriend, but they are much less likely to be victims of the most serious assaults; in the Justice Department survey, 148,000 men were victims of significant domestic violence. Thus, women are almost seven times more likely to be the victim of a serious domestic assault. And although the debate about battered spouse syndrome has focused attention on women who kill their spouses, men are three times more likely than women to kill their spouse or partner.[6]

Wife beating has a long, ignominious history; at one time the common law explicitly granted the husband a legal privilege to chastise and punish his wife.[7] This prerogative disappeared in the nineteenth century, but police and prose-

a. On remand, the prosecution did not challenge the admissibility of the expert's evidence on the battered woman's syndrome. Instead it offered its own experts to support the conclusion that the defendant did not meet the criteria of a battered woman. Apparently the strategy was successful because at the second trial she was again convicted of reckless manslaughter. See Bergen (N.J.) Record, June 27, 1985, p. A21; Elizabeth Schneider, Describing and Changing: Women's Self-Defense Work and the Problem of Expert Testimony on Battering, 9 Women's Rights L. Rptr. 195, 205n.59 (1986). —Eds.

6. U.S. Dept. of Justice, Natl. Institute of Justice, Batterer Programs: What Criminal Justice Agencies Need to Know 2 (July 1998).

7. See Reva B. Siegel, "The Rule of Love": Wife Beating as Prerogative and Privacy, 105 Yale L. J. 2117 (1996).

cutors continued to ignore or tolerate the practice (and more severe physical abuses) until very recent times. Until the 1980s, many police departments had rules expressly discouraging officers from making an arrest in response to a domestic-violence complaint. The battered woman's perception that legal authorities offered no recourse often was well grounded in fact.

This picture began to change, at least to some extent, in the 1980s.[8] Many police departments began to encourage or even mandate an arrest in domestic-violence cases. Advocates for battered women strongly urged the adoption of mandatory-arrest policies and "no-drop" policies to prevent prosecutors from declining to prosecute such cases. An initial empirical study, conducted in Minneapolis, provided strong support for the hypothesis that mandatory arrest would deter battering, but subsequent studies raised concern about possible countervailing effects. Because battered women often are economically dependent on, and fearful of, their male partners, mandatory-arrest policies in some instances seemed to deter reporting and calls for help by women, more than they deterred violence by men. There was also some evidence that mandatory-arrest policies sometimes prompted the arrested men to be to *more* violent toward their spouses afterward, especially over the long run. One scholar who initially supported mandatory arrest cautioned that in light of later studies, the mandatory-arrest approach to domestic violence "may make as much sense as fighting a fire with gasoline."[9]

The jury is still out on this issue, but in the meantime many advocates for battered women also have begun to question mandatory-arrest and no-drop policies, arguing that these approaches give too little weight to the victim's own sense of what kind of official intervention would be best for her.[10] Few professionals in this field believe that vigorous prosecution and punishment of batterers can be sufficient by themselves. Current proposals often seek enhanced possibilities for arrest, prosecution, and court orders of protection, while coordinating these criminal-justice responses with more social and economic support for victims, an improved system of shelters for battered women and their children, and social/psychological treatment for batterers.[11]

Needless to say, implementation of approaches like these and the resources devoted to them vary widely from community to community. Awareness of what help is available can vary among abused women as well. Although substantial progress has been made in the past two decades, the problems of domestic violence are still a long way from being solved. Thus, as in the past, women at times may in some sense be trapped in an abusive relationship, or have reasons to believe they are.

8. See Lawrence W. Sherman, Policing Domestic Violence: Experiments and Dilemmas (1992); Stephen J. Schulhofer, The Feminist Challenge in Criminal Law, 143 U. Pa. L. Rev. 2151, 2158-2170 (1994); Joan Zorza, The Criminal Law of Misdemeanor Domestic Violence, 83 J. Crim. L. & Criminology 46 (1992).

9. Sherman, supra at 210.

10. Linda G. Mills, Killing Her Softly: Intimate Abuse and the Violence of State Intervention, 113 Harv. L. Rev. 550 (1999). Compare Cheryl Hanna, No Right to Choose: Mandated Victim Participation in Domestic Violence Prosecutions, 109 Harv. L. Rev. 1849, 1909 (1996), assessing the problems and concluding that "leaving the choice of prosecution to the victim . . . creates more problems than it solves."

11. See U.S. Dept. of Justice, supra note 6. A related "survivor-centered" approach places the victim's emotional needs at the center of attention. Mills, supra note 10.

2. *When battered women kill.* The idea of a battered woman's syndrome and its use to support a criminal-law defense are subjects discussed in an extensive literature.[12] We focus here on the issues that arise when battered-woman testimony is invoked in connection with a claim of justified self-defense. But we should note that such testimony may also be used in an effort to establish a partial excuse. See page 421 supra, discussing heat-of-passion manslaughter, page 851 infra, discussing duress, and page 919 infra, discussing diminished capacity.

3. *The issue of reasonableness.* Is evidence of battered woman's syndrome relevant to whether the defendant's response to the situation was reasonable? The *Kelly* court appears to say yes, but *not* because the standard is that of the reasonable battered woman. Most courts seem to agree that the syndrome evidence is relevant to reasonableness, but only in a limited way. Explaining the appropriate standard, the California Supreme Court has said (People v. Humphrey, 13 Cal.4th 1073, 1086-1087 (1996)):

> [T]he jury, in determining objective reasonableness, must view the situation from the *defendant's perspective.* [T]he prosecutor argued that, "from an objective, reasonable man's standard, there was no reason for her to go get that gun. This threat that she says he made was like so many threats before. There was no reason for her to react that way." Dr. Browker's testimony supplied a response that the jury might not otherwise receive. As violence increases over time, and threats gain credibility, a battered person might become sensitized and thus able reasonably to discern when danger is real and when it is not. . . .
>
> The Attorney General concedes that Hampton's behavior towards defendant, including prior threats and violence, was relevant to reasonableness, but distinguishes between evidence of this *behavior*—which the trial court fully admitted—and *expert testimony* about its effects on defendant. The distinction is untenable. "To effectively present the situation as perceived by the defendant, and the reasonableness of her fear, the defense has the option to explain her feelings to enable the jury to overcome stereotyped impressions about women who remain in abusive relationships. It is appropriate that the jury be given a professional explanation of the battering syndrome and its effects on the woman through the use of expert testimony." (*State v. Allery* (1984), 682 P.2d 312, 316.)
>
> Contrary to the Attorney General's argument, we are not changing the standard from objective to subjective, or replacing the reasonable "person" standard with a reasonable "battered woman" standard. Our decision would not, in another context, compel adoption of a "'reasonable gang member' standard." . . . The jury must consider defendant's situation and knowledge, which makes the evidence relevant, but the ultimate question is whether a reasonable *person,* not a reasonable battered woman, would believe in the need to kill to prevent imminent harm. Moreover, it is the *jury,* not the expert, that determines whether defendant's belief and, ultimately, her actions, were objectively reasonable.

A few courts have moved closer to a fully subjective standard. According to State v. Leidholm, 334 N.W.2d 811, 818 (N.D. 1983), the jury should be told that the

12. See Regina A. Schuller & Neil Vidmar, BWS Evidence in the Courtroom: A Review of the Literature, 16 Law & Hum. Behav. 273 (1992). For some of the writing see Cynthia Gillespie, Justifiable Homicide: Battered Women, Self Defense and the Law (1989); Lenore Walker, Battered Women Syndrome and Self-Defense, 6 N.D.J.L. Ethics & Pub. Poly. 321 (1992); B. S. Byrd, Till Death Do Us Part: A Comparative Law Approach to Justifying Lethal Self-Defense by Battered Women, 1991 Duke J Comp. & Intl. L. 169; Holly Maguigan, Battered Women and Self-Defense: Myths and Misconceptions in Court Reform Proposals, 140 U. Pa. L. Rev. 379 (1991); Martha R. Mahoney, Legal Images of Battered Women: Redefining the Issue of Separation, 90 Mich. L. Rev. 1 (1991).

"defendant's conduct is not to be judged by what a reasonably cautious person might or might not do"; juries instead should "assume the physical *and psychological* properties peculiar to the accused . . . and then decide whether or not the particular circumstances . . . were sufficient to create [a] reasonable belief that the use of force was necessary. . . ." (emphasis added). This approach, the court said, "allows the jury to judge the reasonableness of the accused's actions against the accused's subjective impressions of the need to use force rather than against those impressions . . . that a hypothetical reasonably cautious person would have."

State v. Edwards, 2000 Mo. App. Lexis 427 (Mo. App. 2000), takes a further step in this direction. The trial judge told the jury to "consider this [battered spouse] evidence in determining . . . whether defendant who was suffering from Battered Spouse's Syndrome reasonably believed she was in imminent danger." The appellate court found this instruction "contradictory . . . and misleading" because it told the jury to assess the question of reasonable belief "based on what a hypothetical reasonable and prudent person would think." The correct approach, the court said, was to weigh the evidence "in light of how an otherwise reasonable person who is suffering from battered spouse syndrome would have perceived and reacted in view of the prolonged history of abuse."

Is it appropriate to individualize the standard to this extent? Professor Stephen Morse thinks not (The "New Syndrome Excuse" Syndrome, Criminal Justice Ethics, pp. 12-13 (Winter/Spring 1995)):

> [I]t is almost impossible to assert sensibly that [barriers to escape] always exist when the syndrome sufferer is in no immediate danger. . . . In response, advocates [for battered women who kill] argue that the battered victim syndrome affects the sufferer's cognitive and volitional functioning, making it difficult or impossible for [her] to recognize or to utilize the alternatives. [I]f these assertions are true, and I believe that they often are, the defendant is really claiming an excuse based on impaired rationality or volition. [P]artial excuses, such as "extreme emotional disturbance" or "imperfect self defense" [can be] employ[ed]. [But killing] was not the right thing to do, and it should not be justified. . . .
>
> To avoid this logic, [advocates for battered women] sometimes argue that the reasonable person standard should be subjectivized to "the reasonable battered victim syndrome sufferer." . . . But this claim makes a mockery of objective standards. . . . Talk of the "the reasonable battered victim syndrome sufferer" is akin to talk of the "reasonable person suffering from paranoia." . . . Such relativization of ethical standards is . . . impossible for the law to adopt if it is to maintain its moral basis.

Do you agree? Consider the following views on the issue:

Elizabeth Schneider, Describing and Changing: Women's Self-Defense Work and the Problem of Expert Testimony on Battering, 9 Women's Right L. Rptr. 195, 211-212 (1986): A battered woman who has been the victim of abuse for many years and has survived it before must credibly explain why it was necessary to act on that occasion. Expert testimony, admitted for the purpose of explaining why the battered woman did not leave, does not help the jury answer the question whether she was reasonable in acting violently in order to save her life. It thus does not address the basic defense problem that the battered woman faces. Indeed, if the testimony is limited, or perceived as limited to the issue of why the woman does not leave, it highlights a contradiction implicit in the message of battered woman syndrome — if the battered woman was so helpless and passive, why did she kill the batterer?

In fairness . . . , the *Kelly* opinion does mention that "the expert's testimony might also enable the jury to find that the battered wife, because of the prior beatings . . . is particularly able to predict accurately the likely extent of violence in any attack on her" and "that conclusion could significantly affect the jury's evaluation of the reasonableness of defendant's fear for her life." This is a crucial point, indeed in most cases this is the real importance of the testimony. Yet the court seems to minimize the importance of this broader and more central understanding of relevance by its statement that the expert testimony is not relevant to the jury's determination of the reasonableness of a person's fear of imminent severe danger because this is "something the jury knows as well as anyone else."

. . . The reasonableness of the woman's fear and the reasonableness of her act are *not* issues which the jury knows as well as anyone else. The jury needs expert testimony on reasonableness precisely because the jury may not understand that the battered woman's prediction of the likely extent and imminence of violence is particularly acute and accurate.

Susan Estrich, Defending Women (Book Review, Cynthia Gillespie, Justifiable Homicide: Battered Women, Self-Defense and the Law (1989)), 88 Mich. L. Rev. 1430, 1434-1437 (1990): The problem here, as always in the criminal law, is striking the balance between the defender's subjective perceptions and those of the hypothetical reasonable person. To apply a purely objective standard is unduly harsh because it ignores the characteristics which inevitably and justifiably shape the defender's perspective, thus holding him (or her) to a standard he simply cannot meet. If the defender is young or crippled or blind, we should not expect him to behave like a strapping, sighted adult. On the other hand, if the reasonable person has all of the defender's characteristics, the standard loses any normative component and becomes entirely subjective. Applying a purely subjective standard in all cases would give free rein to the short-tempered, the pugnacious, and the foolhardy who see threats of harm where the rest of us would not and who blind themselves to opportunities for escape that seem plainly available. These unreasonable people may not be as wicked as (although perhaps more dangerous than) cold-blooded murderers — imperfect self-defense generally reduces murder to manslaughter — but neither are they, in practical or legal terms, justified in causing death. . . .

In this context, "reasonableness" can have two possible meanings. First, a woman's choice may be "reasonable," even if it conflicts with our own (or a mythical other's) assessment of the situation, if the woman is indeed right, or probably right, or at least more likely right than us, in her assessment. [H]er experience as a battered woman, and the syndrome from which she suffers, [may make] her a better judge than us of the seriousness of the situation she actually faces. . . .

But what of the woman who shoots her husband while he is sound asleep, and not, by anyone's account, about to do anything? What of the woman who faces a beating, but not — even within her own or her expert's description of the cycles of violence — serious bodily harm? Put aside the woman who has tried to escape in the past and been beaten for it, or who has called the police and been rebuffed, or who would be leaving her young children defenseless if she left. In these cases, properly applied, the retreat requirement cannot be met with the necessary "complete safety." But what of the woman who has never tried any of these alternatives? What of the woman who could walk out the back door and into a neighbor's house?

In such cases, the "reasonableness" inquiry, and the evidence of battered woman's syndrome, does not really go to the rightness of the woman's belief in the need for deadly force. It is, instead, a request to abandon the limits on self-defense out of empathy for the circumstances of the defender and disgust for the acts of her abuser. We can find her belief in the imminence of danger "reasonable" only by deciding that these standards mean less in the home than outside it, mean less when applied to cruel husbands who torment defenseless wives than to others.

On its face, that is a very uncomfortable request — at least for those of us who see in the rules of self-defense a laudable recognition of the value of human life and a desirable effort to articulate a normative standard which protects even aggressors and wrongdoers from instant execution or vigilante justice.

4. *The issue of scientific reliability.* (*a*) At the time *Kelly* was decided courts were divided over whether the experts' testimony on the battered woman's syndrome was sufficiently reliable to allow it to go to the jury. Today its admissibility is overwhelmingly accepted by courts and legislatures. See Rogers v. State, 616 So. 2d 1098, 1100 (Fla. Ct. App. 1993). In some jurisdictions the issue is resolved by statute. See, e.g., Cal. Evid. Code §1107(b) (1991) ("Expert opinion testimony on battered women's syndrome shall not be considered a new scientific technique whose reliability is unproven"). Texas has the broadest provision inasmuch as it is not restricted to battered woman's cases. Tex. Pen. Code §19.06 (Vernon Supp. 1992):

> In a prosecution for murder or manslaughter . . . the defendant, in order to establish the defendant's reasonable belief that use of force or deadly force was immediately necessary, shall be permitted to offer: (1) relevant evidence that the defendant had been the victim of acts of family violence committed by the deceased, . . . and (2) relevant expert testimony regarding the condition of the mind of the defendant at the time of the offense, including those relevant facts and circumstances relating to family violence that are the basis of the expert's opinion.

(*b*) Concerns about the methodology and reliability of establishing the battered woman's syndrome have been raised. See Note (David L. Faigman), The Battered Woman Syndrome and Self-Defense: A Legal and Empirical Dissent, 72 Va. L. Rev. 619 (1986). The author points to several empirical problems underlying the theory that a syndrome afflicts battered women. He notes that the pivotal research of Lenore Walker leaves unclear the nature of the "loving contrition" phase in the "cycle of violence" and does not indicate whether battered women felt powerless or unable to leave during the periods when intimidation was in abeyance. In addition, he suggests that the Walker research does not specify which groups of women experienced which phases of the cycle of violence, and her data imply that at most only 58 percent of those considered battered women experienced all three phases of the cycle. As a result, he argues, the claim that becomes central in self-defense cases — that battered women develop "learned helplessness" and believe themselves unable to flee — lacks verifiable empirical support. Professor Faigman concludes (id. at 647):

The prevailing theories of battered woman syndrome have little evidentiary value in self-defense cases. The work of Lenore Walker, the leading researcher on battered woman syndrome, is unsound and largely irrelevant to the central issues in such cases. The Walker cycle theory suffers from significant methodological and interpretive flaws that render it incapable of explaining why an abused woman strikes out at her mate when she does. Similarly, Walker's application of learned helplessness to the situation of battered women does not account for the actual behavior of many women who remain in battering relationships.

A comprehensive reassessment of the Walker research and subsequent studies expresses similar misgivings. See Robert F. Schopp, Barbara J. Sturgis & Megan Sullivan, Battered Woman Syndrome, Expert Testimony, and the Distinction Between Justification and Excuse, [1994] U. Ill. L. Rev. 45. The authors find that "Walker's data . . . are inconsistent with the notion that learned helplessness determines whether a battered woman leaves the relationship," and that "[o]ther available research . . . provides no strong support for the proposition that the battered woman syndrome is an accurate description of a syndrome that regularly results from battering relationships" (id. at 58-59). The authors conclude (id. at 63-64):

[T]he currently available data do not justify the claim that the battered woman syndrome, as usually formulated, provides a general portrait of those who have suffered battering relationships. . . .

Perhaps most importantly from the perspective of the criminal courts, learned helplessness has been the aspect of the battered woman syndrome most frequently cited as central to cases of self-defense by battered women, yet it draws very little support from the available data. The complete body of work provides neither any clear conception of learned helplessness nor any good reason to believe that it regularly occurs in battered women. . . . Collectively, the data reviewed supports the proposition that battered women do not suffer learned helplessness, at least as well as it supports the claim that they do. Finally, it would be more consistent with the theoretical and empirical foundations of learned helplessness to contend that battered women who kill their batterers differ from those who remain in the battering relationships without killing their batterers precisely because those who kill do *not* manifest learned helplessness.

5. Feminist perspectives. Much feminist writing tends to be strongly supportive of the battered woman's defense. There is, however, a growing feminist reaction against it. See, e.g., Anne M. Coughlin, Excusing Women, 82 Cal. L. Rev. 1 (1994). The author states (at 4-6):

[T]he battered woman syndrome defense . . . institutionalizes within the criminal law negative stereotypes of women. [T]he defense is objectionable because it relieves the accused woman of the stigma and pain of criminal punishment only if she embraces another kind of stigma and pain: she must advance an interpretation of her own activity that labels it the irrational product of a "mental health disorder."

[Moreover,] the negative implications for women go far beyond the reinforcement of . . . stereotyped gender roles. . . . None of those who advocate, or, for that matter, criticize, adoption of the battered woman syndrome defense has noticed that, for many centuries, the criminal law has been content to excuse women for criminal misconduct on the ground that they cannot be expected to, and, indeed, should not, resist the influence exerted by their husbands. No similar excuse has ever been afforded to men; to the contrary, the criminal law consistently has demanded that men withstand any pressures in their lives that compel them to commit crimes, including pressures exerted by their spouses. In this way, the theory of criminal responsibility has participated in the construction of marriage and, indeed, of gender, as a hierarchical relationship. By construing wives as incapable of choosing lawful conduct when faced with unlawful influence from their spouses, the theory invests men with the authority to govern both themselves and their irresponsible wives.

The battered woman syndrome defense rests on and reaffirms this invidious understanding of women's incapacity for rational self-control.

6. Other syndrome evidence. Many courts that permit the use of battered woman's syndrome to support a claim of self-defense accept similiar evidence in cases involving a battered or abused child who kills the abusive parent.[13] A few, however, do not.[14] How far should the logic of such "syndrome" defenses be extended? See Robert P. Mosteller, Syndromes and Politics in Criminal Trials and Evidence Law, 46 Duke L. J. 461 (1996). In Werner v. State, 711 S.W.2d 639 (Tex. Crim. App. 1986), the defendant appealed his conviction of murder, complaining that the trial court erred in refusing to permit the jury to hear the testimony of his expert witness. He had raised the issue of self-defense, and the witness would have testified that the defendant, as the son of a Nazi concentration camp survivor, was a victim of a so-called "Holocaust Syndrome," which causes people to be unusually assertive in confrontational settings, as a reaction to the memory of Jewish concentration camp victims who did not fight back. The court rejected his argument, stating: "The evidence excluded only tended to show that possibly appellant was not an ordinary and prudent man with respect to self-defense. This did not entitle appellant to an enlargement of the statutory defense on account of his psychological peculiarities" (id. at 646). The dissent made the following observations:

> Dr. Roden's testimony was highly relevant on the issue of the condition of the appellant's state of mind at the time he fired the fatal shot, and would have aided the jury, all of whom were probably totally unfamiliar with this type syndrome, in better deciding . . . how his suffering from "The Holocaust Syndrome" affected the condition of his mind at that time. . . .
>
> When a relatively large number of persons, having the same symptoms, exhibit a combination or variation of functional psychiatric disorders that lead to purely emotional stress that causes intense mental anguish or emotional trauma, . . . the psychiatrists put those persons under one or more labels. Today, we have the following labels: "The Battered Wife Syndrome"; "The Battered Child Syndrome"; "The Battered Husband Syndrome"; "The Battered Parent Syndrome"; "The Battle Fatigue Syndrome"; "The Policeman's Syndrome"; and "The Holocaust Syndrome." Tomorrow, there will probably be additions to the list, such as "The Appellate Court Judge Syndrome." . . .
>
> If scientific, technical, or other specialized knowledge will assist the trier of fact

13. See, e.g., State v. Nemeth, 694 N.E.2d 1332 (Ohio 1998); State v. Janes, 850 P.2d 495 (Wash. 1993).

14. See Jamie H. Sacks, Comment, A New Age of Understanding: Allowing Self-Defense Claims for Battered Children Who Kill Their Abusers, 10 J. Contemp. Health L. & Pol. 349 (1994); Joelle Anne Moreno, Killing Daddy: Developing a Self-Defense Strategy for the Abused Child, 137 U. Pa. L. Rev. 1281 (1989).

to better understand the evidence or determine a fact in issue, a witness . . . qualified as an expert by knowledge, skill, experience, training, or education, . . . should be able to testify in the form of opinion evidence.

In this instance, I find that the subject "The Holocaust Syndrome" was beyond the ken of the average lay person. The jury was entitled to know that when the appellant fired the fatal shot [his] state of mind . . . was affected, not only by that which he visually saw on the night in question, but also [by] his belief that it was necessary for him to defend himself because he comes from a family who did not defend themselves, thus causing them to perish in the Holocaust.

STATE v. NORMAN

Supreme Court of North Carolina
324 N.C. 253, 378 S.E.2d 8 (1989)

MITCHELL, J. The defendant was tried [for] the first degree murder of her husband. The jury found the defendant guilty of voluntary manslaughter. The defendant appealed from the trial court's judgment sentencing her to six years imprisonment. The Court of Appeals granted a new trial, citing as error the trial court's refusal to submit a possible verdict of acquittal by reason of perfect self-defense.

[The defendant's evidence tended to show the following: The 39-year-old defendant was badly abused by her husband during most of their 25-year marriage. He frequently punched and kicked her, threw beer bottles and other objects at her, and burned her with cigarettes or hot coffee. He forced her into prostitution at a local truck stop and then humiliated her in public and at home by calling her "dog," "bitch," or "whore" and forcing her to eat pet food from a bowl on the floor. For years he threatened to maim her and to kill her.

[The day before she killed him, defendant's husband beat her so badly that she called the police. When they arrived, however, they would not arrest him unless she filed a complaint, which she was afraid to do. An hour later she tried to kill herself. When paramedics came to assist her, her husband tried to interfere, insisting that they let her die. He was chased back into the house by a sheriff's deputy but was not arrested.

[The next morning she went to the local mental health center to talk about filing charges and possibly having her husband committed. When she confronted him with this possibility, he threatened to cut her throat before he was taken away. Later, defendant went to the social services office to sign up for welfare so that she would no longer have to prostitute herself to feed her children. Her husband followed her to the office, and dragged her from the interview, forcing her to return home. There he beat her and burned her with cigarettes. He refused to let her eat and forced her to sleep on the floor. When her grandchild began to cry, defendant crept out of the house, and took the baby to her mother's home so that it would not wake up defendant's husband. She returned with a pistol, went to the bedroom, and tried to shoot her husband in the back of the head. The gun jammed, but she fixed it and shot him. After she determined that he was still moving, she fired two more shots into the back of his head.]

Based on the evidence that the defendant exhibited battered wife syndrome, that she believed she could not escape her husband nor expect help from others, that her husband had threatened her, and that her husband's abuse of her had worsened in the two days preceding his death, the Court of Appeals concluded that a jury reasonably could have found that her killing of her husband was justified as an act of perfect self-defense. The Court of Appeals reasoned that the nature of battered wife syndrome is such that a jury could not be precluded from finding the defendant killed her husband lawfully in perfect self-defense, even though he was asleep when she killed him. We disagree. . . .

In North Carolina, a defendant is entitled to have the jury consider acquittal by reason of *perfect* self-defense when the evidence, viewed in the light most favorable to the defendant, tends to show that at the time of the killing it appeared to the defendant and she believed it to be necessary to kill the decedent to save herself from imminent death or great bodily harm. That belief must be reasonable, however, in that the circumstances as they appeared to the defendant would create such a belief in the mind of a person of ordinary firmness. . . . A killing in the proper exercise of the right of *perfect* self-defense is always completely justified in law and constitutes no legal wrong.

Our law also recognizes an *imperfect* right of self-defense in certain circumstances, including, for example, when the defendant is the initial aggressor, but without intent to kill or to seriously injure the decedent, and the decedent escalates the confrontation to a point where it reasonably appears to the defendant to be necessary to kill the decedent to save herself from imminent death or great bodily harm.[a] Although the culpability of a defendant who kills in the exercise of *imperfect* self-defense is reduced, such a defendant is *not justified* in the killing so as to be entitled to acquittal, but is guilty at least of voluntary manslaughter.

The defendant in the present case was not entitled to a jury instruction on either perfect or imperfect self-defense. . . .

The killing of another human being is the most extreme recourse to our inherent right of self-preservation and can be justified in law only by the utmost real or apparent necessity brought about by the decedent. . . . Only [where it is shown that defendant] killed due to a reasonable belief that death or great bodily harm was imminent can the justification for homicide remain clearly and firmly rooted in necessity. . . .

The term "imminent," as used to describe such perceived threats of death or great bodily harm as will justify a homicide by reason of perfect self-defense, has been defined as "immediate danger, such as must be instantly met, such as cannot be guarded against by calling for the assistance of others or the protection of the law." Black's Law Dictionary 676 (5th ed. 1979). . . .

The evidence in this case did not tend to show that the defendant reasonably believed that she was confronted by a threat of imminent death or great bodily harm. [H]er husband had been asleep for some time when she [shot him] three times in the back of the head. [A]ll of the evidence tended to show that the defendant had ample time and opportunity to resort to other means of preventing further abuse by her husband. There was no action underway by the decedent from which the jury could have found that the defendant had reasonable grounds to believe either that a felonious assault was imminent or that it might result in her death or great bodily injury.

a. Imperfect self-defense, as we have seen, supra page 762, more commonly applies when the jury concludes that the defendant truly believed she had to kill to avoid an imminent threat to her life, but that her belief was not reasonable. —Eds.

[T]he lack of any belief by the defendant — reasonable or otherwise — that she faced a threat of imminent death or great bodily harm from the drunk and sleeping victim in the present case was illustrated by the defendant and her own expert witnesses. . . .

Dr. Tyson . . . testified that the defendant "believed herself to be doomed . . . to a life of the worst kind of torture and abuse, degradation that she had experienced over the years in a progressive way; that it would only get worse, and that death was inevitable." . . . [A] defendant's subjective belief of what might be "inevitable" at some indefinite point in the future does not equate to what she believes to be "imminent." Dr. Tyson's opinion that the defendant believed it was necessary to kill her husband for "the protection of herself and her family" was similarly indefinite and devoid of time frame and did not tend to show a threat or fear of *imminent* harm.

The defendant testified that, "I knowed when he woke up, it was going to be the same thing, and I was scared when he took me to the truck stop that night it was going to be worse than he had ever been." She also testified, when asked if she believed her husband's threats: "Yes. . . . [H]e would kill me if he got a chance. If he thought he wouldn't a had to went to jail, he would a done it." Testimony about such indefinite fears concerning what her sleeping husband might do at some time in the future did not tend to establish a fear — reasonable or otherwise — of *imminent death or great bodily harm* at the time of the killing.

We are not persuaded by the reasoning of our Court of Appeals in this case that when there is evidence of battered wife syndrome, neither an actual attack nor threat of attack by the husband at the moment the wife uses deadly force is required to justify the wife's killing of him in perfect self-defense. The Court of Appeals concluded that to impose such requirements would ignore the "learned helplessness," meekness and other realities of battered wife syndrome and would effectively preclude such women from exercising their right of self-defense. . . .

The reasoning of our Court of Appeals in this case proposes to change the established law of self-defense by giving the term "imminent" a meaning substantially more indefinite and all-encompassing than its present meaning. This would result in a substantial relaxation of the requirement of real or apparent necessity to justify homicide. Such reasoning proposes justifying the taking of human life not upon the reasonable belief it is necessary to prevent death or great bodily harm — which the imminence requirement ensures — but upon purely subjective speculation that the decedent probably would present a threat of life at a future time and that the defendant would not be able to avoid the predicted threat.

The Court of Appeals suggests that such speculation would have been particularly reliable in the present case because the jury, based on the evidence of the decedent's intensified abuse during the thirty-six hours preceding his death, could have found that the decedent's passive state at the time of his death was "but a momentary hiatus in a continuous reign of terror by the decedent [and] the defendant merely took advantage of her first opportunity to protect herself." Requiring jury instructions on perfect self-defense in such situations, however, would still tend to make opportune homicide lawful as a result of mere subjective predictions of indefinite future assaults and circumstances. Such predictions of future assaults to justify the defendant's use of deadly force in this case would be entirely speculative, because there was no evidence that her husband had ever inflicted any harm upon her that approached life-threatening injury, even during the "reign of terror." It is far from clear in the defendant's poignant evidence that any abuse by the decedent had ever involved the degree of physical threat required to justify the defendant in using deadly force, even when those threats were imminent. The use of deadly force in self-defense to prevent harm other than death or great bodily harm is excessive as a matter of law.

[The court also ruled that the defendant was not entitled to instructions on *imperfect* self-defense. It held that the imminence requirement applied to both perfect and imperfect self-defense and that the defendant did not meet the requirements for imperfect self-defense because there was no evidence that she actually believed the use of deadly force against her was imminent. The court also noted, however, that the failure to instruct on imperfect self-defense, even if error, was harmless because the defendant was convicted only of voluntary manslaughter; an instruction on imperfect self-defense would have given her nothing more, because in North Carolina killings in cases of imperfect self-defense are treated as voluntary manslaughter.]

[W]e conclude that the defendant's conviction for voluntary manslaughter and the trial court's judgment sentencing her to a six-year term of imprisonment were without error. Therefore, we must reverse the decision of the Court of Appeals which awarded the defendant a new trial.

MARTIN, J., dissenting. . . . Defendant does not seek to expand or relax the requirements of self-defense and thereby "legalize the opportune killing of allegedly abusive husbands by their wives," as the majority overstates. Rather, defendant contends that the evidence as gauged by the existing laws of self-defense is sufficient to require the submission of a self-defense instruction to the jury. . . . I conclude that it was. . . .

Evidence presented by defendant described a twenty-year history of beatings and other dehumanizing and degrading treatment by her husband. In his expert testimony a clinical psychologist . . . described the defendant as a woman incarcerated by abuse, by fear, and by her conviction that her husband was invincible and inescapable:

> Mrs. Norman didn't leave because she believed, fully believed that escape was totally impossible. There was no place to go. He, she had left before; he had come and gotten her. She had gone to the Department of Social Services. He had come and gotten her. The law, she believed the law could not protect her; no one could protect her, and I must admit, looking over the records, that there was nothing done that would contradict that belief. . . .

Evidence presented in the case sub judice revealed no letup of tension or fear, no moment in which the defendant felt released from impending serious harm, even while the decedent slept. . . . For the battered wife, if there is no escape, if there is no window of relief or momentary sense of safety, then the next attack, which could be the fatal one, is imminent. . . . Properly stated, the . . . [question] is not whether the threat was *in fact* imminent, but whether defendant's belief in the impending nature of the threat, given the circumstances as she saw them, was reasonable in the mind of a person of ordinary firmness.

Defendant's intense fear, based on her belief that her husband intended not only to maim or deface her, as he had in the past, but to kill her, was evident in the testimony of witnesses who recounted events of the last three days of the decedent's life. This testimony could have led a juror to conclude that defendant reasonably perceived a threat to her life as "imminent," even while her husband slept. . . . And from this evidence a juror could find defendant's belief in the necessity to kill her husband not merely reasonable but compelling.

DAVID McCORD & SANDRA K. LYONS, MORAL REASONING AND THE CRIMINAL LAW: THE EXAMPLE OF SELF-DEFENSE, 30 Am. Crim. L. Rev. 97, 110 (1992): [Reviewing the *Norman* decision, the authors conclude that it is in accord with traditional law but not with what is morally required. They say:] There are at least ten significant facts which our common sense and life experience tell us are highly significant in this case but which seem not to be considered by the traditional law. In no particular order these ten are: (1) J. T. and Judy [Norman] were not equally matched in terms of physical prowess, as J. T. apparently was significantly more powerful; (2) Judy was distraught because of the actions of J. T.; (3) Judy's mental state was colored not merely by one single incident of abuse, but by the culmination of twenty years of abuse; (4) Because J. T. lived in the same house as Judy, he had virtually constant access to her to inflict abuse on her; (5) Having Judy at his disposal in this manner, J. T. thus was able to decide when, where, and how to inflict the abuse — he took advantage of the option which the law apparently ceded to him to launch nondeadly attacks on her at his whim, without fear of a justifiable deadly response; (6) Judy's future was bleak — there was no basis for her to believe that J. T. would be content to live without her or that he had any intent to stop abusing her; (7) Judy apparently had no viable alternative but to stay in the vicinity — she had no job skills to support herself elsewhere, and her support network was in that community; (8) Judy had no reasonable prospect of being able to stay in that community outside the presence of J. T., since he would find her anywhere in the vicinity; (9) The governmental authorities failed to take any action to protect Judy despite having been contacted by her; and (10) J. T.'s actions prevented Judy from doing anything further to invoke the help of the governmental authorities.

These ignored facts have no place in the moral reasoning mandated by the traditional law of self-defense, yet they cause us to suffer moral disquiet with the result.

Questions: How could the rules of the law of self-defense be formulated to take account of these morally relevant factors? Would it be desirable to add to the traditional rules allowing self-defense in designated circumstances: "or in any other circumstance in which the defendant's killing of the victim was morally justified"?

NOTES ON THE IMMINENT DANGER REQUIREMENT

1. *Nonconfrontational self-defense.* The great majority of battered-spouse prosecutions involve women who kill their abusers in the course of a direct confrontation that they perceive as involving a threat of immediate harm. In one study, only 20 percent of the cases involved abusers killed in nonconfrontational settings — 8 percent while they slept, 8 percent caught unawares during a lull in the violence, and 4 percent killed by a third party at the abused woman's behest. See Holly Maguigan, Battered Women and Self-Defense: Myths and Misconceptions in Current Reform Proposals, 140 U. Pa. L. Rev. 379, 397 (1991).

The nonconfrontational cases nonetheless pose the greatest challenge to traditional conceptions of self-defense. In cases like *Norman,* where the abuser is killed in his sleep, most courts remain unwilling to admit battered-spouse evidence or to permit jury instructions on the possibility of legitimate self-defense.[15] But some flexibility on this issue is beginning to emerge; a few courts have held that the need for lethal self-defense remains a jury issue even in a sleeping-victim case. In Robinson v. State, 417 S.E.2d 88, 91 (S.C. 1992), the court, citing the *Norman* dissent, held that "even when the batterer is absent or asleep . . . , [w]here torture appears interminable and escape impossible, the belief that only the death of the batterer can provide relief may be reasonable in the mind of a person of ordinary firmness."[16] Do you agree? Should such cases go to the jury on the self-defense issue, even when escape *appears* impossible to the battered woman but is possible in fact? What are the dangers of that approach?

2. *When the battered woman seeks help.* A small but significant number of battered-spouse prosecutions (4 percent in Professor Maguigan's study) involve women who hire or persuade a third party to commit the killing. Do the arguments that favor a self-defense instruction for the woman who kills her abuser while he sleeps extend to this situation as well? To date, all the cases addressing the issue have ruled the woman's claim of self-defense untenable.[17] Is this so clear? If "a person of ordinary firmness" can reasonably believe it necessary to shoot her husband in his sleep, why is it unreasonable for her to enlist the help of a third party in catching him unawares? Consider Stephen J. Schulhofer, The Gender Question in Criminal Law, 7 Soc. Phil. & Pol. 105, 119-120 (1990):

> [I]n thinking about non-confrontational cases . . . the Walker approach turns traditional intuitions inside out. In traditional terms, the strongest . . . of the non-confrontational cases [is] that of the woman who filed for divorce, fled, and sought outside help. But such behavior does not fit the typical pattern of learned helplessness. Expert testimony about battered spouse syndrome could be ruled inadmissible, or prosecution experts could testify that the defendant, even if abused, did not display the battered wife *syndrome,* and therefore could be expected to avoid resort to deadly force.
>
> Conversely, . . . the contract killing begins to look like the strongest case of all. The utter passivity, the inability to act even when the abuser is sleeping, the apparent dependence on the intervention of a male support figure, all reinforce a diagnosis of battered wife syndrome. In fact, Lenore Walker is very explicit in challenging traditional assumptions about contract killing. She writes with irritation that under the traditional approach, "hiring someone else to kill an abusive mate is seen as evidence of premeditation, even though many women, because of sex role

15. E.g., Lane v. State, 957 S.W.2d 584 (Tex. App. 1997); State v. Grant, 470 S.W.2d 1 (N.C. 1996) (reaffirming *Norman*); State v. Smith, 481 S.E.2d 747 (W. Va. 1996).

16. See also Commonwealth v. Springer, 998 S.W.2d 439 (Ky. 1999) (relying in part on statute permitting an inference of imminent danger from a past pattern of serious abuse); cf. Commonwealth v. Saiz, 923 P.2d 197 (Colo. App. 1995) (trial judge permitted self-defense instruction, but jury rejected the defense).

17. E.g., People v. Yaklich, 833 P.2d 758 (Colo. App. 1991); State v. Anderson, 785 S.W.2d 596 (Mo. App. 1990); State v. Leaphart, 673 S.W.2d 870 (Tenn. 1983).

> conditioning or other factors, cannot use sufficient force to protect themselves."[47] Walker concludes that this traditional view is just evidence of the criminal law's "[b]iases . . . against women."

Does this argument imply that self-defense should be available both to the battered woman who herself kills and to the one who hires another to do so? Or that, in the absence of an imminent threat of great bodily harm, it should be available to neither?

3. Defense of another. Suppose that Judy Norman had persuaded a neighbor to help her kill her husband. If, as the dissenting judge argues, she could reasonably believe that killing him was necessary, would the neighbor who helps her have a defense as well? If Judy or the neighbor, being poor shots, hire a hitman to do the job (as in People v. Yaklich, 833 P.2d 758 (Colo. App. 1991)), should the hitman have a valid defense?

The widely accepted rule is that someone who comes to the aid of a person in peril can use deadly force to prevent the attack, under the same circumstances that would justify the use of deadly force by the endangered person herself. See, e.g., Model Penal Code §3.05, Appendix.[18] In the context of the prosecution of a third-party helper, how should we assess the facts in *Norman*? If Judy's lethal action was indeed justified, should it matter who carried out the necessary act? Would a belief in the need to kill J. T. Norman, though reasonable for Judy, not be reasonable for someone observing the situation from outside? Or was such a belief equally reasonable for both?

4. Imminence in other contexts. The generally prevailing rule in the law of self-defense is that force can be used only to rebuff an attack that is imminent, in the sense that it is about to happen right then and there. Is this rule subject to special criticism in the context of battered-spouse cases, or is it flawed in a more general way. Consider these situations:

(*a*) In State v. Schroeder, 199 Neb. 822, 261 N.W.2d 759 (1978), a 19-year-old inmate stabbed his older cell-mate at 1 A.M. while the latter was asleep. He was convicted of assault with intent to inflict great bodily harm. The evidence was that the deceased had a reputation for sex and violence, that the defendant had incurred a large gambling debt to the deceased who threatened to make a "punk" out of him by selling his debt to another prisoner, that before going to bed the morning of the incident the deceased said he might walk in his sleep and "collect" some of the money owed.

The majority found no error in the trial court's failure to give any instruction on self-defense. The court said (261 N.W.2d at 761):

47. Lenore E. Walker, A Response to Elizabeth M. Schneider's Describing and Changing, 9 Women's Rights L. Rptr. 223 (1986).

18. Traditionally, the third party is said to "stand in the shoes" of the person in danger. If that person did *not* have the right to use force, then the third party had no defense, even if he was entirely reasonable in thinking (incorrectly) that force was necessary. People v. Young, 183 N.E.2d 319, 319-320 (N.Y. 1962); State v. Weniger, 390 N.E.2d 801 (Ohio 1979). Many jurisdictions now reject this instance of strict liability and allow the mistaken third party a defense, provided that he holds a reasonable belief in the facts necessary to support the use of defensive force. E.g., State v. Beeley, 653 A.2d 722 (R.I. 1995). Conversely, if the third party knows that deadly force is *not* really necessary (for example, if he knows that the assailant is using an unloaded gun), then he would not be justified in killing the assailant, even if the person attacked might be.

> The problem in this case is that there was no evidence to sustain a finding that the defendant could believe an assault was imminent except the threat that Riggs had made before he went to bed. The general rule is that words alone are not sufficient justification for an assault. . . . There is a very real danger in a rule which would legalize preventive assaults involving the use of deadly force where there has been nothing more than threats. We conclude that the trial court did not err in refusing to instruct the jury as requested.

The dissent stated (id. at 761, 762):

> In this case the defendant was faced with a threat by Riggs that he would "collect some of this money I got owed to me tonight." The defendant could not be expected to remain awake all night, every night, waiting for the attack that Riggs had threatened to make. The defendant's evidence here was such that the jury could have found the defendant was justified in believing the use of force was necessary to protect himself against an attack by Riggs "on the present occasion."

(b) In Ha v. State, 892 P.2d 184 (Alaska App. 1995), the victim, Buu, had a violent argument with the defendant and beat him severely, until he was pulled away by bystanders. Buu left, returned with a hammer, and tried to strike the defendant, but again a bystander intervened. Before leaving, Buu shouted several times that he would kill the defendant. Ha spent a sleepless night thinking about the vicious tendencies of Buu's "violent criminal clan" and their reputation for carrying out their threats. He concluded that Buu or the relatives would someday carry out the threat and that "because of his cultural background and poor command of English, . . . it would be useless to go to the police for help" (id. at 191, 195). He then got a rifle, caught Buu unawares and shot him from behind, killing him. At trial the judge withheld the self-defense issue from the jury, and Ha was convicted of murder.

On appeal, the court concluded that "a reasonable person in Ha's position would have feared death or serious physical injury from Buu," and that the evidence could support a conclusion that "there was no escape. . . . Buu comes from . . . a family of thugs who have a reputation for violence and extortion. . . . Today or tomorrow they would stalk him down" (id. at 191). Nonetheless, the court upheld the conviction, stressing that "'inevitable harm' is not the same as 'imminent' harm. [A] reasonable fear of future harm does not authorize a person to hunt down and kill an enemy" (id.).

Is the result sound? If so, does the same principle bar a self-defense claim on the facts of *Norman* and *Schroeder,* or are the situations distinguishable?

5. The Model Penal Code modestly relaxes the imminence requirement, providing that it is sufficient if the actor reasonably believed that the use of defensive force was "immediately necessary" §3.04(1). Several states have adopted similar language. E.g., N.J. §2C:3-4a; Pa. tit. 18, §505. Some courts have loosened the imminence requirement on their own authority. In State v. Janes, 121 Wash. 2d 220, 241-242 (1993), for example, the court interpreted the statutory imminence requirement as follows:

> Imminence does not require an actual physical assault. A threat, or its equivalent, can support self-defense when there is a reasonable belief that the threat will be carried out. Especially in abusive relationships, patterns of behavior become ap-

> parent which can signal the next abusive episode. . . . That the triggering behavior and the abusive episode are divided by time does not necessarily negate the reasonableness of the defendant's perception of imminent harm. Even an otherwise innocuous comment which occurred days before the homicide could be highly relevant when the evidence shows that such a comment inevitably signaled the beginning of an abusive episode.

Question: Would a self-defense instruction have been required in *Norman* if North Carolina had interpreted imminence in this way?

6. For a critique of both the traditional imminence requirement and the more flexible Model Penal Code standard of immediacy, see Richard A. Rosen, On Self-Defense, Imminence, and Women Who Kill Their Batterers, 71 N.C.L. Rev. 371 (1993). Criticizing the result in *Norman,* Professor Rosen argues that neither imminence nor "immediacy" should be required when a killing is necessary, under all the circumstances, to avoid a nonimminent danger.

7. Jahnke v. State, 682 P.2d 991 (Wyo. 1984), involved a 16-year-old boy who waited with his shotgun for an hour and a half for his parents to return from dinner and then shot his father dead as he entered the house. For 14 years the father apparently had subjected the boy to extreme physical and psychological abuse. The boy was rebuffed in his effort to use the "battered person" syndrome to support a self-defense claim. The Supreme Court found no error and upheld a verdict of voluntary manslaughter. The majority opinion observed:

> Although many people, and the public media, seem to be prepared to espouse the notion that a victim of abuse is entitled to kill the abuser[,] that special justification defense is antithetical to the mores of modern civilized society. It is difficult enough to justify capital punishment as an appropriate response of society to criminal acts even after the circumstances have been carefully evaluated by a number of people. To permit capital punishment to be imposed upon the subjective conclusion of the individual that prior acts and conduct of the deceased justified the killing would amount to a leap into the abyss of anarchy.
>
> . . . It is clear that if [battered person] evidence has any role at all it is in assisting the jury to evaluate the reasonableness of the defendant's fear in a case involving the recognized circumstances of self-defense which include a confrontation or conflict with the deceased not of the defendant's instigation.

A concurring judging commented:

> This is a textbook case of first-degree murder. . . . In his defense, appellant employed the oldest, most common and most successful tactic in homicide cases. He put the deceased on trial. . . . There was no one to speak for the deceased. . . . [But by] no stretch of the imagination was this a case of self-defense.

A dissenting opinion stated:

> This case concerns itself with what happens — or can happen — and did happen when a cruel, ill-tempered, insensitive man roams, gun in hand, through his years of family life as a battering bully — a bully who, since his two children were babies, beat both of them and his wife regularly and unmercifully. Particularly, this appeal has to do with a 16-year-old boy who could stand his father's abuse no longer — who could not find solace or friendship in the public services which had

been established for the purpose of providing aid, comfort and advice to abused family members — and who had no place to go or friends to help either him or his sister for whose protection he felt responsible and so — in fear and fright, and with fragmented emotion, Richard Jahnke shot and killed his father. . . .

It is my conception that Richard Jahnke properly came to the courts of Wyoming asking — not that he be judged as one who, at the time and place in question, was *insanely unreasonable* — but that his 14 years of beatings and uncivilized emotional abuse be explained by a qualified expert in order that judgment be passed on the question which asks whether or not his behavior was *sanely reasonable*. . . .

[W]hen the beatings of 14 years have — or may have — caused the accused to harbor types of fear, anxiety and apprehension with which the nonbrutalized juror is unfamiliar and which result in the taking of unusual defensive measures which, in the ordinary circumstances, might be thought about as premature [or] excessive . . . then expert testimony is necessary to explain the battered-person syndrome and the way these people respond to what they understand to be the imminence of danger. . . .

NOTES AND QUESTIONS ON OTHER ISSUES OF SELF-DEFENSE

1. *Limits on the use of deadly force.* Against what kind of threats may deadly force be used? The recent tendency has been to confine its use to narrow bounds. See, e.g., State v. Clay, 297 N.C. 555, 256 S.E.2d 176, 182 (1979):

> We define deadly force as force likely to cause death or great bodily harm.[a] . . . In so holding, we expressly reject defendant's contention, and any implication in our cases in support thereof, that a defendant would be justified by the principles of self-defense in employing deadly force to protect against bodily injury or offensive physical contact. Our decision says, in effect, that where the assault being made upon defendant is insufficient to give rise to a reasonable apprehension of death or great bodily harm, then the use of deadly force by defendant to protect himself from bodily injury or offensive physical contact is excessive force as a matter of law. Although we may hear protestations to the contrary, this decision will not compel anyone "to submit in meekness to indignities or violence to his person merely because such indignities or violence stop short of threatening him with death or great bodily harm." In such cases, a person so accosted may use such force, short of deadly force, as reasonably appears to him to be necessary under the circumstances to prevent bodily injury or offensive physical contact. This decision precludes the use of deadly force to prevent bodily injury or offensive physical contact and in so doing recognizes the premium we place on human life.

The Model Penal Code §3.04(2)(b) limits the use of deadly force to cases where the threatened danger is "death, serious bodily harm, kidnapping or sexual intercourse compelled by force or threat." *Question:* On what theory were the latter two dangers included?

In John Q. La Fond, The Case for Liberalizing the Use of Deadly Force in Self-Defense, 6 U. Puget Sound L. Rev. 237 (1983), the author criticizes the rule that

a. The Model Penal Code defines deadly force as "force which the actor uses with the purpose of causing or which he knows to create a substantial risk of causing death or serious bodily harm." §3.11(2). — Eds.

deadly force can be used only to counter a threat of death or great bodily harm or rape. Because this rule leaves many law-abiding citizens (including most female victims) without a practically effective means of defense against an unlawful, nondeadly assault by an unpredictable or much stronger attacker, the author proposes that resort to deadly force be permissible whenever it is "necessary to protect [the defendant] effectively" against a threat of unlawful physical violence (id. at 280).

In considering the significance of this issue for the battered woman's defense, recall the language of the *Norman* decision that even apart from the absence of an imminent danger, the assaults the defendant suffered during her married life were not deadly, so that she had no ground for fearing a deadly attack at the time she shot her husband.

2. *Motive.* Should a person who was facing an imminent threat be able to invoke the defense of self-defense if he was unaware of his predicament and killed his aggressor for some illicit reason. In his Justification and Excuse in the Criminal Law 38-39 (1989), Professor J. C. Smith puts the following case:

> Peter is now a notorious practical joker. One day, he enters the office of his colleague, Dan, points at Dan what Dan supposes to be a toy pistol and says, "You have got to die." Dan, who has been irritated beyond endurance by Peter's merry japes, responds by throwing his heavy inkstand which hits Peter on the head and kills him. Full of remorse, Dan phones the police and tells them that he has killed a man simply for playing a practical joke on him. But when the police examine the pistol they find that it is a real one and loaded. Further, they find a note in Peter's room, stating that he is going to kill Dan, whom he detests, and then commit suicide. If Dan had not thrown the inkstand, it appears likely that he would have been shot dead. If Dan is charged with murder or manslaughter, can he successfully claim that he was acting in self-defence? Can he rely on unknown circumstances of justification or excuse?

Under the Model Penal Code (and probably under existing American law) a necessary condition for claiming self-defense is that the defendant actually believed in the necessity to use defensive force. See Wayne LaFave & Austin Scott, Criminal Law 458 (2d ed. 1986). Is that a sound position? If the theory of self-defense is excuse, that is, that a reasonable person who believes that his life is about to be taken by another can't be expected simply to permit it to happen, then obviously he should not be permitted to claim self-defense when the condition for the excuse, his belief, is not present. But if the theory of self-defense is that it was right to do what the defendant did, why should it be less right because he was unaware of his right? Wasn't it still a good thing to stop the aggressor from killing an innocent person? For discussion of these issues see Paul Robinson, A Theory of Justification: Societal Harm as a Prerequisite for Criminal Liability, 23 U.C.L.A.L. Rev. 266 (1975), and George Fletcher, The Right Deed for the Wrong Reason: A Reply to Mr. Robinson, 23 U.C.L.A.L. Rev. 293 (1975).

3. *The risk of injury to others.* To what extent is a person who is privileged to use deadly force against an aggressor criminally responsible if his defensive actions cause injury to innocent persons?

In People v. Adams, 9 Ill. App. 3d 61, 291 N.E.2d 54, 55-56 (1972), the defendant, acting in self-defense, shot and killed his assailant, Robinson, who was threatening his life. The deceased, Mary Davis, was at the time sitting in a car with some friends, including Robinson. One of the defendant's bullets passed through Robinson's body and struck and killed Mary Davis, who was sitting next to him. The defendant was convicted of manslaughter of the woman. On appeal, the prosecution contended that:

> [S]elf-defense does not necessarily protect an individual from criminal responsibility for all his acts performed in defending his life against a felonious assault, and that even though defendant's conduct here may have been justified as to Robinson nonetheless it constituted a reckless disregard for the consequences towards Mary Davis, and, as such, supported his conviction for involuntary manslaughter.

The court rejected these arguments and reversed the conviction, stating:

> [I]f the circumstances are such that they would excuse the killing of an assailant in self-defense, the emergency will be held to excuse the person assailed from culpability, if in attempting to defend himself he unintentionally kills or injures a third person. . . .
>
> We are aware that the above rule is not absolute and that . . . , it may be subject to modification depending on the circumstances involved. But we do not believe such circumstances present themselves in the case before us. There were other persons present in the car with defendant's assailant, but it was dark and defendant was being fired on at close range. He had very little time to think or assess the situation. He had to act immediately to protect himself from a man who had been drinking all day and who was not just threatening him but was shooting at him. Even under such circumstances defendant did not shoot wildly or carelessly. From the record it can be inferred that he hit his assailant with every shot and that the innocent victim was killed only as a result of a bullet passing through the body of the assailant. We conclude that under the circumstances of this case the killing of Mary Davis constituted no crime.

Suppose that the defendant knew or should have known that there was a substantial possibility that in shooting at his assailant in self-defense one of the innocent persons in the car would be killed. For example, suppose he were armed only with a shotgun. Would the decision then have been otherwise? Or consider a more extreme situation in which the defendant knew there was a high probability or a virtual certainty that in killing his assailant one or more of the others would also be killed. See the material on choice of evils, page 809 infra and Sanford H. Kadish, Blame and Punishment 122-126 (1987).

Compare §3.09(3) of the Model Penal Code:

> When the actor is justified under Sections 3.03 to 3.08 in using force upon or toward the person of another but he recklessly or negligently injures or creates a risk to injury to innocent persons, the justification afforded by these Sections is unavailable in a prosecution for such recklessness or negligence towards innocent persons.

See Ann E. Barlow, Self-Defense and Reckless Crimes Against Third Parties, 22 Colum. J.L. & Soc. Probs. 417 (1989).

4. *Burden of proof.* Most jurisdictions place the burden on the prosecution to disprove self-defense beyond a reasonable doubt, once the issue is raised by the evidence. Ohio, however, requires the defendant to prove self-defense by a

preponderance of the evidence. In Martin v. Ohio, 480 U.S. 228 (1987), the Supreme Court upheld the constitutionality of this practice, on the ground that the absence of the conditions of self-defense was not among the elements of the crime charged (aggravated murder) as defined by the Ohio statute.

Does this mean that a state could abolish the plea of self-defense completely? Would it be constitutional to punish as a murderer someone who had killed when it was immediately necessary to save herself from an unlawful aggressor? See pages 48-49 supra.

5. *Exceptions to the right of self-defense.* In a number of situations, the law disallows the use of defensive force, even though the defendant faces an imminent threat of injury or death from the unlawful action of another. These situations are explored in the cases that follow.

STATE v. ABBOTT

Supreme Court of New Jersey
36 N.J. 63, 174 A.2d 881 (1961)

WEINTRAUB, C.J. . . . Abbott shared a common driveway with his neighbors, Michael and Mary Scarano. The Scaranos engaged a contractor to pave their portion. Abbott obtained some asphalt from the contractor and made a doorstop to keep his garage door from swinging onto the Scaranos' property. Nicholas Scarano, who was visiting with the Scaranos, his parents, objected to Abbott's innovation. After some words between them a fist fight ensued.

Although Abbott managed to land the first punch, with which he sent Nicholas to the ground, a jury could find Nicholas was the aggressor. At this point Michael Scarano came at Abbott with a hatchet. Michael said the tool had just been returned to him by the contractor, and denied he meant to use it as a weapon. According to Abbott, Mary Scarano followed, armed with a carving knife and large fork. The actors gave varying versions of what happened, but the end result was that all of the Scaranos were hit by the hatchet. Nicholas received severe head injuries. Abbott claimed he too suffered a laceration.

Abbott admitted he finally wrested the hatchet from Michael but denied he wielded it at all. Rather he insisted that the Scaranos were injured during a common struggle for the instrument. A jury could, however, find Abbott intentionally inflicted the blows.

Abbott was separately indicted for atrocious assault and battery upon each of the Scaranos. There was a common trial of these indictments. The jury acquitted Abbott of the charges relating to Michael and Mary, but found him guilty as to Nicholas.

The principal question is whether the trial court properly instructed the jury upon . . . the subject of retreat. . . .

The question whether one who is neither the aggressor nor a party to a mutual combat must retreat has divided the authorities. Self-defense is measured against necessity. . . . From that premise one could readily say there was no necessity to kill in self-defense if the use of deadly force could have been avoided by retreat. The critics of the retreat rule do not quarrel with the theoretical validity of this conclusion, but rather condemn it as unrealistic. The law of course should not denounce conduct as criminal when it accords with the behavior of reasonable men. Upon this level, the advocates of no-retreat say the manly thing is to hold one's ground and hence society should not demand what smacks of cowardice. Adherents of the retreat rule reply it is better that the assailed shall retreat than that the life of another be needlessly spent. They add that not only do right-thinking men agree, but further a rule so requiring may well induce others to adhere to that worthy standard of behavior. . . .

Other justifications are closely divided upon the retreat doctrine. . . . Our Court of Errors and Appeals deliberately adopted the retreat rule with an awareness of the contending views. . . . The Model Penal Code embraces the retreat rule while acknowledging that on numerical balance a majority of the precedents oppose it.

We are not persuaded to depart from the principle of retreat. We think it salutary if reasonably limited. Much of the criticism goes not to its inherent validity but rather to unwarranted applications of the rule. For example, it is correctly observed that one can hardly retreat from a rifle shot at close range. But if the weapon were a knife, a lead of a city block might well be enough. Again, the rule cannot be stated baldly, with indifference to the excitement of the occasion. As Mr. Justice Holmes cryptically put it, "Detached reflection cannot be demanded in the presence of an uplifted knife." Brown v. United States, 256 U.S. 335, 343 (1921). Such considerations, however, do not demand that a man should have the absolute right to stand his ground and kill in any and all situations. . . .

We believe the following principles are sound:

1. The issue of retreat arises only if the defendant resorted to a deadly force. . . . Model Penal Code §3.04(2)(b)(ii). As defined in §3.11(2) a deadly force means "force which the actor uses with the purpose of causing or which he knows to create a substantial risk of causing death or serious bodily harm."

Hence it is not the nature of the force defended against which raises the issue of retreat, but rather the nature of the force which the accused employed in his defense. If he does not resort to a deadly force, one who is assailed may hold his ground whether the attack upon him be of a deadly or some lesser character. Although it might be argued that a safe retreat should be taken if thereby the use of *any* force could be avoided, yet, as the comment in the Model Penal Code observes, "The logic of this position never has been accepted when moderate force is used in self-defense; here all agree that the actor may stand his ground and estimate necessity upon that basis." . . . Hence, in a case like the present one, the jury should be instructed that Abbott could hold his ground when Nicholas came at him with his fists, and also when Michael and Mary came at him with the several instruments mentioned, and that the question of retreat could arise only if Abbott intended to use a deadly force.

2. What constitutes an opportunity to retreat which will defeat the right of self-defense? As §3.04(2)(b)(ii) of the Model Penal Code states, deadly force is not justifiable "if the actor *knows* that he can avoid the necessity of using such force *with complete safety* by retreating. . . ." We emphasize "knows" and "with complete safety." One who is wrongfully attacked need not risk injury by retreating, even though he could escape with something less than serious bodily injury. It would be unreal to require nice calculations as to the amount of hurt, or to ask him to endure any at all. And the issue is not whether in retrospect it can be

found the defendant could have retreated unharmed. Rather the question is whether he knew the opportunity was there, and of course in that inquiry the total circumstances including the attendant excitement must be considered. . . .

[The court reversed the conviction because it found that the trial court's instructions on retreat were ambiguous and confusing.]

NOTES ON THE DUTY TO RETREAT

1. *The traditional view.* The English common law imposed a strict duty to retreat; a person could use deadly force in self-defense only after exhausting every chance to flee, when he had his "back to the wall."[19] In the nineteenth century, American courts began rejecting the English doctrine as unsuited to American values. In a widely quoted decision, Erwin v. State, 29 Ohio St. 186, 199 (1876), the Ohio Supreme Court said that the law "will not permit the taking of [human life] to repel mere trespass, . . . but a true man who is without fault is not obliged to fly from an assailant." Some contemporary scholars continued to defend the retreat requirement; Professor Beale wrote in 1903 that despite the "apparent cowardice, [a] really honorable man . . . would regret ten times more, after the excitement of the contest was past, the thought that he had the blood of a fellow-being on his hands."[20] Many states, especially those on the East coast, retained a retreat requirement, but by the late nineteenth or early twentieth century, the majority had adopted the "true man" or no-retreat rule. Historian Richard Maxwell Brown describes the result:[21]

> The centuries-long English legal severity against homicide was replaced in our country by a proud new tolerance for killing in situations where it might have been avoided. . . . This undoubtedly had an impact on our homicide rate, helping to make it the highest on earth among . . . modern, industrialized nations.

2. *Current controversies.* As the *Abbott* decision notes, most states at that time followed the no-retreat approach. Since then, the law on retreat has been in a state of flux. Ohio, where the "true man" concept originated, rejected that approach in 1979.[22] Tennessee, which had long rejected the no-retreat rule, adopted it by legislation in 1989, and as recently as 1995 its courts approvingly referred to that approach as "the 'true man' doctrine."[23]

Although contemporary cases and commentators continue to identify no-retreat as the majority rule, that is no longer true. About half the states now require retreat when possible, and half a dozen others treat the possibility of retreat as a factor to be considered in judging necessity;[24] only about a third of the states still permit the actor to stand his ground and assess his need for defensive

19. See Richard Maxwell Brown, No Duty to Retreat 4-30 (1991).
20. Joseph Beale, Retreat from a Murderous Assault, 16 Harv. L. Rev. 567, 681 (1903).
21. Brown, supra note 19.
22. State v. Robbins, 388 N.E.2d 755, 758-759 (Ohio 1979).
23. See State v. Renner, 912 S.W.2d 701, 703-704 (Tenn. 1995).
24. E.g., State v. Basting, 572 N.W.2d 281, 285 (Minn. 1997); State v. Bruno, 473 S.E.2d 450, 451 (S.C. 1996); N.D. Code §12.1-05-07 (1997); Pa. Stat. Ann., tit. 18, §505(b)(2)(ii).

force on that basis.[25] Some courts retaining the no-retreat rule expressly reject the old justification for it — that the law should not require what looks like cowardice. Rather, these courts argue that a rule requiring retreat tends to confuse the jury because it is so difficult to determine whether the defendant knew he could retreat with complete safety.[26] Do practical considerations like these justify a rule that permits killings that are not strictly necessary?

3. The "castle" exception. In jurisdictions requiring retreat before deadly force may be used, an exception is commonly made when the defendant is attacked in his own home. Thus, in People v. Tomlins, 107 N.E. 496, 497 (1914), Judge Cardozo stated:

> It is not now and never has been the law that a man assailed in his own dwelling is bound to retreat. If assailed there, he may stand his ground and resist the attack. He is under no duty to take to the fields and the highways, a fugitive from his own home. More than 200 years ago it was said by Lord Chief Justice Hale: In case a man "is assailed in his own house, he need not flee as far as he can, as in other cases of se defendendo, for he hath the protection of his house to excuse him from flying, as that would be to give up the protection of his house to his adversary by flight." Flight is for sanctuary and shelter, and shelter, if not sanctuary, is in the home. That there is, in such a situation, no duty to retreat is, we think, the settled law in the United States as in England.

Is the castle exception sound in principle, or is it just a concession to human instinct? Should it apply only when the aggressor killed in self-defense is an intruder, or should it apply even when the person killed is a co-occupant such as a spouse or child? In *Tomlins,* supra, Judge Cardozo held that a father being threatened by his son could kill the son rather than retreat. Model Penal Code §3.04(2)(b)(ii)(1) endorses this view, as do most of the recent decisions on the issue. E.g., Weiand v. State, 732 So. 2d 1044 (Fla. 1999); State v. Thomas, 673 N.E.2d 1339 (Ohio 1997).[27]

Do you agree? One factor motivating courts that follow this approach is the concern that imposing a duty to retreat would adversely affect women who are victims of domestic violence, because for battered women "escape from the home is rarely possible without the threat of great personal violence or death" (*Thomas,* 673 N.E.2d at 1343), and because "separation or retreat can be the most dangerous time in the relationship for the victims of domestic violence" (*Weiand,* 723 So. 2d at 1053). But will some women (and abused teenage children) be placed in even greater danger by a gender-neutral privilege *not* to retreat? Consider State v. Shaw, 441 A.2d 561 (Conn. 1981). The statute in *Shaw,* patterned after the Model Penal Code, stated: "[T]he actor shall not be required to retreat if he is in his dwelling . . . and was not the initial aggressor. . . ." Nevertheless, the court, noting the overriding policy favoring human life and stressing that in the great majority of homicides the killer and victim are relatives or close acquaintances, chose to read into the statute a requirement of retreat from

25. E.g., State v. Williams, 916 P.2d 445, 448 (Wash. App. 1996); People v. Willner, 879 P.2d 19, 24 (Colo. 1994).

26. See Culverson v. State, 797 P.2d 238, 240 (Nev. 1990).

27. But compare State v. Adams, 727 A.2d 780 (Conn. 1999); State v. Gartland, 694 A.2d 564 (N.J. 1997), both holding that a homeowner must flee if possible when the attacker is a co-occupant.

co-occupants. The court stated: "We cannot conclude that the Connecticut legislature intended to sanction the reenactment of the climactic scene from 'High Noon' in the familial kitchens of this state."

Questions: In jurisdictions that require retreat from one's home when the aggressor is also a lawful occupant, can a battered woman's defense succeed? How could the defendant show that the retreat duty is inapplicable in her situation?

Two in-depth studies of the retreat issue are Richard M. Brown, No Duty to Retreat: Violence and Values in American History and Society (1991); Garrett Epps, Any Which Way But Loose: Interpretive Strategies and Attitudes Toward Violence in the Evolution of the Anglo-American "Retreat Rule," 55 Law & Contemp. Prob. 303 (1992).

UNITED STATES v. PETERSON

United States Court of Appeals, District of Columbia Circuit
483 F.2d 1222 (1973)

ROBINSON, J. Indicted for second-degree murder, and convicted by a jury of manslaughter as a lesser included offense, Bennie L. Peterson urges . . . reversal. . . . He complains . . . that the judge . . . erred in the instructions given the jury in relation to his claim that the homicide was committed in self-defense. . . . After careful study of these arguments in light of the trial record, we affirm Peterson's conviction.

The events immediately preceding the homicide are not seriously in dispute. . . . Charles Keitt, the deceased, and two friends drove in Keitt's car to the alley in the rear of Peterson's house to remove the windshield wipers from the latter's wrecked car. While Keitt was doing so, Peterson came out of the house into the back yard to protest. After a verbal exchange, Peterson went back into the house, obtained a pistol, and returned to the yard. In the meantime, Keitt had reseated himself in his car, and he and his companions were about to leave.

Upon his reappearance in the yard, Peterson paused briefly to load the pistol. "If you move," he shouted to Keitt, "I will shoot." He walked to a point in the yard slightly inside a gate in the rear fence and, pistol in hand, said, "If you come in here I will kill you." Keitt alighted from his car, took a few steps toward Peterson and exclaimed, "What the hell do you think you are going to do with that?" Keitt then made an about-face, walked back to his car and got a lug wrench. With the wrench in a raised position, Keitt advanced toward Peterson, who stood with the pistol pointed toward him. Peterson warned Keitt not to "take another step" and, when Keitt continued onward shot him in the face from a distance of about ten feet. Death was apparently instantaneous. . . .

Peterson's complaint centers upon an instruction that the right to use deadly force in self-defense is not ordinarily available to one who provokes a conflict or is the aggressor in it. Mere words, the judge explained, do not constitute provocation or aggression; and if Peterson precipitated the altercation but thereafter withdrew from it in good faith and so informed Keitt by words or acts, he was justified in using deadly force to save himself from imminent danger of death or grave bodily harm. . . . Peterson contends that there was no evidence that he either caused or contributed to the conflict, and that the instructions on the topic could only [have] misled the jury.

It has long been accepted that one cannot support a claim of self-defense by a self-generated necessity to kill. The right of homicidal self-defense is granted only to those free from fault in the difficulty; it is denied to slayers who incite the fatal attack, encourage the fatal quarrel or otherwise promote the necessitous occasion for taking life. The fact that the deceased struck the first blow, fired the first shot or made the first menacing gesture does not legalize the self-defense claim if in fact the claimant was the actual provoker. In sum, one who is the aggressor in a conflict culminating in death cannot invoke the necessities of self-preservation. Only in the event that he communicates to his adversary his intent to withdraw and in good faith attempts to do so is he restored to his right of self-defense.

This body of doctrine traces its origin to the fundamental principle that a killing in self-defense is excusable only as a matter of genuine necessity. Quite obviously, a defensive killing is unnecessary if the occasion for it could have been averted.

[T]he trial judge's charge fully comported with these governing principles. The remaining question, then, is whether there was evidence to make them applicable to the case. A recapitulation of the proofs shows beyond peradventure that there was. . . .

The evidence is uncontradicted that when Peterson reappeared in the yard with his pistol, Keitt was about to depart the scene. . . . The uncontroverted fact that Keitt was leaving shows plainly that so far as he was concerned the confrontation was ended. [E]ven if he had previously been the aggressor, he no longer was.

Not so with Peterson, however. . . . Emerging from the house with the pistol, he paused in the yard to load it, and to command Keitt not to move. He then walked through the yard to the rear gate and, displaying his pistol, dared Keitt to come in, and threatened to kill him if he did. While there appears to be no fixed rule on the subject, the cases hold, and we agree, that an affirmative unlawful act reasonably calculated to produce an affray foreboding injurious or fatal consequences is an aggression which, unless renounced, nullifies the right of homicidal self-defense. We cannot escape the abiding conviction that the jury could readily find Peterson's challenge to be a transgression of that character.

The situation at bar is not unlike that presented in *Laney* [294 Fed. 412 (1923)]. There the accused, chased along the street by a mob threatening his life, managed to escape through an areaway between two houses. In the back yard of one of the houses, he checked a gun he was carrying and then returned to the areaway. The mob beset him again, and during an exchange of shots one of its members was killed by a bullet from the accused's gun. In affirming a conviction of manslaughter, the court reasoned: "It is clearly apparent . . . that, when defendant escaped from the mob into the back yard . . . he was in a place of comparative safety, from which, if he desired to go home, he could have gone by the back way, as he subsequently did. The mob had turned its attention to a house on the opposite side of the street. According to Laney's testimony, there was shooting going on in the street. His appearance on the street at that juncture could mean nothing but trouble for him. Hence, when he adjusted his gun and stepped out into the areaway, he had every reason to believe that his presence there would provoke trouble. We think his conduct in adjusting his revolver and going into the areaway was such as to deprive him of any right to invoke the plea of self-defense."

Similarly, in Rowe v. United States, 370 F.2d 240 (D.C. Cir. 1966), the accused was in the home of friends when an argument, to which the friends became participants, developed in the street in front. He left, went to his nearby apartment for a loaded pistol and returned. There was testimony that he then made an insulting comment, drew the pistol and fired a shot into the ground. In any event, when a group of five men began to move toward him, he began to shoot at them, killing two, and wounding a third. We observed that the accused "left an apparently safe haven to arm himself and return to the scene," and that "he inflamed the situation with his words to the men gathered there, even though he could have returned silently to the safety of the [friends'] porch." We held that "[t]hese facts could have led the jury to conclude that [the accused] returned to the scene to stir up further trouble, if not actually to kill anyone, and that his actions instigated the men into rushing him. Self-defense may not be claimed by one who deliberately places himself in a position where he has reason to believe "his presence . . . would provoke trouble." We noted the argument "that a defendant may claim self-defense if he arms himself in order to proceed upon his normal activities, even if he realizes that danger may await him"; we responded by pointing out "that the jury could have found that the course of action defendant here followed was for an unlawful purpose." We accordingly affirmed his conviction of manslaughter. . . .

We are brought much the readier to the same conclusion here. We think the evidence plainly presented an issue of fact as to whether Peterson's conduct was an invitation to and provocation of the encounter which ended in the fatal shot. We sustain the trial judge's action in remitting that issue for the jury's determination.

NOTES AND QUESTIONS

1. *Can the non-lethal aggressor respond?* In *Peterson,* the defendant became the initial aggressor when he obtained a pistol, re-entered his yard, and threatened to shoot. Keitt's response (getting the lug wrench) was arguably a legitimate act of self-protection under these circumstances; if so, it is easy to see why Peterson should not have a right to use deadly force in return. But suppose that the initial aggressor, after using only non-lethal force, is met by an excessive, potentially lethal response. Should the initial aggressor still be denied any right to defend his life, when his only initial aggression may have consisted of provocative words, a shove, or a punch?

In a few states, the non-lethal aggressor can regain his right to self-defense if he is met by an excessive, life-threatening response, provided that he then "exhaust[s] every reasonable means to escape such danger other than the use of [deadly] force."[28] But most jurisdictions tend to deny the initial aggressor even this limited means of escape. On the ground that self-defense is available only to the person who is "free from fault," most states hold that the initial aggressor has no self-defense privilege even when his minor provocation is met by a grossly

28. E.g., Ill. Comp. Stat. Ann. ch. 720 §5/7-4(c)(1); Kan. Stat. Ann. §21-3214(3)(a).

excessive response.[29] Apparently, the initial aggressor's only choices are to run (if possible), to forgo self-defense (and be killed) or to fight back unlawfully (and face murder charges if he is forced to kill his attacker). Does this make sense?

Consider Allen v. State, 871 P.2d 79, 92-93 (Okla. Crim. App. 1994). After the defendant and her roommate quarrelled, the roommate, Gloria Leathers, collected her possessions and prepared to move out. As Leathers went to her car, Allen pursued her, asking her to stay, but Leathers grabbed a multiple-pronged garden rake and struck Allen in the face, causing extensive bleeding. Leathers drove off, and Allen got in her own car to pursue Leathers. When Allen caught up, she parked her car and walked toward Leathers' vehicle. At that point Allen saw Leathers coming toward her holding the rake. She returned to her car and retrieved a gun from the glove compartment; when she turned around and saw Leathers standing very near her, holding the rake, she fired. Leathers died from a single gunshot wound to the abdomen. Allen was convicted of first-degree murder and sentenced to death. The appellate court noted that in Oklahoma, "a party has no obligation to retreat from a confrontation; she can stand her ground and defend herself"; nonetheless the court affirmed the conviction and the sentence, after finding the no-retreat privilege unavailable to Allen:

> If a person by provocative behavior initiates a confrontation, even with no intention of killing the other person, she loses the right of self-defense. Here, even assuming Appellant did not intend to provoke an argument when she pursued the decedent . . . , she re-initiated the encounter. . . . She knew the decedent was upset, yet she pursued her anyway, knowing the possibility of a confrontation was strong. [E]ven limiting review to Appellant's version of events, we find the Appellant was not entitled to instructions on self-defense.

Questions: Did Allen commit a punishable offense in pursuing Leathers in order to persuade her to reconsider her decision to move out? Even if Allen had thrown the first punch, what should be the appropriate punishment for that offense?

2. *What kinds of provocation suffice?* How far should courts extend the doctrine that fault forfeits the privilege of self-defense? Suppose that Uriah catches David in flagrante delicto with Uriah's wife. Uriah, enraged, tries to kill David. Can David defend himself with deadly force, or has he become the aggressor, and therefore lost his right to self-defense, by committing this provocative act? What should be the result under Allen v. State, Note 1 supra?

Some courts have held that David could not defend himself with deadly force in this situation. See Dabney v. State, 21 So. 211 (1897). More recent cases addressing the issue tend to reject this approach. See Atkins v. State, 339 S.E.2d 782 (Ga. 1986); Annot., 9 A.L. R.3d 93 (1966). Which is the better view? Is it wrong to permit David to have an affair and then kill the husband who is understandably enraged by his provocative conduct? Or is it worse to permit the enraged husband to kill a provocateur whose most serious offense is adultery?

3. *The Model Penal Code.* The traditional common-law rule reflected in *Peterson*

29. See, e.g., Colo. Rev. Stat. Ann. §18-1-704(3)(b); Ind. Code Ann. §35-41-3-2(d)(3); N.Y. Penal Law §35.15(1)(b), all requiring the nonlethal aggressor to withdraw completely in order to regain his right to self-defense.

and *Allen* differs from the approach of the Model Penal Code, §3.04. The Comments to this provision, Model Penal Code and Commentaries, Comment to §3.04 at 49-51 (1985), state:

> *Use of Protective Force by Initial Aggressor.* Subsection (2)(b)(i) denies justification for the use of deadly force if the actor, with the purpose of causing death or serious bodily harm, provoked the use of force against himself in the same encounter. This is a narrower forfeiture of the privilege of self-defense than commonly obtains. . . . It was believed, however, that it is sufficient to resolve the problem, in view of the adoption in Subsection (2)(b)(ii) of a general duty to retreat before resorting to deadly force.
>
> The typical case to be imagined is this: *A* attacks *B* with his fists; *B* defends himself, and manages to subdue *A* to the extent of pinning him to the floor. *B* then starts to batter *A*'s head savagely against the floor. *A* manages to rise, and since *B* is still attacking him and *A* now fears that if he is thrown again to the floor he will be killed, *A* uses a knife. *B* is killed or seriously wounded.
>
> [Under] this section . . . *B* is entitled to defend himself against *A*'s attack, but only to the extent of using moderate, nondeadly force. He is given this privilege by Subsection (1). *B* exceeds the bounds of "necessary" force under that provision, however, when, after reducing *A* to helplessness, he batters *A*'s head on the floor. Since this excessive force is, in its turn, unlawful, under Subsection (1) *A* is entitled to defend himself against it and, if he believes that he is then in danger of death or serious bodily harm without apparent opportunity for safe retreat, *A* is also entitled to use his knife in self-protection. *A* of course is criminally liable for his initial battery on *B*, but would have a justifying defense that he could raise against prosecution for the ultimate homicide or wounding. Subsection (2)(b)(i), depriving *A* of his justification on the ground of initial aggression, would not become operative unless *A* entered the encounter with the purpose of causing death or serious bodily harm. . . .
>
> So long as the assailant's victim employs moderate force in self-protection, it is not unlawful; the original assailant cannot, therefore, claim a privilege for a response in kind. The problem arises only when the victim goes beyond the necessity by answering moderate force with deadly force. If in such a case there is no opportunity for withdrawal and safe retreat, the fact of the original minor aggression does not warrant the denial of a privilege to defend against deadly force; the initial aggressor can and ought to be convicted of assault.

2. *Protection of Property and Law Enforcement*

PEOPLE v. CEBALLOS

Supreme Court of California
12 Cal. 3d 470, 526 P.2d 241 (1974)

BURKE, J. Don Ceballos was found guilty by a jury of assault with a deadly weapon (Pen. Code, §245). Imposition of sentence was suspended and he was placed on probation. . . .

Defendant lived alone in a home in San Anselmo. The regular living quarters were above the garage, but defendant sometimes slept in the garage and had about $2,000 worth of property there.

In March 1970 some tools were stolen from defendant's home. On May 12,

1970, he noticed the lock on his garage doors was bent and pry marks were on one of the doors. The next day he mounted a loaded .22 caliber pistol in the garage. The pistol was aimed at the center of the garage doors and was connected by a wire to one of the doors so that the pistol would discharge if the door was opened several inches.

The damage to defendant's lock had been done by a 16-year-old boy named Stephen and a 15-year-old boy named Robert. On the afternoon of May 15, 1970, the boys returned to defendant's house while he was away. Neither boy was armed with a gun or knife. After looking in the windows and seeing no one, Stephen succeeded in removing the lock on the garage doors with a crowbar, and, as he pulled the door outward, he was hit in the face with a bullet from the pistol.

Stephen testified: He intended to go into the garage "[f]or musical equipment" because he had a debt to pay to a friend. His "way of paying that debt would be to take [defendant's] property and sell it" and use the proceeds to pay the debt. He "wasn't going to do it [i.e., steal] for sure, necessarily." He was there "to look around," and "getting in, I don't know if I would have actually stolen."

Defendant, testifying in his own behalf, admitted having set up the trap gun. He stated that after noticing the pry marks on his garage door on May 12, he felt he should "set up some kind of a trap, something to keep the burglar out of my home." When asked why he was trying to keep the burglar out, he replied, ". . . Because somebody was trying to steal my property . . . and I don't want to come home some night and have the thief in there . . . usually a thief is pretty desperate . . . and . . . they just pick up a weapon . . . if they don't have one . . . and do the best they can."

When asked by the police shortly after the shooting why he assembled the trap gun, defendant stated that "he didn't have much and he wanted to protect what he did have."

[T]he jury found defendant guilty of assault with a deadly weapon. An assault is "an unlawful attempt, coupled with a present ability, to commit a violent injury on the person of another." (Pen. Code, §240.)

Defendant contends that had he been present he would have been justified in shooting Stephen since Stephen was attempting to commit burglary, that under cases such as United States v. Gilliam, 25 Fed. Cas. p. 1319, No. 15, 205a, defendant had a right to do indirectly what he could have done directly, and that therefore any attempt by him to commit a violent injury upon Stephen was not "unlawful" and hence not an assault. The People argue that the rule in *Gilliam* is unsound, that as a matter of law a trap gun constitutes excessive force, and that in any event the circumstances were not in fact such as to warrant the use of deadly force. . . .

In the United States, courts have concluded that a person may be held criminally liable under statutes proscribing homicides and shooting with intent to injure, or civilly liable, if he sets upon his premises a deadly mechanical device and that device kills or injures another. . . . However, an exception to the rule that there may be criminal and civil liability for death or injuries caused by such a device has been recognized where the intrusion is, in fact, such that the person, were he present, would be justified in taking the life or inflicting the bodily harm with his own hands. . . .

Allowing persons, at their own risk, to employ deadly mechanical devices imperils the lives of children, firemen and policemen acting within the scope of their employment, and others. Where the actor is present, there is always the possibility he will realize that deadly force is not necessary, but deadly mechanical devices are without mercy or discretion. Such devices "are silent instrumentalities of death. They deal death and destruction to the innocent as well as the criminal intruder without the slightest warning. The taking of human life [or infliction of great bodily injury] by such means is brutally savage and inhuman." (See State v. Plumlee, . . . 149 So. 425, 430).

It seems clear that the use of such devices should not be encouraged. Moreover, whatever may be thought in torts, the foregoing rule setting forth an exception to liability for death or injuries inflicted by such devices "is inappropriate in penal law for it is obvious that it does not prescribe a workable standard of conduct; liability depends upon fortuitous results." (See Model Penal Code (Tent. Draft No. 8), §3.06, com. 15.) We therefore decline to adopt that rule in criminal cases.

Furthermore, even if that rule were applied here, as we shall see, defendant was not justified in shooting Stephen. Penal Code section 197 provides:

> Homicide is . . . justifiable . . . 1. When resisting any attempt to murder any person, or to commit a felony, or to do some great bodily injury upon any person; or, 2. When committed in defense of habitation, property, or person, against one who manifestly intends or endeavors, by violence or surprise, to commit a felony. . . .

Since a homicide is justifiable under the circumstances specified in section 197, a fortiori an attempt to commit a violent injury upon another under those circumstances is justifiable.

By its terms subdivision 1 of Penal Code section 197 appears to permit killing to prevent any "felony," but in view of the large number of felonies today and the inclusion of many that do not involve a danger of serious bodily harm, a literal reading of the section is undesirable. People v. Jones, 191 Cal. App. 2d 478, 481, in rejecting the defendant's theory that her husband was about to commit the felony of beating her (Pen. Code §273d) [a] and that therefore her killing him to prevent him from doing so was justifiable, stated that Penal Code section 197 "does no more than codify the common law and should be read in light of it." *Jones* read into section 197, subdivision 1, the limitation that the felony be "some atrocious crime attempted to be committed by force." *Jones* further stated, "the punishment provided by a statute is not necessarily an adequate test as to whether life may be taken for in some situations it is too artificial and unrealistic. We must look further into the character of the crime and the manner of its perpetration. . . . *When these do not reasonably create a fear of great bodily harm,* as they could not if defendant apprehended only a misdemeanor assault, *there is no cause for the exaction of a human life.*" (Italics added. . . .)

Jones involved subdivision 1 of Penal Code section 197, but subdivision 2 of that section is likewise so limited. The term "violence or surprise" in subdivision 2 is found in common law authorities . . . and, whatever may have been the very early common law . . . the rule developed at common law that killing or use of deadly force to prevent a felony was justified only if the offense was a forcible

a. She relied on a statutory amendment that raised a simple assault from a misdemeanor to a felony where committed by a husband upon his wife. —Eds.

and atrocious crime. . . . "Surprise" means an unexpected attack—which includes force and violence . . . and the word thus appears redundant.

Examples of forcible and atrocious crimes are murder, mayhem, rape and robbery. . . . In such crimes "from their atrocity and violence human life [or personal safety from great harm] either is, or is presumed to be, in peril" (see United States v. Gilliam, supra, 25 Fed. Cas. pp. 1319, 1320 . . .).

Burglary has been included in the list of such crimes. . . . However, in view of the wide scope of burglary under Penal Code section 459, as compared with the common law definition of that offense, in our opinion it cannot be said that under all circumstances burglary under section 459 constitutes a forcible and atrocious crime.[2]

Where the character and manner of the burglary do not reasonably create a fear of great bodily harm, there is no cause for exaction of human life . . . or for the use of deadly force. The character and manner of the burglary could not reasonably create such a fear unless the burglary threatened, or was reasonably believed to threaten, death or serious bodily harm.

In the instant case the asserted burglary did not threaten death or serious bodily harm, since no one but Stephen and Robert was then on the premises. A defendant is not protected from liability merely by the fact that the intruder's conduct is such as would justify the defendant, were he present, in believing that the intrusion threatened death or serious bodily injury. . . .

We thus conclude that defendant was not justified under Penal Code section 197, subdivisions 1 or 2, in shooting Stephen to prevent him from committing burglary. . . .

We recognize that our position regarding justification for killing under Penal Code section 197, subdivisions 1 and 2, differs from the position of section 143, subdivision (2), of the Restatement Second of Torts, regarding the use of deadly force to prevent a "felony . . . of a type . . . involving the breaking and entry of a dwelling place" . . . but in view of the supreme value of human life, we do not believe deadly force can be justified to prevent all felonies of the foregoing type, including ones in which no person is, or is reasonably believed to be, on the premises except the would-be burglar.

Defendant also argues that had he been present he would have been justified in shooting Stephen under subdivision 4 of Penal Code section 197, which provides, "Homicide is . . . justifiable . . . 4. When necessarily committed in *attempting*, by lawful ways and means, to *apprehend* any person for any felony committed. . . ." (Italics added.) The argument cannot be upheld. The words "attempting . . . to apprehend" contain the idea of acting for the purpose of apprehending. . . . Here no showing was made that defendant's intent in shooting was to apprehend a felon. Rather it appears from his testimony and extrajudicial statement heretofore recited that his intent was to prevent a burglary, to protect his property, and to avoid the possibility that a thief might get into defendant's house and injure him upon his return. . . .

2. A common law burglary was the breaking and entering of a mansion house in the night with the intent to commit a felony. . . . Burglary under Penal Code section 459 differs from common law burglary in that the entry may be in the daytime and of numerous places other than a mansion house . . . and breaking is not required. . . . For example, under section 459 a person who enters a store with the intent of committing theft is guilty of burglary. . . . It would seem absurd to hold that a store detective could kill that person if necessary to prevent him from committing that offense. . . .

Defendant also does not, and could not properly, contend that the intrusion was in fact such that, were he present, he would be justified under Civil Code section 50 in using deadly force. That section provides, "Any necessary force may be used to protect from wrongful injury the person or property of oneself. . . ." This section also should be read in the light of the common law, and at common law in general deadly force could not be used solely for the protection of property. . . . "The preservation of human life and limb from grievous harm is of more importance to society than the protection of property." (Commonwealth v. Emmons, 157 Pa. Super. 495, 43 A.2d 568, 569.) Thus defendant was not warranted under Civil Code section 50 in using deadly force to protect his personal property. . . .

At common law an exception to the foregoing principle that deadly force could not be used solely for the protection of property was recognized where the property was a dwelling house in some circumstances. "According to the older interpretation of the common law, even extreme force may be used to prevent dispossession [of the dwelling house]." (Model Penal Code, Tent. Draft No. 8 (1958), Comment at pp. 48-51.) Also at common law if another attempted to burn a dwelling the owner was privileged to use deadly force if this seemed necessary to defend his "castle" against the threatened harm. Further, deadly force was privileged if it was, or reasonably seemed, necessary to protect the dwelling against a burglar.

Here we are not concerned with dispossession or burning of a dwelling, and, as heretofore concluded, the asserted burglary in this case was not of such a character as to warrant the use of deadly force.

We conclude that as a matter of law the exception to the rule of liability for injuries inflicted by a deadly mechanical device does not apply under the circumstances here appearing. . . .

The judgment is affirmed.

NOTE ON DEFENSE OF HABITATION

1. Variations on Ceballos. Suppose that instead of using a spring gun, Ceballos had put a curtain over the window to prevent anyone from looking in, had then seated himself inside the garage, facing the door, and had fired at the boys as they raised the door. On these facts would the California court still consider his actions unjustified? Would it matter whether Ceballos knew that the boys were unarmed?

2. Other statutory approaches. (a) Model Penal Code §3.06(3)(d), like the *Ceballos* court, strictly limits the use of deadly force against an intruder in the home. But §3.06(3)(d)(ii)(2) nonetheless permits the use of deadly force when "the use of force other than deadly force to prevent the commission or the consummation of the crime would expose the actor . . . to substantial danger of serious bodily harm." Would Ceballos have a defense under this provision? Aside from the tactic he actually employed, how else could Ceballos have prevented the burglary?

(b) In 1984, ten years after the decision in *Ceballos,* California enacted a "Home Protection Bill of Rights," which provides (Cal. Penal Code §198.5):

> Any person using [deadly] force . . . within his or her residence shall be presumed to have held a reasonable fear of imminent peril of death or great bodily injury . . . when that force is used against another person, not a member of the family or household, who unlawfully and forcibly enters . . . and the person using the force knew or had reason to believe that an unlawful and forcible entry occurred.

Would Ceballos have had a defense under this provision? Would he have a defense if the shooting had occurred as specified in Note 1, supra?

(c) Consider New York Penal Law §35.20(3):

> A person in possession or control of, or licensed or privileged to be in, a dwelling or an occupied building, who reasonably believes that another person is committing or attempting to commit a burglary of such dwelling or building, may use deadly physical force upon such other person when he reasonably believes such to be necessary to prevent or terminate the commission or attempted commission of such burglary.

(d) Many states have gone even further in authorizing the use of deadly force in defense of habitation. Some permit such force to prevent or terminate any felonious entry or even any unlawful entry. And such laws, which appear highly popular, have proliferated in recent years. See Stuart P. Green, Castles and Carjackers: Proportionality and the Use of Deadly Force in Defense of Dwellings and Vehicles, 1999 U. Ill. L. Rev. 1. The Colorado statute, referred to in that state as its "Make-My-Day" law, provides (Colo. Rev. Stat. 18-1-704.5 (1986)):

> (1) [T]he citizens of Colorado have a right to expect absolute safety within their own homes.
>
> (2) [A]ny occupant of a dwelling is justified in using any degree of physical force, including deadly physical force, against another person when that other person has made an unlawful entry . . . , and when the occupant has a reasonable belief that such other person has committed [or intends to commit] a crime in the dwelling in addition to the uninvited entry, . . . and when the occupant reasonably believes that such other person might use any physical force, no matter how slight, against any occupant.
>
> (3) Any occupant of a dwelling using physical force, including deadly force, in accordance with the provisions of subsection (2) of this section shall be immune from criminal prosecution [and civil liability] for the use of such force.

Compare this broad privilege to defend property with the strictly limited privilege to use deadly force in defense of one's life (see supra, Chapter 8A). Under the Colorado approach, if a drunken guest refuses to leave a homeowner's party and takes another beer from the refrigerator, can the homeowner shoot the guest and kill him? What is the rationale for permitting a homeowner to kill a trespasser in circumstances that would not warrant the use of deadly force in self-defense? Some argue that in the event of an unlawful intrusion, the danger of serious injury is so high that it is reasonable to presume such a threat in all cases. Is this convincing? The possible justifications are summarized and criticized in Green, supra, at 18-41.

3. Problem. On the night of October 17, 1992, Rodney Peairs, a manager at a Baton Rouge meat market, killed Yoshihiro Hattori, a 16-year-old Japanese exchange student. He and a friend were looking for a Halloween party, and he was dressed in a "Saturday Night Fever" costume. He mistakenly rang Mr. Peairs' doorbell, and when Mrs. Peairs came to the door and saw them, she became frightened and screamed. Apparently neither Hattori nor his friend could speak enough English to reassure her. At this point Peairs grabbed his laser-scoped .44-magnum handgun from his bedroom and went to the carport door. The two boys had retreated to the sidewalk, but when the carport door opened, Hattori began walking towards Peairs, waving his arms as he often did when trying to communicate. Peairs yelled "freeze," but Hattori did not understand him. Hattori continued forward; he had recently lost a contact lens and presumably did not see the gun. When Hattori was less than five feet away Mr. Peairs fired one shot into his chest. Only a few minutes had passed between the time the doorbell rang, and the time Peairs shot Hattori.

Rodney Peairs was indicted for manslaughter, but he claimed that the shooting, though mistaken, was justified under La. Rev. Stat. Ann. §14:20(3), which allows the use of deadly force based on a reasonable belief that an intruder is "likely to use any unlawful force against a person [in the dwelling] while committing . . . a burglary of that dwelling. . . ." Peairs' lawyer argued that Peairs saw an intruder who was grinning, and who kept advancing "with absolutely no respect for [Peairs'] home, his gun, or his warning." During closing arguments, Peairs' lawyer proclaimed "You have the absolute legal right in this country to answer your door with a gun. In your house, if you want to do it, you have the legal right to answer everybody that comes to your door with a gun." The prosecutor emphasized the fact that Peairs acted without investigating why his wife screamed; Peairs' alleged negligence was "his conduct in going to the closet and getting the biggest handgun made by human beings and never ever asking what it's for." After a seven-day trial and three hours of deliberation, Peairs was acquitted. The acquittal sparked outrage in Japan where owning a handgun is illegal (with minor exceptions), but many people in Peairs' community supported his actions. See N.Y. Times, May 23, 1993, at A1; May 20, 1993, at A10.

In a subsequent development a judge in a civil case found "no justification whatsoever" for the shooting and awarded the estate of Mr. Hattori $650,000 in damages against Mr. Peairs. N.Y. Times, Sept. 16, 1994, at A7.

Questions: Was the result of the criminal prosecution justified under Louisiana law? Would the defendant's case be stronger or weaker if it arose in New York? In Colorado?

DURHAM v. STATE

Supreme Court of Indiana
199 Ind. 567, 159 N.E. 145 (1927)

[Defendant, a deputy game warden, arrested one Long for illegal fishing. Long jumped into his boat in an attempt to escape. Defendant pursued him, grabbing first the gunwale and then the anchor chain. While Long was beating defendant about the head with an oar, defendant shot him in the arm. Defendant was convicted of assault and battery and appealed.]

MARTIN, J. . . . Instruction 12 was to the effect that, if Long resisted arrest, appellant would not be authorized to use such force and instrumentalities as would imperil the life of Long in order to overcome his resistance; that human life is too precious to be imperiled by the arrest of one who is only guilty of a misdemeanor; that, if appellant, in order to overcome Long's resistance, used a dangerous and deadly weapon, and in such manner as to endanger his life, and thereby inflict serious wounds, then the appellant would be guilty of assault and battery, at least. This instruction, standing alone, or considered in conjunction with instruction 15 and the other instructions, did not correctly state the law, and the court erred in giving it.

Our general statutes concerning arrests, and applicable to all classes of criminal cases, provide that:

"The defendant shall not be subject to any more restraint than is necessary for his arrest and detention." Section 2157, Burns' 1926.

"If, after notice of the intention to arrest the defendant, he either flees or forcibly resists, the officer may use all necessary means to effect the arrest." Section 2159, Burns' 1926.

In Plummer v. State (1893) 135 Ind. 308, 34 N.E. 968, the court said:

"The law does not allow a peace officer to use more force than is necessary to effect an arrest. And if he does use such unnecessary force, he . . . may be lawfully resisted. If the officer is resisted before he had used needless force and violence, he may then press forward and overcome such resistance, even to the taking of the life of the person arrested, if absolutely necessary."

The degree or limit of force that lawfully may be employed by an officer in arresting one charged with a misdemeanor (as distinguished from a felony) has been considered in a large number of cases in other jurisdictions. . . .

The general rules deduced therefrom may be stated to be: (a) That an officer having the right to arrest a misdemeanant may use all the force that is reasonably necessary to accomplish the arrest, except (b) that he may not, merely for the purpose of effecting the arrest, kill or inflict great bodily harm, endangering the life of the misdemeanant. Thus an officer may not kill or shed blood in attempting to arrest a misdemeanant who is fleeing, but not resisting.[2] (c) That, if the defendant physically resists, the officer need not retreat but may press forward and repel the resistance with such force, short of taking life, as is necessary to effect the arrest; and, if in so doing the officer is absolutely obliged to seriously wound or take the life of the accused, in order to prevent the accused from seriously wounding, or killing him, he will be justified.[3] . . .

To adopt the rule contended for by the prosecution in the trial below, and stated by the court in instruction 12, would be to paralyze the strong arm of the law, and render the state powerless to use extreme force when extreme resistance is offered, and would permit misdemeanants to stay the power of the state by unlawful resistance.

"To say to a defendant, 'You may measure strength with the arresting officer,

2. The most common examples of this class of cases are those where officers shoot at misdemeanants, their mounts, or their automobile tires, and wound or kill the misdemeanants. "To permit the life of one charged with a mere misdemeanor to be taken when fleeing from the officer would, aside from its inhumanity, be productive of more abuse than good. The law need not go unenforced. The officer can summon his posse, and take the offender." Head v. Martin (1887) 85 Ky. 480, 3 S.W. 622.

3. [T]he protection which an officer is entitled to receive in making an arrest is a different thing from self-defense, for it is his duty to push forward and make the arrest and to secure and retain custody of the prisoner. . . .

and avoid being taken if you are the stronger or after your arrest you may break away unless he can prevail over you in a wrestle,' is to elevate mere brute force to a position of command over the wheels of justice." 1 Bishop's Cr. Proc. (2d Ed.) §16. . . .

The judgment is reversed, with directions to sustain appellant's motion for a new trial, and for further proceedings not inconsistent herewith.

TENNESSEE v. GARNER

Supreme Court of the United States
471 U.S. 1 (1985)

WHITE, J., delivered the opinion of the Court.

This case requires us to determine the constitutionality of the use of deadly force to prevent the escape of an apparently unarmed suspected felon. We conclude that such force may not be used unless it is necessary to prevent the escape and the officer has probable cause to believe that the suspect poses a significant threat of death or serious physical injury to the officer or others.

At about 10:45 P.M. on October 3, 1974, Memphis Police Officers Elton Hymon and Leslie Wright were dispatched to answer a "prowler inside call." Upon arriving at the scene they saw a woman standing on her porch and gesturing toward the adjacent house. She told them she had heard glass breaking and that "they" or "someone" was breaking in next door. While Wright radioed the dispatcher to say that they were on the scene, Hymon went behind the house. He heard a door slam and saw someone run across the back yard. The fleeing suspect, who was appellee-respondent's decedent, Edward Garner, stopped at a 6-feet-high chain link fence at the edge of the yard. With the aid of a flashlight, Hymon was able to see Garner's face and hands. He saw no sign of a weapon, and, though not certain, was "reasonably sure" and "figured" that Garner was unarmed. He thought Garner was 17 or 18 years old and about 5′5″ or 5′7″ tall.[2] While Garner was crouched at the base of the fence, Hymon called out "police, halt" and took a few steps toward him. Garner then began to climb over the fence. Convinced that if Garner made it over the fence he would elude capture,[3] Hymon shot him. The bullet hit Garner in the back of the head. Garner was taken by ambulance to a hospital, where he died on the operating table. Ten dollars and a purse taken from the house were found on his body.

2. In fact, Garner, an eighth-grader, was 15. He was 5′4″ tall and weighed somewhere around 100 or 110 pounds.

3. When asked at trial why he fired, Hymon stated:

> Well, first of all it was apparent to me from the little bit that I knew about the area at the time that he was going to get away because, number 1, I couldn't get to him. My partner then couldn't find where he was because, you know, he was late coming around. He didn't know where I was talking about. I couldn't get to him because of the fence here, I couldn't have jumped this fence and come up, consequently jumped this fence and caught him before he got away because he was already up on the fence, just one leap and he was already over the fence, and so there is no way that I could have caught him.

He also stated that the area beyond the fence was dark, that he could not have gotten over the fence easily because he was carrying a lot of equipment and wearing heavy boots, and that Garner, being younger and more energetic, could have outrun him.

In using deadly force to prevent the escape, Hymon was acting under the authority of a Tennessee statute and pursuant to Police Department policy. The statute provides that "[i]f, after notice of the intention to arrest the defendant, he either flee or forcibly resist, the officer may use all the necessary means to effect the arrest." Tenn. Code Ann. §40-7-108 (1982).[5] The Department policy was slightly more restrictive than the statute, but still allowed the use of deadly force in cases of burglary. The incident was reviewed by the Memphis Police Firearm's Review Board and presented to a grand jury. Neither took any action.

Garner's father then brought this action in the Federal District Court for the Western District of Tennessee, seeking damages under 42 U.S.C. §1983 for asserted violations of Garner's constitutional rights. . . . [T]he district court entered judgment for all defendants. . . . The Court of Appeals reversed and remanded. It reasoned that the killing of a fleeing suspect is a "seizure" under the Fourth Amendment,[6] and is therefore constitutional only if "reasonable." . . .[7] The State of Tennessee, which had intervened to defend the statute, appealed to this Court. . . .

A police officer may arrest a person if he has probable cause to believe that person committed a crime. Petitioners and appellant argue that if this requirement is satisfied the Fourth Amendment has nothing to say about *how* that seizure is made. This submission ignores the many cases in which this Court, by balancing the extent of the intrusion against the need for it, has examined the reasonableness of the manner in which a search or seizure is conducted. . . .

[N]otwithstanding probable cause to seize a suspect, an officer may not always do so by killing him. The intrusiveness of a seizure by means of deadly force is unmatched. The suspect's fundamental interest in his own life need not be elaborated upon. The use of deadly force also frustrates the interest of the individual, and of society, in judicial determination of guilt and punishment. Against these interests are ranged governmental interests in effective law enforcement. It is argued that overall violence will be reduced by encouraging the peaceful submission of suspects who know that they may be shot if they flee. . . . "Being able to arrest such individuals is a condition precedent to the state's entire system of law enforcement."

Without in any way disparaging the importance of these goals, we are not convinced that the use of deadly force is a sufficiently productive means of accomplishing them to justify the killing of nonviolent suspects. . . . [W]hile the meaningful threat of deadly force might be thought to lead to the arrest of more live suspects by discouraging escape attempts, the presently available evidence does not support this thesis. The fact is that a majority of police departments in this country have forbidden the use of deadly force against nonviolent suspects. If those charged with the enforcement of the criminal law have abjured the use of deadly force in arresting nondangerous felons, there is a substantial basis for doubting that the use of such force is an essential attribute of the arrest power in all felony cases. . . . It is not better that all felony suspects die than that they

5. Although the statute does not say so explicitly, Tennessee law forbids the use of deadly force in the arrest of a misdemeanant.

6. "The right of the people to be secure in their persons . . . against unreasonable searches and seizures, shall not be violated. . . ." U.S. Const., Amdt. 4.

7. The Court of Appeals concluded that the rule set out in the Model Penal Code "accurately states Fourth Amendment limitations on the use of deadly force against fleeing felons." . . .

escape. It is no doubt unfortunate when a suspect who is in sight escapes, but the fact that the police arrive a little late or are a little slower afoot does not always justify killing the suspect. A police officer may not seize an unarmed, nondangerous suspect by shooting him dead. The Tennessee statute is unconstitutional insofar as it authorizes the use of deadly force against such fleeing suspects.

It is not, however, unconstitutional on its face. Where the officer has probable cause to believe that the suspect poses a threat of serious physical harm, either to the officer or to others, it is not constitutionally unreasonable to prevent escape by using deadly force. Thus, if the suspect threatens the officer with a weapon or there is probable cause to believe that he has committed a crime involving the infliction or threatened infliction of serious physical harm, deadly force may be used if necessary to prevent escape, and if, where feasible, some warning has been given. As applied in such circumstances, the Tennessee statute would pass constitutional muster.

It is insisted that the Fourth Amendment must be construed in light of the common-law rule, which allowed the use of whatever force was necessary to effect the arrest of a fleeing felon, though not a misdemeanant. . . . Because of sweeping change in the legal and technological context, reliance on the common-law rule in this case would be a mistaken literalism that ignores the purposes of a historical inquiry.

[The common-law rule] arose at a time when virtually all felonies were punishable by death. . . . Courts have also justified the common-law rule by emphasizing the relative dangerousness of felons. Neither of these justifications makes sense today. Almost all crimes formerly punishable by death no longer are or can be. . . . Many crimes classified as misdemeanors . . . at common law are now felonies. These changes have . . . made the assumption that a "felon" is more dangerous than a misdemeanant untenable. Indeed, numerous misdemeanors involve conduct more dangerous than many felonies. . . .

In reversing, the Court of Appeals . . . held that "the facts, as found, did not justify the use of deadly force." We agree. Officer Hymon could not reasonably have believed that Garner — young, slight, and unarmed — posed any threat. Indeed, Hymon never attempted to justify his actions on any basis other than the need to prevent an escape. . . .

The dissent argues that the shooting was justified by the fact that Officer Hymon had probable cause to believe that Garner had committed a nighttime burglary. While we agree that burglary is a serious crime, we cannot agree that it is so dangerous as automatically to justify the use of deadly force. . . . Although the armed burglar would present a different situation, the fact that an unarmed suspect has broken into a dwelling at night does not automatically mean he is physically dangerous. This case demonstrates as much. In fact, the available statistics demonstrate that burglaries only rarely involve physical violence. During the 10-year period from 1973-1982, only 3.8 percent of all burglaries involved violent crime. Bureau of Justice Statistics, Household Burglary, p. 4 (1985). . . .

The judgment of the Court of Appeals is affirmed. . . .

O'CONNOR, J., with whom THE CHIEF JUSTICE and REHNQUIST, J., join, dissenting. . . .

The clarity of hindsight cannot provide the standard for judging the reasonableness of police decisions made in uncertain and often dangerous circumstances. . . .

The public interest involved in the use of deadly force as a last resort to apprehend a fleeing burglary suspect relates primarily to the serious nature of the crime. Household burglaries represent not only the illegal entry into a person's home, but also "pos[e] real risk of serious harm to others." Solem v. Helm, 463 U.S. 277, 315-316 (1983) (Burger, C.J., dissenting). . . . Victims of a forcible intrusion into their home by a nighttime prowler will find little consolation in the majority's confident assertion that "burglaries only rarely involve physical violence." Moreover, even if a particular burglary, when viewed in retrospect, does not involve physical harm to others, the "harsh potentialities for violence" inherent in the forced entry into a home preclude characterization of the crime as "innocuous, inconsequential, minor, or 'nonviolent.'" Solem v. Helm, supra, at 316 (Burger, C.J., dissenting).

Because burglary is a serious and dangerous felony, the public interest in the prevention and detection of the crime is of compelling importance. Where a police officer has probable cause to arrest a suspected burglar, the use of deadly force as a last resort might well be the only means of apprehending the suspect. . . . Although some law enforcement agencies may choose to assume the risk that a criminal will remain at large, the Tennessee statute reflects a legislative determination that the use of deadly force in prescribed circumstances will serve generally to protect the public. . . .

Without questioning the importance of a person's interest in his life, I do not think this interest encompasses a right to flee unimpeded from the scene of a burglary. . . . The legitimate interests of the suspect in these circumstances are adequately accommodated by the Tennessee statute: to avoid the use of deadly force and the consequent risk to his life, the suspect need merely obey the valid order to halt. . . .

The Court's silence on critical factors in the decision to use deadly force invites second-guessing of difficult police . . . decisions that must be made quickly in the most trying of circumstances. Police are given no guidance for determining which objects, among an array of potentially lethal weapons ranging from guns to knives to baseball bats to rope, will justify the use of deadly force. The Court also declines to outline the additional factors necessary to provide "probable cause" for believing that a suspect "poses a significant threat of death or serious physical injury." . . .

Whatever the constitutional limits on police use of deadly force in order to apprehend a fleeing felon, I do not believe they are exceeded in a case in which a police officer has probable cause to arrest a suspect at the scene of a residential burglary, orders the suspect to halt, and then fires his weapon as a last resort to prevent the suspect's escape into the night. I respectfully dissent.

NOTES

1. *Deadly force.* Which police measures for effectuating an arrest constitute the sort of deadly force that *Garner* restricts? Are choke holds, electric cattle prods, night sticks, and pepper spray included? In a recent California incident, a police officer and his K-9 companion observed a suspect tossing objects out from the rear entrance of a fast-food restaurant. When the officer identified himself, the suspect started walking and then running away, ignoring the officer's threat to make use of the dog unless he stopped. The officer then released the dog, who effected the arrest by catching up to the suspect, biting onto his right arm, pulling him to the ground, and holding him there until the officer ordered the dog to release its grip. The suspect sustained severe wounds to his upper arm, requiring surgery and eight days of hospitalization. Was this a use of "deadly force"? Was it permissible under *Garner*? See Vera Cruz v. City of Escondido, 139 F.3d 659 (9th Cir. 1997). Compare the definition of deadly force in Model Penal Code §3.11(2), Appendix.

2. Private citizens. Because the rule announced in *Garner* is based on the Fourth Amendment, this constitutional limit on the use of deadly force applies only to the police and others acting under state authority. (A much-debated question is whether a private person who uses defensive force is "acting under state authority" when state law creates a privilege to use force under those circumstances.) Apart from the technical "state-action" issue under constitutional law, what limits should apply when private citizens use deadly force to protect their property? What limits should apply when the state authorizes conduct that will deprive certain citizens of their life? Reconsider the "Make-My-Day" statutes and other laws permitting homeowners to shoot intruders who do not pose a lethal threat, page 801 supra.

Suppose a teenager cuts a bicycle chain, gets on the bike and starts to ride off on it. May the bicycle's owner, observing from a distance, shoot the teenager in order to recoup his property? See Model Penal Code §3.06(d)(ii), Appendix. If the teenager abandons the bicycle and flees on foot, may the owner shoot to prevent his escape? Should the answer be different if the teenager flees after trying unsuccessfully to rob the owner at gunpoint?

MODEL PENAL CODE

SECTION 3.07(2)(b). USE OF FORCE IN LAW ENFORCEMENT

[See Appendix.]

MODEL PENAL CODE AND COMMENTARIES, COMMENT TO §3.07 AT 111-120 (1985): The common law approach to the problem of deadly force in arrest was based on the distinction between felony and misdemeanor. Deadly force was authorized where necessary to prevent the escape of one fleeing from arrest for felony, but not for misdemeanor. . . .

The extreme breadth of the privilege apparently induced some courts and legislatures to limit its application in the very worst way — by imposing a rule of strict liability. Thus, the privilege was at times said to attach only when the deceased had in fact committed a felony, apart from all considerations of good faith and reasonable belief on the part of the arresting officer. In other jurisdictions, the rule appears to have required that a felony must in fact have been committed, though the deceased need not have committed it if the officer reasonably believed that he did. Such a rule also creates the possibility of an absolute liability. Still other jurisdictions appeared to adhere to a rule of reasonable belief, but the law was in a state of considerable ambiguity and uncertainty on this vital point. . . .

Like the common law rule, Paragraph (i) of Subsection (2)(b) restricts the use of extreme force to arrests for felonies. . . . But unlike the common law rule, Subsection (2)(b) imposes certain additional qualifications on the privilege.

First, the use of deadly force is restricted by Paragraph (ii) of Subsection (2)(b) to those who, under the law of the jurisdiction, are authorized to act as peace officers and to those who are assisting persons whom they believe are authorized to act as peace officers. Where the purpose to be served is the apprehension of persons to answer criminal charges, it has seemed important, in an age of firearms, to restrict the use of deadly force to situations where official personnel are involved, or at least are believed to be involved. . . .

Another difference between the common law and these provisions is stated in Paragraph (iii) of Subsection (2). It is there recognized that the public interest is poorly served if the use of deadly force creates a substantial risk of injury to innocent bystanders. The privilege is accordingly withheld unless the actor believes that there is no such risk. . . .

The third way in which these provisions differ from the common law is contained in Paragraph (iv) of Subsection (2)(b), which is based on the principle that the character of the offender as it can be inferred from the available information, rather than from an abstract classification of the offense he is thought to have committed, should be determinative as to the use of deadly force. Specifically, the judgment is that the use of deadly force should be sanctioned only in cases where the offender is thought to pose such a danger to life or limb that his immediate apprehension overrides competing considerations.

3. *Choice of the Lesser Evil — The Residual Principle of Justification*

PEOPLE v. UNGER

Supreme Court of Illinois
66 Ill. 2d 333, 362 N.E.2d 319 (1977)

RYAN, J. Defendant, Francis Unger, was charged with the crime of escape and was convicted following a jury trial before the circuit court of Will County. Defendant was sentenced to a term of three to nine years to be served consecutively to the remainder of the sentence for which he was imprisoned at the time of the escape. The conviction was reversed upon appeal and the cause was remanded for a new trial. . . . We granted leave to appeal and now affirm the judgment of the appellate court.

At the time of the present offense, the defendant was confined at the Illinois State Penitentiary in Joliet, Illinois. Defendant was serving a one- to three-year term as a consequence of a conviction for auto theft. . . . On February 23, 1972, the defendant was transferred to the prison's minimum security, honor farm. It is undisputed that on March 7, 1972, the defendant walked off the honor farm. Defendant was apprehended two days later in a motel room in St. Charles, Illinois.

At trial, defendant testified that prior to his transfer to the honor farm he had been threatened by a fellow inmate. This inmate allegedly brandished a six-inch knife in an attempt to force defendant to engage in homosexual activities. Defendant was 22 years old and weighed approximately 155 pounds. He testified that he did not report the incident to the proper authorities due to fear of retaliation. Defendant also testified that he is not a particularly good fighter.

Defendant stated that after his transfer to the honor farm he was assaulted and sexually molested by three inmates, and he named the assailants at trial. The attack allegedly occurred on March 2, 1972, and from that date until his escape defendant received additional threats from inmates he did not know. On March 7, 1972, the date of the escape, defendant testified that he received a call on an institution telephone. Defendant testified that the caller, whose voice he did not recognize, threatened him with death because the caller had heard that defendant had reported the assault to prison authorities. Defendant said that he left the honor farm to save his life and that he planned to return once he found someone who could help him. None of these incidents were reported to the prison officials. As mentioned, defendant was apprehended two days later still dressed in his prison clothes. . . .

Defendant's first trial for escape resulted in a hung jury. The jury in the second trial returned its verdict after a five-hour deliberation. The following instruction (People's Instruction No. 9) was given by the trial court over defendant's objection. "The reasons, if any, given for the alleged escape are immaterial and not to be considered by you as in any way justifying or excusing, if there were in fact such reasons." . . .

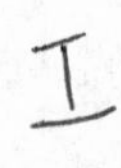

The principal issue in the present appeal is whether it was error for the court to instruct the jury that it must disregard the reasons given for defendant's escape and to conversely refuse to instruct the jury on the statutory defenses of compulsion and necessity. . . . The State contends that, under the facts and circumstances of this case, the defenses of compulsion and necessity are, as a matter of law, unavailable to defendant. . . .

Traditionally, the courts have been reluctant to permit the defenses of compulsion and necessity to be relied upon by escapees. This reluctance appears to have been primarily grounded upon considerations of public policy. Several recent decisions, however, have recognized the applicability of the compulsion and necessity defenses to prison escapes. In People v. Harmon (1974), 53 Mich. App. 482, 220 N.W.2d 212, the defense of duress was held to apply in a case where the defendant alleged that he escaped in order to avoid repeated homosexual attacks from fellow inmates. In People v. Lovercamp (1974), 43 Cal. App. 3d 823, 118 Cal. Rptr. 110, a limited defense of necessity was held to be available to two defendants whose escapes were allegedly motivated by fear of homosexual attacks.

As illustrated by *Harmon* and *Lovercamp,* different courts have reached similar results in escape cases involving sexual abuse, though the question was analyzed under different defense theories. A certain degree of confusion has resulted from the recurring practice on the part of the courts to use the terms "compulsion" (duress) and "necessity" interchangeably, though the defenses are theoretically distinct. . . .

In our view, the defense of necessity, as defined by our statute (Ill. Rev. Stat. 1971, ch. 38, par. 7-13), is the appropriate defense in the present case. In a very real sense, the defendant here was not deprived of his free will by the threat of imminent physical harm which, according to the Committee Comments, appears to be the intended interpretation of the defense of compulsion as set out in section 7-11 of the Criminal Code. . . . Rather, if defendant's testimony is believed, he was forced to choose between two admitted evils by the situation which arose from actual and threatened homosexual assaults and fears of reprisal. Though the defense of compulsion would be applicable in the unlikely event that a prisoner was coerced by the threat of imminent physical harm to perform the specific act of escape, no such situation is involved in the present appeal. . . .

The defendant's testimony was clearly sufficient to raise the affirmative defense of necessity. That defense is defined by statute (Ill. Rev. Stat. 1971, ch. 38, par. 7-13):

> Conduct which would otherwise be an offense is justifiable by reason of necessity if the accused was without blame in occasioning or developing the situation and reasonably believed such conduct was necessary to avoid a public or private injury greater than the injury which might reasonably result from his own conduct.

Defendant testified that he was subjected to threats of forced homosexual activity and that, on one occasion, the threatened abuse was carried out. He also testified that he was physically incapable of defending himself and that he feared greater harm would result from a report to the authorities. Defendant further testified that just prior to his escape he was told that he was going to be killed, and that he therefore fled the honor farm in order to save his life. Though the State's evidence cast a doubt upon the defendant's motives for escape and upon the reasonableness of defendant's assertion that such conduct was necessary, the defendant was entitled to have the jury consider the defense on the basis of his testimony. . . .

The State, however, would have us apply a more stringent test to prison escape situations. The State refers to the *Lovercamp* decision, where only a limited necessity defense was recognized. In *Lovercamp*, it was held that the defense of necessity need be submitted to the jury only where five conditions had been met. Those conditions are: "(1) The prisoner is faced with a specific threat of death, forcible sexual attack or substantial bodily injury in the immediate future; (2) There is no time for a complaint to the authorities or there exists a history of futile complaints which make any result from such complaints illusory; (3) There is no time or opportunity to resort to the courts; (4) There is no evidence of force or violence used towards prison personnel or other 'innocent' persons in the escape; and (5) The prisoner immediately reports to the proper authorities when he has attained a position of safety from the immediate threat."

The State correctly points out that the defendant never informed the authorities of his situation and failed to report immediately after securing a position of safety. Therefore, it is contended that, under the authority of *Lovercamp*, defendant is not entitled to a necessity instruction. We agree with the State and with the court in *Lovercamp* that the above conditions are relevant factors to be used in assessing claims of necessity. We cannot say, however, that the existence of each condition is, as a matter of law, necessary to establish a meritorious necessity defense.

The preconditions set forth in *Lovercamp* are, in our view, matters which go to the weight and credibility of the defendant's testimony. . . . The absence of one or more of the elements listed in *Lovercamp* would not necessarily mandate a finding that the defendant could not assert the defense of necessity.

By way of example, in the present case defendant did not report to the authorities immediately after securing his safety. In fact, defendant never voluntarily turned himself in to the proper officials. However, defendant testified that he intended to return to the prison upon obtaining legal advice from an attorney and claimed that he was attempting to get money from friends to pay for such counsel. Regardless of our opinion as to the believability of defendant's tale, this testimony, if accepted by the jury, would have negated any negative inference which would arise from defendant's failure to report to proper authorities after the escape. The absence of one of the *Lovercamp* preconditions does not alone disprove the claim of necessity and should not, therefore, automatically preclude an instruction on the defense. We therefore reject the contention that the availability of the necessity defense be expressly conditioned upon the elements set forth in *Lovercamp*.

In conclusion, we hold that under the facts and circumstances of the present case the defendant was entitled to submit his defense of necessity to the jury. It was, therefore, reversible error to give People's Instruction No. 9 to the jury and to refuse to give an appropriate instruction defining the defense of necessity, such as the instruction tendered by the defendant. . . .

UNDERWOOD, J., dissenting: My disagreement with my colleagues stems from an uneasy feeling that their unconditional recognition of necessity as a defense to the charge of escape carries with it the seeds of future troubles. Unless narrowly circumscribed, the availability of that defense could encourage potential escapes, disrupt prison discipline, and could even result in injury to prison guards, police or private citizens. For these reasons courts have been quite reluctant to honor the defenses of duress, necessity or compulsion in prison escapes, and, until recent years, they were uniformly held insufficient to justify escapes. . . .

I am not totally insensitive to the sometimes brutal and unwholesome problems faced by prison inmates, and the frequency of sexually motivated assaults. Prisoner complaints to unconcerned or understaffed prison administrations may produce little real help to a prisoner or may actually increase the hazard from fellow inmates of whose conduct complaint has been made. Consequently, and until adequate prison personnel and facilities are realities, I agree that a necessity defense should be recognized. The interests of society are better served, however, if the use of that defense in prison-escape cases is confined within well-defined boundaries such as those in *Lovercamp*. In that form it will be available, but with limitations precluding its wholesale use.

It is undisputed that defendant here did not meet those conditions. . . . Rather, he stole a truck some nine hours after his escape, drove to Chicago, and later drove to St. Charles, using the telephone to call friends in Canada. This conduct, coupled with his admitted intent to leave in order to gain publicity for what he considered an unfair sentence, severely strain the credibility of his testimony regarding his intention to return to the prison.

NOTES

1. In United States v. Bailey, 444 U.S. 394 (1980), the Supreme Court held, contrary to *Unger,* but in accord with *Lovercamp,* that a prerequisite for invoking the necessity defense in a prison escape case is that the defendant make a bona fide effort to surrender or return "as soon as the duress or necessity had lost its coercive force."

2. Consider the bearing of the following comment on the task of weighing the evils in a prison escape case (Model Penal Code and Commentaries, Comments to §3.02 at 12, n.5 (1985)):

> The harm sought to be prevented by the law defining the offense may be viewed broadly enough to permit judicial attention to the effects on law enforcement of allowing the defense in the particular circumstances involved. For example, a court

could consider whether recognition of the defense when a prisoner has escaped to avoid assault would have the effect of substantially encouraging unjustified escapes.

Question: Under this approach could a court deny a necessity defense in an otherwise justified circumstance, on the ground that other defendants might abuse the defense by invoking it when their conduct was *not* justified?

3. The *Unger* case treats the prison escape defense as an issue of justification. The possibility of a defense based on excuse is raised page 845 infra. In considering what difference it might make, consider United States v. Lopez, 662 F. Supp. 1083 (N.D. Cal. 1987). Defendant McIntosh landed a helicopter in the recreation yard of a federal prison and then flew off with Lopez, who had been prisoner there. Prosecuted for escape, Lopez asserted the defenses of duress and necessity, on the basis of her fear that she would have been killed or seriously injured if she had not escaped. McIntosh was charged with aiding and abetting Lopez in her escape. Does he have a good justification defense if Lopez does? Does he have a good duress defense if Lopez does?

4. For commentaries on the prison escape problem, see Martin Gardner, The Defense of Necessity and the Right to Escape from Prison, 49 S. Cal. L. Rev. 110 (1975); Comment, Intolerable Conditions as a Defense to Prison Escapes, 26 U.C.L.A. L. Rev. 1126 (1979).

BOROUGH OF SOUTHWARK v. WILLIAMS, [1971] 2 All E.R. 175: [Defendants were homeless families in dire straits, several among many in London at the time, which was suffering an extreme housing shortage. Obtaining no help from local government, they made an orderly entry into some empty houses belonging to the Borough and became squatters there. The Borough brought an action to oust them. The squatters resisted by raising the defense of necessity. Lord Denning rejected the defense:] There is authority for saying that in case of great and imminent danger, in order to preserve life, the law will permit of an encroachment on private property. . . . The doctrine so enunciated must, however, be carefully circumscribed. Else necessity would open the door to many an excuse. . . . If homelessness were once admitted as a defence to trespass, no one's house could be safe. Necessity would open a door which no man could shut. It would not only be those in extreme need who would enter. . . . There would be others who would imagine that they were in need, or would invent a need, so as to gain entry. Each man would say his need was greater than the next man's. The plea would be an excuse for all sorts of wrongdoing. So the courts must, for the sake of law and order, take a firm stand. They must refuse to admit the plea of necessity to the hungry and the homeless; and trust that their distress will be relieved by the charitable and the good. Applying these principles, it seems to me [the] circumstances of these squatters are not such as to afford any justification or excuse in law for their entry into these houses. We can sympathise with the plight in which they find themselves. We can recognise the orderly way in which they made their entry. But we can go no further. They must make their appeal for help to others, not to us. . . . But, so far as these courts are concerned, we must, in the interest of law and order itself, uphold the title to these properties. . . . The court must exercise its summary jurisdiction and order the defendants to go out.

COMMONWEALTH v. LENO, 415 Mass. 835, 616 N.E.2d 453 (1993): Massachusetts is one of ten States that prohibit distribution of hypodermic needles without a prescription. In the face of those statutes the defendants operated a needle exchange program in an effort to combat the spread of acquired immunodeficiency syndrome (AIDS). As a result, the defendants were charged with and convicted of (1) unauthorized possession of instruments to administer controlled substances, and (2) unlawful distribution of an instrument to administer controlled substances, . . . On appeal, the defendants challenge the judge's refusal to instruct the jury on the defense of necessity. . . . We affirm. . . . The defendants did not show that the danger they sought to avoid was clear and imminent, rather than debatable or speculative. . . . That some States prohibit the distribution of hypodermic needles without a prescription, and others do not, merely indicates that the best course to take to address the long-term hazard of the spread of AIDS remains a matter of debate. The defendants' argument is that, in their view, the prescription requirement for possession and distribution of hypodermic needles and syringes is both ineffective and dangerous. The Legislature, however, has determined that it wants to control the distribution of drug-related paraphernalia and their use in the consumption of illicit drugs. That public policy is entitled to deference by courts. Whether a statute is wise or effective is not within the province of courts. . . . Our deference to legislative judgments reflects neither an abdication of nor unwillingness to perform the judicial role; but rather a recognition of the separation of powers and the undesirability of the judiciary substituting its notions of correct policy for that of a popularly elected Legislature. . . . The defendants argue that the increasing number of AIDS cases constitutes a societal problem of great proportions, and that their actions were an effective means of reducing the magnitude of that problem; they assert that their possession, transportation and distribution of hypodermic needles eventually will produce an over-all reduction in the spread of HIV and in the future incidence of AIDS. The defendants' argument raises the issue of jury nullification, not the defense of necessity. . . . We do not accept the premise that jurors have a right to nullify the law on which they are instructed by the judge, or that the judge must inform them of their power.

[For a thoughtful opinion to the contrary, See People v. Berkowitz, 588 N.Y.S.2d 507 (N.Y. Crim. Ct. 1991).]

COMMONWEALTH v. HUTCHINS, 410 Mass. 726, 575 N.E.2d 741 (1991): [Defendant was charged with illegal possession and cultivation of marijuana. At trial defendant made an offer of proof, supported by affidavits and other material, to show that he was a victim of progressive systemic sclerosis, a serious and sometimes fatal disease with frightful symptoms for which no cure exists, and that ingestion of marijuana had produced a remarkable remission. The judge denied the offer of proof on the ground that the proof offered would not support a necessity defense. The defendant was convicted, and he appealed. The majority of the Supreme Judicial Court of Massachusetts affirmed, stating:] The defendant's proffered evidence does not raise the defense of necessity. In our view, the alleviation of the defendant's medical symptoms, the importance to the defendant of which we do not underestimate, would not clearly and significantly outweigh the potential harm to the public were we to declare that the defendant's cultivation of marihuana and its use for his medicinal purposes may not be punishable. We cannot dismiss the reasonably possible negative impact of such a judicial declaration on the enforcement of our drug laws, including but not limited to those dealing with marihuana, nor can we ignore the government's overriding interest in the regulation of such substances.

[Liacos, C. J., dissenting:] [T]he court . . . fails to give sufficient consideration to the rationale behind the common law defense of necessity. That rationale is based on the recognition that, under very limited circumstances, "the value protected by the law is, as a matter of public policy, eclipsed by a superseding value which makes it inappropriate and unjust to apply the usual criminal rule." The superseding value in a case such as the present one is the humanitarian and compassionate value in allowing an individual to seek relief from agonizing symptoms caused by a progressive and incurable illness in circumstances which risk no harm to any other individual. In my view, the harm to an individual in having to endure such symptoms may well outweigh society's generalized interest in prohibiting him or her from using the marihuana in such circumstances. On a proper offer of proof I would recognize the availability of a necessity defense when marihuana is used for medical purposes.

[The dissent added in footnote 1:] There is no reason to believe, as the court suggests, that allowing a defendant to present evidence of medical necessity to a jury will have a negative impact on the enforcement of drug laws. I am confident that juries would apply their wisdom and common sense in making sure that the necessity defense is not successfully utilized by defendants who use marihuana for purposes other than to alleviate agonizing and painful medical symptoms.

NOTES

1. A story in N.Y. Times, Oct. 11, 1993, §B, at 1, reports the arrest and conviction of Mildred Katz, a 79-year-old grandmother, for growing marijuana in the backyard of her Monticello home in the Catskills. The account states that she did it so that her son would eat properly. It appeared that the son was a victim of chronic multiple sclerosis, and that his failing appetite was restored by ingesting the marijuana. Asked by the police if she would rob a bank if her son needed an operation, she replied, "If it would cure his sickness, I would absolutely. I'd go to jail for life." The local magistrate placed her on probation with an admonition to stay out of trouble.

2. As in *Hutchins,* many courts refuse to permit a necessity defense for medical uses of marijuana. E.g., State v. Poling, 531 S.E.2d 678 (W. Va. 2000). But others have ruled that when marijuana is employed to alleviate the symptoms of serious illness, the common-law defense of necessity can be invoked to bar prosecution for buying or using the drug. See, e.g., Sowell v. State, 738 So. 2d 205 (Fla. App. 1998). Several legislatures have crafted explicit statutory exceptions for such cases, but such exceptions are usually narrow. In Virginia, legislation permits the use of marijuana for glaucoma and cancer patients; because other diseases are not mentioned, the necessity defense was denied in the case of a man who used marijuana to treat debilitating migraine headaches that did not respond to prescription medications. Murphy v. Commonwealth, 521 S.E.2d 301 (Va. App. 1999).

In what may prove to be the most important of these cases, a federal court of appeals recently held that medical necessity can be invoked as a defense to a federal prosecution for buying marijuana, and the U.S. Supreme Court has agreed to review that ruling. See United States v. Oakland Cannabis Buyers' Cooperative, 190 F.3d 1109 (9th Cir. 1999), cert. granted (Nov. 27, 2000). How should the Supreme Court rule? Compare United States v. Bailey, page 812, Note 1, supra.

3. In State v. Rasmussen, 524 N.W.2d 843 (N.D. 1994), the defendant's license to drive had been suspended. On a cold January night, he found himself stranded on a highway in North Dakota. His car had broken down, and the person driving him had left to get help. When the driver did not return, Rasmussen managed to get the car started, took the wheel, and drove away. He was caught and prosecuted for driving while suspended — a strict liability offense. Should he be able to assert a necessity defense when the underlying crime does not require mens rea? Does the necessity defense serve to identify cases in which blame for a wrongful act cannot be imposed (when mens rea is required), or does it identify cases in which the defendant's act was not wrongful at all?

The link between the necessity defense and community judgments on moral culpability is discussed in John T. Parry, The Virtue of Necessity: Reshaping Culpability and the Rule of Law, 36 Houston L. Rev. 397 (1999).

MODEL PENAL CODE

SECTION 3.02. JUSTIFICATION GENERALLY: CHOICE OF EVILS

(1) Conduct which the actor believes to be necessary to avoid a harm or evil to himself or to another is justifiable, provided that:

(a) the harm or evil sought to be avoided by such conduct is greater than that sought to be prevented by the law defining the offense charged; and

(b) neither the Code nor other law defining the offense provides exceptions or defenses dealing with the specific situation involved; and

(c) a legislative purpose to exclude the justification claimed does not otherwise plainly appear.

(2) When the actor was reckless or negligent in bringing about the situation requiring a choice of harms or evils or in appraising the necessity for his conduct, the justification afforded by this Section is unavailable in a prosecution for any offense for which recklessness or negligence, as the case may be, suffices to establish culpability.

MODEL PENAL CODE AND COMMENTARIES, COMMENT TO §3.02 AT 9-14 (1985): This section accepts the view that a principle of necessity, properly conceived, affords a general justification for conduct that would otherwise constitute an offense. It reflects the judgment that such a qualification on criminal liability, like the general requirements of culpability, is essential to the rationality and justice of the criminal law, and is appropriately addressed in a penal code. Under this section, property may be destroyed to prevent the spread of a fire. . . . An ambulance may pass a traffic light. Mountain climbers lost in a storm may take refuge in a house or may appropriate provisions. Cargo may be jettisoned or an embargo violated to preserve the vessel. . . . A druggist may dispense a drug without the requisite prescription to alleviate grave distress in an emergency. A developed legal system must have better ways of dealing with such problems than to refer only to the letter of particular prohibitions, framed without reference to cases of this kind. . . .[3]

The Code's principle of necessity is subject to a number of limitations. First, the actor must actually believe that his conduct is necessary to avoid an evil. . . . It is not enough that the actor believes that his behavior possibly may be conducive to ameliorating certain evils; he must believe it is "necessary" to avoid the evils.[4]

Second, the necessity must arise from an attempt by the actor to avoid an evil or harm that is greater than the evil or harm sought to be avoided by the law defining the offense charged. . . .

Third, the balancing of evils is not committed to the private judgment of the actor; it is an issue for determination at the trial. . . . Subsection (1)(a) . . . requires that the harm or evil sought to be avoided be greater than that which would be caused by the commission of the offense, not that the defendant believe it to be so. What is involved may be described as an interpretation of the law of the offense, in light of the submission that the special situation calls for an exception to the criminal prohibition that the legislature could not reasonably have intended to exclude, given the competing values to be weighed. The Code does not resolve the question of how far the balancing of values should be determined by the court as a matter of law or submitted to the jury. . . .

Fourth, under Subsections (1)(b) and (1)(c), the general choice of evils defense cannot succeed if the issue of competing values has been previously foreclosed by a deliberate legislative choice, as when some provision of the law deals explicitly with the specific situation that presents the choice of evils or a legislative purpose to exclude the claimed justification otherwise appears. . . .

NEW YORK PENAL LAW

Section 35.05. Justification; Generally

Unless otherwise limited by the ensuing provisions of this article defining justifiable use of physical force, or with some other provision of law, conduct which would otherwise constitute an offense is justifiable and not criminal when: . . .

2. Such conduct is necessary as an emergency measure to avoid an imminent public or private injury which is about to occur by reason of a situation occasioned or developed through no fault of the actor, and which is of such gravity that, according to ordinary standards of intelligence and morality, the desirability and urgency of avoiding such injury clearly outweigh the desirability of avoid-

3. A contrary view is expressed in Brown Commn. Final Report §601 Comment, which suggests that any general "choice of evils" codification would be "a potential source of unwarranted difficulty in ordinary cases," and that case by case prosecutive discretion is preferable. But reliance on prosecutorial discretion alone leaves the matter to be decided in the absence of governing principles and by an executive official who must act without legislative guidance or judicial check. . . .

4. This requirement would pose a significant barrier to assertion of the defense both in cases of illegal political protest, see, e.g., United States v. Kroncke, 459 F.2d 697 (8th Cir. 1972), and in cases of illegal governmental action claimed to protect the national security, see, e.g., United States v. Ehrlichman, 546 F.2d 910 (D.C. Cir. 1976).

ing the injury sought to be prevented by the statute defining the offense in issue. The necessity and justifiability of such conduct may not rest upon considerations pertaining only to the morality and advisability of the statute, either in its general application or with respect to its application to a particular class of cases arising thereunder. Whenever evidence relating to the defense of justification under this subdivision is offered by the defendant, the court shall rule as a matter of law whether the claimed facts and circumstances would, if established, constitute a defense.

NOTES

1. New York and Model Penal Code approaches compared. Consider Model Penal Code and Commentaries, Comment to §3.02 at 17, 19-21 (1985):

> [The New York law differs from the Model Code in requiring that the conduct be an "emergency measure to avoid an imminent . . . injury."] Such a requirement unduly emphasizes one ingredient in the judgment that is called for at the expense of others just as important. It is true that genuine necessity rests on the unavailability of alternatives that would avoid both evils, and that typically when the evil is not imminent some such alternative will be available; but it is a mistake to erect imminence as an absolute requirement, since there may be situations in which an otherwise illegal act is necessary to avoid an evil that may occur in the future. . . .
>
> A more important variation from the Model Code is the requirement in the New York provision that the situation that gives rise to the necessity for action be occasioned or developed "through no fault of the actor." Thus, an actor who negligently starts a fire is deprived of any defense for destroying property or breaking traffic regulations in an effort to prevent its spread or to notify the proper authorities. . . .
>
> By contrast, [under] the Code resolution of this matter . . . the actor who negligently starts a fire creating the need for him then to act to stop its spread may be prosecuted for offenses for which negligence would suffice, but would not be deprived of the choice of evils defense for offenses committed in the attempt to put out the fire that require a higher culpability level. . . .

Question: Consider how the previous cases would be decided under the Model Penal Code and New York formulations.

2. Lawrence Tiffany & Carl Anderson, Legislating the Necessity Defense in Criminal Law, 52 Den. L.J. 839, 861-862 (1975), write:

> A question which needs to be clarified is posed by LaFave and Scott: "*A,* driving a car, suddenly finds himself in a predicament where he must either run down *B* or hit *C*'s house and he reasonably chooses the latter, unfortunately killing two people in the house who by bad luck happened to be just at that place inside the house where *A*'s car struck. . . ."
>
> Of course, the defendant in this case is guilty of no crime to begin with. Were defendant charged with manslaughter (reckless homicide), the difficulty would be that recklessness means a conscious disregard of a risk that is "substantial and unjustifiable." The same is true of crimes defined in terms of negligence. Defendant needs no general justification defense when charged with a crime based on recklessness or negligence since it is implicit in the charge itself that the defendant's

conduct was not justified; unjustifiability of conduct becomes an element of the charge itself and must be proved by the state.

3. What perils are created by the elasticity of the defense of necessity? We saw earlier, in the section on the principle of legality, page 290 supra, that vagueness is regarded as a serious evil in the criminal law. Is vagueness less offensive when it affects defenses to, rather than definitions of, criminal conduct? Consider the views of James Fitzjames Stephen on this question. Defending a proposal to eliminate judicial authority to create new crimes while retaining another authorizing judges to develop new defenses, he stated (quoted in Glanville Williams, (2) Necessity, [1978] Crim. L. Rev. 128, 130):

> [T]he reason why the common law definitions of offences should be taken away, whilst the common law principles as to justification and excuse are kept alive, is like the reason why the benefit of a doubt should be given to a prisoner. The worst result that could arise from the abolition of the common law offences would be the occasional escape of a person morally guilty. The only result which can follow from preserving the common law as to justification and excuse is, that a man morally innocent, not otherwise protected, may avoid punishment. In the one case you remove rusty spring-guns and man-traps from unfrequented plantations, in the other you decline to issue an order for the destruction of every old-fashioned drag or life-buoy which may be found on the banks of a dangerous river, but is not in the inventory of the Royal Humane Society.

A modern-day version of Stephen's approach is followed in New Jersey. N.J. Stat. Ann. tit. 2C, §1-5 provides: "Common law crimes are abolished and no conduct constitutes an offense unless the offense is defined by this code or another statute of this State." But §3-2 provides: "a. *Necessity.* Conduct which would otherwise be an offense is justifiable by reason of necessity to the extent permitted by law and as to which neither the code nor other statutory law defining the offense provides exceptions or defenses dealing with the specific situation involved and a legislative purpose to exclude the justification claimed does not otherwise plainly appear." The drafters' commentary states: "The Commission believes it more appropriate to leave the issue to the Judiciary. The rarity of the defense and the imponderables of the particulars of specific cases convince us that the Courts can better define and apply this defense than can be done through legislation." 2 N.J. Crim. Law Rev. Commn., Final Report, The New Jersey Penal Code, Commentary 80 (1971).

Compare Louis B. Schwartz, Reform of the Federal Criminal Laws, [1977] Duke L.J. 171, 217. Responding to a proposal to allow courts to develop new defenses and justifications "in the light of reason and experience," Professor Schwartz observed:

> The open-ended invitation to judges to *add* to the listed defenses is a civil liberties monster. It was earlier urged on the Brown Commission . . . in order to retain all sorts of bad things — for example, the right of police to kill in suppressing riots and the right of a householder to shoot to kill a supposedly burglarious intruder whether or not he is perceived as a threat to life (as where the burglar is shot leaving the house). To leave the judges free to define defenses is virtually to abandon the effort to define crimes, since an offense is defined by the combination of what it prohibits and what is declared to be justified.

UNITED STATES v. SCHOON

United States Court of Appeals, 9th Circuit
971 F.2d 193 (1992)

BOOCHEVER, J.: Gregory Schoon, Raymond Kennon, Jr., and Patricia Manning appeal their convictions for obstructing activities of the Internal Revenue Service Office in Tucson, Arizona, and failing to comply with an order of a federal police officer. Both charges stem from their activities in protest of United States involvement in El Salvador. They claim the district court improperly denied them a necessity defense. Because we hold the necessity defense inapplicable in cases like this, we affirm.

On December 4, 1989, thirty people, including appellants, gained admittance to the IRS office in Tucson, where they chanted "keep America's tax dollars out of El Salvador," splashed simulated blood on the counters, walls, and carpeting, and generally obstructed the office's operation. After a federal police officer ordered the group, on several occasions, to disperse or face arrest, appellants were arrested.

At a bench trial, appellants proffered testimony about conditions in El Salvador as the motivation for their conduct. They attempted to assert a necessity defense, essentially contending that their acts in protest of American involvement in El Salvador were necessary to avoid further bloodshed in that country. While finding appellants motivated solely by humanitarian concerns, the court nonetheless precluded the defense as a matter of law. . . .

To invoke the necessity defense . . . the defendants colorably must have shown that: (1) they were faced with a choice of evils and chose the lesser evil; (2) they acted to prevent imminent harm; (3) they reasonably anticipated a direct causal relationship between their conduct and the harm to be averted; and (4) they had no legal alternatives to violating the law. The district court denied the necessity defense on the grounds that (1) the requisite immediacy was lacking; (2) the actions taken would not abate the evil; and (3) other legal alternatives existed. Because the threshold test for admissibility of a necessity defense is a conjunctive one, a court may preclude invocation of the defense if "proof is deficient with regard to any of the four elements."

While we could affirm substantially on those grounds relied upon by the district court, we find a deeper, systemic reason for the complete absence of federal case law recognizing a necessity defense in an indirect civil disobedience case. As used in this opinion, "civil disobedience" is the wilful violation of a law, undertaken for the purpose of social or political protest. Indirect civil disobedience involves violating a law or interfering with a government policy that is not, itself, the object of protest. Direct civil disobedience, on the other hand, involves protesting the existence of a law by breaking that law or by preventing the execution of that law in a specific instance in which a particularized harm would otherwise follow. This case involves indirect civil disobedience because these protestors were not challenging the laws under which they were charged. In contrast, the civil rights lunch counter sit-ins, for example, constituted direct civil disobedience because the protestors were challenging the rule that prevented them from sitting at lunch counters. . . . Today, we conclude, for the reasons stated below, that the necessity defense is inapplicable to cases involving indirect civil disobedience.

Necessity is, essentially, a utilitarian defense. It therefore justifies criminal acts taken to avert a greater harm, maximizing social welfare by allowing a crime to be committed where the social benefits of the crime outweigh the social costs of failing to commit the crime. Pursuant to the defense, prisoners could escape a burning prison; a person lost in the woods could steal food from a cabin to survive; . . . a crew could mutiny where their ship was thought to be unseaworthy; and property could be destroyed to prevent the spread of fire.

What all the traditional necessity cases have in common is that the commission of the "crime" averted the occurrence of an even greater "harm." In some sense, the necessity defense allows us to act as individual legislatures, amending a particular criminal provision or crafting a one-time exception to it, subject to court review, when a real legislature would formally do the same under those circumstances. For example, by allowing prisoners who escape a burning jail to claim the justification of necessity, we assume the lawmaker, confronting this problem, would have allowed for an exception to the law proscribing prison escapes.

Because the necessity doctrine is utilitarian, however, strict requirements contain its exercise so as to prevent nonbeneficial criminal conduct. . . .

Analysis of three of the necessity defense's four elements leads us to the conclusion that necessity can never be proved in a case of indirect civil disobedience. We do not rely upon the imminent harm prong of the defense because we believe there can be indirect civil disobedience cases in which the protested harm is imminent.

. . . Indirect civil disobedience seeks first and foremost to bring about the repeal of a law or a change of governmental policy, attempting to mobilize public opinion through typically symbolic action. These protestors violate a law, not because it is unconstitutional or otherwise improper, but because doing so calls public attention to their objectives. Thus, the most immediate "harm" this form of protest targets is the existence of the law or policy. However, the mere existence of a constitutional law or governmental policy cannot constitute a legally cognizable harm. *See* Comment, Political Protest and the Illinois Defense of Necessity, 54 U. Chi. L. Rev. 1070, 1083 (1987) ("In a society based on democratic decision making, this is how values are ranked — a protester cannot simply assert that her view of what is best should trump the decision of the majority of elected representatives."). . . . If there is no cognizable harm to prevent, the harm resulting from criminal action taken for the purpose of securing the repeal of the law or policy necessarily outweighs any benefit of the action.

This inquiry requires a court to judge the likelihood that an alleged harm will be abated by the taking of illegal action. In the sense that the likelihood of abatement is required in the traditional necessity cases, there will never be such likelihood in cases of indirect political protest. In the traditional cases, a prisoner flees a burning cell and averts death, or someone demolishes a home to create a firebreak and prevents the conflagration of an entire community. The nexus between the act undertaken and the result sought is a close one. Ordinarily it is the volitional illegal act alone which, once taken, abates the evil.

In political necessity cases involving indirect civil disobedience against congressional acts, however, the act alone is unlikely to abate the evil precisely because the action is indirect. Here, the IRS obstruction, or the refusal to comply with a federal officer's order, are unlikely to abate the killings in El Salvador, or immediately change Congress's policy; instead, it takes another volitional actor not controlled by the protestor to take a further step; Congress must change its mind.

A final reason the necessity defense does not apply to these indirect civil disobedience cases is that legal alternatives will never be deemed exhausted when the harm can be mitigated by congressional action. As noted above, the harm indirect civil disobedience aims to prevent is the continued existence of a law or policy. Because congressional action can always mitigate this "harm," lawful political activity to spur such action will always be a legal alternative. . . .

[T]he "possibility" that Congress will change its mind is sufficient in the context of the democratic process to make lawful political action a reasonable alternative to indirect civil disobedience. . . . [P]etitioning Congress to change a policy is always a legal alternative in such cases, regardless of the likelihood of the plea's success. Thus, indirect civil disobedience can never meet the necessity defense requirement that there be a lack of legal alternatives. . . .

Thus, we see the failure of any federal court to recognize a defense of necessity in a case like ours not as coincidental, but rather as the natural consequence of the historic limitation of the doctrine. Indirect protests of congressional policies can never meet all the requirements of the necessity doctrine. Therefore, we hold that the necessity defense is not available in such cases.

Affirmed.

NOTE

The necessity defense has been raised in many sit-in, vandalism, trespass, and related prosecutions in recent years. The causes have ranged from nuclear power and missile protests to anti-abortion protests. See Matthew Lippman, The Necessity Defense and Political Protest, 26 Crim. L. Bull. 317 (1990); Note (Laura Schulkind), Applying the Necessity Defense, 64 N.Y.U.L. Rev. 79 (1989). Though the defense has sometimes prevailed with juries and magistrates, it has been notably unsuccessful on the appellate level, where courts have overwhelmingly refused necessity instructions or barred defendants from introducing evidence on the issue in civil disobedience situations. See Note, Political Protest and the Illinois Defense of Necessity, 54 U. Chi. L. Rev. 1070 (1987). The *Schoon* case, however, is unusual in flatly denying the necessity defense in any indirect civil disobedience case. See Casenote (James Cavallaro), The Demise of the Political Necessity Defense: Indirect Civil Disobedience and *United States v. Schoon,* 81 Cal. L. Rev. 351 (1993).

REGINA v. DUDLEY AND STEPHENS

Queen's Bench Division
14 Q.B.D. 273 (1884)

[For the opinion in this case, see page 135 supra.]

NOTES

1. James Fitzjames Stephen, Digest of the Criminal Law 25 n. 1 (5th ed. 1894):

I can discover no principle in the judgment in R. v. Dudley. It depends entirely on its peculiar facts. The boy was deliberately put to death with a knife in order that his body might be used for food. This is quite different from any of the following cases — (1) The two men on a plank. Here the successful man does no direct bodily harm to the other. He leaves him the chance of getting another plank. (2) Several men are roped together on the Alps. They slip, and the weight of the whole party is thrown on one, who cuts the rope in order to save himself. Here the question is not whether some shall die, but whether one shall live. (3) The choice of evils. The captain of a ship runs down a boat, as the only means of avoiding shipwreck. A surgeon kills a child in the act of birth, as the only way to save the mother. A boat being too full of passengers to float, some are thrown overboard. Such cases are best decided as they arise.

2. A modern variant on *Dudley and Stephens* occurred in a 1987 tragedy at Zeebrugge, Belgium. The ferry *Herald of Free Enterprise,* lacking an adequate system to signal when its doors were properly shut,[30] suddenly sank as it left port, trapping dozens of passengers inside. Almost 200 passengers drowned, but before the ship went down, many of them attempted to escape by climbing a rope ladder to the deck. At one point a passenger climbing the ladder froze in panic and refused repeated commands to move on. Those below him then pulled him off the ladder, and he drowned. A coroner mentioned the possibility of murder charges but concluded that the actions taken were "a reasonable act of what is known as self-preservation." See Neil Hanson, The Custom of the Sea 301 (2000).

Would Judge Stephen (Note 1, supra) agree? What legal advice would he have given if passengers seeing their escape route blocked had asked whether they had the right to pull the fearful man out of the way? Were those passengers legally (or morally) in the wrong?

3. The American case referred to in Lord Coleridge's opinion was United States v. Holmes, 26 F. Cas. 360, 1 Wall Jr. 1 (C.C.E.D. Pa. 1842). The first mate, 8 seamen and 32 passengers were cast adrift on a life boat following a shipwreck on the high seas. The boat was grossly overcrowded and sprang a leak making it necessary to bail constantly in order to stay afloat. After a day and a half bailing became difficult because of the rough seas and the overcrowding, and the passengers panicked. The first mate ordered all male passengers whose wives were not in the boat to be thrown overboard. Eighteen passengers were jettisoned before a rescue ship arrived. Subsequently Holmes, one of the crew who assisted in ejecting the passengers, was charged with manslaughter, after the grand jury declined to return an indictment for murder. In charging the jury the judge made these points: that generally if two persons face a situation in which only one can survive "neither is bound to save the other's life by sacrificing his own, nor would either commit a crime in saving his own life for the only means of safety"; that while this principle prevailed between sailor and sailor it did not prevail between sailor and passenger because of the special duty owed the latter by the former; that absent this special relationship the choice of who should be sacrificed must be made by lot, since, "In no other way than this or some like way are those having equal rights put on an equal footing, and in no other way is it possible to guard against partiality and oppression, violence and conflict. . . ." Holmes was convicted and sentenced to six months' imprisonment and a fine of $20. Shortly thereafter the penalty was remitted.

30. That problem and related safety failures were attributed to "tough competition" and "the reluctance of the ferry operators . . . to incur extra costs." Jeremy Lovell, Ferry Safety Still an Issue 10 Years After Herald, Journal of Commerce, March 13, 1997, p. 3B.

For accounts of this case see F. Hicks, Human Jettison (1927); Benjamin Cardozo, Law and Literature 110-114 (1930). The latter observes (at 113):

> Where two or more are overtaken by a common disaster, there is no right on the part of one to save the lives of some by the killing of another. There is no rule of human jettison. Men there will often be who, when told that their going will be the salvation of the remnant, will choose the nobler part and make the plunge into the water. In that supreme moment the darkness for them will be illumined by the thought that those behind will ride to safety. If none of such mold are found aboard the boat, or too few to save the others, the human freight must be left to meet the chances of the waters. Who shall choose in such an hour between the victims and the saved? Who shall know when masts and sails of rescue may emerge out of the fog?

4. In his opinion in *Dudley and Stephens* Lord Coleridge argues that it was not certain the defendants had to kill Parker, that the jury's verdict speaks only in terms of probability, that "they might possibly have been picked up next day by a passing ship; they might possibly not have been picked up at all; in either case it is obvious that the killing of the boy would have been an unnecessary and profitless act." But suppose there had been the level of certainty Lord Coleridge was looking for? Professor Glanville Williams supposes the following case in his Textbook of Criminal Law 606 (2d ed. 1983):

> [L]et us suppose that the boat was equipped with an experimental radio transmitter, although radio-telephony was not in general use. The crew were able to make contact with Whitehall, which arranged for a ship to go to the rescue, but it could not arrive for seven days. The boat was lying off the trade routes, so it was unlikely that any other vessel would effect a rescue. The crew had reached such a stage of exhaustion that very soon none of them would be able to wield a knife. In these circumstances they asked to speak to the Home Secretary. They put the question to him: should they all accept death, or may they draw lots, kill the one with the unlucky number, and live on his body? In this way all but one will be saved. What should the Home Secretary reply? What would you reply, if you were Home Secretary?

For a tour de force of hypothetical opinions in a fictional case putting something like the scenario Professor Williams imagines, see Lon Fuller, The Case of the Speluncean Explorers, 62 Harv. L. Rev. 616 (1949).

NOTE ON TAKING LIFE TO SAVE LIFE

May the choice-of-evils principle ever justify the intentional killing of an innocent person who is not an aggressor? The Model Penal Code plainly anticipates an affirmative answer. In the commentary on the necessity proposal, the drafters state (Model Penal Code and Commentaries, Comment to §3.02 at 14-15 (1985)):

> It would be particularly unfortunate to exclude homicidal conduct from the scope of the defense. For, recognizing that the sanctity of life has a supreme place in the hierarchy of values, it is nonetheless true that conduct that results in taking life may promote the very value sought to be protected by the law of homicide. Suppose, for example, that the actor makes a breach in a dike, knowing that this

will inundate a farm, but taking the only course available to save a whole town. If he is charged with homicide of the inhabitants of the farm house, he can rightly point out that the object of the law of homicide is to save life, and that by his conduct he has effected a net saving of innocent lives. The life of every individual must be taken in such a case to be of equal value and the numerical preponderance in the lives saved compared to those sacrificed surely should establish legal justification for the act. So too, a mountaineer, roped to a companion who has fallen over a precipice, who holds on as long as possible but eventually cuts the rope, must certainly be granted the defense that he accelerated one death slightly but avoided the only alternative, the certain death of both. Although the view is not universally held that it is ethically preferable to take one innocent life than to have many lives lost,[15] most persons probably think a net saving of lives is ethically warranted if the choice among lives to be saved is not unfair. Certainly the law should permit such a choice.

How sound is the use of a numerical calculus to justify the intentional killing of an innocent, nonthreatening person? Resistance to such a position is evident in its explicit rejection by statutes and commentators.[31] Professor Andenaes, for example, has observed (Johannes Andenaes, The General Part of the Criminal Law of Norway 169 (1965)): "Even though many lives could be saved by the sacrifice of one, this would hardly be justifiable. It would conflict with the general attitude toward the inviolability of human life to interfere in this way with the course of events." But if it is better, when accidents happen, that fewer lives be lost, why is it wrong for a person to bring this about by his action? How can it be wrong to make things better?

NOTE ON RIGHTS AND LIVES[32]

The one circumstance in which the Model Penal Code (and perhaps prevailing law as well) arguably justifies killing an innocent, nonthreatening bystander is that in which killing him is necessary to avoid the death of several. Under the lesser-evil principle, killing one person is deemed a lesser evil than the death of more than one. To use the example of the Model Penal Code, it is justifiable to deflect flood waters to a farm, even if a family there would be killed, to avert flooding the whole town, which would result in many more deaths. It does not matter that the farm family members are wholly innocent and nonthreatening bystanders, or that deflecting the flood waters to them is itself an act of aggression that violates their rights.

15. Roman Catholic moralists have generally taken the position that one should not cause effects that are directly evil even if they are thought to be a necessary means to a greater good. . . . Thus, it is considered wrong to terminate the life of a fetus even if that is the only way the mother can be saved and even if the fetus will die in any event. On the other hand, an ordinary operation designed directly to protect the mother's health is permissible, even if an inevitable effect is the death of the fetus, under the so-called principle of "double effect" that death is only permitted, not intended, and is not itself a means to saving the mother's life. . . .

31. See John M. Taurek, Should the Numbers Count?, 6 Phil. & Pub. Aff. 293 (1977); Jeffrie G. Murphy, The Killing of the Innocent, 57 Monist 527 (1973); Note, Justification: The Impact of the Model Penal Code on Statutory Reform, 75 Colum. L. Rev. 914, 923 (1975). See also Philippa Foot, Utilitarianism and the Virtues, 94 MIND 196 (1985); Samuel Scheffler, Agent Centered Restrictions, Rationality, and the Virtues, 94 MIND 406 (1985).

32. Drawn from Sanford H. Kadish, Blame and Punishment 122-123 (1987).

But this maximizing-lives principle is not applicable to a case where a person is being threatened by an attacker, even multiple attackers. The privilege of self-defense justifies the person attacked in taking the life of his attacker to save his own life, no matter how many attackers there are. So maximizing lives here yields to the person's right to resist aggression and save himself. Moreover that right exists even if the attackers are innocent: Even when they have a defense of absence of intent, negligence or mental capacity, or a defense of duress or youth, the victim is permitted to kill them if necessary to save his life. See Model Penal Code §3.11(1).

But stories, even farfetched ones, cast doubt on these propositions. Suppose a terrorist and her insane husband and eight-year-old son are operating a machine gun emplacement from a flat in an apartment building. They are about to shoot down a member of the diplomatic corps, whose headquarters the terrorist band is attacking. His only chance is to throw a hand grenade (which he earlier picked up from a fallen terrorist) through his assailants' window. Under the Model Penal Code and American law he will be legally justified in doing so. His right to resist the aggressors' threat is determinative. The value of preserving even the lives of the terrorist, her legally insane husband and their child carry no weight on the scale of rights.

Add to the facts that the victim knows there is one person in an adjoining flat who will surely be killed by the blast. Now the diplomat would *not* be legally justified in throwing the grenade (though he might be excused), for his action will not result in a net saving of nonaggressor lives. The right of the person in the adjoining flat (who is no part of the threat against him) not to be subjected to his aggression is, therefore, determinative.

Finally, assume in addition that the terrorists are directing the machine gun against a companion as well as himself. Under the lesser-evil doctrine the victim will be legally justified in throwing the grenade. The right of the person in the adjoining flat is the same, but that person's claim of right yields to the social valuation that the two other lives are to be preferred over his one life.

This last case reveals the anomaly in the law: that rights prevail over lives in the aggression cases, even multiple or innocent lives, but that lives prevail over rights in the bystander cases like this one or the flood deflection case. We must conclude that, to the extent this is the law, a bystander's right against aggression yields to a utilitarian assessment in terms of net saving of lives. Yet, it should be added, this is not always so, for there are some killings fairly within the net-saving-of-lives, lesser-evil doctrine that we can be sure courts would not permit — for example, killing a person to obtain his organs to save the lives of several other people, or even removing them for that purpose against his will without killing him. This evidences an acute moral unease with reliance on a utilitarian calculus for assessing the justification of intended killings, even when a net savings of lives is achieved.

PROBLEM

A pair of twin girls, Jodie and Mary, were born on August 8 in a Manchester, England hospital. They were joined at the abdomen and share just one heart and one pair of lungs. Their heads are at the opposite ends of their merged bodies and their legs emerge at right angles from each side. Mary depends entirely on Jodie for her blood. The doctors sought the parents' permission to sever the pair. This would mean Mary's instant death and a chance of survival for Jodie. In the absence of surgery both would die shortly. When the parents refused to authorize the surgery, the doctors sought permission from a court. One of the judges commented that the issue was, "Do we save Jodie by murdering Mary?" Is this the question? The barrister appointed to represent Jodie's interest argued, "The purpose of the operation is wholly to maintain life. . . ." The lawyer appointed to represent Mary argued, "Although this is a life of short duration and very severely handicapped, there is insufficient evidence that it is so intolerable as to render it in the child's best interests that it should end." At this writing the Court of Appeal had ordered that the operation proceed; the parents were contemplating an appeal to the House of Lords. CNN.com Web Posting, September 22, 2000. Was the Court of Appeal correct?

PUBLIC COMMITTEE AGAINST TORTURE v. STATE OF ISRAEL

Supreme Court of Israel
H.C. 5100/94 (Sept. 6, 1999)

JUSTICE BARAK, PRESIDENT: The General Security Service (hereinafter, the "GSS") investigates individuals suspected of committing crimes against Israel's security. [Administrative directives] authorize investigators to apply physical means against those undergoing interrogation (for instance, shaking the suspect,[a] [sleep deprivation, and forcing the suspect to wait in painful positions]). The basis for permitting such methods is that they are deemed immediately necessary for saving human lives.

[Israeli authorities had issued "directives" authorizing GSS interrogators to use physical means under restricted circumstances. The directives instructed the officer in charge to weigh the severity and urgency of the attack that an interrogation was intended to prevent and to seek alternative means of averting the danger. They also required that before using such measures, the investigator would evaluate the suspect's health and "ensure that no harm comes to him." The GSS argued that such measures had helped thwart specific bombing attempts in the

a. Elsewhere in its opinion the Court described "shaking" as follows:

"Among the investigation methods outlined in the GSS' interrogation regulations, shaking is considered the harshest. The method is defined as the forceful shaking of the suspect's upper torso, back and forth, repeatedly, in a manner which causes the neck and head to dangle and vacillate rapidly. According to an expert opinion submitted in one of the applications, the shaking method is likely to cause serious brain damage, harm the spinal cord, cause the suspect to lose consciousness, vomit and urinate uncontrollably and suffer serious headaches.

"The State [offered] several countering expert opinions. . . . To its contention, there is no danger to the life of the suspect inherent to shaking; the risk to life as a result of shaking is rare; there is no evidence that shaking causes fatal damage; and medical literature has not to date listed a case in which a person died directly as a result of having been only shaken. In any event, they argue, doctors are present in all interrogation compounds, and instances where the danger of medical damage presents itself are investigated and researched." — EDS.

past and were "indispensable to its ability to thwart deadly terrorist attacks" in the future.

[The applicants, representing suspects arrested and interrogated by the GSS, petitioned the Court for an order prohibiting the use of these physical means against the applicants during their interrogations.]

The State of Israel has been engaged in an unceasing struggle for both its very existence and security, from the day of its founding. Terrorist organizations have established as their goal Israel's annihilation. . . . They carry out terrorist attacks in which scores are murdered in . . . public transportation, city squares and centers, theaters and coffee shops. They do not distinguish between men, women and children. They act out of cruelty and without mercy. . . .

The facts presented before this Court reveal that one hundred and twenty one people died in terrorist attacks between 1.1.96 to 14.5.98. Seven hundred and seven people were injured. A large number of those killed and injured were victims of harrowing suicide bombings in the heart of Israel's cities. Many attacks . . . were prevented due to the measures taken by the authorities responsible for fighting . . . terrorist activities, [mainly] the GSS.

[The Court addressed two issues: whether GSS's general mandate to conduct interrogations encompassed the authority to use physical means and, if not, whether in exceptional situations such an authority could be based on the concept of "necessity." On the first issue, the Court noted that "a reasonable investigation is likely to cause discomfort" for the suspect but concluded nonetheless that in ordinary cases interrogation must be "free of torture, free of cruel, inhuman treatment of the subject and free of any degrading handling whatsoever." Under both Israeli law and International Law, the court said, "[t]hese prohibitions are 'absolute.' There are no exceptions to them and there is no room for balancing."[b] Applying these requirements to the interrogation methods at issue, the court held:]

[Shaking] harms the suspect's body. It violates his dignity. [T]here is no doubt that shaking is not to be resorted to . . . as part of an "ordinary" investigation. [Similarly,] there is no inherent investigative need for seating the suspect on a chair so low and tilted forward towards the ground, in a manner that causes him real pain and suffering [the so-called Shabach position]. These methods . . . impinge upon the suspect's dignity, his bodily integrity and his basic rights in an excessive manner. They are not to be deemed as included within the general power to conduct interrogations.

[Nonetheless,] the authority to employ these interrogation methods . . . can, in the State's opinion, be obtained in specific cases by virtue of the criminal law defense of "necessity" [Penal Law Article 34 (1)]:

> A person will not bear criminal liability for committing any act immediately necessary for the purpose of saving the life, liberty, body or property, of either himself or his fellow person, from substantial danger of serious harm, imminent from the particular circumstances, at the requisite [time], and absent alternative means for avoiding the harm.

b. The court referred here to Ireland v. United Kingdom, 2 EHRR 25 (1978), a case in which the European Court of Human Rights held that similar physical means used by English authorities to investigate suspected terrorism in Northern Ireland constituted "inhuman and degrading" treatment and therefore were prohibited by the European Convention on Human Rights. — Eds.

The State's position is that by virtue of this "defence" to criminal liability, GSS investigators are also authorized to apply physical means, such as shaking, in the appropriate circumstances, in order to prevent serious harm to human life or body, in the absence of other alternatives. The State maintains that an act committed under conditions of "necessity" [is] a deed that society has an interest in encouraging. . . . Not only is it legitimately permitted to engage in the fighting of terrorism, it is our moral duty to employ the necessary means for this purpose. . . . As this is the case, there is no obstacle preventing the investigators' superiors from instructing and guiding them with regard to when the conditions of the "necessity" defence are fulfilled.

[T]he State's attorneys submitted the "ticking time bomb" argument. A given suspect . . . holds information respecting the location of a bomb that [will] imminently explode. There is no way to defuse the bomb without this information. . . . If the bomb is not defused, scores will be killed and maimed. Is a GSS investigator authorized to employ physical means in order to elicit information regarding the location of the bomb? . . .

We are prepared to assume that — although this matter is open to debate — . . . . the "necessity" exception is likely to arise in instances of "ticking time bombs," and that the immediate need [required by the statute] refers to the imminent nature of the act rather than that of the danger. Hence, the imminence criteria is satisfied even if the bomb is set to explode in a few days, or perhaps even after a few weeks, provided the danger is certain to materialize and there is no alternative means of preventing its materialization. . . .

A long list of arguments, from both the fields of Ethics and Political Science, may be raised for and against the use of the "necessity" defence. This matter, however, has already been decided. . . . Israel's Penal Law recognizes the "necessity" defence.

[Thus, we] accept that in the appropriate circumstances, GSS investigators may avail themselves of the "necessity" defence, if criminally indicted. [But here,] we are not dealing with the potential criminal liability of a GSS investigator. . . . The question before us is whether it is possible to infer the authority to, in advance, establish permanent directives setting out the physical interrogation means that may be used under conditions of "necessity." . . .

In the Court's opinion, [the necessity defence] is the result of an improvisation given the unpredictable character of the events. Thus, the very nature of the defence does not allow it to serve as the source of a general administrative power. . . . Moreover, [t]he "necessity" defence does not possess any additional normative value. . . . The very fact that a particular act does not constitute a criminal act (due to the "necessity" defence) does not in itself authorize the administration to carry out this deed, and in doing so infringe upon human rights.

[Therefore,] neither the government nor the heads of security services possess the authority to [authorize] the use of liberty infringing physical means during the interrogation of suspects. . . .

This decision opens with a description of the difficult reality in which Israel finds herself securitywise. . . . We are aware that this decision does not ease dealing with that reality. This is the destiny of democracy, as not all means are acceptable to it, and not all practices employed by its enemies are open before it. Although a democracy must often fight with one hand tied behind its back, it nonetheless has the upper hand. Preserving the Rule of Law and recognition of an individual's liberty constitutes an important component in its understanding of security. At the end of the day, they [add to] its strength. . . . If it will nonetheless be decided that it is appropriate for Israel, in light of its security difficulties, to sanction physical means in interrogations . . . , this is an issue that must be decided by the legislative branch . . . , provided, of course, that a law infringing upon a suspect's liberty "befitting the values of the State of Israel," is enacted for a proper purpose, and to an extent no greater than is required. (Article 8 to the Basic Law: Human Dignity and Liberty). . . .

Our apprehension[,] that this decision will hamper the ability to properly deal with terrorists and terrorism, disturbs us. We are, however, judges. [W]e must act according to our purest conscience when we decide the law. . . . [We have] rejected the "ways of the hypocrites, who remind us of their adherence to the Rule of Law, while being willfully blind to what is being done in practice." . . .

Consequently, it is decided that the order *nisi* [prohibiting physical means of interrogation] be made absolute, as we declare that the GSS does not have the authority to "shake" a man, hold him in the "Shabach" position [or] deprive him of sleep in a manner other than that which is inherently required by the interrogation. . . . Our decision does not negate the possibility that the "necessity" defence be available to GSS investigators . . . if criminal charges are brought against them, as per the Court's discretion.

JUSTICE J'KEDMI: [I]t is difficult for me to accept [that] the State should be helpless from a legal perspective, in those rare emergencies . . . defined as "ticking time bombs." [A]n authority exists in those circumstances, deriving from the basic obligation of being a State . . . to defend its existence, its well-being, and to safeguard its citizens. [I]n those circumstances, the State — as well as its agents — will have the natural right of "self-defence," in the larger meaning of the term.

[Therefore,] I suggest that the judgment be suspended from coming into force for a period of one year. During that year, the GSS could employ exceptional interrogative methods in those rare cases of "ticking time bombs." . . . During the suspension period, the Knesset [legislature] will be given an opportunity to consider the issue. . . . The GSS will be given the opportunity to cope with emergency situations [and] have an opportunity to adapt itself . . . to the new state of things . . . concerning the status and weight of human rights.

I, therefore, join in the judgment of the President subject to my proposal regarding the suspension of the judgment . . . for a period of one year. . . .

[Decided According to the President's Opinion.]

QUESTIONS

1. Do you agree that the necessity defense should be available to an interrogator who uses physical means against a suspected terrorist, in hopes of locating a "ticking time bomb"? If such means fail to elicit the needed information, would the logic of the necessity defense permit the use of even more brutal methods, in order to avert the death of many hundreds of individuals? What should be the result under American law if an FBI agent used brutal torture to get information needed to avert a catastrophic terrorist attack such as the Oklahoma City bombing?

2. If the Court was right to hold that a necessity defense can sometimes be available to an interrogator who uses physical means, wasn't it wrong to hold that administrative authorities should not regulate the use of such methods by rules promulgated in advance? If necessity is a genuine justification, indicating that the action taken is beneficial on balance, why must the circumstances justifying that action always be assessed on an ad hoc basis? Will that approach tend to make the use of "physical means" less frequent or more frequent?

Prior to the decision of the Israeli Supreme Court, the issues raised by the principal case were explored in depth in a report issued by an official commission (the Landau Commission) in 1988. The report and a wide range of commentary on it can be found in Symposium, The Report of the Commission of Inquiry into the Methods of Investigation of the General Security Service Regarding Hostile Terrorist Activity, 23 Israel L. Rev., Nos. 2 & 3 (Spring–Summer 1989).

3. Should the availability of the necessity defense turn in part on the culpability of the person under interrogation? If physical means of interrogation are not justified in the case of someone who is merely a *suspected* terrorist, should such means become permissible when it is known for sure that the person in question is a leader of the terrorist group? Conversely, if the Court was right to allow a possible necessity defense in the interrogation of a suspected terrorist, would the logic of that position also justify the use of physical means against a person known to be innocent — for example a villager who knows where the bomb is but fears that the terrorists will kill him if he reveals its location?

PROBLEM

Can the innocent victim of a lesser-evil choice use force to protect himself? For example, *A*'s house stands just outside the main village. A storm of unusual intensity threatens to break the levee protecting the village from flooding by a nearby river. *B*, seeking to avert the danger to the village and its occupants, prepares to explode a hole in the levee at a point calculated to cause the flood to miss the town but to inundate *A*'s house, which has been evacuated. *A* holds *B* off with a loaded gun, preventing *B* from setting the explosion. The village is flooded, with loss of life and property. Is *A* guilty of assault with a deadly weapon? Of murder or manslaughter of the dead villagers? See Glanville Williams, Criminal Law: The General Part 745 (2d ed. 1961); Peter Glazebrook, The Necessity Plea in English Criminal Law, 30 Camb. L.J. 87, 93 (1972).

Consider 2 James Fitzjames Stephen, History of the Criminal Law of England 108-109 (1883):

> In an American case in which sailors threw passengers overboard to lighten a boat it was held that the sailors ought to have been thrown overboard first unless they were required to work the boat, and that at all events the particular persons to be sacrificed ought to have been decided on by ballot. (Comm. v. Holmes, 1 Wall. Jr. 1.) Such a view appears to me to be over refined. Self-sacrifice may or may not be a moral duty, but it seems hard to make it a legal duty, and it is impossible to state its limits or the principle on which they can be determined. Suppose one of the party in the boat had a revolver and was able to use it, and refused either to draw lots or to allow himself or his wife or daughter to be made to do so or to be thrown

overboard, could any one deny that he was acting in self-defence and the defence of his nearest relations, and would he violate any legal duty in so doing?

For reflections on these problems, see George C. Christie, The Defense of Necessity Considered from the Legal and Moral Points of View, 48 Duke L. J. 975 (1999).

4. *Euthanasia*

INTRODUCTORY NOTE

In the material on omissions, supra page 198, we considered the use of the omission doctrine to avoid criminal liability for physicians who withhold life-sustaining medical measures or withhold treatment from terminally ill patients or those in a permanent vegetative state. Here we revisit the subject of what may loosely be called "euthanasia" to consider how far courts have gone in making legally justified the actions of those who directly take the life of a person who consents, or who help another person take his own life.

CRUZAN v. DIRECTOR, MISSOURI DEPT. OF HEALTH

Supreme Court of the United States
497 U.S. 261 (1989)

CHIEF JUSTICE REHNQUIST delivered the opinion of the Court.

On the night of January 11, 1983, Nancy Cruzan lost control of her car as she traveled down Elm Road in Jasper County, Missouri. The vehicle overturned, and Cruzan was discovered lying face down in a ditch without detectable respiratory or cardiac function. . . . She now lies in a Missouri state hospital in what is commonly referred to as a persistent vegetative state: generally, a condition in which a person exhibits motor reflexes but evinces no indications of significant cognitive function. The State of Missouri is bearing the cost of her care.

After it had become apparent that Nancy Cruzan had virtually no chance of regaining her mental faculties, her parents asked hospital employees to terminate the artificial nutrition and hydration procedures. All agree that such a removal would cause her death. The employees refused to honor the request without court approval. The parents then sought and received authorization from the state trial court for termination. The court found that a person in Nancy's condition had a fundamental right under the State and Federal Constitutions to refuse or direct the withdrawal of "death prolonging procedures." The court also found that Nancy's "expressed thoughts at age twenty-five in somewhat serious conversation with a housemate friend that if sick or injured she would not wish to continue her life unless she could live at least halfway normally suggests that given her present condition she would not wish to continue on with her nutrition and hydration."

The Supreme Court of Missouri reversed by a divided vote. . . . The court found that Cruzan's statements to her roommate regarding her desire to live or die under certain conditions were "unreliable for the purpose of determining her intent," "and thus insufficient to support the co-guardians['] claim to exercise substituted judgment on Nancy's behalf." . . .

We granted certiorari to consider the question whether Cruzan has a right under the United States Constitution which would require the hospital to withdraw life-sustaining treatment from her under these circumstances.

. . . Before the turn of the century, this Court observed that "[n]o right is held more sacred, or is more carefully guarded, by the common law, than the right of every individual to the possession and control of his own person, free from all restraint or interference of others, unless by clear and unquestionable authority of law." Union Pacific R. Co. v. Botsford, 141 U.S. 250, 251 (1891). This notion of bodily integrity has been embodied in the requirement that informed consent is generally required for medical treatment. Justice Cardozo, while on the Court of Appeals of New York, aptly described this doctrine: "Every human being of adult years and sound mind has a right to determine what shall be done with his own body; and a surgeon who performs an operation without his patient's consent commits an assault, for which he is liable in damages." Schloendorff v. Society of New York Hospital, 211 N.Y. 125, 129-130, 105 N.E. 92, 93 (1914). The informed consent doctrine has become firmly entrenched in American tort law . . .

The logical corollary of the doctrine of informed consent is that the patient generally possesses the right not to consent, that is, to refuse treatment. . . .

In [In re Quinlan, 70 N.J. 10, 355 A.2d 647 (1976)], young Karen Quinlan suffered severe brain damage as the result of anoxia and entered a persistent vegetative state. Karen's father sought judicial approval to disconnect his daughter's respirator. The New Jersey Supreme Court granted the relief, holding that Karen had a right of privacy grounded in the Federal Constitution to terminate treatment. . . .

After *Quinlan* . . . most courts have based a right to refuse treatment either solely on the common-law right to informed consent or on both the common-law right and a constitutional privacy right. [The Court then reviewed the state case law developments that followed *Quinlan.*]

As these cases demonstrate, the common-law doctrine of informed consent is viewed as generally encompassing the right of a competent individual to refuse medical treatment. . . . This is the first case in which we have been squarely presented with the issue whether the United States Constitution grants what is in common parlance referred to as a "right to die." . . .

The Fourteenth Amendment provides that no State shall "deprive any person of life, liberty, or property, without due process of law." The principle that a competent person has a constitutionally protected liberty interest in refusing unwanted medical treatment may be inferred from our prior decisions. . . .

But determining that a person has a "liberty interest" under the Due Process Clause does not end the inquiry; "whether respondent's constitutional rights have been violated must be determined by balancing his liberty interests against the relevant state interests." Youngberg v. Romeo, 457 U.S. 307, 321 (1982).

Petitioners insist that under the general holdings of our cases, the forced administration of life-sustaining medical treatment, and even of artificially delivered food and water essential to life, would implicate a competent person's liberty interest. Although we think the logic of the cases discussed above would embrace such a liberty interest, the dramatic consequences involved in refusal of such treatment would inform the inquiry as to whether the deprivation of that interest is constitutionally permissible. But for purposes of this case, we assume that the United States Constitution would grant a competent person a constitutionally protected right to refuse lifesaving hydration and nutrition.

Petitioners go on to assert that an incompetent person should possess the same right in this respect as is possessed by a competent person. . . .

The difficulty with petitioners' claim is that in a sense it begs the question: An incompetent person is not able to make an informed and voluntary choice to exercise a hypothetical right to refuse treatment or any other right. Such a "right" must be exercised for her, if at all, by some sort of surrogate. Here, Missouri has in effect recognized that under certain circumstances a surrogate may act for the patient in electing to have hydration and nutrition withdrawn in such a way as to cause death, but it has established a procedural safeguard to assure that the action of the surrogate conforms as best it may to the wishes expressed by the patient while competent. Missouri requires that evidence of the incompetent's wishes as to the withdrawal of treatment be proved by clear and convincing evidence. The question, then, is whether the United States Constitution forbids the establishment of this procedural requirement by the State. We hold that it does not.

Whether or not Missouri's clear and convincing evidence requirement comports with the United States Constitution depends in part on what interests the State may properly seek to protect in this situation. Missouri relies on its interest in the protection and preservation of human life, and there can be no gainsaying this interest. . . .

We cannot say that the Supreme Court of Missouri committed constitutional error in reaching the conclusion that it did.

The judgment of the Supreme Court of Missouri is affirmed.

WASHINGTON v. GLUCKSBERG

Supreme Court of the United States
521 U.S. 702 (1997)

Chief Justice Rehnquist delivered the opinion of the Court.

[Several terminally ill patients and their physicians sued the state of Washington for a declaratory judgment that the state's ban on assisted suicide was a violation of a fundamental right protected by the Due Process Clause of the Constitution. The federal district court agreed and the 9th Circuit Court of Appeals affirmed.]

The question presented in this case is whether Washington's prohibition against "caus[ing]" or "aid[ing]" a suicide offends the Fourteenth Amendment to the United States Constitution. We hold that it does not. . . .

We begin, as we do in all due-process cases, by examining our Nation's history, legal traditions, and practices. . . . In almost every State — indeed, in almost every western democracy — it is a crime to assist a suicide. The States' assisted-suicide bans are not innovations. Rather, they are longstanding expressions of the States' commitment to the protection and preservation of all human life. . . . More specifically, for over 700 years, the Anglo-American common-law tradition has punished or otherwise disapproved of both suicide and assisting suicide. . . .

Though deeply rooted, the States' assisted-suicide bans have in recent years been reexamined and, generally, reaffirmed. . . . The Washington statute at issue in this case . . . was enacted in 1975 as part of a revision of that State's criminal code. . . . In 1991, Washington voters rejected a ballot initiative which, had it passed, would have permitted a form of physician-assisted suicide. . . . California voters rejected an assisted-suicide initiative similar to Washington's in 1993. On the other hand, in 1994, voters in Oregon enacted, also through ballot initiative, that State's "Death With Dignity Act," which legalized physician-assisted suicide for competent, terminally ill adults. Since the Oregon vote, many proposals to legalize assisted-suicide have been and continue to be introduced in the States' legislatures, but none has been enacted. And just last year, Iowa and Rhode Island joined the overwhelming majority of States explicitly prohibiting assisted suicide. . . . Against this backdrop of history, tradition, and practice, we now turn to respondents' constitutional claim.

The Due Process Clause . . . provides heightened protection against government interference with certain fundamental rights and liberty interests. . . . In a long line of cases, we have held that, in addition to the specific freedoms protected by the Bill of Rights, the "liberty" specially protected by the Due Process Clause includes the rights to marry, to have children, to direct the education and upbringing of one's children, to marital privacy, to use contraception, to bodily integrity, and to abortion, Planned Parenthood v. Casey, 505 U.S. 833 (1992). We have also assumed, and strongly suggested, that the Due Process Clause protects the traditional right to refuse unwanted lifesaving medical treatment. Cruzan v. Director, Missouri Department of Health, 497 U.S. 261 (1990).

But we "ha[ve] always been reluctant to expand the concept of substantive due process because guideposts for responsible decision making in this uncharted area are scarce and open-ended." Collins v. City of Harker Heights, 503 U.S. 115 (1992). By extending constitutional protection to an asserted right or liberty interest, we, to a great extent, place the matter outside the arena of public debate and legislative action. . . .

The Washington statute at issue in this case prohibits "aid[ing] another person to attempt suicide," Wash. Rev. Code §9A.36.060(1) (1994), and, thus, the question before us is whether the "liberty" specially protected by the Due Process Clause includes a right to commit suicide which itself includes a right to assistance in doing so. . . .

. . . To hold for respondents, we would have to reverse centuries of legal doctrine and practice, and strike down the considered policy choice of almost every State. . . .

Respondents contend, however, that the liberty interest they assert is consistent with this Court's substantive-due-process line of cases, if not with this Nation's history and practice. Pointing to *Casey* and *Cruzan,* respondents read our jurisprudence in this area as reflecting a general tradition of "self-sovereignty," . . . and as teaching that the "liberty" protected by the Due Process Clause includes "basic and intimate exercises of personal autonomy." . . .

Respondents contend that in *Cruzan* we "acknowledged that competent, dying persons have the right to direct the removal of life-sustaining medical treatment and thus hasten death," and that "the constitutional principle behind recognizing the patient's liberty to direct the withdrawal of artificial life support applies at least as strongly to the choice to hasten impending death by consuming lethal medication." . . . The right assumed in *Cruzan,* however, was not simply deduced from abstract concepts of personal autonomy. Given the common-law rule that forced medication was a battery, and the long legal tradition protecting the decision to refuse unwanted medical treatment, our assumption was entirely consistent with this Nation's history and constitutional traditions. The decision to commit suicide with the assistance of another may be just as personal and profound as the decision to refuse unwanted medical treatment, but it has never enjoyed similar legal protection. Indeed, the two acts are widely and reasonably regarded as quite distinct. See Vacco v. Quill, 521 U.S. 793 (1997).

Respondents also rely on *Casey*. There . . . [w]e held, first, that a woman has a right, before her fetus is viable, to an abortion "without undue interference from the State"; second, that States may restrict post-viability abortions, so long as exceptions are made to protect a woman's life and health; and third, that the State has legitimate interests throughout a pregnancy in protecting the health of the woman and the life of the unborn child. In reaching this conclusion, the opinion discussed in some detail this Court's substantive-due-process tradition of interpreting the Due Process Clause to protect certain fundamental rights and "personal decisions relating to marriage, procreation, contraception, family relationships, child rearing, and education," and noted that many of those rights and liberties "involv[e] the most intimate and personal choices a person may make in a lifetime." . . . Respondents emphasize the statement in Casey that:

> At the heart of liberty is the right to define one's own concept of existence, of meaning, of the universe, and of the mystery of human life. Beliefs about these matters could not define the attributes of personhood were they formed under compulsion of the State.

By choosing this language, the Court's opinion in *Casey* described, in a general way and in light of our prior cases, those personal activities and decisions that this Court has identified as so deeply rooted in our history and traditions, or so fundamental to our concept of constitutionally ordered liberty, that they are protected by the Fourteenth Amendment. . . . That many of the rights and liberties protected by the Due Process Clause sound in personal autonomy does not warrant the sweeping conclusion that any and all important, intimate, and personal decisions are so protected.

[O]ur decisions lead us to conclude that the asserted "right" to assistance in committing suicide is not a fundamental liberty interest protected by the Due Process Clause. The Constitution also requires, however, that Washington's assisted-suicide ban be rationally related to legitimate government interests. This requirement is unquestionably met here. . . . Washington's assisted-suicide ban implicates a number of state interests.

First, Washington has an "unqualified interest in the preservation of human life." The State's prohibition on assisted suicide, like all homicide laws, both reflects and advances its commitment to this interest. . . . This interest is symbolic and aspirational as well as practical. . . .

> While suicide is no longer prohibited or penalized, the ban against assisted suicide and euthanasia shores up the notion of limits in human relationships. It reflects the gravity with which we view the decision to take one's own life or the life of another, and our reluctance to encourage or promote these decisions." New York State Task Force on Life and the Law, When Death is Sought: Assisted Suicide and Euthanasia in the Medical Context 131-132 (1994)

This remains true, as *Cruzan* makes clear, even for those who are near death.

Relatedly, all admit that suicide is a serious public-health problem, especially among persons in otherwise vulnerable groups. . . . The State has an interest in preventing suicide, and in studying, identifying, and treating its causes. . . . Those who attempt suicide — terminally ill or not — often suffer from depression or other mental disorders. . . . Research indicates, however, that many people who request physician-assisted suicide withdraw that request if their depression and pain are treated.

The State also has an interest in protecting the integrity and ethics of the medical profession. . . . [T]he American Medical Association, like many other medical and physicians' groups, has concluded that "[p]hysician-assisted suicide is fundamentally incompatible with the physician's role as healer." . . . And physician-assisted suicide could, it is argued, undermine the trust that is essential to the doctor-patient relationship by blurring the time-honored line between healing and harming.

Next, the State has an interest in protecting vulnerable groups — including the poor, the elderly, and disabled persons — from abuse, neglect, and mistakes. . . . [T]he New York Task Force warned that "[l]egalizing physician-assisted suicide would pose profound risks to many individuals who are ill and vulnerable. . . . The risk of harm is greatest for the many individuals in our society whose autonomy and well-being are already compromised by poverty, lack of access to good medical care, advanced age, or membership in a stigmatized social group." New York Task Force 120. . . . If physician-assisted suicide were permitted, many might resort to it to spare their families the substantial financial burden of end-of-life health-care costs.

The State's interest here goes beyond protecting the vulnerable from coercion; it extends to protecting disabled and terminally ill people from prejudice, negative and inaccurate stereotypes, and "societal indifference." The State's assisted-suicide ban reflects and reinforces its policy that the lives of terminally ill, disabled, and elderly people must be no less valued than the lives of the young and healthy, and that a seriously disabled person's suicidal impulses should be interpreted and treated the same way as anyone else's. . . .

Finally, the State may fear that permitting assisted suicide will start it down the path to voluntary and perhaps even involuntary euthanasia. The Court of Appeals [below] struck down Washington's assisted-suicide ban only "as applied to competent, terminally ill adults who wish to hasten their deaths by obtaining medication prescribed by their doctors." Washington insists, however, that the impact of the court's decision will not and cannot be so limited. If suicide is protected as a matter of constitutional right, it is argued, "every man and woman in the United States must enjoy it." The Court of Appeals' decision, and its expansive reasoning, provide ample support for the State's concerns. The court noted, for example, that the "decision of a duly appointed surrogate decision maker is for all legal purposes the decision of the patient himself"; that "in some instances, the patient may be unable to self-administer the drugs and . . . administration by the physician . . . may be the only way the patient may be able to receive them"; and that not only physicians, but also family members and loved ones, will inevitably participate in assisting suicide. Thus, it turns out that what is couched as a limited right to "physician-assisted suicide" is likely, in effect, a much broader license, which could prove extremely difficult to police and contain. Washington's ban on assisting suicide prevents such erosion. . . .

We need not weigh exactingly the relative strengths of these various interests. They are unquestionably important and legitimate, and Washington's ban on assisted suicide is at least reasonably related to their promotion and protection. We therefore hold that Wash. Rev. Code §9A.36.060(1) (1994) does not violate the Fourteenth Amendment, either on its face or "as applied to competent, terminally ill adults who wish to hasten their deaths by obtaining medication prescribed by their doctors."

NOTE

An Oregon initiative petition was passed by a majority at the November 8, 1994, election, resulting in the enactment of the Oregon Death with Dignity Act, 1995 Or. Laws ch. 3, the first such legislation in the United States. The ballot description of the act reads as follows:

> This measure would allow an informed and capable adult resident of Oregon, who is terminally ill and within six months of death, to voluntarily request a prescription for medication to take his or her life. The measure allows a physician to prescribe a lethal dose of medication when conditions of the measure are met. . . .
>
> The process begins when the patient makes the request of his or her physician, who shall:
>
> - Determine if the patient is terminally ill, is capable of making health care decisions, and has made the request voluntarily.
> - Inform the patient of his or her diagnosis and prognosis; the risks and results of taking the medication; and alternatives, including comfort care, hospice care, and pain control. . . .
> - Ask that the patient notify next of kin. . . .
> - Refer the patient for counseling, if appropriate.
> - Refer the patient to a consulting physician.
>
> A consulting physician, who is qualified by specialty or experience, must confirm the diagnosis and determine that the patient is capable and acting voluntarily. If either physician believes that the patient might be suffering from a psychiatric or psychological disorder, or from depression causing impaired judgment, the physician must refer the patient to a licensed psychiatrist or psychologist for counseling. The psychiatrist or psychologist must determine that the patient does not suffer from such a disorder before medication may be prescribed. . . .
>
> At least fifteen days must pass from the time of the initial oral request and 48

> hours must pass from the time of the written request before the prescription may be written. Before writing the prescription, the attending physician must again verify the patient is making a voluntary and informed request, and offer the patient the opportunity to rescind the request. . . . Those who comply with the requirements of the measure are protected from prosecution and professional discipline. . . . The measure does not authorize lethal injection, mercy killing or active euthanasia. Actions taken in accordance with this measure shall not constitute suicide, assisted suicide, mercy killing or homicide, under the law.

For various views on the issues see Ronald Dworkin, Life's Dominion 179 (1993); Note, Physician-Assisted Suicide and the Right to Die with Assistance, 105 Harv. L. Rev. 2031 (1992); Comment (E. A. Gifford), *Artes Moriendi:* Active Euthanasia and the Art of Dying, 40 U.C.L.A. L. Rev. 1545 (1993); Yale Kamisar, Physician-Assisted Suicide: The Problems Presented by the Compelling, Heartwrenching Case, 88 J. Crim. L. & Crim. 1121 (1998), and a reply, John Deigh, Physician-Assisted Suicide and Voluntary Euthanasia: Some Relevant Differences, id. at 1155; Symposium on Physician-Assisted Suicide, 109 Ethics 497-642 (April 1999). For a sampling of some of the controversy consider the excerpts that follow.

NEW YORK STATE TASK FORCE ON LIFE AND THE LAW, WHEN DEATH IS SOUGHT — ASSISTED SUICIDE IN THE MEDICAL CONTEXT ix, xiii-xiv (1994): Recent proposals to legalize assisted suicide and euthanasia in some states would transform the right to decide about medical treatment into a far broader right to control the timing and manner of death. After lengthy deliberations, the Task Force unanimously concluded that the dangers of such a dramatic change in public policy would far outweigh any possible benefits. In light of the pervasive failure of our health care system to treat pain and diagnose and treat depression, legalizing assisted suicide and euthanasia would be profoundly dangerous for many individuals who are ill and vulnerable. The risks would be most severe for those who are elderly, poor, socially disadvantaged, or without access to good medical care. . . .

The Task Force members unanimously concluded that legalizing assisted suicide and euthanasia would pose profound risks to many patients. . . .

No matter how carefully any guidelines are framed, assisted suicide and euthanasia will be practiced through the prism of social inequality and bias that characterizes the delivery of services in all segments of our society, including health care. The practices will pose the greatest risks to those who are poor, elderly, members of a minority group, or without access to good medical care.

The growing concern about health care costs increases the risks presented by legalizing assisted suicide and euthanasia. This cost consciousness will not be diminished, and may well be exacerbated, by health care reform.

The clinical safeguards that have been proposed to prevent abuse and errors would not be realized in many cases. For example, most doctors do not have a long-standing relationship with their patients or information about the complex personal factors relevant to evaluating a request for suicide assistance or a lethal injection. In addition, neither treatment for pain nor the diagnosis of and treatment for depression is widely available in clinical practice.

The Task Force members feel deep compassion for patients in those rare cases when pain cannot be alleviated even with aggressive palliative care. They also recognize that the desire for control at life's end is widely shared and deeply felt. As a society, however, we have better ways to give people greater control and relief from suffering than by legalizing assisted suicide and euthanasia.

Depression accompanied by feelings of hopelessness is the strongest predictor of suicide for both individuals who are terminally ill and those who are not. Most doctors, however, are not trained to diagnose depression, especially in complex cases such as patients who are terminally ill. Even if diagnosed, depression is often not treated. In elderly patients as well as the terminally and chronically ill, depression is grossly underdiagnosed and undertreated.

The presence of unrelieved pain also increases susceptibility to suicide. The undertreatment of pain is a widespread failure of current medical practice, with far-reaching implications for proposals to legalize assisted suicide and euthanasia.

If assisted suicide and euthanasia are legalized, it will blunt our perception of what it means for one individual to assist another to commit suicide or to take another person's life. Over time, as the practices are incorporated into the standard arsenal of medical treatments, the sense of gravity about the practices would dissipate.

The criteria and safeguards that have been proposed for assisted suicide and euthanasia would prove elastic in clinical practice and in law. Policies limiting suicide to the terminally ill, for example, would be inconsistent with the notion that suicide is a compassionate choice for patients who are in pain or suffering. As long as the policies hinge on notions of pain or suffering, they are uncontainable; neither pain nor suffering can be gauged objectively, nor are they subject to the kind of judgments needed to fashion coherent public policy. Euthanasia to cover those who are incapable of consenting would also be a likely, if not inevitable, extension of any policy permitting the practice for those who can consent.

These concerns are heightened by experience in the Netherlands, where the practices have been legally sanctioned. Although Dutch law requires an explicit request for euthanasia by the patient, a national study in the Netherlands found that of approximately 3300 deaths annually resulting from mercy killing, 1,000 deaths from euthanasia occurred without an explicit request. Moreover, in some cases, doctors have provided assisted suicide in response to suffering caused solely by psychiatric illness, including severe depression.

JOEL FEINBERG, OVERLOOKING THE MERITS OF THE INDIVIDUAL CASE: AN UNPROMISING APPROACH TO THE RIGHT TO DIE, 4 Ratio Juris. 131, 150-151 (1991): [M]ost of the arguments against the legalization of voluntary euthanasia (or in favour of creating legal impediments to it) are indirect arguments. They don't argue that individual cases judged internally, that is on their own merits, do not warrant euthanasia. Indeed, some of these arguments candidly concede that judged on the merits, many individual cases do deserve euthanasia. Rather, these arguments favour deliberately overlooking the merits of individual cases, and cite extraneous considerations in favour of a blanket prohibition. The most plausible of these arguments is the argument from abusable discretion, which maintains that if legally competent individuals are granted the discretion to decide on their own whether in certain circumstances to continue or to terminate life-sustaining treatment, the inevitability of honest mistakes and not-so-honest abuses will create evils that outweigh the evils of sustaining the comatose and the pain-wracked against their presumed wills. Convincing as the argument from abusable discretion may be in some contexts, . . . it fails in its application to the euthanasia situation, because it cannot be shown that the likely number of mistakenly killed individuals would constitute a greater evil than the likely number of mistakenly sustained individuals. The philosophical problem of voluntary euthanasia is in large part a matter of comparing real risks. The enemy of voluntary euthanasia errs in minimizing the evils of human suffering and overrating the value of merely biological life in the absence of a human person, or in the presence of a human person whose sufferings are too severe for him to have a human life, even though his heart beats on.

SANFORD H. KADISH, LETTING PATIENTS DIE: LEGAL AND MORAL REFLECTIONS, 80 Cal. L. Rev. 857, 867-868 (1992): One ground on which courts have sought to distinguish letting-die situations from conventional suicide is that the latter requires affirmative life-taking actions. On this view a patient refusing to be attached to an apparatus necessary for his survival is not taking his life, but is simply letting nature take its course. Hence death is caused by the disease, not by the person himself, nor by the physician who respects his wishes. [This] distinction between intentionally killing oneself and intentionally submitting to an avoidable death is suspect. . . .

Consider a patient who finds himself attached against his will to some life-sustaining apparatus he had earlier explicitly rejected. He removes it for the same reason he earlier rejected it — he prefers death to living attached to a machine — and dies moments later. Presumably this would constitute suicide, since he achieved his death by positive actions. But could we justifiably say that if the doctors had followed his instructions and he had died, this would not be suicide because his death would then not have been caused by the patient's actions? Or consider an analogous case: a paralyzed man, sitting on a beach threatened by an incoming tide, deliberately, in order to end his life, declines to allow a lifeguard to move him out of harm's way, and drowns in consequence. . . . Would it not be correct to see this as a suicide? Yet the person dying of a disease who chooses not to permit some medical intervention that would save him is in no different a situation. [As a] matter of principle, that a person achieves his goal by refusing necessary medical intervention hardly seems a better reason to treat his action differently than that a person achieves his goal by letting the tide come to him rather than going to it.

[The] basic argument [for] the right to refuse treatment . . . is that the choice between medical treatment and death is so fundamental that it is protected against state control by a constitutional right of autonomy. That being the case, however, there is no principled basis for denying the same freedom of choice to those not dependent on medical treatment for survival. The failure of efforts to distinguish suicide from refusal of treatment is attributable not simply to usage and definition, but to the equivalence between the two. The moral case for autonomy extends to both if it extends to one.

LORD BROWNE-WILKINSON, in AIREDALE NHS TRUST v. BLAND, [1993] 1 All E.R. 821 (sustaining discontinuance of tube-feeding of patient in persistent vegetative state): [T]he conclusion I have reached will appear to some to be almost irrational. How can it be lawful to allow a patient to die slowly, though painlessly, over a period of weeks from lack of food but unlawful to produce his immediate death by a lethal injection, thereby saving his family from yet another ordeal to add to the tragedy that has already struck them? I find it difficult to find a moral answer to that question. But it is undoubtedly the law and nothing I have said casts doubt on the proposition that the doing of a positive act with the intention of ending life is and remains murder.

YALE KAMISAR, A LAW TO STAY THE COLD HAND OF DR. DEATH, Legal Times, Mar. 8, 1993, at 2: The argument for assisted suicide (and for active euthanasia as well) has a certain logical appeal. After all, if one can bring about death by declining medical treatment, why can't one achieve the same result by enlisting the aid of others in committing suicide? Isn't that the next logical step?

But why stop there? Doctor-assisted suicide is not quite active euthanasia, for the final act is performed by the patient herself, not by another. And there is always the possibility that the patient may not carry out the final act. Suppose that a person cannot swallow sleeping pills or trigger a suicide machine or is otherwise unable to perform the final act by herself? Isn't the next logical step, and a short step at that, the right to authorize others to engage in euthanasia?

Of course, doctor-administered euthanasia is the direct, intentional killing of an innocent person. The criminal laws of every state prohibit that — regardless of the consent of the person killed or the motive of the killer. Are all these laws to be struck down, too, insofar as they violate the right to die?

The right to die is a sound principle in certain settings. But it is also a vague, unruly concept. If there really is a broad right to die, why should it be limited to the terminally ill or even the seriously ill? Why should we set any limits on the right to decide the time and manner of one's death?

. . . The right-to-die principle should not be carried to the point where it collides with other principles rubbing against it from other directions — such as the principle that the law protects all human life regardless of the worth or value of a person. . . .

That is why the right to die should be confined to the right to decline or to terminate life-sustaining treatment. A state that so limits the right may be said by some to be acting illogically, but, given our history and our culture, it is not acting unconstitutionally.

C. PRINCIPLES OF EXCUSE

1. *Introduction*[33]

We pointed out earlier (Note on Culpability and Excuse, page 255 supra) the close relation between the mens rea doctrines there explored (mens rea in its special sense) and the general notion of excuse (culpability or mens rea in its general sense). As a prelude to examining specific excuse doctrines, it will be

33. Adapted from Sanford H. Kadish, Excusing Crime, 75 Calif. L. Rev. 257 (1987).

useful to have an overview of the several kinds of excuses the law allows, particularly inasmuch as excuses don't always come bearing that label.

As Austin suggests, page 750, supra, excuses occur when the law allows a defense (either total or partial, though we will here emphasize total defenses) to a wrongful action because the actor has displayed some disability in capacity to know or to choose, which renders the person either free of blame or subject to less blame. The disabilities that ground excuse in our law seem to fall into one of three groups: those disabilities that produce involuntary actions; those that produce deficient but reasonable actions; and those that render all actions irresponsible.

1. Involuntary actions. We have already studied this group of excuses under the label of the defense of the involuntary act. They include situations in which in the most literal sense the person had no control over his bodily movements. Cases of physical compulsion are obvious examples. Others are tumbling downstairs or being pushed. These are easy to deal with because we can see the external force being applied. But the law recognizes some excuses as belonging to this category even when the source of the lack of control is internal, as in the case of reflex movements or epileptic seizures.

Such extreme instances of involuntariness may be viewed as raising a bar to liability more fundamental even than excuse; namely, that there is no *action* at all, only bodily movement, so that there is nothing to excuse — the defendant had no choice in the matter.

2. Deficient but reasonable actions. In the second group of excusing conditions there is power to choose in a literal sense — nothing prevents the person from making a choice — but the choice is so constrained that an ordinary law-abiding person could not be expected to choose otherwise. The constraining circumstances are of two kinds. In the first, the constraint arises from defect of knowledge; in the second, from defect of will.

(*a*) *Cognitive deficiency.* We have already studied the law's excuses based on lack of knowledge earlier in the sections on mens rea, particularly the section on Mistake of Fact, supra page 225. To constitute an excuse it is not enough that the person lacked knowledge of some relevant feature of his action — his lack of knowledge must itself be excusable, in the sense that he was not reckless, or perhaps, negligent in making the mistake.

For example, if you shoot at an object in the forest reasonably thinking it is a game animal, when in fact it is a person dressed in animal costume, you have killed by mistake. Of course, you could have chosen not to shoot at all. But once it is accepted that shooting in the circumstances, as you reasonably took them to be, was a proper action, the mistaken killing was an accident effectively beyond your control.

Explaining mistake or the related concept of accident as excuse is today somewhat unconventional. Like the involuntary-act defense, accident and mistake are more likely to be viewed as precluding liability not because of excuse, but because the elements of the crime have not been proven, thus resulting in failure of the prima facie case. After all, homicidal crimes are defined to require a mens rea of at least culpable negligence. Why, then, in my example, isn't reasonable mistake or accident a defense, not because either one excuses what otherwise would be a crime, but simply because each negates the required culpable mens rea, without which there is no crime to excuse? The answer requires a brief explanation.

Some mens rea requirements are essential elements in the definition of the crime. Take loitering with criminal intent or reckless driving. Without the intent in the first case or recklessness in the second, there is only standing around or driving a car. There is nothing to excuse because we would not expect the person to have acted otherwise. This is the case with all crimes whose definitions, like that of loitering with intent and reckless driving, do not require occurrence of the ultimate harm the crimes seek to prevent. The concern of such crimes is the danger that the harm may occur. The mens rea serves to identify the presence of the danger. This is true of all inchoate crimes.

Other mens rea requirements, on the other hand, are excuses in mens rea clothing. They are excusing conditions because they serve to deny blame for a harm done. That they are cast in the form of mens rea requirements does not change their character. The reasons these particular mental states are required are the very reasons for excusing conditions — if a person could not reasonably be expected to know of some circumstance that made his action harmful, he could not reasonably be said to have effective power of choice to avoid the harm. This is why the defense of reasonable mistake functions as an excuse. True, its presence negates a required element of the crime, but the reason why that element (viz., that the person have acted at least negligently) is included in the definition of the crime is because a reasonable mistake is excusable. This was how mistake and accident were traditionally thought of before the Model Penal Code.[34]

(*b*) *Volitional deficiency*. The law's excuses based on defect of will (short of a total loss of will, as in the defense of involuntary action) are not as well developed as those based on defect of knowledge. Duress is the best established defense of this kind, and even its status is not free of doubt, as we shall shortly see. It is generally established when a person commits a crime under such threats of physical injury that even a person of reasonable fortitude would have yielded to the threat.

3. Irresponsible actions. The excuses in our third category, unlike those in the first, do not involve involuntary actions. And unlike those in the second, they do not rest on circumstances that would lead a person of normal capacities to make the choice the defendant made. The grounds for excuse are simply that this person could not have been expected to act otherwise, given the person's inadequate capacities for making rational judgments.

Our law is grudging with excuses of this kind. The individual's difficulty in complying with the law is a common ground for sentencing mitigation, but it is rarely a ground for a total excuse. Infancy and legal insanity are the only two excuses of this kind the law allows, and because the juvenile court laws have preempted the defense of infancy in practice, legal insanity is the only significant defense remaining in this category.

While the basis for excuses in the second category is that the actor has shown

34. The dual character of accident and mistake defenses may be seen in Cal. Penal Code §26 (West 1993), enacted in 1872:

> All persons are capable of committing crimes except those belonging to the following classes: . . .
>
> Three — Persons who committed the act or made the omission charged under an ignorance or mistake of fact, which disproves any criminal intent. . . .
>
> Five — Persons who committed the act or made the omission charged through misfortune or by accident, when it appears that there was no evil design, intention, or negligence.

herself no different from the rest of us, the basis of the insanity excuse is that she has shown herself *very* different from the rest of us. But how different, and in what respects? After all, those who commit atrocious crimes are certainly very different from the rest of us. That fact alone scarcely excuses them. We will examine these issues in the section on legal insanity.

The three categories of legal excuses just described suggest the common rationale behind them both in the law and in everyday moral judgments; namely, that justice precludes blame where none is deserved. In the first category, people are not to blame because they have no control over their movements; in the second, because they acted in circumstances so constraining that most people would have done the same; in the third, because they suffer from a fundamental deficiency of mind and are therefore not responsible moral agents.

Of course, one might escape excuses altogether by withdrawing the element of blame from a finding of criminality. Indeed there are some who would prefer that the criminal law reject all backward-looking judgments of punishment, blame, and responsibility and concern itself exclusively with identifying and treating those who constitute a social danger. For a leading defense of this approach, see Barbara Wooton, Crime and the Criminal Law (1963). For a critique, see H. L. A. Hart, Book Review, 74 Yale L.J. 1325 (1965). Whatever the merits of this view, it is far from the criminal law we have or are likely to have.

2. *Duress*

STATE v. TOSCANO

Supreme Court of New Jersey
74 N.J. 421, 378 A.2d 755 (1977)

PASHMAN, J. Defendant Joseph Toscano was convicted of conspiring to obtain money by false pretenses in violation of N.J.S.A. 2A:98-1. Although admitting that he had aided in the preparation of a fraudulent insurance claim by making out a false medical report, he argued that he had acted under duress. The trial judge ruled that the threatened harm was not sufficiently imminent to justify charging the jury on the defense of duress. After the jury returned a verdict of guilty, the defendant was fined $500.

The Appellate Division affirmed the conviction. . . . We granted certification to consider the status of duress as an affirmative defense to a crime. . . .

On April 20, 1972, the Essex County Grand Jury returned a 48-count indictment alleging that eleven named defendants and two unindicted co-conspirators had defrauded various insurance companies by staging accidents in public places and obtaining payments in settlement of fictitious injuries. . . . Dr. Joseph Toscano, a chiropractor, was named as a defendant in . . . counts alleging a conspiracy to defraud the Kemper Insurance Company (Kemper). Prior to trial, seven of the eleven defendants pleaded guilty to various charges, leaving defendant as the sole remaining defendant charged with the conspiracy to defraud Kemper. Among those who pleaded guilty was William Leonardo, the architect of the alleged general conspiracy and the organizer of each of the separate incidents. . . .

The State attempted to show that Toscano agreed to fill out the false medical report because he owed money to Richard Leonardo [William's brother] for gambling debts. It also suggested that Toscano subsequently sought to cover up the crime by fabricating office records of non-existent office visits by Hanaway.[a] Defendant sharply disputed these assertions and maintained that he capitulated to William Leonardo's demands only because he was fearful for his wife's and his own bodily safety. Since it is not our function here to assess these conflicting versions, we shall summarize only those facts which, if believed by the jury, would support defendant's claim of duress. . . .

[The court recited a number of overtures made by William Leonardo to defendant, which defendant refused, to prepare a false medical report for submission to a claims adjuster.]

The third and final call occurred on Friday evening. Leonardo was "boisterous and loud" repeating, "You're going to make this bill out for me." Then he said: "Remember, you just moved into a place that has a very dark entrance and you leave there with your wife. . . . You and your wife are going to jump at shadows when you leave that dark entrance." Leonardo sounded "vicious" and "desperate" and defendant felt that he "just had to do it" to protect himself and his wife. He thought about calling the police, but failed to do so in the hope that "it would go away and wouldn't bother me any more."

In accordance with Leonardo's instructions, defendant left a form in his mailbox on Saturday morning for Leonardo to fill in with the necessary information about the fictitious injuries. It was returned that evening and defendant completed it. On Sunday morning he met Hanaway at a prearranged spot and delivered a medical bill and the completed medical report. He received no compensation for his services, either in the form of cash from William Leonardo or forgiven gambling debts from Richard Leonardo. He heard nothing more from Leonardo after that Sunday.

Shortly thereafter, still frightened by the entire episode, defendant moved to a new address and had his telephone number changed to an unlisted number in an effort to avoid future contacts with Leonardo. He also applied for a gun permit but was unsuccessful. His superior at his daytime job with the Newark Housing Authority confirmed that the quality of defendant's work dropped so markedly that he was forced to question defendant about his attitude. After some conversation, defendant explained that he had been upset by threats against him and his wife. He also revealed the threats to a co-worker at the Newark Housing Authority.

After defendant testified, the trial judge granted the State's motion to exclude any further testimony in connection with defendant's claim of duress, and announced his decision not to charge the jury on that defense. . . .

After stating that the defense of duress is applicable only where there is an allegation that an act was committed in response to a threat of present, imminent and impending death or serious bodily harm, the trial judge charged the jury:

> Now, one who is standing and receiving instructions from someone at the point of a gun is, of course, in such peril. . . .

a. Hanaway was an unindicted coconspirator who acted as the victim in a number of staged accidents. — Eds.

> Now, where the peril is not imminent, present and pending to the extent that the defendant has the opportunity to seek police assistance for himself and his wife as well, the law places upon such a person the duty not to acquiesce in the unlawful demand and any criminal conduct in which he may thereafter engage may not be excused. Now, this principle prevails regardless of the subjective estimate he may have made as to the degree of danger with which he or his wife may have been confronted. Under the facts of this case, I instruct you, as members of the jury, that the circumstances described by Dr. Toscano leading to his implication in whatever criminal activities in which you may find he participated are not sufficient to constitute the defense of duress.

. . . Since New Jersey has no applicable statute defining the defense of duress,[b] we are guided only by common law principles which conform to the purposes of our criminal justice system and reflect contemporary notions of justice and fairness.

At common law the defense of duress was recognized only when the alleged coercion involved a use or threat of harm which is "present, imminent and pending" and "of such a nature as to induce a well grounded apprehension of death or serious bodily harm if the act is not done."

It was commonly said that duress does not excuse the killing of an innocent person even if the accused acted in response to immediate threats. Aside from this exception, however, duress was permitted as a defense to prosecution for a range of serious offenses. . . .

To excuse a crime, the threatened injury must induce "such a fear as a man of ordinary fortitude and courage might justly yield to." Although there are scattered suggestions in early cases that only a fear of death meets this test, . . .[8] an apprehension of immediate serious bodily harm has been considered sufficient to excuse capitulation to threats. Thus, the courts have assumed as a matter of law that neither threats of slight injury nor threats of destruction to property are coercive enough to overcome the will of a person of ordinary courage. [The court then referred to cases in which threats of loss of job, denial of food rations, economic need, and prospect of financial ruin were held inadequate.] . . . When the alleged source of coercion is a threat of "future" harm, courts have generally found that the defendant had a duty to escape from the control of the threatening person or to seek assistance from law enforcement authorities.

Assuming a "present, imminent and impending" danger, however, there is no requirement that the threatened person be the accused. [C]oncern for the well-being of another, particularly a near relative, can support a defense of duress if the other requirements are satisfied. . . .

The insistence under the common law on a danger of immediate force causing death or serious bodily injury may be ascribed to . . . judicial fears of perjury and fabrication of baseless defenses. We do not discount [this] concern as a reason for caution in modifying this accepted rule, but we are concerned by its ob-

b. New Jersey does have such a statute at the present time, the legislature having enacted in the meantime the draft proposal referred to subsequently in the court's opinion. —Eds.

8. Several states, by statute, continue to require that the actor have reasonable cause to believe that his life was in danger. . . . Minnesota limits the defense to situations in which "instant death" is threatened. Minn. Stat. 609.08 (1965).

vious shortcomings and potential for injustice. Under some circumstances, the commission of a minor criminal offense should be excusable even if the coercive agent does not use or threaten force which is likely to result in death or "serious" bodily injury. Similarly, it is possible that authorities might not be able to prevent a threat of future harm from eventually being carried out. . . .

[S]ome commentators have advocated a flexible rule which would allow a jury to consider whether the accused actually lost his capacity to act in accordance with "his own desire, or motivation, or will" under the pressure of real or imagined forces. See Newman & Weitzer, "Duress, Free Will and the Criminal Law," 30 S. Cal. L. Rev. 313, 331 (1957); Fletcher, "The Individualization of Excusing Conditions," 47 S. Cal. L. Rev. 1269, 1288-93 (1974). The inquiry here would focus on the weaknesses and strengths of a particular defendant, and his subjective reaction to unlawful demands. Thus, the "standard of heroism" of the common law would give way, not to a "reasonable person" standard, but to a set of expectations based on the defendant's character and situation.

The drafters of the Model Penal code and the New Jersey Penal Code . . . focus[ed] on whether the standard imposed upon the accused was one with which "normal members of the community will be able to comply." . . .

They substantially departed from the existing statutory and common law limitations requiring that the result be death or serious bodily harm, that the threat be immediate and aimed at the accused, or that the crime committed be a non-capital offense. While these factors would be given evidential weight, the failure to satisfy one or more of these conditions would not justify the trial judge's withholding the defense from the jury. . . .

Although they are not entirely identical, under both model codes defendant would have had his claim of duress submitted to the jury.[12] Defendant's testimony provided a factual basis for a finding that Leonardo threatened him and his wife with physical violence if he refused to assist in the fraudulent scheme. Moreover, a jury might have found from other testimony adduced at trial that Leonardo's threats induced a reasonable fear in the defendant. Since he asserted that he agreed to complete the false documents only because of this apprehension, the requisite elements of the defense were established. Under the model code provisions, it would have been solely for the jury to determine whether a "person of reasonable firmness in his situation" would have failed to seek police assistance or refused to cooperate, or whether such a person would have been, unlike defendant, able to resist.

Exercising our authority to revise the common law, we have decided to adopt this approach as the law of New Jersey. Henceforth, duress shall be a defense to a crime other than murder if the defendant engaged in conduct because he was coerced to do so by the use of, or threat to use, unlawful force against his person or the person of another, which a person of reasonable firmness in his situation would have been unable to resist. . . .

Defendant's conviction of conspiracy to obtain money by false pretenses is hereby reversed and remanded for a new trial.

12. The most significant difference between the two provisions is the treatment of duress as a defense to murder. The Model Penal Code permits it as an affirmative defense, while the New Jersey Penal Code allows it only to reduce a crime from murder to manslaughter.

MODEL PENAL CODE

SECTION 2.09. DURESS

[See Appendix for text of this section.]

MODEL PENAL CODE AND COMMENTARIES, COMMENT TO §2.09 AT 372-375 (1985): The problem of how far duress should exculpate conduct that otherwise would constitute a crime is much debated in the literature of the penal law. . . . Stephen argued, for example, that "compulsion by threats ought in no case whatever to be admitted as an excuse for crime, though it may and ought to operate in mitigation of punishment in most though not in all cases." His reason was, in substance, that "it is at the moment when temptation to crime is strongest that the law should speak most clearly and emphatically to the contrary."[29]

Jerome Hall is less hostile to allowing the defense, but he would limit it with rigor to the situation where the actor rightly chose the lesser of two evils; and even then he gives such weight to the moral duty to resist the evil-doing author of the duress that he does not commit himself beyond the proposition that "coercion should not exculpate in the most serious crimes but . . . should be a defense where, e.g., it is a question of imminent death or the commission of relatively minor harm."[30]

Much of the issue posed by these competing views is resolved . . . in Section 3.02, which provides a general defense in cases where the actor believed his conduct necessary to avoid an evil to himself or to another and the evil sought to be avoided is greater than that sought to be prevented by the law defining the offense charged. The Institute saw no reason why this principle should be denied full application when the evil apprehended has its source in the action or the threatened action of another person, rather than the forces and perils of the physical world. The only basis offered for drawing this distinction, that the agent of coercion is an evil-doer who should be resisted, was thought to bear on the necessity of the actor's conduct, rather than the rightness of his choice when the necessity obtains. Surely there are cases where the actor may correctly think resistance on his part to be impossible or doomed to failure. . . . Section 2.09(4) provides, therefore, that Section 3.02 is not superseded by the present section in cases that may seem to give rise to both defenses. . . .

The problem of Section 2.09, then, reduces to the question of whether there are cases where the actor cannot justify his conduct under Section 3.02, as when his choice involves an equal or greater evil than that threatened, but where he nonetheless should be excused because he was subjected to coercion. If he is so far overwhelmed by force that his behavior is involuntary, as when his arm is physically moved by someone else, Section 2.01(1) stands as a barrier to liability, following in this respect the long tradition of the penal law. The case of concern here is that in which the actor makes a choice, but claims in his defense that he was so intimidated that he was unable to choose otherwise. Should such psy-

29. 2 J. Stephen, History of the Criminal Law of England 108 (1883).
30. General Principles of Criminal Law 448 (2d ed. 1960).

chological incapacity be given the same exculpative force as the physical incapacity that may afford a defense under Section 2.01? . . .

In favor of allowing the defense, it may be argued that the legal sanction cannot be effective in the case supposed and that the actor may not properly be blamed for doing what he had to choose to do. It seems clear, however, that the argument in its full force must be rejected. The crucial reason is the same as that which elsewhere leads to an unwillingness to vary legal norms with the individual's capacity to meet the standards they prescribe, absent a disability that is both gross and verifiable, such as the mental disease or defect that may establish irresponsibility. The most that it is feasible to do with lesser disabilities is to accord them proper weight in sentencing. To make liability depend upon the fortitude of any given actor would be no less impractical or otherwise impolitic than to permit it to depend upon such other variables as intelligence or clarity of judgment, suggestibility or moral insight.

Moreover, the legal standard may gain in its effectiveness by being unconditional in this respect. It cannot be known what choices might be different if the actor thought he had a chance of exculpation on the ground of his peculiar disabilities instead of knowing that he does not. No less important, legal norms and sanctions operate not only at the moment of climactic choice, but also in the fashioning of values and of character.

Though, for the foregoing reasons, the submission that the actor lacked the fortitude to make the moral choice should not be entertained as a defense, a different situation is presented if the claimed excuse is based upon the incapacity of men in general to resist the coercive pressures to which the individual succumbed. . . . [L]aw is ineffective in the deepest sense, indeed . . . it is hypocritical, if it imposes on the actor who has the misfortune to confront a dilemmatic choice, a standard that his judges are not prepared to affirm that they should and could comply with if their turn to face the problem should arise. Condemnation in such a case is bound to be an ineffective threat; what is, however, more significant is that it is divorced from any moral base and is unjust. . . .

The Model Code accordingly provides for the defense in cases where the actor was coerced by force or threats of force "that a person of reasonable firmness in his situation would have been unable to resist." The standard is not, however, wholly external in its reference; account is taken of the actor's "situation," a term that should here be given the same scope it is accorded in appraising recklessness and negligence. Stark, tangible factors that differentiate the actor from another, like his size, strength, age, or health, would be considered in making the exculpatory judgment. Matters of temperament would not.

NOTES

1. *Partial vs. Complete Excuse.* Does the rationale for the defense of duress given by the Model Penal Code apply as well to the defense of provocation in the law of homicide? If so, why should provocation only reduce the crime from murder to manslaughter, while duress, where applicable, excuses altogether? See Jeremy Horder, Autonomy, Provocation and Duress, [1992] Crim. L. Rev. 70.

2. *The objective standard.* As the foregoing commentary indicates, the Model Penal Code opposes individualizing the standard of "reasonable firmness" that

a defendant must meet. But as in other areas where a norm of reasonableness is set (for example, in the law defining due care and adequate provocation), it remains necessary to determine how specifically the norm should be tailored to a particular actor's "situation."

In Regina v. Cairns, [1999] Crim. L. Rev. 826, the defendant, described as "a small man and also somewhat timid," committed an assault under alleged duress. His short stature was considered relevant to the amount of resistance to be expected, but his timidity was not. In Regina v. Bowen, [1996] Crim. L. Rev. 577, 578, the defendant claimed that his acts of theft were committed under duress. He argued that because of his low I.Q. (68), he was more easily intimidated. The court held that "the mere fact that the accused was more pliable, vulnerable, timid or susceptible to threats than a normal person were not characteristics with which it was legitimate to invest the reasonable person"; likewise, the court said, "A low I.Q., short of mental impairment or mental defectiveness, could not be said to [make] those who had it . . . less able to withstand threats."

Are these limitations justified? The English Law Commission has argued:[35]

> Threats directed against a weak, immature or disabled person may well be much more compelling than the same threats directed against a normal healthy person. . . . Relative timidity, for example, may be an inseparable aspect of a total personality that is in turn part cause and part product of its possessor's life situation; and thus may itself be one of the "circumstances" in the light of which . . . the duress is to be assessed.

In accord with this approach, see Zelenak v. Commonwealth, 475 S.E.2d 853, 855 (Va. App. 1996). Defendant was convicted for participating in a robbery, despite her claim of duress. The trial court had excluded evidence that her mental state, multiple personality disorder (MPD), made her especially susceptible to intimidation. The appellate court reversed, holding that the MPD evidence was relevant and admissible because the crucial issue was "whether the accused acted out of a subjectively reasonable fear." Do you agree? Compare John Gardner, The Gist of Excuses, 2 Buffalo Crim. L. Rev. 1 (1997), questioning a highly individualized standard.

3. Battered Woman's Syndrome. Courts now uniformly hold that evidence of battered woman's syndrome (BWS) is admissible to support a claim of self-defense when a woman kills her abuser (see page 773 supra), but there is disagreement about whether BWS evidence is relevant when the woman claims duress as an excuse for participating in a robbery or drug deal under pressure from her abuser.[36] Is there a valid basis for this distinction?

Consider State v. Williams, 670 P.2d 122 (N.M. App. 1983). A mother was convicted of child abuse for failing to protect her daughter from beatings inflicted by her husband, a batterer who was abusing both her and her child. Should the criteria for claiming a defense be stricter when the defendant has killed or injured a wholly innocent victim rather than the abuser himself? Or should this consideration be irrelevant?

35. Law Commission, Consultation Paper No. 122, at 55 (1992). See also Alec Buchanan & Graham Virgo, Duress and Mental Abnormality, [1999] Crim. L. Rev. 517; K. L. M. Smith, Duress and Steadfastness, [1999] Crim. L. Rev. 363.

36. Compare United States v. Willis, 38 F.3d 170 (5th Cir. 1994) (BWS inadmissible), with United States v. Marenghi, 893 F. Supp. 85 (D. Me. 1995) (BWS admissible).

Note that the decisive factual question on a claim of duress is identical to that on a claim of self-defense — whether the defendant had a reasonable fear of imminent great bodily harm. Accordingly, most of the recent decisions hold that the logic of the self-defense precedents (which hold BWS evidence admissible) controls in duress cases as well.[37] In contrast, one recent commentator suggests that BWS evidence should weigh heavily at sentencing but not necessarily when duress is claimed as a complete excuse. She argues that on claims of duress, unlike claims of self-defense, the strict imminence requirement should be preserved and the standard of reasonableness should not be adjusted to consider what is reasonable for a woman suffering from BWS. See Laurie Kratky Doré, Downward Adjustment and the Slippery Slope: The Use of Duress in Defense of Battered Offenders, 56 Ohio St. L. J. 665 (1995). Do you agree? The author states (id. at 749):

> One of the primary distinctions between a battered woman's claim of self-defense and that of duress concerns the nature of her response to the perceived deadly threat. In self-defense, the woman avoids the imminent danger by responding in kind against its source — her batterer. In duress, however, the woman avoids her abuser's threat by misconduct directed against an innocent third party.

4. For a comprehensive survey of the elements of a duress defense under the statute law of the various states, see Doré, supra Note 3, at 767-773.

NOTE: NECESSITY AND DURESS COMPARED

The relationship between the defenses of necessity and duress can be confusing. Partly the reason is terminological: Courts and commentators don't always use the terms the same way. But, more significantly, the confusion is analytical. See Claire O. Finkelstein, Duress: A Philosophical Account of the Defense in Law, 37 Ariz. L. Rev. 251 (1995); Miriam Gur-Arye, Should the Criminal Law Distinguish Between Necessity as a Justification and Necessity as an Excuse?, 102 L.Q. Rev. 71 (1986); George Fletcher, Should Intolerable Conditions Generate a Justification or an Excuse for Escape?, 26 U.C.L.A.L. Rev. 1355 (1979).

There are two separate concepts at work here. What is usually called necessity refers to a defense resting on the rationale of justification. One can see this most clearly in the Model Penal Code defense of the choice of evils (§3.02), which we explored in the preceding section: The defendant violated a criminal prohibition, but in the circumstances it was a good thing she did, for to do so was the lesser evil. The other concept rests on the rationale of excuse. The defendant is accorded a defense not because it was right to violate the law, but because the circumstances were so urgent and compelling that otherwise law-abiding people might well have done the same in the circumstances. This is the spirit behind the Model Penal Code formulation of the defense of duress.

But the lines between these two distinguishable concepts are often blurred in the way the law is formulated and talked about. Note the New York defense of

37. E.g., United States v. Brown, 891 F. Supp. 1501 (D. Kan. 1995); State v. Williams, 937 P.2d 1052 (Wash. 1997); People v. Romero, 13 Cal. Rptr. 2d 332 (Cal. App. 1992).

justification, §35.05 of the N.Y. Penal code, supra page 817. While that section is unmistakably a justification provision, the first sentence of the statute requires that the choice be made "as an emergency measure," which is an appropriate consideration for an excuse but not for a justification. The same blurring sometimes occurs in the way duress is defined. See, for example, Wayne LaFave & Austin Scott, Criminal Law 432 (2d ed. 1986), which summarizes the law of duress as requiring not only that the defendant be threatened by another with imminent serious unlawful harm, but that the defendant's choice to break the law was the lesser evil in the circumstances.

In those jurisdictions where the law of duress is as LaFave and Scott summarize it, duress becomes a species of justification. But why is it needed? Wouldn't the defense of justification (necessity) cover all the cases duress covers? The answer might be no, because the law in some jurisdictions accords significance to the source of the peril. Under this view, if the source of the peril was the "do-it-or-else" command of another person, the only possible defense is duress, not necessity; but if the source of the peril is anything else, necessity may be a defense, but not duress. Recall, for example, the dictum in People v. Unger, supra page 810, that the defense of compulsion (duress) would be available only if someone commanded the prisoner to escape by threatening him with serious harm if he did not.

These ways of formulating the defenses of duress and necessity — that *both* are justification defenses and that only a do-it-or-else command of another could establish a defense of duress — are problematical. The Model Penal Code, which has been influential in shaping the law in many jurisdictions, proposes some important changes. Duress is defined in §2.09 purely as an excuse. What establishes the defense is that the defendant acted under a threat a person of reasonable firmness would have been unable to resist; it is not required that he chose the lesser evil. If the circumstances that would make out a defense under this formulation also made the defendant's act the lesser evil, the Model Penal Code permits the justification defense as well. As the Commentary to §3.02 states: "The Institute saw no reason why the [choice-of-evils] principle should be denied full application when the evil apprehended has its source in the action or the threatened action of another person, rather than the forces and perils of the physical world."

But while the Model Penal Code allows the choice-of-evils justification regardless of the source of the peril, it does not allow the duress excuse regardless of the source of the peril. It makes the duress excuse available only when the peril confronting the defendant arises from the do-it-or-else command of another person, not when it arises from some other source, such as a natural condition. To this extent the Model Penal Code adheres to the tradition of differentiating the availability of defenses depending on the source of the peril. Why this should be is explored in the first of the following notes, which sample the major issues in the law of duress.

NOTES ON DURESS

1. *Source of the threat.* What is the basis for the Model Penal Code's distinction depending on the source of the threat? If the peril is great enough that a person of reasonable firmness would be unable to resist, why should it matter whether the peril is from another person or from some natural event. Consider the following cases.

(*a*) *X* is unwillingly driving a car along a narrow and precipitous mountain road which drops off sharply on both sides, under the command of *Y*, an armed escaping felon. The headlights pick out two drunken persons lying across the road in such a position as to make passage impossible without running them over. *X* is prevented from stopping by the threat of *Y* to shoot him dead if he declines to drive straight on. If *X* does go on and kills the drunks in order to save himself, he would not be justified under the lesser evil principle of §3.02, but he will be excused under §2.09 if the jury should find that "a person of reasonable firmness in his situation would have been unable to resist."

(*b*) The same situation as above except that *X* is prevented from stopping by suddenly inoperative brakes. His alternatives are either to run down the drunks or to run off the road and down the mountainside. If *X* chooses the first alternative to save his own life and kills the drunks, he will not be excused under §2.09 even if a jury should find that a person of reasonable firmness would have been unable to do otherwise.

Can the difference between these two cases be defended? Does the logic of the matter necessarily push to a formulation that would excuse an actor whenever she commits a criminal act in such circumstances that most people would lack the fortitude to do otherwise? If so, it would be open in every criminal case for the accused to argue that reasonable people in the defendant's situation would lack the will to act otherwise than as defendant acted. Would such a defense be too easily abused? If so, how could the "person of reasonable firmness" formula be narrowed? Consider California Joint Legislative Committee for Revision of the Penal Code, Penal Code Revision Project §520 (Tent. Draft No. 1, 1967):

> In a prosecution for any offense: (1) it is an affirmative defense that the defendant engaged in the conduct otherwise constituting the offense because he was coerced into doing so by the threatened use of unlawful force against his person or the person of another in circumstances where a person of reasonable firmness in his situation would not have done otherwise; (2) it is an affirmative defense that the defendant engaged in the conduct otherwise constituting the offense in order to avoid death or great bodily harm to himself or another in circumstances where a person of reasonable firmness in his situation would not have done otherwise.[a]

The Model Penal Code, in its final commentary (Model Penal Code and Commentaries, Comment to §2.09 at 378-379 (1985)), justifies its position on hypotheticals (a) and (b) found at the beginning of this Note as follows:

> [T]here is a significant difference between the situations in which an actor makes the choice of an equal or greater evil under the threat of unlawful human force and when he does so because of a natural event. In the former situation, the basic interests of the law may be satisfied by prosecution of the agent of unlawful force; in the latter circumstance, if the actor is excused, no one is subject to the law's application.

a. The Brown Commission, in its proposals for reform of the federal criminal code, adopted this suggestion and influenced a number of states to enact it. See Model Penal Code and Commentaries, Comment to §2.09 at 383 n. 59 (1985).—Eds.

What are the "basic interests of the law" that the Model Penal Code Commentary has in mind? If in principle the defendant in the latter case should be excused, why should it matter that there is no one else to prosecute?

2. Imminence of the threat. Both the *Toscano* decision and Model Penal Code §2.09 treat the imminence of the threatened harm as one factor to be weighed by the jury in determining whether the defendant's conduct was that of "a person of reasonable firmness in his situation." In contrast, many common law decisions treated imminence as an absolute prerequisite to the availability of a duress defense, and some statutes expressly limited the defense to situations involving threats of "instant" death. The great majority of the recent statutory revisions have rejected the Model Penal Code's flexible approach and preserved some requirement that the threatened harm be "immediate," "imminent" or "instant." See Model Penal Code and Commentaries, Comments to §2.09 at 369, 382 (1985). Many of the recent judicial decisions likewise insist on strict temporal imminence. E.g., Anguish v. State, 991 S.W.2d 883 (Tex. App. 1999); People v. Ramsdell, 585 N.W.2d 1 (Mich. App. 1998).

What is the justification for this inflexible imminence requirement? Consider the following cases:

United States v. Fleming, 23 C.M.R. 7 (1957): [Defendant, an Army officer, was court-martialed for violating the Uniform Code of Military Justice while a prisoner of war in Korea. The charges against him rested on his having collaborated with the enemy by helping prepare propaganda designed to promote disaffection among U.S. troops, and by making numerous English language broadcasts criticizing American war objectives and calling upon U.S. authorities to withdraw or surrender. In describing the circumstances leading up to the acts of collaboration, the court noted that after being captured, defendant suffered numerous interrogations, forced marches and physical abuse. It characterized the prison camp conditions as "extremely bad." The court then described specific threats that occurred in response to defendant's initial refusals to cooperate (*id.* at 15-16):]

[T]he accused testified that he was constantly harangued and pressured by Colonel Kim. According to Kim, there were two kinds of people: those for peace and those against peace. Those against peace were war criminals and not fit to live. If the accused fitted into that category he would be put in a "hole" and would never come out. But if he were for peace, he was a friend. . . . When the accused initially refused to do the acts to prove his "friendliness," he was asked if he wanted to return to the previous camp up north. The accused replied in the affirmative and Kim informed him that he could start walking the 150-200 mile distance. It was midwinter, the accused's shoes had been stolen, and he was wearing rags wrapped around his feet. These factors, plus his greatly weakened physical condition, led the accused to the conclusion that he would never reach the north camp alive. Thereafter, on each occasion when the accused objected to Kim's propaganda efforts, he was threatened with the walk north. . . .

Also Kim's subsequent threat of the caves . . . undoubtedly affected prisoner cooperation. [The caves] were recesses in the hillside. They were wet and muddy with little or no heating facilities. The prisoners lived in the muck and mire like animals. . . . The mortality rate in the indescribable filth and privation of these holes in the ground was extremely high. The prisoners felt that a sentence to the caves was almost tantamount to a sentence of death. . . . According to the accused, whenever he balked on the propaganda, Kim reminded him of the Americans in the caves and again took him to see them.

[At the court-martial the trier of fact was instructed that defendant's acts could be excused on grounds of duress only if he had "a well-grounded apprehension of immediate and impending death or of immediate, serious, bodily harm." Defense counsel argued that the insistence on a fear of *immediate* death was error under the circumstances, that fear of "a delayed, or a wasting death from starvation, deprivation or other like conditions can just as well spell coercion and compulsion as the fear of immediate death." Rejecting this argument, the court upheld the conviction (id. at 24-25):]

We are not unmindful of the hardships or the pressures to which the accused and his fellow prisoners were subjected prior to the time of his collaboration with the enemy, [but] we cannot overlook the fact that accused cooperated with his captors upon the mere assertion of the threats. . . . It was not at all certain at the time the threat was made that walking north to Pyoktong would cause death at all, much less immediately. By way of comparison, if, for example, accused's captors had actually made him start on foot for Camp Five, and it then became evident that he could not survive the march, a valid defense of duress might have arisen for capitulation at that point. . . . Here the danger of death was problematical and remote. . . . As the court stated in D'Aquino v. United States. "The person claiming the defense of coercion and duress must be a person whose resistance has brought him to the last ditch" (182 F.2d at 359). Accused's resistance had not "brought him to the last ditch"; the danger of death or great bodily harm was not *immediate.* Accused can not now avail himself of the defense of duress.

United States v. Contento-Pachon, 723 F.2d 691 (9th Cir. 1984): [Defendant, a native of Bogota, Colombia, was employed there as a taxicab driver. One of his passengers, Jorge, proposed] that Contento-Pachon swallow cocaine-filled balloons and transport them to the United States. Contento-Pachon agreed to consider the proposition. He was told not to mention the proposition to anyone, otherwise he would "get into serious trouble." Contento-Pachon testified that he did not contact the police because he believes that the Bogota police are corrupt and that they are paid off by drug traffickers. Approximately one week later, Contento-Pachon told Jorge that he would not carry the cocaine. In response, . . . Jorge told Contento-Pachon that his failure to cooperate would result in the death of his wife and three-year-old child.

The following day the pair met again. Contento-Pachon's life and the lives of his family were again threatened. At this point, Contento-Pachon agreed to take the cocaine into the United States. The pair met two more times. At the last meeting, Contento-Pachon swallowed 129 balloons of cocaine. He was informed that he would be watched at all times during the trip, and that if he failed to follow Jorge's instruction he and his family would be killed.

After leaving Bogota, Contento-Pachon's plane landed in Panama. Contento-Pachon asserts that he did not notify the authorities there because he felt that the Panamanian police were as corrupt as those in Bogota. Also, he felt that any such action on his part would place his family in jeopardy. When he arrived at the customs inspection point in Los Angeles, Contento-Pachon consented to have his stomach x-rayed. The x-rays revealed a foreign substance which was later determined to be cocaine.

[At trial, the government's motion to exclude the duress defense was granted. The District Court held that two necessary elements of the defense are the immediacy and the inescapability of the threat. It concluded that neither element was satisfied. The court of appeals reversed:] [T]he defendant was dealing with a man who was deeply involved in the exportation of illegal substances. Large sums of money were at stake and, consequently, Contento-Pachon had reason to believe that Jorge would carry out his threats. . . . These were not vague threats of possible future harm. According to the defendant, if he had refused to cooperate, the consequences would have been immediate and harsh. . . . Contento-Pachon's contention that he was operating under the threat of immediate harm was supported by sufficient evidence to present a triable issue of fact.

The defendant must show that he had no reasonable opportunity to escape. . . . The trier of fact should decide whether one in Contento-Pachon's position might believe that some of the Bogota police were paid informants for drug traffickers and that reporting the matter to the police did not represent a reasonable opportunity of escape.

If he chose not to go to the police, Contento-Pachon's alternative was to flee. We reiterate that the opportunity to escape must be reasonable. To flee, Contento-Pachon, along with his wife and three year-old child, would have been forced to pack his possessions, leave his job, and travel to a place beyond the reaches of the drug traffickers. A juror might find that this was not a reasonable avenue of escape. Thus, Contento-Pachon presented a triable issue on the element of escapability.

Regina v. Ruzic, [1998] D.L.R.4th 358, involved a defendant who was a 21-year-old woman who had traveled from Belgrade, Yugoslavia, to Toronto with two kilos of heroin strapped to her body. At trial she admitted bringing the heroin into Canada but argued duress. She claimed that a man named Mirkovic, a known killer, had stabbed and burned her arm and had threatened to "do something" to her mother if she would not carry heroin to Canada. She claimed she did not tell the police because she no longer trusted the Yugoslav authorities. A defense expert testified that in Yugoslavia large paramilitary groups engaged in mafia-like coercive activities and that people perceived the police to have lost control.

Section 17 of the Canadian Criminal Code provides:

> A person who commits an offence under compulsion by threats of immediate death or bodily injury from a person who is present when the offense is committed is excused for committing the offense if the person believes that the threats will be carried out.

The trial court instructed the jury on compulsion as a defense but, contrary to the Canadian statute, refused to specify that the threat had to be immediate, had to be made against the defendant herself, and had to be made by a person who was present when the offense was committed. The jury acquitted, and the prosecution appealed. The Ontario Court of Appeal upheld the acquittal on the ground that the restrictive conditions in the duress statute violated Section 7 of the Canadian Charter of Rights and Freedoms, a general provision stating:

Everyone has the right to life, liberty, and security of the person, and the right not to be deprived thereof except in accordance with the principles of fundamental justice.

The court reasoned that if the defendant's story were believed, the threat left her no realistic choice, even though the threat was not immediate and the threatener was not present when she committed the offense. To convict her in such a situation would amount to convicting the innocent in violation of the principles of fundamental justice. She would be innocent because her actions were in effect involuntary, not physically but morally involuntary, since she had no realistic choice but to comply.

Questions: Could an analogous argument be made that conviction in the United States under these circumstances would be unconstitutional under the Due Process Clause? Are immediacy requirements and similar restrictions justified on the ground that a defendant like Ruzic should not be considered morally innocent, or are such restrictions based on practical concerns? As a policy matter, do such practical concerns (if any) justify the conviction of a person who is morally innocent?

3. Duress as a defense to murder. Prior to the Model Penal Code proposals, most jurisdictions held the duress defense inapplicable in prosecutions for murder (and sometimes for other very serious crimes) even when the stringent requirements of an imminent, inescapable lethal threat were satisfied. The Model Penal Code rejected this exclusion of murder cases, as have a few state courts. E.g., Spunaugle v. State, 946 P.2d 246 (Okla. Crim. App. 1997). But the great majority of recent cases and statutory revisions continue to exclude the defense in murder prosecutions. E.g., State v. Getsy, 702 N.E.2d 866 (Ohio 1998); Model Penal Code and Commentaries, Comment to §2.09, at 381 (1985). In England, courts have held that the defense is precluded in cases of murder and attempted murder, but not in cases of aircraft hijacking. See Regina v. Abdul-Hussain, [1999] Crim. L. Rev. 570 (Ct. App.); Regina v. Gotts, [1992] 1 All E.R. 832; Regina v. Howe, [1987] 2 W.L.R. 568.

The issue has assumed new importance in the effort to prosecute individuals involved in perpetrating atrocities in the former Yugoslavia. In several cases, accused soldiers admitted shooting large numbers of unarmed, defenseless civilians but insisted that they had done so under orders; they testified they had been told that if they refused: "[L]ine up with them and we will kill you too."[38] European countries apparently are divided on the scope of the duress defense. France and Germany allow duress as a complete defense, for example, while in Poland and Norway duress is considered only as a mitigating circumstance.[39] The United Nations War Crimes Tribunal for the Former Yugoslavia recently ruled, in a closely divided vote (3-2), that duress is not available as a complete defense to war-crimes charges of this sort. Prosecutor v. Erdemovic, No. IT-96-22-A (Oct. 7, 1997), at 17.

The argument in favor of granting the defense, even to murder, is that the law should not demand a degree of heroism of which the ordinary person is, by definition, incapable. On the other hand, consider the comments of Lord Salmon

38. Prosecutor v. Erdemovic, No. IT-96-22-A (Oct. 7, 1997), at 4.
39. Id., Li, J. (separate and dissenting opinion), at 2-3.

explaining the English position that denies the defense (Abbott v. The Queen, [1976] 3 All E.R. 140, 146):

> In the trials of those responsible for wartime atrocities such as mass killings of men, women or children, inhuman experiments on human beings, often resulting in death, and like crimes, it was invariably argued for the defence that these atrocities should be excused on the ground that they resulted from superior orders and duress; if the accused had refused to do these dreadful things, they would have been shot and therefore they should be acquitted and allowed to go free. This argument has always been universally rejected. Their Lordships would be sorry indeed to see it accepted by the common law of England.
>
> . . . A terrorist of notorious violence might, e.g., threaten death to *A* and his family unless *A* obeys his instructions to put a bomb with a time fuse set by *A* in a certain passenger aircraft and/or in a thronged market, railway station or the like. . . . Is there any limit to the number of people you may kill to save your own life and that of your family?

Question: Suppose that a defendant is compelled to participate in a robbery, and during the course of that crime a bystander is shot and killed by one of the other robbers. If duress is available in a prosecution for robbery but not in a murder prosecution, should the defendant be able to invoke the duress defense in a prosecution for felony murder?[40]

4. The defendant's role in a homicidal offense. Where, as in most jurisdictions, duress cannot be a defense to a murder charge, should the defense nonetheless remain available if the coerced defendant's participation in the crime was relatively minor? Consider the observations of Bray, C.J., dissenting in Regina v. Brown, [1968] S.A.S.R. 467, 494:

> The reasoning generally used to support the proposition that duress is no defence to a charge of murder is, to use the words of Blackstone cited above, that "he ought rather to die himself, than escape by the murder of an innocent." Generally speaking I am prepared to accept this position. Its force is obviously considerably less where the act of the threatened man is not the direct act of killing but only the rendering of some minor form of assistance, particularly when it is by no means certain that if he refuses the death of the victim will be averted, or conversely when it is by no means certain that if he complies the death will be a necessary consequence. It would seem hard, for example, if an innocent passer-by seized in the street by a gang of criminals visibly engaged in robbery and murder in a shop and compelled at the point of a gun to issue misleading comments to the public, or an innocent driver compelled at the point of a gun to convey the murderer to the victim, were to have no defence. . . .

When is a defendant's role sufficiently limited to justify the availability of a duress defense to homicide?

Consider the following case (San Francisco Chronicle, Dec. 24, 1985, at 1): A young man, despairing over his father's suffering from cancer and distraught because the father had said he did not want a lingering death, allegedly strode into

40. Courts are divided. Compare People v. Serrano, 676 N.E.2d 1011 (Ill. App. 1997) (duress available); State v. Hunter, 740 P.2d 559 (Kan. 1987) (same); with People v. Gimotty, 549 N.W.2d 39 (Mich. App. 1996) (duress not available); State v. Berndt, 672 P.2d 1311 (Ariz. 1983) (same).

felony murder

the hospital's intensive care unit, held a pistol to a nurse's head, and threatened to kill her unless she allowed his father to "die with dignity." The nurse disconnected a mechanical respirator and the father, who had been in a coma, died a few minutes later. If the son has no defense to a murder charge, should the nurse nonetheless have a duress defense? On what theory? Should it matter whether the nurse is characterized as the "actual killer" or instead merely as a person guilty of an omission — namely the failure to continue rendering aid?

5. Nature of the threat. At common law the threat had to be one of death or serious bodily harm before it could ground a duress defense. The Model Penal Code requires a threat of unlawful force against the person. What is the reason for these limitations? Consider the comment of Lord Simon dissenting in D. P. P. for Northern Ireland v. Lynch, [1975] A.C. 653, 686:

> [A] threat to property may, in certain circumstances, be as potent in overbearing the actor's [will] as a threat of physical harm. For example, the threat may be to burn down his house unless the householder merely keeps watch against interruption while a crime is committed. Or a fugitive from justice may say, "I have it in my power to make your son bankrupt. You can avoid that merely by driving me to the airport." Would not many ordinary people yield to such threats . . . ?

6. Contributory fault. Should it make any difference whether the defendant is in some way to blame for being in a position that leads to duress? Consider the following situations.

(*a*) *Gang membership.* The defendant joins a gang engaged in petty thefts. When the leader decides to rob a bank, the defendant refuses to go along, but is threatened with death if he fails to cooperate. If the defendant participates in the robbery, should he have a duress defense? A common approach is to hold that where a defendant "voluntarily, and with knowledge of its nature, joined a criminal organization or gang which he knew might bring pressure on him to commit an offense and was an active member when he was put under such pressure, he cannot avail himself of the defense of duress." Regina v. Sharp, [1987] 3 W.L.R. 1, 8-9. If, however, the nature of the criminal enterprise is such that the defendant has no reason to suspect he will be forcibly prevented from withdrawing, and if trouble materializes unexpectedly, the defense remains available. Regina v. Shepherd, 86 Cr. App. R. 47 (1988). See also Model Penal Code §2.09(2), withdrawing the defense where the defendant "recklessly placed himself in a situation in which it is probable that he would be subjected to duress."

Questions: Is it fair for the defense to remain available, as it does under the Model Penal Code, even though the defendant has negligently run an unreasonable risk of incurring duress? Conversely, is the Model Penal Code exception overly broad in relation to crimes that require a culpability level higher than recklessness? For example, suppose that a defendant was aware that his involvement with a gang exposed him to a vague risk that he might be pressured to participate in various unspecified crimes. If in the future the defendant is threatened with death if he does not help in a bank robbery, is it fair to deny him the duress defense to a bank robbery charge?

(*b*) *Problem.* Williams became involved with a gang of drug dealers and voluntarily made several "drug runs" in which he transported drugs from Maryland to New York. Subsequently, three men who knew of his involvement with the gang kidnapped Williams and threatened to kill him if he did not reveal the location of the gang's "stash" of money and drugs. Williams, who apparently did not know where the stash was kept, led the gang to the apartment of a third party (one Hale, a minister as it turned out). The gang broke into Hale's apartment, held him at gunpoint and carefully searched it, but when the stash could not be found, they tied up Hale and left without taking anything.

After the trial judge ruled that Williams could not claim duress, he was convicted of attempted armed robbery. The appellate court affirmed, holding that duress was not available as a defense in view of several factors: (1) "[n]o one forced him to go to the Reverend's house and demand money"; (2) his own prior conduct "contributed mightily to the predicament" because it was through his reckless involvement that others became aware of his connection to the gang; and (3) the situation "would not have occurred but for [his] association with the drug organization." Williams v. State, 646 A.2d 1101, 1103, 1110 (Md. App. 1994).

Questions: Should Williams have a duress defense? What would be the result under Model Penal Code §2.09?

(*c*) *Mistaken threats.* The defendant drives a couple of would-be bank robbers to a bank and serves as lookout, believing they will beat him up badly if he refuses. In fact, the robbers never actually made any such threat, either explicitly or implicitly; defendant is just an abnormally timid soul with a lively imagination. Does the defendant qualify for the duress defense even though he was unreasonable in believing he was being threatened? The language of Model Penal Code §2.09(1) is not clear; the Commentary states that in such a case he would have a defense to robbery, although not to a crime of recklessness or negligence. Model Penal Code and Commentaries, Comment to §2.09 at 380 (1985). Most jurisdictions today appear to follow the common law rule requiring the defendant to have a "well-grounded" fear, Wayne LaFave & Austin Scott, Criminal Law 439 (2d ed. 1986), so that in our hypothetical the defendant would not have a duress defense to the robbery.

Which is the better view? Recall that the provocation defense to murder contains an objective standard. Does it follow that an objective standard should also apply to the duress defense, especially since duress is a complete defense while provocation only reduces the crime to manslaughter?

3. *Intoxication*

REGINA v. KINGSTON

Court of Appeal, Criminal Division
[1993] 4 All E.R. 373,
rev'd,
House of Lords
[1994] 3 All E.R. 353

LORD TAYLOR OF GOSFORTH, C.J. [for the Court of Appeal]: [In order to blackmail defendant, Penn lured a 15-year-old boy to his (Penn's) flat and then invited defendant over to abuse the boy sexually. Penn photographed and audiotaped defendant committing the act. At trial for indecent assault, defendant said he could not remember drinking anything before going to the bedroom, but stated that he sometimes drank coffee at Penn's flat. In addition defendant could be heard to say on the tape "I don't know why, am I falling asleep?" and "Have you put something in my coffee?"

[At trial, the judge instructed the jury it should acquit the defendant only if it found that because of the drug he did not intend to commit an indecent assault upon the boy, but so long as he did have that intent, it is irrelevant that he had been drugged, because "a drugged intent is still an intent." The jury convicted.

[Defendant's counsel argued on appeal that "an accused person may be entitled to be acquitted if there is a possibility that although his act was intentional, the intent itself arose out of circumstances for which he bears no blame." After noting that there was little authority for this proposition, the court turned to first principles:]

[T]he purpose of the criminal law is to inhibit, by proscription and by penal sanction, anti-social acts which individuals may otherwise commit. . . . Having paedophiliac inclinations and desires is not proscribed; putting them into practice is. If the sole reason why the threshold between the two has been crossed is or may have been that the inhibition which the law requires has been removed by the clandestine act of a third party, the purposes of the criminal law are not served by nevertheless holding that the person performing the act is guilty of an offence. A man is not responsible for a condition produced "by stratagem, or the fraud of another." If therefore drink or drug, surreptitiously administered, causes a person to lose his self-control and for that reason to form an intent which he would not otherwise have formed, . . . the law should exculpate him because the operative fault is not his. [I]nvoluntary intoxication negatives the mens rea. . . .

By . . . summing up as he did, the judge effectively withdrew the issue from the jury. In our judgment, that amounted to a material misdirection. . . . [Conviction set aside and appellant discharged.]

LORD MUSTILL [for the House of Lords]: . . . In ordinary circumstances the respondent's paedophiliac tendencies would have been kept under control. . . . The ingestion of the drug (whatever it was) brought about a temporary change in the mentality or personality of the respondent which lowered his ability to resist temptation so far that his desires overrode his ability to control them. Thus we are concerned here with a case of disinhibition. The drug is not alleged to have created the desire to which the respondent gave way, but rather to have enabled it to be released.

. . . The decision [below] was explicitly founded on [the] general principle . . . that if blame is absent the necessary mens rea must also be absent.

My Lords, with every respect I must suggest that no such principle exists or, until the present case, had ever in modern times been thought to exist. . . . [T]o assume that contemporary moral judgments affect the criminality of the act, as distinct from the punishment appropriate to the crime once proved, is to be misled by the expression "mens rea." [T]he epithet "rea" refers to the criminality of the act in which the mind is engaged, not to its moral character. . . . I would therefore reject . . . the respondent's argument which treats the absence of moral fault on the part of the appellant as sufficient in itself to negative the necessary mental element of the offence. . . .

To recognize a new defense of this type would be a bold step. . . . So one must turn to consider just what defence is now to be created. The judgment under appeal implies [several] characteristics.

1. The defence applies to all offences, except perhaps to absolute offences.

It therefore differs from other defences such as provocation and diminished responsibility.

2. The defence is a complete answer to a criminal charge. If not rebutted it leads to an outright acquittal, and unlike provocation and diminished responsibility leaves no room for conviction and punishment for a lesser offence. The underlying assumption must be that the defendant is entirely free from culpability. . . .

5. The defence is subjective in nature. Whereas provocation and self-defence are judged by the reactions of the reasonable person in the situation of the defendant, here the only question is whether this particular defendant's inhibitions were overcome by the effect of the drug. The more susceptible the defendant to the kind of temptation presented, the easier the defence is to establish.

[T]he defence appears to run into difficulties at every turn. . . . Before the jury could form an opinion on whether the drug might have turned the scale witnesses would have to give a picture of the defendant's personality and susceptibilities, for without it the crucial effect of the drug could not be assessed; pharmacologists would be required to describe the potentially disinhibiting effect of a range of drugs whose identity would, if the present case is anything to go by, be unknown; psychologists and psychiatrists would express opinions, not on the matters of psychopathology familiar to those working within the framework of the Mental Health Acts but on altogether more elusive concepts. No doubt as time passed those concerned could work out techniques to deal with these questions. Much more significant would be the opportunities for a spurious defence. Even in the field of road traffic the "spiked" drink as a special reason for not disqualifying from driving is a regular feature. Transferring this to the entire range of criminal offences is a disturbing prospect. The defendant would only have to assert, and support by the evidence of well-wishers, that he was not the sort of person to have done this kind of thing, and to suggest an occasion when by some means a drug might have been administered to him for the jury to be sent straight to the question of a possible disinhibition. The judge would direct the jurors that if they felt any legitimate doubt on the matter — and by its nature the defence would be one which the prosecution would often have no means to rebut — they must acquit outright, all questions of intent, mental capacity and the like being at this stage irrelevant.

My Lords, the fact that a new doctrine may require adjustment of existing principles to accommodate it, and may require those involved in criminal trials to learn new techniques, is not of course a ground for refusing to adopt it, if that is what the interests of justice require. Here, however, justice makes no such demands, for the interplay between the wrong done to the victim, the individual characteristics and frailties of the defendant, and the pharmacological effects of whatever drug may be potentially involved can be far better recognised by a tailored choice from the continuum of sentences available to the judge than by the application of a single Yea-or-Nay jury decision. [Court of Appeal reversed.]

NOTE ON INTOXICATION AS AN AFFIRMATIVE DEFENSE

American law, including the Model Penal Code, is in accord with the position announced by the House of Lords. *Involuntary* intoxication is a defense (beyond its possible evidentiary role in negating mens rea elements of the offense) only if it creates in the defendant at the time of the crime a condition (temporary or permanent) that meets the test of legal insanity, that is, a substantial incapacity either to appreciate the criminality of the actor's conduct or to conform to the law. See Model Penal Code §2.08. The Commentaries to this section state (at 363): "The actor whose personality is altered by intoxication to a lesser degree is treated like others who may have difficulty in conforming to the law and yet are held responsible for violation."

Voluntary intoxication is treated even more restrictively. Again, apart from its possible role as evidence negating a mens rea element of an offense, voluntary intoxication is a defense only when it produces a *permanent* condition sufficient to meet the test for legal insanity. As explained in State v. Booth, 169 N.W.2d 869, 873 (Iowa 1989):

> Voluntary temporary intoxication does not excuse one for the criminal consequences of his conduct. . . . A distinction is made when prolonged extensive use of alcohol damages the brain and "settled or established" insanity results therefrom. This is treated the same as insanity from any other cause. However, a temporary condition caused by voluntary intoxication . . . does not excuse one from responsibility for his conduct.

Consider these criticisms of prevailing laws:

Glanville Williams, Criminal Law: The General Part 564 (2d ed. 1961): If a man is punished for doing something when drunk that he would not have done when sober, is he not in plain truth punished for getting drunk?

Jerome Hall, General Principles of Criminal Law 556 (1960): The principle of mens rea limits penal liability to normal persons who intentionally or recklessly commit harms forbidden by penal law. But since drinking is not usually followed by intoxication, and intoxication does not usually lead to the commission of such harms, it follows that normal persons who commit harms while grossly intoxicated, should not be punished unless, at the time of sobriety and the voluntary drinking, they had such prior experience as to anticipate their intoxication and that they would become dangerous in that condition.

ROBERTS v. PEOPLE

Supreme Court of Michigan
19 Mich. 401 (1870)

CHRISTIANCY, J. The defendant was tried in the Circuit Court for the County of Calhoun, upon an information charging him with assaulting, with intent to murder, one Charles E. Greble, by shooting at him with a loaded pistol. . . .

The . . . question raised by the exceptions is whether the voluntary drunkenness of the defendant, immediately prior to and at the time of the assault, to a degree that would render him incapable of entertaining, in fact, the intent charged, would constitute a valid defense, so far as related to the intent, and leave the defendant liable only for what he actually did — the assault, without the aggravation of the intent. . . .

In determining the question whether the assault was committed with the intent charged, it was therefore material to inquire whether the defendant's mental faculties were so far overcome by the effect of intoxication, as to render him incapable of entertaining the intent. And for this purpose, it was the right and duty of the jury — as upon the question of intent of which this forms a part — to take into consideration the nature and circumstances of the assault, the actions, conduct and demeanor of the defendant, and his declaration before, at the time, and after the assault; and especially to consider the nature of the intent and what degree of mental capacity was necessary to enable him to entertain the simple intent to kill, under circumstances of this case. . . . And as a matter of law, I think the jury should have been instructed, that if his mental faculties were so far overcome by intoxication, that he was not conscious of what he was doing, or if he did know what he was doing, but did not know why he was doing it, or that his actions and the means he was using were naturally adapted or calculated to endanger life or produce death; that he had not sufficient capacity to entertain the intent, and in that event they could not infer that intent from his acts. [T]o be capable of entertaining the intent, it was not necessary that he should so far have the possession of his mental faculties as to be capable of appreciating the moral qualities of his actions, or of any intended results, as being right or wrong. He must [be] presumed to have intended the obscuration and perversion of his faculties which followed from his voluntary intoxication. He must be held to have purposely blinded his moral perceptions, and set his will free from the control of reason — to have suppressed the guards and invited the mutiny. . . . If he did entertain [the intent] in fact, though but for the intoxication he would not have done so, he is responsible for the intent as well as the acts. . . .

But the Circuit Court held, in effect, that no extent of intoxication could have the effect to disprove the intent, treating the intent as an inference of law for the Court, rather than a question of fact for the jury. In this we think there was error. . . .

PEOPLE v. HOOD

Supreme Court of California
1 Cal. 3d 444, 462 P.2d 370 (1969)

TRAYNOR, C.J. [The evidence showed that defendant, who had been drinking heavily, resisted an effort by a police officer to subdue and arrest him and in the course of the struggle seized the officer's gun and shot him in the legs. He was convicted on count 1 of assault with a deadly weapon upon a peace officer. The California Supreme Court reversed because of the failure of the trial court to instruct on the lesser-included offense of simple assault. He was also convicted on count 3 of assault with intent to murder the officer. The Supreme Court reversed this conviction because the trial court gave "hopelessly conflicting instructions on the effect of intoxication." In order to guide the trial court on retrial, the supreme court proceeded to consider the effect of intoxication on the crime of assault with a deadly weapon. The Supreme Court noted that the California courts of appeal were in conflict on whether simple assault and assault with a deadly weapon were "specific intent" or "general intent" crimes. It then continued:]

The distinction between specific and general intent crimes evolved as a judicial response to the problem of the intoxicated offender. That problem is to reconcile two competing theories of what is just in the treatment of those who commit crimes while intoxicated. On the one hand, the moral culpability of a drunken criminal is frequently less than that of a sober person effecting a like injury. On the other hand, it is commonly felt that a person who voluntarily gets drunk and while in that state commits a crime should not escape the consequences.

Before the nineteenth century, the common law refused to give any effect to the fact that an accused committed a crime while intoxicated. The judges were apparently troubled by this rigid traditional rule, however, for there were a number of attempts during the early part of the nineteenth century to arrive at a more humane, yet workable, doctrine. The theory that these judges explored was that evidence of intoxication could be considered to negate intent, whenever intent was an element of the crime charged. . . . To limit the operation of the doctrine and achieve a compromise between the conflicting feelings of sympathy and reprobation for the intoxicated offender, later courts both in England and this country drew a distinction between so-called specific intent and general intent crimes.

Specific and general intent have been notoriously difficult terms to define and apply, and a number of text writers recommended that they be abandoned altogether. Too often the characterization of a particular crime as one of specific or general intent is determined solely by the presence or absence of words describing psychological phenomena — "intent" or "malice," for example — in the statutory language defining the crime. When the definition of a crime consists of only the description of a particular act, without reference to intent to do a further act or achieve a future consequence, we ask whether the defendant intended to do the proscribed act. This intention is deemed to be a general criminal intent. When the definition refers to defendant's intent to do some further act or achieve some additional consequence, the crime is deemed to be one of specific intent. There is no real difference, however, only a linguistic one, between an intent to do an act already performed and an intent to do that same act in the future.

The language of Penal Code section 22, drafted in 1872 when "specific" and "general" intent were not yet terms of art, is somewhat broader than those terms:

> No act committed by a person while in a state of voluntary intoxication is less criminal by reason of his having been in such condition. But whenever the actual existence of any particular purpose, motive, or intent is a necessary element to constitute any particular species or degree of crime, the jury may take into consideration the fact that the accused was intoxicated at the time, in determining the purpose, motive, or intent with which he committed the act.

Even this statement of the relevant policy is no easier to apply to particular crimes. We are still confronted with the difficulty of characterizing the mental element of a given crime as a particular purpose, motive, or intent necessary to constitute the offense, or as something less than that to which evidence of intoxication is not pertinent. . . . The difficulty with applying such a test to the crime of assault or assault with a deadly weapon is that no word in the relevant code provisions unambiguously denotes a particular mental element, yet the word "attempt" in Penal Code section 240 strongly suggests goal-directed, intentional behavior.[6] This uncertainty accounts for the conflict over whether assault is a crime only of intention or also of recklessness.

We need not reconsider our position in *Carmen* [footnote 6 supra] that an assault cannot be predicated merely on reckless conduct. Even if assault requires an intent to commit a battery on the victim, it does not follow that the crime is one in which evidence of intoxication ought to be considered in determining whether the defendant had that intent. It is true that in most cases specific intent has come to mean an intention to do a future act or achieve a particular result, and that assault is appropriately characterized as a specific intent crime under this definition. An assault, however, is equally well characterized as a general intent crime under the definition of general intent as an intent merely to do a violent act. Therefore, whatever reality the distinction between specific and general intent may have in other contexts, the difference is chimerical in the case of assault with a deadly weapon or simple assault. Since the definitions of both specific intent and general intent cover the requisite intent to commit a battery, the decision whether or not to give effect to evidence of intoxication must rest on other considerations.

A compelling consideration is the effect of alcohol on human behavior. A significant effect of alcohol is to distort judgment and relax the controls on aggressive and anti-social impulses. Alcohol apparently has less effect on the ability to engage in simple goal-directed behavior, although it may impair the efficiency of that behavior. In other words, a drunk man is capable of forming an intent to do something simple, such as strike another, unless he is so drunk that he has reached the stage of unconsciousness. What he is not as capable as a sober man of doing is exercising judgment about the social consequences of his acts or controlling his impulses toward anti-social acts. He is more likely to act rashly and impulsively and to be susceptible to passion and anger. It would therefore be anomalous to allow evidence of intoxication to relieve a man of responsibility for the crimes of assault with a deadly weapon or simple assault, which are so frequently committed in just such a manner. . . .

Those crimes that have traditionally been characterized as crimes of specific intent are not affected by our holding here. The difference in mental activity between formulating an intent to commit a battery and formulating an intent to commit a battery for the purpose of raping or killing may be slight, but it is sufficient to justify drawing a line between them and considering evidence of intoxication in the one case and disregarding it in the other. Accordingly, on retrial the court should not instruct the jury to consider evidence of defendant's intoxication in determining whether he committed assault with a deadly weapon on a peace officer or any of the lesser assaults included therein. . . .

STATE v. STASIO, 78 N.J. 467, 396 A.2d 1129 (1979): [The defendant was convicted of assault with intent to rob. Conceding that this was a "specific intent" crime, the court nonetheless ruled that evidence of voluntary intoxication was

6. Penal Code, section 240 provides: "An assault is an unlawful attempt, coupled with a present ability, to commit a violent injury on the person of another."

It was the strong suggestion of intent in the ordinary usage of the word "attempt" that was at the basis of this court's remark in People v. Carmen, 36 Cal. 2d 768, 775 [228 P.2d 281], that "[o]ne could not very well 'attempt' or try to 'commit' an injury on the person of another if he had no intent to cause any injury to such other person."

inadmissible:] [D]istinguishing between specific and general intent gives rise to incongruous results by irrationally allowing intoxication to excuse some crimes but not others. In some instances if the defendant is found incapable of formulating the specific intent necessary for the crime charged, such as assault with intent to rob, he may be convicted of a lesser included general intent crime, such as assault with a deadly weapon. In other cases there may be no related general intent offense so that intoxication would lead to acquittal. Thus, a defendant acquitted for breaking and entering with intent to steal because of intoxication would not be guilty of any crime — breaking and entering being at most under certain circumstances the disorderly persons offense of trespass. . . .

The [traditional] approach may free defendants of specific intent offenses even though the harm caused may be greater than in an offense held to require only general intent. This course thus undermines the criminal law's primary function of protecting society from the results of behavior that endangers the public safety. This should be our guide rather than concern with logical consistency in terms of any single theory of culpability, particularly in view of the fact that alcohol is significantly involved in a substantial number of offenses. The demands of public safety and the harm done are identical irrespective of the offender's reduced ability to restrain himself due to his drinking. . . .

Our holding today does not mean that voluntary intoxication is always irrelevant in criminal proceedings. Evidence of intoxication may be introduced to demonstrate that premeditation and deliberation have not been proven so that a second degree murder cannot be raised to first degree murder or to show that the intoxication led to a fixed state of insanity. Intoxication may be shown to prove that a defendant never participated in a crime. Thus it might be proven that a defendant was in such a drunken stupor and unconscious state that he was not a part of a robbery. . . . His mental faculties may be so prostrated as to preclude the commission of the criminal act. Under some circumstances intoxication may be relevant to demonstrate mistake. However, in the absence of any basis for the defense, a trial court should not in its charge introduce that element. A trial court, of course, may consider intoxication as a mitigating circumstance when sentencing a defendant.

[Pashman, J., dissenting:] [T]he majority rules that a person may be convicted of the crimes of assault *with intent* to rob and breaking and entering *with intent* to steal even though he never, in fact, intended to rob anyone or steal anything. The majority arrives at this anomalous result by holding that voluntary intoxication can never constitute a defense to any crime other than first-degree murder even though, due to intoxication, the accused may not have possessed the mental state specifically required as an element of the offense. This holding . . . defies logic and sound public policy. . . .

A person who intentionally commits a bad act is more culpable than one who engages in the same conduct without any evil design. The intentional wrongdoer [also] constitutes a greater threat to societal repose. A sufficiently intoxicated defendant is thus subject to less severe sanctions not because the law "excuses" his conduct but because the circumstances surrounding his acts have been deemed by the Legislature to be less deserving of punishment. . . .

Just as the lack of premeditation, willfulness, or deliberation precludes a conviction for first-degree murder, so should the lack of intent to rob or steal be a defense to assault and battery with intent to rob, or breaking and entering with intent to steal. The principle is the same in both situations. If voluntary intoxication negates an element of the offense, the defendant has not engaged in the conduct proscribed by the criminal statute, and hence should not be subject to the sanctions imposed by that statute.

The majority . . . professes to be concerned with protecting society from drunken offenders. There are several problems with this approach. First, the majority's opinion is not even internally consistent. Although intoxication is not to be given the status of a defense, the majority states that it can be considered to "buttress the affirmative defense of reasonable mistake." It is difficult to comprehend why the public would be less endangered by persons who become intoxicated and, as a result, commit alcohol-induced "mistakes" . . . than by persons who get so intoxicated that they commit the same acts without any evil intent. . . .

The most important consideration, however, is that the standards for establishing the defense are extremely difficult to meet. Contrary to the implications contained in the majority opinion, it is not the case that every defendant who has had a few drinks may successfully urge the defense. The mere intake of even large quantities of alcohol will not suffice. Moreover, the defense cannot be established solely by showing that the defendant might not have committed the offense had he been sober. What is required is a showing of such a great prostration of the faculties that the requisite mental state was totally lacking. That is, to successfully invoke the defense, an accused must show that he was so intoxicated that he did not have the intent to commit an offense. Such a state of affairs will likely exist in very few cases. I am confident that our judges and juries will be able to distinguish such unusual instances. . . .

NOTES ON INTOXICATION AS EVIDENCE NEGATING MENS REA

The approach endorsed in *Roberts* seems straightforward and logical — evidence of intoxication is admissible whenever it is factually relevant. Yet decisions like *Hood* and *Stasio* reflect widespread resistance to this approach: In a number of jurisdictions, courts and legislatures have long specified that evidence of intoxication sometimes is inadmissible even when it is logically relevant. This Note explores the reasons for this reluctance and the doctrinal forms that it takes.

1. Background. Several of the early common law authorities (Hale, Coke, and Blackstone) seem to imply that evidence of intoxication was *never* admissible to negate mens rea, whether or not it was logically relevant to the mens rea at issue. But early in the nineteenth century, English and American courts began to soften this harsh rule; by the end of the nineteenth century most American jurisdictions followed the approach reflected in *Hood:* evidence of intoxication could be considered in determining specific intent, but not in determining a general intent. See Montana v. Egelhoff, 518 U.S. 37, 44-47 (1996) (opinion of Scalia, J.); D. McCord, The English and American History of Voluntary Intoxication to Negate Mens Rea, 11 J. Legal Hist. 372 (1990).

2. Developments after Hood *and* Stasio. In California and New Jersey, new statutes have superceded the specific tests applied in *Hood* and *Stasio.* California, at the time of *Hood,* allowed intoxication evidence to be considered in determining "purpose, motive or intent," and in 1994 the California Supreme Court ruled, applying similar language then in effect, that intoxication evidence was admissible on the question whether a defendant had formed the malice (subjective recklessness) required for second-degree murder. The legislative response was swift. As amended in 1995, Cal. Penal Code §22(b) states that "[e]vidence of voluntary intoxication is admissible solely on the issue of whether or not the defendant actually formed a required specific intent," including, in murder cases, the issues of premeditation, deliberation and express malice (i.e., intent to kill) but not the issue of implied malice (conscious recklessness).

The New Jersey legislature moved in the opposite direction. After *Stasio* held that intoxication evidence was not admissible to negate specific *or* general intent (except in cases of first-degree murder), the legislature enacted a provision specifying that intoxication evidence could be considered in determining purpose or knowledge but not in determining recklessness or negligence. N.J.S.A. §2C:2-8. As a result, the California and New Jersey approaches, though phrased in slightly different terms, now converge: Both states will consider intoxication evidence on issues of specific intent (purpose or knowledge) but not on issues of general intent (recklessness or negligence).

Looking more widely, state law is far from uniform. Roughly two-thirds of the states follow the same approach as California and New Jersey, and this is the rule in England as well (D.P.P. v. Majewski, [1976] 2 All E.R. 142). But states following this approach set a rather high threshold for admissibility of intoxication evidence, even in connection with specific intent crimes. Generally, intoxication evidence is not considered relevant unless it is of such an extremely high degree that it could produce a complete "prostration of the faculties"; intoxication short of this is deemed incapable of negating specific intent and therefore is inadmissible. See State v. Cameron, 514 A.2d 1302 (N.J. 1986); Turrentine v. State, 965 P.2d 955, 968 (Okla. Crim. App. 1998) (accused must be "so intoxicated that his mental abilities were totally overcome [making it] impossible for him to form the requisite criminal intent").[41]

Many states are even more restrictive. Several, following the *Stasio* approach, exclude logically relevant intoxication evidence even on the issue of specific intent, except in first-degree murder cases (e.g., Swisher v. Commonwealth, 506 S.E.2d 763 (Va. 1998)), and ten states bar defense use of intoxication evidence on *all* mens rea issues. Current law in the 50 states is surveyed in Mitchell Keiter, Just Say No Excuse: The Rise and Fall of the Intoxication Defense, 87 J. Crim. L. & Criminology 482, 518-520 (1997).

3. Why should intoxication be treated differently from other logically relevant evidence? Some of the reluctance to give intoxication its normal significance in rebutting evidence of mens rea is explained by the close connection between alcohol consumption and the commission of crime. In a 1997 national survey, 37 percent of state prisoners reported being under the influence of alcohol at the time of their offense, and for those convicted of violent crimes, the figure rose to 42 percent.[42]

41. California law introduces another subtle distinction. As indicated above, Cal. Penal Code §22(b) provides that evidence of voluntary intoxication is admissible to show whether a defendant "actually formed" a required specific intent. But §22(a) provides that such evidence is *not* admissible "to negate the capacity to form" such an intent. The distinction, in essence, is between "couldn't" and "didn't." Section 22(a) appears designed to preclude expert psychiatric testimony to the effect that a defendant *couldn't* form a required specific intent, while §22(b) leaves the defendant free to offer testimony that he *didn't* form a required specific intent. The concern, in part, was that the jury might feel compelled to give undue deference to the former sort of testimony but would consider itself free to evaluate the latter sort of testimony in the ordinary way.

42. U.S. Dept. of Justice, Bureau of Justice Statistics, Substance Abuse and Treatment, State and Federal Prisoners, 1997, at 3 (Jan. 1999).

In one Cincinnati study, 64 percent of arrested felons were intoxicated at the time of their arrest, and for crimes of violence the figures varied from 67 to 88 percent.[43] Numerous studies find a close association between the alcohol consumption rate and the homicide rate.[44]

4. *Identifying "general intent" crimes.* If assault were defined as an act that recklessly creates a risk of injury, all courts would classify the offense as a "general intent" crime, and it would then follow, under the common law rule set out in Note 1 supra, that intoxication evidence would not be admissible to negate the required mens rea. But because statutes in California (and many other states) define assault as a kind of attempt and require proof of an *intent* to inflict injury (not just recklessness), see People v. Carmen, cited in *Hood* at page 867 n. 6 supra, how can assault be classified as a general intent crime? Because assault, like any other attempt, requires proof of a purpose to accomplish a particular result, the offense seems to meet one of the classic definitions of a *specific intent* crime. See the Note on *"specific intent" and "general intent,"* pages 215-217, Chapter 3, page 215 supra. Did the court in *Hood* decide that assault nonetheless was *not* a specific intent crime, or did it decide that intoxication evidence should be inadmissible even though assault *is* a specific intent crime?

In People v. Rocha, 3 Cal. 3d 893, 479 P.2d 372 (1971), the California Supreme Court noted the confusion generated by *Hood* and announced that assault with a deadly weapon is a "general intent" crime as to which intoxication evidence is inadmissible. This approach preserves the traditional "general intent"-"specific intent" test for determining the admissibility of intoxication evidence, but only at the cost of confounding the traditional test for determining what is a general intent crime. In California, assault is considered a general intent crime even though recklessness is insufficient and intention to injure must be proved.

Do the concepts of general and specific intent really aid the analysis, or are they simply labels used to announce conclusions reached on other grounds? Why shouldn't a court focus directly on the question whether intoxication evidence *should* be admissible, without attempting to determine whether the crime is properly classified as one of "general intent"?

The Model Penal Code, and many of the recent court decisions, reject the controlling significance of the general intent-specific intent distinction and instead focus directly on the question of when intoxication evidence should be admissible.

MODEL PENAL CODE

Section 2.08. Intoxication

[See Appendix for text of this section.]

MODEL PENAL CODE AND COMMENTARIES, COMMENT TO §2.08 AT 357-359 (1985): Two major issues are . . . presented by the Model Code's provisions. The first, which seems more readily disposed of, is the question of whether intoxication

43. Robert A. Moore, Legal Responsibility and Chronic Alcoholism, 122 Am. J. Psychiatry, 748, 753 (1966).

44. See Robert N. Parker & Randi S. Cartmill, Alcohol and Homicide in the United States 1934-1995, 88 J. Crim. L. & Criminology 1369, 1374-1377 (1998).

ought to be accorded a significance that is entirely coextensive with its relevance to disprove purpose or knowledge when they are the requisite mental elements of a specific crime. The answer ought to be affirmative. . . . For when purpose or knowledge, as distinguished from recklessness, is made essential for conviction, the reason very surely is that in the absence of such states of mind the conduct involved does not present a comparable danger . . . or, finally, that the ends of legal policy are served by bringing to book or subjecting to graver sanctions those who consciously defy the legal norm. If the mental state that is the basis of the law's concern does not exist, the reason for its nonexistence is usually immaterial. So it is that in the case of crimes of violence against the person, purpose or knowledge rarely is required to establish liability, though their presence may have weight in aggravating the degree of the offense or in sentencing; recklessness or even negligence is ordinarily sufficient.

The second and more difficult question relates to recklessness, where awareness of the risk created by the actor's conduct ordinarily is requisite for liability under Section 2.02. The problem is whether intoxication ought to be accorded a significance coextensive with its relevance to disprove such awareness, as in the case of purpose or knowledge that has previously been discussed. . . .

Those who oppose a special rule for drunkenness in relation to awareness of the risk in recklessness draw strength . . . from the proposition that it is precisely the awareness of the risk in recklessness that is the essence of its moral culpability — a culpability dependent upon the magnitude of the specific risk knowingly created. When that risk is greater in degree than that which the actor perceives at the time of getting drunk, as is frequently the case, the result of a special rule is bound to be a liability disproportionate to culpability. Hence the solution urged is to dispense with any special rule, relying rather on the possibility of proving foresight at the time of drinking and, when this cannot be proved, upon a generalized prohibition of being drunk and dangerous, with sanctions appropriate for such behavior. This approach would also permit prosecution for negligence if negligent commission of the act in question was sufficient to establish criminal liability. With respect to negligence, the essence of the culpability is the failure to perceive a risk that the actor should have perceived. The actor's culpability in failing to perceive a risk would be judged against the standard of a man in normal possession of his faculties. Thus, the fact that the defendant was drunk will not exculpate him from a charge of negligence. . . .

The case thus made is worthy of respect, but there are strong considerations on the other side. There is first the weight of the antecedent law which here, more clearly than in England, has tended toward a special rule for drunkenness in this context. Beyond this, there is the fundamental point that awareness of the potential consequences of excessive drinking on the capacity of human beings to gauge the risks incident to their conduct is by now so dispersed in our culture that it is not unfair to postulate a general equivalence between the risks created by the conduct of the drunken actor and the risks created by his conduct in becoming drunk. Becoming so drunk as to destroy temporarily the actor's powers of perception and judgment is conduct that plainly has no affirmative social value to counterbalance the potential danger. The actor's moral culpability lies in engaging in such conduct. Added to this are the impressive difficulties posed in litigating the foresight of any particular actor at the time when he imbibes and the relative rarity of cases where intoxication really does engender unawareness as distinguished from imprudence. These considerations led to the conclusion, on balance, that the Model Code should declare that unawareness of a risk, of which the actor would have been aware had he been sober, is immaterial. Most states with revised codes have taken a similar position.

STEPHEN J. MORSE, FEAR OF DANGER, FLIGHT FROM CULPABILITY, 4 Psychol., Pub. Pol. & L. 250, 254 (1998): The [Model Penal Code] equates the culpability of becoming drunk with the conscious awareness of anything criminal that the agent might do while drunk. This "equation" permits the state to meet its burden of persuasion concerning recklessness without actually proving that the defendant was ever actually aware that getting drunk created a grave risk that [he] would then commit [a] specific harm. . . . As an empirical matter, however, this equation is often preposterous. An agent will not be consciously aware while becoming drunk that there is a substantial and unjustifiable risk that he or she will commit a particular crime when drunk, unless the person has a previous history of . . . committing this specific crime [while drunk]. If such a prior history . . . exists, then the prosecution is capable of proving and should be required to prove the existence of previous awareness. The prosecution should not be able to rely on what is, in effect, the conclusive presumption that becoming drunk demonstrates the same culpability as the actual conscious awareness of a substantial and unjustifiable risk that the defendant would commit the specific harm.

NOTES

1. *The recklessness "equation."* Suppose that Husband and Wife attend a relative's wedding. Over the course of the evening, Wife has several strong drinks, assuming that she will not have to drive home because Husband, the "designated driver," has agreed to stay sober. On their way home, Husband becomes ill and unable to drive, so Wife reluctantly takes the wheel. Because her judgment is impaired, she drives too fast and causes a fatal accident. Is Wife guilty of murder? Is it clear that her willingness to drink at the party is equivalent to a reckless mens rea — a conscious awareness of creating a substantial and unjustifiable risk of causing a fatality?

2. *Constitutional problems.* Once a state decides to require a particular mens rea (for example, knowledge or recklessness) as an element of an offense, how can the state legitimately deny a defendant the opportunity to present relevant exculpatory evidence that bears on the question whether in fact he had the required mens rea?

(a) Egelhoff. Montana v. Egelhoff, 518 U.S. 37 (1996), involved a state law defining "deliberate homicide" as a killing committed "purposely" or "knowingly." But Mont. Penal Code §45-2-203 provides that "an intoxicated condition . . . may not be taken into consideration in determining the existence of a mental state which is an element of the offense unless [the intoxication was involuntary]." Egelhoff was convicted of deliberate homicide after a trial at which the judge told the jury, in accordance with §45-2-203, that it could not consider his intoxicated condition in determining whether he had acted purposely or knowingly. The Montana Supreme Court reversed and held the statute unconstitutional.

The court said that the evidence of Egelhoff's intoxication was "clear[ly] . . . relevant to the issue of whether [he] acted knowingly and purposely," and that the rule precluding consideration of that evidence had in effect "relieved [the State] of part of its burden to prove [guilt] beyond a reasonable doubt."

Do you agree? The U.S. Supreme Court did not, but the Court produced five separate opinions and was unable to agree on a single rationale. Justice Scalia, writing for four members of the Court, emphasized that the State must still offer evidence sufficient to prove purpose or knowledge beyond a reasonable doubt. He acknowledged that "by excluding a significant line of evidence that might refute *mens rea*, the statute made it easier for the State to meet [that] requirement." "But," Justice Scalia continued, "*any* evidentiary rule can have that effect. 'Reducing' the State's burden in this manner is not unconstitutional, unless the rule of evidence itself violates a fundamental principle of fairness (which . . . this one does not)." (Id. at 55). Justice O'Connor, also writing for four members of the Court, reached the opposite conclusion. She reasoned that "to impede the defendant's ability to throw doubt on the State's case, [makes] the State's burden to prove its case . . . correspondingly easier," and that the statute therefore violated the Due Process requirement that the prosecution prove each element of an offense beyond a reasonable doubt. Id. at 61.

Justice Ginsburg, casting the deciding vote, found it unnecessary to resolve this disagreement and upheld the Montana statute on a different ground. She concluded that the Montana rule did *not* exclude evidence relevant to a required element of the offense, because §45-2-203 had in effect redefined deliberate homicide. As she interpreted Montana law, a deliberate-homicide conviction required the prosecution to prove *either* (1) that the defendant had killed purposely or knowingly, *or* (2) "that the defendant killed under circumstances that would otherwise establish knowledge or purpose 'but for' [the defendant's] voluntary intoxication." (Id. at 58). She reasoned that Montana had not excluded relevant exculpatory evidence, because the intoxication evidence was irrelevant to an accusation based on the second theory and the prosecution had proved all elements of that theory beyond a reasonable doubt.

(b) Questions. Which of the Justices presents the better interpretation of the Montana statute? In the case of an intoxicated actor, how should the jury go about determining whether his act of killing *would have been* knowing or purposeful "'but for' [his] voluntary intoxication"?

Which of the Justices offers the best way of implementing the requirement of proof beyond a reasonable doubt? Under Justice Scalia's view, is there any judicially enforceable content to the *Winship* rule (page 35 supra) that the state must prove beyond a reasonable doubt "every fact necessary to constitute the crime charged"? But conversely, is Justice O'Connor's more restrictive approach pointless, since a state can evade its limits simply by redefining the elements necessary for a deliberate-homicide conviction?

(c) Problems. Consider, for each of the scenarios below, whether a deliberate-homicide conviction would be possible in Montana under Justice Scalia's approach, under Justice Ginsburg's approach, and under basic principles of fairness and just punishment:[45]

45. The examples are drawn from Ronald J. Allen, Forward: Montana v. Egelhoff — Reflections on the Limits of Legislative Imagination and Judicial Authority, 87 J. Crim. L. & Criminology 633, 638 (1997).

(i) A drunk person driving a car blacks out and as a result runs over and kills a pedestrian.

(ii) A drunk person in a bar has a gun in his waist band. Because he is tipsy, he trips and falls. The gun goes off, killing the bartender.

(iii) A drunk person in a bar pulls out his gun and jokingly points it at the bartender. The gun goes off and the bartender is killed, but the defendant says he had no intention to shoot and no recollection of pulling the trigger.

(d) For incisive critiques of the opinions in *Egelhoff,* see Ronald J. Allen, Forward: Montana v. Egelhoff — Reflections on the Limits of Legislative Imagination and Judicial Authority, 87 J. Crim. L. & Criminology 633 (1997); Larry Alexander, The Supreme Court, Dr. Jekyll, and the Due Process of Proof, 1996 Sup. Ct. Rev. 191.

3. *A separate offense?* In his critique of the Model Penal Code's recklessness "equation" (the notion that knowingly drinking to excess is equivalent to knowingly creating a risk of a harmful result), Professor Morse argues that this notion confuses the vague and relatively minor culpability involved in choosing to get drunk with the much more serious culpability involved in the required mens rea of crimes like rape and murder. But what criminal charges would be available if the prosecution must restrict its attention to the defendant's conduct in choosing to get drunk? At present, such behavior usually is not in itself a crime. Should it be? A German statute creates a separate offense applicable to any person who commits a wrongful act after intentionally or negligently getting intoxicated. Although the act of getting drunk must be committed intentionally or negligently, no additional culpability is required with respect to the subsequent wrongful act that brings the statute into play. See George Fletcher, Rethinking Criminal Law 846-848 (1978). Is this kind of law preferable to the American approach?

A similar reform is suggested by the English Law Commission in its Consultation Paper No. 127, Intoxication and Criminal Liability (1993). Under this proposal, anyone who causes the harm proscribed by certain listed offenses while deliberately intoxicated would be guilty of "criminal intoxication." The listed offenses are those which cause substantial harm to persons, public order, or the physical safety of property. To be culpable, the defendant must have voluntarily taken a substance, knowing that the quantity he took might cause his awareness, understanding, or control to be substantially impaired. The suggested punishment for criminal intoxication is based on the underlying offense: two-thirds of the possible sentence, with a maximum of ten years' imprisonment for nonhomicide offenses. Does linking the punishment to the harm caused make sense given that defendant's culpability is based on choosing to become intoxicated? Or should there be a standard punishment for the offense, regardless of the resulting harm?

4. *Mental Disorder*

a. The Defense of Legal Insanity

INTRODUCTORY NOTE

Insanity can become an important legal issue in a variety of circumstances. A contract may be unenforceable if one of the parties was insane when the contract was made. A will may be held void if the testator was insane. In the criminal process, insanity can be relevant at several different stages. Of greatest importance to the substantive criminal law, insanity at the time of the offense is usually a defense to a criminal charge. In addition, a person who is insane may not be tried, convicted, or sentenced. Neither may such a person be executed if convicted of a capital offense. Further, under many state statutes, a person who becomes insane while in prison must be transferred to a mental hospital.

Question: Should the definition of insanity for these varied purposes be the same? Consider the following issues.

1. *Competency to stand trial.* (*a*) Model Penal Code §4.04 states the generally accepted test of insanity for purposes of determining whether an accused may be tried and sentenced: "No person who as a result of mental disease or defect lacks capacity to understand the proceedings against him or to assist in his own defense shall be tried, convicted or sentenced for the commission of an offense so long as such incapacity endures." In Dusky v. United States, 362 U.S. 402 (1960), the Court stated: "[T]he test must be whether [the defendant] has sufficient present ability to consult with his lawyer with a reasonable degree of rational understanding — and whether he has a rational as well as factual understanding of the proceedings against him."

(*b*) Some courts have permitted forcible medication of defendants in order to render them competent to stand trial. E.g., Khiem v. United States, 612 A.2d 160, 168-169 (D.C. 1992). Yet antipsychotic drugs used for this purpose often affect the defendant's demeanor at trial. Does involuntary medication under these circumstances violate a defendant's right to a fair trial? In Riggins v. Nevada, 112 S. Ct. 1810, 1814-1815 (1992), the Court declined to rule that forcible medication was impermissible per se but held that forcible medication in that case was a violation of due process, because the state had not shown that other means to render the defendant competent to stand trial were unavailable.

(*c*) If a judge finds that the defendant is suffering from total amnesia concerning the alleged crime but is otherwise in full command of her faculties, most courts hold that the defendant is competent to stand trial. See State v. Wynn, 490 A.2d 605 (Del. Super. 1985); People v. Francobandera, 33 N.Y.2d 429, 310 N.E.2d 292, 295 (1974). What is the basis for this view? Doesn't an inability to recall the events charged seriously impede a defendant's ability to mount a defense? Compare State v. McClendon, 101 Ariz. 285, 419 P.2d 69 (1966) (improper to hold trial if continuance might enable amnesiac to recover). See also the more careful inquiry required in Colorado. People v. Palmer, 9 P.3d 1156 (Colo. App. 2000).

2. *Execution.* All states bar execution of a condemned prisoner who becomes insane. But how should insanity be defined in this context?

(*a*) The 1951 Pennsylvania Mental Health Act provided for the transfer to a mental hospital of any person detained in a penal institution who is mentally ill, and defined mental illness as "an illness which so lessens the capacity of a person to use his customary self-control, judgment and discretion in the conduct of his affairs and social relations as to make it necessary or advisable for him to be under care." In Commonwealth v. Moon, 383 Pa. 18, 117 A.2d 96 (1955), the court held this test applicable to determine whether to stay execution of a convicted murderer, because such a person is "detained" in a penal institution (pending execution) within the meaning of the act. Is the result sound? Why should execution of a person be stayed until the person is able to take proper care of himself while alive?

(*b*) In Ford v. Wainwright, 477 U.S. 399 (1986), the Supreme Court held that the Eighth Amendment's proscription of "cruel and unusual punishment" bars execution of the insane, but the Court offered no definition of what constitutes insanity for purposes of the Eighth Amendment requirement. Nor did the Court pinpoint the specific reasons *why* execution of the "insane" would be cruel and unusual. Justice Marshall, speaking for five members of the Court, concluded:

> Unanimity of rationale . . . we do not find. "But whatever the reason of the law is, it is plain the law is so." Hawles, [Remarks on the Trial of Mr. Charles Bateman, [1685] 11 HOW. St. Tr. *477 (1816)]. We know of virtually no authority condoning the execution of the insane at English common law. . . . And the intuition that such an execution simply offends humanity is evidently shared across this Nation. Faced with such widespread evidence of a restriction upon sovereign power, this Court is compelled to conclude that the Eighth Amendment prohibits a State from carrying out a sentence of death upon a prisoner who is insane. Whether its aim be to protect the condemned from fear and pain without comfort of understanding, or to protect the dignity of society itself from the barbarity of exacting mindless vengeance, the restriction finds enforcement in the Eighth Amendment.

Justice Powell, in a concurring opinion, commented as follows:

> [S]ome authorities contended that the prohibition against executing the insane was justified as a way of preserving the defendant's ability to make arguments on his own behalf. Other authorities suggest, however, that the prohibition derives from more straightforward humanitarian concerns. . . .
>
> The first of these justifications has slight merit today. Modern practice provides far more extensive review of convictions and sentences than did the common law, including not only direct appeal but ordinarily both state and federal collateral review. . . . It is thus unlikely indeed that a defendant today could go to his death with knowledge of undiscovered trial error that might set him free. . . .
>
> The more general concern of the common law — that executions of the insane are simply cruel — retains its vitality. It is as true today as when Coke lived that most men and women value the opportunity to prepare, mentally and spiritually, for their death. Moreover, today as at common law, one of the death penalty's critical justifications, its retributive force, depends on the defendant's awareness of the penalty's existence and purpose. . . .[a] For precisely these reasons, Florida requires the Governor to stay executions of those who "d[o] not have the mental capacity to understand the nature of the death penalty and why it was imposed" on them. Fla. Stat. §922.07 (1985). A number of States have more rigorous standards, but none disputes the need to require that those who are executed know the fact of their impending execution and the reason for it.
>
> Such a standard appropriately defines the kind of mental deficiency that should trigger the Eighth Amendment prohibition.

(*c*) Most jurisdictions now define insanity for purposes of execution along the lines endorsed by Justice Powell in *Ford.* See, e.g., Ill. Stat. ch. 730, §5/5-2-3 (1993). In Penry v. Lynaugh, 492 U.S. 302, 333 (1989), a majority of the Su-

a. For a detailed development of this theme, see R. A. Duff, Trials and Punishments 16-35 (1986). — Eds.

preme Court assumed that the Powell test stated the correct standard under the Eighth Amendment but held that the test was met in the case of a mentally retarded prisoner described as having a mental age of seven. A few states have adopted stricter tests. The Washington and South Carolina Supreme Courts have declared that sanity for purposes of execution requires that the prisoner not only understand the nature of the death penalty and why it is being imposed, but also have the ability to communicate rationally with defense counsel. See Singleton v. State, 437 S.E.2d 53 (S.C. 1993); State v. Harris, 789 P.2d 60, 64-65 (Wash. 1990). And subsequent to *Penry,* seven states enacted legislation barring execution of offenders who are "seriously mentally retarded." See Vincent J. Aprile, Criminal Justice Matters: Executing the Mentally Retarded, 9 Crim. J. 38, 38-39 (Spring 1994).

(*d*) At least one court has held that the state may not subject an insane death-row prisoner to antipsychotic medication, against his will, in order to restore his sanity so that he may be executed. See State v. Perry, 610 So. 2d 746 (La. 1992). The problem is a recurrent one, because antipsychotic drugs are an increasingly popular means of treating mental disorder, and up to 70 percent of death-row inmates are estimated to suffer some form of mental illness. See Robert Johnson, Death Work 50 (1990). Does the *Perry* approach mean that the incompetent prisoner (or someone acting on his behalf) must choose between continued insanity and death by execution? Is there any way to escape this dilemma? For a useful discussion of the problem, see Kristen Wenstrup Crosby, Comment, *State v. Perry,* 77 Minn. L. Rev. 1193 (1993).

(*e*) What *procedures* should be used to determine whether a condemned prisoner has become insane? Under the California Penal Code, a sentenced prisoner may not be executed if a specially impanelled jury of 12 persons finds that he is presently insane. Under the same code, a woman may not be executed while pregnant, but the determination of her pregnancy is to be made by three physicians. §§3705, 3706.

Questions: How can one account for the difference in procedure? Would it make sense to do the reverse — that is, to have 12 jurors determine whether a woman is pregnant and 3 physicians determine whether a person is too insane to be executed? Why not?

Fla. Stat. §922.07 (1985) provides that when the governor is informed that a condemned inmate may be insane, he must appoint a commission of three psychiatrists who shall examine the prisoner "with all three psychiatrists present at the same time." Each psychiatrist prepares a report for the governor, who then determines whether the convicted person is insane. In Ford v. Wainwright, Note 2(b) supra, the statutory procedure was initiated after Ford exhibited acute symptoms of mental disorder, including extreme delusions and virtually total incoherence of thought and speech. The three psychiatrists concluded that Ford, though severely disturbed, knew he faced the death penalty and understood its implications. The governor considered the three reports, refused to accept oral or written argument or to consider psychiatric evidence proffered by the defense, and found Ford to be sane.

The Supreme Court held this procedure constitutionally inadequate. A majority of the Court concluded that full-scale adversary procedures were not required but that the prisoner must be afforded an opportunity to present evidence and argument before an impartial officer or board independent of the executive branch. Florida subsequently revised its procedures to permit de novo judicial review of the sanity question, with consideration of experts' reports and any other written or oral submissions from the parties, whenever the Governor determines the prisoner to be sane.[46]

(i) *Competing Formulations*

M'NAGHTEN'S CASE

House of Lords
10 Cl. & F. 200, 8 Eng. Rep. 718 (1843)

[Defendant was indicted for the murder of Edward Drummond, secretary to the prime minister, Sir Robert Peel. Apparently M'Naghten had mistaken Drummond for Peel and had shot Drummond by mistake. Upon his arrest he told police that he had come to London to murder the Prime Minister because "[t]he tories in my city follow and persecute me wherever I go, and have entirely destroyed my peace of mind. [T]hey do everything in their power to harass and persecute me; in fact they wish to murder me." The defense introduced extensive expert and lay testimony indicating that M'Naghten was obsessed with delusions and suffered from acute insanity.[a] The presiding judge, Lord Chief Justice Tindal, in his charge to the jury stated:

> The question to be determined is whether at the time the act in question was committed, the prisoner had or had not the use of his understanding, so as to know that he was doing a wrong or wicked act. If the jurors should be of opinion that the prisoner was not sensible, at the time he committed it, that he was violating the laws both of God and man, then he would be entitled to a verdict in his favour: but if, on the contrary, they were of opinion that when he committed the act he was in a sound state of mind, then their verdict must be against him.

JI

[The jury returned a verdict of "not guilty, on the ground of insanity." The verdict attracted great public attention and aroused considerable alarm. The press suggested that the insanity defense left madmen free to kill with impunity. Queen Victoria was particularly concerned: she herself had been the object of three recent assassination attempts, and one of her attackers had also benefited from an insanity acquittal. Both the *M'Naghten* verdict and the general problem of the insanity defense were debated in the House of Lords. As a result, the English judiciary (there were some 15 judges at the time) were invited to attend the House of Lords for the purpose of delivering answers to certain questions propounded to them. The famous *M'Naghten* Rule is found in the answer to the second and third questions delivered by Lord Chief Justice Tindal.]

46. Fla. R. Crim. P. 3.811, 3.812 (1987). See Joy B. Shearer, Insanity of the Condemned: Florida's Response to *Ford,* Fla. Bar. J., Mar. 1988, at 39-41.

a. At the time of his arrest, M'Naghten was found in possession of £750, and as a result he "probably had the best-financed defense in the history of the Old Bailey." He had the assistance of "four of the most able barristers in Britain [and] nine prominent medical experts." No expert witnesses appeared for the prosecution. See Richard Moran, Knowing Right from Wrong 90 (1981), which provides a fascinating, detailed account of M'Naghten's Case. — EDS.

Your Lordships are pleased to inquire of us, secondly, "What are the proper questions to be submitted to the jury, where a person alleged to be afflicted with insane delusion respecting one or more particular subjects or persons, is charged with the commission of a crime (murder, for example), and insanity is set up as a defence?" And, thirdly, "In what terms ought the question to be left to the jury as to the prisoner's state of mind at the time when the act was committed?" And as these two questions appear to us to be more conveniently answered together, we have to submit our opinion to be, that the jurors ought to be told in all cases that every man is to be presumed to be sane, and to possess a sufficient degree of reason to be responsible for his crimes, until the contrary be proved to their satisfaction; and that to establish a defence on the ground of insanity, it must be clearly proved that, at the time of the committing of the act, the party accused was labouring under such a defect of reason, from disease of the mind, as not to know the nature and quality of the act he was doing; or, if he did know it, that he did not know he was doing what was wrong. The mode of putting the latter part of the question to the jury on these occasions has generally been, whether the accused at the time of doing the act knew the difference between right and wrong: which mode, though rarely, if ever, leading to any mistake with the jury, is not, as we conceive, so accurate when put generally and in the abstract, as when put with reference to the party's knowledge of right and wrong in respect to the very act with which he is charged. If the question were to be put as to the knowledge of the accused solely and exclusively with reference to the law of the land, it might tend to confound the jury, by inducing them to believe that an actual knowledge of the law of the land was essential in order to lead to a conviction; whereas the law is administered upon the principle that every one must be taken conclusively to know it, without proof that he does know it. If the accused was conscious that the act was one which he ought not to do, and if the act was at the same time contrary to the law of the land, he is punishable; and the usual course therefore has been to leave the question to the jury, whether the party accused had a sufficient degree of reason to know that he was doing an act that was wrong: and this course we think is correct, accompanied with such observations and explanations as the circumstances of each particular case may require.

THE KING v. PORTER 55 Commw. L.R. 182, 186-188 (1933): [Presiding at the trial, Justice Dixon explained the *M'Naghten* Rule in his charge to the jury:] There is a legal standard of disorder of mind which is sufficient to afford a ground of irresponsibility for crime, and a ground for your finding such a verdict as I have indicated [that is, not guilty on the ground of insanity].

Before explaining what that standard actually is, I wish to draw your attention to some general considerations affecting the question of insanity in the criminal law in the hope that by so doing you may be helped to grasp what the law prescribes. The purpose of the law in punishing people is to prevent others from committing a like crime or crimes. Its prime purpose is to deter people from committing offences. It may be that there is an element of retribution in the criminal law, so that when people have committed offences the law considers that they merit punishment, but its prime purpose is to preserve society from the depredations of dangerous and vicious people. Now, it is perfectly useless for the law to attempt, by threatening punishment, to deter people from committing crimes if their mental condition is such that they cannot be in the least influenced by the possibility or probability of subsequent punishment; if they cannot understand what they are doing or cannot understand the ground upon which the law proceeds. The law is not directed, as medical science is, to curing mental infirmities. The criminal law is not directed, as the civil law of lunacy is, to the care and custody of people of weak mind whose personal property may be in jeopardy through someone else taking a hand in the conduct of their affairs and their lives. This is quite a different thing from the question, what utility there is in the punishment of people who, at a moment, would commit acts which, if done when they were in sane minds, would be crimes. What is the utility of punishing people if they be beyond the control of the law for reasons of mental health? In considering that, it will not perhaps, if you have ever reflected upon the matter, have escaped your attention that a great number of people who come into a Criminal Court are abnormal. They would not be there if they were the normal type of average everyday people. Many of them are very peculiar in their dispositions and peculiarly tempered. That is markedly the case in sexual offences. Nevertheless, they are mentally quite able to appreciate what they are doing and quite able to appreciate the threatened punishment of the law and the wrongness of their acts, and they are held in check by the prospect of punishment. It would be very absurd if the law were to withdraw that check on the ground that they were somewhat different from their fellow creatures in mental make-up or texture at the very moment when the check is most needed. You will therefore see that the law, in laying down a standard of mental disorder sufficient to justify a jury in finding a prisoner not guilty on the ground of insanity at the moment of offence, is addressing itself to a somewhat difficult task. It is attempting to define what are the classes of people who should not be punished although they have done actual things which in others would amount to crime. . . . With that explanation I shall tell you what that standard is.

The first thing which I want you to notice is that you are only concerned with the condition of the mind at the time the act complained of was done. . . .

The next thing which I wish to emphasize is that his state of mind must have been one of disease, disorder or disturbance. Mere excitability of a normal man, passion, even stupidity, obtuseness, lack of self-control, and impulsiveness, are quite different things from what I have attempted to describe as a state of disease or disorder or mental disturbance arising from some infirmity, temporary or of long standing. If that existed it must then have been of such a character as to prevent him from knowing the physical nature of the act he was doing or of knowing that what he was doing was wrong. . . .

NOTES ON ADMINISTERING THE INSANITY DEFENSE

1. Who may raise the defense? In most jurisdictions the decision to raise the insanity issue must be left entirely within the defendant's control. Courts have stressed that a properly counseled defendant may prefer to be found guilty rather than not guilty by reason of insanity, because the latter verdict can lead to longer confinement, more intrusive treatment, or greater stigma. See, e.g., Frendak v. United States, 408 A.2d 364 (D.C. App. 1979) And a competent defendant may decline to plead insanity even against the advice of his attorney. So in Commonwealth v. Federici, 427 Mass. 740, 696 N.E.2d 111 (1998), the court upheld a trial judge's decision to withhold the insanity issue from the jury where the defendant, against the advice of his attorney, so requested. Compare Lord Denning in Bratty v. Attorney-General, [1963] A. C. 386, 411, speaking of the English practice: "The old notion that only the defence can raise a defence of insanity is now gone. The prosecution are entitled to raise it and it is their duty to do so rather than allow a dangerous person to be at large."

2. *Disposition after acquittal.* How should the law deal with defendants who have been acquitted on grounds of legal insanity? As they have been found not guilty, they cannot be blamed for their actions. On the other hand, those actions have done harm and the public demands protection against any repetition. Consider the following:

(*a*) One approach to protecting the public while also respecting the person's innocence is to rely on the processes for civil commitment. In these processes, a judge, after a hearing, decides whether to commit a person indefinitely to a mental institution because he is suffering from a mental disability that makes him a danger to himself or others. In states that adopt this approach, insanity acquittees may be committed only in compliance with the procedural and substantive standards for any mentally disturbed person in the community. But there are constitutional restrictions on civil commitment. For example, the standard of proof is high — both mental illness and dangerousness must be proven by clear and convincing evidence. Addington v. Texas, 441 U.S. 418 (1979). That high threshold in civil commitment serves to reduce the risk of confining members of the public who are simply idiosyncratic. But is that concern equally applicable to those who have been shown to be irresponsible authors of criminal acts? Many states have thought not and have enacted special commitment procedures for insanity acquittees in which the crucial factual findings, mental illness, and dangerousness, can be made by a preponderance of the evidence. See Jan Brakel, After the Verdict: Dispositional Decisions Regarding Criminal Defendants Acquitted by Reason of Insanity, 37 DePaul L. Rev. 181 (1988).

Other jurisdictions follow a different approach: Commitment is automatic and mandatory for all insanity acquittees. In defense of this approach it has been observed that it "not only provides the public with the maximum immediate protection, but may also work to the advantage of mentally diseased or defective defendants by making the defense of irresponsibility more acceptable to the public and to the jury." Model Penal Code and Commentaries, Comment to §4.08 at 256 (1985). But is the finding of insanity at the criminal trial sufficiently probative of present mental illness and dangerousness to justify confinement?

In Jones v. United States, 463 U.S. 354 (1983), the Supreme Court upheld the constitutionality of mandatory commitment. The court asserted as a matter of common sense, that the mental disorder and dangerousness of an insanity acquittee are likely to continue through to the time of trial and thereafter. Do you agree? Even if a presumption of continuing insanity is plausible, what is the justification for making that presumption in effect irrebuttable, by requiring automatic commitment without any hearing on the present mental disorder and dangerousness of the defendant?

The Court in *Jones* also noted that the committed person was given an opportunity to demonstrate his recovery at a hearing within 50 days of commitment. Does this allay the reservations about the justification for the initial commitment? One court noted "the practical difficulties of requiring a mental patient to overcome the effects of his confinement, his closed environment, his possible incompetence and the debilitating effects of drugs or other treatment. . . ." Fasulo v. Arafeh, 173 Conn. 473, 378 A.2d 553, 557 (1997). These practical difficulties often mean that the initial commitment becomes an indefinite one.

(b) Regardless of the procedure used to support an initial commitment, how long may the person committed be held? Under regular civil commitment statutes, the medical facility may release the patient when satisfied he has recovered and is no longer dangerous to himself or others. Provisions for commitment of insanity acquittees, however, require that the appropriate finding be made by a judge, usually with the burden on the inmate to prove that he meets the conditions for release. As a result, the person committed after winning acquittal may in practice be held indefinitely, sometimes for his entire life. Should extended commitment of this sort be permissible even when the crime charged was a minor property offense punishable by no more than a short prison term? In *Jones,* supra, the Supreme Court held that an insanity acquittee subjected to automatic commitment could be held indefinitely, even when the period he had spent in confinement exceeded the maximum sentence authorized for the underlying offense. The Court reasoned that dangerousness warranting indefinite commitment may be established by proof of a nonviolent act against property, in that case, shoplifting. Do you agree? Is there a case for requiring release at the maximum term for the offense of which the person was acquitted, unless the state can then meet the ordinary criteria for civil commitment by establishing by clear and convincing evidence that the inmate continues to be mentally ill and a danger to himself or others? This is the law in some dozen states. See Brakel, supra at 196. In New Jersey, for example, the maximum period of confinement is the maximum sentence that the committed person would have received under customary sentencing principles if he had been convicted. In re Commitment of W.K., 731 A.2d 482 (1999).

(c) One major concern, especially in states using only the limited social protection option of standard civil commitment, is that a committed insanity acquittee may be released too soon. In Michigan, an acquittee committed under the ordinary civil commitment laws was released, as the law required, upon a medical determination that he was no longer mentally ill and dangerous. His recovery, however, was dependent upon his continuing to take his prescribed medicine, which he failed to do, resulting in a crime spree that shocked the community. This led to the enactment in Michigan of the first of the "guilty but mentally ill" statutes, which by now are to be found in some dozen states. See Sharon M. Brown & Nicholas J. Wittner, Criminal Law (1978 Annual Survey of Michigan Law), 25 Wayne L. Rev. 335 (1978); Christopher Slobogin, The Guilty But Mentally Ill Verdict: An Idea Whose Time Should Not Have Come, 53 G.W. L. Rev. 494 (1985). This statute allowed the jury a third option — it could find the defendant guilty, not guilty by reason of insanity, or guilty but mentally ill at the time of the offense. If the jury returns the last mentioned verdict, the court retains the same sentencing authority it has in cases of guilty verdicts, but if the court sentences the defendant to prison he is to be given treatment "as is psychiatrically indicated for his mental illness." What is the practical effect of such laws? They do establish a cap on how long the defendant can be held without a

fresh judicial determination of dangerousness and mental disorder. But in practice are they likely to make an insanity acquittal less likely and thereby make conviction of morally innocent persons more likely?

The experiment with "guilty but medically ill" statutes also suggests a broader problem — the pervasive perception that public safety considerations make some dilution of the insanity defense a practical necessity. Of course, many would dispute this view. But if public opinion in effect insists on some such dilution, what is the best way to achieve it? Is it preferable to dilute the insanity defense in the way that the "guilty but mentally ill" laws do (by encouraging juries not to vote an insanity acquittal) or in the way that *Jones,* supra, does (by depriving insanity acquittees of the full benefits of an ordinary acquittal)? See Stephen J. Schulhofer, Two Systems of Social Protection, 7 J. Contemp. Leg. Issues 69 (1996); Paul H. Robinson, Forward: The Criminal-Civil Distinction and Dangerous Blameless Offenders, 83 J. Crim. L. & Cr. 693 (1993).

3. Instructing the jury on the consequences of an insanity acquittal. In jurisdictions that provide for mandatory commitment following an insanity acquittal, defendants have pressed to have the jury informed of that fact because the jury may otherwise assume that an insanity acquittal will lead to the release of a dangerous, mentally unstable individual. Yet most courts have held that the jury should not be instructed on the procedures that follow an insanity verdict, on the ground that what will happen to the defendant is not relevant to whether the defendant met the test of legal insanity. See, e.g., People v. Goad, 421 Mich. 20, 364 N.W.2d 584 (1984). For federal prosecutions, the Supreme Court has held that juries should not be informed of the mandatory commitment provisions applicable under federal law. Shannon v. United States, 512 U.S. 573 (1994). The Court said that "the principle that juries are not to consider the consequences of their verdicts is a reflection of the basic division of labor in our legal system between judge [as sentencer] and jury [as fact-finder]"; the Court also noted that "[even if] some jurors will harbor the mistaken belief that defendants found [not guilty by reason of insanity] will be released into society immediately . . . [there is] no reason to depart from 'the almost invariable assumption of the law that jurors follow their instructions." However, a number of courts have taken a less formalistic view. For example, in Commonwealth v. Mutina, 366 Mass. 810, 323 N.E.2d 294 (1975), the court stated (323 N.E.2d at 301-302):

> If jurors can be entrusted with responsibility for a defendant's life and liberty in such cases as this, they are entitled to know what protection they and their fellow citizens will have if they conscientiously apply the law to the evidence and arrive at a verdict of not guilty by reason of insanity. . . .
>
> The instant case represents a classic example of the injustice which may occur when such information is withheld from the jury. The jury could have had no doubt that the defendant killed Miss Achorn. The jury also heard overwhelmingly persuasive evidence that the defendant was insane at the time of the killing and that, for a long time into the future, he will remain a menace to himself and to society. . . .
>
> Implicit in the jury's guilty verdict was a determination that the Commonwealth had proven the defendant's sanity beyond a reasonable doubt. On the record before us, we have found no rational justification or basis for such a finding, except the jury's understandable concern for the need to confine an insane and still dangerous killer for the protection of society. The jury, lacking knowledge of the commitment necessarily flowing from a verdict of not guilty by reason of insanity, ap-

plied their own standards of justice in arriving at a verdict designed to ensure the confinement of the defendant for his own safety and that of the community.

Many state courts now hold, in accord with *Mutina,* that where commitment is mandatory, the jury should be informed that a defendant found not guilty by reason of insanity must be detained until it is determined that she is no longer mentally ill and dangerous. See Note (R.L. Sorensen), *Shannon v. United States:* Supreme Court Determines Whether Federal Courts Should Instruct on the Consequences of a Not Guilty By Reason of Insanity Verdict, 21 J. Contemp. Law. 365 (1995).

Question: If commitment is *not* mandatory, should the jury be informed of that fact?

4. *Burden of proof.* All jurisdictions create a presumption of legal sanity at the trial. The effect of this presumption is that, in the absence of evidence on the issue, the sanity of the accused is presumed for all legal purposes. American jurisdictions, however, differ on two issues: (1) How much evidence need be presented before the effect of the presumption disappears and the question of the defendant's insanity becomes an issue that must be established by the evidence? (2) Where the issue must be established by the evidence, who bears the burden of persuasion, and how is that burden defined?

As to the first question, some states require only "some evidence" of legal insanity in order to eliminate the presumption of sanity, e.g., People v. Hill, 934 P.2d 821 (Colo., 1997). Others require more, usually that the evidence raise a reasonable doubt about the sanity of the accused, e.g., Jamezic v. State, 723 So. 2d 355 (Ala. 1996). For discussion of this issue, see Abraham S. Goldstein, The Insanity Defense ch. 8 (1967); Julian Eule, The Presumption of Sanity: Bursting the Bubble, 25 U. C. L.A. L. Rev. 637 (1978).

As to the second question, once insanity becomes an issue, about a dozen states continue to adhere to what once was the majority rule requiring the prosecution to prove the sanity of the defendant beyond a reasonable doubt. See Commonwealth v. Keita, 429 Mass. 843, 853, 712 N.E.2d 65, 73 (1999), where the court supported this rule on the ground that, "There is no theoretical justification for maintaining a lower standard for the proof of sanity than for the proof of guilt." All this has changed in the aftermath of the *Hinckley* verdict, see page 894 infra. As the court in the *Keita* case observed, "Now, thirty-eight jurisdictions, including the federal court system, place the burden of proof of insanity on the defense." Id. At 712 N.E.2d at 71. For the federal courts, the question is governed by 18 U.S.C. §17(b): "The defendant has the burden of proving the defense of insanity by clear and convincing evidence."

BLAKE v. UNITED STATES

United States Court of Appeals Fifth Circuit
407 F.2d 908 (1969)

BELL, Circuit Judge: . . . Blake was charged with bank robbery, 18 U.S.C.A. §2113. He was arrested on the day following the robbery and his trial began some six months later. The evidence that he committed the robbery was overwhelming; his principal defense was insanity at the time of the commission of the offense. He was convicted and his motion for new trial denied. He was thereafter sentenced and this appeal followed. . . . Appellant urges that the definition of insanity given the jury in charge for determining the issue of not guilty by reason of insanity was outmoded and prejudicial. . . .

[T]he evidence respecting Blake's mental condition disclosed a well-to-do background, two years of college, and active duty with the Navy. In 1944, at the age of 21, and while in the Navy, he suffered an epileptic seizure and was thereafter given a medical discharge. . . . He received electro-shock treatment in 1945, and following further mental difficulties in 1945 and 1946, entered a Veterans Administration hospital for a stay of two to three months in 1946. He taught school and coached for a time in 1946. He married in 1947 and three children were born in the ensuing years of that marriage. He was employed by his father in the construction business. Meanwhile, he became a heavy drinker.

In 1948 he was admitted to a private psychiatric institution in Connecticut where he remained for some two months. . . . He thereafter received private outpatient care from psychiatrists, and between 1948 and 1954 spent time in at least three private psychiatric institutions and received further electro-shock treatment.

By 1954 he had left his father's business. From 1955 to 1960, his behavior was characterized by heavy drinking and irrational acts. He began the use of stimulants and drugs. In 1955 he received eight electro-shock treatments. He was adjudged incompetent in 1956 and placed under his father's guardianship to be placed in a private institution in lieu of commitment. He was discharged from the private institution some six months later. He followed his psychiatrist to Indiana and was treated on an outpatient basis for about a year.

He was divorced from his first wife in 1958 and married again shortly afterwards. He was arrested in December 1959 for shooting his second wife. After spending a few days in jail, he was placed in a state mental hospital for several months and was finally placed on probation for the shooting offense. He continued to receive private psychiatric treatment, in and out of hospitals while on probation up to the spring of 1963. In fact, he spent six months in 1962 in a Florida state mental hospital after being declared incompetent and certified for treatment.

Having received a probated sentence in the shooting incident, and still being on probation, Blake in 1963 was sentenced to the Florida state penitentiary after being called up for violation of probation on a charge of aggravated assault. He was released from prison on September 14, 1965. While in prison he was hospitalized three or four times, saw the prison psychiatrist, and complained of blackouts. During this period of confinement he was divorced by his third wife. He married his fourth wife on December 2, 1965. The robbery in question occurred on December 6, 1965. To this point Blake's adult life had been one long round of confinement for mental problems and drinking when not confined.

The facts of the robbery are rather bizarre. Blake committed the robbery within a matter of two or three hours after making an attempt to obtain a legal hearing before the United States District Court for the Middle District of Florida in Jacksonville. Although not clear in the record, he was apparently seeking a writ of habeas corpus to relieve him of certain state prison release restrictions which kept him from going to the Miami area. He was registered at a Jacksonville hotel. He obtained a hotel employee as a chauffeur for the purpose of driving him about town. He stopped by a bar en route to the robbery, had several drinks and told a waitress that he would be back later with a large sum of money. The waitress jokingly asked him if he planned to rob a bank. He said, "That's possible."

The bank which was robbed was one of two under consideration. Each was a member of the bank group which he claimed had mishandled a trust which was established either by or for him several years earlier. His quarrel with the bank over the trust had gone on for some years and was bitter. He did not case the bank. He selected the bank, ordered his driver to take him to the bank and wait, walked in during rush hour, demanded the money, obtained it, and walked out. He had no trouble getting away immediately to Tampa in the same car and with the same driver. He returned from Tampa to Jacksonville the very next day with an attorney to press his petition for the writ in the district court and was arrested for the robbery.

There was psychiatric testimony that Blake was suffering from the mental disease of schizophrenia, marked with psychotic episodes, and that his behavior on the occasion of the robbery indicated that appellant was in a psychotic episode. This was described as a form of severe mental illness. There was testimony that in such a period his actions would not be subject to his will. On the other hand, there was psychiatric testimony that he had a sociopathic personality and was not suffering from a mental disease. [T]he burden was on the prosecution, once the hypothesis of insanity was established, to prove beyond a reasonable doubt that Blake was sane at the time of the commission of the crime. . . .

We come then to the definition of insanity given in charge. The district court charge was based on the dictum in Davis v. United States, 165 U.S. 373, 378 (1897). . . . The real issue is the government's opposition to the substitution of a standard or measure of substantiality for the complete lack of mental capacity measure of *Davis.* It urges that "substantial" is an imprecise and phantom-like term. The other side of the coin is that rarely if ever is one completely lacking in mental capacity. The government insists on the absolutes of *Davis.* . . .

These positions point up the difference between the *Davis* standard and that of the Model Penal Code as adopted by the American Law Institute. The *Davis* standard is as follows:

> The term "insanity" as used in this defense means such a perverted and deranged condition of the mental and moral faculties as to render a person incapable of distinguishing between right and wrong, or unconscious at the time of the nature of the act he is committing, or where, though conscious of it and able to distinguish between right and wrong and know that the act is wrong, yet his will, by which I mean the governing power of his mind, has been otherwise than voluntarily so completely destroyed that his actions are not subject to it, but are beyond his control.

Section 4.01 of the ALI Model Penal Code is as follows:

> (1) A person is not responsible for criminal conduct if at the time of such conduct as a result of mental disease or defect he lacks substantial capacity either to appreciate the criminality (wrongfulness) of his conduct or to conform his conduct to the requirements of law.
>
> (2) As used in this Article, the terms "mental disease or defect" do not include an abnormality manifested only by repeated criminal or otherwise antisocial conduct. . . .

The facts of this case point up the difference in the standards. Here the facts are such, read favorably to the government as they must be, as not to show complete mental disorientation under the absolutes of *Davis*. The record does show evidence which, if believed, would indicate that Blake suffered from a severe mental disease which the jury might have found impaired his control over the conduct in question. He could not prevail under a *Davis* charge. He might have prevailed under a substantial lack of capacity type charge.

We think that a substantiality type standard is called for in light of current knowledge regarding mental illness. A person, as Blake here, may be a schizophrenic or may merely have a sociopathic personality. The evidence could go either way. He may or may not have been in a psychotic episode at the time of the robbery. But, he was not unconscious, incapable of distinguishing right and wrong nor was his will completely destroyed in terms of the *Davis* definition. Modifying the lack of mental capacity by the adjective "substantial," still leaves the matter for the jury under the evidence, lay and expert, to determine mental defect vel non and its relationship to the conduct in question. . . .

The question remains as to the specifics of the standard. . . . We have concluded to adopt the Model Penal Code standard. . . . At the same time, we must notice that the circuits adopting the Model Penal Code standard have varied it in some degree. . . . We follow the Second and Seventh Circuits . . . in substituting the alternative term "wrongfulness" as used in the first paragraph of the Model Penal Code for "criminality." The Second Circuit concluded that it was a broader term in that it would include the case where the perpetrator appreciated that his conduct was criminal but, because of a delusion, believed it to be morally justified.

MODEL PENAL CODE AND COMMENTARIES (1985)

Section 4.01, pp. 164-172

No problem in the drafting of a penal code presents greater intrinsic difficulty than that of determining when individuals whose conduct would otherwise be criminal ought to be exculpated on the ground that they were suffering from mental disease or defect when they acted as they did. The problem is the drawing of a line between the use of public agencies and force (1) to condemn the offender by conviction, with resulting sanctions in which the ingredient of reprobation is present no matter how constructive one may seek to make the sentence and the process of correction, and (2) modes of disposition in which the condemnatory element is absent, even though restraint may be involved. When the sentence may be capital there is, of course, a starker contrast between the punitive reaction and a reaction of the second kind. Stating the matter differently, the problem is to etch a decent working line between the areas assigned to the authorities responsible for public health and those responsible for the correction of offenders. It is important to maintain this separation, not least in order to control the stigma involved in a hospital commitment. . . .

As far as its principle extends, the M'Naghten rule is right. Those who are irresponsible under the test are plainly beyond the reach of the restraining influence of the law, and their condemnation would be both futile and unjust. A deranged person who believes he is squeezing lemons when he chokes his wife, or who kills in supposed self-defense on the basis of a delusion that another is attempting to kill him, is plainly beyond the deterrent influence of the law; he needs restraint but condemnation is meaningless and ineffective. Moreover, the category defined by the rule is so extreme that to the ordinary person the exculpation of those it encompasses bespeaks no weakness in the law. He does not identify such persons with himself; they are a world apart.

The question remains, however, whether the M'Naghten rule goes far enough to draw a fair and workable distinction. In two respects, this question must be answered in the negative. The M'Naghten test addresses itself to the actor's "knowledge," which can naturally be understood as referring to a simple awareness by the actor of his wrongdoing such as would be manifested by a verbal acknowledgment on his part of the forbidden nature of his conduct. One shortcoming of this criterion is that it authorizes a finding of responsibility in a case in which the actor is not seriously deluded concerning his conduct or its consequences, but in which the actor's appreciation of the wrongfulness of his conduct is a largely detached or abstract awareness that does not penetrate to the affective level. Insofar as a formulation centering on "knowledge" does not readily lend itself to application to emotional abnormalities, the M'Naghten test appears less than optimal as a standard of responsibility in cases involving affective disorder.

A second and more pervasive difficulty with the M'Naghten standard appears in cases in which the defendant's disorder prevents his awareness of the wrongfulness of his conduct from restraining his action. Stated otherwise, these are cases in which mental disease or defect destroys or overrides the defendant's power of self-control. . . .

Responding to the M'Naghten formulation's inadequacy in connection with claims that emphasize a defendant's volitional incapacity rather than his inability to understand, a minority of jurisdictions . . . explicitly supplemented the M'Naghten rule by what was commonly called the "irresistible impulse" test. . . .

The Model Code formulation is based on the view that a sense of understanding broader than mere cognition, and a reference to volitional incapacity should be achieved directly in the formulation of the defense. . . . The resulting standard relieves the defendant of responsibility under two circumstances: (1) when, as a result of mental disease or defect, the defendant lacked substantial capacity to appreciate the criminality [wrongfulness] of his conduct; (2) when, as a result of mental disease or defect, the defendant lacked substantial capacity to conform his conduct to the requirements of law.

The use of "appreciate" rather than "know" conveys a broader sense of understanding than simple cognition. . . .

The part of the Model Code test relating to volition is cast in terms of capacity to conform one's conduct to the requirements of the law. Application of the principle calls for a distinction, inevitable for a standard addressed to impairment of volition, between incapacity and mere indisposition. In drawing this distinction, the Model Code formulation effects a substantial improvement over pre-existing standards.

In contrast to the M'Naghten and "irresistible impulse" criteria, the Model Code formulation reflects the judgment that no test is workable that calls for complete impairment of ability to know or to control. The extremity of these conceptions had posed the largest difficulty for the administration of the old standards. Disorientation, psychiatrists indicated, might be extreme and still might not be total; what clinical experience revealed was closer to a graded scale with marks along the way. Hence, an examiner confronting a person who had performed a seemingly purposive act might helpfully address himself to the extent of awareness, understanding and control. If, on the other hand, he had to speak to utter incapacity vel non under the M'Naghten test, his relevant testimony would be narrowly limited to the question of whether the defendant suffered from delusional psychosis, where the act would not be criminal if the facts were as the defendant deludedly supposed them to be. A test requiring an utter incapacity for self-control imposes a comparably unrealistic restriction on the scope of the relevant inquiry. To meet these difficulties, it was thought that the criterion should ask if the defendant, as a result of mental disease or defect, was deprived of "substantial capacity" to appreciate the criminality (or wrongfulness) of his conduct or to conform his conduct to the requirements of law, meaning by "substantial" a capacity of some appreciable magnitude when measured by the standard of humanity in general, as opposed to the reduction of capacity to the vagrant and trivial dimensions characteristic of the most severe afflictions of the mind.

The adoption of the standard of substantial capacity may well be the Code's most significant alteration of the prevailing tests. It was recognized, of course, that "substantial" is an open-ended concept, but its quantitative connotation was believed to be sufficiently precise for purposes of practical administration. The law is full of instances in which courts and juries are explicitly authorized to confront an issue of degree. Such an approach was deemed to be no less essential and appropriate in dealing with this issue than in dealing with the questions of recklessness and negligence.

UNITED STATES v. LYONS

United States Court of Appeals, 5th Circuit, en banc
731 F.2d 243, 739 F.2d 994 (1984)

GEE, J. Defendant Robert Lyons was indicted on twelve counts of knowingly and intentionally securing controlled narcotics. . . . Lyons proffered evidence that in 1978 he began to suffer from several painful ailments, that various narcotics were prescribed to be taken as needed for his pain, and that he became addicted to these drugs. He also offered to present expert witnesses who would testify that his drug addiction affected his brain both physiologically and psychologically and that as a result he lacked substantial capacity to conform his conduct to the requirements of the law. . . .

[The trial court excluded the proffered evidence, and Lyons was convicted.]

Today the great weight of legal authority clearly supports the view that evidence of mere narcotics addiction, standing alone and without other physiological or psychological involvement, raises no issue of such a mental defect or disease as can serve as a basis for the insanity defense. . . .

We do not doubt that actual physical damage to the brain itself falls within the ambit of "mental disease or defect." . . . Because the proffer offers evidence tending to suggest such damage, that evidence should have been submitted to the jury. And although we today withdraw our recognition of the volitional prong of [the insanity defense] — that as to which such evidence has usually been advanced — we also conclude that should Lyons wish to offer such evidence in an attempt to satisfy the remaining cognitive prong, fairness demands that we afford him an opportunity to do so.

. . . We last examined the insanity defense in Blake v. United Sates, 407 F.2d 908 (5th Cir. 1969) (en banc), where we adopted the ALI Model Penal Code definition of insanity. [W]e concluded that then current knowledge in the field of behavioral science supported such a result. Unfortunately, it now appears our conclusion was premature. . . .

Reexamining the *Blake* standard today, we conclude that the volitional prong of the insanity defense — a lack of capacity to conform one's conduct to the requirements of the law — does not comport with current medical and scientific knowledge, which has retreated from its earlier, sanguine expectations. Consequently, we now hold that a person is not responsible for criminal conduct on the grounds of insanity only if at the time of that conduct, as a result of a mental disease or defect, he is unable to appreciate the wrongfulness of that conduct.

We do so for several reasons. First, as we have mentioned, a majority of psychiatrists now believe that they do not possess sufficient accurate scientific bases for measuring a person's capacity for self-control or for calibrating the impairment of that capacity. Bonnie, The Moral Basis of the Insanity Defense, 69 A.B.A.J. 194, 196 (1983). "The line between an irresistible impulse and an impulse not resisted is probably no sharper than between twilight and dusk." American Psychiatric Association Statement on the Insanity Defense, 11 (1982) [APA Statement]. Indeed, Professor Bonnie [supra] states:

> There is, in short, no objective basis for distinguishing between offenders who were undeterrable and those who were merely undeterred, between the impulse that was irresistible and the impulse not resisted, or between substantial impairment of capacity and some lesser impairment.[b]

In addition, the risks of fabrication and "moral mistakes" in administering the insanity defense are greatest "when the experts and the jury are asked to speculate whether the defendant had the capacity to 'control' himself or whether he could have 'resisted' the criminal impulse." Bonnie, supra, at 196. Moreover, psychiatric testimony about volition is more likely to produce confusion for jurors than is psychiatric testimony concerning a defendant's appreciation of the wrongfulness of his act. It appears, moreover, that there is considerable overlap between a psychotic person's inability to understand and his ability to control his behavior. Most psychotic persons who fail a volitional test would also fail a cognitive test, thus rendering the volitional test superfluous for them. Finally, [case law currently] requires that such proof be made by the federal prosecutor beyond a reasonable doubt, an all but impossible task in view of the present murky state of medical knowledge.[c]

b. In accord with this view, a recent analysis of irresistible impulse and related claims about loss of self-control concludes: "No established metric exists to determine the magnitude of impulses, desires, or feelings. . . . [The psychological] studies do not address, and folk psychology does not know, whether and to what degree people are *unable* to refrain from acting. Neither in psychology [nor in] philosophy . . . is there a reasonably uncontroversial understanding of these matters. . . . The strongest contrary claims in the literature fail both conceptually and empirically." Stephen J. Morse, Culpability and Control, 142 U. Pa. L. Rev. 1587, 1657-1658 (1994). — Eds.

c. For recent changes in the law governing the burden of proof, see Note 5, page 885 supra.

[W]e see no prudent course for the law to follow but to treat all criminal impulses — including those not resisted — as resistible. To do otherwise in the present state of medical knowledge would be to cast the insanity defense adrift upon a sea of unfounded scientific speculation, with the palm awarded case by case to the most convincing advocate of that which is presently unknown — and may remain so, because unknowable. . . .

RUBIN, J., with whom TATE, J., joins, dissenting. . . . An adjudication of guilt is more than a factual determination that the defendant pulled a trigger, took a bicycle, or sold heroin. It is a moral judgment that the individual is blameworthy. "Our collective conscience does not allow punishment where it cannot impose blame." . . . "[H]istorically, our substantive criminal law is based on a theory of punishing the [vicious] will. It postulates a free agent confronted with a choice between doing right and wrong, and choosing freely to do wrong."[3] . . . An acquittal by reason of insanity is a judgment that the defendant is not *guilty* because, as a result of his mental condition, he is unable to make an effective choice regarding his behavior.

The majority does not controvert these fundamental principles; indeed it accepts them as the basis for the defense when the accused suffers from a disease that impairs cognition. It rests its decision to redefine insanity and to narrow the defense on "new policy considerations." . . .

The first is the potential threat to society created by the volitional prong of the insanity defense. Public opposition to any insanity-grounded defense is often based, either explicitly or implicitly, on the view that the plea is frequently invoked by violent criminals who fraudulently use it to evade just punishment. . . . This perception depicts an insanity trial as a "circus" of conflicting expert testimony that confuses a naive and sympathetic jury. And it fears insanity acquittees as offenders who, after manipulating the criminal justice system, are soon set free to prey once again on the community.

Despite the prodigious volume of writing devoted to the plea, the empirical data that are available provide little or no support for these fearsome perceptions and in many respects directly refute them. Both the frequency and the success rate of insanity pleas are grossly overestimated by professionals and lay persons alike; the plea is rarely made, and even more rarely successful.[8] The number of insanity pleas based on control defects, as compared to those based on lack of cognition, must have been almost negligible.

The perception that the defendant who successfully pleads insanity is quickly released from custody is also based only on assumption. . . . "The truth is that in almost every case, the acquittee is immediately hospitalized and evaluated for dangerousness. Usually, the acquittee remains hospitalized for an extended time."[9]

3. Morissette v. United States, 342 U.S. 246, 250 n. 4 (1952) (quoting Pound, Introduction to Sayre, Cases on Criminal Law (1927)).

8. For example, one extensive study examined the opinions held by college students, the general public, state legislators, law enforcement officers, and mental health personnel in Wyoming. Estimates of the frequency with which [felony] defendants entered the plea ranged from 13% to 57%. During the time period considered, however, the actual frequency was only 0.47%: one case in 200. Similarly, although estimates of its success rate varied from 19% to 44%, during the relevant period only one of the 102 defendants who entered the plea was acquitted by reason of insanity. . . .

9. Rappeport, The Insanity Plea Scapegoating the Mentally Ill — Much Ado about Nothing?, 24 So. Tex. L.J. 687, 698 (1983). . . .

Another set of objections to the plea is based on the thesis that factfinders — especially juries — are confused and manipulated by the vagueness of the legal standards of insanity and the notorious "battle of the experts" who present conclusory, superficial, and misleading testimony. These conditions, the argument runs, conspire to produce inconsistent and "inaccurate" verdicts.

Let us first put these objections in perspective. Most cases involving an insanity plea do not go to trial; instead, like most other criminal cases, they are settled by a plea bargain. In many of the cases that do go to trial, psychiatric testimony is presented by deposition, without disagreement among experts, and without opposition by the prosecution. And in the few cases in which a contest does develop, the defendant is usually convicted. . . .

The manipulated-jury argument is supported largely by declamation, not data. [N]o source has been cited to the court to support the conclusion that, as an empirical matter, pleas based upon the volitional prong present an especially problematic task for the jury.

Indeed, the majority opinion does not assert that the insanity defense, particularly the control test, *doesn't* work; it contends that the defense *can't* work. The principal basis for this contention is the belief, held by "a majority of psychiatrists," that they lack "sufficient accurate scientific bases for measuring a person's capacity for self-control or for calibrating the impairment of that capacity." . . . [B]ut the absence of useful expert evidence, if indeed there is none, does not obviate the need for resolving the question whether the defendant ought to be held accountable for his criminal behavior. . . .

Our concept of responsibility in this sense is not limited to observable behavior: it embraces *meaningful* choice, and necessarily requires inferences and assumptions regarding the defendant's unobservable mental state. . . . The difference between the concepts of excusing circumstances such as coercion and the insanity defense is that the former is based on objective assumptions about human behavior and is tested against hypothetical-objective standards such as "the reasonable person." "The insanity defense [on the other hand] marks the transition from the adequate man the law demands to the inadequate man he may be."[17]

The relevant inquiry under either branch of the insanity test is a subjective one that focuses on the defendant's actual state of mind. Our duty to undertake that inquiry is not based on confidence in the testimony of expert witnesses, but on the ethical precept that the defendant's mental state is a crucial aspect of his blameworthiness. . . . The availability of expert testimony and the probative value of such testimony are basically evidentiary problems that can be accommodated within the existing test. . . .

[A] defendant pleading insanity typically faces both a judge and a jury who are skeptical about psychiatry in general and the insanity plea in particular. . . . The formal allocation of the persuasion burden notwithstanding, the defendant to prevail must convince the doubting factfinder that, despite present outward appearances, he was insane at the time he committed the crime.

The majority's fear that the present test invites "moral mistakes" is difficult to understand. The majority opinion concedes that some individuals cannot conform their conduct to the law's requirements. . . . [T]he majority embraces a rule

17. A. Goldstein, The Insanity Defense 18 (1967).

certain to result in the conviction of at least some who are not morally responsible and the punishment of those for whom retributive, deterrent, and rehabilitative penal goals are inappropriate. A decision that virtually ensures undeserved, and therefore unjust, punishment in the name of avoiding moral mistakes rests on a peculiar notion of morality. . . .

Judges are not, and should not be, immune to popular outrage over this nation's crime rate. Like everyone else, judges watch television, read newspapers and magazines, listen to gossip, and are sometimes themselves victims. They receive the message trenchantly described in a recent book criticizing the insanity defense: "Perhaps the bottom line of all these complaints is that *guilty people go free*. . . . These are not cases in which the defendant is *alleged* to have committed a crime. *Everyone knows he did it.*"[25] Although understandable as an expression of uninformed popular opinion, such a viewpoint ought not to serve as the basis for judicial decisionmaking; for it misapprehends the very meaning of guilt.

. . . By definition, guilt cannot be attributed to an individual unable to refrain from violating the law. When a defendant is properly acquitted by reason of insanity under the control test, the guilty does not go free. . . .

NOTES ON CHANGES IN THE LAW

The preceding case exemplifies the changing attitudes toward the insanity defense beginning in the early 1980s. Before then, the Model Penal Code's formulation of the defense had captured a good deal of the field. About half the states adopted some version of the Model Penal Code, either by statute or judicial decision, as did all but one of the United States Courts of Appeal. But this trend in favor of the Model Penal Code approach was abruptly reversed following the 1982 trial of John W. Hinckley, Jr., who shot and wounded President Reagan (and several people accompanying the President) in an abortive assassination attempt that was witnessed on national television. When the jury, applying the Model Penal Code test, found Hinckley not guilty by reason of insanity, there were widespread expressions of concern about the insanity defense and an outpouring of outraged reactions to the verdict. See Valerie P. Hans & Dan Slater, John W. Hinckley, Jr. & the Insanity Defense: The Public's Verdict, 47 Pub. Op. Q. 202 (1983).

Proposals to restrict defenses based on mental illness included adjustments in the burden of proof, changes in the disposition of insanity acquittees, introduction of a separate verdict of "guilty but mentally ill," and complete abolition of the insanity defense. The choice of which approach (if any) to take involves a complex mixture of substantive and tactical judgments. For helpful discussions, see Donald H. J. Hermann, Assault on the Insanity Defense, 14 Rutgers L.J. 241 (1983); Ralph Slovenko, The Insanity Defense in the Wake of the *Hinckley* Trial, 14 Rutgers L.J. 373 (1983); Peter Arenella, Reflections on Current Proposals to Abolish or Reform the Insanity Defense, 8 Am. J.L. & Med. 271 (1982).

Developments in each of the areas just mentioned are explored in the appropriate places in this chapter. The present Note focuses on the formulation of the insanity test itself.

25. W. Winslade & J. Ross, The Insanity Plea 2-3 (1983) (emphasis added).

1. State law. Although a substantial minority of the states still adhere to the Model Penal Code test, several important jurisdictions have returned to the *M'Naghten* rule. California adopted the Model Penal Code formulation by judicial decision in 1978 but returned to *M'Naghten* as a result of a voter initiative approved in 1982. See People v. Skinner, 39 Cal. 3d 765, 704 P.2d 752 (1985). At least seven other states, including Texas and Indiana, likewise dropped the Model Penal Code test in the wake of the *Hinckley* verdict and adopted *M'Naghten* in its place. See John Q. LaFond & Mary L. Durham, Back to the Asylum 64 (1992). According to one count, by the end of the 1980s, 21 states used some form of the *M'Naghten* rule, and 22 states used the Model Penal Code test. See John Ogloff, A Comparison of Insanity Defense Standards on Juror Decision Making, 15 L. & Human Behavior 509, 510 (1991).

2. Federal law. As part of the Comprehensive Crime Control Act of 1984, Congress enacted a provision that supercedes the *Lyons* decision and narrows the insanity test even further. 18 U.S.C. §17(a) provides:

> It is an affirmative defense to a prosecution under any Federal statute that, at the time of the commission of the acts constituting the offense, the defendant, as a result of a severe mental disease or defect, was unable to appreciate the nature and quality or the wrongfulness of his acts. Mental disease or defect does not otherwise constitute a defense.

fed law

3. Legislative proposals. Three influential bodies have, in very similar language, proposed retention of the cognitive branch of the Model Penal Code test and rejection of the control branch. See American Bar Association, Criminal Justice Mental Health Standards §7-6.1(a) (approved Feb. 9, 1983); American Psychiatric Association, Statement on the Insanity Defense, 140 Am. J. Psychiatry 6 (1983); National Conf. of Commissioners on Uniform State Laws, Model Insanity Defense and Post-Trial Disposition Act §201 (1984). The ABA standard provides:

> A person is not responsible for criminal conduct if, at the time of such conduct, and as a result of mental disease or defect, that person was unable to appreciate the wrongfulness of such conduct.

The American Psychiatric Association standard provides:

> A person charged with a criminal offense should be found not guilty by reason of insanity if it is shown that as a result of mental disease or mental retardation he was unable to appreciate the wrongfulness of his conduct at the time of the offense.

4. The impact of the insanity defense. As noted in Judge Rubin's dissenting opinion in *Lyons,* supra, the frequency and success rate of insanity pleas are often overestimated. The actual use of the insanity defense varies markedly from jurisdiction to jurisdiction. Colorado had an average of one insanity plea for every 5,000 arrests, while the rate was one in 480 arrests for Michigan and one in 200 arrests for Wyoming. As might be expected, success rates for insanity pleas tend to be higher where the plea is infrequently used. Success rates ranged from 44 percent of all insanity pleas tendered in Colorado to 7 percent in Michigan and 2 percent in Wyoming. The two largest states, California and New York, had only 63 and 88 successful insanity pleas per year, a ratio of one for every 27,000 arrests in California and one for every 11,000 arrests in New York.[47] Nationally, insanity acquittals probably represent no more than 0.25 percent of terminated felony prosecutions.[48] The overall figures have varied very little over time; the overall success rate for the insanity plea was virtually identical in the early 1980s, before the post-*Hinckley* reforms took effect.[49]

STATE v. GREEN

Tennessee Court of Appeals
643 S.W.2d 902 (1982)

DAUGHTREY, J. . . . On the evening of January 18, 1979, Chattanooga police found the body of Officer Harry Wilcox in a restroom at Warner Park. The corpse, clothed in a blue park police uniform, was lying face down in a pool of blood. The victim had been shot twice in the head, and his police revolver was missing. On the victim's back officers found a plastic bag containing a note. The note, addressed to Agent Ray Hanrahan of the FBI, contained a meaningless string of words and phrases, including reference to an "ousiograph." . . .

Police were led to Green by contacting FBI agent Hanrahan. . . . At trial Hanrahan testified that Green had come to the FBI office . . . and told the agent that some people in New York were talking to him, sending messages to his brain, and "directing" him. Green told Hanrahan that a doctor in New York had invented a machine called an "oustograph" or "ousiograph" that could detect these matters. He asked Hanrahan to find out about the oustograph for him. Hanrahan looked up the word in a dictionary and contacted a radio technician, but could not learn anything about such a machine. Hanrahan said he thought the defendant "had [mental] problems," and he suggested to Green at the time that he go to Erlanger Hospital to seek help.

Hanrahan's perception of the precariousness of Green's mental health was indeed accurate. Green had first received psychiatric treatment at the age of seven when as a child in New York City he was suspended from school for picking fights with other children "for no reason at all. . . . , beat[ing] them up really viciously." At that time he began seeing a psychiatrist who diagnosed his problem as paranoia. After treating the defendant for over two years, the psychiatrist pronounced Green "all right" but warned that the condition could recur during his teenage years. At age twelve, Green attacked his mother with a knife and again received psychiatric treatment.

By the time Green was sixteen, he had become a loner. He refused to go to school, remained in bed all day, and stayed out all night. He refused to bathe. He would not talk to anyone, and when spoken to, he would not respond or would laugh hysterically. Green carried a bag around with him, explaining to his par-

47. Hugh McGinley & Richard A. Pasewark, National Survey of the Frequency and Success of the Insanity Plea and Alternate Pleas, 17 J. Psychiatry & L. 205, 208-214 (1989).

48. See Andrew Blum, Debunking Myths of the Insanity Plea, Natl. L.J., Apr. 20, 1992, at 9, reporting a 1992 study by the American Academy of Psychiatry and the Law.

49. See National Commission on the Insanity Defense, Myths and Realities 14-15 (1983); Borum and Fulero, Empirical Research on the Insanity Defense and Attempted Reforms, 23 L. & Human Behavior 375 (1999).

ents that the bag "kept him company." He complained that the television talked back at him. At first Green insisted there was nothing wrong with him, but he eventually agreed to accept psychiatric treatment. After he was hospitalized for more than a month in 1978, his family reached the limits of their insurance coverage, and Green was transferred to an out-patient clinic. During this period he was heavily medicated and "was just like a zombie." Because the medication made Green so drowsy he could not study, he stopped taking the medicine and refused to visit the out-patient clinic.

Green enrolled in a Navy reserve program, returned to school, and managed to graduate from high school in June 1978. Immediately after graduation, he reported for Navy training, but a few weeks later the Navy discharged him for failure to adapt to regulations. When he returned home from the Navy, Green resumed his old behavior patterns. He stayed in bed during the day and walked the streets at night. He had a fight with his brother and cut him on the leg with a knife. He said that other people in the apartment building had a machine that tampered with his brain. . . . Toward the end of August 1978, he stole the family's household money and left home.

. . . Green stayed with his uncle in Memphis for six to seven weeks. At trial Noah Green described his nephew's bizarre behavior during that time. . . . The defendant would stay in his room all day and only went outside when his uncle insisted. . . . Sometimes he locked himself in the bathroom, but ran the shower without bathing. Green laughed at inappropriate times, and he would stare into space and move his mouth without saying anything. Twice the defendant visited a mental health clinic, but each time he refused to cooperate with the doctors. The medical staff told his family that because Green had not yet exhibited violent tendencies, he could not be hospitalized involuntarily. By November 1978, Green's behavior had become so bizarre that Noah Green feared for the safety of his young children and asked his nephew to leave. Green then went to stay with an aunt, Julia McNair, who also lived in Memphis.

Green lived in McNair's home for two weeks. She testified that during that time he never went out, he kept her apartment in darkness, and he refused to bathe. He would not talk to other people but laughed and talked to himself constantly.

When a psychologist at the local mental health center told McNair that the defendant needed to be hospitalized and that he might "go off at any time" and "do anything," she became frightened. She told her nephew that he would have to leave her home if he did not seek medical help immediately. When he refused, she called her brother, the defendant's father, and told him to come get Green and take him back to New York City. When Green's father arrived in Memphis, the defendant insisted that he did not need treatment and refused to return to New York. His father bought him a pair of shoes, paid for a hotel room for him, and gave him some money. . . .

Some two months later, in January 1979, the defendant was arrested and charged with the Wilcox murder. [In July 1979 Green was found incompetent to stand trial and committed to the Middle Tennessee Mental Health Institute, where the staff also found him "insane at the time of the offense, . . . committable and in need of maximum security." After intensive drug therapy, Green's ability to think coherently gradually improved and he was found competent to stand trial. At the trial in November 1980, Green offered both lay and expert testimony to establish insanity, his sole defense. The case was tried under the Model

Penal Code test. The jury found Green guilty of first-degree murder. On appeal, Green argued that there was "overwhelming proof" of insanity. The appellate court summarized the evidence:]

The medical experts [testified] that they and all the other professional staff members who came in contact with Green after his arrest agreed unanimously that he was insane at the time of the offense. . . .

After months of treatment, Green was finally able to recall and communicate to the staff what occurred on the day Wilcox was killed. Although his various recollections of the event were not entirely consistent, the defendant told the staff in effect that he had acted in response to voices telling him that if he killed, he would be Adolf Hitler.

Shanks [a nurse-clinician at the hospital] described Green as initially talking only in "gibberish." (When asked by one hospital staff member what language he was using, Green replied that it was Chinese; however, a Chinese-speaking staff member knew otherwise.) Gradually, under medication, Green's gibberish gave way to coherent language and there was a lessening of both his inappropriate laughter and his tendency to talk to the ceiling. This improvement, Shanks said, was mainly attributable to the medication Green was receiving; the other factor was his presence in a highly structured environment. She said Green showed no signs of "faking," and she concluded that he had been insane at the time of the offense.

The State's rebuttal evidence, offered to establish the defendant's sanity at the time of the offense, consisted of testimony by five Chattanooga police officers and a former county employee. The first of these witnesses was Terry Slaughter, the detective who arrested Green on January 20, [1979], for the Wilcox killing. He described Green as "cooperative," "coherent," and "intelligent," but said that Green did not want to discuss the shooting. In the two hours he spent with Green, Slaughter noticed no bizarre behavior nor any sign that Green was "under delusion." . . . Asked if he had also told Green's lawyer that this would be an "easy case" for him because the accused was "crazy as a loon," the detective responded, "I don't remember expressing it in that way. . . . I remember expressing the thought to you that I thought the party [Green] needed help."

Officer Janus Marlin, a Warner Park patrolman and a colleague of the victim's, found Green huddled in a phone booth in the park on December 27, [1978]. Green had taken refuge there to get out of the cold and told Marlin he had "no place to go." The officer took him to a nearby rescue mission. Asked if there was "anything out of the ordinary" about Green at the time, Marlin said no, but also testified that "he was dirty and he smelled."

[Three other police officers presented testimony similar to that of Officer Marlin. They described incidents in December 1978 and January 1979 when they had found Green loitering in the park or other public places. Green had told them he had no place to go and was "trying to find someplace to stay warm." In these incidents the officers either arrested Green for vagrancy or simply told him to move on. They described him as "coherent," "fairly quiet," and "very polite" but "unkempt and dirty."]

Finally, the State offered testimony by a former county employee, William Cox, who gave Green a ride [on] the day Officer Wilcox was killed. . . . [Green] was carrying what was apparently his only possession at that time, a pair of shiny black shoes. During the 45 minutes they were in the van together, Cox said, they engaged in "small talk." In response to a question by the prosecution, the witness agreed that he noticed nothing out of the ordinary about Green.

From this testimony, the State took the position that Green was "not insane and crazy and bizarre at the time [the Wilcox killing] happened," but was just "a little bit different." However, the testimony of the various State witnesses, all of whom had had only brief contact with Green over a period of several weeks and described him as "normal," is not inconsistent with a determination that Green was insane at the time of the offense. The medical experts testified, and their testimony is unrefuted, that a paranoid schizophrenic can operate in a *seemingly* normal way. . . . Dr. Pieper [noted:]

> Paranoid schizophrenic people have a characteristic of what we call encapsulated delusions. That is they may have some abnormal thoughts that are about a very particular area. . . . When the person is functioning in areas which don't require any thinking about that particular problem, they can look pretty normal. They can get on a bus and ride the bus and no problem. But if somebody asks them a question or says something or makes a movement that they regard as threatening, suddenly all of this bizarre thinking takes charge and at that point they may react in any sort of way that's totally unexpected and totally irrational. . . .

To undercut the weight of the medical testimony, the State tried to establish that Green was faking his symptoms, or, in the alternative, that his psychosis was the result of the Wilcox killing and not its cause. The record clearly and eloquently refutes these theories. . . . [I]t is difficult if not impossible to believe that Green was able to fake the symptoms outlined above successfully enough to fool the highly trained and experienced medical personnel who both evaluated and treated him in this case. Moreover, the extensive history of Green's mental illness, going back over a decade and evidenced by medical and hospital records, as well as the cogent testimony of his family and the experts who diagnosed and treated him, wholly refutes the idea that Green dropped into a sudden psychotic condition upon shooting Officer Wilcox. The disease from which he suffered is a progressive one, and as Dr. Speal [a court-appointed psychologist] noted, . . . "he has been psychotic for most of his life, if not all of his life." . . .

Given the nature of the evidence offered by the defendant, the burden of proof in this case fell squarely on the State to establish the defendant's sanity beyond a reasonable doubt. Graham v. State, 547 S.W.2d at 544. Under the *Graham* standard, it was incumbent upon the State to prove (1) that at the time of the offense the defendant was not suffering from a mental disease or defect, *or* (2) if he was, that his illness was not such as to prevent him from knowing the wrongfulness of his conduct *and* from conforming his conduct to the requirements of the law. . . .

The State sought to discharge its burden of proof at trial by proving . . . that Green was not suffering from mental incapacity at the time of the offense, a theory which was totally demolished by the strength of the defendant's insanity proof at trial.

[B]efore this Court . . . the State argues that the nature of the defendant's condition was not sufficient to meet the remaining two-prong test of *Graham*. First, the State says, evidence that the defendant fled from the scene of the crime and hid the weapon involved in the shooting proves that he knew the wrongfulness of his act. The most obvious response to this argument is that the record shows only that the defendant left the scene at some point after the shooting and that Officer Wilcox's revolver was never recovered; neither of these facts establishes beyond a reasonable doubt that the defendant was attempting to conceal his identity or complicity from police, or that he otherwise was able to appreciate the wrongfulness of what he had done. . . .

But even if it were conceded that by his post-event behavior Green evidenced some appreciation of the wrongfulness of his conduct, the record is wholly devoid of any evidence that at the time he shot Wilcox, Green was able to conform his conduct to the dictates of law. The State's only argument in response to overwhelming evidence of Green's incapacity in this respect is that his failure to react violently toward *other* police officers with whom he came into contact proves that he was able to conform his conduct to the law with respect to Officer Wilcox. . . . This argument, of course, not only begs the question (that is, whether under this analysis any initial violent behavior could ever be the product of insanity), but it also ignores the nature of paranoid schizophrenia, as described by experts in this and other cases. . . .

The State correctly points out that a jury is not bound by expert testimony, even when it is non-conflicting. However, the Tennessee Supreme Court has clearly delineated what proof the State must produce to meet and overcome evidence of insanity:

> Th[e] burden can be met by the state through the introduction of expert testimony on the issue [of insanity], or through lay testimony where a proper foundation for the expressing of an opinion is laid, or through the showing of acts or statements of the petitioner, at or very near the time of the commission of the crime, which are consistent with sanity *and inconsistent with insanity.*

Edwards v. State, 540 S.W.2d 641, 646 (Tenn. 1976) (emphasis added). In this case, although the acts of the defendant at or near the time of the killing were arguably "consistent with sanity," quite obviously they were not also "inconsistent with insanity." Under the *Edwards* rule, the State has failed to meet its burden of establishing sanity, and thus "the evidence is insufficient to support the findings by the trier of fact of guilt beyond a reasonable doubt." . . . [W]e have no choice but to set aside Green's conviction. . . .

NOTES AND QUESTIONS

1. Beyond criminal law. Was the killing of Officer Wilcox preventable? If Green is not to be blamed for the death, who is? Were his parents or relatives at fault? The health insurance system? The lack of a warm place for him to sleep? Or is Agent Hanrahan responsible? (Note that the great majority of severely disturbed schizophrenics remain nonviolent.) Should Green have been subject to involuntary hospitalization because of his incoherent thinking and delusions about mind control and the "ousiograph"? What is the "moral" of the *Green* case?

2. The effect of different versions of the insanity defense. There is little evidence that different formulations of the insanity defense produce different results in practice. In one attempt to study this question empirically,[50] the researcher assembled

50. Rita James Simon, The Jury and the Defense of Insanity (1967).

roughly 100 experimental jury panels from actual jury pools in Chicago, St. Louis, and Minneapolis. The juries listened to the transcript of an actual insanity defense case, then deliberated until they reached a unanimous verdict. One-third of the juries was given the *M'Naghten* instruction, one-third a more liberalized test, and one-third were simply told to find the defendant not guilty by reason of insanity "[i]f you believe the defendant was insane" at the time of the offense. It turned out the differences in instruction made much less difference than the composition of the jury.

Other researchers reached similar conclusions from studies using mock juries to read case summaries. Asked whether to acquit under M'Naghten, the irresistible Impulse test, the Model Penal Code and "their own best lights", no significant differences in acquittal rates were found.[51]

Another approach relies on before-and-after comparisons in jurisdictions that have enacted statutory changes. In Wyoming, legislation replaced *M'Naghten* with the Model Penal Code test; the change had no significant effect on the rate of insanity pleas tendered, the rate of insanity acquittals, or in the characteristics of defendants invoking the defense.[52] California moved in the opposite direction, replacing the Model Penal Code test with *M'Naghten;* again, there was no significant change in the rate of insanity pleas and acquittals or in the types of defendants invoking the defense.[53]

3. *Prospects for Reform:* Professor Alan A. Stone, who served on the committee that prepared the American Psychiatric Association's formulation of a proposed insanity defense, supra page 895, has offered some sober reflections on the possibility of successfully reforming the insanity defense. He writes in his Law, Psychiatry, and Morality 94-96 (1984):

> Despite the endless attempts of law to define precise tests of criminal responsibility, the ordinary psychiatrist typically asks: Is the person psychotic? If the diagnosis is psychosis, particularly schizophrenia, the person is insane. If a personality disorder is diagnosed, the person is sane. The new APA proposal has gone back to that time-honored clinical distinction, noting that we now have 80 percent reliability [in diagnosis] of psychosis. But . . . Hinckley apparently fell into the 20 percent non-reliability category. We should not be surprised by that. Rather, we should expect that in most cases where the prosecution would want to contest an insanity defense, the defendant will not be obviously psychotic. The obviously psychotic defendant can be readily identified even by a prosecutor. Thus it may be that contested cases raising the insanity defense will be those about which we can expect diagnostic disagreement by psychiatrists. . . .
>
> [The] APA proposal involves going back to an essentially cognitive test — again in part because psychiatric testimony relevant to cognitive matters such as appreciation and understanding "is more reliable, and has a stronger scientific base" than testimony relevant to volition. Here again the hopes of the APA proposal fail. The defense [in Hinckley] found ample evidence of thought disorder, including ideas of reference, magical thinking, bizarre ideas, and a break with reality. The prose-

51. See Norman J. Finkel, The Insanity Defense: A Comparison of Verdict Schemas, 15 L. & Human Behavior 533 (1991); Norman J. Finkel, The Insanity, Defense Reform Act of 1984: Much Ado About Nothing, 7 Behavioral Sciences & L. 399 (1989).

52. Paseward & Bieber, Insanity Plea: Statutory Language and Trial Procedure, 12 J. Psychiatry & L. 399 (1984).

53. McGreevy, Steadman & Callahan, The Negligible Effects of California's 1982 Reform of the Insanity Defense Test, 148 Am. J. Psychiatry 744 (1991).

cution found none of this. Thus testimony limited to the cognitive issue did not prove reliable in the courtroom. . . .

Changing the insanity defense is like chipping away at the tip of the iceberg. . . . An exchange between defense and prosecution psychiatrists will illustrate one aspect of these deeper and more basic theoretical problems. Doctor Biological Psychiatry said that the Valium Hinckley took may well have produced "paradoxical rage," thus causing him to be unable to control himself. Doctor Corrections said it was "appropriate" for Hinckley to take Valium if he was anxious about assassinating the President. Put aside the fact that these are both conjectures. They are conjectures which are part of two quite different kinds of discourse.

The theory of paradoxical rage is part of a discourse about organisms with brains, enzymes, and physical chemical reactions. The theory of appropriate behavior is part of a discourse about persons with minds, intentions, and motivated actions. In the discourse about organisms, the self disappears and paradoxical rage is *caused* by the chemical release of the inhibitory neural system. In the discourse about persons, the self is the agent who chooses, who intends, and who assumes a firing position and pulls the trigger. Morality does not enter the discourse of organisms because free will and choice are not part of that language. To say that a *person* had a paradoxical rage reaction is to confuse the two discourses. . . . Psychiatry has not yet found a unified discourse about organisms and persons. That is the giant iceberg against which the insanity defense inevitably is wrecked. Neither psychiatry nor law nor moral philosophy has found a sure way past this barrier. It does no good to pretend the barrier does not exist or to ask the jury to deal with it. These are not questions for which common sense has an answer.

4. Abolition. While the defense of legal insanity has long been an established feature of American law, there have been movements to abolish it. Several states attempted to do so in the early decades of the past century, but these efforts were usually held to be unconstitutional under state constitutions guaranteeing a jury trial and due process of law. See State v. Lange, 168 La. 958, 123 So. 639 (1929); Sinclair v. State, 161 Miss. 142, 132 So. 581 (1931); State v. Strasburg, 60 Wash. 106, 110 Pac. 1020 (1910). There was a renewal of interest in abolition in the latter decades of the century, leading to abolition of the defense in four states. These later statutes differed from the earlier ones in that they allowed evidence of mental disease to be introduced on the issue of whether the defendant possessed the mens rea required by the crime with which he was charged. Some also authorized the court at the sentencing stage after conviction to determine whether defendant suffered from a mental disease, and if so, to commit him for institutional care and treatment for a period not to exceed the maximum sentence. See, e.g., Kansas Stat. Ann. §22-3220 (1995); Mont. Code Ann. §§46-14-311, 46-14-312(3). All of these statutes have passed constitutional muster. See State v. Korell, 213 Mont. 316, 690 P.2d 992 (1984); State v. Searcy, 188 Idaho 632, 798 P.2d 914 (1990); State v. Herrara, 895 P.2d 359 (Utah 1995).

The desirability of abolition remains controversial, and the issue tends to flare up with widespread media coverage of an insanity acquittal of a highly unsympathetic defendant, like Hinckley. Is abolition a good idea? Will it promote or impair public safety?[54] Consider these comments:

54. For a criticism of the arguments for abolishing the insanity defense, see Stephen J. Morse, Excusing the Crazy: The Insanity Defense Reconsidered, 58 S. Cal. L. Rev. 777 (1985). A recent proposal would consider mental disorder only if relevant to other excuse doctrines, such as lack of mens rea. See Christopher Slobogin, An End to Insanity: Recasting the Role of Mental Illness in Criminal Cases 86 Va. L. Rev. 1199 (2000). For debates on the proposal to abolish the insanity de-

Chief Justice Joseph Weintraub, Insanity as a Defense: A Panel Discussion, 37 F.R.D. 365, 369-372 (1964): [I]nsanity should have nothing to do with the adjudication of guilt but rather should bear upon the disposition of the offender after conviction[;] the contest among *M'Naghten* and its competitive concepts . . . is simply a struggle over an irrelevancy. . . . Upon the psychiatric view the distinction between the sick and the bad is I think an illusion. . . . The thrust of the psychiatric thesis must be to reject insanity as a defense and to deal with all transgressors as unfortunate mortals. . . . The difficulty I think is that the psychiatry-based critics of *M'Naghten* will not accept the inevitable answer, which, I think, psychiatry gives but rather they urge that *M'Naghten* be abandoned in favor of some other concept of insanity which will excuse. . . . And I think that debate just has to be fruitless. It's a quixotic attempt to draw a line that just doesn't exist. No definition of criminal responsibility and hence of legal insanity can be valid unless it truthfully separates the man who is personally blameworthy for his makeup from the man who is not, and I submit to you that there is just no basis in psychiatry to make a differentiation between the two.

Professor Herbert Wechsler, id at 381-383: I suggest you think about [the distinction between the sick and the bad] not in terms of the effort to do absolute justice to individuals (we must agree with the Chief Justice, this is for God and not for man) but rather in terms of asking ourselves this question: how would you feel about living in a society in which a differentiation of this sort were not attempted? For example, your elderly father in an advanced arteriosclerotic state is taken to the hospital and while in the hospital experiences a tantrum, a delusion, delusional phase, and knocks over a lamp, with the result that an attendant is killed. Now, would you be satisfied with a legal system in which he could be indicted and convicted of a homicidal crime and his condition regarded as relevant only on the question of what to do with him? Everybody would say no to this. That is why the criterion of responsibility as affected by disease or a defect parallels the traditional mens rea rules in requiring a determination of blameworthiness in the ordinary moral sense, in the sense of working morality, not in the sense of man's responsibility for his nature or his nurture but in the sense that the afflictive sanctions of the law will not be visited on anyone unless he does something which is the product of a choice, unless in traditional jurisprudential terms he performs a juridical act. Now, general confidence that this is so seems to me quite central to the sense of security that is one of the greatest values in a law abiding society. It is a very important thing for all of us to know that if we should be afflicted and in the course of affliction should be the physical agent of harm to others, that the legal system will conduct an inquiry in which the nature of that affliction can be adduced for an estimate of its bearing on blameworthiness in the ordinary sense. . . . So I don't think that it's just a question of whether you get sent away and for how long. I rather think that the distinctive feature of the entire criminal process is the element of condemnation that it marshals, of social condemnation. And, indeed, is it not the mark of a healthy society that the criminal law marshal an appropriate moral condemnation?

---

fense and to defer inquiry into the mental condition of the defendant until after conviction, compare Barbara Wootton, Crime and the Criminal Law, chs. 2 & 3 (1963), with H. L. A. Hart, The Morality of the Criminal Law 12-29 (1964); and Norval Morris, Psychiatry and the Dangerous Criminal, 41 S. Cal. L. Rev. 514 (1968), with Sanford H. Kadish, The Decline of Innocence, 26 Camb. L. J. 273 (1968). See also John Monahan, Abolish the Insanity Defense?—Not Yet, 26 Rutgers L. Rev. 719 (1973).

Norval Morris, Psychiatry and the Dangerous Criminal, 41 S. Cal. L. Rev. 514, 519-521 (1968): Overwhelmingly, criminal matters are disposed of by pleas of guilty and by bench trials. Only the exceptional case goes to trial by jury. And of these exceptional cases, in only two of every hundred is this defense raised. Does anyone believe that this percentage measures the actual significance of gross psychopathology to crime? Let him visit the nearest criminal court or penitentiary if he does. Clearly this defense is a sop to our conscience, a comfort for our failure to address the difficult arena of psychopathology and crime.

. . . It too often is overlooked that one group's exculpation from criminal responsibility confirms the inculpation of other groups. . . . You argue that insanity destroys, undermines, diminishes man's capacity to reject what is wrong and to adhere to what is right. So does the ghetto — more so. But surely, you reply, I would not have us punish the sick. Indeed I would, if you insist on punishing the grossly deprived. To the extent that criminal sanctions serve punitive purposes, I fail to see the difference between these two defenses. To the extent that they serve rehabilitative, treatment, and curative purposes I fail to see the need for the difference. . . .

Model Penal Code and Commentaries, Comment to §4.01, at 182-186 (1985): A variety of reasons for abolition have been advanced from quite different ideological perspectives. . . . The first position is perhaps epitomized by President Nixon's support of abolition, which he said was "the most significant feature" of the codification of general defenses in the Administration's proposed criminal code and was designed to curb "unconscionable abuse" of the insanity defense. . . . This position . . . has little empirical support. The insanity defense is in fact infrequently invoked and then only for very serious crimes. When it has been invoked, jurors have not shown themselves ready to accept attenuated claims. Those who do successfully claim the defense are often committed for long periods of time. Unfounded fears of "abuse" are hardly a sufficient reason for abolishing a defense that has properly come to be viewed as fundamental.

The other attack on the insanity defense is more complex and it goes to the roots of the criminal law. It shares with the first position a skepticism that distinctions can sensibly be made between those who are responsible and those who are not. Critics taking this view cite the rarity of the employment of the defense as evidence that most mentally ill defendants are being convicted despite the availability of the defense. They doubt that the stigma of those convicted and subsequently treated as mentally disturbed is any worse than the stigma of those who commit criminal acts and are committed to high security institutions for the mentally ill without undergoing trial or after being acquitted on grounds of insanity. They argue that there is little basis for withholding condemnation of those whose mental illness causes them to act criminally when those whose deprived economic and social background causes them to act criminally are condemned. They regard the adversarial debate over the responsibility of particular defendants as wasteful, confusing for the jury, and possibly harmful for those defendants who are mentally disturbed. They think psychiatric diagnosis should be employed primarily after conviction to determine what sort of correctional treatment is appropriate instead of prior to conviction to determine criminal responsibility. Ideally, in the view of some of these critics, criminal convictions generally should not be regarded as stigmatizing, but as determinants of dangerousness to which the community must respond.

When properly understood, this attack is a challenge to the basic notion that a criminal conviction properly reflects moral condemnation by the community of the act performed. Yet those who advance the attack do not provide persuasive reasons for believing it would benefit society if the association between moral wrongdoing and criminal conviction were dissipated. Nor do they give reasons for supposing that the association will be dissipated in the near future. Yet they propose labeling as criminal many persons whom society at large would clearly not regard as morally blameworthy.

7. *Transitional note.* Despite the differences in the prevailing formulations of the defense of legal insanity, they all incorporate two basic concepts. First, all these tests excuse when the defendant is unable to know (or appreciate) that her action was wrong; second, they all require that the disabling condition, however they define it, be attributable to a mental disease or defect. The following two sections are devoted to exploring the meaning of these concepts.

(ii) The Meaning of Wrong

STATE v. CRENSHAW

Washington Supreme Court
98 Wash. 2d 789, 659 P.2d 488 (1983)

BRACHTENBACH, J. . . . While defendant and his wife were on their honeymoon in Canada, petitioner was deported as a result of his participation in a brawl. He secured a motel room in Blaine, Washington and waited for his wife to join him. When she arrived 2 days later, he immediately thought she had been unfaithful — he sensed "it wasn't the same Karen . . . she'd been with someone else."

Petitioner did not mention his suspicions to his wife, instead he took her to the motel room and beat her unconscious. He then went to a nearby store, stole a knife, and returned to stab his wife 24 times, inflicting a fatal wound. He left again, drove to a nearby farm where he had been employed and borrowed an ax. Upon returning to the motel room, he decapitated his wife with such force that the ax marks cut into the concrete floor under the carpet and splattered blood throughout the room.

Petitioner then proceeded to conceal his actions. He placed the body in a blanket, the head in a pillowcase, and put both in his wife's car. Next, he went to a service station, borrowed a bucket and sponge, and cleaned the room of blood and fingerprints. Before leaving, petitioner also spoke with the motel manager about a phone bill, then chatted with him for a while over a beer.

When Crenshaw left the motel he drove to a remote area 25 miles away where he hid the two parts of the body in thick brush. He then fled, driving to the Hoquiam area, about 200 miles from the scene of the crime. There he picked up two hitchhikers, told them of his crime, and enlisted their aid in disposing of his wife's car in a river. The hitchhikers contacted the police and Crenshaw was apprehended shortly thereafter. He voluntarily confessed to the crime.

The defense of not guilty by reason of insanity was a major issue at trial. Crenshaw testified that he followed the Moscovite religious faith, and that it would be improper for a Moscovite not to kill his wife if she committed adultery. Crenshaw also has a history of mental problems, for which he has been hospitalized in the past. The jury, however, rejected petitioner's insanity defense, and found him guilty of murder in the first degree. . . .

Petitioner assigned error to insanity defense instruction 10 which reads: . . .

> For a defendant to be found not guilty by reason of insanity you must find that, as a result of mental disease or defect, the defendant's mind was affected to such an extent that the defendant was unable to perceive the nature and quality of the acts with which the defendant is charged or was unable to tell right from wrong with reference to the particular acts with which defendant is charged.
>
> What is meant by the terms "right and wrong" refers to knowledge of a person at the time of committing an act that he was acting contrary to the law.

But for the last paragraph, this instruction tracks the language of . . . the *M'Naghten* test as codified in RCW 9A.12.-010. Petitioner contends, however, that the trial court erred in defining "right and wrong" as legal right and wrong rather than in the moral sense. . . .

The definition of the term "wrong" in the *M'Naghten* test has been considered and disputed by many legal scholars. . . . This court's view has been that "when *M'Naghten* is used, all who might possibly be deterred from the commission of criminal acts are included within the sanctions of the criminal law." State v. White, 60 Wash. 2d 551, 592, 374 P.2d 942 (1962).

> [O]nly those persons "who have lost contact with reality so completely that they are beyond any of the influences of the criminal law," may have the benefit of the insanity defense in a criminal case.

State v. McDonald, 89 Wash. 2d 256, 272, 571 P.2d 930 (1977). Given this perspective, the trial court could assume that one who knew the illegality of his act was not necessarily "beyond any of the influences of the criminal law," thus finding support for the statement in instruction 10.

Alternatively, the statement in instruction 10 may be approved because, in this case, legal wrong is synonymous with moral wrong. [I]t is important to note that it is society's morals, and not the individual's morals, that are the standard for judging moral wrong under *M'Naghten.* If wrong meant moral wrong judged by the individual's own conscience, this would seriously undermine the criminal law, for it would allow one who violated the law to be excused from criminal responsibility solely because, in his own conscience, his act was not morally wrong. . . .

There is evidence on the record that Crenshaw knew his actions were wrong according to society's standards, as well as legally wrong. Dr. Belden testified:

> I think Mr. Crenshaw is quite aware on one level that he is in conflict with the law *and with people.* However, this is not something that he personally invests his emotions in.

We conclude that Crenshaw knew his acts were morally wrong from society's viewpoint and also knew his acts were illegal. His personal belief that it was his duty to kill his wife for her alleged infidelity cannot serve to exculpate him from legal responsibility for his acts.

A narrow exception to the societal standard of moral wrong has been drawn for instances wherein a party performs a criminal act, knowing it is morally and legally wrong, but believing, because of a mental defect, that the act is ordained by God: such would be the situation with a mother who kills her infant child to whom she is devotedly attached, believing that God has spoken to her and decreed the act. Although the woman knows that the law and society condemn the act, it would be unrealistic to hold her responsible for the crime, since her free will has been subsumed by her belief in the deific decree.

This exception is not available to Crenshaw, however. Crenshaw argued only that he followed the Moscovite faith and that Moscovites believe it is their duty to kill an unfaithful wife. This is not the same as acting under a deific command. Instead, it is akin to "[t]he devotee of a religious cult that enjoins . . . human sacrifice as a duty [and] is *not* thereby relieved from responsibility before the law." (Italics ours.) [People v. Schmidt, 216 N.Y. 324, 340, 110 N.E. 945, 950 (1915).] Crenshaw's personal "Moscovite" beliefs are not equivalent to a deific decree and do not relieve him from responsibility for his acts. . . .

NOTES

1. Legal vs. moral wrong. American courts appear sharply divided on the issue presented in *Crenshaw.* Several jurisdictions hold, in accord with *Crenshaw,* that an insanity acquittal requires the defendant to be unaware that his conduct was *legally* wrong. Although ignorance of the law is not, of course, a defense, *knowledge* of the law will be sufficient in these jurisdictions to defeat any claim under *M'Naghten.* See, e.g., State v. Hollis, 731 P.2d 260 (Kan. 1987); State v. Hamann, 285 N.W.2d 180 (Iowa 1979). In contrast, a number of recent decisions hold that "wrong" means "morally wrong." E.g., People v. Serravo, 823 P.2d 128 (Colo. 1992); State v. Worlock, 117 N.J. 596, 569 A.2d 1314 (1990); People v. Skinner, 39 Cal. 3d 765, 704 P.2d 752 (1985).

Which approach to the *Crenshaw* issue is more consistent with the purposes of an insanity defense? If a defendant has sufficient awareness to realize the illegality of his conduct and to attempt to conceal his crime, doesn't he fall, by definition, among those whose behavior is potentially deterrable? Compare James F. Stephen, 2 History of the Criminal Law of England 167 (1883):

> [T]he question whether "wrong" means "morally wrong," or only "illegal," may be important. In Hadfield's case, for instance, knowledge of the illegality of his act was the very reason why he did it. He wanted to be hung for it. He no doubt knew it to be wrong in the sense that he knew that other people would disapprove of it, but he would also have thought, had he thought at all, that if they knew all the facts (as he understood them) they would approve of him, and see that he was sacrificing his own interest for the common good. I could not say that such a person knew that such an act was wrong. His delusion would prevent anything like an act of calm judgment in the character of the act.

Consider also Justice Dixon's instructions to the jury in The King v. Porter, 55 Commw. L.R. 182, 188-190 (1933):

> We are not dealing with right or wrong in the abstract. The question is whether [the defendant] was able to appreciate the wrongness of the particular act he was

> doing at the particular time. . . . If through the disordered condition of the mind he could not reason about the matter with a moderate degree of sense and composure it may be said that he could not know that what he was doing was wrong. What is meant by "wrong"? What is meant by wrong is wrong having regard to the everyday standards of reasonable people. If you think that at the time when he administered the poison to the child he had such a mental disorder or disturbance or derangement that he was incapable of reasoning about the right or wrongness, according to ordinary standards, of the thing which he was doing, not that he reasoned wrongly, or that being a responsible person he had queer or unsound ideas, but that he was quite incapable of taking into account the considerations which go to make right or wrong, then you should find him not guilty upon the ground that he was insane at the time he committed the acts charged.

In *Serravo,* supra, expert testimony established that due to either brain damage or paranoid schizophrenia, defendant suffered from the delusion that God had told him to construct a multimillion dollar sports facility to teach people the path to perfection and that he believed he had to stab his wife to achieve that goal. At his trial for her murder, psychiatric experts for both the state and the defense agreed that Serravo was unable to distinguish moral right from wrong, though he probably knew that his act was illegal. Holding that knowledge of the act's illegality will not defeat a defense under *M'Naghten,* the court said (823 P.2d at 135-139):

> We acknowledge that some cases subsequent to *M'Naghten* have interpreted the right-wrong test as limiting the insanity defense to a cognitive inability to distinguish legal right from legal wrong, with the result that a person's simple awareness that an act is illegal is a sufficient basis for finding criminal responsibility. We believe, however, that such an analysis injects a formalistic legalism into the insanity equation to the disregard of the psychological underpinnings of legal insanity. A person in an extremely psychotic state, for example, might be aware that an act is prohibited by law, but due to the overbearing effect of the psychosis may be utterly without the capacity to comprehend that the act is inherently immoral. A standard of legal wrong would render such a person legally responsible and subject to imprisonment for the conduct in question notwithstanding the patent injustice of such a disposition. Conversely, a person who, although mentally ill, has the cognitive capacity to distinguish right from wrong and is aware that an act is morally wrong, but does not realize that it is illegal, should nonetheless be held responsible for the act, as ignorance of the law is no excuse. . . . A clarifying instruction on the definition of legal insanity, therefore, should clearly state that, as related to the conduct charged as a crime, the phrase "incapable of distinguishing right from wrong" refers to a person's cognitive inability, due to a mental disease or defect, to distinguish right from wrong as measured by a societal standard of morality, even though the person may be aware that the conduct in question is criminal. Any such instruction should also expressly inform the jury that the phrase "incapable of distinguishing right from wrong" does not refer to a purely personal and subjective standard of morality.

Why should it not be enough for an insanity acquittal that the action of the defendant was in accordance with his own personal conscience, even if he knew it was against the prevailing moral code, so long as his perverted conscience is the product of his mental disease or defect? Two of the concurring opinions in State v. Wilson, 242 Conn. 605, 700 A.2d 633 (1997) argue that it should be enough. See B. V. Ranade (Note), Conceptual Ambiguities in the Insanity Defense: State v. Wilson and the new "Wrongfulness" Standard, 30 Conn. L. Rev. 1377 (1998).

For a helpful review of the possible meaning of "wrongful" as contrary to law, against prevailing morality, or against one's conscience, see Herbert Fingarette, The Meaning of Criminal Insanity 123 (1972).

2. *The "deific decree" exception.* Why does the court in *Crenshaw* suggest that the result would be different if the defendant had said that his acts were "ordained by God" rather than merely by his "Moscovite" religious tenets? So long as Crenshaw's delusion was the product of a mental disease, why should it matter whether God gave the order directly or indirectly through the tenets of the Moscovite religion? In a later case, State v. Cameron, 100 Wash. 2d 20, 674, P.2d 650 (1983), where there was evidence the defendant believed God was instructing him, the court reversed for failure to give a "deific decree" instruction. A concurring judge observed, "Both *Crenshaw* and the subject case were almost factually identical; both involved outrageous, vicious, messy murders. . . . I frankly don't see much or any distinction, however, in carrying out or executing a murder under the direction of God or Crenshaw's Moscovite religious beliefs, or under the beliefs of a prophet, Buddha, etc. . . ." See Christopher Hawthorne (Comment), "Deific Decree, The Short, Happy Life of a Pseudo-Doctrine," 33 Loyola L.A. Rev. 1755 (2000).

(iii) The Meaning of "Mental Disease or Defect"

STATE v. GUIDO

New Jersey Supreme Court
40 N.J. 191, 191 A.2d 45 (1993)

WEINTRAUB, C.J., Adele Guido was convicted of murder in the second degree and sentenced to imprisonment for a minimum of 24 years and a maximum of 27 years. She appeals directly to this Court. . . .

The victim was defendant's husband. When they first met, she was a young girl and he a professional fighter of some success. . . .

All the details of the marital discord need not be stated. [Defendant] wanted a divorce, while decedent insisted upon holding on to her notwithstanding he would not or could not end his extra marital romance and assume the role of a responsible husband and parent. . . . In the early morning of April 17, 1961, after deceased fell asleep on a couch in the living room while watching television, defendant, according to her testimony, took the gun and went into her room, intending to end her life. Deciding that suicide would be no solution, she returned to the living room to put the weapon back in the suitcase, but when her eyes fell upon Guido, she raised the weapon and fired until it was empty.

With respect to physical abuse, the jury could find that although there were only a few incidents of actual injury, there was the constant threat of it from a man who had to have his way and who would not let go of a woman who had had her fill. It appears that on several occasions shortly before the homicide defendant called the local police to express her fear of harm. . . .

Defendant . . . was examined by two court-appointed psychiatrists. [Their] report contained sundry medical findings and ultimately the opinion that defendant was "legally" sane at the time of the shooting. Mr. Saltzman [defense counsel] met with the psychiatrists, and after some three hours of debate the psychiatrists changed their opinion as to "legal" insanity although their underlying medical findings remained the same. They then retyped the last page of their report.

On cross-examination of the first defense psychiatrist, it was developed that the original report had been revised. We do not know how the prosecutor learned of the change. The record shows that on its own initiative the court immediately directed that "Counsel shall produce the original report to the prosecutor." . . . What followed was some high drama that the occasion did not warrant.

Mr. Saltzman . . . returned from his office with the original report. The court undertook to interrogate him [out of the presence of the jury] with respect to the receipt of the changed last page. . . . With much formality the trial court . . . elicited step by step the receipt and transmittal of the papers. . . . The trial then resumed before the jury. . .

Defense counsel and defense psychiatrists were thus subjected to a humiliating experience. Later the prosecutor berated them in his summation. He said "the defense in this case — I am sorry to say this — has been concocted"; . . . that Mr. Saltzman was "in cahoots with Doctors Galen and Chodosh and perpetrated a fraud on this Court"; and "how, how can you believe a woman who lends herself to the deception that was practiced on the Court, on this Court by the doctors and her attorney? Certainly she knew about it."

The trial judge did not stop this unjustifiable attack. On the contrary he intervened in a way that tended to sustain it. . . .

When the basis of the change in the experts' opinion was explored, it quickly appeared that the change was thoroughly consistent with honesty however mistaken it might be. In the minds of the witnesses the change involved no alteration whatever in their medical findings. Rather it stemmed from an altered understanding of the law's concept of insanity. Specifically, the doctors originally understood that the "disease of the mind" required by the *M'Naghten* concept of legal insanity to which we adhere, means a *psychosis* and not some lesser illness or functional aberration. As the result of their pretrial debate with Mr. Saltzman, the doctors concluded they had had too narrow a view of *M'Naghten* and that the "anxiety neurosis" they had found did qualify as a "disease" within the legal rule, and hence when the anxiety reached a "panic" state, "meaning simply a severe disorganizing degree of anxiety," defendant did not know right from wrong and she did not know what she was doing was wrong because of that "disease." . . .

The change in the opinions of the defense psychiatrists simply focuses attention upon an area of undeniable obscurity. As we have said, the *M'Naghten* rule requires a "disease of the mind." The competing concepts of legal insanity also require a disease (or defect) of the mind. . . . But the hard question under any concept of legal insanity is, What constitutes a "disease"? . . . The postulate is that some wrongdoers are sick while others are bad, and that it is against good morals to stigmatize the sick. Who then are the sick whose illness shows they are free of moral blame? We cannot turn to the psychiatrist for a list of illnesses which have that quality because, for all his insight into the dynamics of behavior, he has not solved the riddle of blame. The question remains an ethical one, the answer to which lies beyond scientific truth.

The *M'Naghten* rule does not identify the disease which will excuse, but rather stresses a specific effect of disease, i.e., that at the time of the committing of the act the accused was laboring under a defect of reason such as not to know the nature and quality of the act he was doing, or, if he did know it, that he did not know what he was doing was wrong. But although emphasis is thus upon a state of mind, it is nonetheless required that that state be due to "disease" and not something else. So our cases contrast that concept of insanity with "emotional insanity" or "moral insanity" which, upon the dichotomy mentioned above, is attributed to moral depravity or weakness and hence will not excuse the offender even if his rage was so blinding that he did not really appreciate what he was doing or that it was wrong. . . . Yet the traditional charge of the *M'Naghten* rule to the jury does not attempt to say what is meant by "disease," and [there is a] rather universal reluctance to assay a definition. . . .

We have described the problem, not to resolve it, but simply to reveal the room for disputation, to the end of demonstrating the unfairness of charging defendant, her attorney, and her witnesses with a fraud when the change in the experts' opinion, however frivolous it may be in law, involved no departure from prior medical findings but rather a change in the witnesses' understanding of what the law means by "disease." . . .

The judgment is reversed. . . .

NOTES AND QUESTIONS

1. Questions on Guido. Is "mental disease" a medical or a legal concept? If the former, why was it legitimate for defense counsel to tell the psychiatrists what it meant? But if the latter, why were the psychiatrists allowed to express their conclusions about it at all? In what sense were they "experts" in the meaning of a legal concept?

2. A legal definition of "disease." Most courts seem to assume that "mental disease" for purposes of the insanity defense is a legal, not a medical concept. But then how should the legal concept of disease be defined? Few courts have supplied a definition, or even indicated the general criteria that help determine when this legal element is present. Consider whether the following formulation is helpful (McDonald v. United States, 312 F.2d 847, 850-851 (D.C. Cir. 1962)):

> What psychiatrists may consider a "mental disease or defect" for clinical purposes, where their concern is treatment, may or may not be the same as mental disease or defect for the jury's purpose in determining criminal responsibility. Consequently, for that purpose the jury should be told that a mental disease or defect includes any abnormal condition of the mind which substantially affects mental or emotional processes and substantially impairs behavior controls.

Compare the definition proposed by the American Psychiatric Association (140 Am. J. of Psychiatry 6 (1980)):

> [T]he terms mental disease or mental retardation include only those severely abnormal mental conditions that grossly and demonstrably impair a person's perception or understanding of reality and that are not attributable primarily to the voluntary ingestion of alcohol or other psychoactive substances.

Another attempt at definition, offered by the American Bar Association, states (A.B.A., Crim. Just. Mental Health Stand. §7-6.1(a) (1983)):

> [The term mental disease or defect] refers to impairments of mind, whether enduring or transitory, or to mental retardation which substantially affected the mental or emotional processes of the defendant at the time of the alleged offense.

3. The disease concept. How helpful are these definitions? Suppose that psychiatric examination indicates that the defendant, because of "explosive personality disorder," lacks the capacity to "appreciate" the wrongfulness of his aggressive, violent reactions. Does he qualify for the insanity defense? Should the answer depend on whether the psychiatric profession classifies this abnormality as a "personality disorder" rather than as a psychosis? Consider whether the *McDonald* definition helps resolve the difficulties. The defendant's situation presumably is "abnormal," but is it a "condition of the mind" within the meaning of *McDonald*? Is this a legal or a medical question? Apart from the *McDonald* formulation, what is the "right" result in a case like this one? If a defendant suffers from an impairment of cognition or control sufficiently serious to satisfy the prevailing insanity test, why should it matter that the impairment results not from disease but only from a "personality disorder"? Isn't blame inappropriate (and deterrence unlikely) in either case? In other words, why *bother* to define disease?

The requirement of a mental disease has served as an obstacle to be overcome in defense efforts to introduce evidence of a great variety of mental abnormalities, including battered spouse syndrome,[55] compulsive gambling disorder,[56] premenstrual syndrome,[57] postpartum disorders,[58] multiple personality,[59] post-traumatic stress disorders,[60] and alcohol and drug addictions.[61] Is the existence of this legal obstacle to the introduction of evidence of this kind a good thing or a bad thing?

NOTES ON THE PSYCHOPATH

A major issue of policy for the insanity defense concerns its application to the psychopath — the offender with a long history of antisocial conduct. Many persistent offenders "know" (in a purely verbal way) that their conduct is illegal, but they experience little or no empathy and have no apparent capacity to "understand" (at the "affective," emotional level) the rights of others. Their behavior brings them repeatedly into conflict with others and with the law. Often, psychiatrists diagnose them as suffering from "psychopathic personality" or "sociopathic personality," now more commonly designated "antisocial personality dis-

55. E.g., Bechtel v. State, 840 P.2d 1,7 (Okla. Cr. App. 1992); State v. Myers, 570 A.2d 1260, 1266 (N.J. Super. 1990).

56. E.g., United States v. Gould, 741 F.2d 45 (4th Cir. 1984) (attempted bank robbery); United States v. Torniero, 735 F.2d 725 (2d. Cir. 1984 (interstate transportation of stolen jewelry).

57. See Christopher Boorse, Premenstrual Syndrome and Criminal Responsibility, in Premenstrual Syndrome 81-124 (B. E. Ginsburg and B. F. Carter, eds. 1987).

58. See Laura E. Reece (Comment), Mothers Who Kill: Postpartum Disorders and Criminal Infanticide, 38 U.C.L.A. L. Rev. 699 (1991).

59. See Elyn R. Saks, Jekyll on Trial: Multiple Personality Disorder and Criminal Law (1997).

60. E.g., People v. Babbitt, 755 P.2d 252 (Cal. 1998). See C. Peter Erlinder, Paying the Price for Vietnam: Post-Traumatic Stress Disorder and Criminal Behavior, 25 B.C.L. Rev. 305 (1984).

61. E.g., United States v. Moore, 486 F.2d 1139 (D.C. Cir. 1973); Commonwealth v. Sheehan, 383 NE.2d 1115 (Mass. 1978).

order," and many mental health professionals regard the disorder as a "mental disease." Is such an offender legally insane?

The Model Penal Code §4.01(2), commonly referred to as the "caveat paragraph," was designed to exclude from the concept of "mental disease or defect" the case of the so-called psychopathic personality. It states that "the terms 'mental disease or defect' do not include an abnormality manifested only by repeated criminal or otherwise antisocial conduct." Consider State v. Werlein, 401 N.W.2d 848 (Wis. Ct. App. 1987), decided in a state which had adopted the caveat paragraph. The defendant, for no apparent reason, opened fire with a semiautomatic rifle, inflicting serious injury on the victim. He was convicted of attempted first-degree murder. At trial, he had called Dr. Albert Lorenz, who diagnosed him as suffering from antisocial personality disorder:

> Lorenz testified that Werlein's [symptoms] included an inability to handle work, squandering money, lack of attachment to people or groups, and reckless behavior. Lorenz stated that Werlein has no personality of his own, cannot plan for the future, and follows others much like a little child would. Lorenz concluded that as a result of Werlein's illness, he could not conform his conduct to the requirements of law.

The trial court struck Dr. Lorenz's testimony and precluded the jury from considering whether Werlein was mentally irresponsible. The court of appeals reversed, holding that caveat paragraph was inapplicable, since Dr. Lorenz's diagnosis went far beyond that of an abnormality manifested only by repeated criminal or otherwise antisocial conduct. Cf. Wade v. United States, 426 F.2d 64, 73 (9th Cir. 1970): "[I]t is practically inconceivable that a mental disease or defect would, in the terms of paragraph (2), be 'manifested *only* by repeated criminal or otherwise antisocial conduct'" (emphasis added). If the Model Penal Code text is inadequate to achieve the broad exclusion intended by its drafters, should it be amended? How?

For differing perspectives on whether psychopathy should be regarded as a mental disease for purposes of the defense of legal insanity consider the following contrasting views:

United States v. Currens, 290 F.2d 751, 761-763 (3d Cir. 1961):

> [A] psychopath is very distinguishable from one who merely demonstrates recurrent criminal behavior. . . . One of the most respected, perhaps the leading, modern work on psychopathy is The Mask of Sanity by Hervey Cleckley, M.D. (1941). Dr. Cleckley's findings are best summarized in Professor Robert W. White's, The Abnormal Personality (1948) at p. 401 as follows: "He [Cleckley] rules out . . . those cases in which delinquency and crime have been adopted as a positive way of life — in which the person is an enemy of society but is capable of being a loyal and stable member of a delinquent gang. There remains a group characterized by a diffuse and chronic incapacity for persistent, ordered living of any kind. These are, in Cleckley's view, the true psychopathic personalities. . . . Although the patient outwardly presents a 'convincing mask of sanity' and a 'mimicry of human life,' he has lost contact with the deeper emotional accompaniments of experience and with its purposiveness. To this extent he may be said to have an incomplete contact with reality, and it is certainly very hard to approach him and influence him therapeutically." . . . It would not be proper for this court in this case to deprive a large het-

> erogeneous group of offenders of the defense of insanity by holding blindly and indiscriminately that a person described as psychopathic is always criminally responsible. [A]ll the pertinent symptoms of the accused should be put before the court and jury and the accused's criminal responsibility should be developed from the totality of his symptoms. A court of law is not an appropriate forum for a debate as to the meaning of abstract psychiatric classifications.

Samuel Perry, Allen Frances & John Clarkin, A DSM-111 Casebook of Differential Therapeutics 304-305 (1985), speaking of Tom, a patient with the classic symptoms of an antisocial (psychopathic) personality:

> This 21-year-old man . . . has already been arrested 50 times and been in scrapes with the law on another 15 occasions. He is a barroom brawler, a thief, and a runaway who has never formed meaningful attachments to anyone. . . .
>
> His behavioral problems have a long and consistent history. In childhood he couldn't or wouldn't tell the truth. He was truant from school and stole from both his family and others. He set fires, killed animals needlessly, and frequently vandalized property, always covering his tracks with alibis. Throughout his childhood and during his entire adolescence, multiple attempts have been made to alter his behavior by psychiatric treatment or confinement. All these efforts have failed.
>
> . . . Because Tom has limited control of his behavior, the consultant might understandably wish to protect him from legal action and to help him overcome rather than be punished for emotional problems. At present, however, there is no treatment for Tom's disorder that is very effective — and the provision of an ineffective treatment will make it even worse. Once Tom is offered the opportunity to become a psychiatric patient as a refuge from legal responsibility, he will have even less reason to apply whatever controls are within his power. In addition, if Tom is sent to a hospital instead of a jail, he is likely to become a wolf, preying on the weaknesses of mental patients who are especially unable to protect themselves. He might also study the other patients to learn the particular signs and symptoms of mental illness that will provide him with even more convincing excuses in the future and enable him to be transferred to a hospital and avoid going to jail. . . . The consultant's best contribution in this case is to make clear to the legal and correctional authorities that our capacity to treat antisocial personality disorders is extremely limited and that these individuals should not avoid punishment by being referred for a treatment that does not exist.

For a discussion of psychopathic behavior and current psychiatric views concerning the diagnosis of the condition, see Comment, The Psychopath and the Definition of "Mental Disease or Defect" Under the Model Penal Code Test of Insanity: A Question of Psychology or a Question of Law?, 69 Neb. L. Rev. 190 (1990).

b. Automatism — Sane and Insane

McCLAIN v. STATE

Supreme Court of Indiana, 1997
678 N.E.2d 104

BOEHM, Justice. This is an interlocutory appeal from the Marion Superior Court [where defendant was being tried for aggravated battery on a police officer and resisting arrest]. The question for decision is whether the trial court erred in granting the State's motion in limine excluding expert testimony on sleep disorders and dissociative states because the defendant, David M. McClain, withdrew his insanity defense. The Court of Appeals held that evidence McClain seeks to present on automatism and sleep deprivation is a species of the insanity defense and, accordingly, is subject to the notice requirements of Indiana Code §35-36-2-1 [precluding defendants from introducing evidence of legal insanity if they have not given notice to the court before trial of their intention to interpose the defense].

[J]urisdictions are split between recognizing insanity and automatism as separate defenses and classifying automatism as a species of the insanity defense. [W]e think the approach required under Indiana's criminal statutes is to distinguish automatism from insanity and allow McClain's evidence to be presented as bearing on the voluntariness of his actions. . . .

Indiana Code §35-41-2-1(a) provides that "[a] person commits an offense only if he voluntarily engages in conduct in violation of the statute defining the offense." This section was enacted in 1976 pursuant to the recommendations of the Indiana Criminal Law Study Commission. . . . As the Commission explained: "The term voluntary is used in this Code as meaning behavior that is produced by an act of choice and is capable of being controlled by a human being who is in a conscious state of mind."

The evidence McClain seeks to present on automatism bears on the voluntariness of his actions within the meaning of the statute. In essence McClain claims he was unable to form criminal intent on the night in question due to an automatistic state of mind that precluded voluntary behavior. Although the jury is obviously not required to accept this explanation, permitting McClain to make the argument is consistent with the statute's general purpose that criminal conduct be an "act of choice" by a person in a "conscious state of mind." . . . Accordingly, at trial McClain can call expert witnesses and otherwise present evidence of sleep deprivation and automatism. . . .

Both the language of the insanity statute and the policies underlying the insanity defense counsel against classifying evidence of automatism as a mental disease or defect. Indiana Code §35-41-3-6 provides:

> (a) A person is not responsible for having engaged in prohibited conduct if, as a result of mental disease or defect, he was unable to appreciate the wrongfulness of the conduct at the time of the offense.
>
> (b) As used in this section, "mental disease or defect" means a severely abnormal mental condition that grossly and demonstrably impairs a person's perception, but the term does not include an abnormality manifested only by repeated unlawful or antisocial conduct.

Read expansively, this statute could encompass a broad range of conduct. As McClain argues, intoxication alters a person's state of mind and perception, but it is not recognized as a form of insanity. . . . While automatistic behavior could be caused by insanity, "unconsciousness at the time of the alleged criminal act need not be the result of a disease or defect of the mind." State v. Caddell, 287 N.C. 266, 215 S.E.2d 348, 360 (1975)[; see] Automatism, 27 A.L.R.4th 1067 at §3(b) (collecting cases). . . . Consistent with this view, we hold that McClain's

evidence of automatism as pleaded does not need to be presented under the insanity defense. We understand McClain's defense to consist of automatism manifested in a person of sound mind. To the extent involuntary behavior is contended to result from a mental disease or defect, the insanity statute would apply.

[T]o merge the automatism and insanity defenses as the State urges us to do in this case . . . would produce consequences that we believe were not intended by the framers of Indiana's insanity statute. The requirement that criminal defendants in Indiana be forced into commitment proceedings if found "not responsible by reason of insanity" reinforces our conclusion. [A] sane but automatistic defendant forced to plead the insanity defense faces a choice of possible commitment or effectively presenting no defense to the crime. A defendant intending to plead the insanity defense must give notice to the court so that the court can appoint independent experts to examine that defendant's particular psychiatric characteristics and offer an opinion on the validity of the claim. For an automatistic defendant, as here, there is no need for independent experts at public expense. The issue turns on a series of historical events and the factual circumstances bearing on the defendant's voluntariness, as opposed to the defendant's mental fitness. Although expert testimony may be helpful . . . automatism presents an issue qualitatively the same as any other factual determination.

One important policy underlying the insanity defense is ensuring that mentally-ill criminal defendants receive treatment for their condition. This raises a second and equally important consideration why automatism should not be regarded by the courts as a species of insanity. Although automatism could be the product of a diseased mind in need of treatment and rehabilitation, nothing in the record indicates that McClain presents such a case and McClain does not assert that he does. [M]erging the automatism and insanity defenses could result in confinement, at least temporarily, not of the insane but of the sane. This is a significant deprivation of liberty for an automatistic defendant where the outcome of the commitment hearing is a foregone conclusion. Even apart from the defendant's interest, in the absence of grounds for believing an automatistic defendant suffers from a recurring mental disorder, it is reasonable to infer that legislators did not intend to occupy the courts with commitment hearings for defendants whose sanity is not in question. . . .

[The legal insanity defense] does not deal with every "medical condition." Rather, it turns on the presence of a "mental disease or defect," which connotes a disorder naturally occurring or condition of the mind, as opposed to an induced condition (whether self-induced or otherwise). McClain seems uncertain exactly how to describe his allegedly automatistic condition, calling it "sleep deprivation," "sleep violence," "sleepwalking" and even a state of sleep itself. The gravamen of McClain's argument, however, is that but for a lack of sleep over the course of several days, he would not have been in this state at the time he allegedly involuntarily struck police officers on December 20, 1993. McClain's condition thus is more analogous to intoxication than insanity because it had an external cause. Unlike intoxication, the Legislature has presented no specific standard for dealing with or assessing this defense. Automatism is simply a denial of one element — voluntary action — that the Legislature has required for most crimes. It is not a disease or defect within the meaning of Indiana Code § 35-41-3-6. . . . This case is remanded for proceedings in the trial court consistent with this opinion.

NOTES

1. *Defendant's option?* Most American courts hold that the defendant may elect to plead either insanity, involuntariness, or both. See, e.g., State v. Massey, 747 P.2d 802 (Kan. 1987); People v. Grant, 71 Ill. 2d 551, 377 N.E.2d 4, 8 (1978). The English rule, in contrast, holds that when automatism results from a mental disease or defect, the only defense available is the plea of not guilty by reason of insanity. See Bratty v. Attorney-General for Northern Ireland, [1963] A.C. 386. A few American jurisdictions appear to follow the English approach. See, e.g., Wyo. Stat. §7-11-304(c) (1977):

> Evidence that a person is not responsible for criminal conduct by reason of mental illness or deficiency is not admissible at the trial of the defendant unless a plea of "not guilty by reason of mental illness or deficiency" is made.

2. *Distinguishing sane from insane automatisms.* Where insanity and automatism are mutually exclusive defenses, courts must decide whether the claimed automatism results from a mental disorder. Consider the following treatments of the issue.

(*a*) In Wyoming, the insanity defense is available for impairments resulting from "mental illness or deficiency." "Mental deficiency" is defined as "a defect attributable to mental retardation, brain damage and learning disabilities." Wyo. Stat. §7-11-301(a)(iii) (1977). In Fulcher v. State, 633 P.2d 142 (Wyo. 1981), the defendant was charged with aggravated assault. With the support of expert medical testimony, he claimed that his actions were committed in a state of automatism resulting from traumatic head injuries inflicted in a brawl shortly before the alleged offense. Should such injuries be regarded as a form of "brain damage," which Wyoming law would require to be raised solely in terms of the insanity defense? The Wyoming Supreme Court held that the defendant's injuries did not represent "brain damage" within the meaning of the statute and accordingly that the automatism defense remained available. The court said (id. at 146):

> It is our view that the "brain damage" contemplated in the statute is some serious and irreversible condition having an impact upon the ability of the person to function. It is undoubtedly something far more significant than a temporary and transitory condition.

A dissenting judge commented (id. at 155, 162-163):

> There is no basis whatsoever that supports the proposition the majority espouses that, . . . "the 'brain damage' contemplated in the statute is some serious and irreversible condition . . ." To the contrary, the only material condition is that which exists at the moment of the crime. How long should the condition exist before it comes within the cloak of the statute — a minute, an hour, a day, a week, two weeks, a month, a year, five years, a lifetime? The statute says nothing about a temporary condition or one that is "serious and irreversible."

Question: What considerations might have led the majority to reach this restrictive interpretation of the statute?

(*b*) The problem of distinguishing sane from insane automatisms has generated extensive litigation in England. In *Bratty,* supra Note 1, a defendant accused of murder claimed that his act was committed in a state of automatism resulting from an attack of psychomotor epilepsy. The House of Lords held that this defense could be raised only through a plea of insanity. In explaining why epilepsy should be classified as a mental disease, Lord Denning suggested the following approach:

> The major mental diseases, which the doctors call psychoses, such as schizophrenia, are clearly diseases of the mind. But in Reg. v. Charlson [1955] 1 W.L.R. 317, Barry, J., seems to have assumed that other diseases such as epilepsy or cerebral tumour are not diseases of the mind, even when they are such as to manifest themselves in violence. I do not agree with this. It seems to me that any mental disorder which has manifested itself in violence and is prone to recur is a disease of the mind. At any rate it is the sort of disease for which a person should be detained in hospital rather than be given an unqualified acquittal.

Subsequent cases suggested anomalies in Lord Denning's approach. In Regina v. Quick, [1973] 3 W.L.R. 26, defendant was a diabetic who committed an assault during a state of unconsciousness due to hypoglycaemia (low blood sugar), a condition that resulted from his taking either too much insulin or too little food just prior to the attack. The court recognized that by Lord Denning's test, Quick would be restricted to a defense of legal insanity because his condition "manifested itself in violence and [was] prone to recur." The court rejected that approach and held that Quick was entitled to rely on the involuntary act defense, explaining:

> No mental hospital would admit a diabetic merely because he had a low blood sugar reaction; and common sense is affronted by the prospect of a diabetic being [detained in] such a hospital, when in most cases the disordered mental condition can be rectified quickly by pushing a lump of sugar or a teaspoonful of glucose into the patient's mouth.
>
> . . . A malfunctioning of the mind of transitory effect caused by the application to the body of some external factor such as violence, drugs, including anaesthetics, alcohol and hypnotic influences cannot fairly be said to be due to disease. . . .
>
> In this case Quick's alleged mental condition, if it ever existed, was not caused by his diabetes but by his use of the insulin prescribed by his doctor. Such malfunctioning of his mind as there was, was caused by an external factor and not by a bodily disorder in the nature of a disease which disturbed the working of his mind. It follows in our judgment that Quick was entitled to have his defence of automatism left to the jury. . . .

(c) People v. Grant, 46 Ill. App. 3d 125, 360 N.E.2d 809 (1977). During a disturbance outside a bar, Grant struck a police officer violently in the face and was later charged with aggravated battery. At trial, a defense expert testified that, in his opinion, Grant was suffering from a psychomotor seizure that prevented his conscious mind from controlling his actions. The trial judge instructed the jury on the insanity defense but did not instruct on the requirement of a voluntary act. Grant was convicted of aggravated battery and sentenced to three to nine years' imprisonment. The appellate court reversed:

> [The insanity] instruction . . . fails to distinguish behavior by a person lacking ". . . substantial capacity either to appreciate the criminality of his conduct or to conform his conduct to the requirements of the law . . ." from automatic behavior by an individual who possesses the requisite capacity. . . . [N]o Illinois court has

[previously] determined [whether] a person's actions during a psychomotor epileptic seizure are the actions of an insane person or merely the involuntary or automatic actions of a sane person. . . .

The term automatism is defined as the state of a person who, though capable of action, is not conscious of what he is doing. Automatism is not insanity. . . .

We are not troubled by . . . Bratty v. Attorney-General for Northern Ireland (1961), 3 All E.R. 535 [where] Lord Denning . . . felt that any mental disorder manifesting itself in a form of violence that is prone to recur is a disease of the mind. He stated that it is the sort of disease requiring detention rather than an unqualified acquittal.

. . . Our legislature has provided that a person found not guilty of an offense by reason of insanity can be committed to a mental health facility for treatment, although no such provision applies to an alleged offender who commits an involuntary act. . . . If the jury finds that the defendant was sane but not responsible for the attack on Officer Vonderahe, then he cannot be committed for the offenses. We find this course to be mandated by our legislature which only provided for the commitment of persons who are criminally insane.[a]

3. *Sleep states.* Relatively few cases have dealt with criminal conduct during various states of sleep. The courts appear to be divided on the question whether the defendant in such a case is entitled to outright acquittal due to the absence of a volitional act, or whether the defendant must plead insanity and face commitment to a mental hospital. As we saw, in *State v. McClain,* the principal case, the court held that sleep disturbances would qualify for an automatism defense. An English case reached the opposite conclusion. In Regina v. Burgess, [1991] 2 All E.R. 769, defendant fell asleep while watching a videotape with his neighbor. He awoke to find himself hitting her on the head with a bottle and attempting to strangle her. He quickly came to his senses and called an ambulance for her, but he was charged with assault. He had no history of mental illness and had been on completely friendly terms with the victim. Applying the "internal-external" test used in England to determine whether an involuntary act is the result of "mental disease," the court held that the defendant could not raise a defense of noninsane automatism, and he was found not guilty by reason of insanity. For a trenchant criticism of the result, see Irene Mackay, The Sleepwalker Is Not Insane, 55 Mod. L. Rev. 714 (1992).

Under the Model Penal Code a defendant charged with conduct during a somnambulistic state would be entitled to an outright acquittal for lack of a voluntary act. See §2.01(2)(b). In this connection reconsider the *Cogden* case, page 179 supra. Is an outright acquittal appropriate in such a case?

c. Diminished Capacity

UNITED STATES v. BRAWNER

United States Court of Appeals, District of Columbia Circuit
471 F.2d 969 (1972)

LEVENTHAL, J. [After examining the test of legal insanity as a complete defense, the court considered whether mental health evidence should be admis-

a. Reversed on other grounds, 377 N.E.2d 4 (1978).—EDS.

sible apart from its bearing on the insanity issue.][E]xpert testimony as to a defendant's abnormal mental condition may be received and considered, as tending to show, in a responsible way, that defendant did not have the specific mental state required for a particular crime or degree of crime — even though he was aware that his act was wrongful and was able to control it, and hence was not entitled to complete exoneration.

Some of the cases following this doctrine use the term "diminished responsibility," but we prefer [to] avoid this term, for its convenience is outweighed by its confusion: Our doctrine has nothing to do with "diminishing" responsibility of a defendant because of his impaired mental condition, but rather with determining whether the defendant had the mental state that must be proved as to all defendants.

Procedurally, the issue of abnormal mental condition negativing a person's intent may arise in different ways: For example, the defendant may offer evidence of mental condition not qualifying as mental disease. . . . Or he may tender evidence that qualifies [as a mental disease], yet the jury may conclude from all the evidence that defendant has knowledge and control capacity sufficient for responsibility. . . .

The issue often arises with respect to mental condition tendered as negativing the element of premeditation in a charge of first degree premeditated murder. . . . An offense like deliberated and premeditated murder requires a specific intent that cannot be satisfied merely by showing that defendant failed to conform to an objective standard. This is plainly established by the defense of voluntary intoxication. In Hopt v. Utah, 104 U.S. 631 (1881), the Court, after stating the familiar rule that voluntary intoxication is no excuse for crime, said: "[W]hen a statute establishing different degrees of murder requires deliberate premeditation in order to constitute murder in the first degree, the question of whether the accused is in such a condition of mind, by reason of drunkenness or otherwise, as to be capable of deliberate premeditation, necessarily becomes a material subject of consideration by the jury. . . ."

Neither logic nor justice can tolerate a jurisprudence . . . such that one defendant can properly argue that his voluntary drunkenness removed his capacity to form the specific intent but another defendant is inhibited from a submission of his contention that an abnormal mental condition, for which he was in no way responsible, negated his capacity to form a particular specific intent, even though the condition did not exonerate him from all criminal responsibility. . . .

The pertinent reasoning was succinctly stated by the Colorado Supreme Court as follows [Battalino v. People, 118 Colo. 587, 199 P.2d 897, 901 (1948)]:

> The question to be determined is not whether defendant was insane, but whether the homicidal act was committed with deliberation and premeditation. The evidence offered as to insanity may or may not be relevant to that issue. . . . "A claim of insanity cannot be used for the purpose of reducing a crime of murder in the first degree to murder in the second degree or from murder to manslaughter. If the perpetrator is responsible at all in this respect, he is responsible in the same degree as a sane man; and if he is not responsible at all, he is entitled to an acquittal in both degrees. However, . . . *evidence of the condition of the mind* of the accused at the time of the crime, together with the surrounding circumstances, may be introduced, not for the purpose of establishing insanity, but to prove that the situation was such that a specific intent was not entertained — that is, *to show absence of any deliberate or premeditated design.*" (Emphasis in original.) . . .

Our rule permits the introduction of expert testimony as to abnormal condition if it is relevant to negative, or establish, the specific mental condition that is an element of the crime. The receipt of this expert testimony to negative the mental condition of specific intent requires careful administration by the trial judge. . . . The judge will . . . determine whether the testimony is grounded in sufficient scientific support to warrant use in the courtroom, and whether it would aid the jury in reaching a decision on the ultimate issues. . . .

STATE v. WILCOX

Supreme Court of Ohio
70 Ohio St. 182, 436 N.E.2d 523 (1982)

[Defendant participated in a burglary in which the victim was shot and killed. He was charged with aggravated felony murder, a charge requiring a purpose to kill, and aggravated burglary, a charge requiring a purpose to commit a felony. Before trial, a court-appointed psychiatrist found defendant to be borderline retarded, schizophrenic, dyslexic, and to be suffering from organic brain syndrome. At trial he was permitted to introduce some psychiatric testimony to support his insanity defense, but the trial judge excluded other psychiatric testimony and refused to charge the jury that defendant's mental condition could negate the specific intents required for aggravated murder and aggravated burglary. Defendant was convicted on both counts and sentenced to life imprisonment. The intermediate court of appeals reversed, and the prosecution appealed.]

SWEENEY, J. The question before the court in the instant appeal is whether appellee is entitled to a new trial at which he may present expert psychiatric testimony relating to his alleged incapacity to form the requisite specific intent to commit aggravated murder and aggravated burglary. . . .

If the *Brawner* rule [see page 919 supra] were applied to the case at bar, then appellee, even though legally sane, could present psychiatric testimony as to his abnormal mental condition (diminished capacity) to show that he did not have the specific mental state — in this instance, the purpose — required to commit the crimes with which he stands charged. However, our review of the history and policies underlying the diminished capacity concept and the experience of jurisdictions that have attempted to apply the doctrine militate against the adoption of a *Brawner*-type rule in Ohio. . . .

The diminished capacity defense developed as a covert judicial response to perceived inequities in the criminal law. The purported justifications for the doctrine include the following:

> (1) it ameliorates defects in a jurisdiction's insanity test criteria; (2) it permits the jury to avoid imposing the death penalty on mentally disabled killers who are criminally responsible for their acts; and (3) it permits the jury to make more accurate individualized culpability judgments.

[Peter Arenella, The Diminished Capacity and Diminished Responsibility Defenses: Two Children of a Doomed Marriage, 77 Colum. L. Rev. 827 (1977)] at page 853. . . .

Upon examination, however, we find none of the foregoing justifications for the defense of diminished capacity sufficiently compelling as to warrant its adoption, particularly in light of the problems posed by the doctrine. . . .

The diminished capacity defense does serve to ameliorate the limitations of the traditional, *M'Naghten,* right from wrong test for insanity. It is no coincidence that California, which pioneered the diminished capacity defense, for many years adhered to a strict *M'Naghten* standard. . . .

The ameliorative argument loses much of its force, however, in jurisdictions that have abandoned or expanded upon the narrow *M'Naghten* standard. The test for insanity in Ohio is . . . as follows:

> One accused of criminal conduct is not responsible for such criminal conduct if, at the time of such conduct, as a result of mental disease or defect, he does not have the capacity either to know the wrongfulness of his conduct or to conform his conduct to the requirements of law. . . .

While this standard is arguably less expansive than that espoused by the drafters of the Model Penal Code, see Section 4.01, it is considerably more flexible than the *M'Naghten* rule. [W]e see no reason to fashion a halfway measure, e.g., diminished capacity, when an accused may present a meaningful insanity defense in a proper case.

The interplay between the diminished capacity doctrine and the insanity defense, moreover, is not limited to the supposed ameliorative effect of the former on the latter. Rather, as Dr. Diamond, among others, has observed, . . . "this defense does not just supplement the insanity defense, but tends to supersede it. . . ." . . .

Professor Arenella notes that "[s]eriously disturbed defendants can avoid an indefinite commitment to a mental hospital for the criminally insane by relying on the diminished responsibility defense which frequently leads to a reduced term in prison." Arenella, supra, at page 854. According to this view, the principal practical effect of the diminished capacity defense is to enable mentally ill offenders to receive shorter and more certain sentences than they would receive if they were adjudged insane. Having satisfied ourselves that Ohio's test for criminal responsibility adequately safeguards the rights of the insane, we are disinclined to adopt an alternative defense that could swallow up the insanity defense and its attendant commitment provisions.

We can quickly dispose of the argument that the diminished capacity defense alleviates the harshness of the death penalty when mentally ill but nonetheless sane defendants are convicted of capital crimes. . . . Mental capacity is a formal mitigating factor in capital cases under current Ohio law at the punishment stage of the now bifurcated proceedings. Thus the ameliorative purpose served by the diminished capacity defense in capital cases has largely been accomplished by other means.

The justifications for diminished capacity . . . are based largely on analogies to the insanity defense and the defense of intoxication, respectively. . . .

As Professor Arenella notes, at page 860,

> [t]he analogy to the insanity defense is misleading because the diminished responsibility doctrine asks the expert witness and the jury to make a far more subtle distinction. The insanity defense asks both to distinguish between a large group of offenders who are punishable for their acts despite their mental deficiencies, and a

> small class of offenders who are so mentally disabled that they cannot be held accountable because they lack the minimal capacity to act voluntarily. The diminished responsibility doctrine attempts to divide the first large group of responsible sane offenders into two subgroups: a group of "normal" fully culpable criminal offenders, and a group of mentally abnormal but sane offenders with reduced culpability.

In light of the line-drawing difficulties courts and juries face when assessing expert evidence to make the "bright line" insanity determination, we are not at all confident that similar evidence will enable juries, or the judges who must instruct them, to bring the blurred lines of diminished capacity into proper focus so as to facilitate principled and consistent decision-making in criminal cases. In short, the fact that psychiatric evidence is admissible to prove or disprove insanity does not necessarily dictate the conclusion that it is admissible for purposes unrelated to the insanity defense.

The *Brawner* court emphasized the apparent illogic of permitting evidence of voluntary intoxication to be introduced to negate specific intent while precluding the introduction of evidence of an abnormal mental condition not amounting to insanity for the same purpose. While we concede that there is a superficial attractiveness to the intoxication-diminished capacity analogy, upon closer examination we . . . find the concepts to be quite disparate. . . .

It takes no great expertise for jurors to determine whether an accused was "so intoxicated as to be mentally unable to intend anything (unconscious)," whereas the ability to assimilate and apply the finely differentiated psychiatric concepts associated with diminished capacity demands a sophistication (or as critics would maintain a sophistic bent) that jurors (and officers of the court) ordinarily have not developed. We are convinced . . . that these "significant evidentiary distinctions" preclude treating diminished capacity and voluntary intoxication as functional equivalents for purposes of partial exculpation from criminal responsibility. . . .

The open-endedness of the diminished capacity doctrine troubles us as well. Under the California rule evidence of diminished capacity could only be introduced to negate the mental element in crimes requiring specific intent. The specific intent limitation imposed by the California courts did not, however, flow from the theory underlying the diminished capacity doctrine and, indeed, may have been in direct conflict therewith. The *Bethea* court [Bethea v. United States, 365 A.2d 64 (D.C. App. 1976)] acknowledged this theoretical incongruity in its discussion of *Brawner:*

> . . . Assuming the competency of experts to testify as to an accused's capacity for specific intent we see no logical bar to their observations as to the possible existence or lack of malice or general intent. . . .

If however, in the interests of doctrinal purity, evidence of diminished capacity were admitted to disprove the mental element in general intent crimes, then "successful application of the diminished capacity doctrine . . . would create the anomalous result of a 'partial defense' leading to outright acquittal of the defendant because of the absence of a lesser included offense." Arenella, supra, at fn. 25. [T]he potential applicability of diminished capacity as a complete defense to crimes of general intent dramatically highlights the paradox inhering in the doctrine. "[It] would discard the traditional presumptions concerning mens rea without providing for a corresponding adjustment in the means whereby society is enabled to protect itself from those who cannot or will not conform their conduct to the requirements of the law." *Bethea* supra, at page 90. . . .

We hold, therefore, that the partial defense of diminished capacity is not recognized in Ohio and consequently, a defendant may not offer expert psychiatric testimony, unrelated to the insanity defense, to show that the defendant lacked the mental capacity to form the specific mental state required for a particular crime or degree of crime.

[Conviction affirmed.]

NOTES ON USE OF MENTAL DISORDER TO NEGATE MENS REA

1. Contemporary trends. Many of the recent decisions hold, in accord with *Bethea* and *Wilcox,* that expert psychiatric evidence is never admissible for purposes of proving that the defendant lacked a required mental state, even when the objective is solely to reduce first-degree to second-degree murder. See, e.g., State v. Provost, 490 N.W.2d 93 (Minn. 1992); Chestnut v. State, 538 So. 2d 820 (Fla. 1989). In contrast, the federal courts and about half the states continue to favor the *Brawner* view that expert psychiatric evidence should be admissible whenever relevant to negate the mens rea of a specific intent crime. See, e.g., United States v. Schneider, 111 F.3d 197 (1st Cir. 1997); People v. Saille, 54 Cal.3d 1103, 820 P.2d 588, 595-596 (1991). For a review of the issues, see United States v. Pohlot, 827 F.2d 889 (3rd Cir. 1987). In a few instances, courts or legislatures have gone even further than *Brawner* and have held such evidence admissible to negate the mens rea of *any* crime, e.g., Hendershott v. People, 653 P.2d 385 (Colo. 1985); N.J. Stat. Ann. §2C:4-2. The Model Penal Code adopts this last approach. See §4.02. See Model Penal Code and Commentaries, Comment to §4.02 at 219 (1985):

> If states of mind are accorded legal significance, psychiatric evidence should be admissible when relevant to prove or disprove their existence to the same extent as any other relevant evidence. It is true that when a claim is successfully made that the defendant did not have the state of mind necessary for an offense, there is no provision for automatic commitment, as there is under Section 4.08 for those who successfully claim the defense of irresponsibility of Section 4.01. But procedures for civil commitment remain available, and often the defendant who lacks the state of mind for a more serious offense will still be guilty of a lesser offense based on recklessness or negligence.

2. Problem. Defendant barricaded himself in his home. His wife called the police and when they arrived, he fired several shots at them before eventually surrendering. At his trial for attempted murder of the officers, he offered the testimony of a psychiatrist to support his claim that he had been suffering from severe depression, that he wanted to commit suicide but lacked the strength to do so, and that he had shot at the police not to harm them but solely to goad them into returning his fire and killing him. Applying Minnesota cases that hold, in accord with *Wilcox,* that expert evidence is inadmissible for purposes of negating specific intent, the court ruled the psychiatrist's testimony inadmissible. State v. Brink, 500 N.W.2d 799 (Minn. App. 1993). Is the result sound?

3. Mitigation versus exoneration. In McCarthy v. State, 372 A.2d 180, 183 (Del. 1977), the Delaware Supreme Court held that an instruction on diminished capacity was not appropriate in a prosecution for kidnapping and attempted rape. The court stated:

> This specific intent — general intent dichotomy explains not only the application of the [diminished capacity] doctrine in the first degree murder cases wherein the specific intent element of premeditation and deliberation are negated, . . . but also the seemingly more liberal application of the doctrine in such cases as assault and battery with intent to kill; first degree forgery, requiring specific intent to defraud; . . . and entering a building with intent to commit theft. In each of these instances, the requisite specific intent constituted an aggravating factor to an otherwise general mens rea offense and the doctrine was applied to permit a finding of the lesser offense.
>
> As the above cases illustrate, acceptance of the doctrine requires that there be some lesser-included offense which lacks the requisite specific intent of the greater offense charged. Otherwise, the doctrine of diminished responsibility becomes an impermissible substitute test of criminal responsibility. . . .
>
> In the instant case, there are no such lesser-included offenses within those for which the defendant was charged and tried. The acceptance of the doctrine in this case, therefore, would be inconsistent with the theory's basic purpose.

Compare People v. Wetmore, 22 Cal. 3d 318, 583 P.2d 1308, 1315 (1978):

> [I]f a crime requires specific intent, a defendant who, because of mental disease or defect lacks that intent, cannot commit that crime. The presence or absence of a lesser included offense within the charged crime cannot affect the result. [W]e do not perceive how a defendant who has in his possession evidence which rebuts an element of the crime can logically be denied the right to present that evidence merely because it will result in his acquittal.

The court in *Wetmore* recognized the practical danger of the defense so interpreted — namely, that mentally disordered persons acquitted on a diminished-capacity defense would be set free, since only persons acquitted on a legal insanity defense are subject to the state's confinement and treatment provisions. It responded (id. at 1315):

> The solution to this problem . . . does not lie in barring the defense of diminished capacity when the charged crime lacks a lesser included offense, but in providing [legislation] for the confinement and treatment of defendants with diminished capacity arising from mental disease or defect.

4. The nature of the evidence. Some jurisdictions have attempted to limit the kinds of mental impairment evidence that can be admitted for purposes other than the insanity defense. Consider the following provisions of the California Penal Code:

> 28. (a) Evidence of mental disease, mental defect, or mental disorder shall not be admitted to show or negate the capacity to form any mental state, including, but not limited to, purpose, intent, knowledge, premeditation, deliberation, or malice aforethought, with which the accused committed the act. Evidence of mental disease, mental defect, or mental disorder is admissible solely on the issue of whether

or not the accused actually formed a required specific intent, premeditated, deliberated, or harbored malice aforethought, when a specific intent crime is charged.

(b) As a matter of public policy there shall be no defense of diminished capacity, diminished responsibility, or irresistible impulse in a criminal action. . . .

29. In the guilt phase of a criminal action, any expert testifying about a defendant's mental illness, mental disorder, or mental defect shall not testify as to whether the defendant had or did not have the required mental states, which include, but are not limited to, purpose, intent, knowledge, or malice aforethought, for the crimes charged. The question as to whether the defendant had or did not have the required mental states shall be decided by the trier of fact.

Note that the California statute "abolishes" the diminished capacity defense, but only in the sense that evidence of mental disorder cannot be introduced to negate a defendant's "capacity" to form a required mental state; such evidence is still admissible on the question whether the accused actually formed the required mental state. See People v. Saille, 54 Cal. 3d 1103, 820 P.2d 588, 595-596 (1991); Miguel A. Mendez, Diminished Capacity in California: Premature Reports of Its Demise, 3 Stan. L. & Pol. Rev. 216 (1991). But what, precisely, is the distinction between *capacity* to form the mens rea and *actually* forming the mens rea? Consider Stephen J. Morse, Undiminished Confusion in Diminished Capacity, 75 J. Crim. L. & Criminology 1, 42-43 (1984):

[One] cause of trouble with expert testimony . . . is the conceptualization of the issue in terms of the defendant's *capacity* to form a mens rea, rather than whether he formed it *in fact*. In California, this distinction is colloquially referred to as the difference between "capacity" and "actuality" evidence. On the face of it, the capacity conceptualization appears to make sense. Although the law requires proof of whether a defendant formed a mens rea in fact, if he lacked the capacity to form it, he could not have formed it in fact. . . .

[But] mental disorder . . . seldom negates the capacity to form [mens rea]. A mens rea is a relatively simple mental state; it requires little cognitive capacity to intend to do something or to know legally relevant facts, such as that the car one is driving across the border contains contraband in a hidden compartment. A mentally abnormal person may not form a requisite intent or have the required knowledge, but it will rarely be because he lacked the capacity to form the mens rea. For example, suppose a mentally disordered person abroad in the streets becomes disorganized and lost in a deserted part of town on a cold evening. Lacking the resources to find his way to proper shelter, he breaks into a building to get out of the cold. Caught by the police while doing so, he is charged with burglary on the theory that he intended to steal. Our poor defendant is innocent of burglary because he lacks the mens rea for theft — he only wanted to stay warm, not to steal — but he does not lack mens rea because he did not have the capacity to form it. He was perfectly capable of intending to steal; it is simply the case, however, that he did not intend to do so on this occasion. The defendant's mental disorder is relevant to proving that he lacked mens rea, for it is the reason he became disorganized, got lost, and needed to get warm, but his mental disorder did not affect his capacity to form the mens rea.

5. Problem. In United States v. Busic, 592 F.2d 13 (2d Cir. 1978), the defendant was convicted of aircraft piracy, defined in 49 U.S.C. §1472(i) to mean "any seizure or exercise of control, by force or violence or threat of force or violence, or by any other form of intimidation, and with wrongful intent, of an aircraft within the special aircraft jurisdiction of the United States."

On appeal, the defendant contended that the trial court had improperly excluded psychiatric testimony offered to show that he was incapable of forming the requisite intent to commit the offense. His counsel had offered the testimony of Dr. Bernard L. Diamond, who was prepared to testify as follows (id. at 21):

> Zvanko Busic was in an abnormal mental state on September 10, 1976 when he is alleged to have committed air piracy, homicide, and other criminal acts. . . . It is also my opinion that this abnormal mental state was of such a quality and degree that it prevented the defendant from exercising the ordinary, reasonable and rational powers of free will, choice and decision that constitute the intent required by the definitions of the crimes of which he is charged. Hence, I conclude that Zvanko Busic lacked the capacity for such criminal intent.
>
> I am of the opinion that this abnormal mental state was not caused by mental disease, illness or defect. I do not find the defendant insane or mentally ill in any sense of those terms. . . .
>
> He did what he did out of psychological necessity, not free choice.

The court upheld the exclusion of the testimony on the ground that the availability of such a defense as defendant tendered (id. at 21)

> turns upon whether the offense in question, like deliberated and premeditated murder, requires a specific intent that cannot be satisfied merely by showing that defendant failed to conform to an objective standard. The offense of aircraft piracy, however, requires a showing of general criminal intent, not a showing of specific criminal intent.

Questions: Is the court's reason convincing? Suppose that Dr. Diamond was prepared to testify that the defendant's abnormal mental state prevented him from intending to seize the aircraft because he was under a delusion that the aircraft was his own car. Would the psychiatric testimony still be inadmissible? In *Busic* itself, is the difficulty with the defendant's position the fact that the crime charged was a general-intent rather than a specific-intent crime, or does the difficulty lie in the relevance of the proffered testimony? Would Dr. Diamond's testimony be admissible in jurisdictions that permit the use of diminished capacity evidence in prosecutions for both general-intent and specific-intent crimes? Does the mens rea of aircraft piracy require Dr. Diamond's conception of free will, or just an intent to seize an aircraft?

NOTE ON DIMINISHED RESPONSIBILITY AS GROUNDS FOR MITIGATION

The diminished capacity doctrine at issue in cases like *Brawner* and *Wilcox* involves the use of evidence of mental disorder to negate a required mens rea. That doctrine therefore must be distinguished from what has sometimes been called "diminished responsibility" or "partial responsibility." According to the latter doctrine, the fact that the defendant was mentally disturbed has the effect of entitling him to a reduction in the severity of the sentence, even though the prosecution has proved all the legal elements technically required for conviction. Such a doctrine has been recognized by some European countries. For example, the German Criminal Code provides in §21 that if a defendant's capacity to appreciate the wrongfulness of his or her act or to act in accordance with such understanding was severely impaired at the time of the act as a result of mental illness or serious mental abnormality, the defendant is subject to a lesser punishment. In the United Kingdom, a partial-responsibility doctrine has been adopted, applicable solely to murder. The English Homicide Act, 1957, 5 & 6 Eliz. II, ch. II, §2(1) provides:

> Where a person kills or is a party to the killing of another, he shall not be convicted of murder if he was suffering from such abnormality of mind (whether arising from a condition of arrested or retarded development of mind or any inherent causes or induced by disease or injury) as substantially impaired the mental responsibility for acts and omissions in doing or being a party to the killing. . . . A person who but for this section would be liable . . . to be convicted of murder shall be liable instead to be convicted of manslaughter.

For a discussion of the English experience, see Suzanne Dell, Diminished Responsibility Reconsidered, [1982] Crim. L. Rev. 809.

Is there a case for adopting such an approach in the United States? Since the American doctrine tends to serve some of the same purposes as the less technical German and English approaches, would it be more straightforward to create an explicit affirmative defense for cases in which mens rea requirements are technically present but mental disorder is sufficient to suggest greatly reduced culpability?

The nearest thing to a comparable doctrine in American law appears in sentencing provisions authorizing courts to use their discretion to impose a lesser sentence in cases of reduced capacity. An example is §5K.2.13 of the Federal Sentencing guidelines, which provides (U.S. Sentencing Guidelines Manual (1997)):

> If the defendant committed a non-violent offense while suffering from significantly reduced mental capacity not resulting from voluntary use of drugs or other intoxicants, a lower sentence may be warranted to reflect the extent to which reduced mental capacity contributed to the commission of the offense, provided that the defendant's criminal history does not indicate the need for incarceration to protect the public.

A recent case interpreting this provision, United States v. Leandre, 132 F.3d 796, 803 (D.C. Cir., 1998), held:

> [T]he departure for "significantly reduced mental capacity" under section 5K2.13 does not require a showing of insanity. Neither does it require a defendant's diminished capacity to have prevented formation of the legally defined mental state associated with an offense. Nor must a defendant demonstrate that he or she is severely mentally retarded. The departure . . . applies to all crimes equally and may be considered by the sentencing judge even if the fact-finder has rejected a defense of insanity or diminished capacity.

Question: If the principle behind §5K.2.13 is sound, why should the possibility of a reduced sentence be limited to cases of *non*-violent crimes?

The Model Penal Code chose to conform to the traditional principle rejecting statutorily authorized reduction of punishment for reduced levels of mental capacity. The Commentary reasons as follows, Model Penal Code and Commentaries, Comment to §210, 3 at 71-72 (1980):

[D]iminished responsibility is entirely subjective in character. It looks into the actor's mind to see whether he should be judged by a lesser standard than that applicable to ordinary men. It recognizes the defendant's own mental disorder or emotional instability as a basis for partially excusing his conduct. This position undoubtedly achieves a closer relation between criminal liability and moral guilt. Moral condemnation must be founded, at least in part, on some perception of the capacities and limitations of the individual actor. To the extent that the abnormal individual is judged as if he were normal, to the extent that the drunk man is judged as if he were sober, to the extent, in short, that the defective person is judged as if he were someone else, the moral judgment underlying criminal conviction is undermined. The doctrine of diminished responsibility resolves this conflict in favor of an individualistic and subjective determination of criminal liability. But this approach has its costs. By evaluating the abnormal individual on his own terms, it decreases the incentives for him to behave as if he were normal. It blurs the law's message that there are certain minimal standards of conduct to which every member of society must conform. By restricting the extreme condemnation of liability for murder to cases where it is fully warranted in a relativistic sense, diminished responsibility undercuts the social purpose of condemnation. And the factors that call for mitigation under this doctrine are the very aspects of an individual's personality that make us most fearful of his future conduct. In short, diminished responsibility brings formal guilt more closely into line with moral blameworthiness, but only at the cost of driving a wedge between dangerousness and social control.[a]

5. *Changing Patterns of Excuse*

ROBINSON v. CALIFORNIA

Supreme Court of the United States
370 U.S. 660 (1962)

JUSTICE STEWART delivered the opinion of the Court.

A California statute makes it a criminal offense for a person to "be addicted to the use of narcotics." This appeal draws into question the constitutionality of that provision of the state law, as construed by the California courts in the present case. . . .

[The prosecution's evidence was principally the testimony of policemen that defendant had scar tissue, discoloration and needle marks which indicated his frequent use of narcotics.]

The judge . . . instructed the jury that the appellant could be convicted under a general verdict if the jury agreed *either* that he was of the "status" *or* had committed the "act" denounced by the statute. "All that the People must show is either that the defendant did use a narcotic in Los Angeles County, or that while in the City of Los Angeles he was addicted to the use of narcotics. . . ."

Under these instructions the jury returned a verdict finding appellant "guilty of the offense charged." . . .

The broad power of a State to regulate the narcotic drugs traffic within its

a. For further discussion of these issues, see Stephen J. Morse, Diminished Capacity, in Stephen Shute, et al., eds., Action and Value in Criminal Law 239-278 (1993); Joshua Dressler, Reaffirming the Moral Legitimacy of the Doctrine of Diminished Capacity: A Brief Reply to Professor Morse, 75 J. Crim. L. & Criminology 953 (1984); Peter Arenella, The Diminished Capacity and Diminished Responsibility Defenses: Two Children of a Doomed Marriage, 77 Colum. L. Rev. 827 (1977). — EDS.

borders is not here in issue. . . . This statute is not one which punishes a person for the use of narcotics, for their purchase, sale or possession, or for antisocial or disorderly behavior resulting from their administration. It is not a law which even purports to provide or require medical treatment. Rather, we deal with a statute which makes the "status" of narcotic addiction a criminal offense, for which the offender may be prosecuted "at any time before he reforms." California has said that a person can be continuously guilty of this offense, whether or not he has ever used or possessed any narcotics within the State, and whether or not he has been guilty of any antisocial behavior there.

It is unlikely that any State at this moment in history would attempt to make it a criminal offense for a person to be mentally ill, or a leper, or to be afflicted with a venereal disease. A State might determine that the general health and welfare require that the victims of these and other human afflictions be dealt with by compulsory treatment, involving quarantine, confinement, or sequestration. But, in the light of contemporary human knowledge, a law which made a criminal offense of such a disease would doubtless be universally thought to be an infliction of cruel and unusual punishment in violation of the Eighth and Fourteenth Amendments.

We cannot but consider the statute before us as of the same category. In this Court counsel for the State recognized that narcotic addiction is an illness. Indeed, it is apparently an illness which may be contracted innocently or involuntarily.[9] We hold that a state law which imprisons a person thus afflicted as a criminal, even though he has never touched any narcotic drug within the State or been guilty of any irregular behavior there, inflicts a cruel and unusual punishment in violation of the Fourteenth Amendment. To be sure, imprisonment for ninety days is not, in the abstract, a punishment which is either cruel or unusual. But the question cannot be considered in the abstract. Even one day in prison would be a cruel and unusual punishment for the "crime" of having a common cold. . . .

Reversed.

JUSTICE DOUGLAS, concurring. . . .

The addict is a sick person. He may, of course, be confined for treatment or for the protection of society. Cruel and unusual punishment results not from confinement, but from convicting the addict of a crime. . . . A prosecution for addiction, with its resulting stigma and irreparable damage to the good name of the accused, cannot be justified as a means of protecting society, where a civil commitment would do as well. . . . We would forget the teachings of the Eighth Amendment if we allowed sickness to be made a crime and permitted sick people to be punished for being sick. The age of enlightenment cannot tolerate such barbarous action.

JUSTICE HARLAN, concurring.

I am not prepared to hold that on the present state of medical knowledge it is completely irrational and hence unconstitutional for a State to conclude that narcotics addiction is something other than an illness, nor that it amounts to cruel and unusual punishment for the State to subject narcotics addicts to its criminal law. . . . But in this case the trial court's instructions permitted the jury to find the appellant guilty on no more proof than that he was present in Cali-

9. Not only may addiction innocently result from the use of medically prescribed narcotics, but a person may even be a narcotics addict from the moment of his birth. . . .

fornia while he was addicted to narcotics. Since addiction alone cannot reasonably be thought to amount to more than a compelling propensity to use narcotics, the effect of this instruction was to authorize criminal punishment for a bare desire to commit a criminal act. . . .

JUSTICE WHITE, dissenting. . . .

The Court clearly does not rest its decision upon the narrow ground that the jury was not expressly instructed not to convict if it believed appellant's use of narcotics was beyond his control. The Court recognizes no degrees of addiction. The Fourteenth Amendment is today held to bar any prosecution for addiction regardless of the degree of frequency of use, and the Court's opinion bristles with indications of further consequences. If it is "cruel and unusual punishment" to convict appellant for addiction, it is difficult to understand why it would be any less offensive to the Fourteenth Amendment to convict him for use on the same evidence of use which proved he was an addict. . . .

The Court has not merely tidied up California's law by removing some irritating vestige of an outmoded approach to the control of narcotics. At the very least, it has effectively removed California's power to deal effectively with the recurring case under the statute where there is ample evidence of use but no evidence of the precise location of use. Beyond this it has cast serious doubt upon the power of any State to forbid the use of narcotics under threat of criminal punishment. I cannot believe that the Court would forbid the application of the criminal laws to the use of narcotics under any circumstances. But the States, as well as the Federal Government, are now on notice. They will have to await a final answer in another case. . . .

POWELL v. TEXAS

Supreme Court of the United States
392 U.S. 514 (1968)

JUSTICE MARSHALL announced the judgment of the Court and delivered an opinion in which THE CHIEF JUSTICE, JUSTICE BLACK, and JUSTICE HARLAN join.

In late December 1966, appellant was arrested and charged with being found in a state of intoxication in a public place, in violation of Texas Penal Code, Art. 477 (1952), which reads as follows: "Whoever shall get drunk or be found in a state of intoxication in any public place, or at any private house except his own, shall be fined not exceeding one hundred dollars." . . .

The trial judge in the county court, sitting without a jury, made certain findings of fact, . . . but ruled as a matter of law that chronic alcoholism was not a defense to the charge. He found appellant guilty, and fined him $50. There being no further right to appeal within the Texas judicial system, appellant appealed to this Court. . . .

The principal testimony was that of Dr. Davis Wade, a Fellow of the American Medical Association, duly certified in psychiatry. . . . Dr. Wade sketched the outlines of the "disease" concept of alcoholism; noted that there is no generally accepted definition of "alcoholism"; alluded to the ongoing debate within the medical profession over whether alcohol is actually physically "addicting" or merely psychologically "habituating"; and concluded that in either case a "chronic alcoholic" is an "involuntary drinker," who is "powerless not to drink," and who "loses his self-control over his drinking." He testified that he had examined appellant, and that appellant is a "chronic alcoholic," who "by the time he has reached [the state of intoxication] is not able to control his behavior, and [who] has reached this point because he has an uncontrollable compulsion to drink." . . . He added that in his opinion jailing appellant without medical attention would operate neither to rehabilitate him or lessen his desire for alcohol.

On cross-examination, Dr. Wade admitted that when appellant was sober he knew the difference between right and wrong, and he responded affirmatively to the question whether appellant's act of taking the first drink in any given instance when he was sober was a "voluntary exercise of his will." Qualifying his answer, Dr. Wade stated that

> these individuals have a compulsion, and this compulsion, while not completely overpowering, is a very strong influence, an exceedingly strong influence, and this compulsion, coupled with the firm belief in their mind that they are going to be able to handle it from now on causes their judgment to be somewhat clouded.

Appellant testified concerning the history of his drinking problem. He reviewed his many arrests for drunkenness; testified that he was unable to stop drinking; stated that when he was intoxicated he had no control over his actions and could not remember them later, but that he did not become violent; and admitted that he did not remember his arrest on the occasion for which he was being tried. On cross-examination, appellant admitted that he had had one drink on the morning of the trial and had been able to discontinue drinking. . . .

Evidence in the case then closed. The State made no effort to obtain expert psychiatric testimony of its own, or even to explore with appellant's witness the question of appellant's power to control the frequency, timing, and location of his drinking bouts, or the substantial disagreement within the medical profession concerning the nature of the disease, the efficacy of treatment and the prerequisites for effective treatment. . . . Instead, the State concerned itself with a brief argument that appellant had no defense to the charge because he "is legally sane and knows the difference between right and wrong."

Following this abbreviated exposition of the problem before it, the trial court indicated its intention to disallow appellant's claimed defense of "chronic alcoholism." Thereupon defense counsel submitted, and the trial court entered, the following "findings of fact":

> (1) That chronic alcoholism is a disease which destroys the afflicted person's will power to resist the constant, excessive consumption of alcohol.
>
> (2) That a chronic alcoholic does not appear in public by his own volition but under a compulsion symptomatic of the disease of chronic alcoholism.
>
> (3) That Leroy Powell, a defendant herein, is a chronic alcoholic who is afflicted with the disease of chronic alcoholism.

Whatever else may be said of them, those are not "findings of fact" in any recognizable, traditional sense in which that term has been used in a court of law; they are the premises of a syllogism transparently designed to bring this case within the scope of this Court's opinion in Robinson v. California, 370 U.S. 660 (1962). Nonetheless, the dissent would have us adopt these "findings" without critical examination; it would use them as the basis for a constitutional holding that "a person may not be punished if the condition essential to constitute the defined crime is part of the pattern of his disease and is occasioned by a compulsion symptomatic of the disease."

The difficulty with that position, as we shall show, is that it goes much too far on the basis of too little knowledge. In the first place, the record in this case is utterly inadequate to permit the sort of informed and responsible adjudication which alone can support the announcement of an important and wide-ranging new constitutional principle. We know very little about the circumstances surrounding the drinking bout which resulted in this conviction, or about Leroy Powell's drinking problem, or indeed about alcoholism itself. . . .

Furthermore, the inescapable fact is that there is no agreement among members of the medical profession about what it means to say that "alcoholism" is a "disease." One of the principal works in this field states that the major difficulty in articulating a "disease concept of alcoholism" is that "alcoholism has too many definitions and disease has practically none." This same author concludes that "*a disease is what the medical profession recognizes as such.*" In other words, there is widespread agreement today that "alcoholism" is a "disease," for the simple reason that the medical profession has concluded that it should attempt to treat those who have drinking problems. There the agreement stops. Debate rages within the medical profession as to whether "alcoholism" is a separate "disease" in any meaningful biochemical, physiological or psychological sense, or whether it represents one peculiar manifestation in some individuals of underlying psychiatric disorders. . . .

The trial court's "finding" that Powell "is afflicted with the disease of chronic alcoholism, which destroys the afflicted person's will power to resist the constant, excessive consumption of alcohol" covers a multitude of sins. Dr. Wade's testimony that appellant suffered from a compulsion which was an "exceedingly strong influence," but which was "not completely overpowering" is at least more carefully stated, if no less mystifying. Jellinek insists that conceptual clarity can only be achieved by distinguishing carefully between "loss of control" once an individual has commenced to drink and "inability to abstain" from drinking in the first place. Presumably a person would have to display both characteristics in order to make out a constitutional defense, should one be recognized. Yet the "findings" of the trial court utterly fail to make this crucial distinction, and there is serious question whether the record can be read to support a finding of either loss of control or inability to abstain.

Dr. Wade did testify that once appellant began drinking he appeared to have no control over the amount of alcohol he finally ingested. Appellant's own testimony concerning his drinking on the day of the trial would certainly appear, however, to cast doubt upon the conclusion that he was without control over his consumption of alcohol when he had sufficiently important reasons to exercise such control. . . . Dr. Wade testified that when appellant was sober, the act of taking the first drink was a "voluntary exercise of his will," but that this exercise of will was undertaken under the "exceedingly strong influence" of a "compulsion" which was "not completely overpowering." Such concepts, when juxtaposed in this fashion, have little meaning. . . .

It is one thing to say that if a man is deprived of alcohol his hands will begin to shake, he will suffer agonizing pains and ultimately he will have hallucinations; it is quite another to say that a man has a "compulsion" to take a drink, but that he also retains a certain amount of "free will" with which to resist. It is simply impossible, in the present state of our knowledge, to ascribe a useful meaning to the latter statement. This definitional confusion reflects, of course, not merely the undeveloped state of the psychiatric art but also the conceptual difficulties inevitably attendant upon the importation of scientific and medical models into a legal system generally predicated upon a different set of assumptions. . . .

Despite the comparatively primitive state of our knowledge on the subject, it cannot be denied that the destructive use of alcoholic beverages is one of our principal social and public health problems. . . .

There is as yet no known generally effective method for treating the vast number of alcoholics in our society. . . . [I]t is entirely possibly that, even were the manpower and facilities available for a full-scale attack upon chronic alcoholism, we would find ourselves unable to help the vast bulk of our "visible"— let alone our "invisible"— alcoholic population. . . . The medical profession cannot, and does not, tell us with any assurance that, even if the buildings, equipment and trained personnel were made available, it could provide anything more than slightly higher-class jails for our indigent habitual inebriates. Thus we run the grave risk that nothing will be accomplished beyond the hanging of a new sign — reading "hospital"— over one wing of the jailhouse.

One virtue of the criminal process is, at least, that the duration of penal incarceration typically has some outside statutory limit; this is universally true in the case of petty offenses, such as public drunkenness, where jail terms are quite short on the whole. "Therapeutic civil commitment" lacks this feature; one is typically committed until one is "cured." Thus, to do otherwise than affirm might subject indigent alcoholics to the risk that they may be locked up for an indefinite period of time under the same conditions as before, with no more hope than before of receiving effective treatment and no prospect of periodic "freedom."

Faced with this unpleasant reality, we are unable to assert that the use of the criminal process as a means of dealing with the public aspects of problem drinking can never be defended as rational. . . .

Appellant claims that his conviction on the facts of this case would violate the Cruel and Unusual Punishment Clause of the Eighth Amendment as applied to the States through the Fourteenth Amendment. [He] seeks to come within the application of the Cruel and Unusual Punishment Clause announced in Robinson v. California, 370 U.S. 660 (1962), which involved a state statute making it a crime to "be addicted to the use of narcotics." . . .

On its face the present case does not fall within that holding, since appellant was convicted, not for being a chronic alcoholic, but for being in public while drunk on a particular occasion. The State of Texas thus has not sought to punish a mere status, as California did in *Robinson;* nor has it attempted to regulate appellant's behavior in the privacy of his own home. Rather, it has imposed upon appellant a criminal sanction for public behavior which may create substantial health and safety hazards, both for appellant and for members of the general public, and which offends the moral and aesthetic sensibilities of a large segment of the community. This seems a far cry from convicting one for being an addict, being a chronic alcoholic, being "mentally ill or a leper. . . ."

Robinson so viewed brings this Court but a very small way into the substantive criminal law. And unless *Robinson* is so viewed it is difficult to see any limiting principle that would serve to prevent this Court from becoming, under the aegis of the Cruel and Unusual Punishment Clause, the ultimate arbiter of the standards of criminal responsibility, in diverse areas of the criminal law, throughout the country.

It is suggested in dissent that *Robinson* stands for the "simple" but "subtle" principle that "[c]riminal penalties may not be inflicted on a person for being in a condition he is powerless to change." . . . In that view, appellant's "condition" of public intoxication was "occasioned by a compulsion symptomatic of the disease" of chronic alcoholism, and thus, apparently, his behavior lacked the critical element of mens rea. Whatever may be the merits of such a doctrine of criminal responsibility, it surely cannot be said to follow from *Robinson*. The entire thrust of *Robinson*'s interpretation of the Cruel and Unusual Punishment Clause is that criminal penalties may be inflicted only if the accused has committed some act, has engaged in some behavior, which society has an interest in preventing, or perhaps in historical common law terms, has committed some actus reus. It thus does not deal with the question of whether certain conduct cannot constitutionally be punished because it is, in some sense, "involuntary" or "occasioned by a compulsion." . . . The only relevance of *Robinson* to this issue is that because the Court interpreted the statute there involved as making a "status" criminal, it was able to suggest that the statute would cover even a situation in which addiction had been acquired involuntarily. 370 U.S., at 667, n. 9. That this factor was not determinative in the case is shown by the fact that there was no indication of how *Robinson* himself had become an addict.

Ultimately, then, the most troubling aspects of this case, were *Robinson* to be extended to meet it, would be the scope and content of what could only be a constitutional doctrine of criminal responsibility. In dissent it is urged that the decision could be limited to conduct which is "a characteristic and involuntary part of the pattern of the disease as it afflicts" the particular individual, and that "it is not foreseeable" that it would be applied "in the case of offenses such as driving a car while intoxicated, assault, theft, or robbery." That is limitation by fiat. . . . If Leroy Powell cannot be convicted of public intoxication, it is difficult to see how a State can convict an individual for murder, if that individual, while exhibiting normal behavior in all other respects, suffers from a "compulsion" to kill, which is an "exceedingly strong influence," but "not completely overpowering." Even if we limit our consideration to chronic alcoholics, it would seem impossible to confine the principle within the arbitrary bounds which the dissent seems to envision. . . .

Traditional common-law concepts of personal accountability and essential considerations of federalism lead us to disagree with appellant. We are unable to conclude, on the state of this record or on the current state of medical knowledge, that chronic alcoholics in general, and Leroy Powell in particular, suffer from such an irresistible compulsion to drink and to get drunk in public that they are utterly unable to control their performance of either or both of these acts and thus cannot be deterred at all from public intoxication. And in any event this Court has never articulated a general constitutional doctrine of mens rea.

We cannot cast aside the centuries-long evolution of the collection of interlocking and overlapping concepts which the common law has utilized to assess the moral accountability of an individual for his antisocial deeds. The doctrines of actus reus, mens rea, insanity, mistake, justification, and duress have historically provided the tools for a constantly shifting adjustment of the tension between the evolving aims of the criminal law and changing religious, moral, philosophical, and medical views of the nature of man. This process of adjustment has always been thought to be the province of the States.

Nothing could be less fruitful than for this Court to be impelled into defining some sort of insanity test in constitutional terms. Yet, that task would seem to follow inexorably from an extension of *Robinson* in this case. If a person in the "condition" of being a chronic alcoholic cannot be criminally punished as a constitutional matter for being drunk in public, it would seem to follow that a person who contends that, in terms of one test, "his unlawful act was the product of mental disease or mental defect," Durham v. United States, 214 F.2d 862, 875 (C.A.D.C. Cir. 1954), would state an issue of constitutional dimension with regard to his criminal responsibility had he been tried under some different and perhaps lesser standard, e.g., the right-wrong test of *M'Naghten*'s Case. . . . But formulating a constitutional rule would reduce, if not eliminate, that fruitful experimentation, and freeze the developing productive dialogue between law and psychiatry into a rigid constitutional mold. It is simply not yet the time to write into the Constitution formulas cast in terms whose meaning, let alone relevance, are not yet clear either to doctors or to lawyers.

Affirmed.

JUSTICE BLACK, whom JUSTICE HARLAN joins, concurring. . . .

I agree with Justice Marshall that the findings of fact in this case are inadequate to justify the sweeping constitutional rule urged upon us. I could not, however, consider any findings that could be made with respect to "voluntariness" or "compulsion" controlling on the question whether a specific instance of human behavior should be immune from punishment as a constitutional matter. When we say that appellant's appearance in public is caused not by "his own" volition but rather by some other force, we are clearly thinking of a force that is nevertheless "his" except in some special sense.[1] The accused undoubtedly commits the proscribed act and the only question is whether the act can be attributed to a part of "his" personality that should not be regarded as criminally responsible. Almost all of the traditional purposes of the criminal law can be significantly served by punishing the person who in fact committed the proscribed act, without regard to whether his action was "compelled" by some elusive "irresponsible" aspect of his personality. [P]unishment of such a defendant can clearly be justified in terms of deterrence, isolation, and treatment. On the other hand, medical decisions concerning the use of a term such as "disease" or "volition," based as they are on the clinical problems of diagnosis and treatment, bear no necessary correspondence to the legal decision whether the overall objectives of the criminal law can be furthered by imposing punishment. For these reasons, much as I think that criminal sanctions should in many situations be applied only to those whose conduct is morally blameworthy, see Morissette v. United States, 342 U.S. 246 (1951), I cannot think the States should be held constitutionally required to make the inquiry as to what part of a defendant's personality is responsible for his actions and to excuse anyone whose action was, in some complex, psychological sense, the result of a "compulsion." . . .

1. If an intoxicated person is actually carried into the street by someone else, "he" does not do the act at all, and of course he is entitled to acquittal. E.g., Martin v. State, 31 Ala. App. 334, 17 So. 2d 427 (1944) [page 173 supra].

The rule of constitutional law urged by appellant is not required by Robinson v. California, 370 U.S. 660 (1962). In that case we held that a person could not be punished for the mere status of being a narcotics addict. We explicitly limited our holding to the situation where no conduct of any kind is involved. . . .

Punishment for a status is particularly obnoxious, and in many instances can reasonably be called cruel and unusual, because it involves punishment for a mere propensity, a desire to commit an offense; the mental element is not simply one part of the crime but may constitute all of it. This is a situation universally sought to be avoided in our criminal law; the fundamental requirement that some action be proved is solidly established even for offenses most heavily based on propensity, such as attempt, conspiracy, and recidivist crimes. . . .

The rule of constitutional law urged upon us by appellant would have a revolutionary impact on the criminal law. . . . If the original boundaries of *Robinson* are to be discarded, any new limits too would soon fall by the wayside and the Court would be forced to hold the States powerless to punish any conduct that could be shown to result from a "compulsion," in the complex, psychological meaning of that term. The result, to choose just one illustration, would be to require recognition of "irresistible impulse" as a complete defense to any crime; this is probably contrary to present law in most American jurisdictions.

The real reach of any such decision, however, would be broader still, for the basic premise underlying the argument is that it is cruel and unusual to punish a person who is not morally blameworthy. I state the proposition in this sympathetic way because I feel there is much to be said for avoiding the use of criminal sanctions in many such situations. See Morissette v. United States [, 342 U.S. 246 (1952), reprinted at page 237 supra.] But the question here is one of constitutional law. The legislatures have always been allowed wide freedom to determine the extent to which moral culpability should be a prerequisite to conviction of a crime. E.g., United States v. Dotterweich, 320 U.S. 277 (1943). The criminal law is a social tool that is employed in seeking a wide variety of goals, and I cannot say the Eighth Amendment's limits on the use of criminal sanctions extend as far as this viewpoint would inevitably carry them. . . .

JUSTICE WHITE, concurring in the result.

If it cannot be a crime to have an irresistible compulsion to use narcotics, Robinson v. California, 370 U.S. 660, I do not see how it can constitutionally be a crime to yield to such a compulsion. Punishing an addict for using drugs convicts for addiction under a different name. Distinguishing between the two crimes is like forbidding criminal conviction for being sick with flu or epilepsy but permitting punishment for running a fever or having a convulsion. Unless *Robinson* is to be abandoned, the use of narcotics by an addict must be beyond the reach of the criminal law. Similarly, the chronic alcoholic with an irresistible urge to consume alcohol should not be punishable for drinking or for being drunk. [But] I cannot say that the chronic who proves his disease and a compulsion to drink is shielded from conviction when he has knowingly failed to take feasible precautions against committing a criminal act, here the act of going to or remaining in a public place. On such facts the alcoholic is like a person with smallpox, who could be convicted for being on the street but not for being ill, or like the epileptic, punishable for driving a car but not for his disease.

JUSTICE FORTAS, with whom JUSTICE DOUGLAS, JUSTICE BRENNAN, and JUSTICE STEWART join, dissenting. . . .

Robinson stands upon a principle which, despite its subtlety, must be simply stated and respectfully applied because it is the foundation of individual liberty and the cornerstone of the relations between a civilized state and its citizens: Criminal penalties may not be inflicted upon a person for being in a condition he is powerless to change. In all probability, Robinson at some time before his conviction elected to take narcotics. But the crime as defined did not punish this conduct. The statute imposed a penalty for the offense of "addiction"— a condition which Robinson could not control. Once Robinson had become an addict, he was utterly powerless to avoid criminal guilt. He was powerless to choose not to violate the law.

In the present case, appellant is charged with a crime comprised of two elements — being intoxicated and being found in a public place while in that condition. The crime, so defined, differs from that in *Robinson.* The statute covers more than a mere status. But the essential constitutional defect here is the same as in *Robinson,* for in both cases the particular defendant was accused of being in a condition which he had no capacity to change or avoid. The trial judge sitting as trier of fact found, upon the medical and other relevant testimony, that Powell is a "chronic alcoholic." He defined appellant's "chronic alcoholism" as "a disease which destroys the afflicted person's will power to resist the constant, excessive consumption of alcohol." He also found that "a chronic alcoholic does not appear in public by his own volition but under a compulsion symptomatic of the disease of chronic alcoholism." I read these findings to mean that appellant was powerless to avoid drinking; that having taken his first drink, he had "an uncontrollable compulsion to drink" to the point of intoxication; and that, once intoxicated, he could not prevent himself from appearing in public places. . . . The findings in this case, read against the background of the medical and sociological data to which I have referred, compel the conclusion that the infliction upon appellant of a criminal penalty for being intoxicated in a public place would be "cruel and inhuman punishment." . . .

I would reverse the judgment below.

STATE EX REL. HARPER v. ZEGEER, 296 S.E.2d 873 (W. Va. 1982): We believe that criminally punishing alcoholics for being publicly intoxicated violates the prohibition against cruel and unusual punishment. W. Va. Const. art. III, §5. In Powell v. Texas, 392 U.S. 514 (1968), five Justices [were] unwilling to extend *Robinson*'s rationale to public intoxication. . . . Since *Powell,* no state court has held that alcoholics could not be punished criminally for public intoxication, except Minnesota.[a]

Most states have adopted the Uniform Alcoholism and Intoxication Treatment Act that deals with alcoholism as a disease. Others stopped short of decriminalization, and instead developed diversionary systems for both alcoholics and public drunks. . . . We urge our Legislature to enact a comprehensive plan for dealing with alcoholics in a humane and beneficial manner.

Criminal punishment of chronic alcoholics violates constitutional prohibitions against cruel and unusual punishment. However, their public presence is

a. State v. Fearon, 283 Minn. 90, 166 N.W.2d 720 (1969). — Eds.

a potential threat to their own and others' well-being, is often offensive, even obnoxious to other people, and the State has a legitimate right to get them off the streets or out of whatever public area in which they may be gamboling.[10] . . .

If the arresting officer has knowledge that the accused has a previous history of arrests for public intoxication, he has a duty to bring these facts to the attention of the judicial officer, or to make application for involuntary hospitalization for examination of an accused who, because of his inebriated state, is likely to harm himself or others if allowed to remain at liberty. . . . Upon a showing that an accused is a chronic alcoholic, he is to be accorded all of the procedural safeguards that surround those with mental disabilities who are accused of crime.

NOTES

1. The medical and scientific premises of the defense position in *Powell* are questioned in Herbert Fingarette, Heavy Drinking (1988). Professor Fingarette characterizes the disease concept of alcoholism as a "myth" that attained ever wider public acceptance just at the time that its empirical foundations were being discredited by researchers. He notes that E. M. Jellinek's early articles and his influential 1960 book, The Disease Concept of Alcoholism, upon which Justice Fortas relied heavily in *Powell,* drew on preliminary data subject to limitations that Jellinek himself acknowledged. The research of the next two-and-a-half decades consistently contradicted Jellinek's hypotheses, and Fingarette states (id. at 3) that today "*no* leading research authorities accept the classic disease concept."

The notion that alcoholics cannot "control" their drinking similarly has gained wide acceptance, and Fingarette observes (id. at 32) that "[a]nyone who has ever observed the behavior of a chronic heavy drinker cannot help feeling a sense of powerful momentum at work." Nonetheless, Fingarette notes (id. at 34), researchers have published "decisive evidence disproving the myth." The studies show that on any particular occasion heavy drinkers, including those labeled chronic alcoholics, may drink heavily, moderately, or not at all, and the choice depends on a wide variety of situational factors including the rewards or penalties the drinker believes likely to follow.

For studies more sympathetic to the view of alcoholism as a disease, see George E. Vaillant, The Natural History of Alcoholism (1983); L. Tiffany & M. Tiffany, Nosologic Objection to the Criminal Defense of Pathological Intoxication: What Do the Doubters Doubt?, 13 Intl. J.L. & Psych. 49 (1990).

For further consideration of these issues, see Herbert Fingarette, The Perils of *Powell:* In Search of a Factual Foundation for the "Disease Concept of Alcoholism," 83 Harv. L. Rev. 793 (1970); Kent Greenawalt, "Uncontrollable" Actions and the Eighth Amendment: Implications of *Powell v. Texas,* 69 Colum. L. Rev. 927 (1969).

10. The State has a right and duty to prosecute people who, while drunk, commit crimes: drunken drivers, for example, and peace breachers, assaulters, and such. This opinion is about people who are charged solely with public intoxication. . . .

UNITED STATES v. MOORE

United States Court of Appeals, District of Columbia Circuit
486 F.2d 1139 (1973)

WILKEY, J. . . . Appellant contends that his conviction [for possession of heroin] was improper because he is a heroin addict with an overpowering need to use heroin and should not, therefore, be held responsible for being in possession of the drug. After careful consideration, we must reject appellant's contention. . . .

[The prosecution conceded that Moore was an addict. The evidence was in conflict as to whether he was a trafficking addict. The trial court refused to permit defendant's expert witnesses to testify on the nature of defendant's heroin addiction, and declined to instruct the jury that a nontrafficking addict could not be convicted under the statutes charged.]

We believe it is clear from the evidence that Moore was not a mere nontrafficking addict but was in fact engaged in the drug trade. Yet even if we were to assume that appellant was a simple addict and nothing more, we believe that his conviction must be sustained. . . .

According to appellant this case has one central issue:

> Is the proffered evidence of Appellant's long and intensive dependence on (addiction to) injected heroin, resulting in substantial impairment of his behavior controls and a loss of self-control over the use of heroin, relevant to his criminal responsibility for unlawful possession . . . ?

In other words, is appellant's addiction a defense to the crimes, involving only possession, with which he is charged? Arguing that he has lost the power of self-control with regard to his addiction, appellant maintains that by applying "the broad principles of common law criminal responsibility" we must decide that he is entitled to dismissal of the indictment or a jury trial on this issue. The gist of appellant's argument here is that "the common law has long held that the capacity to control behavior is a prerequisite for criminal responsibility." . . .

Drug addiction of varying degrees may or may not result in loss of self-control, depending on the strength of character opposed to the drug craving. Under appellant's theory, adopted by the dissenters, only if there is a resulting loss of self-control can there be an absence of *free will* which, under the extension of the common law theory, would provide a valid defense to the addict. If there is a demonstrable absence of free will (loss of self-control), the illegal acts of possession and acquisition cannot be charged to the user of the drugs.

But if it is absence of free will which excuses the mere possessor-acquirer, the more desperate bank robber for drug money has an even more demonstrable lack of free will and derived from precisely the same factors as appellant argues should excuse the mere possessor. . . . [T]he peculiar nature of the problem of the heroin traffic makes certain policies necessary that should not be weakened by the creation of this defense. There is no compelling policy requiring us to intervene here. . . .

Robinson is no authority for the proposition that the Eighth Amendment prevents punishment of an addict for acts he is "compelled" to do by his addiction. . . . *Robinson* simply illustrates repugnance at the prospect of punishing one for his status as an addict. . . .

The Eighth Amendment defense for chronic alcoholics advanced by some members of the Court in Powell v. Texas, that is, the interpretation that *Robinson* held that it was not criminal to give in to the irresistible compulsions of a "disease," weaves in and out of the *Powell* opinions, but there is definitely no Supreme Court holding to this effect. . . .

[Conviction affirmed.]

LEVENTHAL, J., with whom MCGOWAN, J., concurs. . . .

Appellant's presentation rests, in essence, on the premise that the "mental disease or defect" requirement of [the insanity defense] is superfluous. He discerns a broad principle that excuses from criminal responsibility when conduct results from a condition that impairs behavior control. . . . The broad assertion is that in general the mens rea element of criminal responsibility requires freedom of will, which is negatived by an impairment of behavioral control and loss of self-control. . . .

It does not follow that because one condition (mental disease) yields an exculpatory defense if it results in impairment of and lack of behavioral controls the same result follows when some other condition impairs behavior controls. . . . By long tradition of the penal law, an actor's behavior is "involuntary" and there is no criminal responsibility, when he is overwhelmed by force, as when his arm is physically moved by someone else. By long tradition, too, the criminal law reaches only acts that are not only voluntary but also accompanied by a mental element, a "mens rea" (Law latin for guilty mind). . . . The elements that our basic jurisprudence requires for criminal responsibility — a voluntary act, and a mental state — are plainly fulfilled by an offense of knowing possession of a prohibited article.

The legal conception of criminal capacity cannot be limited to those of unusual endowment or even average powers. A few may be recognized as so far from normal as to be entirely beyond the reach of criminal justice, but in general the criminal law is a means of social control that must be potentially capable of reaching the vast bulk of the population. Criminal responsibility is a concept that not only extends to the bulk of those below the median line of responsibility, but specifically extends to those who have a realistic problem of substantial impairment and lack of capacity due, say, to weakness of intellect that establishes susceptibility to suggestion; or to a loss of control of the mind as a result of passion, whether the passion is of an amorous nature or the result of hate, prejudice or vengeance; or to a depravity that blocks out conscience as an influence on conduct.

The criminal law cannot "vary legal norms with the individual's capacity to meet the standards they prescribe, absent a disability that is both gross and verifiable, such as the mental disease or defect that may establish irresponsibility. The most that it is feasible to do with lesser disabilities is to accord them proper weight in sentencing."[65]

Only in limited areas have the courts recognized a defense to criminal responsibility, on the basis that a described condition establishes a psychic incapacity negativing free will in the broader sense. These are areas where the courts

65. ALI Model Penal Code §2.09, Comment (Tent. Draft No. 10, 1960), at 6.

have been able to respond to a deep call on elemental justice, and to discern a demarcation of doctrine that keeps the defense within verifiable bounds that do not tear the fabric of the criminal law as an instrument of social control. . . .

Our analysis has revealed that there is no broad common law principle of exculpation on ground of lack of control, but rather a series of particular defenses staked out in manageable areas, with the call for justice to the individual confined to ascertainable and verifiable conditions, and limited by the interest of society in control of conduct. . . .

WRIGHT, J., dissenting: . . . I suggest that the development of the common law of mens rea has reached the point where it should embrace a new principle: a drug addict who, by reason of his use of drugs, lacks substantial capacity to conform his conduct to the requirements of the law may not be held criminally responsible for mere possession of drugs for his own use. . . .

The concept of criminal responsibility is, by its very nature, "an expression of the moral sense of the community." United States v. Freeman, 2 Cir., 357 F.2d 606, 615 (1966). . . . Thus criminal responsibility is assessed only when through "free will" a man elects to do evil, and if he is not a free agent, or is unable to choose or to act voluntarily, or to avoid the conduct which constitutes the crime, he is outside the postulate of the law of punishment. . . .

Moreover, recognition of a defense of "addiction" for crimes such as possession of narcotics is consistent . . . with the traditional goals of penology — retribution, deterrence, isolation and rehabilitation. . . . Revenge, if it is ever to be legitimate, must be premised on moral blameworthiness, and what segment of our society would feel its need for retribution satisfied when it wreaks vengeance upon those who are diseased because of their disease? It is of course true that there may have been a time in the past before the addict lost control when he made a conscious decision to use drugs. But imposition of punishment on this basis would violate the longstanding rule that "[t]he law looks to the immediate, and not to the remote cause; to the actual state of the party, and not to the causes, which remotely produced it." . . .

The most widely employed argument in favor of punishing addicts for crimes such as possession of narcotics is that such punishment or threat of punishment has a substantial deterrent effect. Given our present knowledge, however, the merits of this argument appear doubtful. Deterrence presupposes rationality — it proceeds on the assumption that the detriments which would inure to the prospective criminal upon apprehension can be made so severe that he will be dissuaded from undertaking the criminal act. In the case of the narcotic addict, however, the normal sense of reason, which is so essential to effective functioning of deterrence, is overcome by the psychological and physiological compulsions of the disease. As a result, it is widely agreed that the threat of even harsh prison sentences cannot deter the addict from using and possessing the drug.

A similar situation prevails insofar as deterrence of *potential* addicts is concerned. [N]othing in this opinion would in any way affect the criminal responsibility of non-addict users for crimes they may commit — including illegal possession of narcotics. . . .

Shifting our focus now to the goal of isolating the offender, we arrive here at not only a justifiable basis for action but one which, in some cases at least, may be vital to the interests of society. . . . This does not mean, however, that the goal of isolation justifies infliction of criminal punishment upon the addict. On the contrary, this interest may be fully vindicated through a program of civil commitment with treatment as well as by criminal incarceration. . . .

This, then, brings us to the final and most important goal of modern penology — to rehabilitate the offender. In this age of enlightened correctional philosophy, we now recognize that society has a responsibility to both the individual and the community to treat the offender so that upon his release he may function as a productive, law-abiding citizen. . . .

Perhaps the most troublesome question arising out of recognition of the addiction defense I suggest is whether it should be limited only to those acts — such as mere possession for use — which are inherent in the disease itself. It can hardly be doubted that, in at least some instances, an addict may in fact be "compelled" to engage in other types of criminal activity in order to obtain sufficient funds to purchase his necessary supply of narcotics. . . . Nevertheless, I am convinced that Congress has manifested a clear intent to preclude common law extension of the defense beyond those crimes which, like the act of possession, cause direct harm only to the addict himself. . . .

The basic question of criminal responsibility under the addiction defense is a legal, and not a purely medical, determination. . . . The essential inquiry, then, is simply whether, at the time of the offense, the defendant, as a result of his repeated use of narcotics, lacked substantial capacity to conform his conduct to the requirements of the law.

BAZELON, C.J. (concurring in part and dissenting in part): . . . On the issue of guilt or innocence, Judge Wright's views are closest to my own. I cannot, however, accept his view that the addiction/responsibility defense should be limited to the offense of possession. I would also permit a jury to consider addiction as a defense to a charge of, for example, armed robbery or trafficking in drugs, to determine whether the defendant was under such duress or compulsion, because of his addiction, that he was unable to conform his conduct to the requirements of the law. . . .

MEIR DAN-COHEN, ACTUS REUS, in Encyclopedia of Criminal Justice 15, 18-19 (1983): For punishment to serve as an effective deterrent, the law must preserve a sufficiently wide range of cases where punishment can be imposed. The law, therefore, can and does recognize involuntariness only when the defendant's determinist account of the criminal event is both of a rare kind and is generally perceived to be clearly convincing. By insisting on these two conditions, the law affirms its commitment to fairness (or justice) without significantly diminishing its effectiveness.

From this perspective, the compromise struck by the law is extremely precarious. There is no escaping the recognition that the requirement of voluntariness is locked in a deadly, and possibly losing, battle with determinism. Scientific (psychological, biological, or medical) explanations, it is argued, almost invariably increase the deterministic element in our view of human conduct. An epileptic seizure supports a claim of involuntariness because the acts in question are accounted for by a determinist medical theory. The more such accounts we possess, the greater the encroachment on the presupposition of voluntariness that underlies the criminal law. Any recognition of a case of involuntariness is bound to take us down a slippery slope, at the end of which we would have nullified the entire criminal law. On the other hand, a refusal to go down the slope, or any attempt to stop somewhere along the way, is bound to be arbitrary and unfair. . . .

NOTES

1. For a close analysis of the opinions in the *Moore* case, see Richard Boldt, The Construction of Responsibility in the Criminal Law, 140 U. Pa. L. Rev. 2245 (1992), especially 2285-2294. The author observes:

> In the nearly two decades since *Moore,* other state courts have considered the question referred to them in general terms by Justice Marshall in the *Powell* case. With few significant exceptions, they have declined to recognize any version of the involuntariness or lack-of-choice defense pressed by alcoholic or drug-addicted defendants. The relative paucity of cases in which defendants have pressed a loss-of-control defense, together with the near universal hostility accorded such arguments by the few courts to reach the issue, is significant evidence that a judicially created involition doctrine is unlikely to emerge in the foreseeable future.

A review of the cases is contained in Phillip Hassman, Annot., Drug Addiction or Related Mental State as Defense to Criminal Charge, 73 A.L.R.3d 16 (1991). For commentary on these issues, see Herbert Fingarette, Addiction and Criminal Responsibility, 843 Yale L. J. 413 (1975).

2. Earlier we considered proposals to eliminate the defense of legal insanity, supra page 902 as well as to enlarge the defense by expansive interpretations of the requirement of a "mental disease" to include such conditions as the battered woman's syndrome, compulsive gambling disorder, and others, supra page 912. Those proposals should be reconsidered at this point as further manifestations of changes in thought about the proper contours of legal responsibility. Assessments of these proposals include Alan Dershowitz, The Abuse Excuse (1994); Stephen Morse, The New Syndrome Excuse Syndrome, Criminal Justice Ethics, Winter/Spring 1995 at p. 3; Joshua Dressler, Reflections on Excusing Wrongdoers: Moral Theory, New Excuses and the Model Penal Code, 19 Rutgers L. J. 671 (1988).

NOTE ON ENVIRONMENTAL DEPRIVATION

RICHARD DELGADO, "ROTTEN SOCIAL BACKGROUND": SHOULD THE CRIMINAL LAW RECOGNIZE A DEFENSE OF SEVERE ENVIRONMENTAL DEPRIVATION? 3 Law & Inequality 9, 20-23 (1985): Judge Bazelon first raised the possibility that extreme poverty might give rise to an RSB [Rotten Social Background] defense in United States v. Alexander.[73] . . . In *Alexander,* one of the defendants shot and killed a marine in a tavern after the marine called him a "black bastard." The defense attempted to show that the youth's action stemmed

73. 471 F.2d 923 957-965 (D.C. Cir. 1973).

from an irresistible impulse to shoot, which they, in turn, traced to an emotionally and economically deprived childhood in Watts, California. The defendant reported that when he was young, his father deserted the family and the boy grew up with little money or attention. He was subjected to racist treatment and learned to fear and hate white persons.

A psychiatrist testified that the defendant suffered from impaired behavior controls rooted in his "rotten social background." The psychiatrist refused to label the defendant insane, however. The trial judge instructed the jury to disregard the testimony about the defendant's deprived background and to consider only whether or not his mental condition met the legal standard of insanity. The jury found him sane and the defendant was sentenced to twenty years to life.

The court of appeals affirmed. In a lengthy, troubled opinion that concurred in part and dissented in part, Judge Bazelon laid out his early thoughts on the RSB defense. For Bazelon, the trial judge erred in instructing the jury to disregard the testimony about defendant's social and economic background. That testimony might well have persuaded the jury that the defendant's behavioral controls were so impaired as to require acquittal, even though that impairment might not render him clinically insane. Apart from this, exposure to the testimony would benefit society. As a result of learning about the wretched conditions in which some of its members live, society would presumably decide to do something about them.

Nevertheless, Bazelon was not prepared to abandon all the trappings of the "disease" model. Among other things, that model provides a rationale for detaining dangerous persons following acquittal. Bazelon reviewed other possible dispositions for the RSB defendant — outright release, preventive detention, and psychological reprogramming — finding each unacceptable. According to Bazelon, the ultimate solution to the problem of violent crime in our society is some form of income redistribution coupled with other social reform measures. The current narrow insanity test conceals the need for such reform and thus should be broadened, although disposition of offenders not "sick" in any classic sense remained a problem for Bazelon. Judge Bazelon further developed his views on an RSB defense in his Hoover lecture[87] and in a reply article.[88] . . .

In a response to Judge Bazelon[95] and a short rejoinder,[96] Professor Stephen Morse argued against Judge Bazelon's position. For Morse, all environments affect choice, making some choices easy and others hard. Rarely, however, will environmental adversity completely eliminate a person's power of choice. Poor persons are free to choose or not choose to commit crimes, and the criminal law may justifiably punish them when they give in to temptation and break the law. Although he conceded a statistical correlation between poverty and crime, Morse denied that poverty causes crime. He pointed out that some poor persons are law-abiding, while some wealthy persons break the law, and that economic

87. David Bazelon, The Morality of the Criminal Law, 49 S. Cal. L. Rev. 385 (1976).
88. David Bazelon, The Morality of the Criminal Law: A Rejoinder to Professor Morse, 49 S. Cal. L. Rev. 1269 (1976).
95. Stephen Morse, The Twilight of Welfare Criminology: A Reply to Judge Bazelon, 49 S. Cal. L. Rev. 1247 (1976).
96. Stephen Morse, The Twilight of Welfare Criminology: A Reply to Judge Bazelon, 49 S. Cal. L. Rev. 1275 (1976).

improvements often result in more, not less, crime. Moreover, Bazelon's social-welfare suggestions would be impractical because there is not enough money to eradicate all poverty; giving money to the poor would entail higher taxation, thus endangering such goals as free accumulation and disposition of wealth; and though eradicating poverty may eliminate some crime, it is a wasteful way to do it. Consequently, Bazelon's broadened inquiry into culpability could exonerate dangerous criminals without generating socially useful knowledge or experience. Indeed, Bazelon's defense skirts paternalism. When an individual has freely broken the law, respect for that individual's personhood *demands* punishment; any other treatment demeans the defendant, and treats him or her as something less than an autonomous individual.

The Bazelon-Morse debate thus raises, but does not answer, a number of key questions concerning a "rotten social background" defense. Does economic and cultural disadvantage impair controls or otherwise cause crime, and if so, how? If severe impairment can be shown in a particular case, what effect should this have on criminal responsibility? What should be done with the successful RSB defendant?

[Professor Delgado argues for an affirmative answer to the question his title asks. The case has also been made by George Wright, The Progressive Logic of Criminal Responsibility and the Circumstances of the Most Deprived, 43 Cath. U.L. Rev. 459 (1994). Professor Wright argues that in failing to make allowances for the dire economic and social circumstances of the most deprived elements of the population, the criminal law is departing from its professed principle that only the morally responsible may be punished for their acts. On whether it is just to blame and punish an individual who commits criminal acts because his genes or his upbringing, or both, were the cause of his bad character, see generally Sanford H. Kadish, Blame and Punishment 102-103 (1987); Peter Arenella, Convicting the Morally Blameless: Reassessing the Relationship Between Legal and Moral Accountability, 39 U.C.L.A. L. Rev. 1511 (1992); Samuel H. Pillsbury, The Meaning of Deserved Punishment: An Essay on Choice, Character, and Responsibility, 67 Ind. L. J. 719 (1992); Stephen J. Morse, Culpability and Control, 142 U. Pa. L. Rev. 1587, 1652 (1994).]

H. L. A. HART, PUNISHMENT AND RESPONSIBILITY 31-33 (1968): [N]o legal system in practice admits without qualification the principle that *all* criminal responsibility is excluded by *any* of the excusing conditions. . . . This is so for a variety of reasons.

For one thing, it is clear that not only lawyers but scientists and plain men differ as to the relevance of some excusing conditions, and this lack of agreement is usually expressed as a difference of view regarding what kind of factor limits the human *capacity* to control behaviour. Views so expressed have indeed changed with the advance of knowledge about the human mind. Perhaps most people are now persuaded that it is possible for a man to have volitional control of his muscles and also to know the physical character of his movements and their consequences for himself and others, and yet be *unable* to resist the urge or temptation to perform a certain act; yet many think this incapacity exists only if it is associated with well-marked physiological or neurological symptoms or independently definable psychological disturbances. . . .

Another reason limiting the scope of the excusing conditions is difficulty of *proof.* Some of the mental elements involved are much easier to prove than others. It is relatively simple to show that an agent lacked, either generally or on a particular occasion, volitional muscular control; it is somewhat more difficult to show that he did not know certain facts . . . ; it is much more difficult to establish whether or not a person was deprived of "self-control" by passion provoked by others, or by partial mental disease. As we consider these different cases not only do we reach much vaguer concepts, but we become progressively more dependent on the agent's own statements about himself, buttressed by inferences from "common-sense" generalizations about human nature, such as that men are capable of self-control when confronted with an open till but not when confronted with a wife in adultery. The law is accordingly much more cautious in admitting "defects of the will" than "defect in knowledge" as qualifying or excluding criminal responsibility.

CLARENCE THOMAS, CRIME AND PUNISHMENT — AND PERSONAL RESPONSIBILITY, The Natl. Times, Sept. 1994, at 31: We can see . . . how the intellectual currents of the legal revolution in individual rights affected the management of community institutions such as schools and the civility of our streets, parks and other common spaces. But how did the ideas underlying this revolution affect the functioning of the criminal justice system?

Many began questioning whether the poor and minorities could be blamed for the crimes they committed. Our legal institutions and popular culture began identifying those accused of wrongdoing as victims of upbringing and circumstances. The point was made that human actions and choices, like events in the natural world, are often caused by factors outside of one's control. No longer was an individual identified as the cause of a harmful act. Rather, societal conditions or the actions of institutions and others in society became the responsible causes of harm. These external causes might be poverty, poor education, a faltering family structure, systemic racism or other forms of bigotry, and spousal or child abuse, just to name a few. The consequence of this new way of thinking about accountability and responsibility — or lack thereof — was that a large part of our society could escape being held accountable for the consequences of harmful conduct. The law punishes only those who are responsible for their actions: and in a world of countless uncontrollable causes of aggression or lawlessness, few will have to account for their behavior.

As a further extension of these ideas, some began challenging society's moral authority to hold many of our less fortunate citizens responsible for their harmful acts. Punishment is an expression of society's disapproval or reprobation. In other words, punishment is a way of directing society's moral indignation toward persons responsible for violating its rules. Critics insisted, though, that an individual's harmful conduct is not the only relevant factor in determining whether punishment is morally justified. The individual's conduct must be judged in relation to how society has acted toward that individual in the past. In this regard, many began appearing hesitant to hold responsible those individuals whose conduct might be explained as a response to societal injustice. How can we hold the poor responsible for their actions, some asked, when our society does little to remedy the social conditions of the ill-educated and unemployed in our urban areas? In a similar vein, others questioned how we could tell blacks in our inner cities to face the consequences for breaking the law when the very legal system and society which will judge their conduct perpetuated years of racism and unequal treatment under the law.

Once our legal system accepted the general premise that social conditions and upbringing could be excuses for harmful conduct, the range of cases that might prevent society from holding anyone accountable for his actions became potentially limitless. Do we punish a drunk driver who has a family history of alcoholism? A bigoted employer reared in a segregationist environment, who was taught that blacks are inferior? A thief or drug pusher who was raised in a dysfunctional family and who received a poor education? A violent gang member, rioter or murderer who attributes his rage, aggression and lack of respect for authority to a racist society that has oppressed him since birth? Which of these individuals, if any, should be excused for their conduct? Can we really distinguish among them in a principled way?

An effective criminal justice system — one that holds people accountable for harmful conduct — simply cannot be sustained under conditions where there are boundless excuses for violent behavior and no moral authority for the state to punish. If people know that they are not going to be held accountable because of a myriad of excuses, how will our society be able to influence behavior and provide incentives to follow the law? How can we teach future generations right from wrong if the idea of criminal responsibility is riddled with exceptions and our governing institutions and courts lack the moral self-confidence? A society that does not hold someone accountable for harmful behavior can be viewed as condoning — or even worse, endorsing — such conduct. In the long run, a society that abandons personal responsibility will lose its moral sense. And it is the urban poor whose lives are being destroyed the most by this loss of moral sense.

This is not surprising. A system that does not hold individuals accountable for their harmful acts treats them as less than full citizens. In such a world, people are reduced to the status of children or, even worse, treated as though they are animals without a soul. There may be a hard lesson here: In the fact of injustice on the part of society, it is natural and easy to demand recompense or a dispensation from conventional norms. But all too often, doing so involves the individual accepting diminished responsibility for his future. Does the acceptance of diminished responsibility assure that the human spirit will not rise above the tragedies of one's existence? When we demand something from our oppressors — more lenient standards of conduct, for example — are we merely going from a state of slavery to a more deceptive, but equally destructive, state of dependency?

It also bears noting that contemporary efforts to rehabilitate criminals will never work in a system that often neglects to assign blame to individuals for their harmful acts. How can we encourage criminals not to return to crime if our justice system fosters the idea that it is society that has perpetuated racism and poverty — not the individuals who engaged in harmful conduct — that is to blame for aggression and crime, and thus, in greatest need of rehabilitation and reform.

The transformation of the criminal justice system has had and will continue to have its greatest impact in our urban areas. It is there that modern excuses for criminal behavior abound — poverty, substandard education, faltering families, unemployment, a lack of respect for authority because of deep feelings of oppression.

I have no doubt that the rights revolution had a noble purpose: to stop society from threatening blacks, the poor and others, many of whom today occupy our urban areas — as if they were invisible, not worthy of attention. But the revolution missed a larger point by merely changing their status from invisible to victimized. Minorities and the poor are humans — capable of dignity as well as shame, folly as well as success. [They] should be treated as such.

CHAPTER 9

THEFT OFFENSES

A. THE MEANS OF ACQUISITION

MODEL PENAL CODE AND COMMENTARIES

Comment to §223.1 at 127-132 (1980)

Distinctions among larceny, embezzlement, obtaining by false pretenses, extortion, and the other closely related theft offenses are explicable in terms of a long history of expansion of the role of the criminal law in protecting property. That history begins with a concern for crimes of violence — in the present context, the taking of property by force from the possession of another, i.e., robbery. The criminal law then expanded, by means of the ancient quasi-criminal writ of trespass, to cover all taking of another's property from his possession without his consent, even though no force was used. This misconduct was punished as larceny. The law then expanded once more, through some famous judicial manipulation of the concept of possession, to embrace misappropriation by a person who with the consent of the owner already had physical control over the property, as in the case of servants and even bailees in certain particularly defined situations.

At this point in the chronology of the law of theft, about the end of the 18th century, a combination of circumstances caused the initiative in the further development of the criminal law to pass from the courts to the legislature. . . .

The earliest statutes dealt with embezzlement by such narrowly defined groups as bank clerks. Subsequent laws extended coverage to agents, attorneys, bailees, fiduciaries, public officers, partners, mortgagors in possession, etc., until at last a few American legislatures enacted fraudulent-conversion statutes penalizing misappropriation by anyone who received or had in his possession or control the property of another or property which someone else "is entitled to receive and have." Indeed, some modern embezzlement statutes go so far as to penalize breach of faith without regard to whether anything is misappropriated. Thus, the fiduciary who makes forbidden investments, the official who deposits public funds in an unauthorized depository, the financial advisor who betrays his client into paying more for a property than the market value, may be designated an embezzler. Although this kind of coverage is relatively new for Anglo-American penal law, certain foreign codes have long recognized criminal "breach of trust" as a distinct entity.

The fraud aspects of theft, never regarded with such abhorrence as larceny, begin with the common-law misdemeanor of cheat. This offense required use of false weights or similar "tokens," thus limiting criminal deception to certain special techniques conceived as directed against the public generally. One may suspect that this development was an outgrowth of guild regulation of unfair competition as much as it reflected a desire to protect the buying public. At any rate, the use of false tokens was a technique against which it would be difficult for even a cautious yeoman to guard himself. A mere lie for the purpose of deceiving another in a business transaction did not become criminal until the Statute of 30 Geo. 2, ch. 24 (1757), created the misdemeanor of obtaining property by false pretenses. Even this statute was not at first believed to make mere misrepresentation criminal. Instead, it was thought to require some more elaborate swindling stratagem, such as French law to this day requires. Eventually it was settled in Anglo-American law that false representations of "fact," if "material," would suffice. Today's battleground is over such matters as misrepresentation of "opinion," "law," or "value," as well as "misleading omissions" and "false promises." . . .

If history were the whole explanation of the existence of distinctive theft crimes, there would be little reason to preserve differentiations whose subtleties have occasioned serious procedural difficulties. The problem is not so simple. History has its own logic. The criminal law reached larceny first and embezzlement later because of real distinctions between theft by a stranger and the peculations of a trusted agent. If the move to punish embezzlement was a natural one, it was nevertheless a momentous step when the exceptional liability of servants for stealing from their masters was generalized into fraudulent conversion by anyone who had goods of another in his possession. The ordinary trespass-theft was committed by a stranger, an intruder with no semblance of right even to touch the object taken. The offender was easily recognized by the very taking, surreptitious or forceful, and so set apart from the law-abiding community. No bond of association in joint endeavor linked criminal and victim. In contrast, the embezzler stands always in a lawful as well as in an unlawful relation to the victim and the property. He is respectable; indeed, some tend to identify with him rather than with the bank or insurance company from which he embezzles. The line between lawful and unlawful activity is for the embezzler a question of the scope of his authority, which may be ill-defined. Not every deviation from the authority conferred will be civilly actionable, much less a basis for criminal liability. Sometimes the scope of the authority may be so broad, e.g., as in the case of a revocable inter-vivos trust where the grantor is trustee, as to be hardly distinguishable from ownership. The agent or bailee may actually be part of a co-proprietorship, being entitled to a commission or satisfaction of a lien out of funds in his hands. A man who is psychologically the absolute "owner" may be in the legal position of a bailee with extremely circumscribed freedom to deal with the property, as a result of modern methods of selling consumer goods on credit arrangements involving retention of title by the seller.

The embezzlement problem is complicated further by the necessity of distinguishing between defalcation by one who has "property of another" and failure of a debtor to pay his debts. Modern society is opposed to imprisonment for debt, however committed it may be to punishment for betrayal of trust. Yet when property is entrusted to a dealer for sale, with the expectation that he will receive the proceeds, deduct his commission, and remit the balance, the dealer's criminal liability if he fails to remit may turn on refinements of the civil law of contracts, agency, sales, or trusts. Such refinements, designed to allocate financial risks or to determine priorities among creditors of an insolvent, are hardly a relevant index to the harm done the owner or to the character of the defaulting dealer and thus may be entirely inappropriate as a measure of criminal liability.

It may nevertheless be true that theft by a stranger and a suitably delimited offense of theft by a fiduciary represent similar dangers requiring approximately the same treatment and characterization. . . . To that extent, at least, consolidation conforms to the common understanding of what is substantially the same kind of undesirable conduct. Consolidation also has advantages in the administration of the criminal law if it eliminates procedural problems arising from nice distinctions between closely related types of misbehavior. Differences in the treatment of thieves can be determined on an individual basis by taking into account many factors which are at least as significant as whether fraud or stealth was the means employed to deprive another of his property.

NOTE

Professor George Fletcher has presented a different view of the traditional common law distinctions and technicalities in the law of theft. Fletcher, The Metamorphosis of Larceny, 89 Harv. L. Rev. 469 (1976). His article is worth consulting in connection with the various categories of theft discussed in the following portions of this chapter.

1. *Trespassory Takings*

COMMONWEALTH v. TLUCHAK

Superior Court of Pennsylvania
166 Pa. Super. 16, 70 A.2d 657 (1950)

Reno, J. Appellants, husband and wife, separately appealed from convictions for larceny. The court below overruled their motions for new trials and arrest of judgment. The husband was sentenced to pay a fine of $50 and make restitution. Sentence was suspended in the wife's case.

The case arose out of a real estate transaction. By a written instrument appellants agreed to sell their farm to the prosecutor and his wife. The agreement did not include any personal property but it did cover: "All buildings, plumbing, heating, lighting fixtures, screens, storm sash, shades, blinds, awnings, shrubbery and plants." The purchasers took possession on June 14, 1946, and discovered that certain articles which had been on the premises at the time the agreement of sale was executed were missing. They were a commode which had never been attached and lay on the back porch in its shipping crate, an unattached washstand which had been stored in a bedroom, a hay carriage used in the barn, an electric stove cord extending from the switch box in the cellar to the kitchen, and 30 or 35 peach trees. These articles were charged in the indictment as subjects of the larceny.

The Commonwealth contended that the articles which were not covered by the written contract had been sold by an oral agreement between the parties.

Appellants denied the oral agreement; denied the sale of the personal property; denied taking the trees; admitted they took the hay carriage; and as to all the articles which they took they contended that they were taken under a claim of right and therefore not feloniously. The jury found against them and, although they contend that the evidence is not sufficient in law to sustain a conviction, we shall assume, for the purpose of this decision, that the testimony established a *sale* of the personal property by appellants to the prosecutor and his wife. That is, that appellants sold but failed or refused to deliver the goods to the purchasers. Are sellers who refuse or fail to deliver goods sold to their purchasers guilty of larceny?

. . . Appellants had possession of the goods, not mere custody of them. The evidence indicates that they were allowed to retain possession without trick or artifice and without fraudulent intent to convert them. Presumably title passed upon payment of the purchase price; nevertheless appellants had lawful possession thereafter. "One who is in lawful possession of the goods or money of another cannot commit larceny by feloniously converting them to his own use, for the reason that larceny, being a criminal trespass on the right of possession, . . . cannot be committed by one who, being invested with that right, is consequently incapable of trespassing on it." 52 C.J.S., Larceny, §31; and see §1.

An extensive research failed to uncover a Pennsylvania case in which the rule was applied to a factual situation similar to that at bar. But the principle has been recognized; e.g., in Com. v. Quinn, 144 Pa. Super. 400, 408, 19 A.2d 526, 530, this Court approved instructions to a jury wherein it was said:

> But a person may come into possession of somebody else's property in a legal way and if he, being so in possession of the property in a legal way converts it to his own use or withholds it from the owner so that the owner is deprived of the use thereof which he should have, then, though the defendant could not be guilty of larceny because he received it legally, he may be guilty of fraudulent conversion because after having received it he has deprived the owner of his use of it. . . .

As suggested, appellants may have been guilty of fraudulent conversion, or of larceny by bailee *if* the theory is accepted that a vendor retaining possession of goods sold by him becomes constructively a bailee of the purchaser, and criminally culpable for a failure to deliver them to his purchaser. Appellants were indicted for larceny only, and of that they clearly were not guilty. . . .

Judgments and sentences reversed and appellants discharged without delay.

NOTES

1. *Traditional asportation and its statutory variants.* Larceny, both at common law and under statutory formulations, requires a carrying away (asportation) as well as a trespassory taking. While courts have substantially minimized the significance of this requirement by holding that any movement of the thing, no matter how slight, is sufficient, problems still may arise. Consider State v. Patton, 364 Mo. 1044, 271 S.W.2d 560 (1954). The defendant purported to sell concrete building blocks, not his own, to an innocent purchaser, who himself carried the blocks away. May the defendant be held for larceny? A few courts would answer in the negative because of the absence of an asportation. See, e.g., State v. Laborde, 202 La. 59, 11 So. 2d 404 (1942); Ridgell v. State, 110 Ark. 606, 162 S.W. 773 (1914). The majority, however, as in State v. Patton, supra, turn the trick by finding the purchaser to be the innocent agent of the seller and imputing his acts to defendant. See Annot., 144 A.L.R. 1383 (1942). Can this be analytically defended?

The New York Court of Appeals in People v. Alamo, 34 N.Y.2d 453, 358 N.Y.S.2d 375 (1974), dispensed with the requirement of an actual movement of the object in a case where defendant entered a stranger's car, turned on the lights and started the engine. The court upheld the trial court's instruction that the jury might find theft of the car in these circumstances even if defendant had not moved the vehicle (assuming, of course, they found the requisite intent to steal it). The court read the traditional doctrine requiring an asportation as reflecting a concern that the crucial elements of possession and control were established. Comparing pickpocket cases where some movement of the seized object had been held to be required, the court stated (358 N.Y.S.2d at 379, 381):

> The actions needed to gain possession and control over a wallet, including movement of the wallet which, in itself, is merely an element tending to show possession and control, are not necessarily the actions needed to gain possession and control of an automobile. A wallet, or a diamond ring, or a safe are totally inert objects susceptible of movement only by physical lifting or shoving by the thief. An automobile, however, is itself an instrument of transportation and when activated comes within the total possession and control of the operator. In this situation movement or motion is not essential to control. Absent any evidence that the vehicle is somehow fastened or immovable because of a mechanical defect, the thief has taken command of the object of the larceny. He has, in the words of subdivision 1 of section 155.05 of the Penal Law, wrongfully "taken" the property from its owner surely as much so as had the thief in [the pickpocket case]. . . .

The Model Penal Code eliminates the requirement of an asportation and substitutes the requirement that the defendant "exercise unlawful control" over the movable property. Section 223.2(1). Model Penal Code and Commentaries, Comment to §223.2(1), at 164 (1980) states:

> Since larceny was generally a felony and attempt a misdemeanor, important differences in procedure and punishment turned on the criminologically insignificant fact of slight movement of the object of the theft. Under §5.01 of the Model Code, and in modern criminal law generally, differences in penal consequences between attempt and completed crime are minimized, so that it becomes less important where the line is drawn between them. It is clear, moreover, that similar penalties for the attempt and the completed offense make obsolete any reference to the concept of "asportation"; the same penal consequences follow whether or not an "asportation" has occurred.

Most revised codes follow this lead. Id. at 165.

2. Problems. The defendant removed a price label for £2.73 from a piece of meat in a supermarket and affixed the label to a piece of meat that should have cost £6.91. His act was detected at the checkout counter before he paid for the second piece of meat. Could the defendant be convicted of larceny? This situation was presented in Regina v. Morris, [1983] 3 All E.R. 288 (H.L. 1983). The

English Theft Act of 1968 defines theft as "dishonestly appropriating" another's property (§1(1)); appropriation is defined as, "Any assumption of the rights of an owner" (§3(1)). The House of Lords held that appropriation takes place when the defendant does an act that adversely interferes with or usurps the right of the owner, and that the switching of the price labels was such an appropriation, since it usurped the right of the owner to ensure that the goods were sold and paid for at the greater price. By contrast, removing articles from the shelves, unlike switching labels, would not amount to an appropriation, since a supermarket consents to that much handling of its merchandise. The decision is criticized in J. C. Smith, The Law of Theft, para. 34 (5th ed. 1984); L. H. Leigh, Some Remarks on Appropriation in the Law of Theft after *Morris,* 48 Mod. L. Rev. 167 (1985).

An American counterpart is People v. Olivo, 52 N.Y.2d 309, 420 N.E.2d 40 (1981). The case involved a consolidated appeal from several petit larceny convictions for shoplifting from department stores and a bookstore. In one case the defendant took objects on display and secreted them in his clothing, while furtively looking around. In another case the defendant removed a sensor device from a jacket, put the jacket on, and leaving his own jacket on the table, walked toward the exit. In a third case the defendant furtively concealed a book in his case while appearing to browse. N.Y. Pen. Code §155.05 provides that one commits larceny when "he wrongfully takes" another's property, with the intent to steal. The defendant argued that a customer cannot "wrongfully take" an article in a self-service store so long as he remains in the store. The court disagreed and affirmed all the convictions, holding that these defendants could be held for larceny even though they were apprehended before leaving the store. The court stated (52 N.Y.2d at 317-318):

> [I]n modern self-service stores customers are impliedly invited to examine, try on, and carry about the merchandise on display. Thus in a sense, the owner has consented to the customer's possession of the goods for a limited purpose. That the owner has consented to that possession does not, however, preclude a conviction for larceny. If the customer exercises dominion and control wholly inconsistent with the continued rights of the owner, and the other elements of the crime are present, a larceny has occurred. Such conduct on the part of a customer satisfies the "taking" element of the crime.

Compare People v. Davis, 965 P.2d 1165 (Cal. 1998). The defendant took a shirt off the hanger at a department store, carried it to the service counter, and then told the cashier that he had previously purchased it but wanted to return it because it didn't fit. The cashier gave him a credit voucher, but as he walked away, he was stopped and detained by a security guard who had observed his actions. Is the defendant guilty of larceny?

TOPOLEWSKI v. STATE

Supreme Court of Wisconsin
130 Wis. 244, 109 N.W. 1037 (1906)

[The accused arranged with Dolan, who owed him money and was an employee of the Plankinton Packing Company, to place three barrels of the company's meat on the loading platform, the plan being that accused would load the barrels on his wagon and drive away as if he were a customer. Dolan carried out his end of the plan after informing the company's representatives and receiving their instructions to feign cooperation. Accused took the barrels as planned and was arrested, charged, and convicted of stealing the barrels of meat.]

MARSHALL, J. . . . Did the agreement in legal effect with the accused to place the property of the packing company on the loading platform, where it could be appropriated by the accused, if he was so disposed and was not interfered with in so doing, though his movements in that regard were known to the packing company, and his taking of the property, his efforts to that end being facilitated as suggested, constitute consent to such appropriation?

The case is very near the border line, if not across it, between consent and nonconsent to the taking of the property. [In] Reg. v. Lawrence, 4 Cox C.C. 438, it was held that if the property was delivered by a servant to the defendant by the master's direction the offense cannot be larceny, regardless of the purpose of the defendant. In this case the property was not only placed on the loading platform, as was usual in delivering such goods to customers, with knowledge that the accused would soon arrive, having a formed design to take it, but the packing company's employé in charge of the platform, Ernst Klotz, was instructed that the property was placed there for a man who would call for it. Klotz from such statement had every reason to infer, when the accused arrived and claimed the right to take the property, that he was the one referred to and that it was proper to make delivery to him and he acted accordingly. While he did not physically place the property, or assist in doing so, in the wagon, his standing by, witnessing such placing by the accused, and then assisting him in arranging the wagon, as the evidence shows he did, and taking the order, in the usual way, from the accused as to the disposition of the fourth barrel, and his conduct in respect thereto amounted, practically, to a delivery of the three barrels to the accused.

In Rex v. Egginton, 2 P. & P. 508, we have a very instructive case on the subject under discussion here. A servant informed his master that he had been solicited to aid in robbing the latter's house. By the master's direction the servant opened the house, gave the would-be thieves access thereto and took them to the place where the intended subject of the larceny had been laid in order that they might take it. All this was done with a view to the apprehension of the guilty parties after the accomplishment of their purpose. The servant by direction of the master not only gave access to the house but afforded the would-be thieves every facility for taking the property, and yet the court held that the crime of larceny was complete, because there was no direction to the servant to deliver the property to the intruders or consent to their taking it. [T]he way was made easy for them to do so, but they were neither induced to commit the crime, nor was any act essential to the offense done by any one but themselves.

[W]here the owner of property by himself or his agent, actually or constructively, aids in the commission of the offense, as intended by the wrongdoer, by performing or rendering unnecessary some act in the transaction essential to the offense, the would-be criminal is not guilty of all the elements of the offense. . . .

The logical basis for the doctrine above discussed is that there can be no larceny without a trespass. So if one procures his property to be taken by another intending to commit larceny, or delivers his property to such other, the latter purposing to commit such crime, the element of trespass is wanting and the crime not fully consummated however plain may be the guilty purpose of the one possessing himself of such property. That does not militate against a person's being free to set a trap to catch one whom he suspects of an intention to commit the crime of larceny, but the setting of such trap must not go further than to afford the would-be thief the amplest opportunity to carry out his purpose, formed without such inducement on the part of the owner of the property, as to put him in the position of having consented to the taking. If I induce one to come and take my property and then place it before him to be taken, and he takes it with criminal intent, or if knowing that one intends to take my property I deliver it to him and he takes it with such intent, the essential element of trespass involving nonconsent requisite to a completed offense of larceny does not characterize the transaction, regardless of the fact that the moral turpitude involved is no less than it would be if such essential were present. Some writers in treating this subject give so much attention to condemning the deception practiced to facilitate and encourage the commission of a crime by one supposed to have such a purpose in view, that the condemnation is liable to be viewed as if the deception were sufficient to excuse the would-be criminal, or to preclude his being prosecuted; that there is a question of good morals involved as to both parties to the transaction and that the wrongful participation of the owner of the property renders him and the public incapable of being heard to charge the person he has entrapped with the offense of larceny. That is wrong. It is the removal from the completed transaction, which from the mental attitude of the would-be criminal may have all the ingredients of larceny, from the standpoint of the owner of the property of the element of trespass or nonconsent. When such element does not characterize a transaction involving the full offense of larceny so far as concerns the mental purpose of such would-be criminal is concerned, is often not free from difficulty and courts of review should incline quite strongly to support the decision of the trial judge in respect to the matter and not disturb it except in a clear case. It seems that there is such a case before us.

The judgment is reversed, and the cause remanded for a new trial.

NOTES

1. The police had been troubled by a large number of car thefts in a particular locality. An informer approached a police officer and told him that the defendant, Jarrott, proposed that he join him in the theft and sale of automobiles. The informer was instructed to play along. Later the informer informed the police officer that Jarrott stated he wanted to get a 1925 coupé and indicated the general time and place that Jarrott, with his ostensible help, planned to steal a car. The police officer thereupon arranged for his own coupé to be present at that time and place. He left it with its parking lights on and with the key in the ignition, concealing himself in the back end. This was known to the informer. Jarrott and the informer later appeared. Jarrott saw the car and proposed they steal it. They entered and drove the car to a car lot, the informer doing the driving on Jarrott's protestation that he could not drive. While Jarrott and the buyer were haggling over the price, the policeman climbed out from the car and made his arrest. Defendant appealed a conviction of larceny on the grounds (1) that the car was never taken from the personal possession of the owner and (2) that the taking occurred with the consent of the owner. What should be the result? Jarrott v. State, 108 Tex. Crim. 427, 1 S.W.2d 619 (1927). Could the defendant have also argued that since the informer drove the car it was he who took it and not the defendant because the acts of the informer, as a feigned accomplice, could not be attributed to the defendant? See State v. Hayes, page 633 supra.

Concerning the defense of entrapment by police agents, see Model Penal Code §2.13, Appendix.

2. In United States v. Bryan, 483 F.2d 88 (3d Cir. 1973), the U.S. Lines, on the instruction of the FBI, permitted its agents to deliver a shipment of whiskey to Echols, who was believed to be posing as an agent of the consignee. The court rejected the argument that Echols committed no crime because the U.S. Lines consented to the taking, stating (at 90-92):

> The crime alleged here is violation of 18 U.S.C. §659, which provides penalties for, inter alia, "[w]hoever embezzles, steals, or unlawfully takes, carries away, or conceals . . . from any . . . platform or depot . . . with intent to convert to his own use any goods . . . which constitute an interstate . . . shipment of freight." The crime of stealing under 18 U.S.C. §659 has been given a broad construction, free from the technical requirements of common law larceny. United States v. DeNormand, 149 F.2d 622, 624 (2d Cir. 1945). A trial court instruction that the jury need only find "an unlawful taking of the goods by the defendants," was found sufficient in *DeNormand.* The consent to the removal of the goods by U.S. Lines personnel in this case does not demonstrate the absence of an unlawful taking. In reviewing the record to determine if there was an unlawful taking, the relevant question involves not the state of mind of personnel of U.S. Lines, but rather the state of mind of defendants.
>
> We therefore find no difficulty in reconciling our conclusion that a crime was committed here with the statements in United States v. Cohen, 274 F. 596, 597 (3d Cir. 1921):
>
>> To constitute "stealing" there must be an unlawful taking . . . with intent to convert to the use of the taker and permanently deprive the owner.
>
> and in Vaughn v. United States, 272 F. 451, 452 (9th Cir. 1921), that in a case of larceny, the corpus delicti consists of two elements:
>
>> First, that the property was lost by the owner; and, second, that it was lost by a felonious taking.
>
> Both formulations of the elements of stealing concentrate on the state of mind of the criminal, not upon that of the possessor of the goods taken. In cases where the lawful possessor indicated to the taker that permission was granted for the taking, a finding of commission of a crime would be unlikely. That, however, is not the case sub judice. There is no proof that U.S. Lines led defendants to believe they had permission to take the goods.

3. In the *Topolewski* case, would it have been possible to convict the defendant of an attempt to commit larceny? See Regina v. Miller and Page, 49 Crim. App. 241 (1965), holding affirmatively. See The Case of Lady Eldon's French Lace, page 594 supra.

4. See George Fletcher, The Metamorphosis of Larceny, 89 Harv. L. Rev. 469, 491-498 (1976), for an interpretation of the *Topolewski* case as a modern survival of the common law commitment to the requirement of "manifest criminality" ("acting like a thief"). The problem in *Topolewski* is also illuminatingly discussed in Glanville Williams, Theft, Consent and Illegality: Some Problems, [1977] Crim. L. Rev. 327, 330 et seq.

NOTE ON ROBBERY AND EXTORTION

Note, A Rationale of the Law of Aggravated Theft, 54 Colum. L. Rev. 84-86 (1954): Obviously, larceny may be perpetrated in many ways: a pocket may be picked or a man may be killed to obtain a bankroll. In the former situation, the sole evil is the misappropriation of property; in the latter, bodily injury also results. Consequently, to protect not only against misappropriation but also against injuries which may result from peculiarly dangerous means devised for accomplishing misappropriation, there developed the law of aggravated theft. At common law the only substantive crime embodied within this law was robbery, a larceny accomplished by violence or threat of immediate violence to the person of the victim. In time it was acknowledged that men may be intimidated by threats other than those foreboding bodily harm. As a result, modern legislation has extended the substantive content of aggravated theft, complementing robbery with the crime of extortion. . . .

Entirely a creature of legislative enactment, extortion now exists as a substantive crime in forty-seven states, and in each there is also a robbery statute. The first inquiry, then, concerns the manner in which these crimes differ. The statutory definitions of robbery restate in essence the common law definition: the felonious and forcible taking of property from the person of another or in his presence, against his will, by violence or putting in fear. Extortion statutes are generally of two types. The majority of jurisdictions treat as the substantive crime of extortion the making of certain specified threats for the purpose of obtaining property, but a substantial number require an actual misappropriation with the owner's consent. The differences between the robbery and extortion statutes, therefore, depend to a certain extent on the particular jurisdiction. In jurisdictions following either extortion pattern, robbery requires a taking from the person or in his presence, while for extortion the intimidation is crucial and the place of the taking immaterial. In states which do not require more than the threat for extortion, the fact of misappropriation is relevant only to robbery. In those states where misappropriation is essential to extortion, there is a distinction based on the factor of consent. The robbery statutes speak of the absence of consent; the extortion statutes require its presence. However, the willingness to surrender the property in any case is only an apparent willingness since in both instances the victim must choose between alternative evils, namely, the surrender of his property or the execution of the threat. Only if the taking is accomplished by violence to the person of the victim is this apparent consent precluded, for then the victim is presented with no choice. Thus the definitional distinctions between robbery and extortion are extremely tenuous. . . .

California Penal Code: Section 211. Definition. Robbery Defined. Robbery is the felonious taking of personal property in the possession of another, from his person or immediate presence, and against his will, accomplished by means of force or fear.

Section 212. Fear Defined. The fear mentioned in Section 211 may be either:

1. The fear of an unlawful injury to the person or property of the person robbed, or of any relative of his or member of his family; or,
2. The fear of an immediate and unlawful injury to the person or property of anyone in the company of the person robbed at the time of the robbery.

Section 518. Definition. Extortion is the obtaining of property from another, with his consent, or the obtaining of an official act of a public officer, induced by a wrongful use of force or fear, or under color of official right.

Section 519. Fear Used to Extort: Threats Inducing. Fear, such as will constitute extortion, may be induced by a threat, either:

1. To do an unlawful injury to the person or property of the individual threatened or of a third person; or,
2. To accuse the individual threatened, or any relative of his, or member of his family, of any crime; or,
3. To expose, or to impute to him or them any deformity, disgrace or crime; or,
4. To expose any secret affecting him or them.

Model Penal Code: Section 222.1. Robbery. [See Appendix.]

Model Penal Code: Section 223.4. Theft by Extortion.[a] [See Appendix.]

Further on extortion (also called blackmail), see page 990, infra.

2. *Misappropriation*

NOLAN v. STATE

Maryland Court of Appeals
213 Md. 298, 131 A.2d 851 (1957)

[Defendant was convicted of embezzlement on the following facts. He was the office manager of the Federal Discount Corporation, a finance company engaged in the business of making loans and collections. The evidence showed that he appropriated money from his employer as follows: As payments were received from customers, the payments would be placed in the cash drawer. At the end of the day, an accomplice would prepare a report showing the daily cash re-

a. Model Penal Code and Commentaries, Comment to §223.4 at 202 n. 1 (1980), observes: "At common law, robbery included taking not only by force but also by threat of force or even by threat of certain other serious harms. To be guilty of robbery under the Model Penal Code, the defendant must threaten immediate and serious harm. Other coercive deprivation falls under §223.4."—Eds.

See also id. at 208: "There is no requirement in Section 223.4 that the threatened harm be 'unlawful.' The actor may be privileged or even obligated to inflict the harm threatened; yet, if he employs the threat to coerce a transfer of property for his own benefit, he clearly belongs among those who should be subject to punishment for theft. The case of the policeman who has a duty to arrest illustrates the point. His threat to arrest unless the proposed subject of the arrest pays him money should be treated as extortionate even though the failure to arrest would be dereliction of duty."—Eds.

ceipts. Defendant would then appropriate some of the cash from the drawer, and his accomplice would recompute the adding tapes to equal the remaining cash.]

COLLINS, J. . . . The appellant . . . contends that . . . the evidence produced made the crime larceny and not embezzlement, as charged in the indictment.

. . . It is stated in 2 Wharton's Criminal Law, 12th Ed., pgs. 1589, 1590, that, if the case is larceny at common law because the money was taken from the prosecutor's possession, the charge for embezzlement fails. The embezzlement statutes were passed, not to cover any cause within the common law range of larceny, but to cover new cases outside of that range. If the goods were taken from the owner's possession, the crime is larceny, not embezzlement. Goods which have reached their destination are constructively in the owner's possession although he may not yet have touched them and, hence, after such termination of transit, the servant who converts them is guilty of larceny, not of embezzlement. It is there stated at page 1591: "No inconvenience can arise from the maintenance of this distinction, since it is allowable *as well as prudent* to join a count for larceny to that for embezzlement. But great inconvenience would follow from the acceptance of the principle that the embezzlement statutes absorb all cases of larceny by servants." (Italics supplied.) . . .

From the testimony offered by the State, Federal had provided a cash drawer in which the money was deposited as received. Mr. Abrams and Mr. Wolk, officers of the company, also accepted payments and had access to the money drawer in which all the money was placed. The money was not taken by Mr. Nolan until it had been placed in the cash drawer and balanced at the end of the day. When taken by appellant, as alleged, the cash was in the possession of Federal. We must therefore conclude that under the authorities cited and under the testimony in this case there was not sufficient evidence to find the defendant guilty of embezzlement. The case will be remanded for further proceedings in order that the State, if it deems proper, may try the defendant on an indictment for embezzlement and larceny, if such an indictment is returned against the defendant.

PRESCOTT, J. (concurring). It is unfortunate not to be able to concur fully in such an able and carefully prepared opinion as that filed by a majority of this Court. However, as it seems to me that it reestablishes many of the tenuous niceties between larceny and embezzlement with which the early English cases are replete, and that it unnecessarily will embarrass many future prosecutions although the accused palpably may be guilty, I have decided to state the reasons that prevent my complete concurrence.

It seems as though the present case properly can be decided by reference to our present statute on embezzlement alone, without the necessity of the citation of other authorities. . . . Our statute, Art. 27, §154 of the Maryland Code 1951, reads:

> Whosoever being a . . . servant . . . shall fraudulently embezzle any money . . . which . . . shall be . . . taken into possession by him, for . . . his master or employer, shall be deemed to have feloniously stolen the same from his master or employer, although such money . . . was not received into the possession of such master . . . otherwise than by the actual possession of his . . . servant. . . .

A simple down-to-earth application of the facts presented in the record discloses that every element required in the statute is fully and completely covered. It is conceded that the nature of his employment is within the terms of the statute, and the evidence established to the satisfaction of the jury that the money was taken into his possession for and on behalf of his employer, and that he fraudulently appropriated it to his own use. The statute seems to require no more.

But the majority of the Court feel that the English decisions and other authorities (although apparently there is no Maryland case so ruling) require a holding that because the money went into the drawers before its fraudulent conversion, the offense was larceny and not embezzlement. If this be so, it seems to place the law in an unfortunate and somewhat indefensible position. When a man is in complete charge and control of an office and the law says to him: "If you steal your employer's money before it is placed in a drawer (under your charge and control) you are guilty of embezzlement, but, if you or someone under you places the money in that drawer (still under your charge and control) and then you steal it, you are guilty of larceny, and larceny alone," does it seem right? Could not it be said with just as much reason, logic and justification that if you steal money and place it in your left pocket, you are guilty of embezzlement, but, if you place it in your right pocket, you are guilty of larceny and larceny alone? Would it not be a sounder policy to follow the example of such cases as Calkins v. State, 18 Ohio St. 366. [T]he Ohio Court was requested to make a rather tenuous holding under its embezzlement statute as to whether or not certain property was "under (the) care" of the defendant, but the Court refused to do so, and said: "There is no more reason why courts should allow themselves to be misled by mere names and shadows in the administration of justice in criminal, than in civil cases." . . .

The apprehension that I have concerning the ruling in this case is aptly stated in Komito v. State, 90 Ohio St. 352, 107 N.E. 762, 763, where it is said:

"Courts sometimes indulge in an *ethereal refinement* between larceny and embezzlement that in practical operation very often nullifies these statutes. The only benefit accruing from such a policy results in the rather doubtful advantage of the *criminal escaping his just punishment.*" (Emphasis supplied.)

Thus, we find ourselves in the peculiar position of following the subtle reasoning developed in the English decisions for the purpose of bringing the guilty to the bar of justice; but, in so doing, we directly come to their aid and comfort. Probably the solution of this rather difficult problem lies in the course followed by several of our sister States (and as was done in England) where the legislative power has provided that under an indictment for larceny, or for larceny in one count and embezzlement in another, there may be a conviction of either offense.

NOTE ON EMBEZZLEMENT

The very early conception of larceny as a *vi et armis* (with force and arms) trespassory taking from the possession of the owner *invito domino* (against the will of the owner) was thought to preclude conviction of persons who physically and lawfully held property of the owner, as, for example, servants, guests, and employees. Since they themselves had "possession" of the owner's goods, their making off with them could not constitute larceny.

This was changed through the course of adjudication by development of the concept of "legal" (or "constructive") possession as distinguished from mere custody. The development was gradual, and there was considerable disputation as to whether, for example, a servant had mere custody or possession when the master entrusted property to him to be taken a distance from the house, as to a market, or when certain property, perhaps jewels, were expressly entrusted to a servant. See Holmes, J., in Commonwealth v. Ryan, 155 Mass. 523, 528, 30 N.E. 364, 365 (1892). Such doubts were resolved by statute in 1529 (21 Hen. VIII, ch. 7) and by later cases so that it soon became established that "a servant, whether at the master's home or elsewhere, never has legal possession of such property of his master as he controls in his capacity as servant." 2 W. O. Russell, Crime 1035 (11th ed., Turner, 1958). A servant, therefore, who made off with his master's goods, committed larceny from the possession of the master. By analogous reasoning, similar results were reached with guests.

What of the case in which the servant is given goods by a third party for delivery to his master? Could it be said that here as well, when a servant misappropriated the goods, he was taking them from the possession of the master and was hence guilty of larceny? The answer was no, since the master did not have possession and the third party voluntarily gave up possession. See 1 M. Hale, Pleas of the Crown 667.

A distinction was soon developed where the servant deposited the goods or money so received in a place provided by the master and subject to the master's control prior to the act of misappropriation. In such a case, the possession passed to the master, and the servant retained only custody; hence a dishonest appropriation was larceny. There was again much disputation as to precisely what manner and place of deposit sufficed to justify such a conclusion. In Nolan v. State, supra, for example, defendant's placement of the receipts in the cash drawer was held to transfer "possession" to the employer. Holmes, J., in Commonwealth v. Ryan, supra, reached a contrary result on similar facts (except that the money was picked up by defendant just a few minutes after he deposited it) and sustained an embezzlement conviction, stating (30 N.E. at 364):

> [T]he judge was right in charging the jury that, if the defendant, before he placed the money in the drawer, intended to appropriate it, and with that intent simply put it in the drawer for his own convenience in keeping it for himself, that would not make his appropriation of it just afterwards larceny. The distinction may be arbitrary, but, as it does not affect the defendant otherwise than by giving him an opportunity, whichever offense he was convicted of, to contend that he should have been convicted of the other, we have the less uneasiness in applying it.

A subsequent statutory development of great importance was precipitated by the decision in Bazeley's Case, 168 Eng. Rep. 517 (1799). Bazeley was a bank teller who pocketed a £1000 note received from a customer for deposit. The court found no larceny since the employer did not acquire possession of the note but only a right to possess it; at the time of the conversion, it was in the legal possession of the teller. It would have been otherwise, it was said, if Bazeley had first deposited the note in a drawer kept for this purpose by the employer. Largely to fill the gap in the law dramatized by this case, the first embezzlement statute was passed in 1799 (39 Geo. III, ch. 85) providing:

> if any servant or clerk, or any person employed for the purpose in the capacity of a servant or clerk, to any person or persons whomsoever, or to any body corporate or politick, shall, by virtue, of such employment, receive or take into his possession

> any money, goods, bond, bill, note, banker's draft, or other valuable security, or effects, for or in the name or on the account of his master or masters, or employer or employers, and shall fraudulently embezzle, secrete, or make away with the same, or any part thereof, every such offender shall be deemed to have feloniously stolen the same.

Modern cases, such as Nolan v. State, supra, are products of and explicable in terms of, if not justified by, this history.

Additional enactments following the original embezzlement statute gradually extended the categories of persons capable of embezzling to others than servants or clerks: brokers, merchants, bankers, attorneys, and other agents in 1812; factors in 1827; trustees under express trusts in 1857; etc. American embezzlement statutes still bear the mark of this piecemeal legislative development. See State v. Riggins, page 970 infra.

BURNS v. STATE

Supreme Court of Wisconsin
145 Wis. 373, 128 N.W. 987 (1911)

[A constable upon taking an insane man in charge after pursuit received from another of the pursuers a roll of money that had been thrown away by the man in his flight. The jury, having heard evidence supporting the accusation that the constable had misappropriated the funds, convicted him of larceny by bailee under a Wisconsin statute, which is reproduced in the text of the opinion.]

MARSHALL, J. . . . Error is assigned because the court instructed the jury to the effect that, if the accused converted to his own use any of Adamsky's money, he did so as bailee. It is suggested that the court should have defined the term "bailee," as used in the statute, and left it to the jury to find the fact as to whether the circumstances satisfied such statute or not.

A court may properly instruct a jury in a criminal case, as well as any other, respecting any fact, or facts, established by the evidence beyond any room for reasonable controversy, and when such evidentiary facts exist establishing, beyond any room for reasonable controversy, an essential of any ultimate conclusion sought, it is not harmful error, if error at all, to treat such essential as having been proven, as the court here did in saying that the accused was a bailee of whatever of Adamsky's money came to his possession.

It seems to be thought that a bailment was not established by the evidence because some sort of contract inter partes was essential thereto. No particular ceremony or actual meeting of minds is necessary to the creation of a bailment. If one, without the trespass which characterizes ordinary larceny, comes into possession of any personalty of another and is in duty bound to exercise some degree of care to preserve and restore the thing to such other or to some person for that other, or otherwise account for the property as that of such other, according to circumstances, — he is a bailee. It is the element of lawful possession, however created, and duty to account for the thing as the property of another, that creates the bailment, regardless of whether such possession is based on contract in the ordinary sense or not.

It is said, generally, in the books, that a bailment is created by delivery of the personalty to one person by another to be dealt with in specie as the property of such other person under a contract, express or implied, but the word "contract" is used in a broad sense. The mutuality essential to the contractual feature may be created by operation of law as well as by the acts of the parties with intention to contract.

So it makes no difference whether the thing be intrusted to a person by the owner, or another, or by some one for the owner or by the law to the same end. Taking possession without present intent to appropriate raises all the contractual elements essential to a bailment. So the person who bona fide recovers the property of another which has been lost, or irresponsibly cast away by an insane man, as in this case, is a bailee as much as if the same property were intrusted to such person by contract inter partes. In the latter case the contract creates the duty. In the former the law creates it. Such a situation is to be distinguished from that where one knowingly receives money paid him by mistake and fraudulently retains it. There the element of bona fide possession may be said not to exist and so the duty accompanied by such possession essential to a bailment not to have been created. . . .

The finder of property who voluntarily bona fide takes it into his possession, immediately, thereupon, has imposed upon him by law the duties of a depositary, the mildest type, as regards degree of duty, of bailee.

So the finder here of the cast-away money was clearly a bailee, and when his duties were voluntarily assumed by the accused he became such, and as there was no controversy in respect to such finding and assumption, the court's reference to the matter was proper.

The next suggestion in behalf of plaintiff in error is that, if the accused was guilty of any offense, it was that of having broken the package and extracted therefrom part of the contents for the purpose of appropriating it to his own use, and executed such purpose, thus committing the offense of larceny, not of conversion by a bailee. It is a sufficient answer thereto that the purpose of the statute [containing provisions on traditional larceny and on takings by bailees] was to abolish the distinction between conversion by a bailee of an entire thing, as a quantity of property in a package of some kind, and the unlawful breaking of the package and conversion of part or all of the contents — whether preceded by the element of breaking bulk with intent to permanently deprive the owner of the thing appropriated or not, — making the latter a statutory class of larcenies, differing only from ordinary larcenies, by absence in the former of the element of trespass in gaining original possession, which is essential to the latter. The meaning of the statute, as indicated, seems very plain:

> Whoever being a bailee of any chattel, money or valuable security shall fraudulently take or fraudulently convert the same to his own use or to the use of any person other than the owner thereof, although he shall not break bulk or otherwise determine the bailment, shall be guilty of larceny. . . .

It follows that acquittal of the accused of the offense of larceny is not inconsistent with his conviction of the statute offense of larceny as bailee. . . .

NOTE ON THE MISAPPROPRIATING BAILEE

In the Note following Nolan v. State, supra, we briefly described the development of the possession-custody distinction as a means whereby certain kinds of misappropriation by persons lawfully holding the property of another came to be treated as larceny prior to the enactment of the embezzlement statutes, which eliminated the need for such judicial gap-filling. However, just as this distinction proved inadequate to deal with the servant who received goods for his master from a third person, it proved inadequate to deal with the bailee who misappropriated his bailor's property, because the crucial significance of a bailment relation was the transfer of possession and not mere custody. See 5 Words and Phrases, Bailment, 48 (perm. ed.); 2 W. O. Russell, Crime 916 (12th ed., Turner, 1964). The resources of the early common law, however, were up to the task of bringing at least some bailee misappropriations within the scope of larceny. In the Carrier's Case, decided in 1473 (Y.B. 13 Edw. IV, f. 9, pl. 5), a carrier to whom a foreign merchant delivered a shipment for delivery to a consignee broke into the bales and decamped with the contents. The judges of the Star Chamber produced a variety of opinions but apparently reached no conclusion. The case was again argued before the judges in the Exchequer Chamber, who expressed several opinions as to the theory to govern the case. The majority apparently agreed that if the bailment has terminated, the former bailee who then takes the goods may be guilty of larceny. What was unclear was the theory on which the defendant should be said to have terminated the bailment. Finally the judges, without stating their reasons, reported that a majority found that in the circumstances defendant committed larceny (2 W. O. Russell, Crime 917-918 (12th ed., Turner, 1964)). As Russell observes (at 918),

> Much later we find accepted by the courts the proposition that by breaking bulk the bailee determined [terminated] the bailment and having ceased thereby to be a bailee, in some strange manner lost possession of the property which had been bailed to him and so became a trespasser when he took any portion of the contents.

Stephen observed:

> This has always appeared an extraordinary decision, as, to all common apprehension, theft of the whole thing bailed must determine the bailment quite as much as a theft of part of it. I think it obvious from the report that the decision was a compromise intended to propitiate the chancellor and perhaps the King. This required a deviation from the common law, which was accordingly made, but was as slight as the judges could make it.

3 James Fitzjames Stephen, History of the Criminal Law 139 (1883). The pragmatic basis for the decision suggested by Stephen was further developed by Professor Jerome Hall in his classic study of the case in Theft, Law and Society (2d ed. 1952), where the political, social and economic interests are explored. Hall concludes (at 93):

> On the one hand, the criminal law at the time is clear. On the other hand, the whole complex aggregate of political and economic conditions described above thrusts itself upon the court. The more powerful forces prevailed — that happened which in due course must have happened under the circumstances. The most powerful forces of the time were interrelated very intimately and at many points: the New Monarchy and the nouveau riche — the mercantile class; the business interests of both and the consequent need for a secure carrying trade; the wool and textile industry, the most valuable, by far, in all the realm; wool and cloth,

> the most important exports; these exports and the foreign trade; this trade and Southampton, chief trading city with the Latin countries for centuries; the numerous and very influential Italian merchants who bought English wool and cloth inland and shipped them from Southampton. The great forces of an emerging modern world, represented in the above phenomena, necessitated the elimination of a formula which had outgrown its usefulness. A new set of major institutions required a new rule. The law, lagging behind the needs of the times, was brought into more harmonious relationship with the other institutions by the decision rendered in the Carrier's Case.

At all events, the breaking-bulk device proved only a stopgap. It left without criminal sanction appropriations without breaking bulk as well as cases where the requirement of breaking was difficult to establish, as where the shipment consisted of separable units. The remedy was again statutory, an act of 1857 (20 & 21 Vict., ch. 54, §4) creating the new crime of larceny by bailee, which placed the dishonest bailee on a par with the dishonest servant. American statutes today either retain similar provisions as a separate crime of larceny by bailee or include misappropriation by a bailee as an instance of embezzlement.

NOTES ON APPROPRIATION OF LOST PROPERTY AND PROPERTY TRANSFERRED BY MISTAKE

Where property dishonestly appropriated by a defendant comes into his or her possession through a mistake of the transferor, as by a mistake in the identity of the transferee, the character of the property, or the quantity being delivered, or through the defendant's finding property which the owner has lost, there is apparently no trespassory interference with possession required for larceny. Neither is there the employee or fiduciary relationship or the element of "entrusting" required by the usual embezzlement statute. Of what crime, then, may the dishonest accused be convicted?

1. As for lost property, an early partial solution was the distinction between lost property (that property unintentionally placed where found) and mislaid property (that property deliberately placed where found, the owner forgetting where he or she put it). In the latter case, the courts often found that "possession" never left the owner, so that when the finder appropriated it, the finder "took" it from the owner's possession. State v. Courtsol, 89 Conn. 564, 94 A. 973 (1915). Even as to the former, however, it was eventually determined that the finder took from the constructive possession of the owner, and if at the time the finder appropriated the lost property he or she intended to convert it, knowing or having reason to believe he or she might discover the owner's identity, the finder was guilty of larceny. Penny v. State, 109 Ark. 343, 159 S.W. 1127 (1913). It is generally held, however, that the felonious intent (to appropriate in the face of knowledge or means of knowing the owner's identity) must accompany the original finding and appropriation — otherwise there is no felonious taking. Long v. State, 33 Ala. App. 334, 33 So. 2d 382 (1948).

Consider the solution to this problem proposed by the Model Penal Code and now adopted by many states. Section 223.5 provides:

A person who comes into control of property of another that he knows to have been lost, mislaid, or delivered under a mistake as to the nature or amount of the property or the identity of the recipient is guilty of theft if, with purpose to deprive the owner thereof, he fails to take reasonable measures to restore the property to a person entitled to have it.

See Model Penal Code and Commentaries, Comment to §223.5 at 228 (1980):

The common-law view of larceny as an infringement of the possession of another required a determination of the actor's state of mind at the moment of finding. . . . The search for an initial fraudulent intent appears to be largely fictional, and in any event poses the wrong question. The realistic objective in this area is not to prevent initial appropriation but to compel subsequent acts to restore to the owner. The section therefore permits conviction even where the original taking was honest in the sense that the actor then intended to restore; if he subsequently changes his mind and determines to keep the property, he will then be guilty of theft.

2. In the case of dishonest appropriation of property delivered by mistake, there is again a twofold problem: first, finding the necessary taking from possession and second, finding a felonious intent coincident with the taking. The solution of the Model Penal Code, also now followed in many states, is §223.5, just quoted. The supporting Commentary states as follows (Model Penal Code and Commentaries, Comment to §223.5 at 225-226 (1980)):

[O]ne who accepts a $10 bill knowing that the other person thinks he is handing over a $1 bill acquires it without trespass or false pretense. Moreover, he may not be in any of the employee or fiduciary relations that were enumerated in the typical older embezzlement statutes. Consequently, special legislation or judicial sleight-of-hand was required to reach persons taking advantage of such mistakes. Similarly, if the owner or his agent voluntarily hands the property over to the accused while laboring under a misapprehension as to the identity of the recipient, it requires strenuous manipulation of concepts to disregard the apparent transfer of title as well as possession and to hold that the accused is guilty of larceny because he committed a trespass against the transferor's possession. A prosecution for false pretenses may also be frustrated because the actor may not have created or reinforced the misimpression. Yet the recipient, knowing that the transfer to him is inadvertent, is in a moral and physical situation with respect to the property much like that of the finder of lost property. Moreover, he knows who is rightfully entitled to the property and can easily take steps to restore the property. Accordingly, Section 223.5 imposes theft sanctions against one in this situation who fails to take reasonable measures to restore. Most recent codes and proposals also specifically cover theft of misdelivered property. Some, however, are restricted to theft of lost or mislaid property.

It is necessary to limit the reach of Section 223.5, on the other hand, in order to avoid impinging on certain types of tolerated sharp trading. For example, it is not proposed to punish the purchase of another's property at a bargain price on a mere showing that the buyer was aware that the seller was misinformed regarding the value of what he sold. The language of Section 223.5 is accordingly limited to situations where the mistake is as to "the nature or amount of the property or the identity of the recipient."

PROBLEM

S.F. Chronicle, Nov. 14, 1964, at 4, contained the following story:

MONTGOMERY, Ala.—A man who withdrew $43,000 mistakenly credited to his bank account and refused to give it back was convicted yesterday by a jury in Federal Court.

T. L. (Cotton) Thaggard of Montgomery faces a possible maximum sentence of 10 years in prison and a $5,000 fine. He will be sentenced Friday.

It was Thaggard's second trial. The first ended with a deadlocked jury.

Thaggard was tried under a Federal law which prohibits taking anything worth more than $100 from a bank "with intent to steal or purloin."

In his argument to the jury Thursday, defense attorney Calvin Whitesell contended that as far as the defendant knew, the balance in his account was just what the bank told him it was.

"You can't steal what is yours," Whitesell argued.

The dispute began in March 1963 when the Union Bank & Trust Co. erroneously credited a $43,000 deposit to the account of Alabama Motors, a used car business operated by Thaggard. The money belonged to Alabama Power Co.

On March 6, Thaggard asked for his balance, then drew out the $43,000 after the teller had three times verified the amount, at his request.

He finally signed a withdrawal slip and tellers spent 30 minutes counting out the bills and putting them in a brown paper sack.

In the first trial, Thaggard's lawyer, Ira De Ment, contended his client was not guilty of larceny since the money was voluntarily handed over. "I'm not saying he did right. I'm saying he's not guilty of larceny," De Ment said.

U.S. Attorney Ben Hardeman said, "Cotton Thaggard entered that bank with a heart full of larceny and left there with a sack full of money."

Thaggard has spent the time since carrying the bag of money from the bank in and out of jail and court.

He was locked up by a circuit judge on contempt charges when he refused to tell where he put the money, saying he would incriminate himself by answering.

Thaggard was first arrested on a state charge of false pretense. But that charge was dropped when the State Supreme Court ruled that it wasn't false pretense to get the money after three times asking the bank to recheck his balance.

Later, a Federal grand jury indicted Thaggard on a larceny charge involving a bank whose funds were insured by the Federal Deposit Insurance Corporation.

The bank has won a civil judgment against Thaggard in state court and some $10,575 worth of property belonging to him has been sold to satisfy the judgment.[a]

STATE v. RIGGINS

Supreme Court of Illinois
8 Ill. 2d 78, 132 N.E.2d 519 (1956)

HERSHEY, C.J. The defendant, Marven E. Riggins, was indicted in the circuit court of Winnebago County for embezzlement. After a verdict of guilty by a jury, the court sentenced him to a term in the penitentiary of not less than two nor more than seven years. . . .

a. For a recent prosecution based on similar facts, see United States v. Kossair, 1995 U.S. App. LEXIS 37737 (9th Cir. 1995).—EDS.

At the time of the indictment (January, 1955), the defendant was the owner and operator of a collection agency in Rockford, called the Creditors Collection Service, and had been so engaged for about five years. He maintained an office, had both full- and part-time employees, and during 1953 and 1954 had a clientele of some 500 persons and firms for whom he collected delinquent accounts.

In February, 1953, he called on the complaining witness, Dorothy Tarrant, who operated a firm known as Cooper's Music and Jewelry. He said he was in the collection business and asked to collect the firm's delinquent accounts. As a result, they reached an oral agreement whereby the defendant was to undertake the collections.

By this agreement, the defendant was to receive one third on city accounts and one half on out-of-city accounts. It was further agreed that he need not account for the amounts collected until a bill was paid in full, at which time he was to remit by check.

There is a conflict in the evidence as to whether the defendant was to give a check for the whole amount collected and then receive his commission, or whether he was authorized to deduct his commission and account only for the net amount due.

It was further agreed that the defendant would be liable for court costs in the event he chose to file suit on any of the accounts, but the first money collected was to be applied to those costs. If no collection was made, however, the defendant was to stand the loss.

The parties operated under this agreement for almost two years. During that time the complaining witness exercised no control over the defendant as to the time or manner of collecting the accounts, and with her knowledge he commingled funds collected for all his clients in a single bank account. He also used this as a personal account, from which he drew for business, family and personal expenses.

In October, 1954, the complaining witness became aware that the defendant had collected several accounts for her in full, but had not accounted to her. . . . Thereafter, the complaining witness preferred the charges against the defendant which resulted in his indictment and conviction for embezzlement.

To decide whether the defendant, a collection agent, can be guilty of embezzlement in Illinois, it is helpful to consider our embezzlement statutes in the historical context of this crime.

Embezzlement, unknown at common law, is established by statute, and its scope, therefore, is limited to those persons designated therein. . . .

Viewed in their entirety, our laws relating to embezzlement are broad and comprehensive. The following persons are included in those statutes making the crime of embezzlement a felony: "Whoever embezzles or fraudulently converts to his own use" (Ill. Rev. Stat. 1953, chap. 38, par. 207); "a clerk, agent, servant or apprentice of any person" (par. 208); "any banker or broker, or his agent or servant, or any officer, agent or servant of any banking company, or incorporated bank" (par. 209); "any clerk, agent, servant, solicitor, broker, apprentice or officer . . . receiving any money . . . in his fiduciary capacity" (par. 210); "public officers" (par. 214); "administrators, guardians, conservators and other fiduciaries" (par. 216); and certain members and officers of fraternal societies (par. 218). . . .

In this instance we are particularly interested in the general embezzlement statute (par. 208), and the special statute under which defendant was indicted (par. 210). The former, applying to any "clerk, agent, servant or apprentice of any person," was originally enacted in 1827, and has existed in its present form since 1874. The latter, however, refers to "any clerk, agent, servant, solicitor, broker, apprentice or officer . . . receiving any money, . . . in his fiduciary capacity" and was not passed until 1919. For present purposes, this latter enactment is very significant, for it also provides as follows: such person

> shall be punished as provided by the criminal statutes of this state for the punishment of larceny, *irrespective of whether any such* officer, agent, clerk, servant, solicitor, broker or apprentice *has or claims to have any commission or interest in such money,* substitute for money, or thing of value so received by him.

(Italics added.)

In Commonwealth v. Libbey, 11 Metc., Mass., 64 decided in 1846, it was held that a collecting agent, who followed that as an independent business and who had the right to commingle funds, could not be convicted as an "agent" under a general embezzlement statute. This was predicated on the idea that he had a joint interest in the property said to be embezzled.

Similarly, a 1903 decision of this court reversed the conviction of an agent who was employed to solicit subscriptions on commission and who was authorized to deduct her commissions from the amounts collected, for the reason that she was joint owner with the principal in the amounts collected. McElroy v. People, 202 Ill. 473, 66 N.E. 1058. . . .

Briefly, then, this was the status of the law in 1919 when the special statute (par. 210) . . . expressly abrogated the doctrine enunciated in the foregoing cases and relied upon by the defendant here.[a] . . .

[I]t can hardly be disputed but that the defendant acted as agent for the complaining witness in collecting her accounts. He undertook the collections on her behalf by virtue of authority which she delegated to him. He had no right to collect from anyone except as authorized by her and was required to render a full account of all matters entrusted to him, the same as any agent. . . . The prevailing view of the courts in construing embezzlement statutes is succinctly expressed in 18 Am. Jur., Embezzlement, §30, as follows: "The term 'agent' as used in embezzlement statutes is construed in its popular sense as meaning a person who undertakes to transact some business or to manage some affair for another by the latter's authority and to render an account of such business or affair. . . ."

We conclude that the defendant was an "agent" of the complaining witness, receiving money in a "fiduciary capacity" and, therefore, within the purview of said embezzlement statute. . . .

Reversed and remanded.

SCHAEFER, J., dissenting. . . . The critical question is whether the defendant was the agent of the complaining witness. Upon the record it seems to me that he was not. He maintained his own office, had his own employees, and collected accounts for approximately 500 other individuals and firms. He was subject to

a. Many cases have taken the view (contrary to that of the cases cited by the court) that, even absent such a specific statute, the fact that a collector is entitled to deduct a commission out of the funds collected does not preclude an embezzlement conviction for appropriation of the entire proceeds. See, e.g., Commonwealth v. Hutchins, 232 Mass. 285, 122 N.E. 275 (1919). —EDS.

no control whatsoever by any of his customers in making his collections. His customers knew that he kept all of his collections in a single account. That the defendant was not an agent would be clear, I think, if vicarious liability was sought to be asserted against Dorothy Tarrant on account of the defendant's conduct in the course of his collection activities.

The conclusion of the majority that the defendant was an agent rests upon the assertion that "[t]he term 'agent' as used in embezzlement statutes is construed in its popular sense. . . ." That generalization runs counter to the basic rule that criminal statutes are strictly construed.

More important than generalized statements as to the proper approach to the problem of construction, however, is the language to be construed. The statute under which the defendant was indicted (Ill. Rev. Stat. 1953, chap. 38, par. 210), refers to "any clerk, agent, servant, solicitor, broker, apprentice, or officer." If "agent" has the broad meaning which the majority gives it, each of the other terms is superfluous because all are embraced within the single term "agent." Many of the specific enumerations in the other statutes referred to by the majority likewise become largely, if not entirely, meaningless, for the particular relationships they seek to reach are also swallowed up in the expanded definition of the term "agent."

It is arguable of course that the conduct of the defendant in this case should be regarded as criminal. The General Assembly might wish to make it so. But it might not. It might regard the collection agency as a desirable service enterprise which should not be made unduly perilous. If the defendant in this case, with his little agency, is guilty of one embezzlement, he is guilty of 500. The General Assembly might not want to make the enterprise so hazardous. It has not done so, in my opinion, by the statute before us.[b]

MODEL PENAL CODE

Section 223.8. Theft by Failure to Make Required Dispositions of Funds Received

[See Appendix.]

MODEL PENAL CODE AND COMMENTARIES, COMMENT TO §223.8 AT 255-262 (1980): The challenge is to distinguish default that should be assimilated to theft from non-performance that should be left to the traditional remedies for breach of contract.

The difficulty that has troubled courts in the past may be illustrated by the decisions in Commonwealth v. Mitchneck[1] and State v. Polzin.[2] The *Mitchneck* case involved a mine operator whose employees signed written authorizations for him to deduct from their wages the amounts of their grocery bills. Mitchneck made the deductions but failed to pay the grocer. He was convicted under the Pennsylvania fraudulent-conversion statute, which at the time covered anyone who

b. The various statutes relevant to embezzlement at issue in these opinions have been replaced by §5/16-1 of the Illinois Revised Criminal Code, reprinted at page 1000 infra. How should this case be decided under the new provisions? —Eds.

1. 130 Pa. Super. 433, 198 A. 463 (1938).
2. 197 Wash. 612, 85 P.2d 1057 (1939).

> having received or having possession, in any capacity or by any means or manner whatever, of any money or property, of any kind whatsoever, of or belonging to any other person, firm, or corporation, or which any other person, firm, or corporation is entitled to receive and have, who fraudulently withholds, converts, or applies the same, or any part thereof, . . . to and for his own use and benefit, or to and for the use and benefit of any other person.

The conviction was reversed on the ground that Mitchneck did not have in his possession

> any money *belonging* to his employees. True he owed them money. . . . Defendant's liability for the unpaid wages due his employees was, and remained, civil, not criminal. His liability for the amount due Vagnoni after his agreement to accept or honor the assignments of his employees' wages was likewise civil and not criminal.

If the miners in the *Mitchneck* case had drawn their pay at one window and passed part of it back to Mitchneck's cashier at the next window, conviction for embezzlement or fraudulent conversion could have been obtained. The premise of Section 223.8 is that liability should also follow on the facts of the case as they occurred. The bookkeeping shortcut actually used hardly serves as a rational basis for exculpating Mitchneck from criminal liability.

The *Polzin* case presents a more complex variation of the same situation. Polzin was a money lender who took a note from a Mrs. Braseth under an arrangement by which, instead of paying the cash to her, he agreed to pay off certain of her creditors. Instead of doing so, he made out a check to a collection agency which he owned. He then approached the creditors with a proposal to act for them in collecting their claim from Mrs. Braseth for a 33 percent collection fee. They accepted the arrangement, after which Polzin paid the creditors and withheld $19 as his agreed-upon collection fee.

Polzin was convicted of petty larceny, the jury having evidently taken the view that what was stolen was the $19 fee which Polzin had withheld. The Supreme Court of Washington reversed the conviction. The court held first that there could be no misappropriation of any "property" belonging to Mrs. Braseth, because she never gave Polzin anything other than her note. Since Polzin held no "property" belonging to Mrs. Braseth but had merely promised to make certain payments, he was her debtor rather than her trustee. Second, with respect to the $19 withheld from the creditors, Mrs. Braseth "lost nothing"; the bills had been completely discharged and Polzin had therefore performed his agreement as far as she was concerned.

Section 223.8 was designed in part to provide a theory for reaching cases like *Mitchneck* and *Polzin*. Both were thought to illustrate situations that properly should be assimilated to theft rather than treated as mere breach of contract. . . .

There is a long tradition, deriving to some extent from the harsh days of the debtors' prison and to some extent enshrined in constitutional provisions, against enforcing individual consensual obligations by criminal sanctions. . . . Among the valid objections to the employment of criminal sanctions to enforce debts, as distinct from protecting "ownership" of "property," may be included the following: . . . a feeling that it is up to the contract maker to select his risks and that the invocation of criminal sanctions in cases of non-performance involves the impairment of the incentive to make wise risk selections and thus impairment of the social functions of contract-making . . . ; the unlikelihood of deterring honest insolvency by criminal threats, since insolvency is so often a result of factors beyond the control of the individual; the dangers, in attempting to punish insolvency for which the actor may properly be viewed as at fault, of discouraging the kind of speculation that is properly a part of a free-enterprise system and of securing unjust convictions by hindsight; and the futility, from the creditors' standpoint, of imprisoning a debtor who is unable to pay.

None of the foregoing considerations was thought applicable to cases such as *Mitchneck* and *Polzin.* In neither of those cases was there an ordinary credit transaction or an understanding that involves an assessment of risks at some future date. Mitchneck and Polzin were not supposed to use the funds in any way for their own purposes nor even to retain them for any substantial period. They were merely conduits for the transmission of money to persons designated by the real owner of the money. [A] proprietary use of the money should properly be regarded as theft, much as a guardian may be guilty of embezzlement when he commingles fiduciary funds with his own and reduces the account below the level of his fiduciary obligation in order to satisfy his personal financial needs. . . .

It should be noted, however, that the *Mitchneck* and *Polzin* situations are not free from difficulty even under such a formulation as Section 223.8. The text of the offense requires that the actor "obtain" property from another. The term "obtain" is defined in Section 223.0(5) to mean, in relation to property, "to bring about a transfer or purported transfer of a legal interest in the property, whether to the obtainer or another." The problem in both *Mitchneck* and *Polzin* was that the defendant was not perceived as having "obtained" anything from the victim in this sense, and that perception might be no less applicable to Section 223.8. Indeed, if the property were regarded as having been "obtained" as that term is defined, Section 223.2(1) would be an adequate basis for prosecution. If Mitchneck and Polzin obtained property of another under an understanding and then "exercised unlawful control over" that property, there would seem to be no bar to an ordinary embezzlement prosecution. Even if this is true, however, there may be an important value in addressing a specific formulation to situations of this kind. Convictions of embezzlement are not easily obtained under the broader standards embodied in the general definition of theft.

It is important, nevertheless, to emphasize the point that Section 223.8 must not be construed so broadly that a bright line between theft and breach of contract is obscured. [Consider] credit-card purchases, a practice that has assumed enormous proportions in today's economy. Typically, the purchaser of goods "obtains" property by becoming the drawee-acceptor of a draft, drawn by the merchant in favor of the credit-card company as payee. If unauthorized use of the card is involved, or if forged or stolen cards are used, Section 224.6 is adequate to handle the problem. If the actor intended from the beginning not to pay, Section 223.3 covers the situation. But if the actor is engaged in authorized use and simply cannot pay his bills, it is inappropriate to make him a thief; the risk that he cannot pay is a cost of doing business that credit-card companies should assume. . . .

The path to avoiding such undue extensions of Section 223.8 is to accord proper weight to the limitation embodied in the words "to be reserved," so that Section 223.8 is deemed applicable only in cases of a promise to turn over property actually received in kind or an equivalent sum of money specifically reserved in the sense that a trustee reserves a fiduciary account. It is true that such a construction would seem to limit Section 223.8 to classic instances of embezzlement. [T]here may be some cases beyond ordinary embezzlement to which the provision could be applied by a broad construction of "obtains" to deal with situations where property was not physically exchanged. But in order to eliminate application of the section to cases where civil remedies alone should be permitted, something approaching an explicit agreement to "reserve" would seem to be required.

NOTE

Only some nine states followed the Model Penal Code's lead in this section. See Model Penal Code and Commentaries, Comment to §223.8 at 266 (1980). What might have been the reasons for the reluctance?

3. Fraud

INTRODUCTORY NOTE

The deposit of history is no less substantial in crimes dealing with the use of fraud to acquire another's property than in crimes dealing with misappropriation by one in lawful possession, previously discussed. In both situations, the common law judges through some remarkable reasoning brought certain species of these nontrespassory takings within the scope of the basic common law crime of larceny, while in parallel developments Parliament expressly dealt with these nontrespassory situations by creating new statutory crimes to cover them. This uncoordinated judicial and legislative development left parallel crimes to cover fundamentally similar kinds of theft. The necessity to distinguish which of these kinds of theft were within the stretched judicial definition of larceny and which within the statutory definitions of new crimes is the legacy of this history.

The early common law, influenced by the ethic of caveat emptor, declined to treat as criminal, situations in which a person acquired another's property through simple deception. The classic justification was given by Holt, C.J., in 1703: "[W]e are not to indict one for making a fool of another." Regina v. Jones, 91 Eng. Rep. 330.[1] But through the development of common law "cheats," the principle was modified as to certain kinds of fraud, which were aimed indiscriminately at any member of the public rather than at a particular person and which were thought to be such that ordinary prudence was an insufficient protection: for example, using a false token, false weights or measures, etc. See Rex. v. Wheatley, 97 Eng. Rep. 746, 748 (1761). This common law development was supplemented and amplified by a statute in 1541 that made criminal the acquisition of another's property by deceit in situations doubtfully reached by common law cheats: where accomplished "by colour and means of any [privy] false token or counterfeit letter made in any other man's name." 33 Hen. VIII, ch. 1.

A more far-reaching legislative innovation came in 1757 with the enactment of what subsequently became the prototype false pretense statute, 30 Geo. II, ch. 24, making it a misdemeanor to obtain "money, goods, wares or merchan-

1. Cf. 1 W. Hawkins, Pleas of the Crown 344 (6th ed. 1788): "[It is] needless to provide severe laws for such mischiefs, against which common prudence and caution may be a sufficient security."

dizes" from any person by false pretenses with intent to cheat or defraud. There originally appeared to be some doubt whether the false pretense statute reached any and all misrepresentations or was to be narrowly read in the light of the common law of cheats and the earlier cheating statutes. It was not until 1789 that the broader meaning was established in Young v. The King, 100 Eng. Rep. 475. See Jerome Hall, Theft, Law and Society 45-52 (2d ed. 1952). In the meantime the landmark case of The King v. Pear had been decided in 1779, I Leach 211, 168 Eng. Rep. 208, creating the crime of what came to be known as "larceny by trick" as a distinct form of common law larceny. The following report of the case is taken from 168 Eng. Rep. 208:

> The prisoner was indicted for stealing a black horse, the property of Samuel Finch. It appeared in evidence that Samuel Finch was a Livery-Stablekeeper in the Borough; and that the prisoner, on the 2d of July 1779, hired the horse of him to go to Sutton, in the county of Surry, and back again, saying on being asked where he lived, that he lodged at No. 25 in King-street, and should return about eight o'clock the same evening. He did not return; and it was proved that he had sold the horse on the very day he had hired it, to one William Hollist, in Smithfield Market; and that he had no lodging at the place to which he had given the Prosecutor directions.
>
> The learned Judge said: There had been different opinions on the law of this class of cases; that the general doctrine then was that if a horse be let for a particular portion of time, and after that time is expired, the party hiring, instead of returning the horse to its owner, sell it and convert the money to his own use, it is felony, because there is then no privity of contract subsisting between the parties; that in the present case the horse was hired to take a journey into Surry, and the prisoner sold him the same day, without taking any such journey; that there were also other circumstances which imported that at the time of the hiring the prisoner had it in intention to sell the horse, as his saying that he lodged at a place where in fact he was not known. He therefore left it with the Jury to consider, Whether the prisoner meant at the time of the hiring to take such journey, but was afterwards tempted to sell the horse? for if so he must be acquitted; but that if they were of opinion that at the time of the hiring the journey was a mere pretense to get the horse into his possession, and he had no intention to take such journey but intended to sell the horse, they would find that fact specially for the opinion of the Judges.
>
> The Jury found that the facts above stated were true; and also that the prisoner had hired the horse with a fraudulent view and intention of selling it immediately.
>
> The question was referred to the Judges, Whether the delivery of the horse by the prosecutor to the prisoner, had so far changed the possession of the property, as to render the subsequent conversion of it a mere breach of trust, or whether the conversion was felonious?
>
> The Judges differed greatly in opinion on this case; and delivered their opinions seriatim upon it at Lord Chief Justice De Gray's house on 4th February 1780 and on the 22nd of the same month Mr. Barron Perryn delivered their opinion on it. The majority of them thought, That the question, as to the original intention of the prisoner in hiring the horse, had been properly left to the jury; and as they had found, that his view in so doing was fraudulent, the parting with the property had not changed the nature of the possession, but that it remained unaltered in the prosecutor at the time of the conversion; and that the prisoner was therefore guilty of felony.

The reason the judges thought the false pretense statute, 30 Geo. II, was inapplicable to *Pear* appears in the report of the case in 2 E. H. East, Pleas of the Crown 685, 688-689 (1806):

> [T]he next question was, Whether this offence were within or at all affected by the statutes of Hen. 8 and Geo. 2. Seven of the Judges were of the opinion, that it was not. That the statute of Hen. 8 was confined to the cases of obtaining goods in other men's names, by false tokens or counterfeit letters, made in any other man's name. The statute of Geo. 2 extended that law to all cases where goods were obtained by false pretences of any kind. But both these statutes were confined to cases where credit was obtained in the name of a third person; and did not extend to cases where a man, on his own account, got goods with an intention to steal them.

Use was made, therefore, of the notion that possession never passes to a fraudulent bailee to stretch the concept of larceny to include an act otherwise unamenable to proper criminal sanction. "Fraud in securing possession joined breaking bulk and custody in servants to extend the definition of larceny far beyond its original traditional meaning." Jerome Hall, Theft, Law and Society 42 (2d ed. 1952).

When the false pretense statute was subsequently extended to all misrepresentations of fact, regardless of the technique of deception, there were two crimes, larceny by trick (a felony) and statutory false pretenses (only a misdemeanor), covering very much the same kind of criminal conduct. Perhaps the first hint of the theory on which the crimes would be distinguished appears in the *Pear* case itself, as reported in 2 E. H. East, Pleas of the Crown 685, 689 n. (a) (1806):

> On the debate in this case Eyre, B., adverting to these statutes, said he doubted if there was a distinction in this respect between the owner's parting with the possession and with the property in the thing delivered. That where goods were delivered upon a false token, and the owner meant to part with the property absolutely and never expected to have the goods returned again, it might be difficult to reach the case otherwise than through the statutes; aliter, where he parted with the possession only: for there if the possession were obtained by fraud, and not taken according to the agreement; it was on the whole a taking against the will of the owner; and if done animo furandi, it was felony.

Question: Is there any logical reason why "the deceit which eliminated the consent which the owner intended to give when he regarded himself as parting with merely the possession of his chattel would not have the same effect when he regarded himself as parting with something greater, namely, the ownership of it?" 2 W. O. Russell, Crime 1089 (10th ed. 1950).

HUFSTETLER v. STATE

Alabama Court of Appeals
37 Ala. App. 71, 63 So. 2d 730 (1953)

CARR, J. The accused was convicted by the court without a jury on a charge of petit larceny. The property involved was 6½ gallons of gasoline.

The defendant did not testify nor offer any evidence.

The undisputed facts are narrated by a witness [Peter Whorton] as follows.

> . . . I own and operate a store and service station at Forney, Alabama. On March 29, 1952, the defendant drove an automobile up to my gasoline tanks. There were

> some two or three other men in the car with him, and a man in the back seat got out and started in the store and asked if I had a telephone. When I told him I did not have a telephone, he said he wanted some gasoline and went back and got in the car. I asked him how much and he said "fill it up." I put 6½ gallons of gasoline in the car and this man said to get a quart of oil, and when I went for the oil, the defendant drove off in the automobile together with the man who ordered the gas and the others in the car without paying for the gasoline. This 6½ gallons of gas belonged to me and was of the value of $1.94. . . .

The only question of critical concern is whether, on the basis of the above proof, the judgment of conviction can be sustained.

Appellant's attorney in brief urges that Whorton voluntarily parted with the possession and ownership of the gasoline.

Confusion sometimes arises in an effort to distinguish the kindred criminal offenses of larceny, false pretenses, and embezzlement.

The Massachusetts Supreme Court in Commonwealth v. Barry, 124 Mass. 325, gave a distinction that is clear and comprehensive:

> If a person honestly receives the possession of the goods, chattels or money of another upon any trust, express or implied, and, after receiving them, fraudulently converts them to his own use, he may be guilty of the crime of embezzlement, but cannot be of that of larceny, except as embezzlement is by statute made larceny. If the possession of such property is obtained by fraud, and the owner of it intends to part with his title as well as his possession, the offence is that of obtaining property by false pretenses, provided the means by which they are acquired are such as, in law, are false pretenses. If the possession is fraudulently obtained, with intent on the part of the person obtaining it, at the time he received it, to convert the same to his own use, and the person parting with it intends to part with his possession merely, and not with his title to the property, the offence is larceny.

In the case at bar the circumstances disclose that by the application of the well-known doctrine of aid and abet the appellant secured the possession of the gasoline by a trick or fraud. The obtaining of the property by the consent of the owner under such conditions will not necessarily prevent the taking from being larceny. In other words, an actual trespass is not always required to be proven. The trick or fraud vitiates the transaction, and it will be deemed that the owner still retained the constructive possession.

What we have said related to the possession. It is certainly a logical conclusion that Whorton had no intention of parting with the ownership of the property until he had received pay therefor.

The element of the intent of the appellant is inferable from the factual background. . . .

Affirmed. Remanded for proper sentence.

GRAHAM v. UNITED STATES

United States Court of Appeals, District of Columbia Circuit
187 F. 2d 87 (1950)

WASHINGTON, J. The appellant, an attorney, was indicted in two counts for grand larceny under section 2201 of Title 22 of the District of Columbia Code

(1940 ed.). He was charged with having stolen money from Francisco Gal in the amounts of $100 and $1,900. He appeals from a judgment and conviction entered upon a verdict of guilty.

The complaining witness, Francisco Gal, consulted appellant in his professional capacity. Gal had been arrested and charged with disorderly conduct, and had forfeited $25 as collateral. He was seeking American citizenship and was apprehensive that the arrest would impede or bar his attainment of that goal. An immigrant employed as a cook, his command of the English language was far from complete. He testified that appellant Graham told him that he wasn't sure what he could do, that Graham would "have to talk to the policeman. You have to pay money for that, because the money is talk." He further testified that Graham told him he would charge him $200 for a fee; that he would have to pay an additional $2,000 for the police; that Graham said "don't mention the money for nobody and for the police either." As a result, Gal testified that he paid the appellant $300 on February 2, 1950 (of which, he said, $200 was paid as a legal fee), and $1,900 on February 3, 1950. The police officer who originally had arrested Gal testified that he came to appellant's office, and after talking with Graham, told Gal that he wasn't in any trouble. Gal testified to substantially the same effect. The officer testified that Graham did not then or at any other time offer or give him money. The appellant testified that the entire payment was intended as a fee for legal services; that he had never mentioned money for the police; that no part of the money was in fact paid to the police or anyone else, but was kept by the appellant.

Appellant's principal contentions are: First, that the evidence supports the proposition that Gal voluntarily gave Graham complete title to the money and therefore appellant is entitled to a directed verdict; and, second, that the trial court's charge to the jury was erroneous in not sufficiently distinguishing between the situation where one obtains complete title to another's property by fraud or trick and the case where possession only is obtained.

Section 2201 of Title 22 of the District of Columbia Code provides as follows:

> Whoever shall feloniously take and carry away anything of value of the amount or value of $50 or upward, including things savoring of the realty, shall suffer imprisonment of not less than one nor more than ten years.

Interpreting this statute, this court has held that "one who obtains money from another upon the representation that he will perform certain service therewith for the latter, intending at the time to convert the money, and actually converting it, to his own use, is guilty of larceny." In classic terminology, "the distinction drawn by the common law is between the case of one who gives up possession of a chattel for a special purpose to another who by converting it to his own use is held to have committed a trespass, and the case of one who, although induced by fraud or trick, nevertheless actually intends that title to the chattel shall pass to the wrongdoer." United States v. Patton, 3 Cir., 1941, 120 F.2d 73, 76.

We now turn to appellant's first contention, that under the evidence in the case the court should have directed a verdict for the defendant. We think this contention without merit. If the jury believed Gal's testimony, and did not believe that of the defendant, it was possible for the jury to conclude beyond a reasonable doubt that the defendant fraudulently induced Gal to give him $2,000 to be used for a special purpose, i.e., to bribe the police, that the defendant did not intend so to use the money, and converted it to his own use. Under the rule stated above, this would be larceny by trick.

Thus, in the *Means* case [Means v. United States, 65 F.2d 206], the defendant was convicted of the crime of larceny under the following circumstances: After the kidnapping of the infant son of Charles Lindbergh, the defendant in an interview with Mrs. McLean persuaded her that he could assist in locating and recovering the kidnapped baby, stating that if Mrs. McLean would give him $100,000 he would use that sum to pay the ransom and secure the return of the child. On the basis of these representations he secured the money from Mrs. McLean. His representations were fraudulent and he intended at the time to convert the money to his own use, and actually so converted it. People v. Edwards, 236 P. 944, provides an even closer precedent. There the defendant took money from the complainant, representing to her that it would be used to bribe officers investigating criminal activities by her husband. The complainant did not know exactly how the defendant was going to use the money but understood that it was going to be used in some manner to corrupt the police. The court, in sustaining a conviction for larceny, held that under these circumstances "title would remain in [the complainant] until the accomplishment of the purpose for which she gave [the defendant] the money, i.e., until its final delivery by [him] to the officers whom she was led to believe were to be bribed." . . .

The judgment of the District Court is affirmed.

NOTES AND QUESTIONS

1. Because on Gal's testimony the money was handed to the defendant to be given to the police officer as a bribe, how can the court defend its decision that Gal did not intend to pass his whole interest in the money to the defendant, title and all? On the other hand, if the court had held otherwise, thus precluding a larceny-by-trick conviction, could the defendant have been convicted of obtaining money by false pretenses? Note that a false promise is often regarded as inadequate to sustain a false pretense conviction, although it suffices for larceny by trick. See People v. Ashley, page 983 infra.

2. In Bourbonnaise v. State, 248 P.2d 640 (1952), the defendant bootlegger obtained money from Bean as payment for a bottle of whiskey; he stated he would return with the bottle within 30 minutes after purchasing same from another bootlegger. He never returned. Affirming a conviction of larceny, the court stated (248 P.2d at 642):

> This money was not given the defendant to consummate a purchase of liquor represented by defendant to be in his possession. . . . If such had been the case, then the money would have become defendant's money, and if the defendant had failed to turn over the liquor, then supposed to be in his possession either on his person or somewhere outside, such facts would have supported a charge of obtaining money under false pretense. But here defendant . . . merely agreed to take Bean's money and go purchase the liquor from another bootlegger. The money was not his. He was to pay it over for Bean. It was Bean's money until paid over, and then the whiskey would be Bean's.

3. R. Pearce, Theft by False Promises, 101 U. Pa. L. Rev. 967, 987-989 (1953), writes:

> Although some legal scholars have treated larceny by trick as closely related functionally to false pretenses, or even as completely engulfing it, the offenses are respectively aimed at quite different acquisitive techniques. False pretenses is theft by deceit. The misappropriation it punishes must be effected by communication to the owner. Larceny by trick is theft by stealth. It punishes misappropriation effected by unauthorized disposition of the owner's property. The former focuses on defendant's behavior while face to face with the owner: did it amount to a false pretense? The focus of the latter is upon defendant's behavior behind the owner's back: did it amount to an unauthorized appropriation?
>
> One cause of confusion of the offenses is that larceny by trick requires some deceit in addition to the unauthorized disposition of property which is its gravamen. It is thus thought of as a type of theft by fraud. However, the requirement of deceit in larceny by trick stems from its history rather than its function and plays a minor role. . . .
>
> It should be apparent that deceit had little to do with the offensiveness of Pear's behavior. It can hardly be said that being a servant is offensive, yet being a servant plays the same role in larceny by servants as deceit plays in larceny by trick. Each permits a circumvention of the requirement of a "trespassory taking" in order to reach a misappropriation by a person in possession as common law larceny. Fraud for this highly technical purpose need not be subjected to close scrutiny or held to an exacting standard, for there is adequate external evidence of the defendant's antisocial bent in his subsequent misappropriation. Indeed it is true generally, as it was in Pear's Case, that the only substantial evidence of the initial fraud is found in the subsequent unauthorized appropriation.
>
> In contrast, the antisocial act defined by the crime of false pretenses consists entirely of deceit. It consists of so deceiving the owner of the property that he is induced to consent to the defendant's treating the property as his own. This being so, it is unnecessary as well as impossible for the defendant to subsequently misappropriate property which he has stolen by false pretenses. If the behavior by which he induced consent amounts to a false pretense, he has completed his form of theft at the moment the bargain is struck. . . .
>
> Thus it is said that a defendant cannot be convicted of larceny if his deceit induces the owner to transfer his entire interest in the property, whereas he can be if it induces consent merely to his possession or use of the property. This creates the often troublesome paradox that larceny punishes the lesser fraud and exempts the greater. The apparent contradiction disappears with the realization that larceny by trick does not punish *deceit*— it punishes unauthorized appropriation. This functional distinction between larceny and false pretenses suggests a simple test by which specific fact situations can be distributed between the two offenses. If the deceit be eliminated from the transaction by which the property initially came into the defendant's hands, would his subsequent behavior with respect to the property constitute a conversion? If so, the offense may be larceny by trick; it cannot be false pretenses. If not, the offense may be false pretenses; it cannot be larceny by trick.

4. Problem. Defendant went to an auto dealership, took a vehicle for a test drive, and failed to return it. He was convicted of larceny by false pretenses. Should the conviction be affirmed? See Baker v. Commonwealth, 300 S.E.2d 788 (Va. 1983).

PEOPLE v. ASHLEY

Supreme Court of California
42 Cal. 2d 246, 267 P.2d 271 (1954)

Traynor, J. . . . [Defendant, the business manager of a corporation chartered for the purpose of "introducing people," was charged with feloniously taking money from two women and convicted of grand theft under §404 of the California Penal Code. The evidence revealed that defendant obtained a loan of $7,200 from a Mrs. Russ, a woman 70 years of age, by promising that the loan would be secured by a first mortgage on certain improved property of the corporation and that the money would be used to build a theater on other property owned by the corporation. In fact the corporation leased but did not own the improved property, and no theater was ever built, the money having been used to meet the corporation's operating expenses. After defendant received the money, Mrs. Russ frequently quarreled with him over his failure to deliver the promised first mortgage. She finally received a note of the corporation secured by a second trust deed on some unimproved property owned by the corporation. She testified that she accepted this security because defendant had told her to "take that or nothing." She subsequently received four postdated checks in payment of the loan. After it became apparent that these checks would not be paid, defendant requested an extension. Mrs. Russ granted the extension after defendant had threatened to destroy himself if she refused, so that she might be paid from the proceeds of his life insurance policies.

[Defendant obtained $13,590 from a Mrs. Neal representing that the corporation intended to use the money to buy the El Patio Theatre. She was initially told that the loan would be secured by a trust deed on the theater building and that she would have good security for her loan because the corporation was worth a half million dollars. However, after obtaining the money, defendant issued Mrs. Neal a note of the corporation for $13,500. Subsequently, she loaned the corporation an additional $4,470, receiving a note for $17,500 in exchange for the previous note. Mrs. Neal testified that when she hesitated in making the additional loan, defendant placed a gun on his desk and said: "Now look here, Mrs. Neal, I don't want no monkey business out of you. Do you understand that?" The corporation did not buy the theater; Mrs. Neal never received the trust deed; and the money was deposited to the corporation's account.

[Evidence was introduced indicating that the corporation was in a strained financial condition and was worth nothing like a half million dollars. There was also evidence showing that the defendant received no salary from the corporation, but that he drove an expensive automobile paid for by the corporation, and that he had drawn numerous checks on corporation funds for the payment of expenses.]

. . . The case went to the jury with instructions relating to larceny by trick and device and obtaining property by false pretenses. The jurors were instructed that all would have to agree on the type of theft, if any, that was committed. . . .

Although the crimes of larceny by trick and device and obtaining property by false pretenses are much alike, they are aimed at different criminal acquisitive techniques. Larceny by trick and device is the appropriation of property, the possession of which was fraudulently acquired; obtaining property by false pretenses is the fraudulent or deceitful acquisition of both title and possession. In this state, these two offenses, with other larcenous crimes, have been consolidated into the single crime of theft (Pen. Code, §484), but their elements have not been changed thereby. The purpose of the consolidation was to remove the technicalities that existed in the pleading and proof of these crimes at common law. Indictments and informations charging the crime of "theft" can now simply allege an "unlawful taking." Pen. Code, §§951, 952. Juries need no longer be concerned with the technical differences between the several types of theft, and can return a general verdict of guilty if they find that an "unlawful taking" has been proved. The elements of the several types of theft included within section 484 have not been changed, however, and a judgment of conviction of theft, based on a general verdict of guilty, can be sustained only if the evidence discloses the elements of one of the consolidated offenses. In the present case, it is clear from the record that each of the prosecuting witnesses intended to pass both title and possession, and that the type of theft, if any, in each case, was that of obtaining property by false pretenses. [Defendant's] defense was not based on distinctions between title and possession, but rather he contends that there was no unlawful taking of any sort.

To support a conviction of theft for obtaining property by false pretenses, it must be shown that the defendant made a false pretense or representation with intent to defraud the owner of his property, and that the owner was in fact defrauded. It is unnecessary to prove that the defendant benefited personally from the fraudulent acquisition. People v. Jones, 36 Cal. 2d 373, 377, 381, 224 P.2d 353. The false pretense or representation must have materially influenced the owner to part with his property, but the false pretense need not be the sole inducing cause. If the conviction rests primarily on the testimony of a single witness that the false pretense was made, the making of the pretense must be corroborated. Pen. Code, §1110.

The crime of obtaining property by false pretenses was unknown in the early common law, and our statute, like those of most American states, is directly traceable to 30 Geo. 11, ch. 24, section 1. In an early Crown Case Reserved, Rex v. Goodhall, Russ. & Ry. 461 (1821), the defendant obtained a quantity of meat from a merchant by promising to pay at a future day. The jury found that the promise was made without intention to perform. The judges concluded, however, that the defendant's conviction was erroneous because the pretense "was merely a promise of future conduct, and common prudence and caution would have prevented any injury arising from it." Russ. & Ry. at 463. . . . By stating that the "promise of future conduct" was such that "common prudence and caution" could prevent any injury arising therefrom, the new offense was confused with the old common law "cheat." The decision also seems contrary to the plain meaning of the statute, and was so interpreted by two English writers on the law of crimes. Archbold, Pleading and Evidence in Criminal Cases 183 [3d ed. 1828]; Roscoe, Digest of the Law of Evidence in Criminal Cases 418 [2d Amer. ed. 1840]. The opinion of Rex v. Goodhall, supra, was completely misinterpreted in the case of Commonwealth v. Drew, 1837, 19 Pick. 179, 185, 36 Mass. 179, 185, in which the Supreme Judicial Court of Massachusetts declared by way of dictum, that under the statute "naked lies" could not be regarded as "false pretences." On the basis of these two questionable decisions, Wharton formulated the following generalization: ". . . the false pretense to be within the statute, must relate to a state of things averred to be at the time existing, and not to a state of things thereafter to exist." Wharton, American Criminal Law 542 [1st ed. 1846]. This generalization has been followed in the majority of American cases, almost all of which can be traced to reliance on Wharton or the two cases mentioned above. The rule has not been followed in all jurisdictions, however. Some courts have avoided the problems created by the rule by blurring the distinctions between larceny by trick and device and obtaining property by false pretenses. See generally, Pearce, "Theft by False Promises," 101 U. of Pa. L. Rev. 967. . . . Other courts have repudiated the majority rule. . . .[3]

The Court of Appeals for the District of Columbia has however, advanced the following reasons in defense of the majority rule: "It is of course true that then [at the time of the early English cases cited by Wharton, supra], as now, the intention to commit certain crimes was ascertained by looking backward from the act and finding that the accused intended to do what he did do. However, where, as here, the act complained of — namely, failure to repay money or use it as specified at the time of borrowing — is as consonant with ordinary commercial default as with criminal conduct, the danger of applying this technique to prove the crime is quite apparent. Business affairs would be materially incumbered by the ever present threat that a debtor might be subjected to criminal penalties if the prosecutor and jury were of the view that at the time of borrowing he was mentally a cheat. The risk of prosecuting one who is guilty of nothing more than a failure or inability to pay his debts is a very real consideration. . . ." Chaplin v. United States, 157 F.2d 697, 698-699.

. . . We do not find this reasoning persuasive. In this state, and in the majority of American states as well as in England, false promises can provide the foundation of a civil action for deceit. In such actions something more than nonperformance is required to prove the defendant's intent not to perform his promise. Nor is proof of nonperformance alone sufficient in criminal prosecutions based on false promises. In such prosecutions the People must, as in all criminal prosecutions, prove their case beyond a reasonable doubt. Any danger, through the instigation of criminal proceedings by disgruntled creditors, to those who have blamelessly encountered "commercial defaults" must, therefore, be predicated upon the idea that trial juries are incapable of weighing the evidence and understanding the instruction that they must be convinced of the defendant's fraudulent intent beyond a reasonable doubt, or that appellate courts will be derelict in discharging their duty to ascertain that there is sufficient evidence to support a conviction. . . .

Moreover, in cases of obtaining property by false pretenses, it must be proved that any misrepresentations of fact alleged by the People were made knowingly and with intent to deceive. If such misrepresentations are made innocently or inadvertently, they can no more form the basis for a prosecution for obtaining property by false pretenses than can an innocent breach of contract. . . .

If false promises were not false pretences, the legally sophisticated, without fear of punishment, could perpetrate on the unwary fraudulent schemes like that

3. The majority rule was also rejected by the United States Supreme Court in the construction of the federal mail fraud statute. See Durland v. United States, 161 U.S. 306, 313. . . .

divulged by the record in this case. . . . The inclusion of false promises within sections 484 and 532 of the Penal Code will not "materially encumber" business affairs. . . .

The judgment and the order denying the motion for a new trial are affirmed.

SCHAUER, J. I concur in the judgment solely on the ground that the evidence establishes, with ample corroboration, the making by the defendant of false representations as to existing facts. On that evidence the convictions should be sustained pursuant to long accepted theories of law. . . . I dissent from all that portion of the opinion which discusses and pronounces upon the theories which in my view are extraneous to the proper disposition of any issue actually before us. . . .

In a prosecution for obtaining property by the making of a false promise, knowingly and with intent to deceive, the matter to be proved, as to its criminality, is purely subjective. It is not, like the specific intent in such a crime as burglary, a mere element of the crime; it is, in any significant sense, all of the crime. The proof will necessarily be of objective acts, entirely legal in themselves, from which inferences as to the ultimate illegal subjective fact will be drawn. But, whereas in burglary the proof of the subjective element is normally as strong and reliable as the proof of any objective element, in this type of activity the proof of such vital element can almost never be reliable; it must inevitably (in the absence of confession or something tantamount thereto) depend on inferences drawn by creditors, prosecutors, jurors, and judges from facts and circumstances which by reason of their nature cannot possibly exclude innocence with any certainty. . . . Such inferences as proof of the alleged crime have long been recognized as so unreliable that they have been excluded from the category of acceptable proof.

. . . I am unwilling to accept as a premise the scholastic redaction of the majority that rules of proof may be set aside because appellate judges will always know when a jury has been misled and the proof is not sufficient. . . .

With the rule that the majority opinion now enunciates, no man, no matter how innocent his intention, can sign a promise to pay in the future, or to perform an act at a future date, without subjecting himself to the risk that at some later date others, in the light of differing perspectives, philosophies and subsequent events, may conclude that, after all, the accused *should* have known that at the future date he could not perform as he promised — and if he, as a "reasonable" man from the point of view of the creditor, district attorney and a grand or trial jury — *should* have known, then, it may be inferred, he did know. And if it can be inferred that he knew, then this court and other appellate courts will be bound to affirm a conviction. . . .

NOTE

In accord with *Ashley,* see Commonwealth v. Parker, 564 A.2d 246 (Pa. Super. 1989); Kennedy v. State, 342 S.E.2d 251 (W. Va. 1986). In contrast, some courts continue to hold that a false promise cannot constitute false pretenses. E.g., State v. Allen, 505 So. 2d 1024 (Miss. 1987); People v. Reigle, 566 N.W.2d 21, 24 (Mich. App. 1997). See Annot., 19 A.L.R.4th 959 (Supp. 1993).

NEW YORK PENAL LAW

SECTION 155.05(2)(d)

A person obtains property by false promise when, pursuant to a scheme to defraud, he obtains property of another by means of a representation, express or implied, that he or a third person will in the future engage in particular conduct, and when he does not intend to engage in such conduct or, as the case may be, does not believe that the third person intends to engage in such conduct.

In any prosecution for larceny based upon a false promise, the defendant's intention or belief that the promise would not be performed may not be established by or inferred from the fact alone that such promise was not performed. Such a finding may be based only upon evidence establishing that the facts and circumstances of the case are wholly consistent with guilty intent or belief and wholly inconsistent with innocent intent or belief, and excluding to a moral certainty every hypothesis except that of the defendant's intention or belief that the promise would not be performed. . . .

MODEL PENAL CODE

SECTION 223.3. THEFT BY DECEPTION

[See Appendix.]

NELSON v. UNITED STATES

United States Court of Appeals, District of Columbia Circuit
227 F.2d 21 (1955)

DANAHER, J. This is an appeal from a conviction for obtaining goods by false pretenses in violation of D.C. Code §22-1301 (1951). The trial court entered judgment of acquittal on a second count charging grand larceny. Evidence was offered to show that appellant from time to time over a period of months, for purposes of resale, had purchased merchandise from Potomac Distributors of Washington, D.C., Inc. (hereinafter referred to as Potomac Distributors). By September 18, 1952, his account was said to be in arrears more than thirty days. Late that afternoon, appellant sought immediate possession of two television sets and a washing machine, displayed his customers' purchase contracts to support his statement that he had already sold such merchandise and had taken payment therefor, and told one Schneider, secretary-treasurer of Potomac Distributors, "I promised delivery tonight." Appellant was told no further credit could be extended to him because of his overdue indebtedness in excess of $1800, whereupon appellant offered to give security for the desired items as well as for the delinquent account. He represented himself as the owner of a Packard car for which he had paid $4,260.50, but failed to disclose an outstanding prior indebtedness on the car of $3,028.08 secured by a chattel mortgage in favor of City Bank. Instead, he represented that he owed only one payment of some $55, not then due. Relying upon such representations, Potomac Distributors delivered to appellant two television sets each worth $136, taking in return a demand note for the entire indebtedness, past and present, in the total, $2,047.37, secured by a chattel mortgage on the Packard and the television sets. Appellant promised to make a cash payment on the note within a few days for default of which the holder was entitled to demand full payment. When the promised payment was not forthcoming, Schneider, by telephone calls and a personal visit to appellant's home, sought to locate appellant but learned he had left town. The Packard about that time was in a collision, incurring damage of about $1,000, and was thereupon repossessed in behalf of the bank which held the prior lien for appellant's car purchase indebtedness. . . .

Appellant argues that Potomac Distributors could not have been defrauded for the car on September 18, 1952, "had an equity of between $900 and $1000 and roughly five times the value of the two television sets." That fact is immaterial. . . .

This appellant has sold two television sets, and apparently had taken payment therefor although he had no television sets to deliver to his customers. He could not get the sets from Potomac Distributors without offering security for his past due account as well as for his present purchase. In order to get them he lied. He represented that his car acquired at a cost of more than $4000 required only one further payment of $55. He now complains because his victim believed him when he lied. He argues that the misrepresentations were not material although the victim testified, and the jury could properly find, that he would not have parted with his goods except in reliance upon appellant's statements. . . .

He argues that there was no proof of an intent upon his part to defraud his victim.

> Wrongful acts knowingly or intentionally committed can neither be justified nor excused on the ground of innocent intent. The intent to injure or defraud is presumed when the unlawful act, which results in loss or injury, is proved to have been knowingly committed. It is a well-settled rule, which the law applies in both criminal and civil cases, that the intent is presumed and inferred from the result of the action.

This quotation from a challenged charge was found by the Supreme Court to be "unexceptionable as matter of law" in Agnew v. United States, 1897, 165 U.S. 36, 53. . . .

Affirmed.

MILLER, J. (dissenting). . . . Nelson did make a false representation; but the question is whether there was evidence from which the jury could properly be permitted to infer that he intended to defraud, and to conclude that Potomac was thereby defrauded. . . .

Differing definitions of the word "defraud" probably cause the difference in opinion between the majority and me. They seem to think it means, in connection with a purchase, to make a false pretense in the process of obtaining goods even though the purchase price is well secured. I think the word means, in connection with a purchase, to make a false pretense as a result of which the seller is deprived of his goods or of the purchase price. The difference is particularly important in a case like this one where a purchaser is charged with defrauding a seller. A purchaser can be said to have defrauded the seller of his goods only if he intended to defraud him of the purchase price for which the seller was willing to exchange them. It seems to me to follow that a purchaser who makes a false statement in buying on credit has not defrauded the seller of his goods if he nevertheless amply secures the debt. . . .

In considering the criminality vel non of the false statement, it must be remembered that the past due indebtedness of $1,697.87 is to play no part. That credit had already been extended generally, and with respect to it Potomac parted with nothing on September 18. Nelson was only charged with defrauding Potomac by obtaining through false pretense the articles then delivered, which had a total value of only $349.50.

What was the actual value on September 18 of the property upon which Potomac took a lien, on the strength of which it parted with property worth $349.50? The bank collection manager, testifying for the Government, said that although on September 18 Nelson still owed the bank $3,028.08, he had on that day an equity in the car worth from $900 to $1,000. The mortgaged television sets were, I suppose, worth their price of $272. Adding to this the minimum equity in the automobile proved by the prosecution, it appears that Potomac had a lien on property worth at least $1,172 to protect a debt of $349.50. The proportion was more than three to one.

Such is the evidence as to what happened September 18, from which the jury was permitted to infer that Nelson then intended to defraud, and to conclude that he then did fraudulently obtain from Potomac the three articles purchased. As to intent, I suggest that it is wholly irrational to presume or infer that one intends to defraud when he buys goods on credit and safeguards that credit by giving more than triple security for it — no matter if he does falsely pretend that the security is even greater. It is equally illogical to conclude that the creditor was thereby defrauded. For that reason, my opinion is that the proof I have outlined — which was the only pertinent proof — did not warrant the trial court in submitting the case to the jury. . . .

As I have said, Nelson was guilty of a moral wrong in falsely and grossly misrepresenting his debt to the bank, but in the circumstances he should not have been indicted and convicted because of it. The District of Columbia statute under which he was prosecuted does not make mere falsehood felonious; it only denounces as criminal a false pretense which was intended to defraud and which in fact had that result. Even a liar is entitled to the full protection of the law. I am afraid a grave injustice has been done in this case.

NOTES AND QUESTIONS

1. The defendant contractor applied to the owner of the house he was in the process of constructing for an advance to meet the weekly payroll. Periodic advances were provided for in the construction contract. Since the owner had just been notified that the defendant was indebted to a material-man and requested not to make further advancements, he informed the defendant he would make no further payments until the debt was paid. The defendant then assured him that he had that morning discharged the debt (in fact, he had not done so), whereupon the owner paid over the requested advance and defendant paid the employees their wages. May the defendant be convicted of obtaining money by false pretenses? See Sanson v. Commonwealth, 313 Ky. 631, 233 S.W.2d 258 (1950); Annot., 20 A.L.R.2d 1266 (1951). Would the prosecutor's case be stronger if the defendant's false representation had been that he needed the money to obtain from a carrier a recently arrived shipment of materials for the house? See the material on mens rea, page 1020 infra.

2. Cf. Rex v. Clucas, [1949] 2 All E.R. 40, 41-42, per Lord Goddard, C.J.:

> The evidence showed that these two men, who obviously were dishonest, induced bookmakers to bet with them by representing that they were commission agents acting on behalf of a large number of workmen who were making small bets on various races, whereas, in fact, they were making bets in considerable sums of money for themselves alone. The main question which arises . . . can be stated in this way. Does a man who induces a bookmaker to bet with him by making false pretences as to his identity or as to the capacity in which he is making the bets obtain money by false pretences if he is fortunate enough to back a winning horse and so receives money from the bookmaker? In the opinion of the court it is impossible to say that there was here an obtaining of the money by the false pretences which were alleged, because the money was obtained, not by reason of the fact that the accused persons falsely pretended that they were somebody or acting in some capacity which they were not, but because they backed a winning horse as a result of which the bookmaker paid them the sums obtained. No doubt, the bookmaker might never have opened an account with these men if he had known the true facts, but we must distinguish between a contributing cause and the effective cause which led the bookmaker to pay the money, namely, the fact that these men had backed a winning horse.

4. *Blackmail*

STATE v. HARRINGTON

Supreme Court of Vermont
128 Vt. 242, 260 A.2d 692 (1969)

HOLDEN, C.J. [The respondent, John B. Harrington, was a Vermont attorney retained by Mrs. Norma Morin to obtain a divorce from her husband, Mr. Armand Morin. As Mrs. Morin was without funds, respondent agreed to work on a contingent fee basis. The couple owned assets worth approximately $50,000, including a motel in New Hampshire where the two had previously lived.

[Together with his client, Harrington arranged to obtain evidence of Mr. Morin's infidelity by hiring a woman, armed with a tape recorder, to entice him into having sex with her in one of his motel rooms. She succeeded, and at the appropriate moment Harrington and his associates entered the room and took pictures of Mr. Morin and the woman naked in bed.

[Several days later Harrington, in the presence of Mrs. Morin, dictated a letter to Mr. Morin proposing a settlement of the divorce action in which Mrs. Morin would receive her divorce, give up her interest in the marital assets, waive alimony, and receive a lump sum of $175,000. The letter also provided that

> any such settlement would include the return to you of all tape recordings, all negatives, all photographs and copies of photographs that might in any way, bring dis-

> credit upon yourself. Finally, there would be an absolute undertaking on the part of your wife not to divulge any information of any kind or nature which might be embarrassing to you in your business life, your personal life, your financial life, or your life as it might be affected by the Internal Revenue Service, the United States Customs Service, or any other governmental agency.

The letter stressed Mrs. Morin's current state of insolvency, and requested a prompt reply. The letter went on to say that]

> Unless the writer has heard from you on or before March 22, we will have no alternative but to withdraw the offer and bring immediate divorce proceedings in Grafton County. This will, of course, require the participation by the writer's correspondent attorneys in New Hampshire. If we were to proceed under New Hampshire laws, without any stipulation, it would be necessary to allege, in detail, all of the grounds that Mrs. Morin has in seeking the divorce. The writer is, at present, undecided as to advising Mrs. Morin whether or not to file for "informer fees" with respect to the Internal Revenue Service and the United States Customs Service. In any event, we would file, alleging adultery, including affidavits, alleging extreme cruelty and beatings, and asking for a court order enjoining you from disposing of any property, including your stock interests, during the pendency of the proceeding. . . . With absolutely no other purpose than to prove to you that we have all of the proof necessary to prove adultery beyond a reasonable doubt, we are enclosing a photograph taken by one of my investigators on the early morning of March 8. The purpose of enclosing the photograph as previously stated, is simply to show you that cameras and equipment were in full operating order.

13 V.S.A. §1701 provides: "A person who maliciously threatens to accuse another of a crime or offense, or with an injury to his person or property, with intent to extort money or other pecuniary advantage, or with intent to compel the person so threatened to do an act against his will, shall be imprisoned in the state prison not more than two years or fined not more than $500.00." . . .

[T]he respondent maintains his letter does not constitute a threat to accuse Morin of the crime of adultery. He argues the implicit threats contained in the communication were "not to accuse of the CRIME of adultery but to bring an embarrassing, reputation-ruining divorce proceeding in Mr. Morin's county of residence unless a stipulation could be negotiated."

In dealing with a parallel contention in State v. Louanis, 79 Vt. 463, 467, 65 A. 532, 533, the Court answered the argument in an opinion by Chief Judge Rowell. "The statute is aimed at blackmailing, and a threat of any public accusation is as much within the reason of the statute as a threat of a formal complaint, and is much easier made, and may be quite as likely to accomplish its purpose. There is nothing in the statute that requires such a restricted meaning of the word 'accuse'; and to restrict it thus, would well nigh destroy the efficacy of the act."

The letter, marked "personal and confidential," makes a private accusation of adultery in support of a demand for a cash settlement. An incriminating photograph was enclosed for the avowed purpose of demonstrating "we have all of the proof necessary to prove adultery beyond a reasonable doubt." According to the writing itself, cost of refusal will be public exposure of incriminating conduct in the courts of New Hampshire where the event took place.

In further support of motion for acquittal, the respondent urges that the totality of the evidence does not exclude the inference that he acted merely as an attorney, attempting to secure a divorce for his client on the most favorable terms possible. This, of course, was the theory of the defense. . . .

At the time of the writing, the respondent was undecided whether to advise his client to seek "informer fees." One of the advantages tendered to Morin for a "quiet" and "undamaging" divorce is an "absolute undertaking" on the part of the respondent's client not to inform against him in any way. The Internal Revenue Service, the United States Customs Service and other governmental agencies are suggested as being interested in such information. Quite clearly, these veiled threats exceeded the limits of the respondent's representation of his client in the divorce action. Although these matters were not specified in the indictment, they have a competent bearing on the question of intent.

Apart from this, the advancement of his client's claim to the marital property, however well founded, does not afford legal cause for the trial court to direct a verdict of acquittal in the background and context of his letter to Morin. A demand for settlement of a civil action, accompanied by a malicious threat to expose the wrongdoer's criminal conduct, if made with intent to extort payment, against his will, constitutes the crime alleged in the indictment.

The evidence at hand establishes beyond dispute the respondent's participation was done with preconceived design. The incriminating evidence which his letter threatens to expose was wilfully contrived and procured by a temptress hired for that purpose. These factors in the proof are sufficient to sustain a finding that the respondent acted maliciously and without just cause, within the meaning of our criminal statutes. The sum of the evidence supports the further inference that the act was done with intent to extort a substantial contingent fee to the respondent's personal advantage. . . . The evidence of guilt is ample to support the verdict and the trial was free from errors in law.

Judgment affirmed.

NOTES AND QUESTIONS

1. Consider whether the Vermont statute quoted in the principal case makes criminal the following threats.

(a) Employee, who has been directing a crucial project for employer, to employer: "Give me a raise, or I will quit." Without employee the project will likely fail, possibly placing employer in bankruptcy.

(b) *A* to his lover *B:* "If you stop having sexual relations with me, I will require that you leave my house and sue you for all of that money you owe me." See Lovely v. Cunningham, 796 F.2d 1 (1st Cir. 1986).

(c) Storeowner to shoplifter: "I saw you steal that radio last week. Pay me the $50 it costs, or I'll report you to the police." See People v. Fichtner, 118 N.Y.S.2d 392 (1952), reprinted infra page 994.

(d) Customer to garage mechanic: "Every time you fix my car it breaks within two weeks. Now my car has broken down so many times it's worthless. Buy me a new one, or I'll write to the newspapers about your lousy practices, and you'll never see another customer."

2. Model Penal Code. Consider how the foregoing hypotheticals and the *Harrington* case would come out under Model Penal Code §223.4, Appendix, and the California Penal Code, supra pages 960-961.

3. Consider the following criticism of the decision in *Harrington:*

> Taking the opinion at face value, very serious problems are created for every lawyer. Any time a cause of action involves behavior that is either criminal or embarrassing, a threat to bring the action would be extortionate. Obviously this would effectively preclude many lawyer demand letters. Anomalously, it would be permissible to destroy reputation by bringing suit but not to allow the defendant to avoid that destruction by paying the claim. Not only would this mean a net loss to the privacy that the extortion statute is, in part, aimed at protecting, but it would also involve significantly expanded litigation costs and burdens on efficient utilization of judicial resources. So read, the *Harrington* rule is obviously absurd.

Joseph M. Livermore, Lawyer Extortion, 20 Ariz. L. Rev. 403, 406 (1978).

Question: How else could that decision be read?

4. Lawyers threatening lawsuits. Should what John Harrington did be considered a crime, or merely aggressive advancement of his client's interests? Consider Rex v. Dymond, [1920] 2 K.B. 260, where defendant, who had been sexually assaulted, demanded that her attacker pay her reparations upon threat of "let[ting] the town knowed all about your going on." Glanville Williams criticized her conviction for blackmail:

> The matter assumes a somewhat surprising aspect when it is realised how fine is the line dividing proper from improper threats. Dymond was an illiterate girl, trying to obtain what she may have believed to be her rights without legal aid. Had she the [money] . . . with which to consult a solicitor, instead of writing herself, he would have written a letter to the [attacker] on her behalf in something like the following terms. "Dear Sir, We have been consulted by . . . who states that . . . Our client claims the sum of ______ as compensation for the wrong committed against her, and unless we have your cheque for this amount we are instructed to commence legal proceedings against you." Such a letter would not constitute a criminal offense.

Glanville Williams, Blackmail, [1954] Crim. L. Rev. 162, 165-166.

5. If it is problematic to find extortion in the threat to sue for divorce on the basis of adultery, can the same be said of Harrington's threats to reveal Morin's tax evasion to the Internal Revenue Service and the Customs Service? We are told that for some reason these allegations were not included in the indictment. If they were, should they be regarded as not extortionate because made by a lawyer in the course of representing the interests of his client?

6. American blackmail (often termed extortion) statutes vary a great deal. A useful review may be found in the Commentaries to Model Penal Code §223.4 at 201-224 (1980). There are important variations in the types of threats required. Threats of personal and property injury or to accuse of crime are always enough. Common also are threats to make disclosures that would defame the victim. But how about threats to expose matters that are not defamatory? Some statutes include threats of this nature. See, e.g., Cal. Penal Code §519 (threats to expose any secret affecting the victim); Ill. Cons. Stat. ch. 720, §5/15-5 (threats to reveal any information sought to be concealed by the victim). The Model Penal Code would seem also to exclude such threats, unless they are picked up in the catchall provision that includes "any other harm which would not benefit the actor."

Statutes also vary in how they define what the blackmailer seeks to obtain by his threats. Many statutes, like the Model Penal Code, limit the purpose of the threats to obtaining property or other things of value and rely on other code provisions to deal with the use of coercive threats to obtain other benefits for the threatener. See, e.g., Model Penal Code §212.5 (Criminal Coercion). Some statutes, on the other hand, define the object of the threat more comprehensively; e.g., Fla. Penal Code §836.05 (threats made to compel person to do any act or refrain from doing any act against his will); Minn. Penal Code §609.27 (threats that cause another against his will to do any act or forbear doing a lawful act).

PEOPLE v. FICHTNER

New York Supreme Court, Appellate Division, Second Department
281 A.D. 159, 118 N.Y.S.2d 392, aff'd without opinion,
305 N.Y. 864, 114 N.E.2d 212 (1952)

JOHNSTON, J. Section 850 of the Penal Law provides: "Extortion is the obtaining of property from another . . . , with his consent, induced by a wrongful use of . . . fear. . . ."

Section 851 of the Penal Law provides:

> Fear, such as will constitute extortion, may be induced by an oral or written threat: . . . 2. To accuse him, or any relative of his or any member of his family, of any crime; or, 3. To expose, or impute to him, or any of them, any . . . disgrace. . . .

Defendant Fichtner is the manager, and defendant McGuinness the assistant manager, of the Hill Supermarket in Freeport, Nassau County. On January 30, 1951, an indictment was filed against both defendants, charging them in two counts with the crime of extortion in that on January 18, 1951, defendants, aiding and abetting each other, obtained $25 from one Smith, with his consent, which consent defendants induced by a wrongful use of fear by threatening to accuse Smith of the crime of petit larceny, and to expose and impute to him a disgrace unless Smith paid them $25.

Smith testified that on January 18, 1951, he purchased a number of articles in the Hill store for a total of about $12, but left the store without paying for a fifty-three-cent jar of coffee, which he had concealed in his pocket. After Smith left the store he returned at defendant Fichtner's request. Defendants then threatened to call a policeman, to arrest Smith for petit larceny, with resulting publicity in the newspapers and over the radio, unless he paid $75 and signed a paper admitting that during the course of several months he had unlawfully taken merchandise from the store in that amount. Although Smith admitted he had shopped in Hill's Freeport store about sixteen times and in Hill's Merrick store for about two years, he insisted that the only merchandise he had ever stolen was the fifty-three-cent jar of coffee on the evening in question, and a sixty-five-cent roll of bologna one week previously. However, he finally signed the paper admitting that he had unlawfully taken $50 worth of merchandise from the store during a period of four months. That evening Smith paid $25 in cash and promised to pay the balance in weekly installments of $5. He testified he was induced to sign the paper and make the payment because defendants threatened to accuse him of petit larceny and to expose him to the disgrace of the criminal charge and the resulting publicity. It is not disputed that the $25 taken from Smith was "rung up" on the store register; that the money went into the company funds and that defendants received no part of the money. During the following week Smith reported the incident to the police, and defendants were arrested on January 25, 1951, when Smith, accompanied by a detective, returned to the store and paid the first $5 installment.

Defendants testified that over the course of several weeks, they saw Smith steal merchandise amounting to $5.61, and they honestly believed that during the several months that Smith had been shopping, he had stolen merchandise of the value of $75; that on January 18, 1951, Smith freely admitted that during the four-month period he stole merchandise of the value of $50, and that he voluntarily signed the paper admitting thefts in that amount; that on that date he paid $25 on account and promised to pay the balance in weekly installments.

That the Smith incident was not an isolated one, but rather part of a course of conduct pursued by defendants, even after warning by the police to discontinue the practice, was not only clearly established but admitted by defendant Fichtner. . . .

In my opinion, the verdict is amply supported by the evidence. Implicit in the verdict is a finding that Smith stole only $1.18 in merchandise as he admitted, or at most the $5.61 which defendants claimed they actually saw him steal, and that he was induced to pay the $25 on January 18, 1951, by defendants' threats to accuse him of crime and to expose him to disgrace. By its verdict, the jury rejected defendants' contention that Smith voluntarily admitted having stolen $50 worth of merchandise and that they demanded from Smith only what was rightfully due.

Defendants requested the court to charge that

> if in the judgment of the jury the defendants honestly believed that the amount which the complainant paid or agreed to pay represented the approximate amount of the merchandise which he or they had previously stolen from the Hill Supermarket, then the defendants must be acquitted.

The court refused the request "except as already charged." Although two members of the court are of the opinion that for the reason stated the trial court was justified in refusing to charge as requested, four members of the court are of the further opinion that the request was legally incorrect and, therefore, should have been refused. In other words, we believe that the portion of the main charge to the effect that, under the circumstances of this case, extortion is committed only when one obtains property from another by inducing fear in that other by threatening to accuse him of crime unless he pays an amount over and above what was rightfully due was more favorable to defendants than that which they were entitled to receive. In our opinion, the extortion statutes were intended to prevent the collection of money by the use of fear induced by means of threats to accuse a debtor of crime, and it makes no difference whether the debtor stole any goods, nor how much he stole, and that defendants may properly be convicted even though they believed that the complainant was guilty of the theft of their employer's goods in an amount either equal to or less, or greater than any sum of money obtained from the complainant. Nor is defendants' good faith in thus enforcing payment of the money alleged to be due to their employer a defense. . . .

The law does not authorize the collection of just debts by threatening to accuse the debtor of crime, even though the complainant is in fact guilty of the crime. In my opinion, it makes no difference whether the indebtedness for which a defendant demands repayment is one arising out of the crime for the prosecution of which he threatens the complainant, or is entirely independent and having no connection with the crime which forms the basis of the accusation. The result in both cases is the concealment and compounding of a felony to the injury of the State. It is that result which the extortion statutes were intended to prevent.

[Conviction affirmed.]

WENZEL, J. (dissenting). [T]he jury was permitted to convict defendants of the crime of extortion on proof that they had induced complainant, by the threats alleged, to pay to defendants more than he rightfully owed for goods which he had stolen, even though defendants might have honestly believed that the amount demanded from complainant was the amount which he rightfully owed. In my opinion, although the question is one as to which there is a conflict of authority, if defendants, acting without malice and in good faith, made an honest mistake, they were not guilty of the crime charged. There would then be no criminal intent. The defendants were not acting in their own behalf but in that of their employer, in recovering what they believed to be rightfully due it. . . .

NOTE

Under the New York Penal Law enacted subsequent to *Fichtner,* extortion remains excluded from the class of larceny-type crimes for which a claim of right is a defense. See People v. Reid, page 1027 infra. However, a special provision applicable to extortion, N.Y. Pen. Law §155.15(2) provides:

> In any prosecution for larceny by extortion committed by instilling in the victim a fear that he or another person would be charged with a crime, it is an affirmative defense that the defendant reasonably believed the threatened charge to be true and that his sole purpose was to compel or induce the victim to take reasonable action to make good the wrong which was the subject of such threatened charge.

Section 215.45 provides:

> 1. A person is guilty of compounding a crime when: (a) He solicits, accepts or agrees to accept any benefit upon an agreement or understanding that he will refrain from initiating a prosecution for a crime; or (b) He confers, or offers or agrees to confer, any benefit upon another person upon an agreement or understanding that such other person will refrain from initiating a prosecution for a crime.
>
> 2. In any prosecution under this section, it is an affirmative defense that the benefit did not exceed an amount which the defendant reasonably believed to be due as restitution or indemnification for harm caused by the crime.

NOTE ON THE RATIONALE OF BLACKMAIL

In Unraveling the Paradox of Blackmail, 84 Colum. L. Rev. 670 (1984), James Lindgren identifies the puzzle about blackmail:

Most crimes do not need theories to explain why the behavior is criminal. The wrongdoing is self-evident. But blackmail is unique among major crimes: no one has yet figured out why it ought to be illegal. Recognizing the magnitude of the problem, one theorist wondered whether we can find a principled distinction (or indeed any interesting distinction) between blackmail and permissible behavior that is not blackmail.

In blackmail, the heart of the problem is that two separate acts, each of which is a moral and legal right, can combine to make a moral and legal wrong. For example, if I threaten to expose a criminal act unless I am paid money, I have committed blackmail. Or if I threaten to expose a sexual affair unless I am given a job, once again I have committed blackmail. I have a legal right to expose or threaten to expose the crime or affair, and I have a legal right to seek a job or money, but if I combine these rights it is blackmail. If both a person's ends — seeking a job or money — and his means — threatening to expose — are otherwise legal, why is it illegal to combine them? Therein lies what has been called the "paradox of blackmail."

Following is a sampling of the attempts that have been made to deal with this apparent paradox.

James Lindgren, Unraveling the Paradox of Blackmail, 84 Colum. L. Rev. 670, 692 (1984): [T]he key to the wrongfulness of the blackmail transaction is its triangular structure. The transaction implicitly involves not only the blackmailer and his victim but always a third party as well. This third party may be, for example, the victim's spouse or employer, the authorities or even the public at large. When a blackmailer tries to use his right to release damaging information, he is threatening to tell others. If the blackmail victim pays the blackmailer, it is to avoid the harm that those others would inflict. Thus blackmail is a way that one person requests something in return for suppressing the actual or potential interests of others. To get what he wants, the blackmailer uses leverage that is less his than someone else's. Selling the right to go to the police involves suppressing the state's interests. Selling the right to tell a tort victim who committed the tort involves suppressing the tort victim's interests. And selling the right to inform others of embarrassing (but legal) behavior involves suppressing the interests of those other people.

Noninformational blackmail involves the same misuse of a third party's leverage for the blackmailer's own benefit. For example, when a labor leader threatens to call a strike unless he is given a personal payoff, he is using the leverage of third parties to bargain for his own benefit. Thus the criminalization of informational and noninformational blackmail represents a principled decision that advantages may not be gained by extra leverage belonging more to a third party than to the threatener. Recognizing the triangular structure of the blackmail transaction makes clear the parasitic nature of the blackmailer's conduct. Once this structure is understood, it becomes easier to find in blackmail the kind of behavior that concerns the other theorists: immorality, invasiveness, and economic waste.

George P. Fletcher, Blackmail: The Paradigmatic Crime, 141 U. Pa. L. Rev. 1617, 1626, 1635 (1993): The proper test, I submit, is whether the transaction with the suspected blackmailer generates a relationship of dominance and subordination. If *V*'s paying money or rendering a service to *D* creates a situation in which *D* can or does dominate *V*, then the action crosses the line from permissible commerce to criminal wrongdoing. The essence of *D*'s dominance over *V* is the prospect of repeated demands. . . . Blackmail occurs when, by virtue of the demand and the action satisfying the demands, the blackmailer knows that she can repeat the demand in the future. Living with that knowledge puts the victim of blackmail in a permanently subordinate position. . . .

In order to counteract the power of the criminal over the victim, the state must intervene by exercising power over the criminal. It is not enough to make the offender pay damages or a fine, for all this means is that she purchases her ongoing status exempt from the prohibitions that apply to others. The state must dominate the criminal's freedom, lest the criminal continue her domination of the victim. The deprivation of liberty and the stigmatization of the offense and the offender — these means counteract the criminal's dominance by reducing his capacity to exercise power over others and symbolically lowering his status.

Douglas H. Ginsburg & Paul Shechtman, Blackmail: An Economic Analysis of the Law, 141 U. Pa. L. Rev. 1849, 1873-1874 (1993): [T]he apparent paradox of blackmail, that one may not threaten to do what one has a lawful right to do, is an economically rational rule. If such threats were lawful, there would be an incentive for people to expend resources to develop embarrassing information about others in the hope of then selling their silence. In that case, some people would be deterred from engaging in embarrassing (but lawful) conduct, while some others who were undeterred would find that their business or social acquaintances or family were informed of their activity. Neither such deterrence nor such information can be counted as a good in many situations, however. These particularly include social and family relations in which the concern of one individual for another is altruistic rather than self-interested; i.e., where one might be distressed to learn another's secret, but was not harmed by ignorance of it. It is precisely these relationships that are threatened with disruption by the prototypical blackmail threat, and that would be protected by an economically rational law. The general principle of the Model Penal Code closely approximates this result by prohibiting threats that it would not benefit the actor to carry out.

Wendy J. Gordon, Truth and Consequences: The Force of Blackmail's Central Case, 141 U. Pa. L. Rev. 1741, 1758, 1770, 1775, 1776, 1777 (1993):

> [P]olicymakers prohibit blackmail less because of economic waste or inefficiency than because of they perceive the act of blackmail to be wrong in itself. . . . One person deliberately seeks to harm another to serve her own ends — to exact money or other advantage — and does so in a context where she has no conceivable justification for her act. . . .
>
> Libertarians who recommend the legalization of blackmail sometimes claim that there is no way to distinguish blackmail from an ordinary commercial transaction. . . . I suggest [these] distinctions . . . : first, that the blackmailer intends to harm; and second, that regardless of intent, the buyer of silence in an extortion transaction suffers a net harm, while the buyer in an ordinary commercial transaction is benefitted. . . .
>
> It is important to note that criminalization also has an impact on blackmail victims, providing them with . . . tools to encourage and assist them in resisting the blackmailer's demands. . . . By threatening to go to the authorities if and only if disclosure is made, victims can discourage blackmailers from disclosing the contested information. This is what Joel Feinberg terms "counterblackmail."

For a careful critique of the preceding arguments, see Mitchell N. Berman, The Evidentiary Theory of Blackmail: Taking Motives Seriously, 65 U. Chi. L. Rev. 795 (1998). Professor Berman argues that none of these efforts provides a persuasive account of why blackmail is a crime. He notes, however, that unconditional disclosure of information ordinarily is not illegal because it may be done for legitimate reasons. In contrast, he argues, a conditional threat to disclose (in the event of nonpayment) is made illegal because it provides strong evidence that any disclosure would be morally blameworthy — "the actor would be inflicting harm knowingly and without good motives" (id. at 848).

5. *Consolidation*

INTRODUCTORY NOTE

Insofar as the pattern of discrete theft offenses covering fundamentally similar kinds of acquisitive conduct has left gaps in the law — for example, where deliberately false promises are employed to induce another to transfer his property — only legislative or judicial revision of the definitions of criminal conduct can supply an effective remedy. Another and more direct consequence of this condition of the law of theft is procedural in character. A defendant convicted of one of these theft offenses, embezzlement, say, may be able to obtain a reversal on appeal through the curious device of proving that the evidence technically established another offense, say, larceny. See, e.g., Nolan v. State, page 961 supra. There are some dramatic examples of this tactic succeeding altogether in frustrating conviction of acknowledged thieves. See, e.g., Commonwealth v. O'Malley, 97 Mass. 584 (1867). In all cases the possibility is a constant threat to the efficient administration of criminal justice. The problem is not with the general principles that a person may not be convicted of a crime with which he has not been charged or that a conviction may not stand on appeal where the proof shows the commission of a different crime than the one charged. It is rather that the distinctions between many of the discrete theft offenses (1) are without criminological significance, and (2) turn on highly technical legal characterizations of basically similar fact situations rather than real differences in conduct, so that in these cases a defendant is not likely to be prejudiced (though, of course, he may be) by a variance between charge and proof.

The principal means of reform, which has gained widespread acceptance, is to consolidate the variety of common law forms of wrongful acquisition of another's property into one single crime, which might be called "theft" or "larceny," and to deprive the differences in modes of acquisition of any legal significance. Some examples follow.

MODEL PENAL CODE: *Section 223.1.* Consolidation of Theft Offenses; Grading; Provisions Applicable to Theft Generally. [See Appendix.]

NEW YORK PENAL LAW: *Section 155.05.* Larceny; Defined. 1. A person steals property and commits larceny when, with intent to deprive another of property or to appropriate the same to himself or to a third person, he wrongfully takes, obtains or withholds such property from an owner thereof.

2. Larceny includes a wrongful taking, obtaining or withholding of another's

property, with the intent prescribed in subdivision one of this section, committed in any of the following ways:

(a) By conduct heretofore defined or known as common law larceny by trespassory taking, common law larceny by trick, embezzlement, or obtaining property by false pretenses;

(b) By acquiring lost property. . . .

(c) By committing the crime of issuing a bad check. . . .

(d) By false promise. . . .

(e) By extortion. . . .

Section 155.45. Larceny; Pleading and Proof. 1. Where it is an element of the crime charged that property was taken from the person or obtained by extortion, an indictment for larceny must so specify. In all other cases, an indictment, information or complaint for larceny is sufficient if it alleges that the defendant stole property of the nature or value required for the commission of the crime charged without designating the particular way or manner in which such property was stolen or the particular theory of larceny involved.

2. Proof that the defendant engaged in any conduct constituting larceny as defined in section 155.05 is sufficient to support any indictment, information or complaint for larceny other than one charging larceny by extortion. An indictment charging larceny by extortion must be supported by proof establishing larceny by extortion.

ILLINOIS ANNOTATED STATUTES chapter 720: *Section 5/16 — 1.* Theft. (a) A person commits theft when he knowingly:

(1) Obtains or exerts unauthorized control over property of the owner; or

(2) Obtains by deception control over property of the owner; or

(3) Obtains by threat control over property of the owner; or

(4) Obtains control over stolen property knowing the property to have been stolen or under such circumstances as would reasonably induce him to believe that the property was stolen . . . and

(A) Intends to deprive the owner permanently of the use or benefit of the property; or

(B) Knowingly uses, conceals or abandons the property in such manner as to deprive the owner permanently of such use or benefit; or

(C) Uses, conceals, or abandons the property knowing such use, concealment or abandonment probably will deprive the owner permanently of such use or benefit. . . .

CALIFORNIA PENAL CODE: *Section 484.* Every person who shall feloniously steal, take, carry, lead, or drive away the personal property of another, or who shall fraudulently appropriate property which has been entrusted to him, or who shall knowingly and designedly, by any false or fraudulent representation or pretense, defraud any other person of money, labor or real or personal property, . . . is guilty of theft.

Section 952. In charging an offense, each count shall contain, and shall be sufficient if it contains in substance, a statement that the accused has committed some public offense therein specified. . . . In charging theft it shall be sufficient to allege that the defendant unlawfully took the labor or property of another.

B. THE PROPERTY SUBJECT TO THEFT

1. *Traditional Theft*

STATE v. MILLER

Supreme Court of Oregon
192 Or. 188, 233 P.2d 786 (1951)

LUSK, J. [Defendant induced complaining witness to agree to guarantee his indebtedness to another on his false representation that he owned a tractor free of encumbrance and on his executing a chattel mortgage thereto as security. In fact defendant was purchasing the tractor under a conditional sales contract. He was convicted of obtaining property by false pretenses.]

The statute under which this prosecution is attempted to be maintained is §23-537, O.C.L.A., and, so far as in any way material, reads:

> If any person shall, by any false pretenses or by any privity [sic] or false token, and with intent to defraud, obtain or attempt to obtain, from any other person any money or property whatsoever, or shall obtain or attempt to obtain with the like intent the signature of any person to any writing, the false making whereof would be punishable as forgery, such person, upon conviction thereof, shall be punished by imprisonment. . . . The making of a bill of sale, or assignment, or mortgage of personal property, by any person not the owner thereof, for the purpose of obtaining money or credit, or to secure an existing indebtedness, shall be deemed a false pretense within the meaning of this section.

. . . Reduced to its simplest terms, this indictment means that by false pretenses the defendant induced the Hub Lumber Company to agree to pay his indebtedness to the Howard Cooper Corporation if he should fail to pay it. The question is whether this amounts to an allegation that, in the sense of the statute, the defendant obtained "any property" from the Hub Lumber Company. If not, then the indictment does not charge a crime. . . . There is no claim that the case falls within the provision of the statute which denounces the making of a bill of sale or assignment or mortgage of personal property by any person not the owner thereof for the purpose of obtaining money or credit or securing an existing indebtedness. Under this latter provision the person in whose favor the false instrument is made must also be the person from whom the money or credit is sought to be obtained or to whom the existing indebtedness is owing. So much is not disputed. . . .

The source of the false pretenses statute in this country is the common law and the statute law of England. The English courts hold that the thing obtained must be the subject of larceny at common law, and accordingly a conviction for obtaining two dogs by false pretenses was quashed because at common law dog stealing is not larceny; so likewise of an indictment for obtaining food and lodging by false pretenses. Under statutes like ours many of the courts of this country take the same view of the law. The California statute covers "money or property." Pen. Code, §532. The court in People v. Cummings, 114 Cal. 437, 46 P. 284, in holding that the word "property" did not include real property, said: "And the offense of false pretenses, under the English statutes, has always been construed as largely analogous to, and closely bordering upon, that of larceny, and as applying only to personal property, which was capable of manual delivery. . . . Real property under the English law was never the subject of the offense either of cheating or of false pretenses." . . .

It should be observed at this point that our statute in respect of the present question is not as broad as those in some of the other states. It reads "any money or property whatsoever." In some of the states, as stated in Burdick [Law of Crime], 481, §640, the statutes, "after enumerating various classes of personal property, conclude the list with what is apparently intended as an all inclusive term, such as 'other things of value,' 'any other valuable thing,' or 'any other valuable thing or effects whatsoever.'" The Kansas statute includes "any money, personal property, right in action, or any other valuable thing or effects whatsoever." G.S. 1949, 21-551. Notwithstanding the comprehensiveness of this provision, the [Kansas] court held, in the light of the origin and history of the crime of false pretenses, that obtaining an extension of time in which to pay a matured debt was not a "valuable thing" within the meaning of the section. [State v. Tower, 251 Pac. 401.] The term "personal property" was said "to denote personal movable things generally." "Mere pecuniary advantage, devoid of any physical attribute of money, chattel, or valuable security, in the sense of the English statute, was not included."

The Louisiana statute refers to "money or any property." In State v. Eicher, 174 La. 344, 140 So. 498, 499, the defendant was charged with obtaining credit from a bank by falsely representing that a certain note had value and was secured by a chattel mortgage. The indictment was held bad, the court saying that "The privilege of having a note renewed or the time of its payment extended may be and frequently is a valuable one to the debtor. But such privilege or advantage is neither money nor property in the sense those terms are ordinarily used and understood." The court further said: "'Property,' as that term is used in this statute, means worldly goods or possessions, tangible things, and things which have an exchangeable or commercial value."

These are not isolated holdings, but in their conception of the meaning of the word "property," as used in statutes of this sort, represent the current of authority. . . .

The provisions of the statute which make unlawful the obtaining of the signature of any person with intent to defraud, and the making of a bill of sale or assignment or mortgage of personal property for the purpose of obtaining money or credit or to secure an existing indebtedness, rather definitely indicate that such an intangible thing as credit was not considered by the legislature to be property.

Moreover, this court [has] recognized that "property" under the statute must be something capable of being possessed and the title to which can be transferred. . . . It need hardly be said that the thing which the defendant is charged with obtaining in the present indictment, the guaranty, or, to be more accurate, the benefit of the guaranty which the Hub Lumber Company gave to the Howard Cooper Corporation, could not be possessed, and that there could be no such thing as holding title to it.

Had the indictment alleged that the defendant obtained the signature of the Hub Lumber Company or its agent to a guaranty of the defendant's indebtedness, we would have had an entirely different question. The failure so to allege was not due to an oversight of the pleader but to the facts themselves, for the proof is that no written guaranty was ever executed but merely an oral one. . . .

Even though our statute included "a thing in action," it would avail the prosecution nothing, for the guaranty was not, so far as the defendant was concerned, a "thing in action." It is doubtless true, as the state's brief asserts, that "a guaranty is a chose in action, a right to indemnity from the guarantor," but it is the right of the creditor who extends credit on the faith of the guaranty, not of the debtor to whom credit is given. The defendant did not receive even a chose in action from the Hub Lumber Company. . . .

The state argues that by the weight of authority the obtaining of a loan by fraud is a violation of the statute and asserts that this is a similar case. But in the loan cases, as the state's brief itself points out, the victim parts with his money. And, while it is true (although not alleged in the indictment) that, just as in the loan cases, the accused obtained credit, he obtained it, not from the victim of his false representations, but from another.

The state's argument of "policy" that the public are entitled to the protection of the law against immoral and reprehensible conduct such as that with which the accused was charged, and of which, no doubt, he was guilty, is appealing, but should be addressed to the legislature, not to the courts. The legislature has not undertaken to make every fraud a crime, but has set boundaries around the crime of false pretenses which the courts must respect and have no authority to pass.

The indictment, in our opinion, does not allege a crime, and the judgment must therefore be reversed and the action dismissed.

NOTES

1. What should be the result under the following formulations:

Model Penal Code, §223.0(6):

> "Property" means anything of value, including real estate, tangible and intangible personal property, contract rights, choses-in-action and other interests in or claims to wealth, admission or transportation tickets, captured or domestic animals, food and drink, electric or other power.

Or. Rev. Stat. §164.005(5):

> "Property" any article, substance or thing of value, including, but not limited to, money, tangible and intangible personal property, real property, choses-in-action, evidence of debt or of contract.

2. Theft of services. In Chappell v. United States, 270 F.2d 274 (9th Cir. 1959), the defendant, an Air Force sergeant, was convicted of knowingly converting property of the United States by making use of the services and labor of an airman to paint his own private dwellings during the airman's on-duty hours. The statute, 18 U.S.C. §641, making it criminal to knowingly convert to one's own use anything of value of the United States (the same statute involved in Morissette v. United States, 342 U.S. 246 (1952), page 237 supra), was construed as intending no such revolutionary change in the common law as would be entailed, in the court's view, in holding that an employee's services were property which could be stolen. The conviction was reversed.

The Seventh Circuit reached a contrary conclusion in a case involving a professor who used the services of a research assistant, hired and paid for out of his grant from the Environmental Protection Agency, to perform work for him on a private research contract unrelated to his E.P.A. grant. United States v. Croft, 750 F.2d 1354 (7th Cir. 1984). Affirming his conviction under 18 U.S.C. §641, the court held that the section is designed to punish "intentional conduct by which a person either misappropriates or obtains a wrongful advantage from government property," and that the defendant "obtained a wrongful advantage by converting and misappropriating the services of [the assistant] for his personal research project while allowing those services to be paid for by the E.P.A." In accord, see United States v. Schwartz, 785 F.2d 673, 681 n.4 (9th Cir. 1986), where the court expressed agreement with *Croft* and overruled its earlier decision in *Chappell.* For a criticism of such results as an unwarranted judicial extension of a statute concerned with traditional property offenses, see Note, Theft of Employee Services Under the United States Penal Code, 23 San Diego L. Rev. 897 (1986).

With respect to theft of services, see Model Penal Code §223.7, Appendix; cf. Ill. Cons. Stat. ch. 720, §5/16-3; N.Y. Penal Law §165.15; Or. Rev. Stat. §164.125.

Under the Illinois provision, a person commits theft of services when he obtains "labor or services of another which are available only for hire, by means of threat or deception or knowing that such use is without the consent of the person providing the . . . labor or services." In People v. Davis, 203 Ill.App.3d 838, 561 N.E.2d 165 (1990), defendants were city officials who were supervising a construction project being performed for the city by an independent contractor. They were responsible for giving job assignments to the contractor's employees daily when the employees reported for work. Defendants asked several of the employees to participate in political campaigning instead of working on the construction project. The employees willingly agreed to do so, but their employer was not aware of the arrangement and lost the value of their services. Are the defendants guilty of theft under the Illinois statute? The court held in the negative. Was there any way, under this statute, to support the opposite result?

3. Theft of use of property. In State v. McGraw, 480 N.E.2d 552 (Ind. 1985), a city employee used a city computer and services for his personal business and was convicted of theft under Ind. Code §35-43-4-2: "A person who knowingly or intentionally exerts unauthorized control over property of another person with intent to deprive the other of its value or use, commits theft. . . ." It appeared that the defendant's unauthorized use cost the city nothing, since the computer service was leased at a fixed charge and the tapes and discs he had used could be erased and reused. The court held that these facts could not support a conviction, even assuming arguendo that the use of the computer was "property" under the theft statute. The court reasoned that the city was not deprived of any part of the value or use of the property. The court said (id. at 554):

> We find no distinction between Defendant's use of the City's computer and the use, by a mechanic, of the employer's hammer or a stenographer's use of the employer's typewriter, for other than the employer's purposes. Under traditional con-

> cepts, the transgression is in the nature of a trespass, a civil matter — and a de minimis one, at that. Defendant has likened his conduct to the use of an employer's vacant bookshelf, for the temporary storage of one's personal items, and to the use of an employer's telephone facilities for toll-free calls. The analogies appear to us to be appropriate.

The court noted a conversion statute, Ind. Code §35-43-4-3: "A person who knowingly or intentionally exerts unauthorized control over property of another person commits criminal conversion, a class A misdemeanor." The evidence might have supported a conviction under this statute, in the court's view.

Question: What should be the result under the Model Penal Code?

UNITED STATES v. GIRARD

United States Court of Appeals, 2d Circuit
601 F.2d 69 (1969)

VAN GRAAFEILAND, J. Appellants have appealed from judgments convicting them of the unauthorized sale of government property (18 U.S.C. §641) and of conspiring to accomplish the sale (18 U.S.C. §371). . . .

In May 1977, appellant Lambert was an agent of the Drug Enforcement Administration, and Girard was a former agent. During that month, Girard and one James Bond began to discuss a proposed illegal venture that involved smuggling a planeload of marijuana from Mexico into the United States. Girard told Bond that for $500 per name he could, through an inside source, secure reports from the DEA files that would show whether any participant in the proposed operation was a government informant. Unfortunately for Mr. Girard, Bond himself became an informant and disclosed his conversations with Girard to the DEA. Thereafter, dealings between Bond and Girard were conducted under the watchful eye of the DEA. Bond asked Girard to secure reports on four men whose names were furnished him by DEA agents. DEA records are kept in computerized files, and the DEA hoped to identify the inside source by monitoring access to the four names in the computer bank. In this manner, the DEA learned that Girard's informant was Lambert, who obtained the reports through a computer terminal located in his office. The convictions on Counts One and Two are based on the sale of this information.

Section 641, so far as pertinent, provides that whoever without authority sells any "record . . . or thing of value" of the United States or who "receives . . . the same with intent to convert it to his use or gain, knowing it to have been embezzled, stolen, purloined or converted," shall be guilty of a crime. Appellants contend that the statute covers only tangible property or documents and therefore is not violated by the sale of information. This contention was rejected by District Judge Daly. . . . We agree with the District Judge's decision. . . .

Like the District Judge, we are impressed by Congress' repeated use of the phrase "thing of value" in section 641 and its predecessors. These words are found in so many criminal statutes throughout the United States that they have in a sense become words of art. The word "thing" notwithstanding, the phrase is generally construed to cover intangibles as well as tangibles. For example, amusement is held to be a thing of value under gambling statutes. . . . Sexual intercourse, or the promise of sexual intercourse, is a thing of value under a bribery statute. . . . So also are a promise to reinstate an employee . . . and an agreement not to run in a primary election. . . . The testimony of a witness is a thing of value under 18 U.S.C. §876. . . .

The existence of a property in the contents of unpublished writings was judicially recognized long before the advent of copyright laws. . . . Although we are not concerned here with the laws of copyright, we are satisfied, nonetheless, that the Government has a property interest in certain of its private records which it may protect by statute as a thing of value. It has done this by the enactment of section 641. [If] conversion is the "misuse or abuse of property" or its use "in an unauthorized manner," the defendants herein could properly be found to have converted DEA's computerized records.

The District Judge also rejected appellants' constitutional challenge to section 641 based upon alleged vagueness and overbreadth, and again we agree with his ruling. Appellants, at the time of the crime a current and a former employee of the DEA, must have known that the sale of DEA confidential law enforcement records was prohibited. The DEA's own rules and regulations forbidding such disclosure may be considered as both a delimitation and clarification of the conduct proscribed by the statute. . . . Where, as here, we are not dealing with defendants' exercise of a First Amendment freedom, we should not search for statutory vagueness that did not exist for the defendants themselves. . . . Neither should we find a constitutional infirmity simply because the statute might conceivably trespass upon the First Amendment rights of others. In view of the statute's plainly legitimate sweep in regulating conduct, . . . any overbreadth that may exist [can] be cured on a case by case basis.

The judgments . . . are affirmed.

NOTES

1. Mr. Anthony Lewis, of the New York Times, had some harsh things to say about such an interpretation of §641. Speaking about the same theory sanctioned by a federal trial court in another case, he said (N.Y. Times, June 19, 1978, at 19, col. 1):

> The two men were charged — and convicted — under Section 641 of the federal criminal code, which makes it a crime to steal government property. What was the property? The Justice Department said it was information, and Judge Albert V. Bryan Jr. followed that view of the law when he charged the jury.
>
> "Information may be government property," the judge said, "apart from the document or the sheets of paper themselves." Thus it does not matter if the original government document remains in the files. Anyone who copies it or makes notes from it without official approval has still stolen "property."
>
> For advocates of secrecy, the beauty of that legal theory is that it applies to no matter what kind of government information is involved. National security need not have a thing to do with it. The price of food in the White House mess, the Amtrak deficit — any fact that leaked could be the subject of a criminal prosecution.
>
> In short, the government-property theory of information would give this country an Official Secrets Act. It would be potentially as devastating to the press and public knowledge as Britain's secrecy law, which Americans and a good many Britons have for years condemned.

2. Jones was visiting the United States Attorney's office when he overheard conversations between government personnel concerning an ongoing criminal investigation of an employee at Barclays Bank. The conversations took place in a reception area and in an individual office. Jones subsequently told officials at Barclays that he had information relating to a criminal investigation and offered to sell it to them for $100; ultimately he received $60 for revealing what he knew. The court held that these facts were sufficient to support an indictment for larceny under 18 U.S.C. §641. United States v. Jones, 677 F. Supp. 238 (S.D.N.Y. 1988). Do you agree?

3. Dreiman repeatedly called and harassed his ex-girlfriend. In defense she obtained an unlisted telephone number. Dreiman then broke into her trailer, so that he could copy down the unlisted number. He was convicted of burglary, on the theory that he had entered with the intent to commit a crime (larceny). The court held that copying the unlisted number constituted larceny, and it therefore upheld the burglary conviction. Dreiman v. State, 825 P.2d 758 (Wyo. 1992). Is the result sound? If so, does the same principle justify the results in *Girard* and in the *Jones* case (Note 2 supra), or are those situations distinguishable?

4. In United States v. Bottone, 365 F.2d 389, 393-394 (2d Cir. 1966), the defendants purchased documents, for ultimate exportation to Europe, from several former employees of Lederle Laboratories, knowing that the employees had temporarily removed and copied the documents. The documents described secret processes for manufacturing antibiotics. The court, per Friendly, J., upheld their conviction of a federal receiving charge, stating (at 393-394):

> The only serious point of law raised by appellants is whether the transportation of papers describing the Lederle processes constituted the transportation in interstate or foreign commerce of "any goods, wares, merchandise, securities or money, of the value of $5,000 or more, knowing the same to have been stolen, converted or taken by fraud." 18 U.S.C. §2314. The problem is not any doubt on our part that papers describing manufacturing procedures are goods, wares, or merchandise, as was held with respect to geophysical maps in United States v. Seagraves, 265 F.2d 876 (3d Cir. 1959), and United States v. Lester, 282 F.2d 750 (3d Cir. 1960). Neither do we have any concern over the value of these papers, since we dismiss out of hand the contentions that secret processes for which European drug manufacturers were willing to pay five and six figures and in whose illicit exploitation appellants eagerly invested a large portion of their time and an appreciable amount of their fortunes were not worth the $5,000 required to subject them to federal prosecution. . . . The serious question is whether, on the facts of this case, the papers showing Lederle processes that were transported in interstate or foreign commerce were "goods" which had been "stolen, converted or taken by fraud" in view of the lack of proof that any of the physical materials so transported came from Lederle's possession. The standard procedure was for Fox and Cancelarich to remove documents from Lederle's files at Pearl River, N.Y., take these to Fox' home within New York state, make photocopies, microfilms or notes, and then restore the purloined papers to the files; only the copies and notes moved or were intended to move in interstate or foreign commerce. The case differs in this respect from the Third Circuit cases of *Seagraves* and *Lester* where, as the records on appeal show, the photostats and tracings delivered by the Gulf Oil geologist were the property of the company, having been made in the company's office, on its paper and with its equipment.
>
> We are not persuaded, however, that a different result should obtain simply because the intangible information that was the purpose of the theft was transformed

and embodied in a different physical object. To be sure, where no tangible objects were ever taken or transported, a court would be hard pressed to conclude that "goods" had been stolen and transported within the meaning of §2314; the statute would presumably not extend to the case where a carefully guarded secret formula was memorized, carried away in the recesses of a thievish mind and placed in writing only after a boundary had been crossed. The situation, however, is quite different where tangible goods are stolen and transported and the only obstacle to condemnation is a clever intermediate transcription or use of a photocopy machine. In such a case, when the physical form of the stolen goods is secondary in every respect to the matter recorded in them, the transformation of the information in the stolen papers into a tangible object never possessed by the original owner should be deemed immaterial. It would offend common sense to hold that these defendants fall outside the statute simply because, in efforts to avoid detection, their confederates were at pains to restore the original papers to Lederle's files and transport only copies or notes, although an oversight would have brought them within it.

5. In Carpenter v. United States, 484 U.S. 19 (1987), the Supreme Court upheld the view, reflected in cases like *Girard* and *Bottone,* that confidential information is protected by the law of theft. Consider John C. Coffee, Hush! The Criminal Status of Confidential Information After *McNally* and *Carpenter* and the enduring Problem of Overcriminalization, 26 Am. Crim. L. Rev. 121, 122-123, 140-142 (1988):

[These cases rest] on an analogy that broadly characterizes the unauthorized communication of trade secrets as equivalent to the crime of embezzlement. [T]his view of "confidential information" as a form of property covered by the laws against larceny is (a) historically unsound, [and] (b) inconsistent with most statutory law dealing with the subject of trade secrets. [The] logic [of these cases] has the potential to alter significantly the relationship between employers and employees across the landscape of American business life. . . .

To see this, consider the case of . . . a broker at a major securities firm [who] is fired [and told that] he may not take with him any list or address book listing his clients, as such information is a trade secret belonging to the firm. As a practical matter, if this broker cannot contact his former clients, he is unemployable with other firms and forfeits valuable "human capital" that he may have developed over a career. [I]t is clear as a civil law matter that the customer lists are confidential trade secrets. To criminalize this civil law rule then effectively arms the employer with a weapon that the legislature never intended to grant. . . .

The point here is not just that civil wrongs are being casually converted into criminal offenses, but that the equivalent of a covenant not to compete is being created by operation of law. [S]uch covenants are . . . generally enforceable only if they have a brief duration and limited scope. [If *Carpenter* and similar cases] mean that, in order to avoid potential entanglement with the criminal law, the employee . . . must desist from using any particularized knowledge about his customers that he gained in his former employment, then [these cases have] given the employer a very powerful weapon to stifle competition, one that does not even require that the employee sign a binding covenant.

A third illustration raises an even darker prospect. . . . Suppose a corporate employee reveals to the press that internal corporate studies show some serious environmental consequences of a specific corporate activity. [G]ood motives do not excuse embezzlement. Under [the] logic [of these cases,] the employee is arguably in the same position as if he stole corporate funds to aid a worthy cause.

[M]ost adult Americans are employees; most possess some form of confidential information about their employer; and most will at some point in their careers change employers. Do all departing employees potentially face entanglement with the federal criminal law?

6. In an effort to strengthen federal protection of trade secrets, Congress in 1996 enacted the Economic Espionage Act, 18 U.S.C. §1831-1839. The Act prohibits unauthorized obtaining, destroying, or conveying of trade secrets either (1) with intent to provide economic or strategic benefit to a foreign government, or (2) with intent to provide economic benefit to a third party and to harm the owner of the trade secret. Trade secrets are broadly defined to include "all forms and types of financial, business, scientific, technical, economic, or engineering information." Id., §1839(3). For an overview of the statute and its enforcement to date, see Kent B. Alexander & Kristen L. Wood, The Economic Espionage Act: Setting the Stage for a New Commercial Code of Conduct, 15 Ga. St. L. Rev. 907 (1999).

REGINA v. STEWART

Supreme Court of Canada, 1988
50 D.L.R.4th 1, 41 C.C.C.3d 481

LAMER, J.: . . . A union attempting to organize the approximately 600 employees of the Constellation Hotel, in Toronto, was unable to obtain the names, addresses and telephone numbers of the employees because of a hotel policy that such information be treated as confidential. . . . The appellant, Wayne John Stewart, a self-employed consultant, was hired by somebody he assumed to be acting for the union to obtain the names and addresses of the employees. Stewart offered a security guard [Hart] at the hotel a fee to obtain this information. . . . The security guard reported the offer to his security chief and the police; as a result, a subsequent telephone conversation between Hart and Stewart was recorded, and Stewart was indicted for, [inter alia, counselling the offense of theft, defined in s.283 of the Criminal Code as the taking of "anything whether animate or inanimate" with the required intention. The accused was acquitted by a single judge court, but on appeal the Ontario Court of Appeal reversed and entered a verdict of conviction.[a] The defendant then appealed to the Supreme Court of Canada.]

We are here dealing not with the theft of a list or any other tangible object containing confidential information, but with the theft of confidential information per se, a pure intangible. . . . [T]he assumption that no tangible object would have been taken was part of the agreed statement of facts, and the case was argued throughout on that basis. The word "anything" is not in itself a bar to including any intangible, whatever its nature. However, its meaning must be determined within the context of s.283 of the Code. . . .

[I]t is clear that to be the object of theft, "anything" must be property in the

a. In Canada, unlike the United States, a prosecutor may appeal such an acquittal and have the appellate court enter a judgment of conviction. —EDS.

sense that to be stolen, it has to belong in some way to someone. For instance, no conviction for theft would arise out of a taking or converting of the air that we breathe, because air is not property. . . .

It is possible that, with time, confidential information will come to be considered as property in the civil law or even be granted special legal protection by statutory enactment. Even if confidential information were to be considered as property under civil law, it does not, however, automatically follow that it qualifies as property for the purposes of criminal law. Conversely, the fact that something is not property under civil law is likewise not conclusive for the purpose of criminal law. Whether or not confidential information is property under the Criminal Code should be decided in the perspective of the criminal law. . . .

[T]he qualification of confidential information as property must be done in each case by examining the purposes and context of the civil and criminal law. It is understandable that one who possesses valuable information would want to protect it from unauthorized use and reproduction. In civil litigation, this protection can be afforded by the courts because they simply have to balance the interests of the parties involved. However, criminal law is designed to prevent wrongs against society as a whole. From a social point of view, whether confidential information should be protected requires a weighing of interests much broader than those of the parties involved. As opposed to the alleged owner of the information, society's best advantage may well be to favour the free flow of information and greater accessibility by all. Would society be willing to prosecute the person who discloses to the public a cure for cancer, although its discoverer wanted to keep it confidential?

The criminalization of certain types of conduct should not be done lightly. If the unauthorized appropriation of confidential information becomes a criminal offence, there would be far-reaching consequences that the courts are not in a position to contemplate. For instance, the existence of such an offence would have serious implications with respect to the mobility of labour. . . .

Moreover, because of the inherent nature of information, treating confidential information as property simpliciter for the purposes of the law of theft would create a host of practical problems. For instance, what is the precise definition of "confidential information"? Is confidentiality based on the alleged owner's intent or on some objective criteria? At what point does information cease to be confidential and would it therefore fall outside the scope of the criminal law? Should only confidential information be protected under the criminal law, or any type of information deemed to be of some commercial value? I am of the view that, given recent technological developments, confidential information, and in some instances, information of a commercial value, is in need of some protection through our criminal law. Be that as it may, in my opinion, the extent to which this should be done and the manner in which it should be done are best left to be determined by Parliament rather than by the courts.

Indeed, the realm of information must be approached in a comprehensive way, taking into account the competing interests in the free flow of information and in one's right to confidentiality or again, one's economic interests in certain kinds of information. The choices to be made rest upon political judgments that, in my view, are matters of legislative action and not of judicial decision. . . .

Appeal allowed; acquittal restored.

NOTES AND QUESTIONS

1. Intangible property. In Oxford v. Moss, 68 Crim. App. 183 (Eng. Div. Ct. 1978), the defendant, an engineering student, managed to obtain the page proof to the Civil Engineering exam to be given at his university the following month. He was caught and charged with theft. It was stipulated that the defendant intended only to "borrow" the proofs and hoped to return them undetected after acquiring advance knowledge of the questions to be asked. Section 1(1) of the English Theft Act of 1968 provided that "[a] person is guilty of theft if he dishonestly appropriates property belonging to another with the intention of permanently depriving the other of it." Section 4(1) defined "property" to include "money and all other property, real or personal, including things in action and other intangible property." The court held that the confidential information contained in the exam paper was not "intangible property" within the meaning of the statute. As the *Girard* case indicates, however, the result could be different in the United States, at least if the test had been a federal Civil Service Examination or some other test sponsored by a federal agency. And those who obtain confidential information from private companies arguably could be subject to prosecution for theft of "property" by stealth or fraud. See Coffee, page 1008, Note 5, supra; Geraldine Szott Moohr, Federal Criminal Fraud and the Development of Intangible Property Rights in Information, 2000 U. Ill. L. Rev. 683.

Questions. Are Oxford v. Moss and the *Stewart* cases distinguishable? Consider whether the following defendants should be found guilty of theft: (1) Defendant 1 "borrows" *A*'s season pass to the ice hockey rink and returns it after the season is over. (2) Defendant 2 "borrows" *B*'s car battery and returns it after the battery's power is exhausted.

Model Penal Code §223.0(1) provides that temporarily withholding property from its owner can be treated as a permanent deprivation when the effect is "to appropriate a major portion of [the property's] economic value." This provision would probably suffice to permit conviction of defendants 1 and 2 above. Under the Model Penal Code approach, what would be the result in Oxford v. Moss?

2. Jointly owned property. Can a partner be convicted of larceny or embezzlement for appropriating partnership funds to her personal use? The common law answer was no, although today courts are divided. The New York Court of Appeals recently reaffirmed its negative answer to that question, People v. Zinke, 76 N.Y.2d 8, 555 N.E.2d 263 (1990), stating:

> At common law, no less than today, the requirement that the victim of a theft be an "owner" of the stolen property was an indispensable element of the crime of larceny. . . . From this principle emerged the rule that if property was owned by two or more persons, none of the owners could commit larceny from the others.
>
> Consistent with this principle was the common-law view that a partner could not be convicted of larceny for the misappropriation of partnership assets; because each partner held title to an undivided interest in the partnership, the theory was that partners could not misappropriate what was already theirs. . . . As in other States, the courts of this State consistently regarded the common-law definition of owner as controlling, concluding that partners could not be prosecuted for stealing firm property. . . .
>
> The Model Penal Code, completed in 1962, had rejected the common-law view

> by defining larceny as stealing "property of another," which was in turn defined as property "in which any person other than the actor has an interest . . . regardless of the fact that the actor also has an interest in the property." (Model Penal Code §223.0[7].) The purpose of this provision was to permit "a person ordinarily considered the owner of a property . . . [to] be convicted of theft. . . . Thus, a partner may be convicted of theft of partnership property." (Model Penal Code §223.2, revised comment, at 169 [1980].) In enacting the present Penal Law in 1965, however, the New York Legislature chose to reject the Model Penal Code approach and instead codified its own existing rule. . . . [T]he Legislature was concerned both about the effects of criminalizing conduct arising out of legitimate business activities — where there can often be close questions as to intent — and the effects of offering defeated litigants in civil suits the opportunity to seek retaliation by criminal actions. Allowing larceny prosecutions against partners is, of course, contrary to those legislative concerns.

Theft from a spouse raises related problems. In this area, the traditional common law dogmas have disappeared. See, e.g., Stewart v. Commonwealth, 252 S.E.2d 329 (Va. 1979). One spouse normally remains free to draw on their joint checking account and use other common assets without the other spouse's knowledge or even against the other's wishes. But if one of the spouses conceals the location of jointly owned assets, this action has the effect of defeating the other spouse's equal right to access and to the use of the assets, and the deprivation of this "property" (the marital interest) constitutes theft. See LaParle v. State, 957 P.2d 330 (Alaska App. 1998).

3. Secured property. In cases where the actual owner of property wrongfully takes it from the possession of another who has a special interest therein, such as a lienor, e.g., State v. Marsala, 59 Conn. App. 135 (2000), or a pledgee, e.g., Rose v. Matt, [1951] 1 All E.R. 361, the prevailing view is that such action constitutes theft. What is the difference between these cases and the partnership and spouse cases?

A somewhat different problem is presented if a person rightfully in possession of goods transfers them with intent to defeat the interests of a secured creditor. For example, someone who purchases an electrical appliance under a conditional sales contract may default on the payments due, but conceal the appliance or transfer it to a friend to avoid repossession. Some states have enacted statutes that specifically treat such conduct as theft, at least when certain kinds of security interests are involved. See, e.g., Cal. Penal Code §504a.[2] The Model Penal Code chose to treat these situations not as theft but rather as a separate misdemeanor of defrauding secured creditors. See §§223.0(7), 224.10, Appendix. The reason for separate treatment of those who impair security interests is stated to be that such conduct "deviates less from social norms than does the conduct of thieves who take property to which they have no claim. Moreover, sellers can guard against this kind of fraud by caution in extending credit." Model Penal Code and Commentaries, Comment to §224.10 at 347-348 (1980).

2. The section reads: "Every person who shall fraudulently remove, conceal or dispose of any goods, chattels or effects, leased or let to him by any instrument in writing, or any personal property or effects of another in his possession, under a contract of purchase not yet fulfilled, and any person in possession of such goods, chattels, or effects knowing them to be subject to such lease or contract of purchase who shall so remove, conceal or dispose of the same with intent to injure or defraud the lessor or owner thereof, is guilty of embezzlement."

Question: Is the rationale persuasive? Compare the treatment of theft by deception. Section 223.3, Appendix.

4. Unsecured property. Does it follow from the decision to criminalize the defrauding of secured creditors that defrauding unsecured creditors should also be made criminal? See, e.g., Cal. Penal Code §154: "Every debtor who fraudulently removes his property or effects out of this state, or fraudulently sells, conveys, assigns or conceals his property with intent to defraud, hinder or delay his creditors of their rights, claims or demands, is" guilty of a misdemeanor. The Model Penal Code rejected such provisions on the ground that they present a

> problem of punishing conduct that is not itself indicative of any criminal purpose. This problem is analogous to the distinction between preparation and attempt. Section 5.01(2) provides that conduct shall not be held to constitute a substantial step toward completion of the crime, as is required for conviction for attempt, "unless it is strongly corroborative of the actor's criminal purpose." The sale of one's own unencumbered property is itself a neutral and entirely legal act, distinguishable from legitimate business transactions only if intent to defraud creditors can be shown. It is not conduct "strongly corroborative" of any intent to defraud. To permit such interest to be shown in the absence of some corroboration from the act itself comes dangerously close to punishing evil intention alone.

Model Penal Code and Commentaries, Comment to §224.10 at 346-347 (1980).

2. *Mail and Wire Fraud*

UNITED STATES v. SIEGEL

United States Court of Appeals, 2d Circuit
717 F.2d 9 (1983)

George C. Pratt, J. . . . [Abrams and Siegel were officers and directors of Mego International, a publicly held manufacturer and distributor of toys and games. They were charged with and convicted of violating the wire fraud statute by engaging in a scheme to defraud Mego and its stockholders by violating their fiduciary duties to act honestly and faithfully in the best interest of the corporation and to account for the sale of all Mego property entrusted to them. The fraudulent scheme involved the creation of a hidden cash fund derived from cash sales of merchandise that had been closed out, marked down for clearance, or returned as damaged. These "off the books" sales all together generated in excess of $100,000 in cash. The indictment charged that the defendants used the cash for bribery and self-enrichment. There was much evidence of use of the cash for pay-offs to union officials and to other persons dealing with the corporation. Whether there was evidence of self-enrichment was an issue on appeal, which dealt generally with the sufficiency of the evidence to prove violations of the wire fraud statute.]

The wire fraud statute, 18 U.S.C. §1343 (1976), provides:

> Whoever, having devised or intending to devise any scheme or artifice to defraud, or for obtaining money or property by means of false or fraudulent pretenses, representations, or promises, transmits or causes to be transmitted by

> means of wire, radio, or television communication in interstate or foreign commerce, any writings, signs, signals, pictures, or sounds for the purpose of executing such scheme or artifice, shall be fined not more than $1,000 or imprisoned not more than five years, or both.

While we have described this provision, as well as the mail fraud statute, 18 U.S.C. §1341 (1976), which has been identically construed with respect to the issues before us, as "seemingly limitless," United States v. Von Barta, 635 F.2d at 1001, we have also recognized that "a mere breach of fiduciary duty, standing alone, may not necessarily constitute a mail fraud," United States v. Bronston, 658 F.2d 920, 926 (2d Cir. 1981).

However, we have held that the statute is violated when a fiduciary fails to disclose material information "which he is under a duty to disclose to another under circumstances where the non-disclosure could or does result in harm to the other." United States v. Newman, 664 F.2d 12, 19 (2d Cir. 1981). While the prosecution must show that some harm or injury was contemplated by the scheme, it need not show that direct, tangible economic loss resulted to the scheme's intended victims. In this record there is sufficient evidence from which the jury could reasonably have concluded that defendants received the cash proceeds and used them for non-corporate purposes in breach of their fiduciary duties to act in the best interest of the corporation and to disclose material information to Mego and its stockholders. . . .

Defendants do not seriously contend that the wire fraud statute is not violated when a corporate officer or employee breaches his fiduciary duty to the corporation by taking the proceeds from unrecorded cash sales and using them for his own benefit. Rather, they argue that even if they did participate in the unrecorded cash sales, the record is devoid of any evidence that the money was used for other than corporate purposes and thus fails to support a finding of a breach of fiduciary duty. Defendants claim that at best the evidence merely shows that Abrams and Siegel received the proceeds from the cash sales and that Siegel periodically placed the money in the corporate safe deposit box. While neither Abrams nor Siegel testified, they argue that they received none of it for personal use and that any use of the proceeds for labor payoffs served a legitimate corporate purpose and was not in violation of any fiduciary duty.

While there is little, if any, direct evidence to show that Siegel and Abrams used the cash proceeds for other than corporate purposes, we conclude that the record as a whole does support the determination that Abrams and Siegel used the money for their own enrichment. We reach this conclusion by considering several factors. . . .

[T]here was testimony which showed that Abrams and Siegel personally received the proceeds from the cash sales and either pocketed them or placed them in the corporate safe deposit box. Further, although the cash sales generated in excess of $100,000, the testimony concerning the use to which the money was put accounted for approximately $31,000, used mainly for illicit payoffs. The reasonable mind can think of several destinations for the more than $69,000 that was missing, and, since we have rejected the view that a jury may not rely upon an inference to support an essential allegation unless no opposite inference may be drawn from the proof, we conclude that the jury could have inferred that Abrams and Siegel used some or all of the remainder of the proceeds for their own benefit, and could have fairly concluded beyond a reasonable doubt that theirs was a scheme to misappropriate the proceeds from the sale of Mego assets for self-enrichment. . . .

We do not need to consider whether use of the cash for bribery on behalf of the corporation breached defendants' fiduciary duties, for . . . the jury's verdict establishes that it found beyond a reasonable doubt that the funds were misappropriated for both bribery and self-enrichment. . . .

In affirming defendants' convictions on the wire fraud counts, we in no way wish to encourage the type of indictment prosecuted here. Twenty counts were brought against five defendants, all but two of whom were acquitted of all charges. Siegel and Abrams, although convicted of the wire fraud charges (which might more properly have been redressed in a shareholder's derivative suit or in a state criminal prosecution), were acquitted on several other counts. . . . While we applaud the government's concentration on unrecorded cash sales, a particularly common form of criminal activity, we nevertheless urge the government to think carefully before instituting other massive prosecutions having such slender foundations as this one.

Defendants' convictions on counts one through fifteen are affirmed. . . .

WINTER, J., dissenting. . . .

Once again sailing against the wind in mail or wire fraud cases (or so they are called), I dissent.

In United States v. Margiotta, 688 F.2d 108 (2d Cir. 1982), we read the mail fraud statute to create a regulatory code subjecting public officials, candidates and party leaders to criminal prosecution for allegedly deceptive political speech. Today we read the wire fraud statute to create a federal law of fiduciary obligations imposed on corporate directors and officers, thereby setting the stage for the development of an expandable body of criminal law regulating intracorporate affairs.

The majority's legal theory is that wire fraud occurred because some of Mego's funds were diverted "for noncorporate purposes in breach of [the defendants'] fiduciary duties to act in the best interest of the corporation and to disclose material information to Mego and its stockholders." The evidence is that Mego, a corporation with sales ranging between $30 million and $109 million, during the relevant period, had off-book transactions engineered by the defendants averaging slightly over $11,000 per year. There is no evidence — *none*— that any of the money was diverted to the personal use of either Siegel or Abrams. The government's *prima facie* case is thus made out solely by a showing of improper corporate record keeping. . . .

There is nothing in the language or legislative history of the wire fraud statute remotely suggesting that it was intended as a vehicle for the enforcement of fiduciary duties imposed upon corporate directors or officers by state law. To allow it to be so used would thus be a grave error. However, what the majority does is infinitely worse, for it holds that the wire fraud statute creates a *federal* law of fiduciary obligations. There is no pretense that the source of the fiduciary duty at issue in this case was anything but federal law. There is no reference in the majority opinion to state law or even to Mego's state of incorporation. The jury simply was told that it was up to it to decide whether, as part of the obligation "to act in the best interest of the corporation," the defendants were under a duty to disclose the off-book transactions to shareholders.

The creation of this federal fiduciary duty is no minor step. The relationship of federal and state law in the governance of corporations is a matter of great debate, in which the proponents of federal regulation have strenuously argued that state law governing the conduct of corporate directors and officers is too lax. Over the years, Congress has responded by mandating disclosure through the various securities laws, but has generally declined to enact substantive regulation of corporate transactions.

Notwithstanding the lack of even a hint of relevant Congressional intent in enacting the wire fraud laws, notwithstanding Congress' repeated rejection of pleas to strengthen the fiduciary obligations imposed on corporate directors and officers by state law, and notwithstanding the existence of precise federal legislation requiring disclosure of particular corporate matters, we read the wire fraud statute to embody a federal law of fiduciary obligations, including an undefined duty of yet further disclosure, enforceable by the sanctions of the criminal law.

It will be up to later juries and later panels to define what actions by corporate directors and officers are or are not "in the best interest of the corporation." The elasticity of the concept and the potential for infinite expansion, however, are foreshadowed by the facts of the present case. The "material" information not disclosed to shareholders in the instant case is a series of transactions of roughly \$11,000 annually over nine years, a wholly trivial sum in light of Mego's sales. In holding that these transactions "would be important to a Mego stockholder," the majority simply closes its eyes to investment realities, for there is not a shred of evidence that such a sum would affect share price in the slightest. It requires little imagination to foresee future application of the theory of this case to the use of corporate airplanes, the size of executive salaries, expense accounts, etc.

Moreover, there is no evidence — again, *none*— that the transactions in question harmed the corporation. By allowing an inference of diversion to personal use to be drawn solely from the lack of proper records, the majority has in effect dropped the element of a scheme to defraud from the offense. Courts long ago eliminated the need to show a substantial connection between the scheme to defraud and the use of the mails or wires. Now we are eliminating the need to show fraud. In effect, a new crime — corporate improprieties — which entails neither fraud nor even a victim, has been created.

Other aspects of the majority decision also trouble me. Adequate notice to those affected by such elastic concepts is simply not possible, for even the wisest counsel cannot foresee what corporate acts may after the fact attract a prosecutor's suspicion (or ire) and a judicial stamp of impropriety. The key act of the defendants here was the arousal of prosecutorial suspicions. The government's argument brims with innuendo of other crimes: embezzlement, bribery of a union official, commercial bribery, tax evasion, and securities law violations, all of which go to prove only that the criminal charges in issue are a surrogate for ones which the prosecutor lacked either evidence or jurisdiction to make. The overtones of the majority opinion suggest that the defendants here have been convicted essentially of stealing or embezzling funds from Mego. Had those been the crimes actually charged, however, verdicts would likely have been directed in their favor, for there is no evidence that the cash in question was diverted to any purpose other than increasing the profits of the corporation.

Finally, as in *Margiotta,* a crime is created which by its nature will be prosecuted infrequently and in a highly selective manner. If judges perceive a need for a catch-all federal common law crime, the issue should be addressed explicitly with some recognition of the dangers, rather than continue an inexorable expansion of the mail and wire fraud statutes under the pretense of merely discharging Congress' will.

Quite apart from the self-evident danger in creating vast areas of discretion for prosecutors to single out individuals for improper reasons, there is a real question as to whether the costs in resources equal the benefits achieved. The trial here, involving five defendants, each with his own counsel, lasted seven weeks, consuming substantial prosecutorial, private and judicial resources. Only two of the five defendants were convicted, and total jail sentences amounted to only seven months. In truth, the law enforcement results from society's point of view are as trivial as the off-book transactions were to Mego. Even had the government been more successful, however, there is reason to doubt that much would have been gained. Ill-defined crimes which are necessarily prosecuted on an infrequent and selective basis probably have little deterrent value. Were we to restrict the mail and wire fraud statutes to swindling and fraud, as originally intended, rather than extend them to perceived political or corporate improprieties, we would not only perform the judicial function correctly but probably also make a sensible policy judgment in terms of costs and benefits.

NOTES

1. What was the real controversy between the majority and the dissent? Was it solely a difference over whether the facts supported an inference of personal enrichment, or was it a disagreement about the proper reach of the statute, that is, about whether under the statute personal enrichment was required? The Second Circuit decided another "cash fund" case two years later and pronounced further on the issue of the import of personal enrichment by the defendant. United States v. Weiss, 752 F.2d 777 (2d Cir. 1985). Weiss, an officer of Warner Communications Inc., created a secret cash fund for the corporation from cash refunds on stock purchases, concealing these transactions and the existence of the fund by creating false documents. He was convicted of mail fraud.[3] The circuit court affirmed, stating:

> Appellant's argument that he did not violate the mail fraud statute because his creation of the cash fund was not illegal, was not intended to harm Warner or its shareholders, and did not lead to any personal gain presents a close question. . . .
>
> In *Siegel* defendants defrauded the corporation and its shareholders by deliberately concealing and by failing to account for the sales of all corporate property and merchandise. The government theorized that such acts by top corporate officers defrauded the corporation and its shareholders, and violated the executives' fiduciary duty to act honestly and faithfully. . . .
>
> Our case is within the ambit of the holding in *Siegel.* There is no requirement that the government prove that the misappropriated funds were used by Weiss for

3. Section 1341 prohibits use of the mails in "any scheme or artifice to defraud, or for obtaining money or property by means of false or fraudulent pretense or promises." 18 U.S.C. §1341 (1976).

his own enrichment. Rather, evidence of a non-corporate purpose, explicitly or implicitly derived, will satisfy the requirements of *Siegel.* There was no direct evidence offered concerning the final destination of the misappropriated funds. However the jury could reasonably have concluded that the disbursement of corporate funds for fake feasibility studies and fake invoices for non-rendered services established non-corporate use of the funds. Indeed the record here, as in *Siegel,* allowed the jury to "have drawn a justifiable inference that defendants used the scheme for their own benefit." With the evidence presented here, a jury could, at the very least, infer that the diversion of corporate funds by Weiss was for a non-corporate purpose. This is sufficient to bring the case within the holding in *Siegel.*

2. Note, Peter R. Ezersky, Intra-Corporate Mail and Wire Fraud: Criminal Liability for Fiduciary Breach, 94 Yale L.J. 1427 (1985), makes a critical assault on the *Siegel* and *Weiss* cases, along the lines of Judge Winter's dissent in *Siegel.* The opening paragraphs of the Note state its conclusions:

> Mail/wire fraud law has evolved from its origins as an antidote to "lottery swindles" into a vehicle for attacking a wide range of conduct. Recently, a national standard of fiduciary liability, developed by federal courts in mail/wire fraud cases, has been held to govern the obligations of corporate directors and officers to their shareholders. Public, criminal enforcement under mail/wire fraud thus overlaps the private, civil enforcement of corporate fiduciary obligations. . . . [T]his use of the criminal law to police corporate fiduciary obligations is injurious to corporate shareholders — the supposed beneficiaries, contrary to principles of federalism that apply with special force in the corporate law context, and inconsistent with the principle that criminal proscriptions should be certain and knowable in advance.
>
> This recent use of mail/wire fraud law to enforce fiduciary duties has little to do with fraud. The new corporate fiduciary standard is untenable on theoretical grounds, as is the use of criminal sanctions to enforce essentially contractual duties. Furthermore, this development in mail/wire fraud clashes with the congressional and judicial policy of minimizing federal involvement in intra-corporate affairs. . . . [C]ontrary to accepted notions of legality, courts have used mail/wire fraud law to create a virtual common law crime.

3. A penetrating assessment of the expansion of mail fraud as a threat to rule-of-law values may be found in two articles by Professor John Coffee: From Tort to Crime: Some Reflections on the Criminalization of Fiduciary Breaches and the Problematic Line Between Law and Ethics, 19 Am. Crim. L. Rev. 117 (1981), and The Metastasis of Mail Fraud: The Continuing Story of the "Evolution" of a White-Collar Crime, 21 Am. Crim. L. Rev. 1 (1983).

4. In McNally v. United States, 483 U.S. 350 (1987), the Supreme Court took a step toward narrowing the mail-fraud statute. The case involved the prosecution of a public official for a patronage scheme in which he obtained kickbacks from a private insurance agency to which he had steered state business. The prosecution failed to prove that the state suffered any financial loss, but it nonetheless obtained a conviction on the theory that the defendant had deprived the state's citizens of their "intangible right" to obtain his honest services. The Supreme Court reversed, holding that the mail-fraud statute applied only to deprivations of money or "property" but not to deprivations of the intangible right to honest services. This restriction on federal prosecutorial power proved short-lived, however. A year after *McNally,* Congress enacted 18 U.S.C. §1346, which provides that the mail-fraud statute extends to any "scheme or artifice to deprive another of the intangible right to honest services." See Geraldine Szott Moohr, Mail Fraud and the Intangible Rights Doctrine, 21 Harv. J. Leg. 153 (1994).

In Cleveland v. United States, 121 Sup. Ct. 365 (2000), the Supreme Court reviewed a mail-fraud conviction based on a fraudulent attempt to obtain a license from a state authority. The Court unanimously reversed the conviction. The prosecution had not claimed that the applicant owed the state any fiduciary duty to provide "honest services," and the Court held that the license (which served only a regulatory purpose) was not "property" within the meaning of the mail-fraud statute. The Court stressed that to hold otherwise would excessively broaden federal criminal jurisdiction. Nonetheless, federal courts retain expansive jurisdiction to pass judgment on whether disclosures or non-disclosures amount to fraud, whenever the defendant *has* obtained "property" or can be considered in breach of a duty to provide "honest services."

5. Consider Francis A. Allen, The Erosion of Legality in American Criminal Justice: Some Latter-Day Adventures of the *Nulla Poena* Principle, 29 Ariz. L. Rev. 387, 410-411 (1987):

> [T]he expansion of judicial doctrine in these [mail fraud] cases has at times ignored the restraints of the *nulla poena* principle in the area of its most basic application: that of requiring the criminal law to give fair notice to potential offenders of the threat of criminal punishment. It can hardly be supposed that the lawyer Bronston,[a] aware as he was of his involvement in an unprofessional conflict of interests and presumably of possible professional discipline, could, nevertheless, have contemplated his behavior risked conviction for a federal felony. Nor can it be doubted that the conviction, when it occurred, engendered a powerful sense of injustice in the accused and in those bound to him by ties of family and friendship. . . .
>
> The expansion of coverage of the Mail Fraud Act by the courts assaults the values of legality in another way: it exacerbates the problems of prosecutorial discretion, an area of power surely among the most resistent to regulation by authoritative norms within the range of criminal justice administration. These problems are particularly troublesome, as some dissenting judges have observed, in cases involving immoral and corrupt behavior by persons engaged in state and local governments. The incidents of serious improprieties in these areas are so numerous and ubiquitous that federal prosecution is incapable of responding to more than a small fraction of the total. Because choosing cases for prosecution must necessarily be highly selective, there is the ever-present danger of choices being made that promise the greatest political advantage to the national administration or to political and economic groups at the local level. Almost equally serious, suspicions of politicizing the processes of justice are engendered, whether or not justified in the particular case.
>
> The last category of costs to be mentioned involves definition of the proper ju-

a. At 407, the author states "In Bronston v. United States, [658 F.2d 920 (2d Cir. 1981)] the accused, a state senator and member of a large New York law firm, gave secret assistance to a personal client who was competing for a franchise from the city with a company already being represented by defendant's law firm. Bronston thus wrongfully created and concealed a serious conflict of interest. On the other hand, there is no evidence the accused made use of confidential information supplied by the firm's client to advance the interests of his own client. Nevertheless, the accused's conviction under the Mail Fraud Act was affirmed in the Court of Appeals, principally on the ground that, as a partner, he breached a fiduciary obligation of loyalty owed by him to the firm's clients." — Eds.

dicial role in these cases. . . . A basic element in the legitimacy of law is the perception that in making law, the law-giver acted within the limits of its designated authority. The recent decisions under the Mail Fraud Act surely strain at the limits and may, indeed, exceed them. . . . Converting the federal district courts into a national tribunal to test the political morality of local officials, or precipitately enlarging the fiduciary obligations of corporate managers in their relations with the corporation, may be sound courses for public policy to pursue, but confidence in that conclusion is seriously weakened by the absence of legislative consideration and contribution.

C. MENS REA

PEOPLE v. BROWN

Supreme Court of California
105 Cal. 66, 38 P. 518 (1894)

Garoute, J. [Appellant, a 17-year-old boy, was convicted of burglary on an information charging that he entered a house with intent to commit larceny. The facts revealed that he entered an acquaintance's house and took a bicycle. He testified: "I took the wheel to get even with the boy, and, of course, I didn't intend to keep it. I just wanted to get even with him. The boy was throwing oranges at me in the evening, and he would not stop when I told him to, and it made me mad. I intended to take it back Sunday night; but, before I got back, they caught me."]

Upon the foregoing state of facts, the court gave the jury the following instruction:

> I think it is not necessary to say very much to you in this case. I may say, generally, that I think counsel for the defense here stated to you in his argument very fairly the principles of law governing this case, except in one particular. In defining to you the crime of grand larceny, he says it is essential that the taking of it must be felonious. That is true; the taking with the intent to deprive the owner of it; but he adds the conclusion that you must find that the taker intended to deprive him of it permanently. I do not think that is the law. I think in this case, for example, if the defendant took this bicycle, we will say for the purpose of riding twenty-five miles, for the purpose of enabling him to get away, and then left it for another to get it, and intended to do nothing else except to help himself away for a certain distance, it would be larceny, just as much as though he intended to take it all the while. A man may take a horse, for instance, not with the intent to convert it wholly and permanently to his own use, but to ride it to a certain distance, for a certain purpose he may have, and then leave it. He converts it to that extent to his own use and purpose feloniously.

This instruction is erroneous, and demands a reversal of the judgment. If the boy's story be true, he is not guilty of larceny in taking the machine; yet, under the instruction of the court, the words from his own mouth convicted him. The court told the jury that larceny may be committed, even though it was only the intent of the party taking the property to deprive the owner of it temporarily. We think the authorities form an unbroken line to the effect that the felonious intent must be to deprive the owner of the property permanently. The illustration contained in the instruction as to the man taking the horse is too broad in its terms as stating a correct principle of law. Under the circumstances depicted by the illustration, the man might, and again he might not, be guilty of larceny. It would be a pure question of fact for the jury, and dependent for its true solution upon all the circumstances surrounding the transaction. But the test of law to be applied in these circumstances for the purpose of determining the ultimate fact as to the man's guilt or innocence is, did he intend to permanently deprive the owner of his property? If he did not intend so to do, there is no felonious intent, and his acts constitute but a trespass. While the felonious intent of the party taking need not necessarily be an intention to convert the property to his own use, still it must in all cases be an intent to wholly and permanently deprive the owner thereof.

For the foregoing reasons, it is ordered that the judgment and order be reversed, and the cause remanded for a new trial.

NOTE

Some limited exceptions to the requirement of an intent to take permanently have been made judicially and by statute. The courts early found that, where the thing taken was abandoned or recklessly exposed to loss by the taker, this fact was not only evidentiary of an intent to effect a permanent deprivation but would sustain larceny even if a permanent taking was not the object of the defendant's acts. State v. Davis, 38 N.J.L. 176 (1875). See N.Y. Penal Law §155.00(3): "To 'deprive' another of property means . . . (b) to dispose of the property in such manner or under such circumstances as to render it unlikely that an owner will recover such property." Likewise, where the intent to return the thing taken is conditional, as upon receipt of a reward, the requisite mens rea has been found. State v. Hauptman, 180 A. 809, 819 (1935). The risk-of-loss rationale has also supported larceny convictions where the defendant intends to pledge, though ultimately to redeem and return, the property taken. Regina v. Phetheon, 9 Car. & P. 552, 173 Eng. Rep. 952 (1840). Many states have long enacted "joy ride" statutes which make criminal the temporary taking of an automobile, and sometimes other vehicles. See, e.g., Cal. Penal Code §499(b).

Question: Why should the law of theft confine itself to cases where the intent of the taker is to effect a permanent deprivation? As Holmes observed (The Common Law 71 (1881)): "A momentary loss of possession is not what has been guarded against with such severe penalties. What the law means to prevent is the loss of it wholly and forever. . . ." But should interference with possession which is more than momentary, though less than permanent, be protected against by the law of theft? Following Model Penal Code §223.0(1), N.Y. Penal Law §155.00(3) now provides: "To 'deprive' another of property means (a) to withhold it or cause it to be withheld . . . for so extended a period or under such circumstances that the major portion of its economic value or benefit is lost to him. . . ." §155.00(4) provides: "To 'appropriate' property of another to oneself or a third person means (a) to exercise control over it . . . permanently or for so extended a period or under such circumstances as to acquire the major portion of its economic value or benefit, . . ." These provisions were construed in the following case.

People v. Jennings, 69 N.Y.2d 103, 504 N.E.2d 1079 (1986). [Defendants, Sentry Armored Courier Corp. and its officers, had an agreement with its client, Chemical Bank, to pick up, "fine count" and deliver Chemical's bulk deposits to Chemical's account at the Federal Reserve Bank within 72 hours. Since it took only 24 hours to count the money, defendants used the extra 48 hours to obtain interest on the money by arrangement with the Hudson Valley Bank. The scheme involved little risk, since a "loan," which was a key element in the arrangement, was secured by A-rated bonds. The majority found these facts not to constitute a deprivation or appropriation of Chemical's money under the New York larceny provisions.]

. . . What is lacking here from the People's proof is evidence demonstrating an "intent to deprive . . . or to appropriate." The gist of the People's claim is that by investing Chemical's money for periods up to 48 hours, defendants evinced an intent to deprive its true owner of the money's "economic value or benefit," that is, the interest that the money was capable of generating. The mens rea element of larceny, however, is simply not satisfied by an intent temporarily to use property without the owner's permission, or even an intent to appropriate outright the benefits of the property's short-term use.

The problem presented in this case is similar to that presented in "joy-riding" cases, in which it was held that the intent merely to borrow and use an automobile without the owner's permission cannot support a conviction for larceny. An analysis of the evidence before the Grand Jury in this case indicates only that defendants exercised control over Chemical's money to the extent of using it to make short-term, profitable investments and, as a result, appropriated some portion of its economic benefit for themselves. However, in light of the fact that their unauthorized use of Chemical's money extended over no more than a series of discrete 48-hour periods, the proof was insufficient to show that they intended to use Chemical's money "for so extended a period or under such circumstances as to acquire the *major portion* of its economic value or benefit" (emphasis supplied).

Moreover, the "economic value or benefit" to be derived from the money was the interest or other financial leverage that could be gained by the party who possessed it. Inasmuch as Chemical had ceded possession of its money to Sentry for various 72-hour periods, it had no legal rights during those periods to the money's "economic value or benefit," which is an incident of possession. Thus, to the extent that defendants intended to appropriate to themselves the "economic value or benefit" of Chemical's money, it cannot be said that their intentions were unlawful or even inconsistent with the terms of the bailment. . . .

For similar reasons it cannot be said that defendants committed larceny by intentionally and permanently stealing the interest earned on Chemical's money, as distinguished from the money itself. First, absent proof of an agreement to the contrary, Chemical cannot be deemed the true owner of the interest earned while its money was in defendants' custody pursuant to the parties' "fine counting" agreement. Indeed, there is really no practical difference between the contention that defendants stole the interest on Chemical's money and the contention that they stole the money itself by intentionally appropriating its "economic value or benefit."

Second, it would be inconsistent with the statutory design to treat defendants' concededly permanent taking of the interest earned on Chemical's funds as a larceny within the meaning of Penal Law §§155.00, 155.05 and 155.35. It is clear that an individual who "joy-rides" and thereby deprives the automobile's owner of the value arising from its temporary use is not liable in larceny for stealing that intangible "value" under article 155 of the Penal Law. By parity of reasoning, an individual who temporarily invests another's money and thereby gains interest or profit cannot be deemed guilty of larceny for appropriating that interest or profit. Consistent with our long-held view that criminal liability "cannot be extended beyond the fair scope of the statutory mandate," we hold that in these circumstances the statute must be read to apply only to a taking of the property itself and not to a permanent taking of what is, in essence, only the economic value of its use during the short time the property has been withheld. . . .

Finally, we note that neither Sentry's patently false response to Chemical's inquiry concerning the rerouting of its money through Hudson nor Sentry's disobedience when ordered by Chemical to deliver the money directly are sufficient to establish that Sentry was acting with the larcenous intent required by Penal Law §155.05(3), (4) and §155.05(1). At worst, Sentry's conduct demonstrates its unwillingness to relinquish what was obviously a profitable short-term use of Chemical's money. It does not, however, alter the inescapable and uncontradicted inference that Sentry was merely emulating the behavior of many reputable financial institutions by taking advantage of the "float" on the temporarily idle money in its possession.

Having determined that the People's proof did not establish a larceny, we turn now to the question whether it was sufficient to establish the lesser crime of misapplication of property, which is defined in Penal Law §165.00(1) as follows: "A person is guilty of misapplication of property when, knowingly possessing personal property of another pursuant to an agreement that the same will be returned to the owner at a future time, he loans, leases, pledges, pawns or otherwise encumbers such property without the consent of the owner thereof in such manner as to create a risk that the owner will not be able to recover it or will suffer pecuniary loss."

The obvious thrust of this statute, which we have not previously construed, is to make it a crime to alienate in any way property belonging to another under circumstances creating a risk of loss. While the created risk of loss need not rise to the level of "likelihood" or even mere "probability," the statute does require proof of a risk that is more than a far-fetched or wholly speculative possibility. . . .

There was no actual risk here that the money would not be repaid, since even in the unlikely event of a default by Hudson, the "loans" to Hudson were secured by A-rated bonds held in Hudson's Federal Reserve Bank vault. . . .

In short, however unethical defendants' conduct may have been, it did not constitute the crimes of larceny or misapplication of property. Accordingly, the indictments charging those crimes were properly dismissed.

REGINA v. FEELY

Court of Appeal
[1973] 2 W.L.R. 201

LAWTON, L.J. . . . The appeal raises an important point of law, namely, can it be a defence *in law* for a man charged with theft and proved to have taken money to say that when he took the money he intended to repay it and had reasonable grounds for believing and did believe that he would be able to do so.

Defendant was a branch manager for a firm of bookmakers. In September 1971 the firm sent a circular to all branch managers that the practice of borrowing from tills was to stop. Defendant nevertheless took about £30 from a branch safe on October 4. On October 8 he was transferred to another branch. His successor discovered a cash shortage of about £40, and defendant gave him an IOU for that amount. Though his successor did not report the deficiency, a member of the firm's security staff did and asked defendant for an explanation. Defendant accounted for about £10 by reference to some bets he had paid out, but as to the balance he said that he had taken it because he was "stuck for cash." Defendant stated he borrowed the £30 intending to pay it back and that his employers owed him about £70 from which he wanted them to deduct the money. Trial testimony showed that the firm did owe him that amount. He was convicted of theft of the £30.

[The trial judge directed the jury] that if the defendant had taken the money from either the safe or the till . . . it was no defence for him to say that he had intended to repay it and that his employers owed him more than enough to cover what he had taken. The trial judge put his direction in stark terms: . . .

> As a matter of law, members of the jury, I am bound to direct you, even if he were prepared to pay back the following day and even if he were a millionaire, it makes no defence in law to this offence. If he took the money, that is the essential matter for you to decide.

At no stage of his summing up did he leave the jury to decide whether the prosecution had proved that the defendant had taken the money dishonestly. This was because he seems to have thought that he had to decide as a matter of law what amounted to dishonesty and he expressed his concept of dishonesty as follows: ". . . if someone does something deliberately knowing that his employers are not prepared to tolerate it, is that not dishonest?"

Should the jury have been left to decide whether the defendant had acted dishonestly? The search for an answer must start with the Theft Act 1968, under section 1 of which the defendant had been indicted. . . . The design of the new Act is clear; nearly all the old legal terms to describe offences of dishonesty have been left behind; larceny, embezzlement and fraudulent conversion have become theft; receiving stolen goods has become handling stolen goods; obtaining by false pretences has become pecuniary advantage by deception. Words in everyday use have replaced legal jargon in many parts of the Act. That is particularly noticeable in the series of sections (1 to 6) defining theft.

"Theft" itself is a word known and used by all and is defined . . . as follows: "A person is guilty of theft if he dishonestly appropriates property belonging to another with the intention of permanently depriving the other of it. . . ."

In section 1(1) of the Act of 1968, the word "dishonestly" can only relate to the state of mind of the person who does the act which amounts to appropriation. . . . The Crown did not dispute this proposition, but it was submitted that in some cases (and this, it was said, was such a one) it was necessary for the trial judge to define "dishonestly." . . .

We do not agree that judges should define what "dishonestly" means. This word is in common use whereas the word "fraudulently" which was used in section 1(1) of the Larceny Act 1916 had acquired as a result of case law a special meaning. Jurors, when deciding whether an appropriation was dishonest can be reasonably expected to, and should, apply the current standards of ordinary decent people. . . .

[T]he jury should have been left to decide whether the defendant's alleged taking of the money had been dishonest. They were not, with the result that a verdict of guilty was returned without their having given thought to what was probably the most important issue in the case.

This would suffice for the appeal were it not for . . . two decisions. . . . In Reg. v. Williams [1953] 1 Q.B. 660, the two appellants, who were husband and wife, carried on a general shop, part of which was a sub-post office. The wife was the sub-postmistress. The business of the shop got into difficulties and in order to get out of them the wife, with the knowledge of her husband, took money from the Post Office till to discharge some of the debts of the business. In her evidence, which was supported by that of her husband, she said that she thought she would be able to repay the money out of her salary from the Post Office and from sales from the business. The husband said that he knew it was wrong to do what they had done, but he thought that it would all come right in the end. They were found guilty on a number of counts and in respect of two the jury added a rider that the appellants had intended to repay the money and honestly believed that they would be able to do so, but in respect of three counts, although they intended to repay, they had no honest belief that they would be able to do so.

. . . The question in the case which is relevant for the purposes of this appeal was whether the facts found by the jury and recorded in their riders afforded any defence. [The court held they did not, stating]: "They knew that they had no right to take the money which they knew was not their money. The fact that they may have had a hope or expectation in the future of repaying that money is a matter which at most can go to mitigation and does not amount to a defence."

It is possible to imagine a case of taking by an employee in breach of instructions to which no one would, or could reasonably, attach moral obloquy; for example, that of a manager of a shop, who having been told that under no circumstances was he to take money from the till for his own purposes, took 40p from it, having no small change himself, to pay for a taxi hired by his wife who had arrived at the shop saying that she only had a £5 note which the cabby could not change. . . .

We find it impossible to accept that a conviction for stealing, whether it be called larceny or theft, can reveal no moral obloquy. A man so convicted would have difficulty in persuading his friends and neighbours that his reputation had not been gravely damaged. He would be found to be lowered in the estimation of right thinking people. . . .

If the principle enunciated in Reg. v. Cockburn [1968] 1 W.L.R. 281 was right, there would be a strange divergence between the position of a man who obtains cash by passing a cheque on an account which has no funds to meet it and one who takes money from a till. The man who passes the cheque is deemed in law not to act dishonestly if he genuinely believes on reasonable grounds that when it is presented to the paying bank there will be funds to meet it. . . . But, according to the decision in Reg. v. Cockburn, the man who takes money from a till intending to put it back and genuinely believing on reasonable grounds that he will be able to do so should be convicted of theft. Lawyers may be able to appreciate why one man should be adjudged to be a criminal and the other not; but we doubt whether anyone else would. People who take money from tills and the like without permission are usually thieves, but if they do not admit that they are by pleading guilty, it is for the jury, not the judge, to decide whether they have acted dishonestly. . . .

For these reasons we allowed the appeal.

NOTES AND QUESTIONS ON INTENT TO RESTORE OR PAY

1. In State v. Pratt, 114 Kan. 660, 220 P. 505, 506, 507 (1923), the defendant was convicted of embezzlement on the following facts:

> [T]he Building & Loan Association purchased $10,000 worth, face value, of the Second Liberty Loan bonds of the United States, which passed into the custody of the appellant as secretary-treasurer of the association. Without any authority to do so, and without the knowledge of the directors and other officers of the association, appellant sold these bonds in January, 1920, in Kansas City. The money was not used for the benefit of the association. In fact, appellant concealed his disposition of these bonds from the association until some time in May or June, 1921. At two or three of the meetings of the board of directors of the association held in the meantime, in which they were checking up the assets of the association, appellant substituted other bonds, which he had taken without authority from the envelopes of private boxes of depositors of the bank of which he was president, and counted those at the board meeting as the bonds of the association.

On appeal the defendant contended "that before he could be convicted of the crime of embezzlement the state must prove beyond a reasonable doubt that at the time he wrongfully converted the bonds he had the intent to deprive the owner, not temporarily, but permanently, of its property," and that error was committed in refusing evidence of his intent to restore the bonds or their equivalent and in failing to instruct that such an intent was a good defense. The court affirmed, resting on the weight of authority that "While to constitute . . . embezzlement it is necessary that there be a criminal intent, yet where the money of the principal is knowingly used by the agent in violation of his duty, it is none the less embezzlement because at the time he intended to restore it." Cf. Cal. Penal Code §512 (intent to restore no defense or mitigation in embezzlement if property not restored before indictment or information); §513 (restoration prior to indictment or information mitigates punishment for embezzlement). *Questions:* Does the holding and reasoning of the court mean that defendant could also have been convicted of embezzlement of the depositors' bonds, which he removed temporarily from the bank of which he was president to cover his misappropriation of the savings and loan association bonds? Why not, if intent to restore is not a defense to embezzlement?

2. The intent to restore is likewise held to be no defense to a false pretense charge. See People v. Weiger, 100 Cal. 352, 34 P. 826 (1893). The defendant obtained goods on credit from the complaining witness on false representations concerning his financial position. The court affirmed a conviction of obtaining by false pretenses, holding immaterial that defendant intended to pay for the goods which he purchased.

Questions: Suppose the goods defendant obtained in the *Weiger* case were a set of law books and that her defense was as follows: The defendant was a young attorney, expecting a visit from a potential client of substance whom she wanted to impress. She obtained the books for this purpose, fully intending to ship them back to the seller after the client's visit. Would it follow from *Weiger* that she would be guilty of obtaining by false pretenses? If so, consider the liability of the young attorney if she took the books from another attorney's office for the same purpose and with the same intent to return them after the client's visit. Would this not be a clear temporary taking inconsistent with larceny? Why is the same defense not available whether she obtained the books by a false representation or by a taking?

3. In connection with the issues raised in this Note, consider the following observations in Model Penal Code §206.1(2)(c), Comment at 72-73 (Tent. Draft No. 1, 1953):

> As under present law, it is no defense that the actor intends to reimburse the owner later for property presently misappropriated. . . . Deprivation accompanied by an intent to make good later, by payment of money or by the actor's repurchasing an equivalent article for restoration to the owner, is quite different in effect from the taking of a thing for temporary use of the taker. In the latter situation, the actor's retention of the property offers some assurance of his ability to restore, beyond his general credit. In the former situation, the man who takes money intending to repay or the broker who sells his client's bonds meaning to repurchase and restore the bonds later, substitutes his own credit for the owner's property in hand. Even if the actor carries out his intent to restore, he is simply paying off a liability from his own assets, rather than restoring property which has continued to belong to the owner during the interval of deprivation.

PEOPLE v. REID

New York Court of Appeals
69 N.Y.2d 469, 508 N.E.2d 661 (1987)

SIMONS, J. . . . [Appellants Reid and Riddles were convicted of armed robberies of money from their victims, despite evidence that they were only trying to recover money owed to them. In one case, the trial court, conducting a trial without a jury, stated that it credited the testimony of defendant that he had taken the money to satisfy a debt, but the court denied him the defense of claim of right because he used force.]

The common issue presented by these two appeals is whether a good-faith claim of right, which negates larcenous intent in certain thefts (see, Penal Law §155.15[1]), also negates the intent to commit robbery by a defendant who uses force to recover cash allegedly owed him. We hold that it does not. Accordingly, we affirm the order of the Appellate Division in each case. . . .

A person "commits robbery when, in the course of committing a larceny, he uses or threatens the immediate use of physical force." The larceny statute, in turn, provides that an assertion that "property was appropriated under a claim of right made in good faith" is a defense to larceny.[a] Since a good-faith claim of right is a defense to larceny, and because robbery is defined as forcible larceny, defendants contend that claim of right is also a defense to robbery. They concede the culpability of their forcible conduct, but maintain that because they acted under a claim of right to recover their own property, they were not guilty of robbery, but only some lesser crime, such as assault or unlawful possession of a weapon.

Defendants' general contention is not without support. Several jurisdictions have held that one who acts under a claim of right lacks the intent to steal and should not be convicted of robbery. That logic is tenable when a person seeks to recover a specific chattel: it is less so when asserted under the circumstances presented in these two cases: in *Reid* to recover the proceeds of crime, and in *Riddles,* to recover cash to satisfy a debt.

We have not had occasion to address the issue but the Appellate Divisions to which it has been presented have uniformly ruled that claim of right is not a defense to robbery. Their determinations have been based upon the interpretation of the applicable statutes and a policy decision to discourage self-help and they are consistent with what appears to be the emerging trend of similar appellate court decisions from other jurisdictions. For similar reasons, we conclude that the claim of right defense is not available in these cases. We need not decide the quite different question of whether an individual who uses force to recover a specific chattel which he owns may be convicted of robbery. It should be noted, however, that because taking property "from an owner thereof" is an element of robbery, a person who recovers property which is his own (as compared to the fungible cash taken to satisfy a claimed debt in the cases before us) may not be guilty of robbery. . . .

The claim of right defense is found in the larceny article of the Penal Law, which provides that a good-faith claim of right is a defense to trespassory larceny or embezzlement (see Penal Law §155.15[1]). The defense does not apply to all forms of larceny. For example, extortion is a form of larceny, but the Legislature, consistent with a prior decision of this court, has not authorized a claim of right defense to extortion (see People v. Fichtner, 118 N.Y.S.2d 159). The exception is significant for extortion entails the threat of actual or potential force or some form of coercion. Thus, the inference may reasonably be drawn that in failing to authorize a claim of right defense for extortion in Penal Law §155.15(1), and by failing to incorporate it in article 160 of the statute, which governs robbery, the Legislature recognized that an accused should not be permitted to invoke it in crimes involving force. We assume that if the Legislature intended to excuse forcible taking, it would have said so.

Our decision also rests upon policy considerations against expanding the area of permissible self-help. Manifestly, a larceny, in which the accused reacquires property belonging to him without using force, differs from a robbery in which the defendant obtains money allegedly owed to him by threatening or using force. "The former is an instance of mistake, not subjected to penal sanctions because the threat to private property is not so serious as to warrant interven-

a. N.Y. Penal Law §155.15 provides: "1. In any prosecution for larceny committed by trespassory taking or embezzlement, it is an affirmative defense that the property was appropriated under a claim of right made in good faith."—Eds.

tion by the criminal law. The latter is a species of self help and whether or not the exponent of force or threats is correct in estimating his rights, he is resorting to extra-judicial means in order to protect a property interest" (Note, A Rationale of the Law of Aggravated Theft, 54 Colum. L. Rev. 84, 98 [1954]). Since such forcible conduct is not merely a transgression against property, but also entails the risk of physical or mental injury to individuals, it should be subjected to criminal sanctions. Consequently, we find the courts in both [cases] correctly denied defendants' requests to assert claim of right defenses.

NOTES

1. In accord with *Reid,* courts routinely distinguish between the use of force to reclaim a specific chattel and the use of force to obtain cash as repayment for an alleged debt. A claim-of-right defense is normally available in the former situation but not in the latter. See People v. Tufunga, 987 P.2d 168 (Cal. 1999).

2. Section 223.1(3) of the Model Penal Code provides:

> It is an affirmative defense to prosecution for theft that the actor (a) was unaware that the property or service was that of another; or (b) acted under an honest claim of right to the property or service involved or that he had a right to acquire or dispose of it as he did; or (c) took property exposed for sale, intending to purchase and pay for it promptly, or reasonably believing that the owner, if present, would have consented.

Model Penal Code and Commentaries, Comment to §223.1(3) at 155-157 (1980):

> There is debate in the cases over several situations to which the defense provided in Subsection (3)(b) will apply. One occurs where the actor believes himself privileged to appropriate the property of another in satisfaction of a debt, without any special claim to the particular property appropriated. . . .
>
> Even more doubt as to the defense of claim of right exists in a second situation, namely that of an agent or a fiduciary who profits from dealing with his principal but who believes himself entitled to the profit because, ignorantly or mistakenly, he supposed that he was under no legal obligation to refrain from such dealing or to turn over such profits to his principal. The defense was recognized in one case, where an agent was given $1,450 to buy some land, bought it for $1,150, and kept the difference. On the other hand, the Supreme Court of Indiana affirmed the conviction of a fiduciary who bought bonds for $430 and resold them the same day to the estate for $2,000, the trial court having refused to instruct that the defendant might be acquitted if he had a *bona fide* belief that he was entitled to make a profit in dealing with the estate. . . .
>
> Subsection (3)(b) would permit a defense of claim of right in all of these situations, as well as others. The general principle is that the actor should have a defense where, although he is not in a position to claim that the property belongs to him, he honestly believes that he is entitled to acquire it and that his privilege extends to the use of force or other unlawful method of acquisition. A further example might be where an employee threatens his employer in some way covered by Section 223.4 on theft by extortion, but only for the purpose of compelling the employer to pay wages which the employee believes to be due. If the employee

acted with the prescribed belief in his right to acquire the property "as he did," he would not be guilty of theft although he might be punishable under other sections of the Code for assault or coercion.

. . . Subsection (3)(b) provides a defense . . . premised on the view that a genuine belief in one's legal right should in all cases be a defense to theft. Persons who take only property to which they believe themselves entitled constitute no significant threat to the property system and manifest no character trait worse than ignorance.

3. The argument for allowing a claim of right as a defense to robbery is expressed in the Commentaries at page 157n.99:

[I]t should be emphasized that the provisions of Article 211 dealing with assault and Section 212.5 dealing with criminal coercion would be fully applicable to such conduct. . . . It ought to be the objective of the criminal law to describe the character deficiencies of those subjected to it in accord with the propensities that they actually manifest. One who is prepared to use violence to regain what he regards as his own property is, properly viewed, one who should be subjected to the laws designed to regulate violence and not to the laws designed to regulate the misappropriation of property of another.

Apparently that view has not proved popular. The California Supreme Court in State v. Barnett, 17 Cal. 4th 1044 (1998), overruled a prior decision that had allowed such a defense. The court drew support from recent cases from other jurisdictions that also rejected the Model Penal Code's position, arguing (17 Cal. 4th at 1144) that the position that claim of right negates the felonious intent in robbery:

. . . has no place in an ordered and orderly society such as ours, which eschews self help through violence. Adoption of the proposition would be but one step short of accepting lawless reprisal as an appropriate means of redressing grievances, real or fancied.

Who has the better of the argument? See Comment (Danielle R. Newton), What's Right With a Claim of Right?, 33 U.S. F. L. Rev. 673 (1999).

APPENDIX

AMERICAN LAW INSTITUTE MODEL PENAL CODE OFFICIAL DRAFT, 1962

PART I. GENERAL PROVISIONS

PART I. GENERAL PROVISIONS

Article 1. Preliminary

SECTION 1.01. TITLE AND EFFECTIVE DATE [omitted]

SECTION 1.02. PURPOSES; PRINCIPLES OF CONSTRUCTION

(1) The general purposes of the provisions governing the definition of offenses are:

(a) to forbid and prevent conduct that unjustifiably and inexcusably inflicts or threatens substantial harm to individual or public interests;

(b) to subject to public control persons whose conduct indicates that they are disposed to commit crimes;

(c) to safeguard conduct that is without fault from condemnation as criminal;

(d) to give fair warning of the nature of the conduct declared to constitute an offense;

(e) to differentiate on reasonable grounds between serious and minor offenses.

(2) The general purposes of the provisions governing the sentencing and treatment of offenders are:

(a) to prevent the commission of offenses;

(b) to promote the correction and rehabilitation of offenders;

(c) to safeguard offenders against excessive, disproportionate or arbitrary punishment;

(d) to give fair warning of the nature of the sentences that may be imposed on conviction of an offense;

(e) to differentiate among offenders with a view to a just individualization in their treatment;

(f) to define, coordinate and harmonize the powers, duties and functions of the courts and of administrative officers and agencies responsible for dealing with offenders;

(g) to advance the use of generally accepted scientific methods and knowledge in the sentencing and treatment of offenders;

(h) to integrate responsibility for the administration of the correctional system in a State Department of Correction [or other single department or agency].

(3) The provisions of the Code shall be construed according to the fair import of their terms but when the language is susceptible of differing constructions it shall be interpreted to further the general purposes stated in this Section and the special purposes of the particular provision involved. The discretionary powers conferred by the Code shall be exercised in accordance with the criteria stated in the Code and, insofar as such criteria are not decisive, to further the general purposes stated in this Section.

Section 1.03. Territorial Applicability

(1) Except as otherwise provided in this Section, a person may be convicted under the law of this State of an offense committed by his own conduct or the conduct of another for which he is legally accountable if:

(a) either the conduct which is an element of the offense or the result which is such an element occurs within this State; or

(b) conduct occurring outside the State is sufficient under the law of this State to constitute an attempt to commit an offense within the State; or

(c) conduct occurring outside the State is sufficient under the law of this State to constitute a conspiracy to commit an offense within the State and an overt act in furtherance of such conspiracy occurs within the State; or

(d) conduct occurring within the State establishes complicity in the commission of, or an attempt, solicitation or conspiracy to commit, an offense in another jurisdiction which also is an offense under the law of this State; or

(e) the offense consists of the omission to perform a legal duty imposed by the law of this State with respect to domicile, residence or a relationship to a person, thing or transaction in the State; or

(f) the offense is based on a statute of this State which expressly prohibits conduct outside the State, when the conduct bears a reasonable relation to a legitimate interest of this State and the actor knows or should know that his conduct is likely to affect that interest.

(2) Subsection (1)(a) does not apply when either causing a specified result or a purpose to cause or danger of causing such a result is an element of an offense and the result occurs or is designed or likely to occur only in another jurisdiction where the conduct charged would not constitute an offense, unless a legislative purpose plainly appears to declare the conduct criminal regardless of the place of the result.

(3) Subsection (1)(a) does not apply when causing a particular result is an element of an offense and the result is caused by conduct occurring outside the State which would not constitute an offense if the result had occurred there, unless the actor purposely or knowingly caused the result within the State.

(4) When the offense is homicide, either the death of the victim or the bodily impact causing the death constitutes a "result," within the meaning of Subsection (1)(a) and if the body of the homicide victim is found within the State, it is presumed that such result occurred within the State.

(5) This State includes the land and water and the air space above such land and water with respect to which the State has legislative jurisdiction.

Section 1.04. Classes of Crimes; Violations

(1) An offense defined by this Code or by any other statute of this State, for which a sentence of [death or of] imprisonment is authorized, constitutes a crime. Crimes are classified as felonies, misdemeanors or petty misdemeanors.

(2) A crime is a felony if it is so designated in this Code or if persons convicted thereof may be sentenced [to death or] to imprisonment for a term which, apart from an extended term, is in excess of one year.

(3) A crime is a misdemeanor if it is so designated in this Code or in a statute other than this Code enacted subsequent thereto.

(4) A crime is a petty misdemeanor if it is so designated in this Code or in a statute other than this Code enacted subsequent thereto or if it is defined by a statute other than this Code which now provides that persons convicted thereof may be sentenced to imprisonment for a term of which the maximum is less than one year.

(5) An offense defined by this Code or by any other statute of this State constitutes a violation if it is so designated in this Code or in the law defining the offense or if no other sentence than a fine, or fine and forfeiture or other civil penalty is authorized upon conviction or if it is defined by a statute other than this Code which now provides that the offense shall not constitute a crime. A violation does not constitute a crime and conviction of a violation shall not give rise to any disability or legal disadvantage based on conviction of a criminal offense.

(6) Any offense declared by law to constitute a crime, without specification of the grade thereof or of the sentence authorized upon conviction, is a misdemeanor.

(7) An offense defined by any statute of this State other than this Code shall be classified as provided in this Section and the sentence that may be imposed upon conviction thereof shall hereafter be governed by this Code.

Section 1.05. All Offenses Defined by Statute: Application of General Provisions of the Code

(1) No conduct constitutes an offense unless it is a crime or violation under this Code or another statute of this State.

(2) The provisions of Part I of the Code are applicable to offenses defined by other statutes, unless the Code otherwise provides.

(3) This Section does not affect the power of a court to punish for contempt or to employ any sanction authorized by law for the enforcement of an order or a civil judgment or decree.

SECTION 1.06. TIME LIMITATIONS

(1) A prosecution for murder may be commenced at any time.

(2) Except as otherwise provided in this Section, prosecutions for other offenses are subject to the following periods of limitation:

(a) a prosecution for a felony of the first degree must be commenced within six years after it is committed;

(b) a prosecution for any other felony must be commenced within three years after it is committed;

(c) a prosecution for a misdemeanor must be commenced within two years after it is committed;

(d) a prosecution for a petty misdemeanor or a violation must be commenced within six months after it is committed.

(3) If the period prescribed in Subsection (2) has expired, a prosecution may nevertheless be commenced for:

(a) any offense a material element of which is either fraud or a breach of fiduciary obligation within one year after discovery of the offense by an aggrieved party or by a person who has legal duty to represent an aggrieved party and who is himself not a party to the offense, but in no case shall this provision extend the period of limitation otherwise applicable by more than three years; and

(b) any offense based upon misconduct in office by a public officer or employee at any time when the defendant is in public office or employment or within two years thereafter, but in no case shall this provision extend the period of limitation otherwise applicable by more than three years.

(4) An offense is committed either when every element occurs, or, if a legislative purpose to prohibit a continuing course of conduct plainly appears, at the time when the course of conduct or the defendant's complicity therein is terminated. Time starts to run on the day after the offense is committed.

(5) A prosecution is commenced either when an indictment is found [or an information filed] or when a warrant or other process is issued, provided that such warrant or process is executed without unreasonable delay.

(6) The period of limitation does not run:

(a) during any time when the accused is continuously absent from the State or has no reasonably ascertainable place of abode or work within the State, but in no case shall this provision extend the period of limitation otherwise applicable by more than three years; or

(b) during any time when a prosecution against the accused for the same conduct is pending in this State.

SECTION 1.07. METHOD OF PROSECUTION WHEN CONDUCT CONSTITUTES MORE THAN ONE OFFENSE

(1) *Prosecution for Multiple Offenses; Limitation on Convictions.* When the same conduct of a defendant may establish the commission of more than one offense, the defendant may be prosecuted for each such offense. He may not, however, be convicted of more than one offense if:

(a) one offense is included in the other, as defined in Subsection (4) of this Section; or

(b) one offense consists only of a conspiracy or other form of preparation to commit the other; or

(c) inconsistent findings of fact are required to establish the commission of the offenses; or

(d) the offenses differ only in that one is defined to prohibit a designated kind of conduct generally and the other to prohibit a specific instance of such conduct; or

(e) the offense is defined as a continuing course of conduct and the defendant's course of conduct was uninterrupted, unless the law provides that specific periods of such conduct constitute separate offenses.

(2) *Limitation on Separate Trials for Multiple Offenses.* Except as provided in Subsection (3) of this Section, a defendant shall not be subject to separate trials for multiple offenses based on the same conduct or arising from the same criminal episode, if such offenses are known to the appropriate prosecuting officer at the time of the commencement of the first trial and are within the jurisdiction of a single court.

(3) *Authority of Court to Order Separate Trials.* When a defendant is charged with two or more offenses based on the same conduct or arising from the same criminal episode, the Court, on application of the prosecuting attorney or of the defendant, may order any such charge to be tried separately, if it is satisfied that justice so requires.

(4) *Conviction of Included Offense Permitted.* A defendant may be convicted of an offense included in an offense charged in the indictment [or the information]. An offense is so included when:

(a) it is established by proof of the same or less than all the facts required to establish the commission of the offense charged; or

(b) it consists of an attempt or solicitation to commit the offense charged or to commit an offense otherwise included therein; or

(c) it differs from the offense charged only in the respect that a less serious injury or risk of injury to the same person, property or public interest or a lesser kind of culpability suffices to establish its commission.

(5) *Submission of Included Offense to Jury.* The Court shall not be obligated to charge the jury with respect to an included offense unless there is a rational basis for a verdict acquitting the defendant of the offense charged and convicting him of the included offense.

SECTION 1.08. WHEN PROSECUTION BARRED BY FORMER PROSECUTION FOR THE SAME OFFENSE [OMITTED]

SECTION 1.09. WHEN PROSECUTION BARRED BY FORMER PROSECUTION FOR DIFFERENT OFFENSE [OMITTED]

SECTION 1.10. FORMER PROSECUTION IN ANOTHER JURISDICTION: WHEN A BAR [OMITTED]

SECTION 1.11. FORMER PROSECUTION BEFORE COURT LACKING JURISDICTION OR WHEN FRAUDULENTLY PROCURED BY THE DEFENDANT [OMITTED]

SECTION 1.12. PROOF BEYOND A REASONABLE DOUBT; AFFIRMATIVE DEFENSES; BURDEN OF PROVING FACT WHEN NOT AN ELEMENT OF AN OFFENSE; PRESUMPTIONS

(1) No person may be convicted of an offense unless each element of such offense is proved beyond a reasonable doubt. In the absence of such proof, the innocence of the defendant is assumed.

(2) Subsection (1) of this Section does not:

(a) require the disproof of an affirmative defense unless and until there is evidence supporting such defense; or

(b) apply to any defense which the Code or another statute plainly requires the defendant to prove by a preponderance of evidence.

(3) A ground of defense is affirmative, within the meaning of Subsection (2)(a) of this Section, when:

(a) it arises under a section of the Code which so provides; or

(b) it relates to an offense defined by a statute other than the Code and such statute so provides; or

(c) it involves a matter of excuse or justification peculiarly within the knowledge of the defendant on which he can fairly be required to adduce supporting evidence.

(4) When the application of the Code depends upon the finding of a fact which is not an element of an offense, unless the Code otherwise provides:

(a) the burden of proving the fact is on the prosecution or defendant, depending on whose interest or contention will be furthered if the finding should be made; and

(b) the fact must be proved to the satisfaction of the Court or jury, as the case may be.

(5) When the Code establishes a presumption with respect to any fact which is an element of an offense, it has the following consequences:

(a) when there is evidence of the facts which give rise to the presumption, the issue of the existence of the presumed fact must be submitted to the jury, unless the Court is satisfied that the evidence as a whole clearly negatives the presumed fact; and

(b) when the issue of the existence of the presumed fact is submitted to the jury, the Court shall charge that while the presumed fact must, on all the evidence, be proved beyond a reasonable doubt, the law declares that the jury may regard the facts giving rise to the presumption as sufficient evidence of the presumed fact.

(6) A presumption not established by the Code or inconsistent with it has the consequences otherwise accorded it by law.

Section 1.13. General Definitions

In this Code, unless a different meaning plainly is required:

(1) "statute" includes the Constitution and a local law or ordinance of a political subdivision of the State;

(2) "act" or "action" means a bodily movement whether voluntary or involuntary;

(3) "voluntary" has the meaning specified in Section 2.01;

(4) "omission" means a failure to act;

(5) "conduct" means an action or omission and its accompanying state of mind, or, where relevant, a series of acts and omissions;

(6) "actor" includes, where relevant, a person guilty of an omission;

(7) "acted" includes, where relevant, "omitted to act";

(8) "person," "he" and "actor" include any natural person and, where relevant, a corporation or an unincorporated association;

(9) "element of an offense" means (i) such conduct or (ii) such attendant circumstances or (iii) such a result of conduct as

(a) is included in the description of the forbidden conduct in the definition of the offense; or

(b) establishes the required kind of culpability; or

(c) negatives an excuse or justification for such conduct; or

(d) negatives a defense under the statute of limitations; or

(e) establishes jurisdiction or venue;

(10) "material element of an offense" means an element that does not relate exclusively to the statute of limitations, jurisdiction, venue or to any other matter similarly unconnected with (i) the harm or evil, incident to conduct, sought to be prevented by the law defining the offense, or (ii) the existence of a justification or excuse for such conduct;

(11) "purposely" has the meaning specified in Section 2.02 and equivalent terms such as "with purpose," "designed" or "with design" have the same meaning;

(12) "intentionally" or "with intent" means purposely;

(13) "knowingly" has the meaning specified in Section 2.02 and equivalent terms such as "knowing" or "with knowledge" have the same meaning;

(14) "recklessly" has the meaning specified in Section 2.02 and equivalent terms such as "recklessness" or "with recklessness" have the same meaning;

(15) "negligently" has the meaning specified in Section 2.02 and equivalent terms such as "negligence" or "with negligence" have the same meaning;

(16) "reasonably believes" or "reasonable belief" designates a belief which the actor is not reckless or negligent in holding.

Article 2. General Principles of Liability

SECTION 2.01. REQUIREMENT OF VOLUNTARY ACT; OMISSION AS BASIS OF LIABILITY; POSSESSION AS AN ACT

(1) A person is not guilty of an offense unless his liability is based on conduct which includes a voluntary act or the omission to perform an act of which he is physically capable.

(2) The following are not voluntary acts within the meaning of this Section:

(a) a reflex or convulsion;

(b) a bodily movement during unconsciousness or sleep;

(c) conduct during hypnosis or resulting from hypnotic suggestion;

(d) a bodily movement that otherwise is not a product of the effort or determination of the actor, either conscious or habitual.

(3) Liability for the commission of an offense may not be based on an omission unaccompanied by action unless:

(a) the omission is expressly made sufficient by the law defining the offense; or

(b) a duty to perform the omitted act is otherwise imposed by law.

(4) Possession is an act, within the meaning of this Section, if the possessor knowingly procured or received the thing possessed or was aware of his control thereof for a sufficient period to have been able to terminate his possession.

SECTION 2.02. GENERAL REQUIREMENTS OF CULPABILITY

(1) *Minimum Requirements of Culpability.* Except as provided in Section 2.05, a person is not guilty of an offense unless he acted purposely, knowingly, recklessly or negligently, as the law may require, with respect to each material element of the offense.

(2) *Kinds of Culpability Defined.*

(a) *Purposely.* A person acts purposely with respect to a material element of an offense when:

(i) if the element involves the nature of his conduct or a result thereof, it is his conscious object to engage in conduct of that nature or to cause such a result; and

(ii) if the element involves the attendant circumstances, he is aware of the existence of such circumstances or he believes or hopes that they exist.

(b) *Knowingly.* A person acts knowingly with respect to a material element of an offense when:

(i) if the element involves the nature of his conduct or the attendant circumstances, he is aware that his conduct is of that nature or that such circumstances exist; and

(ii) if the element involves a result of his conduct, he is aware that it is practically certain that his conduct will cause such a result.

(c) *Recklessly.* A person acts recklessly with respect to a material element of an offense when he consciously disregards a substantial and unjustifiable risk that the material element exists or will result from his conduct. The risk must be of such a nature and degree that, considering the nature and purpose of the actor's conduct and the circumstances known to him, its disregard involves a gross deviation from the standard of conduct that a law-abiding person would observe in the actor's situation.

(d) *Negligently.* A person acts negligently with respect to a material element of an offense when he should be aware of a substantial and unjustifiable risk that the material element exists or will result from his conduct. The risk must be of such a nature and degree that the actor's failure to perceive it, considering the nature and purpose of his conduct and the circumstances known to him, involves a gross deviation from the standard of care that a reasonable person would observe in the actor's situation.

(3) *Culpability Required Unless Otherwise Provided.* When the culpability sufficient to establish a material element of an offense is not prescribed by law, such element is established if a person acts purposely, knowingly or recklessly with respect thereto.

(4) *Prescribed Culpability Requirement Applies to All Material Elements.* When the law defining an offense prescribes the kind of culpability that is sufficient for the commission of an offense, without distinguishing among the material elements thereof, such provision shall apply to all the material elements of the offense, unless a contrary purpose plainly appears.

(5) *Substitutes for Negligence, Recklessness and Knowledge.* When the law provides that negligence suffices to establish an element of an offense, such element also is established if a person acts purposely, knowingly or recklessly. When recklessness suffices to establish an element, such element also is established if a person acts purposely or knowingly. When acting knowingly suffices to establish an element, such element also is established if a person acts purposely.

(6) *Requirement of Purpose Satisfied if Purpose Is Conditional.* When a particular purpose is an element of an offense, the element is established although such purpose is conditional, unless the condition negatives the harm or evil sought to be prevented by the law defining the offense.

(7) *Requirement of Knowledge Satisfied by Knowledge of High Probability.* When knowledge of the existence of a particular fact is an element of an offense, such knowledge is established if a person is aware of a high probability of its existence, unless he actually believes that it does not exist.

(8) *Requirement of Wilfulness Satisfied by Acting Knowingly.* A requirement that an offense be committed wilfully is satisfied if a person acts knowingly with respect to the material elements of the offense, unless a purpose to impose further requirements appears.

(9) *Culpability as to Illegality of Conduct.* Neither knowledge nor recklessness or negligence as to whether conduct constitutes an offense or as to the existence, meaning or application of the law determining the elements of an offense is an element of such offense, unless the definition of the offense or the Code so provides.

(10) *Culpability as Determinant of Grade of Offense.* When the grade or degree of an offense depends on whether the offense is committed purposely, knowingly, recklessly or negligently, its grade or degree shall be the lowest for which the determinative kind of culpability is established with respect to any material element of the offense.

Section 2.03. Causal Relationship Between Conduct and Result; Divergence Between Result Designed or Contemplated and Actual Result or Between Probable and Actual Result

(1) Conduct is the cause of a result when:

(a) it is an antecedent but for which the result in question would not have occurred; and

(b) the relationship between the conduct and result satisfies any additional causal requirements imposed by the Code or by the law defining the offense.

(2) When purposely or knowingly causing a particular result is an element of an offense, the element is not established if the actual result is not within the purpose or the contemplation of the actor unless:

(a) the actual result differs from that designed or contemplated, as the case may be, only in the respect that a different person or different property is injured or affected or that the injury or harm designed or contemplated would have been more serious or more extensive than that caused; or

(b) the actual result involves the same kind of injury or harm as that designed or contemplated and is not too remote or accidental in its occurrence to have a [just] bearing on the actor's liability or on the gravity of his offense.

(3) When recklessly or negligently causing a particular result is an element of an offense, the element is not established if the actual result is not within the risk of which the actor is aware or, in the case of negligence, of which he should be aware unless:

(a) the actual result differs from the probable result only in the respect that a different person or different property is injured or affected or that the probable injury or harm would have been more serious or more extensive than that caused; or

(b) the actual result involves the same kind of injury or harm as the probable result and is not too remote or accidental in its occurrence to have a [just] bearing on the actor's liability or on the gravity of his offense.

(4) When causing a particular result is a material element of an offense for which absolute liability is imposed by law, the element is not established unless the actual result is a probable consequence of the actor's conduct.

Section 2.04. Ignorance or Mistake

(1) Ignorance or mistake as to a matter of fact or law is a defense if:

(a) the ignorance or mistake negatives the purpose, knowledge, belief, recklessness or negligence required to establish a material element of the offense; or

(b) the law provides that the state of mind established by such ignorance or mistake constitutes a defense.

(2) Although ignorance or mistake would otherwise afford a defense to the offense charged, the defense is not available if the defendant would be guilty of another offense had the situation been as he supposed. In such case, however, the ignorance or mistake of the defendant shall reduce the grade and degree of the offense of which he may be convicted to those of the offense of which he would be guilty had the situation been as he supposed.

(3) A belief that conduct does not legally constitute an offense is a defense to a prosecution for that offense based upon such conduct when:

(a) the statute or other enactment defining the offense is not known to the actor and has not been published or otherwise reasonably made available prior to the conduct alleged; or

(b) he acts in reasonable reliance upon an official statement of the law, afterward determined to be invalid or erroneous, contained in (i) a statute or other enactment; (ii) a judicial decision, opinion or judgment; (iii) an administrative order or grant of permission; or (iv) an official interpretation of the public officer or body charged by law with responsibility for the interpretation, administration or enforcement of the law defining the offense.

(4) The defendant must prove a defense arising under Subsection (3) of this Section by a preponderance of evidence.

Section 2.05. When Culpability Requirements Are Inapplicable to Violations and to Offenses Defined by Other Statutes; Effect of Absolute Liability in Reducing Grade of Offense to Violation

(1) The requirements of culpability prescribed by Sections 2.01 and 2.02 do not apply to:

(a) offenses which constitute violations, unless the requirement involved is included in the definition of the offense or the Court determines that its application is consistent with effective enforcement of the law defining the offense; or

(b) offenses defined by statutes other than the Code, insofar as a legislative purpose to impose absolute liability for such offenses or with respect to any material element thereof plainly appears.

(2) Notwithstanding any other provision of existing law and unless a subsequent statute otherwise provides:

(a) when absolute liability is imposed with respect to any material element of an offense defined by a statute other than the Code and a conviction is based upon such liability, the offense constitutes a violation; and

(b) although absolute liability is imposed by law with respect to one or more of the material elements of an offense defined by a statute other than the Code, the culpable commission of the offense may be charged and proved, in which event negligence with respect to such elements constitutes sufficient culpability and the classification of the offense and the sentence that may be imposed therefor upon conviction are determined by Section 1.04 and Article 6 of the Code.

Section 2.06. Liability for Conduct of Another; Complicity

(1) A person is guilty of an offense if it is committed by his own conduct or by the conduct of another person for which he is legally accountable, or both.

(2) A person is legally accountable for the conduct of another person when:

(a) acting with the kind of culpability that is sufficient for the commission of the offense, he causes an innocent or irresponsible person to engage in such conduct; or

(b) he is made accountable for the conduct of such other person by the Code or by the law defining the offense; or

(c) he is an accomplice of such other person in the commission of the offense.

(3) A person is an accomplice of another person in the commission of an offense if:

(a) with the purpose of promoting or facilitating the commission of the offense, he

(i) solicits such other person to commit it; or

(ii) aids or agrees or attempts to aid such other person in planning or committing it; or

(iii) having a legal duty to prevent the commission of the offense, fails to make proper effort so to do; or

(b) his conduct is expressly declared by law to establish his complicity.

(4) When causing a particular result is an element of an offense, an accomplice in the conduct causing such result is an accomplice in the commission of that offense, if he acts with the kind of culpability, if any, with respect to that result that is sufficient for the commission of the offense.

(5) A person who is legally incapable of committing a particular offense himself may be guilty thereof if it is committed by the conduct of another person for which he is legally accountable, unless such liability is inconsistent with the purpose of the provision establishing his incapacity.

(6) Unless otherwise provided by the Code or by the law defining the offense, a person is not an accomplice in an offense committed by another person if:

(a) he is a victim of that offense; or

(b) the offense is so defined that his conduct is inevitably incident to its commission; or

(c) he terminates his complicity prior to the commission of the offense and

(i) wholly deprives it of effectiveness in the commission of the offense; or

(ii) gives timely warning to the law enforcement authorities or otherwise makes proper effort to prevent the commission of the offense.

(7) An accomplice may be convicted on proof of the commission of the offense and of his complicity therein, though the person claimed to have committed the offense has not been prosecuted or convicted or has been convicted of a different offense or degree of offense or has an immunity to prosecution or conviction or has been acquitted.

Section 2.07. Liability of Corporations, Unincorporated Associations and Persons Acting, or Under a Duty to Act, in Their Behalf

(1) A corporation may be convicted of the commission of an offense if:

(a) the offense is a violation or the offense is defined by a statute other than the Code in which a legislative purpose to impose liability on corporations plainly appears and the conduct is performed by an agent of the corporation acting in behalf of the corporation within the scope of his office or employment, except that if the law defining the offense designates the agents for whose conduct the corporation is accountable or the circumstances under which it is accountable, such provisions shall apply; or

(b) the offense consists of an omission to discharge a specific duty of affirmative performance imposed on corporations by law; or

(c) the commission of the offense was authorized, requested, commanded, performed or recklessly tolerated by the board of directors or by a high managerial agent acting in behalf of the corporation within the scope of his office or employment.

(2) When absolute liability is imposed for the commission of an offense, a legislative purpose to impose liability on a corporation shall be assumed, unless the contrary plainly appears.

(3) An unincorporated association may be convicted of the commission of an offense if:

(a) the offense is defined by a statute other than the Code which expressly provides for the liability of such an association and the conduct is performed by an agent of the association acting in behalf of the association within the scope of his office or employment, except that if the law defining the offense designates the agents for whose conduct the association is accountable or the circumstances under which it is accountable, such provisions shall apply; or

(b) the offense consists of an omission to discharge a specific duty of affirmative performance imposed on associations by law.

(4) As used in this Section:

(a) "corporation" does not include an entity organized as or by a governmental agency for the execution of a governmental program;

(b) "agent" means any director, officer, servant, employee or other person authorized to act in behalf of the corporation or association and, in the case of an unincorporated association, a member of such association;

(c) "high managerial agent" means an officer of a corporation or an unincorporated association, or, in the case of a partnership, a partner, or any other agent of a corporation or association having duties of such responsibility that his conduct may fairly be assumed to represent the policy of the corporation or association.

(5) In any prosecution of a corporation or an unincorporated association for the

commission of an offense included within the terms of Subsection (1) (a) or Subsection (3) (a) of this Section, other than an offense for which absolute liability has been imposed, it shall be a defense if the defendant proves by a preponderance of evidence that the high managerial agent having supervisory responsibility over the subject matter of the offense employed due diligence to prevent its commission. This paragraph shall not apply if it is plainly inconsistent with the legislative purpose in defining the particular offense.

(6) (a) A person is legally accountable for any conduct he performs or causes to be performed in the name of the corporation or an unincorporated association or in its behalf to the same extent as if it were performed in his own name or behalf.

(b) Whenever a duty to act is imposed by law upon a corporation or an unincorporated association, any agent of the corporation or association having primary responsibility for the discharge of the duty is legally accountable for a reckless omission to perform the required act to the same extent as if the duty were imposed by law directly upon himself.

(c) When a person is convicted of an offense by reason of his legal accountability for the conduct of a corporation or an unincorporated association, he is subject to the sentence authorized by law when a natural person is convicted of an offense of the grade and the degree involved.

SECTION 2.08. INTOXICATION

(1) Except as provided in Subsection (4) of this Section, intoxication of the actor is not a defense unless it negatives an element of the offense.

(2) When recklessness establishes an element of the offense, if the actor, due to self-induced intoxication, is unaware of a risk of which he would have been aware had he been sober, such unawareness is immaterial.

(3) Intoxication does not, in itself, constitute mental disease within the meaning of Section 4.01.

(4) Intoxication which (a) is not self-induced or (b) is pathological is an affirmative defense if by reason of such intoxication the actor at the time of his conduct lacks substantial capacity either to appreciate its criminality [wrongfulness] or to conform his conduct to the requirements of law.

(5) *Definitions.* In this Section unless a different meaning plainly is required:

(a) "intoxication" means a disturbance of mental or physical capacities resulting from the introduction of substances into the body;

(b) "self-induced intoxication" means intoxication caused by substances which the actor knowingly introduces into his body, the tendency of which to cause intoxication he knows or ought to know, unless he introduces them pursuant to medical advice or under such circumstances as would afford a defense to a charge of crime;

(c) "pathological intoxication" means intoxication grossly excessive in degree, given the amount of the intoxicant, to which the actor does not know he is susceptible.

SECTION 2.09. DURESS

(1) It is an affirmative defense that the actor engaged in the conduct charged to constitute an offense because he was coerced to do so by the use of, or a threat to use, unlawful force against his person or the person of another, which a person of reasonable firmness in his situation would have been unable to resist.

(2) The defense provided by this Section is unavailable if the actor recklessly placed himself in a situation in which it was probable that he would be subjected to duress. The

defense is also unavailable if he was negligent in placing himself in such a situation, whenever negligence suffices to establish culpability for the offense charged.

(3) It is not a defense that a woman acted on the command of her husband, unless she acted under such coercion as would establish a defense under this Section. [The presumption that a woman, acting in the presence of her husband, is coerced is abolished.]

(4) When the conduct of the actor would otherwise be justifiable under Section 3.02, this Section does not preclude such defense.

SECTION 2.10. MILITARY ORDERS

It is an affirmative defense that the actor, in engaging in the conduct charged to constitute an offense, does no more than execute an order of his superior in the armed services which he does not know to be unlawful.

SECTION 2.11. CONSENT

(1) *In General.* The consent of the victim to conduct charged to constitute an offense or to the result thereof is a defense if such consent negatives an element of the offense or precludes the infliction of the harm or evil sought to be prevented by the law defining the offense.

(2) *Consent to Bodily Harm.* When conduct is charged to constitute an offense because it causes or threatens bodily harm, consent to such conduct or to the infliction of such harm is a defense if:

(a) the bodily harm consented to or threatened by the conduct consented to is not serious; or

(b) the conduct and the harm are reasonably foreseeable hazards of joint participation in a lawful athletic contest or competitive sport; or

(c) the consent establishes a justification for the conduct under Article 3 of the Code.

(3) *Ineffective Consent.* Unless otherwise provided by the Code or by the law defining the offense, assent does not constitute consent if:

(a) it is given by a person who is legally incompetent to authorize the conduct charged to constitute the offense; or

(b) it is given by a person who by reason of youth, mental disease or defect or intoxication is manifestly unable or known by the actor to be unable to make a reasonable judgment as to the nature or harmfulness of the conduct charged to constitute the offense; or

(c) it is given by a person whose improvident consent is sought to be prevented by the law defining the offense; or

(d) it is induced by force, duress or deception of a kind sought to be prevented by the law defining the offense.

SECTION 2.12. DE MINIMIS INFRACTIONS

The Court shall dismiss a prosecution if, having regard to the nature of the conduct charged to constitute an offense and the nature of the attendant circumstances, it finds that the defendant's conduct:

(1) was within a customary license or tolerance, neither expressly negatived by the person whose interest was infringed nor inconsistent with the purpose of the law defining the offense; or

(2) did not actually cause or threaten the harm or evil sought to be prevented by the law defining the offense or did so only to an extent too trivial to warrant the condemnation of conviction; or

(3) presents such other extenuations that it cannot reasonably be regarded as envisaged by the legislature in forbidding the offense.

The Court shall not dismiss a prosecution under Subsection (3) of this Section without filing a written statement of its reasons.

Section 2.13. Entrapment

(1) A public law enforcement official or a person acting in cooperation with such an official perpetrates an entrapment if for the purpose of obtaining evidence of the commission of an offense, he induces or encourages another person to engage in conduct constituting such offense by either:

(a) making knowingly false representations designed to induce the belief that such conduct is not prohibited; or

(b) employing methods of persuasion or inducement which create a substantial risk that such an offense will be committed by persons other than those who are ready to commit it.

(2) Except as provided in Subsection (3) of this Section, a person prosecuted for an offense shall be acquitted if he proves by a preponderance of evidence that his conduct occurred in response to an entrapment. The issue of entrapment shall be tried by the Court in the absence of the jury.

(3) The defense afforded by this Section is unavailable when causing or threatening bodily injury is an element of the offense charged and the prosecution is based on conduct causing or threatening such injury to a person other than the person perpetrating the entrapment.

Article 3. General Principles of Justification

Section 3.01. Justification an Affirmative Defense; Civil Remedies Unaffected

(1) In any prosecution based on conduct which is justifiable under this Article, justification is an affirmative defense.

(2) The fact that conduct is justifiable under this Article does not abolish or impair any remedy for such conduct which is available in any civil action.

Section 3.02. Justification Generally: Choice of Evils

(1) Conduct which the actor believes to be necessary to avoid a harm or evil to himself or to another is justifiable, provided that:

(a) the harm or evil sought to be avoided by such conduct is greater than that sought to be prevented by the law defining the offense charged; and

(b) neither the Code nor other law defining the offense provides exceptions or defenses dealing with the specific situation involved; and

(c) a legislative purpose to exclude the justification claimed does not otherwise plainly appear.

(2) When the actor was reckless or negligent in bringing about the situation requiring a choice of harms or evils or in appraising the necessity for his conduct, the justification afforded by this section is unavailable in a prosecution for any offense for which recklessness or negligence, as the case may be, suffices to establish culpability.

Section 3.03. Execution of Public Duty

(1) Except as provided in Subsection (2) of this Section, conduct is justifiable when it is required or authorized by:

(a) the law defining the duties or functions of a public officer or the assistance to be rendered to such officer in the performance of his duties; or

(b) the law governing the execution of legal process; or

(c) the judgment or order of a competent court or tribunal; or

(d) the law governing the armed services or the lawful conduct of war; or

(e) any other provision of law imposing a public duty.

(2) The other sections of this Article apply to:

(a) the use of force upon or toward the person of another for any of the purposes dealt with in such sections; and

(b) the use of deadly force for any purpose, unless the use of such force is otherwise expressly authorized by law or occurs in the lawful conduct of war.

(3) The justification afforded by Subsection (1) of this Section applies:

(a) when the actor believes his conduct to be required or authorized by the judgment or direction of a competent court or tribunal or in the lawful execution of legal process, notwithstanding lack of jurisdiction of the court or defect in the legal process; and

(b) when the actor believes his conduct to be required or authorized to assist a public officer in the performance of his duties, notwithstanding that the officer exceeded his legal authority.

Section 3.04. Use of Force in Self-Protection

(1) *Use of Force Justifiable for Protection of the Person.* Subject to the provisions of this Section and of Section 3.09, the use of force upon or toward another person is justifiable when the actor believes that such force is immediately necessary for the purpose of protecting himself against the use of unlawful force by such other person on the present occasion.

(2) *Limitations on Justifying Necessity for Use of Force.*

(a) The use of force is not justifiable under this Section:

(i) to resist an arrest which the actor knows is being made by a peace officer, although the arrest is unlawful; or

(ii) to resist force used by the occupier or possessor of property or by another person on his behalf, where the actor knows that the person using the force is doing so under a claim of right to protect the property, except that this limitation shall not apply if:

(1) the actor is a public officer acting in the performance of his duties or a person lawfully assisting him therein or a person making or assisting in a lawful arrest; or

(2) the actor has been unlawfully dispossessed of the property and is making a re-entry or recaption justified by Section 3.06; or

(3) the actor believes that such force is necessary to protect himself against death or serious bodily harm.

(b) The use of deadly force is not justifiable under this Section unless the actor believes that such force is necessary to protect himself against death, serious bodily harm, kidnapping or sexual intercourse compelled by force or threat; nor is it justifiable if:

(i) the actor, with the purpose of causing death or serious bodily harm, provoked the use of force against himself in the same encounter; or

(ii) the actor knows that he can avoid the necessity of using such force with complete safety by retreating or by surrendering possession of a thing to a person asserting a claim of right thereto or by complying with a demand that he abstain from any action which he has no duty to take, except that:

(1) the actor is not obliged to retreat from his dwelling or place of work, unless he was the initial aggressor or is assailed in his place of work by another person whose place of work the actor knows it to be; and

(2) a public officer justified in using force in the performance of his duties or a person justified in using force in his assistance or a person justified in using force in making an arrest or preventing an escape is not obliged to desist from efforts to perform such duty, effect such arrest or prevent such escape because of resistance or threatened resistance by or on behalf of the person against whom such action is directed.

(c) Except as required by paragraphs (a) and (b) of this Subsection, a person employing protective force may estimate the necessity thereof under the circumstances as he believes them to be when the force is used, without retreating, surrendering possession, doing any other act which he has no legal duty to do or abstaining from any lawful action.

(3) *Use of Confinement as Protective Force.* The justification afforded by this Section extends to the use of confinement as protective force only if the actor takes all reasonable measures to terminate the confinement as soon as he knows that he safely can, unless the person confined has been arrested on a charge of crime.

Section 3.05. Use of Force for the Protection of Other Persons

(1) Subject to the provisions of this Section and of Section 3.09, the use of force upon or toward the person of another is justifiable to protect a third person when:

(a) the actor would be justified under Section 3.04 in using such force to protect himself against the injury he believes to be threatened to the person whom he seeks to protect; and

(b) under the circumstances as the actor believes them to be, the person whom he seeks to protect would be justified in using such protective force; and

(c) the actor believes that his intervention is necessary for the protection of such other person.

(2) Notwithstanding Subsection (1) of this Section:

(a) when the actor would be obliged under Section 3.04 to retreat, to surrender the possession of a thing or to comply with a demand before using force in self-protection, he is not obliged to do so before using force for the protection of another person, unless he knows that he can thereby secure the complete safety of such other person; and

(b) when the person whom the actor seeks to protect would be obliged under Section 3.04 to retreat, to surrender the possession of a thing or to comply with a demand if he knew that he could obtain complete safety by so doing, the actor is obliged to try to cause him to do so before using force in his protection if the actor knows that he can obtain complete safety in that way; and

(c) neither the actor nor the person whom he seeks to protect is obliged to retreat when in the other's dwelling or place of work to any greater extent than in his own.

Section 3.06. Use of Force for the Protection of Property

(1) *Use of Force Justifiable for Protection of Property.* Subject to the provisions of this Section and of Section 3.09, the use of force upon or toward the person of another is justifiable when the actor believes that such force is immediately necessary:

(a) to prevent or terminate an unlawful entry or other trespass upon land or a trespass against or the unlawful carrying away of tangible, movable property, provided that such land or movable property is, or is believed by the actor to be, in his possession or in the possession of another person for whose protection he acts; or

(b) to effect an entry or re-entry upon land or to retake tangible movable property, provided that the actor believes that he or the person by whose authority he acts or a person from whom he or such other person derives title was unlawfully dispossessed of such land or movable property and is entitled to possession, and provided, further, that:

(i) the force is used immediately or on fresh pursuit after such dispossession; or

(ii) the actor believes that the person against whom he uses force has no claim of right to the possession of the property and, in the case of land, the circumstances, as the actor believes them to be, are of such urgency that it would be an exceptional hardship to postpone the entry or re-entry until a court order is obtained.

(2) *Meaning of Possession.* For the purposes of Subsection (1) of this Section:

(a) a person who has parted with the custody of property to another who refuses to restore it to him is no longer in possession, unless the property is movable and was and still is located on land in his possession;

(b) a person who has been dispossessed of land does not regain possession thereof merely by setting foot thereon;

(c) a person who has a license to use or occupy real property is deemed to be in possession thereof except against the licensor acting under claim of right.

(3) *Limitations on Justifiable Use of Force.*

(a) *Request to Desist.* The use of force is justifiable under this Section only if the actor first requests the person against whom such force is used to desist from his interference with the property, unless the actor believes that:

(i) such request would be useless; or

(ii) it would be dangerous to himself or another person to make the request; or

(iii) substantial harm will be done to the physical condition of the property which is sought to be protected before the request can effectively be made.

(b) *Exclusion of Trespasser.* The use of force to prevent or terminate a trespass is not justifiable under this Section if the actor knows that the exclusion of the trespasser will expose him to substantial danger of serious bodily harm.

(c) *Resistance of Lawful Re-entry or Recaption.* The use of force to prevent an entry or re-entry upon land or the recaption of movable property is not justifiable under this Section, although the actor believes that such re-entry or recaption is unlawful, if:

(i) the re-entry or recaption is made by or on behalf of a person who was actually dispossessed of the property; and

(ii) it is otherwise justifiable under paragraph (1)(b) of this Section.

(d) *Use of Deadly Force.* The use of deadly force is not justifiable under this Section unless the actor believes that:

(i) the person against whom the force is used is attempting to dispossess him of his dwelling otherwise than under a claim of right to its possession; or

(ii) the person against whom the force is used is attempting to commit or consummate arson, burglary, robbery or other felonious theft or property destruction and either:

(1) has employed or threatened deadly force against or in the presence of the actor; or

(2) the use of force other than deadly force to prevent the commission or the consummation of the crime would expose the actor or another in his presence to substantial danger of serious bodily harm.

(4) *Use of Confinement as Protective Force.* The justification afforded by this Section extends to the use of confinement as protective force only if the actor takes all reasonable

measures to terminate the confinement as soon as he knows that he can do so with safety to the property, unless the person confined has been arrested on a charge of crime.

(5) *Use of Device to Protect Property.* The justification afforded by this Section extends to the use of a device for the purpose of protecting property only if:

(a) the device is not designed to cause or known to create a substantial risk of causing death or serious bodily harm; and

(b) the use of the particular device to protect the property from entry or trespass is reasonable under the circumstances, as the actor believes them to be; and

(c) the device is one customarily used for such a purpose or reasonable care is taken to make known to probable intruders the fact that it is used.

(6) *Use of Force to Pass Wrongful Obstructor.* The use of force to pass a person whom the actor believes to be purposely or knowingly and unjustifiably obstructing the actor from going to a place to which he may lawfully go is justifiable, provided that:

(a) the actor believes that the person against whom he uses force has no claim of right to obstruct the actor; and

(b) the actor is not being obstructed from entry or movement on land which he knows to be in the possession or custody of the person obstructing him, or in the possession or custody of another person by whose authority the obstructor acts, unless the circumstances, as the actor believes them to be, are of such urgency that it would not be reasonable to postpone the entry or movement on such land until a court order is obtained; and

(c) the force used is not greater than would be justifiable if the person obstructing the actor were using force against him to prevent his passage.

Section 3.07. Use of Force in Law Enforcement

(1) *Use of Force Justifiable to Effect an Arrest.* Subject to the provisions of this Section and of Section 3.09, the use of force upon or toward the person of another is justifiable when the actor is making or assisting in making an arrest and the actor believes that such force is immediately necessary to effect a lawful arrest.

(2) *Limitations on the Use of Force.*

(a) The use of force is not justifiable under this Section unless:

(i) the actor makes known the purpose of the arrest or believes that it is otherwise known by or cannot reasonably be made known to the person to be arrested; and

(ii) when the arrest is made under a warrant, the warrant is valid or believed by the actor to be valid.

(b) The use of deadly force is not justifiable under this Section unless:

(i) the arrest is for a felony; and

(ii) the person effecting the arrest is authorized to act as a peace officer or is assisting a person whom he believes to be authorized to act as a peace officer; and

(iii) the actor believes that the force employed creates no substantial risk of injury to innocent persons; and

(iv) the actor believes that:

(1) the crime for which the arrest is made involved conduct including the use or threatened use of deadly force; or

(2) there is a substantial risk that the person to be arrested will cause death or serious bodily harm if his apprehension is delayed.

(3) *Use of Force to Prevent Escape from Custody.* The use of force to prevent the escape of an arrested person from custody is justifiable when the force could justifiably have been employed to effect the arrest under which the person is in custody, except that a guard or other person authorized to act as a peace officer is justified in using any force, including deadly force, which he believes to be immediately necessary to prevent the es-

cape of a person from a jail, prison, or other institution for the detention of persons charged with or convicted of a crime.

(4) *Use of Force by Private Person Assisting an Unlawful Arrest.*

(a) A private person who is summoned by a peace officer to assist in effecting an unlawful arrest, is justified in using any force which he would be justified in using if the arrest were lawful, provided that he does not believe the arrest is unlawful.

(b) A private person who assists another private person in effecting an unlawful arrest, or who, not being summoned, assists a peace officer in effecting an unlawful arrest, is justified in using any force which he would be justified in using if the arrest were lawful, provided that (i) he believes the arrest is lawful, and (ii) the arrest would be lawful if the facts were as he believes them to be.

(5) *Use of Force to Prevent Suicide or the Commission of a Crime.*

(a) The use of force upon or toward the person of another is justifiable when the actor believes that such force is immediately necessary to prevent such other person from committing suicide, inflicting serious bodily harm upon himself, committing or consummating the commission of a crime involving or threatening bodily harm, damage to or loss of property or a breach of the peace, except that:

(i) any limitations imposed by the other provisions of this Article on the justifiable use of force in self-protection, for the protection of others, the protection of property, the effectuation of an arrest or the prevention of an escape from custody shall apply notwithstanding the criminality of the conduct against which such force is used; and

(ii) the use of deadly force is not in any event justifiable under this Subsection unless:

(1) the actor believes that there is a substantial risk that the person whom he seeks to prevent from committing a crime will cause death or serious bodily harm to another unless the commission or the consummation of the crime is prevented and that the use of such force presents no substantial risk of injury to innocent persons; or

(2) the actor believes that the use of such force is necessary to suppress a riot or mutiny after the rioters or mutineers have been ordered to disperse and warned, in any particular manner that the law may require, that such force will be used if they do not obey.

(b) The jurisdiction afforded by this Subsection extends to the use of confinement as preventive force only if the actor takes all reasonable measures to terminate the confinement as soon as he knows that he safely can, unless the person confined has been arrested on a charge of crime.

SECTION 3.08. USE OF FORCE BY PERSONS WITH SPECIAL RESPONSIBILITY FOR CARE, DISCIPLINE OR SAFETY OF OTHERS

The use of force upon or toward the person of another is justifiable if:

(1) the actor is the parent or guardian or other person similarly responsible for the general care and supervision of a minor or a person acting at the request of such parent, guardian or other responsible person and:

(a) the force is used for the purpose of safeguarding or promoting the welfare of the minor, including the prevention or punishment of his misconduct; and

(b) the force used is not designed to cause or known to create a substantial risk of causing death, serious bodily harm, disfigurement, extreme pain or mental distress or gross degradation; or

(2) the actor is a teacher or a person otherwise entrusted with the care or supervision for a special purpose of a minor and:

(a) the actor believes that the force used is necessary to further such special purpose, including the maintenance of reasonable discipline in a school, class or other group, and that the use of such force is consistent with the welfare of the minor; and

(b) the degree of force, if it had been used by the parent or guardian of the minor, would not be unjustifiable under Subsection (1)(b) of this Section; or

(3) the actor is the guardian or other person similarly responsible for the general care and supervision of an incompetent person; and:

(a) the force is used for the purpose of safeguarding or promoting the welfare of the incompetent person, including the prevention of his misconduct, or, when such incompetent person is in a hospital or other institution for his care and custody, for the maintenance of reasonable discipline in such institution; and

(b) the force used is not designed to cause or known to create a substantial risk of causing death, serious bodily harm, disfigurement, extreme or unnecessary pain, mental distress, or humiliation; or

(4) the actor is a doctor or other therapist or a person assisting him at his direction, and:

(a) the force is used for the purpose of administering a recognized form of treatment which the actor believes to be adapted to promoting the physical or mental health of the patient; and

(b) the treatment is administered with the consent of the patient or, if the patient is a minor or an incompetent person, with the consent of his parent or guardian or other person legally competent to consent in his behalf, or the treatment is administered in an emergency when the actor believes that no one competent to consent can be consulted and that a reasonable person, wishing to safeguard the welfare of the patient, would consent; or

(5) the actor is a warden or other authorized official of a correctional institution, and:

(a) he believes that the force used is necessary for the purpose of enforcing the lawful rules or procedures of the institution, unless his belief in the lawfulness of the rule or procedure sought to be enforced is erroneous and his error is due to ignorance or mistake as to the provisions of the Code, any other provision of the criminal law or the law governing the administration of the institution; and

(b) the nature or degree of force used is not forbidden by Article 303 or 304 of the Code; and

(c) if deadly force is used, its use is otherwise justifiable under this Article; or

(6) the actor is a person responsible for the safety of a vessel or an aircraft or a person acting at his direction, and

(a) he believes that the force used is necessary to prevent interference with the operation of the vessel or aircraft or obstruction of the execution of a lawful order, unless his belief in the lawfulness of the order is erroneous and his error is due to ignorance or mistake as to the law defining his authority; and

(b) if deadly force is used, its use is otherwise justifiable under this Article; or

(7) the actor is a person who is authorized or required by law to maintain order or decorum in a vehicle, train or other carrier or in a place where others are assembled, and:

(a) he believes that the force used is necessary for such purpose; and

(b) the force used is not designed to cause or known to create a substantial risk of causing death, bodily harm, or extreme mental distress.

Section 3.09. Mistake of Law as to Unlawfulness of Force or Legality of Arrest; Reckless or Negligent Use of Otherwise Justifiable Force; Reckless or Negligent Injury or Risk of Injury to Innocent Persons

(1) The justification afforded by Sections 3.04 to 3.07, inclusive, is unavailable when:

(a) the actor's belief in the unlawfulness of the force or conduct against which he employs protective force or his belief in the lawfulness of an arrest which he endeavors to effect by force is erroneous; and

(b) his error is due to ignorance or mistake as to the provisions of the Code, any other provision of the criminal law or the law governing the legality of an arrest or search.

(2) When the actor believes that the use of force upon or toward the person of another is necessary for any of the purposes for which such belief would establish a justification under Sections 3.03 to 3.08 but the actor is reckless or negligent in having such belief or in acquiring or failing to acquire any knowledge or belief which is material to the justifiability of his use of force, the justification afforded by those Sections is unavailable in a prosecution for an offense for which recklessness or negligence, as the case may be, suffices to establish culpability.

(3) When the actor is justified under Sections 3.03 to 3.08 in using force upon or toward the person of another but he recklessly or negligently injures or creates a risk of injury to innocent persons, the justification afforded by those Sections is unavailable in a prosecution for such recklessness or negligence towards innocent persons.

Section 3.10. Justification in Property Crimes

Conduct involving the appropriation, seizure or destruction of, damage to, intrusion on or interference with property is justifiable under circumstances which would establish a defense of privilege in a civil action based thereon, unless:

(1) the Code or the law defining the offense deals with the specific situation involved; or

(2) a legislative purpose to exclude the justification claimed otherwise plainly appears.

Section 3.11. Definitions

In this Article, unless a different meaning plainly is required:

(1) "unlawful force" means force, including confinement, which is employed without the consent of the person against whom it is directed and the employment of which constitutes an offense or actionable tort or would constitute such offense or tort except for a defense (such as the absence of intent, negligence, or mental capacity; duress; youth; or diplomatic status) not amounting to a privilege to use the force. Assent constitutes consent, within the meaning of this Section, whether or not it otherwise is legally effective, except assent to the infliction of death or serious bodily harm.

(2) "deadly force" means force which the actor uses with the purpose of causing or which he knows to create a substantial risk of causing death or serious bodily harm. Purposely firing a firearm in the direction of another person or at a vehicle in which another person is believed to be constitutes deadly force. A threat to cause death or serious bodily harm, by the production of a weapon or otherwise, so long as the actor's purpose is limited to creating an apprehension that he will use deadly force if necessary, does not constitute deadly force.

(3) "dwelling" means any building or structure, though movable or temporary, or a portion thereof, which is for the time being the actor's home or place of lodging.

Article 4. Responsibility

Section 4.01. Mental Disease or Defect Excluding Responsibility

(1) A person is not responsible for criminal conduct if at the time of such conduct as a result of mental disease or defect he lacks substantial capacity either to appreciate the

criminality [wrongfulness] of his conduct or to conform his conduct to the requirements of law.

(2) As used in this Article, the terms "mental disease or defect" do not include an abnormality manifested only by repeated criminal or otherwise anti-social conduct.

SECTION 4.02. EVIDENCE OF MENTAL DISEASE OR DEFECT ADMISSIBLE WHEN RELEVANT TO ELEMENT OF THE OFFENSE; [MENTAL DISEASE OR DEFECT IMPAIRING CAPACITY AS GROUND FOR MITIGATION OF PUNISHMENT IN CAPITAL CASES]

(1) Evidence that the defendant suffered from a mental disease or defect is admissible whenever it is relevant to prove that the defendant did or did not have a state of mind which is an element of the offense.

[(2) Whenever the jury or the Court is authorized to determine or to recommend whether or not the defendant shall be sentenced to death or imprisonment upon conviction, evidence that the capacity of the defendant to appreciate the criminality [wrongfulness] of his conduct or to conform his conduct to the requirements of law was impaired as a result of mental disease or defect is admissible in favor of sentence of imprisonment.]

SECTION 4.03. MENTAL DISEASE OR DEFECT EXCLUDING RESPONSIBILITY IS AFFIRMATIVE DEFENSE; REQUIREMENT OF NOTICE; FORM OF VERDICT AND JUDGMENT WHEN FINDING OF IRRESPONSIBILITY IS MADE

(1) Mental disease or defect excluding responsibility is an affirmative defense.

(2) Evidence of mental disease or defect excluding responsibility is not admissible unless the defendant, at the time of entering his plea of not guilty or within ten days thereafter or at such later time as the Court may for good cause permit, files a written notice of his purpose to rely on such defense.

(3) When the defendant is acquitted on the ground of mental disease or defect excluding responsibility, the verdict and the judgment shall so state.

SECTION 4.04. MENTAL DISEASE OR DEFECT EXCLUDING FITNESS TO PROCEED

No person who as a result of mental disease or defect lacks capacity to understand the proceedings against him or to assist in his own defense shall be tried, convicted or sentenced for the commission of an offense so long as such incapacity endures.

SECTION 4.05. PSYCHIATRIC EXAMINATION OF DEFENDANT WITH RESPECT TO MENTAL DISEASE OR DEFECT

(1) Whenever the defendant has filed a notice of intention to rely on the defense of mental disease or defect excluding responsibility, or there is reason to doubt his fitness to proceed, or reason to believe that mental disease or defect of the defendant will otherwise become an issue in the cause, the Court shall appoint at least one qualified psychiatrist or shall request the Superintendent of the ___ Hospital to designate at least one qualified psychiatrist, which designation may be or include himself, to examine and report upon the mental condition of the defendant. The Court may order the defendant to be committed to a hospital or other suitable facility for the purpose of the examination for a period of not exceeding sixty days or such longer period as the Court deter-

mines to be necessary for the purpose and may direct that a qualified psychiatrist retained by the defendant be permitted to witness and participate in the examination.

(2) In such examination any method may be employed which is accepted by the medical profession for the examination of those alleged to be suffering from mental disease or defect.

(3) The report of the examination shall include the following: (a) a description of the nature of the examination; (b) a diagnosis of the mental condition of the defendant; (c) if the defendant suffers from a mental disease or defect, an opinion as to his capacity to understand the proceedings against him and to assist in his own defense; (d) when a notice of intention to rely on the defense of irresponsibility has been filed, an opinion as to the extent, if any, to which the capacity of the defendant to appreciate the criminality [wrongfulness] of his conduct or to conform his conduct to the requirements of law was impaired at the time of the criminal conduct charged; and (e) when directed by the Court, an opinion as to the capacity of the defendant to have a particular state of mind which is an element of the offense charged.

If the examination can not be conducted by reason of the unwillingness of the defendant to participate therein, the report shall so state and shall include, if possible, an opinion as to whether such unwillingness of the defendant was the result of mental disease or defect.

The report of the examination shall be filed [in triplicate] with the clerk of the Court, who shall cause copies to be delivered to the district attorney and to counsel for the defendant.

Section 4.06. Determination of Fitness to Proceed; Effect of Finding of Unfitness; Proceedings if Fitness is Regained[; Post-Commitment Hearing]

(1) When the defendant's fitness to proceed is drawn in question, the issue shall be determined by the Court. If neither the prosecuting attorney nor counsel for the defendant contests the finding of the report filed pursuant to Section 4.05, the Court may make the determination on the basis of such report. If the finding is contested, the Court shall hold a hearing on the issue. If the report is received in evidence upon such hearing, the party who contests the finding thereof shall have the right to summon and to cross-examine the psychiatrists who joined in the report and to offer evidence upon the issue.

(2) If the Court determines that the defendant lacks fitness to proceed, the proceeding against him shall be suspended, except as provided in Subsection (3) [Subsections (3) and (4)] of this Section, and the Court shall commit him to the custody of the Commissioner of Mental Hygiene [Public Health or Correction] to be placed in an appropriate institution of the Department of Mental Hygiene [Public Health or Correction] for so long as such unfitness shall endure. When the Court, on its own motion or upon the application of the Commissioner of Mental Hygiene [Public Health or Correction] or the prosecuting attorney, determines, after a hearing if a hearing is requested, that the defendant has regained fitness to proceed, the proceeding shall be resumed. If, however, the Court is of the view that so much time has elapsed since the commitment of the defendant that it would be unjust to resume the criminal proceeding, the Court may dismiss the charge and may order the defendant to be discharged or, subject to the law governing the civil commitment of persons suffering from mental disease or defect, order the defendant to be committed to an appropriate institution of the Department of Mental Hygiene [Public Health].

(3) The fact that the defendant is unfit to proceed does not preclude any legal objection to the prosecution which is susceptible of fair determination prior to trial and without the personal participation of the defendant.

[Alternative: (3) At any time within ninety days after commitment as provided in Subsection (2) of this Section, or at any later time with permission of the Court granted for good cause, the defendant or his counsel or the Commissioner of Mental Hygiene [Public Health or Correction] may apply for a special post-commitment hearing. If the application is made by or on behalf of a defendant not represented by counsel, he shall be afforded a reasonable opportunity to obtain counsel, and if he lacks funds to do so, counsel shall be assigned by the Court. The application shall be granted only if the counsel for the defendant satisfies the Court by affidavit or otherwise that as an attorney he has reasonable grounds for a good faith belief that his client has, on the facts and the law, a defense to the charge other than mental disease or defect excluding responsibility.

[(4) If the motion for a special post-commitment hearing is granted, the hearing shall be by the Court without a jury. No evidence shall be offered at the hearing by either party on the issue of mental disease or defect as a defense to, or in mitigation of, the crime charged. After hearing, the Court may in an appropriate case quash the indictment or other charge, or find it to be defective or insufficient, or determine that it is not proved beyond a reasonable doubt by the evidence, or otherwise terminate the proceedings on the evidence or the law. In any such case, unless all defects in the proceedings are promptly cured, the Court shall terminate the commitment ordered under Subsection (2) of this Section and order the defendant to be discharged or, subject to the law governing the civil commitment of persons suffering from mental disease or defect, order the defendant to be committed to an appropriate institution of the Department of Mental Hygiene [Public Health].]

Section 4.07. Determination of Irresponsibility on Basis of Report; Access to Defendant by Psychiatrist of His Own Choice; Form of Expert Testimony When Issue of Responsibility Is Tried

(1) If the report filed pursuant to Section 4.05 finds that the defendant at the time of the criminal conduct charged suffered from a mental disease or defect which substantially impaired his capacity to appreciate the criminality [wrongfulness] of his conduct or to conform his conduct to the requirements of law, and the Court, after a hearing if a hearing is requested by the prosecuting attorney or the defendant, is satisfied that such impairment was sufficient to exclude responsibility, the Court on motion of the defendant shall enter judgment of acquittal on the ground of mental disease or defect excluding responsibility.

(2) When, notwithstanding the report filed pursuant to Section 4.05, the defendant wishes to be examined by a qualified psychiatrist or other expert of his own choice, such examiner shall be permitted to have reasonable access to the defendant for the purposes of such examination.

(3) Upon the trial, the psychiatrists who reported pursuant to Section 4.05 may be called as witnesses by the prosecution, the defendant or the Court. If the issue is being tried before a jury, the jury may be informed that the psychiatrists were designated by the Court or by the Superintendent of the _____ Hospital at the request of the Court, as the case may be. If called by the Court, the witness shall be subject to cross-examination by the prosecution and by the defendant. Both the prosecution and the defendant may summon any other qualified psychiatrist or other expert to testify, but no one who has not examined the defendant shall be competent to testify to an expert opinion with respect to the mental condition or responsibility of the defendant, as distinguished from the validity of the procedure followed by, or the general scientific propositions stated by, another witness.

(4) When a psychiatrist or other expert who has examined the defendant testifies concerning his mental condition, he shall be permitted to make a statement as to the na-

ture of his examination, his diagnosis of the mental condition of the defendant at the time of the commission of the offense charged and his opinion as to the extent, if any, to which the capacity of the defendant to appreciate the criminality [wrongfulness] of his conduct or to conform his conduct to the requirements of law or to have a particular state of mind which is an element of the offense charged was impaired as a result of mental disease or defect at that time. He shall be permitted to make any explanation reasonably serving to clarify his diagnosis and opinion and may be cross-examined as to any matter bearing on his competency or credibility or the validity of his diagnosis or opinion.

Section 4.08. Legal Effect of Acquittal on the Ground of Mental Disease or Defect Excluding Responsibility; Commitment; Release or Discharge

(1) When a defendant is acquitted on the ground of mental disease or defect excluding responsibility, the Court shall order him to be committed to the custody of the Commissioner of Mental Hygiene [Public Health] to be placed in an appropriate institution for custody, care and treatment.

(2) If the Commissioner of Mental Hygiene [Public Health] is of the view that a person committed to his custody, pursuant to paragraph (1) of this Section, may be discharged or released on condition without danger to himself or to others, he shall make application for the discharge or release of such person in a report to the Court by which such person was committed and shall transmit a copy of such application and report to the prosecuting attorney of the county [parish] from which the defendant was committed. The Court shall thereupon appoint at least two qualified psychiatrists to examine such person and to report within sixty days, or such longer period as the Court determines to be necessary for the purpose, their opinion as to his mental condition. To facilitate such examination and the proceedings thereon, the Court may cause such person to be confined in any institution located near the place where the Court sits, which may hereafter be designated by the Commissioner of Mental Hygiene [Public Health] as suitable for the temporary detention of irresponsible persons.

(3) If the Court is satisfied by the report filed pursuant to paragraph (2) of this Section and such testimony of the reporting psychiatrists as the Court deems necessary that the committed person may be discharged or released on condition without danger to himself or others, the Court shall order his discharge or his release on such conditions as the Court determines to be necessary. If the Court is not so satisfied, it shall promptly order a hearing to determine whether such person may safely be discharged or released. Any such hearing shall be deemed a civil proceeding and the burden shall be upon the committed person to prove that he may safely be discharged or released. According to the determination of the Court upon the hearing, the committed person shall thereupon be discharged or released on such conditions as the Court determines to be necessary, or shall be recommitted to the custody of the Commissioner of Mental Hygiene [Public Health], subject to discharge or release only in accordance with the procedure prescribed above for a first hearing.

(4) If, within [five] years after the conditional release of a committed person, the Court shall determine, after hearing evidence, that the conditions of release have not been fulfilled and that for the safety of such person or for the safety of others his conditional release should be revoked, the Court shall forthwith order him to be recommitted to the Commissioner of Mental Hygiene [Public Health], subject to discharge or release only in accordance with the procedure prescribed above for a first hearing.

(5) A committed person may make application for his discharge or release to the Court by which he was committed, and the procedure to be followed upon such appli-

cation shall be the same as that prescribed above in the case of an application by the Commissioner of Mental Hygiene [Public Health]. However, no such application by a committed person need be considered until he has been confined for a period of not less than [six months] from the date of the order of commitment, and if the determination of the Court be adverse to the application, such person shall not be permitted to file a further application until [one year] has elapsed from the date of any preceding hearing on an application for his release or discharge.

SECTION 4.09. STATEMENTS FOR PURPOSES OF EXAMINATION OR TREATMENT INADMISSIBLE EXCEPT ON ISSUE OF MENTAL CONDITION

A statement made by a person subjected to psychiatric examination or treatment pursuant to Sections 4.05, 4.06 or 4.08 for the purposes of such examination or treatment shall not be admissible in evidence against him in any criminal proceeding on any issue other than that of his mental condition but it shall be admissible upon that issue, whether or not it would otherwise be deemed a privileged communication [, unless such statement constitutes an admission of guilt of the crime charged].

SECTION 4.10. IMMATURITY EXCLUDING CRIMINAL CONVICTION; TRANSFER OF PROCEEDINGS TO JUVENILE COURT

(1) A person shall not be tried for or convicted of an offense if:

(a) at the time of the conduct charged to constitute the offense he was less than sixteen years of age [, in which case the Juvenile Court shall have exclusive jurisdiction]; or

(b) at the time of the conduct charged to constitute the offense he was sixteen or seventeen years of age, unless:

(i) the Juvenile Court has no jurisdiction over him, or,

(ii) the Juvenile Court has entered an order waiving jurisdiction and consenting to the institution of criminal proceedings against him.

(2) No court shall have jurisdiction to try or convict a person of an offense if criminal proceedings against him are barred by Subsection (1) of this Section. When it appears that a person charged with the commission of an offense may be of such an age that criminal proceedings may be barred under Subsection (1) of this Section, the Court shall hold a hearing thereon, and the burden shall be on the prosecution to establish to the satisfaction of the Court that the criminal proceeding is not barred upon such grounds. If the Court determines that the proceeding is barred, custody of the person charged shall be surrendered to the Juvenile Court, and the case, including all papers and processes relating thereto, shall be transferred.

Article 5. Inchoate Crimes

SECTION 5.01. CRIMINAL ATTEMPT

(1) *Definition of Attempt.* A person is guilty of an attempt to commit a crime if, acting with the kind of culpability otherwise required for commission of the crime, he:

(a) purposely engages in conduct which would constitute the crime if the attendant circumstances were as he believes them to be; or

(b) when causing a particular result is an element of the crime, does or omits to do anything with the purpose of causing or with the belief that it will cause such result without further conduct on his part; or

(c) purposely does or omits to do anything which, under the circumstances as he believes them to be, is an act or omission constituting a substantial step in a course of conduct planned to culminate in his commission of the crime.

(2) *Conduct Which May Be Held Substantial Step Under Subsection (1)(c).* Conduct shall not be held to constitute a substantial step under Subsection (1)(c) of this Section unless it is strongly corroborative of the actor's criminal purpose. Without negativing the sufficiency of other conduct, the following, if strongly corroborative of the actor's criminal purpose, shall not be held insufficient as a matter of law:

(a) lying in wait, searching for or following the contemplated victim of the crime;

(b) enticing or seeking to entice the contemplated victim of the crime to go to the place contemplated for its commission;

(c) reconnoitering the place contemplated for the commission of the crime;

(d) unlawful entry of a structure, vehicle or enclosure in which it is contemplated that the crime will be committed;

(e) possession of materials to be employed in the commission of the crime, which are specially designed for such unlawful use or which can serve no lawful purpose of the actor under the circumstances;

(f) possession, collection or fabrication of materials to be employed in the commission of the crime, at or near the place contemplated for its commission, where such possession, collection or fabrication serves no lawful purpose of the actor under the circumstances;

(g) soliciting an innocent agent to engage in conduct constituting an element of the crime.

(3) *Conduct Designed to Aid Another in Commission of a Crime.* A person who engages in conduct designed to aid another to commit a crime which would establish his complicity under Section 2.06 if the crime were committed by such other person, is guilty of an attempt to commit the crime, although the crime is not committed or attempted by such other person.

(4) *Renunciation of Criminal Purpose.* When the actor's conduct would otherwise constitute an attempt under Subsection (1)(b) or (1)(c) of this Section, it is an affirmative defense that he abandoned his effort to commit the crime or otherwise prevented its commission, under circumstances manifesting a complete and voluntary renunciation of his criminal purpose. The establishment of such defense does not, however, affect the liability of an accomplice who did not join in such abandonment or prevention.

Within the meaning of this Article, renunciation of criminal purpose is not voluntary if it is motivated, in whole or in part, by circumstances, not present or apparent at the inception of the actor's course of conduct, which increase the probability of detection or apprehension or which make more difficult the accomplishment of the criminal purpose. Renunciation is not complete if it is motivated by a decision to postpone the criminal conduct until a more advantageous time or to transfer the criminal effort to another but similar objective or victim.

Section 5.02. Criminal Solicitation

(1) *Definition of Solicitation.* A person is guilty of solicitation to commit a crime if with the purpose of promoting or facilitating its commission he commands, encourages or requests another person to engage in specific conduct which would constitute such crime or an attempt to commit such crime or which would establish his complicity in its commission or attempted commission.

(2) *Uncommunicated Solicitation.* It is immaterial under Subsection (1) of this Section that the actor fails to communicate with the person he solicits to commit a crime if his conduct was designed to effect such communication.

(3) *Renunciation of Criminal Purpose.* It is an affirmative defense that the actor, after soliciting another person to commit a crime, persuaded him not to do so or otherwise prevented the commission of the crime, under circumstances manifesting a complete and voluntary renunciation of his criminal purpose.

Section 5.03. Criminal Conspiracy

(1) *Definition of Conspiracy.* A person is guilty of conspiracy with another person or persons to commit a crime if with the purpose of promoting or facilitating its commission he:

(a) agrees with such other person or persons that they or one or more of them will engage in conduct which constitutes such crime or an attempt or solicitation to commit such crime; or

(b) agrees to aid such other person or persons in the planning or commission of such crime or of an attempt or solicitation to commit such crime.

(2) *Scope of Conspiratorial Relationship.* If a person guilty of conspiracy, as defined by Subsection (1) of this Section, knows that a person with whom he conspires to commit a crime has conspired with another person or persons to commit the same crime, he is guilty of conspiring with such other person or persons, whether or not he knows their identity, to commit such crime.

(3) *Conspiracy With Multiple Criminal Objectives.* If a person conspires to commit a number of crimes, he is guilty of only one conspiracy so long as such multiple crimes are the object of the same agreement or continuous conspiratorial relationship.

(4) *Joinder and Venue in Conspiracy Prosecutions.*

(a) Subject to the provisions of paragraph (b) of this Subsection, two or more persons charged with criminal conspiracy may be prosecuted jointly if:

(i) they are charged with conspiring with one another; or

(ii) the conspiracies alleged, whether they have the same or different parties, are so related that they constitute different aspects of a scheme of organized criminal conduct.

(b) In any joint prosecution under paragraph (a) of this Subsection:

(i) no defendant shall be charged with a conspiracy in any county [parish or district] other than one in which he entered into such conspiracy or in which an overt act pursuant to such conspiracy was done by him or by a person with whom he conspired; and

(ii) neither the liability of any defendant nor the admissibility against him of evidence of acts or declarations of another shall be enlarged by such joinder; and

(iii) the Court shall order a severance or take a special verdict as to any defendant who so requests, if it deems it necessary or appropriate to promote the fair determination of his guilt or innocence, and shall take any other proper measures to protect the fairness of the trial.

(5) *Overt Act.* No person may be convicted of conspiracy to commit a crime, other than a felony of the first or second degree, unless an overt act in pursuance of such conspiracy is alleged and proved to have been done by him or by a person with whom he conspired.

(6) *Renunciation of Criminal Purpose.* It is an affirmative defense that the actor, after conspiring to commit a crime, thwarted the success of the conspiracy, under circumstances manifesting a complete and voluntary renunciation of his criminal purpose.

(7) *Duration of Conspiracy.* For purposes of Section 1.06(4):

(a) conspiracy is a continuing course of conduct which terminates when the crime or crimes which are its object are committed or the agreement that they be committed is abandoned by the defendant and by those with whom he conspired; and

(b) such abandonment is presumed if neither the defendant nor anyone with whom he conspired does any overt act in pursuance of the conspiracy during the applicable period of limitation; and

(c) if an individual abandons the agreement, the conspiracy is terminated as to him only if and when he advises those with whom he conspired of his abandonment or he informs the law enforcement authorities of the existence of the conspiracy and of his participation therein.

SECTION 5.04. INCAPACITY, IRRESPONSIBILITY OR IMMUNITY OF PARTY TO SOLICITATION OR CONSPIRACY

(1) Except as provided in Subsection (2) of this Section, it is immaterial to the liability of a person who solicits or conspires with another to commit a crime that:

(a) he or the person whom he solicits or with whom he conspires does not occupy a particular position or have a particular characteristic which is an element of such crime, if he believes that one of them does; or

(b) the person whom he solicits or with whom he conspires is irresponsible or has an immunity to prosecution or conviction for the commission of the crime.

(2) It is a defense to a charge of solicitation or conspiracy to commit a crime that if the criminal object were achieved, the actor would not be guilty of a crime under the law defining the offense or as an accomplice under Section 2.06(5) or 2.06(6)(a) or (b).

SECTION 5.05. GRADING OF CRIMINAL ATTEMPT, SOLICITATION AND CONSPIRACY; MITIGATION IN CASES OF LESSER DANGER; MULTIPLE CONVICTIONS BARRED

(1) *Grading.* Except as otherwise provided in this Section, attempt, solicitation and conspiracy are crimes of the same grade and degree as the most serious offense which is attempted or solicited or is an object of the conspiracy. An attempt, solicitation or conspiracy to commit a [capital crime or a] felony of the first degree is a felony of the second degree.

(2) *Mitigation.* If the particular conduct charged to constitute a criminal attempt, solicitation or conspiracy is so inherently unlikely to result or culminate in the commission of a crime that neither such conduct nor the actor presents a public danger warranting the grading of such offense under this Section, the Court shall exercise its power under Section 6.12 to enter judgment and impose sentence for a crime of lower grade or degree or, in extreme cases, may dismiss the prosecution.

(3) *Multiple Convictions.* A person may not be convicted of more than one offense defined by this Article for conduct designed to commit or to culminate in the commission of the same crime.

SECTION 5.06. POSSESSING INSTRUMENTS OF CRIME; WEAPONS

(1) *Criminal Instruments Generally.* A person commits a misdemeanor if he possesses any instrument of crime with purpose to employ it criminally. "Instrument of crime" means:

(a) anything specially made or specially adapted for criminal use; or

(b) anything commonly used for criminal purposes and possessed by the actor under circumstances which do not negative unlawful purpose.

(2) *Presumption of Criminal Purpose from Possession of Weapon.* If a person possesses a firearm or other weapon on or about his person, in a vehicle occupied by him, or otherwise readily available for use, it shall be presumed that he had the purpose to employ it criminally, unless:

(a) the weapon is possessed in the actor's home or place of business;

(b) the actor is licensed or otherwise authorized by law to possess such weapon; or

(c) the weapon is of a type commonly used in lawful sport.

"Weapon" means anything readily capable of lethal use and possessed under circumstances not manifestly appropriate for lawful uses which it may have; the term includes a firearm which is not loaded or lacks a clip or other component to render it immediately operable, and components which can readily be assembled into a weapon.

(3) *Presumptions as to Possession of Criminal Instruments in Automobiles.* Where a weapon or other instrument of crime is found in an automobile, it is presumed to be in the possession of the occupant if there is but one. If there is more than one occupant, it shall be presumed to be in the possession of all, except under the following circumstances:

(a) where it is found upon the person of one of the occupants;

(b) where the automobile is not a stolen one and the weapon or instrument is found out of view in a glove compartment, car trunk, or other enclosed customary depository, in which case it shall be presumed to be in the possession of the occupant or occupants who own or have authority to operate the automobile;

(c) in the case of a taxicab, a weapon or instrument found in the passengers' portion of the vehicle shall be presumed to be in the possession of all the passengers, if there are any, and, if not, in the possession of the driver.

Section 5.07. Prohibited Offensive Weapons

A person commits a misdemeanor if, except as authorized by law, he makes, repairs, sells, or otherwise deals in, uses or possesses any offensive weapon. "Offensive weapon" means any bomb, machine gun, sawed-off shotgun, firearm specially made or specially adapted for concealment or silent discharge, any blackjack, sandbag, metal knuckles, dagger, or other implement for the infliction of serious bodily injury which serves no common lawful purpose. It is a defense under this Section for the defendant to prove by a preponderance of evidence that he possessed or dealt with the weapon solely as a curio or in a dramatic performance, or that he possessed it briefly in consequence of having found it or taken it from an aggressor, or under circumstances similarly negativing any purpose or likelihood that the weapon would be used unlawfully. The presumptions provided in Section 5.06(3) are applicable to prosecutions under this Section.

Article 6. Authorized Disposition of Offenders

Section 6.01. Degrees of Felonies

(1) Felonies defined by this Code are classified, for the purpose of sentence, into three degrees, as follows:

(a) felonies of the first degree;

(b) felonies of the second degree;

(c) felonies of the third degree.

A felony is of the first or second degree when it is so designated by the Code. A crime declared to be a felony, without specification of degree, is of the third degree.

(2) Notwithstanding any other provision of law, a felony defined by any statute of this State other than this Code shall constitute for the purpose of sentence a felony of the third degree.

Section 6.02. Sentence in Accordance with Code; Authorized Dispositions

(1) No person convicted of an offense shall be sentenced otherwise than in accordance with this Article.

[(2) The Court shall sentence a person who has been convicted of murder to death or imprisonment, in accordance with Section 210.6.]

(3) Except as provided in Subsection (2) of this Section and subject to the applicable provisions of the Code, the Court may suspend the imposition of sentence on a person who has been convicted of a crime, may order him to be committed in lieu of sentence, in accordance with Section 6.13, or may sentence him as follows:

(a) to pay a fine authorized by Section 6.03; or

(b) to be placed on probation [, and, in the case of a person convicted of a felony or misdemeanor to imprisonment for a term fixed by the Court not exceeding thirty days to be served as a condition of probation]; or

(c) to imprisonment for a term authorized by Sections 6.05, 6.06, 6.07, 6.08, 6.09, or 7.06; or

(d) to fine and probation or fine and imprisonment, but not to probation and imprisonment [, except as authorized in paragraph (b) of this Subsection].

(4) The Court may suspend the imposition of sentence on a person who has been convicted of a violation or may sentence him to pay a fine authorized by Section 6.03.

(5) This Article does not deprive the Court of any authority conferred by law to decree a forfeiture of property, suspend or cancel a license, remove a person from office, or impose any other civil penalty. Such a judgment or order may be included in the sentence.

Section 6.03. Fines

A person who has been convicted of an offense may be sentenced to pay a fine not exceeding:

(1) $10,000, when the conviction is of a felony of the first or second degree;

(2) $5,000, when the conviction is of a felony of the third degree;

(3) $1,000, when the conviction is of a misdemeanor;

(4) $500, when the conviction is of a petty misdemeanor or a violation;

(5) any higher amount equal to double the pecuniary gain derived from the offense by the offender;

(6) any higher amount specifically authorized by statute.

Section 6.04. Penalties Against Corporations and Unincorporated Associations; Forfeiture of Corporate Charter or Revocation of Certificate Authorizing Foreign Corporation to Do Business in the State

(1) The Court may suspend the sentence of a corporation or an unincorporated association which has been convicted of an offense or may sentence it to pay a fine authorized by Section 6.03.

(2) (a) The [prosecuting attorney] is authorized to institute civil proceedings in the appropriate court of general jurisdiction to forfeit the charter of a corporation organized under the laws of this State or to revoke the certificate authorizing a foreign corporation to conduct business in this State. The Court may order the charter forfeited or the certificate revoked upon finding (i) that the board of directors or a high managerial agent acting in behalf of the corporation has, in conducting the corporation's affairs, purposely engaged in a persistent course of criminal conduct and (ii) that for the prevention of future criminal conduct of the same character, the public interest requires the charter of the corporation to be forfeited and the corporation to be dissolved or the certificate to be revoked.

(b) When a corporation is convicted of a crime or a high managerial agent of a corporation, as defined in Section 2.07, is convicted of a crime committed in the conduct of the affairs of the corporation, the Court, in sentencing the corporation or the agent, may direct the [prosecuting attorney] to institute proceedings authorized by paragraph (a) of this Subsection.

(c) The proceedings authorized by paragraph (a) of this Subsection shall be conducted in accordance with the procedures authorized by law for the involuntary dissolution of a corporation or the revocation of the certificate authorizing a foreign corporation to conduct business in this State. Such proceedings shall be deemed additional to any other proceedings authorized by law for the purpose of forfeiting the charter of a corporation or revoking the certificate of a foreign corporation.

Section 6.05. Young Adult Offenders

(1) *Specialized Correctional Treatment.* A young adult offender is a person convicted of a crime who, at the time of sentencing, is sixteen but less than twenty-two years of age. A young adult offender who is sentenced to a term of imprisonment which may exceed thirty days [alternatives: (1) ninety days; (2) one year] shall be committed to the custody of the Division of Young Adult Correction of the Department of Correction, and shall receive, as far as practicable, such special and individualized correctional and rehabilitative treatment as may be appropriate to his needs.

(2) *Special Term.* A young adult offender convicted of a felony may, in lieu of any other sentence of imprisonment authorized by this Article, be sentenced to a special term of imprisonment without a minimum and with a maximum of four years, regardless of the degree of the felony involved, if the Court is of the opinion that such special term is adequate for his correction and rehabilitation and will not jeopardize the protection of the public.

[(3) *Removal of Disabilities; Vacation of Conviction.*

(a) In sentencing a young adult offender to the special term provided by this Section or to any sentence other than one of imprisonment, the Court may order that so long as he is not convicted of another felony, the judgment shall not constitute a conviction for the purposes of any disqualification or disability imposed by law upon conviction of a crime.

(b) When any young adult offender is unconditionally discharged from probation or parole before the expiration of the maximum term thereof, the Court may enter an order vacating the judgment of conviction.]

[(4) *Commitment for Observation.* If, after pre-sentence investigation, the Court desires additional information concerning a young adult offender before imposing sentence, it may order that he be committed, for a period not exceeding ninety days, to the custody of the Division of Young Adult Correction of the Department of Correction for observation and study at an appropriate reception or classification center. Such Division of the

Department of Correction and the [Young Adult Division of the] Board of Parole shall advise the Court of their findings and recommendations on or before the expiration of such ninety-day period.]

Section 6.06. Sentence of Imprisonment for Felony; Ordinary Terms

A person who has been convicted of a felony may be sentenced to imprisonment, as follows:

(1) in the case of a felony of the first degree, for a term the minimum of which shall be fixed by the Court at not less than one year nor more than ten years, and the maximum of which shall be life imprisonment;

(2) in the case of a felony of the second degree, for a term the minimum of which shall be fixed by the Court at not less than one year nor more than three years, and the maximum of which shall be ten years;

(3) in the case of a felony of the third degree, for a term the minimum of which shall be fixed by the Court at not less than one year nor more than two years, and the maximum of which shall be five years.

Alternate Section 6.06. Sentence of Imprisonment for Felony; Ordinary Terms

A person who has been convicted of a felony may be sentenced to imprisonment, as follows:

(1) in the case of a felony of the first degree, for a term the minimum of which shall be fixed by the Court at not less than one year nor more than ten years, and the maximum at not more than twenty years or at life imprisonment;

(2) in the case of a felony of the second degree, for a term the minimum of which shall be fixed by the Court at not less than one year nor more than three years, and the maximum at not more than ten years;

(3) in the case of a felony of the third degree, for a term the minimum of which shall be fixed by the Court at not less than one year nor more than two years, and the maximum at not more than five years.

No sentence shall be imposed under this Section of which the minimum is longer than one-half the maximum, or, when the maximum is life imprisonment, longer than ten years.

Section 6.07. Sentence of Imprisonment for Felony; Extended Terms

In the cases designated in Section 7.03, a person who has been convicted of a felony may be sentenced to an extended term of imprisonment, as follows:

(1) in the case of a felony of the first degree, for a term the minimum of which shall be fixed by the Court at not less than five years nor more than ten years, and the maximum of which shall be life imprisonment;

(2) in the case of a felony of the second degree, for a term the minimum of which shall be fixed by the Court at not less than one year nor more than five years, and the maximum of which shall be fixed by the Court at not less than ten nor more than twenty years;

(3) in the case of a felony of the third degree, for a term the minimum of which shall be fixed by the Court at not less than one year nor more than three years, and the maximum of which shall be fixed by the Court at not less than five nor more than ten years.

Section 6.08. Sentence of Imprisonment for Misdemeanors and Petty Misdemeanors; Ordinary Terms

A person who has been convicted of a misdemeanor or a petty misdemeanor may be sentenced to imprisonment for a definite term which shall be fixed by the Court and shall not exceed one year in the case of a misdemeanor or thirty days in the case of a petty misdemeanor.

Section 6.09. Sentence of Imprisonment for Misdemeanors and Petty Misdemeanors; Extended Terms

(1) In the cases designated in Section 7.04, a person who has been convicted of a misdemeanor or a petty misdemeanor may be sentenced to an extended term of imprisonment, as follows:

(a) in the case of a misdemeanor, for a term the minimum of which shall be fixed by the Court at not more than one year and the maximum of which shall be three years;

(b) in the case of a petty misdemeanor, for a term the minimum of which shall be fixed by the Court at not more than six months and the maximum of which shall be two years.

(2) No such sentence for an extended term shall be imposed unless:

(a) the Director of Correction has certified that there is an institution in the Department of Correction, or in a county, city [or other appropriate political subdivision of the State] which is appropriate for the detention and correctional treatment of such misdemeanants or petty misdemeanants, and that such institution is available to receive such commitments; and

(b) the [Board of Parole] [Parole Administrator] has certified that the Board of Parole is able to visit such institution and to assume responsibility for the release of such prisoners on parole and for their parole supervision.

Section 6.10. First Release of All Offenders on Parole; Sentence of Imprisonment Includes Separate Parole Term; Length of Parole Term; Length of Recommitment and Reparole After Revocation of Parole; Final Unconditional Release

(1) *First Release of All Offenders on Parole.* An offender sentenced to an indefinite term of imprisonment in excess of one year under Section 6.05, 6.06, 6.07, 6.09 or 7.06 shall be released conditionally on parole at or before the expiration of the maximum of such term, in accordance with Article 305.

(2) *Sentence of Imprisonment Includes Separate Parole Term; Length of Parole Term.* A sentence to an indefinite term of imprisonment in excess of one year under Section 6.05, 6.06, 6.07, 6.09 or 7.06 includes as a separate portion of the sentence a term of parole or of recommitment for violation of the conditions of parole which governs the duration of parole or recommitment after the offender's first conditional release on parole. The minimum of such term is one year and the maximum is five years, unless the sentence was imposed under Section 6.05(2) or Section 6.09, in which case the maximum is two years.

(3) *Length of Recommitment and Reparole After Revocation of Parole.* If an offender is recommitted upon revocation of his parole, the term of further imprisonment upon such recommitment and of any subsequent reparole or recommitment under the same sentence shall be fixed by the Board of Parole but shall not exceed in aggregate length the unserved balance of the maximum parole term provided by Subsection (2) of this Section.

(4) *Final Unconditional Release.* When the maximum of his parole term has expired or he has been sooner discharged from parole under Section 305.12, an offender shall be deemed to have served his sentence and shall be released unconditionally.

Section 6.11. Place of Imprisonment

(1) When a person is sentenced to imprisonment for an indefinite term with a maximum in excess of one year, the Court shall commit him to the custody of the Department of Correction [or other single department or agency] for the term of his sentence and until release in accordance with law.

(2) When a person is sentenced to imprisonment for a definite term, the Court shall designate the institution or agency to which he is committed for the term of his sentence and until released in accordance with law.

Section 6.12. Reduction of Conviction by Court to Lesser Degree of Felony or to Misdemeanor

If, when a person has been convicted of a felony, the Court, having regard to the nature and circumstances of the crime and to the history and character of the defendant, is of the view that it would be unduly harsh to sentence the offender in accordance with the Code, the Court may enter judgment of conviction for a lesser degree of felony or for a misdemeanor and impose sentence accordingly.

Section 6.13. Civil Commitment in Lieu of Prosecution or of Sentence

(1) When a person prosecuted for a [felony of the third degree,] misdemeanor or petty misdemeanor is a chronic alcoholic, narcotic addict [or prostitute] or person suffering from mental abnormality and the Court is authorized by law to order the civil commitment of such person to a hospital or other institution for medical, psychiatric or other rehabilitative treatment, the Court may order such commitment and dismiss the prosecution. The order of commitment may be made after conviction, in which event the Court may set aside the verdict or judgment of conviction and dismiss the prosecution.

(2) The Court shall not make an order under Subsection (1) of this Section unless it is of the view that it will substantially further the rehabilitation of the defendant and will not jeopardize the protection of the public.

Article 7. Authority of Court in Sentencing

Section 7.01. Criteria for Withholding Sentence of Imprisonment and for Placing Defendant on Probation

(1) The Court shall deal with a person who has been convicted of a crime without imposing sentence of imprisonment unless, having regard to the nature and circumstances of the crime and the history, character and condition of the defendant, it is of the opinion that his imprisonment is necessary for protection of the public because:

(a) there is undue risk that during the period of a suspended sentence or probation the defendant will commit another crime; or

(b) the defendant is in need of correctional treatment that can be provided most effectively by his commitment to an institution; or

(c) a lesser sentence will depreciate the seriousness of the defendant's crime.

(2) The following grounds, while not controlling the discretion of the Court, shall be accorded weight in favor of withholding sentence of imprisonment:

(a) the defendant's criminal conduct neither caused nor threatened serious harm;

(b) the defendant did not contemplate that his criminal conduct would cause or threaten serious harm;

(c) the defendant acted under a strong provocation;

(d) there were substantial grounds tending to excuse or justify the defendant's criminal conduct, though failing to establish a defense;

(e) the victim of the defendant's criminal conduct induced or facilitated its commission;

(f) the defendant has compensated or will compensate the victim of his criminal conduct for the damage or injury that he sustained;

(g) the defendant has no history of prior delinquency or criminal activity or has led a law-abiding life for a substantial period of time before the commission of the present crime;

(h) the defendant's criminal conduct was the result of circumstances unlikely to recur;

(i) the character and attitudes of the defendant indicate that he is unlikely to commit another crime;

(j) the defendant is particularly likely to respond affirmatively to probationary treatment;

(k) the imprisonment of the defendant would entail excessive hardship to himself or his dependents.

(3) When a person who has been convicted of a crime is not sentenced to imprisonment, the Court shall place him on probation if he is in need of the supervision, guidance, assistance or direction that the probation service can provide.

Section 7.02. Criteria for Imposing Fines

(1) The Court shall not sentence a defendant only to pay a fine, when any other disposition is authorized by law, unless having regard to the nature and circumstances of the crime and to the history and character of the defendant, it is of the opinion that the fine alone suffices for protection of the public.

(2) The Court shall not sentence a defendant to pay a fine in addition to a sentence of imprisonment or probation unless:

(a) the defendant has derived a pecuniary gain from the crime; or

(b) the Court is of opinion that a fine is specially adapted to deterrence of the crime involved or to the correction of the offender.

(3) The Court shall not sentence a defendant to pay a fine unless:

(a) the defendant is or will be able to pay the fine; and

(b) the fine will not prevent the defendant from making restitution or reparation to the victim of the crime.

(4) In determining the amount and method of payment of a fine, the Court shall take into account the financial resources of the defendant and the nature of the burden that its payment will impose.

Section 7.03. Criteria for Sentence of Extended Term of Imprisonment; Felonies

The Court may sentence a person who has been convicted of a felony to an extended term of imprisonment if it finds one or more of the grounds specified in this Section. The finding of the Court shall be incorporated in the record.

(1) The defendant is a persistent offender whose commitment for an extended term is necessary for protection of the public.

The Court shall not make such a finding unless the defendant is over twenty-one years of age and has previously been convicted of two felonies or of one felony and two misdemeanors, committed at different times when he was over [insert Juvenile Court age] years of age.

(2) The defendant is a professional criminal whose commitment for an extended term is necessary for protection of the public.

The Court shall not make such a finding unless the defendant is over twenty-one years of age and:

(a) the circumstances of the crime show that the defendant has knowingly devoted himself to criminal activity as a major source of livelihood; or

(b) the defendant has substantial income or resources not explained to be derived from a source other than criminal activity.

(3) The defendant is a dangerous, mentally abnormal person whose commitment for an extended term is necessary for protection of the public.

The Court shall not make such a finding unless the defendant has been subjected to a psychiatric examination resulting in the conclusions that his mental condition is gravely abnormal; that his criminal conduct has been characterized by a pattern of repetitive or compulsive behavior or by persistent aggressive behavior with heedless indifference to consequences; and that such condition makes him a serious danger to others.

(4) The defendant is a multiple offender whose criminality was so extensive that a sentence of imprisonment for an extended term is warranted.

The court shall not make such a finding unless:

(a) the defendant is being sentenced for two or more felonies, or is already under sentence of imprisonment for felony, and the sentences of imprisonment involved will run concurrently under Section 7.06; or

(b) the defendant admits in open court the commission of one or more other felonies and asks that they be taken into account when he is sentenced; and

(c) the longest sentences of imprisonment authorized for each of the defendant's crimes, including admitted crimes taken into account, if made to run consecutively would exceed in length the minimum and maximum of the extended term imposed.

Section 7.04. Criteria for Sentence of Extended Term of Imprisonment; Misdemeanors and Petty Misdemeanors

The Court may sentence a person who has been convicted of a misdemeanor or petty misdemeanor to an extended term of imprisonment if it finds one or more of the grounds specified in this Section. The finding of the Court shall be incorporated in the record.

(1) The defendant is a persistent offender whose commitment for an extended term is necessary for protection of the public.

The Court shall not make such a finding unless the defendant has previously been convicted of two crimes, committed at different times when he was over [insert Juvenile Court age] years of age.

(2) The defendant is a professional criminal whose commitment for an extended term is necessary for protection of the public.

The Court shall not make such a finding unless:

(a) the circumstances of the crime show that the defendant has knowingly devoted himself to criminal activity as a major source of livelihood; or

(b) the defendant has substantial income or resources not explained to be derived from a source other than criminal activity.

(3) The defendant is a chronic alcoholic, narcotic addict, prostitute or person of abnormal mental condition who requires rehabilitative treatment for a substantial period of time.

The Court shall not make such a finding unless, with respect to the particular category to which the defendant belongs, the Director of Correction has certified that there is a specialized institution or facility which is satisfactory for the rehabilitative treatment of such persons and which otherwise meets the requirements of Section 6.09, Subsection (2).

(4) The defendant is a multiple offender whose criminality was so extensive that a sentence of imprisonment for an extended term is warranted.

The Court shall not make such a finding unless:

(a) the defendant is being sentenced for a number of misdemeanors or petty misdemeanors or is already under sentence of imprisonment for crimes of such grades, or admits in open court the commission of one or more such crimes and asks that they be taken into account when he is sentenced; and

(b) maximum fixed sentences of imprisonment for each of the defendant's crimes, including admitted crimes taken into account, if made to run consecutively, would exceed in length the maximum period of the extended term imposed.

Section 7.05. Former Conviction in Another Jurisdiction; Definition and Proof of Conviction; Sentence Taking into Account Admitted Crimes Bars Subsequent Conviction for Such Crimes

(1) For purposes of paragraph (1) of Section 7.03 or 7.04, a conviction of the commission of a crime in another jurisdiction shall constitute a previous conviction. Such conviction shall be deemed to have been of a felony if sentence of death or of imprisonment in excess of one year was authorized under the law of such other jurisdiction, of a misdemeanor if sentence of imprisonment in excess of thirty days but not in excess of a year was authorized and of a petty misdemeanor if sentence of imprisonment for not more than thirty days was authorized.

(2) An adjudication by a court of competent jurisdiction that the defendant committed a crime constitutes a conviction for purposes of Sections 7.03 to 7.05 inclusive, although sentence or the execution thereof was suspended, provided that the time to appeal has expired and that the defendant was not pardoned on the ground of innocence.

(3) Prior conviction may be proved by any evidence, including fingerprint records made in connection with arrest, conviction or imprisonment, that reasonably satisfies the Court that the defendant was convicted.

(4) When the defendant has asked that other crimes admitted in open court be taken into account when he is sentenced and the Court has not rejected such request, the sentence shall bar the prosecution or conviction of the defendant in this State for any such admitted crime.

Section 7.06. Multiple Sentences; Concurrent and Consecutive Terms

(1) *Sentences of Imprisonment for More Than One Crime.* When multiple sentences of imprisonment are imposed on a defendant for more than one crime, including a crime for which a previous suspended sentence or sentence of probation has been revoked, such multiple sentences shall run concurrently or consecutively as the Court determines at the time of sentence, except that:

(a) a definite and an indefinite term shall run concurrently and both sentences shall be satisfied by service of the indefinite term; and

(b) the aggregate of consecutive definite terms shall not exceed one year; and

(c) the aggregate of consecutive indefinite terms shall not exceed in minimum or maximum length the longest extended term authorized for the highest grade and degree of crime for which any of the sentences was imposed; and

(d) not more than one sentence for an extended term shall be imposed.

(2) *Sentences of Imprisonment Imposed at Different Times.* When a defendant who has previously been sentenced to imprisonment is subsequently sentenced to another term for a crime committed prior to the former sentence, other than a crime committed while in custody:

(a) the multiple sentences imposed shall so far as possible conform to Subsection (1) of this Section; and

(b) whether the Court determines that the terms shall run concurrently or consecutively, the defendant shall be credited with time served in imprisonment on the prior sentence in determining the permissible aggregate length of the term or terms remaining to be served; and

(c) when a new sentence is imposed on a prisoner who is on parole, the balance of the parole term on the former sentence shall be deemed to run during the period of the new imprisonment.

(3) *Sentence of Imprisonment for Crime Committed While on Parole.* When a defendant is sentenced to imprisonment for a crime committed while on parole in this State, such term of imprisonment and any period of reimprisonment that the Board of Parole may require the defendant to serve upon the revocation of his parole shall run concurrently, unless the Court orders them to run consecutively.

(4) *Multiple Sentences of Imprisonment in Other Cases.* Except as otherwise provided in this Section, multiple terms of imprisonment shall run concurrently or consecutively as the Court determines when the second or subsequent sentence is imposed.

(5) *Calculation of Concurrent and Consecutive Terms of Imprisonment.*

(a) When indefinite terms run concurrently, the shorter minimum terms merge in and are satisfied by serving the longest minimum term and the shorter maximum terms merge in and are satisfied by discharge of the longest maximum term.

(b) When indefinite terms run consecutively, the minimum terms are added to arrive at an aggregate minimum to be served equal to the sum of all minimum terms and the maximum terms are added to arrive at an aggregate maximum equal to the sum of all maximum terms.

(c) When a definite and an indefinite term run consecutively, the period of the definite term is added to both the minimum and maximum of the indefinite term and both sentences are satisfied by serving the indefinite term.

(6) *Suspension of Sentence or Probation and Imprisonment; Multiple Terms of Suspension and Probation.* When a defendant is sentenced for more than one offense or a defendant already under sentence is sentenced for another offense committed prior to the former sentence:

(a) the Court shall not sentence to probation a defendant who is under sentence of imprisonment [with more than thirty days to run] or impose a sentence of probation and a sentence of imprisonment [, except as authorized by Section 6.02(3)(b)]; and

(b) multiple periods of suspension or probation shall run concurrently from the date of the first such disposition; and

(c) when a sentence of imprisonment is imposed for an indefinite term, the service of such sentence shall satisfy a suspended sentence on another count or a prior suspended sentence or sentence to probation; and

(d) when a sentence of imprisonment is imposed for a definite term, the period of a suspended sentence on another count or a prior suspended sentence or sentence to probation shall run during the period of such imprisonment.

(7) *Offense Committed While Under Suspension of Sentence or Probation.* When a defendant is convicted of an offense committed while under suspension of sentence or on probation and such suspension or probation is not revoked:

(a) if the defendant is sentenced to imprisonment for an indefinite term, the service of such sentence shall satisfy the prior suspended sentence or sentence to probation; and

(b) if the defendant is sentenced to imprisonment for a definite term, the period of the suspension or probation shall not run during the period of such imprisonment; and

(c) if sentence is suspended or the defendant is sentenced to probation, the period of such suspension or probation shall run concurrently with or consecutively to the remainder of the prior periods, as the Court determines at the time of sentence.

Section 7.07. Procedure on Sentence; Pre-sentence Investigation and Report; Remand for Psychiatric Examination; Transmission of Records to Department of Correction

(1) The Court shall not impose sentence without first ordering a pre-sentence investigation of the defendant and according due consideration to a written report of such investigation where:

(a) the defendant has been convicted of a felony; or

(b) the defendant is less than twenty-two years of age and has been convicted of a crime; or

(c) the defendant will be [placed on probation or] sentenced to imprisonment for an extended term.

(2) The Court may order a pre-sentence investigation in any other case.

(3) The pre-sentence investigation shall include an analysis of the circumstances attending the commission of the crime, the defendant's history of delinquency or criminality, physical and mental condition, family situation and background, economic status, education, occupation and personal habits and any other matters that the probation officer deems relevant or the Court directs to be included.

(4) Before imposing sentence, the Court may order the defendant to submit to psychiatric observation and examination for a period of not exceeding sixty days or such longer period as the Court determines to be necessary for the purpose. The defendant may be remanded for this purpose to any available clinic or mental hospital or the Court may appoint a qualified psychiatrist to make the examination. The report of the examination shall be submitted to the Court.

(5) Before imposing sentence, the Court shall advise the defendant or his counsel of the factual contents and the conclusions of any pre-sentence investigation or psychiatric examination and afford fair opportunity, if the defendant so requests, to controvert them. The sources of confidential information need not, however, be disclosed.

(6) The Court shall not impose a sentence of imprisonment for an extended term unless the ground therefor has been established at a hearing after the conviction of the defendant and on written notice to him of the ground proposed. Subject to the limitation of Subsection (5) of this Section, the defendant shall have the right to hear and controvert the evidence against him and to offer evidence upon the issue.

(7) If the defendant is sentenced to imprisonment, a copy of the report of any pre-sentence investigation or psychiatric examination shall be transmitted forthwith to the Department of Correction [or other state department or agency] or, when the defendant is committed to the custody of a specific institution, to such institution.

Section 7.08. Commitment for Observation; Sentence of Imprisonment for Felony Deemed Tentative for Period of One Year; Re-sentence on Petition of Commissioner of Correction

(1) If, after pre-sentence investigation, the Court desires additional information concerning an offender convicted of a felony or misdemeanor before imposing sentence, it may order that he be committed, for a period not exceeding ninety days, to the custody of the Department of Correction, or, in the case of a young adult offender, to the custody of the Division of Young Adult Correction, for observation and study at an appropriate reception or classification center. The Department and the Board of Parole, or the Young Adult Divisions thereof, shall advise the Court of their findings and recommendations on or before the expiration of such ninety-day period. If the offender is thereafter sentenced to imprisonment, the period of such commitment for observation shall be deducted from the maximum term and from the minimum, if any, of such sentence.

(2) When a person has been sentenced to imprisonment upon conviction of a felony, whether for an ordinary or extended term, the sentence shall be deemed tentative, to the extent provided in this Section, for the period of one year following the date when the offender is received in custody by the Department of Correction [or other state department or agency].

(3) If, as a result of the examination and classification by the Department of Correction [or other state department or agency] of a person under sentence of imprisonment upon conviction of a felony, the Commissioner of Correction [or other department head] is satisfied that the sentence of the Court may have been based upon a misapprehension as to the history, character or physical or mental condition of the offender, the Commissioner, during the period when the offender's sentence is deemed tentative under Subsection (2) of this Section shall file in the sentencing Court a petition to re-sentence the offender. The petition shall set forth the information as to the offender that is deemed to warrant his re-sentence and may include a recommendation as to the sentence to be imposed.

(4) The Court may dismiss a petition filed under Subsection (3) of this Section without a hearing if it deems the information set forth insufficient to warrant reconsideration of the sentence. If the Court is of the view that the petition warrants such reconsideration, a copy of the petition shall be served on the offender, who shall have the right to be heard on the issue and to be represented by counsel.

(5) When the Court grants a petition filed under Subsection (3) of this Section, it shall re-sentence the offender and may impose any sentence that might have been imposed originally for the felony of which the defendant was convicted. The period of his imprisonment prior to re-sentence and any reduction for good behavior to which he is entitled shall be applied in satisfaction of the final sentence.

(6) For all purposes other than this Section, a sentence of imprisonment has the same finality when it is imposed that it would have if this Section were not in force.

(7) Nothing in this Section shall alter the remedies provided by law for vacating or correcting an illegal sentence.

Section 7.09. Credit for Time of Detention Prior to Sentence; Credit for Imprisonment Under Earlier Sentence for the Same Crime

(1) When a defendant who is sentenced to imprisonment has previously been detained in any state or local correctional or other institution following his [conviction of] [arrest for] the crime for which such sentence is imposed, such period of detention fol-

lowing his [conviction] [arrest] shall be deducted from the maximum term, and from the minimum, if any, of such sentence. The officer having custody of the defendant shall furnish a certificate to the Court at the time of sentence, showing the length of such detention of the defendant prior to sentence in any state or local correctional or other institution, and the certificate shall be annexed to the official records of the defendant's commitment.

(2) When a judgment of conviction is vacated and a new sentence is thereafter imposed upon the defendant for the same crime, the period of detention and imprisonment theretofore served shall be deducted from the maximum term, and from the minimum, if any, of the new sentence. The officer having custody of the defendant shall furnish a certificate to the Court at the time of sentence, showing the period of imprisonment served under the original sentence, and the certificate shall be annexed to the official records of the defendant's new commitment.

PART II. DEFINITION OF SPECIFIC CRIMES

Offenses Involving Danger to the Person

Article 210. Criminal Homicide

SECTION 210.0. DEFINITIONS

In Articles 210-213, unless a different meaning plainly is required:

(1) "human being" means a person who has been born and is alive;

(2) "bodily injury" means physical pain, illness or any impairment of physical condition;

(3) "serious bodily injury" means bodily injury which creates a substantial risk of death or which causes serious, permanent disfigurement, or protracted loss or impairment of the function of any bodily member or organ;

(4) "deadly weapon" means any firearm, or other weapon, device, instrument, material or substance, whether animate or inanimate, which in the manner it is used or is intended to be used is known to be capable of producing death or serious bodily injury.

SECTION 210.1. CRIMINAL HOMICIDE

(1) A person is guilty of criminal homicide if he purposely, knowingly, recklessly or negligently causes the death of another human being.

(2) Criminal homicide is murder, manslaughter or negligent homicide.

SECTION 210.2. MURDER

(1) Except as provided in Section 210.3(1)(b), criminal homicide constitutes murder when:

(a) it is committed purposely or knowingly; or

(b) it is committed recklessly under circumstances manifesting extreme indifference to the value of human life. Such recklessness and indifference are presumed if the actor is engaged or is an accomplice in the commission of, or an attempt to commit, or flight after committing or attempting to commit robbery, rape or deviate sexual intercourse by force or threat of force, arson, burglary, kidnapping or felonious escape.

(2) Murder is a felony of the first degree [but a person convicted of murder may be sentenced to death, as provided in Section 210.6.].

SECTION 210.3. MANSLAUGHTER

(1) Criminal homicide constitutes manslaughter when:

(a) it is committed recklessly; or

(b) a homicide which would otherwise be murder is committed under the influence of extreme mental or emotional disturbance for which there is reasonable explanation or excuse. The reasonableness of such explanation or excuse shall be determined from the viewpoint of a person in the actor's situation under the circumstances as he believes them to be.

(2) Manslaughter is a felony of the second degree.

SECTION 210.4. NEGLIGENT HOMICIDE

(1) Criminal homicide constitutes negligent homicide when it is committed negligently.

(2) Negligent homicide is a felony of the third degree.

SECTION 210.5. CAUSING OR AIDING SUICIDE

(1) *Causing Suicide as Criminal Homicide.* A person may be convicted of criminal homicide for causing another to commit suicide only if he purposely causes such suicide by force, duress or deception.

(2) *Aiding or Soliciting Suicide as an Independent Offense.* A person who purposely aids or solicits another to commit suicide is guilty of a felony of the second degree if his conduct causes such suicide or an attempted suicide, and otherwise of a misdemeanor.

[SECTION 210.6. SENTENCE OF DEATH FOR MURDER; FURTHER PROCEEDINGS TO DETERMINE SENTENCE*

(1) *Death Sentence Excluded.* When a defendant is found guilty of murder, the Court shall impose sentence for a felony of the first degree if it is satisfied that:

(a) none of the aggravating circumstances enumerated in Subsection (3) of this Section was established by the evidence at the trial or will be established if further proceedings are initiated under Subsection (2) of this Section; or

(b) substantial mitigating circumstances, established by the evidence at the trial, call for leniency; or

(c) the defendant, with the consent of the prosecuting attorney and the approval of the Court, pleaded guilty to murder as a felony of the first degree; or

(d) the defendant was under 18 years of age at the time of the commission of the crime; or

(e) the defendant's physical or mental condition calls for leniency; or

(f) although the evidence suffices to sustain the verdict, it does not foreclose all doubt respecting the defendant's guilt.

*. . . The brackets are meant to reflect the fact that the Institute took no position on the desirability of the death penalty. . . .

(2) *Determination by Court or by Court and Jury.* Unless the Court imposes sentence under Subsection (1) of this Section, it shall conduct a separate proceeding to determine whether the defendant should be sentenced for a felony of the first degree or sentenced to death. The proceeding shall be conducted before the Court alone if the defendant was convicted by a Court sitting without a jury or upon his plea of guilty or if the prosecuting attorney and the defendant waive a jury with respect to sentence. In other cases it shall be conducted before the Court sitting with the jury which determined the defendant's guilt or, if the Court for good cause shown discharges that jury, with a new jury empanelled for the purpose.

In the proceeding, evidence may be presented as to any matter that the Court deems relevant to sentence, including but not limited to the nature and circumstances of the crime, the defendant's character, background, history, mental and physical condition and any of the aggravating or mitigating circumstances enumerated in Subsections (3) and (4) of this Section. Any such evidence not legally privileged, which the Court deems to have probative force, may be received, regardless of its admissibility under the exclusionary rules of evidence, provided that the defendant's counsel is accorded a fair opportunity to rebut any hearsay statements. The prosecuting attorney and the defendant or his counsel shall be permitted to present argument for or against sentence of death.

The determination whether sentence of death shall be imposed shall be in the discretion of the Court, except that when the proceeding is conducted before the Court sitting with a jury, the Court shall not impose sentence of death unless it submits to the jury the issue whether the defendant should be sentenced to death or to imprisonment and the jury returns a verdict that the sentence should be death. If the jury is unable to reach a unanimous verdict, the Court shall dismiss the jury and impose sentence for a felony of the first degree.

The Court, in exercising its discretion as to sentence, and the jury, in determining upon its verdict, shall take into account the aggravating and mitigating circumstances enumerated in Subsections (3) and (4) and any other facts that it deems relevant, but it shall not impose or recommend sentence of death unless it finds one of the aggravating circumstances enumerated in Subsection (3) and further finds that there are no mitigating circumstances sufficiently substantial to call for leniency. When the issue is submitted to the jury, the Court shall so instruct and also shall inform the jury of the nature of the sentence of imprisonment that may be imposed, including its implication with respect to possible release upon parole, if the jury verdict is against sentence of death.

Alternative formulation of Subsection (2):

(2) *Determination by Court.* Unless the Court imposes sentence under Subsection (1) of this Section, it shall conduct a separate proceeding to determine whether the defendant should be sentenced for a felony of the first degree or sentenced to death. In the proceeding, the Court, in accordance with Section 7.07, shall consider the report of the pre-sentence investigation and, if a psychiatric examination has been ordered, the report of such examination. In addition, evidence may be presented as to any matter that the Court deems relevant to sentence, including but not limited to the nature and circumstances of the crime, the defendant's character, background, history, mental and physical condition and any of the aggravating or mitigating circumstances enumerated in Subsections (3) and (4) of this Section. Any such evidence not legally privileged, which the Court deems to have probative force, may be received, regardless of its admissibility under the exclusionary rules of evidence, provided that the defendant's counsel is accorded a fair opportunity to rebut any hearsay statements. The prosecuting attorney and the defendant or his counsel shall be permitted to present argument for or against sentence of death.

The determination whether sentence of death shall be imposed shall be in the discretion of the Court. In exercising such discretion, the Court shall take into account the aggravating and mitigating circumstances enumerated in Subsections (3) and (4) and any other facts that it deems relevant but shall not impose sentence of death unless it finds one of the aggravating circumstances enumerated in Subsection (3) and further finds that there are no mitigating circumstances sufficiently substantial to call for leniency.

(3) *Aggravating Circumstances.*

(a) The murder was committed by a convict under sentence of imprisonment.

(b) The defendant was previously convicted of another murder or of a felony involving the use or threat of violence to the person.

(c) At the time the murder was committed the defendant also committed another murder.

(d) The defendant knowingly created a great risk of death to many persons.

(e) The murder was committed while the defendant was engaged or was an accomplice in the commission of, or an attempt to commit, or flight after committing or attempting to commit robbery, rape or deviate sexual intercourse by force or threat of force, arson, burglary or kidnapping.

(f) The murder was committed for the purpose of avoiding or preventing a lawful arrest or effecting an escape from lawful custody.

(g) The murder was committed for pecuniary gain.

(h) The murder was especially heinous, atrocious or cruel, manifesting exceptional depravity.

(4) *Mitigating Circumstances.*

(a) The defendant has no significant history of prior criminal activity.

(b) The murder was committed while the defendant was under the influence of extreme mental or emotional disturbance.

(c) The victim was a participant in the defendant's homicidal conduct or consented to the homicidal act.

(d) The murder was committed under circumstances which the defendant believed to provide a moral justification or extenuation for his conduct.

(e) The defendant was an accomplice in a murder committed by another person and his participation in the homicidal act was relatively minor.

(f) The defendant acted under duress or under the domination of another person.

(g) At the time of the murder, the capacity of the defendant to appreciate the criminality [wrongfulness] of his conduct or to conform his conduct to the requirements of law was impaired as a result of mental disease or defect or intoxication.

(h) The youth of the defendant at the time of the crime.]

Article 211. Assault; Reckless Endangering; Threats

Section 211.0. Definitions

In this Article, the definitions given in Section 210.0 apply unless a different meaning plainly is required.

Section 211.1. Assault

(1) *Simple Assault.* A person is guilty of assault if he:

(a) attempts to cause or purposely, knowingly or recklessly causes bodily injury to another; or

(b) negligently causes bodily injury to another with a deadly weapon; or

(c) attempts by physical menace to put another in fear of imminent serious bodily injury.

Simple assault is a misdemeanor unless committed in a fight or scuffle entered into by mutual consent, in which case it is a petty misdemeanor.

(2) *Aggravated Assault.* A person is guilty of aggravated assault if he:

(a) attempts to cause serious bodily injury to another, or causes such injury purposely, knowingly or recklessly under circumstances manifesting extreme indifference to the value of human life; or

(b) attempts to cause or purposely or knowingly causes bodily injury to another with a deadly weapon.

Aggravated assault under paragraph (a) is a felony of the second degree; aggravated assault under paragraph (b) is a felony of the third degree.

Section 211.2. Recklessly Endangering Another Person

A person commits a misdemeanor if he recklessly engages in conduct which places or may place another person in danger of death or serious bodily injury. Recklessness and danger shall be presumed where a person knowingly points a firearm at or in the direction of another, whether or not the actor believed the firearm to be loaded.

Section 211.3. Terroristic Threats

A person is guilty of a felony of the third degree if he threatens to commit any crime of violence with purpose to terrorize another or to cause evacuation of a building, place of assembly, or facility of public transportation, or otherwise to cause serious public inconvenience, or in reckless disregard of the risk of causing such terror or inconvenience.

Article 212. Kidnapping and Related Offenses; Coercion

Section 212.0. Definitions

In this Article, the definitions given in Section 210.0 apply unless a different meaning plainly is required.

Section 212.1. Kidnapping

A person is guilty of kidnapping if he unlawfully removes another from his place of residence or business, or a substantial distance from the vicinity where he is found, or if he unlawfully confines another for a substantial period in a place of isolation, with any of the following purposes:

(a) to hold for ransom or reward, or as a shield or hostage; or

(b) to facilitate commission of any felony or flight thereafter; or

(c) to inflict bodily injury on or to terrorize the victim or another; or

(d) to interfere with the performance of any governmental or political function.

Kidnapping is a felony of the first degree unless the actor voluntarily releases the victim alive and in a safe place prior to trial, in which case it is a felony of the second degree. A removal or confinement is unlawful within the meaning of this Section if it is accomplished by force, threat or deception, or, in the case of a person who is under the age of 14 or incompetent, if it is accomplished without the consent of a parent, guardian or other person responsible for general supervision of his welfare.

Section 212.2. Felonious Restraint

A person commits a felony of the third degree if he knowingly:

(a) restrains another unlawfully in circumstances exposing him to risk of serious bodily injury; or

(b) holds another in a condition of involuntary servitude.

Section 212.3. False Imprisonment

A person commits a misdemeanor if he knowingly restrains another unlawfully so as to interfere substantially with his liberty.

Section 212.4. Interference with Custody

(1) *Custody of Children.* A person commits an offense if he knowingly or recklessly takes or entices any child under the age of 18 from the custody of its parent, guardian or other lawful custodian, when he has no privilege to do so. It is an affirmative defense that:

(a) the actor believed that his action was necessary to preserve the child from danger to its welfare; or

(b) the child, being at the time not less than 14 years old, was taken away at its own instigation without enticement and without purpose to commit a criminal offense with or against the child.

Proof that the child was below the critical age gives rise to a presumption that the actor knew the child's age or acted in reckless disregard thereof. The offense is a misdemeanor unless the actor, not being a parent or person in equivalent relation to the child, acted with knowledge that his conduct would cause serious alarm for the child's safety, or in reckless disregard of a likelihood of causing such alarm, in which case the offense is a felony of the third degree.

(2) *Custody of Committed Persons.* A person is guilty of a misdemeanor if he knowingly or recklessly takes or entices any committed person away from lawful custody when he is not privileged to do so. "Committed person" means, in addition to anyone committed under judicial warrant, any orphan, neglected or delinquent child, mentally defective or insane person, or other dependent or incompetent person entrusted to another's custody by or through a recognized social agency or otherwise by authority of law.

Section 212.5. Criminal Coercion

(1) *Offense Defined.* A person is guilty of criminal coercion if, with purpose unlawfully to restrict another's freedom of action to his detriment, he threatens to:

(a) commit any criminal offense; or

(b) accuse anyone of a criminal offense; or

(c) expose any secret tending to subject any person to hatred, contempt or ridicule, or to impair his credit or business repute; or

(d) take or withhold action as an official, or cause an official to take or withhold action.

It is an affirmative defense to prosecution based on paragraphs (b), (c) or (d) that the actor believed the accusation or secret to be true or the proposed official action justified and that his purpose was limited to compelling the other to behave in a way reasonably related to the circumstances which were the subject of the accusation, exposure or proposed official action, as by desisting from further misbehavior, making good a wrong done, refraining from taking any action or responsibility for which the actor believes the other disqualified.

(2) *Grading.* Criminal coercion is a misdemeanor unless the threat is to commit a felony or the actor's purpose is felonious, in which cases the offense is a felony of the third degree.

Article 213. Sexual Offenses

Section 213.0. Definitions

In this Article, unless a different meaning plainly is required:

(1) the definitions given in Section 210.0 apply;

(2) "Sexual intercourse" includes intercourse per os or per anum, with some penetration however slight; emission is not required;

(3) "Deviate sexual intercourse" means sexual intercourse per os or per anum between human beings who are not husband and wife, and any form of sexual intercourse with an animal.

Section 213.1. Rape and Related Offenses

(1) *Rape.* A male who has sexual intercourse with a female not his wife is guilty of rape if:

(a) he compels her to submit by force or by threat of imminent death, serious bodily injury, extreme pain or kidnapping, to be inflicted on anyone; or

(b) he has substantially impaired her power to appraise or control her conduct by administering or employing without her knowledge drugs, intoxicants or other means for the purpose of preventing resistance; or

(c) the female is unconscious; or

(d) the female is less than 10 years old.

Rape is a felony of the second degree unless (i) in the course thereof the actor inflicts serious bodily injury upon anyone, or (ii) the victim was not a voluntary social companion of the actor upon the occasion of the crime and had not previously permitted him sexual liberties, in which cases the offense is a felony of the first degree. Sexual intercourse includes intercourse per os or per anum, with some penetration however slight; emission is not required.

(2) *Gross Sexual Imposition.* A male who has sexual intercourse with a female not his wife commits a felony of the third degree if:

(a) he compels her to submit by any threat that would prevent resistance by a woman of ordinary resolution; or

(b) he knows that she suffers from a mental disease or defect which renders her incapable of appraising the nature of her conduct; or

(c) he knows that she is unaware that a sexual act is being committed upon her or that she submits because she mistakenly supposes that he is her husband.

Section 213.2. Deviate Sexual Intercourse by Force or Imposition

(1) *By Force or Its Equivalent.* A person who engages in deviate sexual intercourse with another person, or who causes another to engage in deviate sexual intercourse, commits a felony of the second degree if:

(a) he compels the other person to participate by force or by threat of imminent death, serious bodily injury, extreme pain or kidnapping, to be inflicted on anyone; or

(b) he has substantially impaired the other person's power to appraise or control his conduct, by administering or employing without the knowledge of the other person drugs, intoxicants or other means for the purpose of preventing resistance; or

(c) the other person is unconscious; or

(d) the other person is less than 10 years old.

Deviate sexual intercourse means sexual intercourse per os or per anum between human beings who are not husband and wife, and any form of sexual intercourse with an animal.

(2) *By Other Imposition.* A person who engages in deviate sexual intercourse with another person, or who causes another to engage in deviate sexual intercourse, commits a felony of the third degree if:

(a) he compels the other person to participate by any threat that would prevent resistance by a person of ordinary resolution; or

(b) he knows that the other person suffers from a mental disease or defect which renders him incapable of appraising the nature of his conduct; or

(c) he knows that the other person submits because he is unaware that a sexual act is being committed upon him.

Section 213.3. Corruption of Minors and Seduction

(1) *Offense Defined.* A male who has sexual intercourse with a female not his wife, or any person who engages in deviate sexual intercourse or causes another to engage in deviate sexual intercourse, is guilty of an offense if:

(a) the other person is less than [16] years old and the actor is at least [4] years older than the other person; or

(b) the other person is less than 21 years old and the actor is his guardian or otherwise responsible for general supervision of his welfare; or

(c) the other person is in custody of law or detained in a hospital or other institution and the actor has supervisory or disciplinary authority over him; or

(d) the other person is a female who is induced to participate by a promise of marriage which the actor does not mean to perform.

(2) *Grading.* An offense under paragraph (a) of Subsection (1) is a felony of the third degree. Otherwise an offense under this section is a misdemeanor.

Section 213.4. Sexual Assault

A person who has sexual contact with another not his spouse, or causes such other to have sexual conduct with him, is guilty of sexual assault, a misdemeanor, if:

(1) he knows that the contact is offensive to the other person; or

(2) he knows that the other person suffers from a mental disease or defect which renders him or her incapable of appraising the nature of his or her conduct; or

(3) he knows that the other person is unaware that a sexual act is being committed; or

(4) the other person is less than 10 years old; or

(5) he has substantially impaired the other person's power to appraise or control his or her conduct, by administering or employing without the other's knowledge drugs, intoxicants or other means for the purpose of preventing resistance; or

(6) the other person is less than [16] years old and the actor is at least [four] years older than the other person; or

(7) the other person is less than 21 years old and the actor is his guardian or otherwise responsible for general supervision of his welfare; or

(8) the other person is in custody of law or detained in a hospital or other institution and the actor has supervisory or disciplinary authority over him.

Sexual contact is any touching of the sexual or other intimate parts of the person for the purpose of arousing or gratifying sexual desire.

SECTION 213.5. INDECENT EXPOSURE

A person commits a misdemeanor if, for the purpose of arousing or gratifying sexual desire of himself or of any person other than his spouse, he exposes his genitals under circumstances in which he knows his conduct is likely to cause affront or alarm.

SECTION 213.6. PROVISIONS GENERALLY APPLICABLE TO ARTICLE 213

(1) *Mistake as to Age.* Whenever in this Article the criminality of conduct depends on a child's being below the age of 10, it is no defense that the actor did not know the child's age, or reasonably believed the child to be older than 10. When criminality depends on the child's being below a critical age other than 10, it is a defense for the actor to prove by a preponderance of the evidence that he reasonably believed the child to be above the critical age.

(2) *Spouse Relationships.* Whenever in this Article the definition of an offense excludes conduct with a spouse, the exclusion shall be deemed to extend to persons living as man and wife, regardless of the legal status of their relationship. The exclusion shall be inoperative as respects spouses living apart under a decree of judicial separation. Where the definition of an offense excludes conduct with a spouse or conduct by a woman, this shall not preclude conviction of a spouse or woman as accomplice in a sexual act in which he or she causes another person, not within the exclusion, to perform.

(3) *Sexually Promiscuous Complainants.* It is a defense to prosecution under Section 213.3. and paragraphs (6), (7) and (8) of Section 213.4 for the actor to prove by a preponderance of the evidence that the alleged victim had, prior to the time of the offense charged, engaged promiscuously in sexual relations with others.

(4) *Prompt Complaint.* No prosecution may be instituted or maintained under this Article unless the alleged offense was brought to the notice of public authority within [3] months of its occurrence or, where the alleged victim was less than [16] years old or otherwise incompetent to make complaint, within [3] months after a parent, guardian or other competent person specially interested in the victim learns of the offense.

(5) *Testimony of Complainants.* No person shall be convicted of any felony under this Article upon the uncorroborated testimony of the alleged victim. Corroboration may be circumstantial. In any prosecution before a jury for an offense under this Article, the jury shall be instructed to evaluate the testimony of a victim or complaining witness with special care in view of the emotional involvement of the witness and the difficulty of determining the truth with respect to alleged sexual activities carried out in private.

Offenses Against Property

Article 220. Arson, Criminal Mischief, and Other Property Destruction

SECTION 220.1. ARSON AND RELATED OFFENSES

(1) *Arson.* A person is guilty of arson, a felony of the second degree, if he starts a fire or causes an explosion with the purpose of:

(a) destroying a building or occupied structure of another; or

(b) destroying or damaging any property, whether his own or another's, to collect insurance for such loss. It shall be an affirmative defense to prosecution under this paragraph that the actor's conduct did not recklessly endanger any building or occupied structure of another or place any other person in danger of death or bodily injury.

(2) *Reckless Burning or Exploding.* A person commits a felony of the third degree if he purposely starts a fire or causes an explosion, whether on his own property or another's, and thereby recklessly:

(a) places another person in danger of death or bodily injury; or

(b) places a building or occupied structure of another in danger of damage or destruction.

(3) *Failure to Control or Report Dangerous Fire.* A person who knows that a fire is endangering life or a substantial amount of property of another and fails to take reasonable measures to put out or control the fire, when he can do so without substantial risk to himself, or to give a prompt fire alarm, commits a misdemeanor if:

(a) he knows that he is under an official, contractual, or other legal duty to prevent or combat the fire; or

(b) the fire was started, albeit lawfully, by him or with his assent, or on property in his custody or control.

(4) *Definitions.* "Occupied structure" means any structure, vehicle or place adapted for overnight accommodation of persons, or for carrying on business therein, whether or not a person is actually present. Property is that of another, for the purposes of this section, if anyone other than the actor has a possessory or proprietory interest therein. If a building or structure is divided into separately occupied units, any unit not occupied by the actor is an occupied structure of another.

Section 220.2. Causing or Risking Catastrophe

(1) *Causing Catastrophe.* A person who causes a catastrophe by explosion, fire, flood, avalanche, collapse of building, release of poison gas, radioactive material or other harmful or destructive force or substance, or by any other means of causing potentially widespread injury or damage, commits a felony of the second degree if he does so purposely or knowingly, or a felony of the third degree if he does so recklessly.

(2) *Risking Catastrophe.* A person is guilty of a misdemeanor if he recklessly creates a risk of catastrophe in the employment of fire, explosives or other dangerous means listed in Subsection (1).

(3) *Failure to Prevent Catastrophe.* A person who knowingly or recklessly fails to take reasonable measures to prevent or mitigate a catastrophe commits a misdemeanor if:

(a) he knows that he is under an official, contractual or other legal duty to take such measures; or

(b) he did or assented to the act causing or threatening the catastrophe.

Section 220.3. Criminal Mischief

(1) *Offense Defined.* A person is guilty of criminal mischief if he:

(a) damages tangible property of another purposely, recklessly, or by negligence in the employment of fire, explosives, or other dangerous means listed in Section 220.2(1); or

(b) purposely or recklessly tampers with tangible property of another so as to endanger person or property; or

(c) purposely or recklessly causes another to suffer pecuniary loss by deception or threat.

(2) *Grading.* Criminal mischief is a felony of the third degree if the actor purposely causes pecuniary loss in excess of $5,000, or a substantial interruption or impairment of public communication, transportation, supply of water, gas or power, or other public service. It is a misdemeanor if the actor purposely causes pecuniary loss in excess of $100, or a petty misdemeanor if he purposely or recklessly causes pecuniary loss in excess of $25. Otherwise criminal mischief is a violation.

Article 221. Burglary and Other Criminal Intrusion

Section 221.0. Definitions

In this Article, unless a different meaning plainly is required:

(1) "occupied structure" means any structure, vehicle or place adapted for overnight accommodation of persons, or for carrying on business therein, whether or not a person is actually present.

(2) "night" means the period between thirty minutes past sunset and thirty minutes before sunrise.

Section 221.1. Burglary

(1) *Burglary Defined.* A person is guilty of burglary if he enters a building or occupied structure, or separately secured or occupied portion thereof, with purpose to commit a crime therein, unless the premises are at the time open to the public or the actor is licensed or privileged to enter. It is an affirmative defense to prosecution for burglary that the building or structure was abandoned.

(2) *Grading.* Burglary is a felony of the second degree if it is perpetrated in the dwelling of another at night, or if, in the course of committing the offense, the actor:

(a) purposely, knowingly or recklessly inflicts or attempts to inflict bodily injury on anyone; or

(b) is armed with explosives or a deadly weapon.

Otherwise burglary is a felony of the third degree. An act shall be deemed "in the course of committing" an offense if it occurs in an attempt to commit the offense or in flight after the attempt or commission.

(3) *Multiple Convictions.* A person may not be convicted both for burglary and for the offense which it was his purpose to commit after the burglarious entry or for an attempt to commit that offense, unless the additional offense constitutes a felony of the first or second degree.

Section 221.2. Criminal Trespass

(1) *Buildings and Occupied Structures.* A person commits an offense if, knowing that he is not licensed or privileged to do so, he enters or surreptitiously remains in any building or occupied structure, or separately secured or occupied portion thereof. An offense under this Subsection is a misdemeanor if it is committed in a dwelling at night. Otherwise it is a petty misdemeanor.

(2) *Defiant Trespasser.* A person commits an offense if, knowing that he is not licensed or privileged to do so, he enters or remains in any place as to which notice against trespass is given by:

(a) actual communication to the actor; or

(b) posting in a manner prescribed by law or reasonably likely to come to the attention of intruders; or

(c) fencing or other enclosure manifestly designed to exclude intruders.

An offense under this Subsection constitutes a petty misdemeanor if the offender defies an order to leave personally communicated to him by the owner of the premises or other authorized person. Otherwise it is a violation.

(3) *Defenses.* It is an affirmative defense to prosecution under this Section that:

(a) a building or occupied structure involved in an offense under Subsection (1) was abandoned; or

(b) the premises were at the time open to members of the public and the actor complied with all lawful conditions imposed on access to or remaining in the premises; or

(c) the actor reasonably believed that the owner of the premises, or other person empowered to license access thereto, would have licensed him to enter or remain.

Article 222. Robbery

SECTION 222.1. ROBBERY

(1) *Robbery Defined.* A person is guilty of robbery if, in the course of committing a theft, he:

(a) inflicts serious bodily injury upon another; or

(b) threatens another with or purposely puts him in fear of immediate serious bodily injury; or

(c) commits or threatens immediately to commit any felony of the first or second degree.

An act shall be deemed "in the course of committing a theft" if it occurs in an attempt to commit theft or in flight after the attempt or commission.

(2) *Grading.* Robbery is a felony of the second degree, except that it is a felony of the first degree if in the course of committing the theft the actor attempts to kill anyone, or purposely inflicts or attempts to inflict serious bodily injury.

Article 223. Theft and Related Offenses

SECTION 223.0. DEFINITIONS

In this Article, unless a different meaning plainly is required:

(1) "deprive" means: (a) to withhold property of another permanently or for so extended a period as to appropriate a major portion of its economic value, or with intent to restore only upon payment of reward or other compensation; or (b) to dispose of the property so as to make it unlikely that the owner will recover it.

(2) "financial institution" means a bank, insurance company, credit union, building and loan association, investment trust or other organization held out to the public as a place of deposit of funds or medium of savings or collective investment.

(3) "government" means the United States, any State, county, municipality, or other political unit, or any department, agency or subdivision of any of the foregoing, or any corporation or other association carrying out the functions of government.

(4) "movable property" means property the location of which can be changed, including things growing on, affixed to, or found in land, and documents although the rights represented thereby have no physical location. "Immovable property" is all other property.

(5) "obtain" means: (a) in relation to property, to bring about a transfer or purported transfer of a legal interest in the property, whether to the obtainer or another; or (b) in relation to labor or service, to secure performance thereof.

(6) "property" means anything of value, including real estate, tangible and intangible personal property, contract rights, choses-in-action and other interests in or claims to wealth, admission or transportation tickets, captured or domestic animals, food and drink, electric or other power.

(7) "property of another" includes property in which any person other than the actor has an interest which the actor is not privileged to infringe, regardless of the fact that the actor also has an interest in the property and regardless of the fact that the other person might be precluded from civil recovery because the property was used in an unlawful transaction or was subject to forfeiture as contraband. Property in possession of the actor shall not be deemed property of another who has only a security interest therein, even if legal title is in the creditor pursuant to a conditional sales contract or other security agreement.

Section 223.1. Consolidation of Theft Offenses; Grading; Provisions Applicable to Theft Generally

(1) *Consolidation of Theft Offenses.* Conduct denominated theft in this Article constitutes a single offense. An accusation of theft may be supported by evidence that it was committed in any manner that would be theft under this Article, notwithstanding the specification of a different manner in the indictment or information, subject only to the power of the Court to ensure fair trial by granting a continuance or other appropriate relief where the conduct of the defense would be prejudiced by lack of fair notice or by surprise.

(2) *Grading of Theft Offenses.*

(a) Theft constitutes a felony of the third degree if the amount involved exceeds $500, or if the property stolen is a firearm, automobile, airplane, motorcycle, motorboat or other motor-propelled vehicle, or in the case of theft by receiving stolen property, if the receiver is in the business of buying or selling stolen property.

(b) Theft not within the preceding paragraph constitutes a misdemeanor, except that if the property was not taken from the person or by threat, or in breach of a fiduciary obligation, and the actor proves by a preponderance of the evidence that the amount involved was less than $50, the offense constitutes a petty misdemeanor.

(c) The amount involved in a theft shall be deemed to be the highest value, by any reasonable standard, of the property or services which the actor stole or attempted to steal. Amounts involved in thefts committed pursuant to one scheme or course of conduct, whether from the same person or several persons, may be aggregated in determining the grade of the offense.

(3) *Claim of Right.* It is an affirmative defense to prosecution for theft that the actor:

(a) was unaware that the property or service was that of another; or

(b) acted under an honest claim of right to the property or service involved or that he had a right to acquire or dispose of it as he did; or

(c) took property exposed for sale, intending to purchase and pay for it promptly, or reasonably believing that the owner, if present, would have consented.

(4) *Theft from Spouse.* It is no defense that theft was from the actor's spouse, except that misappropriation of household and personal effects, or other property normally accessible to both spouses, is theft only if it occurs after the parties have ceased living together.

Section 223.2. Theft by Unlawful Taking or Disposition

(1) *Movable Property.* A person is guilty of theft if he unlawfully takes, or exercises unlawful control over, movable property of another with purpose to deprive him thereof.

(2) *Immovable Property.* A person is guilty of theft if he unlawfully transfers immovable

property of another or any interest therein with purpose to benefit himself or another not entitled thereto.

SECTION 223.3. THEFT BY DECEPTION

A person is guilty of theft if he purposely obtains property of another by deception. A person deceives if he purposely:

(1) creates or reinforces a false impression, including false impressions as to law, value, intention or other state of mind; but deception as to a person's intention to perform a promise shall not be inferred from the fact alone that he did not subsequently perform the promise; or

(2) prevents another from acquiring information which would affect his judgment of a transaction; or

(3) fails to correct a false impression which the deceiver previously created or reinforced, or which the deceiver knows to be influencing another to whom he stands in a fiduciary or confidential relationship; or

(4) fails to disclose a known lien, adverse claim or other legal impediment to the enjoyment of property which he transfers or encumbers in consideration for the property obtained, whether such impediment is or is not valid, or is or is not a matter of official record.

The term "deceive" does not, however, include falsity as to matters having no pecuniary significance, or puffing by statements unlikely to deceive ordinary persons in the group addressed.

SECTION 223.4. THEFT BY EXTORTION

A person is guilty of theft if he obtains property of another by threatening to:

(1) inflict bodily injury on anyone or commit any other criminal offense; or

(2) accuse anyone of a criminal offense; or

(3) expose any secret tending to subject any person to hatred, contempt or ridicule, or to impair his credit or business repute; or

(4) take or withhold action as an official, or cause an official to take or withhold action; or

(5) bring about or continue a strike, boycott or other collective unofficial action, if the property is not demanded or received for the benefit of the group in whose interest the actor purports to act; or

(6) testify or provide information or withhold testimony or information with respect to another's legal claim or defense; or

(7) inflict any other harm which would not benefit the actor.

It is an affirmative defense to prosecution based on paragraphs (2), (3) or (4) that the property obtained by threat of accusation, exposure, lawsuit or other invocation of official action was honestly claimed as restitution or indemnification for harm done in the circumstances to which such accusation, exposure, lawsuit or other official action relates, or as compensation for property or lawful services.

SECTION 223.5. THEFT OF PROPERTY LOST, MISLAID, OR DELIVERED BY MISTAKE

A person who comes into control of property of another that he knows to have been lost, mislaid, or delivered under a mistake as to the nature or amount of the property or the identity of the recipient is guilty of theft if, with purpose to deprive the owner thereof, he fails to take reasonable measures to restore the property to a person entitled to have it.

Section 223.6. Receiving Stolen Property

(1) *Receiving.* A person is guilty of theft if he purposely receives, retains, or disposes of movable property of another knowing that it has been stolen, or believing that it has probably been stolen, unless the property is received, retained, or disposed with purpose to restore it to the owner. "Receiving" means acquiring possession, control or title, or lending on the security of the property.

(2) *Presumption of Knowledge.* The requisite knowledge or belief is presumed in the case of a dealer who:

(a) is found in possession or control of property stolen from two or more persons on separate occasions; or

(b) has received stolen property in another transaction within the year preceding the transaction charged; or

(c) being a dealer in property of the sort received, acquires it for a consideration which he knows is far below its reasonable value.

"Dealer" means a person in the business of buying or selling goods including a pawnbroker.

Section 223.7. Theft of Services

(1) A person is guilty of theft if he purposely obtains services which he knows are available only for compensation, by deception or threat, or by false token or other means to avoid payment for the service. "Services" includes labor, professional service, transportation, telephone or other public service, accommodation in hotels, restaurants or elsewhere, admission to exhibitions, use of vehicles or other movable property. Where compensation for service is ordinarily paid immediately upon the rendering for such service, as is the case of hotels and restaurants, refusal to pay or absconding without payment or offer to pay gives rise to a presumption that the service was obtained by deception as to intention to pay.

(2) A person commits theft if, having control over the disposition of services of others, to which he is not entitled, he knowingly diverts such services to his own benefit or to the benefit of another not entitled thereto.

Section 223.8. Theft by Failure to Make Required Disposition of Funds Received

A person who purposely obtains property upon agreement, or subject to a known legal obligation, to make specified payment or other disposition, whether from such property or its proceeds or from his own property to be reserved in equivalent amount, is guilty of theft if he deals with the property obtained as his own and fails to make the required payment or disposition. The foregoing applies notwithstanding that it may be impossible to identify particular property as belonging to the victim at the time of the actor's failure to make the required payment or disposition. An officer or employee of the government or of a financial institution is presumed: (i) to know any legal obligation relevant to his criminal liability under this Section, and (ii) to have dealt with the property as his own if he fails to pay or account upon lawful demand, or if an audit reveals a shortage or falsification of accounts.

Section 223.9. Unauthorized Use of Automobiles and Other Vehicles

A person commits a misdemeanor if he operates another's automobile, airplane, motorcycle, motorboat, or other motor-propelled vehicle without consent of the owner. It is an affirmative defense to prosecution under this Section that the actor reasonably believed that the owner would have consented to the operation had he known of it.

Article 224. Forgery and Fraudulent Practices

Section 224.0. Definitions

In this Article, the definitions given in Section 223.0 apply unless a different meaning plainly is required.

Section 224.1. Forgery

(1) *Definition.* A person is guilty of forgery if, with purpose to defraud or injure anyone, or with knowledge that he is facilitating a fraud or injury to be perpetrated by anyone, the actor:

(a) alters any writing of another without his authority; or

(b) makes, completes, executes, authenticates, issues or transfers any writing so that it purports to be the act of another who did not authorize that act, or to have been executed at a time or place or in a numbered sequence other than was in fact the case, or to be a copy of an original when no such original existed; or

(c) utters any writing which he knows to be forged in a manner specified in paragraphs (a) or (b).

"Writing" includes printing or any other method of recording information, money, coins, tokens, stamps, seals, credit cards, badges, trade-marks, and other symbols of value, right, privilege, or identification.

(2) *Grading.* Forgery is a felony of the second degree if the writing is or purports to be part of an issue of money, securities, postage or revenue stamps, or other instruments issued by the government, or part of an issue of stock, bonds or other instruments representing interests in or claims against any property or enterprise. Forgery is a felony of the third degree if the writing is or purports to be a will, deed, contract, release, commercial instrument, or other document evidencing, creating, transferring, altering, terminating, or otherwise affecting legal relations. Otherwise forgery is a misdemeanor.

Section 224.2. Simulating Objects of Antiquity, Rarity, Etc.

A person commits a misdemeanor if, with purpose to defraud anyone or with knowledge that he is facilitating a fraud to be perpetrated by anyone, he makes, alters or utters any object so that it appears to have value because of antiquity, rarity, source, or authorship which it does not possess.

Section 224.3. Fraudulent Destruction, Removal or Concealment of Recordable Instruments

A person commits a felony of the third degree if, with purpose to deceive or injure anyone, he destroys, removes or conceals any will, deed, mortgage, security instrument or other writing for which the law provides public recording.

Section 224.4. Tampering with Records

A person commits a misdemeanor if, knowing that he has no privilege to do so, he falsifies, destroys, removes or conceals any writing or record, with purpose to deceive or injure anyone or to conceal any wrongdoing.

Section 224.5. Bad Checks

A person who issues or passes a check or similar sight order for the payment of money, knowing that it will not be honored by the drawee, commits a misdemeanor. For the purposes of this Section as well as in any prosecution for theft committed by means of a bad check, an issuer is presumed to know that the check or order (other than a postdated check or order) would not be paid, if:

(1) the issuer had no account with the drawee at the time the check or order was issued; or

(2) payment was refused by the drawee for lack of funds, upon presentation within 30 days after issue, and the issuer failed to make good within 10 days after receiving notice of that refusal.

Section 224.6. Credit Cards

A person commits an offense if he uses a credit card for the purpose of obtaining property or services with knowledge that:

(1) the card is stolen or forged; or

(2) the card has been revoked or cancelled; or

(3) for any other reason his use of the card is unauthorized by the issuer.

It is an affirmative defense to prosecution under paragraph (3) if the actor proves by a preponderance of the evidence that he had the purpose and ability to meet all obligations to the issuer arising out of his use of the card. "Credit card" means a writing, or other evidence of an undertaking to pay for property or services delivered or rendered to or upon the order of a designated person or bearer. An offense under this Section is a felony of the third degree if the value of the property or services secured or sought to be secured by means of the credit card exceeds $500; otherwise it is a misdemeanor.

Section 224.7. Deceptive Business Practices

A person commits a misdemeanor if in the course of business he:

(1) uses or possesses for use a false weight or measure, or any other device for falsely determining or recording any quality or quantity; or

(2) sells, offers or exposes for sale, or delivers less than the represented quantity of any commodity or service; or

(3) takes or attempts to take more than the represented quantity of any commodity or service when as buyer he furnishes the weight or measure; or

(4) sells, offers or exposes for sale adulterated or mislabeled commodities. "Adulterated" means varying from the standard of composition or quality prescribed by or pursuant to any statute providing criminal penalties for such variance, or set by established commercial usage. "Mislabeled" means varying from the standard of truth or disclosure in labeling prescribed by or pursuant to any statute providing criminal penalties for such variance, or set by established commercial usage; or

(5) makes a false or misleading statement in any advertisement addressed to the public or to a substantial segment thereof for the purpose of promoting the purchase or sale of property or services; or

(6) makes a false or misleading written statement for the purpose of obtaining property or credit; or

(7) makes a false or misleading written statement for the purpose of promoting the sale of securities, or omits information required by law to be disclosed in written documents relating to securities.

It is an affirmative defense to prosecution under this Section if the defendant proves by a preponderance of the evidence that his conduct was not knowingly or recklessly deceptive.

SECTION 224.8. COMMERCIAL BRIBERY AND BREACH OF DUTY TO ACT DISINTERESTEDLY

(1) A person commits a misdemeanor if he solicits, accepts or agrees to accept any benefit as consideration for knowingly violating or agreeing to violate a duty of fidelity to which he is subject as:

(a) partner, agent, or employee of another;

(b) trustee, guardian, or other fiduciary;

(c) lawyer, physician, accountant, appraiser, or other professional adviser or informant;

(d) officer, director, manager or other participant in the direction of the affairs of an incorporated or unincorporated association; or

(e) arbitrator or other purportedly disinterested adjudicator or referee.

(2) A person who holds himself out to the public as being engaged in the business of making disinterested selection, appraisal, or criticism of commodities or services commits a misdemeanor if he solicits, accepts or agrees to accept any benefit to influence his selection, appraisal or criticism.

(3) A person commits a misdemeanor if he confers, or offers or agrees to confer, any benefit the acceptance of which would be criminal under this Section.

SECTION 224.9. RIGGING PUBLICLY EXHIBITED CONTEST

(1) A person commits a misdemeanor if, with purpose to prevent a publicly exhibited contest from being conducted in accordance with the rules and usages purporting to govern it, he:

(a) confers or offers or agrees to confer any benefit upon, or threatens any injury to a participant, official or other person associated with the contest or exhibition; or

(b) tampers with any person, animal or thing.

(2) *Soliciting or Accepting Benefit for Rigging.* A person commits a misdemeanor if he knowingly solicits, accepts or agrees to accept any benefit the giving of which would be criminal under Subsection (1).

(3) *Participation in Rigged Contest.* A person commits a misdemeanor if he knowingly engages in, sponsors, produces, judges, or otherwise participates in a publicly exhibited contest knowing that the contest is not being conducted in compliance with the rules and usages purporting to govern it, by reason of conduct which would be criminal under this Section.

SECTION 224.10. DEFRAUDING SECURED CREDITORS

A person commits a misdemeanor if he destroys, removes, conceals, encumbers, transfers or otherwise deals with property subject to a security interest with purpose to hinder enforcement of that interest.

SECTION 224.11. FRAUD IN INSOLVENCY

A person commits a misdemeanor if, knowing that proceedings have been or are about to be instituted for the appointment of a receiver or other person entitled to administer property for the benefit of creditors, or that any other composition or liquidation for the benefit of creditors has been or is about to be made, he:

(a) destroys, removes, conceals, encumbers, transfers, or otherwise deals with any property with purpose to defeat or obstruct the claim of any creditor, or otherwise to obstruct the operation of any law relating to administration of property for the benefit of creditors; or

(b) knowingly falsifies any writing or record relating to the property; or

(c) knowingly misrepresents or refuses to disclose to a receiver or other person entitled to administer property for the benefit of creditors, the existence, amount or location of the property, or any other information which the actor could be legally required to furnish in relation to such administration.

SECTION 224.12. RECEIVING DEPOSITS IN A FAILING FINANCIAL INSTITUTION

An officer, manager or other person directing or participating in the direction of a financial institution commits a misdemeanor if he receives or permits the receipt of a deposit, premium payment or other investment in the institution knowing that:

(1) due to financial difficulties the institution is about to suspend operations or go into receivership or reorganization; and

(2) the person making the deposit or other payment is unaware of the precarious situation of the institution.

SECTION 224.13. MISAPPLICATION OF ENTRUSTED PROPERTY AND PROPERTY OF GOVERNMENT OR FINANCIAL INSTITUTION

A person commits an offense if he applies or disposes of property that has been entrusted to him as a fiduciary, or property of the government or of a financial institution, in a manner which he knows is unlawful and involves substantial risk of loss or detriment to the owner of the property or to a person for whose benefit the property was entrusted. The offense is a misdemeanor if the amount involved exceeds $50; otherwise it is a petty misdemeanor. "Fiduciary" includes trustee, guardian, executor, administrator, receiver and any person carrying on fiduciary functions on behalf of a corporation or other organization which is a fiduciary.

SECTION 224.14. SECURING EXECUTION OF DOCUMENTS BY DECEPTION

A person commits a misdemeanor if by deception he causes another to execute any instrument affecting, purporting to affect, or likely to affect the pecuniary interest of any person.

Offenses Against the Family

Article 230. Offenses Against the Family

SECTION 230.1. BIGAMY AND POLYGAMY

(1) *Bigamy.* A married person is guilty of bigamy, a misdemeanor, if he contracts or purports to contract another marriage, unless at the time of the subsequent marriage:

(a) the actor believes that the prior spouse is dead; or

(b) the actor and the prior spouse have been living apart for five consecutive years throughout which the prior spouse was not known by the actor to be alive; or

(c) a Court has entered a judgment purporting to terminate or annul any prior disqualifying marriage, and the actor does not know that judgment to be invalid; or

(d) the actor reasonably believes that he is legally eligible to remarry.

(2) *Polygamy.* A person is guilty of polygamy, a felony of the third degree, if he marries or cohabits with more than one spouse at a time in purported exercise of the right of plural marriage. The offense is a continuing one until all cohabitation and claim of marriage with more than one spouse terminates. This section does not apply to parties to a polygamous marriage, lawful in the country of which they are residents or nationals, while they are in transit through or temporarily visiting this State.

(3) *Other Party to Bigamous or Polygamous Marriage.* A person is guilty of bigamy or polygamy, as the case may be, if he contracts or purports to contract marriage with another knowing that the other is thereby committing bigamy or polygamy.

Section 230.2. Incest

A person is guilty of incest, a felony of the third degree, if he knowingly marries or cohabits or has sexual intercourse with an ancestor or descendant, a brother or sister of the whole or half blood [or an uncle, aunt, nephew or niece of the whole blood]. "Cohabit" means to live together under the representation or appearance of being married. The relationships referred to herein include blood relationships without regard to legitimacy, and relationship of parent and child by adoption.

Section 230.3. Abortion [omitted]

Section 230.4. Endangering Welfare of Children

A parent, guardian, or other person supervising the welfare of a child under 18 commits a misdemeanor if he knowingly endangers the child's welfare by violating a duty of care, protection or support.

Section 230.5. Persistent Non-Support

A person commits a misdemeanor if he persistently fails to provide support which he can provide and which he knows he is legally obliged to provide to a spouse, child or other dependent.

Offenses Against Public Administration

Article 240. Bribery and Corrupt Influence [omitted]

Article 241. Perjury and Other Falsification in Official Matters [omitted]

Article 242. Obstructing Governmental Operations; Escapes [omitted]

Article 243. Abuse of Office [omitted]

Offenses Against Public Order and Decency

Article 250. Riot, Disorderly Conduct, and Related Offenses

Section 250.1. Riot; Failure to Disperse

(1) *Riot.* A person is guilty of riot, a felony of the third degree, if he participates with [two] or more others in a course of disorderly conduct:

(a) with purpose to commit or facilitate the commission of a felony or misdemeanor;

(b) with purpose to prevent or coerce official action; or

(c) when the actor or any other participant to the knowledge of the actor uses or plans to use a firearm or any other deadly weapon.

(2) *Failure of Disorderly Persons to Disperse Upon Official Order.* Where [three] or more persons are participating in a course of disorderly conduct likely to cause substantial harm or serious inconvenience, annoyance or alarm, a peace officer or other public servant engaged in executing or enforcing the law may order the participants and others in the immediate vicinity to disperse. A person who refuses or knowingly fails to obey such an order commits a misdemeanor.

Section 250.2. Disorderly Conduct

(1) *Offense Defined.* A person is guilty of disorderly conduct if, with purpose to cause public inconvenience, annoyance or alarm, or recklessly creating a risk thereof, he:

(a) engages in fighting or threatening, or in violent or tumultuous behavior; or

(b) makes unreasonable noise or offensively coarse utterance, gesture or display, or addresses abusive language to any person present; or

(c) creates a hazardous or physically offensive condition by any act which serves no legitimate purpose of the actor.

"Public" means affecting or likely to affect persons in a place to which the public or a substantial group has access; among the places included are highways, transport facilities, schools, prisons, apartment houses, places of business or amusement, or any neighborhood.

(2) *Grading.* An offense under this section is a petty misdemeanor if the actor's purpose is to cause substantial harm or serious inconvenience, or if he persists in disorderly conduct after reasonable warning or request to desist. Otherwise disorderly conduct is a violation.

Section 250.3. False Public Alarms

A person is guilty of a misdemeanor if he initiates or circulates a report or warning of an impending bombing or other crime or catastrophe, knowing that the report or warning is false or baseless and that it is likely to cause evacuation of a building, place of assembly, or facility of public transport, or to cause public inconvenience or alarm.

Section 250.4. Harassment

A person commits a petty misdemeanor if, with purpose to harass another, he:

(1) makes a telephone call without purpose of legitimate communication; or

(2) insults, taunts or challenges another in a manner likely to provoke violent or disorderly response; or

(3) makes repeated communications anonymously or at extremely inconvenient hours, or in offensively coarse language; or

(4) subjects another to an offensive touching; or

(5) engages in any other course of alarming conduct serving no legitimate purpose of the actor.

Section 250.5. Public Drunkenness; Drug Incapacitation

A person is guilty of an offense if he appears in any public place manifestly under the influence of alcohol, narcotics or other drugs, not therapeutically administered, to the degree that he may endanger himself or other persons or property, or annoy persons in his vicinity. An offense under this Section constitutes a petty misdemeanor if the actor has been convicted hereunder twice before within a period of one year. Otherwise the offense constitutes a violation.

Section 250.6. Loitering or Prowling

A person commits a violation if he loiters or prowls in a place, at a time, or in a manner not usual for law-abiding individuals under circumstances that warrant alarm for the safety of persons or property in the vicinity. Among the circumstances which may be considered in determining whether such alarm is warranted is the fact that the actor takes flight upon appearance of a peace officer, refuses to identify himself, or manifestly endeavors to conceal himself or any object. Unless flight by the actor or other circumstances makes it impracticable, a peace officer shall prior to any arrest for an offense under this section afford the actor an opportunity to dispel any alarm which would otherwise be warranted, by requesting him to identify himself and explain his presence and conduct. No person shall be convicted of an offense under this Section if the peace officer did not comply with the preceding sentence, or if it appears at trial that the explanation given by the actor was true and, if believed by the peace officer at the time, would have dispelled the alarm.

Section 250.7. Obstructing Highways and Other Public Passages

(1) A person, who, having no legal privilege to do so, purposely or recklessly obstructs any highway or other public passage, whether alone or with others, commits a violation, or, in case he persists after warning by a law officer, a petty misdemeanor. "Obstructs" means renders impassable without unreasonable inconvenience or hazard. No person shall be deemed guilty of recklessly obstructing in violation of this Subsection solely because of a gathering of persons to hear him speak or otherwise communicate, or solely because of being a member of such a gathering.

(2) A person in a gathering commits a violation if he refuses to obey a reasonable official request or order to move:

(a) to prevent obstruction of a highway or other public passage; or

(b) to maintain public safety by dispersing those gathered in dangerous proximity to a fire or other hazard.

An order to move, addressed to a person whose speech or other lawful behavior attracts an obstructing audience, shall not be deemed reasonable if the obstruction can be readily remedied by police control of the size or location of the gathering.

SECTION 250.8. DISRUPTING MEETINGS AND PROCESSIONS

A person commits a misdemeanor if, with purpose to prevent or disrupt a lawful meeting, procession or gathering, he does any act tending to obstruct or interfere with it physically, or makes any utterance, gesture or display designed to outrage the sensibilities of the group.

SECTION 250.9. DESECRATION OF VENERATED OBJECTS [OMITTED]

SECTION 250.10. ABUSE OF CORPSE [OMITTED]

SECTION 250.11. CRUELTY TO ANIMALS [OMITTED]

SECTION 250.12. VIOLATION OF PRIVACY [OMITTED]

Article 251. Public Indecency

SECTION 251.1. OPEN LEWDNESS

A person commits a petty misdemeanor if he does any lewd act which he knows is likely to be observed by others who would be affronted or alarmed.

SECTION 251.2. PROSTITUTION AND RELATED OFFENSES

(1) *Prostitution.* A person is guilty of prostitution, a petty misdemeanor, if he or she:

(a) is an inmate of a house of prostitution or otherwise engages in sexual activity as a business; or

(b) loiters in or within view of any public place for the purpose of being hired to engage in sexual activity.

"Sexual activity" includes homosexual and other deviate sexual relations. A "house of prostitution" is any place where prostitution or promotion of prostitution is regularly carried on by one person under the control, management or supervision of another. An "inmate" is a person who engages in prostitution in or through the agency of a house of prostitution. "Public place" means any place to which the public or any substantial group thereof has access.

(2) *Promoting Prostitution.* A person who knowingly promotes prostitution of another commits a misdemeanor or felony as provided in Subsection (3). The following acts shall, without limitation of the foregoing, constitute promoting prostitution:

(a) owning, controlling, managing, supervising or otherwise keeping, alone or in association with others, a house of prostitution or a prostitution business; or

(b) procuring an inmate for a house of prostitution or a place in a house of prostitution for one who would be an inmate; or

(c) encouraging, inducing, or otherwise purposely causing another to become or remain a prostitute; or

(d) soliciting a person to patronize a prostitute; or

(e) procuring a prostitute for a patron; or

(f) transporting a person into or within this state with purpose to promote that person's engaging in prostitution, or procuring or paying for transportation with that purpose; or

(g) leasing or otherwise permitting a place controlled by the actor, alone or in association with others, to be regularly used for prostitution or the promotion of prostitution, or failure to make reasonable effort to abate such use by ejecting the tenant, notifying law enforcement authorities, or other legally available means; or

(h) soliciting, receiving, or agreeing to receive any benefit for doing or agreeing to do anything forbidden by this Subsection.

(3) *Grading of Offenses Under Subsection (2).* An offense under Subsection (2) constitutes a felony of the third degree if:

(a) the offense falls within paragraph (a), (b) or (c) of Subsection (2); or

(b) the actor compels another to engage in or promote prostitution; or

(c) the actor promotes prostitution of a child under 16, whether or not he is aware of the child's age; or

(d) the actor promotes prostitution of his wife, child, ward or any person for whose care, protection or support he is responsible.

Otherwise the offense is a misdemeanor.

(4) *Presumption from Living off Prostitutes.* A person, other than the prostitute or the prostitute's minor child or other legal dependent incapable of self-support, who is supported in whole or substantial part by the proceeds of prostitution is presumed to be knowingly promoting prostitution in violation of Subsection (2).

(5) *Patronizing Prostitutes.* A person commits a violation if he hires a prostitute to engage in sexual activity with him, or if he enters or remains in a house of prostitution for the purpose of engaging in sexual activity.

(6) *Evidence.* On the issue whether a place is a house of prostitution the following shall be admissible evidence: its general repute; the repute of the persons who reside in or frequent the place; the frequency, timing and duration of visits by non-residents. Testimony of a person against his spouse shall be admissible to prove offenses under this Section.

Section 251.3. Loitering to Solicit Deviate Sexual Relations

A person is guilty of a petty misdemeanor if he loiters in or near any public place for the purpose of soliciting or being solicited to engage in deviate sexual relations.

Section 251.4. Obscenity [omitted]

PART III. TREATMENT AND CORRECTION [OMITTED]

PART IV. ORGANIZATION OF CORRECTION [OMITTED]

TABLE OF CASES

Italics indicate principal cases or cases otherwise prominently treated.

BIBLIOGRAPHIC REFERENCES

This table lists books, articles, reports and other secondary authorities extracted or referred to in the casebook. Anonymous student notes and comments follow alphabetical listing by author.

Materials of General Import

American Law Institute, Model Penal Code and Commentaries (1980-1985).
J. Dressler, Understanding Criminal Law (1987).
Encyclopedia of Crime and Justice (S. H. Kadish ed. 1983)
G. Fletcher, Rethinking Criminal Law (1978).
J. Hall, General Principles of the Criminal Law (1960).
H. L. A. Hart, The Morality of the Criminal Law (1964).
H. L. A. Hart, Punishment and Responsibility (1968).
O. W. Holmes, The Common Law (1881).
S. H. Kadish, Blame and Punishment (1987).
W. LaFave & A. Scott, Criminal Law (2d ed. 1986).
National Commission on Reform of Federal Criminal Laws, Working Papers (1970).
H. Packer, The Limits of the Criminal Sanction (1968).
President's Commission on Law Enforcement and the Administration of Justice, The Challenge of Crime in a Free Society (1967).
J. F. Stephen, A History of the Criminal Law of England (1883).
G. Williams, Criminal Law: The General Part (2d ed. 1961).
G. Williams, Textbook of Criminal Law (2d ed. 1983).

Chapter 1
How Guilt Is Established

R. Allen, The Restoration of In re Winship: A Comment on Burdens of Persuasion in Criminal Cases After Patterson v. New York, 76 Mich. L. Rev. 30 (1977).
A. Alschuler, Courtroom Misconduct by Prosecutors and Trial Judges, 50 Tex. L. Rev. 629 (1972).
A. Alschuler, The Prosecutor's Role in Plea Bargaining, 36 U. Chi. L. Rev. 50 (1968).
American Bar Association, Annotated Model Rules of Professional Conduct (2d ed. 1992).

American Bar Association, Model Code of Professional Responsibility.
M. Angel, Substantive Due Process and the Criminal Law, 9 Loy. U. Chi. L.J. 61 (1977).
H. Ashford & D. Risinger, Presumptions, Assumptions, and Due Process in Criminal Cases: A Theoretical Overview, 79 Yale L.J. 165 (1969).
K. K. Baker, Once a Rapist? Motivational Evidence and Relevancy in Rape Law, 110 Harv. L. Rev. 563 (1997).
S. Beale, Prior Similar Acts in Prosecutions for Rape and Child Sex Abuse, 4 Crim. L. Forum 307 (1993).
D. Bress, Professional Ethics in Criminal Trials: A View of Defense Counsel's Responsibility, 64 Mich. L. Rev. 1493 (1966).
D. Broeder, The Functions of the Jury — Facts or Fictions?, 21 U. Chi. L. Rev. 386 (1947).
D. K. Brown, Jury Nullification Within the Rule of Law, 81 Minn. L. Rev. 1149, 1185-91, (1997).
D. Bryden & R. C. Park, "Other Crimes" Evidence in Sex Offense Cases, 78 Minn. L. Rev. 529 (1994).
W. Burger, Standards of Conduct for Prosecution and Defense Personnel: A Judge's Viewpoint, 5 Am. Crim. L.Q. 11 (1966).
P. Butler, Racially Based Jury Nullification: Black Power in the Criminal Justice System, 105 Yale L. J. 677 (1995).
R. Charrow & V. Charrow, Making Legal Language Understandable: A Psycholinguistic Study of Jury Instructions, 79 Colum. L. Rev. 1306 (1979).
S. J. Clark, The Courage of Our Convictions, 97 Mich. L. Rev. 2381 (1999).
J. Conley, W. O'Barr, & E. Lind, The Power of Language: Presentational Style in the Courtroom, [1978] Duke L.J. 1375.
W. Cornish & A. Sealy, Juries and the Rules of Evidence, [1973] Crim. L. Rev. 208.
E. Dauer & A. Leff, Correspondence: The Lawyer as Friend, 86 Yale L.J. 573 (1977).
F. Dutile, The Burden of Proof in Criminal Cases: A Comment on the *Mullaney-Patterson* Doctrine, 55 Notre Dame Law. 380 (1980).
A. Elwork, B. Sales, & J. Alfini, Making Jury Instructions Understandable (1982).
A. Enker, Perspectives on Plea Bargaining, in President's Commission on Law Enforcement and the Administration of Justice, Task Force Report: The Courts (1967).
N. J. Finkel, Commonsense Justice: Jurors' Notions of the Law (1995).
G. Fletcher, Two Kinds of Legal Rules: A Comparative Study of Burden-of-Persuasion Practices in Criminal Cases, 77 Yale L.J. 880 (1968).
M. Freedman, The Aftermath of Nix v. Whiteside, 23 Crim. L. Bull. 25 (1987).
M. Freedman, Lawyers' Ethics in an Adversary System (1975).
M. Freedman, Professional Responsibility of the Criminal Defense Lawyer: The Three Hardest Questions, 64 Mich. L. Rev. 1469 (1966).
C. Fried, The Lawyer as Friend: The Moral Foundations of the Lawyer-Client Relation, 85 Yale L.J. 1060 (1976).
M. Friedland, Double Jeopardy (1969).
A. Goldman, The Moral Foundations of Professional Ethics (1980).
G. C. Harris, The Communitarian Function of the Criminal Jury Trial and the Rights of the Accused, 74 Neb. L. Rev. 804 (1995).

G. Hazard, Jr., Criminal Justice System: Overview, in 2 Encyclopedia of Crime and Justice 450 (1983).

J. Jeffries & P. Stephan, Defenses, Presumptions and Burdens of Proof in the Criminal Law, 88 Yale L.J. 1325 (1979).

M. Kadish & S. Kadish, Discretion to Disobey (1973).

M. Kadish & S. Kadish, On Justified Rule Departures by Officials, 59 Calif. L. Rev. 905, 914 (1971).

H. Kalven & H. Zeisel, The American Jury (1966).

J. Kaplan & J. Waltz, The Trial of Jack Ruby (1965).

S. Kassin & S. Wrightsman, Coerced Confessions, Judicial Instruction and Mock Juror Verdicts, 11 J. Applied Soc. Psych. 489 (1981).

R. L. Kennedy, Race, Crime, and the Law (1996).

N. J. King, The American Criminal Jury, 62 L. & Contemp. Prob. 41 (1999).

N. J. King, Silencing Nullification Advocacy Inside and Outside the Courtroom, 65 U. Chi. L. Rev. 433 (1998).

N. Lefstein, The Criminal Defendant Who Proposes Perjury, 6 Hofstra L. Rev. 665 (1978).

N. Lefstein, Legal Ethics, 1 Crim. Justice 27 (ABA 1986).

A. D. Leipold, Rethinking Jury Nullification, 82 Va. L. Rev. 253 (1996).

A. D. Leipold, The Dangers of Race-Based Jury Nullification, 44 UCLA L. Rev. 109 (1996).

L. Levin & H. Cohen, The Exclusionary Rules in Nonjury Criminal Cases, 119 U. Pa. L. Rev. 905 (1971).

P. Low & J. Jeffries, DICTA: Constitutionalizing the Criminal Law?, 29 Va. L. Weekly, No. 18, p.1 (1977).

D. Luban, Are Criminal Defenders Different?, 91 Mich. L. Rev. 1729 (1993).

G. Lynch, RICO: The Crime of Being a Criminal, Parts III & IV, 87 Colum. L. Rev. 920 (1987).

N. S. Mardear, The Myth of the Nullifying Jury, 93 Nw. U. L. Rev. 877 (1999).

R. Markus, A Theory of Trial Advocacy, 56 Tulane L. Rev. 95 (1981).

M. McLane, The Burden of Proof in Criminal Cases: *Mullaney* and *Patterson* Compared, 15 Crim. L. Bull. 346 (1979).

M. Mendez, California's New Law on Character Evidence: Evidence Code Section 352 and the Impact of Recent Psychological Studies, 31 U.C.L.A.L. Rev. 1003 (1984).

E. L. Muller, The Hobgoblin of Little Minds? Our Foolish Law of Inconsistent Verdicts, 111 Harv. L. Rev. 771 (1998).

D. Newman, Conviction 216 (1966).

C. J. Ogletree, Jr., Beyond Justifications: Seeking Motivations to Sustain Public Defenders, 106 Harv. L. Rev. 1239 (1993).

M. Orkin, Defence of One Known to Be Guilty, 1 Crim. L.Q. 170 (1958).

R. Reed, Jury Simulation: The Impact of Judge's Instructions and Attorney Tactics on Decisionmaking, 71 J. Crim. L. & Criminology 68 (1980).

C. Rieger, Client Perjury: A Proposed Resolution of the Constitutional and Ethical Issues, 70 Minn. L. Rev. 121 (1985).

S. Saltzburg, Burdens of Persuasion in Criminal Cases, 20 Am. Crim. L. Rev. 393 (1983).

S. Saltzburg, The Unnecessarily Expanding Role of the American Trial Judge, 64 Va. L. Rev. 1 (1978).

A. Scheflin, Jury Nullification: The Right to Say "No," 45 S. Cal. L. Rev. 168 (1972).

A. Scheflin & J. Van Dyke, Jury Nullification: The Contours of a Controversy, 43 L. & Contemp. Prob. 51 (1980).

W. Schwartzer, Communicating with Juries: Problems and Remedies, 69 Calif. L. Rev. 731 (1981).

L. Severance, E. Greene, & E. Loftus, Toward Criminal Jury Instructions That Jurors Can Understand, 75 J. Crim. L. & Criminology 198 (1984).

R. Simon, The Effects of Newspapers on the Verdicts of Potential Jurors, in R. Simon, The Sociology of Law (1968).

R. Simon & L. Mahan, Quantifying Burdens of Proof, 5 L. & Socy. Rev. 319 (1971).

W. Simon, The Ethics of Criminal Defense, 91 Mich. L. Rev. 1703 (1993).

W. Simon, Homo Psychologicus: Notes on a New Legal Formalism, 32 Stan. L. Rev. 487 (1980).

W. Simon, The Ideology of Advocacy, [1978] Wis. L. Rev. 29.

G. Simpson, Jury Nullification in the American System: A Skeptical View, 54 Tex. L. Rev. 488 (1976).

D. Strawn & R. Buchanan, Jury Confusion: A Threat to Justice, 59 Jud. 478 (1976).

S. Stuart, Evidentiary Use of Other Crime Evidence: A Survey of Recent Trends in Criminal Procedure, 20 Ind. L. Rev. 183 (1987).

S. Sue, R. Smith, & C. Caldwell, Effects of Inadmissible Evidence on the Decisions of Simulated Jurors: A Moral Dilemma, 3 J. Applied Soc. Psych. 345 (1973).

S. E. Sunby, The Reasonable Doubt Rule and the Meaning of Innocence, 40 Hastings L.J. 457 (1989).

S. Tanford & S. Penrod, Social Inference Processes in Juror Judgments of Multiple Offense Trials, 47 J. Personality & Soc. Psych. 749 (1984).

B. Underwood, The Thumb on the Scales of Justice: Burdens of Persuasion in Criminal Cases, 86 Yale L.J. 1299 (1977).

R. Uviller, Evidence of Character to Prove Conduct: Illusion, Illogic and Injustice in the Courtroom, 130 U. Pa. L. Rev. 845 (1982).

J. Van Dyke, The Jury as a Political Institution, The Center Magazine 17 (Mar.-Apr. 1970).

M. Vitiello, Reconsidering Rehabilitation, 65 Tulane L. Rev. 1011 (1991).

M. Walsh, The American Jury: A Reassessment, 79 Yale L.J. 142 (1969).

R. Wasserstrom, Lawyers as Professionals: Some Moral Issues, 5 Human Rights 1 (1975).

S. Wax, Inconsistent and Repugnant Verdicts in Criminal Trials, 24 N.Y.L. Sch. L. Rev. 713 (1979).

G. Williams, The Proof of Guilt (3d ed. 1963).

I. Younger, The Facts of a Case, 3 Ark. L. Rev. 345 (1980).

Comment, Inconsistent Verdicts in a Federal Criminal Trial, 60 Colum. L. Rev. 999 (1960).

Comment, Jury Nullification in Historical Perspective: Massachusetts as a Case Study, 12 Suffolk U.L. Rev. 968 (1978).

Note, Improper Evidence in Nonjury Trials: Basis for Reversal?, 79 Harv. L. Rev. 407 (1965).

Note, Winship on Rough Waters, The Erosion of the Reasonable Doubt Standard, 106 Harv. L. Rev. 1093 (1993).
President's Commission on Law Enforcement and the Administration of Justice, The Challenge of Crime in a Free Society (1967).

Chapter 2
The Justification of Punishment

H. Acton, ed., The Philosophy of Punishment (1969).
F. Allen, The Decline of the Rehabilitative Ideal — Penal Policy and Social Policy (1981).
J. Andenaes, General Prevention, 43 J. Crim. L. & Criminology 176 (1952).
J. Andenaes, The General Preventive Effects of Punishment, 114 U. Pa. L. Rev. 949 (1960).
K. Armstrong, The Retributivist Hits Back, 70 Mind 471 (1961).
T. Baker & F. Baldwin, Eighth Amendment Challenges to the Length of a Criminal Sentence: "From Precedent to Precedent," 27 Ariz. L. Rev. 25 (1985).
J. Bentham, An Introduction to the Principles of Morals and Legislation, in Bentham & Mill, The Utilitarians 162 (Dolphin Books 1961).
J. Bentham, Principles of Penal Law, in 1 J. Bentham's Works, pt. II (J. Bowring ed. 1843).
A. Blumstein & J. Cohen, Estimation of Individual Crime Rates from Arrest Records, 70 J. Crim. L. & Criminology 561 (1979).
J. Cederblom and W. Blizek, eds., Justice and Punishment (1977).
M. Clark, The Moral Gradation of Punishment, 21 Phil. Q. 132 (1971).
J. Cohen, Incapacitating Criminals: Recent Research Findings, U.S. Department of Justice, National Institute of Justice, Research in Brief (Dec. 1983).
J. Cohen, Selective Incapacitation: An Assessment, [1984] U. Ill. L. Rev. 253.
J. Cohen & J. A. Canela-Cacho, Incapacitation and Violent Crime (Natl. Academy of Sciences 1994).
M. Cohen, Moral Aspects of the Criminal Law, 49 Yale L.J. 987 (1940).
A. Denning, Freedom Under the Law (1949).
P. Devlin, The Enforcement of Morals (1965).
E. Durkheim, The Division of Labor in Society (Simpson trans. 1933).
R. Dworkin, Lord Devlin and the Enforcement of Morals, 75 Yale L.J. 986 (1966).
A. Ewing, The Morality of Punishment (1929).
A. Ewing, A Study of Punishment II: Punishment as Viewed by the Philosopher, 21 Canadian B. Rev. 102 (1943).
G. Ezorsky, ed., Philosophical Perspectives on Punishment (1972).
J. Feinberg, The Moral Limits of the Criminal Law (1984).
L. Ferrajoli & D. Zolo, Marxism and the Criminal Question, 4 L. & Phil. 71 (1985).
M. Frankel, Criminal Sentences: Law Without Order (1973).
D. Galligan, The Return to Retribution in Penal Theory, in Crime, Proof, and Punishment 144 (C. Tapper ed. 1981).
R. Gerber & P. McAnany, eds., Contemporary Punishment: Views, Explanations and Justifications (1972).
R. Gerber & P. McAnany, Punishment: Current Survey of Philosophy and Law, 11 St. Louis U.L.J. 491 (1967).

K. Greenawalt, Punishment, in Encyclopedia of Crime and Justice 1336 (1983).
P. Greenwood, with A. Abrahams, Selective Incapacitation: Report to the National Institute of Justice (1982).
S. Grupp, ed., Theories of Punishment (1971).
J. Gussfield, On Legislating Morals: The Symbolic Process of Designating Deviancy, 56 Calif. L. Rev. 54 (1968).
H. L. A. Hart, The Aims of the Criminal Law, 23 L. & Contemp. Prob. 401 (1958).
H. L. A. Hart, Law, Liberty, and Morality (1963).
H. L. A. Hart, Review of Wootton, Crime and the Criminal Law (1963), 74 Yale L.J. 1325 (1965).
H. L. A. Hart, Social Solidarity and the Enforcement of Morality, 35 U. Chi. L. Rev. 1 (1967).
D. Hoekema, Punishment, the Criminal Law, and Christian Social Ethics, 5 Crim. Just. Ethics 31 (1986).
O. W. Holmes, The Path of the Law, 10 Harv. L. Rev. 457 (1897).
G. Hughes, Criminal Responsibility, 16 Stan. L. Rev. 470 (1964).
G. Hughes, Morals and the Criminal Law, 71 Yale L.J. 662 (1962).
J. Junker, Criminalization and Criminogenesis, 19 U.C.L.A.L. Rev. 697 (1972).
S. Kadish, More on Overcriminalization: A Reply to Professor Junker, 19 U.C.L.A.L. Rev. 719 (1972).
I. Kant, The Philosophy of Law (W. Hastie trans. 1887).
L. J. Long, Rethinking Selective Incapacitation: More at Stake than Controlling Violent Crime, 62 U.M.K.C.L. Rev. 107 (1993).
J. L. Mackie, Retribution: A Test Case For Ethical Objectivity, in J. Feinberg & Hyman Gross, eds., Philosophy of Law 677 (1991).
R. Martinson, New Findings, New Views: A Note of Caution Regarding Sentencing Reform, 7 Hofstra L. Rev. 243 (1979).
R. Martinson, What Works? — Questions and Answers About Prison Reform, 36 Pub. Interest (1974).
M. Moore, Law and Psychiatry (1984).
M. Moore, The Moral Worth of Retribution, in Character, Emotions and Responsibility (F. Schoeman ed. 1988).
H. Morris, ed., Freedom and Responsibility 546 (1961).
H. Morris, On Guilt and Innocence (1976).
H. Morris, Persons and Punishment, 52 Monist 475 (1968).
N. Morris & G. Hawkins, The Honest Politician's Guide to Crime Control 4 (1970).
J. Murphy, Marxism and Retribution, 2 Phil. & Pub. Aff. 217 (1973).
K. Pecarovich, Bibliography of Responsibility, 49 L. & Contemp. Prob. 277 (1986).
E. Pincoffs, The Rationale of Legal Punishment (1966).
R. Posner, An Economic Theory of the Criminal Law, 85 Colum. L. Rev. 1193 (1985).
L. Radzinowicz & J. Turner, A Study of Punishment I: Introductory Essay, 21 Canadian B. Rev. 91 (1943).
M. Raeder, Gender and Sentencing: Single Moms, Battered Women and Other Sex-Based Anomalies in the Gender-Free World of the Federal Sentencing Guidelines, 20 Pepp. L. Rev. 905 (1993).

N. Rafter, Partial Justice: Women, Prisons, and Social Control (2d ed. 1990).
J. Reiman, The Marxian Critique of Criminal Justice, 6 Crim. Just. Ethics 30 (1987).
D. E. Roberts, Punishing Drug Addicts Who Have Babies: Women of Color, Equality, and the Right of Privacy, 104 Harv. L. Rev. 1419 (1991).
S. Schulhofer, Due Process of Sentencing, 128 U. Pa. L. Rev. 733 (1980).
L. Seidman, Soldiers, Martyrs, and Criminals: Utilitarian Theory and the Problem of Crime Control, 94 Yale L.J. 315 (1984).
T. Sellin, The Law and Some Aspects of Criminal Conduct, in Aims and Methods of Legal Research (A. Conard ed. 1955).
S. Shavell, Criminal Law and the Optimal Use of Nonmonetary Sanctions as a Deterrent, 85 Colum. L. Rev. 1232 (1985).
J. Skolnick, Criminalization and Criminogenesis: A Reply to Professor Junker, 19 U.C.L.A.L. Rev. 715 (1972).
Steinberger, Hegel on Crime and Punishment, 77 Am. Pol. Sci. Rev. 858 (1983).
J. Stephen, Liberty, Equality, Fraternity (R. J. White ed. 1967).
G. Sykes, The Society of Captives (1971).
M. Tonry, Sentencing Reform Impacts (1987).
A. Von Hirsch, K. Knapp, & M. Tonry, The Sentencing Commission and Its Guidelines (1987).
N. Walker, The Efficacy and Morality of Deterrents, [1979] Crim. L. Rev. 129.
N. Walker, Punishment, Danger and Stigma: The Morality of Criminal Justice (1980).
R. Wasserstrom, Philosophy and Social Issues (1980).
A. Wertheimer, Should Punishment Fit the Crime?, 3 Soc. Theory & Prac. 403 (1975).
F. Zimring, Making the Punishment Fit the Crime: A Consumer's Guide to Sentencing Reform, Hastings Center Rep. (Dec. 1976).
F. Zimring & G. Hawkins, Deterrence: The Legal Threat in Crime Control (1973).
F. Zimring & G. Hawkins, Incapacitation: Penal Confinement and the Restraint of Crime (1995).

California Assembly Committee on Criminal Procedure, Progress Report, Deterrent Effects of Criminal Sanctions (May 1968).
Home Office Scottish Home Department, Report of the Committee on Homosexual Offenses and Prostitution (Wolfenden Report 1957).
Note, Selective Incapacitation: Reducing Crime Through Prediction of Recidivism, 96 Harv. L. Rev. 511 (1982).
Note, Survey on the Constitutional Right to Privacy in the Context of Homosexual Activity, 40 Miami U.L. Rev. 521 (1986).
Royal Commission on Capital Punishment, Minutes of Evidence (1949).

Chapter 3
Defining Criminal Conduct

N. Abrams, Criminal Liability of Corporate Officers for Strict Liability Offenses — A Comment on *Dotterweich* and *Park,* 28 U.C.L.A.L. Rev. 463 (1981).

A. Ashworth & E. Steiner, Criminal Omissions and Public Duties: The French Experience, 10 Leg. Stud. 153 (1990).

J. Beale, Consent in the Criminal Law, 8 Harv. L. Rev. 317 (1895).

J. C. Blue, High Noon Revisited: Commands of Assistance by Peace Officers in the Age of the Fourth Amendment, 101 Yale L.J. 1475 (1992).

V. Bolgar, the Present Function of the Maxim Ignorantia Juris Neminem Excusat — A Comparative Study, 52 Iowa L. Rev. 626 (1967).

J. Brady, Strict Liability Offenses: A Justification, 8 Crim. L. Bull. 217 (1973).

P. Brett, An Inquiry into Criminal Guilt (1963).

P. Brett, Mistake of Law as a Criminal Defense, 5 Melb. U.L. Rev. 179 (1966).

K. Brickey, Criminal Liability of Corporate Officers for Strict Liability — Another View, 35 Vand. L. Rev. 1337 (1982).

K. Brickey, Developments in the Law — Corporate Crime: Regulating Corporate Behavior Through Criminal Sanctions, 92 Harv. L. Rev. 1227 (1979).

M. Budd & J. Lynch, Voluntariness, Causation and Strict Liability, [1978] Crim. L. Rev. 74.

J. Campbell, A Strict Accountability Approach to Criminal Responsibility, 29 Fed. Prob. 333 (1965).

R. Charlow, Wilful Ignorance and Criminal Culpability, 70 Tex. L. Rev. 1351 (1992).

D. Cowley, The Retreat from *Morgan*, [1982] Crim. L. Rev. 200.

E. Curley, Excusing Rape, 5 Phil. & Pub. Aff. 325 (1976).

M. Davis, Strict Liability: Deserved Conduct for Faultless Conduct, 33 Wayne L. Rev. 1393 (1987).

F. R. Denton, The Case Against a Duty to Rescue, 4 Can. J. L. & Juris. 101 (1991).

R. Dresser, Culpability and Other Minds, 2 Law and: 41 (1992).

G. Dworkin & G. Blumenfeld, Punishment for Intentions, 75 Mind 396 (1966).

S. Estrich, Real Rape (1987).

F. Feldbrugge, Good and Bad Samaritans — A Comparative Survey of Criminal Law Provisions Concerning Failure to Rescue, 14 Am. J. Comp. L. 630 (1966).

P. Foot, Life and Death, Lond. Rev. of Books, Aug. 7, 1986.

M. Gardner, The Mens Rea Enigma: Observations on the Role of Motive in the Criminal Law Past and Present, 1993 Utah L. Rev. 635.

A. Goldstein, Conspiracy to Defraud the United States, 68 Yale L.J. 405 (1959).

A. Goodhart, Possession of Drugs and Absolute Liability, 84 L.Q. Rev. 382 (1968).

H. L. A. Hart & A. Honoré, Causation in the Law (2d ed. 1985).

S. J. Heyman, Foundations of the Duty to Rescue, 47 Vand. L. Rev. 673 (1994).

L. Houlgate, Ignorantia Juris: A Plea for Justice, 78 Ethics 32 (1967).

D. Husak, Motive and Criminal Liability, 8 Crim. Just. Ethics 3 (1989).

D. Husak & C. Callender, Wilful Ignorance, Knowledge, and the "Equal Culpability Thesis": A Study of the Deeper Significance of the Principle of Legality, 1994 Wis. L. Rev. 26.

D. Husak & A. von Hirsch, Culpability and Mistake of Law, in Action and Value in Criminal Law 157-174 (J. Gardner, J. Horder, and S. Shute, eds., 1993).

J. Jeffries, Legality, Vagueness and the Construction of Penal Statutes, 71 Va. L. Rev. 189 (1985).

J. Jeffries & P. Stephan, Defenses, Presumptions, and Burden of Proof in the Criminal Law, 88 Yale L.J. 1325 (1979).

P. Johnson, Strict Liability: The Prevalent View, in Encyclopedia of Crime and Justice 1518 (1983).
S. Kadish, The Decline of Innocence, 26 Cambridge L.J. 273 (1968).
M. Kelman, Interpretive Construction in the Substantive Criminal Law, 33 Stan. L. Rev. 591 (1981).
M. Kelman, Strict Liability: An Unorthodox View, in Encyclopedia of Crime and Justice 1512 (1983).
D. Kiesel, Who Saw This Happen — States Move to Make Crime Bystanders Responsible, 69 A.B.A.J. 1208 (1983).
J. Kleinig, Good Samaritanism, 5 Phil. & Pub. Aff. 382 (1975).
R. Leng, Death and the Criminal Law, 45 Mod. L. Rev. 206 (1982).
L. L. Levenson, Good Faith Defenses: Reshaping Strict Liability Crimes, 78 Cornell L. Rev. 401 (1993).
J. Lindgren, Death by Default, 56 Law & Contemp. Prob. 185 (1993).
J. Marshall, Intention — in Law and Society (1968).
J. Michael & H. Wechsler, A Rationale of the Law of Homicide, 37 Colum. L. Rev. 701 (1937).
B. Mitchell, Law, Morality and Religion in a Secular Society (1967).
M. S. Moore, Act and Crime — The Philosophy of Action and Its Implications for the Criminal Law (1993).
N. Morris, Somnambulistic Homicide: Ghosts, Spiders, and North Koreans, 5 Res Judicatae 29 (1951).
J. Murphy, Involuntary Acts and Criminal Liability, 81 Ethics 332 (1971).
M. Orne, Review of Reiter, Antisocial or Criminal Acts and Hypnosis: A Case Study, 46 A.B.A.J. 81 (1960).
E. Puttkammer, Consent in Criminal Assault, 19 Ill. L. Rev. 617 (1925).
J. Rachels, Active and Passive Euthanasia, 292 New Eng. J. Med. 78 (1975).
I. Robbins, The Ostrich Instruction: Deliberate Ignorance as a Criminal Mens Rea, 81 J. Crim. L. & Criminology 191 (1990).
D. E. Roberts, Motherhood and Crime, 79 Iowa L. Rev. 95 (1993).
P. Robinson, A Brief History of Distinctions in Criminal Culpability, 31 Hastings L. Rev. 815 (1980).
P. Robinson, Criminal Liability for Omissions: A Brief Summary and Critique of the Law in the United States, 29 N.Y.L. Sch. L. Rev. 101 (1984).
P. Robinson, Hate Crimes: Crimes of Motive, Character, or Group Terror?, 1992/1993 Annual Survey of American Law 605.
P. Robinson & J. Grall, Element Analysis in Defining Criminal Liability: The Model Penal Code and Beyond, 35 Stan. L. Rev. 681 (1983).
J. Sams, The Availability of the "Cultural Defense" as an Excuse for Criminal Behavior, 16 Ga. J. Intl. & Comp. L. 335 (1986).
F. Sayre, Public Welfare Offenses, 33 Colum. L. Rev. 55 (1933).
S. Schulhofer, Harm and Punishment: A Critique of Emphasis on the Results of Conduct in the Criminal Law, 122 U. Pa. L. Rev. 1497 (1974).
L. Schwartz, Reform of the Federal Criminal Laws: Issues, Tactics and Prospects, [1977] Duke L.J. 171.
K. W. Simons, Rethinking Mental States, 72 B.U.L. Rev. 463 (1992).
J. Smith, Liability for Omissions in Criminal Law, 14 Leg. Stud. 88 (1984).
M. Thornton, Intention in Criminal Law, 5 Can. J.L. & Juris. 177 (1992).
M. Vitiello, Does Culpability Matter?: Statutory Construction Under 42 U.S.C. §6928, 6 Tulane Env. L.J. 187 (1993).

R. Wasserstrom, Strict Liability in the Criminal Law, 12 Stan. L. Rev. 731 (1960).
T. Weinstein, Visiting the Sins of the Child on the Parent: The Legality of Criminal Parental Liability Statutes, 64 S. Cal. L. Rev. 859 (1991).
G. Williams, Consent and Public Policy, [1962] Crim. L. Rev. 74.
G. Williams, Euthanasia, 41 Med.-Leg. J. 14 (1973).
G. Williams, The Mental Element in Crime (1965).
G. Williams, Oblique Intention, 46 Camb. L.J. 417 (1987).
G. Williams, The Unresolved Problem of Recklessness, 8 Leg. Studies 74 (1988).
B. Wootton, Crime and the Criminal Law (1963).
D. B. Yaeger, A Radical Community of Aid: A Rejoinder to Opponents of Affirmative Duties to Help Strangers, 71 Wash. U.L.Q. 1, 15 (1993).

Annot., Consent as defense to charge of mayhem, 86 A.L.R.2d 268 (1962).
Annot., Homicide: Physician's withdrawal of life supports from comatose patient, 47 A.L.R.4th 19 (1986).
California Joint Legislative Committee for Revision of the Penal Code, Penal Code Revision Project (Tent. Draft No. 2, 1968).
Comment, United States v. Barker: Misapplication of the Reliance on an Official Interpretation of the Law Defense, 66 Calif. L. Rev. 809 (1978).
Note, Common Law Crimes in the United States, 47 Colum. L. Rev. 1332 (1947).
Note, Criminal Liability Without Fault: A Philosophical Perspective, 75 Colum. L. Rev. 1517 (1975).
Note, Cultural Defenses: One Person's Culture Is Another Person's Crime, 9 Loy. L.A. Intl. & Comp. L.J. 751 (1987).
Note, The Cultural Defense in the Criminal Law, 99 Harv. L. Rev. 1293 (1986).
Note, Declaratory Relief in the Criminal Law, 80 Harv. L. Rev. 1490 (1967).
Note, Developments in the Law — Corporate Crime: Regulating Corporate Behavior Through Criminal Sanctions, 92 Harv. L. Rev. 1227 (1979).
Note (J. DeMarco), A Funny Thing Happened on the Way to the Courthouse: Mens Rea, Document Destruction, and the Federal Obstruction of Justice Statute, 67 N.Y.U.L. Rev. 570 (1992).
Note, Hypnotism and the Law, 14 Vand. L. Rev. 1509 (1961).
Note (J. Marcus), Model Penal Code Section 2.02(7) and Willful Blindness, 102 Yale L.J. 2231 (1993).
Note, Sports Violence as Criminal Assault: Development of the Doctrine by Canadian Courts, [1986] Duke L.J. 1030.
Note, The Tragic Choice: Termination of Care for Patients in a Permanent Vegetative State, 51 N.Y.U.L. Rev. 285 (1976).
Note (A. F. Brooke), When Ignorance of the Law Became an Excuse: *Lambert* and Its Progeny, 19 Am. J. Crim. L. 279 (1992).
A Symposium on Punishment: Critique and Justification, 33 Rutgers L. Rev. 607 (1981).

Chapter 4
Rape

M. Amir, Patterns in Forcible Rape (1971).
M. J. Anderson, Reviving Resistance in Rape Law, 1998 U. Ill. L. Rev. 953.

V. Berger, Man's Trial, Woman's Tribulation: Rape Cases in the Courtroom, 77 Colum. L. Rev. 1 (1977).
V. Berger, Not So Simple Rape, 7 Crim. J. Ethics 69 (1988).
D. P. Bryden, Redefining Rape, 3 Buffalo Crim. L. Rev. 317 (2000).
R. Cavallaro, A Big Mistake: Eroding the Defense of Mistake of Fact About Consent in Rape, 86 J. Crim. L. & Criminology 815 (1996).
M. Chamallas, Consent, Equality and the Legal Control of Sexual Conduct, 61 S. Cal. L. Rev. 777 (1988).
K. C. Connerton, The Resurgence of the Marital Rape Exemption, 61 Alb. L. Rev. 237 (1997).
Developments in the Law — Domestic Violence, 106 Harv. L. Rev. 1498 (1993).
D. A. Dripps, Beyond Rape: An Essay on the Difference Between the Presence of Force and the Absence of Consent, 92 Colum. L. Rev. 1780 (1992).
S. Estrich, Palm Beach Stories, 11 Law & Phil. 5 (1992).
S. Estrich, Real Rape (1987).
S. Estrich, Teaching Rape Law, 102 Yale L.J. 509 (1992).
P. J. Falk, Rape by Fraud and Rape by Coercion, 64 Brooklyn L. Rev. 39 (1998).
S. Friedland, Date Rape and the Culture of Acceptance, 43 Fla. L. Rev. 487 (1991).
I. Frieze, Investigating the Causes and Consequences of Marital Rape (1983).
N. Gilbert, The Phantom Epidemic of Sexual Assault, The Public Interest 54 (Spring 1991).
S. Gordon, Reckless and Inconsiderate Rape, [1991] Crim. L. Rev. 172.
M. Gordon & S. Riger, The Female Fear: The Social Cost of Rape (1991).
V. Hans & N. Vidmar, Judging the Jury (1986).
L. Henderson, Getting to Know: Honoring Women in Law and in Fact, 2 Tex. J. Women & L. 41 (1993).
M. Hilf, Marital Privacy and Spousal Rape, 16 New Eng. L. Rev. 31 (1980).
D. Husak & G. C. Thomas III, Date Rape, Social Convention and Reasonable Mistakes, 11 Law & Phil. 95 (1992).
M. Koss, et al., The Scope of Rape, 55 J. Consulting & Clinical Psych. 162 (1987).
J. Larson, "Women Understand So Little, They Call My Good Nature 'Deceit'": A Feminist Rethinking of Seduction, 93 Colum. L. Rev. 374 (1993).
W. Loh, The Impact of Common Law and Reform Rape Statutes on Prosecution: An Empirical Study, 55 Wash. L. Rev. 543 (1980).
C. MacKinnon, Feminism, Marxism, Method, and the State: Toward a Feminist Jurisprudence, 8 Signs 635 (1983).
C. MacKinnon, Feminism Unmodified (1987).
J. Marsh, A. Geist & N. Caplan, Rape and the Limits of Law Reform (1982).
L. Pineau, Date Rape: A Feminist Analysis, 8 Law & Phil. 217 (1989).
D. Russell, Rape in Marriage (2d ed. 1990).
S. J. Schulhofer, Unwanted Sex (1998).
S. Schulhofer, The Gender Question in Criminal Law, 7 Soc. Phil. & Pol. 105 (1990).
S. Schulhofer, Taking Sexual Autonomy Seriously: Rape Law and Beyond, 11 Law & Phil. 35 (1992).
C. C. Spohn, The Rape Reform Movement: The Traditional Common Law and Rape Law Reforms, 39 Jurimetrics 199 (1999).
E. Stanko, Intimate Intrusions (1985).

J. Tanford & A. Bocchino, Rape Victim Shield Laws and the Sixth Amendment, 128 U. Pa. L. Rev. 544 (1980).
R. Weiner, Shifting the Communication Burden: A Meaningful Consent Standard in Rape, 6 Harv. Women's L.J. 143 (1983).
C. Wells, Swatting the Subjectivist Bug, [1982] Crim. L. Rev. 209.
A. Wertheimer, Consent and Sexual Relations, 2 Legal Theory 89 (1996).
R. West, The Difference in Women's Hedonic Lives, 3 Wis. Women's L.J. 81 (1987).

Comment, Towards a Consent Standard in the Law of Rape, 43 U. Chi. L. Rev. 613 (1976).

Chapter 5
Homicide

A. J. Ashworth, The Doctrine of Provocation, 35 Camb. L.J. 292 (1976).
D. C. Baldus, G. G. Woodworth & C. A. Pulaski, Equal Justice and the Death Penalty (1990).
W. C. Bailey & R. D. Peterson, Murder, Capital Punishment, and Deterrence, in The Death Penalty in America: Current Controversies (H. Bedau ed., 1997).
J. Barzun, In Favor of Capital Punishment, 31 Am. Scholar 181 (Spring 1962).
H. A. Bedau, Innocence and the Death Penalty, in The Death Penalty in America: Current Controversies (H. Bedau ed., 1997).
H. Bedau, The Case Against the Death Penalty (1977).
H. Bedau, The Courts, the Constitution, and Capital Punishment (1977).
H. Bedau, Death as Punishment (1964).
H. Bedau, ed., The Death Penalty in America (1964).
H. Bedau & M. Radelet, Miscarriages of Justice in Potentially Capital Cases, 40 Stan. L. Rev. 21 (1987).
R. A. Berk, R. Weiss & J. Boger, Chance and the Death Penalty, 27 Law & Socy. Rev. 89 (1993).
W. Berns, For Capital Punishment (1979).
C. Black, Capital Punishment: The Inevitability of Caprice and Mistake 29 (2d ed. 1981).
S. B. Bright, Counsel for the Poor: The Death Sentence Not for the Worst Crime but for the Worst Lawyer, 103 Yale L. J. 1835 (1994).
B. Cardozo, What Medicine Can Do for Law, in Law and Literature and Other Essays and Addresses (1931).
D. K. Coker, Heat of Passion and Wife Killing: Men Who Batter/Men Who Kill, 2 S. Cal. Rev. L. & Women's Stud. 71 (1992).
K. Cole, Killings During Crime: Toward a Discriminating Theory of Strict Liability, 28 Am. Crim. L. Rev. 73 (1990).
R. A. Collings, Jr., Negligent Murder — Some Stateside Footnotes to D.P.P. v. Smith, 49 Calif. L. Rev. 254 (1961).
P. L. Crocker, Feminism and Defending Men on Death Row, 29 St. Mary's L. J. 981 (1998).
D. Crump & S. W. Crump, In Defense of the Felony-Murder Doctrine, 8 Harv. J.L. & Pub. Pol. 359 (1985).

D. A. Donovan & S. Wildman, Is the Reasonable Man Obsolete? A Critical Perspective on Self-Defense and Provocation, 14 Loy. L.A.L. Rev. 435 (1981).

J. Dressler, Rethinking Heat of Passion: A Defense in Search of a Rationale, 73 J. Crim. L. & Criminology 421 (1982).

J. Dwyer, P. Neufeld & B. Scheck, Actual Innocence (2000).

I. Ehrlich, The Deterrent Effect of Capital Punishment: A Question of Life and Death, 65 Am. Econ. Rev. 397 (1975).

G. Fletcher, Reflections on Felony-Murder, 12 Sw. U.L. Rev. 413 (1981).

G. Fletcher, The Theory of Criminal Negligence: A Comparative Analysis, 119 U. Pa. L. Rev. 401 (1971).

S. R. Gross, Lost Lives: Miscarriages of Justice in Capital Cases, 61 L. & Contemp. Prob. 125 (1998).

S. Gross, Race and Death: The Judicial Evaluation of Evidence of Discrimination in Capital Sentencing, 18 U.C. Davis L. Rev. 1275 (1985).

J. Horder, Provocation and Responsibility (1992).

P. E. Johnson, Foreword: The Accidental Decision and How It Happens, 65 Calif. L. Rev. 231 (1977).

R. Lempert, Deterrence and Desert: An Assessment of the Moral Bases for Capital Punishment, 79 Mich. L. Rev. 1177 (1981).

L. S. Lustberg & J. V. Jacobi, The Battered Woman as a Reasonable Person: A Critique of the Appellate Division Decision in *State v. McClain,* 22 Seton Hall L. Rev. 365 (1992).

T. B. Macaulay, A Penal Code Prepared by the Indian Law Commissioners (1837).

M. Meltsner, Cruel and Unusual: The Supreme Court and Capital Punishment (1973).

J. Michael & H. Wechsler, A Rationale of the Law of Homicide, 37 Colum. L. Rev. 1261 (1937).

S. J. Morse, Diminished Capacity: A Moral and Legal Conundrum, 2 Intl. J.L. & Psych. 271 (1979).

S. J. Morse, Undiminished Confusion in Diminished Capacity, 75 J. Crim. L. & Criminology 1 (1984).

S. H. Pillsbury, Evil and the Law of Murder, 24 U.C. Davis L. Rev. 437 (1990).

M. L. Radelet, H. A. Bedau & C. E. Putnam, In Spite of Innocence: Erroneous Convictions in Capital Cases (1993).

E. Rapaport, The Death Penalty and Gender Discrimination, 25 Law & Socy. Rev. 367 (1991).

R. A. Rosen, Felony Murder and the Eighth Amendment Jurisprudence of Death, 31 B.C.L. Rev. 1103 (1990).

N. E. Roth & S. E. Sunby, The Felony-Murder Rule: A Doctrine at Constitutional Crossroads, 70 Cornell L. Rev. 446 (1985).

J. W. Salmond, Jurisprudence (8th ed. 1930).

S. Schulhofer, Harm and Punishment: A Critique of Emphasis on the Results of Conduct in the Criminal Law, 122 U. Pa. L. Rev. 1497 (1974).

T. Sellin, The Death Penalty, A Report for the Model Penal Code Project of the American Law Institute (1959).

R. Singer, The Resurgence of Mens Rea: I — Provocation, Emotional Disturbance, and the Model Penal Code, 27 B.C.L. Rev. 243 (1986).

J. C. Smith, The Element of Chance in Criminal Liability, [1971] Crim. L. Rev. 63.

C. S. Steiker & J. M. Steiker, Sober Second Thoughts: Reflections on Two Decades of Constitutional Regulation of Capital Punishment, 109 Harv. L. Rev. 355 (1995).

J. F. Stephen, A History of the Criminal Law (Vol. 3) (1883).

S. E. Sunby, The Lockett Paradox: Reconciling Guided Discretion and Unguided Mitigation in Capital Sentencing, 38 U.C.L.A.L. Rev. 1147 (1991).

E. Van Den Haag, On Deterrence and the Death Penalty, 60 J. Crim. L. & Criminology 141 (1969).

E. Van Den Haag, Punishing Criminals (1975).

H. Wechsler, The Challenge of a Model Penal Code, 65 Harv. L. Rev. 1097 (1952).

W. White, Capital Punishment's Future, 91 Mich. L. Rev. 1429 (1993).

W. White, The Death Penalty in the Eighties (1987).

W. White, Life in the Balance (1984).

G. Williams, Provocation and the Reasonable Man, [1954] Crim. L. Rev. 740.

F. Zimring & G. Hawkins, Capital Punishment and the American Agenda (1986).

Annot., Unintentional killing of or injury to third person during attempted self-defense, 55 A.L.R.3d 620 (1974).

Comment (R. Mison), Homophobia in Manslaughter: The Homosexual Advance as Insufficient Provocation, 80 Cal. L. Rev. 133 (1992).

Note, Merger and the California Felony-Murder Rule, 20 U.C.L.A.L. Rev. 250 (1972).

Note, The California Supreme Court Assaults the Felony-Murder Rule, 22 Stan. L. Rev. 1059 (1970).

Report of the Royal Commission on Capital Punishment, 1949-1953, 25-28 (1953).

Chapter 6
The Significance of Resulting Harm

T. Arnold, Criminal Attempts — The Rise and Fall of an Abstraction, 40 Yale L.J. 53 (1930).

S. Brenner, Undue Influence in the Criminal Law: A Proposed Analysis of the Criminal Offense of Causing Suicide, 47 Albany L. Rev. 62 (1982).

R. Buxton, Circumstances, Consequences and Attempted Rape, [1984] Crim. L. Rev. 25.

M. Dan-Cohen, Causation, in 1 Encyclopedia of Crime and Justice 165 (1983).

R. A. Duff, The Circumstances of an Attempt, 50 Camb. L.J. 100 (1991).

F. Dutile & H. Moore, Mistake and Impossibility: Arranging a Marriage Between Two Difficult Partners, 74 Nw. U.L. Rev. 166 (1979).

I. Elliott, Australian Letter, [1969] Crim. L. Rev. 511.

A. Enker, Mens Rea and Criminal Attempt, [1977] Am. B. Found. Res. J. 845.

R. P. Faulkner & D. H. Hsiao, And Where You Go I'll Follow: The Constitutionality of Antistalking Laws and Proposed Model Legislation, 31 Harv. J. Legis. 1 (1994).

G. Fletcher, Constructing a Theory of Impossible Attempts, 5 Crim. J. Ethics 53 (1986).

K. Greenawalt, Speech and Crime, [1980] Am. B. Found. Res. J. 645.

H. L. A. Hart & A. Honoré, Causation in the Law (1958).

P. Hasset, Absolutism in Causation, 38 Syracuse L. Rev. 683 (1987).
G. Hughes, One Further Footnote on Attempting the Impossible, 42 N.Y.U.L. Rev. 1005 (1967).
D. Husak, Transferred Intent, 10 Notre Dame J. L. Ethics & Pub. Poly. 65 (1996).
S. H. Kadish, The Criminal Law and the Luck of the Draw, 84 J. Crim. L. & Criminology 679 (1994).
M. Kelman, Interpretive Construction in the Substantive Criminal Law, 33 Stan. L. Rev. 591 (1981).
D. Lanham, Murder by Instigating Suicide, [1980] Crim. L. Rev. 213.
G. Marston, Contemporaneity of Act and Intention in Crimes, 86 L.Q. Rev. 208 (1970).
A. McIntyre, Guilty Bystanders? On the Legitimacy of Duty to Rescue Statutes, 23 Phil. & Pub. Aff. 157 (1994).
R. Misner, The New Attempt Laws: An Unsuspected Threat to the Fourth Amendment, 33 Stan. L. Rev. 201 (1981).
M. Moore, Act and Crime — The Philosophy of Action and Its Implications for Criminal Law (1993).
M. Moore, Foreseeing Harm Opaquely, In Action and Value in Criminal Law (S. Shute et al., eds. 1993).
M. S. Moore, Causation and Responsibility, 16 So. Philos. & Policy 1 (Summer 1999).
D. G. Moriarty, Extending the Defense of Renunciation, 62 Temple L. Rev. 1 (1989).
R. Perkins, An Analysis of Assault and Attempts to Assault, 47 Minn. L. Rev. 71 (1962).
R. Perkins, Criminal Attempt and Related Problems, 2 U.C.L.A.L. Rev. 319 (1955).
I. Robbins, Attempting the Impossible: The Emerging Consensus, 23 Harv. J. Legisl. 377 (1986).
I. Robbins, Double Inchoate Crimes, 26 Harv. J. Legis. 1 (1989).
P. Robinson, Imputed Criminal Liability, 93 Yale L.J. 609 (1984).
S. Schulhofer, Attempt, in 1 Encyclopedia of Crime and Justice 97 (1983).
S. Schulhofer, Harm and Punishment: A Critique of Emphasis on the Results of Conduct in the Criminal Law, 122 U. Pa. L. Rev. 1497 (1974).
S. Shavell, Deterrence and the Punishment of Attempts, 19 J. Legal Stud. 435 (1990).
J. Smith, The Element of Chance in Criminal Liability, [1971] Crim. L. Rev. 63.
J. C. Smith & B. Hogan, Criminal Law 46 (7th ed. 1992).
J. Waite, The Prevention of Repeated Crime (1943).
T. Weigend, Why Lady Eldon Should be Acquitted: The Social Harm in Attempting the Impossible, 27 De Paul L. Rev. 231 (1979).
G. Williams, *Finis* for *Novus Actus,* 48 Camb. L.J. 391 (1989).
G. Williams, Police Control of Intending Criminals, [1955] Crim. L. Rev. 66.
G. Williams, The Problem of Reckless Attempts, [1983] Crim. L. Rev. 365.
D. B. Yeager, Dangerous Games and the Criminal Law, Crim. J. Ethics 3 (Winter/Spring 1997).

Comment on *Stephenson,* 31 Mich. L. Rev. 659 (1933).
Note (M. J. Gilligan), Stalking the Stalker: Developing New Laws to Thwart Those Who Terrorize Others, 27 Ga. L. Rev. 285 (1992).

Chapter 7
Group Criminality

J. Arlen, The Potentially Perverse Effects of Corporate Criminal Liability, 23 J. Legal Stud. 833 (1994).

M. B. Bixby, Workplace Homicide: Trends, Issues, and Policy, 70 Or. L. Rev. 333 (1991).

S. W. Brenner, RICO, CCE, and Other Complex Crimes: The Transformation of American Criminal Law?, 2 Wm. & Mary Bill of Rights J. 239 (1993).

K. Brickey, Corporate Criminal Liability, A Primer for Corporate Counsel, 40 Bus. Law. 129 (1984).

K. Brickey, Corporate Criminal Liability: A Treatise on the Criminal Liability of Corporations, Their Officers and Agents (2d ed. 1992).

K. Brickey, Death in the Workplace: Corporate Liability for Criminal Homicide, 2 Notre Dame J. L., Ethics & Pub. Pol. 753 (1987).

P. H. Bucy, Corporate Ethos: A Standard for Imposing Corporate Criminal Liability, 75 Minn. L. Rev. 1095 (1991).

D. Burgman, Unilateral Conspiracy: Three Critical Perspectives, 29 De Paul L. Rev. 75 (1979).

S. Burke, RICO, 24 Am. Crim. L. Rev. 651 (1987).

J. Coffee, Corporate Criminal Responsibility, in Encyclopedia of Crime and Justice 253 (1983).

P. Cook, The Use of Criminal Sanctions to Regulate Product Safety: Comment on Wheeler, 13 J. Leg. Stud. 619 (1984).

T. Cousens, Agreement as an Element of Conspiracy, 23 Va. L. Rev. 898 (1937).

F. Cullen, Corporate Crime Under Attack: The Ford Pinto Case and Beyond (1987).

J. Dressler, Reassessing the Theoretical Underpinnings of Accomplice Liability: New Solutions to an Old Problem, 37 Hastings L. Rev. 91 (1985).

R. A. Duff, "Can I Help You?" Accessorial Liability and the Intention to Assist, 10 Legal Stud. 167 (1990).

R. Farrell & V. Swigert, Corporate Homicide: Definitional Processes in the Creation of Deviance, 15 L. & Socy. Rev. 161 (1980).

D. Fischel & A. Sykes, Civil RICO after *Reves:* An Economic Commentary, [1993] Sup. Ct. Rev. 157.

B. Fisse, Reconstructing Corporate Criminal Law: Deterrence, Retribution, Fault and Sanctions, 56 S. Cal. L. Rev. 114 (1983).

M. Goldsmith, RICO and Enterprise Criminality: A Response to Gerard E. Lynch, 88 Colum. L. Rev. 774 (1988).

A. Goldstein, Conspiracy to Defraud the United States, 68 Yale L.J. 405 (1959).

P. J. Henning, Individual Liability for Conduct by Criminal Organizations in the United States, 44 Wayne L. Rev., 1305 (1998).

J. F. Holderman, Reconciling RICO's Conspiracy and "Group" Enterprise Concepts with Traditional Conspiracy Doctrine, 52 U. Cin. L.R. 385 (1983).

D. Husak, Justifications and the Criminal Liability of Accessories, 80 J. Crim. L. & Criminology 491 (1989).

P. Johnson, The Unnecessary Crime of Conspiracy, 61 Calif. L. Rev. 1137 (1973).

S. Kadish, Some Observations on the Use of Criminal Sanctions in Enforcing Economic Regulations, 30 U. Chi. L. Rev. 423 (1963).

S. Kadish, A Theory of Complicity, in Issues in Contemporary Legal Philosophy: The Influence of H. L. A. Hart 288 (Ruth Gavison ed. 1987).
D. Lanham, Drivers, Control and Accomplices, [1982] Crim. L. Rev. 419.
E. Lederman, Criminal Law, Perpetrator and Corporations: Rethinking a Complex Triangle, 76 J. Crim. L. & Criminology 285 (1985).
G. Lynch, RICO: The Crime of Being a Criminal, 87 Colum. L. Rev. 920 (1987).
G. E. Lynch, A Reply to Michael Goldsmith, 88 Colum. L. Rev. 802 (1988).
P. Marcus, Criminal Conspiracy Law: Time to Turn Back from an Ever Expanding, Ever More Troubling Area, 1 Wm. & Mary Bill of Rights J. 1 (1992).
J. Moore, Corporate Culpability and the Federal Sentencing Guidelines, 34 Ariz. L. Rev. 743 (1992).
C. Morris, Punitive Damages in Personal Injury Cases, 21 Ohio St. L.J. 216 (1960).
R. Posner, Retribution and Related Concepts of Punishment, 9 J. Leg. Stud. 71 (1980).
I. Robbins, Double Inchoate Crimes, 26 Harv. J. Legis. 1 (1989).
D. E. Roberts, Motherhood and Crime, 79 Iowa L. Rev. 95 (1993).
F. Sayre, Criminal Responsibility for the Acts of Another, 43 Harv. L. Rev. 689 (1930).
D. Sentelle, RICO: The Monster That Ate Jurisprudence (1989).
J. C. Smith, Commentary, [1991] Crim. L. Rev. 134.
J. C. Smith & B. Hogan, Criminal Law (7th ed. 1992).
W. Spurgeon & T. Fagan, Criminal Liability for Life-Endangering Corporate Conduct, 72 J. Crim. L. & Criminology 400 (1981).
B. Tarlow, RICO: The New Darling of the Prosecutor's Nursery, 49 Fordham L. Rev. 165 (1980).
B. Tarlow, RICO Revisited, 17 Ga. L. Rev. 291 (1983).
C. Wells, Corporations and Criminal Responsibility (1993).
M. Wheeler, Products Liability: Manufacturers, Wrong Targets for Threat of Criminal Sanctions?, Natl. L.J. (Dec. 22, 1980).
M. Wheeler, The Use of Criminal Statutes to Regulate Product Safety, 13 J. Leg. Stud. 593 (1984).
S. Whitzman, Proof of Conspiracy: The Co-Conspirator's Exception to the Hearsay Rule, 28 Crim. L.Q. 203 (1986).
G. Williams, Victims and Other Exempt Parties in Crime, 10 Legal Stud. 245 (1990).
S. Zipperman, The Park Doctrine — Application of Strict Criminal Liability to Corporate Individuals for Violation of Environmental Crimes, 10 U.C.L.A.J. Environ. L. 123 (1991).

Comment (J. D. Heep), Adapting the Responsible Corporate Officer Doctrine in Light of *United States v. MacDonald & Watson Waste Oil Co.,* 78 Minn. L. Rev. 699 (1994).
Comment, Corporate Homicide: Will Michigan Follow Suit?, 62 U. Det. L. Rev. 65 (1984).
Comment (D. J. Miester, Jr.), Criminal Liability for Corporations That Kill, 64 Tul. L. Rev. 919 (1990).
Comment, Whose Head Is in the Sand? Problems with the Use of the Ostrich Instruction in Conspiracy Cases, 13 W. New Eng. L. Rev. 35 (1991).

National Commission on Reform of Federal Criminal Laws, Working Papers, Vol. 1 (1970).
Note, An Analysis of Wharton's Rule, 71 Nw. U.L. Rev. 547 (1976).
Note, Conspiracy: Statutory Reform Since the Model Penal Code, 75 Colum. L.R. 1122 (1975).
Note, Conspiracy to Violate RICO: Expanding Traditional Conspiracy Law, 58 Notre Dame Law 587 (1983).
Note, Corporate Criminal Liability for Homicide, 17 Cal. West. L. Rev. 465 (1981).
Note, Corporate Homicide: A New Assault on Corporate Decision-Making, 54 Notre Dame Law. 911 (1979).
Note, Corporate Homicide: The Stark Realities of Artificial Beings and Legal Fictions, 8 Pepperdine L. Rev. 367 (1981).
Note, Developments in the Law — Corporate Crime: Regulating Corporate Behavior Through Criminal Sanctions, 92 Harv. L. Rev. 1227 (1979).
Note, Developments in the Law — Criminal Conspiracy, 72 Harv. L. Rev. 920 (1959).
Note, Economic Inefficiency of Corporate Criminal Liability, 73 J. Crim. L. & Criminology 582 (1982).
Note, The Unnecessary Rule of Consistency in Conspiracy Trials, 135 U. Pa. L. Rev. 246 (1986).
Note, The Withdrawal Defense to Criminal Conspiracy: An Unconstitutional Allocation of the Burden of Proof, 51 Geo. Wash. L. Rev. 420 (1981).

Chapter 8
Exculpation

R. Aldridge & B. Stark, Nuclear War, Citizen Intervention, and the Necessity Defense, 26 Santa Clara L. Rev. 299 (1986).
L. Alexander, The Supreme Court, Dr. Jekyll, and the Due Process of Proof, 1996 Sup. Ct. Rev. 191.
R. J. Allen, Forward: Montana v. Egelhoff — Reflections on the Limits of Legislative Imagination and Judicial Authority, 87 J. Crim. L. & Criminology 633 (1997).
V. J. Aprile, Criminal Justice Matters: Executing the Mentally Retarded, 9 Crim. L.J. 38 (Spring 1994).
P. Arenella, Convicting the Morally Blameless: Reassessing the Relationship Between Legal and Moral Accountability, 39 U.C.L.A.L. Rev. 1511 (1992).
P. Arenella, The Diminished Capacity and Diminished Responsibility Defenses: Two Children of a Doomed Marriage, 77 Colum. L. Rev. 827 (1977).
P. Arenella, Reflections on Current Proposals to Abolish or Reform the Insanity Defense, 8 Am. J.L. & Med. 271 (1982).
J. D. Armour, Race Ipsa Loquitur: Of Reasonable Racists, Intelligent Beyesians, and Involuntary Negrophobes, 46 Stan. L. Rev. 781 (1994).
E. Arnolds & N. Garland, The Defense of Necessity in Criminal Law, 65 J. Crim. L. & Criminology 289 (1974).
R. Aronson, Should the Privilege Against Self-Incrimination Apply to Compelled Psychiatric Examinations?, 26 Stan. L. Rev. 55 (1973).
J. Austin, A Plea for Excuses, 57 Proceedings Aristotelian Socy. 1 (1956-1957).

A. E. Barlow, Self-Defense and Reckless Crimes Against Third Parties, 22 Colum. J.L. & Soc. Probs. 417 (1989).
J. Blackman, Potential Uses for Expert Testimony: Ideas Toward the Representation of Battered Women Who Kill, 9 Women's Rights L. Rptr. 227 (1986).
A. Blum, Debunking Myths of the Insanity Plea, Natl. L. J., Apr. 20, 1992, at 9.
R. Boldt, The Construction of Responsibility in the Criminal Law, 140 U. Pa. L. Rev. 2245 (1992).
R. Bonnie, The Moral Basis of the Insanity Defense, 69 A.B.A.J. 194 (1983).
R. Bonnie & C. Slobogin, The Role of Mental Health Professionals in the Criminal Process: The Case for Informed Speculation, 66 Va. L. Rev. 427 (1980).
C. Boorse & R. Sorensen, Ducking Harm, 85 J. Phil. 115 (1988).
C. Boorse, Premenstrual Syndrome and Criminal Responsibility, in Premenstrual Syndrome (B. Ginsburg & B. Carter eds. 1987).
R. M. Brown, No Duty to Retreat: Violence and Values in American History and Society (1991).
B. Cardozo, Law and Literature (1930).
S. Carter, When Victims Happen to Be Black, 97 Yale L.J. 420 (1988).
R. Cipparone, The Defense of Battered Women Who Kill, 135 U. Pa. L. Rev. 427 (1987).
A. M. Coughlin, Excusing Women, 82 Cal. L. Rev. 1 (1994).
D. Creach, Partially Determined Imperfect Self-Defense, 34 Stan. L. Rev. 615 (1982).
P. L. Crocker, The Meaning of Equality for Battered Women Who Kill in Self-Defense, 8 Harv. Women's L.J. 121 (1985).
R. Cross, Reflections on *Bratty*'s Case, 78 L.Q. Rev. 236 (1962).
M. Dan-Cohen, Actus Reus, in Encyclopedia of Crime and Justice 15 (1983).
R. Delgado, Ascription of Criminal States of Mind: Toward a Defense Theory for the Coercively Persuaded ("Brainwashed") Defendant, 63 Minn. L. Rev. 1 (1978).
R. Delgado, "Rotten Social Background": Should the Criminal Law Recognize a Defense of Severe Environmental Deprivation?, 3 L. & Inequality 9 (1985).
S. Dell, Diminished Responsibility Reconsidered, [1982] Crim. L. Rev. 809.
D. Denno, Considering Lead Poisoning as a Criminal Defense, 20 Ford. Urb. L.J. 377 (1993).
A. Dershowitz, The Abuse Excuse (1994).
G. Dix, Psychological Abnormality as a Factor in Grading Criminal Liability: Diminished Capacity, Diminished Responsibility, and the Like, 62 J. Crim. L., Criminology & P.S. 313 (1971).
L. K. Doré, Downward Adjustment and the Slippery Slope: The Use of Duress in Defense of Battered Offenders, 56 Ohio St. L. J. 665 (1995).
J. Dressler, Reaffirming the Moral Legitimacy of the Doctrine of Diminished Capacity: A Brief Reply to Professor Morse, 75 J. Crim. L. & Criminology 953 (1984).
R. Dworkin, Life's Dominion 179 (1993).
J. Ellis, The Consequences of the Insanity Defense: Proposals to Reform Post-Acquittal Commitment Laws, 35 Catholic U.L. Rev. 961 (1986).
G. Epps, Any Which Way But Loose: Interpretive Strategies and Attitudes Toward Violence in the Evolution of the Anglo-American "Retreat Rule," 55 Law & Contemp. Prob. 303 (1992).

C. Erlinder, Paying the Price for Vietnam: Post-Traumatic Stress Disorder and Criminal Behavior, 25 B.C.L. Rev. 305 (1984).

S. Estrich, Defending Women (Book Review, Cynthia Gillespie, Justifiable Homicide: Battered Women, Self-Defense and the Law (1989)), 88 Mich. L. Rev. 1430 (1990).

J. Eule, The Presumption of Sanity: Bursting the Bubble, 25 U.C.L.A.L. Rev. 637 (1978).

C. P. Ewing, Battered Women Who Kill: Psychological Self-Defense as Legal Justification (1987).

D. L. Faigman, Discerning Justice When Battered Women Kill, 39 Hastings L.J. 207 (1987).

J. Feinberg, Overlooking the Merits of the Individual Case: An Unpromising Approach to the Right to Die, 4 Ratio Juris. 131 (1991).

L. Fentiman, "Guilty But Mentally Ill": The Real Verdict Is Guilty, 26 B.C.L. Rev. 601 (1985).

H. Fingarette, Addiction and Criminal Responsibility, 84 Yale L.J. 413 (1975).

H. Fingarette, Heavy Drinking (1988).

H. Fingarette, The Meaning of Criminal Insanity (1972).

H. Fingarette, The Perils of *Powell:* In Search of a Factual Foundation for the "Disease Concept of Alcoholism," 83 Harv. L. Rev. 793 (1970).

G. Fletcher, A Crime of Self Defense: Bernhard Goetz and the Law on Trial (1988).

G. Fletcher, The Individualization of Excusing Conditions, 47 S. Cal. L. Rev. 1269 (1974).

G. Fletcher, Proportionality and the Psychotic Aggressor: A Vignette in Comparative Criminal Theory, 8 Israel L. Rev. 367 (1973).

G. Fletcher, Should Intolerable Conditions Generate a Justification or an Excuse for Escape?, 26 U.C.L.A.L. Rev. 1355 (1979).

S. Fox, Physical Disorder, Consciousness, and Criminal Liability, 63 Colum. L. Rev. 645 (1963).

L. Fuller, The Case of the Speluncean Explorers, 62 Harv. L. Rev. 616 (1949).

J. Gardner, The Gist of Excuses, 2 Buffalo Crim. L. Rev. 1 (1997).

M. Gardner, The Defense of Necessity and the Right to Escape from Prison, 49 S. Cal. L. Rev. 110 (1975).

P. Glazebrook, The Necessity Plea in English Criminal Law, 30 Camb. L.J. 87 (1972).

S. P. Green, Castles and Carjackers: Proportionality and the Use of Deadly Force in Defense of Dwellings and Vehicles, 1999 U. Ill. L. Rev. 1.

K. Greenawalt, "Uncontrollable" Actions and the Eighth Amendment: Implications of Powell v. Texas, 69 Colum. L. Rev. 927 (1969).

M. Gur-Arye, Should the Criminal Law Distinguish Between Necessity as a Justification and Necessity as an Excuse?, 102 L.Q. Rev. 71 (1986).

C. Hanna, No Right to Choose: Mandated Victim Participation in Domestic Violence Prosecutions, 109 Harv. L. Rev. 1849, 1909 (1996).

V. Hans & D. Slater, John W. Hinckley, Jr. & the Insanity Defense: The Public's Verdict, 47 Public Opinion Q. 202 (1983).

P. Hassman, Annot., Drug Addiction or Related Mental State as Defense to Criminal Charge, 73 A.L.R.3d 16 (1991).

D. Hermann, Assault on the Insanity Defense, 14 Rutgers L.J. 241 (1983).

F. Hicks, Human Jettison (1927).

E. Holtzman, Premenstrual Symptoms: No Legal Defense, 60 St. John's L. Rev. 712 (1986).
J. Horder, Autonomy, Provocation and Duress, [1992] Crim. L. Rev. 70.
P. Johnson, The Turnabout in the Insanity Defense, in 6 Crime and Justice 221 (M. Tonry & N. Morris eds. 1985).
R. Johnson, Death Work 50 (1990).
M. Kadish & S. Kadish, Discretion to Disobey (1973).
S. Kadish, The Decline of Innocence, 26 Camb. L.J. 273 (1968).
S. Kadish, Letting Patients Die: Legal and Moral Reflections, 80 Cal. L. Rev. 857 (1992).
Y. Kamisar, A Law to Stay the Cold Hand of "Dr. Death," Legal Times, Mar. 8, 1993.
J. Kaplan, The Hardest Drug (1983).
J. Q. La Fond, The Case for Liberalizing the Use of Deadly Force in Self-Defense, 6 U. Puget Sound L. Rev. 237 (1983).
C. K. Y. Lee, Race and Self-Defense: Toward a Normative Conception of Reasonableness, 81 Minn. L. Rev. 367 (1996).
M. Lippman, The Necessity Defense and Political Protest, 26 Crim. L. Bull. 317 (1990).
D. Lunde & R. Wilson, Brainwashing as a Defense to Criminal Liability: Patty Hearst Revisited, 13 Crim. L. Bull. 341 (1977).
I. Mackay, The Sleepwalker Is Not Insane, 55 Mod. L. Rev. 714 (1992).
R. D. Mackay, The Consequences of Killing Very Young Children, [1993] Crim. L. Rev. 21.
C. MacKinnon, Toward Feminist Jurisprudence, 34 Stan. L. Rev. 703 (1982).
H. Maguigan, Battered Women and Self-Defense: Myths and Misconceptions in Current Reform Proposals, 140 U. Pa. L. Rev. 379 (1991).
V. M. Mather, The Skeleton in the Closet: The Battered Woman Syndrome, Self-Defense and Expert Testimony, 39 Mercer L. Rev. 545 (1988).
D. McCord, The English and American History of Voluntary Intoxication to Negate Mens Rea, 11 J. Legal Hist. 372 (1990).
D. McCord & S. K. Lyons, Moral Reasoning and the Criminal Law: The Example of Self-Defense, 30 Am. Crim. L. Rev. 97 (1992).
H. McGinley & R. A. Pasewark, National Survey of the Frequency and Success of the Insanity Pleas and Alternate Pleas, 17 J. Psychiatry & L. 205 (1989).
M. Mihajlovich, Does Plight Make Right: The Battered Woman Syndrome, Expert Testimony and the Law of Self-Defense, 62 Ind. L.J. 1253 (1987).
S. Milgram, Obedience to Authority (1974).
L. G. Mills, Killing Her Softly: Intimate Abuse and the Violence of State Intervention, 113 Harv. L. Rev. 550 (1999).
M. H. Mitchell, Does Wife Abuse Justify Homicide?, 24 Wayne L. Rev. 1705 (1978).
J. Monahan, Abolish the Insanity Defense?—Not Yet, 26 Rutgers L. Rev. 719 (1973).
M. Moore, Law and Psychiatry: Rethinking the Relationship (1984).
R. Moore, Legal Responsibility and Chronic Alcoholism, 122 Am. J. Psych. 748 (1966).
J. A. Moreno, Killing Daddy: Developing a Self-Defense Strategy for the Abused Child, 137 U. Pa. L. Rev. 1281 (1989).
N. Morris, Madness and the Criminal Law (1982).

N. Morris, Psychiatry and the Dangerous Criminal, 41 S. Cal. L. Rev. 514 (1968).
S. Morse, Diminished Capacity: A Moral and Legal Conundrum, 2 Intl. J. L. & Psych. 271 (1979).
S. J. Morse, Fear of Danger, Flight from Culpability, 4 Psychol., Pub. Pol. & L. 250 (1998).
S. Morse, Diminished Capacity, in S. Shute et al., eds., Action and Value in Criminal Law 239 (1993).
S. Morse, Failed Explanations and Criminal Responsibility: Experts and the Unconscious, 68 Va. L. Rev. 971 (1982).
S. Morse, Undiminished Confusion in Diminished Capacity, 75 J. Crim. L. & Criminology 1 (1984).
T. P. Myers, Halcion Made Me Do It: New Liability and a New Defense — Fear and Loathing in the Halcion Paper Chase, 62 U. Cin. L. Rev. 603 (1993).
D. Neely, Legal Necessity and Civil Disobedience, 74 Ill. B.J. 596 (1986).
R. Nozick, Anarchy, State and Utopia (1974).
J. Ogloff, A Comparison of Insanity Defense Standards on Juror Decision Making, 15 Law & Human Behavior 509 (1991).
J. T. Parry, The Virtue of Necessity: Reshaping Culpability and the Rule of Law, 36 Houston L. Rev. 397 (1999).
R. Pasewark, Insanity Plea: A Review of the Research Literature, 9 J. Psych. & L. 357 (1981).
S. H. Pillsbury, The Meaning of Deserved Punishment: An Essay on Choice, Character, and Responsibility, 67 Ind. L.J. 719 (1992).
L. E. Reece, Comment, Mothers Who Kill: Postpartum Disorders and Criminal Infanticide, 38 U.C.L.A.L. Rev. 699 (1991).
R. A. Rosen, On Self-Defense, Imminence, and Women Who Kill Their Batterers, 71 N.C.L. Rev. 371 (1993).
W. Roth, General Versus Specific Intent: A Time for Terminological Understanding in California, 7 Pepperdine L. Rev. 67 (1979).
L. Rubin, Quiet Rage: Bernie Goetz in a Time of Madness (1988).
E. M. Schneider, Describing and Changing: Women's Self-Defense Work and the Problem of Expert Testimony on Battering, 9 Women's Rights L. Rptr. 195 (1986).
R. F. Schopp, Automatism, Insanity and the Psychology of Criminal Responsibility (1991).
R. F. Schopp, B. J. Sturgis & M. Sullivan, Battered Woman Syndrome, Expert Testimony, and the Distinction Between Justification and Excuse, [1994] U. Ill. L. Rev. 45.
S. J. Schulhofer, The Feminist Challenge in Criminal Law, 143 U. Pa. L. Rev. 2151 (1994).
S. J. Schulhofer, The Gender Question in Criminal Law, 7 Soc. Phil. & Pol. 105 (1990).
L. Schwartz, Reform of the Federal Criminal Laws, [1977] Duke L.J. 171.
L. W. Sherman, Policing Domestic Violence: Experiments and Dilemmas (1992).
R. Simon, The Jury and the Defense of Insanity (1967).
A. Singer, The Imposition of the Insanity Defense on an Unwilling Defendant, 41 Ohio St. L.J. 637 (1980).
R. Slovenko, The Insanity Defense in the Wake of the *Hinckley* Trial, 14 Rutgers L.J. 373 (1983).
J. C. Smith, Justification and Excuse in the Criminal Law (1989).

H. J. Steadman, et al., Maintenance of an Insanity Defense Under Montana's "Abolition" of the Insanity Defense, 146 Am. J. Psychiatry 357 (1989).
A. Stone, Law, Psychiatry, and Morality (1984).
G. R. Sullivan, Bad Thoughts and Bad Acts, [1990] Crim. L. Rev. 559.
L. Taylor, Provoked Reason in Men and Women: Heat-of-Passion Manslaughter and Imperfect Self-Defense, 33 U.C.L.A.L. Rev. 1679 (1986).
C. Thomas, Crime and Punishment — and Personal Responsibility, The National Times, Sept. 1994, at 31.
L. Tiffany & C. Anderson, Legislating the Necessity Defense in Criminal Law, 52 Den. L.J. 839 (1975).
L. Tiffany & M. Tiffany, Nosologic Objection to the Criminal Defense of Pathological Intoxication: What Do the Doubters Doubt?, 13 Intl. J.L. & Psych. 49 (1990).
P. Wald, Alcohol, Drugs, and Criminal Responsibility, 63 Geo. L.J. 69 (1974).
H. Wales, An Analysis of the Proposal to "Abolish" the Insanity Defense in S. 1: Squeezing a Lemon, 124 U. Pa. L. Rev. 687 (1976).
A. Wallach & L. Rubin, The Premenstrual Syndrome and Criminal Responsibility, 19 U.C.L.A.L. Rev. 209 (1971).
D. Wasserman, Justifying Self-Defense, 16 Phil. & Pub. Aff. 356 (1987).
D. Wexler, An Offense-Victim Approach to Insanity Defense Reform, 26 Ariz. L. Rev. 17 (1984).
G. Williams, A Commentary on Regina v. Dudley and Stephens, 8 Cambrian L. Rev. 94 (1977).
W. Winslade & J. Ross, The Insanity Plea (1983).
B. Wootton, Crime and the Criminal Law (1963).
J. Zorza, The Criminal Law of Misdemeanor Domestic Violence, 83 J. Crim. L. & Criminology 46 (1992).

California Special Commission on Insanity and Criminal Offenders, First Report 30 (1962).
Casenote (James Cavallaro), The Demise of the Political Necessity Defense: Indirect Civil Disobedience and *United States v. Schoon,* 81 Cal. L. Rev. 351 (1993).
Comment (E. A. Gifford), *Artes Moriendi:* Active Euthanasia and the Art of Dying, 40 U.C.L.A.L. Rev. 1545 (1993).
Comment, The Battered Wife's Dilemma: To Kill or To Be Killed, 32 Hastings L.J. 895 (1981).
Comment, From Duress to Intent: Shifting the Burden in Prison-Escape Prosecutions, 127 U. Pa. L. Rev. 1142 (1979).
Comment, Intolerable Conditions as a Defense to Prison Escapes, 26 U.C.L.A.L. Rev. 1126 (1979).
Comment, The Law of Necessity as Applied in the Bisbee Deportation Case, 13 Ariz. L. Rev. 264 (1961).
Insanity as a Defense: A Panel Discussion, Annual Judicial Conference, Second Judicial Circuit of the United States, 37 F.R.D. 365 (1964).
The Law Commission Consultation Paper No. 127, Intoxication and Criminal Liability (1993).
The Law Commission, Consultation Paper No. 122, Legislating the Criminal Code, Offenses Against the Person and General Principles (1992).

New York State Task Force on Life and the Law, When Death Is Sought—Assisted Suicide in the Medical Context (1994).
Note, Amnesia, A Case Study in the Limits of Particular Justice, 71 Yale L.J. 109 (1961).
Note, Antinuclear Demonstrations and the Necessity Defense, 5 Vt. L. Rev. 103 (1980).
Note (Laura Schulkind), Applying the Necessity Defense, 64 N.Y.U.L. Rev. 79 (1989).
Note, The Battered Woman Syndrome and Self-Defense: A Legal and Empirical Dissent, 72 Va. L. Rev. 619 (1986).
Note, Does Plight Make Right: The Battered Woman Syndrome, Expert Testimony and the Law of Self-Defense, 62 Ind. L.J. 1263 (1987).
Note, Has the PMS Defense Gained a Legitimate Toehold in Virginia Criminal Law?, 14 Geo. Mason L. Rev. 427 (1991).
Note, Justification: The Impact of the Model Penal Code on Statutory Reform, 75 Colum. L. Rev. 914 (1975).
Note, Limits on the Use of Defensive Force to Prevent Intramarital Assaults, 10 Rut.-Cam. L.J. 643 (1979).
Note, Medical Necessity as a Defense to Criminal Liability: United States v. Randall, 46 Geo. Wash. L. Rev. 273 (1978).
Note, Necessity as a Defense to a Charge of Criminal Trespass in an Abortion Clinic, 48 Cin. L. Rev. 509 (1979).
Note, The Necessity Defense to Prison Escape After United States v. Bailey, 65 Va. L. Rev. 359 (1979).
Note, Physician-Assisted Suicide and the Right to Die with Assistance, 105 Harv. L. Rev. 2031 (1992).
Note, Political Protest and the Illinois Defense of Necessity, 54 U. Chi. L. Rev. 1070 (1987).

Chapter 9
Theft Offenses

F. Allen, A Crisis of Legality in the Criminal Law? Reflections on the Rule of Law, 42 Mercer L. Rev. 811 (1991).
F. Allen, The Erosion of Legality in American Criminal Justice: Some Latter-Day Adventures of the *Nulla Poena* Principle, 29 Ariz. L. Rev. 387 (1987).
M. N. Berman, The Evidentiary Theory of Blackmail: Taking Motives Seriously, 65 U. Chi. L. Rev. 795 (1998).
J. Coffee, Does "Unlawful" Mean "Criminal"?: Reflections on the Disappearing Tort/Crime Distinction in American Law, 71 B.U.L. Rev. 193 (1993).
J. Coffee, From Tort to Crime: Some Reflections on the Criminalization of Fiduciary Breaches and the Problematic Line Between Law and Ethics, 19 Am. Crim. L. Rev. 117 (1981).
J. Coffee, The Metastasis of Mail Fraud: The Continuing Story of the "Evolution" of a White-Collar Crime, 21 Am. Crim. L. Rev. 1 (1983).
J. C. Coffee, Hush! The Criminal Status of Confidential Information After *McNally* and *Carpenter* and the Enduring Problem of Overcriminalization, 26 Am. Crim. L. Rev. 121 (1988).

P. R. Ezersky, Intra-Corporate Mail and Wire Fraud: Criminal Liability for Fiduciary Breach, 94 Yale L.J. 1427 (1985).
G. Fletcher, Blackmail: The Paradigmatic Crime, 141 U. Pa. L. Rev. 1617 (1993).
G. Fletcher, The Metamorphosis of Larceny, 89 Harv. L. Rev. 469 (1976).
D. H. Ginsburg & P. Shechtman, Blackmail: An Economic Analysis of the Law, 141 U. Pa. L. Rev. 1849, 1873-1874 (1993).
W. J. Gordon, Truth and Consequences: The Force of Blackmail's Central Case, 141 U. Pa. L. Rev. 1741 (1993).
J. Hall, Theft, Law and Society (2d ed. 1952).
R. Hammond, Theft of Information, 100 L.Q. Rev. 252 (1984).
J. Lindgren, Unraveling the Paradox of Blackmail, 84 Colum. L. Rev. 670 (1984).
J. M. Livermore, Lawyer Extortion, 20 Ariz. L. Rev. 403 (1978).
G. S. Moohr, Federal Criminal Fraud and the Development of Intangible Property Rights in Information, U. Ill. L. Rev. 683 (2000).
G. Moohr, Mail Fraud and Intangible Rights Doctrine, 31 Harv. J. Leg. 153 (1994).
M. Nimmer, National Secrets v. Free Speech: The Issues Left Undecided in the *Ellsberg* Case, 28 Stan. L. Rev. 311 (1974).
R. Pearce, Theft by False Promises, 101 U. Pa. L. Rev. 967 (1953).
G. Williams, Forgery and Falsity, [1974] Crim. L. Rev. 71.
G. Williams, Theft, Consent and Illegality: Some Problems, [1977] Crim. L. Rev. 327.

Note, A Rationale of the Law of Aggravated Theft, 54 Colum. L. Rev. 84 (1954).

INDEX